UNIVERSITY CASEBOOK SERIES®

ENERGY, ECONOMICS AND THE ENVIRONMENT

CASES AND MATERIALS

FOURTH EDITION

by

JOEL B. EISEN
Professor of Law
University of Richmond School of Law

EMILY HAMMOND
Professor of Law
The George Washington University Law School

JIM ROSSI
Professor of Law
Vanderbilt University Law School

DAVID B. SPENCE
Professor of Law, Politics & Regulation
McCombs School of Business and School of Law, University of Texas at
Austin

JACQUELINE L. WEAVER
A.A. White Professor of Law
University of Houston Law Center

HANNAH J. WISEMAN
Attorneys' Title Professor of Law
Florida State University College of Law

FOUNDATION
PRESS

University Casebook Series is a trademark registered in the U.S. Patent and Trademark Office.

Printed in the United States of America

ISBN: 978-1-60930-307-5

INTRODUCTION

PREFACE TO PREVIOUS EDITIONS

In both law and business schools, energy courses were common after the oil price shocks of the 1970s. A number of fine casebooks were written in the early 1980s, responding to the sense of "energy crisis" and "environmental crisis" during that period.

As the 1980s progressed, however, declining energy prices, improving economic and environmental conditions, and diminishing Cold War tensions alleviated the sense of crisis. Gradually, schools began to lose interest. However, the 1990s saw renewed attention to a new set of energy issues. The collapse of communism created worldwide interest in the privatization and deregulation of monopolies. Information technology facilitated international business combinations and more trading of energy as a commodity. International environmental concerns grew in importance with worries about the ozone layer, climate change, Asian dust plumes reaching California's shores, an asthma epidemic, loss of rainforests and biogenetics. The United States seemed unable to control air and water pollution from small sources.

During the 1990s, law schools created an increasing number of courses on "regulated industries"—an ironic title given the diminishing role of economic regulation. The law and economics movement continued to expand its influence. Environmental law programs spawned a growing number of subspecialties, and interest in international law boomed. Natural resources law continued to be dominated by intense political and ideological controversy over the use of public lands, by concern about the long-term supply of resources, and by worries over our reliance on unfriendly overseas suppliers.

By 2000, climate change started to influence the course of energy law in earnest. Many law schools offered courses on climate change law in addition to international environmental law. However, despite many new materials addressing these trends, no new casebooks on energy law had been created. All of these factors contributed to the authors' belief that the beginning of the new century was an appropriate time for a new casebook on energy, economics and the environment. The first edition of this casebook, published in 2000, by Fred Bosselman, Jim Rossi and Jacqueline Weaver, responded to that need.

Joel Eisen and David Spence joined the second edition of the casebook (published in 2006), which expanded the book's emphasis on environmental concerns surrounding the use of energy resources, renewable energy, and energy markets. The third edition, published in 2010, extended the book's coverage with more significant integration of topics related to climate change and efficiency and conservation.

PREFACE TO THE FOURTH EDITION

This fourth edition of this casebook significantly expands on and updates our previous efforts. It also reflects some changes in the composition of the book's authors.

Emily Hammond and Hannah Wiseman joined this new edition, expanding the book's attention to administrative law, risk theory, and nuclear law; as well as state and local law, hydraulic fracturing, and renewables integration.

The 2013 death of Fred Bosselman, one of the book's founding authors, was a significant loss for all of us. Fred was a pioneer in many areas of legal scholarship, and it was he who first had the idea to put together an energy law book in the mid-1990s. His vision continues to influence how we approach the topic, such as locating energy law at the intersection of traditional economic issues and more contemporary environmental concerns. We hope that the new edition continues to reflect his passion for sharing ideas about energy and environmental regulation by connecting the past and the present with a new generation of students.

We dedicate this edition of the casebook to Fred Bosselman, our coauthor, colleague and friend.

OVERVIEW OF THE CASEBOOK

While this casebook does not (and cannot) present every issue in energy law, its approach is to embrace many of the practical challenges and problems energy law faces into the next decade by drawing out the recurring themes across multiple resources. If students can develop an appreciation for the richness and adaptation of the recurring themes across multiple energy resources and technologies, they will be well equipped to adapt to the new challenges they will face as energy lawyers in the coming decades.

We believe that the material can be taught in many different ways, depending on whether your professor presents it as an Energy Law survey course, as a course focused on energy markets, as a survey of environmental issues associated with energy, as a course themed around electricity regulation, or as a course focused on renewable and clean energy issues.

In response to new developments in energy, we have changed the organization of the book and have made efforts to focus the presentation of materials around recurring themes in energy law, as are presented in Chapter 1. We also have expanded the problems and case studies, allowing students to better examine energy law topics in context.

The chapters and organizational structure of this book proceed as follows:

Chapter 1 presents energy law as organized around four recurring themes, which we return to throughout the book.

Chapter 2 discusses "public utility" law principles and presents the basic structure of the electric power industry. While they have a long history, these principles remain central to many modern issues surrounding competition and innovation in energy regulation.

Chapter 3 addresses the production of coal, the fossil fuel resource on which the United States depends most heavily for electric power production.

Chapter 4 focuses on the production of oil and gas, the other fossil fuels that predominate in the electric power and transportation sectors of the United States. This chapter covers conventional drilling techniques for production, as well as legal issues surrounding newer approaches such as hydraulic fracturing.

Chapter 5 discusses policy issues and the federal and state systems of regulating externalities produced by fossil fuels in electric power combustion. These externalities include conventional pollutants that cause local and regional harms, as well as greenhouse gas pollutants associated with harms such as climate change and sea level rise.

Chapter 6 addresses hydroelectric power—one of the earliest technologies for generating electric power and the energy technology that is most closely tied with the use and development of navigable rivers.

Chapter 7 discusses policy and legal issues surrounding nuclear power—an energy source that provides approximately 20% of the electric power in the United States.

Chapter 8 presents a hypothetical problem to introduce and survey some of the issues surrounding rate regulation of electric and natural gas utilities.

Chapter 9 addresses oil and gas regulation, with a focus on pipelines and "open access" principles for interstate oil and gas markets.

Chapter 10 addresses basic issues related to electric power markets. These include the application of "open access" principles to electric power transmission, energy trading practices and their regulation, and retail competition in electric power.

Chapter 11 addresses the emerging law and policies relating to development of renewable power (wind, solar, and other renewable energy resources).

Chapter 12 presents two case studies of specific hypothetical renewable power projects, as a way of discussing basic principles related to project development and financing, and surveying the range of legal issues related to large-and small-scale wind and solar projects.

Chapter 13 discusses energy conservation and efficiency, with a particular focus on the "Smart Grid" (the modernized electricity network) and regulatory strategies and new technologies associated with it. The chapter includes a case study on demand response, which involves incentives for reduced consumption of electricity.

Chapter 14 addresses international issues related to energy, particularly human rights issues associated with energy production abroad and international trade issues in energy resources.

Chapter 15 discusses the legal issues concerning energy use for transportation. These include land use and planning issues, and vehicle fuel emissions standards.

WEBSITE AND UPDATES

We have established a website for the book, www.energylawbook. com, where we will make available periodic updates.

A NOTE ON EDITING

In common with traditional casebook practice, excerpts from cases, books and other sources have usually been edited to eliminate material not directly relevant to the topic of discussion. Ellipses are routinely used to designate omitted material, but footnotes and citations have often been excised without so indicating. Asterisks may also be used to indicate the deletion of substantial amounts of material. Where footnotes have been included, the footnote number from the original is noted in brackets and precedes our footnote number. Where multiple citations are found in the original, only the official reporter or source has been included. A reader who plans to rely on any of the excerpted material for research purposes is advised to consult the original.

ACKNOWLEDGMENTS

Joel Eisen would like to thank Daniel Savage and Andy Flavin for assistance in locating materials and updating chapters. He also thanks the University of Richmond School of Law for its continuing support.

Emily Hammond would like to thank her Fall 2014 students in Energy Law at the George Washington University Law School for their helpful comments and suggestions on an earlier draft of this book. She also thanks the George Washington University Law School for its generous research support.

Jacqueline Weaver thanks Christopher Dykes, her reference librarian, for his always-timely responses to her requests for updated material and proper citations to input into this casebook. Amanda Parker's skills and cheerful patience in solving word processing mysteries greatly eased the task of editing draft upon draft. Professor Weaver also thanks Kirk K. Weaver for his superb proofreading skills. Finally, she thanks the University of Houston Law Foundation for providing summer research grants to complete this edition.

Jim Rossi thanks Colton Michael Peterson for assistance with research and Vanderbilt Law School for its administrative support.

All of the authors thank those students and faculty who have used the book over the past 15 years for their many suggestions for improvement.

Karen Berry deserves particular recognition for her diligent support in coordinating the manuscript. Emily Padget helped to obtain copyright permissions for the materials excerpted in the book.

SUMMARY OF CONTENTS

TABLE OF CONTENTS

TABLE OF CASES

The principal cases are in bold type.

UNIVERSITY CASEBOOK SERIES®

ENERGY, ECONOMICS AND THE ENVIRONMENT

CASES AND MATERIALS

FOURTH EDITION

CHAPTER 1

INTRODUCTION: THEMES IN ENERGY LAW

A. THE IMPORTANCE OF ENERGY

It is an exciting time to be working in energy law. Old systems of regulation are being supplanted by policies that emphasize competitive markets. Rapid changes in science and technology stand to impact the availability of energy resources as well as our means for tackling the most pressing issues of scarcity, environmental degradation, and climate change presented by the production and use of energy resources. Wildly fluctuating markets, changes in energy companies' structures, and the emergence of new, entrepreneurial market entrants make long-range planning challenging both for corporate entities and the government institutions with which they interact. Add in the impacts of consumer behavior and demand and one can quickly see that a multitude of catalysts influence the way we extract, distribute, process, and use energy resources.

Given the massive breadth and depth of the issues in energy law, we recognize (and often hear from our own students) that approaching the topic is intimidating. Part of what makes energy law overwhelming is the ever-evolving range of issues it addresses. Even in this broad and quickly changing field, however, we believe that energy law can be organized and understood through the lens of four recurring themes: (1) ownership of energy resources, (2) basic decisions regarding markets versus regulation and their interaction in allocating energy resources, (3) how to address the externalities and risks associated with energy resources, and (4) in the public governance arena, deciding who (the federal government,

1

states, or someone else?) will regulate energy resources and their use. These four themes have defined energy law since the area developed in the early twentieth century. Although the particular issues on which modern energy lawyers focus might differ from those that may have been the most important to energy lawyers thirty years ago, there is a durability to these themes: They will inform the future of energy law too, even as the particular energy resources, technologies, and issues that hold the attention of lawyers inevitably change.

This chapter provides an overview and examples of each theme, grounding their presentation in the context of energy use and resources in the United States as well as the history of the U.S. approach to regulating energy resources. As you study the topics in more depth later in this course, you may find it helpful to refer back to these themes.[1] The next two subsections provide an overview of the structure of the energy industry and the historical development of energy law.

1.   ENERGY RESOURCES AND DEMAND

Energy industries increasingly employ highly entrepreneurial and creative people. But they do not "create" energy. The laws of thermodynamics tell us that we cannot create energy; we can only *transform* it. We must start with the resources found in nature and convert them to forms suitable to meet our needs.

The energy resources used in the United States include fossil fuels, such as coal, oil and natural gas; nuclear power; and renewable resources, such as hydropower, wind, solar, biomass and geothermal energy. Over 80% of our energy now comes from fossil fuels. Roughly two-thirds of these primary energy resources are converted into electricity or used in transportation. The other third is used in the industrial, commercial or residential sectors of the economy. *See* **Figure 1–1**. Policy initiatives aimed at reducing reliance on fossil fuels have tended to focus particularly on the electricity and transportation sectors of the economy.

---

[1]   In addition, the governmental agency websites referenced throughout this book are important sources of information and updates. In studying energy law, it is inevitable that you will confront some new technical, economic, and legal terminology. One particularly helpful resource to expanding your vocabulary is the energy glossary provided by the Energy Information Administration: http://www.eia.gov/tools/glossary/.

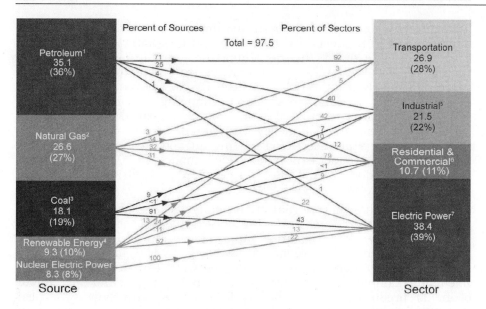

Figure 1–1
Source: U.S. Energy Info. Admin. (EIA),
U.S. Primary Energy Consumption by Source and Sector, 2013 (Quadrillion Btu),
http://www.eia.gov/totalenergy/data/monthly/pdf/flow/css_2013_energy.pdf

In **Figure 1–1** above, the left-hand number on each arrow shows the percentage of each resource used for a particular sector—e.g., 71% of petroleum used in the United States is used for transportation. The right-hand number on that same arrow shows how much each sector relies on that particular resource—e.g., 92% of all energy used in transportation comes from petroleum, for example.

Before introducing the legal and policy themes addressed in this book, it is useful to review some facts. The United States is the largest consumer of energy resources in the world, consuming about nineteen percent of worldwide energy each year. One author notes, "[c]ompared with people elsewhere, Americans are less self-conscious about how unsustainable a high-energy society is and, historically speaking, less aware of the anomaly of high energy use. . . ." David E. Nye, Path Insistence: Comparing European and American Attitudes Toward Energy, 53 J. Intl. Affairs 129, 130 (1999). According to the same author, "Americans have become so 'path dependent' that they only become aware of energy during a blackout or gasoline shortage." *Id.* If this is true, policy-makers need to reflect seriously on how individuals' behaviors will change in reaction to legal and economic incentives.

To meet this massive demand for energy, the United States has historically had abundant and accessible energy resources, a fact that has no doubt contributed to our economic growth. All of the coal and almost 90 percent of the natural gas consumed in the United States is produced from domestic sources. The United States was self-sufficient in energy until the late 1950s, when energy consumption began to outpace domestic production. By the 1970s, rising demand and falling supply sharply increased oil imports, in particular, and, combined with the OPEC oil crisis, drew attention to the fact that the United States had become highly dependent on fossil fuel imports, particularly oil. Over a fourth of the oil produced in the world is still consumed in the United States. Although events in the Middle East in the past few decades remind us that the United States remained reliant on international sources for much of its oil well past the 1970s, **Figure 1–2** shows that the U.S. trade imbalance in energy is changing as the United States ramps up its own production of oil and as shale natural gas grows in its significance as a source of energy. Indeed, EIA, which compiles a wide range of energy statistics, released this unexpected headline in 2012: "U.S. petroleum product exports exceeded imports in 2011 for first time in over six decades." EIA, Today in Energy, Mar. 7, 2011, www.eia.gov/todayinenergy/detail.cfm?id=5290.

One important concept that drives many discussions in energy policy is the concern over *peak oil,* or the notion that the production of any nonrenewable energy resource supply faces finite limits and will eventually decline. The urgency of peak oil is widely debated, in part because neither energy resources nor the ways they are produced are fixed. For example, new forms of oil are often discovered, and the number of fields producing oil in the world changes with new geological discoveries and technological advancements in drilling technologies. Some have argued that peak oil has already occurred, but others argue that it will not occur for several decades. Debates over peak oil have been renewed by new sources of energy from shale oil. This oil is now produced in large quantities within the United States due to a particular technological advancement that has been used to extract oil as well as natural gas—the use of horizontal drilling and "slick water" hydraulic fracturing, which uses larger volumes of water and reaches through larger portions of underground formations than previous fracturing techniques. Some maintain that the growth of shale oil production has the potential to offset any reductions in oil supply from conventional sources of petroleum. Energy efficiency innovations have also challenged the idea that concerns about the finite nature of energy resources should drive energy policy discussions. Debates over the urgency of peak oil continue, but one reality is clear: Because energy resources are finite and demand continues to increase, total energy supplies are declining.

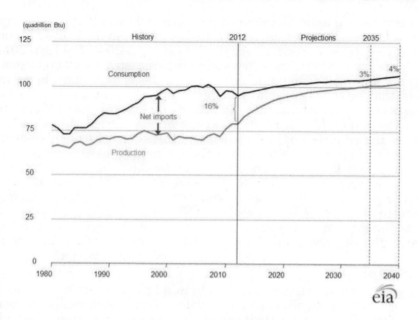

Figure 1–2
Source: EIA, Annual Energy Outlook 2014,
http://www.eia.gov/forecasts/aeo/er/early_production.cfm

The fact that the United States has been so dependent on imported petroleum means that in setting energy policy, much of the focus is on the sector of the economy that uses most of that petroleum—the transportation sector. Automobiles, trucks, airplanes and trains all run on fuels derived from petroleum. The transportation sector in the United States uses a much higher amount of petroleum per person than in any other country. This has led to a reexamination of our standards for engines, motor vehicles, and fuels, and even to a reconsideration of the land use patterns of "urban sprawl" that make us so dependent on the automobile.

Although transportation is often the point of focus in discussions of energy resources, **Figure 1–1** shows that electric power makes up an even larger portion of our energy portfolio. Electricity generation utilizes more than one-third of the primary energy resources consumed in the United States, and this sector will become increasingly important. Think of all the devices and equipment that rely on electricity—heating and cooling, refrigeration, computers, and so on. It is not a stretch to say that modern life as we know it would be impossible without large quantities of electricity. Debates about the choice of resources used to produce electricity have been some of the most volatile in American politics, and have produced a complex array of laws that attempt to balance the economic benefits, safety risks, and environmental attributes of the competing fuels: coal, oil, natural gas, uranium, hydropower, solar, wind, and other renewable resources. Recently, the emergence of "distributed generation" (small-scale, decentralized, customer-based production of electricity) has challenged the electric utility industry, leading to still more efforts to encourage this trend.

In contrast to many developing countries, where per capita energy demand is increasing, average energy use per person in the United States is actually expected to decline over the period 2010–2040. *See* EIA, 2014 Annual Energy Outlook, http://www.eia.gov/forecasts/aeo/pdf/0383-2014 %29.pdf. Yet overall demand in the United States is increasing, and EIA projects that electricity use will increase by 29% from 2012 to 2040. Forecasts of energy demand into the future are dependent on population growth, the geographic distribution of populations, the level of industrial activities, the efficiency of production, and the expected price of energy. Given the widespread dependence of the United States on energy, it is not at all surprising that energy resources have had an extensive influence on economic growth and development in this country. The estimated value of primary energy sources (inputs) in the U.S. economy is 5 percent of Gross National Product (GNP). With end-use products and services, energy sources comprise as much as 12 percent of GNP. Although the materials in this book may seem focused on a narrow industry at times, its impact is widespread and reverberates throughout the economy.

In your study of energy law, keep in mind the relationship between energy price and demand. Economists refer to the relationship between price and demand according to its *elasticity*—that is, the extent to which demand will change in response to a change in price. Demand for many goods and services is fairly price elastic, with demand decreasing as price increases and vice versa. Perhaps because energy is considered such a vital commodity, many energy policy decisions over the years have been driven by the idea that demand for energy resources, such as electric power, is inelastic. That is, changes in price have small effects on the quantity of the resource demanded. However, in recent years it has increasingly been recognized that consumers are more responsive to price changes in energy markets and that demand for many energy resources is elastic—at least to a point.

2. THE ERAS OF ENERGY LAW

Energy law did not develop in a vacuum but grew alongside technological innovations in energy production (such as the development of nuclear power) and economic and world events (such as the 1970s worldwide oil crisis). Assumptions about the optimal mix of energy resources, economics, and environmental policy have influenced—or been influenced by—the various energy policy choices reflected in each era.

Our understanding and use of energy resources over time can be mapped onto five overlapping eras of energy law from the 1800s to the present, each of which had different law and policy focuses:

(1) a pre-regulatory phase, during which private property and common law principles ordered the use of energy resources;

(2) a demand growth era that followed World War II and continued into the early 1970s;

(3) a rise in environmental and risk regulation, focusing on primarily on local pollution impacts, beginning in the 1960s;

(4) increasing competition in energy markets beginning in the middle 1970s; and

(5) attention to global pollution impacts and climate change, from around 2000 to the present.

Excluding the pre-regulatory phase, each era produced a distinct set of statutes and regulatory initiatives affecting energy resources and their use. **Figure 1–3** illustrates each of these eras with a timeline of major federal energy statutes, identifying the major state and federal statutory and regulatory initiatives that each era produced:

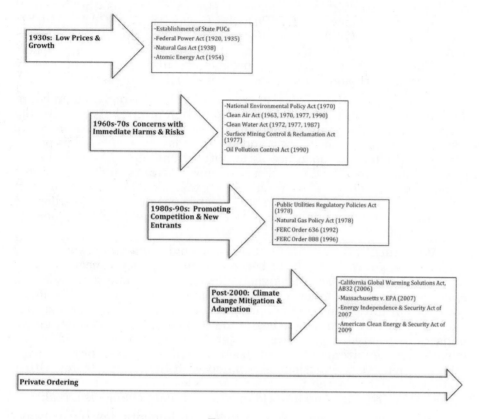

Figure 1–3

During the pre-regulatory phase, energy resources were governed primarily by private property concepts, including private transactions and property-related tort law such as trespass and nuisance. For example, early in the development of hydropower resources in the United States, common-law concepts ordered the rights between mill owners and neighboring property owners whose land was flooded by mill ponds. Eventually, government regulation tended to displace the use of private law in resolving these disputes. Nevertheless, as described below, ownership conflicts continue influence energy policy.

From the New Deal until the later 1970s, energy policy focused on regulating energy prices and growing infrastructure. This era saw a significant emphasis on infrastructure expansion by monopolistic firms and public regulation of the prices charged for electricity and fuel resources to meet consumer protection goals—a set of issues primarily within the subfield of regulated industries. State agencies regulated the delivery of natural gas and electric power to consumers during this era, which also saw the rise of federal regulation of interstate natural gas and electric power markets. Nuclear energy came of age during this era as well. Overall, the major policy emphasis was on encouraging energy resources to be abundantly available and inexpensive for consumers.

During the 1960s and 1970s, mounting awareness of environmental externalities gave rise to significant growth in environmental and risk regulation, including the passage of statutes such as the National Environmental Policy Act (NEPA), the Clean Air Act (CAA), and the Clean Water Act (CWA). These statutes challenged the energy industry and related regulators to be mindful of the environmental impacts associated with the extraction, production, and delivery of energy resources, even though many impacts were local and domestic.

Beginning in the 1980s, energy policy increasingly emphasized deregulation, competition, and the introduction of markets to drive the investment in, allocation of, and pricing of energy resources—a set of issues that emphasized contract and antitrust law principles. This period saw federal efforts to open access to natural gas pipelines and electric power transmission and to encourage new entrants and competition. Some states, such as California and Texas, also experimented with restructuring (partial deregulation of electric power delivery)—allowing new entrants to supply electric power and also enabling consumers to choose suppliers.

At the turn of the twenty-first century, environmental law shifted as climate change and its effects became a major policy concern driving regulation. As discussed throughout this book, the energy sector is a major source of greenhouse gas emissions, but it also holds much potential for mitigating and adapting to climate change. Several states, most notably California, have begun to regulate carbon and other global impacts associated with energy. Federal agencies have turned to the major federal environmental statutes, primarily the CAA, for regulating the greenhouse gas emissions associated with the energy sector. Other regulatory efforts at the federal and state level focus on how to better adapt energy resources to a world in which climate change is a reality.

More recently, although energy and environmental law have always been connected, attention to climate change has increasingly led lawyers to integrate energy and environmental concerns in their approaches to solving legal problems. Good energy lawyers today cannot ignore environmental law concerns, but neither can good environmental lawyers ignore the themes of energy law.

B. RECURRING THEMES IN ENERGY LAW

While the five eras introduced above reflect varying emphases on laws and policies, several distinct themes recur throughout the history of energy law. These themes inform and help define energy law as a distinct and coherent conceptual approach to evaluating legal problems. Energy lawyers will confront new technologies and new challenges in the future. But history often repeats itself. As we move forward into the next era of energy law, attention to the same themes will ensure that energy law continues to play a significant role as a distinct field in addressing energy issues into our future.

The first theme is resource ownership. Rooted in ancient common law, concepts of private property explain much of energy law's history and exert considerable force on current energy law and policy issues. Although private property ownership tends to be the default approach in the United States, public ownership is an equally important property regime for energy law. Each regime raises some basic opportunities and challenges for energy resources, raising the perennial question whether the government or private sector is better equipped to develop, deliver, and conserve energy resources.

A second theme relates to how energy resources are priced and allocated. Many energy resources are price regulated for obvious consumer protection purposes, but price regulation often goes hand-in-hand with government endorsement of a monopoly franchise for energy resources. Much of energy law's history involves government bodies interacting with the private sectors to form regulatory commitments to attract investment and promote innovation in energy resources. Once major investments are made in energy infrastructure, careful attention must be paid to who bears the risks of these investments and the incentives this creates for new market entrants and innovation.

The third theme, which has risen in prevalence in the past several decades, is that of externalities and concepts of risk in the regulation of energy resources. As described in more detail below, externalities are costs or benefits that are not internalized (paid for) by the entity that creates the costs or receives the benefits. Instead, these costs or benefits are transferred to the public. What mechanisms are most effective in resolving issues related to externalities produced by energy resource production, delivery and use? How should the uncertainties associated with various energy-related risks be accounted for in structuring risk management schemes?

The fourth theme relates to public governance: Which regulatory bodies will make decisions about energy resources—the federal government, state or local governments, or regional or international regulatory bodies? For modern energy lawyers, this theme encompasses traditional questions related to economic regulation and federalism (the distribution of power under the U.S. Constitution between the federal government and the states), but also includes the nuanced division of governmental authority established in environmental laws.

1. Ownership of Energy Resources

The twin concepts of property and ownership are fundamental to American law. Deeply held notions of what it means to "own" something both provide explanatory power for much of energy law and raise challenges to innovation in energy technology, law, and policy. Furthermore, the choice whether energy resources are privately or publicly owned holds consequences for their management and regulation. This section provides a brief overview of some fundamental concepts; you will find numerous detailed examples throughout the book.

Not surprisingly, energy law frequently assumes that energy resources are privately owned. Although much oil and gas production occurs on public lands, the United States is the only major oil and gas producing country in which such interests are commonly held as private property. This private property interest is rooted in the *ad coelum* doctrine,[2] reinforcing ancient common-law concepts of near-absolute dominion over the resource. Other private property concepts modify the doctrine and shape the transferability, extraction, and use of such interests. Consider, for example, the rule of capture, which confers the right to produce all the oil and gas that flows through a well on one's own land, even if the minerals flowed from under another's land. This rule has been critical to oil and gas production for decades, and remains so today. *See* Coastal Oil & Gas Corp. v. Garza Energy Trust, 268 S.W.3d 1 (Tex. 2008) (extending doctrine in hydraulic fracturing context); *cf.* Stone v. Chesapeake Appalachia, No. 512–CV–102, 2013 WL 2097397 (N.D. W. Va. Apr. 10, 2013), *vacated on joint mot. due to settlement*, 2013 WL 7863861 (Jul. 30, 2013) (rejecting doctrine's extension in hydraulic fracturing context).

To what extent should private property concepts be extended from one resource to another? For example, should the rule of capture similarly apply to wind? Like oil and gas, wind is fugacious—it flows across properties without regard to ownership—and it is not valuable as an energy resource until it is captured. To the extent that the rule of capture rewards the initiative and labor necessary to bring value to an energy resource, applying it to wind may promote increased development of this renewable energy resource. On the other hand, an unfettered rule of capture leads to economic and physical waste, as described in more detail in Section 3 below. Relatedly, mineral interests may be severed from the land they underlie, but owners of mineral rights retain an easement to use the surface as is reasonably necessary to access the minerals. Many landowners in areas with plentiful wind have executed deeds severing wind rights that are modeled on such transfers in the oil and gas context. But there is uncertainty whether this approach is permissible; many jurisdictions permit wind easements and leases, but some have enacted statutes banning wind severance, and others have not addressed the issue. Uncertain property rights, of course, may deter investors and slow development of alternative energy resources.

The dominant private property pedigree for energy resources strongly influences legal and policy decisions in other contexts as well. For example, a consequence of making energy resources subject to private ownership is that government regulation of those resources can lead to takings challenges. The classic regulatory takings case, *Pennsylvania Coal Co. v. Mahon*, 260 U.S. 393 (1922), involved energy resources; there the Supreme Court held that an exercise of the police power that prevented mining severed mineral rights in coal violated the Constitution. Suppose that a city ordinance prohibits drilling new oil and gas wells near a lake that serves as the city's primary drinking water supply. Should the holders of mineral rights who are now unable to extract those minerals be compensated under a regulatory takings theory? *See* City of Houston v. Trail Enters., Inc., 377 S.W.3d 873 (Tex. Ct. App. 2012) (no taking given strong government interest and low investment-backed expectations, even given significant economic impact on claimants).

---

[2] The full statement of the doctrine is *cujus est solum, ejus est usque ad coelum et ad inferos* (to whomever the soil belongs, he owns also to the sky and to the depths).

Indeed, the police power and other sources of law limit common-law property doctrine and accompanying rights, and thus narrow property rights and reasonable expectations associated with those rights. Many of these limits are described in the following sections, and are imposed to promote certainty, encourage investment, and manage externalities and risks. Although the default may be private ownership, the public interest may justify numerous inroads into the traditional private property rights to exclude, possess, use, and transfer. For example, owners of electrical transmission lines operating in the wholesale market must make transmission services available to others on a non-discriminatory basis. To what extent should concepts of open access reach even further?

Of course, not all energy resources are considered private property. Early in the development of hydropower, a major debate concerned whether the government or the private sector is better positioned to develop hydroelectric dams. The United States favored public ownership and development of dams, which stands in contrast to most other energy resources. Government ownership of federal land, moreover, has important implications for such energy resources as minerals and wind, as well as siting electricity transmission lines and oil and gas pipelines. Although private ownership gives rise to numerous challenges described in the sections below, public ownership presents its own set of problems. How should government decisionmaking with respect to public property operate to ensure transparency, avoid capture, and foster fairness and accountability?

Ownership as a theme of energy law goes beyond corporeal property. Consider, for example, that intellectual property law and policy relate deeply to energy as well. As scarce resources, opening markets, and environmental concerns highlight the need for new technologies, a fundamental promise of intellectual property law is that inventors may receive limited monopolies, thereby allowing them to profit from their work, in exchange for disclosure of their inventions. But what if the promise of the intellectual property system is insufficient to spur innovation? To what extent should public funds be expended on this goal—and if funds are expended, to whom should the resulting property belong? On the other hand, is more regulation needed to open markets to innovators? Or less?

2. MONOPOLY VS. COMPETITION

Energy projects are often major infrastructure undertakings that require an enormous commitment of financial capital. Throughout the history of the United States the development of new types of energy resources raised questions about whether the development and delivery of these resources is best approached by the government granting a monopoly to a single firm, or whether a competitive market would be a fairer and more efficient way of developing and delivering the resource. John D. Rockefeller's success in monopolizing the oil business led to the antitrust laws in the nineteenth century. Samuel Insull's similar success in the electric power business encouraged strict regulation of that industry, including the development of the public utility approach to regulating electric power that was prevalent for much of the twentieth century.

Regulation of energy resources by state and local governments began late in the nineteenth century. Oil and gas production was initially regulated by state agencies to avoid physical waste and, not coincidentally, to keep prices high. Local governments typically granted a monopoly to a private company to sell gas and electricity to consumers by issuing a public utility franchise that provided that the company's rates and service were subject to local regulation. As these franchises proliferated, state legislatures often preempted the local regulation of rates and services by creating a public utility commission (PUC)—a single agency to regulate the delivery of energy to consumers. Most energy resources were regulated at the state or local level, if at all. This early regulation, primarily by state PUCs, focused on setting the rates for a local monopoly-franchised utility and protecting the utility from competing firms. The need for such regulation was largely perceived as a response to the market failures associated with monopolies: that left unregulated, a single firm operating as a monopoly will charge higher prices and produce less of a service than a competitive firm would. Regulators, by contrast, could mimic the result of the competitive market by setting rates based on the cost of service and requiring the utility to serve customers within its geographic franchise service area.

In this sense, a major regulatory objective in energy law is protecting consumers from the ills of monopoly and ensuring that, where appropriate, suppliers face an even playing field in energy production and delivery. As you will learn in Chapter 8, the cost-of-service approach to utility regulation is often termed a "regulatory compact," a contract of sorts whereby regulators ensure the firm would be able to recover the costs of the infrastructure in which it had invested; in return, the firm would subject itself to regulation to ensure its rates are reasonable. Not surprisingly, this regulatory compact has produced some mistakes, in no small part due to the lag time between the decision to favor a particular technology, the actual deployment of that technology, and the window of time it takes to pay for it. Over time, technological advances have made competition among different parts of the energy sector more feasible.

For example, nuclear power plants—once anticipated to be "too cheap to meter"—produced notorious cost overruns in the 1970s. Nuclear power seemed less necessary and desirable, yet regulators had already approved utilities charging customers for some of these plants. The resultant "stranded costs" posed a significant policy issue to consumer and industry interests alike. A challenge that energy law consistently must confront is how to balance these kinds of regulatory commitments—necessary to induce investment in infrastructure—with the adoption of new technologies. The theme is recurring: Today some coal plants may be facing similar stranded-cost issues given the availability of much lower-cost natural gas resources in many parts of the United States.

Economic regulation of utilities and other entities involved in providing energy resources may fall short of its intended goals for several reasons. First, the regulatory process itself is imperfect, especially if regulated firms are able to capture or control the outcome of the process. Some argue that this is a recurring problem in the energy regulatory sector, where large corporations have wielded enormous influence on the political and regulatory process. Yet much of energy law is focused on ensuring that the public interest does not yield to private interests.

Second, regulation may cause regulated firms to incur excessive costs or adopt inefficient methods of operation. Some economists have suggested that price regulation has induced many public utilities to artificially inflate their rate base and to overinvest in capital assets upon which they can earn a regulated rate of return—e.g., to build too many power plants for their customer base. The effect of this is to create a surplus of power and to inflate the ultimate costs to consumers.

Finally, in recent years public choice theory, which applies critical economic analysis to government institutions and the decision-making processes of politicians and bureaucracies, has raised the concern that government regulation itself is prone to certain failures. If the purpose of government regulation is to correct market failures, but regulation as implemented results in solutions that do not approximate the results of a well-functioning market, then regulation itself may have imposed unnecessary costs or inhibited self-correcting incentives. Competition among rent-seeking private investors, imperfect though it may be, may be better at pricing and allocating energy resources than regulation by rent-seeking government officials and lawmakers. On the other hand, regulation exists for a reason, and private choices about energy resources may impose unnecessary costs on consumers.

These kinds of issues have revived age-old questions about the proper approach to economic regulation. Many markets that impose cost-of-service regulation on the public utility model share a common trait: the services provided in them are in fact several different markets with varying characteristics. For example, consider the natural gas market. There are thousands of gas producers and literally millions of consumers of natural gas. Apart from the need to transport gas, the gas sales market is as close to the economist's competitive ideal as any market can be. Transportation of gas through pipelines, however, is subject to large economies of scale and is a natural monopoly. Yet historically, sales of natural gas and its transportation have been bundled within a single rate-regulated service. Similarly, electric power generation and electricity transmission have traditionally been bundled into a single rate-regulated service, even though power generation, like natural gas sales, possesses characteristics of a competitive market.

Congress began restructuring the natural gas industry in the late 1980s by unbundling gas sales from pipeline transportation services and providing equal access to the latter. FERC then undertook to restructure the electric utility industry in a similar fashion. Again, this approach has two steps: first, recognizing that there are two or more distinct markets bundled together, only one of which is a natural monopoly (i.e., the "pipes and wires," or transmission service); second, after unbundling the two distinct markets, then implementing an equal access regulatory scheme that applies only to the natural monopoly market so that all gas producers and electricity generators can ship their gas or electrons to the buyer who offers them the best deal. However, because FERC's jurisdiction over electric utilities does not extend as far as its jurisdiction over natural gas pipelines, the states retain jurisdiction over many aspects of the electric power industry. Some states, such as California, Texas, and Pennsylvania, have introduced new regulatory regimes that give some consumers a choice of their retail electricity supplier, much as consumers are able to choose their long-distance phone provider.

In addition, FERC and state PUCs have embarked on a series of incremental changes to traditional utility price regulation. More than thirty states have instituted competitive bidding regimes for electric utilities, which require utilities to consider and solicit bids before building new power plants. FERC has approved market-based rates, which displace traditional cost-of-service filings, for power sellers that meet certain conditions. FERC and many PUCs have also adopted incentive regulation to encourage a variety of non-traditional utilities to enter into power markets. Together, these new regulatory efforts have sparked considerable growth of new firms in traditional markets and have led to the emergence of new pricing markets, such as spot and futures markets in which electricity or other energy resources are traded on a short-term basis.

In the United States, there are a wide range of well-established markets for stocks and commodities that have continued to enjoy investor confidence, despite economic cycles and occasional financial scandal. When energy markets are mentioned, however, the ghost of Enron looms. The manipulation of the California energy market by Enron and other traders in 2000–2001 is not easily forgotten. And even respected markets like the NYMEX oil trading market have been accused of being a playground for speculators during the volatile 2007–09 period.

Current efforts to monitor energy markets are overlapping, expensive, and hampered by the speed of trading technologies and the energy buyers' needs for fast delivery. Will it be possible to regulate energy trading—and carbon emission trading—to prevent speculators from profiting from commodity or price "bubbles" that do not reflect underlying economic realities—or to prevent the traders from demanding government aid because they are deemed too important to fail? Will stable contract and property norms exist to attract energy project financing for massive capital investments designed for the long term in light of regulatory transitions in the industry and volatile markets?

Even though competition is an enduring theme for energy, the reality is that vital components of the industry remain heavily regulated. Most regulators still consider gas and oil pipelines and electric power transmission and distribution lines to be natural monopolies—better provided to customers by a single firm than two or more firms. These essential network facilities play a crucial role in modern energy markets. Without pipelines or power transmission lines, energy commodities cannot be delivered to consumers in the first place. The history of energy law focused on control of these network resources, as they were crucial to preserving the market power of energy firms. For example, early in the expansion of electricity transmission to rural communities, pursuant to a program sponsored by the federal government, private utilities battled with rural electric cooperatives over customers. Today regulators are struggling with how to attract sufficient investment in this infrastructure, how to regulate access to it, and how to price it. Again, history repeats itself: New entrants generating electric power by wind want to have similar access to transmission as incumbents have, many of which are generating electric power via conventional fuels. How to provide for access to infrastructure is one of the major issues facing energy industries today, even where energy is freely traded as a commodity in a competitive market.

3. MANAGING ENERGY EXTERNALITIES AND RISKS

Increasingly, society has become aware of additional consequences of ownership structures, market failures, and policy choices favoring incumbents over new entrants. As illustrated in **Figure 1–3**, the environmental regulatory era produced an important source of new law and policy impacting energy resources. Today, concerns about greenhouse gas emissions from fossil fuels and the urgency of climate change have created a convergence in environmental and energy law. The wide variety of energy externalities—which are essentially market failures—is often used to justify regulation going beyond price controls. However, other tools for reducing negative externalities include market-based mechanisms, technological and financial assistance, and private law remedies. In addition, the concepts of uncertainty as well as risk assessment, perception, and management inform and even dictate modern approaches to energy law and policy.

a. EXTERNALITIES

As noted above, an externality is produced where an entity engaged in an activity produces a cost or benefit that is not borne within that entity, but rather is transferred to others. Externalities can be negative, or positive. An example of a negative externality is the air pollution released by a coal-fired power plant that is exempted from compliance with the CAA. Such pollution imposes a cost on society for which the power plant producing does not pay. An example of a positive externality is a homeowner's green rooftop. Her neighbors might enjoy aesthetic value from the greenery, but they do not pay for that enjoyment. Externalities represent a form of market failure; in the case of negative externalities, correction of this market failure is often offered as a justification for regulation.

Negative energy externalities include overuse of resources, physical waste, and environmental harm, among others. The classic resource paradigm of the "tragedy of the commons" bears on this discussion, and often is used to frame energy policy issues. In a 1968 article in the journal *Science*, ecologist Garrett Hardin recounted the story of the tragedy of the commons as an allegory explaining the need for regulation of environmental pollution and natural resource use. Herdsmen sharing a common grazing area, said Hardin, face an ever-present temptation to increase the size of their herds because they capture all the benefits of using the common grazing land (through ownership of their individual herds), but shift some of the costs of use to others. Each herdsman acts in his own self-interest, continually increasing the size of his herd, but collectively they produce "ruin," the destruction of the commons. Hardin's prescription for this problem was "mutual coercion, mutually agreed upon"—in other words, government regulation. *See* Garrett Hardin, The Tragedy of the Commons, 162 Science 1243 (1968). Extending the tragedy of the commons to energy law, ask yourself whether, without government regulation, individual economic actors might burn coal without pollution controls, thereby "consuming" clean air; harvest biomass at unsustainable rates; or pump oil from a reservoir in inefficient and wasteful ways. Imposing limits on these activities, by issuing permits for example, is thus a way of controlling the externalities that the activities produce.

Regulation through permits is not the only method of managing negative externalities. Common law causes of action such as nuisance, negligence, and trespass can allocate costs and benefits. These private mechanisms have a long history and remain relevant today. *See* Prah v. Maretti, 321 N.W.2d 182 (Wis. 1982) (recognizing common-law cause of action in nuisance for claim of interference with plaintiff's solar collector). The relationship between private law and public law in the energy field is constantly in flux. Advocates of stronger action to address externalities often pursue both strategies, particularly if one appears to be momentarily stymied. For example, facing a lack of comprehensive federal climate change legislation, many plaintiffs sought common-law remedies from oil and gas companies, electricity generators, and states for contributing to climate change or failing to take measures to mitigate it. *See, e.g.*, Am. Electric Power Co. v. Connecticut, 131 S. Ct. 2527 (2011) (holding federal common-law nuisance claims were displaced by Congress's delegation of regulatory power over greenhouse gases to a federal agency under the CAA).

Market-based mechanisms can also assist in managing negative externalities—though markets often depend as much on government regulation as do permits or more explicit regulatory commands. Recent climate bills considered by Congress included cap-and-trade schemes that would have created markets for carbon allowances and credits—an approach California and the Northeastern region of the United States have already adopted. Others argue a carbon tax would most efficiently reduce greenhouse gas emissions. This approach, called a Pigovian tax, is meant to force internalization of negative externalities by requiring the generator of the externality to pay a tax equal to the externality's cost.

Other tools for managing negative externalities and spurring economic growth include technology- and information-sharing, education, and funding for research and development. These tools are part of the existing global and domestic landscape for climate change mitigation and adaptation, and have been used in many other contexts. Often, they can be first steps towards a more robust legal framework. For example, the Atomic Energy Act of 1954 represented a deliberate choice by Congress to shift information, technology, and property rights involving atomic energy from the military to the civilian sector. This shift, overseen by the Atomic Energy Commission (now the Nuclear Regulatory Commission, or NRC), enabled the development of civilian electricity generation using nuclear power and closely followed President Eisenhower's announcement of the Atoms for Peace program. This program offered sharing of nuclear technology for peaceful purposes like medical uses and electricity generation while attempting to stall nuclear weapons proliferation. Though the program is criticized (for example, it gave political cover to the United States in its own buildup of a nuclear arsenal), it also led to the creation of the International Atomic Energy Agency and various new treaties and laws governing the nuclear resource.

In sum, negative externalities are a feature of the world of energy. Regulation, private remedies, market-based mechanisms, and technology development are the most common approaches to correcting externalities. Determining the impacts of these externalities from a scientific or technical standpoint, however—and developing a mix of strategies that are effective—requires an understanding of concepts of risk.

b. THE ROLES OF RISK AND UNCERTAINTY

Economically efficient outcomes are difficult to obtain, and moreover, individuals seldom behave as the purely rational economic actors that economic theory posits. Energy law and policy challenges can be understood through a framework of risk theory that includes risk assessment, risk perception, and risk management. Each of these components makes an important contribution to our understanding of energy law and policy.

Risk assessment refers to mathematical or engineering approaches of quantifying the likelihood that a particular hazard will cause harm. Assessing risk is a core component of many energy policy decisions. For example, how likely are security breaches in the electric grid, and what harms might be caused? (See Chapter 13.) How likely is it that hydraulic fracturing will contaminate groundwater supplies? (See Chapter 4.) How likely is it that radioactive materials from spent nuclear fuel will escape from a given repository and harm human health? (See Chapter 7.) Each of these questions is framed in such a way as to invite a scientific and technical assessment that can provide decision makers with information about probabilities and the magnitude of harm.

Many areas of energy policy are susceptible to "punctuating events"—significant events, sometimes even catastrophes, that prompt close attention to how we manage particular risks. A first step in responding to such events is to update risk assessments. For example, after the September 11, 2001 terrorist attacks in the United States, many federal energy agencies conducted assessments of the risks that terrorist attacks would pose to important energy infrastructure. And after the 2011 earthquake that triggered the nuclear disaster in Fukushima, Japan (see Chapter 7), NRC considered whether to revise its risk assessment requirements for nuclear power facilities regarding earthquake risks. Concepts of risk assessment also inform the minutiae of the energy landscape; for example, risk assessments are fundamental to creating design standards such as those for hydroelectric dams, nuclear reactor vessels, and oil and gas pipelines.

But risk assessment is only part of the story of energy law and policy. For a variety of reasons, people frequently *perceive* risks as being of larger or lesser magnitude than an engineering risk assessment would indicate. Researchers have documented, for example, that in simple gambling situations, people will over-predict their odds of winning and under-predict their odds of losing. We are also more likely to perceive risks to be great if they seem urgent and imminent as opposed to remote in time or space. Risks that seem catastrophic and unfamiliar—"dread risks" like radiation and chemical contamination—are perceived as greater even than those that present themselves with much more frequency, like deaths due to smoking or bicycle accidents. *See* Paul Slovic, Perception of Risk, 236 Science 280, 281 (1987).

Other risk perception mechanisms are inextricably linked to individuals' views about social ordering, their obligations towards future generations, and the role of government in society. For example, people with strong individualistic tendencies may be less likely to perceive climate change as a serious risk because doing so would invite government regulation. On the other hand, when presented with market-based mechanisms as a way of mitigating climate change, individualists may be more likely to perceive the risk itself more seriously. People with strong egalitarian tendencies may be more likely to perceive nuclear power as a serious risk because they believe it means that disadvantaged groups or future generations will be singled out to bear the brunt of nuclear policy decisions. But when compared to the risks associated with coal-fired power's greenhouse gas emissions and contributions to climate change, egalitarians may perceive the risks of nuclear power as diminished in magnitude. *See* Dan M. Kahan, Hank Jenkins-Smith, & Donald Braman, Cultural Cognition of Scientific Consensus, 9 J. Risk Res. 1 (2010).

A major concern about risk perception is that it can lead to inefficient levels of regulation, but as a practical matter, perceptions about risk cannot be ignored because they factor so strongly into energy policy decisions. Deciding whether and how to address a particular risk relates to risk *management*. Because hazards always exist, it is impossible to entirely eliminate a risk. But risk management mechanisms are meant to decrease the likelihood of a harm, its magnitude, or both. There is considerable overlap in the means of reducing externalities set forth above, and the potential options for risk management. The risk concepts described here, however, add nuances that both help explain energy policy choices that have already been made, and suggest additional ways of thinking about the policy choices that must be made going forward. As should be evident, risk assessments can give probabilities. However, they cannot eliminate uncertainty about the unknown or unknowable. The energy choices society makes may be informed by risk assessments, but the ultimate decisions in light of uncertainty reflect perceptions, values, and broader views about appropriate means of governance.

4.   PUBLIC GOVERNANCE OF ENERGY RESOURCES

A final theme that recurs throughout the history of energy law is who governs these problems: Is federal regulation necessary and when? Do the land use implications of many energy issues, and the localized nature of the impacts of electricity generation and fuel extraction, mean that state and local governments will always play a major role? Are some problems presented by energy resources international in scale, and what does that mean? Can any one regulator solve complex energy issues, or will a hybrid governance model always be necessary?

a.   FEDERAL AGENCIES

The twentieth century saw a significant growth in the expansion of federal regulation of energy resources. At the federal level, no single agency has plenary authority to address the full range of issues presented by energy resources. At the national level, energy policy is managed by DOE, a Cabinet-level agency which sponsors energy research and plays a key role in addressing international issues involving energy. While the Secretary of DOE is appointed by the President, and has a seat at the highest level of the executive branch, DOE exercises powers delegated by Congress and is constrained by limited statutory authority, leaving it unable to solve most issues on its own. DOE also must work with some independent agencies such as FERC, which administers the Natural Gas Act and Federal Power Act (FPA), among others. FERC also regulates the construction of hydroelectric facilities and oversees the rates of natural gas and electricity to the extent they are transported in interstate commerce. Further, FERC articulates policies for the structure of natural gas and electric power markets. NRC, as mentioned above, regulates the construction and operation of nuclear power plants.

Since their creation, these agencies have focused heavily on promoting stability in economic aspects of energy resources, but increasingly federal agencies are also being challenged to address some externality and risk issues associated with energy resources. Environmental pollution issues are largely regulated by agencies such as the Environmental Protection Agency (EPA) (which administers the CAA and CWA). EPA administers a variety of environmental programs that affect energy: for example, the CAA has a major impact on electric power plants and oil refineries, and the Oil Pollution Act affects the operation of oil tankers. Since many energy resources involve mineral rights or the rights to develop on public lands, the Department of Interior (DOI) plays a major role in formulating energy policy. DOI controls the federal lands, both onshore and offshore, from which much of our coal, oil and gas resources is extracted, and regulates the surface mining of coal.

This list is by no means a complete description of federal regulatory agencies that affect the energy industry. For example, the Department of Transportation plays a role in regulating oil pipelines, and the Department of Labor implements safety standards for coal mines. The Commodity Futures Trading Commission has jurisdiction over trading certain energy futures contracts. Most larger energy companies maintain Washington, D.C. offices, or employ legal counsel, to keep track of these regulatory programs. Energy industry lobbyists also abound.

Any major energy project, such as a new pipeline, faces challenges working with this myriad of federal agencies. Energy law practitioners need to be familiar with basic administrative law principles, but to be effective they need to be especially sensitive to the obligations and opportunities that federal agencies have to coordinate, or work together, in resolving disputes. For example, building a transmission line may require the approval of as many as nine different federal agencies. Conversely, the failure of federal regulation with respect to many energy issues might be described as a coordination failure—a good example might be the worst oil spill in U.S. history, which polluted the Gulf of Mexico during 2010, and which was traced in part to a failure in cooperation between the activities of various federal agencies (see Chapter 4).

b.   STATE AND LOCAL AGENCIES

Energy law is also immersed in federalism issues. State and local regulation of energy resources has always been important because energy has a major impact on land in its production and delivery. Although federal programs have expanded significantly, state systems of public utility regulation have not been replaced by federal regulation. State PUCs continue to regulate the rates, facilities, and services of the private utilities that supply natural gas and electricity within the state.

Defining the precise line between state and federal jurisdiction has produced a great deal of litigation—with respect to almost every type of energy resource. The climate change context raises particularly difficult governance issues in deciding whether federal or state agencies—or both—should address this complex set of problems.

State governments also have environmental regulatory agencies that administer state programs and cooperate with EPA in administering federal programs. For example, in cooperation with EPA, state agencies set water quality standards that have a major impact on the disposal of wastes from energy resource production. In some instances, federal statutes may give even greater power to states. State oil and gas conservation commissions regulate most aspects of well drilling and production under state laws designed to control the wasteful aspects of the common-law rule of capture. State natural resource agencies also participate in many energy resource decisions, such as developing hydropower, that may affect wildlife. In the West, where many states own large tracts of land, state land agencies are also major players.

At the local level (where municipal governments or counties have regulatory authority), energy companies often must comply with a wide range of land use regulations. Construction of new power lines, for example, is likely to run into local concerns that may be expressed through prohibitory regulations. Even rooftop solar panels or backyard wind generators have sometimes run afoul of local zoning laws. In some states, state laws have preempted these local regulations. Where permitted, many local governments also have detailed ordinances addressing safety and environmental issues associated with oil and gas drilling.

Some local governments operate their own electricity or gas distribution systems. Historically, federal and state legislatures have often granted incentives such as tax exemptions and inexpensive loans to municipal electric facilities and rural cooperatives, and have relieved them from some forms of regulation.

Local governments also exercise power over electric and gas companies through control over the local street that the companies need to use for delivery of services. In many places, local governments use regulatory programs as a revenue-raising device by adding various fees to consumers' utility bills. For people in many local communities, both in the United States and in rapidly developing countries like China, India and Brazil, the presence of urban sprawl, dying species, traffic congestion and unhealthy air arouse a public desire for greener communities, better mass transit, energy-saving appliances—and perhaps even a less frantic pace of life?

When are we likely to see state or local regulation favored over national or international approaches? State or local regulation makes sense in contexts where the impacts of energy activities are likely to vary based on geography, where they are focused on a particular jurisdiction, or where the expertise needed to manage these activities is geographically confined. In addition, local regulation has been favored over federal regulation because local governments might be more "adaptive" in their ability to solve problems. For example, state and local agencies have been quicker out of the gate in addressing problems such as climate change—a trend some in environmental law have praised as "adaptive federalism." *See* David E. Adelman & Kirsten Engel, Adaptive Federalism: The Case Against Reallocating Environmental Regulatory Authority, 92 Minn. L. Rev. 1796 (2008).

In instances where there is light-handed federal regulation of an activity—in hydraulic fracturing, for example—local regulation plays a significant role in managing energy resources and their externalities. Even where there is federal regulation, local governments often play an overlapping role with federal regulators. For example, many federal statutes envision local governments providing input to federal regulators, and in some instances local governments may have veto authority over energy projects, even where the federal government favors them.

c.   FEDERALISM CHALLENGES

Where state or local governments continue to play a role in energy resource management, challenging legal issues can be presented. Subnational regulation may create negative spillover costs—a type of externality, albeit one created by jurisdictional lines—for other states or regions that outweigh any benefits associated with state or local control. In the Northeast, for example, pollution from automobiles may spill over from one state to another, and this may invite some type of federal or regional solution. In addition, economies of scale in production may transcend state borders. For example, although the pollution from automobiles may not drift from one state to another outside of the densely populated Northeast, automobile production does exhibit significant economies of scale: the cost per vehicle of meeting one uniform regulation is much lower than the costs of meeting multiple regulations in multiple states. *See* Margaret A. Walls, U.S. Energy and Environmental Policies: Problems of Federalism and Conflicting Goals, in Making National Energy Policy 95 (Hans H. Landsberg, ed. 1993). *But see* Richard L. Revesz, Rehabilitating Interstate Competition: Rethinking the 'Race to the Bottom' Rationale for Federal Environmental Regulation, 67 N.Y.U. L. Rev. 1210 (1992). Where these spillover effects are international, they may demand a federal or even international response. Mining wastes from Canada may flow downstream to the United States; power plants in Mexico may pollute Texas air and U.S. plants may pollute Canadian air. Greenhouse gases emitted anywhere on the globe affect all of its inhabitants.

Several federalism issues have been litigated across a range of energy resources, and inform the ongoing significance of federalism to resolving many issues in energy law.

First, how much judicial deference is appropriate to a Congressional determination that an activity is within its commerce power? In *United States v. Lopez*, 514 U.S. 549 (1995), a 5–4 decision decided in 1995, the U.S. Supreme Court held invalid a federal statute that criminalized the possession of a gun in a local school zone as beyond Congress's power under the Commerce Clause of the Constitution. The Court reasoned that the statute did not regulate an economic activity that had a "substantial effect" on interstate commerce. After *Lopez*, can the federal government require states to consider certain conservation criteria in approving power plant expansion plans for municipal utilities selling power locally? In some cases, the Tenth Amendment, which reserves to the states those powers not given to the federal government, remains an important mechanism for challenging energy regulation. *See, e.g.*, New York v. United States, 505 U.S. 144 (1992); FERC v. Mississippi, 456 U.S. 742 (1982).

Second, a state regulatory program may favor one state's economic interests at the expense of the citizens of another state. Such action may violate the "dormant" commerce clause—a judicially created doctrine that has been inferred from the text of the Commerce Clause. For example, in *New England Power Co. v. New Hampshire*, 455 U.S. 331 (1982), the Supreme Court held that a state prohibition on the export of locally generated hydropower was unconstitutional because it favored New Hampshire citizens at the expense of out-of-state citizens. In another case, the Illinois legislature passed a law that required air quality compliance plans filed by large in-state utilities to consider scrubber installation at their power plants, favoring the usage of Illinois coal in electricity generation facilities. The Court of Appeals for the Seventh Circuit struck the statute down because it discriminated against out-of-state coal producers. *See* Alliance for Clean Coal v. Miller, 44 F.3d 591 (7th Cir. 1995). As the states become more concerned about air pollution flowing between the states and about promoting renewable energy resources, dormant commerce clause challenges are likely to become more common in the electricity regulation context—especially as states attempt to regulate externalities associated with activities in other jurisdictions.

Third, a state's regulatory initiatives may be preempted by a federal law or regulatory program. *See, e.g.*, Pacific Gas & Electric Co. v. Energy Resources and Development Comm'n, 461 U.S. 190 (1983). Under the Supremacy Clause of the U.S. Constitution, the federal law takes precedence over the state regulation. Since the 1930s, Congress has had the authority to regulate purely intrastate activities that affect interstate commerce, such as electricity generation and natural gas production, transmission, and distribution. In many instances, Congress has chosen not to regulate certain energy resource uses. For example, FERC's rate jurisdiction over electricity rates under the FPA extends only to wholesale transactions; Congress has left most matters of retail rate regulation to the states. This dual regulatory scheme inevitably creates a conflict and has led to much litigation.

Even absent any federal regulation, local governments may face challenges to their own authority within a particular state jurisdiction— a form of federalism internal to each state. For example, local governments have faced challenges over bans on hydraulic fracturing activities based on whether a state legislature must delegate such authority or has the power to prohibit such bans, or whether this is an inherently local power in states that recognize home rule for municipal governments.

d.   THE RISE OF REGIONAL AND INTERNATIONAL GOVERNANCE OF ENERGY

With increased recognition that many problems associated with energy are global rather than local, the ability of state and national regulators to solve these problems on their own is increasingly called into question. Some of the most effective responses to these problems recognize that the scale of many modern energy problems transcends the power of individual jurisdictions to solve them on their own.

Within the United States, one response to this jurisdictional mismatch has been to recognize that energy disputes are increasingly regional in scope, or require some kind of hybrid governance solution. For example, some energy issues such as the disposal of low-level nuclear waste have been addressed through Interstate Compacts, or agreements between states that are authorized by Congress (see Chapter 7). Less formal cooperation between state governors and regulators has also been pursued as ways for states to resolve issues on their own at the regional level. A good example of this is the Regional Greenhouse Gas Initiative in the Northeastern United States—a cooperative agreement among nine states to cap and reduce carbon dioxide emissions from the electric power sector. In the electric power sector, there are also significant private agreements between utilities operating across multiple state jurisdictions that allow private governance between firms to solve some federalism problems.

Another response to the jurisdictional mismatch problem with national regulation has been an expansion of international law in steering energy policy. International law has played several distinct roles for energy resources. One prominent role has been using treaties as a way for nation states to share information, as occurs in the context of nuclear power risk assessment.

Another role for international law has been to help set goals and aspirations, as has occurred in the assessment of climate change risks by the Intergovernmental Panel on Climate Change (IPCC). International law has also shaped norms, especially with respect to climate change regulation, where individual nation states have made commitments that later influenced the adoption of domestic targets and policies.

These information-sharing and aspirational roles have been significant, but the binding nature of international law in setting a course for energy policy cannot be underestimated. Examples abound: The International Energy Program Agreement, which commits the United States to plan for energy emergencies by maintaining strategic oil reserves and to provide assistance through the International Energy Agency in case of emergency situations; and the Nuclear Non-Proliferation Treaty and the programs of the International Atomic Energy Agency, which require the United States to restrict certain nuclear and related exports to nonsignatory countries and provide for international inspection systems. The United States also has entered into bilateral treaties and agreements with significant obligations concerning energy resources with Canada, Mexico, Venezuela, and Israel.

Notably, international law is also being used to limit domestic law regarding energy policy; for example, international trade law has been deployed as a limit on domestic subsidies for a variety of energy industries, including, most recently, renewable energy. Federal or state regulation of energy resources may conflict with U.S. obligations under international law. Among these obligations are the General Agreement on Tariffs and Trade (GATT) and the North American Free Trade Agreement (NAFTA), which prevent the United States from unilaterally imposing impediments to trade with most of its energy trading partners (see Chapter 14).

C. TOWARDS A PORTFOLIO OF ENERGY STRATEGIES

The environmental consequences of energy resources are significant, and the challenges in addressing them are daunting. For example, developing energy resources in the tropical rainforest affects global biodiversity. Massive tanker spills know no national boundaries. Dust clouds and pollution from China reach California's shores. The most troublesome issue for the energy sector is the increasingly strong evidence that the combustion of fossil fuels will increase global temperatures and cause rising sea levels. How are the nearly two billion people on earth who are currently living a subsistence lifestyle, without any access to electricity, to be provided an acceptable standard of living as climate change threatens to bring increased droughts and floods in many of the poorest areas of the world? Adaptation to climate change is a new job for land use planners, agronomists, and levee builders.

For energy users and producers, the first major issue is whether and how greenhouse gas emissions can be slowed down or leveled off. The second issue is how people and all other living things will adapt to what many see as the inevitable changes in the earth's landscape caused by global warming, even if strong efforts are made to lower greenhouse gas emissions, particularly emissions of carbon dioxide.

There is no simple energy solution to the problem of climate change. In an important article, Robert Socolow and Stephen Pacala illustrate how, with current technologies, it may be possible to stabilize carbon emissions at or below current levels. Stephen Pacala and Robert Socolow, Stabilization Wedges: Solving the Climate Problem for the Next 50 Years With Current Technologies, Science, Aug. 13, 2004, at 968. To begin, they highlight how a significant change in behavior represented by a "stabilization triangle"—maintaining emissions flat for 50 years—will require cutting projected carbon output significantly. **Figure 1–4** illustrates the "stabilization triangle" that is created by the gap between the world's current path of increased carbon emissions (the "ramp" up) and the flat line representing no additional tons emitted after 2004.

What technologies will enable the world to follow the flat path versus the ramp up? Prior to the publication of their article, much focus was on finding a "silver bullet" to avert climate change. But climate change will require a multifaceted solution. According to Socolow and Pacala, at least 15 strategies are available today, each of which can reduce carbon emissions by about 1 billion tons per year by 2054. Each of these 15 technologies is called a "carbon wedge" that, when added together, form the stabilization triangle of avoided emissions—the emissions that do not occur. To stabilize emissions, only 8 wedges of 1 billion tons of avoided carbon are needed. To reduce emissions rather than merely stabilize them, policies can be adopted to use all the technologies. Many experts now believe that so much carbon dioxide is already in the atmosphere (where it lingers for more than 100 years) that the developed countries must actually reduce their emissions by an astounding 50% to 80% by 2050, in conjunction with significant reductions by countries such as China, India and Brazil.

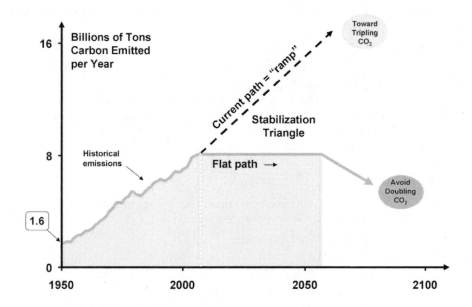

Figure 1–4
Carbon Stabilization Triangle
Source: Princeton Carbon Mitigation Initiative:
http://cmi.princeton.edu/wedges/intro.php

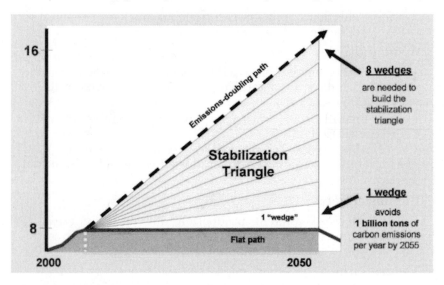

Figure 1–5
Stabilization Triangle With "Wedges"
Source: Princeton Carbon Mitigation Initiative:
http://cmi.princeton.edu/wedges/intro.php

The task is daunting, but Socolow and Pacala insist that it is possible with existing technologies, and urge the adoption of policies that will put many of these stabilization wedges in place. Here is a list of the 15 wedges, each of which reduce emissions by 1 billion tons of carbon per year:

Efficiency

1. Double fuel efficiency of 2 billion cars from 30 miles per gallon (mpg) to 60 mpg.
2. Decrease the number of car miles traveled by half.
3. Use best efficiency practices in all residential and commercial buildings.
4. Produce coal-based electricity with twice today's efficiency.

Fuel Switching

5. Replace 1,400 coal-powered electric-generating plants with natural gas-powered facilities.

Carbon Capture and Storage

6. Capture and permanently store underground the CO_2 emissions from 800 coal-fired electric plants.
7. Produce hydrogen from coal at six times today's rate and store the captured CO_2, using the hydrogen as clean-burning fuel.
8. Produce synthetic fuels from 180 coal-to-synfuels plants and capture and store the CO_2.

Nuclear

9. Add double the current global nuclear capacity to replace coal-based electricity.

Wind and Solar

10. Increase wind electricity capacity by 50 times relative to today, for a total of 2 million large windmills by 2054.
11. Install 700 times the current capacity of solar electricity.
12. Use 40,000 square kilometers of solar panels (or 4 million windmills) to produce hydrogen for fuel cell cars.

Biomass Fuels

13. Increase ethanol production 50 times by creating biomass plantations with an area equal to 1/6th of the world's current cropland.

Natural Sinks

14. Eliminate tropical deforestation and double the current rate of new forest planting.
15. Adopt conservation tillage in all agricultural soils worldwide.

Not everyone is as optimistic that we can reduce carbon emissions so readily. Since the publication of the initial Socolow and Pacala article, carbon emissions have increased. Pacala and Socolow's premise was that stabilizing emissions at 2004 levels would be sufficient to meet a target of 500 parts per million, but emissions have increased over the past seven years from about seven gigatons to about nine gigatons annually. Thus, it is no longer a matter of stabilizing emissions, but of lowering them to meet the target of 500 parts per million. This would require more than twice the number of wedges Socolow and Pacala initially envisioned. In addition, many in the global community have begun to call into question the idea of a carbon emissions target of 500 parts per million, suggesting that the challenge is even more onerous. For these reasons, some have questioned Socolow and Pacala's conclusion that existing technologies are sufficient to address climate change and have argued that there is an urgent need for new innovation. *See* Steve Davis, et al., Rethinking Wedges, 8 Envtl. Res. Letters 1 (2013).

Whether it draws from existing technologies or new innovations, any carbon wedge solution will come with its own set of environmental and economic problems. The Socolow/Pacala article does not offer cost comparisons or environmental effects to help policymakers choose among the wedges. Their wedges simply represent what current technologies could do, if implemented, regardless of cost or externalities. Yet, many of the wedges require the use of large amounts of water and land and some require large amounts of additional energy to transport and store CO_2 underground in what is called carbon capture and sequestration (CCS). No path to addressing the effects of climate change is completely carbon neutral or without some of its own impacts on carbon emissions.

Climate change is indeed a daunting problem. Slowing its pace and adapting to its reality will have a pervasive influence on energy law in the coming decades. To add to the complexity, addressing climate change is not the only goal that the United States is focusing on as it develops its energy strategies for the future. It is also focused on keeping energy prices low. Ensuring a reliable and stable energy supply is a priority too. Promoting domestic industries, including energy resources and firms that use them, also is a priority for many. And goals like energy independence and sustainability in energy resources often take precedence as well. Sometimes these goals converge with addressing climate change but that is rare. The tension among these goals across various issues in energy law adds richness to our discussions about our energy future, and ensures the need for informed lawyers to navigate the path to solutions for decades to come.

CHAPTER 2

PUBLIC UTILITY PRINCIPLES AND AN OVERVIEW OF THE ELECTRIC POWER INDUSTRY

A. HISTORICAL DEVELOPMENT OF THE ELECTRIC UTILITY

Historically, the United States relied largely upon fossil fuels to power industrial processes and to heat homes. The twentieth century saw a major shift toward electricity as a source of energy for households and many industrial uses, rather than primary energy resources such as oil and gas. After introducing basic principles of public utility regulation, this chapter will present the electric power industry as a context for addressing them. The electric industry is in the midst of rapid and ongoing changes, as later chapters illustrate. Later chapters in the book will address the economic and environmental changes confronting the modern electric power industry. An appreciation of the role and scope of public utility regulation is fundamental to understanding how the legal and regulatory system has influenced infrastructure and innovation in the electric power industry.

1. EARLY ELECTRIC TECHNOLOGY

Water power, wind, sunlight, geothermal heat, wood, coal, oil, and natural gas are "primary" forms of energy resources. They are found in nature, and their energy can be used directly. When energy is used to directly power something or to produce heat, such as burning oil in a furnace to heat a building or gasoline in a gas tank to move a car, this is called "primary" energy use.

By contrast common forms of production for electricity is what is known as a "secondary" energy use—to the extent it depends on primary energy uses such as burning fuel. Electricity is also found in nature, as Benjamin Franklin proved in the mid-18th century with his famous experiment in which he flew a kite during a thunderstorm to determine whether lightning was in fact electricity. But our ability to harness natural electricity for useful residential and commercial purposes has been very limited. For all practical purposes, we make our electricity from one of the primary energy resources listed above or from nuclear fission, to be discussed in Chapter 7.

James Trefil, A Scientist in the City
(Doubleday, 1994).

Electricity is different from other kinds of energy. When you turn on a light or use an electric tool, you don't need the source of the energy in the same building. In fact, the energy that drives the lights that allow you to read this book was probably generated some tens (if not hundreds) of miles from where you are sitting. Electricity provides a way of separating the generation of energy from its use.

Our modern electrically driven society owes its existence to an English scientist named Michael Faraday. In a series of experiments in 1831, he discovered that when a magnet is moved, an electric current will flow in wires near it. This discovery, part of Faraday's basic research into the nature of electricity, made it possible to build machines that could convert the energy stored in coal into electric energy carried in wires.

A simple generator [is] the device that carries out this conversion. A loop of wires is spun around between the poles of a magnet. From the point of view of someone on the loop, the magnet is always moving, so a current will always flow—first one way, then the other. This so-called alternating current (AC) can be run through wires to the place where it is to be used. To get the electricity from a power plant to your house may require that it travel through many miles of wire, from huge power lines on pylons to the smaller wires that bring it into your home to the little cord that runs from the wall to your lamp.

So long as you have an energy source that can make a shaft spin, you can use that energy to produce electricity. The most common technique is to boil water to make high-pressure steam and then squirt that steam against curved blades attached to the spinning shaft (a device like this is called a steam turbine). It makes no difference how you make the steam—it can be (and is) done routinely by burning coal, oil, or gas, or by extracting heat from a nuclear reactor. You can also turn the shaft by damming a river and then letting water fall from a great height onto the turbine blades.

Today, the advantages of electricity for supplying a city's energy are so obvious that there would seem little point in arguing about them. When electricity was first produced commercially in the late nineteenth century, however, it was far from clear that it would prevail over its competitors. The first use of electricity was for lighting, one of the landmarks of urban electrification occurring in Chicago on April 25, 1878, when a jury-rigged system of batteries and lamps lit up Michigan Avenue for the first time. The demonstration showed up both the strengths and weaknesses of the new technology. The lights used weren't the steady incandescent lights we're accustomed to today but, rather, the kind of carbon arc lights now used only for searchlights and stage lighting. They produce light by passing an electric spark between two cone-shaped carbon rods. In the Chicago demonstration, the result was an intense light: the two electric lamps produced an illumination equivalent to over 600 gas lamps. But they required constant adjustment as the carbon rods burned down. In addition, electrical systems in those days were unreliable in the extreme. The night after that first successful illumination in Chicago, for example, the whole system burned out, and it was months before another demonstration could take place.

The first people to use electrical power in a big way were stores and hotels in downtown business districts. At this stage of development, the main question was whether electricity would be generated locally, by each user, or whether there would be a central utility selling electricity to customers. Many businesses (Wanamaker's store in Philadelphia and the Palmer House hotel in Chicago, for example) installed their own generators. The first central power station was built by Charles Brush in San Francisco in 1879, but at that time the price of copper wire was so high that it was only economical to deliver electricity about half a mile— 8 city blocks.

You can't imagine a city with generating plants every 16 blocks. Before our modern system could emerge, with its far-flung power plants and long transmission lines, a huge number of engineering advances had to take place. There's no single thing you can point to and say, "Here's the invention that made it all happen." Instead, there was a steady progression of nickel-and-dime developments that made it possible to generate electricity in large amounts and send it out over long distances—a better valve on a generator here, a better switch on a transmission line there. In the end, such developments wound up not only beating out gas lamps but giving our cities an entirely new shape.

There is no question that electricity is the energy form of choice for urban America. The energy history of our cities over the past century has seen the constant displacement of direct burning of fuels by electricity. The gas lamps were the first to go, except in "olde townes," where they are kept for their historical associations. They were followed by steam-powered factories and steam locomotives, and it probably won't be long before the gasoline-powered automobile joins the list. Let's face it: there's something very attractive about having energy available when you want it, while someone else has to deal with the pollution and other social costs of its generation. ∎

When we think of the history of electricity in the United States the first name on everybody's lips is that of Thomas Alva Edison. After hundreds of hours of failed experiments with different materials, cotton sewing thread was carefully carbonized, inserted into a glass evacuated by suction pump and connected to electricity supply form a dynamo. The light bulb "burned like an evening star," and we have the exact beginning of a new era for civilization: October 21, 1879. Vaclav Smil, Energies 158–159, The MIT Press (1999).

The great inventor of the light bulb, the phonograph and countless other products was also a pioneer in the generation and distribution of electricity. In 1882, when his company's Pearl Street generating station first delivered electric light to buildings throughout Wall Street, he became a national hero. Neil Baldwin, Edison: Inventing the Century (Hyperion, 1995).

Edison's talents were more on the creative side than on the management side. Credit for the development of the management model for delivering electricity that prevailed throughout the 20th century—the vertically integrated public utility monopoly—is generally given to one of Edison's lieutenants, Samuel Insull, who left Edison's employ in 1892 to assume the presidency of Chicago Edison Co. The great depression of 1893 hit the company hard, but Insull handled it well and led the company, which became Commonwealth Edison, until the depression of the 1930s, turning it into a widely copied model of corporate organization.

As you read the following excerpts from Harold Platt's book on Insull and his successors (a book that is well worth reading in full) ask yourself whether the key ideas that Insull developed are still appropriate to today's conditions; in particular, (1) the "central station" concept, in which electricity is generated at a central power plant and distributed to customers by wires, and (2) the demand/commodity rate design, which is discussed further in Chapter 8.

Harold L. Platt, The Electric City
(University of Chicago Press, 1991).

In spite of Edison's faith in the central station concept, electrical technology seemed to contain inherent diseconomies of scale. Practical experience continued to accumulate in favor of the self-contained, "isolated" plant for the large consumer of electric lighting. Unit costs (and hence rates) were highest for small consumers, since they made the least efficient use of the station's generating equipment. As more lights were burned for longer periods, the cost of a unit of electricity—expressed as a kilowatt-hour (kWh)—declined. When the equipment was used more fully, the utility's huge capital costs were spread over more units of electricity, making each unit cheaper to generate. The resulting equation between rates and costs appeared to point irreversibly toward the eventual triumph of the self-contained system. As a customer's use increased, it would reach a point where significant savings could be gained from disconnecting the utility lines and purchasing a self-contained system of the appropriate size. In response, utility companies could offer discounts to large consumers, but at the expense of shifting a heavier burden of capital costs onto the small consumers. The result would be rates beyond the reach of most city dwellers who badly wanted to install the new technology.

More than any other individual, Samuel Insull solved the problems inherent in electrical technology and put the central station on a sound economic footing. Great ambition, international background, apprenticeship with Edison, and faith in technological progress combined to give the English immigrant a unique perspective on the problems facing local utility operators . . . in the years leading up to his arrival in Chicago in 1892. . . .

The state of the electrical industry in Chicago at the time of Insull's arrival can be described simply as one of chaotic growth. He would have to use all his considerable skills and talents to prove the superiority of the central station approach to meeting the city's electrical energy needs. . . . Within municipal borders alone, the city inspector's report of 1892 listed 18 central stations and 498 self-contained systems that were powering a total of 273,600 incandescent lights and 16,415 arc lamps . . .

The resulting crazy quilt of small distribution grids growing out from jerry-built central stations raised serious doubts about the ability of any single utility company to attain the economies of scale necessary to beat the competition of the self-contained system and cheaper sources of light and power. Perhaps the greatest shortcoming of the Edison system was its DC distributors. They used low voltage or "pressure," which made transmission at a distance extremely costly in terms of copper wiring and energy losses. The DC grid works much like a system of water mains. Larger and larger mains are needed to pump water to more distant points at a constant pressure. In a similar way, the diameter of the copper cables had to be enlarged in proportion to increases in both the size of the electrical load and the distance of transmission. . . .

Operators of Edison systems faced a challenge even more threatening to their futures after the appearance in 1886 of an entirely new electrical technology using alternating current (AC). As the name implies, a generator creates a flow of electricity that rapidly alternates back and forth in a circuit. In contrast, in a DC system electricity flows in a single direction around a circuit. The critical, practical difference between the two was the unequivocal superiority of AC for transmitting electricity at a distance. Alternating current could be sent efficiently at high voltage or "pressure," which meant that comparatively inexpensive thin copper cables could be used without suffering unacceptable energy losses. The transmission of energy became increasingly efficient as the voltage was raised. To achieve high-voltage transmission, a passive device called a transformer was used, first to boost the voltages at the generator station for long-distance transmission and then to reduce it for local distribution at the service area.

Championed by George Westinghouse, the AC system threatened a fatal economic blow to the backers of Edison's DC technology. In the late 1880s, local companies using Westinghouse equipment began operating in middle-class communities such as Englewood on the South Side and Evanston on the northern border of the city. The applications of the early AC systems were restricted to incandescent lights and did not include practical motors or streetlamps, but the obvious advantages of the AC distribution grids made the technology ideal for the metropolitan area's vast expanse of low-density residential housing.

Over the next five years of depression and crisis between 1893 and 1898, Insull completed his plan to acquire all the central stations and their franchises in the Loop. Hard times undoubtedly helped persuade the small companies to sell out, especially since Insull followed a policy of offering generous terms. In most cases the equipment of these shoestring operators was simply junked, and the customers were connected to the Edison company lines. Added together with new light and power business in the Loop, the growth of the utility was extremely impressive during a period of general economic distress. For example, the Harrison Street Station had to be expanded by 167 percent from a maximum output of 2,400 to 6,400 KW to keep up with the peak demand. The use of electricity rose from 6.6 million kWh in 1893 to almost 11 million kWh in 1897, an average annual increase in consumption of about 18 percent.

But to Insull's dismay, generating all the CBD's [Central Business District of Chicago's] electric business by a modern central station did not save enough to undercut the competition of self-contained systems, let alone gas lighting in the home. To be sure, the Harrison Street Station, with its more economical engines, generators, and fuel-handling equipment, could be expected to reduce the company's operating costs. And the growth of demand in the Loop would probably repay the investment capital sunk in the copper transmission line to link the riverfront plant to the Adams Street building. Yet, as Insull admitted, "no one in the central station business at that time really understood its fundamental economics."

During the depression, rates remained at luxury levels. Complaints from businessmen about high prices replaced the initial enthusiasm for the novel technology. Even in the homes of the affluent middle classes, the common practice was to use electric illumination only in the parlor when guests were present. After they left the light bulbs would be turned off, leaving the gas jets lit in the living quarters. The popularity of dual gas-electric chandeliers was a testament to the high cost of better lighting in the home.

The World's Fair of 1893, however, provided important clues on how to remove these supply-side constraints. For the electricians and the scientists, Chicago's exposition had technical as well as cultural lessons [that] demonstrated the principles of a universal system of distribution. Westinghouse employed a recent invention, the rotary convertor, to convert AC to DC for use by the intramural elevated railway. When coupled with the transformer, the rotary convertor provided a technological means of removing the constraints of restricted distribution areas. Electricity generated at a central station could now be boosted to high voltage by a transformer for long-distance transmission and then changed at local substations by transformers and convertors to meet the particular needs of the distribution area. The model city of 1893 taught Insull and other electrical men in Chicago that there was no real "battle of the systems" between AC and DC. The most important lesson of the World's Fair was that the two systems could be harnessed together to deliver a complete range of electrical services throughout the city.

Insull soon applied the lessons of the model city to the real one, making Chicago Edison first or second to put the rotary convertor into commercial use. In August 1897 electricity from the Harrison Street Station was transmitted at 2,300 volts to the Twenty-seventh Street Station, converted back to DC, and fed to the homes and businesses of the Near South Side. Two years later the first true substation, containing no generating equipment, was jerry-built on the North Side to help handle periods of peak demand from 4:00 p.m. to midnight. Within a few months, the cost efficiencies convinced Insull to shut down the nearby Clark Street Station and convert it into a full-time substation.

More important, these experiments proved the feasibility of a metropolitan power network. Insull was quick to appreciate the economic implications of the new technology for supplying electrical energy at a price lower than previously possible. The combined AC–DC system suggested a hierarchy composed of a few efficient power plants and a citywide network of substations where electricity would be transformed to meet the needs of each local district. This novel concept of central station service led Insull almost immediately to expand his monopoly plans from the CBD to encompass the entire city. In just two years between 1897 and 1898, he was able to achieve this major goal owing to his control of key patent licenses and a measure of incredible good luck. . . . The resulting concept of a central station hierarchy, together with the monopoly he had obtained, put Insull on the threshold of creating a metropolitan network of power. Yet all this technical and business success would mean little unless Insull also found an answer to the riddle of rates for the large consumer as well as the small residential customer. Electric rates had to be cut sufficiently to compete with the self-contained system and cheaper sources of artificial illumination. Only then would the demand for electrical energy reach a point where true economies of scale could be achieved.

As with the rotary convertor, an invention helped Insull solve the equation of utility costs and consumer rates. But in contrast to the hardware displayed at the World's Fair, the Wright demand meter did not directly answer the question of how to undersell both the self-contained plant and the alternative sources of artificial illumination. Instead, this ingenious device provided Insull with an "aha" experience that suddenly made the pieces of the puzzle fit together. All the economic requirements to beat the competition fell into place once he grasped the peculiar, instantaneous relationship between supply and demand that is inherent in electrical systems. As Insull testified, the demand meter "first taught us how to sell electricity."

Insull first heard about the innovative measuring instrument in 1894 while visiting his homeland. Recently invented by Arthur Wright of Brighton, England, the meter recorded not only a customer's amount of consumption but also the timing and the maximum level of his demand. Intrigued by the device, Insull returned to Chicago but sent his chief electrician, Louis Ferguson, to make a thorough study of its use in Brighton. The engineer returned with an enthusiasm for the metering system that soon infected Insull. In September 1897 the Chicago Edison Company started making a practical test of the measuring device. Within a few years, Wright's invention replaced most of the utility's other meters.

The demand meter showed Insull that electric companies did not work "just as the gas companies do." On the contrary, the two were fundamentally different. The storage tanks of the gas companies allowed them to even out their production schedules and make maximum use of the equipment on a twenty-four hour cycle. In this way gas companies could keep their capital investments in central station machinery to a minimum, because there was no need for expensive but little-used equipment to meet brief periods of peak demand on the system. In contrast, electric companies had to keep an instant balance between demand and supply or suffer service blackouts and equipment damage. To be sure, storage batteries could help meet periods of peak demand, but they had serious drawbacks of their own: they were expensive, cumbersome, dangerous, and very inefficient. Whether to purchase batteries or extra generating equipment to meet periods of maximum demand remained a problem.

Helping Insull break free of his mentor's teachings, the demand meter gave him the insight to recalculate the equation between the electric utility's costs and the customers' bills. Wright's invention suggested a new method of ratemaking with a two-part bill to replace the traditional flat charge. A customer's energy consumption (the number of kilowatt-hours of electricity recorded by the meter) corresponded to the company's operating expenses. The measure of peak demand on the meter represented the customer's share of the capital invested in generating equipment that had to stand ready to serve him. The utility would use each customer's maximum demand to apportion equally the cost of financing the utility's plants and equipment. This primary charge serviced the interest payments on the company's bonded indebtedness, which constituted about 70 percent of its total expenses. The demand meter would determine the number of kilowatt-hours for which to charge each customer at the higher primary rate. A much lower secondary charge would be levied for any consumption beyond that monthly minimum number of units of electricity. The primary rates were fixed for all customers, but the secondary rates were discounted on a sliding scale to encourage greater consumption.

In this way a two-tier rate structure promised to cut the bills of both the small household and the large commercial enterprise. In effect, residential customers would pay a smaller proportion of the utility's financial costs because they had relatively small peak demands. The net result of the two-tier system would be a lower effective rate for each kilowatt-hour of energy. For the most part, the heavy burden of the utility's interest payments would be absorbed by the large consumers of light and power. At the same time, they would benefit from the discounts for heavy use of the equipment, which would progressively reduce their net rate of charge for each kilowatt-hour of electricity. In this way a two-tier system of ratemaking was structured to encourage every type of consumer to use more energy.

During the second half of 1899, Insull not only talked about the future, he began taking practical steps to get there as soon as possible. . . . The Chicago utility announced a two-tier system of rates for light and power. For the average residential customer, the new method of billing translated into an immediate 32 percent savings, or a net reduction from 19.5¢ per kWh to 13.33¢. At the same time, the utility extended a special incentive to new customers by offering to install six lighting outlets free of charge. . . . During the crisis of the nineties, rapid improvements in central station service offered comforting reassurance to a nation torn with doubt about the power of technology to promote social justice and democracy. ∎

NOTES AND COMMENTS

1.   Two physical features of electricity present serious challenges for engineers, regulators and any effort to use law to regulate it. First, on a large-scale basis it cannot be stored for long period of times. More or less, it must be consumed as it is used—requiring a constant balancing of supply and demand in managing the electric power system. Second, electrons put into the transmission and distribution system flow in the path of least resistance and, absent a dedicated distribution or transmission line for that customer, cannot be directed to a particular user. This means that, for all practical purposes, once electric power is generated and put into the grid, those electrons intermingle with other electrons, and as a physical matter users draw power from the grid independent from the source that produced it.

2.   Samuel Insull eventually built up a complex of holding companies that exercised operating control over most of the electric utilities in the United States by the 1920s. By making a large share of the stock in the actual operating companies nonvoting, Insull controlled half a billion dollars' worth of electric utility assets in 1930 with a capital investment of about 27 million dollars. Leonard S. Hyman, America's Electric Utilities: Past, Present and Future 106 (Public Utilities Reports, Inc., 6th ed. 1997).

3.   The Insull empire collapsed in the depression of the 1930s. Many of the operating companies went bankrupt and their stockholders lost their entire investment. In response, Congress passed the Public Utility Holding Company Act of 1935 (PUHCA), which gave the Securities and Exchange Commission oversight responsibility for companies that owned ten percent or more of the shares of an electric or gas utility. 15 U.S.C. § 79. This Act required utilities to obtain SEC approval before offering certain securities and conducting certain structural acquisitions and reorganizations, and to comply with various reporting requirements, among other mandates. Congress repealed PUHCA in the Energy Policy Act of 2005 (EPAct 2005).

4.   Westinghouse's alternating current (AC) system prevailed in the so-called "war of the currents" because it was considered the more economical of the two systems. Nikola Tesla, a brilliant inventor who worked for Westinghouse for a time, was a very early booster of the AC distribution system, and is credited with inventing several of the key pieces of equipment that ultimately made the system so efficient and economical.

2.   WHY TREAT ELECTRIC POWER AS A "PUBLIC UTILITY"?

The "public utility" is a very important legal concept for energy lawyers—not only in confronting the history of energy infrastructure and its regulation but also in addressing modern issues such as energy markets and their regulation and especially the development of renewable energy projects. Understanding the bedrock principles of public utility law can be helpful in framing issues today as old infrastructure is challenged by new technologies.

Public utilities are often privately owned. Yet, in contrast to other privately-owned businesses, public utilities are controlled by a different set of economic and legal expectations. These privately owned companies are called "public" because they are "affected with a public interest," in that they provide a service of great public need and tend to require expensive, centralized, shared infrastructure to provide this service. The phrase "affected with a public interested" was used in early English legal writings and endorsed in *Munn v. Illinois*, 94 U.S. 113 (1877), which involved grain elevators—a business once viewed as essential to the public.

Today, statutes and regulations largely determine the benefits and burdens that attach to public utilities, but the concept of the public utility has a rich history in the common law and regulation. The principle characteristics of public utilities are of relevance in determining the extent of benefits and burdens for many modern energy firms and how these firms are regulated.

Infrastructure projects such as ferries, sewers, mills, bridges, and railroads provide the historical origins for modern public utility regulation. Although sometimes these were government owned and operated, in many, if not most instances, they were privately owned in England and early America.

As the concept of the public utility is introduced, it is helpful to ask why for most of the twentieth century electric power was considered a public utility and was regulated in this manner. Was Insull's central station approach a necessity for electric power and why? What assumptions does this depend on?

As a contrasting example, consider whether governments should regulate retail gasoline prices. As prices at the pump have risen, some politicians have suggested that gasoline prices should be regulated. Such proposals for regulation would treat gasoline distributed at the pump as a public utility, setting limits on the price of gasoline. Hawaii, for example, has passed a law that places a cap on gasoline prices. While proposals to regulate the price of gas at the pump have been floated in political discussions—and some have been passed into law—their success is questionable.

So why is gasoline distribution not generally considered a public utility? Why would its treatment differ from other energy resources, such as natural gas and electric power, which most state regulators treated as public utilities? Looking to the historical examples of public utilities, can you identify aspects of these business services that differ from other private businesses, such as farming, smartphone manufacturing, or hotel and restaurant operation? Think about these questions as you are studying the historical development of the legal principles regarding public utilities.

a.   THE ROLE OF EXCLUSIVE MONOPOLY

Public utilities are often treated as exclusive monopolies. On one hand, this means that the public utility is protected from competition by other firms, at least insofar as those other firms are encroaching on the utility's monopoly. On the other hand, granting a monopoly franchise entails a responsibility to society. These privileges and responsibilities were frequently the subject of litigation in the development of public utility law.

Tripp v. Frank

100 Eng. Rep. 1234 (1792).

■ This was an action on the case, wherein the plaintiff declared, that he was possessed of South Ferry, over the Humber; and that the defendant wrongfully carried persons and cattle from Kingston upon Hull to Barton, and other parts of the coast, whereby the plaintiff was injured in his right to his ferry, and lost his tolls. . . . At the trial before Buller, J. at the last assizes for York, it appeared that the defendant, who was the owner of a marketboat at Barrow, had carried over persons. . . . from Kingston upon Hull to Barrow, to which place they were going, and which lies two miles lower down the Humber than Barton, upon the same coast. It was shown that there was a daily ferry between Kingston and Barton, but none to any other part of the Lincolnshire coast. A verdict was taken for the plaintiff of 1 shilling with liberty for the defendant to enter a nonsuit in case the Court should be of opinion that the plaintiff was not entitled to recover under these circumstances.

[Plaintiff's counsel argued] that if the conduct of the defendant could be justified in this instance, it would render a right of ferry perfectly nugatory. Every person then, by going a little to the right or left of the usual track of the ferry, may equally avoid the ferry: but that would annihilate the right itself. Ferries in general must have some considerable extent upon which their right may operate, otherwise the exclusive privilege would be of no avail. . . . The owners of ferries are bound at their peril to supply them for the public use; and are therefore fairly entitled to preserve the exclusive advantage arising from them. But they admitted, on a question being asked by the Court, that the ferryman was not compellable to provide boats to any place on the Lincolnshire coasts besides Barton.

LORD KENYON, CH.J.—It seems to me that the evidence does not support this action. If certain persons wishing to go to Barton had applied to the defendant, and he had carried them at a little distance above or below the ferry, it would have been a fraud on the plaintiff's right, and would be the ground of an action. But here these persons were substantially, and not colourably merely, carried over to a different place; and it is absurd to say that no person shall be permitted to go to any other place on the Humber than that to which the plaintiff chooses to carry them. It is now admitted that the ferryman cannot be compelled to carry passengers to any other place than Barton: then his right must be commensurate with his duty.

■ ASHHURST. J.—The plaintiff's claim is so unreasonable, that it cannot be supported. According to his argument, if a passenger wishes to cross over from Kingston to the Lincolnshire coast three miles eastward, he must necessarily be first carried to Barton, where he would be many miles distant from his place of destination; whereas, if it were not for this ferry, he might go over directly. But the admission which the counsel have made is decisive against the plaintiff.

■ BULLER, J.—The question here is, what right the plaintiff has established by evidence; and that extends only from Hull to Barton, and back again. The question of fraud might arise in this way; by saying that, though the defendant really meant to go to Barton, he went in fraud of the plaintiff's claim a little above or below the ferry. But in this case the defendant had no intention of going to Barton: his place of destination was Barrow, at the distance of two miles from Barton; to which place the plaintiff's right does not extend, and to which he says he is not compellable to go.

■ GROSE, J. of the same opinion.

Rule discharged. ■

NOTES AND COMMENTS

1.   What is the remedy where a monopoly franchise owner's legal rights have been invaded? What is the benefit of granting an exclusive monopoly and why would the government do this? Why wouldn't it want to encourage competitors to carry passengers across a river, rather than authorize a single ferry to do so?

2.   The feudal system in England allowed the monarchy and the aristocracy to grant themselves and their friends a wide range of privileges. These frequently included the privilege of operating some type of business, such as a flour mill or a ferry, on a monopoly basis—with no competition allowed. *See* Matthew Hale, Prerogatives of the King (edited for the Selden Society by D.E.C. Yale, 1976). The courts tempered these privileges by requiring the monopolist to serve all potential customers that requested service.

Consider the following account of the duty to serve in American law:

> [T]he common law duty to serve is as ancient as the Anglo-American concept of equality and, indeed, predates the equal protection language of the federal Constitution by more than seven hundred years of conscious judicial effort. The veneration of the equality norm . . . can be traced to the writings of Henry de Bracton, legal counselor to Henry III. Here we first discover the judge-created concept that, at a fundamental level of social organization, all persons similarly situated in terms of need have an enforceable claim of equal, adequate, and nondiscriminatory access to essential services; in addition, this doctrine makes such access largely a governmental responsibility. . . .

> The founding of—the American Republic coincided with a second great upheaval . . .—the Industrial Revolution. The energy harnessed by Watt transformed the law as it remade the industrial world. Turnpike interests may have doomed the steam coaches, or "teakettles," which sought to traverse conventional road surfaces, but this triumph stamped upon them new obligations to the public. The railroads then emerged as the focus of legal and ideological struggles concerning the duty to serve, much as even now their tracks often divide the more from the less desirable parts of town. . . .

> The emergence of legislative action, and even dominance in railway affairs, did not undercut the doctrine of the duty to serve. The courts remained the prophets of the equality norm. In fact, the appearance of state and, with the 1887 Interstate Commerce Act,

federal regulatory legislation meant the enhancement, not eclipse of the common law duty to serve, as the new branch of government drew on common law precedents for its regulatory activities.

Charles M. Haar & Daniel W. Fessler, The Wrong Side of the Tracks 21–23 (Simon & Schuster 1986).

This requirement still plays an important part in American law: The common law "duty to serve" is presumed to apply to any charter or franchise from the government to operate as a monopoly. *See* Jim Rossi, The Common Law 'Duty to Serve' and Protection of Consumers in an Age of Competitive Retail Public Utility Restructuring, 51 Vand. L. Rev. 1233 (1998). Today, however, the nature and extent of the duty is often spelled out in statutes and regulations, and the company often charges customers for the cost of extending service to remote areas. *See, e.g., Deerfield Estates, Inc. v. Township of East Brunswick*, 286 A.2d 498 (N.J. 1972).

3.   Whenever the government grants someone a monopoly to provide a particular service, the extent or scope of the monopoly becomes an issue. The problem addressed by the court in *Tripp v. Frank* commonly occurs today in the context of increasing urbanization or technological advancements. For example, when a city expands into formerly rural areas, does the company that provided service to the city automatically expand its territory too? Or does the company that provided service to the rural area retain that privilege? *See, e.g., City of Wichita v. State Corporation Commission*, 592 P.2d 880 (Kan. 1979).

4.   During the seventeenth and eighteenth centuries, the power of the English crown diminished. Following the "glorious revolution" of the seventeenth century, parliament became the supreme power in the English government. *See* Christopher Hill, The Century of Revolution, 1603–1714 (New York, Norton, rev. ed. 1980). The result was the loss of privilege for many of the old monopolists whose powers were granted by the king. The term "monopoly" began to carry connotations of decadence. *See* Vernon A. Mund, Open Markets: An Essential of Free Enterprise (Harper 1948).

b.   MONOPOLY AND INNOVATION

In America, most state courts endorsed basic public utility principles such as the duty to serve. One of the early issues courts were required to address during the early industrial age was whether the grant of a monopoly franchise guaranteed the monopolist protection against the competition provided by new entrants. While this may have been attractive for the monopolist who was granted a franchise, it also disfavored competition and innovation in some infrastructure contexts. The U.S. Supreme Court spoke to the issue in the classic *Charles River Bridge* case in 1837. Today, the case and the principles it stands for remain of great importance; we will return to them in later chapters.

The Proprietors of the Charles River Bridge v. The Proprietors of the Warren Bridge

36 U.S. 420 (1837).

■ TANEY, J.: [In 1785], a petition was presented to the legislature, by Thomas Russell and others, stating the inconvenience of the transportation by ferries, over Charles river, and the public advantages that would result from a bridge; and praying to be incorporated, for the purpose of erecting a bridge in the place where the ferry between Boston and Charlestown was then kept. Pursuant to this petition, the legislature, on the 9th of March 1785, passed an act incorporating a company, by the name of 'The Proprietors of the Charles River Bridge,' for the purposes mentioned in the petition. Under this charter, the company were empowered to erect a bridge, in 'the place where the ferry was then kept;' certain tolls were granted, and the charter was limited to forty years from the first opening of the bridge for passengers; and from the time the toll commenced, until the expiration of this term . . . and at the expiration of the forty years, the bridge was to be the property of the commonwealth [of Massachusetts].

The bridge was accordingly built, and was opened for passengers on the 17th of June 1786. In 1792, the charter was extended to seventy years from the opening of the bridge; and at the expiration of that time, it was to belong to the commonwealth.

In 1828, the legislature of Massachusetts incorporated a company by the name of 'The Proprietors of the Warren Bridge,' for the purpose of erecting another bridge over Charles river. This bridge is only sixteen rods, at its commencement, on the Charlestown side, from the commencement of the bridge of the plaintiffs; and they are about fifty rods apart, at their termination on the Boston side.

The Warren bridge, by the terms of its charter, was to be surrendered to the state, as soon as the expenses of the proprietors in building and supporting it should be reimbursed; but this period was not, in any event, to exceed six years from the time the company commenced receiving toll.

The bill, among other things, charged as a ground for relief, that the act for the erection of the Warren bridge impaired the obligation of the contract between the commonwealth and the proprietors of the Charles River bridge; and was, therefore, repugnant to the constitution of the United States.

In the argument here, it was admitted, that since the filing of the supplemental bill, a sufficient amount of toll had been reserved by the proprietors of the Warren bridge to reimburse all their expenses, and that the bridge is now the property of the state, and has been made a free bridge; and that the value of the franchise granted to the proprietors of the Charles River bridge, has by this means been entirely destroyed.

The plaintiffs in error insist [t]hat the acts of the legislature of Massachusetts, of 1785 and 1792, by their true construction, necessarily implied, that the legislature would not authorize another bridge, and especially, a free one, by the side of this, and placed in the same line of travel, whereby the franchise granted to the 'Proprietors of the Charles River Bridge' should be rendered of no value.

The act of the legislature of Massachusetts, of 1785, by which the plaintiffs were incorporated . . . is the grant of certain franchises, by the public, to a private corporation, and in a matter where the public interest is concerned. The rule of construction in such cases is well settled, both in England, and by the decisions of our own tribunals. In the case of the *Proprietors of the Stourbridge Canal v. Wheeley and others*, 2 B. & Ad.

793, the court say, 'the canal having been made under an act of parliament, the rights of the plaintiffs are derived entirely from that act. This, like many other cases, is a bargain between a company of adventurers and the public, the terms of which are expressed in the statute; and the rule of construction in all such cases, is now fully established to be this, that any ambiguity in the terms of the contract, must operate against the adventurers, and in favor of the public, and the plaintiffs can claim nothing that is not clearly given them by the act.'

Borrowing, as we have done, our system of jurisprudence from the English law; and having adopted, in every other case, civil and criminal, its rules for the construction of statutes; is there anything in our local situation, or in the nature of our political institutions, which should lead us to depart from the principle, where corporations are concerned? We think not; and it would present a singular spectacle, if, while the courts in England are restraining, within the strictest limits, the spirit of monopoly, and exclusive privileges in nature of monopolies, and confining corporations to the privileges plainly given to them in their charter, the courts of this country should be found enlarging these privileges by implication and construing a statute more unfavorably to the public, and to the rights of community, than would be done in a like case in an English court of justice.

Adopting the rule of construction above stated as the settled one, we proceed to apply it to the charter of 1785, to the proprietors of the Charles River bridge. This act of incorporation is in the usual form, and the privileges such as are commonly given to corporations of that kind. It confers on them the ordinary faculties of a corporation, for the purpose of building the bridge; and establishes certain rates of toll, which the company are authorized to take: this is the whole grant. There is no exclusive privilege given to them over the waters of Charles river, above or below their bridge; no right to erect another bridge themselves, nor to prevent other persons from erecting one, no engagement from the state, that another shall not be erected; and no undertaking not to sanction competition, nor to make improvements that may diminish the amount of its income. Upon all these subject, the charter is silent; and nothing is said in it about a line of travel, so much insisted on in the argument, in which they are to have exclusive privileges.

Can such an agreement be implied? The rule of construction before stated is an answer to the question: in charters of this description, no rights are taken from the public, or given to the corporation, beyond those which the words of the charter, by their natural and proper construction, purport to convey.

Indeed, the practice and usage of almost every state in the Union, old enough to have commenced the work of internal improvement, is opposed to the doctrine contended for on the part of the plaintiffs in error. Turnpike roads have been made in succession, on the same line of travel; the later ones interfering materially with the profits of the first. These corporations have, in some instances, been utterly ruined by the introduction of newer and better modes of transportation and traveling. In some cases, railroads have rendered the turnpike roads on the same line of travel so entirely useless, that the franchise of the turnpike corporation is not worth preserving. Yet in none of these cases have the corporation supposed that their privileges were invaded, or any contract violated on the part of the state. The absence of any such controversy, when there must have been so many occasions to give rise to it, proves, that neither states, nor individuals, nor corporations, ever imagined that such a contract could be implied from such charters.

And what would be the fruits of this doctrine of implied contracts, on the part of the states, and of property in a line of travel, by a corporation, if it would now be sanctioned by this court? To what results would it lead us? If it is to be found in the charter to this bridge, the same process of reasoning must discover it, in the various acts which have been passed, within the last forty years, for turnpike companies. If this court should establish the principles now contended for, what is to become of the numerous railroads established on the same line of travel with turnpike companies; and which have rendered the franchises of the turnpike corporations of no value? Let it once be understood, that such charters carry with them these implied contracts, and give this unknown and undefined property in a line of traveling; and you will soon find the old turnpike corporations awakening from their sleep, and calling upon this court to put down the improvements which have taken their place. The millions of property which have been invested in railroads and canals, upon lines of travel which had been before occupied by turnpike corporations, will be put in jeopardy. We shall be thrown back to the improvements of the last century, and obliged to stand still, until the claims of the old turnpike corporations shall be satisfied; and they shall consent to permit these states to avail themselves of the lights of modern science, and to partake of the benefit of those improvements which are now adding to the wealth and prosperity, and the convenience and comfort, of every other part of the civilized world.

The judgment of the supreme judicial court of the commonwealth of Massachusetts, dismissing the plaintiffs' bill, must, therefore, be affirmed, with costs.

■ STORY, J., dissenting: [W]ith a view to induce the court to withdraw from all the common rules of reasonable and liberal interpretation in favor of grants, we have been told at the argument, that this very charter is a restriction upon the legislative power; that it is in derogation of the rights and interests of the state, and the people; that it tends to promote monopolies and exclusive privileges; and that it will interpose an insuperable barrier to the progress of improvement. Now, upon every one of these propositions, which are assumed, and not proved, I entertain a directly opposite opinion; and if I did not, I am not prepared to admit the conclusion for which they are adduced. If the legislature has made a grant, which involves any or all of these consequences, it is not for courts of justice to overturn the plain sense of the grant, because it has been improvidently or injuriously made.

But I deny the very ground-work of the argument. This charter is not any restriction upon the legislative power; unless it be true, that because the legislature cannot grant again, what it has already granted, the legislative power is restricted. If so, then every grant of the public land is a restriction upon that power; a doctrine, that has never yet been established, nor (so far as I know) ever contended for. Every grant of a franchise is, so far as that grant extends, necessarily exclusive; and cannot be resumed or interfered with.

Then, again, how is it established, that this is a grant in derogation of the rights and interests of the people? No individual citizen has any right to build a bridge over navigable waters; and consequently, he is deprived of no right, when a grant is made to any other persons for that purpose. . . .

The erection of a bridge may be of the highest utility to the people. It may essentially promote the public convenience, and aid the public interests, and protect the public property. And if no persons can be found willing to undertake such a work, unless they receive in return the exclusive privilege of erecting it, and taking toll; surely, it cannot be said, as of course, that such a grant, under such circumstances, is, per se, against the interests of the people.

Again, it is argued, that the present grant is a grant of a monopoly, and of exclusive privileges; and therefore, to be construed by the most narrow mode of interpretation.

There is great virtue in particular phrases; and when it is once suggested, that a grant is of the nature or tendency of a monopoly, the mind almost instantaneously prepares itself to reject every construction which does not pare it down to the narrowest limits. It is an honest prejudice, which grew up, in former times, from the gross abuses of the royal prerogatives; to which, in America, there are no analogous authorities. But what is a monopoly, as understood in law? It is an exclusive right, granted to a few, of something which was before of common right. Thus, a privilege granted by the king for the sole buying, selling, making, working or using a thing, whereby the subject, in general, is restrained from that liberty of manufacturing or trading, which before he had, is a monopoly.

No sound lawyer will, I presume, assert that the grant of a right to erect a bridge over a navigable stream is a grant of a common right. It was neither a monopoly; nor, in a legal sense, had it any tendency to a monopoly. It took from no citizen what he possessed before; and had no tendency to take it from him. It took, indeed, from the legislature the power of granting the same identical privilege or franchise to any other persons. But this made it no more a monopoly, than the grant of the public stock or funds of a state for a valuable consideration.

But it has been argued, and the argument has been pressed in every form which ingenuity could suggest, that if grants of this nature are to be construed liberally, as conferring any exclusive rights on the grantees, it will interpose an effectual barrier against all general improvements of the country. This is a subject upon which different minds may well arrive at different conclusions, both as to policy and principle. For my own part, I can conceive of no surer plan to arrest all public improvements, founded on private capital and enterprise, that to make the outlay of that capital uncertain and questionable, both as to security and as to productiveness. No man will hazard his capital in any enterprise, in which, if there be a loss, it must be borne exclusively by himself; and if there be success, he has not the slightest security of enjoying the rewards of that success, for a single moment. If the government means to invite its citizens to enlarge the public comforts and conveniences, to establish bridges, or turnpikes, or canals, or railroads, there must be some pledge, that the property will be safe; that the enjoyment will be co-extensive with the grant; and that success will not be the signal of a general combination to overthrow its rights and to take away its profits. And yet, we are told, that all such exclusive grants are to the detriment of the public.

But if there were any foundation for the argument itself, in a general view, it would totally fail in its application to the present case. Here, the grant, however exclusive, is but for a short and limited period, more than two-thirds of which have already elapsed; and when it is gone, the whole property and franchise are to revert to the state. The legislature exercised a wholesome foresight on the subject; and within a reasonable period, it will have an unrestricted authority to do whatever it may choose, in the appropriation of the bridge and its tolls. There is not, then, under any fair aspect of the case, the slightest reason to presume that public improvements either can, or will, be injuriously retarded by a liberal construction of the present grant.

In order to entertain a just view of this subject, we must go back to that period of general bankruptcy, and distress and difficulty. The constitution of the United States was not only not then in existence, but it was not then even dreamed of. The union of the states was crumbling into ruins, under the old confederation. Agriculture, manufactures and commerce were at their lowest ebb. There was infinite danger to all the states, from local interests and jealousies, and from the apparent impossibility of a much longer adherence to that shadow of a government, the continental congress.

This is not all. It is well known, historically, that this was the very first bridge ever constructed, in New England, over navigable tide-waters so near the sea. The rigors of our climate, the dangers from sudden thaws and freezing, and the obstructions from ice in a rapid current, were deemed by many persons to be insuperable obstacles to the success of such a project. . . .

Now, I put it to the common sense of every man, whether if, at the moment of granting the charter, the legislature had said to the proprietors; you shall build the bridge; you shall bear the burdens; you shall be bound by the charges; and your sole reimbursement shall be from the tolls of forty years: and yet we will not even guaranty you any certainty of receiving any tolls; on the contrary; we reserve to ourselves the full power and authority to erect other bridges, toll or free bridges, according to our own free will and pleasure, contiguous to yours, and having the same termini with yours; and if you are successful, we may thus supplant you, divide, destroy your profits, and annihilate your tolls, without annihilating your burdens: if, I say, such had been the language of the legislature, is there a man living, of ordinary discretion or prudence, who would have accepted such a charter, upon such terms?

But it is said, if this is the law, what then is to become of turnpikes and canals? Is the legislature precluded from authorizing new turnpikes or new canals, simply because they cross the path of the old ones, and incidentally diminish their receipt of tolls? The answer is plain. Every turnpike has its local limits and local termini; its points of beginning and of end. No one ever imagined, that the legislature might grant a new turnpike, with exactly the same location and termini. That would be to rescind its first grant. And the opinion of Mr. Chancellor Kent, and all the old authorities on the subject of ferries, support me in the doctrine.

But then again, it is said, that all this rests upon implication, and not upon the words of the charter. What objection can there be to implications, if they arise from the very nature and objects of the grant? If it be indispensable to the full enjoyment of the right to take toll, that it should be exclusive within certain limits, is it not just and reasonable, that it should be so construed? . . . If the public exigencies and interests require that the franchise of Charles River bridge should be taken away, or impaired, it may be lawfully done, upon making due compensation to the proprietors.

I maintain, that, upon the principles of common reason and legal interpretation, the present grant carries with it a necessary implication, that the legislature shall do no act to destroy or essentially to impair the franchise; that (as one of the learned judges of the state court expressed it) there is an implied agreement that the state will not grant another bridge between Boston and Charlestown, so near as to draw away the custom from the old one; and (as another learned judge expressed it) that there is an implied agreement of the state to grant the undisturbed use of the bridge and its tolls, so far as respects any acts of its own, or of any persons acting under its authority. . . .

Upon the whole, my judgment is, that the act of the legislature of Massachusetts granting the charter of Warren Bridge, is an act impairing the obligation of the prior contract and grant to the proprietors of Charles River bridge; and, by the constitution of the United States, it is, therefore, utterly void. I am for reversing the decree to the state court (dismissing the bill); and for remanding the cause to the state court for further proceedings, as to law and justice shall appertain. ∎

Stanley I. Kutler, Privilege and Creative Destruction: The Charles River Bridge Case
(Lippincott 1971).

On Bunker Hill Day, 1786, residents of Boston and Charlestown gathered to celebrate their new fortune. At last the two areas were linked by a bridge across the Charles River. Technical skills and entrepreneurial resources, encouraged by the state, had mastered formidable barriers to construct the span. While men had envisioned such a bridge for nearly a century, the costs and physical hazards always made it a risky proposition. But in 1785 the Massachusetts legislature granted a charter to a group of Charlestown businessmen who assumed the risks in exchange for a forty-year guarantee of tolls. With the bridge's completion a year later, the proprietors and townspeople alike could well congratulate themselves on their happy circumstance. There was a steady and sizable flow of goods and persons between the two towns. In place of the old and unreliable ferry, and despite the tolls, communications now were faster and cheaper. And with the successful engineering feat, the proprietors knew that their bridge would continue to provide them with lucrative profits.

Six years later the state extended the charter for another thirty years. The proprietors almost immediately realized their anticipated profits, and then some; by 1814, stock in the corporation sold for over $2,000 per share, up more than 600 percent from the original price.

But in December 1828 there was new cause for rejoicing among some of the townspeople and businessmen, but certainly not among the proprietors and their friends. It was then that a second Charlestown bridge was completed. Overriding the proprietors' claims for exclusive privileges, the Massachusetts legislature had chartered the Warren Bridge Corporation in March 1828 to construct a new bridge nearly adjacent to the existing facility, terminating on the Charlestown side less than ninety yards from the Charles River Bridge. The new company could charge the same tolls as the old, but with a six-year time limit, after which its bridge was to revert to the Commonwealth and become a free avenue.

Constitutional rhetoric and considerations of public policy dominated the controversy over a new bridge. The advocates of a free bridge insisted that the state had never bartered away its right to charter competing franchises, and that the state retained the power to provide improvements for public necessities. In response, the proprietors argued that their charter guaranteed them a vested and exclusive right that could be abrogated only upon the payment of proper compensation. Constitutional principles aside, the antagonists pitched their battle lines around competing views of the state's public policy role. The proponents of a free bridge contended that charter rights should be strictly construed so that privilege would not hamper opportunity or the pressing needs of the community. The Charles River Bridge supporters maintained that the state must scrupulously respect existing titles and interpret their rights liberally in order to ensure a favorable investment climate for future private enterprises.

Defeated in the legislature, the proprietors turned to the courts in defense of their rights. First, in 1828, they sought an injunction from the state supreme court to prevent the completion of the bridge. Daniel Webster and Lemuel Shaw, their distinguished counsel, argued that the Charles River Bridge charter granted exclusive privileges to the corporation, and therefore the legislative act of 1828 impaired the obligation of the contract and was repugnant to the federal constitution. They further contended that the chartering of a new bridge destroyed the tolls—in effect, the property—of the old structure and thus constituted the taking of private property for public use without compensation, in violation of the Massachusetts constitution. The court refused to grant the injunction, however, primarily because of the proprietors' ambiguous claims to exclusive rights. The state court subsequently heard the case on its merits, but in January 1830 dismissed the complainants' bill. The proprietors immediately appealed to the United States Supreme Court.

The Charles River Bridge case was first argued in Washington in 1831, with John Marshall presiding. Despite a determined effort by Justice Joseph Story to secure a judgment for the Charles River Bridge proprietors, the Supreme Court divided on the issue. Subsequent absences and vacancies prevented a decision by the Marshall Court before the Chief Justice's death in 1835. After the appointment of his successor, Roger B. Taney, and before a fully constituted bench, the case was reargued in January 1837. The Court's opinion followed the next month. A clear majority of the Court sustained the state's action and denied the appeal of the proprietors. For Justice Story it was a sad occasion, symbolizing in his mind the evil days that had come upon the court and the law he revered. "With a pained heart, and subdued confidence," Story found himself almost alone as "the last of the old race of judges.". . . .

The Charles River Bridge case had much more at stake than a relatively petty local dispute over a new, free bridge. The Warren Bridge was a symbol for the rapid technological developments competing for public acceptance against existing, privileged property forms. The destruction of vested interest in favor of beneficial change reflected a creative process vital to ongoing development and progress. Within its contemporary setting, and for its historical significance, the case assumes greater meaning if railroads and the development of a new and improved transportation infrastructure—or even the benefits the community could derive from all inventions and scientific knowledge— are substituted for bridges. The competing principles of the parties in the bridge case fundamentally involved the state's role and power of encouraging or implementing innovations for the advantage of the community. . . . ■

NOTES AND COMMENTS

1.   One distinguished legal historian summarizes the Charles River Bridge case in the following way: "On one side of the case were the old-money Federalists, who owned many monopoly franchises and argued that private construction of public improvements required monopoly protection for the investors. On the other side was a new group of entrepreneurs, poised to enter American markets. They believed that all markets should be competitive." Herbert Hovenkamp, Enterprise and American Law 1836– 1937 110 (Harv. U. Press 1991). Who won?

2.   With monopoly comes a concern about corruption and capture of the regulatory process. Stanley Kutler discusses how corruption may have been present in the initial grant to the proprietors of Charles River bridge over the alternative charter proposal:

> That the legislature chose to grant a charter to the Russell group for purposes of profit, rather than to the Cabot brothers who had proposed a schedule of tolls that merely would recoup their investment and development costs raises obvious questions of economic ideology and legislative behavior. Beginning in 1792, and in recurring years afterward, critics of the Charles River Bridge company charged that the proprietors had gained their charter under fraudulent conditions, an allegation never proved. But what motivated the legislature to select the group that frankly sought a long-standing profit arrangement? There may have been some vague, but conscious, perception that the pursuit of profit, even at the public's expense, was a desirable good, one that would regularly attract further investments in behalf of the community. But, more practically, the legislature's decision probably stemmed from the intensive lobbying activities of the Charleston community which was involved most directly, and whose need was clearly greater than that of its neighbors who would have benefited most from the Cabot's proposal.

Stanley I. Kutler, Privilege and Creative Destruction: The Charles River Bridge Case 11 (1971). In recognizing a public utility and granting a monopoly, how can regulators protect against corruption and capture?

3.   In a concurrence to the Supreme Court's opinion, Justice John McLean characterized the relationship between the state of Massachusetts and the proprietors of the Charles River Bridge as a contract:

> Where the Legislature, with a view of advancing the public interest by the construction of a bridge, a turnpike road, or any other work of public utility, grants a charter, no reason is perceived why such a charter should not be construed by the same rule that governs contracts between individuals. . . .

36 U.S. at 557 (McLean, J., concurring). This regulatory contract rationale for regulation contains an appealing logic. The utility agrees to serve customers and, in return, the state provides the utility protection against new entrants and guarantees recovery of its costs through regulated rates. Judge Kenneth Starr, when sitting on U.S. Court of Appeals for the D.C. Circuit, also endorsed this view of regulation:

> The utility business represents a compact of sorts: a monopoly on service in a particular geographic area (coupled with state conferred rights of eminent domain or condemnation) is granted to the utility in exchange for a regime of intensive regulation, including price regulation, quite alien to the free market. Each party to the contract gets something in the bargain.

Jersey Central Power & Light v. FERC, 810 F.2d 1168, 1189 (D.C. Cir. 1987) (Starr, J., concurring). Should the same rules regarding construction of contracts between individuals apply where one of the contracting parties is the government? What incentives do these rules create for the private sector? What approach does the Supreme Court appear to take in the Charles River Bridge case?

4.   The Charles River bridge case and its principles remain of considerable importance to issues in energy regulation today, as natural gas and electric utilities are confronted with new entrants and competition from new technologies, including distributed solar and other renewable energy technologies. For example, are incumbent distribution utilities somehow protected from new entrants, such as companies offering to lease solar rooftop panels to residential customers? This topic is discussed further in Chapters 11 and 12.

5.   Why did the Commonwealth of Massachusetts grant a monopoly franchise to initial investors in the Charles River Bridge? Does the same rationale apply in the following case?

Munn v. Illinois

94 U.S. 113 (1877).

■ WAITE, C.J.: The question to be determined in this case is whether the general assembly of Illinois can, under the limitations upon the legislative power of the States imposed by the Constitution of the United States, fix by law the maximum of charges for the storage of grain in warehouses at Chicago and other places in the State having not less than one hundred thousand inhabitants, 'in which grain is stored in bulk, and in which the grain of different owners is mixed together, or in which grain is stored in such a manner that the identity of different lots or parcels cannot be accurately preserved.'

It is claimed that such a law is repugnant . . . to that part of amendment 14 which ordains that no State shall "deprive any person of life, liberty, or property, without due process of law, nor deny to any person within its jurisdiction the equal protection of the laws."

While this provision of the amendment is new in the Constitution of the United States, as a limitation upon the powers of the States, it is old as a principle of civilized government. It is found in Magna Carta, and, in substance if not in form, in nearly or quite all the constitutions that have been from time to time adopted by the several States of the Union. By the Fifth Amendment, it was introduced into the Constitution of the United States as a limitation upon the powers of the national government, and by the Fourteenth, as a guaranty against any encroachment upon an acknowledged right of citizenship by the legislatures of the States.

When one becomes a member of society, he necessarily parts with some rights or privileges which, as an individual not affected by his relations to others, he might retain. 'A body politic,' as aptly defined in the preamble of the Constitution of Massachusetts, 'is a social compact by which the whole people covenants with each citizen, and each citizen with the whole people, that all shall be governed by certain laws for the common good.' This does not confer power upon the whole people to control rights which are purely and exclusively private, *Thorpe v. R. & B. Railroad Co.*, 27 Vt. 143; but it does authorize the establishment of laws requiring each citizen to so conduct himself, and so use his own property, as not unnecessarily to injure another.

This is the very essence of government, and has found expression in the *maxim sic utere tuo ut alienum non laedas*. From this source come the police powers, which, as was said by Mr. Chief Justice Taney in the *License Cases*, 5 How. 583, 'are nothing more or less than the powers of government inherent in every sovereignty, . . . that is to say, . . . the power to govern men and things.' Under these powers the government regulates the conduct of its citizens one towards another, and the manner in which each shall use his own property, when such regulation becomes necessary for the public good. In their exercise it has been customary in England from time immemorial, and in this country from its first colonization, to regulate ferries, common carriers, hackmen, bakers, millers, wharfingers, innkeepers, & c., and in so doing to fix a maximum of charge to be made for services rendered, accommodations furnished, and articles sold.

To this day, statutes are to be found in many of the States on some or all these subjects; and we think it has never yet been successfully contended that such legislation came within any of the constitutional prohibitions against interference with private property. With the Fifth Amendment in force, Congress, in 1820, conferred power upon the city of Washington 'to regulate . . . the rates of wharfage at private wharves, . . . the sweeping of chimneys, and to fix the rates of fees therefore, . . . and the weight and quality of bread,' 3 Stat. 587, sect. 7; and, in 1848, 'to make all necessary regulations respecting hackney carriages and the rates of fare of the same, and the rates of hauling by cartmen, wagoners,

carmen, and draymen, and the rates of commission of auctioneers,' 9 *id.*
224, sect. 2.

. . . Looking, then, to the common law, from whence came the right
which the Constitution protects, we find that when private property is
'affected with a public interest, it ceases to be juris privati only.' This was
said by Lord Chief Justice Hale more than two hundred years ago, in his
treatise De Portibus Maris, 1 Harg. Law Tracts, 78, and has been
accepted without objection as an essential element in the law of property
ever since. Property does become clothed with a public interest when
used in a manner to make it of public consequence, and affect the
community at large. . . .

Thus, as to ferries, Lord Hale says, in his treatise De Jure Maris, 1
Harg. Law Tracts, 6, the king has 'a right of franchise or privilege, that
no man may set up a common ferry for all passengers, without a
prescription time out of mind, or a charter from the king. He may make
a ferry for his own use or the use of his family, but not for the common
use of all the king's subjects passing that way; because it doth in
consequence tend to a common charge, and is become a thing of public
interest and use, and every man for his passage pays a toll, which is a
common charge, and every ferry ought to be under a public regulation,
viz., that it give attendance at due times, keep a boat in due order, and
take but reasonable toll; for if he fail in these he is finable.' So if one owns
the soil and landing places on both banks of a stream, he cannot use them
for the purposes of a public ferry, except upon such terms and conditions
as the body politic may from time to time impose; and this because the
common good requires that all public ways shall be under the control of
the public authorities. This privilege or prerogative of the king, who in
this connection only represents and gives another name to the body
politic, is not primarily for his profit, but for the protection of the people
and the promotion of the general welfare.

And the same has been held as to warehouses and warehousemen.
In *Aldnutt v. Inglis*, 12 East, 527, decided in 1810, it appeared that the
London Dock Company had built warehouses in which wines were taken
in store at such rates of charge as the company and the owners might
agree upon. Afterwards the company obtained authority, under the
general warehousing act, to receive wines from importers before the
duties upon the importation were paid; and the question was, whether
they could charge arbitrary rates for such storage, or must be content
with a reasonable compensation. . . .

But we need not go further. Enough has already been said to show
that, when private property is devoted to a public use, it is subject to
public regulation. It remains only to ascertain whether the warehouses
of these plaintiffs in error, and the business which is carried on there,
come within the operation of this principle.

From [a brief filed by plaintiffs] it appears that 'the great producing
region of the West and Northwest sends its grain by water and rail to
Chicago, where the greater part of it is shipped by vessel for
transportation to the seaboard by the Great Lakes, and some of it is
forwarded by railway to the Eastern ports. . . . Vessels, to some extent,
are loaded in the Chicago harbor, and sailed through the St. Lawrence
directly to Europe. . . . The quantity [of grain] received in Chicago has
made it the greatest grain market in the world. This business has created

a demand for means by which the immense quantity of grain can be handled or stored, and these have been found in grain warehouses, which are commonly called elevators, because the grain is elevated from the boat or car, by machinery operated by steam, into the bins prepared for its reception, and elevated from the bins, by a like process, into the vessel or car which is to carry it on. . . . In this way the largest traffic between the citizens of the country north and west of Chicago and the citizens of the country lying on the Atlantic coast north of Washington is in grain which passes through the elevators of Chicago. In this way the trade in grain is carried on by the inhabitants of seven or eight of the great States of the West with four or five of the States lying on the sea-shore, and forms the largest part of interstate commerce in these States. . . . It has been found impossible to preserve each owner's grain separate, and this has given rise to a system of inspection and grading, by which the grain of different owners is mixed, and receipts issued for the number of bushels which are negotiable, and redeemable in like kind, upon demand. This mode of conducting the business was inaugurated more than twenty years ago, and has grown to immense proportions. The railways have found it impracticable to own such elevators, and public policy forbids the transaction of such business by the carrier; the ownership has, therefore, been by private individuals, who have embarked their capital and devoted their industry to such business as a private pursuit.'

In this connection it must also be borne in mind that, although in 1874 there were in Chicago fourteen warehouses adapted to this particular business, and owned by about thirty persons, nine business firms controlled them, and that the prices charged and received for storage were such 'as have been from year to year agreed upon and established by the different elevators or warehouses in the city of Chicago, and which rates have been annually published in one or more newspapers printed in said city, in the month of January in each year, as the established rates for the year then next ensuing such publication.' Thus it is apparent that all the elevating facilities through which these vast productions 'of seven or eight great States of the West' must pass on the way 'to four or five of the States on the seashore' may be a 'virtual' monopoly.

Under such circumstances it is difficult to see why, if the common carrier, or the miller, or the ferryman, or the innkeeper, or the wharfinger, or the baker, or the cartman, or the hackney coachman, pursues a public employment and exercises 'a sort of public office,' these plaintiffs in error do not. They stand, to use again the language of their counsel, in the very 'gateway of commerce,' and take toll from all who pass. Their business most certainly 'tends to a common charge, and is become a thing of public interest and use.' Every bushel of grain for its passage 'pays a toll, which is a common charge,' and, therefore, according to Lord Hale, every such warehouseman 'ought to be under public regulation, viz., that he . . . take but reasonable toll.' Certainly, if any business can be clothed 'with a public interest, and cease to be juris privati only,' this has been. It may not be made so by the operation of the Constitution of Illinois or this statute, but it is by the facts.

In matters not in this case that these plaintiffs in error had built their warehouses and established their business before the regulations complained of were adopted. What they did was from the beginning subject to the power of the body politic to require them to conform to such regulations as might be established by the proper authorities for the common good. They entered upon their business and provided themselves with the means to carry it on subject to this condition. If they did not wish to submit themselves to such interference, they should not have clothed the public with an interest in their concerns. The same principle applies to them that does to a proprietor of a hackney-carriage, and as to him it has never been supposed that he was exempt from regulating statutes or ordinances because he had purchased his horses and carriage and established his business before the statute or the ordinance was adopted.

It is insisted, however, that the owner of property is entitled to a reasonable compensation for its use, even though it be clothed with a public interest, and that what is reasonable is a judicial and not a legislative question.

As has already been shown, the practice has been otherwise. In countries where the common law prevails, it has been customary from time immemorial for the legislature to declare what shall be a reasonable compensation under such circumstances, or, perhaps more properly speaking, to fix a maximum beyond which any charge made would be unreasonable. Undoubtedly, in mere private contracts, relating to matters in which the public has no interest, what is reasonable must be ascertained judicially. But this is because the legislature has no control over such a contract. So, too, in matters which do affect the public interest, and as to which legislative control may be exercised, if there are no statutory regulations upon the subject, the courts must determine what is reasonable. The controlling fact is the power to regulate at all. If that exists, the right to establish the maximum of charge, as one of the means of regulation, is implied. In fact, the common-law rule, which requires the charge to be reasonable, is itself a regulation as to price. Without it the owner could make his rates at will, and compel the public to yield to his terms, or forego the use.

We conclude, therefore, that the statute in question is not repugnant to the Constitution of the United States, and that there is no error in the judgment. In passing upon this case we have not been unmindful of the vast importance of the questions involved. This and cases of a kindred character were argued before us more than a year ago by most eminent counsel, and in a manner worthy of their well earned reputations. We have kept the cases long under advisement, in order that their decision might be the result of our mature deliberations.

Judgment affirmed.

▪ FIELD, J., with whom STRONG J., concurs, dissenting: I am compelled to dissent from the decision of the court in this case, and from the reasons upon which that decision is founded. The principle upon which the opinion of the majority proceeds is, in my judgment, subversive of the rights of private property, heretofore believed to be protected by constitutional guaranties against legislative interference, and is in conflict with the authorities cited in its support. . . .

The declaration of the Constitution of 1870, that private buildings used for private purposes shall be deemed public institutions, does not make them so. The receipt and storage of grain in a building erected by private means for that purpose does not constitute the building a public warehouse. There is no magic in the language, though used by a constitutional convention, which can change a private business into a public one, or alter the character of the building in which the business is transacted. A tailor's or a shoemaker's shop would still retain its private character, even though the assembled wisdom of the State should declare, by organic act or legislative ordinance, that such a place was a public workshop, and that the workmen were public tailors or public shoemakers. One might as well attempt to change the nature of colors, by giving them a new designation. The defendants were no more public warehousemen, as justly observed by counsel, than the merchant who sells his merchandise to the public is a public merchant, or the blacksmith who shoes horses for the public is a public blacksmith; and it was a strange notion that by calling them so they would be brought under legislative control.

If [the majority's approach] be sound law, if there be no protection, either in the principles upon which our republican government is founded, or in the prohibitions of the Constitution against such invasion of private rights, all property and all business in the State are held at the mercy of a majority of its legislature. The public has no greater interest in the use of buildings for the storage of grain than it has in the use of buildings for the residences of families, nor, indeed, any thing like so great an interest; and, according to the doctrine announced, the legislature may fix the rent of all tenements used for residences, without reference to the cost of their erection. If the owner does not like the rates prescribed, he may cease renting his houses. He has granted to the public, says the court, an interest in the use of the buildings, and 'he may withdraw his grant by discontinuing the use; but, so long as he maintains the use, he must submit to the control.' . . .

The power of the State over the property of the citizen under the constitutional guaranty is well defined. The State may take his property for public uses, upon just compensation being made therefore. It may take a portion of his property by way of taxation for the support of the government. It may control the use and possession of his property, so far as may be necessary for the protection of the rights of others, and to secure to them the equal use and enjoyment of their property. The doctrine that each one must so use his own as not to injure his neighbor sic utere tuo ut alienum non laedas is the rule by which every member or society must possess and enjoy his property; and all legislation essential to secure this common and equal enjoyment is a legitimate exercise of State authority. Except in cases where property may be destroyed to arrest a conflagration or the ravages of pestilence, or be taken under the pressure of an immediate and overwhelming necessity to prevent a public calamity, the power of the State over the property of the citizen does not extend beyond such limits.

It is only where some right or privilege is conferred by the government or municipality upon the owner, which he can use in connection with his property, or by means of which the use of his property is rendered more valuable to him, or he thereby enjoys an advantage over others, that the compensation to be received by him becomes a legitimate matter of regulation. Submission to the regulation of compensation in such cases is an implied condition of the grant, and the State, in exercising its power of prescribing the compensation, only determines the conditions upon which its concession shall be enjoyed. When the privilege ends, the power of regulation ceases.

———

The Supreme Court's increasing willingness to allow government to regulate a wider range of businesses occurred at a point in U.S. history when an array of new technologies for the generation and distribution of energy (and other services) were also being developed, as pointed out in the following excerpt.

Charles M. Haar & Daniel W. Fessler, The Wrong Side of the Tracks 142–49

(Simon & Schuster 1986).

In 1865 the first natural gas utility was opened in Fredonia, New York; in 1892 a 120-mile pipeline from wells in Indiana to Chicago made the long distance transmission of natural gas possible for the first time. Americans in 1878 first saw the electric arc for street and home lighting, followed in 1882 by the first central electric station, with 5500 lamps, at Pearl Street Station, New York. Shortly thereafter, central stations were constructed in Boston, Brooklyn, and Chicago. By 1886, there were forty seven Edison illuminating companies; more than 1,000 central stations were listed in 1890. The proliferation of waterworks was also impressive from 136 in 1860 (when fewer than 400 cities had populations over 2500) to over 3000 systems by the end of the century (when there were over 1737 such cities). In 1852, 23,000 miles of telegraph lines were in operation. The Western Union Telegraph Company completed the first telegraph line to the Pacific Coast in 1861, and in 1866 it merged with the two other large telegraph companies. After Alexander Graham Bell constructed the initial pair of magneto telephones in 1875, it was but three years until first New Haven, then San Francisco, Albany, Chicago, St. Louis, Detroit, and Philadelphia had local service. By 1880 there were over 34,000 miles of wire for the nation's 50,000 telephones; the American Telephone and Telegraph Company was organized in 1885 to develop long distance service. The modern, mechanized American city had been born.

The new utility networks possessed many of the characteristics of common carriers: they provided what were more and more commonly perceived as essential services; they were usually natural or legal monopolies, or both; they exercised the power of eminent domain; and they operated under a franchise from the state or municipality. . . . [But the view that this new type of business] was not a public enterprise that concerned the courts . . . remained the prevailing judicial stance until the United States Supreme Court spoke in *Munn v. Illinois* in 1876.

The *Munn* decision, written by Chief Justice Waite, upheld the Illinois statutes that regulated and set maximum rates for warehouses, grain elevators, and railroads. The decision became most memorable for its now famous delineation of property that becomes "clothed with a public interest when used in a manner to make it of public consequence, and affect the community at large." Waite consulted Lord Hale's famous treatise to support his assertions: "Every bushel of grain for its passage 'pays a toll, which is a common charge,' and, therefore, according to Lord Hale, every such warehouseman 'ought to be under public regulation, viz., that he . . . take but reasonable toll.' Certainly, if any business can be clothed 'with a public interest, and cease to be *juris privati* only,' this has been."

Yet beneath the constitutional catchwords "affected with a public interest," the *Munn* case was more fundamentally grounded in the Court's awareness of the shifting social, political, and economic patterns of the post-Civil War period. . . . In blessing the validity of some governmental control (state regulation by commission) the highest federal judges served as priests of a juridical reformation. The orthodoxy of private competition handed down in the Charles River Bridge decision forty years before had been weakened by the public outcry over abuses and panic attributed to the railroad juggernaut and other malefactors of great power.

By the close of the nineteenth century, courts generally recognized that the common law requirement to proffer equal service should apply to the increasing variety of businesses affected with a public interest whether they were common carriers or not. . . .

Courts have used four different rationales [in imposing] the obligation to furnish adequate supply or service without discrimination:

(1) The imposition of a common right to access drawn from the doctrine of services as *a public calling, essential to individual survival within the community;*

(2) The duty to serve all equally, inferred from and recognized as an essential part of *natural monopoly power;*

(3) The duty to serve all parties alike, as a consequence of the *grant of the privileged power of eminent domain; and, finally,*

(4) The duty to serve all equally, *flowing from consent, expressed or (more frequently) implied.*

A notion of reciprocity informs each of the judge-made justifications of the duty to serve. In each case, the court is presenting the elements of a multifaceted *quid pro quo:* if one wants the power to take private property against the wishes of the owner, one has to assume the responsibility of making the land (or the services that spring forth from the land) available to all members of the society; if one claims an exclusive franchise, one has to abide by the rules of the game and provide equal access; if one were going to act like a government, then one assumes the obligations of the sovereign to act in the common interest of all its citizens.

Whichever the rationale proffered, the courts in a pinch could always rest their argument upon "consent." Consent, to them, meant accepting the responsibilities along with the rest of the bargain: if a company has freely chosen to engage in providing a service to the public, then it has voluntarily assented to the appropriate requirements of a public service. Deducing a sufficient incentive for this free choice was easy, for a corporation "has, or must be supposed to have, an equivalent for its consent." Hence, the corporation, it was reasoned, had sought out and willingly assumed the very burdens it was now seeking to negate or avoid. ∎

NOTES AND COMMENTS

1.   The *Munn* decision arose out of a long and bitter political battle between farmers and food processors in the Midwest. The context of the dispute is analyzed in William Cronon's book, Nature's Metropolis (W.W. Norton 1991). In deciding whether the Chicago grain warehouses were devoted to a public use, the court relied on the warehouse companies' own brief in which they bragged about how important they were to the entire Western United States because they served as the shipping point for all of the area's grain. In the nineteenth century, Chicagoans had the reputation of being insufferable braggarts about their great city. It was this trait, not the climate, that gave Chicago the nickname "the Windy City." Emmett Dedmon, Fabulous Chicago 221 (2d. ed. 1981).

2.   While today the *Munn* decision's result of allowing for government regulation of prices may seem obvious, historically the case was of great significance. After the Civil War, American states that long had promoted and encouraged railroads and utilities also began to regulate their prices. The *Munn* decision grew out of the varied legislative responses states were taking to the "railroad problem"—i.e., large railroad companies that could charge different prices to different customers and control access to transportation markets. It was one of seven cases known as the "Granger cases," historical rulings that tested the constitutional authority of state police power, through legislation, to regulate private businesses.

3.   At the time, the decision in *Munn* also shed some light on the recently enacted Fourteenth Amendment. The Court was not unanimous in *Munn*. Justice Stephen J. Field, in a dissent joined by William Strong, made an early plea for substantive due process limitations on regulation. Later, the Supreme Court endorsed this view in *Lochner v. New York*, 198 U.S. 45 (1905), a case that made the Court the overseer of all kinds of regulatory activity until the mid-1930's.

4.   The Supreme Court expanded the definition of "business affected with a public interest" in *Nebbia v. New York*, 291 U.S. 502 (1934). After dairy prices in New York collapsed as a result of oversupply, the legislature commanded a milk control board to fix both maximum and minimum retail milk prices. Nebbia, a grocer, was convicted for selling milk too cheaply. He contested the conviction under the due process and equal protection clauses, arguing that neither the milk business nor retail grocery sales were monopolies or traditional regulated industries. In affirming Nebbia's conviction, the Court said that "affected with a public interest" means "no more than that an industry, for adequate reason, is subject to control for the public good." 291 U.S. at 536. The Court said that "price control, like any other form of regulation, is unconstitutional only if arbitrary, discriminatory, or demonstrably irrelevant to the policy the legislature is free to adopt." 291 U.S. at 539. The *Nebbia* case was seen as an indication that the Court would no longer actively question the extent to which particular businesses could be subjected to regulation. *Lochner*'s reasoning, of course, was expressly overruled only a few years later, in *West Coast Hotel v. Parrish*, 300 U.S. 379 (1937).

5.   Following *Munn*, most states interpreted the case as granting them broad authority to set up programs to regulate public utilities. The Court had said that states were free to substitute more detailed statutory rules for the common law principles. Originally, many of the states adopted a series

of statutes, one for each type of common public service (e.g., a gas act, an electric act, and a telephone act). But the states usually assigned the power to administer all of these acts to a single board or commission called the "Public Utilities Commission" (PUC), Public Service Commission (PSC), Corporation Commission, or something similar. The concept that the government may regulate the prices or rates charged by an enterprise if it is "clothed with the public interest" remains the basic rule today—any such business is called a "public utility." Thus, many state statutes provide for regulation of electric and natural gas "utilities" by a PUC or PSC. Regulation of public utilities is not exclusively a state law issue. For example, section 205 of the Federal Power Act (FPA), 16 U.S.C. § 824d provides for rate regulation of "any public utility" selling electricity to consumers where the transaction is subject to the Federal Energy Regulatory Commission's (FERC's) jurisdiction. Under FPA section 201 this extends to wholesale sales of energy, but states retain jurisdiction over rates concerning retail sales.

6.   Although the common law is useful in interpreting such language, the definition of a public utility remains a contentious issue of statutory interpretation, which often makes its way to court. Drawing the line between those businesses that are "clothed" with the public interest and those that lack the requisite cloak is no less contentious today than it was when *Munn v. Illinois* was decided. For example, should a natural gas distribution company (a regulated public utility) be allowed to recover from its ratepayers expenses for oil exploration and production (which is unregulated)? *See Comm. of Consumer Servs. v. Pub. Serv. Comm'n*, 595 P.2d 871 (Utah 1979). Or, should a company selling energy conservation and efficiency services have a duty to serve? As competition has grown in the electrical utility industry, many electric utilities now own power marketing or supply companies, which are unregulated. Regulators have been required to police carefully to make sure that ratepayers do not bear the risks of these non-public utility activities.

Summary—The Common Law Principles Affecting Public Utilities:

1.   **Service to public.** It operates a business that is thought to provide a service to the public.

2.   **Monopoly power.** It has the legal or *de facto* authority to prevent other businesses from competing with it.

3.   **Fixed territory.** A geographical boundary is defined, within which the business is required to provide service.

4.   **Technological limits.** As technology changes, the nature of the business's monopoly may be narrowly construed.

5.   **Duty to serve.** The business has a duty to serve all members of the public, but only for the specific service for which it has a monopoly.

6.   **Reasonable prices.** Rates charged by public utilities, which the common law had required be reasonable, could be regulated by the legislative branch. We will consider at some length later what "reasonable" means.

---

c.   A Brief Economic Perspective on Monopoly

The history of enterprise in the U.S. suggests a variety of rationales for regulation. Numerous political, economic, and legal considerations are involved.

Extreme political skeptics of governmental regulation (as well as many public choice economists) may describe regulation as the result of strong political forces—whether industry, environmental groups, or consumers—mustering support to protect their interests.[1] Consider, for example, the debate surrounding the Charles River bridge, and the powerful political and economic interests behind the grant of the monopoly franchise. Was this an example of capture of the regulatory process by powerful interest groups? Or is there something more positive for society in granting a monopoly franchise?

One common view of regulation is that it is a response to the market failures introduced by natural monopoly—that government's main role is to ensure that the prices and quantities produced in monopolistic markets approximate those of a competitive market. Still another theory of regulation is based on prompting broader notions of the "public interest"—that we need government to make sure that private enterprises advance the public good rather than purely private gain.[2]

The neoclassical economic model attempts to approximate the behavior of a firm in a perfectly competitive market. A perfectly competitive market assumes certain conditions: a firm faces many buyers and sellers in the market, all firms and buyers have equal access to information, the costs of transaction between any seller and buyer are extremely low, and there are no significant impediments to market entry and exit. Given such conditions, the neoclassical economic model shows that perfectly competitive firms will price their products or services at marginal cost—the cost to the firm of producing one additional unit of output. If a firm prices above marginal cost, the lure of economic profits will result in new firms entering the market and, as supply increases, driving price downward towards marginal cost. By contrast, if a firm were to price below marginal cost, the cost of each new unit of production or sales would exceed the revenue from the additional unit; since firms cannot stay in operation for long if their costs exceed their revenues, some firms would be likely to exit such a market and, as supply decreases, drive price upward toward marginal cost.

However, most markets that are price regulated are not perfectly competitive. While a perfectly competitive market marks one extreme of the neoclassical market spectrum (indeed, its ideal), at the other end of the spectrum is natural monopoly: a market that can be served at a lower average cost by a single firm than by two or more firms. A market is a natural monopoly if it faces decreasing average costs over its entire range of production; a single firm in such a market could increase its production

    [1] A good summary of this literature is included in George Priest, The Origins of Regulation and the "Theories of Regulation" Debate, 36 J. L. Econ. & Org. 289 (1993). For early works arguing this general thesis see Sam Peltzman, Towards a More General Theory of Regulation, 19 J. L. & Econ. 211 (1976); George Stigler, The Theory of Economic Regulation, 2 Bell J. Econ. & Mgmt. Sci. 3 (1971).

    [2] *See* Paul L. Joskow & Roger Noll, Regulation in Theory and Practice: An Overview, in Studies in Public Utility Regulation (Gary Fromm, ed., MIT Press 1981).

or sales at a lower average cost than if a new entrant were to also compete in the market.

Consider, for example, electricity distribution within an urban area. Assume that one firm serves the entire city of Chicago by building a power distribution network to reach all customers and by centralizing its power generation and distribution decisions. Once a firm has built a network to serve a fraction of the customers throughout this densely populated urban area (say the largest customers, such as factories, hotels, and large retail establishments), it will be cheaper for that same firm to increase its customer base incrementally than for a new firm to begin a network from scratch to serve additional customers (such as smaller residential customers). Indeed, we could imagine the unnecessary duplication that would result if multiple utilities were required to build power distribution lines to the same neighborhoods to provide electricity to different customers. Electricity distribution is characterized by economies of scale: the average cost of distributing electricity decreases over the entire range of production for the market. Thus, it is cheaper for a single firm to expand its operations than for additional firms to enter the market.

In addition to simple production efficiency, recent developments in economics focus on network efficiencies. Network economies, a type of economy of scale, may occur when a single firm is able to more efficiently operate than multiple firms, because it is better able to coordinate interdependent aspects of an industry's operations or because it is able to process information more efficiently. For example, it may be considered more efficient for a single firm to operate a large-scale distribution network for a product. A single firm may be able to coordinate its operations, such as times for delivery, more efficiently than multiple firms. In addition, the single firm may be able to gather and process information about market supply and demand more efficiently than multiple firms.

For these reasons, governments grant certain utilities and common carriers a monopoly franchise to provide service to a specified geographic area. A monopoly is able to provide more reliable and economic service in markets that face significant economies of scale.

However, once a utility has been granted a monopoly franchise, this raises a new problem: the specter of monopoly pricing. It is well established that the monopolist faces strong incentives to charge a price higher and produce less of a good or service than a perfectly competitive market would yield. For this reason, monopoly franchises are typically subject to some sort of price regulation.[3]

The extraction, conversion, and distribution of many energy resources, such as natural gas and electricity, have historically been price regulated to protect customers against abuses by the monopoly owners. As introduced above, since *Munn v. Illinois*, it has been recognized that certain industries are "clothed with the public interest" and subject to an obligation to provide equal service to all. Firms providing natural gas or

---

[3] Some argue that the presence of a single firm need not necessarily lead to monopolistic pricing. *See* Harold Demsetz, Why Regulate Utilities?, 9 J. L. & Econ. 55 (1968). In addition, more modern work in contestable market theory calls into question monopoly pricing. *See* Elizabeth E. Bailey and William J. Baumol, Deregulation and the Theory of Contestable Markets, 1 Yale J. on Reg. 111 (1984).

electricity to end-use customers have traditionally been regulated as "public utilities"—firms granted a monopoly franchise in a geographic area in return for a duty to serve the public.

For example, Florida Power & Light (FP&L), an investor-owned utility, has been granted an exclusive service territory in a large area of Florida in exchange for its promise to provide power to any customer within its service territory at a reasonable rate. This protection against competition within a geographic area is often called a "horizontal monopoly." There are two distinct economic reasons that FP&L is granted this type of a monopoly franchise.

First, FP&L possesses many characteristics of a classic natural "monopoly" (which is described above). It is able to provide electricity to the market at a lower average cost than two or more firms because of economies of scale or other network economies. Second, it may be advantageous to allow a single firm to provide power service because there are efficiencies to be gained by integrating different market services. This is often called "vertical integration," and its economic rationales are discussed further below. In the computer industry, for example, it may be efficient for a manufacturer to bundle computer hardware with basic operating system software. A classic example in the energy industry is an electric utility like FP&L: often, a single firm can more efficiently transport and distribute energy if it serves other market functions, such as power generation, as well.[4]

NOTE ON THE ECONOMICS OF NATURAL MONOPOLY

Not all students will find this material easily accessible, but it is important to know that the basic principle that some markets work better as monopolies has an economic explanation that is grounded in the costs of production. The economic phenomenon of economies of scale can be illustrated by comparing the general cost functions of different types of firms. A firm's costs can be divided into fixed and variable costs. Fixed costs are the costs associated with the firm's plant; assuming the firm remains in business with a constant plant size, they do not vary with the level of production. Variable costs, however, change with the firm's output level. For example, in making a decision to operate a plant 24 hours a day, as opposed to 12 hours a day, a manufacturing firm raises its variable costs significantly. Total costs represent the sum of fixed and variable costs.

Figure 2–1 illustrates the relationship between total costs and a hypothetical firm's output level. Imagine, for example, that the firm in panel A is a power plant with 150 megawatts (MW) capacity. The horizontal axis represents the firm's operation level, in MW. The vertical axis represents the total costs of production, in dollars. Assume that the fixed costs of the plant are $5 million. Since the firm will have to pay these costs even if it chooses not to operate the plant, the vertical axis begins at $5 million. The graph in panel A is drawn to reflect a cost phenomenon observed in most production processes, including power generation. At low levels of operation, such as those below 50 MWs, variable costs rise rapidly, although at a decreasing rate. Initially, it may take a lot of fuel to fire up the power plant's turbines,

---

4   Harold L. Platt, The Electric City 74–82 (University of Chicago Press; 1991); Paul L. Joskow & Richard Schamalensee, Markets for Power: An Analysis of Electric Utility Deregulation (MIT Press 1983).

just as it takes a lot of fuel to quickly accelerate a car from zero to 40 miles per hour. Between the 50 and 100 MW level, variable costs rise more slowly with increased operation levels and output. Once the power plant's turbines are running, additional operation levels are more efficient than the initial startup, for reasons similar to an automobile's improved gas mileage in highway driving. Above the 100 MW level, however, the plant may lose some of its earlier efficiencies. Here costs may climb at a greater rate with each additional unit of output. The shape of this curve suggests that the plant operates most efficiently in the 50 to 100 MW range of output.

The graph in panel B illustrates how this cost phenomenon translates into a relationship between marginal and average costs for the hypothetical firm. Average costs are calculated by dividing total costs by the output level. The average cost curve in panel B is derived from the curve in panel A; each point in the average cost curve represents total costs divided by the corresponding output level, or the slope of the total cost curve. Marginal (or incremental) costs, by contrast, refer to the costs associated with each additional unit of output. When marginal costs are below average costs, average costs fall, and when marginal costs are above average costs, average costs rise. Of course, every law student is familiar with this concept: if a law student's average is 75, her GPA will rise if she receives an 80 in torts but will fall if she receives a 70.

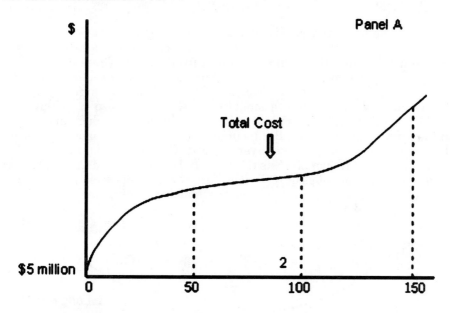

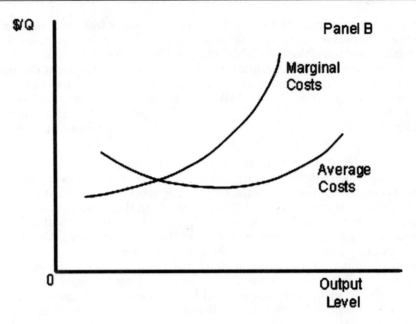

Figure 2–1

Over the long run, nearly all costs are variable. For example, a firm must eventually replace even the plant itself. Cost considerations come into play in determining the optimal size of a firm's plant. These decisions, as well as many regulatory decisions, will depend on the shape of an industry's long run average cost curve. Consider **Figure 2–2**, which represents an entire industry rather than a single firm. A plant of size A has average production costs C1, while a plant of size B has average production costs C2. In the range between A and B, this industry experiences economies of scale: the larger plant produces lower average costs. However, a plant of size C has greater average production costs than size B. Between B and C, the industry experiences diseconomies of scale. The curve connecting these various plant average cost curves corresponds to the industry's long run average cost curve.

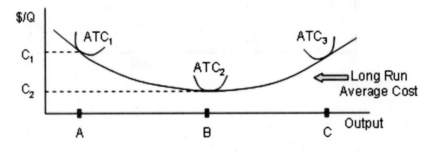

Figure 2–2

What does this long run average cost curve tell us about regulatory policy? A lot depends on the level of demand for an industry's products or services. In an industry with a demand curve similar to that in **Figure 2–3**, firm B would be able to compete more effectively than firm A because firm

B's larger size and production scale give it lower average costs. Over time, firm B would drive firm A out of business. In this industry, a single firm is more efficient than two or more firms. If two or more firms operated in this market, prices would be higher and output would be lower, since the quantity demanded would decrease with higher prices. Such a market is called a *natural monopoly.*

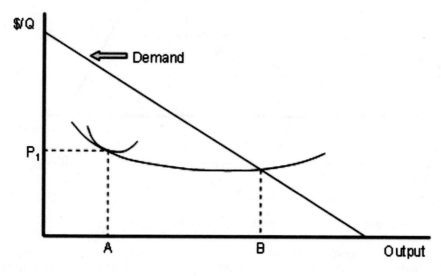

Figure 2–3

Contrast a natural monopoly market with a competitive market. **Figure 2–4** illustrates a very different relationship between market demand and long run average costs. At price P1, this industry could support four firms. The cost characteristics of various industries are determined primarily by technological issues and transactions costs, reflected in the scope of the industry-wide cost curve. Some industries, such as agriculture, have cost curves more like **Figure 2–4** than **Figure 2–3**. These industries are competitive and will be able to support a larger number of firms. The relationship between long run average costs and demand is the major economic factor in determining the optimal number of firms serving a given market and, in turn, whether that market is competitive. For further discussion of industry cost characteristics, see F.M. Scherer & David Ross, Industrial Market Structure and Economic Performance (Houghton Mifflin Co., 3d ed. 1990); W. Kip Viscusi, John M. Vernon & Joseph E. Harrington, Jr., Economics of Regulation and Antitrust (Heath 1992). While technical in nature, the basic cost characteristics of energy firms are very important to issues such as rate regulation (discussed in Chapter 8) and the operation and regulation of modern competitive energy markets (discussed in Chapters 9 and 10).

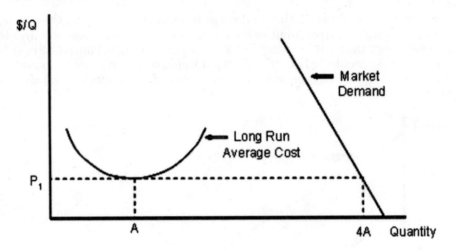

Figure 2–4

B. AN OVERVIEW OF THE ELECTRIC POWER INDUSTRY

Subsequent chapters will discuss the legal issues arising from ongoing changes to the electric power industry. These include the increasing significance of environmental regulation for power generation, the rise of interstate markets in electric power, extensive mergers within the electric industry itself, both in the United States and overseas, as well as combinations of traditional electric companies with gas companies, energy marketers and a wide range of other companies. They also include the entry into the electricity business of a wide range of independent companies that may engage in more limited roles than the traditional vertically integrated electric utility.

As background for these changes, however, it is important to have an understanding of the basic nature of the electric power industry and the major firms that participate in this industry.

1. ELECTRIC POWER BASICS

The physical equipment of a modern electric power system is divided into three basic categories: generation, transmission and distribution. Traditionally, in the territory of an investor-owned utility (IOU) or a large municipal utility, the same entity has owned and operated all three parts of the system. Today, however, an increasing share of the generation facilities is operated by independent power producers. In the future, the transmission and distribution functions for electric power may increasingly be handled by separate entities, as discussed in Chapter 10.

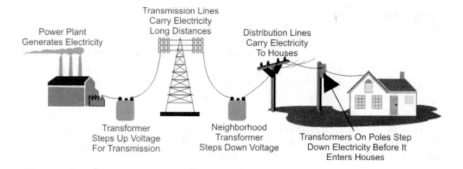

Figure 2–5

a. GENERATION

Most electricity is generated by power plants from fuels such as coal, natural gas, or uranium. Some plants use renewable resources, such as hydro, geothermal, biomass, wind and solar energy to generate electricity. The type of fuel, its cost, and generating plant efficiency can determine the way a particular generating plant is used. The demand for electricity varies considerably on both daily and yearly cycles. A large electric system will usually contain many different types of generating plants. The system operator will try to keep the mix of plants with the lowest operating costs running at any given time.

For purposes of deciding which plants to operate at any given time, power plants are generally classified into four categories: (1) base load plants, mostly nuclear, newer coal plants, and increasingly, natural gas plants, which have low fuel costs and (with the exception of some natural gas plants) cannot be turned off and on rapidly; (2) variable "must run" plants, powered by hydro and wind and sometimes solar, which have virtually no fuel costs but can operate only if the proper amount of water or wind or sun is available; (3) intermediate load plants, often older coal plants that are more costly to operate than newer models; and (4) peaking plants, typically natural gas or diesel fueled, which have higher operating costs but are relatively inexpensive to build and can be taken on and off line quickly.

The need for this kind of careful balancing of the system results from the fact that electricity cannot be easily stored. This means that whenever customers turn the power on or off the generating load must be increased or decreased almost instantaneously to avoid affecting the voltage significantly.[5] Extensive research is underway in advanced battery design and superconducting magnetic energy storage, but progress is slow. See Chapter 13 for FERC's initiatives in adding energy storage to the electric grid.

---

[5] The equivalent of storage can be obtained with "pumped hydro" plants, in which water is pumped up to the reservoir during periods when demand for electricity is low, and then released to generate power at peak times. However, there are few potential sites for such plants and the cost of operating them is not cheap. Electric energy can also be "stored" using flywheels or compressed air, but these technologies remain expensive, both in terms of cost and energy lost.

b.   TRANSMISSION

Most electricity is generated by large and immovable power plants,, making it necessary to transport electricity from the generating plant site to the ultimate consumer. The transmission system (or "grid") accomplishes much of this task with an interconnected system of lines, distribution centers, and control systems. Transmission lines are the lines commonly called "high-voltage" lines placed on high towers along wide rights of way. For example, the Electricity Reliability Council of Texas transmission system, which covers most of Texas, has over 40,000 miles of high-voltage transmission lines, including 9,249 miles of 345KV lines and 19,565 miles of 138KV lines. ERCOT Quick Facts, http://www. ercot.com/content/news/presentations/2013/ERCOT_Quick_Facts_Apr% 202013.pdf. These lines form a spider web-like pattern on the landscape with many points of interconnection. When newly generated electricity is introduced into the network it will flow in whichever direction the lines are most lightly loaded. Similarly, where lines intersect, electricity will flow through the junction in a way that tries to even out the line loads. Thus, if demand increases on a particular line, power will flow toward that line even if the generator assumed it was going to go somewhere else. This concept is known as "loop flow" and is discussed in Chapter 10.

To a degree, transmission expansion is a substitute for generation expansion. For example, if a utility expands its transmission resources, it may not need to build new generation facilities to serve customers but can transmit, or "wheel" power from another utility's generator. Also, the transmission network must be operated in a way that keeps the voltage and frequency constant within very narrow limits. All systems keep a certain ratio of "spinning reserve;" *i.e.,* generating plants that are in operation and ready to be switched onto the network immediately if needed. In addition, a system needs "operating reserve" in the form of generation equipment or curtailable load that can be brought on or off line within ten minutes or so. Finally, to operate properly the transmission system needs voltage control equipment dispersed where voltage support is needed, and an overall system operator with authority to determine which generating units go on and off line at any time. These features of the transmission system are known in the trade as "ancillary services." *See* F.E.R.C. Order No. 888–A, 1997.

Standards for the operation of transmission systems have been set by the North American Electric Reliability Corporation (NERC), a consortium of various electric industry entities representing public and private utilities that account for virtually all of the electricity supplied in the United States and Canada. Standing committees, such as a reliability committee and a critical infrastructure protection (CIP) committee, carry out NERC's technical activities. See http://www.nerc.com/comm/Pages/default.aspx. Pursuant to 2005 legislation FERC reviews NERC's activities and has the power to reject and modify proposed standards and their enforcement. Chapter 13 discusses the CIP committee in connection with cybersecurity protection for the electric grid.

The transmission systems of the United States and Canada are divided into three giant networks. (1) Beginning at about the Rocky Mountains and extending throughout the Western United States and Canada is the Western Interconnection. Its operation is governed by the Western Systems Coordinating Council, a non-profit entity controlled by representatives of the various utilities in the region. (2) Most of Texas has its own Texas Interconnection. These lines are operated by the Electric Reliability Council of Texas, a corporation created pursuant to state statute.[6] (Hawaii and Alaska, due to their geographical position, also have independent networks.) (3) The rest of the United States and Canada is part of the Eastern Interconnection, which is one giant network. Operation of the Eastern Interconnection is not centralized, however, but is managed by seven separate regional reliability councils. The future of the system of management of the transmission network is under considerable discussion (*See* Chapter 10).

Construction of transmission lines increased at a rapid rate during the 1970s but began to slow down after about 1985. Hyman, *supra*, at 144, 161. Construction of new transmission lines today often encounters opposition from neighbors or environmental agencies, and may require a long period of negotiation. For discussion of this topic, see Chapter 11, discussing expansion of transmission to accommodate renewable power suppliers.

c. **DISTRIBUTION**

Substations are located at various points on the transmission system. These substations contain transformers that reduce the voltage and send the power to the 120 and 240 volt lines that serve homes and businesses. (Large industries often bypass the distribution system and take electricity directly from the transmission network if they need higher voltages.)

The distribution system consists of the substations, poles, and wires common to many neighborhoods as well as underground lines found in many other areas. Maintenance of these systems must respond to tree growth, sudden wind or ice storms, nesting eagles, and dozens of other local problems that frequently arise.

The distribution function also includes billing customers, reading meters, customer service, and many of the common activities that the average person associates with the work of an electric utility. As a public utility, the distributing company has an obligation to provide service to all customers at published rates. State laws sometimes make it difficult to terminate service to a customer even when he is not paying his bill.

Many rural cooperatives and small municipal utilities operate only a distribution system without either generating or transmitting power. They purchase power in "wholesale" transactions from other utilities or from Federal marketing entities.

Increasingly, both transmission and distribution systems benefit from "Smart Grid" technologies, which computerize grid functions that previously required human involvement. Distribution wires traditionally have allowed electric power to flow in a single direction, and enabled the

---

[6] Texas has traditionally tried to limit the interconnections between its lines and those of the rest of the country in order to discourage federal jurisdiction. *See generally* Guide to Electric Power in Texas (Center for Global Studies and Energy Institute, University of Houston, 2d. Ed., 1999); David Spence & Darren Bush, Why Does ERCOT Have Only One Regulator?, in Electricity Restructuring: The Texas Story (L. Lynne Keisling and Andrew N. Kleit, Eds.) (AEI Press, 2009).

utility to collect information about consumer use through a meter that measured only the flow of electricity leaving the grid at the site of the customer's use on monthly basis. Smart Grid technologies allow for bi-directional, real-time flows of information, allowing utilities to better predict the flow of electricity through transmission and distribution lines, for example; automatically notify a utility when portions of a transmission or distribution grid are compromised; and relieve congestion in certain lines by automatically rerouting certain electricity flows. Smart Grid technologies can also "island" certain portions of the grid, thus preventing cascading blackouts or brownouts. Further, by providing better "communication" between generation and transmission/distribution systems and easier interconnection of generation to these systems, the Smart Grid also allows a transmission or distribution system to draw from a broader and more diverse set of generators. Some Smart Grid technologies also allow for bidirectional flows of electricity, allowing consumers to add power to the distribution grid, such as electricity generated from roof-top solar panels. Smart Grid approaches to metering and distribution are discussed further in Chapter 12.

2. THE MODERN ELECTRIC ENERGY SYSTEM

The modern electric energy industry is a complex system, and involves several distinct but interconnected entities. Historically, privately-owned utilities generated and sold most of the electric power sold in the United States, though today they produce less than half of the electricity sold to customers. Publicly-owned power systems continue to serve customers in many cities and rural communities, and often own power generation facilities. In recent years the power industry has also had many privately-owned new entrants who produce or sell power but do not operate as public utilities. All of these firms are connected through the power grid, which allows the transmission of electric power over large distances.

The electric power industry today relies heavily on fossil fuels to produce electricity, though nuclear, hydro and renewable energy also hold a significant portion of the power generation portfolio. According to 2013 data, about 40% of the electricity in the United States comes from coal-fired plants. About 20% comes from nuclear power plants. Hydro furnishes less than ten percent, depending on the amount of rainfall that has taken place. The use of natural gas as power plant fuel is increasing and is now more than 25 percent—making it one of the most significant sources of electric power. In fact, when seasonal demand for electricity was low in Spring 2012, coal and natural gas temporarily provided equal amounts of electric power to customers. Power from renewable sources other than hydro is also increasing, and is now up to 6% of total generation. Monthly statistics on power generation by source are on the website of the U.S. Energy Information Administration (EIA), an excellent source of all kinds of energy information. *See* http://www.eia. doe.gov/totalenergy/data/monthly/pdf/sec7_6.pdf.

a. Investor-Owned Utilities

Although referred to as *public* utilities, **investor-owned utilities** (IOUs) are private sector companies owned by their shareholders, ranging in size from small local operations serving a customer base of a few thousand to giant multistate corporations serving millions of customers. The larger IOUs have always been vertically integrated, owning or controlling all the generation, transmission, and distribution facilities required to meet the needs of the customers in their assigned service area, although recent trends suggest that this vertical integration may become less prevalent. See Chapter 10.

IOUs can be found in every state except Nebraska (which does not allow IOUs to sell power to retail customers). Their local operations are typically regulated heavily by state public utility commissions. Except for those relatively few states that have embraced retail competition and market-based retail rates, state regulation includes setting retail rates. However, the wholesale power sales and power transmission contracts for IOUs fall under FERC's jurisdiction.

Control over IOUs is further concentrated because many of them are actually subsidiaries of utility holding companies. Nearly one-quarter of the IOU operating companies are subsidiaries of electric utility holding companies. Consolidation of ownership of electric utilities was regulated under the Public Utility Holding Company Act of 1935 (PUHCA), 15 U.S.C. § 79, by the Securities and Exchange Commission and FERC, until repeal of that statute in the 2005 Energy Policy Act. Major utility holding companies included companies such as American Electric Power Co. and Entergy Corp. FERC continues to regulate market power aspects of utility mergers, and state regulators also continue to regulate their implications for retail customers.

b. Public Power

Many customers purchase power from publicly owned utilities, both federal and state or local, or from consumer-owned cooperatives. This form of utility is often referred to as "public power."

The Federal Government generates electric power at federally owned hydroelectric facilities. It is primarily a wholesaler, marketing its power through five **federal power marketing agencies**: 1) Bonneville Power Administration, 2) Western Area Power Administration, 3) Southeastern Power Administration, 4) Southwestern Power Administration, and 5) The Alaska Power Administration. Federal power systems are generally required under existing legislation to give preference in the sale of their output to other public power systems and to rural electric cooperatives.

Federally owned or chartered power systems also include the Tennessee Valley Authority (TVA),[7] whose service area spans seven states, and facilities operated by the U.S. Army Corps of Engineers, the Bureau of Reclamation, the Bureau of Indian Affairs, and the International Water and Boundary Commission. Jurisdiction over federal power systems operations and the rates charged to their

---

[7] The TVA is an independent government corporation that sells power within its statutory service area. 16 U.S.C. § 831.

customers is established in various authorizing legislative provisions in
Title 16 of the U.S. Code.

The more than 2,000 **public power systems** include local,
municipal, state, and regional public power systems ranging in size from
tiny municipal distribution companies to giant systems like the Los
Angeles Department of Water and Power. Some states, such as Nebraska
and New York, operate electric systems that cover all (in the case of
Nebraska) or part of the state. Many public systems are involved only in
retail power distribution; they purchase power supplies from other
utilities.

The extent of regulation of public power systems varies among
states. In some states the PUC exercises jurisdiction in whole or part over
operations and rates of publicly owned systems. In other states, public
power systems are regulated by local governments, or are self-regulated.
Municipal systems are usually run by the local city council or an
independent board elected by voters or appointed by city officials. Other
public power systems are overseen by public utility districts, irrigation
districts, or special state authorities.

Electric cooperatives are electric systems owned by their members,
each of whom has one vote in the election of a board of directors. The
Rural Electrification Act of 1936, 49 Stat. 1363, created the Rural
Electrification Administration (REA) to bring electricity to rural areas
and subsequently gave it broad lending authority to stimulate rural
electricity use. The Act authorizes federal loans at no interest or very low
interest to cooperatives for the purpose of "financing the construction and
operation of generating plans, electric transmission and distribution
lines or systems for the furnishing of electric energy to persons in rural
areas who are not receiving central station service." 7 U.S.C. § 904.

In the early 1930s, 9 out of 10 rural homes were without electric
service. Today, 99 percent of rural homes have electricity service. Rural
co-ops often act as buying and distribution agents for utility-generated
power or for generation and transmission co-ops (G & Ts), which own
both generating and transmission facilities. Early REA borrowers tended
to be small cooperatives that purchased wholesale power for distribution
to members. Over the past 20 years, however, many expanded into
generating and transmission cooperatives in order to lessen their
dependence on outside power sources.

Regulatory jurisdiction over cooperatives varies among the states,
with some states exercising considerable authority over rates and
operations, and others exempting cooperatives from state regulation. In
addition to state regulation, cooperatives with outstanding federal loans
fall under the jurisdiction of the Rural Utilities Service (RUS), successor
to REA, which imposes various conditions intended to protect the
financial viability of borrowers. *See* 7 U.S.C. § 901 et seq.

c.   NEW ENTRANTS

Today the electric power industry is dynamic and includes many new
entrants in the business of power generation and sales. These include
non-utility independent power producers and privately owned marketers
and brokers who sell electric power.

Most **independent power producers**—also known as "non-utility" generators—began operation because of the Public Utility Regulatory Policies Act of 1978 (PURPA) and its requirement that utilities purchase power from certain defined qualifying facilities (QFs). PURPA prohibited utilities from owning a majority share of QFs. *See* Chapter 10. In addition, many state PUCs helped the independent power business by persuading utilities to put major generating capacity additions out to bid. Independents often found that they could underbid the traditional utilities, which brought even more independents into the business.

The national Energy Policy Act of 1992 extended the conditions under which an independent power producer could build and own projects itself without becoming regulated by FERC as a public utility. It encouraged the regulated utilities to set up their own unregulated subsidiaries to act as independent builders and operators of generating plants outside the utility's jurisdiction. And it gave FERC greater authority to compel utilities to provide transmission services for wholesale transactions between independent power producers and distant distributing utilities.

Since the enactment of the Energy Policy Act of 1992, many new companies have been created to serve as privately owned **marketers and brokers** of electric power. These companies do not own or operate any electric facilities. They buy and sell electricity on the open market—an opportunity that has increased price transparency for both consumers and firms but that has also raised serious concerns about market opportunism and manipulation. Some IOUs have created subsidiaries to operate as marketers, but many marketers are independent. Chapter 10 discusses energy trading by marketers and brokers.

d.   THE GRID

The power transmission grid ties all of these various industry players together, both physically and economically. The grid includes distribution facilities and high voltage transmission lines. Power distribution issues are discussed in chapters 10 and 12. Transmission is one of the most daunting challenges confronting the modern electric power system. A detailed discussion of some of the legal issues surrounding transmission lines is in Chapter 10 and Chapter 11.

e.   DEMAND FOR ELECTRIC POWER

The U.S. uses significantly more electricity than any other country in the world in terms of total kwh consumed. U.S. Energy Info. Admin., International Energy Statistics, http://www.eia.gov/cfapps/ipdbproject/IEDIndex3.cfm?tid=2&pid=2&aid=2 U.S. electricity demand is expected to grow 22% by 2035, with the largest portion of this demand growth stemming from customers in the commercial (28% growth) and residential (18% growth) sectors. U.S. Energy Info. Admin., Market Trends—Electricity, http://www.eia.gov/forecasts/aeo/MT_electric.cfm.

The nature of electric power demand presents challenges for the electric power supply fleet. Because electric power cannot be stored in high quantities or for long periods of time, the demand for electric power must be met instantaneously by power generation supply. Demand is not constant, nor is the production output of many individual power generators or methods of production. Importantly, electricity demand has daily and seasonal cycles. Each day, electricity demand rises and falls in a pattern corresponding with human activities. Each day begins with low demand, which rises steadily throughout the morning and early afternoon, as individuals' activities at home and work continue to intensify. Intra-day demand peaks late in the afternoon as commercial consumption remains significant, but consumers also generate increased residential demand as they return home. Electricity demand also displays a fairly consistent seasonal demand cycle. Annual consumption peaks during the summer as a result of the intense demand due to residential and business cooling needs. A lesser demand peak occurs in winter, in connection with temperatures at the other extreme, which generates demand through electric heat and the electricity needed to run gas-fired heating systems. As a general matter, summer peaks are more profound in warmer climates, whereas the winter peaks are more profound in cooler climates.

Across most of the United States the all-around highest demand occurs when the seasonal peak and the daily peak coincide—that is, during hot summer afternoons for most of the nation. Just as the parking lot of a shopping mall must be large enough to accommodate the peak traffic of the holiday season, the electric power supply system generally must have enough generation to meet the extreme level of demand that occurs only a few times a year, when the grid's demand peaks coincide. (Demand response, described further in Chapter 13, necessitates an asterisk to this overarching rule. Specifically, through demand response, end-users reduce their consumption of electricity at times of high demand, thus reducing the grid's "peak" demand.) Importantly, periods of peak demand are also the time when power is at its most expensive. Generally, the electrical grid is organized so that the least expensive available generation is used to meet the next increment of demand. When demand is modest, the cheapest generators are able to satisfy it, resulting in modest prices. However, during peak periods, all generation resources—even the most expensive—must be called upon. The level of peak demand is thus of critical importance in determining how much power supply, and how many power plants, will be necessary to provide service to customers.

As a general economic principle, demand for most products is somewhat "elastic." That is, for any given product the degree of demand is responsive to price, because consumers demand the product less as its price increases. Demand for electricity is not exempt from this principle. However, the degree of elasticity of demand for electricity is less than that of many other products, for several reasons. First, as is discussed below, consumers are typically shielded from the immediate impacts of changes in the costs of generating electricity by state-level rate regulation, discussed in Chapter 8. Utilities are obliged to file tariffs with state regulators committing to specified rates, and so the utilities—not customers—bear much of the risk of price changes. Second, even to the extent that cost increases are passed on to retail customers, the response is sluggish. Much electricity demand arises from uses like refrigeration, temperature control, and lighting—in other words, uses that are foundational to modern homes and businesses. These uses are unlikely to be curtailed heavily, other than in acute situations. Moreover, in most jurisdictions consumers are not well informed about changes in electricity prices, as a result both of the delay between consumption and billing, and of the fact that electricity typically comprises a modest portion of a consumer's overall budget. Finally, many consumers who live in multi-unit dwellings are removed from electricity prices because those prices are paid by a building owner, or otherwise averaged over a group of residents. Despite these factors that present some inelasticity in the demand for electricity, with new innovations in billing and metering there are considerable opportunities to make the demand for electricity much more responsive to changes in price.

f.   SUPPLY: THE ELECTRIC POWER GENERATION MIX

The United States relies on a diverse portfolio of resources to generate electric power. **Figure 2–6** illustrates the composition of the power generation portfolio in the United States. Though fossil fuels continue to predominate the mix of energy resources to generate electricity, this is rapidly changing. Renewable energy in particular is growing significantly. This is a brief overview, with detailed discussion of legal issues associated with each method of generation in subsequent chapters.

Coal-fired turbines have long represented the largest share of electricity generation. As noted above, they account for the single largest share of the U.S. electric generation portfolio, about 40% but declining. Coal is abundant and inexpensive in the United States, and its price has shown less volatility than other sources of electricity, in part because there are few competing uses for coal. There is considerable regional variation in reliance on coal, however. In some states, like California, Idaho, Maine, and Rhode Island, there is virtually no reliance on coal, whereas in other states, including Indiana, Kentucky, West Virginia, and Wyoming, coal accounts for more than 80% of the electric generation portfolio.

Recently, natural gas has grown substantially and, at least in some months of the year, has surpassed coal as a share of the electricity portfolio in some months. Natural gas's current share of over 25% of the U.S. electricity portfolio is expected to increase. Its proportionate share of generation has grown steadily, for a variety of economic and environmental reasons, since the deregulation of the natural gas transportation industry in 1978, and more recently has risen sharply as a result of a dramatic increase in domestic natural gas production.

Nuclear power's roughly 20% share of overall generation is produced by about 100 reactors in 31 states. U.S. Nuclear Reg. Comm'n, Power Reactors, http://www.nrc.gov/reactors/power.html. Nuclear power is inherently suited to supplying stable, base load power because nuclear fission is a chain reaction that cannot readily be ramped up or down to meet varying load demands.

In the United States, hydroelectric power's 6% share of electricity generation is more than those for all other renewable resources combined. However, the dispersal of hydroelectric power is not uniform; instead, it is concentrated around major river systems. The Pacific Northwest, in particular, features the extensive Columbia River and its tributaries, on which numerous dams have been built. As a result, the

Pacific Northwest enjoys some of the least expensive and cleanest power in the United States.

In recent years, the development of renewables other than hydroelectric power has been accelerated by a combination of federal, state, and local policy drivers, because of the relatively benign environmental and climate change impacts of these generation sources. Federal policies supporting renewables have been meaningful, but ephemeral—far less stable over time than federal subsidies for fossil fuels. State policy initiatives have been a key driver of growth in renewables, but they vary significantly state-to-state. While renewables other than hydroelectric power remain the smallest significant component of the generation portfolio (at less than 6% combined), they comprise the fastest-growing component of the generation portfolio. Yet to date, because of the persistent gap between the cost of renewables and other sources of energy, and because of a relative absence of private investment, growth in installed generation of these sources of energy tends to rise and fall with the presence or absence of government subsidies. See Chapter 11.

Sources of U.S. Electricity Generation, 2012

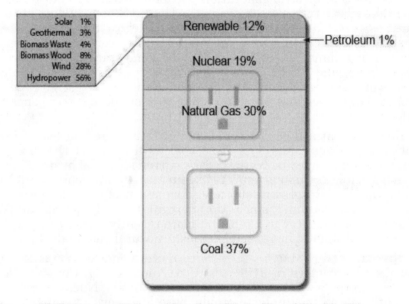

Source: U.S. Energy Information Administration, *Electric Power Monthly* (March 2013). Percentages based on Table 1.1 and 1.1a; preliminary data for 2012.

Figure 2–6

C. THE RISE OF ELECTRIC POWER REGULATION

To understand the legal issues surrounding today's electric power industry, it is important to understand how it is regulated. In large part because of history, today the industry remains regulated by both state and federal regulators—each of which is assigned a distinct role. State regulators focus primarily on regulating distribution utilities and the sale of electricity to retail customers. Federal regulators focus primarily on regulating the electric power transmission system along with wholesale (or "bulk power") sales of electricity in interstate commerce. This divide in jurisdiction between FERC and states (which is discussed much further in chapters 8, 10, 11 and 13) is complex and continues to make energy law challenging today.

1. THE ROLE OF STATE REGULATION

As noted above, state agencies control much public utility regulation. In the early part of the twentieth century most public utilities could not have been effectively regulated by the federal government because at that time the Supreme Court had a fairly restrictive view of the extent of federal power under the Commerce Clause. As a result, the more local aspects of public utility operation would have been constitutionally exempt from federal regulation. This would not necessarily be true today since the companies are more integrated into national networks and the Court takes a more expansive view of federal power under the Commerce Clause.

Local regulation, on the other hand, was widely seen as ineffective. Originally, it was the cities that tried to regulate public utilities: "Transit, gas and electric companies had extensive, and corrupt, influence in . . . city councils," but business consumers and employee unions were also influential. The interests of neighboring municipalities and rival utilities "generated intense legal and political controversy." Morton Keller, Regulating a New Economy: Public policy and Economic Change in America, 1900–1933 58–59 (Harvard Univ. Press, 1990). Many municipal governments offered franchises to private utility operators, subject to a competitive process of franchise review and renewal. Alternatively, the municipal government itself sometimes entered into the utility business, which often left regulatory decisions to big city political machines. The result was a decentralized, piecemeal regulatory process, one that provided little uniformity and made many of the private utilities unhappy with the uncertainty of their franchises. State legislatures were sometimes involved in regulatory decisions, but their ability to address serious regulatory problems was substantially limited. At the state level the growth of regulation by agency officials can be attributed in large part to the failures of municipal regulation of energy utilities. The creation of state PUCs was intended to supersede a pattern of municipal regulation that had proven to be controversial.

"The initiation and development of public service regulation by state commissions owed much to the forces of political reform—under the leadership of men like Charles Evans Hughes of New York and Robert LaFollette of Wisconsin . . . [in] response to the excesses of the public service companies and the inadequacies of other methods of control." Many of the companies themselves "encouraged the movement to vest regulatory powers in state commissions—at the expense of municipal authorities [believing that] their operations and investments would be more secure if insulated from politically motivated interference from uninformed (and often corrupt) state and local political factions." William K. Jones, Origins of the Certificate of Public convenience and Necessity: Developments in the States, 1870–1920, 79 Colum. L. Rev. 426, 432 (1979). Following the leadership of New York and Wisconsin (whose state public service commission legislation was drafted by the University of Wisconsin economist John Commons), many states established state-wide regulatory commissions for public utilities in the early twentieth century. *See* Robert L. Bradley, Jr., The Origins of Political Electricity: Market Failure or Political Opportunism, 17 Energy L.J. 59 (1996).

Although initially skeptical of more government involvement in their businesses, many electric, gas and telephone companies actively began to seek state regulation. One reason for this is that their operation was bedeviled by the inconsistent approaches and demands by local governments. State regulation could provide a more uniform approach, so most state public utilities acts preempted local regulation.

Although the concept of a public utility has common law roots, today most utility regulation begins with a provision of a statute or state constitution that designates the enterprises to be regulated and the type of regulatory powers that may be exercised over them. State regulatory control is exercised by a specialized agency of government which, as mentioned above, may be a PSC or a PUC. Other common agencies are called Railroad Commissions (as in Texas, for example) or Corporation Commissions (as in Virginia and Oklahoma, for example). The practice for selecting commission members varies from state to state: some are elected, while others are appointed by the state governor. Most commissions have a staff of lawyers, accountants, engineers, and economists, although the training and experience of the staff members varies widely from state to state.

While state commissions have the power to initiate actions on their own, they are generally reactive regulatory bodies. A regulated utility will come to the agency to increase its rates or change its existing structure. Alternatively, a prospective entrant may seek to provide service in a regulated market, drawing complaints from customers or competitors. Consumers also might request a review of existing utility rates if they believe they have been overcharged. Agencies will often be asked to resolve such matters.

Although the process varies from state to state and in different contexts at the federal level, most public utility regulation imposes the following general requirements:

1) **Certificate of Convenience and Necessity:** The business must obtain permission to enter into and operate within the regulated market. This is achieved by securing a "certificate of convenience and necessity," also sometimes called a certificate of public convenience and necessity or a certificate of need. Often this includes granting the utility the power of eminent domain.

2) **Monopoly Franchise:** As part of this licensing process, the government often creates a monopoly by establishing an exclusive

geographic franchise. Within this service area, the utility has the right to serve the market without competition.

3) **Duty to Serve:** In return for this exclusive service territory, the government often requires the utility to provide a certain level of service to all customers within the service territory. The utility has a duty to serve customers and cannot selectively choose its customer base for its own private gain.

4) **Price Regulation:** The regulatory body will allow the utility to charge only "just and reasonable" rates to customers. This is normally done on the basis of the cost of providing service to each class of customers (see Chapter 8).

For example, consider two separate industries: food packaging and electricity distribution. A new entrant to the food packaging business (Packco) need not seek government permission to build and operate its plant. However, before building a power transmission line, a power generator (Genco) must obtain a certificate of convenience and necessity from the relevant state authority, usually a PUC. Packco will likely compete with numerous other food packaging companies within the same geographic market. By contrast, Genco may seek an exclusive service territory and may ask the PUC to grant a monopoly franchise. If the PUC has approved Genco's franchise, Genco will no longer face competition in this geographic area. If granted a franchise, the PUC will require Genco to serve all customers within its territory and will ensure that it charges these customers just and reasonable rates. Packco, however, will continue to face competition from other food packaging companies, as well as potential new entrants to the food packaging business. Although certain aspects of the food packaging business may be regulated, such as the information that may be presented on certain products and the materials that may be used, Packco will charge the price that the market yields, not a price set by regulators.

Today every state has some sort of commission or agency charged with regulating different types of public utilities in the energy sector. A utilities commission will typically monitor the prices that utilities charge for natural gas, electricity and telephone service within the state. Visit your state utilities commission web site. Does it set rates for energy companies? Does it otherwise regulate how they price and offer service? How does it do so? What kinds of energy companies does it regulate? Does it treat electricity differently from natural gas or gasoline purchased at the pump?

2. THE RISE OF NATIONAL REGULATION OF ELECTRIC POWER

Although state public utility regulation of electric power spread quickly in the twentieth century, it soon became clear that the state boundary lines often made no economic sense to an electron—especially given technologies for transmitting electricity over long distances. Many communities and businesses found it more efficient to obtain their power from a nearby plant in another state rather than from a plant in their own state that might be farther away or more expensive. To the extent transmission lines crossed state borders, however, electrons were in "interstate commerce"—triggering federalism concerns for electric power regulation.

Public Utilities Comm. of Rhode Island v. Attleboro Steam & Electric Co.

273 U.S. 83 (1927).

■ SANFORD, J.—This case involves the constitutional validity of an order of the Public Utilities Commission of Rhode Island putting into effect a schedule of prices applying to the sale of electric current in interstate commerce

The Narragansett Electric Lighting Company is a Rhode Island corporation engaged in manufacturing electric current at its generating plant in the city of Providence and selling such current generally for light, heat and power. The Attleboro Steam & Electric Company is a Massachusetts corporation engaged in supplying electric current for public and private use in the city of Attleboro and its vicinity in that State.

In 1917, these companies entered into a contract by which the Narragansett Company agreed to sell, and the Attleboro Company to buy, for a period of twenty years, all the electricity required by the Attleboro Company for its own use and for sale in the city of Attleboro and the adjacent territory, at a specified basic rate; the current to be delivered by the Narragansett Company at the State line between Rhode Island and Massachusetts and carried over connecting transmission lines to the station of the Attleboro Company in Massachusetts, where it was to be metered. The Narragansett Company filed with the Public Utilities Commission of Rhode Island a schedule setting out the rate and general terms of the contract and was authorized by the Commission to grant the Attleboro Company the special rate therein shown; and the two companies then entered upon the performance of the contract. Current was thereafter supplied in accordance with its terms; and the generating plant of the Attleboro Company was dismantled.

In 1924 the Narragansett Company—having previously made an unsuccessful attempt to obtain an increase of the special rate to the Attleboro Company—filed with the Rhode Island Commission a new schedule, purporting to cancel the original schedule and establish an increased rate for electric current supplied, in specified minimum quantities, to electric lighting companies for their own use or sale to their customers and delivered either in Rhode Island or at the State line. The Attleboro Company was in fact the only customer of the Narragansett Company to which this new schedule would apply.

The Commission thereupon instituted an investigation as to the contract rate and the proposed rate. After a hearing at which both companies were represented, the Commission found that, owing principally to the increased cost of generating electricity, the Narragansett Company in rendering service to the Attleboro Company was suffering an operating loss, without any return on the investment devoted to such service, while the rates to its other customers yielded a fair return; that the contract rate was unreasonable and a continuance of service to the Attleboro Company under it would be detrimental to the general public welfare and prevent the Narragansett Company from performing its full duty to its other customers; and that the proposed rate was reasonable and would yield a fair return, and no more, for the service to the Attleboro Company. And the Commission thereupon made an order putting into effect the rate contained in the new schedule.

From this order the Attleboro Company prosecuted an appeal to the Supreme Court of Rhode Island which [held] that the order of the Commission imposed a direct burden on interstate commerce and was invalid because of conflict with the commerce clause of the Constitution; and entered a decree reversing the order and directing that the rate investigation be dismissed. 46 R. I. 496.

It is conceded, rightly, that the sale of electric current by the Narragansett Company to the Attleboro Company is a transaction in interstate commerce, notwithstanding the fact that the current is delivered at the State line. The transmission of electric current from one State to another, like that of gas, is interstate commerce, and its essential character is not affected by a passing of custody and title at the state boundary, not arresting the continuous transmission to the intended destination.

The petitioners contend, however, that the Rhode Island Commission cannot effectively exercise its power to regulate the rates for electricity furnished by the Narragansett Company to local consumers, without also regulating the rates for the other service which it furnishes; that if the Narragansett Company continues to furnish electricity to Attleboro Company at a loss this will tend to increase the burden on the local consumers and impair the ability of the Narragansett Company to give them good service at reasonable prices; and that, therefore, the order of the Commission prescribing a reasonable rate for the interstate service to the Attleboro Company should be sustained as being essentially a local regulation, necessary to the protection of matters of local interest, and affecting interstate commerce only indirectly and incidentally.

The order of the Rhode Island Commission is not a regulation of the rates charged to local consumers, having merely an incidental effect upon interstate commerce, but is a regulation of the rates charged by the Narragansett Company for the interstate service to the Attleboro Company, which places a direct burden upon interstate commerce. Being the imposition of a direct burden upon interstate commerce, from which the State is restrained by the force of the Commerce Clause, it must necessarily fall, regardless of its purpose. It is immaterial that the Narragansett Company is a Rhode Island corporation subject to regulation by the Commission in its local business, or that Rhode Island is the State from which the electric current is transmitted in interstate commerce, and not that in which it is received. The forwarding state obviously has no more authority than the receiving State to place a direct burden upon interstate commerce. Nor is it material that the general business of the Narragansett Company appears to be chiefly local. The test of the validity of a state regulation is not the character of the general business of the company, but whether the particular business which is regulated is essentially local or national in character; and if the regulation places a direct burden upon its interstate business it is none the less beyond the power of the State because this may be the smaller part of its general business. Furthermore, if Rhode Island could place a direct burden upon the interstate business of the Narragansett Company because this would result in indirect benefit to the customers of the Narragansett Company in Rhode Island, Massachusetts could, by parity of reasoning, reduce the rates on such interstate business in order to benefit the customers of the Attleboro Company in that State, who would have, in the aggregate, an interest in the interstate rate correlative to that of the customers of the Narragansett Company in Rhode Island. Plainly, however, the paramount interest in the interstate business carried on between the two companies is not local to either State, but is essentially national in character. The rate is therefore not subject to regulation by either of the two States in the guise of protection to their respective local interests; but, if such regulation is required it can only be attained by the exercise of the power vested in Congress.

The decree is accordingly affirmed.

■ BRANDEIS, J., dissenting—The business of the Narragansett Company is an intrastate one. The only electricity sold for use without the State is that agreed to be delivered to the Attleboro Company. That company takes less than 3 per cent. of the electricity produced and manufactured by the Narragansett, which has over 70,000 customers in Rhode Island. The problem is essentially local in character. The Commission found as a fact that continuance of the service to the Attleboro Company at the existing rate would prevent the Narragansett from performing its full duty towards its other customers and would be detrimental to the general public welfare. It issued the order specifically to prevent unjust discrimination and to prevent unjust increase in the price to other customers. The Narragansett, a public service corporation of Rhode Island, is subject to regulation by that State. The order complained of is clearly valid as an exercise of the police power, unless it violates the Commerce Clause.

The power of the State to regulate the selling price of electricity produced and distributed by it within the State and to prevent discrimination is not affected by the fact that the supply is furnished under a long-term contract. If the Commission lacks the power exercised, it is solely because the electricity is delivered for use in another State. That fact makes the transaction interstate commerce, and Congress has power to legislate on the subject. It has not done so, nor has it legislated on any allied subject, so there can be no contention that it has occupied the field. Nor is this a case in which it can be said that the silence of Congress is a command that the Rhode Island utility shall remain free from the public regulation—that it shall be free to discriminate against the citizens of the State by which it was incorporated and in which it does business. That State may not, of course, obstruct or directly burden interstate commerce. But to prevent discrimination in the price of electricity wherever used does not obstruct or place a direct burden upon interstate commerce. . . .

In my opinion the judgment below should be reversed. ■

NOTES AND COMMENTS

1.   What was the constitutional basis used by the Court for invalidating the state law at issue in this case? Would the test proposed by Justice Brandeis, that a state could "prevent discrimination in the price of electricity wherever

used," have been as effective a means of ensuring fair pricing as the creation of a federal regulatory system? Do the principles of rate design seem clear enough that they could serve as a constitutional standard?

2.   After the Supreme Court limited the ability of the states to regulate interstate sales of electricity in the *Attleboro* case, Congress passed the FPA, which in section 201 gave to the Federal Power Commission (FPC)[8] the power to regulate the "sale of electric energy at wholesale in interstate commerce." 16 U.S.C. § 824. This jurisdiction provision is widely seen today as giving FERC jurisdiction over wholesale sales of energy, including wholesale rates. FERC also has jurisdiction over transmission, but retail sales of energy and power distribution and generation facilities are regulated by states.

3.   At the national level, today public utility regulation is implemented by FERC. FERC derives its regulatory powers from three primary statutes: the Natural Gas Act, which regulates natural gas sales; the FPA, which regulates sales of electricity for resale (i.e., wholesale sales) in interstate commerce; and the Interstate Commerce Act (ICA), which gives FERC jurisdiction over the shipment of oil by pipeline. FERC is composed of five commissioners appointed by the President and confirmed by the Senate. Commissioners are appointed for a term of four years, but no more than three members of FERC can be from the same political party. FERC, like the Interstate Commerce Commission and Federal Communications Commission, is an "independent" agency: in addition to limitations on the number of FERC members from a single political party, the President may remove FERC commissioners only for "inefficiency, neglect of duty, or malfeasance in office," not for simple disagreement with policies. 42 U.S.C. § 7171. Along with its five commissioners, FERC employs a staff of approximately 1,500, which includes lawyers, accountants, engineers, and economists as well as "street level" bureaucrats.

4.   While in the electricity sector FERC's jurisdiction over energy sales is limited to wholesale sales by FPA section 201, the same sentence of the statute also gives FERC jurisdiction over the "transmission of electric energy in interstate commerce." Should federal jurisdiction over electric transmission be broader than federal jurisdiction over energy sales, and why?

By the 1950s, the nation was blanketed with a few hundred investor-owned electric utilities on the Insull model. In addition, there were a few large federal electric generation and distribution agencies, such as the TVA, a host of publicly owned municipal electric agencies (the "municipals" or "munis") and hundreds of rural electric cooperatives created under the REA (the "REA co-ops"). Since the 1930s, the interconnection of these separate entities had been overseen by the FPC (now FERC). In the 1960s, the issue of interconnection assumed new importance as rapid economic growth left some areas subject to power shortages.

Throughout the 1950s and 1960s, demand for electricity was constantly increasing. Until approximately 1965, utilities were able to meet this increasing demand simply by expanding their base-load capacity and

---

[8]   The FPC was previously in existence, having been created under the Federal Water Power Act of 1920 to oversee the construction of hydroelectric dams on interstate rivers. See Chapter 6. The new statute was combined with the old into a new Federal Power Act. In a subsequent reorganization, the Commission's name was changed to FERC.

passing through these costs to customers in rate base. During this period, electricity generation was believed by regulators to have been characterized by significant economies of scale. Generation capacity was increased—often without question—to meet this demand. In 1965, the FPC published an extensive survey, the National Power Survey, which suggested that closely coordinated plant constructions and operations by electric utilities could produce power far more cheaply than expansions of capacity and operations by individual utilities.

Many regulators were becoming concerned that sufficient capacity did not exist to meet consumer demand. On November 2, 1965, a relay on the Ontario Hydro system broke. The system was tied into the network of interconnected lines that covered the entire Northeast United States and parts of Canada. Surges of power cascaded through the system, overloading lines and knocking them out of commission. The Northeast Blackout of 1965, as it came to be known, is one of the worst power failures the electric industry has ever seen. Within a quarter-hour over 30 million people lost their electricity. The FPC responded with recommendations to form "reliability councils" on a regional basis with representatives from the various utilities and government agencies. Until 2005, industry wrote and enforced voluntary reliability standards through the North American Electric Reliability Council and its regional sub-groups called "regional entities." NERC is now called the North American Electric Reliability Corporation, many of its reliability standards are now mandatory, and FERC has the authority to review and enforce some of these standards.

Stephen Breyer[9] & Paul MacAvoy, Energy Regulation by the Federal Power Commission
Brookings Institution, 1974.

Electricity service is customarily viewed as consisting of (a) production of power by water or steam turbines, (b) transmission over high-voltage lines of the energy produced, and (c) local distribution for short distances over low-voltage lines to final consumers. By the accounting methods of the industry, more than half the costs are charged to production of electricity, one-eighth to transmission, and the rest to distribution. Several hundred firms owned by private investors provide approximately three-quarters of the nation's electricity supply. The remainder is produced by local, state, or federal installations. Nearly all private firms are vertically integrated, providing generating, transmitting, and distributing services as a single entity or through separate firms controlled by the same holding company . . .

. . . [C]hanging technology [in the electric utility industry] provoked similar change in the pattern of regulation. As technology made large-scale operation more efficient, competition between companies within a single city began to disappear, and municipalities sought to regulate prices and service quantity through their prerogatives in issuing franchises. Then, between 1905 and 1920, local franchising gave way to comprehensive control by state regulatory boards.

---

[9]   Some two decades after co-authoring this book with economist Paul MacAvoy, Stephen Breyer was appointed to the Supreme Court of the United States by President Clinton.

More recently, regulatory control has ceased to mirror the scale of operation that technology makes possible. . . . [T]oday as in the 1930s electricity regulation takes place primarily at the state level; state commissions control the prices of retail sales and review all construction plans. Restraints imposed by the commission or other federal agencies are typically viewed as supplementary forms of regulation.

With the growth of scale in capacity, power companies recognized the importance of coordinating generation and transaction by combining them across regions larger than the single retail distribution area. Recent technological change increasing the size of efficient generating units has in all probability increased the need for coordination. Operation of a group of generating units and a network of interconnecting transmission lines for service to multiple population centers as if the parts were one system can, in principle, produce cost savings in six categories.

Operating costs can be held to a minimum through a program to select for dispatch the power from the generators capable of producing it most cheaply. The program is formulated by tabulating the power stations in ascending order of marginal operating costs the "first" station being the one with lowest marginal costs and then by loading the plants on the system in that order as demand increases. Each plant is "started up" for power production when total demand exceeds full capacity of the operating plants already on line with lower marginal costs.

Costs for meeting peak demands for electricity can be reduced by taking advantage of the fact that demand varies according to the time of day and the season of the year. Two regions in which peak demands occur at different times can save generating capacity by using the peaking capacity in one to supply some part of the peak demand in the other. If in winter demand peaks sharply at about 5:00 P.M., two adjacent systems in different time zones may be able to share the equipment needed to supply their respective peaks. The same principle suggests the possibility of exchanges between areas which have summer peaks because of air conditioning and those where peaks occur in winter because of heating demand. Coordination across companies with different peaks results in what is sometimes referred to as demand-diversity cost savings.

Reserve costs are also reduced by coordination. Reserve generating capacity is kept in case peak demand has been underestimated or in case operating units break down and for use during periods of maintenance. Interconnection can save on the capacity needed to allow maintenance work if firms in a coordination group can stagger their maintenance schedules to allow each to use the same spare generator to substitute for the generator being overhauled. Coordination can also reduce the risk of underforecasting demand. The larger the interconnected system, the more likely that the effect of unusual weather and changes in industrial demand in one place can be absorbed by reserve capacity from another place.

Coordinating the operations of several systems also reduces the need for breakdown reserves. Pooling reserve capacity allows each firm to call upon the reserves of other firms if a generator outage occurs. And the reserves of the others will be available unless several outages occur simultaneously a contingency that becomes more remote the larger the number of generators in the system. Sharing such capacity can reduce investment in reserve capacity by an amount sufficient to compensate for the increased costs of interconnecting transmission lines.

Generating costs can be reduced by coordination if it allows firms to take advantage of economies of scale in generator size. Since capacity depends on boiler and turbine volume while costs very roughly depend on metal surface areas, costs per unit of capacity decline with total outlay. The larger the generator, the more cheaply it can produce electricity at the margin. In fact, in estimating the elasticity of costs with respect to capacity, the consensus seems to be that costs increase by only 8 or 9 percent when capacity increases 10 percent. Thus the most efficient way to make electricity usually is to install the largest generator that technology permits a size that increased from roughly 400 megawatts (400,000 kilowatts) in the early 1960s to approximately 1,000 megawatts in the early 1970s. A large generating unit, however, requires a large backup unit in case it breaks down and recently larger units have tended to break down more frequently. Whereas a smaller firm may not face sufficient demand for its electricity to justify replacing a small generator with a large one, several small firms combined into a single system may be able to do so.

Transmission reliability costs can also be reduced through coordinated planning across a wide geographical area. When a generator breaks down, reserve generators must make up the deficit; but, during the first few seconds after a major breakdown (before the reserve generators can start up), more is needed. Power will rush into the deficit area, and the interconnecting transmission lines must be sufficiently strong to withstand the surge. Similarly, when a major line breaks down, power recoils and spreads itself out through the remaining interconnected lines of the system; those remaining lines must not break down, or they will aggravate the problem. Thus, once firms are interconnected at all, the generating or transmission plans of one will affect the need for lines elsewhere. Company X's installation of a large generator in State A may require the strengthening of Company Y's lines in State B, an area well outside Company X's service area. Unless Companies X and Y and others affected coordinate their plans, there is a risk of power failure, on the one hand, or waste, on the other.

Social costs, such as the adverse environmental effects from power generation, can also be reduced through coordination. Nearly every method of making electricity affects the environment in some way. Fossil-fuel plants pollute the air; nuclear plants heat nearby rivers and lakes; hydroelectric plants and their accompanying transmission lines disturb the biotic equilibrium and scenic attraction of wild areas. Coordinated planning over a wide geographic area can reduce total construction and help to locate the area's plants so as to produce the desired level of power at a lower cost to the environment. ■

NOTES AND COMMENTS

1.   Throughout the late 1960s and the 1970s, blackouts and brownouts began to be a serious concern, especially during periods in which consumer demand peaked—such as summer periods, in which residential and office air conditioning was added to normal demand. Most of us tend to take for granted the ability to throw a switch to provide light, power for appliances, or heat. We tend to underestimate the social impact of energy shortages.

Another blackout, in New York City on July 13 & 14, 1977, in addition to closing most public transportation facilities and businesses, led to communications shutdown (and the closing of Wall Street), riots and looting, prolonged fires, and many injuries and deaths. The Cost of an Urban Blackout, The Consolidated Edison Blackout, July 13–14, 1977, A Study for the Subcommittee on Energy and Power, Committee on Interstate and Foreign Commerce, United State House of Representatives (June 1978) at 4.

2. Writing in 1974 in the above-excerpted book, Breyer and MacAvoy went on to encourage the FPC to use its authority to require utilities to interconnect with each other in order to encourage the economies of scale that come with larger generating plants. They noted: "The most efficient way to make electricity usually is to install the largest generator that technology permits—a size that increased from roughly 400 megawatts (400,000 kilowatts) in the early 1960s to approximately 1,000 megawatts in the early 1970s." At that time, regulators were under intense pressure to increase utility capacity to supply electricity in order to meet expected shortages.

More recent economic studies suggest that the optimal size for coal and gas plants never exceeded 500 MW, although the optimal size for a nuclear plant was in the 900–1,100 MW range. *See* Paul L. Joskow & Richard Schmalansee, Markets for Power: An Analysis of Electric Utility Deregulation 51–54 (1983). If regulators during the 1970s were approving new plant construction on the basis of Breyer & MacAvoy's assumptions, would this be likely to lead to unnecessary capital expansion?

Today, the electric industry is one of the most capital-intensive industries in the US economy: It requires roughly $4 in capital investment for every $1 in annual revenues, as compared to a 3/1 ratio for the telephone industry and 6/1 for the automobile industry.

3. The risks of blackout continue to plague the electric power industry. The size and impact of a major blackout in 2003 eclipsed the 1965 blackout: "On August 14 to August 15 of 2003, the northeastern U.S. suffered the worst electric power blackout in history. Over 50 million people in New York, Connecticut, Massachusetts, Vermont, New Jersey, Pennsylvania, Ohio, Michigan, and Ontario, Canada, went without electric power for up to 48 hours. Within nine seconds, an electric power surge had caused 100 power plants and 61,800 MW of electric generation to trip offline." James W. Moeller, Of Credits and Quotas: Federal Tax Incentives for Renewable Resources, State Renewable Portfolio Standards, and the Evolution of Proposals for a Federal Renewable Portfolio Standard, 51 Fordham Envtl. L. J. 69, 173 (2004). Powerful storms also continue to cause major grid disruptions, as recently demonstrated by Hurricane Sandy and associated power outages in the Northeast.

CHAPTER 3

COAL PRODUCTION

A. THE EVOLUTION OF THE MODERN COAL INDUSTRY

Once commonplace as a fuel for home heating, today coal produces more electric power in the United States than any other fuel source. Historically, coal has been one of the most plentiful and abundant energy sources, but domestic coal production as well as reliance on coal to generate electricity has declined in recent years. The United States holds more coal resources in reserves than any other country in the world, making coal exports an increasingly important energy market for domestic producers. This Chapter focuses primarily on legal issues surrounding the domestic production of coal. The externalities produced by coal in fossil fuel combustion to produce electric power are discussed in Chapter 5. Coal export issues are discussed with other international issues in Chapter 14.

The coal industry has evolved from a highly labor-intensive industry plagued by health and safety problems to a highly mechanized industry heavily dependent on huge surface mining operations that are plagued by environmental problems. The coal industry is one of the most heavily regulated industries in the United States. Legal challenges to federal and state regulations of the coal industry have produced some of the most important decisions in American constitutional history. However, before addressing the regulatory environment of the coal industry, it is necessary to understand the important role that coal has played in the development of the United States, and the changing nature of the coal industry in today's environment.

1.   FROM WOOD TO COAL

Ever since prehistoric humans discovered how to make fire they have been cutting down trees to obtain wood as a fuel. Wood, along with muscles, water and wind, continued to be the dominant source of energy until the mid-nineteenth century. In the United States today, wood is still used as a fuel in fireplaces and wood stoves, and burned to generate some electricity (see Chapter 11's discussion of biomass), but it accounts for only a minute fraction of our energy usage.

Human beings also have a long history of using peat for fuel. Peat is the remains of wetland vegetation that has formed a coherent mass. For centuries it has been dug and used as fireplace fuel in many parts of the world. But peat's heating efficiency is very low, and it produces lots of smoke. When geological changes cause peat to be buried under layers of rock, the peat becomes compressed and turns into coal. This compression packs a lot of potential energy into a small space, with the result that coal is a much more efficient fuel than peat.

Coal varies greatly in heat content and in sulfur content. The relative efficiency of different types and grades of coal can vary significantly depending on differences in original vegetation and, more importantly, in the magnitude and duration of transforming temperatures and pressures.

> Anthracites and the best bituminous coals—ancient fuels derived primarily from the wood of large, scaly-barked trees laid down in immense coastal swamps more than two hundred million years ago—break up to reveal hard, jet-black facets of virtually pure carbon. These fuels contain hardly any water and very little ash, and their heat values are near 30 MJ/kg [megajoules per kilogram] In contrast, the youngest lignites are soft, often crumbly, clayish, fairly wet chunks of brownish hues. They contain large shares of ash and water, often a great deal of sulfur, and their energy density is as low as 10 MJ/kg, inferior to air-dried wood.
>
> Not surprisingly, all large lignite-producing nations call them brown coals. As with their drawbacks, the redeeming qualities of brown coals spring from their relative immaturity: their deposits are often very thick, quite level and close to the surface, conditions making a large-scale extraction in huge open-cast mines very economical.

Vaclav Smil, Energies: An Illustrated Guide to the Biosphere and Civilization 136–137 (1999).

But the switch to coal from fuels like peat was not just a simple matter of replacing one energy base with another. Coal is more difficult to extract and process than wood or peat because it takes a great deal more energy to transform it into a usable state. Jeremy Rifkin suggests that this may reflect a universal principle: the second law of thermodynamics. "The available energy in the world is constantly being dissipated. The more available sources of energy are always the first to be used. Each succeeding environment relies on a less available form of energy than the one preceding it. It is more difficult to mine coal and process it than it is to cut down trees. It's still more difficult to drill and process oil, and even harder to split atoms for nuclear energy." Jeremy Rifkin with Ted Howard, Entropy: A New World View 85 (1985).

2. THE INDUSTRIAL REVOLUTION

Coal provided a more efficient source of heat than wood, and it was a sufficiently concentrated form of energy that it became practical to convert it to motion through the use of the steam engine. The development of the steam engine was the foundation of the dramatic change in living conditions that became known as the Industrial Revolution. Early steam engines burned coal (to produce steam to drive a piston), and were first put to industrial uses, exploiting the mechanical energy they produced in mills, and later, on trains. While these great engines powered the industrial revolution, they could deliver power only on-site:

> Once you pare away the fancy additions, all the bells and whistles, all steam engines share one central property—they deliver energy mechanically, by making a shaft move or a wheel spin. This is a serious limitation on the steam engine's usefulness, because it means that the power must be developed close to the place where it will be used. Whatever is to be moved by the engine has to be connected to it. The great puffs of smoke issuing from a steam locomotive are a reminder of the fact that you have to carry both the coal and the engine along with you if you expect the wheels to turn. You can see the same thing in photos and etchings of turn-of-the-century factories, where long lines of lathes or other machines are run by belts connected to rotating overhead shafts near the factory ceiling. This meant that when the great manufacturing cities of the nineteenth century were built, every factory with power-driven machinery had to have its own steam engine (or engines) and supply of coal.

James Trefil, A Scientist in the City (1994).

3. COAL RESERVES IN THE UNITED STATES

Coal remains one of the major sources of energy in the United States and throughout much of the world today. Converting coal to energy requires four steps: mining, processing, transportation, and combustion. The big coal companies typically operate large mines that often ship their entire output to a few major users such as power plants or large factories, but some coal is mined by smaller companies that sell to wholesalers.

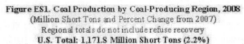

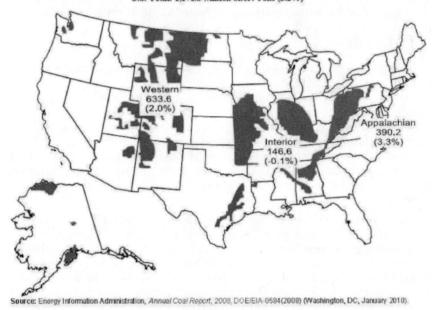

Figure ES1. Coal Production by Coal-Producing Region, 2008
(Million Short Tons and Percent Change from 2007)
Regional totals do not include refuse recovery
U.S. Total: 1,171.8 Million Short Tons (2.2%)

Source: Energy Information Administration, *Annual Coal Report*, 2008, DOE/EIA-0584(2008) (Washington, DC, January 2010).

Figure 3–1
Coal Production By Region
Source: U.S. Energy Info. Admin. (EIA), Annual Coal Report, 2008
http://www.eia.gov/coal/annual/archive/05842008.pdf

In the United States, coal was initially found primarily in the Appalachian Mountains, particularly in Pennsylvania and West Virginia. As the nation expanded westward, coal mines were opened first in the Midwestern states and, more recently, in the Rocky Mountain area. Today, nearly one-fourth of the nation's coal reserves are in Montana, with another 14% in neighboring Wyoming.

It is difficult to estimate the exact amount of coal buried underground, but there is no question that the United States has enormous coal reserves, probably in the neighborhood of five hundred billion tons of readily extractable coal. Almost half of this coal is in the Rocky Mountain area, but significant coal reserves remain in Illinois, West Virginia, Kentucky, Pennsylvania and Ohio. However, the increasing abandonment of small mines in these states has contributed to a significant loss of potential coal reserves.[1]

The predominant type of coal in the eastern United States has a high heat content and usually a high sulfur content as well, which means that

---

[1]   Small blocks of coal are not amenable to the larger-scale, higher-technology mining that can boost average productivity rates. The closing of these small mines has left significant coal reserves unmineable. Some operators choose to extract only the quickest-or easiest-to-mine parts of a coal deposit or only the highest-grade coal that will fetch a premium price, leaving the rest, which will probably be spoiled by caving and weathering. With prices low and competition keen, coal deposits once regarded as reserves at producing properties have been found to be no longer marketable. If reserve blocks contain coal of moderate to high sulfur content, for which markets are shrinking, the chances of permanent closure are high.

it will create high volumes of sulfur dioxide when burned. Typical western coal, on the other hand, has less sulfur and a lower heat content, which means that more tons of coal must be mined and shipped to produce the same energy. Historically, these regional differences have had a major impact on the politics of coal in the United States. Congressional representatives from Eastern states have tended to support requirements for the installation of power plant scrubbers, which would remove sulfur compounds from the emitted stack gas and thus allow the plants to continue to burn high-sulfur coal. Representatives from Rocky Mountain states have tended to support laws that would promote shipment of low-sulfur Western coal to power plants in the East and Midwest. *See* Bruce A. Ackerman and William T. Hassler, Clean Coal/Dirty Air (1981).

4.   CHANGING MARKETS FOR COAL

Iron and steel used to be big consumers of coal in the form of coke. Now, much of our steel is imported, and what is made here does not use much coke any more. Today less than 5% of American coal goes to the steel industry. Electric utilities continue to consume the lion's share of the coal mined in the United States (92% in 2013), though their consumption has declined from a peak of 1.05 billion short tons[2] in 2007 to about 858 million short tons in 2013. *See* EIA, Annual Energy Outlook, May 2014, http://www.eia.gov/forecasts/aeo/. This decline corresponds to increases in domestic shale gas production and the associated decline in domestic natural gas prices. The remainder of the coal mined in the United States is used for industrial purposes, such as cement plants and foundries. The heaviest use of coal tends to be in the Eastern-Central part of the country, from Pennsylvania to Missouri. Less coal is used on the East and West Coasts. But the state that burns the most coal is Texas, mostly lignite that is used for power generation.

Over time, coal production in the United States has shifted sharply to the West from the East, and toward strip mining and away from underground mining. **Table 3–1** shows state-by-state production data for 2010.

---

[2]   A short ton is a unit of mass equal to 2,000 pounds, and, in the United States, is commonly simply referred to as a ton. By contrast, the metric ton, or "tonne," is 1,000 kilograms and 2,240 pounds.

Table 3–1: Top 5 Coal Producing States, 2010
Data Source: EIA, Annual Coal Report, 2011
http://www.eia.gov/coal/annual/

Mine Type	Number of Mines	Production
Wyoming Total	**19**	**442,522**
Underground	1	3,819
Surface	18	438,703
West Virginia Total	**252**	**135,220**
Underground	152	84,544
Surface	100	50,676
Kentucky Total	**392**	**104,960**
Underground	171	63,993
Surface	221	40,967
Pennsylvania Total	**240**	**58,593**
Underground	44	47,667
Surface	196	10,926
Montana Total	**6**	**44,732**
Underground	1	4,389
Surface	5	40,343

Coal exports fell sharply in the early years of the 21st century, but the rate of decline has decreased in the last few years. Recently, some American coal has found a market in Europe, where natural gas prices remain high and tied to oil prices.

B. COAL MINING

Mines are thriving in the West, where mining is less labor-intensive, but they are closing in many coal-mining areas east of the Mississippi. In the last two decades, thousands of small mines have closed. This gradual switch to larger-scale, higher-technology mining has cut the number of jobs in the industry almost by half between 1986 and 2012, from about 155,000 to about 54,000. Huge surface mines in the Powder River Basin of Wyoming have become the primary source of fuel for electricity generation.

The decline in underground mining and the growth of surface mining has aggravated the legal problems of the industry in two key respects: (1) the declining number of companies engaged in underground mining has depleted a potential source of financial support for remedying the health and environmental problems created by these mines; and (2) the increasing number of surface mines has aroused significant opposition to the transformation of the landscape that they create.

1. HEALTH AND SAFETY IN UNDERGROUND MINING

Originally, most coal was mined through underground methods—digging shafts and tunnels spreading out underground from a single minehead. Although this creates highly intensive activity on the surface around the minehead, it does not necessarily appear to have a substantial impact on the surface of most of the land under which the coal lies because most of the work takes place underground. Surface subsidence caused by underground mining, while rare, constitutes an exception to this generalization.

Underground coal mines pose significant health and safety problems for the mine workers. Methane gas, which is commonly found in association with coal, is potentially explosive and can also cause asphyxiation, so underground mines must be carefully ventilated. As the coal is removed from an underground seam there is always a danger that the mine shaft will collapse, crushing anyone who happens to be in it; engineering plans to prevent mine collapse are not always successful. Finally, coal miners inhale large amounts of coal dust that, over a period of years, can cause black lung disease, a progressive loss of lung capacity that can be fatal unless the miner retires promptly after the initial diagnosis. Alan Derickson, Black Lung: Anatomy of a Public Health Disaster (1998). Public attention focused on the hazards of coal mining in the 1960s. Congress passed the Federal Coal Mine Health and Safety Act of 1969 (FCMHSA), 30 U.S.C. § 801, and the Black Lung Benefits Act of 1972, 30 U.S.C. § 900.

The FCMHSA establishes health and safety standards for underground mining and delegates enforcement responsibility to the Federal Mine Safety and Health Administration (MSHA). Readers familiar with the Occupational Safety and Health Act will see a similarity between the Occupational Safety and Health Administration's (OSHA's) standards and MSHA standards in that both prescribe permissible exposure limits for indoor air pollutants in mines (like dust and methane), as well as broader safety standards for miners. (Indeed, both OSHA and MSHA are agencies within the Department of Labor.) More particularly, MSHA rules are divided into equipment standards, 30 C.F.R. Parts 14–36, health standards, 30 C.F.R. Part 70, and safety standards, 30 C.F.R. Part 75.

a.   SAFETY AND MINING FATALITIES

Coal mining fatalities have fallen with declines in coal mining employment, but fatalities per worker have declined as well. According the MSHA data, in 1912 about 2,400 miners died, of about 722,000 employed in coal mining (3 percent). In 2012, 20 of 137,000 miners perished (less than 2/10 of 1 percent). Rates of non-fatal injuries have also declined. Nevertheless, high profile mining disasters still occur in the United States. In 2010, 29 miners were killed at Massey Energy's Upper Big Branch mine in Naoma, West Virginia. In the aftermath of the disaster, Alpha Natural Resources, Massey's successor, settled wrongful death claims with the miners' families for an undisclosed amount, and reached a $210 million settlement with the U.S. Department of Justice that spared the corporation (but not individuals) criminal prosecution. Alpha also faced shareholder litigation over allegations that shareholders were misled by Massey about safety conditions at the mine. The U.S. government has pursued criminal charges against several Massey executives, alleging that company officials disabled methane detectors and falsified safety records. As of this writing the government has secured four convictions, and more charges may be filed. The convictions include a 2013 plea agreement with the mine superintendent under which he was sentenced to 42 months in prison for conspiracy to impede the MSHA and to violate mining safety and health laws. Howard Berkes, Former Massey Exec Gets 42 Months in

Mine Disaster Case, Nat'l Pub. Radio, Sept. 10, 2013, http://www.npr.org/blogs/thetwo-way/2013/09/10/221161240/former-massey-exec-gets-42-months-in-mine-disaster-case.

The Upper Big Branch disaster had been preceded by criticism of the MSHA's enforcement practices. Critics saw the agency's approach as lax and tolerant of patterns of bad behavior by mine owners like Massey. *See, e.g.* Jane Barrett, When Business Conduct Turns Violent: Bringing BP, Massey and Other Scofflaws to Justice, 48 Am. Crim. L. Rev. 287 (2011) (alleging that many serious mining and drilling accidents are caused by employers' failure to follow established rules). In the two years preceding the accident MSHA had issued more than 600 notices of violation against Massey. Indeed, after the accident Secretary of Labor Hilda Solis appointed an independent panel to examine the accident. The panel concluded that if MSHA had done timely enforcement of laws and regulations prior to the explosion, "it would have lessened the chances of—and possibly could have prevented" the accident. The FCMSHA empowers MSHA to enjoin mining operations under certain circumstances, but the agency did not use that power until after the Upper Big Branch accident. In November 2010 it issued an injunction against Freedom Energy Mining and Sidney Coal, Inc. to close a mine for its pattern of safety violations at Mine No. 1 in Pikes County, Kentucky. Solis v. Freedom Energy Mining Co., No. 10–132–ART, 2010 WL 5209239, at 1 (E.D. Ky., 2010).

In addition to this use of its injunction power, the agency responded to the criticism of its prior approach by enacting a new "patterns of violation" (POV) rule for dealing with serial bad actors in the mining industry.

Mine Safety and Health Administration, Pattern of Violations, Final Rule
78 Fed. Reg. 5056 (2013).

In enacting the Federal Mine Safety and Health Act of 1977 (Mine Act), Congress included the pattern of violations (POV) provision in section 104(e) to provide MSHA with an additional enforcement tool to protect miners when the mine operator demonstrated a disregard for the health and safety of miners. The need for such a provision was forcefully demonstrated during the investigation of the Scotia Mine disaster, which occurred in 1976 in Eastern Kentucky (S. Rep. No. 181, 95th Cong., 1st Sess. at 32). As a result of explosions on March 9 and 11, 1976, caused by dangerous accumulations of methane, 23 miners and three mine inspectors lost their lives. The Scotia Mine had a chronic history of persistent, serious violations that were repeatedly cited by MSHA. After abating the violations, the mine operator would permit the same violations to recur, repeatedly exposing miners to the same hazards. The accident investigation showed that MSHA's then existing enforcement program had been unable to address the Scotia Mine's history of recurring violations.

The Mine Act places the responsibility for ensuring the health and safety of miners on mine operators. The legislative history of the Mine Act emphasizes that Congress reserved the POV provision for mine operators with a record of repeated significant and substantial (S&S)

violations. Congress intended the POV provision to be used for mine operators who have not responded to the Agency's other enforcement efforts. The legislative history states that Congress believed that the existence of a pattern would signal to both the mine operator and the Secretary that "there is a need to restore the mine to effective safe and healthful conditions and that the mere abatement of violations as they are cited is insufficient' " (S. Rep. No. 181, supra at 33).

. . . Until mid-2007, POV screening was decentralized; MSHA District offices were responsible for conducting the required annual POV screening of mines. Following the accidents at the Sago, Darby, and Aracoma mines in 2006, MSHA developed a centralized POV screening process.

MSHA initiated a newly developed "Pattern of Violations Screening Criteria and Scoring Model' " in mid-2007, using a computer program based on the screening criteria and scoring model to generate lists of mines with a potential pattern of violations (PPOV). In late 2009, MSHA determined that the Agency needed to revise its POV regulation and placed Part 104—Pattern of Violations on the Agency's 2010 Spring Semi-annual Regulatory Agenda. The safety and health conditions at the Upper Big Branch (UBB) mine that led to the accident on April 5, 2010, further demonstrated the need to update the POV regulation. As one commenter stated, the UBB mine avoided being placed on a POV despite an egregious record of noncompliance.

In order to increase transparency, the Agency also created a user-friendly, "Monthly Monitoring Tool for Pattern of Violations" (on-line Monthly Monitoring Tool) that provides mine operators, on a monthly basis, a statement of their performance with respect to each of the PPOV screening criteria posted on MSHA's Web site.

Prior to MSHA's creation of the on-line Monthly Monitoring Tool, mine operators had to track each mine's compliance performance and calculate the statistics to determine whether the mine met each of the specific screening criteria. Many mine operators relied on MSHA to issue a PPOV notice. Now, with MSHA's on-line Monthly Monitoring Tool, they do not have to calculate the statistics. Operators, including those that own multiple mines, can easily monitor their performance.

. . . Consistent with the Mine Act, the final rule covers all mines. MSHA acknowledges, however, that the majority of mine operators are conscientious about providing a safe and healthful work environment for their miners. The POV regulation is not directed at these mine operators. Consistent with the legislative history, it is directed at those few operators who have demonstrated a repeated disregard for the health and safety of miners and the health and safety standards issued under the Mine Act. The final rule addresses situations where a mine operator allows violations to occur and hazardous conditions to develop repeatedly without taking action to ensure that the underlying causes of the violations are corrected.

. . . MSHA's existing POV rule was developed before the widespread use of the Internet or even computers in many mines. Now, with MSHA's on-line Monthly Monitoring Tool, operators, including those that own multiple mines, can easily and frequently monitor their compliance performance. . . . The final rule encourages mine operators to continually evaluate their compliance performance and respond appropriately. Through MSHA's on-line Monthly Monitoring Tool, mine operators now have information readily available regarding each mine, the level of violations compared with the criteria, and an indication of whether the mine in question has triggered one of the POV criteria. This information eliminates uncertainty surrounding POV status and the need for MSHA to inform mine operators of a PPOV, since mine operators are able to access that information at any time . . .

Mine operators are responsible for operating their mines in compliance with all applicable standards and regulations. The on-line Monthly Monitoring Tool, which is currently available, will continue to provide mine operators, on a monthly basis, their performance status relative to the POV screening criteria posted on MSHA's Web site. MSHA developed the on-line Monthly Monitoring Tool based on feedback from the mining industry. MSHA conducted a stakeholder meeting prior to announcing the implementation of the "Monthly Monitoring Tool for Pattern of Violations" on April 6, 2011. At this meeting, MSHA demonstrated use of the on-line Monthly Monitoring Tool. The POV Single Source Page at http://www.msha.gov/POV/POVsinglesource.asp contains the Monthly Monitoring Tool; Pattern of Violations Screening Criteria; Pattern of Violations (POV) Procedures Summary; a copy of the applicable regulations; and contact information to request assistance. MSHA receives and responds to requests for information about the screening criteria, the procedures, and mine-specific data related to the POV procedures and will continue to do so.

Using the enforcement data and specific POV criteria on MSHA's Web site, mine operators can perform the same review of their compliance and accident data as MSHA. MSHA's on-line Monthly Monitoring Tool is self-effectuating, quick, and easy to use; it does not require extra skill or training, technical assistance, or interpretation. Indeed, MSHA data indicate that operators are already making frequent use of the tool—there are nearly 2,200 hits per month on the on-line Monthly Monitoring Tool on the POV single source page. ∎

NOTES AND COMMENTS

1.   The POV rule seeks to use transparency to promote good behavior by mine operators. As a further part of its effort to promote safety, any time a miner dies on the job the MSHA posts a notice, which it calls a "fatalgram," on its web site. The fatalgram explains the details of the fatal accident, and it lists "best practices" for preventing the type of accident at issue. Each fatalgram also includes a tally of the number of mining deaths to date in the calendar year.

2.   Methane is found in coal seams, and also poses a hazard to miners; indeed, the proverbial "canary in the coal mine" was an early form of methane detector. MSHA's exposure limits for methane can be found at 30 C.F.R. Part 75. Methane is also a potent greenhouse gas. However, MSHA standards do not focus on preventing methane emissions. To the contrary, the statute permits ventilating methane from underground mines to the surface. *See* 30 U.S.C. § 863. Typically, methane is vented either through boreholes drilled into the mine (sometimes called "gob vent boreholes"), or through gas wells drilled directly into gas seams. While the FCMHSA does not regulate mine methane once it leaves the mine, MSHA has approved

plans to capture and use underground mine methane; however, as a rule it does not require such capture.

Flaring (burning off, rather than venting) the methane, or using it for power generation, would produce fewer climate impacts by emitting CO_2 (a less potent greenhouse gas) rather than methane to the atmosphere. However, regulators worry that flaring might jeopardize miners' safety, and have been wary of mandating flaring at underground mines. *See* U.S. Forest Serv., Record of Decision, E Seam Methane Drainage Wells Project, Appx. D (Mar. 2008) (setting forth agency position and concerns). To date, neither MSHA nor the U.S. Environmental Protection Agency (EPA) has established a general requirement that methane from underground coal mining be flared.[3] However, active underground coal mines are a covered source category for EPA's greenhouse gas reporting rule, and EPA rules governing underground coal mining operations are found at 40 C.F.R. Part 98(FF). As with all covered source categories under the reporting rule, mining operations must monitor and report GHG emissions. Specifically, mining operations must submit quarterly reports of methane emissions, methane destruction (for example, through flaring), and CO_2 emissions, where applicable. 40 C.F.R. § 98.322. For more on the greenhouse gas reporting rule, see Chapter 5.

b. BLACK LUNG DISEASE

The resurgence of black lung disease among miners poses yet another regulatory problem for the MSHA. In 2012, National Public Radio published a series of reports chronicling the increase. *See* As Mine Protections Fail, Black Lung Cases Surge, Nat'l Pub. Radio, July 9, 2012, http://www.npr.org/2012/07/09/155978300/as-mine-protections-fail-black-lung-cases-surge. MSHA responded in May of 2014 by revising its standards for miners' occupational exposure to respirable coal dust. Specifically, the agency lowered the permissible exposure limit and tightened monitoring and measuring requirements for mining companies. The rule requires the use of "continuous personal dust monitors" (CPDMs) for underground miners, which, as the name implies, provide a continuous measure of exposure to respirable dust. The CPDM requirement takes effect in 2016, and is optional for surface miners. The revised rules can be found at 30 C.F.R. Parts 70, 71, 72, 75, and 90.

While the new respirable dust exposure rule is forward looking, the Black Lung Benefits Act addresses past harm, requiring coal companies to pay benefits to miners who had contracted the disease, including some who had left the companies' employ long ago. Usery v. Turner Elkhorn Mining Co., 428 U.S. 1 (1976) (upholding retroactive application of Act).

Because the onset of black lung disease and other work-related illnesses may arise long after the miner quits working, the attribution of the injury to a particular employer has proven to be a problem, especially because many mining companies have gone out of business in the period of time between when employees were exposed to coal dust and when they seek health benefits. The Coal Industry Retiree Health Benefit Act

---

[3] For mining development on federal lands, it is conceivable that the obligation to flare or capture methane could be included as a requirement of the lease. For a discussion of the legal authority for the use of leases in this way, *see* Robert A. Bassett, James A. Holtkamp & Rebecca Ryon, U.S. Laws and Policies Regarding Capturing Methane Gas, U.S. Coal Mine Methane Conference (2009).

of 1992, 26 U.S.C. § 9701, increased the responsibility of mining companies to pay lifetime medical benefits to miners. It adopted the policy that coal mining companies were retroactively liable for these health benefits if they had been in the coal business after the point in time when there was a "general understanding" between the industry and the United Mine Workers that lifetime health benefits would be paid. The retroactive elements of the Act were challenged by Eastern Enterprises, a company that had gotten out of the coal business many years ago,[4] but now found itself responsible for the medical costs of some retired miners.

Eastern Enterprises alleged that it had been in the coal business only until 1966, at which time it spun off its coal business to a subsidiary that it later sold. The Act assigned Eastern the responsibility for paying the medical benefits of certain miners if the miners had worked for Eastern prior to 1966 and had not worked for any other currently existing mine operator since that time. In 1998, the case reached the Supreme Court, which held the Act unconstitutional as applied to Eastern in one of the most confusing opinions in recent Court history. The Court considered three potential constitutional defects in the Coal Act and its application to Eastern Enterprises. One option was the Ex Post Facto Clause, but since *Calder v. Bull*, 3 U.S. 386 (1798) the Court had limited the application of that clause primarily to criminal statutes. A second option was the Due Process Clause, and the use of the once-popular notion of "substantive due process" to address the Act's unfairness. The third option was the Takings Clause, which had been more commonly applied to statutes that impose burdens on real property. Although the Court held the application of the Act to Eastern to be unconstitutional, there was no majority agreement on which clause of the Constitution had been violated. Four justices found that the Act constituted a taking of property without just compensation, but refused to consider the issue of substantive due process. One justice, Justice Kennedy, found that there was no taking, but held that the Act violated substantive due process as applied to Eastern Enterprises. Four dissenters would have upheld the Act. They agreed with Justice Kennedy that there was no taking, and they agreed that the Act should be tested on grounds of substantive due process, but they said that the statute did *not* violate substantive due process. *Eastern Enterprises v. Apfel,* 524 U.S. 498 (1998).

In the course of his opinion, Justice Kennedy interpreted the Takings Clause in a new way; he said that a liability to make a monetary payment, such as a tax or a fee, could never be the subject of a taking because it did not involve an "identified property interest" that was protected by the Clause. The four dissenting justices all announced their agreement with Justice Kennedy on this issue. As a result, a majority of the Court now supports an interpretation of the Takings Clause that would appear to make it completely inapplicable to statutes such as the Coal Industry Retiree Health Benefit Act.

Therefore the *Eastern Enterprises* case produced the highly unusual result of a part of a statute being found invalid but with no majority

---

4   Eastern Enterprises is the parent corporation of Boston Gas Company, the largest distributor of natural gas in New England, and of Midland Enterprises, Inc., the leading barge carrier of coal. *See* Note, Nontraditional Takings and the Coal Act, 20 Energy L.J. 117, 123 (1999).

agreeing on the reason for the invalidity. The lack of any consistent rationale for the Court's result has posed difficult problems for the lower courts, as the following case illustrates. The case arose because the *Eastern Enterprises* decision struck down the Act as applied to a coal company that had left the business in 1966, but it left open the issue of the Act's validity to other companies that had continued in business after that time. The companies in the following case stayed in the coal business through the 1970s, but they argued that the precedent of *Eastern Enterprises* should protect them as well.

Unity Real Estate Co. v. Hudson

178 F.3d 649 (3d Cir. 1999).

■ BECKER, C.J. In *Eastern Enterprises v. Apfel,* 524 U.S. 498 (1998), the Supreme Court held unconstitutional the portion of the 1992 Coal Industry Retiree Health Benefit Act (Coal Act), 26 U.S.C. §§ 9701–9722 (1994 & Supp. II), that required former coal mine operators to pay for health benefits for retired miners and their dependents, as applied to a former operator who last signed a coal industry benefit agreement [an "NBCWA"] in 1964. In this case, we are asked to apply *Eastern* to former coal mine operators who were signatories to coal industry agreements in 1978 and thereafter. *Eastern* was decided by a sharply divided Court, and the parties disagree as to what, if any, principles commanded a majority.

The plaintiffs, Unity Real Estate ("Unity") and Barnes & Tucker Co. ("B&T"), challenge the Coal Act as applied to them as both a violation of substantive due process and an unconstitutional uncompensated taking. Although it is an exceedingly close question, and we are highly sympathetic to plaintiffs' unfortunate situation, in which retroactively imposed liability operates to bind them to commitments they had thought satisfied when they left the coal industry, we conclude that the Act is constitutional as applied to these plaintiffs. Accordingly, their recourse must be to Congress rather than to the courts.

First, we conclude, albeit with substantial hesitation, that the Coal Act does not violate due process. Our due process inquiry proceeds in two parts. We acknowledge at the outset that there is a gap between what the contracts between the union and the mining companies required and what the Coal Act now mandates from those former mining companies. Because this is a substantive due process challenge, we accord deference to Congress's judgments, based on the report and recommendations of the Coal Commission. While reasonable minds could differ on the point, we are satisfied that the agreements signed by the plaintiffs in 1978 and thereafter promised that miners and their dependents would receive lifetime benefits from the benefit funds, and that, at all events, these agreements informed reasonable expectations that the benefits would continue for life. Similarly, we conclude that it was reasonable for Congress to conclude that the plaintiffs' withdrawal from the funds contributed to the funds' financial instability, though the agreements themselves permitted withdrawal. The history of coal mining in this country also supports Congress's decision to step in when the funds that provided health benefits to retired miners began to falter.

The question we must then answer is whether those congressional judgments provide enough of a rationale for closing the gap between the contracts and the needs of the benefit funds through the mechanism of the Coal Act. Consistent with our due process jurisprudence, we ask whether the Coal Act was a rational response to the problems Congress identified, taking into account the Act's retroactivity, which is highly disfavored in our legal culture. In light of Congress's findings and in the context of extensive government regulation of the coal industry, we hold that it was not fundamentally unfair or unjust for Congress to conclude that the former coal companies should be responsible for paying for such benefits, even if they were no longer contractually obligated to pay into the benefit funds. The retroactive scope of this enactment, especially as applied to plaintiff Unity (eleven years), approaches the edge of permissible legislative action, but we cannot say that the law is beyond the legislative power.

We also decline to find a compensable taking on the ground that the Coal Act will put the plaintiffs out of business, because it is contrary to the reasoning of a majority of the Supreme Court in *Eastern*. Moreover, granting relief whenever a plaintiff could credibly argue that it would be driven out of business by a regulation would create major difficulties in evaluating the constitutionality of much modern legislation. We therefore decline to construe this regulatory burden as a "categorical taking" analogous to the total destruction of the value of a specific piece of real property.

[The court then analyzed the Supreme Court's *Eastern Enterprises* opinion, noting the unusual split in the Court's rationale (described above), and that Eastern Enterprises (i) was involved in coal mining until 1965, (ii) had signed every NBCWA from 1947 until 1964, (iii) was assigned liability under the Act for over 1000 miners, based on Eastern's status as the pre-1978 signatory for whom the miners had worked for the longest period of time, and (iv) its total liability was estimated to be between $50 and $100 million. The court reasoned that the key issue for its determination was whether companies that had stayed in the coal business through 1981, like the present plaintiffs, were distinguishable from Eastern because the bargaining agreements entered into during the time period between 1978 and 1981 implicitly promised the miners that they would receive lifetime health benefits.]

Unlike Eastern, Unity and B&T, as members of the Bituminous Coal Operators' Association (BCOA), participated in the negotiations that created the post-1978 funding structure. They benefitted from the NBCWAs by obtaining labor peace. Although the contract allowed the companies to unload their obligations to the retirees onto the Trustees, they should reasonably have anticipated that such a strategy would threaten the Funds and might well prompt a congressional response. . . . The question is what reasonable expectations the coal companies' actions created. While an expectation cannot be reasonable without some foundation in the real world, an explicit representation that the companies would provide lifetime benefits is not required, since reasonable expectations may arise from a consistent course of conduct as well.

Plaintiffs and amici argue that the coal companies never made any promises, implicit or explicit, or raised any expectations of lifetime benefits. They first point to the text of the NBCWAs, which did not themselves require the coal companies to provide lifetime benefits under all circumstances. . . . It is true that the funding contribution requirements were limited to the life of the agreement, "ending when this Agreement is terminated," in 1978 and subsequent NBCWAs. Yet all of these arguments have the same fundamental weakness, which is that they go to the contract and not to the reasonable expectations that might have been created by the contract. The United Mine Workers Association ("UMWA") negotiator's testimony is a particularly strong example of this: the parties could have agreed to eliminate benefits in any given negotiation, but there was no realistic chance that they would. . . .

Ultimately, although the issue is close, we conclude that the Coal Act is targeted to address the problem of insufficient resources in the benefit funds and that it puts the burden on those who, in Congress's reasonable judgment, should bear it. The law's retroactivity is troubling, yet given the nature of the commitments at issue and the relationship of Coal Act liabilities to past acts in the industry, we cannot say that the Act violates due process.

■ ALDISERT, J., concurring: As a native of Carnegie, Pennsylvania—a coal mining and steel mill town near Pittsburgh—who is old enough to remember the organizational efforts of John L. Lewis in the coal fields in the 1930s and the 1947 Krug-Lewis Agreement, I no doubt have a unique perspective. I know first-hand the mantra of every coal miner through decades of strikes and picketing: "No Contract, No Work."

To the miner, the actual contract controlled, not the expectation of future agreements. Without the contract in hand, the miners would not pick up their lamps at the lamp house and descend into the shafts. They worked under the precise language in a given contract and under no other representations. The sordid history of the coal company towns that surrounded Carnegie, and the inhumane treatment of the miners and their families prior to effective unionization in the mines, impelled the miners to require thereafter that every representation of working conditions and benefits be set forth in clear language in a hard-fought written collective bargaining agreement.

. . . Without additional and more realistic Congressional intervention, we may see a phenomenon of the "last man standing," as companies disappear from the economic scene and responsibility for paying benefits shifts to surviving companies. If this case is any example and a forerunner of things to come, the operation of the present statutory solution to the vexing health benefit problem of retirees and their dependents may serve as a full employment program for bankruptcy lawyers of companies unable to make prescribed payments. Sadly, I do not believe that this statement is an argumentum ad terrorem.

I join in the judgment of the court. ■

NOTES AND COMMENTS

1. Professor Jan Laitos has been suggesting for some years that retroactivity is one of the Court's half-hidden concerns in all property rights cases, not just takings cases. *See* Jan G. Laitos, Legislative Retroactivity, 52 Wash. U. J. Urb. & Contemp. L. 81 (1997). In his 1999 treatise on property rights, he cites the *Eastern Enterprises* opinion as a vindication of his position. For his extended discussion of the history of the Supreme Court's

retroactivity decisions and their modern relevance, see Jan Laitos, The Law of Property Rights Protection, Chs. 13–16 (1999).

2.   On the other hand, the Supreme Court in *Eastern Enterprises* is certainly not saying that all retroactive legislation is invalid on its face. Both the plurality opinion by Justice O'Connor and Justice Kennedy's concurrence carefully limited their discussion to the specific facts of that particular company's situation. As Justice O'Connor wrote, "[L]egislation might be unconstitutional if it imposes severe retroactive liability on a limited class of parties that could not have anticipated the liability, and the extent of that liability is substantially disproportionate to the parties' experience." 524 U.S. 528 (O'Connor, J.). Legislation that "singles out certain employers to bear a burden that is substantial in amount, based on the employers' conduct far in the past, and unrelated to any commitment that the employers made or to any injury they caused, the governmental action implicates fundamental principles of fairness underlying the Taking Clause." *Id.* at 537. By contrast, it should be noted that Justice Thomas's brief concurrence suggested he may be willing to go so far as to hold all retroactive legislation facially invalid. *See id.* at 538–39 (Thomas, J., conc.).

Professor Mark Tushnet refers to such narrowly limited opinions as "judicial minimalism," and calls *Eastern Enterprises* the best recent example because "it used so many standards and made each important to the conclusion." Mark Tushnet, The New Constitutional Order and the Chastening of Constitutional Aspiration, 113 Harv. L. Rev. 29, 92–93 (1999). Is the most that we can discern from the *Eastern Enterprises* opinions that the Court may be telling us that it will employ some higher level of scrutiny in reviewing laws that have "severe retroactive" effect? Will the Court ever be able to come up with a bright line rule that alerts us to the degree of retroactivity that would be permitted? Should there be retroactive liability for environmental harms from energy-related activities generally? Does your answer change if comprehensive *ex ante* regulation specifies how energy should be produced (as with hydroelectric and nuclear licensing)?

3.   There have been no successful challenges to the Act's constitutionality since the *Unity* opinion. The standard set forth in *Unity* has been applied several times, and no plaintiff has succeeded in meeting the standard. The courts have tended to apply the substantive due process test, concluding that the plaintiffs failed to meet that test. *See, e.g.,* USX Corp. v. Barnhart, 395 F.3d 161 (3d Cir. 2004); Pittston Co. v. United States, 368 F.3d 385 (4th Cir. 2004); Berwind Corp. v. Comm'r of Soc. Sec., 307 F.3d 222 (3d Cir. 2002); A.T. Massey Coal Co., Inc. v. Massanari, 305 F.3d 226 (4th Cir. 2002); Apogee Coal Co. v. Holland, 296 F.3d 1294 (11th Cir. 2002); Coltec Indus., Inc. v. Hobgood, 280 F.3d 262 (3d Cir. 2002); Anker Energy Co. v. Consolidation Coal Co., 177 F.3d 161 (3d Cir. 1999).

4.   The Coal Act does not involve the acquisition of any property or money by the government, but requires the coal companies to pay money directly to a fund for the coal miners. Does the fact that the government is transferring wealth from one group to another, rather than acquiring a property interest itself, suggest the need for an analysis under the due process clause rather than the Taking Clause? *See* John V. Orth, Taking from A and Giving to B: Substantive Due Process and the Case of the Shifting Paradigm, 14 Const. Commentary 337 (1997).

5.   Today, surface mining (also called strip mining) is the most efficient way of mining coal if the coal is relatively near the surface. About three-fifths of

the coal mined in the United States is currently mined by surface mining using huge shovels the size of a multistory building. Surface mining does not create the same health and safety issues for the mine workers as underground mining. Moreover, surface mining is much less labor-intensive, so the productivity of each employee is far higher than in underground mines. On the other hand, the impact of surface mining on the use of the surface of the land is more extensive than the impact of underground mining.

2.   EXTERNALITIES OF COAL MINING

In addition to the health and safety problems of mining workers, coal mining often has serious adverse impacts on other people who are not associated with the coal industry. These impacts have led to extensive legislation designed to regulate these impacts.

a.   UNDERGROUND MINING EXTERNALITIES

Underground mining was the only method of coal mining used in the 19th century and it still accounts for at least a third of the coal produced in the United States. A mine shaft is drilled down to the coal seam. Then tunnels are excavated through the seam. Two specific problems associated with underground mining have posed major regulatory issues:

(1)   Mines cause subsidence of the surface; either intentional, in the case of longwall mining (see *infra* subsection (c)(3)), or accidental, after the mine is abandoned and the support system collapses; and

(2)   Mines tap into seams of minerals and heavy metals that then leak out of the mines into streams or aquifers where they become water pollutants called acid mine drainage.

i.   *Subsidence*

Coal mine subsidence is the lowering of strata overlying a coal mine, including the land surface, caused by the extraction of underground coal. This lowering of the strata can have devastating effects. It can cause substantial damage to foundations, walls, and the structural integrity of houses and buildings. Subsidence frequently causes sinkholes or troughs in land, which make the land difficult or impossible to develop. Its effect on farming has been well documented: many subsided areas cannot be plowed or properly prepared. Subsidence can also cause the loss of groundwater and surface ponds. *Keystone Bituminous Coal Ass'n v. DeBenedictis,* 480 U.S. 470 (1987).

In the famous case of *Pennsylvania Coal Co. v. Mahon,* 260 U.S. 393 (1922), the Supreme Court held that the Kohler Act, a Pennsylvania statute that prevented coal companies from mining coal in a way that caused subsidence to the owner of a surface estate, was invalid as a taking of property without just compensation. Justice Holmes, writing for the majority, acknowledged that while "there is a public interest . . . in every purchase and sale and in all that happens within the commonwealth . . . ," that interest "does not warrant . . . this kind of interference." Balancing the "extent of the public interest" (which Holmes characterized as largely private and "limited") against "the extent of the taking" (which Holmes characterized as "great" in that it rendered commercial mining impracticable), the Court concluded that the statute effected a taking requiring compensation. The *Pennsylvania Coal* decision represented the first time that the Supreme Court had held that a regulation could be "tantamount to a taking." In recent years, the Court has devoted increased attention to the issue of regulatory takings.

Sixty-five years after the initial *Pennsylvania Coal* decision, the Court returned to the issue of coal mine subsidence. In *Keystone Bituminous Coal Ass'n v. DeBenedictis,* 480 U.S. 470 (1987), this time upholding another Pennsylvania statute preventing coal companies from mining coal in a way that caused subsidence to roads, schools and other public facilities. The Court distinguished the earlier case on the ground that it was designed only to rearrange the rights among private parties, while the later statute was designed to protect public safety. Said the Court:

> The holdings and assumptions of the Court in *Pennsylvania Coal* provide obvious and necessary reasons for distinguishing *Pennsylvania Coal* from the case before us today. . . . First, unlike the Kohler Act, the character of the governmental action involved here leans heavily against finding a taking; the Commonwealth of Pennsylvania has acted to arrest what it perceives to be a significant threat to the common welfare. Second, there is no record in this case to support a finding, similar to the one the Court made in *Pennsylvania Coal*, that the Subsidence Act makes it impossible for petitioners to profitably engage in their business, or that there has been undue interference with their investment-backed expectations.
>
> Unlike the Kohler Act, which was passed upon in *Pennsylvania Coal*, the Subsidence Act does not merely involve a balancing of the private economic interests of coal companies against the private interests of the surface owners. The Pennsylvania Legislature specifically found that important public interests are served by enforcing a policy that is designed to minimize subsidence in certain areas.
>
> 480 U.S. at 476.

After Keystone, the courts have had difficulty deciding whether to award damages to coal companies that have been denied permits. Where the federal government refused to issue a permit to mine coal to a company due to a risk of public injury because of large cracks in the ground, collapsing structures, and breaks in gas, water and electrical lines, the federal circuit found that the mining company was not deprived of all beneficial use because "the nature of the owner's estate shows that the prescribed use interests were not part of the title to begin with." M & J Coal Co. v. United States, 47 F.3d 1148 (Fed. Cir. 1995). *But see* Machipongo Land & Coal Co., Inc. v. Commonwealth, 719 A.2d 19 (Pa. Commw. Ct. 1998) (discussing various theories for measuring the extent to which the regulation diminishes the company's interest); Eastern Minerals Int'l, Inc. v. United States, 36 Fed. Cl. 541 (1996) (holding that an inexcusable delay in issuing a mining permit may constitute a taking).

Congress entered the dispute in 1992 by adding a new § 720 to the Mining Act, *see* Energy Policy Act of 1992 (EPAct 1992), Pub. L. No. 102–486, § 2504(a)(1), which provides:

(a) Requirements. Underground coal mining operations conducted after October 24, 1992, shall comply with each of the following requirements:

(1) Promptly repair, or compensate for, material damage resulting from subsidence caused to any occupied residential dwelling and structures related thereto, or non-commercial building due to underground coal mining operations. Repair of damage shall include rehabilitation, restoration, or replacement of the damaged occupied residential dwelling and structures related thereto, or non-commercial building. Compensation shall be provided to the owner of the damaged occupied residential dwelling and structures related thereto or non-commercial building and shall be in the full amount of the diminution in value resulting from the subsidence. Compensation may be accomplished by the purchase, prior to mining, of a noncancellable premium-prepaid insurance policy.

(2) Promptly replace any drinking, domestic, or residential water supply from a well or spring in existence prior to the application for a surface coal mining and reclamation permit, which has been affected by contamination, diminution, or interruption resulting from underground coal mining operations. Nothing in this section shall be construed to prohibit or interrupt underground coal mining operations.

The D.C. Circuit Court of Appeals upheld regulations promulgated under EPAct 1992 requiring coal companies to repair or fully compensate homeowners for property damage caused by subsidence, even if a waiver agreement was in place. Nat'l Mining Ass'n v. Babbitt, 172 F.3d 906 (D.C. Cir. 1999). The National Mining Association (NMA) had challenged the regulation as unreasonable "to the extent it purports to nullify prior agreements between owners of eligible structures and underground mine operators." NMA argued that if the statute authorizes the annulment of waiver agreements, landowners would receive a windfall, and coal mining companies could suffer an unconstitutional taking of contract rights through a double recovery scheme, in which the mining company first pays a landowner for subsidence damage by buying waiver rights and then has to pay again for post-mining damage through the Energy Policy Act.

The government argued in response that there would be no double recovery because the cost of the waiver would be subtracted from the post-mining damage amount. The court agreed with the government's position.

NMA also argued that interference with contract rights is a per se taking. The court disagreed, citing the rule from *Connolly v. Pension Benefit Guar. Corp.,* 475 U.S. 211, 244 (1986): "legislation [that] disregards or destroys existing contractual rights does not always transform the regulation into an illegal taking." NMA should have been prepared to demonstrate why "(1) the economic impact of the regulation on the claimant; (2) the extent to which the regulation has interfered with investment-backed expectations; and (3) the character of the governmental action" show that an unconstitutional taking would result. *Id.* at 225 (quoting *Penn Cent. Transp. Co. v. City of New York*, 438 U.S. 104, 124 (1978)).

At the present time, therefore, coal mining companies are responsible for most significant damages caused by subsidence. Although Justice Holmes' famous opinion in *Pennsylvania Coal* is still widely cited, the factual context on which it was based now appears to be obsolete.

ii.   Acid Mine Drainage

Acid mine drainage (AMD) can be associated with either surface mining or underground mining, and often results in water polluted not only with high acidity but with toxic substances. The purpose of the Clean Water Act (CWA) "is to restore and maintain the chemical, physical, and biological integrity of the nation's waters." 33 U.S.C. § 1251. The idea is to use technology-based effluent limitations and water quality-based ambient standards to achieve swimmable and fishable water throughout the United States. These standards are implemented through the national pollutant discharge elimination system (NPDES) permit. Individual states are responsible for administering the NPDES permitting system. The EPA may administer a program only if the state fails to do so or the state's program is found to be inappropriate.

The CWA makes the discharge of any pollutant into navigable waters by any person unlawful, except when in compliance with designated sections of the statute. *Id.* § 11. A pollutant is basically anything other than sewage from vessels or fluids used to facilitate the production from an oil or gas well.[5] *Id.* § 1362(6). Discharge of a pollutant is the addition of any pollutant to navigable waters from a point source. *Id.* § 1362(12). Navigable waters are "the waters of the United States," including the territorial seas. *Id.* § 1362(7). "Point source" is broadly defined, and includes pipes, tunnels and animal feed lots. *Id.* § 1362(14).

In the following case, the Fourth Circuit attempted to apply the statutory language to AMD from a West Virginia mine.

United States v. Law

979 F.2d 977 (4th Cir. 1992).

■ PER CURIAM. Lewis R. Law and Mine Management, Inc. appeal their felony convictions for violating the Clean Water Act, 33 U.S.C. § 1319(c)(2) ("CWA") by knowingly discharging polluted water into Wolf and Arbuckle Creeks in Fayette County, West Virginia without a National Pollution Discharge Elimination System ("NPDES") permit. Finding no reversible error, we affirm.

In 1977 Lewis R. Law formed Mine Management, Inc. ("MMI"), a West Virginia corporation, to engage in various coal-related business activities. From MMI's inception, Law was its sole officer and stockholder. In 1980, MMI purchased 241 acres from the New River Company ("New River"). The conveyance included an aged coal preparation plant, masses of coal refuse ("gob piles"), and a water treatment system. New River installed this system in the late 1970s to collect, divert, treat, and discharge runoff and leachate from a gob pile that covered a large portion of the subject property.

---

[5]   Pollution from oil and gas wells is dealt with under other statutes. *See* Chapter 4.

The water treatment system was designed to reduce the acidity and metal content of drainage from the gob pile. The system comprised a collection pond near Wolf Creek, a pump, and piping that channeled the collected water over a ridge and through a hopper, which dispensed soda ash briquettes to raise the pH of the water. Iron and manganese then precipitated out as the water flowed through two settling ponds before its discharge into Arbuckle Creek.

The water treatment system was subject to an NPDES permit when MMI purchased the site. Despite repeated notice, however, neither MMI nor Law ever applied for, or was granted, an NPDES permit authorizing discharges into Wolf or Arbuckle Creeks. Due to MMI's failure to operate the water treatment system effectively, acid mine drainage discharged from the collection pond into Wolf Creek, or from the second settling pond into Arbuckle Creek, on at least 16 occasions between March, 1987 and November 15, 1991. Law and MMI were indicted for violating the CWA, 33 U.S.C. § 1319(c)(2), tried to a jury, and found guilty. Law was sentenced to two years in prison and Law and MMI were fined $80,000.00 each.

Law and MMI challenge their convictions on two grounds. They argue, first, that the trial court instructed the jury erroneously on the law governing their case and, second, that the court abused its discretion in barring evidence regarding New River's alleged policy of concealing preexisting environmental problems from prospective purchasers of its property. We reject both grounds of appeal.

Under the CWA, it is a felony to (a) knowingly (b) discharge 8 a pollutant (d) from a point source (e) into a navigable water of the United States (f) without, or in violation of, an NPDES permit. See 33 U.S.C. §§ 1311(a), 1319(c)(2), 1342(a); *Arkansas v. Oklahoma*, 112 S. Ct. 1046, 1054 (1992); see also 33 U.S.C. § 1362(12) (defining "discharge" as "any addition of any pollutant to navigable waters from any point source") (emphases added). Appellants do not contest that they added untreated acid mine drainage to Wolf and Arbuckle Creeks from the collection pond and the settling pond, respectively, knowing that they lacked the requisite NPDES permit.

In challenging the trial court's jury instructions, however, appellants contend that the CWA imposes liability only upon the generators of pollutants discharged into navigable waters of the United States, and not upon persons over whose property preexisting pollutants are passed along to flow finally into navigable waters. They contend that the trial court erred by refusing to instruct the jury that no responsibility lies for discharging pollutants that originate beyond one's own property, and by instructing the jury instead that

> . . . it is not a defense to the charge that the water discharged from the point source came from some other place or places before its discharge from the point source. It is not a defense to this action that some, or all, of the pollutants discharged from a point source originated at places not on the defendants' property. This is because the offense consists of the knowing discharge of a pollutant from a point source into a water of the United States [without, or in violation of, an NPDES permit]. J App 489–90

Appellants rely for this contention upon decisions in *National Wildlife Federation v. Consumers Power Co.,* 862 F.2d 580 (6th Cir. 1988), *National Wildlife Federation v. Gorsuch,* 224 U.S. App. D.C. 41, 693 F.2d 156 (D.C. Cir. 1982), and *Appalachian Power Co. v. Train,* 545 F.2d 1351 (4th Cir. 1976). In these cases, operators of power plants and dams diverted, then released, navigable waters of the United States. The appellate courts held that where "pollutants" existed in the waters of the United States before contact with these facilities, the mere diversion in the flow of the waters did not constitute "additions" of pollutants to the waters. *Consumers Power,* 862 F.2d at 585–86; *Gorsuch,* 693 F.2d at 174–75; *Train,* 545 F.2d at 1377–78. Appellants sought to square their case with these decisions by showing that the headwaters of Wolf and Arbuckle Creeks originated, and were polluted, before entering their water treatment system, so that, like the power plant and dam operators, they had no duty to remove preexisting pollutants.

With respect to pollutants preexisting in the waters of the United States, where the flow of the waters is merely diverted, the trial court's jury instructions did not state the law with strict accuracy ("it is not a defense . . . that some, or all, of the pollutants . . . originated at places not on the defendants' property"). The error was harmless, however, because, as a matter of law, appellants' water treatment system was not part of the waters of the United States; to the contrary, the system constituted a point source.

Unlike the river and lake waters diverted in *Consumers Power, Gorsuch,* and *Train,* appellants' water treatment system collected runoff and leachate subject to an NPDES permit under the CWA, and therefore was not part of the "waters of the United States." *See* 40 C.F.R. § 122.2(g) ("Waste treatment systems, including treatment ponds and lagoons designed to meet the requirements of CWA . . . are not waters of the United States."). The origin of pollutants in the treatment and collection ponds is therefore irrelevant. The proper focus is upon the discharge from the ponds into Wolf and Arbuckle Creeks.

Appellants' treatment system is also unlike the power plants and dams at issue in *Consumers Power, Gorsuch,* and *Train* because it clearly satisfies the statutory definition of "point source." *See* 40 C.F.R. § 122.2 (a "point source" is "any discernible, confined and discrete conveyance, including but not limited to any pipe, ditch, channel, . . . conduit, . . . discrete fissure, . . . [or] landfill leachate collection system . . . from which pollutants are or may be discharged" (emphasis added); "discharge" includes "surface runoff which is collected or channeled by man"); see also *Sierra Club v. Abston Constr. Co.,* 620 F.2d 41, 47 (5th Cir. 1980) (collection and channeling of runoff constitutes a point source). Because appellants' treatment system was, as a matter of law, not part of the waters of the United States but instead a point source, the trial court's instructions to the jury were without prejudicial error.

Appellants also claim that the trial court abused its discretion in excluding evidence concerning New River's alleged policy of concealing existing environmental problems from prospective purchasers. Under the foregoing analysis of the CWA, the relevant *mens rea* issue was Law's knowledge as of March, 1987, that the ponds were discharging pollutants into the creeks without, or in violation of, an NPDES permit. Appellants' attempts to cross-examine former New River employees Louis Briguglio and Don Reedy regarding the alleged policy were therefore properly excluded as irrelevant. Law's testimony regarding his conversations with Briguglio were properly excluded as hearsay.

For the foregoing reasons, we affirm the convictions of Lewis R. Law and Mine Management, Inc. on all counts. ∎

NOTES AND COMMENTS

1.   There are two main categories of NPDES permitting standards under the CWA. Technology-based effluent limits establish discharge requirements from coal mining point sources based on control technology. The regulations require compliance with numerical limits based on the capacities of technologies examined, but do not prescribe the use of a particular technology. Technology-based limits are used to ensure the uniform adoption of advanced effluent standards across entire industry groups without considering the discharge locations or water quality in the receiving water body. 40 C.F.R. § 434. Water quality-based limits are based on the physical qualities of the water body and are designed to protect the designated uses of that water body. Individual states set their own water quality standards, subject to EPA approval. These standards must "protect the public health or welfare, enhance the quality of the water, and serve the purposes of the CWA." 33 U.S.C. § 1313(c)(2)(A). NPDES permit limitations are then established regardless of the availability or effectiveness of treatment technologies. If the existing water quality is above what is necessary to support designated activities, the water quality standards cannot be set lower than what currently exists. Waters that have been designated "special national resources" may not be degraded at all. 40 C.F.R. §§ 131.10, 131.12. The EPA has published regulations governing discharge of acid mine drainage from mines. These "new source performance standards" establish different sets of rules for different subcategories of mines, and, as discussed further in Note 2 directly below, specify the procedures mine owners should use to control discharges of stormwater runoff that contain acids. *See* 40 C.F.R. Part 434.

2.   A mine owner's obligation to secure a NPDES permit may extend beyond the close of operations, if discharges continue to occur. *See* 40 C.F.R. pt. 434(E) (applicable to "post-mining" areas). There is little incentive to comply with a CWA discharge permit once mining is finished if the owner becomes insolvent or no longer exists. For a discussion of post-mining CWA issues, see Mary J. Hackett, Remining and the Water Quality Act of 1987: Operators Beware!, 13 Colum. J. Envtl. L. 99, 115–17 (1987). Under its CWA authority, EPA has established effluent limitations (40 C.F.R. §§ 434.32–434.34) and New Source Performance Standards (40 C.F.R. § 434.35) governing AMD from mines, which specify procedures mine owners must use to control discharges containing acids. Generally, 40 C.F.R. Part 434 addresses a variety of different water discharges from mines, including AMD. To comply with AMD standards, mine operators must use either active or passive treatment systems. An active system may be manual or mechanical and requires the periodic addition of reagents, ongoing support, and maintenance; for example, adding lime to a treatment pool to raise the pH of an acidic discharge. Passive systems are designed to be self-sustaining and use chemical or biological processes that rely on no external support. For example, constructed wetlands are sometimes used to treat mine drainage

because many of the plant species that comprise wetlands thrive on acidic material.

3.   Drainage from abandoned underground coal mines is often a major water pollution problem in those areas where coal has been mined for many years, and many such mines have been placed on the National Priority List under the Comprehensive Environmental Response, Compensation, and Liability Act (CERCLA), 42 U.S.C. § 9601 *et seq* . . . This problem is often aggravated in the East because of the high sulfur content of the coal. *See* William H. Rodgers, Jr., Environmental Law 724 (West Publishing, 2d ed. 1994).

4.   Does *United States v. Law* mean that if anyone owns a point source that is discharging pollutants into water of the United States without a permit, that person is in violation of the CWA, regardless of where the pollutants originated? A review of the joint appendix in the record of the case shows the complexity of the situation faced by Law and MMI.

Law formed Mine Management Company in 1977 to engage in various business activities related to the coal industry. MMI leased the right to recover coal from the property owned by New River Company. Prior to this, New River Company operated the Lochgelly mine on the site. Coal mining activities also took place on the property adjacent to the site. Refuse from New River's coal processing was dumped at the site, resulting in a gob pile that covered approximately 100 acres of the surface, and approximately 100 feet deep. The head waters of the Wolf and Arbuckle Creeks are located near the foot of this gob pile. New River installed a series of collection ponds on the Wolf and Arbuckle Creeks to treat acid mine drainage in 1979. New River acquired an NPDES permit, which was in place when MMI purchased the property.

MMI purchased 241 acres of the surface of the property owned by New River, including the various treatment ponds, in 1980. Between 1980 and 1991, Law was informed on numerous occasions that an NPDES permit was required for the treatment ponds on his property. Law failed to comply.

Conflicting evidence was presented at trial as to how acid mine drainage entered the Wolf Creek collection pond. Prosecution experts testified that AMD leached from the surface of the gob pile as a result of rain and the migration of water through the pile. Defense experts testified that the AMD came from underground springs contaminated as a result of mining activities on other properties adjacent to MMI's site. Law argued that he had no duty to treat the AMD because he was the surface owner and could not be required to treat pollutants generated below the surface. However, Law's argument was unpersuasive because the statute does not require that the defendant create the pollutants. The CWA does not regulate the generation of pollutants, but the addition of pollutants to navigable waters. *See* Los Angeles Cnty. Flood Cntrl. Dist. v. NRDC, 568 U.S. ___, 133 S. Ct. 710 (2013) (conveyance of already-polluted water passing through a flood control and stormwater management system, and ultimately into a navigable river is not a "discharge" requiring an NPDES permit because the system merely transferred polluted water between two parts of the same water body). *See also* Phillip B. Scott, S. Benjamin Bryant, Criminal Enforcement of the Clean Water Act in the Coal Fields: United States v. Law and Beyond, 95 W.Va. L. Rev. 663 (1993).

If Law's argument were accepted, could a mining company discharge pollutants as long as the pollutants were generated by someone else? In the coal fields, could the CWA be circumvented by severing (1) the AMD producing estate, (2) the subsurface from the AMD discharging estate, and (3) the surface? Should there be special treatment of environmental criminal defendants, sometimes called "green collar" criminals, in regard to the criminal intent requirement? *See* Lawrence Friedman & H. Hamilton Hackney III, Questions of Intent: Environmental Crimes and "Public Welfare" Offenses, 10 Villanova Envtl L. J. 1 (1999).

5.   Another one of Law's challenges was that the Wolf and Arbuckle Creeks were polluted before entering the collection ponds. He claimed that the ponds added no additional pollutants and therefore were not regulated by the CWA. This argument was based on evidence that the original headwaters of the stream extended to the area now covered by the gob pile and that the ponds lay in the original stream beds. This argument rested on an analogy to the reservoirs created by power plants and dams. Law relied on a long line of cases holding that power plants and dams, which merely divert or accumulate waters of the United States and then release those waters, do not require an NPDES permit if they do not physically add pollutants from the outside world into those waters, and they are not required to remove pollutants from the waters that were already there. The *Law* court rejected this analogy. The court held that the treatment ponds were a part of Law's water treatment system and the waters in them were not waters of the United States, unlike the reservoir behind the dam in a river. Thus when water was discharged from the treatment pond into a river, it was a discharge into the waters of the United States and therefore subject to the CWA. *See* Rayle Coal Co. v. Chief, Division of Natural Resources, 401 S.E.2d 682 (W.Va. 1990).

6.   Interestingly, the Fourth Circuit Court of Appeals cited the *Law* decision in requiring the West Virginia Department of Environmental Protection (WVDEP) to secure NPDES permits for discharges in connection with the WVDEP's efforts to clean up abandoned coal mines. W. Va. Highlands Conservancy, Inc. v. Huffman, 625 F.3d 159 (4th Cir. 2010). Like Law, the WVDEP claimed that the prior mine owners, not the agency, were the source of the pollutants it discharged. The court cited Law for the proposition that the origin of the pollutants was irrelevant to the question of liability for discharges under Section 402. *Law, supra,* at 978.

7.   Is criminal prosecution the appropriate way to deter environmental crimes? Some contend that its complexity and reliance on detailed prescriptive and proscriptive rules makes application of traditional criminal liability standards frequently unfair in the context of environmental law. This unfairness may be exacerbated by the fact that federal environmental laws typically provide that any responsible officer of a corporation can be held criminally responsible for violations if they knew or should have known that the corporation was violating environmental regulations. For contrasting views on these fairness issues, see Richard Lazarus, Meeting the Demands of Integration in the Evolution of Environmental Law: Reforming Environmental Criminal Law, 83 Geo. L.J. 2407 (1995); Kathleen Brickey, Environmental Crime at the Crossroads: The Intersection of Environmental and Criminal Law Theory, 71 Tulane L. Rev. 487 (1997). For a challenge to the traditional deterrence-based theory of enforcement in environmental

law, see David B. Spence, The Shadow of the Rational Polluter, 89 Calif. L. Rev. 917 (2001).

b.   SURFACE MINING EXTERNALITIES

Although surface mining lacks the pervasive health and safety problems of underground mining, it has a massive impact on the landscape. As mining equipment has grown in size and efficiency, its ability to reach deep into the earth and permanently transform its surface has greatly exceeded the expectations of people familiar only with early forms of strip mining.

Since 1977, the Federal Surface Mining Control and Reclamation Act (SMCRA), 30 U.S.C. § 1201 *et seq.*, has imposed regulations on strip mining to mitigate the adverse effects on the use of the surface of the land. In general, where the land is capable of being farmed, mining companies must restore the original surface; in other cases (where a mountaintop is removed, and restoring the original surface is thus not possible), they must leave it in a way that retards erosion. Land that is classified as prime farmland is not supposed to be mined at all. Agricultural interests were among the strong proponents of tough legislation designed to protect farmland.

Mining companies must get approval of reclamation plans before proceeding to mine. Under these plans the company must: (1) restore the land to a condition capable of supporting uses as good as existed before (this does not apply to mountaintop removal); (2) restore the approximate original contour of the land (this also does not apply to mountaintop removal); (3) stabilize the soil; (4) spread the topsoil back over the area; and (5) revegetate the site.

i.   *Federalism Issues*

From the beginning, questions were raised about whether a national program was the appropriate way to deal with surface mining. First, surface mining for coal was concentrated in a relatively small number of states, and was not on the radar screen of many people outside these areas. Second, the issues associated with surface mining differ greatly depending on the terrain and climate of the particular region; the Appalachian ridges, the Illinois prairies, and the high plains of Montana vary so greatly in terms of geomorphology and climate that the ability to generalize on national standards was in question.

Despite these doubts, Congress passed SMCRA to "establish a nationwide program to protect society and the environment from the adverse effects of surface coal mining operations" while assuring that there is an adequate supply of coal to meet the nation's energy needs. 30 U.S.C. §§ 1202(a), (f). Like the CAA and CWA, SMCRA is a cooperative effort between the federal and state governments to control surface mining. The federal role is administered by the Office of Surface Mining (OSM) in the Department of the Interior.

Congress did provide for a great deal of state participation in the program. Much like the cooperative federalism model described above in the CWA context, states may get federal approval to administer SMCRA themselves. Under the Act, a state may obtain jurisdiction for regulating surface mining on non-federal lands within the state by submitting a program proposal to the Secretary of the Interior. 30 U.S.C. § 1253. Once a state achieves "primacy," OSM acts only as an overseer and its authority is limited.

The adoption of SMCRA was challenged by a number of states that thought the federal government was infringing on states' traditional responsibilities. SMCRA was one of a number of federal environmental statutes passed in the 1970s pursuant to the authority of Congress under the interstate commerce power. Little doubt was expressed about the basic constitutional authority of the federal government to regulate most of the problems addressed by this environmental legislation. It was obvious that air and water moved across state lines, so legislation designed to control the pollution of these media was clearly within the scope of the federal government's power under the Commerce Clause of the Constitution. SMCRA, on the other hand, posed a more complex constitutional issue. The primary externality of surface mining might be characterized as "land pollution," and land is more localized than air or water.

The coal industry initially challenged SMCRA as an overreaching of federal power under the Commerce Clause, and district judges in Indiana and Virginia initially held the statute invalid. A district judge in Indiana, in *Indiana v. Andrus*, 501 F. Supp. 452 (1980), held (1) that the sections of SMCRA designed to protect prime farmland are directed at facets of surface coal mining which have no substantial and adverse effects on interstate commerce; (2) that the prime farmland provisions are not related to the removal of air and water pollution and are, therefore, not reasonably and plainly adapted to the legitimate end of removing any substantial adverse effect on interstate commerce; and (3) that all of these sections are not within powers delegated to Congress and are unlawful as being contrary to the Tenth Amendment to the Constitution. He also held unconstitutional the "approximate original contour provisions, the topsoiling requirements, the areas unsuitable for surface mining provisions, [and those provisions] which combine to require a commitment by an operator to a certain postmining land use" because they "are not directed at the alleviation of water or air pollution, to the extent there are such effects, and are not means reasonably and plainly adapted to removing any substantial and adverse effect on interstate commerce. These sections are outside the enumerated powers of Congress and are, therefore, unconstitutional and unlawful." *Andrus*, 501 F. Supp. at 461.

The district judge went on to hold that these provisions of the statute also violated the Tenth Amendment, which reserves to the states those powers not delegated to the federal government, because (a) land use control and planning is a traditional or integral governmental function or area of State sovereignty, and (b) the statute constituted "displacement, regulation and altering of the management structure and operation of the traditional area of State sovereignty or integral governmental function of land use planning and control" in violation of the Tenth Amendment. 501 F. Supp. 467–68.

The federal government appealed to the U.S. Supreme Court from both the Indiana and Virginia decisions. The Court reversed and upheld the validity of the statute in two separate opinions, *Hodel v. Virginia*

Surface Mining & Reclamation Ass'n, Inc., 452 U.S. 264 (1981) and *Hodel v. Indiana*, 452 U.S. 314 (1981). In the latter case the Court said:

> In our view, Congress was entitled to find that the protection of prime farmland is a federal interest that may be addressed through Commerce Clause legislation. . . . The court incorrectly assumed that the Act's goals are limited to preventing air and water pollution. . . . Congress was also concerned about preserving the productive capacity of mined lands and protecting the public from health and safety hazards that may result from surface coal mining. All the provisions invalidated by the court below are reasonably calculated to further these legitimate goals.

452 U.S. 327. The Supreme Court also rejected summarily the district court's Tenth Amendment analysis:

> The District Court ruled that the real purpose and effect of the Act is land-use regulation, which, in the court's view, is a traditional state governmental function. . . . We hold that the District Court erred in concluding that the challenged provisions of the Act contravene the Tenth Amendment. The sections of the Act under attack in this case regulate only the activities of surface mine operators who are private individuals and businesses, and the District Court's conclusion that the Act directly regulates the States as States is untenable.

452 U.S. 330. Further, the Court reversed the district court on the issues of the Takings and Due Process clauses.

The Court's analysis of the Commerce Clause in the two *Hodel* opinions was almost routine. Between 1937 and 1995, the Court never held a federal statute invalid for exceeding federal power under the Commerce Clause. That string was broken by the Court's decision in *United States v. Lopez*, 514 U.S. 549 (1995), in which the Court struck down a federal statute making it a crime to carry a gun within a certain distance of a school. The crucial votes in the 5–4 decision were provided by Justices Kennedy and O'Connor, who joined in a concurring opinion written by Justice Kennedy, which noted that earlier decisions upholding "the exercise of federal power where commercial transactions were the subject of regulation [is] within the fair ambit of the Court's practical conception of commercial regulation and are not called in question by our decision today. . . ."

> [U]nlike the earlier cases to come before the Court here neither the actors nor their conduct have a commercial character, and neither the purposes nor the design of the statute have an evident commercial nexus. The statute makes the simple possession of a gun within 1,000 feet of the grounds of the school a criminal offense. In a sense any conduct in this interdependent world of ours has an ultimate commercial origin or consequence, but we have not yet said the commerce power may reach so far. If Congress attempts that extension, then at the least we must inquire whether the exercise of national power seeks to intrude upon an area of traditional state concern.
>
> An interference of these dimensions occurs here, for it is well established that education is a traditional concern of the

States. . . . The proximity to schools, including of course schools owned and operated by the States or their subdivisions, is the very premise for making the conduct criminal. In these circumstances, we have a particular duty to insure that the federal-state balance is not destroyed.

Lopez, 514 U.S. at 580–81. Does the standard set forth in Justice Kennedy's opinion threaten SMCRA's continuing validity? Can you think of any federal laws regulating energy that might not have "an evident commercial nexus?"

ii. *Enforcement Issues*

The regulations adopted by the Secretary of Interior under SMCRA were also subjected to numerous challenges in the courts. Final rules setting out the responsibilities of the Office of Surface Mining Reclamation and Enforcement (OSMRE) were challenged by the coal industry, but in 1981 a new Secretary of the Interior took office in the Reagan administration, with the result that the regulations were significantly relaxed, which in turn led to litigation by environmental groups.

On paper, SMCRA is one of the toughest environmental statutes on the books. In practice, there is often little support for enforcing the act to the letter. The cost of restoring the site to permit agricultural use is often much greater than the cost of simply keeping it safe and forested.

The permitting requirements of SMCRA say that a permit is necessary before any person may engage in surface mining operations. 30 U.S.C. § 1256(a). SMCRA requires a permit before any person may engage in surface mining operations. 30 C.F.R. Parts 772–73 (OSMRE permit requirements for coal operations). The permit application requires the mine operators to plan the mining operation in detail, identify adverse effects on the environment, and devise a reclamation plan. OSMRE rules include requirements that mining permittees post a bond to ensure the availability of resources necessary for reclamation at the cessation of mining operations, 30 C.F.R. Part 800, as well as specific performance standards for different categories of surface coal mines, *id.* pts. 810–28.

Reclamation requirements are often the most controversial issues in a SMCRA permit. SMCRA is designed to assure "complete reclamation of mine sites." Cat Run Coal Co. v. Babbitt, 932 F. Supp. 772, 774–5 (S.D. W.Va. 1996). Every operator of a mining operation must post a bond which is calculated to ensure that the commitments set forth in the permit are carried out. 30 U.S.C. § 1259(a). The bond requirement ensures that funds are available to reclaim mined lands if an operator defaults and to give incentive to comply with the reclamation requirements. *See* Barlow Burke, Reclaiming the Law of Suretyship, 21 So. Ill. U. L. J. 449 (1997).

To be released from liability under SMCRA, an operator must apply to the appropriate agency and demonstrate performance of the reclamation work required under SMCRA and the bond. 30 U.S.C. § 1269(c). The appropriate agency inspects the reclamation work. First, the operator must complete backfilling, grading, and drainage control in accordance with the reclamation plan. Then the operator must revegetate the regraded mine lands. Finally, if the agency finds that all reclamation requirements have been met, it will release the reclamation bond.

National Wildlife Federation v. Lujan

950 F.2d 765 (D.C. Cir. 1991).

■ RANDOLPH, J. Surface coal mining is a temporary use of the land. When mining ends the land must be restored. After revegetation is complete, and sufficient time has passed to ensure its success—5 years in the east, 10 years in the arid west—a mine operator who has fulfilled all legal requirements is entitled to have his performance bond released. The principal question in this case is whether under the Surface Mining Control and Reclamation Act of 1977, 30 U.S.C. §§ 1201–1328 (1988), regulatory jurisdiction may then be terminated. The Secretary of the Interior issued regulations so providing. *See* 52 Fed. Reg. 24,092 (1987) (Notice of Proposed Rulemaking); 53 Fed. Reg. 44,356 (1988) (Final Rule). The district court, at the behest of the National Wildlife Federation and others ("NWF"), struck them down. *National Wildlife Fed'n v. Interior Dep't,* 31 Env't Rep. Cas. (BNA) 2034, 2040–41 (D.D.C. 1990). Because we find the Act silent on the issue presented and the Secretary's interpretation permissible, we reverse.

As night follows day, litigation follows rulemaking under this statute. Since the Act's passage in 1977, in cases challenging regulations, our opinions have described in considerable detail the Act's structure and operation. We shall assume familiarity with those opinions. In brief, the Act is intended to protect the environment from the adverse effects of surface coal mining while ensuring an adequate supply of coal to meet the nation's energy requirements. 30 U.S.C. § 1202(a), (f). Section 501(b) directs the Secretary to promulgate regulations establishing regulatory procedures and performance standards "conforming to the provisions of" the Act (30 U.S.C. § 1251(b)). Section 515 contains detailed "environmental protection performance standards" applicable to "all surface coal mining and reclamation operations." 30 U.S.C. § 1265. Through the Office of Surface Mining Reclamation and Enforcement ("OSMRE"), the Secretary is to take steps "necessary to insure compliance with" the Act. 30 U.S.C. § 1211(a), (c)(1). The states too have a significant role to play. After an interim period of federal regulation, states had the option of proposing plans for implementing the Act consistent with federal standards on non-federal lands. When the Secretary approved the programs submitted by the states, those states became primarily responsible for regulating surface coal mining and reclamation in the non-federal areas within their borders. 30 U.S.C. § 1253. In states not having an approved program, the Secretary implemented a federal program. 30 U.S.C. § 1254(a), (b). The "permanent program" regulations issued under section 501(b) set standards for federally-approved state programs and for the federal program that takes effect when a State fails to "implement, enforce, or maintain" its program. 30 U.S.C. § 1254(a). Enforcement is carried out by the "regulatory authority," that is, the state agency administering the federally-approved program, the Secretary administering a federal program, or OSMRE conducting oversight of state programs. *See* 30 C.F.R. § 700.5.

The primary means of ensuring compliance is the permit system established in sections 506 through 514 and section 515(a). 30 U.S.C. §§ 1256–1264, 1265(a). A permit is required for "any surface coal mining operations." 30 U.S.C. § 1256. Summaries of applications for permits must be published, and objections may be submitted by local agencies or by "any person having an interest which . . . may be adversely affected" by a proposed operation. 30 U.S.C. § 1263. Each application must include a reclamation plan. Section 507(d), 30 U.S.C. § 1257(d). A reclamation plan describes the present use of the land, proposed and possible post-mining uses of the land, and what steps the operator will take to ensure the viability of the latter. Among other things, the plan must show how the operator will achieve soil reconstruction and revegetation of the mined area. Section 508, 30 U.S.C. § 1258. A permit application can only be approved if it demonstrates that "all requirements" of the Act have been satisfied and that "reclamation as required by [the Act] . . . can be accomplished." 30 U.S.C. § 1260.

Section 509 requires the operator to post a performance bond in an amount sufficient to secure completion of reclamation. The operator and the surety remain liable under the bond for the duration of the surface mining and reclamation operation and until the end of the "revegetation period" (5 or 10 years) prescribed by section 515(20). 30 U.S.C. § 1259(b). At that time, the operator may petition the regulatory authority for release of the bond. The petition must be published, and is subject to the same opportunities for comment and hearing as the permit application. 30 C.F.R. § 800.40(a)(2), (b)(2). Further, "no bond shall be fully released . . . until reclamation requirements of the Act and the permit are fully met." *Id.* § 800.40(c)(3).

Prior to this rulemaking, the relationship between bond release and continuing regulatory jurisdiction was unclear. 53 Fed. Reg. 44,356 (1988). State authorities would decline to act on violations reported after bond release, even when the allegation was that the bond had been released improperly. In some such cases, OSMRE would re-assert jurisdiction directly. *Id.* This led to confusion about whether a site was or was not subject to the Act. In order to end this confusion, the Secretary promulgated the rules at issue, which specify when regulatory jurisdiction over a site terminates. *Id.* Thus, 30 C.F.R. § 700.11(d)(1) provides that "a regulatory authority may terminate its jurisdiction . . . over [a] reclaimed site" when (and only when) the authority determines (either independently or pursuant to a bond release) that "all requirements imposed" have been completed. *Id.* By tying termination of jurisdiction to bond release, the Secretary sought to resolve doubts about the former, while imposing minimum standards for the latter on the state authorities.

In the district court NWF claimed that it was "premature" to terminate regulatory jurisdiction at the time of bond release. Complaint of National Wildlife Federation at 14, Civ. No. 88–3345 (D.D.C. filed Nov. 17, 1988). The district court interpreted NWF's complaint not simply as an objection to timing, but as an attack on "the concept of terminating jurisdiction." *National Wildlife Federation v. Interior Dept.,* 31 Env't Rep. Cas. (BNA) at 2039. Seizing on language found in section 521 of the Act, 30 U.S.C. § 1271, the court noted that the Secretary was under "an ongoing duty . . . to correct violations . . . without limitation." 31 Env't

Rep. Cas. (BNA) at 2040. The court also believed that allowing termination of jurisdiction would "hinder" the Act's goal of "protecting the environment." *Id.* at 2041. In view of these considerations, the court believed it proper to interpret Congress' silence on the precise question of termination of jurisdiction as a call for perpetual regulation. *Id.*

The district court's opinion and NWF's claim of prematurity suffer from the same flaw. Section 521 cannot be read to express or assume that regulatory jurisdiction over a surface coal mining and reclamation operation must continue forever. It is true that section 521 requires the regulatory authority to "take . . . action" "whenever" a violation occurs, 30 U.S.C. § 1271(a)(1) (emphasis added). But by "action," section 521 means primarily the issuance of an order requiring "cessation of surface coal mining and reclamation operations." 30 U.S.C. § 1271(a)(2). Section 521(a)(2) also empowers the Secretary to impose other "affirmative obligations" on the operator; these, however, are to be exacted "in addition to the cessation order," 30 U.S.C. § 1271(a)(2). It thus appears that Congress contemplated enforcement actions only during mining and reclamation operations. If the site were no longer the scene of a "surface coal mining and reclamation operation," and it could not be by the time the bond is released, it would be difficult to see how section 521 could nevertheless continue to apply. The regulation, then, cannot be upheld or struck down solely by reference to Congress' intent, at least not as that intent was expressed in section 521. . . .

NWF apparently believes that because, under the regulations, it is possible for some operators to avoid liability for violations of the Act that are undiscovered or undiscoverable at the time of bond release, the regulations improperly fail to promote the Act's purpose: protection of the environment. The Act, however, was a compromise, designed both to protect the environment and to ensure an adequate supply of coal to meet the nation's energy requirements. *See* 30 U.S.C. § 1202(a), (f). The Secretary struck a reasonable balance between these competing interests in his interpretation of the Act (and, as noted above, responded to NWF's concerns about unabated environmental harm by adding 30 C.F.R. § 700.11(d)(2)).

The regulation also strikes a reasonable balance between the gradual increase, due to improving technology, in what legitimately may be demanded of an operator, and an operator's need for certainty regarding closed sites. "It would not be appropriate . . . to require operators who had . . . met the standards of their permits and the applicable regulatory program to . . . reclaim [closed sites] in accordance with new technology." 53 Fed. Reg. 44,361 (1988).

In short, we find the regulation consistent with the goals of the Act and a reasonable interpretation of it. Furthermore, the factors supporting "the concept of terminating jurisdiction," 31 Env't Rep. Cas. (BNA) at 2039, buttress the Secretary's decision to use bond release as the point at which termination occurs. Until bond release the operator is still liable, and an attempt to terminate jurisdiction sooner would violate the terms of the Act. Nothing in the statute speaks in fixed temporal terms of regulation after bond release. Under the regulation that is the point at which the regulatory authority must "sign off" on the reclamation project. Bond release also has the advantage of being an independently identifiable point in time. For these reasons the

Secretary's choice was not arbitrary or capricious. Accordingly, we reverse the district court's judgment insofar as it invalidated 30 C.F.R. § 700.11(d). ∎

NOTES AND COMMENTS

1.   The coal industry estimates that more than two million acres of mined lands have been reclaimed in the past twenty years. This represents an area larger than the state of Delaware. Reclamation involves the following steps: leveling off fill soil by bulldozers, placing topsoil or approved substitute over graded area, reseeding with native vegetation, crops and/or trees, and monitoring the area for many years to ensure success of reclamation. Nat'l Coal Mining Ass'n, Fast Facts About Coal, www.nma.org.

Coal mining lands have been restored to a variety of uses. Farming is one of the most common post-mining land uses. Housing development is often used for mined lands located near urban centers. Often, special uses arise out of reclamation projects. For example, the OSM coordinates the use of trees grown on reclaimed coal mine lands in Maryland for the National Christmas Pageant of Peace tree-lighting ceremony in Washington, D.C. A former coal mine in West Virginia now includes a little league baseball field.

2.   Depending on the nature of the soils and terrain and on the desired end use, the time that it takes to determine with some confidence whether reclamation has been successfully accomplished can range from a few years to many decades. In most instances, the mining companies are not enthusiastic about retaining responsibility for sites that are no longer producing income, but once the company's deep pocket disappears, conditions on the site may deteriorate. Can you think of other solutions for the long-term maintenance of reclaimed mining sites?

3.   Definition of the relative powers of the federal and state agencies under SMCRA remains a source of controversy. *See* Robert E. Beck, Water and Coal Mining in Appalachia: Applying the Surface Mining Control and Reclamation Act of 1977 and the Clean Water Act, 106 W. Va. L. Rev. 629 (2004). The D.C. Circuit upheld the OSM regulations under which the agency retains backup authority to issue a notice of violation even though it has delegated to a state agency primary enforcement authority. Nat'l Mining Ass'n v. U.S. Dep't of the Interior, 70 F.3d 1345 (D.C. Cir. 1995).

4.   Approved state programs for administering SMCRA become incorporated into federal OSMRE requirements. 30 C.F.R. Parts 900–955. At times, there has been conflict between OSMRE and state agencies administering SMCRA. SMCRA regulations provide authority for regulators to reassert jurisdiction over mining sites after bond release in cases where the bond release "was based upon fraud, collusion, or misrepresentation of a material fact." 30 C.F.R. § 700.11(d). In a 2007 decision a federal district court in West Virginia granted summary judgment in favor of OSM in a dispute with the WVDEP over reassertion of jurisdiction to address acid mine drainage at a site after release of the bond. After a citizen complaint, OSM provided WVDEP notice of its intention to issue a notice of violation against the mining company for violating SMCRA rules requiring water discharges to comply with Clean Water Act permitting standards for AMD. When WVDEP failed to take action, OSM issued the notice of violation over the WVDEP's objections that jurisdiction had terminated. The court granted summary judgment in OSM's favor, reasoning that the "misrepresentation

of material fact" standard does "not require intentional wrongdoing," Rather, "misrepresentation can be established by objective evidence relating to whether the reclamation plan was fully complied with and completed at the time of bond release." Cheyenne Sales Co., Inc. v. Norton, 2007 WL 773904 (N.D. W.V. 2007), at 16; *see also* Nat'l Mining Ass'n v. U.S. Dep't of the Interior, *supra* (affirming right of OSMRE to issue notice of violation directly to mining company, even though state agency was delegated primary enforcement authority; state agency had declined to act).

c.   MOUNTAIN-TOP MINING

The most controversial form of surface mining has been the so-called "mountain-top mining" that has become prevalent in southern Appalachia. A recent Fourth Circuit opinion affirming the issuance of a Clean Water Act discharge permit as part of a mountaintop mining operation described the process:

> The mountaintop removal method of surface coal mining, pioneered in West Virginia, involves the blasting of the soil and rock atop a mountain to expose coal deposits below. While mining operations are ongoing, the overburden is hauled or pushed into adjacent valleys. This excavated overburden is known as "spoil." Once the coal has been extracted, efforts are made to re-contour the mountaintop by replacing the removed overburden, but stability concerns limit the amount of spoil that can be returned to the area. In its natural state, the spoil material is heavily compacted; once excavated, however, the loosening of the rock and soil and incorporation of air causes significant swelling. As a result, large quantities of the blasted material cannot be replaced, and this excess spoil ("overburden") remains in the valley, creating a "valley fill" that buries intermittent and perennial streams in the process.

> Water that collects in the fill must be moved out to ensure the fill's continued stability. Thus, an underdrain system is constructed by placing large boulders up to and above the ordinary high-water mark of the stream. The collected water is then channeled into a treatment pond, where sediment from the runoff is allowed to settle. Sediment ponds usually are constructed in existing streambeds, using earth and rock to create an embankment. After sediments have settled out of the fill runoff, the treated water is discharged from the sediment pond back into existing streams. When practicable, a sediment pond will be constructed in the streambed immediately adjacent to the end (or "toe") of the fill. But, because West Virginia's steep, mountainous topography often prevents this kind of positioning, a short stream segment is frequently used to move runoff from the fill downstream to the sediment pond. Once a valley fill is stabilized, the embankments of the sediment pond are removed, and the ponds and the stream segments are restored to their pre-project condition.

> Much of the impact of a valley fill project is felt by headwater streams. Headwater streams are small streams that form the origin of larger streams or rivers, and may be intermittent or ephemeral. Intermittent streams receive their

flow from both surface runoff and groundwater discharge, while ephemeral streams rely on major rain or snow events for their flow. The precise role of headwater streams in overall watershed ecology is a matter of some debate in this litigation, as we discuss more below, but all parties agree that these streams perform important ecological functions.

Ohio Valley Envtl. Coal. v. Aracoma, 556 F.3d 177 (4th Cir. 2009).

The deposit of overburden is governed by both the permitting and reclamation provisions of SMCRA and Section 404 of the Clean Water Act, which requires a permit for the deposit of "dredge or fill" material into wetlands. 33 U.S.C. § 1304. SMCRA rules at 30 C.F.R. Parts 773–780 address requirements for obtaining a SMCRA permit for all methods of coal mining. These rules specifically addresses permits for the mountaintop removal mining method. 30 C.F.R. § 785.14. In situations in which the overburden is deposited into a "navigable water" or adjacent wetland, the Clean Water Act prohibition against "discharges" of pollutants without a permit would appear to apply, because the Act defines "dirt" as a pollutant, and (as in *United States v. Law*) its addition to navigable waters and adjacent wetland constitutes a "discharge" requiring a permit under the Act.

However, the Army Corps of Engineers (Corps), which exercises permitting jurisdiction over the deposit of fill into wetlands, has traditionally permitted this activity under its so-called "Nationwide Permit 21," granting general approval for certain kinds of fill activities, including deposit of overburden from mountaintop mining operations. The practice of issuing nationwide permits has long proved controversial and prompted litigation alleging that it is inconsistent with the CWA. *See, e.g.*, Ohio Valley Envtl. Coal. v. Bulen, 429 F.3d 493 (4th Cir. 2005) (overturning and remanding district court decision finding nationwide permit inconsistent with the CWA); Kentuckians for the Commonwealth v. Rivenburgh, 317 F.3d 425 (4th Cir. 2003) (upholding fill activities under the nationwide permit); Ohio Valley Envtl. Coalition v. Hurst, 604 F.Supp.2d 860 (2009) (S.D. W. Va. 2009) (issuance of nationwide permit was arbitrary and capricious).

The presidential succession in 2009 changed the dynamics of this issue dramatically. On July 15, 2009, Corps proposed two changes in Nationwide Permit (NWP) 21:

> First, the Corps proposes to modify NWP 21 to prohibit its use to authorize discharges of dredged or fill material into waters of the United States for surface coal mining activities in the Appalachian region of the following states: Kentucky, Ohio, Pennsylvania, Tennessee, Virginia, and West Virginia until it expires on March 18, 2012. The proposed modification would enhance environmental protection of aquatic resources by requiring surface coal mining projects in the affected region to obtain individual permit coverage under the Clean Water Act (CWA), which includes increased public and agency involvement in the permit review process, including an opportunity for public comment on individual projects. The application of NWP 21 to surface coal mining activities in the rest of the United States would not be affected by this proposed modification.

> Second, the Corps is proposing to suspend NWP 21 to provide an interim means of requiring individual permit reviews in Appalachia, while proposing to undertake the longer-term measure of modifying NWP 21 to prohibit its use to authorize discharges of dredged or fill material into waters of the United States associated with surface coal mining activities in the Appalachian region of these six States. The Corps is also proposing to suspend NWP 21 to provide immediate environmental protection while it evaluates the comments received in response to the proposal to modify NWP 21.

Proposed Suspension and Modification of Nationwide Permit 21, 74 Fed. Reg. 3411 (July 15, 2009). Valley fill activities now require an individual permit. Reissuance of Nationwide Permits, 72 Fed. Reg. 11,092 (July 15, 2009). Also in 2009, EPA and Corps instituted an enhanced coordination procedure through which EPA concluded that most of the pending mountaintop mining projects in Appalachia posed a threat to water quality, resulting in delays in processing those projects' section 404 permit applications. In October 2011, a federal court struck down the enhanced coordination procedure as an improper encroachment by EPA on Corps's permitting authority. Nat'l Mining Ass'n v. Jackson, 816 F. Supp. 2d 37 (D.D.C. 2011). However, the decision did not alter the requirement that mining companies obtain individual section 404 permits for valley fill activities. U.S. Army Corps of Eng'rs, Proposed Suspension and Modification of Nationwide Permit 21, 74 Fed. Reg. 3411 (July 15, 2009). The Corps' suspension regulations require an opportunity for public comment on the suspension before it takes effect.

More recently, a federal district court has confirmed that the EPA has the right to veto the Army Corps' choice of location for the disposal of dredge and fill material even after the Corps has issued an individual permit. Thus, although the EPA and the Corps are constrained in the extent to which they may coordinate permitting, the EPA has the right to prohibit discharges of dredge and fill from mountaintop removal, thus giving it substantial authority in this area. *See* Mingo Logan Coal Co. v. U.S. EPA, 714 F.3d 608 (C.A.D.C. 2013). The EPA has this authority because Section 404 of the Clean Water Act provides: The Administrator is authorized to prohibit the specification (including the withdrawal of specification) of any defined area as a disposal site, and he is authorized to deny or restrict the use of any defined area for specification (including the withdrawal of specification) as a disposal site, whenever he determines, after notice and opportunity for public hearings, that the discharge of such materials into such area will have an unacceptable adverse effect on municipal water supplies, shellfish beds and fishery areas (including spawning and breeding areas), wildlife, or recreational areas. 33 U.S.C. § 1344.

3. MINERAL RIGHTS

The English common law, which was incorporated into American law, gave the owner of the surface of the land the right to all minerals underneath it, but it allowed the "mineral rights" to land to be separated from the right to use the surface of the land. This severance allowed mining companies to control the extraction of the minerals without having to assume all of the responsibility for the uses on the surface.

Indeed, it was this mineral estate that the Court determined to have been "taken" by the State of Pennsylvania in *Pennsylvania Coal v. Mahon*.

The terms defining the mineral rights vary with the needs of the parties. For example, the rights might be to all minerals (including oil and gas; see Chapter 4), just coal, coal in a particular seam, or coal of a particular grade. The landowner and the mining company may define the rights conveyed in any manner they choose. Once the mineral rights are divided as a separate interest, they can be transferred independently from the surface. Often, the mineral rights are leased rather than purchased from the surface owner.

The modern mineral rights deed or lease will spell out the obligations of each party in regard to, among other things: (1) the extent to which a mineral owner has a right to use the surface for mine openings, roads, etc.; (2) the extent to which the mine operator is liable for subsidence of the land; and (3) whether the mineral rights owner has an obligation to explore and develop the minerals within a particular time.

Where underground mining is contemplated, coal mining companies typically purchase only the mineral rights from the landowner rather than purchasing a fee simple interest in the land on which the coal was located. Because the surface owner could continue to farm or develop the land for a profit while the mining was taking place underneath it, she would normally ask a lower price for the mineral rights than for the property as a whole.

Surface mining has become prevalent only since the 1950s. If a coal company purchased the mineral rights from a landowner at a time when the only known method of mining was underground mining, does the coal company now have the right to remove the coal by surface mining, thus effectively destroying the value of the surface owner's interest? This contentious issue has been a source of both legal and political battles in the coal mining states. For example, mineral rights owners in Kentucky acquired rights to mineral estates from surface owners through so-called "broad form" deeds, most of which were created prior to the advent of surface mining. Typically, the deeds granted the mineral owner rights to use the surface to the extent necessary or convenient to gain access to the minerals. In 1956, in *Buchanan v. Watson*, 290 S.W.2d 40 (1956), the Kentucky Supreme Court ruled that surface owners could not prevent mineral rights holders from using strip mining to mine coal pursuant to these broad form deeds. When the Kentucky legislature attempted to overturn this rule by limiting mineral estate holders to the use of techniques common at the time of execution of the deed, the Kentucky Supreme Court invalidated the critical portion of the statute (Ky. Rev. Stat. § 381.940) in *Akers v. Baldwin*, 736 S.W.2d 294 (Ky. 1987). In response, the Kentucky legislature in 1988 ratified an amendment to the Kentucky Constitution, denoted Section 19(2), which stated that:

> In any instrument heretofore or hereafter executed purporting to sever the surface and mineral estates or to grant a mineral estate or to grant a right to extract minerals, which fails to state or describe in express and specific terms the method of coal extraction to be employed, or where said instrument contains language subordinating the surface estate to the mineral estate, it shall be held, in the absence of clear and convincing evidence to the contrary, that the intention of the

parties to the instrument was that the coal be extracted only by the method or methods of commercial coal extraction commonly known to be in use in Kentucky in the area affected at the time the instrument was executed, and that the mineral estate be dominant to the surface estate for the purposes of coal extraction by only the method or methods of commercial coal extraction commonly known to be in use in Kentucky in the area affected at the time the instrument was executed.

The Kentucky Supreme Court reviewed that amendment in the case of *Ward v. Harding*, 860 S.W.2d 280 (Ky. 1993). Reasoning that it is "neither fair nor just to permit surface mining contrary to the wishes of the surface owner and beyond the contemplation of the original parties to [the instrument]," the court upheld the amendment's conclusion that broad form deeds do not authorize strip mining, and expressly overruled all contrary precedent. In so doing, the court rejected arguments that the amendment contravened the Contracts Clause of the U.S. Constitution:

> As we have said hereinabove, at the time of the original mineral conveyance, the parties could not have intended any substantial disturbance of the surface. The original contract did not create a right to surface mine; this right, such as it was, arose by court decision half a century after the conveyance. While appellees acquired their mineral ownership after our decision in Buchanan and with an expectation of the right to strip mine, they acquired no greater right than their vendors possessed.

Ward, 860 S.W.2d at 288. The court also rejected a claim that the amendment amounted to a regulatory taking of the mineral estate.

The longwall method of underground mining is another mining technique that was unknown at the time many mineral rights were granted. This method often produces a great deal of surface subsidence. With the longwall method, entries into the coal seam are made and supported by pillars. The mining equipment is moved to the furthest point on the panel and begins cutting toward the front. As the machine moves forward, the supports collapse, along with the overburden. Extraction is around 90%, but subsidence is usually immediate. S. Peng & H. Chaing, Longwall Mining (1984).

In *Smerdell v. Consolidation Coal Co.*, 806 F. Supp. 1278 (N.D. W. Va. 1992) the owners of the surface had waived all claims for damages from subsidence in 1905. The current owners of the surface claimed that their predecessors' waiver was no longer valid because the coal company had switched to the longwall mining method. The district court held that the effect of changed circumstances, such as the development of new mining techniques, on an unambiguous written instrument was not subject to judicial interpretation, and that the right to subjacent support was waived no matter what method of coal extraction is used.

Today, it is most common for the surface owner to lease the mineral rights to the mining company for a modest cash rental plus a significant percentage of the minerals that are found—this is known as a royalty interest. For example, the surface owner might retain a 1/8 royalty interest in all coal discovered and produced from under the land. The mining company will want the lease to set out its right to erect structures and build roads on the land, if underground mining is contemplated. Whether underground or surface mining is contemplated, the lease should expressly set out the methods of mining that are anticipated. The owner will also want to know what type of land reclamation the mining company contemplates when the mining operation has been completed.

The broad form deeds at issue in *Ward*, and the court's construction of them prior to that decision, reflected the attitude prevalent in the nineteenth century—that because coal was dramatically increasing peoples' ability to produce goods and raise their standard of living, the law ought to construe instruments in a way that encouraged the production of this valuable commodity. *See generally* Morton J. Horwitz, The Transformation of American Law, 1780–1860 (Harvard University Press, 1977). Only much later did people fully realize some of the adverse impacts of coal mining (see Chapter 4 (oil and gas extraction)).

A large part of the remaining coal reserves underlie federal lands in the western states, so companies seeking to mine this coal must comply with the complex laws relating to federal public lands. Coal on federal lands is under the jurisdiction of the Department of the Interior, where different aspects of coal production are handled by different agencies, including the Bureau of Land Management and the Minerals Management Service. For an analysis of these federal regulations, see Marla E. Mansfield, Coal, in James E. Hickey et. al., Energy Law & Policy in the 21st Century, Ch. 9 (2000).

Texas has extensive deposits of brown coal known as lignite, much of which can be mined by surface mining methods. Under Texas law, a landowner's conveyance of the rights to "oil, gas and other minerals" has been construed not to convey the rights to any lignite that is near the surface. Reed v. Wylie, 597 S.W.2d 743 (Tex. 1980).

PROBLEM

The Rith Energy Company's application for a revised mining permit under SMCRA was denied. Its original permit was suspended after regulators decided that the original mining plan posed the risk of water contamination from acid mine drainage. When its application for the revised permit was denied, Rith brought suit in the United States Court of Federal Claims. The government sought to dismiss the complaint, arguing as follows:

> Plaintiff's just compensation claim fails because plaintiff does not possess the compensable expectancy it presumes. First, one of plaintiff's two leases, the Eagle/Boylan lease, allows the mining of coal only by underground methods. As to that lease, plaintiff's "bundle of rights" never included the expectancy to surface mine at all. Lucas v. South Carolina Coastal Council, 505 U.S. 1003, 1027 (1992).

> Second, plaintiff's claim in essence presumes it possesses a constitutionally protected right to mine in a particular manner. However, the property interests under which plaintiff has mined, and seeks to mine further, were created after the enactment of SMCRA. Accordingly, when plaintiff received those interests, its expectancies were already affected by the restrictions of the Act. Thus, it could have acquired no right to mine in a manner which

was in violation of the Act. M & J Coal Co. v. United States, 30 Fed. Cl. 360, 369 (1994), *aff'd,* 47 F.3d 1148 (1995), *cert. denied,* 516 U.S. 808 (1995). In other words, before plaintiff's interests were created, SMCRA required that a permit be denied if the operator would not be able to reclaim the site or if mining operations would cause offsite hydrologic impacts. Plaintiff could have acquired no right to mine in a manner which was already prohibited by the Act. For that reason alone, Rith's just compensation claim must fail . . .

Finally, the governmental action challenged here is itself reactive to plaintiff's seeking to engage in a mining method with nuisance-like impacts. Measured against a variety of factors, including longstanding federal regulation under SMCRA and the risk that the mining practices in which plaintiff sought to engage would have nuisance-like consequences under state law, plaintiff could have acquired no "historically rooted" expectancy—no "property" for purposes of Fifth Amendment compensation—to mine in a manner which would cause nuisance-like impacts. The "background principles" analysis articulated in *Lucas v. South Carolina Coastal Council* confirms that, when acquired, Rith's right to mine could not have included an expectation of being allowed to mine if to do so would cause a nuisance.

Are the government's arguments persuasive? How would you respond on behalf of the plaintiff? What additional facts would you like to know? *See* Rith Energy, Inc. v. United States, 44 Fed. Cl. 108 (1999), *aff'd* Rith Energy v. United States, 247 F.3d 1355 (Fed Cir. 2001).

C. THE FUTURE OF COAL

The market for coal is undergoing seismic shifts. It is facing competition from other fuels (particularly natural gas) and increasingly stringent regulation in the United States; at the same time, demand for coal is increasing in Asia. (Asian coal reserves are substantial; but demand for control in Asia is growing faster than production.) Coal has advantages and disadvantages as an energy source. Its biggest advantage is the sheer volume of it that is available; we will not need to worry about worldwide coal shortages for many generations. Second, the reserves of coal within the United States are sufficiently great that we need not be concerned about interruptions caused by international conflict, which gives coal a major advantage over oil. However, the shale revolution (see Chapter 4) is reducing coal's energy security advantages.

Coal has the disadvantage of being a relatively dirty fuel, which means that much more money must be spent on pollution control equipment if one burns burn coal rather than oil or especially natural gas. The externalities caused by the mining of coal, as described above, are quite significant. And coal has the big disadvantage of being relatively inflexible in the way it can be used. While it can be conveniently burned under boilers, the cost of transforming it into a liquid or gas that can be more easily transported remains prohibitive, and in our increasingly mobile society this limitation is increasingly serious.

Air pollution problems (addressed in Chapter 5) have shifted demand for coal. As air pollution standards have tightened, buyers have sought lower-sulfur coal from western mines. More recently, carbon regulation has undercut demand as well. There are now fewer total active mines, but the active mines are larger in size. The overall production is increasing in surface mines, as well as underground production from longwall mining.

Furthermore, the market for electric generation, on which coal is heavily dependent, is undergoing major structural changes (see Chapter 10). Restructuring of the utility industry intensified the fight over pollution from coal combustion in the 1990s. Initially, some feared that restructuring (i.e., the move to competitive prices rather than administratively-set prices) would lead to increased reliance on coal, as a relatively cheap, plentiful fuel source. These 1996 remarks of an energy industry consultant were typically skeptical about the environmental effects of restructuring:

> [T]he lowest-cost producers of power, by far, are the older, Midwest power plants that have the fewest environmental controls. These plants, which are also incidentally upwind of the Northeast and Midwest population centers of the eastern half of the United States, with no further governmental intervention, will benefit from the greatest consumer demand and will significantly increase production in turn increasing emissions. If a purely free market selling price is the only issue, rather than utilizing clean burning nuclear or gas power or building a new clean generator, customers across the country will favor the cheapest power (typically a coal-based generator) instead of local production—even if the local producer offers cleaner energy.

William G. Rosenberg, Restructuring the Electric Utility Industry and Its Effect on the Environment, 14 Pace Envtl. L. Rev. 69 (1996).

That fear, however, has been overcome by other trends. Governments retain significant leverage over the power generation mix even within restructured electricity markets, and many are already using that leverage to try to ensure that price competition in electricity markets will not squeeze out cleaner sources of power in favor of dirtier ones. Restructuring states have created or strengthened laws and rules favoring the use of cleaner generation sources. New York, California, Texas, and several other states that have opened retail electricity markets to competition in the last decade have instituted renewable portfolio standards requiring that retail service providers purchase a specified percentage of their power from renewable sources. See Chapter 11. More than 30 states now have some sort of renewable energy standard on the books. These laws, along with federal tax credits and decreasing costs for wind and solar generation, have kept renewables in the mix, as Chapters 11 and 12 discuss in more detail.

Even more importantly, coal has lost market share recently to natural gas, supplies of which have become inexpensive and plentiful thanks to hydraulic fracturing. Domestic natural gas prices nosedived with the spread of shale gas production using hydraulic fracturing ("fracking"), allowing natural gas to challenge coal's traditional control of electric generation markets. Figure 3–2 illustrates this point.

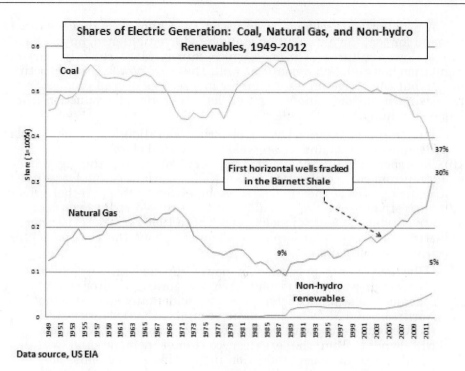

Figure 3–2

Indeed, natural gas and renewables have captured most of the growth in electricity generation over the last two decades. Coal plants require a larger investment than gas plants and other alternatives. Investors eyeing volatile electricity prices in some newly restructured markets may be wary of making such a large investment until these markets mature. The regulatory environment of coal-fired power generation has been changing rapidly, prompting allegations of a "war on coal" in political campaigns. The Energy Policy Act of 2005 provided federal financial assistance for research and development of a wide variety of so-called "clean coal" technologies, including new gasification technologies like and new pollution control technologies for coal emissions. *See* Energy Policy Act, Title IV. Research into these technologies continues, and some may hold the promise of much cleaner coal combustion, though it remains to be seen whether this can be accomplished at competitive costs. For now, the future of coal is uncertain.

CHAPTER 4

OIL AND GAS PRODUCTION

A. PETROLEUM BASICS

1. TERMINOLOGY

"Petroleum" is found in certain geological formations under the surface of the earth. In place, it typically consists of a mixture of liquid hydrocarbons called "crude oil," and various gaseous hydrocarbons, primarily methane, known as "natural gas."[17] Like coal, petroleum is a fossil fuel because it is the byproduct of millennia of decay and compression of organic material. About 62% of the energy used in the United States today is oil and gas, from both domestic and imported sources. For many purposes, the law treats petroleum as a single commodity regardless of whether it consists of crude oil, natural gas or a mixture. For example, standard lease contracts between landowners and oil companies cover both oil and gas and state conservation commissions regulate both oil and gas wells.

However, in two fundamental ways, oil differs from natural gas. First, the price of oil produced and sold in the United States is set on the international market by global market forces, often involving geopolitical events. By contrast, the price for natural gas produced in the United States is largely set by domestic supply and demand forces. The price of gas is far lower in the United States than in Europe or Asia. As yet, there is no single international price for natural gas, although exports of natural gas from the United States in the form of liquefied natural gas (LNG) are expected to reduce the large differential in prices between regions of the world in the coming years. The new U.S. gas supplies are a result of the rise of horizontal drilling and hydraulic fracturing (also called "fracking," "hydrofracking," or "fracing"[18]) in unconventional formations such as shales and tight sandstone around the country.

Second, because oil is a liquid that can be stored in tanks, it is much easier to transport, using pipelines, barges, rail cars, and long-distance oil tankers on the high seas. For decades, natural gas could be transported only by pipelines, which are 30 times as expensive to build as oil pipelines. Natural gas cannot be stored above ground unless it is compressed and contained in highly pressurized vessels (like propane tanks used in rural areas for fuel or in barbeque grills) or unless it is cooled to form LNG. The development of LNG tankers that can travel the world with "frozen" gas in their holds (gas cooled to -161° Centigrade) began only in the 1960s. Susan L. Sakmar, Energy for the 21st Century 55–57 (2013). Because the use of large quantities of gas was so critically tied to having pipeline access in the 1930s, natural gas producers entered into long-term (twenty years or longer) contracts with pipeline owners rather than selling their production at short-term "spot" market prices under thirty-day contracts, as was customary in oil markets. Pipeline

---

[17] The term "gas" is commonly used as a shorthand for "gasoline," the liquid refined from crude oil that is a key transportation fuel. In this book, the term "gas" means natural gas unless the context makes it obvious that gasoline is intended.

[18] Actors in the oil and gas industry tend to criticize the term "fracking" as a pejorative word adopted by the media and environmental groups, although industry insiders often used the term "fracing" or "frac'ing." "Fracking" is now commonly used to describe hydraulic fracturing because it is phonetically intuitive. See Jonathan Fahey, No industry backing for the word "fracking," Wall St. J., Jan. 27, 2012, http://online.wsj.com/article/AP98dcc66f92764ea488 c3211a338ce7c6.html.

companies could not secure financing to build the lines unless they had both a long-term source of gas under contract and a long-term market in which to sell the transported gas. Gas pipelines were (and still are) regulated under the Natural Gas Act of 1938 (NGA) as public utilities and, for several decades, the price of natural gas was also subject to federal price controls under the NGA.

Still, the process of exploring, drilling and producing wells in the field is the same for oil and gas. This chapter focuses on the legal framework for oil and gas production in two contexts: first, development on private land onshore, and second, development on the federally owned Outer Continental Shelf (OCS) offshore. The chapter only tangentially discusses oil and gas development on public onshore lands because many law schools have entire courses on public lands and resource management. Federal land and mineral ownership is highly concentrated in eleven Western states and Alaska. Crude oil production from onshore federal and Indian lands is even more highly concentrated in a few states, notably North Dakota (the Bakken shale), New Mexico and Wyoming. Federal gas production is only somewhat more dispersed among the states. *See* U.S. Energy Information Admin. (EIA), Sales of Fossil Fuels Produced from Federal and Indian Lands, FY 2003 through FY 2013, at 19 & 20 (June 2014). The recent surge in production from shale oil and gas has largely occurred on private lands, often in Eastern or Midwestern states that have little federal land. The federal share of U.S. crude oil production dropped from 33% in 2003 to 23% in 2013, and the federal share of natural gas production fell from 36% in 2003 to 16% in 2013. *Id.* at 2. Even though oil production from federal leases in North Dakota and New Mexico has soared in recent years, the federal share of total U.S. production fell in 2013 because of the high growth rate (15%) in total U.S. crude production that year. Put simply, modest increases in federal oil production in 2013 were outpaced by huge increases in production from non-federal lands. *Id.* at 4.

As to the offshore, the federal Gulf of Mexico produced 69% of all crude oil from federal and Indian lands in 2013. *Id.* at 1. By focusing on federal offshore development, the student will be able to contrast the legal framework of private onshore oil and gas development, dominated by the common law of contract, tort and property rights and by state regulation, with the regulatory framework of one large federal leasing program. Federal development triggers a number of statutes that do not apply on private lands, notably the National Environmental Policy Act (NEPA). Developers on federal land also must interact with the federal agencies that administer the nation's leasing laws under different federal statutes applicable to the type of federal land being leased.

Federal onshore oil and gas permitting is conducted largely by the Bureau of Land Management (BLM) of the Department of Interior (DOI). Industry often complains that federal policies retard efficient development because of lengthy delays in permitting and "needless" regulation by agency bureaucrats. In 2013, the BLM reported an average of 7.5 months to process an application for a permit to drill whereas state agencies claimed that they averaged only 80 days. *See* Office of Inspector Gen., DOI, Onshore Oil and Gas Permitting 6 (June 2014). However, federal lands are managed under a multiple-use mandate that requires federal land use plans, triggering NEPA and much citizen participation over which use should prevail among recreation, grazing, resource extraction, forestry, and wilderness. Moreover, industry personnel often fail to fill out the permits properly, causing delay. *Id.* Some expert commentators, while sympathetic to industry's complaints, point to layers of state and local barriers imposed on federal lands as the major impediment to federal resource extraction. *See* Jan G. Laitos & Elizabeth Getches, Multi-layered and Sequential: State and Local Barriers to Extractive Resource Development, 23 Va. Envtl. L. J. 1 (2004). These same state and local barriers often arise on private lands, as the material in this chapter shows. As long as resource extraction has significant environmental externalities and land impacts, developers will face opposition from some citizens.

The offshore material also discusses oil spills and blowouts. By 2020, deepwater oil production is forecast to supply a third of the world's oil production. Jelena Vidic-Perunovic & Bill Jelena-Heade, Novel Hull Concepts Address Ultradeep Gulf of Mexico Production, Oil & Gas J., Nov. 4, 2013, at 74.

Chapter 9 discusses the regulatory framework that allows oil and gas production to flow to markets through pipelines. It traces the long and ultimately successful effort to restructure the gas pipeline industry by forcing the pipelines to become "open access" carriers of gas owned by third parties rather than gas owned by the pipeline itself. Oil pipeline regulation has always followed an open-access model, but is regulated differently from gas pipelines. Chapter 14 on International Energy Markets looks at trade and security issues, often centered on oil and gas flows among nations.

2. THE LONG-TERM PRICES OF OIL AND GAS

Fluctuations in the price of oil have driven much of the legislation enacted by both state and federal governments in the United States. A long-term view of this key determinant of our energy policies appears below, showing the impact of various geopolitical events. Note that the price of crude oil started to surge around 2001, dropped briefly after the global financial crisis in 2008, and then rebounded rapidly. It has generally hovered around $100 per barrel from 2011 to early 2014:

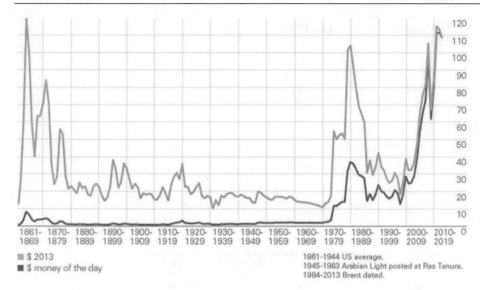

1861-1944 US average.
1945-1983 Arabian Light posted at Ras Tanura.
1984-2013 Brent dated.

Figure 4–1
Crude Oil Prices 1861–2013
Source: BP Statistical Summary,
http://www.bp.com/en/global/corporate/about-bp/energy-economics/statistical-
review-of-world-energy/review-by-energy-type/oil/oil-prices.html

Domestic natural gas prices (at the wellhead) have followed a different price pattern, especially after the 2008 financial crisis, as shown below in Figure 4–2. The large drop in gas prices compared to oil prices reflects the shale gas boom in the United States and the current inability to export large volumes of gas for sale on world markets where prices are much higher.

U.S. Natural Gas Wellhead Price

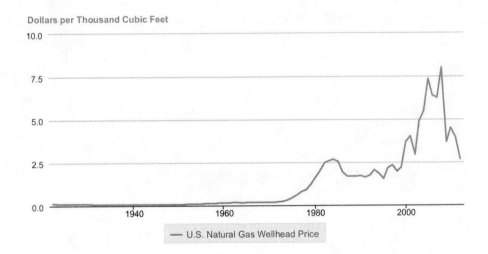

Figure 4–2
U.S. Natural Gas Wellhead Price 1922–2012
Source: EIA, http://www.eia.gov/dnav/ng/hist/n9190us3a.htm

3.   THE RESOURCE BASE: CONVENTIONAL AND UNCONVENTIONAL

a.   CONVENTIONAL

Until the 1990s, petroleum was mainly produced from underground reservoirs composed of sandstone or limestone rock. These sedimentary rocks are porous. If you spill gasoline or motor oil onto a concrete pavement, much of the liquid will seep into the tiny pore spaces of the concrete rather than form a puddle on the surface. Similarly, oil and gas are stored in the microscopic pore spaces of sedimentary rocks, but they are under great pressure caused by the weight of hundreds of feet of overlying silt and rock. In conventional reservoirs, a layer of impervious rock forms a kind of dome or trap that prevents the petroleum from migrating upwards to the surface. If a well bore penetrates this reservoir rock, the oil and gas will naturally flow towards the low-pressure area at the bottom of the well bore. If the well is not carefully controlled, the oil and gas, under great pressure, will rush up the well bore to the surface. Oil spills or gas explosions can result when oil and gas gush from a "blowout," i.e., from an uncontrolled release.

Some fields produce only gas; some produce oil, and some produce both. Some gas production is "dry" gas comprised largely of methane molecules that we recognize as the natural gas flowing in pipelines to various end uses, including residential stove tops. Some gas is "wet gas" and contains other hydrocarbons that are liquid at room temperature. These "natural gas liquids," or NGLs, include ethane, propane, butane, and natural gasoline. As gas production grows, so does the production of

NGLs, which are separated from dry gas at gas processing facilities, usually located near the field. Almost all ethane is used in the petrochemical sector to make products that are then converted into plastics. About half of the propane is used for heating and fuel. Other NGLs are used in oil refining. The growing availability of low-cost natural gas and NGLs from unconventional formations has led to what some call a "manufacturing renaissance" in the United States based on the competitive advantage of access to low-priced feedstocks such as NGLs. Brookings Inst., Natural Gas Liquids (Mar. 2013, Natural Gas Briefing Document #1).

Almost all oil wells also produce gas that flows up the well bore with the oil. This gas was originally dissolved in the oil underground, but when the pressure is lowered, the gas comes out of solution, much like bubbles of carbon dioxide in a soda drink are released when you pop the top off a soda can. This gas is called "casinghead gas." It is usually separated from the crude oil in a simple process near the wellhead. The crude oil can be stored in tanks in the field or put into a pipeline. However, if no gas pipeline is nearby, the accompanying casinghead gas is burned in a flare close to the wellhead.

From 2009 to 2014, the price of crude oil has been many times greater than the price of natural gas on a heating value basis. The ratio between the prices of oil and gas based on the equivalent heating value of each is 6:1, meaning that if gas sells for $4 per million British thermal units (BTUs) (equivalent to about $4 per thousand cubic feet (MCF)), the equivalent amount of oil in heating value would sell for $24 per barrel. The ratio in recent years has been closer to 25:1, i.e., gas sells for $4 per MCF and oil for $100 per barrel. Thus, drillers have a much greater incentive to explore for and produce oil than gas. In two huge shale oil plays in the United States, the Bakken Shale in North Dakota and the Eagle Ford shale in South Texas, large amounts of casinghead gas are being flared because the pipeline infrastructure for gas is not available and the gas is not considered valuable enough to capture. The flares from both of these shale oil fields can be seen in satellite photos of the earth. Meanwhile, the much higher-priced oil is produced and shipped by pipelines or by rail in tank cars. The United States recently entered into the ranks of the top ten gas-flaring countries in the world, joining Russia, Nigeria and others. (Until the shale boom, very little gas was flared in the United States after 1970.)

The unrelenting surge in oil (and gas) prices from 2001 until mid-2008 seemed to prove the existence of "Peak Oil:" that global supplies of oil had peaked and the world would need to learn to live with declining supplies of this vital fuel. In 1956, geologist M. King Hubbert from Shell Oil forecast that oil production would peak in the United States around 1970—and it did. Peak Oil proponents apply Hubbert's model, or variants of it, to global oil production. Hubbert's model is based on the following pattern: Oil discoveries will peak at some point because oil is a finite resource and the big fields that are easy to find are found first. Once discoveries peak, oil production will peak some years later as these new discoveries are exploited and depleted over time. In short, when discoveries start falling, production will ultimately fall too, around 40 years later. At that point, the world will not have "run out of oil," but oil supply will be on an irreversible decline curve. (Picture a bell-shaped curve.) In July 2008, oil prices reached the $140 per barrel mark. The United States was already headed for recession when the U.S. housing bubble burst and financial markets deflated. Many countries of the world plunged into serious financial recession, triggering government bailouts of banks, sharp rises in unemployment, and considerable mistrust of Wall Street.

The debate over the predictive accuracy of the Peak Oil model pits geological pessimism against economic and technological optimism. The Peak Oilers, who included a number of noted physicists and geologists, saw the end of the age of oil because the largest fields in the world were in significant decline, including the giant fields in Saudi Arabia that had been pumping oil for more than 50 years. The anti-Peak Oil proponents argued that energy comes from human ingenuity—a bottomless well. Anything is possible—surely bacteria will be invented to ferment tar sands. The cost of extracting oil will go up slowly, but we will always find more, especially when high prices provide incentives to explore and innovate. Also, it is often governments, not Mother Nature, that create "geological" shortages by restricting access to petroleum reserves, both in the United States and around the world.

The two camps saw very different oil scenarios in the future. One foresaw the possibility of Oil War III, abrupt recessions in oil-consuming countries, and continuous global conflicts between the U.S., Europe, China, and Japan to secure oil supplies unless consumers adapted to a more frugal lifestyle. The other camp said we could "keep the lights on" and enjoy the use of energy as technology, human intelligence and markets brought good things to life.

Any reader might be confused by the jarring dissonance between the competing brainpower on both sides of the Peak Oil issue. However, the "disconnect" is not so large when framed as follows: The Peak Oil debate is largely about conventional oil. All players seemed to recognize that the world has large supplies of unconventional oil and even larger amounts of unconventional gas. Still, when large amounts of oil and gas began to trickle and then pour out of shale fields in the United States from 2008 onwards, the scale of the shale plays stunned virtually every expert in government and in industry itself. Technology had trumped Peak Oil's geological pessimism. Unconventional oil and gas would fuel the future.

b.   UNCONVENTIONAL

Oil and gas are "unconventional" when they cannot be produced economically without special stimulation techniques. In general, unconventional sources are not found in the sandstone and limestone reservoir rocks that characterized the first century of petroleum development, starting in 1859. Conventional oil and gas have been characterized as "hard to find, but easy to produce" because once a well bore has succeeded in penetrating a conventional reservoir, the oil and gas flow up the bore freely. Mother Nature supplies the inherent reservoir pressure that pushes the oil and gas through the rock into the bore without any other stimulation. Conventional reservoir rocks are both porous and permeable. Porosity measures the ability of a rock to hold oil, gas or water. Permeability measures the ability of oil, gas or water to flow through the rock. Without permeability, the hydrocarbons stay trapped underground, with no tiny tunnels or routes to reach the well bore.

While shale oil and gas, found in shale formations, are now the largest unconventional sources, several other kinds of unconventional oil exist, such as:

Oil sands (also called tar sands) and heavy oil. These oil sources are so viscous (i.e., thick and gooey) that they cannot flow unless heated (with steam) or diluted (with lighter crude oil or natural gas) to reduce their viscosity. Heavy oil has long been produced in Venezuela's Orinoco Belt. The oil sands of Canada are vast and are the subject of much controversy as producers there seek pipelines to export the oil. The oil sands consist of bitumen that must be upgraded in on-site processing plants in order to flow in pipelines to refineries, a process that produces significantly greater greenhouse gas emissions than conventional oil production. Citizen opposition to pipelines that ship this upgraded bitumen to refineries along the Gulf Coast of the United States or to export terminals on the Eastern or Western coasts of Canada is intense. Chapter 14 discusses the Keystone XL pipeline proposal to send oil from the oil sands across the Canadian border into the United States.

Oil shale. The United States has the largest oil shale deposit in the world in the Green River formation in Colorado, Utah and Wyoming. Oil shale (not to be confused with shale oil, discussed below) contains kerogen, an organic material that was not buried deep enough at high temperatures to convert into petroleum. Kerogen is not crude oil and the rock containing it is not shale, so "oil shale" is badly misnamed. To date, its extraction has been uneconomic, and it is not commercially produced. Shallow deposits of oil shale can be surface mined and the material is then crushed and heated in a massive retorting process that produces an oil-like liquid that requires upgrading before transport to a refinery. Deeper deposits must be "cooked" in situ (i.e., heated in place underground) to convert them to a liquid that can be removed and upgraded.

Unconventional gas sources, other than shale gas, include the following:

Coalbed methane. Coal seams often contain trapped natural gas that is released when mining the coal. Historically, this gas was seen as a dangerous by-product of coal mining because it can cause explosions that kill miners and collapse the mine tunnels. However, this coalbed gas can be purposefully extracted by dewatering a coal seam to reduce the pressure holding the gas in the porous coal.

Tight gas (and tight oil). Tight gas and tight oil are trapped in sandstone or limestone formations that are atypically impermeable and less porous than usual. The formations must be fractured in order to allow the oil and gas to flow. These tight formations are often more difficult to fracture than shale formations.

Two other sources of natural gas exist in stunningly large amounts, but are not yet able to be commercially produced. *Geopressurized methane* is located in the Gulf Coast region, dissolved at high temperatures in deep aquifers of saline water containing perhaps 60,000 trillion cubic feet (TCF) of methane. For perspective, the United States consumed about 29 TCF of gas in 2013. *Methane hydrates* exist in almost inexhaustible quantities beneath permafrost and under ocean bottoms. The methane is trapped with water in frozen, lattice-like formations. Research is underway by several nations, notably Japan, to find ways to harvest the methane from the hydrate formations without causing methane leakage into the atmosphere, which would contribute greatly to global warming. In May 2012, a consortium of the U.S. Department of Energy (DOE), a Japanese corporation and ConocoPhillips injected a mixture of carbon dioxide and nitrogen into a methane hydrate formation in the North Slope of Alaska. These gases replaced the methane in the structure and allowed the extraction of the methane. The project has potential for carbon sequestration and natural gas production. Clive Schofield, New Marine Resource Opportunities, Fresh Challenges, 35 U. Haw. L. Rev. 715, 724–26 (2013).

c.   THE "SHALE REVOLUTION:" SHALE GAS AND SHALE OIL

Shale rock is a very fine sedimentary rock that naturally consists of thin layers that can be split apart. The shale contains large amounts of oil and gas, but the shale rock is not permeable so oil and gas cannot flow to a well bore. If a well is drilled into the shale formation, nothing will flow out until further treatment. Shale formations cover huge areas and are "easy to find, but hard to produce." Conventional gas reservoirs are created when natural gas migrates from an organic-rich source formation into permeable reservoir rock, where it is trapped by an overlying layer of impermeable rock. In contrast, shale gas resources form within the organic-rich shale source rock. The low permeability of the shale greatly inhibits the gas from migrating to more permeable reservoir rocks. EIA, Energy in Brief: What Is Shale Gas and Why Is it Important?, www.eia. gov/energy_in_brief/article/about_shale_gas.cfm. This EIA document has the following useful graphic:

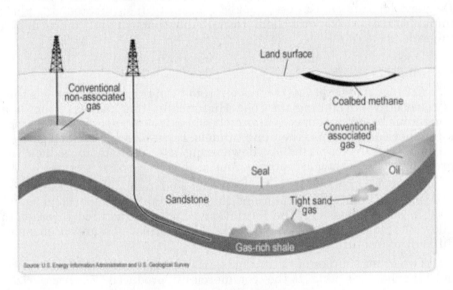

Figure 4–3
The Geology of Natural Gas Resources
Source: EIA, Today in Energy; Feb. 14, 2011
http://www.eia.gov/todayinenergy/detail.cfm?id=110

Two technologies, which to date have primarily been deployed in the United States, have unlocked oil and gas from shale in commercial quantities: horizontal drilling and hydraulic fracturing. To horizontally drill a well, a rig first drills straight down towards the targeted formation and then arcs the drill bit so that it drills sideways through the formation to expose more surface area and thus more gas and/or oil trapped within the formation. Portions of the shale or tight sandstone around the horizontal well bore are then fractured in stages. The most common form of hydraulic fracturing used in wells today is "slick water" fracturing, in which the portions of the well bore within the productive shale are perforated by shooting shaped charges through the steel well bore to allow entry of liquids into the formation. The company then pumps several million gallons of water mixed with small amounts of chemicals down the well at very high pressure, and this mixture is pushed outward through the perforations into the shale or tight sandstone. The pressurized water solution fractures the shale rock as a result of the sheer force of the solution being injected down the well. "Proppants" such as sand are also injected to prop open the fractures so that oil or gas may flow through them. A more detailed, but still brief, description of new techniques used to produce gas today, with photos, appears in Stephen A. Holditch, Getting the Gas Out of the Ground, Am. Inst. of Chem. Eng'rs, CEP J., Aug. 2012, http://energy.tamu.edu/media/90710/hold itch%20-%20hydraulic%20fracturing.pdf. Compared to conventional oil and gas fields, which are like a bulls eye target, shale plays underlie huge areas of land, many of which have not produced oil or gas in decades, as shown in Figure 4–4:

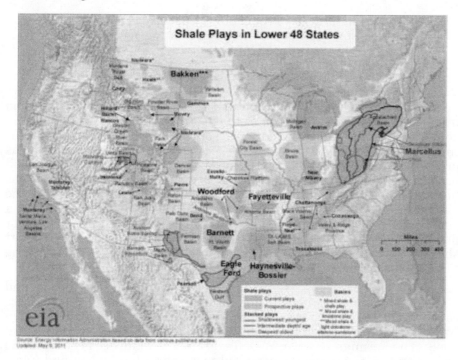

Figure 4–4
Shale Plays in Lower 48 States
Source: EIA, http://www.eia.gov/oil_gas/rpd/shale_gas.pdf

The EIA Energy in Brief shows the importance of shale gas to U.S. gas supplies:

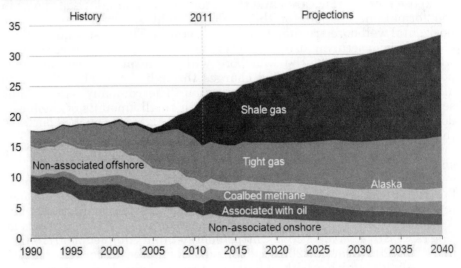

U.S. dry natural gas production trillion cubic feet

Source: U.S. Energy Information Administration, *Annual Energy Outlook 2013 Early Release*

Figure 4–5
U.S. Natural Gas Production By Source, 1990–2040
Source: EIA, http://www.eia.gov/forecasts/aeo/er/pdf/0383er.pdf

Almost all of the increase in U.S. gas production through 2040 is expected to come from growth in shale gas supplies. As Figure 4–5 shows, these are projected to increase from 7.8 TCF in 2011 to 16.7 TCF in 2040. Total U.S. gas production is projected to increase 44% over this time frame, allowing the United States to export gas that it cannot consume domestically. Note how conventional sources of gas are declining over time. The lowest layer in Figure 4–5 is "non-associated onshore" gas production, i.e., gas production from gas fields not associated with oil production. Production from both conventional onshore and offshore gas fields declines over time. Shale gas and tight gas increase to supply the gas market. Note that in 2005, shale gas was barely noticeable as a supply source. Only after 2009 did shale gas come to be seen as a major new fuel source. It literally surprised the world, as two fields, the Barnett shale in the Dallas–Fort Worth area and the Marcellus shale underlying Pennsylvania, ramped up production with astounding growth rates.

Just as surprising, the same technologies of fracturing and horizontal drilling worked to unlock the "light, tight oil" (sometimes called "LTO") in shale rock. Liquid production from the Bakken field in North Dakota and the Eagle Ford field in South Texas took off around 2008. (The Permian Basin in West Texas and New Mexico is now coming on strong and may have the potential to surpass the Bakken and Eagle Ford.) Figure 4–6 shows the ramp-up in the Eagle Ford field, which stunned so many forecasters. By mid-2014, this field was producing about 1.4 million barrels per day:

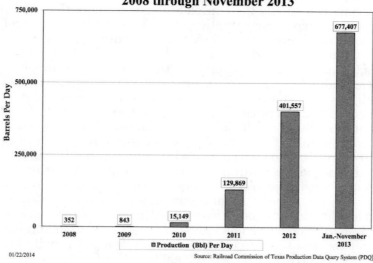

Figure 4–6
Texas Eagle Ford Shale Oil Production
2008 through Nov. 2013
Source: Railroad Commission of Texas, http://www.rrc.state.tx.us/media/7078/eagle
fordproduction_oil_perday.pdf

Estimating the size of U.S. shale oil and gas resources is an ongoing process. Two types of figures are most often used for this purpose. The first measures technically recoverable resources that may or may not be economic to produce. The estimated size of these resources changes as technology changes and better seismic information about geological prospects becomes available. Proved reserves are the "inventory" that oil companies hold and can produce under current economic conditions, operating methods and government regulations. These are smaller than technically recoverable reserves because they represent the oil and gas volumes that have been discovered and defined by wells or other exploratory measures and which can be economically recovered in a relatively short time frame. These reserves decline as they are produced and sold, but also increase as technology allows producers to extract more oil and gas or as prices rise allowing more commercial recovery.

In 2012, EIA estimated that the amount of technically recoverable shale gas in the United States had nearly tripled over the five years since 2008 to a total of 482 TCF, while aggregated estimates from over 130 industry, government and academic groups reported that such reserves had grown to almost 1,000 TCF. U.S. Gov't Accountability Ofc. (GAO), Information on Shale Resources, Development, and Environmental and Public Health Risks 19–25 (Sept. 2012). For shale oil, the U.S. Geological Survey estimated that technically recoverable oil in shale and tight formations had more than tripled between 2006 and 2011, even though it had not evaluated shale plays that had just started up. *Id.* Proven shale reserves for both oil and gas have also risen significantly in the past few years. *Id.*

The conventional wisdom now seems to be that the domestic gas resource base can supply the United States with more than 100 years of natural gas at current consumption rates. Perhaps it is worth reflecting at this point on the history of forecasts of natural gas supply. In 1978, experts estimated that the United States had about 208 TCF of gas reserves, about a ten-year supply at then-current consumption rates. But, as explained in Chapter 9, prices of natural gas had been kept artificially low by federal price controls for decades. When price controls were removed and gas prices increased, producers explored for and found much more gas. By 1999, official estimates of recoverable reserves totaled 60 years of supply. Both the Environmental Law Institute and the National Petroleum Council concluded that the United States could meet increased demand for natural gas to replace more polluting coal-fired power plants with ease. Yet, no sooner had the ink dried on these 1999 reports, than the price of natural gas began a steep, almost relentless climb to heights unanticipated by anyone. In a cold snap in late 2000, the price soared to $8 per MCF and industrial users with switching capability turned off the gas taps. Industrial demand dropped rapidly from 17.1 billion cubic feet (BCF) per day in 2000 to 10.3 BCF in 2002. Along the Gulf Coast, many ammonia and methanol plants that produced fertilizers closed. In an abnormally cold period in late February 2003, gas prices on one day soared to an astounding $22 per MCF, although they dropped again fairly quickly.

Still, natural gas prices stayed high, in the range of $6.50 to $8 per MCF, until the global financial recession hit in 2008. The National Petroleum Council issued gloomy forecasts of natural gas availability in 2003 and 2007. Industry projected that domestic natural gas shortages were such a long-term problem that U.S. energy policy must focus on the rapid permitting of LNG terminals that would allow large-scale imports of natural gas from abroad. Eleven LNG import terminals now exist in the United States, most of which were built in the first decade of this century to import LNG when prices were high. However, given the significant increases in the supply of domestically produced natural gas, these terminals are now seeking permission to convert to LNG export terminals at the cost of billions of additional dollars, to export some of the large supply of natural gas flowing out of shale gas fields. Chapter 9 explains in more detail how natural gas markets were restructured in the United States between 1978 and 1990, resulting in more supply and more price volatility. Chapter 14 continues the story of exporting LNG and oil from U.S. ports to far-flung markets.

4. THE OIL AND GAS BUSINESS

Between the well head and an end user's gasoline tank, boiler, stove top or blast furnace, oil and gas are transported and processed from lower-valued hydrocarbons, often produced in remote areas, to higher-valued products used in populated centers of industrial activity. The largest companies in the industry are often vertically integrated and operate in all five stages of the value chain: (1) exploration; (2) production; (3) refining; (4) distribution; and (5) marketing. However, a large number of small-, medium-, and large-size companies also operate as "independent" producers, refiners, transporters and marketers, active in just one or two of the stages. Natural gas is treated like oil for purposes of exploration and production, but it is distributed and marketed through different networks than those used for oil. Crude oil usually flows to a refinery for processing into gasoline, jet fuel, diesel and other products, while gas is often processed in the field to recover hydrocarbon liquids and to eliminate undesirable elements like sulfur and water. The gas then needs no further refining and is transported by pipeline to markets.

a. EXPLORATION

The exploration staff is led by petroleum geologists who use tools such as seismographs, magnetic surveys from NASA satellites, gravimeters and infrared remote sensors to unlock the earth's buried secrets.

Today's shale and tight sandstone wells are rarely dry holes, although operators still bear the market risk that these high-cost wells will be profitable as market conditions change. Despite technological improvements in seismic imaging, exploratory "wildcat" wells, seeking to tap into conventional reservoirs, remain a geological gamble. In 1975, only three out of 100 exploratory wells drilled were commercially successful. Technical progress in supercomputers in the 1990s now allows the processing of enormous amounts of data from geological surveys. Computers can produce brightly colored 3-D seismic images which virtually shout "drill here" and this greatly increases the probability of successful drilling. Still, even promising locations can result in "dusters," or dry holes, rather than the "gushers" depicted in movies like "Giant." For example, Conoco took a $19 million charge against earnings in early 1999 to write off an unsuccessful deepwater wildcat well drilled in 4,800 feet of water off New Zealand. Many of the most promising areas for big discoveries are in deep offshore waters and in the remote Arctic where the challenges and costs of drilling are great. Many companies have ventured overseas in places like Russia, South America and Nigeria, where large political risks are added to geological risk and the market risk of highly fluctuating oil prices.

b. PRODUCTION

The efficient recovery of crude oil from the tiny pore spaces of conventional reservoir rock is technically rather complicated. When a well bore penetrates a formation holding oil under high pressure, the well bore creates an area of low pressure. Yet, oil cannot expel itself from the rock. It is compressed gas or water trapped in the reservoir with the oil that expands in response to the lower pressure at the well bore. The expanding gas or water forces the oil up and out of the well in a displacement process and provides the continuing pressure essential for producing oil without the use of pumps. If the original field pressure is low or has decreased over time as oil is withdrawn, wells will need to be put "on the pump."

Two factors must be controlled to produce a conventional reservoir efficiently: (1) the rate of production; and (2) the location of wells. A controlled rate of production maintains reservoir pressure by preventing the rapid release of dissolved gas from solution. It also assures that the boundary between the migrating oil and the advancing gas or water front is fairly uniform so that the entire reservoir is effectively flushed without bypassing areas of oil-saturated rock. The proper location of wells also increases recovery rates. No wells should be allowed to produce gas from the "gas cap" that may sit at the top of a layer of oil until all of the oil is flushed out; and oil wells in a water-drive field should be located high on the structure where they will not prematurely produce large amounts of water and dissipate the water drive.

Thus, for each such reservoir there is generally a dominant displacement mechanism, an optimal pattern of well locations, and a "maximum efficient rate" of production (MER) that, if exceeded, will lead to an avoidable loss of ultimate oil recovery. The MER of a field is determined technically through engineering studies. The use of the MER to control production rates is probably the single most important conservation measure for assuring efficient oil recovery.

Further improvements in production efficiency can result from artificial pressure-maintenance activities such as injecting water or gas into the reservoir. The injected gas or water may be recycled from the reservoir or brought in from extraneous sources. Many older fields in West Texas are being repressured with carbon dioxide (CO_2) delivered through a 400-mile pipeline from natural deposits of this gas in Colorado. Transporting anthropogenic sources of CO_2 captured from coal-fired power plants or other large combustion sources to oil fields for use in enhanced recovery operations and then permanently sequestering the CO_2 in the reservoir after the oil is depleted is one possible way of reducing CO_2 emissions. Some companies have business models built on owning CO_2 reserves and infrastructure to increase recovery rates. An example is Denbury Resources, Inc., which received its first anthropogenic source of CO_2 into its Green Line pipeline from an Air Products plant in Port Arthur, Texas in 2012. Denbury, http://www.denbury.com/operations/operations-overview/default.aspx.

The recovery of natural gas is much less complicated than recovering oil because gas is highly expansible. It can be recovered from porous rock simply by allowing it to migrate by expansion into the low-pressure area around the well bore. This process commonly can recover 90 percent or more of the original gas in place. Recovery rates less than this occur only when the permeability of the reservoir rock is so low that gas cannot flow freely into the well bore. As introduced above, operators in shale rock or tight sand formations must use hydraulic fracturing to create cracks in the formation so that the gas can flow freely. Legal and policy issues associated with fracturing are discussed below in Section C.5 of this Chapter.

c.   REFINING

Crude oil in its natural state is of little practical value. It consists of a mixture of hundreds of hydrocarbon compounds, each having its own boiling point. Refining separates these compounds into desired products such as gasoline, jet fuel, kerosene, diesel fuel, heating oil, and asphalt. Petroleum hydrocarbons are also the source of many feedstocks for chemical plants producing everything from nylons to insecticides.

Refining first separates the hydrocarbons in crude oil by heating them and distilling the different vapor streams which result at different temperatures. Heated crude oil is sent to a fractionation tower that may be a hundred feet high. The hydrocarbons with the lowest boiling points, such as gasoline, will vaporize first. As other hydrocarbons rise and then cool, they condense at different heights in the tower and are withdrawn as separate products.

Distillation of crude oil into its fractions does not produce the correct proportion of products demanded by the marketplace. For example, it produces relatively small amounts of gasoline. Therefore, refineries use thermal cracking and catalytic cracking to break larger hydrocarbon molecules into smaller ones that will rise to the top of the fractionation tower.

Oil refineries pose major problems of air and water pollution. Many refineries are located in sensitive coastal areas because they are designed to receive and ship products by tanker. In addition, refineries process tremendous quantities of liquids and vapors at high temperatures and high pressures. Explosions and blasts, while rare, can kill and injure workers and seriously affect the health and property of people living in surrounding neighborhoods.

As noted earlier, the natural gas that flows from a well may require some treatment, such as sulfur removal, but this is a much simpler operation than the refining of crude oil.

d.   TRANSPORTATION AND DISTRIBUTION

In general, the method of distributing petroleum compounds varies with their relative weight. Heavy compounds, like asphalt, usually go by truck, rail or barge. Liquids can vary from heavy crude, which is like molasses, to gasoline, which evaporates readily. Heavy crude usually goes by tanker or barge, although it may go by pipeline if it can flow. Refined products are typically distributed by pipeline to a terminal and then by truck or train to the ultimate user. Natural gas can be liquefied and shipped by LNG tankers, but it is mostly transported by pipeline. Crude oil is a "niche" fuel because its refined products are used mainly by one sector of the economy—transportation, which accounted for almost 70 percent of the oil consumed in the United States in 2013.

A "spaghetti bowl" of pipes underlies cities, like Houston, located near producing fields and refinery complexes. A large network of interstate pipelines moves oil and gas from the producing states to consuming centers. Pipelines are specialized for natural gas and different types of petroleum products. In 1906, oil pipelines were regulated as common carriers by federal law. *See* the Hepburn Act Amendment of 1906, Pub. L. No. 357, 34 Stat. 584 (1906). At that time, the major pipeline companies attempted to circumvent this Act by transporting only oil produced from their own leases or purchased at the wellhead, thereby refusing to hold themselves out as public pipelines for hire. In *The Pipeline Cases*, 234 U.S. 548 (1914), the U.S. Supreme Court held that the 1906 law applied to interstate pipelines, even if the pipeline owned the oil being transported. Justices Holmes wrote: "Availing itself of its monopoly of the means of transportation the Standard Oil Company refused through its subordinates to carry any oil unless the same was sold to it or to them and through them to it on terms more or less dictated by itself. In this way it made itself master of the fields without the necessity of owning them and carried . . . a great subject of international commerce coming from many owners but, by the duress of which the

Standard Oil Company was master, carrying it all as its own." *Id.* at 559; *see* Edwin I. Malet, Oil Pipelines as Common Carriers: Issues of Form and Substance, 20 Hous. L. Rev. 801 (1983); George S. Wolbert, Jr., The Pipe Line Story, 4 Okla. L. Rev. 305–36 (1951).

The technology for gas pipelines did not exist in 1906. Gas pipelines were regulated in 1938 when the NGA was enacted in recognition of the monopoly power of interstate gas pipelines. Gas pipelines were not originally regulated as common carriers; for decades, the pipeline owners carried only their own gas, purchased directly from producers in the fields. The effort to convert these pipelines to "open access" pipelines that would carry gas owned by many other market participants, including competitors' gas, was the primary mission of the Federal Energy Regulatory Commission (FERC) during the 1980s and 1990s. This story of natural gas pipeline restructuring is told in Chapter 9. Oil and carbon dioxide pipeline regulation also appears there.

B. EARLY HISTORY: THE LEASE CONTRACT AND COMMON LAW

1. OIL BEFORE PETROLEUM

In the newly formed United States, the primary source of power for mills and other growing industries was water power. Water could turn wheels, but it could not produce light. For illumination, most people relied on candles and fireplaces. Wealthier people were able to light their homes with oil lamps, which produced a brighter and more reliable flame, but the animal and vegetable fats used to fuel such lamps were expensive. The premium fuel, whale oil, became increasingly expensive as the whalers wiped out the whale populations of the Atlantic and were forced to travel to the Antarctic to obtain supplies.

Around 1800, gas made from coal, called "town gas," was developed and piped into street lamps and the homes of middle-and upper-class families in urban areas. Town gas was too expensive for many households, however. For most of the 19th century, tens of millions of rural households around the world continued to fill their lamps with a biofuel—the oil rendered from the blubber of sperm whales.

Whaling, a poorly paid and dangerous way of life—portrayed so unforgettably in 1851 in Melville's "Moby Dick"—reached its peak just before 1850. The American whaling fleet, by far the largest in the world, had a record total of more than 7,900 vessels in 1846. As the number of sperm whales dwindled, whaling rapidly declined. This was the first Tragedy of the Commons to affect America's energy supplies. What new fuel would take its place?

In the 1850s, a Canadian inventor discovered a way to extract a liquid from natural deposits of tar and asphalt. He called this liquid, which could be burned in existing oil lamps, kerosene. Although expensive, it produced better illumination than vegetable or animal oils, and the kerosene lamp became a common fixture in the homes and offices of the wealthy. The growing market for kerosene increased the interest in learning more about the still mysterious properties of oil.

As storm clouds were gathering for the Civil War, the discovery of oil in Pennsylvania foretold a breakthrough in energy use that would rank with the great technological advances of all time. The tar-like substances that provided the source material for kerosene were scarce and difficult to process, so kerosene remained a luxury. Until 1859, petroleum was gathered from natural seeps and springs or skimmed off ponds. Then, in 1859, the Pennsylvania Rock Oil Company deeded a tract of land to Edwin Drake as "lessee" to drill a well near an old oil spring, using a rig made from an old steam engine and an iron bit attached by a rope to a wooden windlass. The drill bit hit oil at 69 feet below the surface. "Drake's Folly" had proved the practicality of a new technique for tapping liquid petroleum from the earth.

The discovery that oil could be found by drilling sparked a "gold rush" into the northwestern Pennsylvania region. Wild speculation in land followed as prospectors rushed into the area to try their luck. No one knew why oil could be found in one place but not another, so whenever someone struck oil, everyone else scurried to buy up the rights to nearby land. "Close-ology" was the geology of the day. In 1861, the first refinery went into operation in this region, producing mostly kerosene. To supply more distant refineries, railroads built spurs into the region, and in 1865 a railroad tank car was developed especially for carrying crude in two large wooden tanks. As large quantities of Pennsylvania oil reached the market, the price of kerosene dropped dramatically and the kerosene lamp became the basic source of lighting for homes and businesses all over the eastern United States.

2. THE OIL AND GAS LEASE

The United States is unique in that private landowners can own oil and gas and other minerals in the ground as real property. In virtually all other countries of the world, the state owns the mineral resources. In many countries, oil and gas are typically developed by national oil companies, such as Pemex in Mexico or the China National Offshore Oil Corporation, often in joint ventures with multinational corporations such as ExxonMobil, British Petroleum (BP) or Royal Dutch Shell. The relationship between the host country and multinational corporations is discussed in Chapter 14.

In the United States, private ownership of oil and gas has created a body of oil and gas law governed by the common law of property, contract, and tort. This common law operates within a complex framework of state conservation legislation and federal statutes. In addition to this system of private ownership, the federal government owns substantial mineral resources on public lands through its ownership of about 30 percent of the total land area in the United States, located mostly in the Western states and Alaska. (83 percent of Nevada and 68 percent of Alaska are federal land.) The federal government also owns the OCS, which produces much oil and gas from offshore wells drilled in the Gulf of Mexico and other coastal areas. The coastal states usually own the first three miles of offshore lands, at which point federal jurisdiction begins. See Section D of this Chapter.

Despite this diverse system of private, state, and federal ownership of minerals in the United States, the exploration and production of oil and gas are typically done pursuant to an "oil and gas lease" between the landowner as lessor (whether private or public) and an oil company (the "operator") as lessee. This core contract is designed to meet the unique needs of an industry exploring for and producing a substance hidden thousands of feet underground. The lessee wants the right, but not the duty, to develop a leasehold for a certain time. If promising deposits are found, the lessee wants the right to hold the lease for as long as profitable production continues.

The typical lessor does not have the capital or technical expertise to develop the oil and gas himself and does not want to bear the costs and risks of drilling and producing wells. Therefore, the lessor transfers the exclusive right to develop the oil and gas to the lessee in return for a cost-free share of production, called a royalty. In addition, the lessor will bargain with the lessee for a bonus—a one-time cash payment to the lessor for signing the lease. In "hot" territory where discoveries have been found on nearby acreage, the bonus may amount to thousands of dollars an acre. In "wildcat" territory where no operators have yet drilled, the bonus may be far less. If a lessee never drills, or drills only dry holes, the lessor's royalty payments are zero because there is no production, but the lessor has at least received the bonus payment. When the lessor is the state or federal government, leases are usually awarded through competitive auctions to the company that submits the highest bonus bid for a particular tract.

The relationship between the lessor and lessee is the mainstay of courses in oil and gas law, but it is premised on these straightforward economic goals of the two parties to the lease. By 1930, the U.S. oil and gas lease had developed into a standardized document, only a few pages long, and printed on a form to hand to a prospective lessor. Briefly, the typical oil and gas lease includes three basic clauses:

1.   A granting clause that transfers the mineral estate under the described land from the lessor to the lessee.

2.   The habendum clause which reads: "This lease shall be for a primary term of ___ years and as long thereafter as oil or gas is produced from said land."

3.   The royalty clause that, until the high price of oil after 2001, typically granted the lessor a 1/8 royalty on all the oil and gas produced from the lease.

NOTES AND COMMENTS

1.   The lessee under a typical lease never promises to drill a single well. If the lessee never drills and never secures production, the lease will terminate automatically at the end of the primary term because of the habendum clause. Lessors often seek to encourage drilling by contracting for the lessee's payment of annual delay rentals in exchange for the privilege of delaying the commencement of a well. Thus, if a lease has a primary term of 5 years and the lessee does not drill by the end of the first year, the lessee will have to pay delay rentals every year to extend the lease for additional years in the four-year primary term. Nonetheless, it is still the lessee's option to either drill or pay delay rentals; there is no contractual obligation to drill. If the lessee does seismic work and the data indicate an uneconomic drilling prospect, the lessee can simply decide to not pay delay rentals and the lease will end automatically, even before the 5-year term has passed.

During the secondary term, the lease terminates if production stops. "Shut-in" provisions in the lease, however, often allow temporary cessation of production for well maintenance or to allow the lessee to wait for available market opportunities, so long as the lessee pays the lessor shut-in royalties and does not exceed the allowed shut-in period.

2.   Test your knowledge of the lessor/lessee relationship:

(a) If you are the lessee, will you bargain for a three-year or a ten-year primary term in the blank in the habendum clause? If you are the lessor, which will you prefer?

(b) The lessee usually hands the lessor a printed lease form with a fixed royalty printed therein and hopes that the lessor will not bargain for a higher fraction. However, when oil and gas prices are high and leases are valuable, lessors may be able to secure a 1/6 or greater royalty share. The larger the cost-free royalty, the less money remains for the lessee to pay for all the costs of producing the oil and gas. Conversely, when oil prices dip to record lows, why might a lessor grant temporary royalty relief to a lessee and lower royalties until prices rise to an agreed level? *See, e.g.,* the Outer Continental Shelf Deep Water Royalty Relief Act (DWRRA) § 302, 43 U.S.C. § 1337(a)(3), which provides incentives to develop domestic deepwater resources by providing royalty holidays for initial production increments.

(c) If a lessee signs a lease on January 1, 2010 containing a three-year primary term, and has no production on January 1, 2013, what happens to the lease? What if the lessee has no production but is drilling a well on that day? What if the lessee has drilled a number of good wells and discovered a large gas field, but is not yet producing gas because no pipeline connection exists? What if the lessee has drilled some good shale gas wells, but they have not yet been hydraulically fractured?

3.   OWNERSHIP OF OIL AND GAS UNDERGROUND: SPLIT ESTATES

This section discusses ownership in the context of "split estates." Split estates are common in the United States: One owner owns the surface of the land and a second owner owns the minerals on the same tract. The surface owner may be an Alabama cotton farmer, a West Texas rancher, a Utah retiree in a small town near a national park, a hedge-fund manager from New York with vacation homes in upstate New York and Wyoming, or an entire suburban community outside Fort Worth or Denver. The mineral estate owner is most often someone entirely unrelated and often unknown to the surface owner. When an area becomes "hot" for an oil and gas play, operators will search county title records for the owners of the mineral estate, not the surface estate. The mineral estate owner is often happy to grant an oil and gas lease for a healthy bonus in the hundreds of dollars per acre and for the opportunity to receive royalty checks should the lessee find and produce oil or gas beneath the tract. The surface owner, of course, who is not a party to the lease, will often be devastated by the news that a drilling rig will soon be placed in the middle of his cotton crop, grasslands, backyard, or scenic view. The surface owner will not receive any of the bonus money or royalties from the leasing transaction; he or she does not own the severed oil and gas. As discussed in Part 4 *infra*, the surface owner has little control over the operator's reasonable use of the surface to access the minerals, as the mineral estate is dominant. Operators often negotiate with surface owners to avoid disputes, however, and some states have surface damage acts that require negotiation and/or operator payment of damages to surface owners.

Because oil and gas were first produced in the coal country of Pennsylvania, that state's supreme court had to address at an early date whether the term "mineral" included oil and gas. In an 1882 case, this court interpreted an 1870 deed to "minerals" and announced the "Dunham rule." When production from the Marcellus Shale underlying much of Pennsylvania started up in 2003, the ownership of this shale rock and the gas it contained reached the court again:

Butler v. Charles Power Estate

65 A.3d 885 (Pa. 2013).

■ BAER, J. We granted allowance of appeal to consider whether a deed executed in 1881, which reserved to the grantor the subsurface and removal rights of "one-half [of] the minerals and Petroleum Oils" contained beneath the subject property, includes within the reservation any natural gas contained within the shale formation beneath the subject land known as the Marcellus Shale Formation. The trial court in this matter, relying on the 1882 decision of this Court in *Dunham & Shortt v. Kirkpatrick,* 101 Pa. 36 (Pa.1882), and its progeny held that because the deed reservation did not specifically reference natural gas, any natural gas found within the Marcellus Shale beneath the subject land was not intended by the executing parties to the deed to be encompassed within the reservation. The Superior Court reversed that decision and remanded the case with instructions to the trial court to hold an evidentiary hearing complete with expert, scientific testimony to examine whether: (1) the gas contained within the Marcellus Shale is "conventional natural gas;" (2) Marcellus shale is a "mineral;" and (3) the entity that owns the rights to the shale found beneath the property also owns the rights to the gas contained within that shale. For the reasons that follow, we respectfully hold that the Superior Court erred in ordering the remand for an evidentiary hearing and reinstate the order of the trial court.

Appellants in this matter, John and Mary Josephine Butler, own 244 acres of land in Susquehanna County. Appellants' predecessors in title obtained the land in fee simple by deed in 1881 from Charles Powers. The deed contained the following reservation:

> [O]ne-half the minerals and Petroleum Oils to said Charles Powers his heirs and assigns forever together with all and singular the buildings, water courses, ways, waters, water courses, rights, liberties, privileges, hereditaments, and appurtenances, whatsoever there unto belonging or in any wise appertaining and the reversions and remainders rents issues and profits thereof; And also all the estate right, title interest property claimed and demand whatsoever there unto belonging or in any wise appertaining in law equity or otherwise however of in to or out of the same.

On July 20, 2009, Appellants filed a complaint to quiet title in the Susquehanna County Court of Common Pleas, alleging ownership of the property in fee simple and ownership, through adverse possession, of all (as opposed to one-half) of the minerals and petroleum oils contained beneath the property. The Estate of Charles Powers and his heirs and assigns were originally named as defendants. After some initial difficulty in locating representatives of the estate, on September 21, 2009, William and Craig Pritchard (Appellees) surfaced as rightful heirs to the Powers' Estate. Eventually, Appellees filed a motion for declaratory judgment, seeking a holding from the trial court that the deed reservation included one-half of all natural gas located within any Marcellus shale found beneath the property. Appellants filed a preliminary objection in the form of a demurrer, arguing that pursuant to long-standing precedent of this Court, a deed reservation does not contemplate or include natural gas unless expressly stated therein.

The trial court . . . denied Appellees' request for declaratory relief. The court noted that Pennsylvania law has long recognized a rebuttable presumption that "if, in connection with a conveyance of land, there is a reservation or an exception of 'minerals' without any specific mention of natural gas or oil, . . . the word 'minerals' was not intended by the parties to include natural gas or oil." This precept, commonly known as the *Dunham* Rule, may be rebutted by a challenger through clear and convincing evidence that the intent of the parties, at the time of the conveyance, was to include natural gas and/or oil. . . .

Appellees appealed to the Superior Court, a panel of which reversed in a published opinion. The panel also remanded the case to the trial court for an evidentiary hearing replete with expert testimony "on whether Marcellus shale constitutes a type of mineral such that the gas in it falls within the deed reservation." While the court extensively recounted *Dunham, Highland,* and related cases, it determined that those "decisions do not end the analysis" because of a 1983 decision of this Court, *United States Steel Corporation. v. Hoge,* 503 Pa. 140, 468 A.2d 1380 (1983) (*Hoge II*). Briefly, the *Hoge II* Court considered which party controlled access to "coalbed gas," a dangerous by-product of coal mining contained within coal seams, pursuant to reservations contained within various private deeds. Those reservations gave U.S. Steel the exclusive rights to mine and remove coal within a specific coal seam, while keeping with the property owners all oil and natural gas rights below the coal seam. In considering which party possessed the right to the coalbed gas, the *Hoge II* Court noted, "as a general rule, subterranean gas is owned by whoever has title to the property in which the gas is resting." Without discussing the *Dunham* Rule, the *Hoge II* Court concluded, "such gas as is present in coal must necessarily belong to the owner of the coal." Thus, U.S. Steel, as the owner of the coal, possessed the rights to the coalbed gas contained within the coal seam.

The Superior Court in this case found that because of the *Hoge II* decision, the trial court erred [in applying the *Dunham* Rule to Marcellus shale gas]. . . . Marcellus shale itself is a mineral; and Marcellus shale is similar to coal so that the *Hoge II* holding should apply to this case, resulting in Appellees owning one-half of the natural gas rights because of the *situs* of the gas in shale. In effect, the remand order directed the trial court to consider whether the *Hoge II* Court's logic *vis-a-vis* coalbed gas and coal scientifically and legally applied to natural gas contained within the Marcellus Shale. Appellants petitioned this Court for allowance of appeal, which we granted to consider the following issue:

In interpreting a deed reservation for "minerals," whether the Superior Court erred in remanding the case for the introduction of scientific and historic evidence about the Marcellus [S]hale and the natural gas contained therein, despite the fact that the Supreme Court of Pennsylvania has held (1) a rebuttable presumption exists that parties intend the term "minerals" to include only metallic substances, and (2) only the parties' intent can rebut the presumption to include non-metallic substances.

The Dunham Rule and its Progeny

Before delving into the parties' arguments, we find it prudent to recount the history of the *Dunham* Rule to facilitate a full understanding of the issues before us. While *Dunham* was decided in 1882, the doctrine for which that case has become well-known has its genesis in the 1836 decision of *Gibson v. Tyson,* 5 Watts 34 (Pa.1836). In *Gibson,* a deed reserved to the grantor of land "all minerals or magnesia of any kind" contained beneath the property. The Court was tasked with determining whether chrome (also known as chromate of iron) should be encompassed within the "all minerals" portion of the reservation. The Court noted that "the first, and indeed the only matter then is, to ascertain, if possible, what the parties intended and gave their assent to by making the agreement in question." In determining the parties' intent, the court continued, to people "entirely destitute of scientific knowledge in regard to such things . . . [to] the bulk of mankind, . . . [n]othing is thought by [minerals] to be such unless it be of a metallic nature, such as gold, silver, iron, copper, lead, [etc.]. . . ." Reluctantly, the Court determined that chrome would be considered by "the bulk of mankind" as a mineral because it was commonly thought to be of a metallic nature, akin to gold or silver, as demonstrated by parol evidence introduced before the trial court. Thus, the Court held the reservation specifying minerals included chrome based upon a common usage understanding, as opposed to any scientific basis.

* * *

With the notion that the common-man comprehension of terms included in contracts should be used, this Court in *Dunham* examined an 1870 deed, which reserved to the grantor "all the timber suitable for sawing; also all minerals," to determine whether the reservation included oil within the term "all minerals." . . . The Court followed the lead of *Gibson* . . . and held that a common understanding of the word "minerals" should be used. . . . Accordingly, using the common understanding of mankind, the court determined that oil is not a mineral pursuant to the framework laid by the *Gibson* Court that minerals are of a metallic nature. Thus, for the deed reservation to include oil, it must specifically be included within the clause.

* * *

[T]he *Dunham* Rule, a well-established and relied upon rule of property, continues to bind all situations in which a deed reservation does not expressly include oil or natural gas within the reservation. . . .

United States Steel Corp. v. Hoge

As noted, the Superior Court in this case found the *Dunham* progeny did not end the analysis because of *Hoge II.* Thus, we turn next to that decision. In the late 1970s, a question was raised concerning so-called "coalbed gas," which is a combination of methane, ethane, propane and other gases. Within the coal mining and natural gas industries, coalbed gas, which is found within crevices and empty pockets in coal seams and commonly known among miners as "firedamp," bears "little if any distinction [from] the gas found in oil-and-gas-bearing sands (natural gas)."

In the 1970s, various landowners in Greene County obtained deeds to tracts of land that, through a single predecessor, had already relinquished all rights to the coal contained within the Pittsburgh Coal Seam underlying the surface of the subject properties to U.S. Steel. U.S. Steel also possessed "the right of ventilation and drainage and the access to the mines for men and materials." The landowners retained, however, "the right to drill and operate through said coal for oil and gas without being held liable for any damages." In 1977 and 1978, two related events occurred: U.S. Steel began operations of its Cumberland Mine in Greene County to remove the coal contained beneath the landowners' property pursuant to the coal reservations, and the landowners began drilling wells through the property "for the express purpose of recovering coalbed gas contained" within the subject coal seam. The landowners utilized the process of hydrofracturing to obtain the coalbed gas. U.S. Steel sought injunctive and declaratory relief in the Greene County Court of Common Pleas. . . . [On appeal], [w]ithout discussing or, indeed, even citing to the merits of the *Dunham* Rule, this Court began its analysis by noting that "[g]as is a mineral, though not commonly spoken of as such, . . . [and therefore] necessarily belongs to the owner in fee, so long as it remains part of the property. . . ." Thus, we held that when a landowner conveys property rights to another, anything contained within the severed property, including all subterranean minerals, becomes subject to the ownership of the grantee. "In accordance with the foregoing principles governing gas ownership, therefore, *such gas as is present in coal must necessarily belong to the owner of the coal,* so long as it remains within his property and subject to his exclusive dominion and control."

In so holding, however, the *Hoge II* Court went on to make some critical distinctions concerning the unique nature of coalbed gas. It noted that the commercial exploitation of coalbed gas was "very limited and sporadic" because it was generally viewed as a dangerous waste product of coal mining, which had to be vented from a coal seam to allow the coal to be safely mined. This Court therefore questioned why the landowners' predecessor would retain the right to a waste product with well-known explosive and dangerous predispositions? The answer, in this Court's opinion, was in the language of the deed reservations themselves, which explicitly left to the surface owners the unfettered right to all of the oil and gas below the severed coal seam.

* * *

We . . . turn to the continuing viability of the *Dunham* Rule, and we reaffirm that the rule continues to be the law of Pennsylvania. . . . [W]e recognize that the *Dunham* Rule has now been an unaltered, unwavering rule of property law for 131 years; indeed its origins actually date back to the *Gibson* decision, placing the rule's age at 177 years. As noted by this Court in *Highland,* "[a] rule of property long acquiesced in should not be overthrown except for compelling reasons of public policy or the imperative demands of justice."

We next examine whether the *Dunham* Rule applies to this appeal, and, readily hold that it does. At the outset, we note the obvious: the term "natural gas" is contained nowhere in the plain language of the deed reservation. Under the *Dunham* Rule, then, the burden is on Appellees to plead and prove, by clear and convincing parol evidence, that the intent of the parties when executing the deed in 1881 was to include natural gas within the reservation. . . . We hold . . . that Marcellus shale natural gas cannot, consistent with the *Dunham* Rule, be considered a mineral for private deed purposes.

The *Dunham* Rule is clear, dating back to *Gibson,* that the common, layperson understanding of what is and is not a mineral is the only acceptable construction of a private deed. Notwithstanding different interpretations proffered by other jurisdictions, the rule in Pennsylvania is that natural gas and oil simply are not minerals because they are not of a metallic nature, as the common person would understand minerals. . . . [T]he party advocating for the inclusion of natural gas within the deed reservation (here Appellees) bears the burden of pleading and proving by clear and convincing evidence that the intent of the parties who executed the reservation was to include natural gas. Critically, however, such intention may only be shown through parol evidence that indicates the intent of the parties at the time the deed was executed—in this case, 1881.

Finally, we disagree with the Superior Court that because the natural gas at issue in this case is contained within the Marcellus Shale, the *Hoge II* decision and its statement that "such gas as is present in coal must necessarily belong to the owner of the coal" become relevant or controlling. First, . . . we reject any insinuation by Appellee that *Hoge II* limited or overruled the *Dunham* Rule by stating that "gas is a mineral." The *Hoge II* Court made this statement without discussing the *Dunham* Rule, and therefore we find no merit to any averment that *Hoge II sub silentio* abrogated the *Dunham* Rule.

Concerning the *Hoge II* decision itself, the deed reservation at issue there concerned coal rights and the related right of ventilation of coalbed gas. This distinction between *Hoge II,* the *Dunham* line of cases, and the instant appeal is critical for several reasons. First, the right of ventilation would only apply to coalbed gas because of its extremely dangerous and volatile nature. Related thereto, coalbed gas was not commercially viable at the time the deed reservation in *Hoge II* was executed due to its explosive characteristics. Second, the *Hoge II* Court inherently made a legal distinction between coalbed gas and natural gas, despite recognizing the chemical similarities between the two, by upholding the landowners' right to drill through the coal seam to obtain natural gas. To this end, Appellees in the appeal *sub judice* forward no argument that the Marcellus shale natural gas is different than natural gas commonly found in sand deposits. . . .

Lastly, the *situs* of Marcellus shale natural gas and the methods needed and utilized to extract that gas do not support deviation from a

Dunham analysis. While we recognize that hydrofracturing methods are employed to obtain both coalbed gas and Marcellus shale natural gas, the basis of the *Dunham* Rule lies in the common understanding of the substance itself, not the means used to bring those substances to the surface. We therefore find no merit in any contention that because Marcellus shale natural gas is contained within shale rock, regardless of whether shale rock is or is not be a mineral, such consequentially renders the natural gas therein a mineral. . . .

Therefore, under the *Dunham* Rule, the trial court correctly concluded on the averments of record that Marcellus shale natural gas was not contemplated by the private deed reservation presented in this case. ∎

NOTES AND COMMENTS

1.   Many state courts, like the court in *Butler,* define minerals by analyzing what the parties to the transaction intended minerals to include at the time of the transaction. John S. Lowe, What Substances Are Minerals? 30th Ann. Rocky Mtn. Min. L. Inst., ch. 2 (1984). Reliance on intent results in much case-by-case analysis. The case law of 21 states with shale gas plays is collected in Mikal C. Watts & Emily C. Jeffcott, Does He Who Owns the "Minerals" Own the Shale Gas? A Guide to Shale Mineral Classification, 8 Tex. J. Oil, Gas & Energy L. 28 (2012–2013).

2.   Disputes seldom arise over the ownership of conventional oil and gas. These two resources belong to the mineral estate owner, usually as a matter of law. However, the courts in many states have had to settle major litigation over the ownership of other resources which completely destroy the surface during the extraction process. Oil and gas wells can co-exist, albeit not often peacefully, with other surface uses, but a stripmining operation for coal or an open pit mine for copper cannot. Many states, like Texas, developed a rule to determine ownership of these hard minerals that greatly favored the surface owner. If the deed which severed the two estates was silent about which minerals were included in the mineral severance, then the courts applied the "surface destruction" test to determine the ownership of the resource. If extracting the resource (coal, uranium, iron ore, etc.) would destroy the surface, then the courts assumed that the parties could not have intended the mineral estate owner to own it. No surface owner would have bargained for a worthless estate. Therefore, the surface owners of East Texas own vast amounts of low-grade coal, called lignite, which is stripmined and used in power plants, even though everyone may think of coal as a "mineral." Ernest E. Smith & Jacqueline L. Weaver, 1 Texas Law of Oil & Gas § 3.6 (2013)(also discussing the subsequent adoption of the "ordinary and natural meaning" test for the ownership of minerals in Texas). Of course, if the parties expressly granted lignite or another substance as a defined mineral in the deed, the courts follow the intent of the parties.

3.   Split estates also exist on federal lands. Much of the land in the Western states is owned by the federal government and administered by DOI for multiple uses, such as recreation, grazing, timber, wildlife conservation, mining, and oil and gas development. In addition, federal minerals underlie private surface lands on 57 million acres granted to patentees under various land acts intended to encourage homesteaders to settle the West. In other instances, the government owns the surface, but private parties own the underlying minerals.

Starting around 1990, coalbed methane (CBM) production soared in the United States, with a boost from significant federal tax credits. The ownership of millions of dollars of coalbed methane under various land grants soon arose. When decaying plant material at the bottom of swamps turns to peat and then is buried by layers of sediment, the peat transforms into coal. This process generates methane, some of which stays in the porous coal. CBM gas exists in coal in three forms: as free gas; as gas dissolved in the water in coal; and as gas "adsorped" on the solid surface of the coal where it is held by weak forces called van der Waals forces. Because coal pores have large surface areas, a much higher proportion of gas is adsorbed on the surface of coal than is adsorbed on other rock. When pressure is lowered in the coalbed as coal is mined or as the coalbed is dewatered, the gas is released.

Assume these facts: A federal Patentee, under a 1906 Land Sale Act, has been granted a deed to federal land and becomes the owner of everything in the land except coal, which the government reserves to itself as a strategic fuel. Later, the government grants the coal rights to Indiana Jones.

Who owns the right to lease the land for coal? For iron ore? For oil?

Who owns the right to lease the land to produce gas from a conventional gas reservoir? To produce CBM gas trapped in the coal?

Would you look at what the average person in Congress thought the meaning of "coal" was in 1906 when the Land Act was passed? *See* Amoco Production Co. v. Southern Ute Indian Tribe, 526 U.S. 865 (1999).

How will conflicts between Patentee and Indiana Jones be resolved if one party owns the coal and another owns the CBM? Should ownership be determined in a way that minimizes such a conflict by granting Indiana Jones the ownership of both coal and CBM? Does this result avoid conflict between conventional gas development and coal mining? Conflicts between coal owners and gas owners on private lands have been the source of much case law and commentary. *See, e.g.*, Jeff L. Lewin, Coalbed Methane: Recent Court Decisions Leave Ownership "Up in the Air," But New Federal and State Legislation Should Facilitate Production, 96 W.Va. L. Rev. 577 (1994); Nicolle R. Snyder Bagnell, Coal and Oil/Gas Conflicts: Marcellus Shale Development in Coal Country, 2010 No. 5 Rocky Mtn. Min. L. Fdn. Paper 12 (2012).

4.   Depleted sandstone or limestone reservoirs are valuable pieces of rock, even though little native gas is left in them. They are the least expensive way of storing natural gas closer to population centers to meet peak demand for gas during winter cold snaps (for space heating) or summer heat waves (for electricity generation to power air conditioners). There are over 400 underground gas storage reservoirs in the United States—a big business indeed, and one crucial to deregulated electricity markets as you will see later.

In addition, these reservoirs are now being viewed as storage containers for the permanent sequestration of CO_2, the main greenhouse gas. *See* Intergovernmental Panel on Climate Change, Special Report on Carbon Dioxide Capture and Storage (2005), www.climatescience.gov. The Carbon Sequestration Leadership Forum is an international effort of many nations to cooperate in CO_2 capture and storage projects.

When the land containing the depleted reservoir is a split estate, does the surface owner or mineral estate owner own this valuable storage space? To obtain the right to produce the original gas, the developer bargained with the mineral owner. Once production of the native gas has ceased, does this lessee have any rights to continue to use the reservoir in a new way as a storage vessel? What happens to an oil and gas lease when production ends? If a new developer wants to lease the space for storage, with whom should he or she negotiate? Where states have passed eminent domain statutes allowing utilities to condemn underground reservoirs for gas storage, which split-estate owner should receive the compensation payments?

If the analogy to depleted underground coal mines is apt, the surface owner will probably win. The empty tunnels and shafts left by the mining operation typically revert back to the surface owner, perhaps to rent for mushroom growing, tourism, or secure data storage. However, the tiny pore spaces in a depleted gas reservoir are hardly like the tunnels left in coal mining. Since the pore spaces are so closely related to the enjoyment and exploitation of the mineral estate, should ownership go to the mineral owner? Should the depleted reservoir rock be considered a unique "mineral" in and of itself? *See* John Lyckman, Comment, The Underground Natural Gas Storage and Conservation Act of 1977: A Threshold Issue, 29 Baylor L. Rev. 1066 (1977) (yes, especially since it would not destroy or seriously impair the surface estate to so hold). Surprisingly little case law exists on this point, but most commentators appear to think that the surface owner is the proper owner, under the following reasoning:

> Unlike pressure maintenance . . . , underground injections for storage purposes are not directly related to production. Indeed, they are usually not even associated with initial marketing [of the native gas], but with downstream activities more closely connected to final retail sales. From this perspective, it would seem that the right to store [nonnative] gas . . . is roughly analogous to the right to open a service station, a right that belongs more properly to the surface estate than the mineral estate.

Ernest E. Smith & Jacqueline L. Weaver, 1 Texas Law of Oil and Gas § 2.1(B)(3) (2013); *see also* Owen L. Anderson, Geologic CO_2 Sequestration: Who Owns the Pore Space?, 9 Wyo. L. Rev. 97 (2009).

4. MINERAL ESTATE DOMINANCE AND SURFACE ACCOMMODATION

When split-estate conflicts arose in the United States, the British common law was readily adopted to govern the dispute. After all, "royalty" itself meant the payment owed the king or sovereign. The monarchy had once owned all valuable minerals like gold and silver in the kingdom and the common law had early developed the rule that the mineral estate was dominant. If the king no longer owned the surface estate because, e.g., he had granted it to a lord in return for military service, the king nonetheless retained the minerals and had an easement of necessity across the surface to access his mines and assure that he would receive "royalty" payments from those to whom he leased the mines. In short, the mineral estate was dominant and could use the surface freely, without negotiating access rights or payments for damages to crops or other surface uses.

The early Texas case of *Grimes v. Goodman Drilling Co.,* 216 S.W. 202 (1919) illustrates this dominance. The owner of a small, town lot sought an injunction to abate a nuisance against the lessee drilling a well on the tract. Plaintiff had bought the surface of the lot, subject to a prior oil and gas lease, at a time when no well was located thereon, but many wells had already been drilled in the town. Goodman Drilling erected a derrick in the front yard without asking permission or compensating the plaintiff. The court continued:

> The slush pit connected with the well is near to and runs along the side of plaintiff's house, and slush spatters onto the sides of the house, the doors, and windows, and necessitates that side of the house being closed up. The running of the engine is very objectionable to the plaintiff's family and often prevents their sleeping at nights, and is so loud as to require them in ordinary conversation to speak in very loud tones. *Id.* at 204.

The court ruled against the plaintiff: He had purchased the lot on the severed estate burdened with the lease and was presumed to know that drilling a well would make the use of the home "disagreeable, inconvenient, and perhaps dangerous." There was no evidence that the driller was negligent in placing the boiler or slush pit near the house; that is where they could fit.

Over the years, the implied rights of the dominant mineral estate to use the surface have been held to cover a wide range of activities: seismic tests, storage tanks, roads, and use of the surface owners' freshwater (which might be quite scarce in the arid West) for drilling or secondary recovery operations. For example, in Texas, the mineral owner does not have an obligation to protect the surface owner's cattle by fencing the well site or any obligation to restore the surface, absent provisions in the lease requiring such acts. Courts, state legislatures, and city councils have acted to reduce the dominance of the mineral estate in several ways. As you read through these measures, ask yourself if a mineral estate owner could successfully argue that his property rights have suffered an unconstitutional taking.

   a.   *The accommodation doctrine.* The courts themselves have whittled the common law principle of dominance to uses of the surface that are "reasonably necessary" to develop the oil and gas and to non-negligent uses. Thus, if a reasonable operator would have used 2 acres as a drill site, but an operator strews equipment or spills oil over 5 acres of a corn field, then damages are due the surface owner for use of the additional 3 acres. In addition, the lessee must make efforts to reasonably accommodate existing surface uses. The best-known case on the accommodation doctrine involved a surface farmer growing a crop in the nearly rainless Panhandle area of Texas, the "dust bowl." Farming was possible only by using large sprinkler systems that took groundwater from wells through pipes and hoses linked to wheeled sprinklers that moved across the surface of the farm to reach all corners. For many years, farmer Jones had co-existed peacefully with Getty Oil's operations. The sprinklers could roll over the 4-foot high wellheads. However, when pressure in the field decreased, Getty Oil put some of the wells on pumpjacks, mechanical pumping units over 20 feet high. The wheeled sprinkler system was doomed and with it, the farmer's livelihood. The court in *Getty Oil Co. v. Jones,* 470 S.W.2d 618, at 622 (Tex. 1971) held:

[W]here there is an existing use by the surface owner which will otherwise be precluded or impaired, and where under the established practices in the industry there are alternatives available to the lessee whereby the minerals can be recovered, the rules of reasonable usage of the surface may require the adoption of the alternative by the lessee.

Because other operators in the area were putting their pumping units in underground pits or were using smaller electric pumps at an additional cost of just $12,000 per well, the lessee was required to accommodate the farmer's pre-existing use. Both crops and oil would continue to be produced. Query: If no such reasonable alternative existed, who would win this case?

In later cases, the court narrowed the surface owner's protection under the accommodation doctrine: the lessee could never be forced to go off the leased premises to develop an alternative that would mitigate damage to the surface estate overlying the lease, regardless of how reasonable this alternative was. Sun Oil v. Whitaker, 483 S.W.2d 808 (Tex. 1972). Directional drilling from off-lease surfaces is widely practiced in offshore production and onshore in the Arctic. Several wells are clustered in a central spot and then the wells, rather than being drilled straight down, are directionally drilled to radiate out to distant parts of the reservoir, often a mile and sometimes 5 miles from the central platform. This type of drilling significantly decreases surface impacts and reduces the number of expensive offshore platforms required in deep water. However, under Texas law, the accommodation doctrine cannot stretch so far as to force a lessee to seek a surface location adjacent to a leased farm from which the lessee could drill directionally and bottom the well under the farm. Many leases on federal and state lands do have "no surface occupancy" restrictions in environmentally sensitive or scenic areas and these lease stipulations require directional drilling from nonrestricted surface sites. It is also increasingly common for private owners of mineral and surface estates to negotiate non-surface use leases due to the flexibility offered by horizontal drilling technology.

Query: If the town where Grimes owned his small house did not have a drilling ordinance, who would win given the facts in *Grimes v. Goodman Drilling supra* under the accommodation doctrine?

b.   *Surface damages statutes.* Many farming and ranching states (but not Texas) have passed surface damages acts that require the mineral operator to pay for the loss of use of the surface. While the common law has no such compensation requirement, even in states without surface damages acts, operators almost always offer surface owners a pre-set schedule of payments for each well site or rod of pipeline laid on the land. The payments are minimal compared to the cost of drilling. But in states without surface damages acts, if the surface owner refuses to accept the payments, the common law allows the operator to proceed without paying anything. Surface damages acts require the operator to give the surface owner adequate notice of the commencement of drilling operations and compensation for actual damages from the drilling, regardless of fault. The types of damages are often listed, such as loss of crops, lost land value, and lost use of the surface or any surface improvements. Some acts require the operator to pay damages for groundwater contamination from drilling. *See generally* Andrew Miller,

Comment: A Journey Through Mineral Estate Dominance, the Accommodation Doctrine and Beyond, 40 Hous. L. Rev. 461 (2003). These statutes have been sustained against challenges that they are an unconstitutional taking of the mineral estate owner's rights.

c. ***Surface development statutes.*** Some states, particularly those with growing populations of both people and well sites near major cities (like Houston and Dallas), have enacted statutes that offer some protection from backyard wells to housing developments. For example, in Texas, the surface developer in certain populated counties can bind the mineral owner to plats designed by the surface owner to accommodate the residential community. Tex. Nat. Res. Code §§ 92.001–92.007 (Vernon 2008). The purpose of the statute is "to assure proper and orderly development of both the mineral and land resources of this state." The surface owner of a tract of land (no more than 640 acres in size) can create a "qualified subdivision" by securing conservation commission approval of a plat of the subdivision and filing the plat with the county clerk. The plat must contain an oil and gas operations site for each separate 80 acres in the subdivision, with access roads and pipeline easements located for these sites. The operations site is an area of two or more acres, large enough to fit a drilling rig and its accompanying facilities. If the commission approves the plat, the mineral interest owners may use only the surface areas designated as operations sites and access easements. The commission will not approve the plat unless it finds that the application ensures that the mineral resources of the subdivisions can be "fully and effectively exploited." Thus, the commission may approve more than one well site for each 80 acres. This type of statute requires mineral owners on undeveloped land to have considerable foresight in judging what drill sites and easements might be necessary in the future. *See* 2 Smith & Weaver, *supra*, § 9.2.

A 2005 statute in Colorado gave authority to surface owners to request that the Colorado Oil and Gas Conservation Commission conduct an onsite inspection where a proposed well had been applied for. The statute requires that the surface owner and operator conduct good faith consultations, but if they are unable to agree, the surface owner can trigger a request for inspection to determine if the proposed drill site is reasonably located. The inspection does not address surface owner compensation or property value diminution. The purpose of the inspection is to determine if technical or operational conditions of approval should be attached to the drilling permit to mitigate environmental, health, safety or welfare concerns, including: visual or aesthetic impacts, moving the access road, controlling noxious weeds, muffling motors or installing sound barriers, watering roads to reduce dust, analyzing water samples and monitoring wells, sampling for gas that might be collecting in residential crawl spaces, installing fences, and limiting drilling to seasonal periods when wildlife impacts are minimized. Any conditions must be cost-effective, technically feasible and prevent waste, but the commission cannot require an operator to use directional drilling or "otherwise compromise its reasonable geologic and petroleum engineering considerations." Colorado Oil & Gas Conservation Comm'n, Policy for Onsite Inspection (2005), implementing 2 Colo. Code Regs. 401–1, Sec. 201 (2005).

It is not clear under principles of federalism and the Commerce Clause whether surface-protective state acts such as these apply to federal leaseholders whose operations are located on privately owned surface land.

d.   *City zoning ordinances—a preview.* Even though the earliest boom towns in Texas seemed to welcome rigs and wells in backyards, many municipalities later enacted zoning ordinances to protect public health and safety. For example, the city of South Houston passed an ordinance in 1935 that required operators to obtain a city drilling permit and restricted the number and location of wells. The city reserved the right to refuse a permit where the location of the proposed well posed a serious risk to the city's residents—a wise move given that 18 of the 64 existing businesses in the city manufactured and stored explosive fireworks. The court in *Tysco Oil Co. v. Railroad Commission*, 12 F. Supp. 195 (S.D. Tex. 1935) had little difficulty upholding the town's police power to pass this ordinance.

Local land-use ordinances often impose far more restrictions on oil and gas operations than the surface damage acts and surface platting acts discussed *supra*. As shale development has proceeded apace, towns and villages have passed detailed ordinances regulating and, in some instances, banning development. Whether local control of oil and gas activity is preempted by the state is discussed in Section C *infra*, after coverage of the conservation regulation that producing states have enacted to prevent the physical waste of oil and gas and regulate some of the externalities of development.

5.   THE RULE OF CAPTURE: THE TRAGEDY OF THE COMMONS

The discovery of oil and gas from wells tapping underground reservoirs posed a novel legal question: Who owned the oil and gas produced at the well head if some was drained from other tracts? The courts' answer had a major impact on the way that the oil business was conducted.

Barnard v. Monongahela Natural Gas Co.
216 Pa. 362, 65 A. 801 (1907).

[Daniel and Elizabeth Barnard brought a bill in equity against the Monongahela Natural Gas Company for an injunction and an accounting. The plaintiffs owned a 66-acre farm adjoining the 156-acre farm owned by James Barnard. The gas company held leases on both farms. James' farm joined the other Barnards' farm in such a way that one corner of his farm formed an angle of about 12 degrees less than a right angle. A circle large enough to include ten acres with its center at this corner would enclose 2 1/2 acres of James' land and 7 1/2 acres of Daniel and Elizabeth's land. The gas company drilled a well on James' farm near the corner of this angle, only 35 feet from the line dividing the two farms.

On appeal, the Supreme Court dismissed the bill in equity, quoting the opinion of the court below as follows:]

■ The first question stated broadly is this: "Can a landowner in gas territory drill a well on his farm close to the line of his adjoining landowner and draw from the land of the latter three-fourths of the gas that his well may produce without so invading the property rights of the adjoining landowner as to be legally accountable therefore?" There is no doubt that the oil and gas confined in the oil and gas-bearing sands of a farm belong to the one who holds title to the farm, but it is also recognized, both as a question of fact and law, that oil and gas are fugitive in their nature, and will by reason of inherent pressure seek any opening from the earth's surface that may reach the sand where they are confined. . . .

The right of every landowner to drill a well on his own land at whatever spot he may see fit certainly must be conceded. If, then, the landowner drills on his own land at such a spot as best subserves his purposes, what is the standing of the adjoining landowner whose oil or gas may be drained by this well? He certainly ought not to be allowed to stop his neighbor from developing his own farm. There is no certain way of ascertaining how much of the oil and gas that comes out of the well was when in situ under this farm and how much under that. What then has been held to be the law? It is this: . . . every landowner or his lessee may locate his wells wherever he pleases, regardless of the interests of others. He may distribute them over the whole farm or locate them only on one part of it. He may crowd the adjoining farms so as to enable him to draw the oil and gas from them. What then can the neighbor do? Nothing; only go and do likewise. He must protect his own oil and gas. He knows it is wild and will run away if it finds an opening and it is his business to keep it at home. This may not be the best rule; but neither the Legislature nor our highest court has given us any better. No doubt many thousands of dollars have been expended "in protecting lines" in oil and gas territory that would not have been expended if some rule had existed by which it could have been avoided. Injunction certainly is not the remedy. If so, just how far must the landowner be from the line of his neighbor to avoid the blow of "this strong arm of the law"? ■

NOTES AND COMMENTS

1.   The rule of capture adopted for oil and gas was based, perhaps surprisingly, on the principle expressed in the famous case of *Pierson v. Post*, 3 Caines 175 (N.Y. Sup. 1805), involving ownership of a wild fox. In *Westmoreland & Cambria Natural Gas Co. v. De Witt*, 130 Pa. 235, 18 A. 724 (1889), the court wrote:

> Water and oil, and still more strongly gas, may be classed by themselves, if the analogy be not too fanciful, as minerals ferae naturae. In common with animals, and unlike other minerals, they have the power and the tendency to escape without the volition of the owner. Their "fugitive and wandering existence within the limits of a particular tract was uncertain. . . ." They belong to the owner of the land, and are part of it, so long as they are on or in it, and are subject to his control; but when they escape, and go into other land. . . , the title of the former owner is gone. Possession of the land, therefore is not necessarily possession of the gas. . . .

2.   The rule of capture has been adopted in all oil and gas producing states. On January 10, 1901, the greatest gusher the world had ever seen erupted in Spindletop, Texas, spewing over 75,000 barrels of oil a day over the coastal plain. Does it surprise you that Spindletop's Boiler Avenue looked like Figure 4–7 in 1903?

Figure 4–7
Boiler Avenue at Spindletop
Photo courtesy of American Petroleum Institute.

Land that had once been pig pastures sold for as much as $900,000 an acre. A glut of oil dropped the price to as little as 3 cents a barrel, while a cup of water cost 5 cents. The boom, however, was short-lived. Rapid and uncontrolled production depleted the field's pressure so quickly that by 1903 the field had begun to decline and within ten years, Spindletop was a virtual ghost town. Less than 5 percent of the field's oil was produced.

3.   Many natural gas reservoirs have produced all of the native gas originally in the pore spaces of the reservoir formation. These depleted reservoirs are valuable "pieces of rock," especially when they are located near cities or industry, because they can be used to store gas which has been produced and transported from other distant fields. The gas is pumped into the pore spaces of the depleted reservoir and then can be quickly extracted when a cold snap hits and homeowners all turn up the thermostats on their gas furnaces. Underground storage is usually the only feasible and safe method of storing large quantities of natural gas.

In *Lone Star Gas Co. v. Murchison*, 353 S.W.2d 870 (Tex. App. 1962), the plaintiff, Lone Star, was a public utility engaged in the business of distributing natural gas to a large number of customers. Because the demand for gas, especially for residential use, fluctuates widely, Lone Star stored gas during periods of low demand and withdrew it to meet periods of peak demand. Lone Star had acquired the rights to all of the underground formation except for a small amount of acreage underlying the Jackson land. The Jacksons leased this land to Murchison and he drilled a well into the gas formation and started extracting large quantities of gas. Lone Star sought an injunction to prevent the Murchison well from producing gas, and also sued for damages for conversion of its gas.

Should the rule of capture apply to stored gas? The Texas courts said no, holding that stored gas is the personal property of the storer.

Could Murchison then claim that Lone Star was trespassing on his property? Lone Star's gas molecules were invading his mineral estate without his permission. The court ducked this question, writing that "[t]he status of this record is such . . . that we must, as Ulysses 'lash ourselves to the mast and resist Siren's songs' of trespass." *Id.* at 875. How would you be tempted to rule on the trespass issue? If you find a trespass, would you grant Murchison an injunction against the gas storer? What if it is impossible for Lone Star to "fence off" its part of the reservoir? Unlike wild animals, Lone Star cannot corral its molecules into a holding pen to prevent them from escaping on to Murchison's tract. Yet an injunction will destroy the value of the reservoir as a storage device. Lone Star could offer to lease Murchison's subsurface estate. If other landowners had leased for a dollar an acre, do you think Murchison will accept this amount? Or will he demand, say, $1,000 an acre, to buy out his trespass cause of action? Is this "extortion" to allow Murchison to extract monopoly rents from Lone Star?

If you were a state legislator, would you vote for a statute which authorized public utility companies to exercise the right of eminent domain over depleted gas reservoirs which can be used for storage? Why would such a law operate in the public interest? If one person owns the surface of the tract and another owns the mineral estate underlying that tract, which person owns the depleted gas reservoir that has been emptied of its native gas? The ownership of depleted reservoirs on such "split estates" is important if vast amounts of carbon dioxide are to be stored underground in depleted reservoirs as one solution to global warming.

4.   An early Kentucky case held that the rule of capture applied to stored gas. *See* Hammonds v. Central Kentucky Natural Gas Co., 75 S.W.2d 204 (Ky. 1934). In 1987, the Kentucky Supreme Court was asked to render a

declaratory judgment by joint petition of a bank and a gas storer. The bank wanted to loan the gas company $24 million to finance the purchase of gas to be stored in a Kentucky field. The question arose: Should the bank secure its loan with a lien against the gas as personal property under Article 9 of the Uniform Commercial Code, or with a real estate mortgage? In *Texas American Energy Corp. v. Citizens Fidelity Bank & Trust Co.*, 736 S.W.2d 25 (Ky. 1987), the court distinguished the earlier Hammonds case as follows:

> In *Hammonds* there was a known "leak" in the gas storage reservoir inasmuch as Mrs. Hammonds' land was, in fact, a part of the natural reservoir, though not controlled by the storage company. In the case at hand, however, it has been stipulated that the gas reservoir has total integrity, and the gas cannot escape nor can it be extracted by anyone other than [Texas American Energy]. Using the ferae naturae analogy, [Texas American] has captured the wild fox, hence reducing it to personal property. The fox has not been released in another forest, permitting it to revert to the common property of mankind; but rather, the fox has only been released in a private confinement zoo. The fox is no less under the control of [Texas American] than if it were on a leash.

Id. at 28.

Are there any other limits to the rule of capture under the common law in addition to the exception for stored gas? Suppose the driller next door to you negligently causes the well to blow out, creating an enormous low-pressure area to which your gas rapidly flows and erupts in a fiery inferno that can be seen for miles around. Is the driller shielded from liability for draining all of your gas because of the rule of capture?

The following case introduces the common law property concept of "correlative rights" among the owners of a common reservoir.

Elliff v. Texon Drilling Co.

210 S.W.2d 558 (Tex. 1948).

[Plaintiff owned land overlying a gas field. Defendant was engaged in drilling a well on the neighboring tract only 466 feet east of plaintiff's property line. The well struck gas under high pressure and exploded and burned. Plaintiff sought to recover damages for the hydrocarbons lost from underneath plaintiff's land because of the adjacent blowout. The jury found that the drilling company had been negligent.]

■ FOLLEY, J. . . . In our state the landowner is regarded as having absolute title in severalty to the oil and gas in place beneath his land. The only qualification of that rule of ownership is that it must be considered in connection with the law of capture and is subject to police regulations. The oil and gas beneath the soil are considered a part of the realty. Each owner of land owns separately, distinctly and exclusively all the oil and gas under his land and is accorded the usual remedies against trespassers who appropriate the minerals or destroy their market value.

. . . [C]ourts generally have come to recognize that oil and gas, as commonly found in underground reservoirs, are securely entrapped in a static condition in the original pool, and, ordinarily, so remain until disturbed by penetrations from the surface. It is further established, nevertheless, that these minerals will migrate across property lines towards any low pressure area created by production from the common pool. This migratory character of oil and gas has given rise to the so-called rule or law of capture. That rule simply is that the owner of a tract of land acquires title to the oil or gas which he produces from wells on his land, though part of the oil or gas may have migrated from adjoining lands. He may thus appropriate the oil and gas that have flowed from adjacent lands without the consent of the owner of those lands, and without incurring liability to him for drainage. The nonliability is based upon the theory that after the drainage, the title or property interest of the former owner is gone. This rule, at first blush, would seem to conflict with the view of absolute ownership of the minerals in place, but it was otherwise decided in the early case of *Stephens County v. Mid-Kansas Oil & Gas Co.*, 254 S.W. 290, 292 (1923). Mr. Justice Greenwood there stated:

> "The objection lacks substantial foundation that gas or oil in a certain tract of land cannot be owned in place, because subject to appropriation, without the consent of the owner of the tract, through drainage from wells on adjacent lands. If the owners of adjacent lands have the right to appropriate, without liability, the gas and oil underlying their neighbor's land, then their neighbor has the correlative right to appropriate, through like methods of drainage, the gas and oil underlying the tracts adjacent to his own."

Thus it is seen that, notwithstanding the fact that oil and gas beneath the surface are subject both to capture and administrative regulation, the fundamental rule of absolute ownership of the minerals in place is not affected in our state. In recognition of such ownership, our courts, in decisions involving well-spacing regulations of our Railroad Commission, have frequently announced the sound view that each landowner should be afforded the opportunity to produce his fair share of the recoverable oil and gas beneath his land, which is but another way of recognizing the existence of correlative rights between the various landowners over a common reservoir of oil or gas.

It must be conceded that under the law of capture there is no liability for reasonable and legitimate drainage from the common pool. The landowner is privileged to sink as many wells as he desires upon his tract of land and extract therefrom and appropriate all the oil and gas that he may produce, so long as he operates within the spirit and purpose of conservation statutes and orders of the Railroad Commission. These laws and regulations are designed to afford each owner a reasonable opportunity to produce his proportionate part of the oil and gas from the entire pool and to prevent operating practices injurious to the common reservoir. In this manner, if all operators exercise the same degree of skill and diligence, each owner will recover in most instances his fair share of the oil and gas. This reasonable opportunity to produce his fair share of the oil and gas is the landowner's common law right under our theory of absolute ownership of the minerals in place. But from the very nature of this theory the right of each land holder is qualified, and is limited to legitimate operations. Each owner whose land overlies the basin has a like interest, and each must of necessity exercise his right with some regard to the rights of others. No owner should be permitted to carry on his operations in reckless or lawless irresponsibility, but must submit to such limitations as are necessary to enable each to get his own.

* * *

In like manner, the negligent waste and destruction of petitioners' gas and distillate was neither a legitimate drainage of the minerals from beneath their lands nor a lawful or reasonable appropriation of them. [Ed. note: distillate, also called condensate, is a natural gas liquid that drips out of "wet" gas as a liquid at surface temperatures.] Consequently, the petitioners did not lose their right, title and interest in them under the law of capture. At the time of their removal they belonged to petitioner, and their wrongful dissipation deprived these owners of the right and opportunity to produce them. That right is forever lost, the same cannot be restored, and petitioners are without an adequate legal remedy unless we allow a recovery under the same common law which governs other actions for damages and under which the property rights in oil and gas are vested. . . . The fact that the major portion of the gas and distillate escaped from the well on respondents' premises is immaterial. Irrespective of the opening from which the minerals escaped, they belonged to the petitioners and the loss was the same. . . . Being responsible for the loss, [respondents] are in no position to deny liability because the gas and distillate did not escape through the surface of petitioners' lands. ■

C. STATE CONSERVATION REGULATION

1. PREVENTING PHYSICAL WASTE

The rule of capture resulted in pell-mell development that wasted large amounts of petroleum both above and below ground. States sought to regulate the chaotic, dangerous and wasteful conditions. Not surprisingly, operators whose production was crimped by such laws sought refuge in the Takings Clause of the Constitution. A few years after Spindletop, a takings case reached the highest court of the land. The state of Indiana had adopted a statute in 1893 that required the operator of any oil or gas well to confine the flow of oil or gas into a pipeline or other safe receptacle within two days of discovery.

The state attorney general sued the Ohio Oil Company to enjoin it from allowing gas to escape. Ohio Oil had drilled five wells which produced large amounts of casinghead gas, *i.e.,* gas dissolved in oil which separates from the oil when it reaches the reduced pressure at the top of the well, called the casing head. Until the late 1950s, casinghead gas was often flared at the wellhead because no ready market existed for it. However, in this case, nearby cities were using some gas from the field as fuel. The state's complaint alleged that Ohio Oil's flaring was destroying the "back pressure" in the field that prevented an underlying layer of salt water from encroaching into the oil wells. Ohio Oil contended that it was impossible to produce the oil without producing the gas; that the gas had no value to the defendant; and that enforcing the statute deprived it of the right to produce oil in violation of its due process rights. The Supreme Court responded:

Ohio Oil Co. v. Indiana

177 U.S. 190 (1900).

■ WHITE, J. . . . [I]t is apparent, from the admitted facts, that the oil and gas are commingled and contained in a natural reservoir which lies beneath an extensive area of country, and that as thus situated the gas and oil are capable of flowing from place to place, and are hence susceptible of being drawn off by wells from any point, provided they penetrate into the reservoir. . . . From this it must necessarily come to pass that the entire volume of gas and oil is in some measure liable to be decreased by the act of any one who bores wells from the surface and strikes the reservoir containing the oil and gas. And hence, of course, it is certain, . . . that unless laws can prevent it, a single owner could use the unrestrained license to waste the entire contents of the reservoir by allowing the gas to be drawn off and to be dispersed in the atmospheric air, and by permitting the oil to flow without use or benefit to any one. These things being lawful, as they must be if the acts stated cannot be controlled by law, it follows that no particular individual having a right to make borings can complain, and thus the entire product of oil and gas can be destroyed by any one of the surface owners. . . . But it cannot be that property as to a specified thing vests in one who has no right to prevent any other person from taking or destroying the object which is asserted to be the subject of the right of property. . . .

Hence it is that the legislative power, from the peculiar nature of the right and the objects upon which it is to be exerted, can be manifested for the purpose of protecting all the collective owners by preventing waste. This necessarily implied legislative authority is borne out by the analogy suggested by things *ferae naturae* which it is unquestioned the legislature has the authority to forbid all from taking, in order to protect them from undue destruction, so that the right of the common owners, the public, to reduce to possession, may be ultimately efficaciously enjoyed. Viewed, then, as a statute to protect or to prevent the waste of the common property . . . [the law at issue here] is a statute protecting private property and preventing it from being taken by one of the common owners without regard to the enjoyment of the others. . . . ■

NOTES AND COMMENTS

1.   *Ohio Oil Co. v. Indiana* was one of the earliest cases to recognize the doctrine of correlative rights, which appeared in *Elliff v. Texon Drilling Co.*, involving negligent drainage. The doctrine holds that each owner of a common source of supply has both legal rights and legal duties toward the other owners. The strongest right continues to be the rule of capture if exercised properly under common law tort principles and in compliance with a broad range of state conservation laws enacted after 1900. Does the doctrine of correlative rights guarantee that each owner of a common reservoir receives a fair share of the oil and gas in the reservoir, even if that owner never drills a well? Or does it guarantee only the opportunity to produce a fair share, which if unexercised, allows one owner to drain another without liability?

2.   Why wasn't Ohio Oil marketing its gas to the cities nearby? If there was no market for its gas, should Ohio Oil be forced to reinject the gas back

underground, where it can help push more oil out of the reservoir? What if reinjection is uneconomic?

2. PREVENTING ECONOMIC WASTE WITH MARKET DEMAND PRORATIONING

With the discovery of oil at Spindletop in 1901, the mad rush was on to explore for oil in Texas and the neighboring states of Oklahoma and Louisiana. Many large fields were discovered in the next few decades, leading to a sharp increase in oil production in the familiar "boom and bust" pattern caused by the rule of capture. Fortuitously, the invention of the gasoline-powered engine sparked an enormous increase in the demand for gasoline. In the 19th century, the primary use for petroleum had been for kerosene. In the 20th century, the primary use soon became gasoline for the "horseless carriage." Kerosene sales shrank to negligible levels after Thomas Edison's invention of the incandescent light bulb.

The excessive well drilling and wasteful production engendered by the rule of capture were difficult to ignore. States began to enact conservation legislation like that in *Ohio Oil,* and created regulatory agencies to implement the new laws. Many states enacted well spacing rules which provided that no well could be drilled on less than a certain number of acres or closer than so many feet from an existing well. However, these regulations were often not enforced in situations where small tracts of land, often town lots, already existed. Moreover, well spacing alone did not address the most important factor affecting the ultimate percentage of oil recovered from a field: the field's production rate.

Producers were battered by widely fluctuating swings in the price of oil. Flush production from the Seminole field in Oklahoma and the great East Texas field caused the price to drop from $3 a barrel in 1920 to as low as 10 cents a barrel in the early 1930s. Some operators imposed voluntary controls on themselves, such as a moratorium on new drilling until pipeline capacity and storage facilities were enlarged to handle the increased flow. However, most voluntary efforts to conserve were doomed to failure under the inexorable logic of the Tragedy of the Commons. Many operators pressed their state legislators to enact prorationing statutes that would authorize a state agency to restrict production in a field by establishing a maximum "allowable" that each well could produce. Inevitably, such a statute was challenged by other operators and ultimately reached the highest court of the land.

The plaintiff in the case, Champlin Refining Co., was a vertically integrated oil company that produced and refined crude oil and transported and marketed the crude and its products in interstate commerce. Its refinery had a daily capacity of 15,000 barrels of crude. It owned 735 tank cars, operated 470 miles of pipeline, and had 256 wholesale and 263 retail gasoline stations supplied from its refinery. At the refinery, it had gas-tight steel storage tanks which could hold 645,000 barrels of petroleum and its products. It did not use earthen storage and the court acknowledged that it utilized all the crude oil that it could produce for commercial purposes without letting any crude "run at large." Yet, Oklahoma's statute forced Champlin to cut back production from its wells quite drastically so that it only took a "proportional share" of production from the field.

Champlin Refining Co. v. Corporation Commission of Oklahoma

286 U.S. 210 (1932).

■ The refining company by this suit seeks to enjoin the commission, attorney general and other state officers from enforcing certain provisions of c. 25 of the laws of Oklahoma enacted February 11, 1915, . . . , and certain orders of the commission on the ground that they are repugnant to the due process and equal protection clauses of the Fourteenth Amendment and the commerce clause.

The Act prohibits the production of petroleum in such a manner or under such conditions as constitute waste. Section 3 defines waste to include—in addition to its ordinary meaning—economic, underground and surface waste, and waste incident to production in excess of transportation or marketing facilities or reasonable market demands, and empowers the commission to make rules and regulations for the prevention of such wastes. Whenever full production from any common source can only be obtained under conditions constituting waste, one having the right to produce oil from such source may take only such proportion of all that may be produced therefrom without waste as the production of his wells bears to the total. The commission is authorized to regulate the taking of oil from common sources so as to prevent unreasonable discrimination in favor of one source as against others.

The plaintiff has nine wells in the Greater Seminole field which . . . was discovered in 1925 and by June 15, 1931, there were 2,141 producing wells having potential production of 564,908 barrels per day. The wells are separately owned and operated by 80 lessees. About three-fourths of them, owning wells with 40 per cent of the total potential capacity of the field, have no pipelines or refineries and are entirely dependent for an outlet for their crude upon others who purchase and transport oil. Five companies, owning wells with about 13 per cent of the potential production, have pipelines or refinery connections affording a partial outlet for their production. Nineteen other companies own or control pipelines extending into this area having a daily capacity of 468,200 barrels, and most of them from time to time purchase oil from other producers in the field.

Crude oil and natural gas occur together or in close proximity to each other, and the gas in a pool moves the contents toward the point of least resistance. When wells are drilled into a pool, the oil and gas move from place to place. If some of the wells are permitted to produce a greater proportion of their capacity than others, drainage occurs from the less active to the more active. . . . Where proportional taking from the wells in flush pools is not enforced, operators who do not have physical or market outlets are forced to produce to capacity in order to prevent drainage to others having adequate outlets. In Oklahoma prior to the passage of the Act, large quantities of oil produced in excess of transportation facilities or demand therefor were stored in surface tanks, and by reason of seepage, rain, fire and evaporation enormous waste occurred. Uncontrolled flow of flush or semi-flush wells for any considerable period exhausts an excessive amount of pressure, wastefully uses the gas and greatly lessens ultimate recovery. . . .

* * *

The court found that at all times covered by orders involved there was a serious potential overproduction throughout the United States and particularly in the flush and semi-flush pools in the Seminole and Oklahoma City fields; that, if no curtailment were applied, crude oil for lack of market demand and adequate storage tanks would inevitably go into earthen storage and be wasted; that the full potential production exceeded all transportation and marketing facilities and market demands; that accordingly it was necessary, in order to prevent waste, that production of flush and semi-flush pools should be restricted as directed by the proration orders, and that to enforce such curtailment, with equity and justice to the several producers in each pool, it was necessary to enforce proportional taking from each well and lease therein and that, . . . a comprehensive plan of curtailment and proration conforming to the rules prescribed in the Act was adopted by the commission and was set forth in its orders.

[The district court also found that none] of the commission's orders has been made for the purpose of fixing the price of crude oil or has had that effect. When the first order was made the price was more than two dollars per barrel, but it declined until at the time of the trial it was only thirty-five cents. [The commission] has never entered any order under § 2 of the Act [which expressly allowed the commission to set a wellhead price for crude if lack of market demand resulted in a price that did not equal the "actual value" of crude]. It was not shown that the commission intended to limit the amount of oil entering interstate commerce for the purpose of controlling the price of crude oil or its products or of eliminating plaintiff or any producer or refiner from competition, or that there was any combination among plaintiff's competitors for the purpose of restricting interstate commerce in crude oil or its products, or that any operators' committee made up of plaintiff's competitors formulated the proration orders.

* * *

Plaintiff insists that it has a vested right to drill wells upon the lands covered by its leases and to take all the natural flow of oil and gas therefrom so long as it does so without physical waste and devotes the production to commercial uses. But if plaintiff should take all the flow of its wells, there would inevitably result great physical waste, even if its entire production should be devoted to useful purposes. The improvident use of natural gas pressure inevitably attending such operations would cause great diminution in the quantity of crude oil ultimately to be recovered from the pool. Other lessees and owners of land above the pool would be compelled, for self-protection against plaintiff's taking, also to draw from the common source and so to add to the wasteful use of lifting pressure. And because of the lack, especially on the part of the non-integrated operators, of means of transportation or appropriate storage and of market demand, the contest would, as is made plain by the evidence and findings, result in surface waste of large quantities of crude oil. . . .

. . . The court found that none of the proration orders here involved were made for the purpose of fixing prices. The fact that the commission never limited production below market demand, and the great and long continued downward trend of prices contemporaneously with the enforcement of proration, strongly support the finding that the orders assailed have not had that effect. . . . As plaintiff has failed to prove that any order in force at the time of the trial was not in accordance with the rule prescribed by § 4 [granting plaintiff a proportional share of the limited production from the field] or otherwise invalid, the part of the decree from which it appealed will be affirmed. . . . ∎

NOTES AND COMMENTS

1.   How was Champlin wasting oil? Did the court uphold the prorationing statute because it prevented waste by restricting the field's output to its MER? Or because it protected correlative rights by assuring fair shares of production to all operators? Or, because it raised the price of oil (coincidently providing tax revenues to the state treasury) by restricting output far below the field's MER?

2.   What is the relationship between restricting a field's production to its MER to prevent physical waste, and restricting production to meet market demand and prevent economic waste? Suppose that the MER of a field would allow 500,000 barrels per day of production under good reservoir engineering practices, but the market "demands" only half of this amount. With market-demand prorationing, the wells in this field will be allowed to produce a total of 250,000 barrels per day. After market demand prorationing became institutionalized as part of the conservation framework of most large producing states like Oklahoma and Texas during the 1930s, the price of crude oil remained remarkably stable for the next 40 years, save for an increase after World War II when a post-war economic boom increased demand. Return to Figure 4–1. Does market-demand prorationing explain the stable crude price from the mid-1930s until about 1973?

From the earliest years, the price of crude oil has been set by international markets because oil is found in large fields around the world and can be shipped. The big Texas oil fields, discovered in the 1930s, played a pivotal role in world oil supplies and in setting the international price of oil. For years, Texas fields had much "shut in" capacity, meaning that their oil wells were prorated below what they could produce without physical waste. For example, in 1960, wells were prorated to a market demand factor (MDF) of 28% of their capacity by the state conservation commission. Thus, a well that could efficiently produce 100 barrels a day was restricted to 28 barrels. If the nation demanded more crude oil in the post-WWII years, the Texas Railroad Commission could simply raise the MDF to, say, 41%. Producers would turn the valves on their wells, and more oil would flow.

Over these same years, the domestic cost of drilling rose because new fields were generally smaller and deeper than the large discoveries of old. As costs rose, fewer producers drilled new wells. The United States imported increasing quantities of crude oil from giant fields developed abroad, especially in Saudi Arabia, where production costs were so much lower that crude oil could be delivered to U.S. coasts at a lower price than domestic production. As a comparison, in 1996, the average production per well in the United States was 11.2 barrels of oil per day. Wells in Saudi Arabia averaged

6,000 barrels per day. 2 Energy Law & Transactions (David J. Muchow & William A. Mogel, eds., App. 10, at 51–52 (1999)).

In 1973, for the first time, the MDF in Texas was 100%; Texas oil wells were producing at their maximum efficient rate of recovery and no spare capacity was shut in. This marked the first year that the United States was vulnerable to a geopolitical event that curtailed global oil supplies and raised world oil prices. Does it surprise you, then, that some large oil-producing Arab nations in the Mideast chose to embargo imports to U.S. shores in 1973, angered by the U.S. support of Israel in the Arab-Israeli war? The graphic below shows the price of crude oil linked to other geopolitical events over the last 50 years of world history:

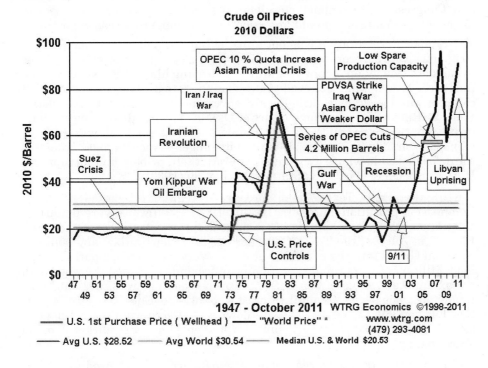

Figure 4–8
Crude Oil Prices 1947–2011
Source: WTRG Economics, http://www.wtrg.com/oil_graphs/oilprice1947.gif

Since 1973, market-demand prorationing has been meaningless for oil production in the United States. Virtually all domestic oil wells produce at their capacity, restricted only by the field's MER. However, as explained in Chapter 14, the Organization of Petroleum Exporting Countries (OPEC), comprised of largely Mideastern nations, has its own form of market-demand prorationing on an international scale. As a cartel, OPEC is sometimes able to control the price of oil on the international market, and this price ultimately sets the domestic price that U.S. producers receive. Does the advent of the shale oil revolution in the United States reduce U.S. vulnerability to geopolitical events, making us energy secure because we are "energy independent?"

3.   If Texas severely prorated its wells to market demand, but other producing states like Oklahoma or Louisiana did not, Texas producers would lose market share to competing states' producers, a clearly unacceptable result. So how was market demand prorationing to be coordinated among the major producing states? In 1934, Secretary of the Interior Harold Ickes was pushing for federal control of the petroleum industry to prevent the rampant waste of oil and gas. His plan used a public utility model to regulate the industry. To forestall federal intervention, the governors of Oklahoma, Texas, and other producing states met to devise an interstate oil compact that authorized voluntary agreements among states to restrict production in place of federally-set, binding production quotas. In 1935, the Interstate Compact to Conserve Oil and Gas was created and approved by the President and Congress. The compact now has 30 member states and 6 associate members, but market demand prorationing is no longer its reason for being.

4.   Support for proration was not universal in the industry. Some smaller companies viewed prorationing as a conspiracy by the major oil companies to bankrupt the independent producer by depriving him of the cash flow from flush production. Some believed that resort to state agencies for production controls was too great a drift toward governmental control. Chief Justice Fletcher Riley of the Supreme Court of Oklahoma, in a dissenting opinion, expressed this viewpoint: "In my opinion, proration of oil was born of monopoly, sired by arbitrary power, and its progeny (such as these orders) is the deformed child whose playmates are graft, theft, bribery and corruption." H.F. Wilcox Oil & Gas Co. v. State, 162 Okla. 89 (1933).

        In the East Texas field, producers regularly ignored Railroad Commission prorationing orders. In July 1931, 1,300 wells were producing 1.4 million barrels of oil per day. The price dropped below 10 cents a barrel. Finally, in August, the Texas Governor declared martial law and sent the National Guard into the field to shut down every well. Troops patrolled the field. Military officers ran a prorationing office and re-opened the wells with a maximum allowable of 225 barrels of oil per day per well. *See* James H. Keahy, Jr., The Texas Mineral Interest Pooling Act: End of an Era, 4 Nat. Res. Lawyer 359, at 360–61. The shutdown was effective in raising the price of oil, and this considerably tamed the opposition to market-demand prorationing.

5.   How is the state conservation agency to determine each producer's "fair share" of the total field allowable? Should every well be allowed to produce the same amount, regardless of how much acreage it drains? (This is the "per well" allowable system which the National Guard used.) Is it fair that the owner of one well on a town lot no bigger than 1/10 of an acre be allowed to produce the same amount of oil as the owner of a well on a 10-acre tract? Should the owner of the 10-acre tract be granted additional wells as exceptions to the field's well-spacing rule requiring at least ten acres for a well permit? If so, won't this encourage unnecessary well drilling, just like occurred under the rule of capture?

6.   As the science of petroleum engineering progressed, state conservation agencies adopted larger and larger spacing units. As a rule of thumb, one well can drain oil from about 40 acres of a conventional reservoir. A gas well can drain gas from about 640 acres. Assume you own a one-acre tract in the Excalibur oil field. The 40-acre spacing rule prohibits you from getting a well permit to drill. Your neighbor owns a 40-acre tract and drills a well close to your boundary in a field that is determined to be 4,000 acres large. The

conservation commission sets the total field allowable at 4,000 barrels a day. The commission allocates this total using a prorationing formula based on acreage. Under this formula your neighbor can produce 40 of these barrels because she owns 40/4000 (or one percent) of the acreage in the field. While your neighbor is selling the 40 barrels for $3 per barrel, (or $120 a day in revenues), you are producing nothing. Are your correlative rights protected in this scenario?

Suppose the commission grants you an exception to the spacing rule so that your oil will not be confiscated through drainage to your neighbor's well. If you drill and produce your own well, you will be granted an allowable of 1/4000, or one barrel of oil per day. If oil is selling for $3 dollars a barrel, you will have revenues of $3 a day. This amount does not cover the costs of drilling and producing the well on your one acre. You will lose money. Are your correlative rights protected in this scenario?

Suppose the commission grants every well in the field the same allowable of 40 barrels of oil per day, whether it drains from 40 acres or from one acre. Now your well on one acre is profitable to drill and produce. Does this prorationing formula protect the correlative rights of your larger neighbor?

Can you think of a better way to run an oil field? Many states enacted compulsory pooling laws. These statutes allow the conservation commission to pool small tracts into acreage large enough to secure a well permit under the spacing rules. All the owners with interests in the pooled acreage share in the production from the one well, usually on a surface-acreage basis. Thus, four owners, owning 1, 5, 10, and 24 acres respectively, could be pooled into a 40-acre unit on which one well would be drilled. The owners would receive 1/40, 5/40, 10/40 and 24/40, respectively, of the production from the single well. Does pooling protect correlative rights and prevent the waste of unnecessary well drilling? Why is compulsory process usually needed to coerce operators into pooling and sharing the production from one well? If you were the owner of the drillsite well, would you voluntarily agree to pool with others?

3.   SECONDARY RECOVERY: THE TRAGEDY OF THE COMMONS AGAIN

Because many U.S. fields were produced so inefficiently under the rule of capture, much oil remained in the reservoirs after the natural reservoir drive was depleted. Secondary recovery can sweep this oil up. In 1979, secondary recovery accounted for about 60 percent of Texas's total oil production and about 38 percent of Oklahoma's. In a typical secondary recovery operation, powerful machines on the surface of a tract inject gas or water down into the pore spaces of the reservoir rock. These high-pressured substances drive oil away from the injection wells toward producing wells. A waterflood operation commonly uses a five-spot pattern that places injection wells at the corners of a square and a producing well at the center. The injected water pushes a bank of oil toward the producing well. In recent decades, advanced forms of secondary recovery—called enhanced oil recovery—have been devised. For example, carbon dioxide is piped from a large natural reservoir of CO_2 in Colorado to large oil fields in West Texas. There it is injected and displaces oil from the pore spaces of the rock. Sometimes chemical surfactants and polymers are added to waterflooding to better "scrub" the rock clean of the clinging oil.

Do conservation laws and the common law maximize the efficiency of these "second chance" operations? Imagine a field comprised of 1000 acres, 900 leased by Big Oil and 100 leased by Little Oil. Big Oil wants to conduct a secondary recovery operation using salt water injection at a cost of several million dollars, but Little Oil refuses to join in the project. If Big Oil conducts the recovery by itself, its 900 acres of leasehold will have higher reservoir pressure than Little's 100 acres. All fluids flow to the area of lowest pressure, and it is virtually impossible for Big Oil to prevent either the oil under its tract or the injected salt water from crossing the lease line and invading Little's lease. In fact, the salt water may "drown out" some of Little's producing oil wells located near the lease line. These wells will begin to produce salt water, not oil.

Can Little bring a cause of action in trespass against Big for injuring Little's underground estate and Little's ability to produce oil? This issue arose in *Railroad Commission of Texas v. Manziel,* 361 S.W.2d 560 (Tex. 1962). Whelan and Manziel were competitive operators in the Vickie Lynn Field. Only 15% of the original oil in place in the field had been recovered because the operators had failed to maintain adequate pressure in the dissolved-gas drive reservoir. Pressures had fallen from 2,650 pounds per square inch (psi) to 371 psi. The remaining oil in the field was essentially "dead" without repressuring.

Whelan applied to the Railroad Commission for approval of waterflooding in its part of the field; Manziel refused to join in the operation. The commission approved the secondary recovery because it was expected to significantly increase oil production from the field. For several years, Manziel benefited from this arrangement as oil flowed slowly under the ground toward the lower-pressure tract. To stop this flow to its rival, Whelan asked the Railroad Commission to allow Whelan to place an injection well very close to the lease line. Since salt water spreads out radially from the injection well, two effects are inevitable: First, the injection well will cause salt water to invade the Manziel tract and drown out Manziel's nearby oil well; second, it will stop the flow of Whelan's oil onto the Manziel tract by pushing oil back towards the Whelan tract.

The injection well location that Whelan sought was only 206 feet from the lease line, necessitating a commission exception to the standard distance of 660 feet. Manziel strongly objected to the placement of the proposed injection well so near the lease line because it spelled an early death to the nearby Manziel well. The commission nonetheless approved the exception location. The commission found that the same amount of oil would ultimately be recovered from the field, whether the injection well was placed 206 feet or 660 feet from the lease line. The issue before the commission was not one of preventing waste, but of protecting correlative rights: What constituted "fair shares" of oil between the two owners of this common reservoir?

The commission estimated that four times as much of the oil beneath the Whelans' lease would be pushed to the Manziel lease if the injection well was located 660 feet from the lease line as opposed to a 206-foot location. On the other hand, the Manziel's nearby well would have an

estimated life of 32 months if the injection well were placed 660 feet from
lease line, but its life would be reduced to 3 1/2 to 8 months if placed
closer.

The Railroad Commission approved the closer location, and the
Texas Supreme Court ultimately upheld this decision on the basis that it
protected correlative rights and was not arbitrary or capricious. The
Manziel tract had originally had no more than 2.4% of the original oil in
place in the field, yet it had recovered more than 5.8% of the field's total
production to date. Clearly, the Manziel tract had been draining oil from
the Whelan tract for several years, and it was now fair to allow the
Whelan tract to place an injection well advantageously to secure its fair
share of the original oil in place in the field.

The Texas Supreme Court then squarely addressed the issue of
trespass raised by the facts in *Manziel*. In the most famous, oft-quoted
part of the decision, the court wrote:

> Secondary recovery operations are carried on to increase
> the ultimate recovery of oil and gas, and it is established that
> pressure maintenance projects will result in more recovery than
> was obtained by primary methods. It cannot be disputed that
> such operations should be encouraged, for as the pressure
> behind the primary production dissipates, the greater is the
> public necessity for applying secondary recovery forces. It is
> obvious that secondary recovery programs could not and would
> not be conducted if any adjoining operator could stop the project
> on the ground of subsurface trespass. . . . The orthodox rules and
> principles applied by the courts as regards surface invasions of
> land may not be appropriately applied to subsurface invasions
> as arise out of the secondary recovery of natural resources. If
> the intrusions of salt water are to be regarded as trespassory in
> character, then under common notions of surface invasions, the
> justifying public policy considerations behind secondary
> recovery operations could not be reached in considering the
> validity and reasonableness of such operations.

> Certainly, it is relevant to consider and weigh the interests
> of society and the oil and gas industry as a whole against the
> interests of the individual operator who is damaged; and if the
> authorized activities in an adjoining secondary recovery unit are
> found to be based on some substantial, justifying occasion, then
> this court should sustain their validity.

> We conclude that if, in the valid exercise of its authority to
> prevent waste, protect correlative rights, or in the exercise of
> other powers within its jurisdiction, the Commission authorizes
> secondary recovery projects, a trespass does not occur when the
> injected, secondary recovery forces move across lease lines, and
> the operations are not subject to an injunction on that basis. The
> technical rules of trespass have no place in the consideration of
> the validity of the orders of the Commission.

NOTES AND COMMENTS

1.   The deliberate invasion of injurious salt water onto another's property
sure looks like a trespass. Why does the court refuse to find that orthodox

rules of trespass apply? Would the holding be different if Whelan had not secured the Railroad Commission's approval of the waterflooding as being in the public interest of increasing production from the field?

2.   Is there then no liability whatsoever when one operator floods out another? Does commission approval of waterflooding immunize an operator from all liability? The court specifically stated that no injunction would issue in this case. Are damages possible in a *Manziel*-type situation? Or has the court adopted a "negative rule of capture" which allows a waterflooder to damage an adjoining owner without liability, much as the "positive rule of capture" allows one owner to drain a neighbor without liability.

Most states, including Texas, have recognized that damages are still possible as a remedy for waterflooding that may unreasonably injure an adjoining operation. The language quoted from *Manziel supra* about weighing "the interests of society and the oil and gas industry as a whole against the interests of the individual operator who is damaged" mimics the law of nuisance. Thus, tort damages are still possible against a neighboring waterflooder, although very few complaining operators have ever been able to prove the unreasonableness of a waterflooding operation that has been approved by the state's conservation commission. For one interesting case in which damages were awarded against a waterflooding operator, see *Tidewater Oil Co. v. Jackson*, 320 F.2d 157 (10th Cir. 1963) (adjacent oil well still in primary recovery drowned out within hours of a waterflooding operation conducted by a rival operator using a commission-approved injection well only 12 feet from the lease line).

3.   Higher oil prices in recent years have spurred secondary recovery in many old oil fields with the help of new supercomputer systems that can read seismics and well data and find pockets of untapped oil in old fields. Generally, only 30 percent of the oil in a field is recovered using traditional secondary recovery methods such as waterflooding. However, engineers are now exploiting new "tertiary" recovery methods, including the use of colonies of microbes, that some experts project will lead to recovery rates of 60 percent or more, doubling the known reserves of oil. Anadarko, for one, has injected CO_2 that was once vented from a gas processing plant operated by Exxon about 125 miles away into an oil field to extract an additional 150 million barrels from the field. The CO_2 will be permanently sequestered underground after production ceases. Otis Port, Tapping Gushers Beneath the Gushers, Bus. Week, July 5, 2005.

4.   UNITIZATION: OVERCOMING THE TRAGEDY OF THE COMMONS

The *Manziel* case illustrates the difficulty that conservation commissions face in their dual role of preventing waste and protecting the correlative rights of all owners of oil and gas in a common field. The operator of a repressuring project does not want to incur tort liability to adjacent owners, but also wants to prevent a holdout or "free rider" from being unjustly enriched by the repressuring operation of the hard-working operator.

The ideal way to both prevent waste and protect correlative rights lies in securing a unitization agreement from all the owners in a common field. Such an agreement binds all the parties to develop the field cooperatively for the good of all. One operator, usually the one with the largest share of the field, becomes the unit operator and produces the field in a manner which minimizes the number of wells drilled and maximizes efficient recovery from the field. All owners then receive a fair share of the production from the entire field, regardless of where the wells are located. A unitization agreement substitutes cooperative development for the competitive rule of capture.

However, all owners in the field are unlikely to be able to agree on the unitization agreement's formula for allocating fair shares among the owners. For example, why didn't Manziel agree to cooperate with Whelan, each operator paying a fair share of the waterflooding operation and each reaping a fair share of the profits from production? With cooperation, the total size of the "pie" would be larger because the two operators would save the costs of drilling unnecessary injection wells along lease lines as barriers to the flow of oil. Did Manziel prefer to be a "free rider" and benefit from the repressuring without paying for it?

Determining the formula to measure each operator's fair share is the same contentious issue that arose under prorationing. A large-tract owner will want shares based on acreage. A small-tract owner will want almost any other factor than acreage in the formula since he has very little acreage. Because securing 100% agreement among all the owners is so difficult, almost all oil and gas producing states have enacted compulsory unitization statutes which allow the state conservation commission to force a minority of owners into a unit agreed to by a supra-majority of owners. The following case illustrates the need for compulsory process.

Gilmore v. Oil and Gas Conservation Commission
642 P.2d 773 (Wyo. 1982).

■ BROWN, JUSTICE. On July 1, 1980, the Wyoming Oil and Gas Conservation Commission (hereinafter referred to as Commission) entered its order approving a plan of unitization of the Hartzog draw field. Appellant appeals the unitization plan approved by the Commission and its affirmance by the district court [alleging that the order does not protect his correlative rights].

We will affirm.

The Hartzog draw field is located in Campbell and Johnson Counties, Wyoming. The field is about 18 miles long and from one to three miles wide, embracing approximately 31,065 acres. At the time of the hearing before the Commission on the application to unitize the field, there were 177 producing wells with working interest ownership held by more than 80 individuals or entities.

The Commission [in 1977], . . . initiated numerous hearings and required the operators to keep the Commission advised of progress in development, production and the nature of the reservoir in the field. Technical committees and subcommittees of operators and their representatives met numerous times. Hearings were held before the Commission pursuant to § 30–5–104(b), W.S.1977. This provision of the law makes it the Commission's duty to investigate and determine whether waste exists or is imminent, or whether other facts justify or require action by the Commission. It eventually became apparent that reservoir pressure was falling to the bubble point. The lower the pressure the more difficult it becomes to recover additional oil. The further the pressure falls below the bubble point, the less likely a successful secondary recovery operation can be accomplished.

A technical committee of operators and their representatives concluded that reservoir pressure had fallen from an original pressure of 5,000 PSIG [pounds per square inch gauge] to slightly below the bubble point of 1,500 PSIG as of January 1979. This committee recommended that the field be unitized as soon as possible. It was estimated that the contemplated secondary recovery operation would recover 30,525,000 barrels of oil. Evidence before the Commission was that 1,800,000 barrels of oil would be wasted by a one-year delay in unitization and secondary recovery and 4,000,200 barrels by a two-year delay. In other words, 5,753.5 barrels of oil would be wasted each day that unitization and secondary recovery was [sic] delayed.

The Commission found that waste was occurring and would continue to occur by delaying secondary recovery, and as a result, after a November 13, 1979, hearing, ordered a curtailment of production pending unitization.

The operators held various meetings at which they voted on formulae to be used in allocating production under unitization. The 81 working interest owners considered a total of 71 formulae. Naturally, each of the owners wanted parameters favorable to them and wanted more weight to be given these parameters. After voting on almost 60 formulae, the owners were frustrated in their attempt to find one that would receive the statutory approval. As a result, they examined their voting records and used a computer to arrive at an equitable compromise formula that could receive the required approval. The resulting formula number 67 at issue here, received 75.89 percent approval. It appeared that no greater percentage would approve any formula proposed.

[The court then quoted the Wyoming compulsory unitization statute, Section 30–5–110(f), which requires the approval of 80% of the lessees and royalty interest owners in the field before the commission can use compulsory process to force the other 20% of the owners into the unit against their will. In certain circumstances, the statute allows the commission to reduce the minimum percentage approval to 75%.]

. . . On July 1, 1980, the Commission approved a unitization plan based on formula 67 and reduced the required approval from 80 to 75 percent. . . . Formula 67 allocated appellant about 1.2 percent of unitized production. Formula 67, which was approved by the Commission, allocated unitization production based on eleven parameters or factors of varying weight [including the number of usable wells, the remaining primary oil under each tract, the porosity of each acre-foot of reservoir rock, and the last six months production ending March 31, 1979].

Appellant complains that some parameters of this formula are unfair, specifically, the last three months and last six months production ending March 31, 1979. He further complains that he receives a net acreage shortage of 33.66 acres. Acreages used in the unitization plan were based on an 1880 survey of the General Land Office (GLO). All parties agree that there were some inaccuracies in this survey. The Commission made extensive findings, together with ultimate findings of fact and conclusions of law. The final finding of fact and conclusion of law states:

> "10. The approval of the proposed unit is in the public interest, will substantially increase the ultimate recovery of hydrocarbons from the Shannon Sandstone Formation in the Hartzog Draw Unit, will assist in the prevention of waste, and will protect the correlative rights of all parties in interest within the Unit Area."

Appellant generally objects to the latter portion of Finding and Conclusion No. 10 that the unitization plan "will protect the correlative rights of all parties in interest within the unit area." More specifically, he objects to the Commission's finding that inaccuracies in the General Land Office survey would affect all working interests indiscriminately, and that the unitization formula gave appellant his fair, just and equitable share of the unit production. He also alleges that no findings were made with respect to his objection before the Commission that the last six months and last three months production parameters were not fair to him [because his wells had suffered undue downtime during the selected periods].

When asked the nature of his objection, appellant stated:

> "A. Well, two of our three tracts are larger than depicted on the GLO maps which were made back in, I believe, 1870. This map is highly inaccurate. And therefore, we do have more acreage than is shown in the parameters that are developed, that are used using the GLO maps. We take a pretty good beating there."

All operators experience some downtime. All operators are naturally going to want their periods of peak production as parameters in the allocation formula or other favorable parameters. They will want more weight to be given to these parameters. Though appellant does not complain that these parameters inaccurately reflect his production for the periods in question, he claims they should be updated. If this were done, the operators would probably never have achieved unitization. Some cutoff date had to be used. With over eighty working interest owners and 177 wells in the field, it would have been difficult, if not impossible, to find a period when someone would not have had excessive downtime.

. . . Regardless of when the downtime occurred, appellant presented no evidence to show how much downtime his wells experienced or how much production suffered because of it. Appellant's Exhibits 2–A, 2–B, and 2–C generally reflect an erratic production history for his three wells. The causes of the fluctuation are unknown. As to the last six and last three months parameters, even if they understated the potential of his wells, these parameters are weighted to account for a total of 3.25 percent of the total allocation. Their effect is insubstantial. [The court then noted that Appellant's Exhibit 1, comparing nonunitized against unitized production indicated that he would be better off by not unitizing.]

    * * *

Appellant concedes that unit operation "was probably the most effective which the Commission had available to it," to prevent waste. He contends that in preventing waste his correlative rights cannot be ignored. We agree, but hold that substantial waste cannot be countenanced by a slavish devotion to correlative rights. We are faced with a delicate balancing problem between prevention of waste and correlative rights, but prevention of waste is of primary importance.

* * *

Here the Commission strived mightily to strike an equitable balance between correlative rights and prevention of waste. We agree with the Commission's acting Chairman, "And when that public interest conflicts with the private interest, the public interest has to come first."

The eleven factor formula used here is fairer because it diminishes the loss caused by coming up a little short on one factor. . . . Coming up short on one of eleven parameters is much less drastic than coming up short on one if there are only two or three parameters.

There is no indication that a more equitable formula could be devised. After three years, formula number 67 appeared to be the fairest that could receive the necessary approval. The operator's technical committee and the Commission, both having experience and expertise at unitization, settled the formula 67 as the fairest and most feasible. Appellant did not suggest a better formula to the Commission, the district court, or to us. . . .

Appellant acknowledges he will receive 321,622 barrels of the additional oil from secondary recovery, which is 321,622 barrels more than he would receive if the field were not unitized.

Appellant's position has not been consistent throughout the history of this unitization plan. Appellant, by offering to lease the lands or by participating in a competitive bid, in effect relied on the survey of the lands by the United States 1880 GLO survey. He accepted the leases, which were subject to the regulations and requirements which might be imposed by the United States Geological Survey. When the unitization plan was proposed, however, appellant tried to avoid the survey. . . .

We do not understand what appellant expects to accomplish by his lawsuit except perhaps force a settlement advantageous to him someplace along the line. A reversal here would not give appellant a larger share of the allocation, but would send the case back to the Commission with a mandate to come up with another formula. We do not believe that even appellant has any real expectation of a different formula that would receive the required approval. If a new formula were found and agreed upon, it could spawn new lawsuits. . . .

The owners and technical committees worked for three years, trying to develop a formula that would get the necessary approval. . . . Appellant seems to expect perfection. Justice was accomplished here, as much as could be under the circumstances. This litigation should end. ■

NOTES AND COMMENTS

1.   Does compulsory unitization solve the tragedy of the commons problem by subjecting some operators to the tyranny of the majority of other operators in the field? To the tyranny of government bureaucrats?

2.   Unitization is the joint, coordinated operation of all, or a substantial part, of a reservoir as a single unit by all the different operators holding leases in the field. This term is distinguished from "pooling" which is the

process of combining small tracts of land into acreage large enough to secure a drilling permit to meet the spacing rules of the conservation commission. Pooling prevents the drilling of unnecessary wells and protects the correlative rights of all the owners being drained by the one well on the spacing unit and usually occurs during primary production. Unitization combines many spacing units into a fieldwide unit, usually to conduct secondary recovery operations. A fieldwide unit may have hundreds of different owners. The more owners, the more difficult it is to reach an agreement voluntarily.

3.   Most states have compulsory unitization statutes like that in *Gilmore* which allow the conservation agency to force holdouts into a unit that is expected to increase the total recovery from the field. Texas, the largest oil producing state, does not. Compulsory unitization was castigated by the Texas independent producers for years as a "substitution of force for persuasion . . . another fetter on the step of Freedom, another move down the road towards confiscation, tyranny, and unmorality" whose advocates were "socialists, bureaucrats, self-seeking politicians [and] fuzzy thinkers of the left." Comment, Prospects for Compulsory Fieldwide Unitization in Texas, 44 Tex. L. Rev. 510, 524 (1966). Independent operators generally received more than their fair share of a reservoir's bounty under the peculiar (and very inefficient) prorationing and drilling permit system used in Texas for decades. These operators felt threatened by a compulsory unitization statute that would give them only fair shares. In 1998, the lack of such a statute was retarding secondary recovery in West Texas fields to such an extent that TIPRO, the Texas Independent Producers and Royalty Association, drafted and supported a compulsory unitization bill. However, it never reached the floor of the legislature, largely because an ideology of private property rights held sway. A substantial number of the largest fields in Texas have been unitized because the Railroad Commission arm-twisted the operators to unitize "voluntarily" by shutting in the fields or prorating them severely under the agency's broad authority to prevent waste. *See* Jacqueline L. Weaver, Unitization of Oil and Gas Fields in Texas: A Study of Legislative, Administrative and Judicial Policies 137–166 (1986).

4.   The rule of capture and the absence of pooling and unitization statutes in the early decades of the oil and gas development in the United States, coupled with private ownership of small tracts of land, have left an enduring legacy. We are a nation of marginal wells, many of which have become idle and orphaned. Abandoned wells that are not properly plugged pose serious hazards, such as escaping gases and salt water migrating into freshwater reservoirs. In recent times, states like Texas have created oilfield cleanup funds from permit fees and taxes on operators and have required higher well-plugging bonds as security against future orphaned wells. The cleanup funds are used to plug abandoned wells whose owners cannot be found or are bankrupt. *See* Jacqueline L. Weaver, The Federal Government as a Useful Enemy: Perspectives on the Bush Energy/Environmental Agenda from the Texas Oilfields, 19 Pace Envtl. L. Rev. 1 (2001).

5.   Because minerals in the United States can be privately owned, mineral estates are often subdivided into fractional interests owned by many cotenants when deeds, wills or intestacy laws transfer the property from one generation to another or to unrelated buyers. The mineral estates also often become subdivided into smaller and smaller physical tracts over time, particularly as ranches and large urban tracts are broken up into residential

subdivisions. The subdivision and fractionalization of privately owned interests cause serious problems for lessees. For example, as early as 1928, a cotenant who owned an undivided 1/768 interest in a tract of land in West Virginia prevented its development; the 131-acre tract would have to be partitioned into separately owned tracts before a lessee could drill. Law v. Heck, 106 W.Va. 296, 145 S.E. 601 (1928). Even though the common law in most states today would allow one cotenant to lease or drill without the consent of all the others, the developing cotenant must still account to the nondeveloping cotenants for their share of profits from any producing operations. Over time, many owners end up being paid a percentage interest that begins in the sixth decimal place to the right of zero. This owner will receive less than $10 a month from a well's oil production worth $1 million a month. Few wells produce that much revenue in one month, so thousands of royalty owners are due only a few pennies. The administrative costs to lessees of accounting to so many owners for their rightful shares of a well's revenues are very high. *See* Owen L. Anderson & Ernest E. Smith, The Use of Law to Promote Domestic Exploration and Production, 50 Inst. of Oil & Gas L. & Tax'n 2–1 (1999). This fractionated ownership is one reason that oil companies have sought to explore in areas where large tracts of land are available owned by a single lessor—the government. Such lands exist offshore the United States on the Outer Continental Shelf, on federal- or state-owned land in the Western United States and Alaska, and throughout the rest of the world where private ownership of minerals is not recognized. Here, the government owns all the oil and gas.

5. HYDRAULIC FRACTURING: THE RULE OF CAPTURE REIGNS AGAIN

The widespread use of hydraulic fracturing and horizontal well drilling today brings novel issues for courts and legislators to resolve. As introduced above, operators today often drill horizontal wells through shales or tight sandstones that stretch for more than a mile and are then fractured. The fractures might extend beyond the limits of the operator's lease on to another's tract, giving rise to the issue of trespass once again, as in the case presented next.

The facts are simply stated: The Salinas family leased their 768-acre tract of land called Share 13 to Coastal. Coastal owned the adjacent Share 12 in fee simple. The Vicksburg T gas reservoir lay under their tracts. Coastal performed a large fracturing operation on a well on its Share 12. Salinas claimed that the fractures extended into Share 13, causing substantial drainage of their tract by their own lessee from its nearby well. The jury found for Salinas and awarded $1 million in lost royalties. In an opinion likely to be influential in fracturing battles in the new shale gas reservoirs found in many other states, the Texas Supreme Court reversed and remanded.

Coastal Oil and Gas Corp. v. Garza Energy Trust
268 S.W.3d 1 (Tex. 2008).

■ HECHT, J., delivered the opinion of the Court. . . .

The primary issue in this appeal is whether subsurface hydraulic fracturing of a natural gas well that extends into another's property is a trespass for which the value of gas drained as a result may be recovered as damages. We hold that the rule of capture bars recovery of such damages. . . .

The Vicksburg T is a "tight" sandstone formation, relatively imporous and impermeable, from which natural gas cannot be commercially produced without hydraulic fracturing stimulation, or "fracing". . . . This is done by pumping fluid down a well at high pressure so that it is forced out into the formation. The pressure creates cracks in the rock that propagate along the azimuth of natural fault lines in an elongated elliptical pattern in opposite directions from the well. Behind the fluid comes a slurry containing small granules called proppants— sand, ceramic beads, or bauxite are used—that lodge themselves in the cracks, propping them open against the enormous subsurface pressure that would force them shut as soon as the fluid was gone. The fluid is then drained, leaving the cracks open for gas or oil to flow to the wellbore. Fracing in effect increases the well's exposure to the formation, allowing greater production. First used commercially in 1949, fracing is now essential to economic production of oil and gas and commonly used throughout Texas, the United States, and the world.

Engineers design a fracing operation for a particular well, selecting the injection pressure, volumes of material injected, and type of proppant to achieve a desired result based on data regarding the porosity, permeability, and modulus (elasticity) of the rock, and the pressure and other aspects of the reservoir. The design projects the length of the fractures from the well measured three ways: the hydraulic length, which is the distance the fracing fluid will travel, sometimes as far as 3,000 feet from the well; the propped length, which is the slightly shorter distance the proppant will reach; and the effective length, the still shorter distance within which the fracing operation will actually improve production. Estimates of these distances are dependent on available data and are at best imprecise. Clues about the direction in which fractures are likely to run horizontally from the well may be derived from seismic and other data, but virtually nothing can be done to control that direction; the fractures will follow Mother Nature's fault lines in the formation. . . .

For the Coastal Fee No. 1, the fracing hydraulic length was designed to reach over 1,000 feet from the well. Salinas's expert, Dr. Michael J. Economides, testified he would have designed the operation to extend at least 1,100 to 1,500 feet from the well. The farthest distance from the well to the Share 13 lease line was 660 feet. The parties agree that the hydraulic and propped lengths exceeded this distance, but they disagree whether the effective length did. The lengths cannot be measured directly, and each side bases its assertion on the opinions of an eminent engineer long experienced in hydraulic fracturing: Economides for Salinas, and Dr. Stephen Allen Holditch for Coastal. Holditch believed that a shorter effective length was supported by post-fracing production data.

All the wells on Shares 12 and 13 were fraced. As measured by the amount of proppant injected into the well, the fracing of the Coastal Fee [well] was, as Economides testified, "massive," much larger than any fracing operation on a well on Share 13.

* * *

[Part II.B of the majority opinion]:

Had Coastal caused something like proppants to be deposited on the surface of Share 13, it would be liable for trespass, and from the ancient common law maxim that land ownership extends to the sky above and the earth's center below, one might extrapolate that the same rule should apply two miles below the surface. But that maxim . . . "has no place in the modern world." Wheeling an airplane across the surface of one's property without permission is a trespass; flying the plane through the airspace two miles above the property is not. Lord Coke, who pronounced the maxim, did not consider the possibility of airplanes. But neither did he imagine oil wells. The law of trespass need no more be the same two miles below the surface than two miles above.

* * *

We need not decide the broader issue [of whether a trespass exists] here. In this case, actionable trespass requires injury, and Salinas's only claim of injury—that Coastal's fracing operation made it possible for gas to flow from beneath Share 13 to the Share 12 wells—is precluded by the rule of capture. That rule gives a mineral rights owner title to the oil and gas produced from a lawful well bottomed on the property, even if the oil and gas flowed to the well from beneath another owner's tract. The rule of capture is a cornerstone of the oil and gas industry and is fundamental both to property rights and to state regulation. Salinas does not claim that the Coastal Fee No. 1 violates any statute or regulation. Thus, the gas he claims to have lost simply does not belong to him. He does not claim that the hydraulic fracturing operation damaged his wells or the Vicksburg T formation beneath his property. In sum, Salinas does not claim damages that are recoverable.

Salinas argues that the rule of capture does not apply because hydraulic fracturing is unnatural. The point of this argument is not clear. If by "unnatural" Salinas means due to human intervention, the simple answer is that such activity is the very basis for the rule, not a reason to suspend its application. Nothing is more unnatural in that sense than the drilling of wells, without which there would be no need for the rule at all. If by "unnatural" Salinas means unusual, the facts are that hydraulic fracturing has long been commonplace throughout the industry and is necessary for commercial production. . . . And if by "unnatural" Salinas means unfair, the law affords him ample relief. He may use hydraulic fracturing to stimulate production from his own wells and drain the gas to his own property—which his operator, Coastal, has successfully done already—and he may sue Coastal for not doing so sooner—which he has also done, in this case, though unsuccessfully, as it now turns out.

Salinas argues that stimulating production through hydraulic fracturing that extends beyond one's property is no different from drilling a deviated or slant well—a well that departs from the vertical significantly—bottomed on another's property, which is unlawful. Both produce oil and gas situated beneath another's property. But the rule of capture determines title to gas that drains from property owned by one person onto property owned by another. It says nothing about the ownership of gas that has remained in place. The gas produced through a deviated well does not migrate to the wellbore from another's property; it is already on another's property. The rule of capture is justified because a landowner can protect himself from drainage by drilling his own well, thereby avoiding the uncertainties of determining how gas is migrating through a reservoir. It is a rule of expedience. One cannot protect against drainage from a deviated well by drilling his own well; the deviated well will continue to produce his gas. Nor is there any uncertainty that a deviated well is producing another owner's gas. The justifications for the rule of capture do not support applying the rule to a deviated well.

We are not persuaded by Salinas's arguments. Rather, we find four reasons not to change the rule of capture to allow one property owner to sue another for oil and gas drained by hydraulic fracturing that extends beyond lease lines.

First, the law already affords the owner who claims drainage full recourse. This is the justification for the rule of capture, and it applies regardless of whether the drainage is due to fracing. If the drained owner has no well, he can drill one to offset drainage from his property. If the minerals are leased and the lessee has not drilled a well, the owner can sue the lessee for violation of the implied covenant in the lease to protect against drainage. If an offset well will not adequately protect against drainage, the owner (or his operator) may offer to pool, and if the offer is rejected, he may apply to the Railroad Commission for forced pooling. The Commission may also regulate production to prevent drainage. No one suggests that these various remedies provide inadequate protection against drainage.

Second, allowing recovery for the value of gas drained by hydraulic fracturing usurps to courts and juries the lawful and preferable authority of the Railroad Commission to regulate oil and gas production. Such recovery assumes that the gas belongs to the owner of the minerals in the drained property, contrary to the rule of capture. While a mineral rights owner has a real interest in oil and gas in place, . . . [t]he mineral owner is entitled, not to the molecules actually residing below the surface, but to "a fair chance to recover the oil and gas in or under his land, *or* their equivalents in kind." The rule of capture makes it possible for the Commission, through rules governing the spacing, density, and allowables of wells, to protect correlative rights of owners with interests in the same mineral deposits while securing "the state's goals of preventing waste and conserving natural resources." But such rules do not allow confiscation; on the contrary, they operate to prevent confiscation. Without the rule of capture, drainage would amount to a taking of a mineral owner's property—the oil and gas below the surface of the property—thereby limiting the Commission's power to regulate production to assure a fair recovery by each owner. The Commission has never found it necessary to regulate hydraulic fracturing, . . . but should it ever choose to do so, permitting fracturing that extended beyond property lines, however reasonable in terms of industry operation, would be met with the objection that the Commission had allowed the minerals in the drained property to be confiscated. While " 'all property is held subject to the valid exercise of the police power' and thus not every regulation is a compensable taking, . . . some are." "Physical possession is categorically, a taking for which compensation is constitutionally mandated." We need not hold here that without the rule of capture, all regulation of drainage would be confiscatory and thus beyond the Commission's power. We observe only that the rule of capture leaves the Commission's historical role unimpeded [to regulate the production of oil and gas for the prevention of waste and the protection of correlative rights]. The Commission's role should not be supplanted by the law of trespass.

Third, determining the value of oil and gas drained by hydraulic fracturing is the kind of issue the litigation process is least equipped to handle. One difficulty is that the material facts are hidden below miles of rock, making it difficult to ascertain what might have happened. Such difficulty in proof is one of the justifications for the rule of capture. But there is an even greater difficulty with litigating recovery for drainage resulting from fracing, and it is that trial judges and juries cannot take into account social policies, industry operations, and the greater good which are all tremendously important in deciding whether fracing should or should not be against the law. While this Court may consider such matters in fashioning the common law, we should not alter the rule of capture on which an industry and its regulation have relied for decades to create new and uncertain possibilities for liability with no more evidence of necessity and appropriateness than this case presents. Indeed, the evidence in this case counsels strongly against such a course. The experts in this case agree on two important things. One is that hydraulic fracturing is not optional; it is essential to the recovery of oil and gas in many areas, including the Vicksburg T formation in this case. . . . The other is that hydraulic fracturing cannot be performed both to maximize reasonable commercial effectiveness and to avoid all drainage. Some drainage is virtually unavoidable. In this context, common law liability for a long-used practice essential to an industry is ill-advised. . . .

Fourth, the law of capture should not be changed to apply differently to hydraulic fracturing because no one in the industry appears to want or need the change. The Court has received amicus curiae brief . . . from every corner of the industry [including the Railroad Commission, the General Land Office, landowners, royalty owners, operators and well service providers and] all oppose liability for hydraulic fracturing, almost always warning of adverse consequences in the direst language. Though hydraulic fracturing has been commonplace in the oil and gas industry for over sixty years, neither the Legislature nor the Commission has ever seen fit to regulate it, though every other aspect of production has been thoroughly regulated. Into so settled a regime the common law need not thrust itself.

Accordingly, we hold that damages for drainage by hydraulic fracturing are precluded by the rule of capture. It should go without saying that the rule of capture cannot be used to shield misconduct that is illegal, malicious, reckless, or intended to harm another without commercial justification, should such a case ever arise. But that certainly did not occur in this case, and no instance of it has been cited to us. ■

NOTES AND COMMENTS

1.   Did the majority of the court decide whether fracturing that extends under lease lines is a trespass? Three justices dissented from Part II.B of the opinion, writing that they "would not address whether the rule of capture

precludes damages when oil and gas is produced through hydraulic fractures that extend across lease lines until it is determined whether [this act] is a trespass." These justices noted that the majority opinion could injure small tract owners because it encouraged operators to capture gas from unleased and unpooled tracts by fracturing wells on nearby leased land, allowing lessees to expand the boundary lines of their leases without paying for additional acreage. Justice Willett's concurring opinion praises fracturing and the increased production it brings at a time of record-high energy prices.

2.   How would you decide to rule when presented with this set of facts:

Plaintiff owned a 200-acre tract and leased it to Axle Oil Company. This lease did not authorize the lessee to pool plaintiff's tract with other property to form a larger drilling unit that combined acreage from several leased tracts. In 2010, Axle Oil requested that Plaintiff amend the lease and allow pooling, but Plaintiff refused. Axle Oil then drilled a horizontal well on the neighboring property, placing its horizontal bore length 35 feet from plaintiff's property line. The well was then fractured. Plaintiff sued for trespass damages and for violation of Axle's duty to protect plaintiff's tract from drainage to other owners (a well-recognized implied duty in oil and gas jurisprudence interpreting a lessee's duty to its lessor). Axle Oil moved for a summary judgment declaring that it owed Plaintiff nothing.

In *Stone v. Chesapeake Appalachia*, 2013 WL 2097397 (N.D. W. Va.) (*vacated due to settlement*, 2013 WL 7863861 (N.D. W. Va. 2013)), the court refused to grant the oil company's motion for summary judgment and refused to follow *Garza* because *Garza* gave "operators a blank check to steal from the small landowner" without even contacting him or her for a lease. The court relied heavily on the *Garza* dissent as well as the Restatement (Second) of Torts § 158 on liability for intentional intrusions on land.

3.   The well at issue in the *Garza* case was drilled vertically and then fractured. Today, most wells using hydraulic fracturing extend horizontally, often passing through tracts leased from many different owners. The lessee must have the consent of all the different mineral interest owners of land invaded by the horizontal well bore to avoid trespass liability. Pooling clauses in leases or compulsory pooling procedures under state law allow lessees to combine acreage from different tracts into a larger-sized unit. How should royalties from the horizontal well be allocated among the different owners in the unit? By surface acreage under lease? By the proportional length of the horizontal well bore under each owner's land? *See* Browning Oil Co. v. Luecke, 38 S.W.3d 625 (Tex. App. 2000).

6.   REGULATING EXTERNALITIES OF DRILLING AND PRODUCTION

Most new onshore oil and gas wells drilled in the United States will require hydraulic fracturing. In addition to raising important common law issues of property rights, fracturing has drawn renewed attention to the regulation of the externalities of oil and gas development. As we have seen, states have long had primary control over such regulation, and they retain this control due to a number of exemptions of oil and gas activity from federal environmental statutes. Most oil and gas exploration and production ("E & P") wastes, even those with hazardous characteristics, are exempt from federal hazardous waste regulation under the Resource Conservation and Recovery Act (RCRA), 40 C.F.R. 261.4(b)(5). Thus, operators need not follow the federal RCRA requirements for labeling and tracking hazardous wastes and disposing of them only at approved disposal facilities. Hydraulic fracturing, with the exception of fracturing with diesel, also does not count as "underground injection" under the Safe Drinking Water Act (SDWA) that is designed to protect underground sources of drinking water from endangerment, so operators conducting fracturing need not obtain an SDWA permit. 42 U.S.C. § 300h (d)(1). A number of federal regulations apply at least partially to oil and gas production, however. *See* GAO, Unconventional Oil and Gas Development: Key Environmental and Public Health Requirements (Sept. 2012), http://www.gao.gov/assets/650/647782.pdf.

The states, which have long shouldered the bulk of regulatory responsibility for oil and gas extraction, initially focused on the conservation of oil and gas by enacting waste-prevention statutes, unitization and other laws discussed above to ensure that operators withdrew oil and gas efficiently and with maximum recovery rates. *See* Ground Water Protection Council, prepared for DOE, State Regulations Designed to Protect Water Resources (May 2009), http://www.gwpc.org/sites/default/files/state_oil_and_gas_regulations_designed_to_protect_water_resources_0.pdf. Beginning in the 1970s, however, states moved toward environmental regulation of oil and gas operations. Some of the most common regulations address the following externalities of oil and gas drilling:

a.   *Air emissions.* Operators often flare off the natural gas that first comes out of a well after it is drilled and fractured in order to "clean out" the well and prepare it for production. Further, some oil wells, such as those in the Bakken Shale of North Dakota, produce large quantities of "associated gas" along with oil throughout the life of the well. Where well operators lack access to pipelines to carry the gas to a market, widespread flaring occurs (as in North Dakota and South Texas in 2013). Mineral owners who leased to operators in North Dakota have brought suit, requesting damages for the lost royalties on the flared gas. They argue that the operators violated a North Dakota statute that requires operators to implement alternatives to flaring, such as connecting gathering lines to the well or powering on-site generators with gas, within the first year of production unless to do so would be economically infeasible. Sorenson v. Burlington Resources Oil & Gas Co., LP, case 4:13–cv–00132–DLH–CSM (D. N.D. 2014); *see* N.D. Cent. Code § 38–08–06.4. Other states' environmental regulations have placed limited restrictions on the timing and amount of flaring that may occur, although most states do allow some flaring. As an alternative to flaring, operators directly vent methane—a potent greenhouse gas—into the air.

Additional sources of air emissions at well sites include the rigs and other on-site equipment that typically run on diesel fuel as well as the substances contained in pits and tanks on site. Condensate, a "light" oil that is produced from some wells and stored temporarily on site, emits substantial quantities of pollutants into the air that contribute to ground-level ozone, better known as smog. In the Denver area in 2008, prior to Colorado's implementation of stricter air quality controls, condensate tanks were the largest source of volatile organic compounds (VOCs), which are precursors to ground-level ozone. These tanks emitted 33% of the total daily VOC emissions. Other oil and gas activities contributed to 16% of the emissions (including "area" and "point" sources of air pollution from oil and gas wells), while highway vehicles caused 17% of emissions. The remaining VOC emissions came from sources such as lawn and garden equipment and consumer solvents. Dale Wells, Colo. Dept. Publ. Health & Envt., Condensate Tank Emissions, Figure 6. 2008 Ozone Nonattainment Area VOC Emission Inventory by Tons Per Day, http://www.epa.gov/ttnchie1/conference/ei20/session6/dwells.pdf.   The city of San Antonio is in danger of becoming a nonattainment area under the Clean Air Act because of increased oil and gas activity and flaring in the Eagle Ford field to its south.

Certain emissions from tanks, as well as venting and flaring activities at gas wells (not oil wells), will be curtailed by a new EPA Clean Air Act regulation, which requires that operators capture VOCs, including methane, that are emitted by newly fractured or refractured gas wells and associated facilities. Oil and Natural Gas Sector: New Source Performance Standards and National Emission Standards for Hazardous Air Pollutants Reviews; Final Rule, 77 Fed. Reg. 49,490 (Aug. 16, 2012) (to be codified at 40 C.F.R. Part 63); and Oil and Natural Gas Sector: Reconsideration of Certain Provisions of New Source Performance Standards, Final Rule, 78 Fed. Reg. 22,125 (Sept. 23, 2013) (codified at 40 C.F.R § 60.5365, § 60.5380, § 60.5395, §§ 60.5410–60.5413, §§ 60.5415–60.5417, § 60.5420, and § 60.5430) (modifications of certain storage vessel rules). Capturing VOCs in the fracturing process is called a "green completion."

b.   *Leakage of methane and other substances from wells into groundwater.* When oil and gas operators drill a well into an underground formation, there is a risk that water will infiltrate the well and contaminate the oil and gas flowing through it. There is also a risk that methane (natural gas) or other substances flowing through the well, such as fracturing fluids, will leak out of the well into underground waters. Some of the earliest state environmental regulations of oil and gas wells were "casing" requirements, which mandated that operators line the well with steel tubing and cement the tubing into place. Certain types of cementing methods were required, and states often mandated that casing extend a minimum depth below groundwater resources.

Even if adequate casing is initially installed in a well, if wells are improperly abandoned when they no longer produce, they can leak methane and other substances. This is a significant problem in states like Texas and Pennsylvania, which are working to properly plug hundreds of old, abandoned wells in an effort to prevent leakage. *See* Railroad Comm'n of Tex., Oil Field Cleanup, State Well Pluggings Remaining by District as of 03/31/2013, http://www.rrc.state.tx.us/environmental/ plugging/Wells_Remaining_0313.pdf; Pa. Dept. of Envtl. Prot., Pennsylvania's Plan for Addressing Problem Abandoned Wells and Orphaned Wells at 4 (2000), http://www.elibrary.dep.state.pa.us/dsweb/ Get/Version-48262/.

c.   *Contamination of well sites, surface water, and underground water from waste storage and disposal.* When an operator drills a well, soil and rock called "cuttings" come out of the ground. These cuttings often contain naturally occurring radioactive materials (NORM). Other wastes include flowback water—the water that flows back up out of a well after it is hydraulically fractured—and brine or produced water, which is the water that was naturally contained within the formation and comes out of the well, along with oil and gas, over the productive lifespan of the well. Flowback and brine also can contain NORM that is picked up from the formation. States now often require that these wastes be stored and disposed of using certain methods. Operators often store wastes temporarily in pits or impoundments dug on the surface of the well site, and states began to require that operators line these pits with clay and/or plastic to prevent wastes from seeping into the soil, surface water, and groundwater. States also specified acceptable disposal methods for these wastes. While some of the dry wastes may be disposed of at the well site by incorporating the wastes into the soil, the liquid wastes typically must be sent to an underground injection control (UIC) well that is regulated under the Safe Drinking Water Act. In many states, the EPA has delegated to the states the authority to permit UIC wells, but some states still rely on the EPA to issue the permits. Certain liquid wastes, particularly brines, are sometimes spread on dirt roads for dust control, or they might be sent to a wastewater treatment plant. However, treatment plants cannot remove NORM contaminants.

Public attention to the environmental externalities of oil and gas operations has grown as hydraulic fracturing has enabled development in more parts of the country. A number of actors participate in regulating these externalities, as discussed next.

Private contractual provisions. In some cases, sophisticated landowners and banks or other lenders that finance well operations have inserted environmental restrictions on drilling in private leases or lending contracts. Such restrictions may prevent drilling on sites that contain a certain percentage of surface water or require that a plastic liner be placed beneath the entire well pad (the flat area on which a well is drilled and pits, tanks, and other facilities temporarily sit). Nonetheless, many citizens rely largely on government entities to protect them from environmental risks.

State regulation. Many states have updated their environmental regulations, although there are ongoing debates about whether these updates adequately control externalities. The most common changes have been the following:

- Requirements that wells or well sites be set back at greater distances from homes and natural resources, such as streams and wetlands.
- Enhanced pit lining requirements, or, more rarely, requirements that wastes be stored in tanks ("closed loop") systems rather than pits.
- Requirements that operators disclose the chemicals used in hydraulic fracturing, although operators typically may claim trade secret status for chemicals when they make this disclosure.
- Requirements that operators test water wells around well sites prior to drilling, or rebuttable presumptions that water contamination within a certain distance of well sites and a certain time after drilling and fracturing was caused by oil and gas operations. A very limited number of states and municipalities even require groundwater monitoring during drilling and fracturing.

- Requirements that well casing be pressure tested before being installed to ensure that it can withstand the maximum pressure that hydraulic fracturing places on the well.

- Requirements that blowout prevention equipment be used on wells to minimize the risks of explosions and releases of polluting substances onto land and into water.

- Requirements that well operators submit water management plans indicating where they will withdraw the approximately one to five or more million gallons of water required for each fracturing treatment and how they will avoid endangering aquatic life in the process.

- Monitoring for induced seismicity (earthquakes) around underground injection control wells, and moratoria on the use of UIC wells in certain areas (Arkansas).

Regional governance. Certain regional governing entities also play a role in addressing the externalities of oil and gas development. Operators withdrawing water for fracturing within the watershed of the Susquehanna River Basin Commission must obtain a permit from the Commission, which contains a number of conditions, including a requirement that operators sometimes stop withdrawing surface waters to assure a minimum streamflow.

Industry voluntary codes. Some companies in the Marcellus Shale region (Pennsylvania and neighboring states) have entered into voluntary agreements to meet performance standards at well sites that are more protective than many existing state regulations. These companies have agreed to be privately audited to confirm compliance with these "gold standards." *See* Center for Sustainable Shale Development, Performance Standards, https://www.sustainableshale. org/performance-standards/. The use of voluntary industry codes of conduct as "private regulation" appears in the offshore section of this chapter (discussing the Center for Offshore Safety) and in the international energy chapter where "soft law" often predominates over the hard law of treaties. In July 2014, the American Petroleum Institute released its first edition of "Community Engagement Guidelines" (ANSI/API Bulletin 100–3) that outline what local communities can expect from operators as good practices.

Some impacts of oil and gas development remain largely unaddressed. The thousands of new wells that are drilled and fractured each year fragment habitat and can substantially impact wildlife, as well as the appearance of landscapes. Although the Endangered Species Act prevents the "take" (harm) of species that have been listed as threatened and endangered, whether on private or public land, it does so on a species-by-species basis and does little to address broader habitat impacts that can affect the many species not yet listed as threatened or endangered. Some states are beginning to address habitat impacts. Maryland is considering a requirement that operators determine how to mitigate landscape impacts when submitting a permit to drill. Md. Dept. of the Env't, Marcellus Shale Safe Drilling Initiative Study Part II Best Practices (Draft for Public Comment), Section III—Comprehensive Gas Development Plans (Aug. 2013). Santa Fe County in New Mexico has completed a sophisticated mapping project to determine sensitive areas where drilling is not suitable, such as wildlife habitats and areas with agriculture and archaeological resources. Bd. of Cnty. Comm'rs of Santa Fe Cnty., Ordinance No. 2008–19, § 9.4.1.1, http://www.santafe countynm.gov/userfiles/SFCOrdinance2008_19.pdf.

The U.S. Fish and Wildlife Service (FWS) has signed a voluntary agreement with the Western Association of Fish and Wildlife Agencies (WAFWA) to protect the lesser prairie chicken whose habitat overlies many of the largest shale plays in Texas and other Western states. The agreement, called the Range-wide Oil and Gas Candidate Conservation Agreement with Assurances, enrolls companies and landowners who pledge to take steps to protect this bird and to pay mitigation fees for harm to its habitat. In exchange, the FWS agrees not to impose further limits on the parties if the bird is listed as threatened under the Endangered Species Act. Five large oil companies were the first to sign the agreement, which requires, for example, that they forego operations during breeding hours and pay mitigation fees to fund the removal of tall trees and bushes that the birds do not tolerate. Enrolled ranchers can earn "chicken credits" for improving habitat for the birds. *See* FWS & WAFWA, Range-Wide Oil and Gas Candidate Conservation Agreement with Assurances for the Lesser Prairie-Chicken, Jan. 28, 2014, http:// www.fws.gov/coloradoes/Lesser_prairie_chicken/02%2028%2014%20 Draft%20CCAA%20with%20CI%20Revised_Clean_WAFWA.pdf.

Local regulation and bans. Overlaying state, regional and federal regulation are many local initiatives enacted by cities, large and small, to regulate oil and gas development within their limits. The court in the *Tysco* case, noted *supra* in Section B(4), upheld a 1935 ordinance enacted by a town where fireworks manufacturing co-existed precariously around oil and gas activity. The ordinance required that operators obtain a city drilling permit (in addition to the state permit) and have fire extinguishment equipment on site. It also limited the number and placement of wells. The ordinance protected correlative rights by conditioning the grant of a permit for each 16-acre "drilling district unit" on the permittee's sharing of production among the different landowners in the unit, a form of early compulsory pooling.

Whether state conservation law preempts a city or town from regulating the oil and gas industry is an important issue. The recent shale boom has spurred more local governments to enact oil and gas ordinances with detailed restrictions on drilling and fracturing. Some local governments have placed moratoria or all-out bans on hydraulic fracturing. Litigation over local control has experienced a boom of its own. The local regulations take the following forms, or a combination of them:

1.   *Zoning and land use.* These ordinances typically prohibit oil and gas development in residential or commercial zones or require an operator to obtain a "special use" permit to drill in any zones. Some ordinances, such as that in Santa Fe County in New Mexico, allow drilling only where a special drilling "overlay" zone has been created. The drilling company must obtain a special use permit and a number of other permits, and the county must complete a detailed environmental review and a determination of the services and infrastructure that will be required for the well. The county may charge the drilling company special assessments for the costs of these services. Santa Fe Cnty., N.M.

Ordinance No. 2008–19. The County also prepared an expensive, computer-based mapping analysis that identified sensitive portions of the County, including those with special archaeological or environmental resources, in which drilling should not occur. *Id*. Regardless of the zone in which development is allowed, local governments often also require setbacks and prohibit the placement of wells within a certain distance of residences or buildings like churches or schools.

2.   *Operational*. Local governments often regulate the operation of oil and gas development in addition to its location, as noted in the *Tysco* case. Operators may be required to use certain equipment, such as blowout preventers, to prevent the uncontrolled release of pressure in a well during drilling and fracturing; or to use closed loop systems rather than pits to store drilling and fracturing wastes, in addition to many other technical requirements. Some local governments have specifically addressed hydraulic fracturing in their regulations. Dallas requires that fracturing companies use "tracers" that will allow identification of where fracturing fluid travels underground and assist in detecting any pollution. *See* Dallas Ordinance 29228 (2013). Several cities and counties in Texas and New Mexico require operators to obtain environmental liability insurance that will cover $5 million to $10 million per incident. *See* City of Fort Worth, Texas, Ordinance No. 18449-02-2009, *available at* http://fortworthtexas.gov/uploadedFiles/Gas_Wells/090120_gas_drill ing_final.pdf; City of Arlington, Texas, Ordinance No. 07-074, http://www.marcellus-shale.us/pdf/Gas-Drill-Ord_Arlington-TX.pdf.

3.   *Bans*. A growing number of local governments, using either their zoning or more general powers, have fully banned oil and gas development and/or hydraulic fracturing within their jurisdictions.

The powers of local governments to take the actions described above all derive from state governments. Under the Tenth Amendment of the U.S. Constitution, the states retain "police powers" as reserved powers that allow them to protect the public health, safety, and welfare. These powers have been interpreted quite broadly. States often delegate certain of these broad powers to local governments. The most common form of delegation is the Standard State Zoning Enabling Act, now adopted in some form by all fifty states. Through zoning enabling acts, state legislatures give local governments the power to designate "zones" within which certain types of land uses may occur. States also often delegate to local governments the powers to conduct comprehensive planning for growth and to approve subdivisions and building permits, among other powers.

To determine the extent of powers granted by states to local governments under the zoning enabling act and other delegating acts within a state, one must first determine whether a state is a "Dillon's Rule" or a "home rule" state, or something in between. In Dillon's Rule states, local governments only have the powers expressly and specifically delegated to them by the state. In home rule states, local governments have broader, bottom-up authority to regulate anything that affects their internal affairs, and this authority need not be expressly delegated to them. Some states only grant home rule powers that impact affairs within the municipal limits and not beyond.

Local power increasingly conflicts with the state's assertion of power over oil and gas activity, resulting in a burgeoning docket of state/local preemption cases. Three types of state preemption of local authority exist: (1) express preemption, in which the state legislature expressly states an intent to preempt local control; (2) conflict preemption, in which the state has not expressly preempted local control, but industry compliance with a local standard would cause violation of a state standard or would otherwise interfere with state law; and (3) field preemption, in which the state has not expressly preempted local control but has enacted so many regulations in an area that the state is found to have impliedly intended to preempt local interference in that area. Courts have decided a number of preemption cases that are creating unique state-by-state results.

As examples, in Louisiana, state political subdivisions are "expressly forbidden, to prohibit or in any way interfere with the drilling of a well or test well" under La. Rev. Stat. Ann. § 30:28(F). In *Energy Management Corp. v. Shreveport*, 467 F.3d 471 (5th Cir. 2006), the Fifth Circuit Court of Appeals held that a Shreveport ordinance preventing drilling within 1,000 feet of a lake and regulating drilling within 5,000 feet of the lake was expressly preempted in its entirety. Contrast this with West Virginia, where the state has not expressly preempted local regulation of oil and gas. Nonetheless, a county court found that the City of Morgantown's ban on natural gas drilling was preempted because the state had a comprehensive set of oil and gas regulations that "occupied" the regulatory field and left no room for local regulation. Northeast Natural Energy, LLC v. Morgantown. Circuit Ct. of Monongalia Cty., WV, Div. No. 1 (Aug. 12, 2011).

In Pennsylvania, prior to 2012, state court decisions had suggested that local regulation of oil and gas development was not completely preempted by a statute governing oil and gas regulation in the state. In a political bargain that appeared to trade greater state environmental protection for the certainty of state preemption of local law, the Pennsylvania Legislature enacted Act 13 in 2012. This Act required local governments to allow oil and gas drilling in all zones, including residential areas. In *Robinson Township v. Commonwealth*, 83 A.3d 901 (Pa. 2013), the Pennsylvania Supreme Court held that Act 13's preemption of local authority was unconstitutional. Two justices stated that requiring local governments to allow drilling in all zones violated substantive due process. Substantive due process grants citizens a right to non-arbitrary zoning decisions as a substantive right, meaning that citizens have a right to a non-arbitrary zoning outcome, regardless of the procedure followed. Act 13 violated substantive due process because it forced local governments to ignore the comprehensive plans they had designed as a blueprint for compatible uses, resulting in arbitrary zoning. Other justices found that Act 13 violated the Environmental Rights Amendment of the state constitution, which requires the Commonwealth to hold Pennsylvania's natural resources in trust for the citizens of Pennsylvania.

Finally, in New York, the state's highest court upheld a home-rule town's complete ban on oil and gas activities in *Norse Energy Corp. v. Town of Dryden*, N.Y. 16 N.E.3d 1188 (N.Y. Ct. App. 2014). Land use in the town of Dryden was governed by a comprehensive plan and zoning ordinance designed to "preserve the rural and small town character of the Town of Dryden, and the quality of life its residents enjoy." Under

Article IX, section 2 of the New York Constitution, "every local government [was granted] power to adopt and amend local laws not inconsistent with the provisions of [the] constitution or any general law relating to its property, affairs or government." New York law expressly preempted "all local laws or ordinances relating to the regulation of the oil, gas and solution mining industries." N.Y. Envtl. Conserv. Law § 23–0303 (commonly known as the Oil, Gas and Solution Mining Law (OGSML)).

While local governments cannot use their home rule authority to enact ordinances that conflict with a "general law," the court in *Norse Energy* stated that it would not "lightly presume preemption where the preeminent power of a locality to regulate land use is at stake." The court then analyzed the state law that arguably preempted "all local laws" related to the "regulation" of the oil and gas industry. The court's task was made easier because it had already decided that similar preemptive language for "extractive mining" activity did not preempt local land use laws in *Matter of Frew Run Gravel Prods. v. Town of Carroll*, 71 N.Y.2d 126 (1987). The court in *Frew Run* considered three factors determinative of whether the Legislature intended state preemption: (1) the plain language of the supersession clause; (2) the statutory scheme as a whole; and (3) the relevant legislative history.

In *Norse Energy,* the court used these three factors and concluded that local *land use*-based bans on oil and gas are not local *regulation* and thus are not preempted. The court's analysis of the three factors proceeded as follows: First, the plain language of the state law was most "naturally read" as preempting only local laws that purported to regulate actual oil and gas operations, not zoning ordinances that restrict or prohibit certain land uses within the town boundaries. Second, the statutory scheme as a whole confirmed this reading of the plain language of the statute. The stated purposes of the Oil, Gas and Solution Mining Law were fourfold: (i) to regulate oil and gas practices to "prevent waste;" (ii) to authorize operation and development so that a "greater ultimate recovery of oil and gas may be had;" (iii) to protect the "correlative rights" of owners; and (iv) to regulate underground gas storage, solution mining of salt and geothermal, and brine disposal wells." "Waste" was found to be a term of art in the OGSML, meaning the "inefficient, excessive or improper use" of reservoir energy and preventing inefficient drilling practices. The third factor, legislative history, also confirmed that the OGSML was designed as classic oil and gas conservation law with roots extending back to 1935 to address overproduction of oil and gas and the waste caused by unchecked drilling.

A dissenting justice strongly disagreed and viewed the town's land use ordinance as regulation of the oil, gas and solution mining industries under the "pretext of zoning:"

> The ordinances here created a blanket ban on an entire industry without specifying the zones where such uses are prohibited. In light of the language of the zoning ordinances at issue—which go into great detail concerning the prohibitions against the storage of gas, . . . and [petroleum-related materials and equipment]—it is evident that [these ordinances] go above and beyond zoning and, instead, regulate those industries, which is exclusively within the purview of the Department of

Environmental Conservation. In this fashion, prohibition of certain activities is, in effect, regulation.

In Texas, although the state has historically allowed relatively extensive local regulation of oil and gas activities, the state has changed its position in response to a recent Denton, Texas referendum banning hydraulic fracturing. The Texas General Land Office sued Denton in county court, arguing that the ban is preempted by state law. Jerry Patterson, Commissioner, Texas General Land Office v. City of Denton, Texas, Plaintiff's Original Petition and Application for Permanent Injunction, Nov. 5, 2014, *available at* http://www.desmogblog.com/sites/ beta.desmogblog.com/files/denton%20filed%20copy.pdf.

The overarching theme of these preemption cases is that home rule status is only the beginning of a court's inquiry. Once courts have addressed home rule issues, they must address the text of the preemption language and statutory interpretation. But variability in the legal reasoning of courts makes it difficult to find grand principles or to predict results in future cases. West Virginia found implied field preemption despite a rather weak state regulatory regime for oil and gas. Pennsylvania did not discuss home rule at all and struck down preemption on constitutional grounds. No one theme has emerged or seems likely to emerge.

Questions about whether the federal government should preempt certain state and local controls over oil and gas and exert more environmental regulatory authority are also at the forefront of a rich legal and policy discussion. *See, e.g.*, John R. Nolon & Steven E. Gavin, Hydrofracking: State Preemption, Local Power, and Cooperative Governance, 63 Case W. Res. L. Rev. 995 (2013); Uma Outka, Intrastate Preemption in a Shifting Energy Sector, 86 U. Colo. L. Rev.— (forthcoming 2015); David B. Spence, The Political Economy of Local Vetoes, 93 Tex. L. Rev. 351 (2014); David B. Spence, Federalism, Regulatory Lags, and the Political Economy of Energy Production, 161 U. Pa. L. Rev. 431 (2012); Hannah J. Wiseman, Urban Energy, 40 Fordham Urb. L.J. 1793 (2013).

While these authors have diverse views, they seem to agree on one principle: that fully preempting local authority over oil and gas matters may not be a good idea. Professor David Spence notes how local governments can engage in bargaining toward a good utilitarian result. Professor Uma Outka observes that local governments, with their many and varied regulations, contribute to national energy policy. Professor John Nolon reminds us that effective regulation can result when states and local governments work together. And Professor Hannah Wiseman notes that impacts of development usually fall more heavily on communities than on the state. These articles suggest that some degree of local authority over oil and gas matters should be retained.

Clearly, public concerns about the externalities of oil and gas development remain, despite an ever-increasing body of regulatory and private law. It is important to note that regulations and private standards still vary substantially among municipalities and states. For descriptions of the regulations and variation among them, as well as maps showing variation, see Nathan Richardson et al., Resources for the Future, The State of State Shale Gas Regulation (2013), http://www.rff.org/rff/ documents/RFF-Rpt-StateofStateRegs_Report.pdf. While some of this variation is justified by differences in geology, climate, and other factors, some is caused because hydraulic fracturing has proceeded so rapidly that regulation has lagged behind. *See, e.g.*, Hannah Wiseman, Risk and Response in Fracturing Policy, 84 U. Colo. L. Rev. 729 (2013). Some scholars believe that courts can and should handle any environmental issues that emerge. *See, e.g.*, Thomas W. Merrill & David M. Schizer, The Shale Oil and Gas Revolution, Hydraulic Fracturing, and Water Contamination: A Regulatory Strategy, 98 Minn. L. Rev. 101 (2013) (proposing tort standards that should apply, depending on factors such as the type of alleged environmental impact and the level of knowledge about causation).

A good summary of "what is known, what is uncertain, and what is unknown" about both the economic and environmental consequences of the shale gas revolution lists 24 critical questions that require further research. *See* Alan J. Krupnick et al., The Natural Gas Revolution: Critical Questions for a Sustainable Energy Future (Resources for the Future, Mar. 2014), http://www.rff.org/Publications/Pages/Publication Details.aspx?PublicationID=22365. The questions range from supply and demand uncertainties to effects on public health, water supplies, and climate change. Whether the answers will be found in time to avoid irreversible and large-scale adverse impacts of shale development by adopting good policies and regulation is the task of scientists, policymakers and industry leaders. *See also* Environmental Impacts of Shale Gas Extraction in Canada (Council of Canadian Academies 2014)(report of the Expert Panel on Harnessing Science and Technology to Understand the Environmental Impacts of Shale Gas Extraction), http://www.scienceadvice.ca/en/assessments/completed/shale-gas.aspx.

D. OFFSHORE OIL AND GAS

1. INTRODUCTION

In 2013, about 24 percent of U.S. oil production and 7 percent of gas production came from wells on the federal Outer Continental Shelf (OCS). A significant share of our nation's oil and gas reserves lies under the OCS, particularly in the Gulf of Mexico. The late 1990s saw a resurgence of drilling offshore in the Gulf due to a number of factors: (1) new knowledge of how sands were deposited far from shore (as far as 130 miles) in the Gulf of Mexico millions of years ago in flood-related currents from the Mississippi River; (2) the use of new 3–D seismic technology; (3) the 1995 Deep Water Royalty Relief Act, which exempted up to 87.5 million barrels of oil from royalty payments from each newly discovered field; and (4) advances in the evolution of offshore oil platforms from towers that rest on the sea bottom to floating or guyed structures, some of which are taller than the Sears Tower in Chicago. Peter Wilson, Science and Technology in the Offshore Oil Industry, Nat. Res. & Env't, Spring 1990, at 552.

Little political opposition exists to drilling in the Western Gulf of Mexico, even after the massive Deepwater Horizon-BP blowout and spill in mid-2010, but in areas of the Eastern Gulf near Florida's tourist industry, opposition is strong. The governors of some Eastern coastal states have campaigned for the start of federal leasing off their shores in recent years, while other states, such as California and Massachusetts,

have not been so welcoming. Alaska and the Arctic present unique
environmental and political challenges, as the following material
demonstrates.

2. THE STATUTORY FRAMEWORK

One event, above all, was the catalyst for the wave of environmental
legislation enacted from 1969 onwards: the Santa Barbara oil spill of
January 28, 1969. In 1966, the first federal leases on the Pacific offshore
were issued in the Santa Barbara Channel. As Union Oil drilled the fifth
well on its Platform A in the channel, the well blew out. Eleven days
passed before the well was plugged and some 24,000 to 71,000 barrels of
oil spilled into the channel and onto nearby beaches. Figure 4–9 depicts
the ensuing tsunami of environmental legislation.

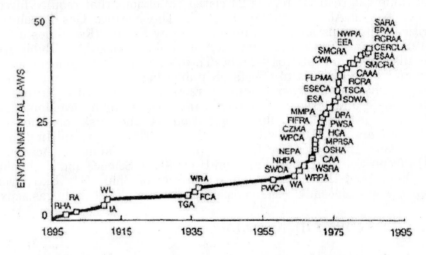

1899 - River and Harbors Act (RHA)
1902 - Reclamation Act (RA)
1910 - Insecticide Act (IA)
1911 - Weeks Law (WL)
1934 - Taylor Grazing Act (TGA)
1937 - Flood Control Act (FCA)
1937 - Wildlife Restoration Act (WRA)
1958 - Fish and Wildlife Coordination Act (FWCA)
1964 - Wilderness Act (WA)
1965 - Solid Waste Disposal Act (SWDA)
1965 - Water Resources Planning Act (WRPA)
1966 - National Historic Preservation Act (NHPA)
1968 - Wild and Scenic Rivers Act (WSRA)
1969 - National Environmental Policy Act (NEPA)
1970 - Clean Air Act (CAA)
1970 - Occupational Safety and Health Act (OSHA)
1972 - Water Pollution Control Act (WPCA)
1972 - Marine Protection, Research and
         Sanctuaries Act (MPRSA)
1972 - Coastal Zone Management Act (CZMA)
1972 - Home Control Act (HCA)
1972 - Federal Insecticide, Fungicide and
         Rodenticide Act (FIFRA)
1972 - Parks and Waterways Safety Act (PWSA)
1972 - Marine Mammal Protection Act (MMPA)

1973 - Endangered Species Act (ESA)
1974 - Deepwater Port Act (DPA)
1974 - Safe Drinking Water Act (SDWA)
1974 - Energy Supply and Environmental
         Coordination Act (ESECA)
1976 - Toxic Substances Control Act (TSCA)
1976 - Federal Land Policy and Management Act (FLPMA)
1976 - Resource Conservation and Recovery Act (RCRA)
1977 - Clean Air Act Amendments (CAAA)
1977 - Clean Water Act (CWA)
1977 - Surface Mining Control and Reclamation Act
         (SMCRA)
1977 - Soil and Water Resources Conservation Act
         (SWRCA)
1978 - Endangered Species Act Amendments (ESAA)
1978 - Environmental Education Act (EEA)
1980 - Comprehensive Environmental Response
         Compensation and Liability Act (CERCLA)
1982 - Nuclear Waste Policy Act (NWPA)
1984 - Resource Conservation and Recovery Act
         Amendments (RCRAA)
1984 - Environmental Programs and Assistance Act (EPAA)
1986 - Safe Drinking Water Act Amendments (SDWAA)
1986 - Superfund Amendments and Reorganization Act
         (SARA)

Figure 4–9
U.S. Environmental Law Growth
Source: Nat'l Acad. of Eng'rg, Energy, Production, Consumption and Consequences
185 (1990), http://www.nap.edu/openbook.php?record_id=1442&page=185

This wave of environmental protection closely coincided with the rocketing price of crude oil following the 1973 Arab oil embargo and its ensuing decade of energy shocks and crises. Energy competed with the environment for national attention. Could a balance be struck? Nowhere was this question more sharply framed than on the OCS and in Alaska, the two areas of highest potential to provide the nation with crude oil so essential to the transportation sector.

After the Santa Barbara spill, Congress enacted, in rapid succession, NEPA, the Marine Protection, Research and Sanctuaries Act of 1972, the Coastal Zone Management Act (CZMA) of 1972, the Marine Mammal Protection Act of 1972, and the Endangered Species Act of 1973, followed by the massive Clean Water and Clean Air Acts of 1977. In 1978, Congress significantly revised the Outer Continental Shelf Lands Act (OCSLA) of 1953, reflecting widespread dissatisfaction with DOI's administration of the earlier law. The 1978 amendments expanded the role of state and local government officials in the federal OCS leasing process in the hopes that this action would quell the unrelenting litigation between many coastal states and DOI, so that OCS oil could be expeditiously developed in the wake of the 1970s price shocks. However, opposition to OCS leasing continued unabated in states like California, except that the states now had additional legal mechanisms to fight the federal government in its attempts to develop domestic oil and gas. The "cooperative federalism" scheme championed in the CZMA was failing miserably.

In 1977, the Interior Department prepared another lease sale off the Santa Barbara coast. In the following case, the U.S. Supreme Court was called upon to interpret the CZMA of 1972 and the OCSLA Amendments of 1978 in the context of this leasing decision. The case provides a good history of the 1972 and 1978 acts and a nice description of the potential adverse impacts of offshore leasing. It also defines the nature of a lessee's property right in a federal offshore lease.

The strong dissenting opinion of four justices may explain why Congress amended the CZMA in 1990 and deleted the word "directly" in the phrase "directly affecting" at issue in this case.

Secretary of Interior v. California

464 U.S. 312 (1984).

■ O'CONNOR, J. This case arises out of the Department of Interior's sale of oil and gas leases on the outer continental shelf off the coast of California. We must determine whether the sale is an activity "directly affecting" the coastal zone under § 307(c)(1) of the Coastal Zone Management Act (CZMA). That section provides in its entirety:

> "Each Federal agency conducting or supporting activities directly affecting the coastal zone shall conduct or support those activities in a manner which is, to the maximum extent practicable, consistent with approved state management programs." 16 U.S.C. § 1456(c)(1).

We conclude that the Secretary of the Interior's sale of outer continental shelf oil and gas leases is not an activity "directly affecting" the coastal zone within the meaning of the statute.

I

CZMA defines the "coastal zone" to include state but not federal land near the shorelines of the several coastal states, as well as coastal waters extending "seaward to the outer limit of the United States territorial sea." 16 U.S.C. § 1453(1). The territorial sea for states bordering on the Pacific or Atlantic Oceans extends three geographical miles seaward from the coastline. *See* 43 U.S.C. § 1301; United States v. California, 381 U.S. 139 (1965). Submerged lands subject to the jurisdiction of the United States that lie beyond the territorial sea constitute the "outer continental shelf" (OCS). *See* 43 U.S.C. § 1331(a). By virtue of the Submerged Lands Act, passed in 1953, the coastal zone belongs to the states, while the OCS belongs to the federal government. 43 U.S.C. §§ 1302, 1311.

CZMA was enacted in 1972 to encourage the prudent management and conservation of natural resources in the coastal zone. Congress found that the "increasing and competing demands upon the lands and waters of our coastal zone" had "resulted in the loss of living marine resources, wildlife, nutrient-rich areas, permanent and adverse changes to ecological systems, decreasing open space for public use, and shoreline erosion." 16 U.S.C. § 1451(c). Accordingly, Congress declared a national policy to protect the coastal zone, to encourage the states to develop coastal zone management programs, to promote cooperation between federal and state agencies engaged in programs affecting the coastal zone, and to encourage broad participation in the development of coastal zone management programs. 16 U.S.C. § 1452.

Through a system of grants and other incentives, CZMA encourages each coastal state to develop a coastal management plan. Further grants and other benefits are made available to a coastal state after its management plan receives federal approval from the Secretary of Commerce. To obtain such approval, a state plan must adequately consider the "national interest" and "the views of the Federal agencies principally affected by such program." 16 U.S.C. §§ 1455(c)(8), 1456(b).

Once a state plan has been approved, CZMA § 307(c)(1) requires federal activities "conducting or supporting activities directly affecting the coastal zone" to be "consistent" with the state plan "to the maximum extent practicable." 16 U.S.C. § 1456(c)(1). The Commerce Department has promulgated regulations implementing that provision. Those regulations require federal agencies to prepare a "consistency determination" document in support of any activity that will "directly affect" the coastal zone of a state with an approved management plan. The document must identify the "direct effects" of the activity and inform state agencies how the activity has been tailored to achieve consistency with the state program. 15 C.F.R. § § 930.34, 930.39 (1983).

II

OCS lease sales are conducted by the Department of the Interior (Interior). Oil and gas companies submit bids and the high bidders receive priority in the eventual exploration and development of oil and gas resources situated in the submerged lands on the OCS. A lessee does not, however, acquire an immediate or absolute right to explore for, develop, or produce oil or gas on the OCS; those activities require separate, subsequent federal authorization.

In 1977, the Department of Commerce approved the California Coastal Management Plan. The same year, Interior began preparing Lease Sale No. 53—a sale of OCS leases off the California coast near Santa Barbara. Interior first asked several state and federal agencies to report on potential oil and gas resources in this area. The Agency then requested bidders, federal and state agencies, environmental organizations, and the public, to identify which of 2036 tracts in the area should be offered for lease. In October 1978, Interior announced the tentative selection of 243 tracts, including 115 tracts situated in the Santa Maria Basin located off western Santa Barbara. Various meetings were then held with state agencies. Consultations with other federal agencies were also initiated. Interior issued a Draft Environmental Impact Statement in April, 1980.

On July 8, 1980 the California Coastal Commission informed Interior that it had determined Lease Sale No. 53 to be an activity "directly affecting" the California coastal zone. The state commission therefore demanded a consistency determination—a showing by Interior that the lease sale would be "consistent" to the "maximum extent practicable" with the state coastal zone management program. Interior responded that the Lease Sale would not "directly affect" the California coastal zone. Nevertheless, Interior decided to remove 128 tracts, located in four northern basins, from the proposed lease sale, leaving only the 115 tracts in the Santa Maria Basin. In September 1980, Interior issued a final Environmental Impact Statement. On October 27, 1980, it published a proposed notice of sale, limiting bidding to the remaining 115 blocks in the Santa Maria Basin. 45 Fed. Reg. 71140 (1980).

On December 16, 1980, the state commission reiterated its view that the sale of the remaining tracts in the Santa Maria Basin "directly affected" the California coastal zone. The commission expressed its concern that oil spills on the OCS could threaten the southern sea otter, whose range was within 12 miles of the 31 challenged tracts. The commission explained that it "has been consistent in objecting to proposed offshore oil development within specific buffer zones around special sensitive marine mammal and seabird breeding areas. . . ." App. 77. The commission concluded that 31 more tracts should be removed from the sale because "leasing within 12 miles of the Sea Otter Range in Santa Maria Basin would not be consistent" with the California Coastal Management Program.

Interior rejected the State's demands. In the Secretary's view, no consistency review was required because the lease sale did not engage CZMA § 307(c)(1), and the Governor's request was not binding because it failed to strike a reasonable balance between the national and local interests. On April 10, 1981, Interior announced that the lease sale of the 115 tracts would go forward, and on April 27 issued a final notice of sale. 46 Fed. Reg. 23674 (1981).

Respondents filed two substantially similar suits in federal district court to enjoin the sale of 29 tracts situated within 12 miles of the Sea Otter range. Both complaints alleged, *inter alia*, Interior's violation of § 307(c)(1) of CZMA. They argued that leasing sets in motion a chain of events that culminates in oil and gas development, and that leasing therefore "directly affects" the coastal zone within the meaning of § 307(c)(1).

The district court entered a summary judgment for respondents on the CZMA claim. The Court of Appeals for the Ninth Circuit affirmed that portion of the district court judgment that required a consistency determination before the sale. We granted certiorari, and we now reverse.

III

Whether the sale of leases on the OCS is an activity "directly affecting" the coastal zone is not self-evident. As already noted, OCS leases involve submerged lands outside the coastal zone, and as we shall discuss, an OCS lease authorizes the holder to engage only in preliminary exploration; further administrative approval is required before full exploration or development may begin. Both sides concede that the preliminary exploration itself has no significant effect on the coastal zone. Both also agree that a lease sale is one . . . in a series of decisions that may culminate in activities directly affecting that zone.

A

We are urged to focus first on the plain language of § 307(c)(1). Interior contends that "directly affecting" means "having a direct, identifiable impact on the coastal zone." Brief for Federal Petitioners 20. Respondents insist that the phrase means "initiating a series of events of coastal management consequence." Brief for Respondents State of California, et al. 10. But CZMA nowhere defines or explains which federal activities should be viewed as "directly affecting" the coastal zone, and the alternative verbal formulations proposed by the parties, both of which are superficially plausible, find no support in the Act itself.

* * *

IV B

* * *

OCSLA was enacted in 1953 to authorize federal leasing of the OCS for oil and gas development. The Act was amended in 1978 to provide for the "expeditious and orderly development, subject to environmental safeguards," of resources on the OCS. 43 U.S.C. § 1332(3) (1976 ed., Supp. III). As amended, OCSLA confirms that at least since 1978 the sale of a lease has been a distinct stage of the OCS administrative process, carefully separated from the issuance of a federal license or permit to explore, develop, or produce gas or oil on the OCS.

Since 1978 there have been four distinct statutory stages to developing an offshore oil well: (1) formulation of a five year leasing plan by the Department of the Interior; (2) lease sales; (3) exploration by the lessees; (4) development and production. Each stage involves separate regulatory review that may, but need not, conclude in the transfer to lease purchasers of rights to conduct additional activities on the OCS. And each stage includes specific requirements for consultation with Congress, between federal agencies, or with the States. Formal review of consistency with state coastal management plans is expressly reserved for the last two stages.

(1) Preparation of a leasing program. The first stage of OCS planning is the creation of a leasing program. Interior is required to prepare a 5-year schedule of proposed OCS lease sales. During the preparation of that program Interior must solicit comments from interested federal agencies

and the governors of affected states, and must respond in writing to all comments or requests received from the state governors. The proposed leasing program is then submitted to the President and Congress, together with comments received by the Secretary from the governor of the affected state. [43 U.S.C. § 1344 (1976 ed., Supp. III).]

Plainly, prospective lease purchasers acquire no rights to explore, produce, or develop at this first stage of OCSLA planning, and consistency review provisions of CZMA § 307(c)(3)(B) are therefore not engaged. There is also no suggestion that CZMA § 307(c)(1) consistency requirements operate here, though we note that preparation and submission to Congress of the leasing program could readily be characterized as "initiat[ing] a [s]eries of [e]vents of [c]oastal [m]anagement [c]onsequence." Br. for Resp. State of Cal., et al., at 10.

(2) *Lease sales.* The second stage of OCS planning—the stage in dispute here—involves the solicitation of bids and the issuance of offshore leases. 43 U.S.C. § 1337(a) (1976 ed., Supp. III). Requirements of the National Environmental Policy Act and the Endangered Species Act must be met first. The governor of any affected state is given a formal opportunity to submit recommendations regarding the "size, timing, or location" of a proposed lease sale. 43 U.S.C. § 1345 (1976 ed., Supp. III). Interior is required to accept these recommendations if it determines they strike a reasonable balance between the national interest and the well-being of the citizens of the affected state. Local governments are also permitted to submit recommendations, and the Secretary "may" accept these. The Secretary may then proceed with the actual lease sale. Lease purchasers acquire the right to conduct only limited "preliminary" activities on the OCS—geophysical and other surveys that do not involve seabed penetrations greater than 300 feet and that do not result in any significant environmental impacts. 30 C.F.R § 250.34–1 (1982).

Again, there is no suggestion that these activities in themselves "directly affect" the coastal zone. But by purchasing a lease, lessees acquire no right to do anything more. Under the plain language of OCSLA, the purchase of a lease entails no right to proceed with full exploration, development, or production that might trigger CZMA § 307(c)(3)(B); the lessee acquires only a priority in submitting plans to conduct those activities. If these plans, when ultimately submitted, are disapproved, no further exploration or development is permitted.

(3) *Exploration.* The third stage of OCS planning involves review of more extensive exploration plans submitted to Interior by lessees. 43 U.S.C. § 1340 (1976 ed., Supp. III). Exploration may not proceed until an exploration plan has been approved. A lessee's plan must include a certification that the proposed activities comply with any applicable state management program developed under CZMA. OCSLA expressly provides for federal disapproval of a plan that is not consistent with an applicable state management plan unless the Secretary of Commerce finds that the plan is consistent with CZMA goals or in the interest of national security. 43 U.S.C. § 1340(c)(2) (1976 ed., Supp. III). The plan must also be disapproved if it would "probably cause serious harm or damage . . . to the marine, coastal, or human environment. . . ." 43 U.S.C. §§ 1334(a)(2)(A)(I), 1340(c)(1) (1976 ed., Supp. III). If a plan is disapproved for the latter reason, the Secretary may "cancel such lease

and the lessee shall be entitled to compensation. . . ." 43 U.S.C. § 1340(c)(1) (1976 ed., Supp. III).

There is, of course, no question that CZMA consistency review requirements operate here. CZMA § 307(c)(3)(B) expressly applies, and as noted, OCSLA itself refers to the applicable CZMA provision.

(4) Development and production. The fourth and final stage is development and production. 43 U.S.C. § 1351 (1976 ed., Supp. III). The lessee must submit another plan to Interior. The Secretary must forward the plan to the governor of any affected state and, on request, to the local governments of affected states, for comment and review. Again, the governor's recommendations must be accepted, and the local governments' may be accepted, if they strike a reasonable balance between local and national interests. Reasons for accepting or rejecting a governor's recommendations must be communicated in writing to the governor. In addition, the development and production plan must be consistent with the applicable state coastal management program. The State can veto the plan as "inconsistent," and the veto can be overridden only by the Secretary of Commerce. 43 U.S.C. § 1351(d) (1976 ed., Supp. III). A plan may also be disapproved if it would "probably cause serious harm or damage . . . to the marine, coastal or human environments." 43 U.S.C. § 1351(h)(1)(D)(I) (1976 ed., Supp. III). If a plan is disapproved for the latter reason, the lease may again be canceled and the lessee is entitled to compensation. 43 U.S.C. § 1351(h)(2)(C) (1976 ed., Supp. III). Once again, the applicability of CZMA to this fourth stage of OCS planning is not in doubt.

Congress has thus taken pains to separate the various federal decisions involved in formulating a leasing program, conducting lease sales, authorizing exploration, and allowing development and production. Since 1978, the purchase of an OCS lease, standing alone, entails no right to explore, develop, or produce oil and gas resources on the OCS. The first two stages are not subject to consistency review; instead input from State governors and local governments is solicited by the Secretary of Interior. The last two stages invite further input from governors or local governments, but also require formal consistency review. States with approved CZMA plans retain considerable authority to veto inconsistent exploration or development and production plans put forward in those latter stages. The stated reason for this four part division was to forestall premature litigation regarding adverse environmental effects that all agree will flow, if at all, only from the latter stages of OCS exploration and production. . . .

It is argued, nonetheless, that a lease sale is a crucial step. Large sums of money change hands, and the sale may therefore generate momentum that makes eventual exploration, development, and production inevitable. On the other side, it is argued that consistency review at the lease sale stage is at best inefficient, and at worst impossible: Leases are sold before it is certain if, where, or how exploration will actually occur.

The choice between these two policy arguments is not ours to make; it has already been made by Congress. In the 1978 OCSLA amendments Congress decided that the better course is to postpone consistency review until the two later stages of OCS planning, and to rely on less formal input from State governors and local governments in the two earlier ones.

It is not for us to negate the lengthy, detailed, and coordinated provisions of CZMA § 307(c)(3)(B), and OCSLA §§ 1344–1346 and 1351, by a superficially plausible but ultimately unsupportable construction of two words in CZMA § 307(c)(1).

* * *

V

Collaboration among state and federal agencies is certainly preferable to confrontation in or out of the courts. In view of the substantial consistency requirements imposed at the exploration, development, and production stages of OCS planning, the Department of the Interior, as well as private bidders on OCS leases, might be well advised to ensure in advance that anticipated OCS operations can be conducted harmoniously with state coastal management programs. But our review of the history of CZMA § 307(c)(1), and the coordinated structures of the amended CZMA and OCSLA, persuades us that Congress did not intend § 307(c)(1) to mandate consistency review at the lease sale stage.

Accordingly, the decision of the Court of Appeals for the Ninth Circuit is reversed insofar as it requires petitioners to conduct a consistency review pursuant to CZMA § 307(c)(1) before proceeding with Lease Sale No. 53.

It is so ordered.

■ JUSTICE STEVENS, with whom JUSTICE BRENNAN, JUSTICE MARSHALL, and JUSTICE BLACKMUN join, dissenting.

* * *

The question in this case is whether the Secretary of the Interior was conducting an activity directly affecting the California Coastal Zone when he sold oil and gas leases in the Pacific ocean area immediately adjacent to that zone. One would think that this question could be easily answered simply by reference to a question of fact—does this sale of leases directly affect the coastal zone? The District Court made a finding that it did, which the Court of Appeals affirmed, and which is not disturbed by the Court. Based on a straightforward reading of the statute, one would think that that would be the end of the case. [The dissent then conducted its own review of the plain language and legislative history of the CZMA.]

The majority's construction of § 307(c)(1) is squarely at odds with [the purpose of the CZMA]. Orderly, long-range, cooperative planning dictates that the consistency requirement must apply to OCS leasing decisions. The sale of OCS leases involves the expenditure of millions of dollars. If exploration and development of the leased tracts cannot be squared with the requirements of the CZMA, it would be in everyone's interest to determine that as early as possible. On the other hand, if exploration and development of the tracts would be consistent with the state management plan, a pre-leasing consistency determination would provide assurances to prospective purchasers and hence enhance the value of the tracts to the Federal Government and, concomitantly, the public. Advance planning can only minimize the risk of either loss or inconsistency that may ultimately confront all interested parties. It is directly contrary to the legislative scheme not to make a consistency determination at the earliest possible point. Such a construction must be rejected.

There is no dispute about the fact that the Secretary's selection of lease tracts and lease terms constituted decisions of major importance to the coastal zone.

[The dissent then quoted from the District Court's summary of the DOI's own 1980 study and the EIS for the lease sale, both of which discussed direct effects on the coastal zone, including DOI's estimate of a 52% overall probability of an oil spill impacting a point within the sea otter range during the life of the project. Impacts on air and water quality, marine ecosystems, fisheries, recreation, and navigation had been documented. Indeed, the EIS stated that normal offshore operations, such as pipelaying and drilling, would have "unavoidable effects" on the quality of the surrounding water and could affect the spot prawn fishery. Additional impacts included risks to the aesthetics of the area, to archeological sites in the area, the in-migration of labor, and competition for onshore land sites used in the OCS activities.]

[The dissent concluded by agreeing with the District Court's opinion that:] "The threshold test under § 307(c)(1) would in fact be satisfied by a finding of a single direct effect upon the coastal zone. Although the evidence of direct effects is substantial, such a showing is not required by the CZMA" (quoting from 520 F.Supp. 1359, 1380–1382 (C.D.Cal.1981)).

■

NOTES AND COMMENTS

1.   In 1950, the Supreme Court ruled that the entire continental shelf was under federal control (*United States v. Texas*, 339 U.S. 707 (1950) and cases cited therein), but, in 1953, Congress passed the Submerged Lands Act, which gave the states the rights to certain offshore waters, typically three miles seaward of the shore. Texas and Florida prevailed in their historical claims to extend their territorial sea jurisdiction to three marine leagues, or about ten miles seaward. This jurisdictional "wrinkle" has enriched Texas state coffers by millions of dollars. *See* Francis J. Gaynor, Beyond All Boundaries—A Study of Marine Jurisdiction of the State of Texas—Past History and Current Issues, 17 Hous. J. Int'l L. 253 (1994).

2.   Section 307(c)(1)(A) of the CZMA currently reads: "Each Federal agency activity within or outside the coastal zone that affects any land or water use or natural resource of the coastal zone shall be carried out in a manner which is consistent to the maximum extent practicable with the enforceable policies of approved State management programs." 16 U.S.C.A. § 1456(c)(1)(A). How does this amendment affect the balance between federal and state power over control of vital OCS resources? Does it give states a veto power over OCS leasing?

Section 307(c)(1)(B) allows the President, under certain conditions, to exempt a specific federal agency activity from compliance with the new consistency requirements if the President determines such a waiver is "in the paramount interest of the United States." What might justify a presidential waiver against a state like Florida that continues to oppose drilling off its shores?

3.   In an omitted footnote in this case, the majority opinion noted that the California Coastal Commission had warned: "Any attempt to explore or develop these tracts will face the strong possibility of an objection to a consistency certification of the Plan of Exploration or Development." What projected rate of return would warrant the political risks of leasing in the Santa Barbara Channel? What property right have lessees bought in exchange for winning bids, which totaled $220 million on the disputed leases in this case? Is the lease little more than a "lottery ticket" that *may* allow the lessee a chance to explore—but may also be worth nothing because the lessee never succeeds in securing consistency approval under the CZMA?

Test your understanding of this property right:

a.   A lessee successfully bid on an offshore tract, paying $1 billion. The coastal state had strongly protested this federal lease sale. The lessee later submitted its Plan of Exploration (POE) to DOI, which reviewed and approved it, despite the coastal state's insistence that the POE was not consistent with its CZMA-approved plan. The Secretary of Commerce also found the POE to be consistent. Is the lessee's decision to spend another $2 billion on exploratory drilling now risk-free under the CZMA (assuming the state does not mount a court challenge to these executive actions)?

b.   Assume the same facts, but either DOI or the Commerce Secretary, or both, refuse to grant a consistency determination for the POE (perhaps because of an upcoming election or a recent election that resulted in a change of control in the White House). Can the lessee proceed to explore? If not, can it get its $1 billion back because the government has breached the terms of the lease?

Find the provisions of OCSLA under which the lessee is entitled to compensation when it can no longer proceed because its plans are not approved.

c.   Assume that DOI refuses to approve the POE because it learns that the blowout preventers being used on exploratory wells in the deep water of the OCS are not capable of preventing blowouts for the high-pressure wells being drilled there. DOI has learned this because of a massive blowout and subsequent oil spill that occurred in the Gulf of Mexico the year before. DOI cancels the lease. Is the lessee entitled to compensation? Is it more likely that DOI will suspend the leases until better blowout preventers are invented and tested for deepwater conditions? After all, royalties on offshore leases make a significant contribution to the federal treasury.

Here is the story of one offshore lessee's journey to the U.S. Supreme Court after being caught in the swirling political climate that arose in the aftermath of the *Exxon Valdez* tanker oil spill in Alaska. Mobil sought restitution of its $156 million in bonus monies paid for a lease acquired in 1981 on tracts about 45 miles from the North Carolina coast. It did not fare well in the Court of Appeals for the Federal Circuit because of this court's reading of *Secretary of Interior v. California*. This court refused to order restitution after finding that the two oil companies were sophisticated lessees who bargained "with their legal eyes wide open." They knew the leases were a gamble: The leases gave the companies the right to explore if they could secure a state consistency certificate under the CZMA or a federal override of a state's refusal to find that the federal leasing was consistent with its approved coastal plan.

The U.S. Supreme Court, with a lone dissent by Justice Stevens, reversed and ordered the restitution of the $156 million in *Mobil Oil Exploration & Producing Southeast, Inc. v. United States*, 530 U.S. 604 (2000). The opinion reads like a treatise in first-year Contracts. The majority used the following lottery ticket example:

> If a lottery operator fails to deliver a purchased ticket, the purchaser can get his money back—whether or not he eventually would have won the lottery. And if one party to a contract, whether oil company or ordinary citizen, advances the other party money, principles of restitution normally require the latter, upon repudiation, to refund that money. Restatement [of Contracts] § 373.

Id. at 624.

How exactly had the federal government repudiated the lease contract? The lessees paid the $156 million in bonus money in 1981. With the ten-year primary term of the leases running out, the companies entered into a memorandum of understanding with both DOI and North Carolina in 1989 to implement a draft Exploration Plan as the next stage in the OCS leasing process. The companies promised to submit their draft Plan to both North Carolina and DOI before submitting a final one. In September 1989, this draft Plan was submitted to the state and DOI. Ten months later, in July 1990, DOI issued an environmental report that all parties conceded had been intensively reviewed. The DOI concluded that the proposed exploration would not "significantly affect" the environment. In August 1990, the companies submitted both their final Exploration Plan and their CZMA consistency certification to DOI. It seemed that all systems were "go" because of the cooperative, extensive review by both the state and DOI.

However, the timetable for processing this Exploration Plan ran into trouble because the *Exxon Valdez* oil spill had occurred in March 1989. As crude oil soaked Alaskan shorelines for hundreds of miles and impacted fishermen, wildlife and tourism, coastal senators remembered how devastating the Santa Barbara platform oil spill of 1969 had been. The Outer Banks off the East coast are a prime fisheries area.

The Congressional reaction resulted in the Outer Banks Protection Act of 1990 (OBPA), Pub. L. 101–380, Title VI, § 6003, 104 Stat. 484, 555 (1990) (codified at 33 U.S.C. § 2753; repealed 1996), which prohibited DOI from approving any Exploration Plan or Development and Production Plan or awarding any drilling permit until (a) a new OBPA-created Environmental Sciences Review Panel had reported to the Secretary, and (b) the Secretary had certified to Congress that he had sufficient information to make all OCSLA-required approval decisions, but, in no event could he issue an approval or permit for the next 13 months (until October 1991). OBPA § 6003(c)(3) (codified at 33 U.S.C. § 2753(c)(3); repealed 1996).

The OBPA came into effect on August 18, 1990, two days before Mobil and its partner companies submitted their final Exploration Plan and their CZMA consistency certification to DOI on August 20, 1990. About five weeks after Plan submission, DOI deemed the final Plan to be "approvable in all respects." The Plan would have only a "negligible effect" on the environment and DOI had no authority to disapprove the Plan—except for the fact that the new OBPA prohibited its approval. Therefore, DOI would suspend the lease, pending the OBPA-required scientific reports.

Eighteen months later, the Interior Secretary received the OBPA's Panel report, which recommended some further studies. The Secretary announced that he would wait for these studies.

Meanwhile, in November 1990, North Carolina objected to the CZMA consistency certificate on the grounds that Mobil had not provided enough information about possible environmental harm. Ultimately, in 1994, the Secretary of Commerce refused to override the state's objection to CZMA consistency.

In light of the company's failure to secure a CZMA consistency certificate, how could the government be liable for breach of contract? Its "lottery ticket" simply did not hold a winning number.

Here is the relevant provision of the CZMA used by the Supreme Court, followed by excerpts showing how the U.S. Supreme Court explained its holding:

> Section § 1340(c)(1) of OCSLA's title 43 requires that the leaseholder submit an exploration plan for approval and that "the Secretary shall approve such plan, as submitted or modified, within 30 days of its submission," unless the Secretary determines that the proposed activity, even if modified, "would probably cause serious harm or damage to life (including fish and other aquatic life), to property, . . . or to the marine, coastal, or human environment" [§ 1334(a)(2)(A)(i)], in which event the Secretary "shall disapprove the plan." This subsection then provides that the Secretary may "cancel such lease and the lessee shall be entitled to compensation."

Mobil Oil Exploration & Producing Southeast, Inc. v. United States

530 U.S. 604 (2000).

[Part II D of the opinion, 530 U.S. at 623–24]:

■ [T]he Government argues that repudiation could not have hurt the companies. Since the companies could not have met the CZMA consistency requirements, they could not have explored (or ultimately drilled) for oil in any event. Hence, OBPA caused them no damage. . . . [Ed. note: Recall that a divided panel of the Court of Appeals for the Federal Circuit held for the government on this basis in 177 F.3d 1331 (Fed. Cir. 1999).] This argument, however, misses the basic legal point. The oil companies do not seek damages for breach of contract. They seek restitution of their initial payments. Because the Government repudiated the lease contracts, the law entitles the companies to that restitution whether the contracts would, or would not, ultimately have produced a financial gain or led them to obtain a definite right to explore.

[Introduction to Part II, 530 U.S. at 614]:

The record makes clear (1) that OCSLA required Interior to approve "within thirty days" a submitted Exploration Plan that satisfies OCSLA's requirements, (2) that Interior told Mobil the companies' submitted Plan met those requirements, (3) that Interior told Mobil it would not approve the companies' submitted Plan for at least 13 months, and likely longer, and (4) that Interior did not approve (or disapprove) the Plan, ever. The Government does not deny that the contracts, made "pursuant to" and "subject to" OCSLA, incorporated OCSLA provisions as promises. The Government further concedes, as it must, that relevant contract law entitles a contracting party to restitution if the other party "substantially" breached a contract or communicated its intent to do so. . . . Yet the Government denies that it must refund the companies' money.

[Part II B of the opinion, 530 U.S. at 620–21]:

The Government next argues that any violation of the contracts' terms was not significant; hence there was no "substantial" or "material" breach that could have amounted to a "repudiation." In particular, it says that OCSLA's 30-day approval period "does not function as the 'essence' of these agreements. . . ."

We recognize that the lease contracts gave the companies more than rights to obtain approvals. They also gave the companies rights to explore for, and to develop, oil. But the need to obtain Government approvals so qualified the likely future enjoyment of the exploration and development rights that the contract, in practice, amounted primarily to an opportunity to try to obtain exploration and development rights in accordance with the procedures and under the standards specified in the cross-referenced statutes and regulations. Under these circumstances, if the companies did not at least buy a promise that the Government would not deviate significantly from those procedures and standards, then what did they buy?

The Government's modification of the contract-incorporated processes was not technical or insubstantial. It did not announce an (OBPA-required) approval delay of a few days or weeks, but of 13 months minimum, and likely much longer. The delay turned out to be at least four years. And lengthy delays matter, particularly where several successive agency approvals are at stake. Whether an applicant approaches Commerce with an Interior Department approval already in hand can make a difference (as can failure to have obtained that earlier approval). Moreover, as we have pointed out, OBPA changed the contract-referenced procedures in several other ways as well. . . . ■

NOTES AND COMMENTS

1. In essence, the government's announcement that it would not approve Mobil's plan within 30 days, even though the Plan met OCSLA requirements, constituted the substantial breach. Under OCSLA, the companies took their leases "subject to" existing laws as of the effective date of their contracts and nothing in OCSLA subjected the lessees to the risks that *new* statutes, like the OBPA, would be able to affect their procedural and substantive rights under their leases. In deciding the case, the Court interpreted this standard lease provision in federal leases:

> This lease is issued pursuant to the Outer Continental Shelf Lands Act of August 7, 1953, 67 Stat. 462[,] 43 U.S.C. § 1331 *et seq.*, as amended (92 Stat. 629), (hereinafter called the "Act"). The lease is issued subject to the Act; all regulations issued pursuant to the Act and in existence upon the Effective Date of this lease; all regulations issued pursuant to the statute in the future which

provide for the prevention of waste and conservation of the natural resources of the Outer Continental Shelf and the protection of correlative rights therein; and all other applicable statutes and regulations.

May the Secretary impose new regulations on lessees with existing leases if the regulations are issued under OCSLA's authority? Under other statutes? Does the "catchall" phrase at the end of this provision sweep in new laws and regulations or only existing ones? Oil companies that venture abroad often seek a "stabilization" clause in their contracts with the host government that freezes existing laws applied to their contracts. Is this overreaching?

2.   How can an OCS lessee be reasonably justified in expecting quick (30-day) approval of a controversial leasing decision? Note that the OBPA-approved Environmental Sciences Panel recommended that further studies be done, even after they had studied possible environmental impacts for more than a year. Should more careful studies have been done before the decision to lease these areas was made? In 1996, Congress repealed the OBPA.

3.   Should the Secretary of Interior, despite the OBPA, have issued his approval to the Exploration Plan? If so, and the state of North Carolina had secured a judicial decree enjoining the Secretary's actions, would the Secretary then have been authorized to suspend the leases? One of the OCSLA regulations reads as follows:

> The Regional Supervisor may also direct . . . suspension of any operation or activity, including production, because . . . (7) [t]he suspension is necessary to comply with judicial decrees prohibiting production or any other operation or activity, or the permitting of those activities. . . .

30 C.F.R. § 250.10(b)(7) (1990).

Would this sequence of events have affected the majority's opinion?

4.   The staged structure of offshore oil development explicated in *Secretary of Interior v. California* has ramifications for the Environmental Impact Statement (EIS) process required for any major federal activity significantly affecting the human environment under NEPA.

In *Village of False Pass v. Clark,* 733 F.2d 605 (9th Cir. 1984), the court explained the interaction among OCSLA, NEPA, and the ESA, in a case involving "an important marine environment, rare whales, large sums of money, [and] a search for increasingly scarce energy resources." *Id.* at 607.

In this case, the Secretary of Interior had approved federal leasing in the St. George Basin, located off the west coast of Alaska in the Bering Sea, "the gateway to virtually every marine mammal, fish, and bird species moving between the North Pacific and the Bering Sea." The Basin potentially held oil reserves of 1.12 billion barrels for which oil companies were willing to spend almost half a billion dollars for the right to investigate the chance (rated at 28 to 37 percent) of discovering commercial quantities.

The Village of False Pass and other intervenors argued that the Secretary had abused his discretion under NEPA by failing to perform a worst-case analysis in the EIS of an oil spill of 100,000 barrels or larger occurring while whales migrated nearby. In response, the court wrote:

The village would have a better argument for the importance of a worst case analysis at the lease sale stage of a 100,000 barrel oil spill if that were the only time the Secretary could review the potential environmental impacts of those leases. . . . As our earlier discussion of OCSLA's three stage process made clear, however, NEPA may require an environmental impact statement at each stage: leasing, exploration, and production and development. Furthermore, each stage remains separate. The completion of one stage does not entitle a lessee to begin the next [citing *Secretary of Interior v. California*].

Id. at 614.

A strong dissent in *False Pass* argued that the *California* case should not affect the interpretation of NEPA's requirements. The earlier case held that the OCSLA lease sale stage did not "directly affect" the coastal zone so as to require a consistency review under the CZMA. But the purposes of NEPA are different, explained the dissent:

Prior to sale, the Secretary has absolute discretion to decline to lease an OCS tract. *See* 43 U.S.C. § 1344(a). He can therefore decline to lease on the ground that exploration or development will run a small but real risk of immense environmental harm. Once the Secretary leases a tract, however, he loses that freedom, and consequently commits himself to incur such a risk. The reasons why the Secretary loses his freedom upon sale of the leases are both legal and practical.

As a legal matter, the Secretary is allowed to cancel an existing lease for environmental reasons only if he determines that:

(i) continued activity . . . *would probably cause* serious harm or damage to . . . [the] environment; (ii) the threat of harm or damage will not disappear or decrease to an acceptable extent within a reasonable period of time; and (iii) the advantages of cancellation outweigh the advantages of continuing such lease or permit in force [citing 43 U.S.C. § 1334(a)(2)(A) (emphasis added); 43 U.S.C. § 1351(h)(1)(D)].

The requirement of a determination that continued activity "would *probably* cause serious harm to the environment" is a forceful restriction on the Secretary's authority. At least under ordinary circumstances, it prohibits cancellation because of the possibility of a major oil spill; . . . a major oil spill is not a *probable* occurrence, but rather is "an event of low probability but catastrophic effects." The effect of the statute, therefore, is that sale of the leases ends the Secretary's right to call a total halt to exploration and development out of concern over remote environmental catastrophes. . . .

It is true that the Secretary's power to *suspend* operations remains broad, but we have held that the power to suspend is exceeded when the suspension is so open-ended as to amount to a cancellation of a lease. *Union Oil Co. of Cal. v. Morton*, 512 F.2d 743, 750–51 (9th Cir. 1975). Suspension is therefore a temporary remedy, and being temporary, cannot eliminate the possibility of a major oil spill. Only cancellation can do that.

Id. at 617–18.

5.   The *Village of False Pass* case also involved the ESA and whales. Section 7(a)(2) of the ESA requires that every federal agency "insure that any action authorized, funded, or carried out by such agency . . . is not likely to jeopardize the continued existence of any endangered species or threatened species" or adversely modify its critical habitat. 16 U.S.C. § 1536(a)(2). The majority opinion states that "ESA appears to apply equally to each stage [of offshore activity] of its own force and effect." False Pass v. Clark, 733 F.2d at 609. The court found no violation of the ESA because the Secretary had placed special disclaimers in the Notice of Lease Sale, stating that the Secretary retained authority to regulate seismic testing and to suspend drilling whenever migrating whales came close enough to be subject to the risk of spilled oil. The opinion continues:

> The Village characterizes these [disclaimers] as "only a plan for later action." We conclude that, given the Fisheries Service's general recommendations about oil spills and exploration stage seismic testing, the Secretary could properly limit his action at the lease sale stage to a plan for later implementation. The ESA applies to every federal action. . . . The lease sale decision itself could not directly place gray or right whales in jeopardy, and the plan insures that the many agency actions that may follow indirectly from the sale will not either.
>
> By choosing this plan, however, the Secretary recognizes his obligation under ESA to implement it. *See generally Conservation Law Found. of New England, Inc. v. Andrus*, 623 F.2d at 715. With each exploration plan, development and production plan, or permit to drill, the Secretary must: implicitly conclude that any approval does not affect an endangered species, *see* 50 C.F.R. § 402.04(a)(2) (1982); take appropriate steps to insure, on the basis of his previous consultation with the Fisheries Service, the absence of jeopardy to an endangered species; or reinitiate formal consultation, *see*, e.g., *Village of False Pass v. Watt*, 565 F. Supp. at 1161 & n.28 (strong suggestion that formal consultation about oil spill risks on whales will be required at the exploration stage); 50 C.F.R. § 402.04(h) (1982).
>
> The monitoring agreement with the Fisheries Service will help the Secretary take these steps and diligently pursue ESA compliance after the lease sale, *see Village of False Pass v. Watt*, 565 F. Supp. at 1161. The Secretary's own regulations require an environmental report from each lessee for each exploration plan, . . . and development and production plan. . . . Approval of these plans may even require a full environmental impact statement. *See* 30 C.F.R. § 250.34–4(a) (1982); *see also* 43 U.S.C. § 1351(e) (OCSLA); 42 U.S.C. § 4332(2)(C) (NEPA). Even if not a full environmental impact statement, these reports and plans must include information about marine mammal use of the area. *See* 30 C.F.R. § 250.34–3(a)(1)(I)(G)(4) (1982). . . . This means that the

Secretary will have precise, site-specific information in each case to insure the best compliance with ESA.

These regulations, promulgated in part under OCSLA, help make the Secretary's plan a real safeguard. Neither the regulations, nor OCSLA itself, dilute the full application of ESA to actions by the Secretary. . . .

Id. at 612.

Could the Secretary of Interior cancel a lease permanently because she found that exploration on the tract would jeopardize an endangered species and no temporary suspension could "unjeopardize" it? Would the lessee be entitled to compensation for lease cancellation? Continue to keep these questions in mind as you approach the material on OCS leasing moratoria.

6.   *Review problem.* Some federal oil and gas leases still exist off the coast of California, the legacy of *Secretary of Interior v. California's* holding that the CZMA, as enacted in 1972, did not allow California to challenge the federal government's decision to conduct a lease sale because such sales did not "directly affect" the coastal zone. The leases were granted between 1968 (even before the CZMA) and 1986, before Congress amended the Coastal Zone Management Act in 1990 to override the holding in *Secretary of Interior v. California*. Some lessees obtained production under their leases; many did not. Those leases without production would expire under their primary terms. However, over many years, DOI granted suspensions to these leases under a provision of OCSLA allowing suspensions that "facilitate proper development of the leases," (43 U.S.C. § 1334(a)(1)), thereby keeping them in effect.

The state of California asserted that it had the authority to review these lease suspensions for consistency with its coastal management plan. The United States argued that the suspensions did not have the potential to affect the coastal environment and so did not require a state's consistency review. California brought suit alleging that the federal government was violating the CZMA, as amended after *Secretary of Interior v. California*. Do you think the federal decision to suspend the leases rather than terminate them requires a CZMA consistency review because a lease suspension is a federal action much like a lease sale? *See* California v. Norton, 311 F.3d 1162 (9th Cir. 2002).

Now assume that the patience of some of these lessees, whose leases have been suspended for decades, finally wears thin. They seek restitution of their bonus payments of $1.1 billion. Under the precedent of *Mobil Oil,* should they win? Explain your reasoning.

7.   In Land Use Planning and Oil and Gas Leasing on Onshore Public Lands 12–13 (1989), the National Research Council was informed by the federal agencies that, as a rule of thumb, about 10 percent of all oil and gas leases issued are ever drilled on, and about 10 percent of those drilled on ever produce oil and gas. Does this rule of thumb bolster the views of the majority? Should NEPA generate paperwork evaluating speculative possibilities that are a long shot? *See* Park County Res. Council, Inc. v. Dep't of Agriculture, 817 F.2d 609 (10th Cir. 1987) (lease issuance not a major federal action significantly affecting the environment in a national forest because, among other factors, future drilling was "nebulous").

Until 1987, federal onshore leasing was conducted under the Mineral Leasing Act of 1920. In 1987, Congress enacted FOOGLRA, the Federal Onshore Oil and Gas Leasing Reform Act, to amend serious deficiencies in the 1920 Act. For a full discussion of onshore leasing, see George C. Coggins & Robert L. Glicksman, 4 Public Natural Resources Law Ch. 39 (2d ed. 2013).

3. MORATORIA AND WITHDRAWALS OF LAND FROM LEASING

The moratorium movement gained momentum when James Watt became Secretary of the Interior under Ronald Reagan in 1981 and proposed to lease virtually the entire federal offshore area of almost one billion acres during the five-year period from 1982–87. This amounted to 25 times as much land as was offered during the entire period from 1954 to 1980. In 1982, Congress responded by writing into the 1982 Interior appropriations bill a prohibition against offering certain areas for lease in California. By 1989, succeeding appropriation bills had extended the moratoria to more than 181 million acres off the coasts of California, the North Atlantic, and the Eastern Gulf of Mexico (near Florida). This "off limits" acreage equaled more than twice the acreage that had been leased in the entire history of the OCS program. The reasons for the Congressional moratoria have been summarized as follows:

> The rapid pace and magnitude of leasing proposed under [Secretary Watt's] program undermined the ability of state and local governments to adequately assess the environmental impact of leasing and to plan for OCS development. The . . . refusal to delete areas of environmental sensitivity and economic importance from lease sales was perceived by coastal states and environmental groups as a resource program weighted heavily toward energy production, irrespective of legitimate state concerns for balanced OCS development. The administration's opposition to continued funding for state coastal management programs, OCS revenue sharing, and consistency requirements lead [sic] states and local citizens to conclude that they were taking all the risks of OCS activity but receiving none of the benefits in return.

G. Kevin Jones, Understanding the Debate over Congressionally Imposed Moratoria on Outer Continental Shelf Leasing, 9 Temp. Envtl L. & Tech. J. 117 at 144 (1990).

The domestic oil industry did not respond kindly to the moratoria: "If a foreign power had managed to do to us what we have done to ourselves, to shape our energy policy so disastrously, we would call it an act of war." Id. at 147. In the first two years of the Watt program, eight of the 15 scheduled lease sales were challenged in court, resulting in major delays and uncertainties in the program rather than Watt's hoped-for acceleration. ARCO forfeited a $30 million investment by abandoning a high potential area off California because of the litigation. Id. at 163.

Subsequent presidents, undoubtedly also influenced by the sharp drop in oil prices in 1981 that crimped demand for federal leases, did not want to repeat the Watt era of turmoil. In 1990, the first President Bush canceled all lease sales pending off California, Washington, Oregon, Florida, and the Georges Bank area off New England (one of the richest fishing areas in the world) and issued moratoria on leasing in these areas until the year 2002. *Id.* at 44–45.

In 1998, President Clinton extended through the year 2012 the Bush moratoria against drilling off most of the U.S. coastline, except in the Central and Western Gulf of Mexico (excluding the Eastern Gulf of Mexico off Florida) and parts of Alaska. The American Petroleum Institute responded: "The extension is unfortunate because it ignores the near-perfect performance of the American petroleum industry in operating offshore in a safe and environmentally sensitive manner. U.S. government statistics show that natural seeps from the ocean floor introduce 100 times more crude oil into U.S. marine waters than do the petroleum industry's offshore activities." In turn, the Natural Gas Supply Association said cleaner air and increased use of affordable, clean-burning natural gas depended on access to the large gas fields off the nation's coasts. The moratoria made projections of a 35 percent growth in U.S. gas consumption by 2010 or 2015 "virtually untenable." Clinton Extends Wide Offshore Drilling Ban, Oil & Gas J., June 22, 1998, at 32.

Even the second President Bush trod lightly in the political arena surrounding OCS development off the East and West coasts. While strongly advocating the development of increased domestic oil and gas sources, his administration focused on opening the federal National Petroleum Reserve in Alaska, spurring more deepwater drilling in the Gulf of Mexico, and providing speedier access to federal lands in the Rockies, Wyoming and Montana. The OCS moratoria on the populated East and West coasts (and opening up the Arctic National Wildlife Refuge) were simply too hot to handle.

However, record-high oil and gas prices from 2003 onwards led Congress to reassess its opposition to broader OCS leasing. In 2009, Congress did not include a leasing prohibition in any appropriation bills. Near the end of his term in 2008, President Bush lifted the Executive Order against OCS leasing except in areas designated as marine sanctuaries. Once lifted, DOI could consider offering lease sales almost everywhere, except in the Eastern Gulf of Mexico off Florida where Congress had imposed a new moratorium in 2006 to continue through June 30, 2022. Cong. Res. Svc., Offshore Oil and Gas Development: Legal Framework (Mar. 21, 2013).

In early 2009, President Obama's Secretary of Interior, Ken Salazar, initiated the development of a new five-year leasing program for 2010–2015 that included once-banned areas of the East and West coasts. In one of the great ironies of history, just as these large areas were opened to leasing, the worst oil spill in the nation's history occurred when the Macondo well being drilled by BP, using a rig called the Deepwater Horizon, blew out and spewed almost 5 million barrels of oil into the Gulf for almost three months before being capped.

In response, a major reorganization of the federal offshore leasing agency occurred, short-term moratoria were placed on any further exploratory drilling in the Gulf, and the Five Year Leasing Plan for 2010–2015 became a plan for 2012–2017, with fewer planning areas included. In early 2014, DOI's new leasing agency, the Bureau of Ocean Energy Management (BOEM), issued a final Programmatic Environmental Review for seismic surveys of the mid-Atlantic coast from Delaware to Florida. Actual lease sales off the Atlantic would not occur until the

2017–22 lease schedule. Seismic ships use air guns to generate sound vibrations that penetrate the seabed. There is increasing evidence that air guns can have injurious effects on marine mammals. BOEM requires that seismic companies suspend air gun blasts when whales and dolphins are sighted. The BOEM website has extensive information on the leasing program. www.boem.gov.

Can recalcitrant coastal states be lured into accepting oil and gas development through a revenue-sharing mechanism that gives them more of the OCS bounty? States currently receive 50 percent of federal onshore oil and gas revenues, but such largesse does not extend to the OCS. Six states with OCS production began to receive 27 percent of OCS revenues in 1986 under section 1337(g) of OCSLA, but only from federal leases directly bordering their submerged lands, *i.e.*, within 3 miles of the border of the state-owned coastal waters. However, much OCS production is now located much further out on the continental shelf, and there is no revenue sharing with the states from these OCS leases. *See generally* Edward A. Fitzgerald, The Conservation and Reinvestment Act of 1999: Outer Continental Shelf Revenue Sharing, 30 Envtl. L. Rptr. 10,165 (Envtl. L. Inst., Mar. 2000). In 2006, the Gulf of Mexico Energy Security Act (GOMESA) (Pub. L. No. 109–432) provided that 37.5% of qualified OCS revenues for new leases in certain areas go to the four Gulf states of Alabama, Louisiana, Mississippi, and Texas through 2017, at which point another revenue-sharing formula will apply through 2055.

Senator Mary Landrieu of Louisiana has been especially active in promoting increased revenue shares to the states. Louisiana's coastline has been severely impacted by a network of canals dredged by pipeline companies for their transportation facilities or by oil companies to float drilling equipment to state-owned coastal lands. These canals have contributed to erosion of Louisiana's coastal wetlands. In short, Louisiana is sinking and shrinking. *See, e.g.,* Terrebonne Parish School Board v. Columbia Gulf Transmission Co., 290 F.3d 303 (5th Cir. 2002). A 2009 report by the federal Minerals Management Service concluded that oil and gas pipelines serving OCS production in the Gulf of Mexico are responsible for severe habitat changes and loss of coastal wetlands. In Louisiana alone, OCS pipelines and canals cover 11% of the state's coast. James B. Johnston, DOI, Outer Continental Shelf (OCS)-Related Pipelines and Navigational Canals in the Western and Central Gulf of Mexico: Relative Impacts on Wetland Habitats and Effectiveness of Mitigation 31, Tab. 1.7 (2009).

In 2006, the state of Louisiana sought to enjoin DOI from moving forward with Lease Sale 200 only weeks after hurricanes Katrina and Rita had ripped through its coasts, arguing that DOI had not analyzed the impacts of these storms on its damaged coastlines. While the state's suit was dismissed by a federal district court, the failed effort to use the CZMA, NEPA, and OCSLA actually resulted in a victory for Louisiana through a favorable settlement agreement with DOI, granting the state considerable oversight of leasing until DOI had completed a new environmental impact statement that included the hurricane impacts. *See* Amy McIntire, Oil and Gas Development on the Outer Continental Shelf: The Uphill Battle for State Input in Federal Policy, 9 Tex. J. Oil, Gas & Energy L. 38 (2014).

Because of the moratoria, there has been little opportunity for agencies, state officials, or courts to test the difference between "directly affecting" and "affecting" in post-1990 consistency certifications. Between 1978 and 2003, DOI approved over 10,600 Exploration Plans and over 6,000 Development Plans, but only 14 instances occurred where a lessee appealed a state's consistency objection to the Secretary of Commerce. In seven of the 14 cases, the Secretary overrode the state objection; in the other seven, he did not. David W. Kaiser, The Coastal Zone Management Act Furthers Offshore Oil and Gas Development and Supports a National Energy Policy, 54 Inst. on Oil & Gas, Ch. 13 at 13–8 (2003).

Withdrawals of onshore federal lands from oil and gas and other resource development have also occurred throughout our nation's history. Congress has often voted to create national parks and wilderness areas in which development is forbidden. When Congress has refused to act quickly to protect areas against commercial activity, presidents have acted unilaterally under the Antiquities Act of 1906. This Act authorizes the President "in his discretion to declare by public proclamation historic landmarks, historic and prehistoric structures and other objects of historic or scientific interest that are situated upon the lands owned or controlled by the Government of the United States to be national monuments." 16 U.S.C. § 431. President Roosevelt withdrew 1,279 square miles of the Grand Canyon from future mining claims under this Act in 1908. A full accounting of the many laws and policies for resource use and management of our federal lands, such as national forests, grazing lands, wildlife refuges and parks, demands its own course. The boom in shale development in the United States since 2003 has largely occurred on privately owned lands.

4.   OFFSHORE WASTES AND THE CLEAN WATER ACT

All too frequently, regulations designed to improve one environmental condition create an environmental problem elsewhere. An offshore platform is a world in microcosm. As waste products are generated, they can be deposited in the ocean, reinjected at the platform, or shipped back to shore for burial.

The EPA, after long study and debate, issued regulations governing waste disposal from offshore operations. Both industry and environmentalists challenged the regulations. In a voluminous decision, the Sixth Circuit addressed the complaints of both sides. The Clean Water Act (CWA), like the Clean Air Act (CAA), presents a maze of almost impenetrable acronyms, largely defining the severity of technological controls that industry must use. Yet the legal issues can be clearly grasped in the excerpted version of this case, which illustrates both the workings of the CWA and the work of judges tackling complex technical issues. As a preface, consider Professor Oliver Houck's ode to BAT—the Best Available Technology standard at issue in the case—as the alternative to an earlier approach that was failing to clean up water:

> [The earlier] Federal Water Pollution Control Act aimed at the attainment of water quality standards. Scientists would establish concentration limits for every pollutant, and when waters exceeded these limits, scientists would determine the cause and require abatement. But concentration limits for what use: swimming, drinking water, or fishing? If for fishing, would

the target be catfish or trout? . . . States lowered their standards to attract industry, which then held them hostage under the threat of moving away.

The "scientific" part of the act . . . involved extrapolating "acceptable" concentration limits from laboratory experiments to natural surroundings; from single pollutants to cocktails of multiple pollutants; and then from rapid, observable, lethal effects to long-term, sublethal, and reproductive effects. . . . When it came next to enforcement, someone had to prove who and what were causing the exceedance of the standards. . . . [W]as it the cattle farming, the shoe tannery, the local sewage system, or Mother Nature?

In 1972, after 15 years of futility with the water quality standards program, during which the Cuyahoga River and the Houston Ship Canal caught fire, . . . Congress changed the rules of the clean water game and adopted a new standard: best available technology (BAT).

The theory of BAT was very simple: If emissions could be reduced, just do it. It did not matter what the impacts were. . . . It didn't matter what scientists said the harm was or where it came from. Just do it.

Oliver Houck, Tales from a Troubled Marriage: Science and Law in Environmental Policy, 302 Science 1926–1929, Dec. 12, 2003.

BP Exploration & Oil, Inc. v. EPA

66 F.3d 784 (6th Cir. 1995).

■ BATCHELDER, J. * * * For the reasons that follow, we affirm the effluent limitations promulgated by the Environmental Protection Agency (EPA) for the offshore oil and gas industry.

I.

The disputed effluent limitations guidelines are the final regulations and standards of performance for the "Offshore Subcategory of the Oil and Gas Extraction Point Source Category," published pursuant to sections 301, 304, and 306 of the Clean Water Act (CWA or "Act"). 33 U.S.C.A. §§ 1311, 1314, 1316 (West 1986). . . . These regulations (the "Final Rule") were also formulated in response to a Consent Decree entered on April 5, 1990, in *NRDC v. Reilly*, C.A. No. 79–3442 (D.D.C.) (subsequently modified on May 28, 1992). The Final Rule became effective on April 5, 1993, ending a process that began in 1975 with EPA's publication of interim guidelines for the offshore oil and gas industry.

[Industry Petitioners BP Exploration & Oil, Inc., the American Petroleum Institute and others] contend that the effluent standards are too stringent. . . . [P]etitioner Natural Resources Defense Council, Inc. (NRDC), representing environmental interests, contends that EPA violated the CWA by promulgating effluent standards that are generally too lenient. . . .

A.   The Clean Water Act

The objective of the CWA "is to restore and maintain the chemical, physical, and biological integrity of the Nation's waters." § 1251.

Congress' original goal was for the discharge of all pollutants into navigable waters to be eliminated by the year 1985. § 1251(a)(1). Consequently, the discharge of any pollutant is illegal unless made in compliance with the provisions of the CWA. . . .

The CWA directs EPA to formulate national effluent limitation guidelines for those entities that discharge pollutants into the navigable waters of the United States. In formulating these guidelines, the CWA directs EPA to institute progressively more stringent effluent discharge guidelines in stages. Congress intended EPA to consider numerous factors in addition to pollution reduction: "The Committee believes that there must be a reasonable relationship between costs and benefits if there is to be an effective and workable program." Clean Water Act of 1972, Pub. L. No. 92–500, 1972 U.S.C.C.A.N. (86 Stat.) 3713.

At the first stage of pollutant reduction, EPA is to determine the level of effluent reduction achievable within an industry with the implementation of the "best practicable control technology currently available" (BPT). § 314(b)(1)(A). In general, BPT is the average of the best existing performances by industrial plants of various sizes, ages, and unit processes within the point source category or subcategory. In arriving at BPT for an industry, EPA is to consider several factors, including the total cost of the application of the technology in relation to the effluent reduction benefits to be achieved from such application.[4][19] For the offshore oil and gas subcategory, BPT was to be achieved by July 1, 1977. § 1311(b)(1)(A).

At the second stage, EPA is to set generally more stringent standards for toxic and conventional pollutants. For toxic pollutants, EPA is to set the standard for the "best available technology economically achievable" (BAT). BAT represents, at a minimum, the best economically achievable performance in the industrial category or subcategory. Compared to BPT, BAT calls for more stringent control technology that is both technically available and economically achievable. Among the factors that EPA must consider and take into account when setting BAT are the cost of achieving such effluent reduction and the non-water quality environmental impact including the energy requirements of the technology. § 1314(b)(2)(B). For the offshore oil and gas subcategory, BAT was to be achieved by July 1, 1987. § 1311(b)(2)(A).

Conventional pollutants[8][20] are treated differently from toxics under the CWA. Pursuant to 1977 amendments to the Act, a new standard was conceived for conventional pollutants entitled "best conventional pollutant control technology" (BCT). This standard is designed to control conventional pollutants about which much is known but for which stringent BAT standards might require unnecessary treatment. Congress intended for BCT to prevent the implementation of technology for technology's sake. BCT is not an additional level of control, but replaces BAT for conventional pollutants. [The court then explained

---

[19] Other factors EPA must consider are the age of equipment and facilities involved, the process employed, the engineering aspects of the application of various types of control techniques, process changes, non-water quality environmental impacts, and such other factors as the Administrator deems appropriate. § 1314(b)(1)(B); *see also EPA v. Nat'l Crushed Stone Ass'n*, 449 U.S. 64, 71 n.10 (1980).

[20] Conventional pollutants include biochemical oxygen demand (BOD), total suspended solids (TSS) (nonfilterable), pH, fecal coliform, oil and grease. 40 C.F.R. § 401.16 (1994).

the BCT standard, which is based on both an explicit "cost reasonableness" test and an additional factor.]

Finally, the CWA directs EPA to establish a separate standard for new sources of pollutants. These "new source performance standards" (NSPS) require application of the technology chosen as BAT to remove all types of pollutants from new sources within each category. § 1316. Factors to be considered in formulating NSPS include the cost of achieving such effluent reduction and any non-water quality environmental impact and energy requirements. § 1316 (b) (1) (B).

* * *

C. The Industry

EPA identified a total of 2,550 offshore structures that will be affected by the Final Rule. Of these structures, 2,517 are located in the Gulf of Mexico, 32 are located off the coast of California, and one is located off the coast of Alaska. Petitioners challenge those portions of EPA's Final Rule relating to (1) produced water, (2) drilling fluids and drill cuttings, and (3) produced sand. Although wastewater originates both from the exploration and development process and from the production phase of the oil and gas industry's offshore operations, drilling fluids make up the majority of the effluent produced from exploration and development, and produced water represents a majority of the effluent from production. Produced sand is a minimal component of the effluent from production.

D. The Standard of Review

[The court reiterated the standard principles of judicial review of agency action. If Congressional intent is clear, it must be given effect. *Chevron, U.S.A., Inc. v. Natural Resources Defense Council, Inc.*, 467 U.S. 837, 842 (1984). If the statute is silent or ambiguous, the question for the court is whether the agency's answer is based on a permissible construction of the statute. Much deference must be given to an agency's construction of a statutory scheme that it is entrusted to administer. A court must set aside agency action, findings, and conclusions if they are found to be "arbitrary, capricious, an abuse of discretion, or otherwise not in accordance with law." 5 U.S.C. § 706(2)(A). The court must be the most deferential in reviewing an agency's scientific determinations within its area of expertise.]

II.A. Produced Water

The bulk of produced water is water trapped in underground reservoirs along with oil and gas that eventually rises to the surface with the produced oil and gas. Most of the oil and gas in the produced water is separated as part of the oil and gas extraction process. The remaining produced water, still containing some oil and grease, is then discharged overboard or otherwise disposed of. Produced water also includes the injection water used for secondary oil recovery and various well treatment chemicals added during production and oil and gas extraction. Produced water is the highest volume waste source in the offshore oil and gas industry.

Under the Final Rule, EPA determined that BAT and NSPS would be set to limit the discharge of oil and grease[21] in produced water to a daily maximum of 42 mg/l and a monthly average of 29 mg/l, based on the improved operating performance of gas flotation technology (otherwise referred to as improved gas flotation). BCT for produced water was set by the Final Rule to equal current BPT limitations (72 mg/l daily maximum, 48 mg/l 30-day average).

Gas flotation is a technology that forces small gas bubbles into the wastewater to be treated. As the bubbles rise through the produced water, they attach themselves to any oil droplets in their paths. As the gas and oil are separated from the wastewater, they rise to the surface, where they are skimmed away. EPA characterizes "improved performance" gas flotation as the gas flotation technology enhanced through improved operation and maintenance, more operator attention to treatment systems operations, chemical pretreatment to enhance system effectiveness, and possible resizing of certain treatment system components for increased treatment efficiency. . . . In setting the limits, EPA used the "median" platform from the 83 Platform Composite Study. In other words, 50 percent of the platforms in the study discharged higher levels of pollutant, and 50 percent of the platforms discharged lower levels of pollutant. The daily maximum limitation was set so that there would be a 99 percent likelihood that a physical composite sample taken from the median platform would have a total oil and grease measurement less than or equal to that limitation. The monthly average was set so that there would be a 95 percent probability that a monthly average taken from the median platform would also be less than or equal to that limitation. EPA estimates that 60 percent of the platforms in the composite of 83 platforms already meet the new BAT limitations. For those platforms that do not already meet the new BAT standard, chemical coagulants can be used to improve the removal of dissolved or soluble oil.

In light of the deference due the EPA, especially concerning scientific and technical data, Industry petitioners have not proven their claim that improved gas flotation does not remove "dissolved" oil or that EPA violated either the CWA or the Administrative Procedure Act (APA) by using Method 413.1 to measure oil and grease in produced water.

[The court also upheld the EPA's refusal to regulate radioactive pollutants (called radionuclides) in produced water on the basis that inadequate information on environmental and health harms existed to issue such rules. The EPA was gathering information and intended to require radium monitoring as part of the permitting process for offshore oil and gas producers.]

3.   Reinjection of Produced Water

The NRDC also contends that EPA illegally refused to require zero discharge of produced waters through reinjection because record evidence shows that reinjection is technologically and economically feasible. . . .

---

[21] Although oil and grease are conventional pollutants rather than toxics, oil and grease are limited under BAT and NSPS as an "indicator" pollutant to measure discharge of toxic and nonconventional pollutants. – Eds.

EPA admits that reinjection may be technologically feasible.[14][22] The only evidence that reinjection may not be feasible is the possibility that geologic formations in some areas may preclude reinjection. However, EPA's rejection of reinjection as a BAT, while based in part on concerns regarding feasibility, was, more importantly, based on several relevant factors, such as unacceptably high economic and nonwater quality environmental impacts.

EPA estimates the cost of implementing reinjection as BAT and NSPS would exceed several billion dollars. The extraordinary cost was one basis for rejecting reinjection, although NRDC is correct that EPA did not conclusively determine that reinjection was not economically attainable. In addition to the high expense of reinjection, the negative impact reinjection would have on air emissions and the loss of production resulting from reinjection combined to cause EPA to reject reinjection for BAT and NSPS.

EPA estimates that the implementation of reinjection at existing platforms in the Gulf and Alaska alone would increase the emission of air pollutants by 1,041 tons/year for BAT and 849 tons/year for NSPS. The existing air quality of Southern California is so bad that reinjection was not considered an option at all. Reinjection was also rejected based on the increased energy required to run the reinjection pumps. According to EPA, reinjection would result in additional energy requirements of 977,000 barrels of oil equivalent (BOE)/year for BAT and 785,000 BOE/year for NSPS. Finally, EPA projected that reinjection would result in a one percent loss in production. (It is worth noting that one percent of oil and gas production from the Gulf of Mexico amounts to several million BOE/year.) The accumulation of these factors led EPA to reject reinjection as BAT and NSPS for produced water.

We think that EPA acted within its statutory authority in rejecting zero discharge based on reinjection. As EPA correctly points out, NRDC's contention that economic, energy, and nonwater quality environmental impacts are less important than achieving zero discharge merely reflects NRDC's disagreement on a policy level. This Court may not substitute NRDC's judgment, any more than our own, for that of the EPA.

* * *

[The court then discussed the EPA standard for disposing of drilling fluids and drill cuttings. EPA's Final Rule prohibited all discharges of these fluids and cuttings from wells located within three nautical miles from shore for the Gulf and California. This "zero discharge" rule required that all such material be barged to shore and disposed in landfills. Beyond three miles, the materials could be discharged under BCT after meeting the "static sheen" test. Industry challenged the three-mile zero discharge limit, arguing that EPA used poor data in its cost analysis. The court found that EPA did indeed make some mistakes, but better data would not effect the ultimate result reached by EPA.

---

[22] A majority of the platforms in California already reinject their produced water to enable recovery of the heavy crude oil that is typically produced in that part of the country. The only offshore rig in Alaska also reinjects its produced water in order to comply with state regulation. Reinjection of produced water is much less common in the Gulf of Mexico, although some studies have shown it to be feasible there as well. It is important to remember, however, that of 2,500 offshore platforms, only 33 platforms are located off the coast of California and Alaska.

Similarly, the court found that EPA may well have erred in classifying drill cuttings as solids suspended in water because a large percentage of the stream of drill cuttings are heavy bits of rock that sink immediately to the ocean floor without disturbing water quality by being suspended in the water. While finding "merit" in industry's argument, the court upheld the EPA's final rule.

Finally the court addressed the NRDC's argument that all drilling muds and cuttings should be barged ashore, even from beyond the three-mile limit, because barging was technologically available and economically achievable. The EPA had rejected the "zero discharge everywhere" rule because of lack of landfill capacity in the Gulf region and air pollution impacts in California. The opinion continues:]

NRDC generally charges that EPA cannot reject zero discharge on the basis of possible increased air emissions. According to NRDC, EPA cannot reject a limit based on non-water quality environmental impacts unless the impacts are "wholly disproportionate" to the possible pollution reduction. NRDC also argues that the estimated addition of 54 tons/year of air pollution off the coast of California is small compared to the present degree of air pollution in California, and that offshore platforms that increase air emissions would be able to purchase pollution offsets to compensate for the increased air pollution. We find each of NRDC's arguments unpersuasive.

The overriding principle in our review of the Final Rule is that the agency has broad discretion to weigh all relevant factors during rulemaking. The CWA does not state what weight should be accorded to the relevant factors; rather, the Act gives EPA the discretion to make those determinations. . . . Compared to the benefit of a zero discharge requirement for all California offshore platforms, EPA views this increase in air pollution to be unjustified.

Furthermore, Southern California is a severe nonattainment area under the measurements of the Clean Air Act (CAA). There is some doubt that emissions offsets are available at any cost. Even if offsets could be purchased by offshore oil producers, they would cost approximately $15,000 per ton of nitrogen dioxide and $5,000 per ton of hydrocarbons. . . .

For the foregoing reasons, we AFFIRM the Final Rule ■

NOTES AND COMMENTS

1.   Do you feel confident in either the EPA's or the judge's ability to understand the technical or economic aspects of an industrial activity? The court repeatedly found that the EPA had erred in its analysis or had used poor data, but still upheld the rule. Is there a better way to formulate control standards than through the rulemaking procedures under the Administrative Procedure Act? Regulatory negotiations, or "reg-negs," are a form of alternative dispute resolution designed to bring together potential litigants to resolve differences before a proposed rule is published. In 1985, Santa Barbara County sued Exxon to force better air pollution controls on its offshore platforms. The federal government held three years of reg-negs with five different caucuses (the oil industry, environmentalists, federal, state, and local governments), but to no avail. The reg-neg process failed because of disputes about factual issues, the complexity of technical issues,

and whipsawing national politics. *See* William Fulton, "Reg-Neg: How California's First Regulatory Negotiations Fell Victim to the Politics of Offshore Drilling," 9 Calif. Lawyer 65 (Nov. 1989). Exxon did agree, however, to fully electrify its Santa Ynez project (in lieu of using diesel fuel) at a cost of millions of dollars. *Id.* at 136. Does this victory for Santa Barbara simply move pollution around, perhaps to the coal-fired power plants near the Grand Canyon? Or to the new Ivanpah solar plant built in the California Mojave desert in 2013? See Chapter 11.

2.   Do you agree with Professor Houck's positive assessment of a technology-based approach to cleaning up pollution? Suppose industry "just does it" and all firms adopt the requisite technologies to reduce water pollution. Yet the Cuyahoga River is still unsafe for human contact or fishing. The Clean Water Act has a second-stage system of pollution control based on water quality standards. States must classify each body of water for particular uses every three years, and then set a Total Daily Maximum Load (TDML) of discharges into that water body by all the parties using that water to dispose of wastes under authorized permits. The goal is to ultimately achieve a fishable/swimmable classification. If the discharges exceed the total maximum load, then some users have to either shut down or adopt better technology to reduce the total discharges. Does this approach remind you of the difficulties of agreeing to "fair shares" in unitizing a common reservoir? For an overview of the Clean Water Act, see Mark Ryan (ed.), The Clean Water Act Handbook (3d ed. 2011).

3.   Note that new platforms are subject to more stringent technological standards than existing sources under the CWA. A similar statutory framework—the CAA's New Source Review provisions—has been a source of contentious litigation. See Chapter 5. Oil companies and environmental organizations joined battle in 2010 over EPA's standards for the cooling water intake structures for new and existing offshore rigs, with an outcome largely favorable to the EPA's defense of its rule. *See* ConocoPhillips Co. v. U.S. EPA, 612 F.3d 822 (5th Cir. 2010).

4.   Virtually all produced water from conventional oil and gas wells onshore is reinjected. The disposal of flowback water and produced water from shale fields is discussed *supra* in section (C)(6).

5.   In 2003, an EPA report found that 25% of major industrial facilities were in "significant noncompliance" with their CWA discharge permits, but few were penalized by the agency. "Significant noncompliance" can indicate discharges above permitted levels or paperwork violations, such as late filing of monitoring reports. In 2001, nearly half of the facilities that violated their permit limits for toxic pollutants had exceedances that were twice the allowable levels. Thirteen percent of exceedances were 1,000 percent above permitted levels for toxic pollutants. The report stated that some EPA staff believe some of these exceedances may be the result of unachievable water quality-based limits due to technical limitations or cost. Susan Bruninga, Most Large Industrial Sites Not Penalized for Violations of their Discharge Permits, Daily Rept. for Executives, June 9, 2003, at A–29. EPA's Clean Water Action Plan issued on October 15, 2009 continued to find significant noncompliance (SNC) defined as "serious violations that are considered to be . . . significant to water quality" at both large discharging facilities (24% in SNC) and at smaller facilities (48% in SNC).

       Are our environmental laws just too complicated for even the best-intentioned firms to ever be in compliance? *See* J.B. Ruhl & James Salzman,

Mozart and the Red Queen: The Problem of Regulatory Accretion in the Administrative State, 91 Georgetown L.J. 757 (2003) (yes); David B. Spence, The Shadow of the Rational Polluter: Rethinking the Role of Rational Actor Models in Environmental Law, 89 Cal. L. Rev. 917 (2001) (yes).

6.   If the EPA determines that a state has failed to impose the best available technology in a permit approving a developer's project (perhaps because the state is more disposed to welcome industry for the jobs and taxes that it brings), can the federal agency overrule the state? In a sharply divided opinion, the U.S. Supreme Court, in *Alaska Dep't of Environmental Conservation v. EPA*, 540 U.S. 461 (2004), upheld an EPA determination that Alaska had not required BAT to control air pollution in a permit issued for expansion of the world's largest zinc mine. The Red Dog mine, 100 miles north of the Arctic Circle, is the largest private employer in northwest Alaska. Alaskan officials had selected a "logistically and economically less onerous" technology as BAT, but the EPA ruled that the state had not justified its refusal to adopt a cleaner technology. The dissent characterized the holding as "relegating states to the role of mere provinces or political corporations, instead of coequal sovereigns." *Id.* at 518.

5. OFFSHORE SPILLS, BLOWOUTS AND SAFETY MANAGEMENT SYSTEMS

As noted, the 1969 Santa Barbara platform blowout has had an enduring legacy in the wave of subsequent federal environmental legislation and in continued opposition to offshore leasing in certain states. Here is a "brief recollection" of the event in an opinion by the Ninth Circuit Court of Appeals some 32 years after the blowout:

> Five miles off the shore of the small beach town of Summerland, California, at 10:45 a.m. on Tuesday, January 28, 1969, crews on Union Oil Company offshore Platform Alpha were pulling the drilling tube out of well A–21 in order to assess their progress. Mud began to ooze up from the depths through the well shaft. . . . Within minutes, tons of mud spewed out of the top of the well propelled by a blast of natural gas. . . . The unlined walls of the well shaft gave way and oil poured into the surrounding geological formation under the sea floor. As the pressure continued to build, the oil burst upward through the roof of the Venture Anticline, ripped five long gashes in the ocean floor, and rose 188 feet through the blue-green waters of the Santa Barbara channel [spreading a tar-black patch seaward over 800 square miles of ocean for a week, after which the wind shifted and drove the oil onto 30 miles of coastal beaches where an "acrid stench" clung to the shoreline for weeks on end].* * *

> The nation was confronted with an environmental disaster of unprecedented proportions that might have been avoided but for a failure of federal oversight. A federal regulator had approved Union Oil's request to waive safety requirements that called for well shafts to be lined with hardened casing to prevent just the type of accident that occurred.

California v. Norton, 311 F.3d 1162 (9th Cir. 2002).

Two other spills, far larger than the Santa Barbara one, are discussed in this next section: the first from the *Exxon Valdez* tanker, the second from the blowout of BP's Macondo well in the Gulf of Mexico in 2010. While the *Exxon Valdez* spill did not involve oil production, the spill triggered enactment of the Oil Pollution Act that now governs both onshore and offshore producers. The reading also previews (rather eerily) the key issue that arises in the BP blowout case, notably: How can the law change human behavior in high-risk situations where an act of simple negligence can cause a disaster? The nuclear and pipeline industries face this same issue. As you read this material, also consider the respective roles of the regulator and the industry actors in these events. If human error, which is almost always a root cause of disasters, cannot be prevented by law, is there a "fool-proof" technology that can safeguard against it?

a.   TANKER SPILLS

Art Davison, In the Wake of the Exxon Valdez: The Story of America's Most Devastating Oil Spill 10–18 (1990)

By 9:00 p.m., [on March 23, 1989] the *Exxon Valdez* was ready to depart. Earlier, Third Mate Gregory Cousins had tested the vessel's navigation equipment: radar, gyro compass, automatic pilot, course indicator, rudder control, and other sophisticated instrumentation. At 9:12 p.m., the tanker's last mooring line was detached from the pier and two tugs nudged the *Exxon Valdez* from its berth. On the bridge were harbor pilot Ed Murphy and Captain Hazelwood. Coast Guard regulations require that harbor pilots—who are trained to know about navigational hazards in local waters—be contracted to guide tankers from port to open water. Earlier, when they were boarding, Murphy had smelled alcohol on Hazelwood's breath but had said nothing about it.

At 9:21 p.m., Murphy, directing the vessel's speed and course settings, began to steer the *Exxon Valdez* out of the harbor toward Valdez Narrows, 7 miles from port. The Narrows, a channel that forms the entrance to Valdez Bay, is 1,700 yards wide. Middle Rock, a rock in the channel sometimes called "the can opener," reduces the minimum usable width to 900 yards. In computer simulations before the route was sanctioned, pilots repeatedly wrecked their imaginary tankers on Middle Rock. However, with the help of escort tugs and harbor pilots, tankers three football fields long had successfully negotiated the Narrows for eleven years. . . .

On this March 23 evening, the *Exxon Valdez* passed through the Narrows without mishap. Fourteen miles out of port, the tanker reached Rocky Point, where harbor pilots normally transfer command of a ship back to the captain. Murphy had to order Hazelwood called back to the bridge. When Hazelwood returned to the control room, Murphy again noticed the smell of alcohol on the captain's breath. However, a Valdez harbor pilot had never challenged a captain's command of his vessel. A pilot's continued employment by a given vessel can depend on the captain's good will. Murphy decided that Hazelwood looked fit and focused enough to assume command. At 11:20 p.m., Captain Joseph Hazelwood took control of the *Exxon Valdez*.

In the dimly lit radar room atop the three-story Coast Guard station in Valdez, civilian radar man Gordon Taylor watched a bright orange ring on the radar scope. The ring represented the *Exxon Valdez* as it moved from the terminal out through the Narrows. At Rocky Point, radar coverage became fainter and Taylor found it difficult to read. . . .

As the *Exxon Valdez* approached the edge of radar coverage, Hazelwood radioed the Coast Guard that he was "heading outbound and increasing speed."

[At 11:24 p.m., harbor pilot Murphy left the tanker on a pilot boat back to Valdez.]

Shortly after Hazelwood notified the Coast Guard that he was going to divert from the Traffic Separation Scheme (designated one-way inbound and outbound tanker lanes), he radioed that he was going to angle left and reduce speed in order to work through some floating ice . . . . However, despite Hazelwood's assurance to the Coast Guard, the ship's speed was not reduced.

. . . Third Mate Gregory Cousins had joined Hazelwood on the bridge to make a navigational fix on the vessel's position in the sound. The night was too dark for the seaman on watch to see any bergs, but ice was silhouetted on the radar screen. It was an extensive floe—thousands of chunks of ice had broken from the Columbia Glacier and were being massed together by the current. Cousins and Hazelwood discussed skirting the ice. Some of the ice, broken into pieces the size of a car and smaller, were of little consequence to a tanker. But the massive bergs—those the size of a house and larger, the ones they called growlers—caused concern. However, Cousins couldn't tell from the radar screen whether there were any growlers out there in the night.

The northern edge of the floe appeared to be two miles dead ahead. At their current course setting, they would run into it. The ice was backed up to Columbia Glacier, so they couldn't pass it to the right. To the left of the ice was a gap of nine-tenths of a mile between the edge of the ice and Bligh Reef. They could wait until the ice moved, or reduce speed and work their way through the ice. Captain Hazelwood chose another option: turn and enter the gap between the ice and the reef.

. . . A well-timed right turn would be necessary to avoid Bligh Reef, which lay six miles ahead in the darkness. There would be little room for error. The vessel needed at least six-tenths of a mile to make the turn, and the gap between the ice and Bligh Reef was only nine-tenths of a mile wide. The tanker itself was nearly two-tenths of a mile long. The tanker would have to start its turn well before the gap between the ice and the reef if it was to make it through.

. . . Helmsman Harry Claar's shift was coming to an end. Claar's job as helmsman was to physically move the steering wheel at the direction of the captain or qualified mates. Hazelwood gave him two last orders: to accelerate to sea speed and to put the ship on automatic pilot. Both commands were highly unusual. Speed was normally reduced when ice was encountered, both to minimize impact with bergs and to allow the crew more time to plot vessel position, make course adjustments, and react to an emergency. The automatic pilot—almost never used in the sound—would have to be released if any course changes had to be made.

Though puzzled by Hazelwood's orders, Claar increased speed and locked the controls on automatic pilot. He was then replaced at the helm by Robert Kagan.

On the bridge, Hazelwood told Cousins he was going below and asked if he felt comfortable navigating alone. Cousins had made only a few voyages with Hazelwood, and he had never maneuvered the *Exxon Valdez* in tight quarters. Nevertheless, he replied, "Yes, I feel I can manage the situation."

Standard Coast Guard procedure dictates that in the presence of danger, two officers must be on the bridge. The junior of the two is responsible for fixing the location of the vessel. The senior officer is responsible for directing the vessel's course based on this navigational information. Before leaving Cousins alone on the bridge, Hazelwood told him to make a right turn when the ship was across from the Busby Island light and to skirt the edge of the ice—but he neither gave Cousins an exact course to follow nor plotted a line on the chart. If he had, Hazelwood might have noticed that it was virtually impossible to turn abeam the Busby light and also miss the ice.

Hazelwood left the bridge at 11:53 p.m. "to send a few messages from [my] cabin." Cousins was now the only officer on the bridge. The chief mate and second mate were off duty, resting. Moments after the captain left, Cousins . . . discovered that the vessel was on automatic pilot, and he shifted it back into manual mode. The ship was still headed toward Bligh Reef, and Cousins faced a critical maneuver: he had to avoid the ice but couldn't wait too long before turning. The vessel was increasing speed.

At 11:55 p.m., Cousins called Hazelwood to say, "I think there's a chance that we may get into the edge of this ice." Hazelwood said, "Okay," and asked if the second mate had made it to the bridge yet. Cousins replied that the second mate hadn't arrived. They talked for less than a minute and neither mentioned slowing the vessel down.

Once more, Cousins assured the captain that he could handle things and then told the helmsman to make a 10-degree right turn. Cousins turned again to the radar, trying to locate the leading edge of ice. As he concentrated on the ice, Cousins may have lost track of time for a few minutes. He was peering at the radar screen when the tanker slipped past the Busby Island light without beginning to turn.

It was nearly midnight, the beginning of Good Friday, March 24, when Maureen Jones, now on watch, noticed that the red light on the Bligh Reef buoy was to the ship's right [instead of to its left, where it should have been]. . . .

At virtually the same moment, though the ship was turning slowly, Cousins concluded that the tanker had not responded to his 10-degree right-turn command. He ordered a 20-degree right turn, and this time he noticed the vessel responding.

Jones called Cousins a second time [to report the light on the wrong side of the ship]. Cousins ordered a hard right and called Hazelwood, saying, "I think we are in serious trouble."

At 12:04 a.m., the *Exxon Valdez* shuddered. Hazelwood raced to the bridge. After first impact, the tanker advanced 600 feet before it ground to a halt on Bligh Reef.

Hazelwood didn't try to back off the reef. With the engines running full speed forward, he ordered a hard right, then a hard left. In the engine room, the chief engineer did not know they had grounded; he couldn't figure out why the system was overloading. ∎

b.   REMEDIAL LEGISLATION: OPA 90

The *Exxon Valdez* spill was to the Oil Pollution Act of 1990 (often called OPA 90) as the Santa Barbara spill was to NEPA and the Coastal Zone Management Act. OPA 90 passed the Senate without a single dissenting vote, even though attempts to strengthen oil spill laws had foundered for years until then.

It seems clear from the account of the *Exxon Valdez* spill that human behavior played a large role in the grounding of this massive tanker. Professor Rodgers, an avid student of evolutionary biology and its interface with environmental law, warns of the "false behavioral assumptions" that underlie laws and cause lawmakers to delude themselves that a law will result in effective compliance. In William H. Rodgers, Jr., Where Environmental Law and Biology Meet: Of Panda's Thumbs, Statutory Sleepers, and Effective Law, 65 U. Colo. L. Rev. 25 (1993), Professor Rodgers discusses the provisions of OPA aimed at the "specter of the drunken captain, personified as Joseph Hazelwood, that drove [OPA's] legislative engine," by creating procedures for what Rodgers terms a "legalized mutiny."

Section 4104 of OPA 90 requires the second-in-command to take charge of a vessel when the two next most senior officers on a vessel "reasonably believe that the master or individual in charge of the vessel is under the influence of alcohol or a dangerous drug and is incapable of commanding the vessel." 46 U.S.C. § 8101(i). Professor Rodgers constructs a "compliancegram" that assesses the likelihood that a junior officer will know of this law, recognize the risk, overcome hesitation to take over the vessel, persuade his colleagues to join in the takeover, and defeat other practical barriers to the takeover. Here is Professor Rodgers' analysis of what he calls the junior officers' "mutiny rights."

> The big problem with risk recognition (R) is in appreciating that the drunken captain is "incapable" of commanding the vessel. The situation is bound to be ambiguous (the captain might be only slightly drunk, . . . or waters could be calm, or the automatic-pilot dependable, etc.), and ambiguity can be resolved as non-threatening in the mind of a junior officer. There is evidence also that self-deception may be at work to convince both the captain and the junior officers that the risks are non-emergent.

> Having recognized the risk, will the mate overcome (O) hesitation to put in motion the machinery of this legalized mutiny? Even with personal safety at stake, the behavioral constraints against this sort of challenge to authority are formidable. Within primate bands, the very idea of a "temporary" takeover of leadership is implausible because of

small rewards and high risks of subsequent retaliation. Sociological studies of modern bureaucracies underscore the difficulties of encouraging communication contrary to established norms,[266][23] much less direct challenges to the authority of the leadership. In the maritime world, of course, centuries of tradition have accorded the captain a role of unquestioned authority, and those in the business are entirely familiar with the career-threatening consequences of challenging these traditions. Junior officers who will rock this boat will be made of stern and unusual stuff.

Id. at 68–69.

The article continues the scenario of the junior officer trying to convince a second junior officer about the need for a takeover. The second officer will also need to contemplate "a course of action under highly ambiguous and stressful conditions that will be of some considerable risk to her career. *Id.* at 69. Then, will the crew cooperate? What if the captain resists with force? Professor Rodgers does not have great faith in Section 4104's mutiny provisions as a bulwark against maritime accidents.

Professor Rodgers similarly has little faith in first responders' ability to contain a large spill. He points to an account of the after-spill events by Professor Plater that documented the behavior of the key actors under the oil spill contingency plans that had been part of the water pollution laws since the 1960s. After the grounding of the tanker, fishermen in Prince William Sound watched as the pool of oil spilling from the tanker spread over the calm seas that fortuitously existed during the first 40 hours of the event. Yet, no one from either government or industry appeared with skimming barges, containment booms or any such equipment. As the second day ended, high winds kicked in and within 24 hours, the spill spread 40 miles to the southeast, "out of control forevermore, as the official players still continued to try to figure out what to do." *Id.* at 70–71 (quoting Zygmunt J.B. Plater, A Modern Political Tribalism, in 13 Natural Resource Management, 11 Pub. Land L. Rev. 1, at 1–9 (1990)).

Rodgers' article continues:

The reasons for this contingency nonresponse are not much in doubt: confusion of authority (all looked to Alyeska [the Alaskan pipeline owners]), lack of preparedness (Exxon took over command of the response operation within twenty-four hours but was untrained for the job), staff limitations (supervision of all operations at the Valdez terminal was assigned to one-half the time of one full-time Alaska Department of Environmental Conservation field person), shortages of equipment (skimming barges, containment booms), lack of expertise (not enough people to operate the equipment,

---

[23] *See* Presidential Comm'n on the Space Shuttle Challenger Accident, Report to the President, chs. 4–5, 95–96, 99, 101, 107 (1986) (the contractors (Morton Thiokol) recommended against the launch because of concerns regarding O-ring temperatures, ran into opposition from middle-level NASA managers and Morton Thiokol's superiors (one key person was told to "take off his engineering hat and put on his management hat"), took another "perspective" under this pressure, identified an "ambiguity" in the data, and caved in by withdrawing the no-launch recommendation; NASA upper-level management responsible for the launch were never informed about the safety concerns or the engineers' opposition).

interpret the tides, etc.). It is another question, of course, and not a trivial one, to ask whether any response would have sufficed to contain the 10.8 million gallons of crude oil that found its way into the waters of Prince William Sound on March 22, 1989.

How did Congress respond to this demonstrated failure of contingency planning? By adding to the Act "an extremely elaborate system of contingency planning, consisting of a national response unit ("NRU"), Coast Guard strike teams, Coast Guard district response groups, area committees, area contingency plans, and individual vessel and facility response plans." The facility and vessel response plans, which have their own histories going back to 1973, must be written to combat a "worst case discharge" and are expected to cover topics such as training, equipment testing, unannounced drills, and planned responses.

Id. at 71.

Professor Rodgers then develops a "compliancegram" for OPA's mandated contingency plans, and concludes that:

[E]ven if the plans are written, they are unlikely to be adequate, and if adequate they are unlikely to be implemented, and if implemented they are unlikely to be successful. . . . A legislator might vote for the measure on symbolic grounds or because it is packaged with other effective provisions or because a plan might be helpful for dealing with small spills in confined waters.

Id. at 70.

NOTES AND COMMENTS

1.   As you read the following summary of other provisions of OPA 90, ask how they might affect the "compliancegram" for preventing oil spills. Which provisions best deal with the problem of human error? OPA applies to both spills from vessels and spills from offshore facilities:

(A) OPA charges the "Responsible Party" (RP) with strict liability for spills without regard to fault (unless the spill was solely caused by an act of God, an act of war, or the act of a very limited set of unaffiliated third parties). OPA defines RPs as the owner or operator of vessels (such as tankers); or, in the case of an offshore facility, the lessee/operator of the federal lease the facility is located on. 33 U.S.C § 2701. Thus, a defined RP has virtually no chance of escaping liability for oil spill damages. 33 U.S.C § 2703.

(B) RPs are strictly liable for all removal costs with no maximum liability cap for these cleanup costs. 33 U.S.C § 2702(a).

(C) RPs are also liable for other specified damages, but some caps on liability exist here. The liability limit for vessels depends on the size (gross ton weight) of the ship. The liability cap for an offshore facility is the "total of all removal costs plus $75 million" per incident. However the limits do not apply if the RP is found to have acted with gross negligence, willful misconduct, or in violation of applicable federal regulations. 33 U.S.C. § 2704.

(D) Six types of damages are recoverable. Three types are recoverable by private claimants: (1) economic losses from destruction of real or personal property caused by the spill (e.g., a shrimper's boat engine is destroyed by oil gunk in its intake); (2) damages equal to "the loss of profits or impairment of earning capacity due to the loss of property or natural resources" (e.g., the loss in income to fisherman and to beach hotel owners and store owners when tourists disappear); and (3) damages due to loss of subsistence use of natural resources (e.g., loss of fish or seal meat used as food sources). Three types of damages are recoverable only by governments: (1) damages for injury or loss of natural resources, recoverable by a government Trustee; (2) damages for the increased cost of public services incurred by the state during removal activities; and (3) damages equal to the net loss of taxes, royalties, rents and fees owed to governments. 33 U.S.C. § 2702(b)(2).

(E) A new Oil Spill Liability Trust fund was created to pay for costs in excess of the liability limits, funded by a cent-per-barrel tax on oil (currently set at 8 cents). The Fund can be used to pay for removal costs and other damages that the RP has not covered, for whatever reason. (Perhaps the RP faces bankruptcy.) The Fund is limited to paying out a maximum of $1 billion per incident. In June 2010, as the Gulf of Mexico spill widened, the Fund held a balance of $1.5 billion. *See* 26 U.S.C. § 9509 *et seq.*

(F) OPA 90 requires more drug and alcohol reporting, testing and retesting of merchant mariners and limits the number of hours worked to prevent exhaustion. 33 U.S.C § 4103.

(G) All newly constructed tankers must have double hulls, and existing tankers must be retrofitted for double hulls under a phased in schedule over 20 years. 33 U.S.C. § 4115.

(H) Civil penalties were dramatically increased, as were criminal sanctions, for failure to report discharges. 33 U.S.C. §§ 4301–4306.

In addition to OPA, criminal liability under the CWA, the Migratory Bird Treaty Act, OCSLA, the Refuse Act and the ESA may arise. Civil penalties are also available under many statutes.

2.   Note that cargo owners are not liable for spills under OPA. If Exxon had chartered a tanker owned by someone else, would Exxon have any liability for a spill of its cargo? What prevents cargo owners from chartering old, poorly maintained, low-cost tankers sailing under foreign "flags of convenience"?

3.   Does the saga of the *Exxon Valdez* affect your opinion about whether a "worst case analysis" of a 100,000 barrel oil spill should have been included in the challenged EIS in *Village of False Pass*, discussed in the notes following *Secretary of Interior v. California* in Section D.2 above? *See* Edward A. Fitzgerald, The Rise and Fall of Worst Case Analysis, 18 Dayton L. Rev. 1 (1992). OPA now requires a "worst case" response plan, defined as a spill of a vessel's entire cargo in adverse weather, as part of the national contingency plan, area contingency plans, and the facility response plan.

Are plans likely to work in the event of a worst-case disaster? In 1999, public health experts role-played a "high-impact" bio-terrorism event using smallpox as the agent to test the epidemic response plans of cities in the United States. The scenario left 15,000 people dead within two months and 80 million dead at the end of the year, primarily because of inadequate vaccine supplies globally. One expert declared: "Whatever planning we had

. . . didn't work." Laurie Garrett, "Smallpox Bioterrorism Exercise Proves Disaster in Preparedness," Houston Chron., Feb. 22, 1999, at 7A.

4.   The Coast Guard is the lead agency for assuring maritime safety. It approves plans for ship construction and inspects vessels and offshore drill ships and Mobile Offshore Drilling Units (MODU) to assure that workers onboard these facilities have a safe working environment. It also acts as one of five armed forces of the United States and is the only military organization under the Department of Homeland Security. The Coast Guard is charged with monitoring LNG tankers as they reach our shores and ports, not just for typical safety issues, but also to protect against terrorist attacks on these vessels.

Art Davidson's account of the *Exxon Valdez* spill excerpted *supra* describes the Coast Guard's actions that night. In 1981, the Valdez Coast Guard Commander had requested improved radar to ensure coverage between Bligh Island and the Columbia Glacier at a cost of $100,000. The request was viewed as "cost prohibitive," and President Reagan's war on drugs had drained the Guard's budget and moved staff to other places. In 1986, a new Valdez commander found no reason to upgrade the system because nothing had gone wrong in 12 years. Without the use of radar, the guardsman on duty that fateful night moved pieces of paper (the tanker traffic data sheets, one for each tanker in the area) around the room to simulate tanker movements so that he could send warnings if he spotted danger. He also left to get a cup of coffee for an unknown period of time. Davidson, *supra*, at 12–14.

5.   How do you prevent people working in areas where safety lapses can have huge consequences from becoming complacent after years of no trouble? The same problem affects any business in which the risk of failure is small but the cost of failure is catastrophic, such as the nuclear power industry, petrochemical facilities or LNG plants.

Has the decrease in oil spills after passage of OPA 90 led to complacency and lack of real situational experience by Oil Spill Response Organizations (OSROs) that must be able to arrive on scene within one hour of spill detection? A chief of port operations in the Coast Guard worried about this aspect of OPA's success. Sharon Grau, Oil Spill Preparedness: Is the Focus Shifting?, Oil & Gas J., May 23, 2005, at 20–25. Boredom is also a problem.

6.   Retrospective analyses of the first ten years of OPA are generally favorable, although Swanson assails the lack of uniformity resulting from OPA 90 because of its failure to preempt state law. *See* Lawrence I. Kiern, Liability, Compensation, and Financial Responsibility under the Oil Pollution Act of 1990: A Review of the First Decade, 24 Tulane Mar. L. J. 481 (2000); Steven R. Swanson, OPA 90 + 10: The Oil Pollution Act of 1990 after Ten Years, 32 J. Mar. & Com. 135 (2001). OPA 90 expressly denies any intent to preempt more stringent state laws regarding oil spills, including state laws imposing unlimited liability. 33 U.S.C. § 2718. Many states have enacted their own oil spill laws. *See, e.g.*, Gary V. Pesko, Comment: Spillover from the Exxon Valdez: North Carolina's New Offshore Oil Spill Statute, 68 Envtl L. 1214 (1990). Following the *Valdez* spill, the state of Washington enacted laws that require tanker operators to comply with the state's "best achievable protection (BAP)" regulations. These regulations consisted of many operating and personnel rules, such as requirements that all deck officers be proficient in English and able to speak a language understood by

the crew, that the crew have completed a comprehensive state training program; and that the navigation watch be composed of at least two licensed deck officers, a helmsman, and a lookout. The International Association of Independent Tanker Owners (Intertanko) brought suit, arguing that 16 of the BAP regulations were federally preempted. The lower courts upheld almost all of the 16 rules, relying on OPA's expression of non-preemption.

However, in *United States v. Locke*, 529 U.S. 89 (2000), the Supreme Court held that reliance on OPA's savings clause was misplaced. OPA's non-preemptive effect was limited to state laws involving oil spill liability, but did not affect the preemptive powers of another federal statute, the Ports and Waterways Safety Act of 1972 (as amended in 1978). The Court found that OPA's non-preemptive clauses applied only to Title I of OPA, captioned Oil Pollution and Compensation, and not to the whole Act. Therefore, a state cannot regulate vessel operation, design, or manning, as Washington's BAP rules tried to do. In short, maritime commerce is largely a matter for federal and international regulation. The Court concluded:

> When one contemplates the weight and immense mass of oil ever in transit by tankers, the oil's proximity to coastal life, and its destructive power even if a spill occurs far upon the open sea, international, federal, and state regulation may be insufficient protection. Sufficiency, however, is not the question before us. The issue is not adequate regulation but political responsibility; and it is, in large measure, for Congress and the Coast Guard to confront whether their regulatory scheme, which demands a high degree of uniformity, is adequate.

529 U.S. at 92.

7.   Under OPA 90, a person operating an onshore facility is liable if the facility has discharged oil or poses a substantial threat of discharging oil into the nation's navigable waters. 33 U.S.C. §§ 2701(32)(B), 2702(a). As noted in Chapter 6, the CWA defines "navigable waters" very broadly, as "waters of the United States" and OPA uses this same definition. The reach of OPA's strict liability provision was tested in *Rice v. Harken Exploration Co.*, 250 F.3d 264 (5th Cir. 2001), when owners of the Big Creek Ranch in the Panhandle of Texas sued Harken, seeking $38 million in damages and remediation for discharging pollutants from drilling operations onto the surface of ranch land near a dry creek bed. The seasonal creek flowed into the Canadian River (which flows into other rivers that ultimately reach the Gulf of Mexico). Under OPA, the ranchers had to prove two elements: (1) that a discharge of oil by Harken occurred, and (2) that it threatened navigable waters. The ranch owners alleged that the navigable Canadian River was threatened by Harken's discharges onto dry land because contaminants seeped into the subsurface flow of groundwater under the ranch and ultimately into the river. The Fifth Circuit ruled against the ranchers' "unwarranted expansion" of OPA to gradual natural seepage from a discharge onto dry land.

Suppose the discharge had been into an intermittent creek bed or a wetland that flows into a navigable river? Would the CWA and OPA then be violated?

8.   On the 25th anniversary of the *Valdez* spill in March 2014, sea otters in Prince William Sound had finally recovered to their pre-spill level, joining 11 other species on the recovered list. Eight species and habitats were still

recovering, including intertidal communities, clams, mussels and one pod of killer whales. Three species were not recovering: the herring, a bird, and a second pod of killer whales that was seen swimming in the spilled oil in 1989. The effects of the spill have lasted much longer than many scientists expected. *See* Nat'l Ocean Svc., The *Exxon Valdez*: 25 Years Later, http://oceanservice.noaa.gov/podcast/mar14/mw122-exxonvaldez.html.   The National Oceanic and Atmospheric Administration (NOAA) was heavily involved in the cleanup, and its website has additional information on the spill. A 2009 study found that about 100 tons of oil remain buried along Alaska's beaches and that low levels of residual pollution continue to cause chronic harm to biota. Daily Report for Executives, Feb. 13, 2009, at A–25.

A volunteer who organized citizens to hand-scrub the oil off hundreds of otters and birds looked back on this effort: "Exxon spent $80,000 per otter that survived the cleaning, but at least half of those are thought to have died soon after they were released. So it was closer to $160,000 per animal. I think that money would have been better spent restoring and protecting habitat." Sierra, Sea of Crude, Legacy of Hope, Mar/April 1999, at 81. Nearly $700 million of Exxon's settlement with the state and federal governments has been used to purchase over half a million acres of spectacular Alaskan coastline to preserve as parks and wildlife refuges.

9.   In 1997, the D.C. Circuit upheld most of the regulations implementing the natural resources damages sections of OPA 90. General Elec. Co. v. U.S. Dep't of Commerce, 128 F.3d 767 (D.C. Cir. 1997). Natural resource damages compensate for injury to or loss of natural resources. Exxon paid a total of $900 million to the state and federal governments for such damages. (Exxon also incurred expenses of $2.2 billion in cleanup costs.) Natural resource damages must be placed in a fund administered by a trustee and can be spent only to restore, replace or acquire the equivalent of the damaged resource. Such damages include compensation for "nonuse values," such as the value of knowing that you or your children might be able to visit Alaska in the future and see a pristine Prince William Sound with otters and seals playing in the water. Economists measure such nonuse values using "contingent valuation" surveys that ask people how much they are willing to pay to experience a resource in a particular environmental condition. Contingent valuation has been attacked as speculative nonsense, e.g., Note, Ask a Silly Question . . . Contingent Valuation of Natural Resource Damages, 105 Harv. L. Rev. 1981 (1992)), and supported as consistent with economists' concept of option values, e.g., Miriam Montesinos, It May Be Silly, but It's an Answer: The Need to Accept Contingent Valuation Methodology in Natural Resource Damage Assessments, 26 Ecology L.Q. 48 (1999).

10.   Litigation arising out of the *Exxon Valdez* spill has matched the size of the spill. The federal district court certified a Commercial Fishing Class, a Native Class, and a Landowner Class for compensatory damages. The district court also certified a mandatory punitive damages class, so the award would not be duplicated in other litigation and would include all punitive damages the jury thought appropriate. For purposes of this litigation, Exxon stipulated that its negligence caused the oil spill. In 1996, a jury awarded $287 million in compensatory damages and $5 billion in punitive damages against Exxon, the largest punitive damages award in American history to that date, as well as $5,000 in punitive damages against Hazelwood. Over the next 14 years, Exxon litigated the punitive damages award. The case finally reached the Supreme Court in *Exxon Shipping Co.*

v. Baker, 554 U.S. 471(2008). At that point, the punitive damages award stood at $2.5 billion. The Supreme Court vacated the award and remanded the case in a 5-to-3 decision with 4 concurrences. The Court created a maximum ratio of punitive damages to compensatory damages of 1:1 in maritime cases, premised on the need for "reasonably predictable" penalties that are fair and consistent. The majority decided that punitive damages could not exceed what Exxon had paid to compensate injured parties for economic losses, a sum of $500 million.

A footnote in one of the earliest cases in this much litigated battle over punitive damages (note 12 in *In re The Exxon Valdez*, 270 F.3d 1215 (9th Cir. 2001)) describes almost 30 cases spawned by the spill. The nightmare spill was a litigator's dream.

11. Perhaps in the hopes of short-circuiting some of the massive litigation it saw coming, and also to moderate hostile 24/7 media coverage, BP executives met with President Obama a few weeks after the Macondo well blew out on April 20, 2010 (see below), and agreed to pay $20 billion into a trust fund, called the Gulf Coast Claims Facility (GCCF) to compensate those who suffered damages from the spill and pay for third-party cleanup costs. The $20 billion is not a capped maximum; if cash in the Fund runs out, BP must pay additional legitimate claims and other costs directly. By late August 2010, the GCCF had begun processing claims and, by June 2012, had paid out $6.2 billion to 220,000 claimants for lost earnings, at which time the GCCF was superseded by a court-supervised settlement agreement (almost 1,000 pages long) called the Economic and Property Damages Settlement.

The billions that BP has paid out for economic losses from the Trust Fund is far in excess of the OPA liability cap of $75 million for economic losses that BP could have asserted (absent a showing of gross negligence) under OPA. BP's strategy of earning back the good will of the communities injured by the spill (by paying claims quickly from a large, dedicated trust fund) has not brought it much peace from litigation, however. BP sought to limit some payments approved by the fund administrator as not meeting the protocols in the settlement agreement, but without much success. Other claims appear to have been fraudulently made by certain Louisiana attorneys and were under review. BP had originally estimated that the Macondo event would cost it a total of about $40 billion, but that number is increasing. Settlement spill claims, once estimated to cost $7.8 billion, are now $9.4 billion and could go higher. An account of the status of the litigation facing BP appears in its 2013 Annual Report Form 20–F.

On November 15, 2012, BP reached an agreement with the U.S. Department of Justice (DOJ) to plead guilty to 11 counts of felony manslaughter (11 workers had died), two misdemeanors, and one felony count of lying to Congress, and agreed to pay $4 billion in fines and penalties, the largest criminal fine in U.S. history. BP also settled claims with the Securities and Exchange Commission for $525,000,000. The 2012 agreement does not resolve the DOJ's civil claims under the CWA or claims for natural resources damages under OPA 90. CWA penalties amount to $1,100 per barrel of oil discharged, but rise to $4,300 per barrel if the discharger is found to have acted in a grossly negligent way. See Chapter 7 of the Environmental Law Handbook (ed. Thomas F.P. Sullivan, 22d ed., 2014) for a good summary of the Oil Pollution Act's many damage provisions.

BP's 2012 settlement agreement with the federal government also imposed equitable relief on BP, administered by the court for a five-year probation period, to enhance BP's risk management and safety practices in the Gulf. A process safety monitor and an ethics and compliance monitor will review BP's actions and report to the court-ordered probation officer. BP will undertake an independent third-party audit of its safety systems. Such an audit is now required of all operators in the Gulf, as discussed below in c.

Many of the hundreds of lawsuits against BP were consolidated into two multi-district litigation proceedings, one in federal district court in New Orleans under Judge Barbier (MDL 2179) and the other in Houston for shareholder-related claims (MDL 2185). MDL 2179 was divided into three trial phases: (1) degree of fault and allocation of fault among the various parties involved in drilling the Macondo well; (2) determining how much oil was spilled; and (3) determining civil penalties under the Clean Water Act. As of September 5, 2014, the first two phases had been tried and hearings on the third phase were scheduled for January 2015.

On September 4, 2014, Judge Barbier issued his lengthy opinion in the first phase of the trial. In re: Oil Spill by the Oil Rig "Deepwater Horizon" in the Gulf of Mexico on April 20, 2010, MDL 2179, Phase One, 2014 WL 4375933,—F.Supp.2d—(E.D. La. Sept. 4, 2014). The opinion traces in great detail the acts of and communications between BP personnel, Transocean crew members and Halliburton cementing specialists. In the end, Judge Barbier found that BP had acted in a grossly negligent manner (*id.* at 114–130), defined as "an extreme departure from the care required under the circumstances or a failure to exercise even slight care." *Id.* at 115 (*see* ¶ 483) and at 121 (*see* ¶ 498). The same conduct was "willful misconduct" and "reckless." *Id.* at 122 (*see* ¶ 499) and 129 (*see* ¶ 519 listing the eight specific BP acts of negligence). Thus, BP may owe CWA penalties of as much as $4,300 per barrel of oil discharged.

The court also allocated comparative fault: BP was 67% liable, Transocean was 30% liable (for negligence, not gross negligence); and Halliburton was 3% liable (for negligence, not gross negligence). *Id.* at 136 (*see* ¶ 544). BP was spared punitive damages for egregious behavior, which the judge otherwise would have awarded, because of precedent from the Fifth Circuit Court of Appeals that, in maritime cases of operational recklessness, punitive damages are not available without additional proof of higher corporate policy approval. *Id.* at 140–142 (noting that other circuits would not require such additional proof). Transocean, even though not a Responsible Party under OPA § 2702(a), was found to be liable for clean-up costs incurred by government agencies because it was an "owner or operator" of an "OCS facility" under OPA § 2704(c)(3). However, its contractual indemnity agreement with BP shifted Transocean's liability to BP. *Id.* at 149–151.

Judge Barbier also ruled that the liability caps in OPA § 2704 did not apply to BP because its conduct in failing to cement the well properly violated a federal safety or operating regulation. *Id.* at 147–48. BP has stated that it will appeal.

12. Almost ten times as much oil was released into the environment from used engine oil dumped into storm sewers and from road runoff as from major tanker spills. *See* Nat'l Res. Council, Oil in the Sea: Inputs, Fates and

Effects 82 (1985). What laws can change the behavior of the weekend "do it yourselfer" who dumps used engine oil down sewers?

13. Outside the jurisdiction of the United States, a complex series of international treaties governs claims for compensation for damage from oil spills. These treaties are administered by the International Maritime Organization, based in London, and claims are paid out of the International Fund for Compensation for Oil Pollution Damage. See Mans Jacobsson, The International Liability and Compensation Regime for Oil Pollution From Ships—International Solutions for a Global Problem, 32 Tulane Mar. L.J. 1 (2007), for a good explanation of the international system.

c.   OFFSHORE BLOWOUTS AND SAFETY MANAGEMENT SYSTEMS

As mentioned above, on April 20, 2010, an explosion ripped through a MODU named the Deepwater Horizon while it was in the final stage of drilling the Macondo exploratory well in deep water about 40 miles from shore. The blast killed 11 workers and led to the worst oil spill in the nation's history. Almost 5 million barrels of oil poured into the Gulf of Mexico from the damaged wellhead that sat on the seabed underneath 5,000 feet of water. The well penetrated the seabed and extended another 2 1/2 miles to tap into a rich reservoir of porous rock, the new frontier sought by many large operators in the Gulf. The gushing oil reached Louisiana's coast within ten days. The Macondo well's flow was not contained for 87 days.

The extensive investigations that followed documented both industry and government failures that were so serious as to be almost incredible to those who thought that the United States was shielded from such disasters by a well-functioning regulatory system and by industry's technical drilling prowess and oil spill response plans. Unlike the *Exxon Valdez* oil spill which triggered quick passage of OPA 90, the Macondo disaster did not result in Congressional passage of any new environmental or safety laws. Rather, the post-Macondo reforms all took place at the agency and industry level, with the creation of new entities, such as BSEE, BOEM, and COS described below. This section of the chapter focuses on the use of industry Recommended Practices as regulations, an increasingly common feature of the modern administrative state.

President Obama quickly charged an independent, nonpartisan commission to investigate the Macondo incident and report back to the nation. Its January 2011 report provides a gripping account of the events leading to the disaster, valuable background on offshore leasing and drilling, and many policy recommendations to better prevent such disasters in the future. Nat'l Comm'n on the BP Deepwater Horizon Oil Spill and Offshore Drilling, Deepwater: The Gulf Oil Disaster and the Future of Offshore Drilling, Report to the President, at ix (2011) (referred to as the Nat'l DWH Commission), http://www.gpo.gov/fdsys/pkg/GPO-OIL COMMISSION/pdf/GPO-OILCOMMISSION.pdf. The Foreword to this Report summarizes its conclusions:

- The explosive loss of the Macondo well could have been prevented.
- The immediate causes of the Macondo well blowout can be traced to a series of identifiable mistakes made by BP,

Halliburton, and Transocean that reveal such systematic failures in risk management that they place in doubt the safety culture of the entire industry.

- Deepwater energy exploration and production, particularly at the frontiers of experience, involve risks for which neither industry nor government has been adequately prepared, but for which they can and must be prepared in the future.

- To assure human safety and environmental protection, regulatory oversight of leasing, energy exploration, and production require reforms even beyond those significant reforms already initiated since the Deepwater Horizon disaster. Fundamental reform will be needed in both the structure of those in charge of regulatory oversight and their internal decisionmaking process to ensure their political autonomy, technical expertise, and their full consideration of environmental protection concerns.

- Because regulatory oversight alone will not be sufficient to ensure adequate safety, the oil and gas industry will need to take its own, unilateral steps to increase dramatically safety throughout the industry, including self-policing mechanisms that supplement governmental enforcement.

The Commission summed up its Report, stating: "The Deepwater Horizon disaster exhibits the culture of complacency." *Id.* The experienced Transocean crew (Transocean was the drilling contractor that owned the Deepwater Horizon MODU and leased it to BP to drill the Macondo well) that was performing the actual operation made serious errors, such as attributing an anomalous pressure reading in the drill pipe to a "bladder effect," a term and condition unknown to professional engineers. BP's onboard Well Site Leader mistakenly concluded that the pressure test confirmed the well's integrity. BP engineers' chose a well design that made proper cementing of the well more difficult, but the engineers at Halliburton, the cement company chosen by BP, had failed to communicate to BP that several lab tests of the cement showed it was unstable and risky to use without further consultation. The drill crew member monitoring pressure in the drill pipe did not notice when the pressure began slowly increasing at 9:01 pm and no one noticed other pressure anomalies. The annular blowout preventer, once activated, did not seal the well. After the first explosion, the crew engaged the Emergency Disconnect System (EDS) that should have closed the blind shear rams, a powerful blowout preventer device that severs the drill pipe and seals the well at seabed level. The EDS system should have also disconnected the MODU from the riser that connected the MODU to the well head so that the MODU could float away from the blowout. The EDS did not work. The men and women on the MODU would have to race for lifeboats or jump 100 feet into Gulf waters in an attempt to escape the raging fire that broke out quickly on the rig.

Professor Jacqueline Weaver has published two articles on "Offshore Safety in the Wake of the Macondo Disaster." The first examines three changes to business as usual stemming from the disaster: rapid technology development (such as the creation and deployment of capping stacks and containment vessels that can fit over damaged wells and capture the oil flow within days rather than weeks); the quick adoption in the United States of global safety practices from abroad; and the recognition of complacency as negligence. *See* Jacqueline L. Weaver, Offshore Safety in the Wake of the Macondo Disaster: Business as Usual or Sea Change?, 36 Hous. J. Int'l L. 147 (2014) (Part I). The second looks closely at the role of the regulator in offshore safety. Jacqueline L. Weaver, Offshore Safety in the Wake of the Macondo Disaster: The Role of the Regulator, 36 Hous. J. Int'l L. 379 (2014) (Part II). The following text mixes slightly modified excerpts from these two articles with notes and comments.

Jacqueline L. Weaver, Offshore Safety in the Wake of the Macondo Disaster: Business as Usual or Sea Change?
36 Hous. J. Int'l L. 147, 161–63 (2014) (Part I).

The National DWH Commission's report bluntly concluded that "the Deepwater Horizon disaster exhibits the costs of a culture of complacency" that extended beyond any one entity to the industry as a whole:

> Though it is tempting to single out one crucial misstep or point the finger at one bad actor as the cause of the Deepwater Horizon explosion, any such explanation provides a dangerously incomplete picture of what happened—encouraging the very kind of complacency that led to the accident in the first place. (DWH Commission Report at viii).

Industry objected to the Commission's insistence that industry as a whole had a "systemic" problem because the data showed that 43,000 wells had been drilled in the Gulf without a Macondo-like accident. Juxtapose this industry defense against this excerpt from Nancy G. Leveson, a professor of Aeronautics and Astronautics Engineering at M.I.T., in her book Engineering a Safer World: Systems Thinking Applied to Safety (2011) at page 383:

> As safety efforts are successfully employed, the feeling grows that accidents cannot occur, leading to a reduction in the safety efforts, an accident, and then increased controls for a while until the system drifts back to an unsafe state and complacency again increases[.]

> This complacency factor is so common that any system safety effort must include ways to deal with it.

Accidents like Macondo, involving complex systems in high-risk environments, are often characterized as "high consequence, low probability" events. Professor Leveson characterizes them otherwise: they are "high consequence, low frequency" events, but such infrequent accidents are quite probable, and complacency is a root causal factor. In Leveson's view, all complex systems migrate towards states of high risk. As time passes, people decrease their estimates of how risky an operation is, lowering their estimates of the probability of an accident occurring. Yet, risks are probably increasing rather than decreasing as the complacency factor sets in.

Guarding against complacency is a critical factor in making offshore operations safer. Yet, it is exceedingly difficult to do because complacency is the product of everyday practical experience. Very few workers ever experience a seriously frightening workplace incident. As Professor Hopkins [another noted safety expert] explains: "The reality is that people learn that so-called complacent behaviour works."[24] The "failure to learn" from previous disasters, especially as time dims the memory of them, is a failure of the managers of organizations to have structures, reporting procedures, and performance incentives in place that embed "lessons learned" from a disaster into the daily routine of the organization itself. ∎

NOTES AND COMMENTS

1.   A Mechanical Risk Index is used by industry to rank wells in terms of riskiness. Only 43 higher-risk wells had been drilled in the Gulf at the time of the Macondo disaster. Is the risk of failure of a deepwater well drilled into a high pressure reservoir better assessed as one well in 43, or one well in 43,000? Or have risks been lowered because of new regulations and practices?

2.   Virtually overnight, DOI eliminated the Minerals Management Service as the federal agency in charge of all offshore operations and created a new agency under the DOI umbrella called the Bureau of Safety and Environmental Enforcement, or BSEE for short, with a sole focus on safety and environmental issues. Leasing would be done by a different agency, the new BOEM. Why is separating the offshore regulatory enforcement agency from the lease-sale agency a good practice?

3.   In the aftermath of the disaster, DOI quickly adopted two new regulations, one called the Drilling Safety Rule and the other called the Workplace Safety Rule, or SEMS rule, where SEMS stands for Safety & Environment Management Systems. The Drilling Safety Rule prescribes technical well design and construction standards and requires that at least two independent barriers exist to flow paths, so that if one barrier fails, the other would act as backstop. The DOI was able to act so quickly because it simply adopted two industry Recommended Practices (called RPs), developed by the standards-setting unit of the American Petroleum Institute (API), and incorporated them into the Code of Federal Regulations as requirements for offshore operators. The Drilling Safety Rule is API RP 65.

    Most Americans know the API as a powerful lobbyist for the oil industry, but it is also an accredited Standards Development Organization for technical practices and operational procedures that are used throughout the industry as representing good practices. The National DWH Commission found that the API's standards too often reflected "consensus" standards that met with the approval of its wide industry membership rather than representing good, much less best, practices. The National DWH Commission report (at 225) bluntly stated that MMS reliance on these API standards to develop its own regulations systematically undermined the entire offshore regulatory system. The incorporation of industry standards into federal rules clearly requires a skilled and well-resourced regulator that is able to understand the standards and evaluate them in terms of whether

---

[24]   Andrew Hopkins, Disastrous Decisions: The Human and Organizational Causes of the Gulf of Mexico Blowout 117 (2011). This slim book is the single best source of reading about the causes of the BP blowout and the safety management systems designed to guard against such disasters.

they meet the agency's statutory mandates. Reports from the National Academy of Sciences, the DWH National Commission, and many others documented serious weaknesses in the capacity of MMS to regulate effectively. Starved of funds for years and out-lobbied by industry, the agency lacked the engineering and technical expertise to participate effectively in standard setting or to enforce required standards that it adopted. Yet, a heretofore obscure federal statute, the National Technology Transfer and Advancement Act of 1995, requires that federal agencies "use technical standards that are developed or adopted by voluntary consensus standards bodies, . . . as a means to carry out policy objectives or activities." 15 U.S.C. § 272 note.

The SEMS rule identifies the procedures and practices that are to prevent managers and workers from becoming complacent about offshore safety in the context of major work hazards like blowouts (as distinct from occupational safety issues, such as slips and falls). After Macondo, DOI quickly adopted API RP 75 as the new SEMS rule:

Jacqueline L. Weaver, Offshore Safety in the Wake of the Macondo Disaster (Part I)
supra at 190–92.

[The SEMS rule] requires offshore operators, for the first time, to have in place a "comprehensive management program for identifying, addressing and managing operational safety hazards and impacts." As explained by BSEE, the SEMS rule gives the agency "oversight and enforcement of SEMS provisions" that address "human factors behind accidents" and provides a "flexible approach to systematic safety that can keep up with evolving technologies."

For many years, the industry had successfully lobbied against even a modest introduction of four of the twelve standard safety management practices, called "SEMS factors," into U.S. offshore regulations, and the Minerals Management Service had failed to follow through with its safety management initiatives. Yet, on May 17, 2010, less than a month after the Macondo blowout, the API's Joint Industry Task Force (JITF) White Paper issued an "immediately actionable" recommendation that a safety management system be adopted for all operations using a subsea blowout preventer stack on the OCS. . . .

This recommendation by the [API]'s Task Force described the "safety case" as a written demonstration that the facility and the operation are "capable of providing a safe working environment for personnel and that there are sufficient barriers to reduce identified hazards and risks to "as low as reasonably practicable" or "ALARP," the common European standard for environmental and safety risk reduction.

* * *

That the MMS had not been able to require earlier what the industry considered as a recommended good practice is an indictment of both of these key actors in the Gulf. ∎

Under the SEMS I rule, operators are required to have a safety management system that addresses 13 mandatory elements found in API RP 75. The elements include: provisions for a facility-level hazard analysis, management of change procedures, operating procedures, manuals on safe work practices, preventive maintenance programs for mechanical integrity, pre-start up review of all systems, emergency response and evacuation plans, safety training, investigation of incidents, audits, and recordkeeping. Later, BSEE adopted SEMS II with a few additional elements.

The SEMS rule is surprisingly short. Here is an excerpt of the new hazards analysis requirement that operators must perform in their SEMS plans, under 30 C.F.R. Section 250.1911(a):

> (1) The hazards analysis must address the following:
>
> (i) Hazards of the operation; (ii) Previous incidents related to the operation you are evaluating, . . . (iii) Control technology applicable to the operation. . . . (iv) A qualitative evaluation of the possible safety and health effects on employees, and potential impacts to the human and marine environments, which may result if the control technology fails.

The SEMS regulations consist of lists of plans and procedures that offshore operators must develop and implement. BSEE does not pre-approve the SEMS plans before issuing permits, but operators must be able to show that they have a SEMS plan upon demand. By contrast, in the U.K. and Norway, the operator must submit its "Safety Case" to the offshore regulator that must review and accept it before the operator can proceed. Without such a review by BSEE, how will BSEE know if the operator's SEMS planning is adequate (i.e., that it has identified major hazards and acted to mitigate their risks), and more importantly, how will BSEE know that the "paper plan" is actually being put into practice by management and workers offshore? Reread the last bullet in the National Commission Report's Foreword *supra*. Industry would have to police itself.

Professor Weaver's second article explains how the Center for Offshore Center came into being to do this job under the umbrella of the API. In late May 2010, President Obama imposed a six-month moratorium on any new deepwater exploratory drilling. The major operators and drilling contractors working offshore realized that industry had to act if the moratorium was to be lifted. They formed the Center for Offshore Safety (COS) with the mission of promoting "the highest level of safety for offshore drilling," just as the nuclear industry had formed the Institute of Nuclear Power Operations (INPO) to promote the "highest levels" of safety after the near-meltdown at the Three Mile Island plant in Pennsylvania. The initial focus of COS was to develop independent, third-party auditing protocols that would allow auditors to determine if operators were implementing the required SEMS procedures. The Center's objective was to better assure that the negligence of one "bad actor" would not again result in stopping all other operators' drilling activities or lead to new moratoria off the East and West coasts.

In April 2013, DOI incorporated the COS auditing protocols into the SEMS II rule, as shown in this excerpt from the SEMS rule at 30 C.F.R. section 250.198:

> (1) COS Safety Publication COS–2–01 Qualification and Competence Requirements for Audit Teams and Auditors

Performing Third-party SEMS Audits of Deepwater Operations, First Edition, Effective Date October 2012 [is] incorporated by reference at sections 250.1900, 250.1903, 250.1094, and 250.1920.

The COS protocols are easily accessed at the Center of Offshore Safety's website, including a SEMS Toolkit. Visit http://www.centerfor offshoresafety.org. The Audit Protocol Checklist created by COS consists of 187 questions (317 including all subparts) that an audit team must address to ascertain whether a facility conforms to SEMS requirements. The operator must submit the audit report to BSEE, along with any Corrective Action Plan. As of June 2014, only operators and contractors active in deepwater (over 1,000 feet deep) are eligible to be COS members under the by-laws and membership requirements adopted by COS. However, because the COS protocols are incorporated into BSEE regulations, they apply to all operators, regardless of water depth. BSEE's jurisdiction under SEMS is limited to operator/lessees, who are in turn responsible for assuring that their drilling contractors have good SEMS systems. BSEE does not regulate drilling contractors under SEMS, even though the contractors may be COS members.

Companies that voluntarily agree to become members of COS must send the same audit reports that they submitted to BSEE to the Center for Offshore Safety, but stripped of any identifying company information. COS will analyze the data to see where its members are having the most problems conforming to SEMS requirements. The Center will then work to address these problems through training and sharing best practices with its members. COS can also analyze the data to benchmark the safety performance of its member companies in terms of SEMS compliance, showing, e.g., that Operator X had an average compliance rate of 78% with all SEMS elements, while Operator Y had a 93% rate. The data and analysis are the property of the API and may not be released to the public without API approval. *See* Weaver, Part II, *supra*, at 430–33.

Here are examples of some of the 317 numbered questions on the COS Audit Protocol Checklist that the auditor must answer with a Yes, No, or Not Applicable, and then identify in a "Findings" column whether the audited company is Conforming or Nonconforming:

RP–1–General

Q 1: Has a SEMS been (a) implemented? (b) maintained?

Q 3: Has management ensured that goals and performance measures are established for the SEMS?

Q 4: Do the safety and environmental objectives and performance measures address the following: (a) a commitment to continuous improvement? (b) responsibilities for achieving objectives and goals at each relevant function and level of the organization? (c) specific means and timeframe by which the goals and objectives are to be achieved? (d) performance measures established to gauge safety and environmental performance?

Q 15: Has the Operator ensured that Contractors are familiar with the SEMS program?

James Watson, the first director of BSEE, characterized the new offshore safety regime as "an operator-driven safety program with BSEE oversight." *See* Weaver, Part II, *supra*, at 402 n.86. This regime is summarized and assessed by Professor Weaver in the following excerpts:

Jacqueline L. Weaver, Offshore Safety in the Wake of the Macondo Disaster: The Role of the Regulator
36 Hous. J. Int'l L. 379 (2014) (Part II).

[T]he SEMS auditing system in the federal regulations today is almost wholly a construct of the offshore industry itself. COS has been and still is the dominant player in creating and implementing an audit system for operators (and other offshore companies) to use in the Gulf of Mexico, a system based almost entirely on its parent API's Recommended Practice 75 and on COS-standardized audit protocols. *Id.* at 413.

BSEE's only formal link to COS is that BSEE "approves" COS as an Accreditation Body. Once approved, . . . COS accredits the external, third-party providers of auditing services, now called Audit Service Providers (ASPs).[25] The operator/lessee retains an ASP, and that company performs the SEMS II audit. *Id.* at 423.

[U]nder SEMS II regulations, the ASP must use the COS-created auditing protocols and reporting templates and must deliver a final audit report to the operator/lessee, using the COS-standardized forms, . . . now incorporated by reference in SEMS rules. *Id.* at 424.

The SEMS II regulatory framework . . . looks like "industry self-regulation through third-party audits." Other than adding several new SEMS elements and mandating that auditors be external, the entire SEMS II system adopted by BSEE is based on industry practices founded in API RP 75 and COS-created protocols and templates. *Id.* at 426.

[The following excerpt appears *id.* at 474–76:]

A large body of literature has discussed and then analyzed the successes and failures of what is called the "new governance:" the trend to use hybrid regulatory systems in many areas of regulation from food safety to greenhouse gas reporting. . . . The results of empirical studies of various self-regulatory or hybrid regimes are decidedly mixed. Deregulation of the financial system in the early 1990s and weak government oversight of banks contributed to the banking collapses and the global financial recession that began in mid-2008 and still continues—a notable failure of the new governance. In other contexts, self-regulation has been quite successful, as in the INPO model, cited by the National Commission on the Deepwater Horizon as a model for what is now the Center for Offshore Safety.

Some academics have reported favorably on one type of this new governance, [particularly] the use of "regulation by third-party verification," which is an apt description of the very system that BSEE is now using to audit offshore operators. In her article so titled, Professor Lesley McAllister proposes greater consideration of government reliance

---

[25] An ASP is a company like Det Norske Veritas that performs offshore safety audits much like Ernst & Young performs financial audits for company clients.

on private auditors to verify the achievement of government objectives.[26] Regulatory failure too often occurs because agencies lack both the expertise and the funding to monitor and detect noncompliance. Third-party verification (3PV) privatizes the verification process by requiring companies to hire independent auditors to determine compliance. The agency does not pay for the audits and does not have to hire or retrain personnel to conduct them. The drivers of this type of new governance are not just lack of funding and expertise of government regulators. The 3PV process can further an approach to a targeted industry member that engages the services of an experienced auditor in a more cooperative, "peer-assist" manner that promotes greater information sharing, better communication, and tailored correction plans. The audit becomes a learning experience that fosters continuous improvement in a way that traditional government audit and inspection processes cannot achieve.

Professor McAllister conditions her proposal for greater reliance on 3PV regimes on having essential safeguards in place to assure that the private verifiers are accountable for achieving the public values expressed in the government regulation. The government agency must set the ground rules for auditor qualifications and for the audit protocols to be used by them in performing the task of enforcing public values. The government must always retain the authority to apply sanctions on non-complying companies that have been audited through third-party verifiers.

One significant disadvantage of using a 3PV system is that the regulator is left outside the "learning loop." Its employees lose expertise in understanding the industry's problems and how the regulations work in practice. Also, there are fewer ways of sanctioning a third-party verifier who does poor work, so the 3PV system is less accountable for advancing the public goals embraced in the laws it is enforcing. Therefore, using a 3PV system requires that the government maintain accountability for these public values in two essential ways. First, the government must actively oversee the 3PV process by monitoring the work of the verifiers (that is, the Audit Service Providers) and by assessing how the system is functioning in terms of actually improving safety. Second, the agency must operate transparently by publicly disclosing the results of its own monitoring of the 3PV system. Thus, the agency must check, for example, that the third-party verifiers are independent from the client company they are auditing; it must deter "shopping around" for auditors; and it must monitor and prevent conflicts of interest that develop when the Audit Service Provider seeks other work from the same client company. COS has built in considerable oversight authority of the ASPs that it certifies, but this cannot substitute for government accountability for meeting the public mandates delegated to specialized regulatory agencies by law. ∎

NOTES AND COMMENTS

1.   How should BSEE audit COS to assure that COS is adequately policing the Audit Service Providers that COS has accredited to be the front-line watchdogs over offshore operators? That is, how should BSEE audit the auditors' auditor?

---

[26]   Lesley McAllister, Regulation by Third Party Verification, 53 B.C. L. REV. 1 (2012).

After the financial scandals of Enron, Tyco International, HealthSouth and others exposed seriously deficient auditing practices by some of the largest accounting firms that had failed to uncover the fraudulent schemes used by company executives, Congress created the Public Company Accounting Oversight Board (PCOAB) to audit the performance of the Big Four accounting firms. Even today the PCOAB's audits of the Big Four companies' audits have found a disturbing lack of auditor independence and competence. Nearly 1 out of 3 audits done by the Big Four firms and then inspected by PCOAB failed to adequately test and evaluate the audited companies' internal controls. Weaver, Part II, *supra*, at 481–82.

2.   What should BSEE do with all the SEMS II audit reports that it receives from operators? BSEE (unlike COS) does know the identity of the operator submitting the audit report. Should BSEE review them for nonconformances and match these reports with BSEE's own reports from its inspectors and from incident investigations? Should BSEE then perform complete or partial audits on certain screened operators? BSEE will need a cadre of trained auditors with special expertise in various aspects of offshore activity, many of which are quite technical. COS audit protocols require that COS-certified auditors (technically called Audit Service Providers) have many years of prior experience in order to qualify for this role. Private industry can outbid BSEE for safety and drilling engineers. The shortage of trained BSEE employees is acute. *See* GAO, Interior Has Begun to Address Hiring and Retention Challenges, but Needs to Do More, GAO–14–2013 (Jan. 1, 2014).

3.   Suppose that an offshore deepwater operator has received a COS certificate (privately issued by COS to a member company as a sort of "Good Housekeeping Seal of Approval") indicating successful SEMS II compliance from its COS-accredited Audit Service Provider and then has a Macondo-like incident. Will COS be in the hot seat at subsequent Congressional hearings as the dominant player in the offshore safety regime? Or will BSEE be faulted as having allowed regulation to be outsourced to COS and to third-party providers? Aren't COS and BSEE allied in the need to assure this new SEMS system works well?

4.   Professor Weaver concludes that it will take a number of years for BSEE to be an effective regulator. Her second article details the critical tasks that BSEE must learn to perform to meet the best practices of experienced U.K. and Norwegian regulators in the North Sea, such as collecting and analyzing "near miss" data from operators of incidents that could have led to disasters (but were ultimately controlled) and learning from them. She warns that operators cannot depend on BSEE to provide competent oversight to help them perform more safely. BSEE cannot (yet) be part of a "defense in depth" in which the regulator acts as a "necessary redundancy" to backstop the operator's self-audits of its safety system and the external audits required by SEMS II. Similarly, the European petroleum industry's trade association, the OGP (formerly the Oil and Gas Producers Forum), undertook many post-Macondo studies and offered this studied message to its members:

> OGP members should be aware that if a regulator is not providing robust oversight. . . . [t]his should be recognized as a reason to carry out a more extensive programme of self-audit to compensate for the lack of competent regulatory oversight.

Weaver, Part II, *supra* at 494.

As shown by the United Kingdom and Norwegian examples documented in her article, a good regulator can be industry's best friend in policing against complacency.

5.   The 1978 amendments to the OCS Lands Act aimed to increase offshore drilling but with strong safeguards, one of which requires using the "best available and safest technologies" found by the Secretary of Interior to be "economically feasible wherever failure of equipment would have a significant effect on safety, health or the environment." Only if the Secretary determines that the "incremental benefits are clearly insufficient to justify the incremental costs of utilizing [the best and safest] technologies," is something less than the best to be used. 43 U.S.C. § 1347. The blowout preventers on the Macondo well failed to seal the well and were later judged to be inadequately designed for deepwater conditions. The BAST standard appeared to have been forgotten as the industry moved into deep waters.

The Arctic is the new frontier. It is estimated to hold 13% of the world's undiscovered oil and 30% of its undiscovered gas deposits, as well as many minerals, such as iron ore, nickel and rare earths. Ofc. of the President, Nat'l Strategy for the Arctic 5 (May 2013) (citing the 2008 U.S. Geological Survey report titled "Circum-Arctic Resource Appraisal: Estimates of Undiscovered Oil and Gas North of the Arctic Circle," which estimated that the total mean undiscovered conventional resources of the Arctic are 90 billion barrels of oil, 1,669 trillion cubic feet of gas, and 44 billion barrels of natural gas liquids). The Alaskan Arctic area holds the largest amount and share of undiscovered oil resources in this USGS survey of the basins of five Arctic nations (Canada, Greenland, Norway, Russia and the United States).

The harsh Arctic climate, in darkness for half of the year, demands even more rigorous equipment testing. A 2013 National Academy of Sciences (NAS) report noted the urgent need for BSEE to develop protocols to determine the "best and safest available technology" (BAST) for use in the Arctic. (Note that the BAST standard applies to all OCS lands, not just the Arctic. The sparkless tools that are used in North Sea offshore regimes could prevent explosions from welding and other operations that have killed offshore workers in the Gulf.)

The NAS report bluntly noted that BSEE needed a "trusted agent" to fulfill its mandates, using the vehicle of a federally funded or university-affiliated R&D center that could pay competitive salaries. Marine Bd. of the Nat'l Acad. of Eng'g & Nat'l Research Council, Best Available & Safest Technologies for Offshore Oil and Gas Operations: Options for Implementation (2013). Shortly thereafter, a new entity, the Offshore Energy Safety Institute (OESI), was created by DOI as an independent "forum for dialogue, shared learning and cooperative research" for all stakeholders. OESI would help BSEE develop BAST protocols and also train and educate government employees.

6.   As of mid-2014, Shell had spent more than $6 billion on as-yet unsuccessful efforts to explore its Chukchi and Beaufort Sea leases, estimated to contain as much as 30 billion barrels of oil equivalent. Margaret Kriz Hobson, Shell Carefully Choreographing its Return to the Arctic, EnergyWire, May 29, 2014. It had bid $2.1 billion to win the leases in 2008. Shell Oil's ill-fated attempt in 2012 to drill exploratory wells in the Beaufort and Chukchi Seas confirmed the urgent need for BAST standards, for better management planning of operations, and for greater operator monitoring of

its contractors. *See* Report to the Secretary of the Interior, Review of Shell's 2012 Alaska Offshore Oil and Gas Exploration Program (Mar. 8, 2013). Shell and other federal lessees in Alaskan Arctic waters have postponed their plans to drill there in the ice-free 2014 season, while waiting for DOI to finalize regulatory requirements based on the lessons learned from Shell's 2012 experience and from the Macondo incident. The Coast Guard also issued an official report on the grounding of Shell's purpose-built MODU (named the Kulluk) that Shell had used in its 2012 drilling effort. As the Kulluk was being towed south by a tow company after the drilling season had closed, tow lines snapped in a heavy storm. The Kulluk ran aground and its crew had to be removed in a dangerous helicopter rescue by the Coast Guard. The report concluded that the leading causal factor of the event was "inadequate assessment and management of risks" and a "failure to adequately understand, respect and not complacently assume past practice will address new risks." U.S. Coast Guard, Report of Investigation into the Circumstances Surrounding the Multiple Related Marine Casualties and Grounding of the MODU Kulluk on December 31, 2012 (Apr. 2, 2014).

The National Research Council of the National Academies of Science issued a report in April 2014, concluding that the Coast Guard was not capable of overseeing a spill response in the Arctic. Nat'l Research Council, Responding to Oil Spills in the U.S. Arctic Environment (2014). It lacked personnel, equipment, transportation, communication, and safety resources. The onshore support infrastructure, such as ports, air access, and storage depots for equipment and dispersants, did not exist to support effective oil spill response.

Supporters of Arctic drilling point to on-going research projects that, in their view, will enable the industry to manage the risks of Arctic drilling, such as the use of unmanned drones (both subsea and in the air) to track oil spills in extreme weather and darkness and new radar systems to track moving ice and oil under or within the ice. *See* Joel Parshall, Opportunity, Challenge Meet on Arctic Horizon, J. of Pet. Tech. 56–60 (May 2012). Many industry and government task forces are working on Arctic oil and gas research.

Meanwhile, Alaskan Arctic drilling ran afoul of the NEPA. In *Native Village of Point Hope v. Jewell*, 740 F.3d 489 (9th Cir. 2014), the Ninth Circuit Court of Appeals held that the Final EIS issued by BOEM for the Chukchi Sea Lease Sale 193 conducted in July 2005 was fatally flawed. The EIS was based on a single scenario that no more than one billion barrels of recoverable oil would be produced, yet resource estimates indicated that much greater production could take place from potentially recoverable oil resources ranging from 3.6 billion to 11.8 billion barrels. So premised, the EIS significantly understated the cumulative impacts of the lease sale. BOEM argued that the one billion barrels was actually a generous estimate because oil development in the region had a less than 10% probability of occurring. Yet, this argument conflicted with BOEM's earlier conclusion that oil production was "reasonably foreseeable" because of the area's high resource potential. Also, the EIS did not consider a 2006 MMS report that the mean estimate of economically recoverable oil climbed steeply as crude prices rose. At $46 a barrel, the mean estimate was 2.37 billion barrels; at $80 a barrel, the mean estimate was 12 billion barrels. The evidence showed that BOEM had selected the one billion barrels by simply assuming that only one project in the lease area would ever be developed, a clearly arbitrary assumption.

BOEM next argued that any errors in the EIS for the lease sale could be corrected through site-specific EISs done later in the development process, citing, *inter alia, Village of False Pass v. Clark,* 733 F.2d 605 (9th Cir. 1984), discussed *supra* in Section D(2) at Note 4. How do you think the Ninth Circuit distinguished its earlier decision in *False Pass*?

The majority opinion in *Native Village of Point Hope* remanded the case to the U.S. District Court for the District of Alaska. Justice Rawlinson dissented, finding that BOEM's EIS analysis met NEPA standards. In his view, the potential size of commercially extractable oil deposits in the Chukchi Sea is a "quintessential example of a predictive judgment uniquely within BOEM's area of expertise." *Id.* at 509. BOEM was due substantial deference in its choice of the one-billion barrel benchmark. BOEM had concluded that substantial obstacles to oil development in the region made future production of the region's full economic potential unlikely. Five earlier exploration tests of some of the best sites had not yet discovered a commercial-size oil field. BOEM's choice of one billion barrels as the benchmark estimate was tied to the minimum size field necessary to support an offshore Arctic platform. This was a realistic benchmark given major uncertainties in geology, engineering and economics.

In April 2014, the Obama Administration asked the federal district court in Alaska to allow BOEM to rewrite the EIS for Lease Sale 193, while simultaneously allowing BOEM to review proposed exploration plans submitted by Sale 193 lessees. BOEM would not approve any such plans nor deem them to be formally submitted. Margaret Kriz Hobson, Shell Highlights Arctic Commitment and Readiness in Annual Sustainability Report, EnergyWire, Apr. 10, 2014. Shell filed a parallel request to proceed in this manner in order to preserve the possibility of a 2015 drilling season. *Id.* Environmentalists and Alaskan native groups argued against the requested order. The district court ruled against these two groups and authorized BOEM to review permits submitted to it for operations on Lease 193. Nathanial Gronewold, Judge Clears Way for Shell to Resume Drilling in Chukchi Sea, EnergyWire, Apr. 25, 2014. BOEM set an October 2014 deadline for release of a draft supplemental EIS on Lease Sale 193. Margaret Kriz Hobson, Interior Timeline Could Allow Shell Exploration Next Summer, EnergyWire, May 27, 2014. Whether Shell will launch another expensive effort to drill in the Chukchi in 2015 is not clear because Shell faced investor opposition to its many high-cost development projects around the world. *Id.*

As of mid-2014, four years after the Deepwater Horizon spill, DOI had still not completed its new rule on blowout preventer standards. DOI was also drafting a new Arctic Drilling Rule, laying the groundwork for a possible auction of Arctic leases in 2016, the first since 2008. Any new leases are likely to face the same onslaught of litigation that has occurred under the 2008 leases. *See* G. Alexander Robertson, Avoiding the Next Deepwater Horizon: The Need for Greater Statutory Restrictions on Offshore Drilling Off the Arctic Coast of Alaska, 4 Geo. Wash. J. Energy & Envtl L. 107 (2013) (describing lawsuits brought under NEPA and OCSLA that sometimes succeeded in temporarily halting exploratory Arctic drilling, mostly on procedural grounds, and recommending substantive changes in OCSLA). In 2014, Canadian regulators were engaged in consultations with Imperial Oil (a subsidiary of ExxonMobil) on an application to drill the deepest and most costly well ever drilled, with a price tag of $10 billion. The exploratory well in the Beaufort Sea will take four years to drill during the ice-free season. Canadian regulators must exempt the well from the rule that operators must be able to complete a relief well to stop a blowout in the same summer drilling season. Chester Dawson, Oil Giants Set Their Sights on Arctic Seas, Wall St. J., May 19, 2014, at R4.

7.   Meanwhile, on April 18, 2014, Gazprom shipped its first tankers of Arctic oil produced from an offshore platform in the Barents Sea oil to Rotterdam. The two ice-class tankers were made in Russian shipyards specifically for this project. The platform, with 36 slant wells drilled from it, had taken 20 years to build. Gazprom stated that the design of the platform "completely excludes an oil spill during extraction, storage and loading." Daily Rep. for Executives, Apr. 22, 2014, at A–11. A 2012 study by Informatica Riska, a Russian risk assessment group that usually works with Western oil companies, concluded that an oil spill from this platform would cause significant pollution in the Pechora Sea coast areas because Gazprom would not be able to contain the spill or recover the oil under conditions of darkness and high winds. Greenpeace and the World Wildlife Fund commissioned the spill study. Daily Rep. for Executives, Aug. 23, 2012, at A–4.

And—as a final April 2014 development: the Alaskan Legislature passed an act authorizing the state to work with ExxonMobil, BP, ConocoPhillips and TransCanada to ship the natural gas trapped in the Prudhoe Bay oil field more than 800 miles south to an LNG liquefaction and export facility. The project is estimated to cost $45 to $65 billion and could ship gas by 2024. Margaret Kriz Hobson, 'Historic Moment for Alaskans' as Legislature OKs Massive Pipeline Project, EnergyWire, Apr. 22, 2014.

Relative to Arctic oil and gas development, onshore shale plays using horizontal wells and hydraulic fracturing seem relatively risk-free.

CHAPTER 5

CONTROLLING THE EXTERNALITIES OF FOSSIL-FUELED GENERATION

We can distinguish the relatively clean electric generation technologies (hydroelectric power, nuclear power, and renewable power) from the relatively dirty fossil-fueled power plants (which use coal-, natural gas-, or oil-fired power). Coal-fired generation has traditionally commanded the lion's share of the American electricity market, but has steadily been losing market share to natural gas and renewables in the 21st Century (see Chapter 3). Oil-fired plants' share of the electric generation mix dwindled sharply after the oil crises of the 1970s.

Coal-fired generators burn coal to produce steam to drive a turbine and generate electricity, discharging air pollutants and warmed water, and producing coal ash as a solid waste product. Gas-fired plants are much cleaner, and are of two major types. Simple combustion turbines (CTs) are essentially jet engines that drive a turbine using pressurized gas, and have no steam cycle. Combined-cycle natural gas turbines (CCNGs, or sometimes NGCCs) operate like CTs, but use waste heat from the gas turbine to create steam to generate additional electricity from an additional turbine.

This Chapter discusses the regulation of externalities from fossil-fueled generation. Most (but not all) of the discussion focuses on air pollution, and much of the focus is on coal-fired power, because much of the regulatory attention and litigation focuses on coal-fired generation. Despite the focus on coal, however, most of the legal principles discussed in this chapter apply to other fossil-fueled power plants, oil refineries, biomass and waste-to-energy facilities.

A. FOSSIL-FUELED GENERATION AND THE CLEAN AIR ACT

Today, coal and natural gas comprise about 70 percent of the U.S. electric generation mix nationally, though there is great regional variation around that average. Coal combustion produces fine dust called particulate matter (PM), which is a source of respiratory problems, heart and lung disease, and haze. Particulates from coal combustion can also contain mercury, a toxic metal that can enter the food chain through deposition of combustion particulates into waterways. Sulfur dioxide (SO_2) mixes with moisture in the upper atmosphere to form sulfuric acid, which falls as acid rain, damaging vegetation and changing the pH of aquatic environments. Nitrogen oxides (NO_x) are a precursor to both acid rain and ground-level ozone (smog), which triggers respiratory problems in some humans. Carbon dioxide (CO_2), another byproduct of coal combustion, is the earth's most plentiful greenhouse gas (GHG), and human contributions of carbon dioxide into the atmosphere are hastening global warming. By contrast, gas-fired plants produce less than half the carbon dioxide, none of the mercury, and a small fraction of the other air pollutants produced by coal-fired plants. The link between coal combustion and pollution problems has long been understood.

Barbara Freese, Coal: A Human History
98–100, 177–73 (2003).

London had long been known for its fogs, including occasional "Great Stinking Fogs," as one seventeenth-century astronomer called them in his weather records. There was, though, a marked increase in the frequency of London fogs between 1750 and 1890. Natural climate fluctuations could have contributed to the increase, but inevitably so did the smoke. The city could barely be seen from above, such as the top of St. Paul's Cathedral. Lord Byron described the London skyline as a "wilderness of steeples peeping on tiptoe through their sea-coal canopy." Smoke was such a quintessential part of London that for a long time the city held the nickname "The Big Smoke."

While the fogs were unnatural, they could also be beautiful. * * * [However, w]ith all its potential for aesthetic appeal, it's quite clear that the pollution of Victorian London could bring confusion and death, particularly when a dense fog planted itself over the city for three or more days. On a Wednesday in December 1873, for example, a thick cold fog settled in and stayed until the following Saturday, at one point stretching fifty miles from the city. Visibility was reduced to a few yards, and according to the brief articles printed in the weather section of the *Times*, "all locomotion, especially to people on foot a the crossings of great thoroughfares, became extremely dangerous." The fog was blamed for a sad and chaotic parade of sometimes fatal accidents that left the hospitals straining to care for the injured: Carriages crashed into light posts and other obstacles, people were run over by omnibuses and Hanson cabs (one poor fellow was run over by both), horses tripped and crushed their riders, and a train struck a man who was putting fog lights along the track. The police were kept busy trying to handle the multitudes of lost children. The most common reported fog-related deaths were the twenty drownings that took place over the four-day period, caused when people simply stumbled into the Thames or the canals of the city, or when barge collisions threw them into the water. The paper failed to report that several cattle, in the city for an exhibition, dropped dead in the fog, and many others were in such distress that they had to be immediately slaughtered.

Amidst the various locomotion related deaths, the *Times* also noted the deaths of two gentlemen who in separate incidents fell into the street and shortly died from "inhaling the fog." In reporting just these two deaths by inhalation, the *Times* was off by two orders of magnitude. An analysis of the city's death statistics performed decades later showed that the 1873 fog quietly killed from 270 to 700 Londoners. Another foggy week in 1880 would kill from 700 to 1,100 people, and one in 1892 would kill about 1,000. These deaths went largely unreported, while people worried instead about the far less deadly but more dramatic confusion in the streets.

* * *

Following coal's emissions through nature is an ongoing scientific odyssey. Already it has forced us to increase our understanding of how the wind blows, how the rain falls, how light scatters, and how chemicals cycle through the air and soil and water. It has also taught us things about our own lungs and hearts and brains, and about the subtle and sometimes not-so-subtle ways that things we release into the world can come back to haunt us. All in all, tracking the smoke has given us ample proof that we're intimately linked, through our economic decisions and through large-scale natural processes, to the broader web of life on Earth and to each other.

The first great wave of environmental sentiment swept through the nation in 1970, marked by the celebration of the first Earth Day. In the wake of this new awareness came the formation of the Environmental Protection Agency ("EPA") and passage of a string of new laws, the most ambitions and far-reaching of which was the 1970 Clean Air Act. The act established the straightforward requirement that the nation's air be cleaned up to healthy levels by 1975. To a nation that had just landed men on the Moon, such a lofty goal must have seemed entirely possible. Three decades later it looks hopelessly naïve, a reflection of how little we knew about air pollution, health and environmental politics.

When the Clean Air Act was passed, the nation's primary concern was the effect of urban air pollution levels on health. The potentially deadly nature of the urban smoke had been demonstrated some years earlier during London's historic "Black Fog" on December 5–9, 1952. A temperature inversion trapped the city's smoke close to the ground. On the first day it was still a white fog, but so extraordinarily dense that cars and buses moved slower than a walk, and the opera had to be cancelled when fog seeped into the theater and made it impossible for the singers to see the conductor. By the last day, the fog had turned black, visibility was limited to a mere eleven inches, and the hospitals were full of Londoners perishing from the smoke. Many of the 4,000 or so people killed by this episode never made it to the hospital but died on the streets; fifty bodies were removed from one small city park. In 1956, after nearly seven hundred years of complains about the coal smoke in London, Parliament finally banned the burning of soft coal in the central city, and the air immediately improved.

The primary culprit in the deaths was a gas called sulfur dioxide. Sulfur dioxide, or SO_2, is not some exotic chemical contrived in a laboratory. Nature spews it out through volcanic eruptions, but we spew out more with our coal fires, our own slow-motion, domesticated little volcanoes. This old-fashioned and surprisingly dangerous pollutant results, quite literally, from mixing fire and brimstone, or, in other words from burning the sulfur that contaminates coal.

In 1970, total SO_2 emissions in the United States were reaching an all-time high. The greatest sources by far were the coal-fired power plant, which doubled their SO_2 emissions every decade between 1940 and 1970. Despite these increasing SO_2 emissions, in most city centers the air probably held much less SO_2 than it had earlier in the century because taller smoke stacks were spewing it farther. Some of the Clean Air Act regulations promoted the continuation of this trend. A common saying among environmental regulators was "the solution to pollution is dilution." Of course, this is only true if your fires are small enough and your planet is big enough, and neither turned out to be the case. In time, the dirtiest air got cleaner but downwind some of the cleanest air got dirtier. Health concerns persisted, but they were soon overshadowed by the other issues, like the mystery of the missing fish.

In the late 1960s, scientists were perplexed over the disappearance of fish that had formerly thrived in certain pristine lakes in southern Sweden and Norway and the Adirondack Mountains of New York. The lakes looked more beautiful than ever because the microorganisms that used to cloud the water were also gone. There were other mysteries, too: High-elevation stands of trees were dying of unknown causes, and, oddly enough, in parts of Sweden people were surprised to find their hair turning green. Researchers finally linked all these problems back to acid-forming pollution, and particularly to SO_2 emissions from the enormous coal fires in Britain and Germany (causing pollution in Scandinavia) and in the industrial Midwest (causing pollution in the northeastern United States and Canada).

Acid rain not only raises the acidity of distant lakes and streams, which directly harms fish, but as it passes through the soils it also leaches out toxic minerals like aluminum and mercury, causing more damage to the ecosystems. By the 1970s the acid had seeped into thousands of shallow wells in southern Sweden, corroding the copper pipes and contaminating the tap water with copper sulfate. The fair-haired Swedes who washed in the contaminated water found that it tinted their hair green, sometimes as "green as a birch in spring," as a Swedish researcher described it in 1981. It was an ironic choice of words, because the same pollutants were causing certain trees to lose their green needles and turn brown.

. . . Finally, in 1990, Congress adopted an Acid Rain Program requiring power plants to cut their SO_2 emissions nearly in half by 2010.

* * *

Even before the evidence of the continuing acid rain problems emerged, coal-burning was being increasingly blamed for a surprising proportion of our other long-standing pollution problems. For example, we know now that SO_2, invisible when it comes out of the smokestack, is the primary reason people can't see great distances in the eastern United States. On an average day in the East, you can see about fourteen miles. If not for human-made air pollution, you could see from forty-five to ninety miles. The main cause of the vista-destroying haze that covers virtually everything east of the Mississippi are tiny sulfate particles that scatter sunlight; the particles are formed from SO_2 emissions, which come mostly from coal fires. In the West, even though SO_2 emissions are much less, there is still enough coal pollution to obscure views: The EPA found that a significant part of the haze problem at the Grand Canyon has been due to SO_2 emissions from a coal plant seventy-five miles away. One economic study found that the Acid Rain Program's improvement of visibility—a benefit barely considered when the law was passed—is alone worth the substantial cost of pollution controls, quite apart from the many other environmental and health benefits.

Of course, vistas are also impaired by what we call "smog." Smog is mainly ozone—a gas we have too little of up in the stratosphere, where it shields us from radiation, but too much of down here. Ozone is a big problem both in rural areas, where it harms the growth of forests and crops, and in urban areas. . . .

Ozone does not come out of smoke stacks. Rather, it forms when gases called nitrogen oxides (NO_x) combine with other air pollutants in the presence of sunshine and heat. Although smog is mainly blamed on road traffic, coal contributes nearly a quarter of the nation's NO_x emissions, which is more than all cars, vans and sport utility vehicles combined. NO_x emissions are also a secondary cause of acid rain, and, because nitrogen is a fertilizer, they contribute to excessive algae growth and the depletion of oxygen in coastal waters such as the Chesapeake Bay.

And then there is the slippery problem of mercury. Many thousands of lakes in the United States contain fish so tainted with mercury that pregnant women and children are warned not to eat them because mercury can damage the developing brain. Most mercury in lakes rains down from the air, and perhaps as much as a third of mercury emissions to the air comes from coal plants, making them the largest source. The public health threat posed by mercury is not trivial: A recent report by the National Academy of Sciences warns that 60,000 babies born in the United States each year may have been exposed to enough mercury in utero to cause poor school performance later in life. Once mercury is introduced into the environment, it is impossible to clean up because it keeps reevaporating and raining down again indefinitely, ping-ponging its way mercurially around the world, posing new risks wherever it lands.

■

Since Freese was writing, the scientific record documenting and measuring the harm produced by coal combustion has continued to grow. We discuss estimates of the considerable costs associated with climate change (to which GHG emissions from coal combustion are a major contributor) at greater length in section D of this chapter. A 2009 National Academy of Sciences study estimated the annual *non-climate* related external damages from 406 coal-fired power plants to be $62 billion, or about 3.2 cents per kilowatt hour (kwh), representing about thirty to fifty percent of the average cost of electricity. *See* News Release, Nat'l Acad. of Sci., Report Examines Hidden Health and Environmental Costs of Energy Production and Consumption in U.S. 1 (Oct. 19, 2009). A 2011 study reported in the Annals of the New York Academy of Sciences (a multidisciplinary scientific journal) examined the health effects of the coal industry on a lifecycle basis. Paul R. Epstein et al., Full Cost Accounting for the Life Cycle of Coal, 1219 Annals N.Y. Acad. Sci. 73 (2011). The authors, comprising a large group of researchers from various public health and academic institutions, estimated that these externalities cost the American public as much as half a trillion dollars each year, and "conservatively" estimated that if these costs were internalized, the price of electricity generated from coal would "double or triple." *Id.* at 93.

Another 2011 study, reported in the American Economic Review, developed a framework for comparing (quantifying) the damages associated with non-GHG air pollution emissions from 820 industries (including all of the major polluting industries) with the value added to the economy by those industries. The authors concluded that the net benefits[1] of seven of those industries (including oil- and coal-fired power plants, but not natural gas-fired power plants) were negative. *See* Nicholas Z. Muller et al., Environmental Accounting for Pollution in the United States Economy, 101 Am. Econ. Rev. 1649, 1665 (2011). The authors further concluded that coal-fired combustion created by far the largest amount of environmental damage, which they estimated to be approximately fifty-three billion dollars per year. By contrast, they estimated environmental damages from natural gas-fired production to be less than one billion dollars per year. The authors estimated the environmental costs of coal-fired generation to be approximately 2.8 cents per kwh (cents/kwh), from oil-fired generation to be 2 cents/kwh, and from natural gas-fired generation to be approximately 0.1 cents/kwh. *Id.* at 1667–69.

---

[1] More precisely, the authors expressed the results in terms of net costs—the ratio of environmental damages to value added for each industry.

This literature suggests that while the climate impacts of fossil fuel combustion draw the most attention, the bulk of the measurable harm caused by fossil fuel combustion is attributable to mortality resulting from emissions of conventional air pollutants, primarily SO_2, PM, and NO_x. By comparison, the dollar value of environmental harm from GHG emissions pales in comparison, representing well under 1 percent of the harm estimated in the American Economic Review analysis. This may be partly because many of lives lost and health effects from GHG emissions occur in the distant future, and so are heavily discounted in economic studies that seek to attach a dollar value to the harm. Nevertheless, the magnitude of the harm done by these other pollutants, which come disproportionately from coal combustion, may explain the sustained regulatory attention the U.S. Environmental Protection Agency (EPA) has devoted to coal-fired power.

B. REGULATION OF CRITERIA POLLUTANTS UNDER THE CLEAN AIR ACT

1. NAAQS AND PERMITTING

One aim of the Clean Air Act of 1970 (CAA), and of its major amendments in 1977 and 1990, was to force plant owners to internalize some of the external costs of fossil fuel combustion by requiring new plants to install pollution controls to limit their emissions. The CAA has significantly reduced emissions of some pollutants into the atmosphere, and has provided a structured backdrop for a four-decade-long process of conflict over the regulation of coal-fired combustion.

The CAA requires new, stationary sources of pollution, like power plants, to secure a permit from state regulators before emitting "criteria" pollutants—lead, carbon monoxide, ozone, SO_2, PM, and NO_x, into the air. The permit must contain emissions limitations for these pollutants that reflect certain technology-based standards, which are described and defined in the CAA itself. The stringency of these standards, in turn, depends upon whether the source is located in area that is in attainment with national ambient air quality standards (NAAQS) for the pollutant in question. If the plant is located in an attainment area, the source must obtain a Prevention of Significant Deterioration (PSD) permit and the emissions limitation must reflect the "best available control technology" (BACT). 42 U.S.C. § 7475(a)(4). In nonattainment areas, the limitation must reflect the "lowest achievable emissions rate" (LAER). 42 U.S.C. § 7503(a)(2). In either case, the emissions limits must be relatively more stringent than levels of pollution control achieved by most other similar sources. Thus, as new permits are issued and old permits expire and are renewed, and as pollution control technology grows more efficient and effective, the statutory technology-based standards—the levels of pollution control that are available, achievable, and better than the industry norm—grow more stringent over time. Permit writers (often state agencies) decide the numeric limits that satisfy these standards subject to EPA-established backstop emissions limits for emissions from particular source categories, called New Source Performance Standards (NSPS).

This CAA permitting regime has resulted in significant reductions in criteria pollutants since its passage, as **Figure 5–1** indicates.

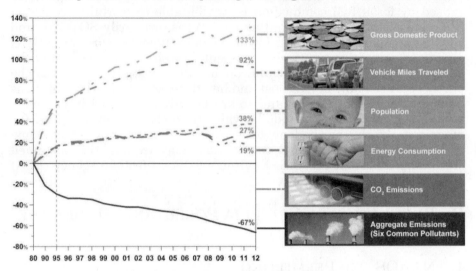

Figure 5–1
Emissions of Criteria Pollutants Since 1980
Source: EPA, Air Quality Trends, http://www.epa.gov/airtrends/aqtrends.html

Even without controlling for economic and population growth, emissions of the criteria pollutants in 2012 were all less than half of what they were in 1980.

CAA sections 108 and 109 authorize EPA to revise the NAAQS for criteria pollutants periodically, but EPA has used this power relatively infrequently. The statute directs that NAAQS be set at a level that will "protect public health with an adequate margin of safety," and the courts have endorsed the notion that EPA may not consider the costs imposed by a new standard when revising the NAAQS. Whitman v. Am. Trucking Ass'ns, 531 U.S. 457, 473–76 (2001). Rather, costs are to be considered under other sections of the statute. *Id.* at 467–68. The Obama Administration has alternated between bold action and caution when it comes to revising NAAQS. In 2010, EPA revised the NAAQS for SO_2. The new SO_2 standard replaces the old 24-hour standard of 140 parts per billion (ppb) with a 1-hour maximum of 75 ppb, which may increase the number of SO_2 nonattainment areas and trigger more stringent emissions limits in permits issued for facilities in those new nonattainment areas. Primary National Ambient Air Quality Standard for Sulfur Dioxide; Final Rule, 75 Fed. Reg. 35,520 (June 10, 2010), codified at 40 C.F.R. § 50.17.

The Obama EPA also proposed revisions of the NAAQS for ozone in 2010. National Ambient Air Quality Standards for Ozone; Proposed Rule, 75 Fed. Reg. 42,938 (Jan. 19, 2010). At the time of the proposal, the D.C. Circuit was considering a legal challenge to the Bush EPA's ozone standard in *Mississippi v. EPA*, in which environmental groups challenged the existing standard as not stringent enough. The proposed Obama EPA ozone standard revision would lower the primary (health-based) standard from its current level of 75 ppb to between 60 to 70 ppb, averaged over 8 hours. This would affect both coal- and gas-fired generation, since both sources emit NO_x and volatile organic chemicals, which are precursors of ozone. However, the White House Office of Information and Regulatory Affairs reviewed the new proposal, voiced concerns over its cost impacts, and—at the President's request—returned the rule to EPA for further risk analyses and study. EPA thereafter withdrew the proposed rule, and the D.C. Circuit subsequently decided *Mississippi v. EPA*, upholding most of the Bush EPA standard. Mississippi v. EPA, 723 F.3d 246 (2013). EPA issued a new proposed rule in December 2014 that would establish a standard of 65 to 70 ppb, which is slightly less stringent than its original proposal but more stringent than the Bush EPA standard. National Ambient Air Quality Standards for Ozone; Proposed Rule, 79 Fed. Reg. 75,234 (Dec. 17, 2014).

Finally, as of this writing the Obama EPA is also considering revising the current annual NAAQS for PM, but has not yet proposed a revision. Its internal review documents indicate it is considering making the standards more stringent. EPA, Policy Assessment for the Review of the Particulate Matter National Ambient Air Quality Standards (Apr. 2011), http://www.epa.gov/ttn/naaqs/standards/pm/data/20110419pmpa final.pdf.

2. NEW SOURCE REVIEW

The CAA's tough permitting provisions apply to "new" sources of air pollution. Therefore, coal-fired power plants that were in existence at the time the permitting requirements took effect—"grandfathered" plants— fall outside the scope of their coverage. However, the CAA calls for application of a "new source" permitting standards to "stationary source[s] the construction *or modification* of which is commenced after" the effective date of the CAA's new source permitting requirements. Congress may have intended that this provision operate gradually to widen the scope of coverage of the new source permitting provisions as old plants were replaced or modified, so that over time the number of exempted plants would dwindle to zero. In any case, older coal-fired power plants, many of them in the Midwest, continued to pollute at essentially unregulated rates long after the Act's passage, depositing acid rain on, and contributing to violations of NAAQS in, downwind (Eastern) states. These unregulated power plants have been the source of long-running disputes between Eastern and Midwestern states, between industry and environmental groups, and between successive Democratic and Republican administrations.

During the 1990s, the transformation of the electric utility industry from price regulation to price competition (see Chapter 10) stoked fears that sellers of electricity would rely more heavily than ever on cheap, reliable power from grandfathered coal-fired plants. The language of CAA section 111 authorizes EPA to apply new source review to any plant that had been "modified"—that is, any plant that has undergone a "physical change" resulting in an increase in emissions. However, in 1978, EPA promulgated a rule defining the term "physical change" to exclude "routine maintenance, repair and replacement," apparently signaling its intention to exempt some repairs that increase emissions from new source review. The Seventh Circuit affirmed the limited nature of the exemption for routing maintenance, repair, and replacement in

Wisconsin Electric Power Co. v. Reilly, 893 F.2d 901 (7th Cir. 1990), popularly known as the "WEPCO" case. WEPCO sought to avoid new source review for a "life extension program" for its Port Washington electric power plant. That program involved extensive renovations, including repair and replacement of the turbine-generators, boilers, mechanical and electrical auxiliaries and the common plant support facilities. The court rejected WEPCO's arguments, noting that, "other courts considering the modification provisions of [the CAA] have assumed that 'any physical change' means precisely that." To permit the definition to be narrowed, said the court, "would open vistas of indefinite immunity from the provisions of [the CAA]." *Wisconsin Electric Power Co.,* 893 F.2d at 908–09.

The other core idea in the CAA's definition of "modification," besides the concept of a physical change, is the requirement that the work *increase* emissions. Deciding whether an emissions increase has taken place, or will take place, as the result of any physical change in the plant, is not always straightforward. Consider an old coal-fired power plant that has operated at less than full capacity for many years, either because of lack of demand for its output or because its old equipment cannot run at full capacity without repairs. At full capacity it emits X tons of pollutant per year, representing y pounds of pollutant per unit of energy generated. But because it operates at less than full capacity it has emitted less than $X/2$ tons of pollutant per year. After repairs and replacement of equipment, the plant is more efficient and durable. It now emits z pounds of pollutant per unit of energy generated ($z<y$), but will certainly operate at closer to full capacity in the future, emitting up to W tons of pollutant next year ($W>X/2$). Is the work producing these changes a "modification" triggering new source review? Should an "increase" in emissions be measured by an increase in pollutant output per year, output of pollutant per hour, or output of pollutant per unit of energy generated?

In *WEPCO*, the court disapproved EPA's practice of deciding whether emissions have increased by comparing a plant's pre-modification *actual* emissions with the plant's post-modification *potential* emissions. Industry complained that the use of this "potential-to-emit" approach compares apples to oranges, since the post-modification emission estimate assumes that the plant will operate at a higher capacity after the modification than it did beforehand. After *WEPCO*, EPA decided to use an "actual-to-projected actual" emissions standard.

In June 2005, however, the Supreme Court upheld EPA's comparison of pre- and post-modification levels of actual *annual* emissions in *Environmental Defense v. Duke Energy Corp.*, 549 U.S. 561 (2007). Duke Energy had replaced boilers and other major parts of several coal-fired power plants, thereby increasing annual but not *hourly* emissions. EPA used an annual emissions comparison in its PSD program, but the agency's NSPS regulations used a comparison of hourly emissions. Both the statutory definition of "modification" and EPA's regulatory definitions were the same in the PSD provisions as in its NSPS provisions, but neither directly addressed the question whether emissions increases are to be measured using hourly or annual rates. The Fourth Circuit interpreted the CAA to require EPA to limit "modifications" to those that produce an increase in hourly emissions rates in both its PSD and NSPS programs, but the Supreme Court reversed. Said the Court:

> Respondent Duke Energy Corporation runs 30 coal-fired electric generating units at eight plants in North and South Carolina. The units were placed in service between 1940 and 1975, and each includes a boiler containing thousands of steel tubes arranged in sets. Between 1988 and 2000, Duke replaced or redesigned 29 tube assemblies in order to extend the life of the units and allow them to run longer each day.

> . . . The United States and intervenor-plaintiffs (collectively, plaintiffs) subsequently stipulated "that they do not contend that the projects at issue in this case caused an increase in the maximum hourly rate of emissions at any of Duke Energy's units." Rather, their claim "is based solely on their contention that the projects would have been projected to result in an increased utilization of the units at issue." . . .

> In applying the 1980 PSD regulations to Duke's conduct, the Court of Appeals thought that, by defining the term "modification" identically in its NSPS and PSD provisions, the Act required EPA to conform its PSD interpretation of that definition to any such interpretation it reasonably adhered to under NSPS. But principles of statutory construction are not so rigid. . . . It is true that the Clean Air Act did not merely repeat the term "modification" or the same definition of that word in its NSPS and PSD sections; the PSD language referred back to the section defining "modification" for NSPS purposes. 42 U.S.C. § 7479(2)(C). But . . . we do not see the distinction as making any difference here. Nothing in the text or the legislative history of the technical amendments that added the cross-reference to NSPS suggests that Congress had details of regulatory implementation in mind when it imposed PSD requirements on modified sources; the cross-reference alone is certainly no unambiguous congressional code for eliminating the customary agency discretion to resolve questions about a statutory definition by looking to the surroundings of the defined term, where it occurs. Absent any iron rule to ignore the reasons for regulating PSD and NSPS "modifications" differently, EPA's construction need do no more than fall within the limits of what is reasonable, as set by the Act's common definition.

See 549 U.S. at 576.

Duke Energy was one of many enforcement actions brought by the Clinton Administration, using precedents like *WEPCO* to try to subject old facilities to new source review. The Bush Administration announced its intention not to initiate new cases, and settled many of the pending cases it inherited on terms that environmental groups charged were too lenient. In December 2002, EPA modified its new source review rules by, among other things, (i) allowing firms to compare post-work actual emissions with pre-work emissions covering any two years in the ten year period prior to the work, and (ii) adding "plantwide applicability limits" (PALs). Prevention of Significant Deterioration (PSD) and Nonattainment New Source Review (NSR): Baseline Emissions Determination, Actual-to-Future-Actual Methodology, Plantwide

Applicability Limitations, Clean Units, Pollution Control Products, 67 Fed. Reg. 80,186 (Dec. 31, 2002). The creation of PALs allows sources to lump together emissions of different pollutants in determining when there has been an emissions increase that could trigger new source review. The 2002 rule changes were upheld, for the most part, in *New York v. EPA*, 413 F.3d 3 (2005).

In 2003 EPA added a new version of the routine maintenance, repair and replacement exemption to its new source review rules. Prevention of Significant Deterioration (PSD) and Non-Attainment New Source Review (NSR): Equipment Replacement Provision of Routine Maintenance, Repair and Replacement Exclusion, 68 Fed. Reg. 61,248 (Oct. 27, 2003). The 2003 rule excluded from the definition of "modification" any work for which "the fixed capital cost of the replaced component" plus other costs "does not exceed 20 percent of the replacement value of the entire process unit," and for which "the replacement does not cause the unit to exceed any emissions limits." The 2003 capital cost rules were overturned in *New York v. EPA*, 443 F.3d 880 (2006).

In spring 2009, the Obama EPA began initiating new enforcement actions against energy companies, charging that past modifications of older facilities triggered new source review. These included actions brought against Westar Energy, Louisiana Energy, Midwest Generation, NRG, American Municipal Power, Ameren, and DTE Energy. Many of these suits, like their predecessors in the new source review program, resulted in settlements. *See* Thomas O. McGarity, When Strong Enforcement Action Works Better Than Weak Regulation: The EPA/DOJ New Source Review Enforcement Initiative, 72 Md. L. Rev. 1204 (2013); Darren Samuelsohn, Obama, Ill. File NSR Lawsuit Against Midwest Generation, N.Y. Times (Aug. 28, 2009).

3. POLLUTANT TRANSPORT

a. THE ACID RAIN PROGRAM

The CAA contemplates the problem of pollution transport across state boundaries, and CAA sections 110 and 126 (42 U.S.C. §§ 7410 & 7426) require states to prohibit emissions that "contribute significantly" to NAAQS violations in other states. For a state to permit such emissions is a violation of the CAA that is enforceable by EPA or by citizen suit, and downwind states may petition EPA under section 126 for a finding that that prohibition has been violated. Northeastern states have attempted to use these provisions to persuade EPA to curb emissions from largely unregulated Midwestern power plants. However, before the 1990s these provisions were narrowly read by EPA and the courts, and were therefore relatively ineffective remedies for downwind states. Furthermore, these provisions offered no help with the problem of acid rain, which does much of its damage without triggering violations of NAAQS. Downwind states received some help with the acid rain problem from Congress in the form of the Clean Air Act Amendments of 1990 (CAAA90), which mandated a sharp, staged decrease in SO_2 emissions from coal-fired power plants, including existing sources left unregulated by the Act's new source permitting requirements.

The acid rain program, 42 U.S.C. §§ 7401–7642, took a new approach to pollution reduction by creating a market for acid rain "allowances" (rights to pollute), which owners may freely trade, buy or sell. The total number of allowances distributed to owners of coal-fired power plants each year is based on a historical baseline of plant emissions, and is gradually reduced over time to achieve the more than 50 percent total emissions reduction called for by the CAAA90. Allowance holders face a combination of the following choices: (1) to simply reduce emissions to match the number of allowances they receive, (2) to buy additional allowances from other allowance holders in order to pollute more, or (3) to reduce their pollution further than required and sell their "excess" allowances to others. In this way, those who can reduce their pollution most cheaply will tend to bear the lion's share of the pollution reduction burden, while those for whom reducing pollution is most expensive, will engage in less pollution control. This creates the potential for pollution "hot spots," or at least an uneven distribution of the pollution reduction burden (measured in tons of pollution reduced). The danger of hot spots is mediated somewhat by the requirement that any applicable preexisting permit or other limits applicable to plants' SO_2 emissions continue to act as a ceiling on individual plant emissions covered by the acid rain program, and by the fact that acid rain allowances grow more scarce over time.

Since the mid-1990s, acid rain allowances have been traded on the Chicago Board of Trade and elsewhere, and EPA tracks the market. The price of allowances, estimated to be in the low thousands of dollars per ton before the creation of the program, hovered in the low hundreds of dollars per ton for the market's first decade. This overestimation has been attributed to reductions in the cost of pollution control and of shipping (cleaner) Western coal to Eastern plants, overstatement of compliance costs by utilities and the coal industry prior to creation of the program, or some combination of the two. The early years of the program saw relatively little trading activity. The Environmental Law Institute attributed this in part to state laws that constrained trading. In states that continue to rely on traditional cost-of-service ratemaking (see Chapter 10), utility owners of coal-fired power plants were sometimes unsure how acid rain allowance transactions might be treated in rate cases. State public utility commissions were slow to develop rules governing allowance transactions, which created uncertainty and presented a significant barrier to risk-averse utilities. In addition, in most states the standard rules governing the allowed rate of return, the depreciation rate, and the risk that expenses, such as allowance purchases, may not be recoverable in electricity rates, are all less favorable to allowance transactions. Furthermore, prohibitions against shareholder earnings on capital gains (but not capital losses) impose one-sided risks on utilities that purchase allowances. Douglas R. Bohi, Utilities and State Regulators Are Failing to Take Advantage of Emission Allowance Trading, Elec. J., Mar. 1994, at 20.

The big losers in the compromise that produced the CAAA90 were the states in which high-sulfur coal was mined. A number of these states sought to adopt laws or regulations that would discourage their local electric companies from switching from local high-sulfur coal to low-sulfur coal from out of state. But it proved difficult to enact such rules without violating the dormant Commerce Clause of the Constitution, as the following case illustrates.[2]

Alliance for Clean Coal v. Miller

44 F.3d 591 (7th Cir. 1995).

■ CUMMINGS, J. Plaintiff Alliance for Clean Coal ("Alliance") is a Virginia trade association whose members include Colorado and Oregon coal companies and three railroads that transport coal. The defendants are the chairman and six commissioners of the Illinois Commerce Commission in charge of the administration and enforcement of the Illinois Public Utilities Act.

Coal has long been and continues to be the most important source of fuel for the generation of electric power in this country, accounting for 56 percent of all electricity generated in 1992. Electric utilities, the primary consumers of domestic coal, burned 78 percent of the 998 million tons of coal produced in the United States in 1992. Coal is produced in over half the states and is sold in a highly competitive national market.

Coal's sulfur content varies greatly depending on its geographical origin. Western coal, mined west of the Rocky Mountains, generally has the lowest sulfur content of any coal produced in the country. Coal mined in the "Illinois Basin," which includes most of Illinois and parts of Indiana and western Kentucky, is relatively high in sulfur. Burning coal emits sulfur dioxide in an amount proportional to the coal's sulfur content. *See generally* Bruce A. Ackerman & William T. Hassler, Clean Coal/Dirty Air (1981).

In the 1970 Amendment to the Clean Air Act, Congress authorized the Environmental Protection Agency ("EPA") to set new standards to regulate various emissions, including sulfur dioxide. *See* 42 U.S.C. § 7411 (1970) (amended 1977). The EPA provided for two methods to control sulfur dioxide emissions: (1) the use of low sulfur coal; and (2) the use of pollution control devices ("scrubbers").

In 1977 Congress again amended the Clean Air Act, requiring new electric plants to build scrubbers. By requiring scrubbers regardless of the sulfur content of the coal burned, Congress essentially eliminated for new facilities the low-sulfur coal compliance option that had been available under the 1970 Amendment.

In 1990 Congress once again amended the Act, this time requiring a drastic two-stage reduction in industrial sulfur dioxide emissions in an attempt to combat acid rain. The 1990 Act implements a market-driven approach to emissions regulation, allowing for the free transfer of emission "allowances." The Act is aimed at reducing sulfur dioxide emissions in the most efficient manner and, like the 1970 Act, allows electric generating plants to meet the emission standards in the cheapest

---

[2]   The term "dormant" references the fact that although the Constitution does not specifically say that the states may not regulate interstate commerce, the Court has held that such a limitation is implicit (i.e., dormant) in the grant of power to Congress to regulate interstate commerce. In the last fifty years, cases arising under the dormant Commerce Clause that contest the validity of state regulation have been far more frequent than cases challenging federal power under the direct application of the Commerce Clause. *See* Dan T. Coenen, Business Subsidies and the Dormant Commerce Clause, 107 Yale L. J. 965 (1998). See Chapter 11 for application of the dormant Commerce Clause to renewable power projects.

way possible. The principal methods of compliance now include installing new scrubbers, using low-sulfur coal, switching to another fuel source, or buying additional emission allowances.

The 1990 amendments meant the end of the salad days for high-sulfur coal-producing states such as Illinois. Low-sulfur western coal once again offered a viable alternative to the continued burning of high-sulfur coal combined with the installation of expensive new scrubbers. Faced with potentially damaging competition for the local coal industry, in 1991 the Illinois General Assembly passed the Coal Act, an addition to the Utilities Act, concerning implementation and compliance with the 1990 Clean Air Act amendments. *See* 220 ILCS 5/8–402.1. Under the Coal Act, utilities must formulate Clean Air Act compliance plans which must be approved by the Illinois Commerce Commission. In preparing and approving these compliance plans, the utilities and the Commerce Commission are required to:

> Take into account the need for utilities to comply in a manner which minimizes to the extent consistent with the other goals and objectives of this Section the impact of compliance on rates for service, the need to use coal mined in Illinois in an environmentally responsible manner in the production of electricity and the need to maintain and preserve as a valuable State resource the mining of coal in Illinois. 220 ILCS 5/8–402.1(a).

The Act encourages the installation of scrubbers to allow the continued burning of Illinois coal, stating that the combination can be an environmentally responsible and cost effective means of compliance when the impact on personal income in this State of changing the fuel used at such generating plants so as to displace coal mined in Illinois is taken into account. *Id.*

The four largest generating plants in Illinois currently burning Illinois coal are required to include the installation of scrubbers in their compliance plans so that they will be able to continue their use of Illinois coal. The cost of these scrubbers will be deemed "used and useful" when placed in operation and the utilities are guaranteed that they will be able to include the costs in their rate base. The Act further provides that the Commerce Commission must approve any 10 percent or greater decrease in the use of Illinois coal by a utility.

Plaintiff asked the district court to declare the Illinois Coal Act repugnant to the Commerce Clause of the federal Constitution and to enjoin its enforcement. In December 1993, District Judge Conlon handed down a memorandum opinion and order granting such relief. *Alliance for Clean Coal v. Craig,* 840 F. Supp. 554 (N.D. Ill. 1993). The court enjoined the Illinois Commerce Commission from enforcing the Illinois Coal Act and voided federal Clean Air Act compliance plans approved in reliance on the Illinois Coal Act.

On appeal, the defendant commissioners request that we dismiss the case for want of jurisdiction or, if we reach the merits, reverse the judgment below . . .

Alliance attacks the constitutionality of the Illinois Coal Act under the Commerce Clause of the Constitution. That clause provides that "the Congress shall have power . . . to regulate commerce . . . among the

several states." Article I,. Section 8, Clause 3. It has long been interpreted
to have a "negative" aspect that denies the states the power to
discriminate against or burden the interstate flow of articles of
commerce. . . . "If a statute discriminates against interstate commerce
either on its face or in its practical effect, it is subject to the strictest
scrutiny . . . 'Where simple economic protectionism is effected by state
legislation, a virtual per se rule of invalidity has been erected.' " *DeHart
v. Town of Austin,* 39 F.3d 718, 723 (7th Cir.1994), *quoting Philadelphia
v. New Jersey,* 437 U.S. 617, 624.

Two recent Supreme Court cases interpreting the negative
Commerce Clause are controlling here. In *Oregon Waste Systems v.
Department of Environmental Quality,* 128 L. Ed. 2d 13, 114 S. Ct. 1345,
the Court held that the negative Commerce Clause prohibited a state
surcharge on the disposal of solid waste generated out of state. In *West
Lynn Creamery, Inc. v. Healy,* 129 L. Ed. 2d 157, 114 S. Ct. 2205, the
Court struck down a Massachusetts milk-pricing order which employed
a tax on all milk sold to fund a subsidy to in-state producers. Because the
Illinois Coal Act, like the milk-pricing order in West Lynn, has the same
effect as a "tariff or customs duty—neutralizing the advantage possessed
by lower cost out of state producers," it too is repugnant to the Commerce
Clause and the principle of a unitary national economy which that clause
was intended to establish. *West Lynn,* 114 S. Ct. at 2212.

The Illinois Coal Act is a none-too-subtle attempt to prevent Illinois
electric utilities from switching to low-sulfur western coal as a Clean Air
Act compliance option. Indeed, the statute itself states that the Illinois
General Assembly determined that there was "the need to use coal mined
in Illinois" and "the need to maintain and preserve as a valuable State
resource the mining of coal in Illinois." 220 ILCS 5/8–402.1(a). The Act
implements this protectionist policy in four ways. First, it tilts the overall
playing field by requiring that commissioners take account of the effect
on the local coal industry when considering compliance plans. *Id.* Second,
the Act requires that certain large generating units install scrubbers "to
enable them to continue to burn Illinois coal." 220 ILCS 5/8–402.1(e).
Third, the Act guarantees that the cost of these scrubbers can be included
in the utility's rate base and passed through to consumers, even where
the use of low-sulfur western coal would be a cheaper compliance option.
220 ILCS 5/8–402.1(e) and 220 ILCS 5/9–212. Finally, the Act requires
Commerce Commission approval before a utility can make a change in
fuel that would result in a 10 percent or greater decrease in the utility's
use of Illinois coal. In determining whether to grant approval, the
Commerce Commission "shall consider the impact on employment
related to the production of coal in Illinois." 220 ILCS 5/8–508. The
intended effect of these provisions is to foreclose the use of low-sulfur
western coal by Illinois utilities as a means of complying with the Clean
Air Act. This of course amounts to discriminatory state action forbidden
by the Commerce Clause.

Illinois seeks to save the Act by claiming that it merely "encourages"
the local coal industry and does not in fact discriminate. This argument
rings hollow. The Illinois Coal Act cannot continue to exist merely
because it does not facially compel the use of Illinois coal or forbid the
use of out-of-state coal. As recognized in *West Lynn Creamery,* even
ingenious discrimination is forbidden by the Commerce Clause. 114 S.

Ct. at 2215. By "encouraging" the use of Illinois coal, the Act discriminates against western coal by making it a less viable compliance option for Illinois generating plants. Moreover, the requirement that certain generators be equipped with scrubbers essentially mandates that these generators burn Illinois coal: that is the purpose of the scrubber requirement, and the Commerce Commission would likely not allow the pass-through of the then-unnecessary additional cost of low-sulfur western coal. Such a mandate runs directly afoul of *Wyoming v. Oklahoma,* 502 U.S. 437 (requirement that Oklahoma generating plants burn 10 percent Oklahoma coal held to violate the Commerce Clause). Similarly, the guaranteed pass-through of the scrubber cost to rate-payers is equivalent to the minimum price fixing for the benefit of local producers held unconstitutional in *Baldwin v. G.A.F. Seelig, Inc.,* 294 U.S. 511.

Illinois argues that it has merely "agreed to 'subsidize' the cost of generating electricity through the use of Illinois coal by requiring its own citizens to bear the cost of pollution control devices." First, the fact that Illinois rate-payers are footing the bill does not cure the discriminatory impact on western coal producers. As the Supreme Court noted in rejecting an identical argument in West Lynn, "the cost of a tariff is also borne primarily by local consumers yet a tariff is the paradigmatic Commerce Clause violation." *West Lynn,* 114 S. Ct. at 2216–2217. Second, Illinois' characterization of the Act as an "agreement to subsidize" does not suffice to fit this case into the "market participant" exception to the negative Commerce Clause created in *Hughes v. Alexandria Scrap Corp.,* 426 U.S. 794. Illinois is not acting as a purchaser of either coal or electricity but as a regulator of utilities. The fact that its regulatory action "has the purpose and effect of subsidizing a particular industry . . . does not transform it into a form of state participation in the free market." *New Energy Co. of Indiana v. Limbach,* 486 U.S. 269, 277 (state tax credit for the use of Ohio-produced ethanol violated the Commerce Clause).

Finally, defendants champion the Illinois Coal Act as a means of protecting Illinois and its citizens from economic harm that would result from a decline in the local coal industry. Such concerns do not justify discrimination against out-of-state producers. "Preservation of local industry by protecting it from the rigors of interstate competition is the hallmark of economic protection that the Commerce Clause prohibit." *West Lynn,* 114 S. Ct. at 2217.

The purpose of the Illinois Coal Act was "to maintain and preserve . . . the mining of coal in Illinois" and to continue "to use Illinois coal as a fuel source." 220 ILCS 5/8–402.1(a). The Illinois Commerce Commission was required to take into account "the need to use coal mined in Illinois." *Id.* The obvious intent was to eliminate western coal use by Illinois generating plants, thus effectively discriminating against western coal. The Commerce Clause compels us to invalidate this statute, and consequently the compliance plans thereunder.

Judgment affirmed.

■ CUDAHY, J., concurring: Although the framework provided by the majority opinion is supportable, I believe that it is incomplete and, at the same time, may overstate the case. When all the conflicting considerations are weighed, there is some basis for concluding that

Illinois has crossed the constitutional line, but its actions are probably only the first in a series of efforts to accommodate conflicting but important and legitimate public policies . . .

The State's most effective argument is that we are dealing with a local (retail) ratemaking and electric operations problem over which the states have plenary authority. *See Arkansas Elec. Coop. v. Arkansas Public Serv. Comm'n,* 461 U.S. 375, 395 (1983) (replacing the bright line distinction between state regulation of retail versus wholesale electricity sales with the balancing test of modern Commerce Clause jurisprudence, but reaffirming the general premise of "leaving regulation of retail utility rates largely to the States.") The basic principle under the Coal Act (as elsewhere) for the conduct of electric operations is to arrive at the "least cost" solution. The State argues, in accordance with unimpeachable economic theory, that "cost" means "social cost" and should include the cost of providing compensation for the sectors of society suffering injury from the lost Illinois coal business (such as the cost of unemployment compensation and loss of tax revenue). This is an "externality" not incorporated in ordinary commercial calculations but is a real cost to society nonetheless.

The answer to this argument seems to be that this is an externality that the states may not recognize since the Commerce Clause effectively precludes consideration of local economic damage as a legitimate reason to handicap interstate commerce. *Wyoming,* 112 S. Ct. at 800 ("When the state statute amounts to simple economic protectionism, a virtually per se rule of invalidity has applied."). Another way of handling this problem would be to offset the externality of damage to the Illinois coal industry with the additional externality of the long-term benefit accruing to Illinois from the free trade bias of the Constitution. In any event, the external cost of damage to the Illinois coal industry is something that presumably may not be recognized in computation of "least cost" for present purposes.

Nonetheless, the assurance of rate base treatment for scrubbers (which provide a capability for using Illinois coal) seems a tenuous basis for finding a violation of the Commerce Clause. I believe no Supreme Court case goes so far as clearly to support the conclusion that this is a violation although the trend of the Court's decisions may point this far. (*See* discussion above of *Wyoming,* 502 U.S. 437; *New Energy,* 486 U.S. 269; *Bacchus Imports,* 468 U.S. 263.) It is difficult to perceive the realities here since, as discussed above, we do not know the price and cost relationships involved and, in addition, it is hard to know how far this statute takes us beyond the already existing commercial and regulatory biases.

In this connection, I assume that both the utilities and the Illinois Commerce Commission may have reason to favor Illinois coal even without this legislation. The utilities are pervasively state regulated and simply as a matter of political prudence one would expect them to be more sensitive to major Illinois political and economic interests—like the coal industry and the labor it employs—than to the needs of the same interests in Wyoming or Montana. Similarly, the members of the Illinois Commerce Commission are appointed by a Governor dependent for votes on Illinois' coal-producing areas. One would not expect them to be hard at work furthering the aims of out-of-state mines or railroads. The mandates of the Coal Act may bring a local bias into more focus, but I doubt that they bring about a fundamental shift in preference.

I am also inclined to consider this legislation as possibly vulnerable under the Supremacy Clause. In contrast to the 1978 law, when Congress ordered scrubbers for all new coal plants, in 1990 . . . there seems to have been a disposition to leave the matter to the markets. It might be argued that Congress intended to "occupy the field" with a market-based approach, eschewing any mandatory measures. If this were the case, any "putting of thumbs on the scale" by the states might be preempted by the prescribed market-oriented methodology. The relevant Court cases, however, seem to make much easier the striking down of state legislation on Commerce Clause grounds, where relatively little burden or interstate commerce need be shown, than on grounds of preemption, where the requirements seem quite exacting. *See English v. General Electric Co.,* 496 U.S. 72 (1990); *Pacific Gas and Electric,* 461 U.S. 190.

These somewhat inconsistent considerations seem to create a conundrum in the case before us, whatever the standard for striking down state "encouragement" to local industry. In the end, I join, but with significant reservations, in the result reached by the majority opinion. ∎

NOTES AND COMMENTS

1. The CAAA90 subjected several hundred existing coal-fired electric generating units to stricter regulation, but gave all power producers greater discretion to create least cost overall strategies to achieve national pollution control targets. The most likely compliance option for the 435, mostly older, electric power units affected by Phase I of the CAAA90 was to switch to low-sulfur coal, and Powder River Basin coal was potentially a less expensive source for many of them. During the 2 to 3 years following CAAA90, legislatures and other authorities in Oklahoma, Illinois, Indiana, and Kentucky passed legislation or took other steps to protect in-state coal mining jobs through legal requirements or economic incentives designed to persuade in-state utilities to burn local high-sulfur coals and to install flue gas scrubbers. By 1995 these approaches had been overturned by decisions, like the preceding case, finding that the laws violated the Commerce Clause. *See also* Alliance for Clean Coal v. Bayh, 72 F.3d 556 (7th Cir. 1995).

2. After hovering in the low hundreds of dollars per ton for more than a decade, the price of SO_2 allowances rose to more than $1500 a ton in 2006; that price spike may have been caused by a disruption in the supply of low-sulfur coal from the Powder River Basin. Since then prices have crashed, particularly after the recession, and have never recovered. Prices fell to less than $50 a ton in 2012.

3. As described *infra* Section E of this chapter, states have created tradable permit regimes for greenhouse gas emissions, and those programs seem likely to grow in the wake of EPA's new guidelines for existing fossil-fueled power plants. As described in Chapter 11, there are also multi-state tradable credit regimes for renewable energy credits. Can you think of reasons why states might wish to restrict trades within those regimes to in-state sources or power plants? And can you imagine that a state might do this in ways that might run afoul of the dormant Commerce Clause? See Chapter 11 for further discussion of this issue.

4.   Is it immoral to trade pollution rights? Some scholars contend that the commodification of pollution rights in programs like the acid rain program removes the stigma that should properly be attached to polluting behavior. *See* Michael J. Sandel, It's Immoral to Buy the Right to Pollute, New York Times, Op-Ed, p. A29 (Dec. 15, 1997); Stephen Kelman, Cost-Benefit Analysis: An Ethical Critique, 5 Reg. 33 (1981). Do you agree with this view? Is pollution immoral? Should there be a moral stigma attached to polluting behavior, legal or illegal?

b.   OZONE TRANSPORT

Since the acid rain program, EPA has struggled to address another pollution transport problem—the transport of ozone precursors, mainly NO_x. Its attempts to address the problem have produced a long saga of litigation and regulatory reversals stretching over two decades. It begins in the 1990s, when many communities struggled to comply with EPA's NAAQS for ground-level ozone. While the lion's share of the problem was attributable to local vehicle emissions, the problem was exacerbated in the Eastern United States by the downwind (mostly eastward) transport of ozone and its precursors, including NO_x, coming from fossil fuel combustion.

In response to pressure from Northeastern states and Congress, EPA began to study the problem of ozone transport with an eye toward imposing further limits on the emission of ozone precursors in the Eastern half of the United States. After concluding that the existing ozone NAAQS was insufficient to protect human health, the Clinton Administration promulgated a new, more stringent ozone standard in 1997,[3] which further exacerbated the ozone compliance problem for the states. The Clinton EPA also issued a rule in 1998 requiring 22 states in the eastern half of the country to further reduce their emissions of ozone precursors, specifically mandating that electric generating units share a significant portion of the burden of those reductions. This rule is known as the "NO_x SIP Call," because it required states to submit revised "state implementation plans" (SIPs) to describe how they planned to implement these additional restrictions on emissions of ozone precursors. Finding of Significant Contribution and Rulemaking for Certain States in the Ozone Transport Assessment Group Region for Purposes of Reducing Regional Transport of Ozone, 63 Fed. Reg. 57,356 (Oct. 27, 1998). It authorized a voluntary cap-and-trade program to achieve the reductions.

In 2005 the Bush EPA replaced the Clinton initiative with its own "Clean Air Interstate Rule" (CAIR), which imposed NO_x emission limits ("budgets") on 28 eastern states and the District of Columbia. Rule to Reduce Interstate Transport of Fine Particulate Matter and Ozone (Clean Air Interstate Rule), 70 Fed. Reg. 25,165 (Mar. 25, 2005). CAIR also addressed certain emissions of other interstate pollutants, and authorized states to achieve the required emission reductions under CAIR either: (1) by requiring power plants to participate in an EPA-administered interstate cap and trade system that caps emissions in two stages, or (2) through measures of the state's choosing. Using the SIP

---

[3]   The existing standard was expressed in terms of a one-hour average limit. That standard was replaced by an 8-hour standard at a level of 0.08 parts per million (ppm), which was generally considered to be a more stringent standard. *See* National Ambient Air Quality Standards for Ozone; Final Rule, 62 Fed. Reg. 38,856 (July 18, 1997).

process, EPA established an interstate NO$_x$ trading program under CAIR. However, in July 2008 the D.C. Circuit Court of Appeals overturned CAIR for, among other things, failing to properly address its stated purpose of reducing upwind contributions to NAAQS violations:

> Because EPA evaluated whether its proposed emissions reductions were "highly cost effective," at the regionwide level assuming a trading program, it never measured the "significant contribution" from sources within an individual state to downwind nonattainment areas. . . . Thus EPA's apportionment decisions have nothing to do with each state's "significant contribution" because under EPA's method of analysis, state budgets do not matter for significant contribution purposes.
>
> But according to Congress, individual state contributions to downwind nonattainment areas do matter. Section 110(a)(2)(D)(i)(I) prohibits sources *"within the State"* from "contribut[ing] significantly to nonattainment *in . . . any other State . . ."* (emphasis added). Yet under CAIR, sources in Alabama, which contribute to nonattainment of PM$_{2.5}$ NAAQS in Davidson County, North Carolina, would not need to reduce their emissions at all. Theoretically, sources in Alabama could purchase enough NO$_x$ and SO$_2$ allowances to cover all their current emissions, resulting in no change in Alabama's contribution to Davidson County, North Carolina's nonattainment. CAIR only assures that the entire region's significant contribution will be eliminated. It is possible that CAIR would achieve section 110(a)(2)(D)(i)(I)'s goals. . . . But EPA is not exercising its section 110(a)(2)(D)(i)(I) duty unless it is promulgating a rule that achieves something measurable toward the goal of prohibiting sources "within the State" from contributing to nonattainment or interfering with maintenance "in any other State."

North Carolina v. EPA, 531 F.3d 896, 907 (D.C. Cir. 2008).

After initially vacating the rule, the court granted EPA's petition to leave it in place pending amendments conforming to the court's decision. In response, the Obama EPA promulgated the Cross State Air Pollution Rule (CSAPR) to address interstate transport of SO$_2$ and NO$_x$ in July 2011. Federal Implementation Plans: Interstate Transport of Fine Particulate Matter and Ozone and Correction of SIP Approvals, 76 Fed. Reg. 48,208 (Aug. 8, 2011). The rule required 27 states to reduce power plant emissions of SO$_2$ and NO$_x$ that contribute to ozone and/or fine particle pollution in other states. Reductions in SO$_2$ emissions under the rule were significant: emissions would decline to 73 percent below 2005 levels in the covered states in 2014. However, in August 2012 the D.C. Circuit Court of Appeals struck down the rule, concluding that the rule violated the CAA by: (i) imposing emissions reductions obligations on upwind states beyond those authorized by the statute; and (ii) establishing a federal implementation plan for the rule, rather than allowing states to issue state plans. The Supreme Court granted certiorari, and issued its decision in 2014.

Environmental Protection Agency v. EME Homer Generation, L.P.

134 S.Ct. 1584 (2014).

■ JUSTICE GINSBURG delivered the opinion of the Court.

These cases concern the efforts of Congress and the Environmental Protection Agency (EPA or Agency) to cope with a complex problem: air pollution emitted in one State, but causing harm in other States. Left unregulated, the emitting or upwind State reaps the benefits of the economic activity causing the pollution without bearing all the costs. Conversely, downwind States to which the pollution travels are unable to achieve clean air because of the influx of out-of-state pollution they lack authority to control. To tackle the problem, Congress included a Good Neighbor Provision in the Clean Air Act (Act or CAA). That provision, in its current phrasing, instructs States to prohibit in-state sources "from emitting any air pollutant in amounts which will . . . contribute significantly" to downwind States' "nonattainment . . . , or interfere with maintenance," of any EPA-promulgated national air quality standard. 42 U.S.C. § 7410(a)(2)(D)(i).

Interpreting the Good Neighbor Provision, EPA adopted the Cross-State Air Pollution Rule (commonly and hereinafter called the Transport Rule). The rule calls for consideration of costs, among other factors, when determining the emission reductions an upwind State must make to improve air quality in polluted downwind areas. The Court of Appeals for the D.C. Circuit vacated the rule in its entirety. It held, 2 to 1, that the Good Neighbor Provision requires EPA to consider only each upwind State's physically proportionate responsibility for each downwind State's air quality problem. That reading is demanded, according to the D.C. Circuit, so that no State will be required to decrease its emissions by more than its ratable share of downwind-state pollution.

In *Chevron U.S.A. Inc.* v. *Natural Resources Defense Council, Inc.,* 467 U.S. 837 (1984), we reversed a D.C. Circuit decision that failed to accord deference to EPA's reasonable interpretation of an ambiguous Clean Air Act provision. Satisfied that the Good Neighbor Provision does not command the Court of Appeals' cost-blind construction, and that EPA reasonably interpreted the provision, we reverse the D.C. Circuit's judgment.

* * *

The statute requires States to eliminate those "amounts" of pollution that "contribute significantly to *nonattainment*" in downwind States. Thus, EPA's task is to reduce upwind pollution, but only in "amounts" that push a downwind State's pollution concentrations above the relevant NAAQS. As noted earlier, however, the nonattainment of downwind States results from the collective and interwoven contributions of multiple upwind States. The statute therefore calls upon the Agency to address a thorny causation problem: How should EPA allocate among multiple contributing up-wind States responsibility for a downwind State's excess pollution?

A simplified example illustrates the puzzle EPA faced. Suppose the Agency sets a NAAQS, with respect to a particular pollutant, at 100 parts per billion (ppb), and that the level of the pollutant in the atmosphere of downwind State A is 130 ppb. Suppose further that EPA has determined that each of three upwind States—X, Y, and Z—contributes the equivalent of 30 ppb of the relevant pollutant to State A's airspace. The Good Neighbor Provision, as just observed, prohibits only upwind emissions that contribute significantly to downwind *nonattainment*. EPA's authority under the provision is therefore limited to eliminating a *total* of 30 ppb, *i.e.,* the overage caused by the collective contribution of States X, Y, and Z.

How is EPA to divide responsibility among the three States? Should the Agency allocate reductions proportionally (10 ppb each), on a per capita basis, on the basis of the cost of abatement, or by some other metric? The Good Neighbor Provision does not answer that question for EPA. Under *Chevron*, we read Congress' silence as a delegation of authority to EPA to select from among reasonable options.

Yet the Court of Appeals believed that the Act speaks clearly, requiring EPA to allocate responsibility for reducing emissions in "a manner proportional to" each State's "contributio[n]" to the problem. Nothing in the text of the Good Neighbor Provision propels EPA down this path. Understandably so, for as EPA notes, the D.C. Circuit's proportionality approach could scarcely be satisfied in practice.

To illustrate, consider a variation on the example set out above. Imagine that States X and Y now contribute air pollution to State A in a ratio of one to five, *i.e.,* State Y contributes five times the amount of pollution to State A than does State X. If State A were the only downwind State to which the two upwind States contributed, the D.C. Circuit's proportionality requirement would be easy to meet: EPA could require State Y to reduce its emissions by five times the amount demanded of State X.

The realities of interstate air pollution, however, are not so simple. Most upwind States contribute pollution to multiple downwind States in varying amounts. Suppose then that States X and Y also contribute pollutants to a second downwind State (State B), this time in a ratio of seven to one. Though State Y contributed a relatively larger share of pollution to State A, with respect to State B, State X is the greater offender. Following the proportionality approach with respect to State B would demand that State X reduce its emissions by seven times as much as State Y. Recall, however, that State Y, as just hypothesized, had to effect five times as large a reduction with respect to State A. The Court of Appeals' proportionality edict with respect to *both* State A and State B appears to work neither mathematically nor in practical application. Proportionality as to one downwind State will not achieve proportionality as to others. Quite the opposite. And where, as is generally true, upwind States contribute pollution to more than two downwind receptors, proportionality becomes all the more elusive.

Neither the D.C. Circuit nor respondents face up to this problem. The dissent, for its part, strains to give meaning to the D.C. Circuit's proportionality constraint as applied to a world in which multiple upwind States contribute emissions to multiple downwind locations. In the dissent's view, upwind States must eliminate emissions by "whatever minimum amount reduces" their share of the overage in each and every one of the downwind States to which they are linked. In practical terms, this means each upwind State will be required to reduce emissions by the amount necessary to eliminate that State's largest downwind contribution. The dissent's formulation, however, does not account for the combined and cumulative effect of each upwind State's reductions on attainment in multiple downwind locations. The result would be costly overregulation unnecessary to, indeed in conflict with, the Good Neighbor Provision's goal of attainment.

In response, the dissent asserts that EPA will "simply be required to make allowance for" the overregulation caused by its "proportional-reduction" approach. What criterion should EPA employ to determine which States will have to make those "allowance[s]" and by how much? The dissent admits there are "multiple ways" EPA might answer those questions. But proportionality cannot be one of those ways, for the proportional-reduction approach is what led to the overregulation in the first place. And if a nonproportional approach can play a role in setting the final allocation of reduction obligations, then it is hardly apparent why EPA, free to depart from proportionality at the back end, cannot do so at the outset.

Persuaded that the Good Neighbor Provision does not dictate the particular allocation of emissions among contributing States advanced by the D.C. Circuit, we must next decide whether the allocation method chosen by EPA is a "permissible construction of the statute." *Chevron*, 467 U.S. at 843. As EPA interprets the statute, upwind emissions rank as "amounts [that] . . . contribute significantly to nonattainment" if they (1) constitute one percent or more of a relevant NAAQS in a nonattaining downwind State and (2) can be eliminated under the cost threshold set by the Agency. In other words, to identify which emissions were to be eliminated, EPA considered both the magnitude of upwind States' contributions and the cost associated with eliminating them.

The Industry respondents argue that, however EPA ultimately divides responsibility among upwind States, the final calculation cannot rely on costs. The Good Neighbor Provision, respondents and the dissent emphasize, "requires each State to prohibit only those '*amounts*' of air pollution emitted within the State that 'contribute significantly' to another State's nonattaintment." The cost of preventing emissions, they urge, is wholly unrelated to the actual "amoun[t]" of air pollution an upwind State contributes. Because the Transport Rule considers costs, respondents argue, "States that contribute identical 'amounts' . . . may be deemed [by EPA] to have [made] substantially *different*" contributions.

But, as just explained, the Agency cannot avoid the task of choosing which among equal "amounts" to eliminate. The Agency has chosen, sensibly in our view, to reduce the amount easier, *i.e.*, less costly, to eradicate, and nothing in the text of the Good Neighbor Provision precludes that choice.

Using costs in the Transport Rule calculus, we agree with EPA, also makes good sense. Eliminating those amounts that can cost-effectively be reduced is an efficient and equitable solution to the allocation problem the Good Neighbor Provision requires the Agency to address. Efficient because EPA can achieve the levels of attainment, *i.e.*, of emission reductions, the proportional approach aims to achieve, but at a much lower overall cost. Equitable because, by imposing uniform cost thresholds on regulated States, EPA's rule subjects to stricter regulation those States that have done relatively less in the past to control their pollution. Upwind States that have not yet implemented pollution controls of the same stringency as their neighbors will be stopped from free riding on their neighbors' efforts to reduce pollution. They will have to bring down their emissions by installing devices of the kind in which neighboring States have already invested.

Suppose, for example, that the industries of upwind State A have expended considerable resources installing modern pollution-control devices on their plants. Factories in upwind State B, by contrast, continue to run old, dirty plants. Yet, perhaps because State A is more populous and therefore generates a larger sum of pollution overall, the two States' emissions have equal effects on downwind attainment. If State A and State B are required to eliminate emissions proportionally (*i.e.*, equally), sources in State A will be compelled to spend far more per ton of reductions because they have already utilized lower cost pollution controls. State A's sources will also have to achieve greater reductions than would have been required had they not made the cost-effective reductions in the first place. State A, in other words, will be tolled for having done more to reduce pollution in the past. EPA's cost based allocation avoids these anomalies.

Obligated to require the elimination of only those "amounts" of pollutants that contribute to the nonattainment of NAAQS in downwind States, EPA must decide how to differentiate among the otherwise like contributions of multiple upwind States. EPA found decisive the difficulty of eliminating each "amount," *i.e.*, the cost incurred in doing so. Lacking a dispositive statutory instruction to guide it, EPA's decision, we conclude, is a "reasonable" way of filling the "gap left open by Congress."

* * *

For the reasons stated, the judgment of the United States Court of Appeals for the D.C. Circuit is reversed, and the cases are remanded for further proceedings consistent with this opinion.

It is so ordered.

■ JUSTICE ALITO took no part in the consideration or decision of these cases.

■ JUSTICE SCALIA, with whom JUSTICE THOMAS joins, dissenting.

Too many important decisions of the Federal Government are made nowadays by unelected agency officials exercising broad lawmaking authority, rather than by the people's representatives in Congress. With the statute involved in the present cases, however, Congress did it right. It specified quite precisely the responsibility of an upwind State under the Good Neighbor Provision: to eliminate those *amounts of pollutants* that it contributes to downwind problem areas. But the Environmental Protection Agency was unsatisfied with this system. Agency personnel, perhaps correctly, thought it more efficient to require reductions not in proportion to the *amounts of pollutants* for which each upwind State is responsible, but on the basis of how *cost-effectively* each can decrease emissions.

Today, the majority approves that undemocratic revision of the Clean Air Act. The Agency came forward with a textual justification for its action, relying on a farfetched meaning of the word "significantly" in the statutory text. That justification is so feeble that today's majority does not even recite it, much less defend it. The majority reaches its result ("Look Ma, no hands!") without benefit of text, claiming to have identified a remarkable "gap" in the statute, which it proceeds to fill (contrary to the plain logic of the statute) with cost-benefit analysis—and then, with no pretended textual justification at all, simply extends cost-benefit analysis beyond the scope of the alleged gap. . . .

I would affirm the judgment of the D.C. Circuit that EPA violated the law both in crafting the Transport Rule and in implementing it. ■

NOTES AND COMMENTS

1.   The Court also reversed the D.C. Circuit's conclusion that EPA failed to give states ample opportunity to prepare SIPs. The CAA requires EPA to promulgate a Federal Implementation Plan (FIP) for a state "at any time within two years" after finding that the state has failed to submit a SIP or a finding that an existing SIP is inadequate. 42 U.S.C. § 7410(c)(1). The D.C. Circuit had interpreted this provision to require EPA to give the states "a reasonable period of time" to submit a SIP after EPA established the emissions budget for the state. In this instance the agency declared the state SIP inadequate long before establishing an emissions budget for the state. Interpreting the Act mechanically, the Supreme Court concluded that:

> The Act does not require EPA to furnish upwind States with information of any kind about their good neighbor obligations before a FIP issues. Instead, a SIP's failure to satisfy the Good Neighbor Provision, without more, triggers EPA's obligation to issue a federal plan within two years. § 7410(c). After EPA has disapproved a SIP, the Agency can wait up to two years to issue a FIP, during which time the State can "correc[t] the deficiency" on its own. But EPA is not obliged to wait two years or postpone its action even a single day: The Act empowers the Agency to promulgate a FIP "at any time" within the two-year limit.

134 S. Ct. at 1601.

2.   EPA estimates that the CSAPR will impose compliance costs on the power sector of about $2.4 billion annually when fully implemented, and render about 4.8 GW of coal-fired electric generating capacity uneconomic. 76 Fed. Reg. at 48,346. By virtue of these changes, the CSAPR is projected to *reduce emissions of CO_2* from electrical generating units by about 25 million metric tons annually. *Id.* at 48,311. This is one of several CAA rules that promote incidental GHG emissions reductions by targeting other pollutants. Similarly, a rule targeting emissions of volatile organic compounds from natural gas facilities will yield significant reductions in emission of methane, another GHG. *See* Oil and Natural Gas Sector: New Source Performance Standards and National Emission Standards for Hazardous Air Pollutants Reviews, 77 Fed. Reg. 49,490 (Aug. 16, 2012). Should the benefits of reducing emissions of pollutant Y be part of the cost-benefit analysis of a rule mandating reduced emissions of pollutant X?

3. Justice Scalia's dissent expresses concern about "unelected bureaucrats" making policy decisions. However, according to some scholars, political polarization in Congress has rendered Congress increasingly unable to agree on legislative solutions to important policy decisions like those presented in the *EME Homer* case. As a consequence, EPA and other federal agencies seem likely to face increasing pressure to make difficult policy decisions without the input of Congress. Should courts reviewing agency decisions be more deferential to agency interpretations of their enabling laws knowing that Congress is paralyzed by gridlock? *See* Jody Freeman & David B. Spence, Old Statutes, New Problems, 161 U. Penn. L. Rev. 431 (2014) (arguing for judicial deference to agency decisions in an era of unprecedented gridlock).

C. REGULATING TOXIC POLLUTANTS UNDER THE CLEAN AIR ACT

Sulfur dioxide and NO_x are regulated as criteria pollutants under the CAA. However, the Act reserves its most stringent technology-based permitting standards for emissions of *toxic* pollutants, also known as "hazardous air pollutants" (HAPs). CAA § 112 specifies that permits for toxic pollutants must reflect "maximum achievable control technology" (MACT). The Act defines MACT as:

> Emission standards promulgated under this subsection *for existing sources* in a category or subcategory may be less stringent than standards for new sources in the same category or subcategory but shall not be less stringent, and may be more stringent than (A) the average emission limitation achieved by the best performing 12 percent of the existing sources (for which the Administrator has emissions information), excluding those sources that have, within 18 months before the emission standard is proposed or within 30 months before such standard is promulgated, whichever is later, first achieved a level of emission rate or emission reduction which complies, or would comply if the source is not subject to such standard, with the lowest achievable emission rate . . . or (B) the average emission limitation achieved by the best performing 5 sources (for which the Administrator has or could reasonably obtain emissions information) in the category or subcategory for categories or subcategories with fewer than 30 sources.

42 U.S.C. § 7412(d)(3) (emphasis added). Note that for toxic pollutants, unlike conventional pollutants like SO_2 and NO_x, the CAA's stringent permitting standards apply to new and existing sources of emissions alike.

As with ozone, the fight over how (and how stringently) to regulate mercury emissions from power plants has consumed decades. Despite longstanding awareness that the accumulation of mercury in the food chain might be responsible for an increased incidence of birth defects and neurological damage in humans, by the 1990s EPA had not yet regulated mercury emissions from coal-fired power plants. The CAAA90 directed EPA to study, and report to Congress on, the risks associated with toxic emissions from coal-fired power plants. The Sierra Club and Natural Resources Defense Council sued EPA for missing the statutory deadline for submitting its mercury report to Congress, and for failing to include coal-fired power plants on its list of sources of toxic pollution to be regulated under CAA § 112. EPA subsequently submitted two reports to Congress on this issue in the late 1990s: a study of the effects of mercury required by section 112(n)(1)(B) of the Act, and a second study focusing specifically on power plant emissions, required by section 112(n)(1)(A). *See* EPA, Mercury Study: Report to Congress, (EPA–452/R–97–003, Dec. 1997); EPA, Study of Hazardous Air Pollutant Emissions from Electric Steam Generating Units: Final Report to Congress (EPA–453/R–98–004a, Feb. 1998).

EPA's 1998 report to Congress on toxics emissions from coal-fired power plants concluded that regulating these emissions was both "appropriate and necessary." That conclusion, in turn, led to a December 2000 proposal by the Clinton EPA to regulate mercury emissions from coal-fired power plants as a toxic pollutant under § 112 of the CAA, and to create a MACT standard for mercury emissions from coal-fired power plants. However, the Bush Administration reversed the finding that regulating mercury emissions under § 112 is appropriate and necessary, and imposed a less stringent "cap and trade" system for mercury emissions, one that did not include establishing a MACT standard for mercury emissions from coal-fired power plants. Revision of December 2000 Regulatory Finding on the Emissions of Hazardous Air Pollutants From Electric Utility Steam Generating Units and the Removal of Coal- and Oil-Fired Electric Utility Steam Generating Units From the Section 112(c) List, 70 Fed. Reg. 15,994 (Mar. 29, 2005).

Various states and environmental groups filed suit in federal court to challenge the legality of EPA's new approach to regulating mercury emissions from coal-fired power plants. The D.C. Circuit Court of Appeals struck down the rule in *New Jersey v. EPA*, 517 F.3d 574 (D.C. Cir. 2008). The court said:

> Environmental Petitioners contend that EPA violated Section 112's plain text and structure when it did not comply with the requirements of section 112(c)(9) in delisting EGUs. . . . Petitioners contend that once the Administrator determined in 2000 that EGUs should be regulated under Section 112 and listed them under section 112(c)(1), EPA had no authority to delist them without taking the steps required under section 112(c)(9). We agree.

> Section 112(c)(9) provides that:

>> The Administrator may delete *any* source category from the [section 112(c)(1) list] . . . whenever the Administrator . . . [determines] that emissions from no source in the category or subcategory concerned . . . exceed a level which is adequate to protect public health with an ample margin of safety and no adverse environmental effect will result from emissions from any source. [emphasis added]

> EPA concedes that it listed EGUs under section 112 [and] EPA concedes that it never made the findings section 112(c)(9) would require in order to delist EGUs. EPA's purported removal of EGUs from the section 112(c)(1) list therefore violated the

CAA's plain text and must be rejected under step one of *Chevron*.

EPA maintains that it possesses authority to remove EGUs from the section 112 list under the "fundamental principle of administrative law that an agency has inherent authority to reverse an earlier administrative determination or ruling where an agency has a principled basis for doing so." An agency can normally change its position and reverse a decision, and prior to EPA's listing of EGUs under section 112(c)(1), nothing in the CAA would have prevented it from reversing its determination about whether it was "appropriate and necessary" to do so. Congress, however, undoubtedly can limit an agency's discretion to reverse itself, and in section 112(c)(9) Congress did just that, unambiguously limiting EPA's discretion to remove sources, including EGUs, from the section 112(c)(1) list once they have been added to it.

517 F.3d at 582.

In February 2012, EPA finalized its MACT standard for the emissions of HAPs from coal-fired power plants. National Emission Standards for Hazardous Air Pollutants From Coal and Oil-Fired Electric Utility Steam Generating Units and Standards of Performance for Fossil-Fuel-Fired Electric Utility, Industrial-Commercial-Institutional, and Small Industrial-Commercial-Institutional Steam Generating Units, 77 Fed. Reg. 9304 (Feb. 16, 2012). The rule is variously referred to as the "MATS rule" (mercury and air toxics rule) or the "Utility MACT" rule. A broad array of industry and environmental petitioners challenged the rule in court. Part of the D.C. Circuit's response to those challenges follows.

White Stallion Energy Center, LLC v. EPA

748 F.3d 1222 (D.C. Cir. 2014).

■ PER CURIAM. In 2012, the Environmental Protection Agency promulgated emission standards for a number of listed hazardous air pollutants emitted by coal- and oil-fired electric utility steam generating units. In this complex case, we address the challenges to the Final Rule by State, Industry, and Labor petitioners, by Industry petitioners to specific aspects of the Final Rule, by Environmental petitioners, and by Julander Energy Company. For the following reasons, we deny the petitions challenging the Final Rule.

II.

State, Industry, and Labor petitioners challenge EPA's interpretation and application of the "appropriate and necessary" requirement in § 112(n)(1)(A). . . . Apart from the instruction to "consider the results of the [Utility Study]" on public health hazards from [Electric Generating Unit ("EGU")] emissions, the statute offers no express guidance regarding what factors EPA is required or permitted to consider in deciding whether regulation under § 112 is "appropriate and necessary." Neither does it define the words "appropriate" or "necessary.". . . If, however, the statute is silent or ambiguous with respect to the specific issue, the court will uphold the agency's interpretation so long as it constitutes "a permissible construction of the statute. . . . To the extent petitioners' challenge concerns EPA's change in interpretation from that in 2005, our approach is the same because "[a]gency inconsistency is not a basis for declining to analyze the agency's interpretation under the *Chevron* framework." *Nat'l Cable & Telecomms. Ass'n v. Brand X Internet Servs.*, 545 U.S. 967, 981 (2005). That is, "if the agency adequately explains the reasons for a reversal of policy, change is not invalidating, since the whole point of *Chevron* is to leave the discretion provided by the ambiguities of a statute with the implementing agency." *Id.*

Reliance on delisting criteria. In the Final Rule, EPA concluded that it is "appropriate and necessary" to regulate HAP emissions on the basis, *inter alia*, that EGU emissions of certain HAPs pose a cancer risk higher than the standard set forth in the § 112(c)(9) delisting criteria (i.e., greater than one in a million for the most exposed individual). Petitioners contend that by so doing EPA wrongly conflated the delisting criteria with the "appropriate and necessary" determination. "By applying the delisting provisions of § 112(c)(9) in making the initial, pre-listing determination whether it is 'appropriate and necessary' to regulate EGUs, EPA has unlawfully imposed requirements on itself the Congress chose not to impose at the listing stage." They maintain that EPA's approach "would treat EGUs the same as all other major source categories—as a category that must be listed unless the delisting criteria are met." EPA explained that it was relying upon the delisting criteria to interpret an ambiguous term in § 112(n)(1)(A), namely, "hazards to public health," because the phrase "hazards to public health" is nowhere defined in the CAA. EPA looked to the delisting criteria, which specify the risk thresholds below which a source category need not be regulated, as evidence of congressional judgment as to what degree of risk constitutes a health hazard.

EPA explained:

> Although Congress provided no definition of hazard to public health, section 12(c)(9)(B) is instructive. In that section, Congress set forth a test for removing source categories from the section 112(c) source category list. That test is relevant because it reflects Congress' view as to the level of health effects associated with HAP emissions that Congress thought warranted continued regulation under section 112.

NPRM, 76 Fed. Reg. at 24,993 (emphasis added) . . .

EPA reasonably relied on the § 112(c)(9) delisting criteria to inform its interpretation of the undefined statutory term "hazard to public health." Congress did not specify what types or levels of public health risks should be deemed a "hazard" for purposes of § 112(n)(1)(A). By leaving this gap in the statute, Congress delegated to EPA the authority to give reasonable meaning to the term. EPA's approach does not, as petitioners contend, "treat EGUs the same as all other major source categories." Other major source categories must be listed unless the delisting criteria are satisfied; EPA's approach treats EGUs quite differently. For EGUs, EPA reasonably determined that it may look at a broad range of factors—only one of which concerned the § 112(c)(9) benchmark levels—in assessing the health hazards posed by EGU HAPs. Nowhere does EPA state or imply that the delisting criteria provide the sole basis for determining whether it is "appropriate and necessary" to regulate EGUs under § 112. Because EPA's approach is based on a permissible construction of § 112(n)(1)(A), it is entitled to deference and must be upheld.

Costs of regulation. Noting that in 2005 EPA construed § 112(n)(1)(A) to allow consideration of costs in determining whether regulation of EGU HAP emissions is "appropriate," petitioners contend that EPA's new interpretation to "preclude consideration of costs unreasonably constrains the language of § 112(n)(1)(A)." They point to the dictionary definition of "appropriate" and to the differences between regulation of EGUs under § 112(n)(1)(A) and regulating other sources under § 112(c), and to this court's precedent that "only where there is 'clear congressional intent to preclude consideration of cost' [do] we find agencies barred from considering costs." . . .

On its face, § 112(n)(1)(A) neither requires EPA to consider costs nor prohibits EPA from doing so. Indeed, the word "costs" appears nowhere in subparagraph A. In the absence of any express statutory instruction regarding costs, petitioners rely on the dictionary definition of "appropriate"—meaning "especially suitable or compatible" or "suitable or proper in the circumstances"—to argue that EPA was required "to take into account costs to the nation's electricity generators when deciding whether to regulate EGUs." Yet these definitions, which do not mention costs, merely underscore that the term "appropriate" is "open-ended," "ambiguous," and "inherently context-dependent." *Sossamon v. Texas*, 131 S. Ct. 1651, 1659 (2011); *cf. Nat'l Ass'n of Clean Air Agencies v. EPA*, 489 F.3d 1221, 1229 (D.C. Cir. 2007). Even if the word "appropriate" might require cost consideration in some contexts, such a reading of "appropriate" is unwarranted here, where Congress directed EPA's attention to the conclusions of the study regarding public health hazards from EGU emissions. Throughout § 112, Congress mentioned costs explicitly where it intended EPA to consider them. Indeed, in the immediately following subparagraph of § 112(n), Congress expressly required costs to be considered. The contrast with subparagraph A could not be more stark. "Where Congress includes particular language in one section of a statute but omits it in another section of the same Act, it is generally presumed that Congress acts intentionally . . . in the disparate inclusion or exclusion." *Russello v. United States*, 464 U.S. 16, 23 (1983) (alterations omitted); *cf. Catawba Cnty., N.C. v. EPA*, 571 F.3d 20, 36 (D.C. Cir. 2009). Petitioners offer no compelling reason why Congress, by using only the broad term "appropriate," would have intended the same result—that costs be considered—in § 112(n)(1)(A). The legislative history the dissent claims "establishes" the point, consists of a Floor statement by a single congressman that at best is ambiguous.

For these reasons, we conclude that the statute does not evince unambiguous congressional intent on the specific issue of whether EPA was required to consider costs in making its "appropriate and necessary" determination under § 112(n)(1)(A). EPA's . . . position that "nothing about the definition of ['appropriate'] compels a consideration of costs," Final Rule, is clearly permissible.

Environmental harms. Petitioners also contend that EPA was constrained to consider only public health hazards, not environmental or other harms, in making its "appropriate and necessary" determination.

In their view, § 112(n)(1)(A) unambiguously forecloses the consideration of non-health effects because the statute requires EPA to make its "appropriate and necessary" determination after considering the results of the Utility Study, which is focused exclusively on identifying "hazards to public health" caused by EGU HAP emissions. Petitioners insist that in 2005 EPA followed the health-only approach.

EPA reasoned that "nothing in the statute suggests that the [EPA] should ignore adverse environmental effects in determining whether to regulate EGUs under section 112." To the contrary, EPA concluded that the purpose of the CAA and the statute's express instruction to assess environmental effects in the Mercury Study suggest "it is reasonable to consider environmental effects in evaluating the hazards posed by HAP emitted from EGUs." EPA explained in response to comments that restricting it from considering environmental harms would "incorrectly conflate the requirements for the Utility Study with the requirement to regulate EGUs under CAA section 112 if EPA determines it is appropriate and necessary to do so."

EPA did not err in considering environmental effects alongside health effects for purposes of the "appropriate and necessary" determination. Although petitioners' interpretation of § 112(n)(1)(A) is plausible, the statute could also be read to treat consideration of the Utility Study as a mere condition precedent to the "appropriate and necessary" determination. EPA has consistently adopted this latter interpretation, including in 2005. In the absence of any limiting text, and considering the context (including § 112(n)(1)(B)) and purpose of the CAA, EPA reasonably concluded that it could consider environmental harms in making its "appropriate and necessary" determination. . . .

Regulation under § 112(d). Petitioners contend that even if it is "appropriate and necessary" to regulate EGU HAP emissions, such regulation should be effected under § 112(n)(1)(A) to the degree appropriate and necessary—not under § 112(d) through the imposition of MACT standards. They maintain that regulation of EGU HAPs that do not pose health hazards, or regulation at a level higher than needed to eliminate such hazards, is not regulation that is "appropriate and necessary." Petitioners contend that § 112(n)(1)(A)'s instruction to "regulate electric steam generating units under this section" (emphasis added)—rather than "under § 112(d)"—evinces congressional intent that EGU HAPs should be regulated differently than other sources. EPA expressly considered and dismissed petitioners' proposed interpretation. EPA concluded that the phrase "under this section" presumptively refers to regulation under section 112, not to regulation under subparagraph 112(n)(1)(A). Thus, the plain statutory language suggests "EGUs should be regulated in the same manner as other categories for which the statute requires regulation." . . . EPA acted properly in regulating EGUs under § 112(d). Section 112(n)(1)(A) directs the Administrator to "regulate electric steam generating units under this section, if the Administrator finds such regulation is appropriate and necessary." EPA reasonably interprets the phrase "under this section" to refer to the entirety of section 112.

■ KAVANAUGH, CIRCUIT JUDGE, concurring in part and dissenting in part.

Suppose you were the EPA Administrator. You have to decide whether to go forward with a proposed air quality regulation. Your only statutory direction is to decide whether it is "appropriate" to go forward with the regulation. Before making that decision, what information would you want to know? You would certainly want to understand the benefits from the regulations. And you would surely ask how much the regulations would cost. You would no doubt take both of those considerations—benefits and costs—into account in making your decision. That's just common sense and sound government practice.

So it comes as a surprise in this case that EPA excluded any consideration of costs when deciding whether it is "appropriate"—the key statutory term—to impose significant new air quality regulations on the Nation's electric utilities. In my view, it is unreasonable for EPA to exclude consideration of costs in determining whether it is "appropriate" to impose significant new regulations on electric utilities. To be sure, EPA could conclude that the benefits outweigh the costs. But the problem here is that EPA did not even consider the costs. And the costs are huge, about $9.6 billion a year—that's billion with a b—by EPA's own calculation. ∎

NOTES AND COMMENTS

1. EPA estimates that annual compliance costs for the electric power industry will be about $9.6 billion, but that the rule will have negligible overall impacts on jobs. Most of these costs represent what EPA describes as "co-benefits," or damages done by PM emissions, not damage unique to mercury particles. 77 Fed. Reg. at 9425–26. Industry estimates much more significant job losses and slightly higher costs. *See* Anne E. Smith et al., An Economic Impact Analysis of EPA's Mercury and Air Toxics Standards Rule, NERA Econ. Consulting (Mar. 1, 2012), http://www.nera.com/67_7631.htm. The agency estimates that the benefits of the new rule will greatly exceed its costs, and that most of those benefits will consist of averted deaths, neurological disorders, diseases and environmental effects associated with coal-fired power emissions. Industry and some states have claimed that the new mercury MACT standard will interfere with electric power reliability, as coal-fired power plants are taken off-line faster than they can be replaced. EPA rejects this contention, concluding that "industry is well-positioned to comply with EPA's proposed air regulations without threatening electric system reliability." 77 Fed. Reg. at 9407.

2. As the name implies, the Utility MACT rule regulates more than mercury missions from coal-fired power plants. It establishes MACT standards for emissions of several air toxics—specifically mercury (Hg), arsenic (As), chromium (Cr), and nickel (Ni); and acid gases, including hydrochloric acid (HCl) and hydrofluoric acid (HF)—from coal-fired and oil-fired facilities. It simultaneously revised NSPS limits on NO_x, PM and other conventional pollutants for fossil-fueled power plants generally. Petitioners in *White Stallion* objected to the coverage of toxic emissions that were not considered as part of the original 2000 "necessary and appropriate" finding. The D.C. Circuit rejected that challenge, citing precedent that once EPA regulates toxic/HAP emissions from a source category, it should regulate all such emissions. 748 F.3d at 1244.

3. The majority opinion in *White Stallion* comprises more than 60 pages, responds to a wide variety of technical challenges to the rule, and concludes that certain plaintiffs lacked standing to challenge certain parts of the rule because they fall outside the zone of interests protected by the Clean Air Act.

The Supreme Court has agreed to hear an appeal on the issue of whether EPA improperly refused to consider costs when deciding whether it was "appropriate" to regulate toxic emissions from electric utility generators. As of this writing the Court had scheduled oral argument in March 2015.

D. REGULATING GREENHOUSE GAS EMISSIONS UNDER THE CLEAN AIR ACT

1. CLIMATE CHANGE AND GREENHOUSE GAS EMISSIONS

There is a consensus among climate scientists that emissions of GHGs are transforming the Earth's climate, and that the potential damage to human communities and natural ecosystems is likely to be far-reaching and long-lasting. The "greenhouse effect" is the name given to the process that occurs when GHGs accumulate in the atmosphere and trap heat at the surface of the earth, thus contributing to increases in temperature levels. Jean-Baptiste-Joseph Fourier hypothesized its existence in the 1820s, *see* Gale E. Christianson, Greenhouse: The 200-Year Story of Global Warming 11–12 (1999), and the Swedish chemist Svante Arrhenius was awarded the Nobel prize for his calculations of the greenhouse effect as early as 1903. *Id.* at 105–115. Climatologists have been focusing intently on this problem for many decades, and in 1992 the United Nations Framework Convention on Climate Change (UNFCCC) represented the developed world's first collective attempt to address the problem. The United States signed and ratified the UNFCCC; it signed but did not ratify the later Kyoto Protocol, which went into force in 2005. Indeed, until recently the United States lagged behind Europe in its efforts to regulate GHG emissions. This chapter covers legal regimes being employed in the United States to address this problem. For a source on international climate change law, see Duncan French & Lavanya Rajamani, Climate Change and International Environmental Law: Musings on a Journey to Somewhere, 25 J. Envt'l L. 437 (2013).

In addition to CO_2, other greenhouse gases include N_2O, SO_2, chlorofluorocarbons (CFCs) and tropospheric ozone. Methane, the primary component of natural gas, is itself a powerful greenhouse gas that on a molecule-for-molecule basis has over twenty times the heat retention power of carbon dioxide. The net effect of the GHG accumulation is that the earth's atmosphere acts as a blanket to retain the sun's heat and maintain the earth's average surface temperature of about 15ËC. This heat retention is principally due to the action of the particles and gases that give rise to the greenhouse effect. A certain amount of greenhouse gas is needed to keep a planet at a habitable temperature; the earth would be much colder in the absence of any greenhouse warming. But when the amount of GHGs increases, there is an increase in the planet's temperature because more heat is trapped. Temperature increases are not uniform at the earth's surface, and GHGs trapped in the atmosphere cause some places to become cooler. The term "climate change" is therefore more accurate than global warming, although both terms are in common use.

Much of global warming science has been developed and organized by the Intergovernmental Panel on Climate Change (IPCC), established in 1988 by the World Meteorological Organization and the United

Nations Environment Programme. *See* http://www.ipcc.ch/. The IPCC includes thousands of scientists from around the world, representing the model builders and other academic and governmental agencies with expertise in climate science. The IPCC was directed to prepare a report every five years that would indicate the consensus of the views of the expert community about the extent of climate change that was likely to take place, and its causes. The IPCC reports are based on sophisticated computer climate models that seek to replicate the forces that affect climate on a global basis and distinguish between natural and anthropogenic influences on climate. The models are updated and recalibrated through a constant process of comparing modeled and observed spatial and temporal patterns of climate change.

In 2013, the Fifth Assessment Report of the IPCC (IPCC AR5) reaffirmed that the planet is warming, and that it is extremely likely that human-generated emissions are the cause:

> Warming of the climate system is unequivocal, and since the 1950s, many of the observed changes are unprecedented over decades to millennia. The atmosphere and ocean have warmed, the amounts of snow and ice have diminished, sea level has risen, and the concentrations of greenhouse gases have increased. Each of the last three decades has been successively warmer at the Earth's surface than any preceding decade since 1850. In the Northern Hemisphere, 1983–2012 was likely the warmest 30-year period of the last 1400 years. . . .
>
> Understanding recent changes in the climate system results from combining observations, studies of feedback processes, and model simulations. Evaluation of the ability of climate models to simulate recent changes requires consideration of the state of all modelled climate system components at the start of the simulation and the natural and anthropogenic forcing used to drive the models. Compared to AR4, more detailed and longer observations and improved climate models now enable the attribution of a human contribution to detected changes in more climate system components. Human influence on the climate system is clear. This is evident from the increasing greenhouse gas concentrations in the atmosphere, positive radiative forcing, observed warming, and understanding of the climate system. . . .
>
> Human influence has been detected in warming of the atmosphere and the ocean, in changes in the global water cycle, in reductions in snow and ice, in global mean sea level rise, and in changes in some climate extremes. This evidence for human influence has grown since AR4. *It is extremely likely that human influence has been the dominant cause of the observed warming* since the mid-20th century.[4]

IPCC, Climate Change 2013: The Physical Basis (2013) (emphasis added).

---

[4] In the IPCC assessment reports, terms such as "extremely likely" are associated with specific probabilities. For example, the term "virtually certain" means 99–100% probability, "extremely likely means as 95–100% probability, and "very likely" (the term used in the Fourth Assessment Report) means a 90–100% probability.

Climatological science presents policymakers with three key propositions: (1) atmospheric levels of GHGs are increasing because of human activities; (2) GHGs absorb and re-radiate infrared radiation in a way that heats the planet; and (3) atmospheric changes are long-lasting because: the major GHGs remain in the atmosphere for periods ranging from a decade to centuries, and the climate itself has considerable inertia, mainly because of the high heat capacity of the world ocean. While climatologists continue to debate the speed and impacts of these changes, there seems little doubt that these changes will be momentous. The risks these changes pose are by now familiar to most informed observers: inundation of low-lying areas and associated loss of assets and displacement of people, increased global conflict over resources associated with climate-induced migration, increased incidence of drought and severe weather, and associated property and human losses, etc.

Economists and geoscientists employ a variety of models, including "integrated assessment models" (IAMs), to measure the costs and benefits of reducing greenhouse gas emissions. These models try to determine the optimal emissions path for society, taking into consideration a wide variety of characteristics about the natural carbon cycle, the impacts of human activity on that cycle, predictions about how natural and human systems will respond to climate change, and more. *See, e.g.*, Lawrence H. Goulder and William A. Pizer, The Economics of Climate Change, Resources for the Future Discussion Paper 06–06 (2006); Michael D. Mastrandrea, Calculating the Benefits of Climate Policy: Examining the Assumptions of Integrated Assessment Models, Pew Ctr. on Global Climate Change (2004). These kinds of models try to estimate a wide variety of impacts of increasing global temperatures, including damage to markets (such as changing crop yields) and property (such as the inundation of land), direct and indirect costs associated with the reduced availability of fresh water (such as health effects and relocation costs), damage from more extreme weather events or sea level rise (such as flooding), lost ecosystem services, and lost biodiversity. Some of these costs are far easier to quantify than others, and researchers must sometimes make assumptions about how (and how successfully) humans and ecosystems will adapt to change. Likewise, estimating the cost of reducing GHG emissions requires assumptions about how the public and private sectors will pursue this goal. Will governments mandate emissions reductions? If so, how? Will the U.S. government impose a tradable permitting system? Will it impose environmental taxes? There are also questions about how modelers should discount the future, given that GHGs remain in the atmosphere for a very long time, and that the benefits of reducing emissions will accrue mostly to future generations while the costs will be borne by the current generation.

Different models answer these questions differently, employing different assumptions and discount rates. Naturally, this has led to varying estimates of the net benefits of reducing greenhouse gas emissions. Certainly, the worst-case scenarios are bleak, but there is disagreement over the probability of encountering the worst-case scenario. One 2005 meta-analysis, by Richard Tol, looked at 28 climate change IAM studies and attempted to summarize conclusions they reached. Tol concluded that the 90 percent confidence interval for estimates of the benefits of reducing climate change ranged from-$10 per ton of carbon (implying that climate change represents a net benefit to society) to $350 per ton of carbon. Richard S.J. Tol, The Marginal Damage Costs of Carbon Dioxide Emissions: an Assessment of the Uncertainties, 33 Energy Pol'y 2064 (2005). We can ascribe some of this variation to the difficulty of predicting how the climate system will react to temperature increases, and how (and how effectively) humans will react and adapt to physical changes in the environment. On the other hand, there is much more certainty about (and much smaller confidence intervals around estimates of) the costs of reducing GHG emissions. For example, we are developing better data about the cost of capturing carbon and storing it, though this technology remains in its infancy. We also have much more experience with lower-polluting combined cycle natural gas plants and renewable energy, and are learning more about the costs of electric cars and hybrid cars, for example.

Despite the uncertainty, the vast majority of economic studies of climate change conclude that the benefits of reducing emissions exceed the costs. A 2014 analysis estimated the damages from climate change in Europe to be at least 190 billion, representing a loss of almost 2 percent of GDP. A prominent meta-analysis commissioned by the British government, called the "Stern Review," reaches this conclusion, and argues further that recent experience with temperature change implies that the costs of warming will be far greater than earlier models anticipated. The Stern Review concludes that:

- The world will be unlikely to stabilize greenhouse gases concentrations at the equivalent of 450 ppm of CO_2; rather, a concentration in the neighborhood of 500 to 550 ppm is more likely.

- Stabilizing emissions at the 550 ppm level will cost approximately 1% of GDP, but will avoid costs that are likely to be five to 10 times greater than that.

Nicholas Stern, The Stern Review: the Economics of Climate Change (2006). *But see* Richard S. J. Tol, The Stern Review of the Economics of Climate Change: A Comment (Oct. 30, 2006) (disputing elements of the Stern analysis).

Of course, the United States is a major contributor to the problem. In 2012, U.S. total GHG emissions were 6,526 million metric tons CO_2 equivalent, of which more than 5,000 million metric tons were emitted by fossil fuel combustion. About 40 percent of that number, in turn, represents fossil-fueled electric generating facilities, with the remainder attributed to transportation uses, industrial uses, and miscellaneous other uses. EPA, Inventory of U.S. Greenhouse Gas Emissions and Sinks: 1990–2012 (2014). The amount of GHGs a power plant emits depends upon the type of fossil fuel it burns to generate electricity. Coal-fired power—which accounted for more than three-fourths of electric power industry's CO_2 emissions in 2012—has the highest rate of CO_2 emissions per unit of energy used among fossil fuels. Natural gas, itself primarily the GHG methane, also produces CO_2 during combustion.

Neither the Clinton Administration (whose representatives signed the Kyoto Agreement) nor the Bush Administration made serious efforts to regulate GHG emissions. Rather, it has been the Obama EPA that has spearheaded the effort to regulate GHG emissions in the United States using the tools available to it under the CAA. This was not the Administration's preferred approach. It developed regulations under the CAA only after failing to secure new legislation addressing GHG emissions. Energy bills introduced by the Democratic majority during the 111th Congress represented by far the most comprehensive and fundamental attempt at regulatory reform in quite some time. In the Summer of 2009, the House of Representatives passed H.R. 2454, the American Clean Energy and Security Act of 2009, also known as the "Waxman-Markey bill." H.R. 2454 (111th Cong.).

Among other things, the Waxman-Markey bill:

- required the EPA administrator to promulgate regulations creating a marketable permit system for GHG emissions effective in 2012 (with an ultimate goal of reducing emissions to 17% of 2005 levels by the year 2050),
- required a 65% reduction in carbon dioxide emissions from electric generating units by 2020, and
- authorized the EPA administrator to establish GHG emissions standards for new heavy-duty vehicles.

However, the Senate took no final action on energy legislation in the 111th Congress. The bill that garnered the most attention in the media was S.1733, the Clean Energy Jobs and American Power Act, also known as the "Kerry-Boxer" bill, S. 1733 (111th Cong.). But Kerry-Boxer was never reported out of committee in the Senate, and the Waxman-Markey bill (which passed narrowly in the House) was pronounced "dead on arrival" in the Senate by various commentators. Opposition from Republicans and coal-state Democrats has left the prospects for climate change legislation bleak in subsequent Congresses.

2.   THRESHOLD QUESTIONS UNDER THE CLEAN AIR ACT

a.   MASSACHUSETTS V. EPA

It is probably safe to say that the CAA regulatory regime was not designed with GHG emissions in mind. Humans are harmed by exposure to criteria and toxic pollutants, by ingesting or inhaling them directly or indirectly (as when we ingest fish tainted by mercury). Therefore, the CAA establishes NAAQS and NSPS standards that are designed to minimize harmful exposures. By contrast, GHGs are not "toxic" to humans, nor is it easy to conceive of how one might develop a NAAQS for GHGs. Nonetheless, despite the awkward fit between the statute and the problem, GHG emissions do cause harm to humans, and the CAA does offer EPA tools with which to address the problem. The Bush EPA resisted their use, however. In 2003, EPA's general counsel, Robert Fabricant, reversed a position taken by the agency's two previous general counsels on this issue. Fabricant declared that CO_2 does not fall under the CAA's definition of an air pollutant and that EPA did not have the authority to regulate. On the same day, EPA denied a rulemaking petition filed by 19 individuals asking EPA to regulate CO_2 emissions from new motor vehicles, using its authority to control emissions from mobile sources under Title II of the CAA, § 202 (42 U.S.C. § 7521). *See* Control of Emissions From New Highway Vehicles and Engines, 68 Fed. Reg. 52,922 (2003). The denial stated that EPA did not have the authority to regulate CO_2 emissions from automobiles, and would refuse to exercise it even if it did.

Twelve states and numerous other parties challenged these actions in the D.C. Circuit. A divided panel of the D.C. Circuit upheld EPA's decision. Circuit Judge Randolph's opinion for the court stated that EPA properly exercised the discretion given to it under CAA § 202(a)(1) in denying the petition for rulemaking. Circuit Judge Sentelle wrote separately in a concurring opinion that the plaintiffs did not have standing to bring the lawsuit.[5]

The Supreme Court granted certiorari and addressed both issues: the plaintiffs' standing and the underlying challenge to EPA's refusal to regulate CO_2 emissions. First, the Court held that Massachusetts had standing to challenge EPA's refusal to regulate GHG emissions from motor vehicles. Next, the Court turned to the remaining two questions: whether EPA has the statutory authority to regulate GHG emissions from new motor vehicles; and if so, whether its stated reasons for refusing to do so were consistent with the CAA.

Massachusetts v. EPA

549 U.S. 497 (2007).

■ JUSTICE STEVENS delivered the opinion of the Court.

Section 202(a)(1) of the Clean Air Act provides:

"The [EPA] Administrator shall by regulation prescribe (and from time to time revise) in accordance with the provisions of this section, standards applicable to the emission of any air pollutant from any class or classes of new motor vehicles or new motor vehicle engines, which in his judgment cause, or contribute to, air pollution which may reasonably be anticipated to endanger public health or welfare. . . ."

The Act defines "air pollutant" to include "any air pollution agent or combination of such agents, including any physical, chemical, biological, radioactive . . . substance or matter which is emitted into or otherwise enters the ambient air." § 7602(g). "Welfare" is also defined broadly: among other things, it includes "effects on . . . weather . . . and climate." § 7602(h). . . .

In concluding that it lacked statutory authority over greenhouse gases, EPA observed that Congress "was well aware of the global climate change issue when it last comprehensively amended the [Clean Air Act] in 1990," yet it declined to adopt a proposed amendment establishing binding emissions limitations. EPA further reasoned that Congress' "specially tailored solutions to global atmospheric issues,"—in particular, its 1990 enactment of a comprehensive scheme to regulate pollutants that depleted the ozone layer—counseled against reading the general authorization of § 202(a)(1) to confer regulatory authority over greenhouse gases.

EPA stated that it was "urged on in this view" by this Court's decision in FDA v. Brown & Williamson Tobacco Corp., 529 U.S. 120

---

[5] The standing requirement comes from Article III of the Constitution, which limits federal court jurisdiction to "Cases" and "Controversies." *See* Lujan v. Defenders of Wildlife, 504 U.S. 555 (1992).

(2000). In that case, relying on "tobacco['s] unique political history," we invalidated the Food and Drug Administration's reliance on its general authority to regulate drugs as a basis for asserting jurisdiction over an "industry constituting a significant portion of the American economy," ibid.

EPA reasoned that climate change had its own "political history": Congress designed the original Clean Air Act to address local air pollutants rather than a substance that "is fairly consistent in its concentration throughout the world's atmosphere." Because of this political history, and because imposing emission limitations on greenhouse gases would have even greater economic and political repercussions than regulating tobacco, EPA was persuaded that it lacked the power to do so. In essence, EPA concluded that climate change was so important that unless Congress spoke with exacting specificity, it could not have meant the agency to address it.

Having reached that conclusion, EPA believed it followed that greenhouse gases cannot be "air pollutants" within the meaning of the Act. The agency bolstered this conclusion by explaining that if carbon dioxide were an air pollutant, the only feasible method of reducing tailpipe emissions would be to improve fuel economy. But because Congress has already created detailed mandatory fuel economy standards subject to Department of Transportation (DOT) administration, the agency concluded that EPA regulation would either conflict with those standards or be superfluous.

Even assuming that it had authority over greenhouse gases, EPA explained in detail why it would refuse to exercise that authority. The agency began by recognizing that the concentration of greenhouse gases has dramatically increased as a result of human activities, and acknowledged the attendant increase in global surface air temperatures. EPA nevertheless gave controlling importance to the NRC Report's statement that a causal link between the two " 'cannot be unequivocally established.' " Given that residual uncertainty, EPA concluded that regulating greenhouse gas emissions would be unwise.

The agency furthermore characterized any EPA regulation of motor-vehicle emissions as a "piecemeal approach" to climate change, and stated that such regulation would conflict with the President's "comprehensive approach" to the problem. According to EPA, unilateral EPA regulation of motor-vehicle greenhouse gas emissions might also hamper the President's ability to persuade key developing countries to reduce greenhouse gas emissions. Id., at 52931.

Because EPA believes that Congress did not intend it to regulate substances that contribute to climate change, the agency maintains that carbon dioxide is not an "air pollutant" within the meaning of the provision.

The statutory text forecloses EPA's reading. The Clean Air Act's sweeping definition of "air pollutant" includes "any air pollution agent or combination of such agents, including any physical, chemical . . . substance or matter which is emitted into or otherwise enters the ambient air. . . ." § 7602(g) (emphasis added). On its face, the definition embraces all airborne compounds of whatever stripe, and underscores that intent through the repeated use of the word "any." Carbon dioxide, methane, nitrous oxide, and hydrofluorocarbons are without a doubt "physical [and] chemical . . . substance[s] which [are] emitted into . . . the ambient air." The statute is unambiguous.

Rather than relying on statutory text, EPA invokes postenactment congressional actions and deliberations it views as tantamount to a congressional command to refrain from regulating greenhouse gas emissions. Even if such postenactment legislative history could shed light on the meaning of an otherwise-unambiguous statute, EPA never identifies any action remotely suggesting that Congress meant to curtail its power to treat greenhouse gases as air pollutants.

EPA's reliance on Brown & Williamson Tobacco Corp., 529 U.S. 120, is similarly misplaced. In holding that tobacco products are not "drugs" or "devices" subject to Food and Drug Administration (FDA) regulation pursuant to the Food, Drug and Cosmetic Act (FDCA), we found critical at least two considerations that have no counterpart in this case.

First, we thought it unlikely that Congress meant to ban tobacco products, which the FDCA would have required had such products been classified as "drugs" or "devices." Here, in contrast, EPA jurisdiction would lead to no such extreme measures. EPA would only regulate emissions. Second, in Brown & Williamson we pointed to an unbroken series of congressional enactments that made sense only if adopted "against the backdrop of the FDA's consistent and repeated statements that it lacked authority under the FDCA to regulate tobacco." We can point to no such enactments here. Prior to the order that provoked this litigation, EPA had never disavowed the authority to regulate greenhouse gases, and in 1998 it in fact affirmed that it had such authority. There is no reason, much less a compelling reason, to accept EPA's invitation to read ambiguity into a clear statute.

EPA finally argues that it cannot regulate carbon dioxide emissions from motor vehicles because doing so would require it to tighten mileage standards, a job (according to EPA) that Congress has assigned to DOT. The two obligations may overlap, but there is no reason to think the two agencies cannot both administer their obligations and yet avoid inconsistency.

While the Congresses that drafted § 202(a)(1) might not have appreciated the possibility that burning fossil fuels could lead to global warming, they did understand that without regulatory flexibility, changing circumstances and scientific developments would soon render the Clean Air Act obsolete. The broad language of § 202(a)(1) reflects an intentional effort to confer the flexibility necessary to forestall such obsolescence. . . . Because greenhouse gases fit well within the Clean Air Act's capacious definition of "air pollutant," we hold that EPA has the statutory authority to regulate the emission of such gases from new motor vehicles. . . .

The alternative basis for EPA's decision—that even if it does have statutory authority to regulate greenhouse gases, it would be unwise to do so at this time—rests on reasoning divorced from the statutory text. While the statute does condition the exercise of EPA's authority on its formation of a "judgment," 42 U.S.C. § 7521(a)(1), that judgment must relate to whether an air pollutant "cause[s], or contribute[s] to, air pollution which may reasonably be anticipated to endanger public health or welfare," ibid. Put another way, the use of the word "judgment" is not a roving license to ignore the statutory text. It is but a direction to exercise discretion within defined statutory limits.

Once EPA has responded to a petition for rulemaking, its reasons for action or inaction must conform to the authorizing statute. Under the clear terms of the Clean Air Act, EPA can avoid taking further action only if it determines that greenhouse gases do not contribute to climate change or if it provides some reasonable explanation as to why it cannot or will not exercise its discretion to determine whether they do. Ibid. To the extent that this constrains agency discretion to pursue other priorities of the Administrator or the President, this is the congressional design.

EPA has refused to comply with this clear statutory command. Instead, it has offered a laundry list of reasons not to regulate. Although we have neither the expertise nor the authority to evaluate these policy judgments, it is evident they have nothing to do with whether greenhouse gas emissions contribute to climate change. Still less do they amount to a reasoned justification for declining to form a scientific judgment. In particular, while the President has broad authority in foreign affairs, that authority does not extend to the refusal to execute domestic laws. . . .

Nor can EPA avoid its statutory obligation by noting the uncertainty surrounding various features of climate change and concluding that it would therefore be better not to regulate at this time. If the scientific uncertainty is so profound that it precludes EPA from making a reasoned judgment as to whether greenhouse gases contribute to global warming, EPA must say so. That EPA would prefer not to regulate greenhouse gases because of some residual uncertainty—which, contrary to Justice Scalia's apparent belief, is in fact all that it said—is irrelevant. The statutory question is whether sufficient information exists to make an endangerment finding.

In short, EPA has offered no reasoned explanation for its refusal to decide whether greenhouse gases cause or contribute to climate change. Its action was therefore "arbitrary, capricious, . . . or otherwise not in accordance with law." 42 U.S.C. § 7607(d)(9)(A). We need not and do not reach the question whether on remand EPA must make an endangerment finding, or whether policy concerns can inform EPA's actions in the event that it makes such a finding. Cf. *Chevron* . . . We hold only that EPA must ground its reasons for action or inaction in the statute. . . .

The judgment of the Court of Appeals is reversed, and the case is remanded for further proceedings consistent with this opinion.

It is so ordered.

■ JUSTICE SCALIA, dissenting.

Global warming may be a "crisis," even "the most pressing environmental problem of our time." Indeed, it may ultimately affect nearly everyone on the planet in some potentially adverse way, and it may be that governments have done too little to address it. It is not a problem, however, that has escaped the attention of policymakers in the Executive and Legislative Branches of our Government, who continue to consider regulatory, legislative, and treaty-based means of addressing global climate change.

Apparently dissatisfied with the pace of progress on this issue in the elected branches, petitioners have come to the courts claiming broad-ranging injury, and attempting to tie that injury to the Government's alleged failure to comply with a rather narrow statutory provision. I would reject these challenges as nonjusticiable. Such a conclusion involves no judgment on whether global warming exists, what causes it, or the extent of the problem. Nor does it render petitioners without recourse. This Court's standing jurisprudence simply recognizes that redress of grievances of the sort at issue here "is the function of Congress and the Chief Executive," not the federal courts. *Lujan* . . . I would vacate the judgment below and remand for dismissal of the petitions for review. [Eds. note: The dissent goes on to criticize the majority's holding on standing.]

. . . As the Court recognizes, the statute "condition[s] the exercise of EPA's authority on its formation of a 'judgment.' " There is no dispute that the Administrator has made no such judgment in this case.

The question thus arises: Does anything require the Administrator to make a "judgment" whenever a petition for rulemaking is filed? Without citation of the statute or any other authority, the Court says yes. Why is that so? When Congress wishes to make private action force an agency's hand, it knows how to do so. Where does the CAA say that the EPA Administrator is required to come to a decision on this question whenever a rulemaking petition is filed? The Court points to no such provision because none exists.

Instead, the Court invents a multiple-choice question that the EPA Administrator must answer when a petition for rulemaking is filed. The Administrator must exercise his judgment in one of three ways: (a) by concluding that the pollutant does cause, or contribute to, air pollution that endangers public welfare (in which case EPA is required to regulate); (b) by concluding that the pollutant does not cause, or contribute to, air pollution that endangers public welfare (in which case EPA is not required to regulate); or (c) by "provid[ing] some reasonable explanation as to why it cannot or will not exercise its discretion to determine whether" greenhouse gases endanger public welfare (in which case EPA is not required to regulate).

The Court, with no basis in text or precedent, rejects all of EPA's stated "policy judgments" as not "amount[ing] to a reasoned justification," effectively narrowing the universe of potential reasonable bases to a single one: Judgment can be delayed only if the Administrator concludes that "the scientific uncertainty is [too] profound." The Administrator is precluded from concluding for other reasons "that it would . . . be better not to regulate at this time." Such other reasons—perfectly valid reasons—were set forth in the agency's statement.

When the Administrator makes a judgment whether to regulate greenhouse gases, that judgment must relate to whether they are air pollutants that "cause, or contribute to, air pollution which may reasonably be anticipated to endanger public health or welfare." But the statute says nothing at all about the reasons for which the Administrator may defer making a judgment—the permissible reasons for deciding not to grapple with the issue at the present time. Thus, the various "policy" rationales that the Court criticizes are not "divorced from the statutory text" except in the sense that the statutory text is silent, as texts are often silent about permissible reasons for the exercise of agency discretion. The reasons the EPA gave are surely considerations executive agencies regularly take into account (and ought to take into account) when deciding whether to consider entering a new field: the impact such entry would have on other Executive Branch programs and on foreign policy. There is no basis in law for the Court's imposed limitation.

EPA's interpretation of the discretion conferred by the statutory reference to "its judgment" is not only reasonable, it is the most natural reading of the text. The Court nowhere explains why this interpretation is incorrect, let alone why it is not entitled to deference under *Chevron*. . . . As the Administrator acted within the law in declining to make a "judgment" for the policy reasons above set forth, I would uphold the decision to deny the rulemaking petition on that ground alone.

Even on the Court's own terms, however, the same conclusion follows. As mentioned above, the Court gives EPA the option of determining that the science is too uncertain to allow it to form a "judgment" as to whether greenhouse gases endanger public welfare. Attached to this option (on what basis is unclear) is an essay requirement: "If," the Court says, "the scientific uncertainty is so profound that it precludes EPA from making a reasoned judgment as to whether greenhouse gases contribute to global warming, EPA must say so." But EPA has said precisely that—and at great length, based on information contained in a 2001 report by the National Research Council (NRC) entitled Climate Change Science: An Analysis of Some Key Questions. I simply cannot conceive of what else the Court would like EPA to say. . . .

Even before reaching its discussion of the word "judgment," the Court makes another significant error when it concludes that "§ 202(a)(1) of the Clean Air Act authorizes EPA to regulate greenhouse gas emissions from new motor vehicles in the event that it forms a 'judgment' that such emissions contribute to climate change." For such authorization, the Court relies on what it calls "the Clean Air Act's capacious definition of 'air pollutant.'"

"Air pollutant" is defined by the Act as "any air pollution agent or combination of such agents, including any physical, chemical, . . . substance or matter which is emitted into or otherwise enters the ambient air." 42 U.S.C. § 7602(g). The Court is correct that "[c]arbon dioxide, methane, nitrous oxide, and hydrofluorocarbons" fit within the second half of that definition: They are "physical, chemical, . . . substance[s] or matter which [are] emitted into or otherwise ente[r] the ambient air." But the Court mistakenly believes this to be the end of the analysis. In order to be an "air pollutant" under the Act's definition, the "substance or matter [being] emitted into . . . the ambient air" must also meet the first half of the definition—namely, it must be an "air pollution agent or combination of such agents." The Court simply pretends this half of the definition does not exist.

It is perfectly reasonable to view the definition of "air pollutant" in its entirety: An air pollutant can be "any physical, chemical, . . . substance or matter which is emitted into or otherwise enters the ambient air," but only if it retains the general characteristic of being an "air pollution agent or combination of such agents." This is precisely the conclusion EPA reached. Once again, in the face of textual ambiguity, the Court's application of Chevron deference to EPA's interpretation of the word "including" is nowhere to be found.[2][6]

Evidently, the Court defers only to those reasonable interpretations that it favors.

. . . Using (as we ought to) EPA's interpretation of the definition of "air pollutant," we must next determine whether greenhouse gases are "agent[s]" of "air pollution." If so, the statute would authorize regulation; if not, EPA would lack authority.

Unlike "air pollutants," the term "air pollution" is not itself defined by the CAA; thus, once again we must accept EPA's interpretation of that ambiguous term, provided its interpretation is a "permissible construction of the statute." *Chevron.* . . . In deciding whether it had authority to regulate, EPA had to determine whether the concentration of greenhouse gases assertedly responsible for "global climate change" qualifies as "air pollution." EPA began with the commonsense observation that the [p]roblems associated with atmospheric concentrations of CO_2 bear little resemblance to what would naturally be termed "air pollution." Regulating the buildup of CO_2 and other greenhouse gases in the upper reaches of the atmosphere, which is alleged to be causing global climate change, is not akin to regulating the concentration of some substance that is polluting the air.

We need look no further than the dictionary for confirmation that this interpretation of "air pollution" is eminently reasonable. The definition of "pollute," of course, is "[t]o make or render impure or unclean." Webster's New International Dictionary 1910 (2d ed. 1949). And the first three definitions of "air" are as follows: (1) "[t]he invisible, odorless, and tasteless mixture of gases which surrounds the earth"; (2) "[t]he body of the earth's atmosphere; esp., the part of it near the earth, as distinguished from the upper rarefied part"; (3) "[a] portion of air or of the air considered with respect to physical characteristics or as affecting the senses." Id., at 54. EPA's conception of "air pollution"—focusing on impurities in the "ambient air" "at ground level or near the surface of the earth"—is perfectly consistent with the natural meaning of that term.

Once again, the Court utterly fails to explain why this interpretation is incorrect, let alone so unreasonable as to be unworthy of Chevron deference.

The Court's alarm over global warming may or may not be justified, but it ought not distort the outcome of this litigation. This is a

---

[6] Not only is EPA's interpretation reasonable, it is far more plausible than the Court's alternative. As the Court correctly points out, "all airborne compounds of whatever stripe" would qualify as "physical, chemical, . . . substance[s] or matter which [are] emitted into or otherwise ente[r] the ambient air," 42 U.S.C. § 7602(g). It follows that everything airborne, from Frisbees to flatulence, qualifies as an "air pollutant." This reading of the statute defies common sense.

straightforward administrative-law case, in which Congress has passed a malleable statute giving broad discretion, not to us but to an executive agency. No matter how important the underlying policy issues at stake, this Court has no business substituting its own desired outcome for the reasoned judgment of the responsible agency. ∎

NOTES AND COMMENTS

1.   What is the impact of the *Massachusetts* decision on private rights to bring tort claims against emitters of GHGs? The decision represented the first time plaintiffs in a climate change lawsuit established standing. Some hoped that *Massachusetts* would open the door to a flood of climate change litigation, but those hopes rested on the answers to two questions. Was the Court's standing analysis limited to the special context of that case, in which Massachusetts was given "special solicitude" as a state bringing suit? And what preemptive effect, if any, did the CAA exert over public nuisance claims under federal common law? The Supreme Court answered the latter question in *American Electric Power v. Connecticut,* 582 F.3d 309 (2011). In that case, several states and land trusts brought a public nuisance claim against a group of large GHG emitters. The Court concluded that Congress, by delegating to EPA responsibility for regulating GHG emissions, displaced federal common law nuisance claims. As for the former question, lower courts have rejected a variety of state common-law claims on standing grounds, distinguishing *Massachusetts. See, e.g.*, Comer v. Murphy Oil USA, Inc., 839 F. Supp. 2d 849, 861 (S.D. Miss. 2012); Native Village of Kivalina, 663 F. Supp. 2d 863, 880 (N.D. Cal. 2009). For an overview of common-law litigation in the climate change context, see generally Emily Hammond & David L. Markell, Civil Remedies, *in* Global Climate Change and U.S. Law (Michael B. Gerrard & Jody Freeman, eds., 2d ed. 2014).

2.   On the subject of GHG controls under Title II, what exactly did the plaintiffs *win*? After this decision, was EPA required to regulate CO_2 emissions from automobiles? Not necessarily. While the definition of "air pollutant" encompassed CO_2 and the grounds available to EPA for refusing to regulate under Title II were limited, the agency could still decline to do so provided its reasons were permissible. For the remainder of the Bush Administration, EPA held off on regulating automobile CO_2 emissions. Following the remand of *Massachusetts*, EPA issued an advance notice of proposed rulemaking calling the CAA "an outdated law originally enacted to control regional pollutants that cause direct health effects [that] is ill-suited for the task of regulating global greenhouse gases." Regulating Greenhouse Gas Emissions Under the Clean Air Act, 73 Fed. Reg. 44,354 (July 30, 2008). Once again, however, EPA policy changed with the presidential transition.

b.   EPA'S INITIAL REGULATION OF GHG EMISSIONS

The Obama EPA made a formal endangerment finding in 2009, in which it concluded that GHGs from new cars and trucks endanger public health and welfare. Endangerment and Cause or Contribute Findings for Greenhouse Gases Under Section 202(a) of the Clean Air Act, 74 Fed. Reg. 66,496 (Dec. 15, 2009). That decision, in EPA's view, triggered a succession of additional rulemakings that subjected both mobile *and* stationary sources to GHG permitting obligations under the Act. As described in more detail later in this section, the D.C. Circuit upheld the endangerment finding, mobile source standards, and triggering rule. The Supreme Court granted certiorari on the triggering decision, and had this to say:

Utility Air Regulatory Group v. EPA

134 S.Ct. 2427 (2014).

■ JUSTICE SCALIA announced the judgment of the Court.

Acting pursuant to the Clean Air Act, the Environmental Protection Agency recently set standards for emissions of "greenhouse gases" (substances it believes contribute to "global climate change") from new motor vehicles. We must decide whether it was permissible for EPA to determine that its motor-vehicle greenhouse-gas regulations automatically triggered permitting requirements under the Act for stationary sources that emit greenhouse gases.

I. Background

i. Stationary-Source Permitting

The Clean Air Act regulates pollution-generating emissions from both stationary sources, such as factories and powerplants, and moving sources, such as cars, trucks, and aircraft. This litigation concerns permitting obligations imposed on stationary sources under Titles I and V of the Act.

Title I charges EPA with formulating national ambient air quality standards (NAAQS) for air pollutants. §§ 7408–7409. To date, EPA has issued NAAQS for six pollutants: sulfur dioxide, particulate matter, nitrogen dioxide, carbon monoxide, ozone, and lead. [S]ee generally 40 CFR pt. 50 (2013). . . . Stationary sources in areas designated attainment or unclassifiable are subject to the Act's provisions relating to "Prevention of Significant Deterioration" (PSD). §§ 7470–7492. EPA interprets the PSD provisions to apply to sources located in areas that are designated attainment or unclassifiable for *any* NAAQS pollutant, regardless of whether the source emits that specific pollutant. Since the inception of the PSD program, every area of the country has been designated attainment or unclassifiable for at least one NAAQS pollutant; thus, on EPA's view, all stationary sources are potentially subject to PSD review.

It is unlawful to construct or modify a "major emitting facility" in "any area to which [the PSD program] applies" without first obtaining a permit. §§ 7475(a)(1), 7479(2)(C). To qualify for a permit, the facility must not cause or contribute to the violation of any applicable air-quality standard, § 7475(a)(3), and it must comply with emissions limitations that reflect the "best available control technology" (or BACT) for "each pollutant subject to regulation under" the Act. § 7475(a)(4). The Act defines a "major emitting facility" as any stationary source with the potential to emit 250 tons per year of "any air pollutant" (or 100 tons per year for certain types of sources). § 7479(1). It defines "modification" as a physical or operational change that causes the facility to emit more of "any air pollutant." § 7411(a)(4).

In addition to the PSD permitting requirements for construction and modification, Title V of the Act makes it unlawful to *operate* any "major source," wherever located, without a comprehensive operating permit. § 7661a(a). . . . The permit must include all "emissions limitations and standards" that apply to the source, as well as associated inspection, monitoring, and reporting requirements. § 7661c(a)–(c). Title V defines a "major source" by reference to the Act-wide definition of "major stationary source," which in turn means any stationary source with the potential to emit 100 tons per year of "any air pollutant." §§ 7661(2)(B), 7602(j).

ii.   EPA's Greenhouse-Gas Regulations

. . . Under EPA's view, once greenhouse gases became regulated under any part of the Act, the PSD and Title V permitting requirements would apply to all stationary sources with the potential to emit greenhouse gases in excess of the statutory thresholds: 100 tons per year under Title V, and 100 or 250 tons per year under the PSD program depending on the type of source. 73 Fed. Reg. 44,420, 44,498, 44,511 (2008). Because greenhouse-gas emissions tend to be "orders of magnitude greater" than emissions of conventional pollutants, EPA projected that numerous small sources not previously regulated under the Act would be swept into the PSD program and Title V, including "smaller industrial sources," "large office and residential buildings, hotels, large retail establishments, and similar facilities." *Id.* at 44,498– 99. The Agency warned that this would constitute an "unprecedented expansion of EPA authority that would have a profound effect on virtually every sector of the economy and touch every household in the land," yet still be "relatively ineffective at reducing greenhouse gas concentrations." *Id.* at 44,355.

In 2009, EPA announced its determination regarding the danger posed by motor-vehicle greenhouse-gas emissions. EPA found that greenhouse-gas emissions from new motor vehicles contribute to elevated atmospheric concentrations of greenhouse gases, which endanger public health and welfare by fostering global "climate change." 74 Fed. Reg. 66,523, 66,537 (hereinafter Endangerment Finding). It denominated a "single air pollutant" the "combined mix" of six greenhouse gases that it identified as "the root cause of human-induced climate change": carbon dioxide, methane, nitrous oxide, hydrofluorocarbons, perfluorocarbons, and sulfur hexafluoride. *Id.* at 66,516, 66,537. A source's greenhouse-gas emissions would be measured in "carbon dioxide equivalent units" (CO_2e), which would be calculated based on each gas's "global warming potential." Id. at 66,499 n.4.

Next, EPA issued its "final decision" regarding the prospect that motor-vehicle greenhouse-gas standards would trigger stationary-source permitting requirements. 75 Fed. Reg. 17,004 (2010) (hereinafter Triggering Rule). EPA announced that beginning on the effective date of its greenhouse-gas standards for motor vehicles, stationary sources would be subject to the PSD program and Title V on the basis of their potential to emit greenhouse gases. As expected, EPA in short order promulgated greenhouse-gas emission standards for passenger cars, light-duty trucks, and medium-duty passenger vehicles to take effect on January 2, 2011. 75 Fed. Reg. 25,324 (hereinafter Tailpipe Rule).

EPA then announced steps it was taking to "tailor" the PSD program and Title V to greenhouse gases. 75 Fed. Reg. 31,514 (hereinafter Tailoring Rule). Those steps were necessary, it said, because the PSD program and Title V were designed to regulate "a relatively small number of large industrial sources," and requiring permits for all sources with greenhouse-gas emissions above the statutory thresholds would radically expand those programs, making them both unadministrable and "unrecognizable to the Congress that designed" them. *Id.* at 31,555, 31,562. EPA nonetheless rejected calls to exclude greenhouse gases entirely from those programs, asserting that the Act is not "ambiguous with respect to the need to cover [greenhouse-gas] sources under either the PSD or title V program." *Id.* at 31,548 n.31. Instead, EPA adopted a "phase-in approach" that it said would "appl[y] PSD and title V at threshold levels that are as close to the statutory levels as possible, and do so as quickly as possible, at least to a certain point." *Id.* at 31,523.

The phase-in, EPA said, would consist of at least three steps. During Step 1, from January 2 through June 30, 2011, no source would become newly subject to the PSD program or Title V solely on the basis of its greenhouse gas emissions; however, sources required to obtain permits anyway because of their emission of conventional pollutants (so-called "anyway" sources) would need to comply with BACT for greenhouse gases if they emitted those gases in significant amounts, defined as at least 75,000 tons per year CO_2e. *Ibid.* During Step 2, from July 1, 2011, through June 30, 2012, sources with the potential to emit at least 100,000 tons per year CO_2e of greenhouse gases would be subject to PSD and Title V permitting for their construction and operation and to PSD permitting for modifications that would increase their greenhouse-gas emissions by at least 75,000 tons per year CO_2e. *Id.* at 31,523–24. At Step 3, beginning on July 1, 2013, EPA said it might (or might not) further reduce the permitting thresholds (though not below 50,000 tons per year CO_2e), and it might (or might not) establish permanent exemptions for some sources. *Id.* at 31,524. Beyond Step 3, EPA promised to complete another round of a joint rulemaking by April 30, 2016, in which it would "take further action to address small sources," which might (or might not) include establishing permanent exemptions. *Id.* at 31,525. . . .

iii. Decision Below

Numerous parties, including several States, filed petitions for review in the D.C. Circuit under 42 U.S.C. § 7607(b), challenging EPA's greenhouse-gas-related actions. The Court of Appeals dismissed some of the petitions for lack of jurisdiction and denied the remainder. Coalition for Responsible Regulation, Inc. v. EPA, 684 F. 3d 102 (2012) (*per curiam*). First, it upheld the Endangerment Finding and Tailpipe Rule. Next, it held that EPA's interpretation of the PSD permitting requirement as applying to "any regulated air pollutant," including greenhouse gases, was "compelled by the statute." The court also found it "crystal clear that PSD permittees must install BACT for greenhouse gases." Because it deemed petitioners' arguments about the PSD program insufficiently applicable to Title V, it held they had "forfeited any challenges to EPA's greenhouse gas-inclusive interpretation of Title V." Finally, it held that petitioners were without Article III standing to challenge EPA's efforts to limit the reach of the PSD program and Title V through the Triggering and Tailoring Rules. . . .

We granted six petitions for certiorari but agreed to decide only one question: "Whether EPA permissibly determined that its regulation of greenhouse gas emissions from new motor vehicles triggered permitting requirements under the Clean Air Act for stationary sources that emit greenhouse gases."

II. Analysis

. . . We first decide whether EPA permissibly interpreted the statute to provide that a source may be required to obtain a PSD or Title V permit on the sole basis of its potential greenhouse-gas emissions.

EPA thought its conclusion that a source's greenhouse-gas emissions may necessitate a PSD or Title V permit followed from the Act's unambiguous language. The Court of Appeals agreed and held that the statute "compelled" EPA's interpretation. We disagree. The statute compelled EPA's greenhouse-gas-inclusive interpretation with respect to neither the PSD program nor Title V.

The Court of Appeals reasoned by way of a flawed syllogism: Under *Massachusetts*, the general, Act-wide definition of "air pollutant" includes greenhouse gases; the Act requires permits for major emitters of "any air pollutant"; therefore, the Act requires permits for major emitters of greenhouse gases. The conclusion follows from the premises only if the air pollutants referred to in the permit-requiring provisions (the minor premise) are the same air pollutants encompassed by the Act-wide definition as interpreted in *Massachusetts* (the major premise). Yet no one—least of all EPA—endorses that proposition, and it is obviously untenable.

The Act-wide definition says that an air pollutant is "any air pollution agent or combination of such agents, including any physical, chemical, biological, [or] radioactive . . . substance or matter which is emitted into or otherwise enters the ambient air." § 7602(g). In *Massachusetts*, the Court held that the Act-wide definition includes greenhouse gases because it is all-encompassing; it "embraces all airborne compounds of whatever stripe." 549 U.S. at 529. But where the term "air pollutant" appears in the Act's operative provisions, EPA has routinely given it a narrower, context-appropriate meaning.

That is certainly true of the provisions that require PSD and Title V permitting for major emitters of "any air pollutant." Since 1978, EPA's regulations have interpreted "air pollutant" in the PSD permitting trigger as limited to *regulated* air pollutants, a class much narrower than *Massachusetts'* "all airborne compounds of whatever stripe," 549 U.S. at 529. And since 1993 EPA has informally taken the same position with regard to the Title V permitting trigger, a position the Agency ultimately incorporated into some of the regulations at issue here. *See* Memorandum from Lydia N. Wegman, Deputy Director, Office of Air Quality Planning and Standards, to Air Division Director, Regions I–X, pp. 4–5 (Apr. 26, 1993); Tailoring Rule 31,607–31,608 (amending 40 CFR §§ 70.2, 71.2). Those interpretations were appropriate: It is plain as day that the Act does not envision an elaborate, burdensome permitting process for major emitters of steam, oxygen, or other harmless airborne substances. It takes some cheek for EPA to insist that it cannot possibly give "air pollutant" a reasonable, context-appropriate meaning in the PSD and Title V contexts when it has been doing precisely that for decades. [Examples omitted] . . .

We need not, and do not, pass on the validity of all the limiting constructions EPA has given the term "air pollutant" throughout the Act.

We merely observe that taken together, they belie EPA's rigid insistence that when interpreting the PSD and Title V permitting requirements it is bound by the Act-wide definition's inclusion of greenhouse gases, no matter how incompatible that inclusion is with those programs' regulatory structure.

In sum, there is no insuperable textual barrier to EPA's interpreting "any air pollutant" in the permitting triggers of PSD and Title V to encompass only pollutants emitted in quantities that enable them to be sensibly regulated at the statutory thresholds, and to exclude those atypical pollutants that, like greenhouse gases, are emitted in such vast quantities that their inclusion would radically transform those programs and render them unworkable as written. . . .

Having determined that EPA was mistaken in thinking the Act *compelled* a greenhouse-gas-inclusive interpretation of the PSD and Title V triggers, we next consider the Agency's alternative position that its interpretation was justified as an exercise of its "discretion" to adopt "a reasonable construction of the statute." Tailoring Rule 31,517. We conclude that EPA's interpretation is not permissible. . . .

EPA itself has repeatedly acknowledged that applying the PSD and Title V permitting requirements to greenhouse gases would be inconsistent with—in fact, would overthrow—the Act's structure and design. In the Tailoring Rule, EPA described the calamitous consequences of interpreting the Act in that way. Under the PSD program, annual permit applications would jump from about 800 to nearly 82,000; annual administrative costs would swell from $12 million to over $1.5 billion; and decade-long delays in issuing permits would become common, causing construction projects to grind to a halt nationwide. The picture under Title V was equally bleak: The number of sources required to have permits would jump from fewer than 15,000 to about 6.1 million; annual administrative costs would balloon from $62 million to $21 billion; and collectively the newly covered sources would face permitting costs of $147 billion. Moreover, "the great majority of additional sources brought into the PSD and title V programs would be small sources that Congress did not expect would need to undergo permitting." EPA stated that these results would be so "contrary to congressional intent," and would so "severely undermine what Congress sought to accomplish," that they necessitated as much as a 1,000-fold increase in the permitting thresholds set forth in the statute.

Like EPA, we think it beyond reasonable debate that requiring permits for sources based solely on their emission of greenhouse gases at the 100- and 250-tons-per-year levels set forth in the statute would be "incompatible" with "the substance of Congress' regulatory scheme." *Brown & Williamson*, 529 U.S. at 156. A brief review of the relevant statutory provisions leaves no doubt that the PSD program and Title V are designed to apply to, and cannot rationally be extended beyond, a relative handful of large sources capable of shouldering heavy substantive and procedural burdens.

Start with the PSD program, which imposes numerous and costly requirements on those sources that are required to apply for permits. Among other things, the applicant must make available a detailed scientific analysis of the source's potential pollution-related impacts, demonstrate that the source will not contribute to the violation of any applicable pollution standard, and identify and use the "best available control technology" for each regulated pollutant it emits. § 7475(a)(3), (4), (6), (e). The permitting authority (the State, usually) also bears its share of the burden: It must grant or deny a permit within a year, during which time it must hold a public hearing on the application. § 7475(a)(2), (c). Not surprisingly, EPA acknowledges that PSD review is a "complicated, resource-intensive, time-consuming, and sometimes contentious process" suitable for "hundreds of larger sources," not "tens of thousands of smaller sources." 74 Fed. Reg. 55,304, 55,321–22.

Title V contains no comparable substantive requirements but imposes elaborate procedural mandates. It requires the applicant to submit, within a year of becoming subject to Title V, a permit application and a "compliance plan" describing how it will comply with "all applicable requirements" under the Act; to certify its compliance annually; and to submit to "inspection, entry, monitoring, . . . and reporting requirements." §§ 7661b(b)–(c), 7661c(a)–(c). The procedural burdens on the permitting authority and EPA are also significant. The permitting authority must hold a public hearing on the application, § 7661a(b)(6), and it must forward the application and any proposed permit to EPA and neighboring States and respond in writing to their comments, § 7661d(a), (b)(1). If it fails to issue or deny the permit within 18 months, any interested party can sue to require a decision "without additional delay." §§ 7661a(b)(7), 7661b(c). An interested party also can petition EPA to block issuance of the permit; EPA must grant or deny the petition within 60 days, and its decision may be challenged in federal court. § 7661d(b)(2)–(3). As EPA wrote, Title V is "finely crafted for thousands," not millions, of sources.

The fact that EPA's greenhouse-gas-inclusive interpretation of the PSD and Title V triggers would place plainly excessive demands on limited governmental resources is alone a good reason for rejecting it; but that is not the only reason. EPA's interpretation is also unreasonable because it would bring about an enormous and transformative expansion in EPA's regulatory authority without clear congressional authorization. When an agency claims to discover in a long-extant statute an unheralded power to regulate "a significant portion of the American economy," *Brown & Williamson*, 529 U.S. at 159, we typically greet its announcement with a measure of skepticism. We expect Congress to speak clearly if it wishes to assign to an agency decisions of vast "economic and political significance." *Id.* at 160. . . .

EPA thought that despite the foregoing problems, it could make its interpretation reasonable by adjusting the levels at which a source's greenhouse-gas emissions would oblige it to undergo PSD and Title V permitting. Although the Act, in no uncertain terms, requires permits for sources with the potential to emit more than 100 or 250 tons per year of a relevant pollutant, EPA in its Tailoring Rule wrote a new threshold of *100,000* tons per year for greenhouse gases. Since the Court of Appeals thought the statute unambiguously made greenhouse gases capable of triggering PSD and Title V, it held that petitioners lacked Article III standing to challenge the Tailoring Rule because that rule did not injure petitioners but merely relaxed the pre-existing statutory requirements. Because we, however, hold that EPA's greenhouse-gas-inclusive interpretation of the triggers was *not* compelled, and because EPA has essentially admitted that its interpretation would be unreasonable without "tailoring," we consider the validity of the Tailoring Rule.

We conclude that EPA's rewriting of the statutory thresholds was impermissible and therefore could not validate the Agency's interpretation of the triggering provisions. An agency has no power to "tailor" legislation to bureaucratic policy goals by rewriting unambiguous statutory terms. . . .

Were we to recognize the authority claimed by EPA in the Tailoring Rule, we would deal a severe blow to the Constitution's separation of powers. . . . The power of executing the laws necessarily includes both authority and responsibility to resolve some questions left open by Congress that arise during the law's administration. But it does not include a power to revise clear statutory terms that turn out not to work in practice.

In the Tailoring Rule, EPA asserts newfound authority to regulate millions of small sources-including retail stores, offices, apartment buildings, shopping centers, schools, and churches- and to decide, on an ongoing basis and without regard for the thresholds prescribed by Congress, how many of those sources to regulate. We are not willing to stand on the dock and wave goodbye as EPA embarks on this multiyear voyage of discovery. We reaffirm the core administrative-law principle that an agency may not rewrite clear statutory terms to suit its own sense of how the statute should operate. EPA therefore lacked authority to "tailor" the Act's unambiguous numerical thresholds to accommodate its greenhouse-gas-inclusive interpretation of the permitting triggers. Instead, the need to rewrite clear provisions of the statute should have alerted EPA that it had taken a wrong interpretive turn. . . . ∎

∎ JUSTICE BREYER, with whom JUSTICE GINSBURG, JUSTICE SOTOMAYOR, and JUSTICE KAGAN join, concurring in part and dissenting in part.

These cases take as a given our decision in *Massachusetts* that the Act's *general definition* of "air pollutant" includes greenhouse gases. One of the questions posed by these cases is whether those gases fall within the scope of the phrase "any air pollutant" as that phrase is used in the more specific provisions of the Act. The Court's answer is "no." I disagree.

The Clean Air Act provisions at issue here are Title I's Prevention of Significant Deterioration (PSD) program, § 7470 *et seq.*, and Title V's permitting regime, § 7661 *et seq.* . . . These cases concern the definitions of "major emitting facility" and "major source," each of which is defined to mean any stationary source that emits more than a threshold quantity of "any air pollutant." *See* § 7479(1) ("major emitting facility"); §§ 7602(j), 7661(2)(B) ("major source"). To simplify the exposition, I will refer only to the PSD program and its definition of "major emitting facility"; a parallel analysis applies to Title V.

. . . In effect, we are dealing with a statute that says that the PSD program's regulatory requirements must be applied to "any stationary source that has the potential to emit two hundred fifty tons per year or more of any air pollutant."

The interpretive difficulty in these cases arises out of the definition's use of the phrase "two hundred fifty tons per year or more," which I will call the "250 tpy threshold." When applied to greenhouse gases, 250 tpy is far too low a threshold. As the Court explains, tens of thousands of stationary sources emit large quantities of one greenhouse gas, carbon dioxide. To apply the programs at issue here to all those sources would be extremely expensive and burdensome, counterproductive, and perhaps impossible; it would also contravene Congress's intent that the programs' coverage be limited to those large sources whose emissions are substantial enough to justify the regulatory burdens. The EPA recognized as much, and it addressed the problem by issuing a regulation-the Tailoring Rule-that purports to raise the coverage threshold for greenhouse gases from the statutory figure of 250 tpy to 100,000 tpy in order to keep the programs' coverage limited to "a relatively small number of large industrial sources."

The Tailoring Rule solves the practical problems that would have been caused by the 250 tpy threshold. But what are we to do about the statute's language? The statute specifies a definite number—250, not 100,000—and it says that facilities that are covered by that number must meet the program's requirements. The statute says nothing about agency discretion to change that number. What is to be done? How, given the statute's language, can the EPA exempt from regulation sources that emit more than 250 but less than 100,000 tpy of greenhouse gases (and that also do not emit other regulated pollutants at threshold levels)?

The Court answers by (1) pointing out that regulation at the 250 tpy threshold would produce absurd results, (2) refusing to read the statute as compelling such results, and (3) consequently interpreting the phrase "*any* air pollutant" as containing an implicit exception for greenhouse gases. (Emphasis added.) Put differently, the Court reads the statute as defining "major emitting facility" to mean "stationary sources that have the potential to emit two hundred fifty tons per year or more of any air pollutant *except for those air pollutants, such as carbon dioxide, with respect to which regulation at that threshold would be impractical or absurd or would sweep in smaller sources that Congress did not mean to cover.*" . . .

I agree with the Court that the word "any," when used in a statute, does not normally mean "any in the universe." Rather, "[g]eneral terms as used on particular occasions often carry with them implied restrictions as to scope," and so courts must interpret the word "any," like all other words, in context. As Judge Learned Hand pointed out when interpreting another statute many years ago, "[w]e can best reach the meaning here, as always, by recourse to the underlying purpose, and, with that as a guide, by trying to project upon the specific occasion how we think persons, actuated by such a purpose, would have dealt with it, if it had been presented to them at the time." Borella v. Borden Co., 145 F. 2d 63, 64 (2d Cir. 1944). The pursuit of that underlying purpose may sometimes require us to "abandon" a "literal interpretation" of a word like "any."

The law has long recognized that terms such as "any" admit of unwritten limitations and exceptions. Legal philosophers like to point out that a statute providing that "[w]hoever shall willfully take the life of another shall be punished by death" need not encompass a man who kills in self-defense; nor must an ordinance imposing fines upon those who occupy a public parking spot for more than two hours penalize a driver who is unable to move because of a parade. The maxim *cessante ratione legis cessat ipse lex*—where a law's rationale ceases to apply, so does the law itself—is not of recent origin.

I also agree with the Court's point that "a generic reference to air pollutants" in the Clean Air Act need not "encompass every substance falling within the Act-wide definition" that we construed in *Massachusetts*, § 7602(g). . . . But I do not agree with the Court that the only way to avoid an absurd or otherwise impermissible result in these cases is to create an atextual greenhouse gas exception to the phrase "any air pollutant." After all, the word "any" makes an earlier appearance in the definitional provision, which defines "major emitting facility" to mean "*any* . . . source with the potential to emit two hundred and fifty tons per year or more of any air pollutant." § 7479(1) (emphasis added). As a linguistic matter, one can just as easily read an implicit exception for small-scale greenhouse gas emissions into the phrase "any source" as into the phrase "any air pollutant." And given the purposes of the PSD program and the Act as a whole, as well as the specific roles of the different parts of the statutory definition, finding flexibility in "any source" is far more sensible than the Court's route of finding it in "any air pollutant."

. . . [T]he interpretation I propose leaves the EPA with the sort of discretion as to interstitial matters that Congress likely intended it to retain. My interpretation gives the EPA nothing more than the authority to *exempt* sources from regulation insofar as the Agency reasonably determines that applying the PSD program to them would expand the program so much as to contravene Congress's intent. That sort of decision, which involves the Agency's technical expertise and administrative experience, is the kind of decision that Congress typically leaves to the agencies to make. ∎

∎ JUSTICE ALITO, with whom JUSTICE THOMAS joins, concurring in part and dissenting in part.

In *Massachusetts v. EPA*, 549 U.S. 497 (2007), this Court considered whether greenhouse gases fall within the Clean Air Act's general definition of an air "pollutant." The Environmental Protection Agency cautioned us that "key provisions of the [Act] cannot cogently be applied to [greenhouse gas] emissions," but the Court brushed the warning aside and had "little trouble" concluding that the Act's "sweeping definition" of a pollutant encompasses greenhouse gases. I believed Massachusetts v. EPA was wrongly decided at the time, and these cases further expose the flaws with that decision. ∎

NOTES AND COMMENTS

1. The Court's decision did not overturn the agency's assertion of PSD permitting jurisdiction over GHG emissions from facilities otherwise subject to PSD review (because of their non-GHG emissions). In the *UARG* decision the Court also decided the question whether EPA's decision to require BACT for greenhouse gases emitted by those sources is, as a general matter, a permissible interpretation of the statute. The Court concluded that it is, based on the observation that the BACT requirement, at 42 U.S.C. § 7475(a)(4), applies to "each pollutant subject to regulation under this chapter" (meaning the entire Clean Air Act). Furthermore, the Court authorized EPA to limit the application of BACT to already-covered sources "only if the source emits more than a *de minimis* amount of greenhouse gases." EPA, said the Court, may establish an appropriate *de minimis* threshold below which BACT is not required; however, the Tailoring Rule's

75,000 tons per year CO_2e threshold was not intended to establish that *de minimis* level, so it remains for EPA establish the threshold.

The Supreme Court left standing a variety of other holdings contained in the D.C. Circuit's decision in *Coalition for Responsible Regulation, Inc. v. EPA*, 684 F.3d 115 (2014). Petitioners originally challenged EPA's issuance of the endangerment finding, claiming (among other things) that (1) EPA improperly failed to consider the benefits of activities that's result in the admission of greenhouse gases, (2) the scientific record does not support EPA's endangerment finding, and (3) EPA failed to quantify or measure a concentration of greenhouse gases that endangers public health and welfare. The D.C. Circuit rejected the first contention, noting that the statute requires the agency to focus on harm caused by emissions of air pollutants, and that nothing in the statute requires the agency to perform a cost-benefit analysis and making its endangerment finding. The court also rejected the latter two arguments, citing its deference to the agency's expert judgment about these matters. 684 F.3d at 118.

2. The D.C. Circuit court also dismissed petitioners' challenges to the Tailpipe Rule, including a challenge to EPA's conclusion that CAA § 202 requires the agency to regulate motor vehicle emissions of greenhouse gases once the endangerment finding is made. Noting that section 202 is expressed in mandatory language ("The administrator shall . . . prescribe"), the court concluded that the plain text of the statute refutes the petitioners claims. 684 F.3d at 126.

The standards apply for model years 2012 through 2016 (the standard and the target date conforming with California's as well, as noted above), and more recent Tier 3 Motor Vehicle Emission and Fuel Standards have been issued for models 2017 through 2025, as discussed in more detail in Chapter 15. Like other federal vehicle emissions standards, the 2012–2016 standards are expressed in grams per mile of CO_2 emissions. However, because the agencies expected that automakers would meet the new targets largely by making higher mileage cars and trucks, the targets also translate to a miles per gallon (mpg) equivalent. The Tier 3 standards are more complex, incorporating regulations for both fuel content and tailpipe controls in order to further reduce emissions.

The combined 2012–2016 standard would require vehicles to meet an estimated combined average emissions level of 250 grams of CO_2 per mile in 2016, or the equivalent of 35.5 mpg if automakers met the standard solely through fuel economy improvements. As described in more detail in Chapter 15, the 2017–2025 rules aim for an average of 55.3 to 56.2 miles per gallon for passenger vehicles. *See* Jody Freeman, The Obama Administration's National Auto Policy: Lessons from the Car Deal, 35 Harv. Envtl. L. Rev. 343 (2011) (describing the unique rulemaking process and the variety of compliance flexibilities made available by the government).

3. In addition to promulgating the Tailpipe Rule, EPA also granted California's waiver to implement its own auto GHG emissions standards. If EPA's Tailpipe Rule had imposed a different GHG emissions standard, automakers might have been subject to three different standards: the California GHG standards, the new CAFE standards, and the new EPA GHG standards. EPA and NHTSA dealt with this by negotiating an agreement with California and the automakers on a unified national program to establish a combined national fuel economy standard and GHG emissions

standard that meshes with the California standards. California agreed to amend its own standards to conform to the new federal standard from 2012 to 2016, retaining flexibility to set its own standards before 2012 and after 2016. Automakers got a benefit, too: the ability to build cars and trucks that simultaneously satisfy both the national standards and the California standards (in the states where they apply). See Chapter 15 for further discussion of transportation issues.

4. In September 2009, EPA announced its final rule for mandatory reporting of GHG emissions. The Reporting Rule requires certain direct GHG emitters, fossil fuel and industrial gas suppliers, and manufacturers of vehicles and engines to collect and report information about GHG emissions of their operations and/or products. The rule covers about 85 percent of the nation's GHG emissions, and has enabled EPA to develop a more accurate and complete emissions inventory for GHGs.

3. REGULATING GREENHOUSE GAS EMISSIONS FROM POWER PLANTS

a. NEW POWER PLANTS

Despite the Supreme Court's rejection of the Tailoring Rule, another part of the CAA, Section 111, authorizes EPA to set standards for power plants under the CAA's New Source Performance Standards (NSPS) program. The NSPS provisions requires the agency to set baseline pollution standards for all industrial categories that emit pollution found to endanger public health. NSPS standards are set by EPA, not the states; and they apply uniformly to industrial categories rather than individual sources. The PSD program, by contrast, is implemented by the states, and the application of "best available control technology," varies across sources and across states. In addition, NSPS standards are based on "best demonstrated technology."

EPA's proposed rule for *new* power plants—its first step in regulating power plant GHG emissions—went through two very controversial and highly visible iterations. The initial proposed rule proposed a single standard for both coal and natural gas-fired electricity generating units, treating them as a single source category for standard-setting purposes (a departure from the agency's past practice in the NSPS program). Standards of Performance for Greenhouse Gas Emissions for New Stationary Sources: Electric Utility Generating Units, 77 Fed. Reg. 22,392 (proposed Apr. 13, 2012). This proposed rule required all new fossil-fuel-fired EGUs to emit no more than 1000 pounds of CO_2/ megawatt hour (MWH) on an average annual basis, which is based on the CO_2 emissions from a highly efficient, natural gas combined cycle facility. The 1000 lb/MWH standard was set at a level that only the most efficient new gas plants could meet, but that coal units could not meet without carbon capture and sequestration technology. Thus, the uniform standard for coal- and natural gas-fired plants would seem likely to ensure that no new coal fired power plants will be built without being carbon capture-ready.

Industry argued that this standard is a major obstacle to the construction and development of any new coal-fired generation capacity because, as EPA concedes, the limits cannot be achieved by a new coal-

fired EGU using currently available technology. *See* Hearing Before the
H.R. Comm. on Energy and Commerce, 111th Cong. (2012) (testimony of
Thomas F. Farrell II, Chairman, President, and CEO, Dominion).
Whether in response to that criticism or not, EPA withdrew this proposal
and submitted a new one. The revised proposed standard for new power
plants now sets *separate* targets for natural gas-fired and coal-fired units,
and has eased stringency somewhat for the latter—though only slightly.
The second proposed rule retains the 1000 lb/MWH standard for gas-fired
plants, but establishes a new 1100 lb/MWH standard for new coal-fired
plants. *See* Standards for Performance for Greenhouse Gas Emissions for
New Stationary Sources: Electric Utility Generating Units, 79 Fed. Reg.
1429 (Jan. 8, 2014).

Why did the agency abandon its single source category proposal for
coal- and gas-fired plants? While EPA has always enjoyed considerable
flexibility to define industrial categories under section the NSPS
program, it may have worried that the initial decision to conflate the
categories rendered the original proposal legally vulnerable. Industry
objected that the agency's approach essentially dictated which fuels can
be used for electricity generation, which is not authorized by the Act.
Industry also viewed the original proposal as a weakly veiled effort to
circumvent the statutory requirement that technology be both
demonstrated and available, arguing that the agency could never have
required carbon capture as the best demonstrated technology standard
for coal units as a separate category, since the technology is not yet
commercially competitive. However, carbon capture will continue to be
necessary for new coal-fired power plants to comply with the second
proposed rule.

The rule has not yet been reviewed by the courts, and its fate is
important because it is the first of many anticipated standards EPA
expects to set, sector-by-sector, for stationary sources of GHGs. Indeed, a
number of consent decrees now require the agency to promulgate
additional standards for GHG pollution from other new sources, such as
oil and gas refineries. A reversal in the D.C. Circuit would delay
implementation of these regulations, but more importantly, it would
delay the next step in the agency's implementation strategy—setting
standards for *existing* power plants, which depends upon the existence of
standards for new plants.

Is carbon capture an "adequately demonstrated" technology for coal-
fired power plants? EPA thinks so, but industry disagrees, and has
mounted ferocious opposition to the proposal. The American Public
Power Association calls for a 1950 lb/MWH standard. And EPA has
recently declined to require carbon capture as "best available control
technology" in certain PSD permitting contexts. *See* In the Matter of
ExxonMobil Chemical Co., Envtl. App. Bd., PSD Permit No. PSD–TX–
102982–GHG (2014) (upholding EPA's refusal to require carbon capture).
This issue will undoubtedly be central to any judicial challenge to the
new power plants rule.

b.   EXISTING POWER PLANTS

As we have noted throughout this book, the prospects for new coal-
fired power plants were uncertain at best before EPA proposed its GHG
NSPS for power plants, thanks to market pressure from natural gas-fired

power and the numerous other regulatory pressures described in this chapter. Regulating GHGs from *existing* power plants is a far more important aspect of U.S. climate policy. As described elsewhere in this chapter, grandfathered power plants have defied congressional expectations and lived much longer, and higher-polluting, lives than anyone ever anticipated. Interestingly, however, the CAA's NSPS program provides an avenue to control GHG emissions from these older sources in the form of Section 111(d).

Under Section 111(d), once EPA sets a standard for *new* sources of GHGs, the states are obligated to set standards for *existing* sources as well. To avoid duplicative regulation, this requirement applies to pollutants other than the six criteria pollutants for which states already submit NAAQS compliance plans (SIPs), and which are not emitted from a source category already regulated under the Act's hazardous air pollutant regulations. 42 U.S.C. §§ 7411(b), (d). Because GHGs are not criteria pollutants, and not hazardous pollutants either, they appear to qualify for regulation under 111(d). EPA elected not to set a NAAQS for GHGs, explaining that in its view, relying on performance standards under the NSPS program is the more effective approach. *See* Regulating Greenhouse Gas Emissions Under the Clean Air Act, 73 Fed. Reg. 44,354, 44,363–4 (2008). EPA's decision not to set NAAQS may eventually lead to litigation over just this question. *See* NRDC v. Train, 545 F.2d. 320 (2nd Cir. 1976) (requiring EPA to set a NAAQS for lead under § 109 notwithstanding EPA's preference to reduce lead emissions by regulating gasoline under the Act's mobile source provisions).

The statute requires EPA to issue "guidelines" under which the states are required to set "standards of performance" for the existing sources under their jurisdiction. States must then submit plans for meeting those standards (akin to SIPs). Section 111 defines a "standard of performance" as a "standard for emissions of air pollutants which reflects the degree of emission limitation achievable *through application of the best system of emission reduction. . . .*" 42 U.S.C. § 7411(g)(4)(B) (emphasis added).

The hard legal question is whether EPA can approve "systems" that combine different kinds of greenhouse gas reduction strategies in lieu of setting and enforcing rate-based performance standards source-by-source. For example, could states comply by setting a standard that reflects a level of emissions reduction *equivalent* to what would have been achieved by applying source-specific emissions standards to existing power plants, while achieving the standard through a variety of non-source specific measures? Might the "best system of emissions reduction" allow trading among sources? Might states go further, counting toward compliance any reductions from the electricity sector more broadly, including reductions achieved through investments in renewable energy, energy efficiency or demand response?

These approaches would require a flexible interpretation of what it means to set an emission standard, which has traditionally consisted of rate-based limits applicable to individual facilities (or a small group of facilities treated as a "bubbled" group) but which in this context might admit of a more elastic interpretation. Indeed, the most ambitious reading of section 111(d) would authorize EPA to implement a national cap-and-trade system for reducing GHG emissions. *See* Jeremy M. Tarr et al., Regulating Carbon Dioxide under Section 111 of the Clean Air Act, Options, Limits, Impacts, Nicholas Inst. for Pol'y Solutions, Jan. 2013.

EPA published its proposed guidelines in the summer of 2014:

Proposed Rule: Carbon Pollution Emission Guidelines for Existing Stationary Sources: Electric Utility Generating Units (Executive Summary)

79 Fed. Reg. 34,829 (June 18, 2014).

Under the authority of Clean Air Act (CAA) section 111(d), the EPA is proposing emission guidelines for states to follow in developing plans to address greenhouse gas (GHG) emissions from existing fossil fuel-fired electric generating units (EGUs). . . .

Nationwide, by 2030, this rule would achieve CO_2 emission reductions from the power sector of approximately 30 percent from CO_2 emission levels in 2005. This goal is achievable because innovations in the production, distribution and use of electricity are already making the power sector more efficient and sustainable while maintaining an affordable, reliable and diverse energy mix. This proposed rule would reinforce and continue this progress. The EPA projects that, in 2030, the significant reductions in the harmful carbon pollution and in other air pollution, to which this rule would lead, would result in net climate and health benefits of $48 billion to $82 billion. At the same time, coal and natural gas would remain the two leading sources of electricity generation in the U.S., with each providing more than 30 percent of the projected generation.

Based on evidence from programs already being implemented by many states as well as input received from stakeholders, the agency recognizes that the most cost-effective system of emission reduction for GHG emissions from the power sector under CAA section 111(d) entails not only improving the efficiency of fossil fuel-fired EGUs, but also addressing their utilization by taking advantage of opportunities for lower-emitting generation and reduced electricity demand across the electricity system's interconnecting network or grid.

The proposed guidelines are based on and would reinforce the actions already being taken by states and utilities to upgrade aging electricity infrastructure with 21st century technologies. The guidelines would ensure that these trends continue in ways that are consistent with the long-term planning and investment processes already used in this sector, to meet both region- and state-specific needs. The proposal provides flexibility for states to build upon their progress, and the progress of cities and towns, in addressing GHGs. It also allows states to pursue policies to reduce carbon pollution that: 1) continue to rely on a diverse set of energy resources, 2) ensure electric system reliability, 3) provide affordable electricity, 4) recognize investments that states and power companies are already making, and 5) can be tailored to meet the specific energy, environmental and economic needs and goals of each state. Thus, the proposed guidelines would achieve meaningful CO_2 emission reduction while maintaining the reliability and affordability of electricity in the U.S.

The proposal has two main elements: 1) state-specific emission rate-based CO_2 goals and 2) guidelines for the development, submission and implementation of state plans. To set the state-specific CO_2 goals, the EPA analyzed the practical and affordable strategies that states and utilities are already using to lower carbon pollution from the power sector. These strategies include improvements in efficiency at carbon-intensive power plants, programs that enhance the dispatch priority of, and spur private investments in, low emitting and renewable power sources, as well as programs that help homes and businesses use electricity more efficiently. In addition, in calculating each state's CO_2 goal, the EPA took into consideration the state's fuel mix, its electricity market and numerous other factors. Thus, each state's goal reflects its unique conditions.

While this proposal lays out state-specific CO_2 goals that each state is required to meet, it does not prescribe how a state should meet its goal. CAA section 111(d) of creates a partnership between the EPA and the states under which the EPA sets these goals and the states take the lead on meeting them by creating plans that are consistent with the EPA guidelines. Each state will have the flexibility to design a program to meet its goal in a manner that reflects its particular circumstances and energy and environmental policy objectives. Each state can do so alone or can collaborate with other states on multi-state plans that may provide additional opportunities for cost savings and flexibility.

To facilitate the state planning process, this proposal lays out guidelines for the development and implementation of state plans. The proposal describes the components of a state plan, the latitude states have in developing compliance strategies, the flexibility they have in the timing for submittal of their plans and the flexibility they have in determining the schedule by which their sources must achieve the required CO_2 reductions. The EPA recognizes that each state has differing policy considerations—including varying emission reduction opportunities and existing state programs and measures—and that the characteristics of the electricity system in each state (e.g., utility regulatory structure, generation mix and electricity demand) also differ. Therefore, the proposed guidelines provide states with options for meeting the state-specific goals established by the EPA in a manner that accommodates a diverse range of state approaches. This proposal also gives states considerable flexibility with respect to the timeframes for plan development and implementation, providing up to two or three years for submission of final plans and providing up to fifteen years for full implementation of all emission reduction measures, after the proposal is finalized.

Addressing a concern raised by both utilities and states, the EPA is proposing that states could choose approaches in their compliance plans under which full responsibility for actions achieving reductions is not placed entirely upon emitting EGUs; instead, state plans could include measures and policies (e.g., demand-side energy efficiency programs and renewable portfolio standards) for which the state itself is responsible. Of course, individual states would also have the option of structuring programs (e.g., allowance-trading programs) under which full responsibility rests on the affected EGUs. . . .

The proposed guidelines are designed to build on and reinforce progress by states, cities and towns, and companies on a growing variety of sustainable strategies to reduce power sector CO2 emissions. At the same time, the EPA believes that this proposal provides flexibility for states to develop plans that align with their unique circumstances, as well as their other environmental policy, energy and economic goals. All states will have the opportunity to shape their plans as they believe appropriate for meeting the proposed CO2 goals. This includes states with long-established reliance on coal-fired generation, as well as states with a commitment to promoting renewable energy (including through sustainable forestry initiatives). It also includes states that are already participating in or implementing CO2 reduction programs, such as the Regional Greenhouse Gas Initiative (RGGI), California's "Global Warming Solutions Act" and Colorado's "Clean Air, Clean Jobs Act".

States would be able to rely on and extend programs they may already have created to address the power sector. Those states committed to Integrated Resource Planning (IRP) would be able to establish their CO2 reduction plans within that framework, while states with a more deregulated power sector system could develop CO2 reduction plans within that specific framework. Each state, including states without an existing program, would have the opportunity to take advantage of a wide variety of strategies for reducing CO2 emissions from affected EGUs. . . .

States would be able to address the economic interests of their utilities and ratepayers by using the flexibilities in this proposed action to: 1) reduce costs to consumers, minimize stranded assets, and spur private investments in renewable energy and energy efficiency technologies and businesses; and 2) if they choose, work with other states on multi-state approaches that reflect the regional structure of electricity operating systems that exists in most parts of the country and is critical to ensuring a reliable supply of affordable energy. The proposed rule gives states the flexibility to provide a broad range of compliance options that recognize that the power sector is made up of a diverse range of companies that own and operate fossil fuel-fired EGUs, including vertically integrated companies in regulated markets, independent power producers, rural cooperatives and municipally-owned utilities, all of which are likely to have different ranges of opportunities to reduce GHG emissions while facing different challenges in meeting these reductions.

Both existing state programs (such as RGGI, the California Global Warming Solutions program and the Colorado Clean Air, Clean Jobs program) and ideas suggested by stakeholders show that there are a number of different ways that states can design programs that achieve required reductions while working within existing market mechanisms used to dispatch power effectively in the short term and to ensure adequate capacity in the long term. These programs and programs for conventional pollutants, such as the Acid Rain Program under Title IV of the CAA, have demonstrated that compliance with environmental programs can be monetized such that it is factored into power sector economic decision making in ways that reduce the cost of controlling pollution, maintain electricity system reliability and work within the least cost dispatching principles that are key to operation of our electric power grid. The proposal would also allow states to work together with individual companies on potential specific challenges. ∎

NOTES AND COMMENTS

1.   Note that the EPA proposal focuses on reducing emissions from power plants, and contemplates a variety of different "systems of emissions reductions" under § 111, including participation in state permit trading programs. *See* Erika Martinson, Cap and Trade Lives On Through the States, Politico (May 27, 2014). We examine these programs in the next section of this Chapter.

2.   EPA's proposal contemplates that some states will submit plans that do not rely fully on cutting emissions from power plants. Instead, these states might adopt measures that promote cleaner sources of energy (such as initiatives for the production of more renewable power) or programs to bring about more energy efficiency and other "demand-side" improvements that reduce demand for electricity and thereby reduce emissions. *See* Joel B. Eisen & Todd S. Aagaard, Tackling Climate Change: Don't Forget Energy Efficiency, N.Y.L.J., July 10, 2014, http://www.newyorklawjournal.com/id= 1202662613538/Tackling-Climate-Change-Dont-Forget-Energy-Efficiency? slreturn=20140711151725. Chapters 11 and 12 discuss renewable power; Chapter 13 discusses energy efficiency and other demand-side measures. In a portion of the *UARG* decision not excerpted above, the Court noted that in establishing BACT limits under the PSD program, EPA may not require "fundamental redesign" of an emitting facility or reductions in energy demand. This is because BACT is about "control technology." May a "system of emissions reduction" include demand reduction under the Act?

3.   Some of these measures would require action by other federal agencies to implement them. As an example, the Federal Energy Regulatory Commission (FERC), which regulates the electric grid, has attempted to assert jurisdiction over some demand-side measures that affect the wholesale electricity markets. See Chapter 13 for a fuller discussion of this issue. At a 2014 Congressional hearing, Congressman Henry Waxman asserted FERC's right to impose "carbon adders" in wholesale electricity markets (administratively-determined increases in the wholesale price of fossil-fueled power in competitive wholesale markets). If the Federal Power Act requires wholesale prices to be "just and reasonable" (as it does), does the administrative addition of carbon adders make prices more or less "just" or "reasonable"? See Chapter 10 for a fuller discussion of this issue. *See also* Steven Weissman, The Federal Energy Regulatory Commission Can Do A Lot to Reduce Greenhouse Gas, Legal Planet, July 22, 2014, http://legal-planet.org/2014/07/22/the-federal-energy-regulatory-commission-can-do-a-lot-to-reduce-greenhouse-gas/.

4.   Note also that EPA's proposal establishes state-specific emissions reduction goals. Under this proposal, each state will submit a plan for achieving its goals. While the proposal offers the states flexibility as to the means of compliance and the distribution of the burden across covered sources within the state, the state plans must include "enforceable CO2 emission limits that apply to affected EGUs." Given the ways states reacted to the burdens of the acid rain program, how do you think states might differ in their approaches to this requirement?

5. There is little precedent on § 111(d). EPA has used it in only limited circumstances. As described earlier in this chapter, during the George W. Bush administration, EPA sought to use § 111(d) to create a cap-and-trade regime for mercury and other pollutants. In striking down that rule, the D.C. Circuit did not reach the question whether a cap-and-trade approach would be lawful under § 111(d). *New Jersey v. EPA*, 517 F.3d 574, 583 (D.C. Cir. 2008), held that because Congress listed mercury as a hazardous air pollutant under § 112, it must be regulated under that section. EPA has also promulgated standards under 111(d) for non-NAAQS pollutants emitted by municipal waste facilities, but that scheme does not approach the scope envisioned by some of the creative proposals for using § 111(d) to regulate existing sources of GHGs. It is thus an open question whether EPA now can take a flexible approach to defining the word "standard" under the NSPS program, when it has traditionally treated standards as rate-based numerical limits.

6. Recall that the text of § 111(d) requires states to set standards for existing sources of pollutants only if the pollutants are not from *sources* already subject to regulation under the air toxics program in § 112. After promulgation of the mercury and air toxics rule, described earlier in this chapter, existing power plants are regulated under § 112. Read literally, the statute appears to foreclose regulating GHG emissions from these sources. However, EPA interprets 111(d) to preclude it from regulating only *pollutants* already listed as hazardous under the air toxic program regardless of whether the *sources* of those pollutants are subject to regulation under that program for emitting other pollutants. Why? In enacting the CAAA90, the House and Senate each approved a different amendment to § 111(d)—one that precludes regulation of *pollutants* subject to § 112 and another that precludes regulation of *sources*. Oddly, the Conference Committee never resolved the differences between the two amendments and *both* were enacted in Public Law 101–549 as parenthetical options. The U.S. Code mysteriously omits the parenthetical reference to the Senate amendment, but EPA has concluded that the Statutes at Large constitute the legal evidence of the laws. EPA argues that the best reconciliation of the two amendments, in light of the legislative history from both the 1977 and 1990 amendments, is to read the provision as precluding *duplicative* regulation, meaning that EPA may not set standards under § 111(d) for pollutants already regulated under § 112. Should EPA's interpretation of the statute be entitled to *Chevron* deference in this instance?

E. STATE REGULATION OF GREENHOUSE GAS EMISSIONS

For over two decades, states, regions and localities have adopted a wide variety of laws, regulations, and policies to reduce GHG emissions, including cap-and-trade programs, state and local climate action plans, and other initiatives. In the 1990s, some states used "environmental adder" procedures to require planners to factor in the environmental costs of CO_2 emissions in decisions to build power plants. In 1998, for example, a Minnesota court upheld a utility commission rule that required utilities to quantify the externalities associated with CO_2 emissions in procedures for choosing among potential power plant types. In the Matter of the Quantification of Envtl. Costs, 578 N.W.2d 794 (Minn. App. 1998). The Minnesota Public Utilities Commission reopened the proceeding in 2014 to determine whether the value for CO_2 should be updated. Dan Haugen, Coal giant Peabody Energy enters Minnesota pollution debate, Midwest Energy News, Feb. 20, 2014, http://www.mid westenergynews.com/2014/02/20/coal-giant-peabody-energy-enters-minnesota-pollution-debate/.

Contemporary state GHG laws and programs range from hortatory state action plans to mandatory GHG emission reduction standards. Some, such as net metering (see Chapter 13), renewable portfolio standards (see Chapter 11), and incentives for low-carbon fuels and vehicles (see Chapter 15) have multiple goals besides GHG reduction. Others aim more directly at reducing GHG emissions. Several states and some localities now have GHG targets and binding emissions standards. California has a comprehensive law and regulations designed to limit GHG emissions throughout the state's economy. The first section below presents various state and local strategies. The second section covers the two major cap-and-trade emissions reduction programs.

1. STATE AND LOCAL STRATEGIES

The following excerpt is from a guide to state CO_2 strategies; many individual types of emissions reduction measures mentioned in this guide are covered in more depth in other Chapters. Local initiatives are discussed in the note material following the excerpt.

Center for Climate and Energy Solutions, Climate Change 101: State Action (2011)

http://www.c2es.org/science-impacts/climate-change-101/states.

TAKING THE INITIATIVE

Two trends are apparent with regard to state and regional efforts that address climate change: 1) more states are taking action and 2) they are adopting more types of policies. In this way, states and regions are acting as both leaders and innovators of climate change policy. State and regional efforts are wide ranging, including high-profile policies such as cap-and-trade programs, renewable portfolio standards, and climate action plans. The states and regions are acting as "policy laboratories," developing initiatives that can serve as models for federal action, as well as for other states.

Since many individual states are major sources of greenhouse gas (GHG) emissions, state-level policies have the potential to produce significant reductions. Texas, for example, emits twice the amount of GHGs as Spain while California's emissions exceed those of Italy. As state-level policies proliferate, so too do the climate benefits associated with these actions. Moreover, state actions are important because state governments have decision-making authority over many issues and economic sectors—such as power generation and agriculture—that are critical to addressing climate change.

A wide range of policies have been adopted at the state and regional levels to reduce greenhouse gas emissions, develop clean energy resources, and promote more energy-efficient vehicles, buildings, and appliances, among other things.

WORKING ACROSS STATE BORDERS

In working to address climate change, many states have reached beyond their borders to enlist their neighbors in collaborative efforts. Across the United States, climate-related regional initiatives have been designed to reduce GHG emissions, develop clean energy sources, and achieve other goals. Regional initiatives can be more efficient and effective than actions taken by individual states because they cover a broader geographic area (and, in turn, more sources of GHG emissions), eliminate duplication of work among the states, and help businesses by bringing greater uniformity and predictability to state rules and regulations.

Regional climate initiatives, including three cap-and-trade programs, are being developed and implemented among U.S. states and Canadian provinces. Cap-and-trade programs set an overall emissions cap while allowing companies to trade emission allowances so they can achieve their reductions as cost effectively as possible. Similar programs have been successfully implemented in the United States and elsewhere to control other pollutants in an environmentally sound, cost-effective manner.

Regional Greenhouse Gas Initiative. In December 2005, the governors of seven Northeastern and Mid-Atlantic states signed an agreement formalizing the first U.S. GHG cap-and-trade program, the Regional Greenhouse Gas Initiative (RGGI). RGGI now consists of ten Northeastern and Mid-Atlantic states that are implementing a cap-and-trade program to reduce carbon dioxide (CO2) emissions from power plants in the region. The RGGI cap-and-trade program began in January 2009 and is administered with the technical assistance of a regional organization called RGGI, Inc. The successful implementation of RGGI has been an example for other states and national governments.

Western Climate Initiative. In February 2007, five western governors signed an agreement establishing the Western Climate Initiative (WCI), a joint effort to reduce GHG emissions and address climate change. The WCI has since grown to include seven U.S. states and four Canadian provinces that have jointly set a regional GHG emissions target of 15 percent below 2005 levels by 2020.

REDUCING ELECTRICITY EMISSIONS

States have considerable authority over how electricity is generated and used in the United States. With the generation of electricity accounting for 33 percent of all U.S. GHG emissions and 40 percent of U.S. CO2 emissions, states can play a crucial role in reducing the power sector's climate impacts by promoting low-carbon energy solutions and energy efficiency.

The two major options for reducing GHG emissions from electricity are energy efficiency and low-carbon electricity production. Energy efficiency policies come in many forms, including funding and requirements for energy efficient products, buildings, appliances, and transportation and utility programs that reduce their customers' energy demand. State actions to promote low-carbon electricity include incentives and mandates that reduce emissions by promoting a cleaner energy supply, for example by supporting renewable energy.

Renewable Portfolio Standards. Twenty-seven states and the District of Columbia have established mandatory Renewable Portfolio Standards (RPS), policies that require a certain percentage or amount of electricity generation from eligible renewable sources by a given date. An additional five states have renewable energy goals. RPS design varies significantly across the states. The standards range from modest to ambitious, and what qualifies as "renewable energy" can vary from state to state. While the use of renewable electricity can deliver significant reductions in GHG emissions, a variety of factors can drive the implementation of an RPS, including job creation in the renewables industry, diversification of energy sources, and improved air quality.

Public Benefit Funds. Almost half of U.S. states have funds, often called "public benefit funds," that are dedicated to supporting energy efficiency and renewable energy projects. The funds are collected either through a small charge on the bill of every electric customer or through specified contributions from utilities. Having a steady stream of funding ensures that money is available to pay for these projects, which often include low-income household energy assistance, weatherization programs, investment in renewable technologies, and subsidies for efficient appliances.

Net Metering. Forty-five U.S. states have at least one utility that permits customers to sell electricity back to the grid; this is referred to as "net metering." Eighteen of these states offer net metering on a statewide basis for all utilities, 24 others have statewide net metering for certain utility types, and the remaining three have individual utilities that offer net metering.

Limits on Power Plant Emissions. Oregon and Washington require that new power plants offset a certain portion of their anticipated CO2 emissions—for example, by reducing emissions on their own or by paying a specified fee to a designated organization that will then select and fund offset projects. California, Montana, Oregon, and Washington also require new power plants to meet a GHG emissions performance standard.

Carbon Capture and Storage. Carbon capture and storage is an emerging technology for reducing GHG emissions from large sources, primarily coal-fueled power plants. Colorado, Florida, Illinois, Indiana, Kansas, Kentucky, Louisiana, Minnesota, Mississippi, Montana, New Mexico, North Dakota, Rhode Island, Texas, Virginia and Wyoming have direct financial incentives for carbon capture and storage, including state bonds for construction, tax incentives, and utility cost recovery mechanisms. Many states also provide incentives for the development and use of technologies that may make carbon capture easier, such as integrated gasification combined cycle (IGCC) power plants.

Energy Efficiency Resource Standards. Twenty-six states have Energy Efficiency Resource Standards (EERS), which establish a target for utilities to increase energy savings by a specified amount over time from electricity and/or heating fuels. This encourages utilities to either promote energy-efficient technology for consumers or integrate more efficient technology for generation. In addition, some states allow savings from energy efficiency measures to count toward their RPS requirements rather than having a separate EERS.

Appliance Efficiency Standards. The federal government has established minimum efficiency standards for approximately 30 kinds of residential and commercial products, including washers and dryers, refrigerators and freezers, dishwashers, and air conditioners. Numerous states—including Arizona, California, Connecticut, Maryland, New Jersey, New York, Rhode Island, and Washington—have set standards on products not covered by federal standards. Many states have also implemented a variety of incentive programs, including rebates and tax exemptions, to promote energy efficiency.

TRANSPORTATION POLICIES

Transportation accounts for 27 percent of all U.S. GHG emissions and 32 percent of U.S. CO2 emissions. State options for reducing these emissions range from adopting more stringent emission standards for cars and trucks to offering incentives for alternative fuels and fuel-efficient vehicles.

New Vehicle Standards. California adopted a requirement for GHG emissions from new light-duty vehicles that would reduce new vehicle emissions on average 30 percent by 2016. California has unique authority among the states to set vehicle emissions standards because of a provision in the federal Clean Air Act that allows it to set stricter standards if granted a waiver by the EPA. Under the provision, other states have the option of either following federal or California standards. Rather than grant a waiver, the Obama administration opted to move federal standards to match California's fuel economy requirements—35.5 mpg by 2016.

Alternative Fuels. More than half of U.S. states provide incentives for alternative fuels, gasoline/ethanol blends, alternative-fuel vehicles, and low-emission vehicles; there are also state incentives for converting traditional vehicles to run on alternative fuels. These incentives to promote biofuel production and use include excise tax exemptions, tax credits, and grants. In addition to these incentives, 13 states have established Renewable Fuels Standards.

Incentives for Low-Carbon Fuels and Vehicles. In January 2007, California announced the first low-carbon fuel standard, which set a goal of reducing the life-cycle carbon intensity of transportation fuels by a minimum of 10 percent by 2020. The California LCFS was formally adopted in January 2010 and took effect in January 2011. Market-based mechanisms, such as credit trading, will allow fuel providers to meet the standard in a cost-effective manner.

EMISSION TARGETS AND CLIMATE ACTION PLANS

Many states are taking a comprehensive approach to climate policy by establishing statewide GHG emission reduction targets and developing climate action plans that provide a range of policy recommendations to address climate change, including measures to reduce emissions and respond to impacts.

Emission Targets. Twenty-three states have adopted statewide emission targets and goals. The stringency and timelines associated with these targets varies by state. The first enforceable statewide GHG emissions target was established in 2006 by California with A.B. 32, the Global Warming Solutions Act.

Climate Action Plans. Thirty-six states have completed comprehensive climate action plans or are in the process of revising or developing one. In addition, more than half of the states have set up advisory boards or commissions to develop and/or implement climate action plans. The process of developing a climate action plan can help state decision-makers identify cost-effective opportunities to reduce GHG emissions in ways that are most appropriate for their states, taking into account the individual characteristics of each state's economy, resource base, and political structure. In addition to addressing measures to reduce GHG emissions, a number of climate action plans have also focused on what the state must do to adapt to some degree of climate change.

LEARNING FROM THE STATES

In recent years, states have acted as leaders on climate action. Climate-friendly policies have emerged across the country to address key sectors, from electricity to transportation to agriculture, with significant variation in design. By acting as policy laboratories, states have been able to tailor policies to their own circumstances, test innovative approaches, and build experience with program design and implementation. The experiences of early acting states have already helped shape other state policies and will similarly be able to inform future state, regional, and federal action.

For example, state and regional experience to date suggests that some programs, such as emission inventories or cap-and-trade programs, should be designed so they can easily be expanded, linked to, or integrated with other programs at the regional and national levels. Since regional action can be more efficient and effective than individual state programs, designing easily expandable programs or joining a regional program can be an effective way to deal with climate change within the strict budget requirements that states face.

A key issue is the appropriate respective roles of different levels of government. The history of environmental protection in the United States shows that very few areas have been vested in the exclusive control of either the state or federal governments alone; rather, most are areas of overlapping or shared competence. Thus, policy makers need to ensure that state-level efforts are taken into account in the design of federal programs. ■

NOTES AND COMMENTS

1. Numerous U.S. cities (including Seattle, Miami, Cincinnati, Portland and others) and counties have comprehensive GHG emissions reduction plans. Over 1,000 cities and municipalities have signed the U.S. Conference of Mayors' Climate Protection Agreement, which calls for cities to reduce their GHG emissions. *See* U.S. Conf. of Mayors Climate Protection Agreement, http://www.usmayors.org/climateprotection/agreement.htm. In 1993, Portland, Oregon was the first U.S. city to adopt a climate action plan, and has updated and expanded it since then, with perhaps the most aggressive target in the nation: reducing local carbon emissions by 80 percent by 2050. City of Portland, Bureau of Planning & Sustainability, http://www.portlandoregon.gov/bps/28534. Many cities also have created

sustainability departments, which act as focal points for GHG mitigation strategies and other environmental programs.

2.   Several hundred universities have signed the American College & University Presidents' Climate Commitment, which calls for campus climate plans designed to achieve climate neutrality. *See* Am. Coll. & Univ. Presidents' Climate Commitment, http://www.presidentsclimatecommitment.org/about/ commitment. Has your institution signed the Commitment? What actions is it taking to reduce emissions from fossil fuel generation?

3.   This table includes measures discussed above that are designed to mitigate climate impacts, and the Chapters of this book that discuss them in more depth:

Climate Mitigation Measure	Chapter Discussed
Renewable Portfolio Standards	Chapter 13
Public Benefit Funds	Chapter 13
Net Metering	Chapter 12
Energy Efficiency Resource Standards	Chapter 13
Appliance Standards (federal)	Chapter 13
Alternative Vehicle Fuels/California LCFS	Chapter 15

2.   CAP-AND-TRADE PROGRAMS (RGGI, CALIFORNIA AB 32)

Two GHG cap-and-trade emissions programs operate in the United States: California's "AB32" program and the Northeast region's cap-and-trade scheme, the Regional Greenhouse Gas Initiative (RGGI).

Section B.3 above, dealing with the CAA's acid rain program, discussed the basic mechanics of cap-and-trade programs. To review, the government determines which facilities or emissions are covered and sets an overall target (the "cap") for covered emissions. Emissions allowances, each generally equal to one allowance per ton of emissions, are either auctioned or freely distributed, or some combination of these. The total number of allowances equals the cap number. Covered facilities must hold allowances equivalent to their emissions at the end of each compliance period (typically, one year). As noted above, covered firms can choose to (1) reduce emissions to match the number of allowances they receive, (2) buy additional allowances to pollute more, or (3) make deeper pollution reductions and sell "excess" allowances.

The cap-and-trade program takes advantage of the fact that firms face different costs for reducing emissions. Those that can reduce their pollution most cheaply will do so, while others will purchase allowances. The cap-and-trade program therefore gives firms flexibility to determine how and when to reduce emissions, and reductions are envisioned to take place at the lowest overall cost.

a.   REGIONAL GREENHOUSE GAS INITIATIVE

The RGGI cap-and-trade program began with ten Northeastern and Mid-Atlantic states, and covers CO_2 reductions from power plants. New Jersey's withdrawal from RGGI became effective in 2012, but the other states (listed below) are still participating.

Regional Greenhouse Gas Initiative Overview and Summary of Model Rule Changes (2013)

RGGI Inc., http://www.rggi.org.

The Regional Greenhouse Gas Initiative (RGGI) is the first market-based regulatory program in the United States to reduce greenhouse gas emissions. RGGI is a cooperative effort among the states of Connecticut, Delaware, Maine, Maryland, Massachusetts, New Hampshire, New York, Rhode Island, and Vermont to cap and reduce CO_2 emissions from the power sector.

RGGI is composed of individual CO_2 Budget Trading Programs in each RGGI participating state. Each participating state's CO_2 Budget Trading Program is based on the Model Rule, which was developed to provide guidance to states as they implemented the RGGI program. Each RGGI State's CO_2 Budget Trading Program is based upon its own statutory and/or regulatory authority. The RGGI CO2 Budget Trading Programs regulate emissions from fossil fuel-fired power plants with a capacity of 25 MW or greater located within the RGGI States ("CO_2 budget sources" or "sources").

Sources are required to possess CO_2 allowances equal to their CO_2 emissions over a three-year control period. The first three-year control period took effect on January 1, 2009 and extended through December 31, 2011 for the states of Connecticut, Delaware, Maine, Maryland, Massachusetts, New Hampshire, New Jersey, New York, Rhode Island, and Vermont. The second three-year control period took effect on January 1, 2012 and extends through December 31, 2014 for the states of Connecticut, Delaware, Maine, Maryland, Massachusetts, New Hampshire, New York, Rhode Island, and Vermont.

To reduce emissions of greenhouse gases, the RGGI States use a market-based cap-and-trade approach that includes:

- A multi-state CO_2 emissions budget ("cap").
- Requirements for fossil fuel-fired electric power generators with a capacity of 25 megawatts (MW) or greater ("regulated sources") to hold allowances equal to their CO_2 emissions over a three-year control period.
- Allocating CO_2 allowances through quarterly, regional CO_2 allowance auctions. A CO_2 allowance represents a limited authorization to emit one short ton of CO_2 from a regulated source, as issued by a participating state. CO_2 allowances are issued by each state in an amount defined in each state's applicable statute and/or regulations.
- Investing proceeds from the CO_2 allowance auctions in consumer benefit programs to improve energy efficiency and accelerate the deployment of renewable energy technologies.
- Allowing offsets (greenhouse gas emissions reduction or carbon sequestration projects outside the electricity sector) to help companies meet their compliance obligations.
- An emissions and allowance tracking system to record and track RGGI market and program data, including CO_2

emissions from regulated power plants and CO_2 allowance transactions among market participants.

Guided by the Model Rule, each state's regulations limit emissions of CO_2 from electric power plants, establish participation in CO_2 allowance auctions, create CO_2 allowances and determine appropriate allowance allocations. Regulated power plants can use a CO_2 allowance issued by any participating state to demonstrate compliance with an individual state program. In this manner, the state programs, in aggregate, function as a single regional compliance market for CO_2 emissions.

RGGI participating states have completed a 2012 Program Review, which is a comprehensive evaluation of program successes, program impacts, the potential for additional reductions, imports and emissions leakage, and offsets. Following the Program Review, the RGGI states implemented a new 2014 RGGI cap of 91 million short tons. The RGGI CO_2 cap then declines 2.5 percent each year from 2015 to 2020.

States sell nearly all emission allowances through auctions and invest proceeds in energy efficiency, renewable energy, and other consumer benefit programs. These programs are spurring innovation in the clean energy economy and creating green jobs in the RGGI states. ■

NOTES AND COMMENTS

1.   The RGGI Model Rule contained core provisions but was not comprehensive. Some decisions (such as flexibility in decisions about applicability and source exemptions, allowance allocations and set-asides, and permitting) were made on a state-by-state basis. Because the RGGI is not a government, it also had to rely on each state to change its environmental protection laws and regulations to incorporate RGGI content. This required different administrative processes in different states, and states sometimes had to change existing laws to conform to the Model Rule.

2.   For the first several years of the RGGI program, the number of available allowances was greater than market demand, resulting in a surplus of unsold allowances and low allowance prices. There were several reasons for this. First, the initial cap was set higher than historical emissions, because it was expected that electricity demand and emissions would grow. Instead, the Great Recession and greater use of energy efficiency programs led to decreased demand for electricity in the RGGI region and lower demand for allowances. Lower natural gas prices prompted generators to switch from coal to natural gas, resulting in lower emissions and demand for allowances.

Thus, between 2010 and 2013, many allowances went unsold and unused. *See* Ctr. For Climate And Energy Solutions, Regional Greenhouse Gas Initiative, http://www.c2es.org/us-states-regions/regional-climate-initiatives/rggi. Demand for allowances increased dramatically after the reduced 2014 cap of 91 million tons went into place, and clearing prices nearly doubled. *Id.*

3.   Even with relatively low clearing prices, proceeds of RGGI allowance auctions totaled over $1.75 billion as of mid-2014. *See* Regional Greenhouse Gas Initiative, Auction Results, http://rggi.org/market/co2_auctions/results.

RGGI states agreed that at least 25% of emission allowance proceeds would be invested in energy efficiency or clean energy technologies to benefit consumers and lessen the impacts of the cap-and-trade program on them. Member states have plans in place to use the proceeds for energy efficiency and renewable energy programs, and worker training for clean energy industries. A RGGI report from November 2012 estimates that these investments had avoided 12 million tons of CO_2 emissions. *See* Regional Greenhouse Gas Initiative, Regional Investment of RGGI CO_2 Allowance Proceeds, 2011 (2012), http://www.rggi.org/docs/Documents/2011-Investment-Report.pdf.

4.   "Emissions leakage" has been identified as a problem in RGGI, whose members border on states and regions that do not participate in the program. For this reason, some utilities can import "dirty" electricity instead of paying a higher price for "clean" electricity generated in the RGGI region. William Funk, Constitutional Implications of Regional CO_2 Cap-and-Trade Programs: The Northeast Regional Greenhouse Gas Initiative as a Case in Point, 27 UCLA J. Envtl. L. & Pol'y 353, 363–64 (2009). As part of the 2012 Program Review, member states committed to continue working to develop a mechanism for combating this problem.

5.   In a cap-and-trade program, projects that reduce emissions from non-regulated entities create "offsets" that covered sources can use to satisfy all or part of their reduction requirements. To some, offsets are a "feel-good" way of appearing to care about the environment while actually doing nothing to solve the problem. David A. Fahrenthold, There's a Gold Mine In Environmental Guilt, Wash. Post (Oct. 6, 2008). You can "offset" the emissions you generate on a cross-country airplane trip, but you are still taking the trip. Some counter that offsets "provide important additional benefits by creating incentives for the adoption of low- and no-carbon technologies and forest preservation." Nat'l Comm. on Energy Pol'y, Domestic and International Offsets: Forging the Climate Consensus (2009).

Then there is the problem of "additionality": offsets depend on the counter-factual of proving that reductions would not have happened if offsets were not available. RGGI requires any offset to be "real, additional, verifiable, enforceable, and permanent." Regional Greenhouse Gas Initiative, CO_2 Offsets, http://www.rggi.org/market/offsets.

How might an offsets program ensure "real" and "additional" GHG reductions? The RGGI limits offsets to five project categories that serve as proxies for "pure" additionality and minimize the need for case-by-case administrative decisions:

— Landfill methane capture and destruction

— Reduction in emissions of sulfur hexafluoride in the electric power sector

— Sequestration of carbon due to afforestation

— Reduction or avoidance of CO_2 emissions from natural gas, oil, or propane end-use combustion due to end-use energy efficiency in the building sector; and

— Avoided methane emissions from agricultural manure management operations.

Regional Greenhouse Gas Initiative, Offset Project Categories, http://rggi.org/offsets.

All offsets must take place in a RGGI member state, and offsets can account for 3.3 percent of a regulated power plant's total compliance obligation. *Id.*

b.   CALIFORNIA AB 32 (GLOBAL WARMING SOLUTIONS ACT)

If California were a separate economy, it would be the fifteenth largest emitter of GHGs in the world, accounting for about two percent of worldwide emissions. In 2006, it enacted a landmark law—the Global Warming Solutions Act (AB32)—to establish a GHG reduction scheme. As shown in **Figure 5–2**, AB32's cap-and-trade program is only one part of a larger, more comprehensive effort to address GHG emissions in the state's entire economy. AB 32's goal is reducing the state's GHG emissions to 1990 levels by 2020 and an 80% reduction from 1990 levels by 2050.

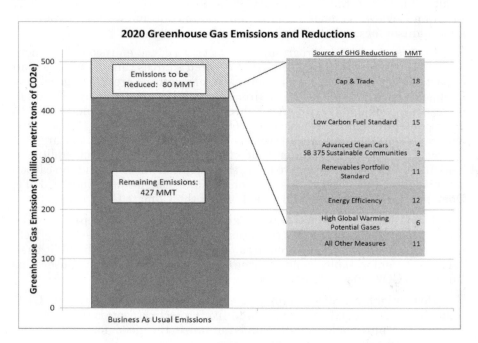

Figure 5–2
2020 Greenhouse Gas Emissions and Reductions
Source: Cal. Air Res. Bd,
Cap-and-Trade Auction Proceeds Investment Plan 9 (2013) http://www.arb.ca.gov/
cc/capandtrade/auctionproceeds/final_investment_plan.pdf

AB 32 directed the state's air pollution control agency, the California Air Resources Board (CARB), to implement a cap-and-trade program, and CARB put the program into effect in 2013. The first of three compliance periods between 2013 and 2020 caps emissions from electric generating utilities, electricity importers and large industrial facilities. By 2020, the program will cover an estimated 85% of the state's emissions. The initial cap will decrease by about 2% each year during the first compliance period.

California Air Resources Board Overview of ARB
Emissions Trading Program (2011)

http://www.arb.ca.gov/newsrel/2011/cap_trade_overview.pdf.

AB 32 requires California to return to 1990 levels of greenhouse gas emissions by 2020. All programs developed under AB 32 contribute to the reductions needed to achieve this goal, and will deliver an overall 15% reduction in greenhouse gas emissions compared to the 'business-as-usual' scenario in 2020 if we did nothing at all.

The cap and trade program is a key element in California's climate plan. It sets a statewide limit on sources responsible for 85 percent of California's greenhouse gas emissions, and establishes a price signal needed to drive long-term investment in cleaner fuels and more efficient use of energy. The program is designed to provide covered entities the flexibility to seek out and implement the lowest-cost options to reduce emissions.

Scope

• Program covers about 350 businesses, representing 600 facilities
• Starts in 2013 for electric utilities and large industrial facilities
• Starts in 2015 for distributors of transportation, natural gas and other fuels
• Designed to link with similar trading programs in other states and regions

The cap

• Set in 2013 at about 2 percent below the emissions level forecast for 2012
• Declines about 2 percent in 2014
• Declines about 3 percent annually from 2015 to 2020

Allowances

• Large industrial facilities
• Start with free allocation but must buy auctioned allowances later in program
• Allowances for each industrial sector to be set at about 90 percent of average emissions, based on a benchmark that rewards efficient facilities
• Distribution of allowances to be updated annually for industries according to the production and efficiency of each facility
• Electric utilities
• Free distribution, with value of allowances to benefit ratepayers
• Allowances to be set at about 90 percent of average emissions computed from recent data

Cost containment and market flexibility mechanisms

• Trading allowances allowed, to minimize cost of pollution controls
• Banking of allowances, to guard against shortages and price swings
• 4 percent of allowances will be held in a strategic reserve, to contain costs
• Three-year compliance periods, to buffer annual variations in product output

Offsets

• Allowed for up to 8 percent of a facility's compliance obligation

• Limited to emission-reduction projects in U.S.

• Initially restricted to projects in four areas: forestry, urban forestry, dairy digesters, and destruction of ozone-depleting substances

• Offsets must be independently verified

• Provisions to credit offsets registered with entities outside ARB

• Framework for future inclusion of international offset programs

Emissions reporting and verification

• Capped industries must continue to report emissions annually (as required since 2008)

• These industries must register with ARB to participate in emissions trading market

• Independent third-party verification of reported emissions

Compliance and enforcement

• Every year, capped industries provide allowances and offsets for 30 percent of previous year's emissions

• Every three years, these industries provide allowances and offsets covering the remainder of emissions in that three-year compliance period

• If deadline is missed or there is a shortfall, four allowances must be provided for every ton of emissions that was not covered in time

• The program includes mechanisms to prevent market manipulation

Next Steps:

• January 1, 2012: Cap-and-trade regulation becomes effective.

• August and November, 2012: first auctions will be held.

• January 1, 2013: Compliance obligation for greenhouse gas emissions begins. ■

NOTES AND COMMENTS

1.   How are the following handled—the same, or differently in RGGI and California: Determination of covered sources? Distribution of allowances? Offsets?

2.   California has held several quarterly AB32 allowance auctions since 2012. Much of the auction revenue has gone to finance climate change mitigation programs. As of mid-2013, roughly 50 million allowances had been sold, raising $256 million. A 2013 Investment Plan details the uses of the revenues for clean energy investments and other purposes. CARB, Cap-and-Trade Auction Proceeds Investment Plan (2013), http://www.arb.ca.gov/cc/capandtrade/auctionproceeds/final_investment_plan.pdf.

In 2013, in a move criticized as potentially unlawful under state law, Governor Jerry Brown proposed borrowing $500 million of auction revenue to balance the state's budget (which was later done), which led to speculation about how much future revenue would be used for climate mitigation purposes.

3.   In early 2014, California linked its cap-and-trade system with that of the Canadian province Quebec. This linkage was all that was left of the

Western Climate Initiative (see Section E.1 above) following the withdrawal of all U.S. states except for California. *See* Shawn McCarthy, Quebec-California partnership blazes trail for carbon trading, The Globe and Mail, Jan. 2, 2014.

4.   California attempted to address the leakage problem by imposing GHG control requirements on any plant selling electricity in the California market, regardless of whether the electricity was generated in California. While this approach reduces movement of electricity producers across borders, it may not reduce emissions. One logical response to the California rule for plant owners is "resource shuffling," explained in a forthcoming article by Jim Rossi and Andrew James Dearing Smith:

> At the outset an illustration of shuffling may be helpful to understanding its significance as a problem and California's response to it. Suppose that there are two power plants with equal production capacity, both located outside of California's borders. Plant A burns high-carbon coal, while Plant B uses relatively low-carbon natural gas. For years, Plant A has operated under a contract to sell power to a California utility (for delivery to customers within California's borders), while Plant B has a contract to sell power to a Nevada utility. Since the California utility has to buy permits for its GHG emissions, Plant A becomes more expensive. Shuffling occurs when the CA utility swaps contracts with the NV utility, thus lowering its compliance costs. Both plants continue operating and producing the same amount of electric power. In this example there is no overall emissions reduction, but if Plant A is located further from the Nevada utility than Plant B, the Nevada utility may need to purchase a greater amount of electric power from Plant A to cover the line losses associated with transmission, and there could actually be an increase in the overall GHG emissions associated with delivering the same amount of electricity to customers.

Jim Rossi and Andrew James Dearing Smith, Electric Power Resource 'Shuffling' and Subnational Carbon Regulation: Looking Upstream for a Solution, 5 San Diego J. Climate & Energy L. 43 (2013–2014).

5.   Should power plants' emissions reductions under the AB32 or RGGI program count toward the state targets in the federal rule regulating existing power plants under CAA section 111(d) (discussed above in Section D.3)? For a discussion of the complex issues this raises, see Megan Herzog, Part III—EPA's Proposed 111(d) Rule: Some Insights & Open Legal Questions, Legal Planet, June 6, 2014, http://legal-planet.org/2014/06/06/part-iii-epas-proposed-111d-rule-some-insights-open-legal-questions/.

F. OTHER EXTERNALITIES OF FOSSIL FUEL GENERATION

Most of this chapter has focused on the air emissions implications of fossil-fueled electricity generation. But combusting fossil fuels generates other negative externalities as well. This section provides an overview of two of the most prominent externalities: coal combustion residuals (CCRs), and cooling water. Like the GHG emissions issues above, these two externalities are facing increased scrutiny from regulators, who are

evaluating the need and ability of older environmental statutes to
address these very current challenges.

1.   COAL COMBUSTION RESIDUALS

As the name implies, coal combustion residuals (CCRs, commonly
known as "coal ash") are a by-product of coal combustion. When coal is
burned for electricity generation, it creates both "fly ash"—the PM that
is collected in pollution control equipment under the CAA—and "bottom
ash"—the heavier ashes that are too heavy to be airborne and that are
collected through the bottom of coal furnaces. Other solids from the coal
combustion process include slag and materials generated in the process
of removing other air pollutants, like SO2, from the exhaust gas.
Combined, these residuals amount to a large component of the waste
stream in coal-fired power plants; in 2012, for example, coal-fired power
plants in the United States generated over 109 million tons of CCRs. *See*
Am. Coal Ash Ass'n, 2012 Coal Combustion Product (CCP) Production &
Use Survey Report, http://www.acaa-usa.org/Portals/9/Files/PDFs/
revisedFINAL2012CCPSurveyReport.pdf.

CCRs contain a variety of heavy metals like lead, arsenic, and
chromium, which can be toxic at sufficient concentrations. CCRs are
typically disposed of in one of three ways: (1) wet disposal in unlined "ash
ponds," (2) wet disposal in lined ash ponds; or (3) dry disposal in lined
landfills. Of these three, the first option is the cheapest, but it also poses
the greatest risk to human health and the environment. Unlined disposal
methods permit toxics to contaminate the soil, groundwater, and surface
water and such disposal is disfavored today. Nevertheless, the legacy of
past practices has caused several high-profile incidents—two of which
are described in the following sections—and invited increasing
regulatory scrutiny.

a.   REGULATION UNDER THE RESOURCE CONSERVATION AND RECOVERY ACT

Despite being a solid waste that includes toxic components, until
December 2014, CCRs were not regulated under the federal Resource
Conservation and Recovery Act (RCRA), which governs the generation,
transportation, and disposal hazardous wastes (subtitle C) and the
disposal of solid wastes (subtitle D). To qualify for subtitle C regulation,
CCRs would have to either exhibit hazardous characteristics, or be listed
as a hazardous waste by EPA. *See* 42 U.S.C. § 6921. Because CCRs have
small amounts of heavy metals relative to large waste streams, they
generally do not qualify as having hazardous characteristics under the
applicable testing procedures. But RCRA also prohibits regulating CCRs
under subtitle C until EPA provides a report to Congress and makes a
determination that regulation is warranted. *Id.* § 6921(b)(3)(A)(i).

After years of delay and litigation, EPA completed a report to
Congress in 1999 and made a regulatory determination in 2000 in which
it concluded that regulation under subtitle C was not warranted. EPA
stated that it would continue to collect information, however, and would
develop regulations for CCRs under subtitle D. But the agency never
developed subtitle D regulations, and in 2008, a major release of CCRs
(detailed in the excerpt below) brought renewed attention to CRRs'

potential to cause environmental harms. Various environmental groups petitioned EPA to promulgate rules that would regulate CCRs under RCRA, and EPA announced its intent to regulate CCRs under either subtitle C or D:

Proposed Rule, Hazardous and Solid Waste Management System: Identification and Listing of Special Wastes; Disposal of Coal Combustion Residuals from Electric Utilities
75 Fed. Reg. 35,128 (June 21, 2010).

On December 22, 2008, a failure of the northeastern dike used to contain fly ash occurred at the dewatering area of the [Tennesee Valley Authority's (TWA's)] Kingston Fossil Plant in Harriman, Tennessee. Subsequently, approximately 5.4 million cubic yards of fly ash sludge was released over an approximately 300-acre area. The ash slide disrupted power, ruptured a gas line, knocked one home off its foundation and damaged others. A root-cause analysis report developed for TVA, accessible at http://www.tva.gov/kingston/rca/index.htm, established that the dike failed because it was expanded by successive vertical additions, to a point where a thin, weak layer of fly ash ("slime") on which it had been founded, failed by sliding. The direct costs to clean up the damage from the TVA Kingston incident are well into the billions, and [are] currently estimated to exceed $1.2 billion.

Although the TVA spill was the largest, it was not the only damage case to involve impoundment stability. A smaller, but still significant incident occurred in August 2005, when a gate in a dam confining a 40-acre CCR surface impoundment in eastern Pennsylvania failed. The dam failure, a violation of the facility's state-issued solid waste disposal permit and Section 402 of the Clean Water Act, resulted in the discharge of 0.5 million cubic yards of coal-ash and contaminated water into the Oughoughton Creek and the Delaware River.

Moreover, documented cases of the type of damage that EPA originally identified to result from improper management of CCR have continued to occur, leading EPA to question whether the risks that EPA originally identified have been sufficiently mitigated since our May 2000 Regulatory Determination. . . . [T]here is a growing record of proven damage cases to groundwater and surface water, as well as a large number of potential damage cases. Since the May 2000 Regulatory Determination, EPA has documented an additional 13 proven damage cases and 4 potential damage cases.

Further, recently collected information regarding the existing state regulatory programs calls into question whether those programs, in the absence of national minimum standards, have sufficiently improved to address the gaps that EPA had identified in its May 2000 Regulatory Determination such that EPA can continue to conclude that in the absence of federal oversight, the management of these wastes will be adequate to protect human health and the environment. Many state regulatory programs for the management of CCRs, including requirements for liners and groundwater monitoring, are lacking, and while industry practices may be improving, EPA continues to see cases of inappropriate management or cases in which key protections (e.g., groundwater monitoring at existing units) are absent. Although . . . most new units appear to be better designed, in that they are lined and have installed groundwater monitoring systems, and therefore the total percentages of unprotected units have decreased, it appears that a large amount of waste is still being disposed into units that lack the necessary protections of liners, and groundwater monitoring. Furthermore, while corrective action has generally been taken at the proven damage cases, the RCRA regulatory program is designed to prevent contamination in the first place, if at all practicable, rather than one in which contamination is simply remedied after discovery. This information also highlights that EPA still lacks details regarding the manner and degree to which states are regulating the management of this material. All of these factors emphasize the need for prompt federal rulemaking and have led EPA to reconsider its May 2000 Regulatory Determination.

In sum, as a result of the significant new information . . . , the Agency has determined that reevaluation of its original conclusions in light of all of the [applicable] factors is necessary. Based on its consideration of these statutory factors, EPA has not yet reached a decision on whether to revise the . . . Regulatory Determination. Rather, EPA has summarized the information available for each of the factors, and identifies those considerations on which EPA believes that critical information is lacking. Accordingly, EPA is soliciting further information and public input on each of these considerations that will factor into the Agency's determination as to whether regulation under RCRA subtitle C or D is warranted. ∎

NOTES AND COMMENTS

1.   Although CCRs contain various toxic constituents, they can be put to beneficial use in concrete, road surfaces, construction materials, and the like. The American Coal Ash Association (ACAA) estimates significant potential revenues from selling CCRs for reuse. It has also catalogued a variety of environmental benefits from their reuse, including saving landfill space and avoiding GHG emissions by substituting fly ash for Portland cement. *See* ACAA, Frequently Asked Questions, http://www.acaa-usa.org/AboutCoal Ash/CCPFAQs.aspx#Q5. Would regulating CCRs under RCRA hinder the industry's ability to realize these financial and environmental benefits?

2.   In EPA's May 2000 regulatory determination, the agency supported its decision not to regulate CCRs under subtitle C by explaining that many states already regulate CCR disposal as a matter of state law. As described in the excerpt above, however, EPA continued to document cases of harm to the environment and has now stated its view that federal oversight is necessary. On December 19, 2014, EPA issued a final rule under subtitle D. The rule includes structural integrity requirements for containment structures, and mandates that facilities maintain compliance information on publicly available websites. *See* Final Rule, Disposal of Coal Combustion Residuals from Electric Utilities, ___ Fed. Reg ___ (2014).

3.   Compare this relative inaction on the part of both the states and EPA with the variety of state and federal initiatives described above in the materials on GHG emissions. Why would states be more proactive with respect to GHG emissions than with CCR disposal? Is federal involvement easier or harder to justify in either arena? Are other sources of law better

suited to addressing CCR externalities? Consider the materials in the following section.

b. OTHER FEDERAL AND STATE LAW: A CASE STUDY

Although RCRA is the most obvious candidate for regulation of CCRs at the federal level, other sources of law may be applicable in certain circumstances. Below is a case study involving Duke Energy's numerous unlined coal ash ponds in North Carolina. As you read, ask yourself the following questions:

(1) From a governance standpoint, which sources of law (that is, primarily federal or primarily state law) seem most consistent with other governance schemes?

(2) From a policy standpoint, what are the competing issues inherent in using each of these other sources of law to address CCR externalities?

(3) After you've covered Chapter 8 (ratemaking), return to this Case Study and consider who should bear the costs of these externalities: Ratepayers? Utilities and their shareholders? The general public?

Case Study: Duke Energy's Coal Ash

Duke Energy, an investor-owned utility that operates in a number of Southern and Mid-Atlantic states, reported in February 2014 that between 50,000 and 80,000 tons of coal ash had been released from an unlined ash pond at its retired coal-fired power plant in Eden, North Carolina. The release lasted for five days and contaminated the Dan River, which serves as the drinking water supply for several communities, including Danville, Virginia's 18,000 customers. The release was caused when a stormwater pipe beneath the pond broke and acted as a conduit from the pond to the river. In the wake of this incident, the President of Duke Energy North Carolina was quoted on the company's website, stating, "We will do the right thing for the river and surrounding communities. We are accountable." Duke also pledged not to ask customers to pay the costs of cleanup.

Prior to the 2014 release, various environmental groups had filed a lawsuit against Duke challenging its disposal practices at a different site and alleging violations of the CWA. Other facts are detailed in the following two excerpts.

Cape Fear River Watch, Inc. v. Duke Energy Progress, Inc.

No. 7–13–CV–200–FL (E.D.N.C. June 9, 2014).

This matter comes before the court on defendant's motion to dismiss for failure to state a claim and for lack of subject matter jurisdiction. . . .

[Plaintiffs, various environmental groups, brought this action against Duke in September 2013, alleging violations of the CWA by: unauthorized surfacewater discharges to Lake Sutton; violations of Duke's existing NPDES permit; and unauthorized groundwater discharges to Lake Sutton.]

A.   Allegations in the Complaint

In 1971, North Carolina authorized, through statute and easement, defendant's predecessor to dam Catfish Creek, a navigable stream, in order to create the 1,100-acre Sutton Lake. Since then, the lake has been managed by the North Carolina Wildlife Resources Commission ("WRC") as a public fishery. Sutton Lake is a popular fishing destination, frequented by sport and subsistence fishermen for consumption. WRC manages the Sutton Lake fishery with financial support from federal funds and grants from the U.S. Fish and Wildlife Service's Sport Fish Restoration Program. These entities encourage the public to fish at the Lake and recently renovated its boat ramps and fishing pier to provide greater public access. North Carolina Department of Justice, in correspondence attached to the complaint, suggested that Sutton Lake is a water of the state, as defined under North Carolina law.

Pursuant to its delegated authority under the CWA, 33 U.S.C. § 1342(b), the North Carolina Department of Environment and Natural Resources (DENR) issued a National Pollutant Discharge Elimination System ("NPDES") permit (the "Sutton NPDES permit"). The Sutton NPDES permit authorizes only one point source discharge into the Cape Fear River from the Sutton Site. Defendant does not have a NPDES permit for discharges into Sutton Lake.

The Sutton facility includes two coal ash settling lagoons, known as the Old Ash Pond Area (approximately 54 acres, constructed in 1972) and New Ash Pond (approximately 82 acres, constructed in 1984), which border Sutton Lake and discharge into it. The lagoons contain coal ash stored in a wet state. Neither of the lagoons has a synthetic liner. A sinkhole opened beneath one of the berms of the New Ash Pond in 2000, and there was a partial collapse and spill from another of the New Ash Pond berms in 2010. EPA noted that some of the Old Ash Pond berms may be constructed on a foundation of coal ash, as was the case with a 2008 Kingston, Tennessee, coal ash spill. The berms of both Sutton coal ash lagoons have been given a "Significant" Hazard rating by EPA based on the potential for economic and environmental losses due to a spill.

Defendant has dumped and is dumping polluted water from its coal ash lagoons directly into Sutton Lake and its public fishery. These discharges include coal ash sluice water, coal pile runoff, chemical metal cleaning wastes, and other wastewater. As a result, Sutton Lake has become heavily contaminated with toxic pollutants including arsenic, selenium, mercury, antimony, cadmium, chromium, lead and zinc; and other pollutants including sulfate, copper, ammonia, nitrogen, phosphorus, iron, manganese, total dissolved solids, and total suspended solids.

Taking selenium as an example, decades of sampling reveal that concentrations in Sutton Lake have increased dramatically over time, such that in recent years the selenium concentrations in the surface water reached levels that cause reproductive failure of fish and waterfowl and have far exceeded those levels in the lake sediments and in fish tissue itself. WRC determined that the sediment and fish tissue concentrations of selenium represent a "High" hazard for reproductive failure of fish and waterfowl. WRC staff commented that defendant has been withholding selenium data from WRC, despite multiple requests for updated concentration information. Once selenium levels reach a certain point, the fishery could be killed off entirely. Selenium is also bioaccumulative, meaning it is passed up the food chain in increasing concentrations, and excessive amounts have been found in water snakes, small mammals, birds and humans.

As summarized by the parties, the Sutton NPDES permit treats discharges from the waste streams of the coal ash lagoons into Sutton Lake as "internal outfalls" within a waste treatment system. These discharges are termed "internal" in the permit because they are considered not to discharge to waters of the United States. Accordingly, the Sutton NPDES permit contains no limits on the discharges to Sutton Lake for toxic pollutants such as selenium and arsenic. Thus, the permit does not protect water quality in Sutton Lake. In addition, defendant has allowed pollutants and coal ash materials to escape from its coal ash lagoons into the groundwater at Sutton. These discharges are prohibited by the Sutton NPDES permit. The resulting plume of contaminated groundwater is migrating towards drinking water supply wells that provide drinking water to the community around Flemington Road. These Flemington wells are located approximately half a mile from the Sutton coal ash lagoons. As described in the complaint, a recent "Source Water Assessment Program Report" prepared by the North Carolina Division of Environmental Health, Public Water Supply Section, for the water system served by the Flemington wells assigned them an "Inherent Vulnerability Rating," "Contaminant Rating," and "Susceptibility Rating" the highest risk ratings, and the report listed the Sutton facility numerous times as a "Potential Contaminant Source" for these wells. The report also confirms that many of the highly contaminated groundwater wells at Sutton are within the area that contributes groundwater to the Flemington wells. The contaminated groundwater at Sutton is also flowing directly into a canal that is connected to and flows into Sutton Lake. As a result, the coal ash lagoons are discharging pollutants into Sutton Lake via this hydrologic connection.

Defendant had plans to retire its coal-fired generating operation at Sutton by the end of 2013, but had not submitted a closure plan for the ash lagoons to DENR and planned to leave the ash in place and continue using the ash lagoons to receive waste streams and discharge into Sutton Lake. As long as the coal ash remains in these leaking lagoons, it will continue to discharge pollutants into Sutton Lake and place the public fishery at risk of a coal ash spill into the Lake.

B. Recent Developments at Coal Ash Facilities Statewide

Before plaintiffs filed complaint in this court, DENR sued defendant in state court, on August 16, 2013, alleging violations of state environmental laws at Sutton and five other facilities in North Carolina. State of North Carolina v. Duke Energy Progress, Inc., C.A. No. 13–CVS–11032, Aug. 16, 2013, (Wake Co.). DENR notes in its complaint that groundwater sampling is required, and groundwater standards . . . are alleged to be violated pursuant to state law. Thus, the claims in DENR's complaint before Wake County Superior Court are different from the claims brought by plaintiffs in this case.

On February 10, 2014, the United States Attorney's Office in the Eastern District of North Carolina issued a subpoena to DENR requiring testimony before the court's grand jury regarding defendant's Dan River facility, which discharges coal ash and wastewater to the Dan River and recently had a catastrophic spill onsite. Defendant was also subpoenaed on that date. On February 11, 2014, eighteen DENR employees were subpoenaed concerning payments or other things of value they may have received from defendant or its related companies, and DENR was subpoenaed again for personnel records of twenty current and former employees. Notably, Sergei Chernikov is one of the employees subpoenaed and also the DENR contact person for the Fact Sheet on the Sutton NPDES Permit.

On February 18, 2014, DENR was subpoenaed for documents and information relating to fourteen facilities owned by defendant, including Sutton. The February 18, 2014, subpoena specifically seeks documents related to the activities of defendant and DENR and their handling of the state court enforcement proceedings that includes the Sutton facility.

On February 20, 2014, DENR indicated that it was assembling a task force in response to the Dan River ash spill, which would revisit the terms of a then-proposed consent order regarding that site in state superior court. The consent order was subsequently withdrawn in that case. On February 28, 2014, DENR issued a Notice of Violation to Duke Energy-Dan River Steam Station for its violations at the Dan River facility. In that notice, DENR cites the discharge of coal ash pollutants from the ash pond at the Dan River facility into waters of the state, and as a result claims a violation of the Removed Substances Permit Provision of that NPDES permit. The Removed Substances Provision for the Dan River facility's permit is one of the standard conditions that is also contained in the Sutton NPDES permit.

On March 12, 2014, defendant responded to an inquiry from Governor Pat McCrory regarding its recommendations for actions concerning coal ash basins in North Carolina. DENR found this response to be inadequate, and on March 13, 2014, DENR issued two press releases. First, DENR indicated that it plans to modify permits at three facilities, including Sutton. Second, DENR claimed that defendant's response to an information request on coal ash facilities was inadequate, specifically listing Sutton as high-priority. On March 14, 2014, DENR sent defendant a notice of modification regarding the Sutton NPDES permit. That same day, DENR invited EPA to "partner with DENR in the responsible resolution of not only the Dan River matter, but other environmental issues at the thirteen additional Duke Energy sites in North Carolina." On March 17, 2014, EPA responded that such a joint approach was "a desirable way to proceed for both of our agencies," and also suggested "crafting an over-all solution to outstanding CWA concerns at Duke Energy facilities."

[The court went on to deny defendants' motion to dismiss as to the unauthorized surface discharges and the violation of the NPDES permit. It granted the motion to dismiss as to the groundwater claim. (Why? See the "navigable waters" issue under the CWA, discussed in Chapter 6.)] ∎

Tansey v. Good et al. and Duke Energy Corp.

Verified Shareholder Derivative Complaint for Breach of Fiduciary Duty, Waste of
Corporate Assets, and Unjust Enrichment (Del. Chancery Ct. filed May 1, 2014).

NATURE AND SUMMARY OF THE ACTION

1.   This is a verified shareholder derivative action brought by plaintiffs
on behalf of nominal defendant Duke Energy Corporation against certain
of its officers and directors for breaches of fiduciary duties and violations
of law. These wrongs have exposed the Company to billions of dollars in
potential liability.

2.   Duke Energy is the largest provider of electricity in the United
States. The company generates power from a variety of sources, with 41%
of its energy generated from coal. When coal is burned for fuel, coal ash
is generated as a byproduct. Coal ash contains numerous chemicals that
are toxic to humans and wildlife, including lead, arsenic, and mercury,
among others. North Carolina's Department of Environment and
Natural Resources (DENR) requires companies producing coal ash, such
as Duke Energy, to create and implement proper coal ash disposal
systems, and also to obtain various permits from the DENR to legally
discharge rainwater draining from coal plants into public waterways.
These permits help to ensure that proper testing and inspections are
implemented at the facilities, and further insure that the rainwater
discharge is within acceptable environmental limits.

3.   Duke Energy has at least thirty-three unlined ash ponds in North
Carolina. . . .

4.   Of the three major energy suppliers in North and South Carolina,
Duke Energy is the only company that has refused to remove their coal
ash from unlined ponds and store it in lined landfills or recycle it. Worse,
certain of the Company's ash ponds were installed over local stormwater
runoff pipes, which allow excess rainwater to run unimpeded into local
rivers. Thus, any breach in the pipes allows the coal ash to enter the pipe
and flow directly into nearby rivers.

5.   On February 2, 2014, one of the stormwater pipes broke below an
ash pond at the Company's retired Dan River Steam Station in Eden,
North Carolina (the Dan River Station). The pipe was positioned only
three feet under the twenty-seven acre coal ash pond. As a result, over
the next few days, at least 39,000 tons of coal ash and twenty-seven
million gallons of contaminated water spilled into the Dan River, making
it the third largest coal ash spill in the nation's history. The spill coated
the river bottom with coal ash for at least seventy miles in North Carolina
and Virginia. On February 14, 2014, government investigators
discovered that a second, smaller stormwater pipe at the Dan River
Station was also releasing coal ash into the Dan River.

6.   As detailed herein, subsequent investigations have revealed that at
a minimum, the Individual Defendants (as defined herein) have known
for years that the Duke Energy's coal ash ponds were seeping toxic
chemicals into the soil and rivers, yet took no action to remedy the
problems. The Individual Defendants also knew since at least 2010 that
the Company was illegally operating without proper permits in several
Duke Energy facilities, including at the Dan River Station. Even a major
disaster such as the Dan River Station spill, however, did not motivate

the Individual Defendants to cause Duke Energy to obey environmental laws. As a result of the Individual Defendant's failure, Duke Energy has received eight permit violations since the Dan River Station spill, including: (i) six violations for failing to obtain proper permits at various coal plants, including at the Dan River Station; (ii) one violation specifically relating to the environmental destruction caused by the Dan River Station spill; and (iii) one violation for illegally and intentionally dumping millions of gallons of contaminated coal ash water into local rivers just one month after the Dan River Station disaster occurred.

7.   On March 6, 2014, Judge Paul C. Ridgeway, a Superior Court Judge for the Wake County General Court of Justice, ordered Duke Energy to "take immediate action to eliminate sources of contamination" at all fourteen of the Company's coal plants in North Carolina, which include thirty-three ash ponds. To date, the Individual Defendants have refused to cause Duke Energy to comply with the order. Instead, the Company has proposed to leave the majority of the coal ash in place and simply cap the ponds.

8.   In the wake of the disaster, the U.S. Attorney's Office in Raleigh, North Carolina, opened a criminal investigation of Duke Energy and the DENR. According to news reports, the investigation is focused on DENR's relationship with Duke Energy and Duke Energy's influence on DENR's regulatory actions. Federal prosecutors have issued at least twenty-three grand jury subpoenas to Duke Energy executives and various state employees. The subpoenas demand documents, emails, and reports related to the Dan River Station spill and the state's oversight of Duke Energy's thirty-three North Carolina coal ash ponds. The subpoenas also suggest that the Company is being investigated for bribery as they demand documents involving any investments, cash, or items of value that state employees received from anyone at Duke Energy.

9.   Plaintiffs now bring this action against the Individual Defendants to repair the harm that they caused the Company with their faithless actions and prevent the future harm that is occurring. ■

NOTES AND COMMENTS

1.   Count the various claims and investigations against Duke. In what jurisdictions do they arise? To what extent do they overlap? How many specialty areas of law are implicated?

2.   *Cape Fear* is an order on a motion to dismiss; the *Tansey* Complaint presents shareholders' allegations. Thus, in neither case has a party yet come forward with evidence sufficient to survive a motion for summary judgment. Imagine you are Duke's general counsel. With respect to *Cape Fear*, how would you start developing a record in support of your eventual motion for summary judgment? With respect to *Tansey*, which allegations would you want to deny? Which would you admit? Which allege conclusions of law rather than facts?

3.   Should Duke be forced to handle this multitude of litigation and investigation in so many different fora? What about the doctrine of preemption (which displaces certain state lawsuits in favor of federal ones) or issue preclusion (which bars litigating the same issue more than once)? Note that the *Cape Fear* court held that the pending litigation brought by DENR against Duke did not bar the plaintiffs' CWA claims. The "diligent

prosecution bar" in the CWA prohibits citizens from bringing suit when either the federal or state government is "diligently prosecuting" a civil or criminal action regarding the same violations. 33 U.S.C. §§ 1365(b)(1)(B), 1319(g)(6). In this case, however, the court reasoned that the state court claims were not based on the same underlying alleged violations as the plaintiffs' CWA claims, making the diligent prosecution bar inapplicable.

2. COOLING WATER

Thermoelectric power plants boil water to generate steam, which turns turbines to create electricity. Thermoelectric power, therefore, can be generated by fossil fuels, nuclear, or even some types of renewable energy like biomass and geothermal (see Chapters 7, 11). Many thermoelectric power plants use an adjacent body of water as the steam source, for cooling the steam for reuse, or both.

Water discharged from these processes is typically warmer than the original body of water. Heat is considered a pollutant under the CWA; therefore, thermoelectric power plants have long been subject to the CWA NPDES program for point-source discharges of pollutants to navigable waters. In addition, the CWA directs EPA to promulgate regulations for cooling water intake structures. *See* 33 U.S.C. § 1326(b). The environmental concerns associated with such structures are primarily related to fish and other aquatic organisms, which can be killed by entrainment (capture in the intake structures) and impingement (pressing against intake screens).

In 2014, EPA issued final rules after decades of litigation. *See* National Pollutant Discharge Elimination System—Final Regulations to Establish Requirements for Cooling Water Intake Structures at Existing Facilities and Amend Requirements at Phase I Facilities, ___ Fed. Reg. ___ (May 19, 2014), http://water.epa.gov/lawsregs/lawsguidance/cwa/316b/upload/316b-prepub-preamble.pdf. These rules apply to both existing and new facilities but distinguish between such facilities depending on how much water they use and whether they are existing or new.

For a sampling of litigation involving cooling water intake structures, see *Entergy Corp v. EPA*, 556 U.S. 208 (2009); *Riverkeeper, Inc. v. EPA*, 552 U.S. 1309 (2007); *Conoco Phillips Co. v. EPA*, 612 F.3d 822 (5th Cir. 2010). Note the water-use and water-quality implications of thermoelectric power generation; what other examples of a water-energy nexus can you think of? See Chapters 3, 4, 6, and 7. For symposium treatment, see the articles collected in the Energy-Water Nexus, 48 U. Rich. L. Rev. (2014).

CHAPTER 6

HYDROELECTRIC POWER

Hydroelectric power is one of the oldest methods of electricity generation in the United States. As a consequence, most of the locations that are best suited to large-scale transformation of the stored energy from water into electricity have already been developed, restricting growth opportunities for traditional hydroelectric development. However, the relicensing of old projects, which often involves retrofitting dams with more efficient turbine technologies, as well as the licensing of new projects using non-traditional hydroelectric generation technologies (often referred to as "hydrokinetic" projects) promise growth opportunities for the industry and future work for regulatory lawyers. This chapter explains the historical, technical and legal/regulatory development of the hydroelectric industry in the United States.

A. WATER AS A SOURCE OF ENERGY

If water is located at any place higher than the level of the area towards which it seeks to flow, it has potential gravitational energy. From the dawn of recorded history, humans have experimented with ways to turn that potential energy into useful kinetic energy.

One of the first devices to utilize the force of falling water as a source of energy was the simple water mill. Flowing water in a river turned some sort of paddle wheel attached to a drive shaft that connected it to some type of machinery. The earliest examples were mills to grind grain. Both windmills and watermills were common in the medieval world, but watermills were far more abundant; in the Domesday Book count of 1086 (a survey and census of England undertaken by William the Conqueror), there were 5624 mills in southern and eastern England, or one for every 350 people.

By the eighteenth century, water mills were widely used in England to run factories that created textiles, tools, and other commodities. To the English settlers of North America, the search for water provided great opportunities for transportation and also great challenges, particularly as it was recognized that water could be harnessed into power. After the revolutionary war, Americans wanted to establish their economic independence from England by manufacturing their own goods, such as clothing and tools, which had traditionally been imported from England. To do so, they needed to utilize the energy potential of the rivers flowing into the Atlantic Ocean, which proved easiest in the rolling terrain of New England.

This New England regional complex had an interdependence and an inner dynamic that shaped the role of the textile industry in the national economy. Geographically, the industry spread inward along the rivers of New England, eventually studding the great waterpower sites with clusters of large mills and housing for workers. Mill towns were connected by river, canal, turnpike, and eventually railroad to major mercantile centers, which imported the raw cotton, shipped the finished goods, and served as general supply centers and managerial and financial headquarters. D.W. Meinig, II The Shaping of America 377 (1993).

Most of America's first important industrial facilities were located along Northeastern rivers at locations where dams could be built to run mills powered by water wheels. Even after coal-fired steam engines became common in New England in the mid-1850s, steam was still about three times more expensive than water as a prime mover. Vaclav Smil, Energy in World History 108 (1994).

Effective use of water power usually required the construction of a dam that would store large quantities of water. As the needs of industry grew, higher and higher dams were needed to provide the power. The difference in the height of the water above and below the dam is called the "head" of the dam. As the height of the head increased, flooding of lands behind the dam increased, which often created conflict between mill owners and farmers whose land was flooded.

When a mill dam was built and the reservoir filled, the water was then released in a steady flow so that the water mill would run continuously and evenly. Water that naturally would have flowed freely downstream was therefore captured and held by the dam so that its potential energy could be used to turn the mill's machinery. The dam reduced the amount of water (and potential energy) that would otherwise be available to downstream landowners. Because the construction of a dam affected the landowners both above and below the dam, legal rules were needed for determining the rights of the various landowners. These rules set precedents that influenced the development of energy law as new and more powerful sources of potential energy came into operation later in the century.

American courts wrestled with the legal issues arising out of these energy transfers. In *Fiske v. Framingham Manufacturing Co.*, 29 Mass. (12 Pick.) 68 (1831), the plaintiff, the owner of land near a pond, claimed that the defendants, by drawing water from the pond, overflowed his land, damaging his crops. Massachusetts had enacted a statute that limited the rights of such plaintiffs to seek common law remedies, thereby favoring public improvements like mills. In resolving the dispute, the court discussed the balance of private property rights and the public benefits provided by mills.

The statute . . . is somewhat at variance with that absolute right of dominion and enjoyment which every proprietor is supposed by law to have in his own soil; and in ascertaining their extent, it will be useful to inquire into the principle upon which they are founded. We think they will be found to rest for their justification, partly upon the interest which the community at large has in the use and employment of mills, and partly upon the nature of the property, which is often so situated, that it could not be beneficially used without the aid of this power. A stream of water often runs through the lands of several proprietors. One may have a sufficient mill-site on his own land, with ample space on his own land for a mill pond or reservoir, but yet, from the operation of the well known physical law, that fluids will seek and find a level, he cannot use his own property without flowing the water back more or less on the lands of some other proprietor. We think the power given by statute was intended to apply to such cases, and that the legislature meant to provide, that as the public interest in such case coincides with that of the mill-owner, and as the mill-owner and the owner of lands to be flowed cannot both enjoy their full rights, without some interference, the latter shall yield to the former, so far that the former may keep up his mill and head of water, notwithstanding the damage done to the latter, upon payment of an equitable compensation for the real damage sustained, to be ascertained in the mode provided by the statute.

From this view of the object and purpose of the statute, we think it quite manifest, that it was designed to provide for the most useful and beneficial occupation and enjoyment of natural streams and water-courses, where the absolute right of each proprietor to use his own land and water privileges, at his own pleasure, cannot be fully enjoyed, and one must of necessity, in some degree, yield to the other. But we think it would be an extension of the principle not warranted by the statute, if it were so construed as to authorize one person to make a canal or artificial stream in such manner as to lead the water into the lands of another; and in such case, therefore, the right of the party whose lands are flowed, to recover damages by an action at common law, is not taken away or impaired.

The court ultimately concluded that the Massachusetts statute limiting common law remedies did not apply because the flooding was caused not by the mere construction of a dam, but by construction of a "sluice and gate, through which the water was drawn which flooded the plaintiff's meadow." The following excerpt offers more historical context on these kinds of conflicts.

Morton J. Horwitz, The Transformation of American Law
1780–1860 (1977).

The various acts to encourage the construction of mills offer some of the earliest illustrations of American willingness to sacrifice the sanctity of private property in the interest of promoting economic development. The first such statute, enacted by the Massachusetts colonial legislature in 1713, envisioned a procedure for compensating landowners when a "small quantity" of their property was flooded by the raising of waters for mill dams. The statutory procedure was rarely used, however, since the Massachusetts courts refused to construe the act to eliminate the traditional common law remedies for trespass or nuisance. After the act was amended in 1795 and 1798, mill owners began to argue that it provided an exclusive remedy for the flooding of lands. As a result, the mill acts adopted in a large number of states and territories on the model of the Massachusetts law were, more than any other legal measure, crucial in dethroning landed property from the supreme position it had occupied in the eighteenth century world view, and ultimately, in transforming real estate into just another cash-valued commodity. The history of the acts is a major source of information on the relationship of law to economic change. For reasons of convenience the discussion that follows concentrates on the Massachusetts experience which, though particularly rich, is not atypical.

Under the 1795 Massachusetts statute, Act of Feb. 27, 1795, ch. 74, [1794–96] Mass. Acts & Resolves 443, an owner of a mill situated on any nonnavigable stream was permitted to raise a dam and flood the land of his neighbor, so long as he compensated him according to the procedures established by the act. The injured party was limited to yearly damages, instead of a lump sum payment, even if the land was permanently flooded, and the initial estimate of annual damages continued from year to year unless one of the parties came into court and showed that circumstances had changed. The act conferred extensive discretion on the jury, which, in addition to determining damages, could prescribe the height to which a dam could be raised as well as the time of year that lands could be flooded. The Massachusetts law authorized the mill owner to flood neighboring lands without seeking prior court permission. Thus, except for the power of the jury to regulate their future actions, there was no procedure for determining in advance the utility of allowing mill owners to overflow particular lands.

The exclusive remedial procedures of the mill acts foreclosed four important alternative avenues to relief:

First, they cut off the traditional action for trespass to land, in which a plaintiff was not required to prove actual injury in order to recover. In a mill act proceeding a defendant could escape all liability by showing that, on balance, flooding actually benefitted the plaintiff.

Second, the statutory damage formula removed the possibility of imposing punitive damages in trespass or nuisance. The common law view had been that unless punitive damages could be imposed, it might pay the wrongdoer to "keep it up forever; and thus one individual will be enabled to take from another his property against his consent, and detain it from him as long as he pleases."

A third form of relief at common law allowed an affected landowner to resort to self-help to abate a nuisance. Indeed, there are a number of reported cases in which mill dams not covered by the protection of the mill acts were torn down by neighbors claiming to enforce their common law rights.

Finally, the acts foreclosed the possibility of permanently enjoining a mill owner for having created a nuisance.

In the early nineteenth century the need to provide a doctrinal rationale for the extraordinary power that the mill acts delegated to a few individuals was acute. Not only had the use of water power vastly expanded in the century since the original Massachusetts act, but there was also a major difference between the eighteenth century grist mill, which was understood to be open to the public, and the more recently established saw, paper, and cotton mills, many of which served only the proprietor.

By 1814, the significance of the growing separation between public and private enterprise was only beginning to penetrate the judicial mind. Some still conceived of mills as a form of public enterprise in which competition was impermissible. Business corporations were only beginning to upset the old corporate model, in which the raison d'etre of chartered associations was their service to the public. Nor is there any evidence that the increasingly private nature of mills, which was painfully evident to everyone fifteen years later, had as yet caused judges the slightest conceptual difficulty. At this time in Virginia, for example, where the old corporate model still prevailed, judges were also clear that the state's mill act could be defended on the ground that "the property of another is, as it were, seized on, or subjected to injury, to a certain extent, it being considered in fact for the public use." Skipwith v. Young, 19 Va. (5 Munf.) 276, 278 (1816).

The dramatic growth of cotton mills after 1815 provided the greatest incentive for mill owners to flood adjoining land and, in turn, brought to a head a heated controversy over the nature of property rights. The original mill dams were relatively small operations that caused some upstream flooding when proprietors held back water in order to generate power. With the growth of large integrated cotton mills, however, the flooding of more lands became necessary not only because larger dams held back greater quantities of water but also because of the need to generate power by releasing an enormous flow of water downstream. In light of this fact, the Massachusetts legislature amended the mill act in 1825 to allow the flooding of "lands . . . situated either above or below any mill dam." Act of Feb. 26, 1825, ch. 153, § 1 [1822–25] Mass. Laws 658.

Extension of the mill act to manufacturing establishments brought forth a storm of bitter opposition. One theme—that manufacturing establishments were private institutions—appeared over and over again. . . . The nearly unanimous denunciation of the mill acts soon brought forth a degree of change. From 1830, when Lemuel Shaw began his thirty year tenure as chief justice, the Massachusetts court began a marked retreat away from its earlier reluctant, but expansive, interpretation of the act. Conceding that the mill acts "are somewhat at variance with that absolute right of dominion and enjoyment which every proprietor is supposed by law to have in his own soil," Fiske v. Framingham Mfg. Co., 29 Mass. (12 Pick.) 68, 70 (1832), Shaw nevertheless proceeded to offer a dual justification for the acts. The legislation could be defended, he wrote, "partly upon the interest which the community at large has, in the use and employment of mills"—a theory of eminent domain—"and partly upon the nature of the property, which is often so situated, that it could not be beneficially used without the aid of this power." *Id.* at 70–71. However artificial it may have been in the existing context, Shaw argued that the mill act "was designed to provide for the most useful and beneficial occupation and enjoyment of natural streams and water-courses, where the absolute right of each proprietor, to use his own land and water privileges, at his own pleasure, cannot be fully enjoyed, and one must of necessity, in some degree, yield to the other." *Id.* at 71–72.

The main contribution of Shaw's formulation was to force courts to see that a conception of absolute and exclusive dominion over property was incompatible with the needs of industrial development. Whether the rationale for state intervention was eminent domain or a more explicit recognition of the relativity of property rights, under the influence of the mill acts men had come to regard property as an instrumental value in the service of the paramount goal of promoting economic growth. ∎

NOTES AND COMMENTS

1.   When the mill owner's dam flooded the farmer's land, a natural resource (i.e., agricultural land) was lost that could have converted the sun's energy into crops. On the other hand, the stored water in the dam was potential energy that could be converted to kinetic energy that would grind corn or convert cotton into textiles. Was the dam's conversion of energy more efficient (i.e., did it create less entropy (lost energy)) than the farmer's conversion of solar energy into corn or cotton? How would such efficiency be measured? Did the rules of law created in Massachusetts to resolve the conflicts between the mill owner and the farmer take into account any differences in relative efficiency of energy conversion?

2.   If the mill owner were required to pay the farmer the value of her land, would the relative market values of the respective parcels of land automatically take into account the relative efficiency of the mill owner's and the farmer's conversion of energy?

3.   "The Virginia Mill Act provided significant protection for landowners against incursions by the mills and was interpreted in a way that made it quite difficult to construct a mill. . . . First, the Act protected landowners directly by requiring millers to obtain permission from a court before flooding nearby land and by ensuring that the millers paid adequate damages. Second, judges added extra protection for landowners by construing the act very strictly, often finding technical reasons to forbid construction of a mill. Thus, the Virginia Mill Act did allow for some industrial development, but without enriching 'men of commerce and industry' at the expense of less powerful groups or running roughshod over other interests." Note: Water Law and Economic Power: A Reinterpretation of Morton Horwitz's Subsidy Thesis, 77 Va. L. Rev. 397 (1991). What differences between the conditions in Massachusetts and Virginia might have contributed to the development of different laws governing the balance of power between mill owners and farmers?

4.   The Mill Acts effectively gave mill owners a power of private eminent domain to flood their neighbors' land as long as they paid damages (a power now granted to licensees of hydroelectric projects under the Federal Power Act). In 1991, Peter Dorey, who had purchased an old mill near Foster Pond in Bridgton, Maine, sought a declaratory judgment that he was entitled to increase the height of the dam under the Maine Mill Act, which was similar to the Massachusetts Act. His action would cause flooding for forty-four

owners of waterfront property on the pond. How should the court have decided the case? *See* Dorey v. Estate of Spicer, 715 A.2d 182 (Me. 1998).

B. PUBLIC VS. PRIVATE POWER

Early in the twentieth century, the technology for the use and distribution of electricity became readily available (see Chapter 2), leading to a search for the most efficient way of generating electricity. One of the earliest technologies to be developed was a relatively simple one; the rotating movement of the traditional water mill was transferred to a turbine, which generated electric current. Such electricity became known as hydroelectric power (also called hydropower or simply hydro).

Considerable hydropower development had occurred by the time Congress passed a series of statutes to govern hydroelectric development, beginning with the Federal Water Power Act of 1920 and continuing with the Federal Power Act of 1935 (FPA). Part I of the FPA, which amended and broadened the Federal Water Power Act, created the modern federal hydropower licensing program. 16 U.S.C. § 792 *et seq.* In the FPA, Congress delegated licensing responsibility to the Federal Power Commission (FPC or the Commission), predecessor to the modern Federal Energy Regulatory Commission (FERC or the Commission), and authorized the FPC to grant licenses for developing hydroelectric facilities that are "best adapted to a comprehensive plan for development of the waterway," consistent with "the public interest." The FPC set out to license a tremendous variety of new and existing hydro facilities, including large dams with hundreds of megawatts of generating capacity and very small dams with only a few kilowatts of capacity, old facilities that generated power for paper and textile mills, utility generators, municipal power facilities, and more.

While the FPC was granted broad authority to manage the licensing of privately- and municipally-owned hydroelectric facilities, Congress sometimes directly authorized the construction of federally owned hydroelectric facilities outside the FPA licensing process. Indeed, the builders of some of the largest dams were two federal agencies, the Bureau of Reclamation and the U.S. Army Corps of Engineers (Corps). Projects such as the Colorado River's Boulder Dam (later renamed Hoover Dam after the President who was one of its strongest backers) and the Columbia River's Grand Coulee Dam were triumphs of engineering that still awe people by their size. These agencies also built hundreds of smaller dams as congressional delegations sought to bring federal money into their districts.

With the election of President Franklin Roosevelt and the "New Deal" policies he espoused, the role of the federal government in hydroelectric power was intensified. Congress created the Tennessee Valley Authority as a federal agency with a monopoly on electric generation in the valley of the Tennessee River and its tributaries, and it began constructing a whole series of dams to produce power. In the northwest, another federal agency, the Bonneville Power Authority, was created to harness the power potential of the Columbia River. The reservoirs created by these dams displaced thousands of people, but the promised economic benefits of the new technology were so great that the minor hardship (Congress provided fairly generous compensation) was widely seen as simply the price of progress. Although these dams represented impressive engineering feats and continued to be constructed, environmental groups like the Sierra Club opposed them for decades (beginning in the 1920s), citing the impacts to aesthetics, aquatic life, and recreation. The political controversy surrounding hydroelectric dams is explored in fictional writings such as Edwards Abbey's The Monkey Wrench Gang and nonfictional accounts such as Encounters with the Archdruid by John McPhee. Despite opposition, policies supporting hydroelectric dams were generally successful, as shown in the following excerpt.

Robert L. Bradley, Jr., The Origins of Political Electricity: Market Failure or Political Opportunism

17 Energy L.J. 59 (1996).

As governor of New York in the 1920s, Franklin Roosevelt endorsed municipal provision of electric power to ensure that more Americans gained access to power and to use as a "yardstick" enterprise to compete against investor-owned utilities. Power provision to FDR was "a national problem," and in his first term as president he formulated a National Power Policy not only to bring interstate electricity under federal public utility regulation but also to make electricity "more broadly available at cheaper rates to industry, to domestic and to agricultural consumers." Hydropower as a federal public works program and rural subsidy program was key.

Three major laws . . . would follow as part of FDR's public works program to promote economic recovery during the Great Depression.

1. **Tennessee Valley Authority.** On April 10, 1933, FDR proposed a major hydro project to Congress to rectify "the continued idleness of a great national investment in the Tennessee Valley." The next month, Congress approved the Tennessee Valley Act (TVA) "in the interest of national defense and for agricultural and industrial development, and to improve navigation in the Tennessee River and to control the destructive flood waters." The Act established a three-member board with eminent domain powers to "construct dams, reservoirs, power houses, power structures, transmission lines . . . and to unite the various power installations into one or more systems by transmission lines." The agency was empowered to "produce, distribute, and sell electric power" with preference to "States, counties, municipalities, and cooperative organizations of citizens and farmers, not organized or doing business for profit, but primarily for the purpose of supplying electricity to its own citizens or members." Contracts could be for up to twenty years, and agreements with for-profit entities could be voided with five years' notice if the power was needed on the non-profit side. . . . The fateful decision made by Congress was to construct and operate the facilities as a public project. Numerous applications for private development languished before Congress between 1903 and 1933 without approval. Two Tennessee utilities applied for federal permits to invest between $60 and $100 million to develop eleven waterpower sites only to encounter years of inaction. The result of government provision was a competitive antagonism between TVA and neighboring private systems who were discriminated against under the preference system and feared taxpayer-

funded raiding that led to litigation and obstructionism that retarded rural electrification. Facilities were also duplicated.

2.   Rural Electrification Act of 1936. In early 1935, FDR endorsed a program to subsidize rural electrification to which Congress responded with a $100 million appropriation. On May 11, 1935, FDR issued an executive order creating a new agency to transmit electricity "to as many farms as possible in the shortest possible time, and to have it used in quantities sufficient to affect rural life." The Rural Electrification Administration (REA) was empowered to make loans to private and public parties to finance connections with farms. As a public works program, 90% of involved workers had to originate from the relief rolls unless an exemption was granted by the REA. The next year the program was put on a more permanent basis with the passage of the Rural Electrification Act. The REA was instructed to "make loans in the several States and Territories of the United States for rural electrification and the furnishing of electric energy to persons in rural areas [defined as residing in population centers under 1,500 persons] who are not receiving central station service." The REA was appropriated $50 million for fiscal year 1937 and $40 million for each of the next eight years to finance generation, transmission, and distribution facilities. Loans for such assets could not exceed 85% of the principal amount and had to be fully amortized over a twenty-five-year period (with a maximum five-year extension) at an interest rate paid by the government on long term debt. Financing preference was given to governmental bodies and private cooperatives and nonprofits. . . .

3.   Bonneville Power Administration Act of 1937. Federal monies to develop the water resources of the Pacific Northwest were first allocated by Congress in 1933 as part of the employment program of the Public Works Administration. An additional allocation followed two years later in the Rivers and Harbors Improvement Act. The final push was the Bonneville Power Administration Act of 1937 (BPA), which authorized the Secretary of War to "provide, construct, operate, maintain, and improve at [the dam projects under construction at Bonneville, Oregon and North Bonneville, Washington] such machines, equipment, and facilities for the generation of electric energy . . . to develop such electricity as rapidly as markets may be found therefor." To "encourage the widest possible use of all electricity," the Bonneville Power Administrator was authorized to construct transmission facilities to interconnect with other markets. Eminent domain rights were granted to facilitate land requisition associated with the above. . . .

FDR's policy of "direct and indirect competition in reducing electricity prices . . . including yardstick federal power projects, birch rod potential competition from municipalities and rural cooperatives, [and] well-publicized annual rate surveys" has been found by one business historian to be "quite sound." This analysis adds the caveats, however, that (1) rates could have fallen further still without FDR's activism, and (2) the "administrative costs, rent-seeking costs, price discrimination practices, government subsidies, and other factors" related to his activism would have to be assessed. While the first point can probably be discounted—more generation and distribution investment would surely increase supply to lower prices compared to its absence—the second point raises a very obvious issue: a large dedication of taxpayer resources amid Depression scarcity was not a free lunch. But the foregone opportunity of FDR's action was not so much his inaction. It was the deregulation of electric utilities and privatized electric provision to let market forces guide the industry where, by definition, no taxpayer or regulatory costs would be incurred. ■

Part I of the FPA (which governs hydroelectric power projects) was enacted at a time of national ambivalence over the question whether the private sector or the public sector should take the lead in the development and control of electric power. This conflict was heightened in the context of hydroelectric dam development because many viewed the nation's waterways as a public resource, the flows of which ought not to be subjected to private control, irrespective of riparian property rights regimes. Beyond the general requirement that licensing decisions be made "in the public interest," the FPA favored governmental influence over hydropower development in several ways. First, Section 4 gave federal agencies directly affected by a proposed project the authority to specify conditions to be included in any license granted to that project. Thus, for example, if a private applicant seeks a license to build a hydroelectric project at a dam owned by the Corps or on land owned by the U.S. Forest Service or Bureau of Land Management, the Commission was required (and still is required) to include in the license conditions specified by those agencies. (However, this power has been weakened somewhat by the passage of the Energy Policy Act of 2005. *See infra* section D.1.). Second, Section 7(a) established the so-called "municipal preference" at licensing,[1] which acted as a tie-breaker in favor of municipal license applicants in any competitive licensing proceeding between municipal and private sector applicants. Third, Section 7(b) established a mechanism by which FPC might deny license applications and recommend development of the site by the federal government.

In *Udall v. Federal Power Comm'n*, 387 U.S. 428 (1967), the Supreme Court faced an attempted exercise of this Section 7(b) authority. In that case, both a private power company and a municipality applied for a license to construct the High Mountain Sheep Dam on the Snake River. During the licensing process, the Secretary of the Interior urged the Commission to postpone the licensing of either project while means of protecting the salmon and other fisheries were studied. FPC opted to move forward with the licensing process without the benefit of the requested study, after which the Secretary of the Interior wrote FPC urging it to recommend to Congress the consideration of federal construction of High Mountain Sheep. After an FPC hearing on the license application, the hearing examiner recommended that Pacific Northwest Power Company, one of the two applicants, receive the license. He disposed of the issue of federal development by noting that there "is no evidence in this record that Federal development will provide greater flood control, power benefits, fish passage, navigation or recreation; and there is substantial evidence to the contrary." FPC affirmed the Examiner's decision, noting "that the record supports no reason why

---

[1]   Section 7(a) of the Act provides: "In issuing preliminary permits hereunder or licenses where no preliminary permit has been issued and in issuing licenses to new licensees under section 15 hereof the Commission shall give preference to applications therefor by States and municipalities, provided the plans for the same are deemed by the Commission equally well adapted, or shall within a reasonable time to be fixed by the Commission be made equally well adapted, to conserve and utilize in the public interest the water resources of the region. . . ." 16 U.S.C. § 800(a).

federal development should be superior," and that it found "nothing in this record to indicate" that the public purposes of the dam (flood control, etc.) would not be served as adequately by Pacific Northwest as they would under federal development.

When the Secretary's appeal of FPC's decision reached the Supreme Court, the Court remanded the decision for further consideration of the federal development option. The Court noted the lack of an evidentiary record to justify FPC's rejection of federal takeover:

> The issue was of course briefed and argued; yet no factual inquiry was undertaken. Section 7(b) says "Whenever, in the judgment of the Commission, the development of any water resources for public purposes should be undertaken by the United States itself," the Commission shall not approve other applications. Yet the Commission by its rulings on the applications of the Secretary to intervene and to reopen precluded it from having the informed judgment that § 7(b) commands.

> We indicate no judgment on the merits. We do know that on the Snake-Columbia waterway between High Mountain Sheep and the ocean, eight hydroelectric dams have been built and another authorized. These are federal projects; and if another dam is to be built, the question whether it should be under federal auspices looms large. Timed releases of stored water at High Mountain Sheep may affect navigability; they may affect hydroelectric production of the downstream dams when the river level is too low for the generators to be operated at maximum capacity; they may affect irrigation; and they may protect salmon runs when the water downstream is too hot or insufficiently oxygenated. Federal versus private or municipal control may conceivably make a vast difference in the functioning of the vast river complex.

> Beyond that is the question whether any dam should be constructed. . . . Section 10(a) of the Act provides that "the project adopted" shall be such "as in the judgment of the Commission will be best adapted to a comprehensive plan for improving or developing a waterway . . . and for other beneficial public uses, including recreational purposes."

> The objective of protecting "recreational purposes" means more than that the reservoir created by the dam will be the best one possible or practical from a recreational viewpoint. There are already eight lower dams on this Columbia River system and a ninth one authorized; and if the Secretary is right in fearing that this additional dam would destroy the waterway as spawning grounds for anadromous fish (salmon and steelhead) or seriously impair that function, the project is put in an entirely different light. The importance of salmon and steelhead in our outdoor life as well as in commerce is so great that there certainly comes a time when their destruction might necessitate a halt in so-called "improvement" or "development" of waterways. The destruction of anadromous fish in our western waters is so notorious that we cannot believe that Congress through the present Act authorized their ultimate demise.

. . . In his letter of November 21, 1960, the Secretary noted that, due to increased power resources, the projects could be safely deferred. . . . By 1980 nuclear energy "should represent a significant proportion of world power production." By the end of the century "nuclear energy may account for about one-third of our total energy consumption." Ibid. "By the middle of the next century it seems likely that most of our energy needs will be satisfied by nuclear energy." Some of these time schedules are within the period of the 50-year licenses granted by the Commission.

. . . The need to destroy the river as a waterway, the desirability of its demise, the choices available to satisfy future demands for energy—these are all relevant to a decision under § 7 and § 10 but they were largely untouched by the Commission. On our remand there should be an exploration of these neglected phases of the cases, as well as the other points raised by the Secretary.

387 U.S. 428, 432–5.

The opinion of the Supreme Court in the *Udall* case came at the beginning of a decade of heightened environmental sensitivity that produced much federal environmental legislation. The case, along with the *Scenic Hudson* decision (discussed in the next section) is often cited as one of the earliest examples of the "hard look" doctrine, which was used extensively by federal courts in the 1970s to force federal agencies to examine the environmental implications of their decisions. *See* James Oakes, The Judicial Role in Environmental Law, 52 N.Y.U. L. Rev. 498 (1977). The FPA continues to contemplate the possibility of federal projects of the kind proposed by the Secretary of the Interior in *Udall*, but the courts, Congress and FPC (now FERC) have opted to promote environmental values in different ways (see section C). Eight years after *Udall*, Congress included the proposed dam site in the Hells Canyon National Recreation Area, thereby prohibiting the construction of dams and preserving the area's free-flowing rivers and salmon habitat. However, the "designation did nothing to restore the spring fish flows that young Idaho salmon needed to survive the eight federal dams that now obstructed their journey from their spawning grounds to the ocean." Michael C. Blumm and F. Lorraine Bodi, in The Northwest Salmon Crisis: A Documentary History (Joseph Cone and Sandy Ridlington, eds., Oregon State University Press 1996).

There are many dams in the Columbia and Snake River basin, eight of which are operated by the Corps. The Corps implemented several mechanisms in efforts to preserve the existing fish population. Adult fish ladders are used to assist the adult salmon in forging their way upstream to places to spawn. Juvenile fish bypass systems are also in place, to allow juvenile fish to make their way to the ocean. However, these bypass systems involve the fish going through a turbine or over a dam spillway, which can be detrimental to the fish. Another measure being used to aid in the preservation of fish species is the trap and haul method. Fish are caught and transported by truck around the hydropower projects and then released back into the river. For a discussion of how these issues are being addressed in proceedings governing the relicensing of Snake River dams, see *infra* section D.2.

The *Udall* Court's predictions that nuclear power would replace the need for traditional sources of power generation now seems rather ironic. Not only has such power proven to be more expensive than was then anticipated, but the environmental opposition to it has been even more intense than to hydroelectric projects. Nuclear power is discussed in Chapter 7. This is not the last example you will see of a confidently voiced energy prediction that proves widely off the mark.

C. HYDROELECTRIC LICENSING AND THE PUBLIC INTEREST

In addition to the question of *who* should develop hydroelectric sites, the Commission also faced the question of *whether* and *how* such sites should be developed. The FPA gave the Commission precious little guidance on the question of how to answer these questions. Section 4 of the FPA authorized the Commission to issue licenses "in the public interest." 16 U.S.C. §§ 797(a), (e). Section 10 directed the agency to license projects which are "best adapted to a comprehensive plan for improving or developing a waterway," which might include hydropower development or "other beneficial public uses, including recreational purposes . . ." *Id.* § 803(a). The task of balancing these various values was left entirely to the Commission. In order to fulfill this mission, the agency faced the question whether and how to license not only new proposed projects, but already-built hydroelectric facilities as well.

1. JURISDICTION

A hydroelectric project needs the approval of FERC if it is located on a river over which FERC has jurisdiction. In the following case, a publicly owned water authority in Fairfax County, Virginia, had built two dams on the Occoquan River to store water for public water supply. It included hydroelectric power generating facilities to supplement its own need for electricity to run its water pumping operations. The Authority did not think it needed to get a license from FERC, but FERC's Director of Hydropower Licensing disagreed. The Authority appealed his decision to the full Commission:

Fairfax County Water Authority
43 F.E.R.C. ¶ 61,062 (1988).

By orders issued January 21, 1987 and March 16, 1987, the Director, Office of Hydropower Licensing (Director), determined that the Fairfax County Water Authority's (Authority) Upper and Lower Occoquan Projects, located on the Occoquan River in Fairfax County, Virginia, are required to be licensed pursuant to Section 23(b)(1) of the Federal Power Act, 16 U.S.C. § 817(1) (1982) (FPA). The Director concluded that the projects are located on a stretch of the Occoquan River that is navigable within the meaning of Section 3(8) of the FPA, 16 U.S.C. § 796(8). Accordingly, the orders required the Authority to file license applications for the Occoquan projects.

The Authority filed timely appeals of the January 21 and March 16 orders, arguing that the Director erred in concluding that the stretch of the Occoquan River where the projects are located is navigable. The

Authority also claims that the projects do not affect the interests of interstate or foreign commerce. . . .

Section 23(b)(1) of the FPA would require licensing of the Occoquan projects if: (1) they are located on a navigable water of the United States; (2) they occupy lands of the United States; (3) they utilize surplus water or water power from a government dam; or (4) they are located on a body of water over which Congress has Commerce Clause jurisdiction, project construction occurred on or after August 26, 1935, and the projects affect the interests of interstate commerce. Since the Authority's projects do not occupy lands of the United States or utilize surplus water or water power from a government dam, whether the projects are required to be licensed depends on whether they are located on a navigable water or come within the scope of (4) above.

Navigability. Under Section 3(8) of the FPA,[3][2] navigable waters are generally those streams which in their natural or improved condition are used or suitable for use for the transportation of persons or property in interstate or foreign commerce, including any interrupting falls, shallows, or rapids compelling land carriage. *See United States v. Appalachian Elec. Power Co.,* 311 U.S. 377 (1940).

The Occoquan River rises in Loudoun, Fairfax, and Fauquier Counties and drains the upper part of Prince William County. It is formed by the junction, about a mile south of Brentsville, Virginia, of Broad Run and Cedar Run, and thence flows northeast to where it is joined by Bull Run and continues in a generally southeast direction for approximately 14 miles to the Potomac River. The Occoquan River crosses the fall-line[5][3] just before it reaches the town of Occoquan, which is the head of tidewater, and up to which there is a navigable depth of five feet at low tide and seven feet at high tide. A fall, now partially inundated by the dams of the Occoquan projects, begins approximately three miles above the head of tidewater and continues down to tide, falling about 80 feet in that distance. At its mouth, the Occoquan River is five miles wide. At the head of tide, approximately six to seven miles above, it narrows to 75 yards.

The Director relied on a 1938 Federal Power Commission Report on the Potomac River Basin to conclude that the Occoquan projects are located on a stretch of the Occoquan River that is navigable. The 1938 Report indicates, and the Authority agrees, that for six miles above its mouth the river is navigable. However, the Authority claims that the

---

    [2]   Section 3(8) provides: "navigable waters" means those parts of streams or other bodies of water over which Congress has jurisdiction under its authority to regulate commerce with foreign nations and among the several States, and which either in their natural or improved condition notwithstanding interruptions between the navigable parts of such streams or waters by falls, shallows, or rapids compelling land carriage, are used or suitable for use for the transportation of persons or property in interstate or foreign commerce, including therein all such interrupting falls, shallows, or rapids, together with such other parts of streams as shall have been authorized by Congress for improvement by the United States or shall have been recommended to Congress for such improvement after investigation under its authority. 16 U.S.C. § 796(8).

    [3]   The fall-line [separates] . . . the middle and western water-shed divisions from the eastern division, which extends from the coast to the head of tidewater and navigation. It marks the last considerable fall on the rivers. *See* United States Department of the Interior, Report on the Water Power of the United States, Middle-Atlantic Water-Shed 520 (1885).

projects are located above the navigable tidal reach, which extends to the town of Occoquan just below the falls.

Staff inspection reveals that the upper project is located where the falls once existed, approximately one and one-half miles above the head of tidewater. Nevertheless, the falls are navigable waters if the river above the falls is navigable. *See Rochester Gas Elec. Corp. v. Fed. Power Comm'n*, 344 F.2d 594, 595 (2d Cir. 1965). However, the 1938 Report does not indicate any use of the river above the town of Occoquan for transportation of commerce, and additional research regarding this stretch has uncovered no substantial evidence to support a finding that the river, in the vicinity of the upper project, is navigable.

Effect on Interstate Commerce. The Occoquan River is a body of water that Congress has authority to regulate under the Commerce Clause,[7][4] and project construction at the site occurred after 1935. Accordingly, a license is required to operate the Occoquan projects if they affect the interests of interstate or foreign commerce.

The Authority states that all of the energy from the Occoquan projects is used to serve its own power needs and that therefore the projects do not affect the interests of interstate commerce. The Authority claims in the alternative that, while it admittedly purchases less power from its supplier, Virginia Electric and Power Company ("VEPCO"), because of the projects' generation, any resultant effect on interstate commerce is too minimal to meet the "real and substantial" standard used in *City of Centralia v. FERC*, 661 F.2d 787 (9th Cir. 1981).

In *Federal Power Comm'n v. Union Elec. Co.*, 381 U.S. 90, 96 (1965), the Supreme Court interpreted Section 23(b)'s reference to "affecting the interests of interstate commerce," finding that Congress had invoked "its full authority over commerce, without qualification, to define what projects on non-navigable streams are required to be licensed." The Court held that the central purpose of the FPA to provide comprehensive control over uses of the nation's water resources would be more fully served if the Commission "considers the impact of the project on the full spectrum of commerce interests." *Id.* at 98, 101. Since Part I of the FPA thus embodies the full reach of the Commerce Clause, whether projects generate to transmit energy across state lines or feed into an interstate power system for distribution is not dispositive of the effect on interstate commerce issue. Rather, the relevant point of inquiry is the relationship between the activity to be regulated and interstate commerce. Thus, if a project on a Commerce Clause water with post-1935 construction affects any of the broad range of Commerce Clause interests, it is required to be licensed under Section 23(b)(1) of the FPA. Moreover, as noted by the *Centralia* court, *supra,* 661 F.2d at 789, even if the project itself does not substantially affect the interests of commerce, it can nevertheless be reached if it belongs to a class of projects whose activities affect interstate commerce, [and] a substantial effect can be measured by the cumulative effect of a class of activities. *See Wickard v. Filburn,* 317 U.S. 111 (1942).

The Authority operates the Occoquan projects to provide power generation for its water supply pumping station located in the town of Occoquan. The upper project contains two 500-kW synchronous

---

4   The Occoquan River is a tributary of the Potomac, a navigable river, and thus comes within the scope of the Commerce Clause. *See* FPC v. Union Electric Co., 381 U.S. 90, 97 (1965).

generating units, and the lower project contains a single 350-kW synchronous generating unit. The generators' 4.16-kV terminals are continuously paralleled with the 4.16-kV incoming utility circuit from VEPCO's 34.5/4.16-kV, 16.2-MVA Aqua Substation. Direction of power flow over this utility circuit is always toward the project, since the project load always exceeds its generating capability. The magnitude of this flow varies, depending upon the relative levels of project generation and load. The respective estimated average annual output of the upper and lower projects is 4,320,000 kwh and 1,296,000 kwh. The projects supply an estimated 24.29 percent of the Authority's needs on an annual basis. The remainder of the Authority's energy needs is met with purchases from VEPCO. VEPCO's system serves load in Virginia, North Carolina, and West Virginia, and is directly connected with Allegheny Power, Appalachian Power Company, Carolina Power and Light Company, and Potomac Electric Power Company.

The units within this interstate system are interlocked electromagnetically, and thus the actions of one unit within the system affect every other generating unit in the system. *See Federal Power Comm'n v. Florida Power & Light Co.,* 404 U.S. 453 (1972). . . . To the extent the projects do or do not generate, they affect the functioning of the interstate energy and thus interstate commerce, because they increase or decrease the amount of power that other resources must produce to keep the system balanced.

An interconnected project that generates to supply its own power needs, thereby displacing power that would otherwise be purchased from the interstate system, affects the operation of the system as does the project that generates to directly sell energy, because both affect the supply of and the demand for energy.

The foregoing demonstrates the effect of the Occoquan projects on electricity as a basic element of interstate commerce.

Since the projects are located on Commerce Clause waters, involve post-1935 construction, and affect the interests of interstate or foreign commerce, they are required to be licensed pursuant to Section 23(b)(1) of the FPA.

The Commission orders: (A) The appeals filed by the Fairfax County Water Authority on February 9, 1987, in Docket No. UL87–3–001, and on April 10, 1987, in Docket No. UL87–9–001, are denied. (B) Fairfax County Water Authority must file with the Secretary of the Commission, within 45 days of the date of this order, an expeditious schedule for submitting a license. . . . ■

NOTES AND COMMENTS

1.   The FPA definition of the term "navigable water" is specific to that act only. The various statutory and judge-made definitions of navigability have created a long history of legal puzzles. *See generally* A. Dan Tarlock, Law of Water Rights and Resources § 9.03 (1995).

Federal jurisdiction over navigable waterways has evolved since the formation of our country. The distinction between navigable and non-navigable waterways first arose in a Commerce Clause context under the Constitution, where the primary issue is what power Congress possesses vis-à-vis the states. The Commerce Clause "comprehends navigation, within the limits of every state in the Union; so far as that navigation may be, in any manner, connected with 'commerce with foreign nations, or among the several states, or with the Indian Tribes.' " Gibbons v. Ogden, 22 U.S. (19 Wheat.) 1, 197 (1824). For some time after this decision, federal policies dealt only with protection and enhancement of navigation, a power that was exercised often, usually to improve the navigable capacity of water bodies. The Report of the President's Water Resources Policy Commission, Vol. 3 Water Resources Law 87–91 (1950).

The first challenge to the definition of navigable waterways involved the effects that tidal movements had on navigability. Until 1851, inland lake and river systems were not considered navigable waterways. In 1851, the Supreme Court adopted "suitability for commercial navigation" as the test for federal jurisdiction. The Propeller Genesee Chief v. Fitzhugh, 53 U.S. (12 How.) 443 (1851). This test worked well for the larger bodies of water, but did not include smaller rivers and lakes. Several years later, the test changed to include rivers that are "navigable in fact"—that is when in their ordinary condition as highways of commerce, over which trade and travel are or may be conducted in the customary modes of trade and travel over water. The Daniel Ball, 77 U.S. (10 Wall.) 557, 563 (1871).

The "navigation in fact" test is still used today, and has been expanded by the Supreme Court. Federal jurisdiction was first extended to obstructions and diversions on non-navigable portions of navigable rivers. United States v. Rio Grande Dam & Irrigation Co., 174 U.S. 690 (1899). Federal jurisdiction then extended to rivers that could be made navigable by "reasonable improvement." United States v. Appalachian Elec. Power Co., 311 U.S. 377 (1940). Currently, courts must consider whether a river (1) is presently in use or suitable for use, or (2) was used or suitable for use in the past, or (3) could be made usable by reasonable improvements. Rochester Gas and Elec. Corp. v. Federal Power Comm'n, 344 F.2d 594, 596 (2d Cir.), cert. denied, 382 U.S. 832 (1965). This is the controlling test for FERC jurisdiction.

The environmental movement of the 1960s created confusion in the definition of navigable waters. Environmentalists exerted pressure on the federal government to regulate the protection of shallow water bodies and wetlands. During this period, courts were split as to whether small streams were navigable or not. Those that denied federal jurisdiction did so if the parties could not produce substantial evidence of past commercial navigation or that navigation is possible by reasonable improvements. United States v. Crow, Pope & Land Enters., Inc., 340 F. Supp. 25 (N.D. Ga. 1972). Other courts allowed federal jurisdiction if the river served commercial recreational purposes. United States v. Underwood, 344 F. Supp. 486 (M.D. Fla. 1972). Commerce Clause opinions were cited by courts for support that federal jurisdiction did not hinge upon a water body being navigable in fact. Id.

As noted in Chapter 3, the Clean Water Act (CWA) defines navigable waters as "the waters of the United States." 33 U.S.C. § 1362(7). Federal jurisdiction has been extended to small tributaries and associated groundwater, and lagoons separated from the ocean, to land-locked lakes and associated wetlands. See Quivira Mining Co. v. EPA, 765 F.2d 126 (10th Cir. 1985); Boone v. United States, 944 F.2d 1489 (9th Cir. 1991); United States v. Byrd, 609 F.2d 1204 (7th Cir. 1979); Slagle v. United States, 809 F.Supp. 704 (D. Minn. 1992). However, the Supreme Court placed new limits on the reach of federal jurisdiction in 2001 when it adopted a more restrictive interpretation of the Clean Water Act definition, in *Solid Waste Agency of Cook County v. U.S. Army Corps of Engineers*, 531 U.S. 159 (2001), concluding that the definition did not cover isolated wetlands. The Court restricted the definition further in *Rapanos v. United States*, 547 U.S. 715 (2006), in which a plurality of the court limited CWA jurisdiction over wetlands to wetlands with a "continuous surface connection" to navigable surface waters, such as rivers and lakes. Five members of the court (one concurring and four dissenting) seemed to reject the plurality's definition as contrary to Congress's intent, however.

2.   In *Federal Power Comm'n v. Florida Power & Light Co.*, cited by FERC in the above opinion, the Supreme Court held that any electric system that is connected to a network of power lines that crosses state lines is subject to federal regulation pursuant to the Interstate Commerce Clause. The power flow within state lines is subject to federal regulation if a utility is connected to an interstate grid, even if the utility does not transmit energy beyond the state's borders because the power has the potential to be in interstate commerce. *Id.* This ruling was reaffirmed in *New England Power Co. v. New Hampshire*, 455 U.S. 331 (1982), where the court held that FERC has regulatory jurisdiction over transmission service performed by a utility connected to the interstate network. Virtually all electric systems are so connected, other than those in Hawaii, Alaska and arguably Texas. Congress, however, has never chosen to exercise fully the federal regulatory power, so by far the largest share of the regulation of the electric industry remains with the state governments. See Chapter 10.

3.   Once approved by FERC, an eminent domain power attaches to a hydroelectric dam licensee under the FPA:

> When any licensee cannot acquire by contract or pledges an unimproved dam site or the right to use or damage the lands or property of others necessary to the construction, maintenance, or operation of any dam, reservoir, diversion structure, or the works appurtenant or accessory thereto, in conjunction with any improvement which in the judgment of the commission is desirable and justified in the public interest for the purpose of improving or developing a waterway or waterways for the use or benefit of interstate or foreign commerce, it may acquire the same by the exercise of the right of eminent domain in the district court of the United States for the district in which such land or other property may be located, or in the State courts.

16 U.S.C § 814. Does "works appurtenant of accessory thereto" include transmission lines to serve hydroelectric dams? Expanded eminent domain authority for hydroelectric projects contrasts with FERC's authority over other power generation and transmission projects. As is discussed in Chapter 11, FERC ordinarily cannot exercise eminent domain powers for transmission lines, which must be approved by state regulators.

2.   DEVELOPMENT VS. THE ENVIRONMENT

Since the beginning of the hydro licensing program, the licensing process has provoked disputes over environmental issues. Conservation organizations, Indian tribes, governmental agencies, and others raised concerns about the impacts of hydro projects on fisheries and recreation long before the advent of the modern environmental movement, and

FERC imposed conditions on project licenses in response to these concerns. As early as 1953, the Commission rejected a license application for a proposed project on environmental grounds. In the Matter of Namekagon Hydro Company, 12 F.P.C. 203 (1953), *aff'd* 216 F.2d 509 (7th Cir. 1954). The Commission denied Namekagon's application for a license because its project would be located on a river with special and unique scenic and recreational values and explicitly acknowledged that environmental amenities can sometimes trump development interests in the licensing process.

However, application denials have been the exception rather than the rule, and by the 1960s environmental groups were lamenting the Commission's apparent lack of attention to environmental values. In 1963 one commissioner took his colleagues to task in an order issuing a license for an existing project:

> We should not lose sight of our obligation to properly utilize and conserve our natural resources. . . . For an agency merely to say we have no objection . . . is not the searching type of review I consider necessary or appropriate. Would recreation be increased, would stream flow regulation be improved, would stream pollution be lessened, would fish runds [*sic*] be restored, would fish and wildlife be benefited by either the removal of the project or conversion to nonpower uses? These questions and similar ones should be asked each time an applicant for a constructed project comes before us.

S. C. Electric & Gas Co., 30 F.P.C. 1338, 1342–43 (1963) (Ross, Comm'r, dissenting).

Of course, hydroelectric projects have a wide variety of environmental impacts on project sites in addition to aesthetic and recreational impacts. The construction of dams disrupts migratory fish patterns: fish cannot survive downstream migration either over a dam or through a turbine, and the dam completely blocks upstream migration. Fish passage facilities like fish ladders or so-called "trap and truck" methods restore only a fraction of the unimpeded migration. The replacement of moving water with a warmer, still water reservoir behind the dam and a dewatered or reduced flow stretch of river between the dam and the tailrace also disrupts and changes fisheries. Unless the project is operated in "run of river" mode, such that the reservoir height stays constant and downstream flows (through the generators and over the dam) always equal natural inflows from upstream, shifts in reservoir height can damage wetland habitats adjacent to the reservoir. The creation and operation of a hydro project can affect dissolved oxygen levels and other indices of water quality in the river. By the 1960s advances in the science of ecology and the embryonic national environmental movement had heightened concerns about impacts like these, prompting Commissioner Ross's objections.

Environmental groups were particularly unhappy with a special category of hydroelectric project called "pumped storage" projects. These projects did not require falling water to generate head to produce power; rather, pumped storage projects created new reservoirs at uphill locations near a body of water, so that power could be pumped up to the reservoir when electricity demand was low (and so electricity was plentiful and cheap), and released back downhill through the turbines to the river or lake when electricity demand was high (and so electricity was scarce and valuable). These pumped storage projects were energy inefficient in that they consumed more power (pumping water uphill to the reservoir) than they generated, but they made economic sense because the price difference between peak power and nonpeak power more than compensated for this energy inefficiency. Environmentalists' dissatisfaction with one such pumped storage project led to the D.C. Circuit's landmark *Scenic Hudson* decision.

Scenic Hudson Preservation Conference v. Federal Power Commission

354 F.2d 608 (D.C. Cir. 1965).

■ HAYS, CIRCUIT JUDGE. In this proceeding the petitioners . . . Scenic Hudson Preservation Conference, an unincorporated association consisting of a number of non-profit, conservationist organizations . . . ask us . . . to set aside . . . an order of March 9, 1965 granting a license to the intervener, the Consolidated Edison Company of New York, Inc., to construct a pumped storage hydroelectric project on the west side of the Hudson River at Storm King Mountain in Cornwall, New York . . .

A pumped storage plant generates electric energy for use during peak load periods, using hydroelectric units driven by water from a headwater pool or reservoir. The contemplated Storm King project would be the largest of its kind in the world. Consolidated Edison has estimated its cost, including transmission facilities, at $162,000,000. The project would consist of three major components, a storage reservoir, a powerhouse, and transmission lines. The storage reservoir, located over a thousand feet above the powerhouse, is to be connected to the powerhouse, located on the river front, by a tunnel 40 feet in diameter. The powerhouse, which is both a pumping and generating station, would be 800 feet long and contain eight pump generators. . . .

During slack periods Consolidated Edison's conventional steam plants in New York City would provide electric power for the pumps at Storm King to force water up the mountain, through the tunnel, and into the upper reservoir. In peak periods water would be released to rush down the mountain and power the generators. Three kilowatts of power generated in New York City would be necessary to obtain two kilowatts from the Cornwall installation. . . .

The Storm King project has aroused grave concern among conservationist groups, adversely affected municipalities and various state and federal legislative units and administrative agencies.

To be licensed by the Commission a prospective project must meet the statutory test of being "best adapted to a comprehensive plan for improving or developing a waterway," Federal Power Act § 10(a), 16 U.S.C. § 803(a). . . .

". . . (a) That the project adopted, * * * shall be such as in the judgment of the Commission *will be best adapted to a comprehensive plan for improving or developing a waterway or waterways for the use or benefit of interstate or foreign commerce, for the improvement and utilization* [* *12] *of water-power development, and for other beneficial public uses, including recreational purposes*; and if necessary in order to secure such plan the Commission shall have authority to require the modification of any project and of the plans and specifications of the project works before approval." (Emphasis added.)

"Recreational purposes" are expressly included among the beneficial public uses to which the statute refers. The phrase undoubtedly encompasses the conservation of natural resources, the maintenance of natural beauty, and the preservation of historic sites. n10 *See Namekagon Hydro Co. v. Fed. Power Comm'n*, 216 F.2d 509, 511–512 (7th Cir. 1954). All of these "beneficial uses," the Supreme Court has observed, "while unregulated, might well be contradictory rather than harmonious." In licensing a project, it is the duty of the Federal Power Commission properly to weigh each factor. . . .

The Commission in its opinion recognized that in connection with granting a license to Consolidated Edison it "must compare the Cornwall project with any alternatives that are available." There is no doubt that the Commission is under a statutory duty to give full consideration to alternative plans. . . .

On January 7, 1965 the testimony of Mr. Alexander Lurkis, as to the feasibility of an alternative to the project, the use of gas turbines, was offered to the Commission by Hilltop Cooperative of Queens, a taxpayer and consumer group. The petition to intervene and present this new evidence was rejected on January 13, 1965 as not "timely." It was more than two months after the offer of this testimony, on March 9, 1965, that the Commission issued a license to Consolidated Edison. When Mr. Lurkis's testimony was subsequently reoffered by the petitioners on April 8, 1965, it was rejected because it represented "at best" a "disagreement between experts." On the other hand, we have found in the record no meaningful evidence which contradicts the proffered testimony supporting the gas turbine alternative. . . .

Mr. Lurkis's analysis was based on an intensive study of the Consolidated Edison system, and of its peaking needs projected year by year over a fifteen year period. He was prepared to make an economic comparison of a gas turbine system (including capital and fuel operating costs) and the Storm King pumped storage plant. Moreover, he was prepared to answer Consolidated Edison's objections to gas turbines . . .

[U]nder the circumstances, we must conclude that there was no significant attempt to develop evidence as to the gas turbine alternative; at least, there is no such evidence in the record. . . .

It is not our present function to evaluate this evidence. Our focus is upon the action of the Commission. The fact that Lurkis's testimony was originally offered by a non-petitioner, Hilltop Cooperative, is irrelevant. A party acting as a "private attorney general" can raise issues that are not personal to it. Especially in a case of this type, where public interest and concern is so great, the Commission's refusal to receive the Lurkis testimony, as well as proffered information on fish protection devices and underground transmission facilities, a disregard of the statute and of judicial mandates instructing the Commission to probe all feasible alternatives. . . .

In this case, as in many others, the Commission has claimed to be the representative of the public interest. This role does not permit it to act as an umpire blandly calling balls and strikes for adversaries appearing before it; the right of the public must receive active and affirmative protection at the hands of the Commission.

This court cannot and should not attempt to substitute its judgment for that of the Commission. But we must decide whether the Commission has correctly discharged its duties, including the proper fulfillment of its planning function in deciding that the "licensing of the project would be in the overall public interest." The Commission must see to it that the record is complete. The Commission has an affirmative duty to inquire into and consider all relevant facts. . . .

In addition to the Commission's failure to receive or develop evidence concerning the gas turbine alternative, there are other instances where the Commission should have acted affirmatively in order to make a complete record. . . .

[The court determined that the Commission had ignored or excluded evidence on fisheries impacts and the availability of power for purchase from other utilities as well.]

On remand, the Commission should take the whole fisheries question into consideration before deciding whether the Storm King project is to be licensed.

The Commission should reexamine all questions on which we have found the record insufficient and all related matters. The Commission's renewed proceedings must include as a basic concern the preservation of natural beauty and of national historic shrines, keeping in mind that, in our affluent society, the cost of a project is only one of several factors to be considered. The record as it comes to us fails markedly to make out a case for the Storm King project on, among other matters, costs, public convenience and necessity, and absence of reasonable alternatives. Of course, the Commission should make every effort to expedite the new proceedings.

Petitioners' application, pursuant to Federal Power Act § 313(b), 16 U.S.C. § 825l(b), to adduce additional evidence concerning alternatives to the Storm King project and the cost and practicality of underground transmission facilities is granted. ∎

NOTES AND COMMENTS

1.   Does the *Scenic Hudson* decision force the Commission to accede to the demands of environmental groups? Does it require the Commission to strike the balance between development and environment in favor of the environment? The subsequent history of the case offers some insight into these questions. After the court remanded the case back to FPC, it issued a license to Consolidated Edison once again. However, changes in project economics killed the project before it was ever built. According to two empirical studies of the licensing program, the Commission's licensing decisions have not been particularly responsive to the demands of environmental groups; but they have been responsive to the demands of state and federal environmental agencies. *See* J.R. DeShazo and Jody Freeman, Public Agencies as Lobbyists, 105 Colum. L. Rev. 2217 (2005); David B. Spence, Using Law to Steer Administrative Agencies, 28 J. Legal Stud. 413 (1999).

2.   While the Commission did license a number of pumped storage projects prior to the 1980s, pumped storage projects subsequently fell out of favor with the Commission and developers alike. But might there be a future for pumped storage in a world where: (1) intermittent sources of power like wind and solar represent a larger share of the energy mix, or (2) increasingly competitive electricity markets in which the ability to "ramp up" or "ramp down" generation quickly is more highly valued (better compensated)? Why might that be? Interestingly, FERC has seen a sharp increase in the number of applications for preliminary permits for pumped storage projects since 2007, a period marked by sharp growth in wind and solar generation and the maturation of wholesale electricity markets.

3.   The *Scenic Hudson* case provided a template for the National Environmental Policy Act (NEPA), 42 U.S.C. § 4331 *et seq.*, which imposed on all federal agencies, including FERC, the obligation to review the environmental impacts of actions they propose to undertake or approve before undertaking or approving such actions. NEPA requires the preparation of an Environmental Impact Statement (EIS) for any "major federal action significantly affecting the quality of the human environment." 42 U.S.C. § 4332(c). If the agency determines that an EIS is unnecessary, a "Finding of No Significant Impact" (FONSI) is prepared giving reasons for this conclusion. At this point, no further action is taken under NEPA. The great majority of agency decisions on NEPA compliance conclude that an EIS is not necessary.[5] In practice, FERC prepares EISs in connection with very few hydroelectric licensing proceedings. However, FERC routinely prepares an "environmental assessment" (EA), a shorter and less procedurally cumbersome analysis of environmental impacts required by NEPA for proposed hydro projects. Nevertheless, NEPA, like the *Scenic Hudson* decision, merely requires the FERC to analyze environmental impacts, not to avoid them.

4.   In the *Fairfax Water Authority* case, discussed *supra* in section C.1 of this chapter, FERC followed its determination of jurisdiction over the project with a licensing order that included the requisite NEPA review. Fairfax Cnty. Water Auth., 54 F.E.R.C. ¶ 62,142 (1991). The Water Authority hired a consultant to prepare a draft EA, which was submitted to FERC in the hope that FERC would adopt it and issue a FONSI. (Many years after the licensing of the project, the Authority surrendered its license after the project

---

[5]   If an EIS is necessary, the agency will publish a "notice of intent" to prepare an EIS. The agency will also note the scope of the EIS and the important issues that will be addressed. A draft EIS is then prepared, giving complete analysis of the project, alternatives, actions to mitigate adverse effects, and possible environmental consequences. Upon completion, a draft EIS must be made available for public comment. Public comments must be included in the record of the final agency decision. The agency must respond to public comments and modify the draft if necessary, and the final EIS is then prepared. Final agency actions are subject to judicial review, usually to review the decision not to prepare an EIS or whether the procedural requirements of NEPA have been met. An EIS must contain several key components. Alternatives to the proposed action must be considered. § 102(2)(C)(iii), 42 U.S.C. § 4332(2)(C)(iii); § 102(2)(E), 42 U.S.C. § 4332(2)(E). Only reasonable alternatives need be identified. These must include a discussion of the "no action" alternative, reasonable alternatives that would eliminate or lessen the need for the proposed action, and alternatives that would mitigate the environmental impacts of the proposed action. Sometimes, there is inadequate scientific information about the environmental effects of a proposed action. At the very least, the agency must disclose what information is lacking. An agency may choose to prepare a "worst case analysis" (EA), as a way of dealing with the unknown. An agency may also be required to prepare a supplemental EIS in the event that new information becomes available or the design of the proposal changes.

became uneconomical to operate). *See* Fairfax Cnty. Water Auth., 129 F.E.R.C. ¶ 62,085 (2009). The great majority of NEPA compliance actions are handled in this way. *See* Rodgers, *supra*, at 893–896. Nowadays, FERC routinely publishes the EA as an appendix to its licensing orders, and the EA often contains a fairly lengthy and systematic analysis of environmental issues, though not nearly as lengthy as an EIS.

5.   One reason why environmental issues have proven so contentious in the hydropower licensing process for so long is that FERC has had an unusual amount of decision-making autonomy over environmental issues, and groups opposing hydro development have unusually little legal recourse outside of the FERC licensing process. This is due in part to U.S. Supreme Court's conclusion that the FPA's broad grant of authority to FERC preempts state and local environmental laws (by operation of the Supremacy Clause). *See* California v. FERC, 495 U.S. 490 (1990); First Iowa Hydro-Elec. Coop. v. Fla. Power Comm'n, 328 U.S. 152 (1946); *see also* Simmons v. Sabine River Auth. State of La., 732 F.3d 469 (5th Cir. 2013) (FPA preempts damage claims based in state tort law where damage caused by operation of hydro project in compliance with its license). While state and local environmental agencies routinely participate in the licensing process (and private interests may intervene as well), they cannot force FERC to adopt their point of view.[6]

6.   This concentration of environmental policy-making authority in the hands of a single agency has made for persistent conflict over environmental issues in the licensing process. After the 1965 *Scenic Hudson* decision, politicians (particularly those in Congress) attempted to influence FERC's resolution of environmental issues in a variety of ways. Statutes like NEPA in 1970, the Wild and Scenic Rivers Act in 1968, 16 U.S.C. § 1271 *et seq.,* and the CWA in 1972, 33 U.S.C. § 1251 *et seq.,* were aimed at least partly at FERC and were intended to create more environmentally protective agency decisions and policies. The Wild and Scenic Rivers Act of 1968 prohibited hydroelectric development at waterways designated by Congress as "wild or scenic" under the statute. That is, the statute established a system for removing FERC's decision-making authority over projects on river segments designated by Congress as environmentally sensitive. However, designation of river segments as "wild" or "scenic" required Congressional action, and could not be accomplished by agencies or environmental groups without this legislative help.

7.   The Public Utility Regulatory Policies Act of 1978 (PURPA), 16 U.S.C. § 2601 *et seq.* sparked an explosion of hydroelectric licensing activity in the 1980s by providing financial incentives for the development of alternative sources of energy, including hydro power, by nonutility developers. Specifically, the statute required electric utilities to purchase power from independently owned hydroelectric (and other) power producers at full "avoided cost" rates. As a result of this statute, FERC began to process hundreds of license applications for much smaller hydroelectric projects from a new class of applicants. Prior to the 1980s, most FERC licensees used hydroelectric power either to service retail customers or for on-site industrial operations. The former category included investor-owned and state or municipal utilities; the latter category comprised mostly paper and textile mills. The passage of PURPA introduced independent entrepreneurs into the

---

[6]   As noted, federal agencies have more leverage by way of Section 4 of the FPA, but that section grants no such leverage to state and local agencies. State environmental agencies have one source of leverage on water quality issues in Section 401 of the CWA, discussed *infra.*

licensing mix. Now many small hydroelectric projects are owned and operated by merchant generating companies who neither use the power they generate, nor sell it at retail.

D. THE CHANGING LANDSCAPE OF HYDROELECTRIC DEVELOPMENT

1. THE ENVIRONMENT VS. DEVELOPMENT BALANCE TODAY

If anything, the increased licensing activity spurred by PURPA's passage only accelerated conflict over environmental issues. To environmental groups, the *Namekagon* and *Scenic Hudson* decisions were the exceptions that proved the rule: namely, that FERC was insufficiently attentive to environmental concerns in its licensing decisions. They pressed Congress to require FERC to give more weight to environmental concerns in its licensing decisions. Meanwhile, during the 1990s hundreds of existing hydroelectric licenses were set to expire, which would require relicensing proceedings. Existing licensees urged Congress to abolish the municipal preference at relicensing, fearing that the municipal preference would force licenses (and projects) to change hands as municipalities simply copied licensees' project plans and submitted those plans as their own license applications during the relicensing proceedings. These twin desires set the stage for the legislative bargain that produced the Electric Consumers Protection Act of 1986 (ECPA), Pub. L. No. 99–495, amending 16 U.S.C. § 791 *et seq.* (1986).

ECPA. ECPA abolished the municipal preference at relicensing, ensuring that competing proposals would have to be superior to the incumbent's proposal in order to secure the new license. At the same time, ECPA added teeth to the environmental provisions of the FPA's previously-vague licensing standards, admonishing FERC to "give equal consideration" not only to "power and development purposes" but "energy conservation, . . . fish and wildlife . . . recreational opportunities, and the preservation of other aspects of environmental quality." 16 U.S.C. § 797(e). ECPA also added two important procedural requirements to the licensing process, both of which were designed to benefit environmental interests. One sought to force FERC to consider the impacts of multiple dams on a single river basin by requiring the use of a "cumulative impact assessment procedure" (CIAP) in such situations. *See* FERC's Cluster Impact Assessment Procedure (CIAP), 18 C.F.R. § 2.23 (1998). The other requirement, found in section 10(j) of the statute, required FERC to accept and include in hydroelectric licenses any conditions recommended by state or federal "resource agencies" (including environmental regulatory agencies) or to explain in writing why it was rejecting the recommended conditions. That section states, in pertinent part:

> All licenses issued under this subchapter shall be on the following conditions: . . . (j) . . . *each license issued under this subchapter shall include conditions for protection, mitigation, and enhancement [of fish and wildlife]. . . . Such conditions shall be based on recommendations received . . . from the National Marine Fisheries Service, the United States Fish and Wildlife Service, and State fish and wildlife agencies.* Whenever the

Commission believes that any [such] recommendation . . . may be inconsistent with the purposes and requirements of . . . applicable law, the Commission and the agencies shall attempt to resolve any such inconsistency, giving due weight to the recommendations, expertise, and statutory responsibilities of such agencies. If, after such attempt, the commission does not adopt in whole or in part a recommendation of any such agency, the commission shall publish each of the following findings (together with a statement of the basis for each of the findings): (A) A finding that adoption of such recommendation is inconsistent with the purposes and requirements of this subchapter or with other applicable provisions of law. (B) A finding that the conditions selected by the commission comply with the requirements of [the statute].

16 U.S.C. § 803(j) (1998) (emphasis added).

Note that while Section 10(j) does not impose a mandatory requirement of the kind found in Section 4 of the statute, it does increase the transaction costs of ignoring the wishes of environmental agencies in the licensing process. It is not clear whether Section 10(j) has made FERC any more receptive to environmental concerns. One study of FERC's licensing decisions concludes that the passage of ECPA did not produce any durable change in the FERC's decision-making on environmental issues. *See* David B. Spence, Managing Delegation Ex Ante: Using Law to Steer Administrative Agencies, 28 J. Legal Stud. 413 (1999). On the other hand, it may have had an impact on relicensing decisions. *See* discussion of relicensing issues, *infra*, at § D.2. As for the ECPA-added requirement that FERC consider "not only" development concerns but environmental concerns as well, both FERC and the courts have interpreted the language as merely procedural, rejecting the notion that environmental concerns be accorded any particular weight. *See, e.g.,* U.S. Dept. of the Interior v. FERC, 952 F.2d 538 (D.C. Cir. 1992).

The "Integrated" Licensing Process. As a practical matter, applicants for hydroelectric licenses are required by FERC to put a great deal of effort into addressing potential environmental concerns prior to filing their license applications. The primary mechanisms by which this occurs are FERC's pre-filing consultation requirements and NEPA. Under the pre-filing consultation process, prospective license applicants are required to seek input on their project plans from local, state, and federal resource agencies, and to incorporate responses to those agencies' concerns in their project proposals. Indeed, failure to do so can result in the FERC's refusal to accept the license application for processing. Once the application is accepted, federal resource agencies retain significant leverage over FERC's consideration of environmental issues by virtue of Section 4 of the FPA (described above). Furthermore, NEPA requires FERC to prepare an EA or EIS for each project proposal, guaranteeing that, at a minimum, FERC must do as the *Scenic Hudson* court directed it to do, namely, consider the environmental impacts of the proposed project.

In response to concerns about the large transaction costs associated with these review processes, FERC issued in July of 2003 a rule establishing its so-called "Integrated Licensing Process" (ILP). *See* FERC, Hydroelectric Licensing Under the Federal Power Act, 104 FERC

¶ 61,109 (July 23, 2003), 68 Fed. Reg. 51,069 (Aug. 25, 2003). After July 25, 2005, ILP became the default licensing process under FERC's rules. The ILP tries to streamline the licensing process by permitting the pre-filing consultation process, and the early stages of NEPA review (called the "scoping" process) to occur concurrently rather than sequentially. The ILP applies to both licensing and relicensing applications, and is outlined at 18 C.F.R. Part 5. At the heart of the process are (a) the required pre-application notification of all parties potentially affected by the proposed project, including federal resource agencies, described at 18 C.F.R. § 5.5, and (b) the circulation of the "pre-application document," described at 18 C.F.R. § 5.6:

§ 5.5   Notification of intent.

(b) *Requirement to Notify.* . . . a potential license applicant must file with the Commission . . . an original and eight copies of a letter that contains the following information:

(1) The potential applicant or existing licensee's name and address.

(2) The project number, if any.

(3) The license expiration date, if any.

(4) An unequivocal statement of the potential applicant's intention to file an application for an original license, or, in the case of an existing licensee, to file or not to file an application for a new or subsequent license.

(5) The type of principal project works licensed, if any, such as dam and reservoir, powerhouse, or transmission lines.

(6) The location of the project by state, county, and stream, and, when appropriate, by city or nearby city.

(7) The installed plant capacity, if any.

(8) The names and mailing addresses of:

(i) Every county in which any part of the project is located, and in which any Federal facility that is used or to be used by the project is located;

(ii) Every city, town, or similar political subdivision;

(A) In which any part of the project is or is to be located and any Federal facility that is or is to be used by the project is located, or

(B) That has a population of 5,000 or more people and is located within 15 miles of the existing or proposed project dam;

(iii) Every irrigation district, drainage district, or similar special purpose political subdivision:

(A) In which any part of the project is or is proposed to be located and any Federal facility that is or is proposed to be used by the project is located; or

(B) That owns, operates, maintains, or uses any project facility or any Federal facility that is or is proposed to be used by the project;

(iv) Every other political subdivision in the general area of the project or proposed project that there is reason to believe would be likely to be interested in, or affected by, the notification; and

(v) Affected Indian tribes.

§ 5.6   Pre-Application document.

(a) *Pre-Application Document.* (1) Simultaneously with the filing of its notification of intent to seek a license as provided for in § 5.5, . . . a potential applicant for a license . . . must file with the Commission and original and eight copies and distribute to the appropriate Federal, state, and interstate resource agencies, Indian tribes, local governments, and members of the public likely to be interested in the proceeding, the Pre-Application Document provided for in this section. . . .

(b) *Purpose of Pre-Application Document.*

(1) The Pre-Application document provides the Commission and the entities identified in paragraph (a) of this section with existing information relevant to the project proposal. . . .

The notice and circulation of the pre-application document set in motion a process of give and take between the applicant, FERC staff, and the commenting agencies. The recipients of the pre-application document must submit comments on the document within a specified period of time. These comments, in turn, are used by FERC staff to initiate the EA (scoping) process and by the applicant to construct a "study plan" according to which it will provide more detailed information about the environmental impacts of its proposal. The product of these efforts is a "preliminary licensing proposal" which, if satisfactory, will lead, finally, to the submission of the license application to FERC. Once the application has been accepted, interested parties may intervene before FERC to contest environmental or other issues. FERC will then resolve those disputes before making its final decision whether to issue a license, and if so, under what conditions.

401 Certification. While the *First Iowa* principle reserves for FERC the lion's share of authority to balance development interests against the environmental concerns raised by states, municipalities, and interest groups, states do have one source of leverage in the process: namely, Section 401 of the CWA. Section 401 requires "any applicant for a Federal license or permit" to secure from the appropriate state environmental agency a "certification . . . that any . . . discharge [from the project] will comply with the [the Clean Water Act]." 33 U.S.C. § 1341(a). Hydroelectric projects are not required to secure permits under the CWA because they do not "add" pollutants to waterways. *See supra* section C.1. One might suspect, then, that securing a so-called "401 certification" under this section might be a relatively straightforward matter. However, over the years state environmental agencies lacking any other means of exerting influence in the hydroelectric licensing process have used the 401 certification process to attempt to extract concessions from license applicants. Throughout the 1980s and early 1990s these attempts were unsuccessful. Courts interpreted the 401 certification requirement as one aimed only at ensuring that the hydroelectric project in question would not impair water quality, narrowly defined, and overturned attempts by state environmental agencies to impose broader environmental protection conditions in 401 certificates. *See, e.g.,* In the Matter of Niagara Mohawk Power Corp. v. N.Y. State Dep't of Envtl. Conservation, 624 N.E.2d 146 (N.Y. 1993). However, in 1994 the Supreme Court broadened the meaning of the 401 certification process in *PUD No. 1 of Jefferson County v. Washington Department of Ecology,* 511 U.S. 700 (1994).

Petitioners in *PUD No. 1,* applicants for a license to build a hydroelectric project, sought a 401 certificate from the Washington Department of Ecology (DEQ). DEQ issued a certification requiring that the petitioners maintain a minimum stream flow in order to protect fisheries in the areas to be affected by the dam. Petitioners argued that under the CWA the state had only the authority to regulate discharges, not stream flow. The Court disagreed with this position, quoting 401(d) of the CWA, which provides "any certification shall set forth 'any effluent limitations and other limitations . . . necessary to assure that any applicant' will comply with various provisions of the Act and appropriate state law requirements." The Court held that this section of the CWA applies to the applicant, not to the particular discharge, which allows the state to impose other limitations as needed. The Court stated:

> In many cases, water quantity is closely related to water quality; a sufficient lowering of the water quantity in a body of water could destroy all of its designated uses, be it for drinking water, recreation, navigation or, as here, as a fishery. In any event, there is recognition in the Clean Water Act itself that reduced stream flow, *i.e.,* diminishment of water quantity, can constitute water pollution. First, the Act's definition of pollution as 'the man-made or man induced alteration of the chemical, physical, biological, and radiological integrity of the water' encompasses the effects of reduced water quantity. 33 U.S.C. § 1362(19). This broad conception of pollution—one which expressly evinces Congress' concern with the physical and biological integrity of water—refutes petitioners' assertion that the Act draws a sharp distinction between the regulation of water 'quantity' and water 'quality.' Moreover, § 304 of the Act expressly recognizes that water 'pollution' may result from 'changes in the movement, flow, or circulation of any navigable waters . . . , including changes caused by the construction of dams.' 33 U.S.C. § 1314(f). This concern with the flowage effects of dams and other diversions is also embodied in EPA regulations, which expressly require existing dams to be operated to attain designated uses. 40 C.F.R. § 131.10(g)(4) (1992).

511 U.S. at 719–20.

The Court concluded that minimum stream flow requirements were acceptable state water quality standards. The result was to substantially increase the power of the states in hydropower licensing.

Following that decision, the Second Circuit Court of Appeals had occasion to consider some limits imposed in a 401 certificate by the State of Vermont on certain hydropower projects in that state that were on FERC's licensing agenda.

American Rivers, Inc. v. FERC
129 F.3d 99 (2d Cir. 1997).

■ WALKER, J. Petitioners, the State of Vermont and American Rivers, Inc., seek review of several orders issued by the Federal Energy Regulatory Commission ("FERC" or "Commission") licensing six hydropower projects located on rivers within the State of Vermont. The dispute surrounds (1) the authority of the State under § 401 of the Clean Water Act ("CWA"), 33 U.S.C. § 1341, to certify—prior to the issuance of a federal license—that such projects will comply with federal and state water quality standards and (2) the appropriate route for review of a state's certification decisions. The Commission argues that, when it determines that a state has exceeded the scope of its authority under § 401 in imposing certain pre-license conditions, it may refuse to include the ultra vires conditions in its license as it did in each of the proceedings at issue.

Petitioners contend that the Commission is bound by the language of § 401 to incorporate all state-imposed certification conditions into hydropower licenses and that the legality of such conditions can only be challenged by the licensee in a court of appropriate jurisdiction. We agree with petitioners and, thus, grant the petition for review, vacate the Commission's orders, and remand.

The principal order under review in this proceeding arises from the efforts of the Tunbridge Mill Corporation ("Tunbridge") to obtain a license from FERC for the operation of a small hydroelectric facility on the First Branch of the White River in Orange County, Vermont, restoring an historic mill site in Tunbridge Village. Pursuant to § 401(a)(1) of the CWA, 33 U.S.C. § 1341(a)(1), an applicant for a federal license for any activity that may result in a discharge into the navigable waters of the United States must apply for a certification from the state in which the discharge originates (or will originate) that the licensed activity will comply with state and federal water quality standards. *See P.U.D. No. 1 of Jefferson County v. Washington Dep't of Ecology*, 511 U.S. 700 (1994). Such certifications, in accordance with § 401(d), 33 U.S.C. § 1341(d), shall

> set forth any effluent limitations and other limitations, and monitoring requirements necessary to assure that any applicant for a Federal license or permit will comply with any applicable effluent limitations and other limitations, under section 1311 or 1312 of this title, standard of performance under section 1316 of this title, or prohibition, effluent standard, or pretreatment standard under section 1317 of this title, and with any other appropriate requirement of State law set forth in such certification. . . .

The CWA further provides that the state certification "shall become a condition on any Federal license or permit subject to the provisions of this section." *Id.*

The [Vermont natural resources agency] issued a draft certification on September 18, 1991, for public notice and comment in compliance with § 401(a)(1), 33 U.S.C. § 1341(a)(1), and Vermont law. A week later, on September 25, 1991, the certification was issued. No one challenged the ruling through the state's process of administrative and judicial review, and thus the certification became final fifteen days later. *See* 10 Vt. Stat. Ann. § 1024(a).

As issued, the certification contained eighteen conditions (designated by letters "A" through "R"), three of which, P, J, and L, are relevant for our purposes. Condition P reserves the right in Vermont to amend (or "reopen") the certification when appropriate. Condition J requires Tunbridge to submit to the state for review and approval any plans for significant changes to the project. Finally, condition L requires Tunbridge to seek clearance from the state before commencing construction so that the state may ensure that plans are in place to control erosion and manage water flows.

Certificate in hand, Tunbridge sought a license from FERC, which is vested with authority under 4(e) of the Federal Power Act ("FPA"), 16 U.S.C. § 797(e), to issue licenses for "the development, transmission, and utilization of power across, along, from, or in any of the streams or other bodies of water over which Congress has jurisdiction. . . . "FERC may issue such licenses "whenever the contemplated improvement is, in the judgment of the Commission, desirable and justified in the public interest," *id.*, and "best adapted to a comprehensive plan . . . for the improvement and utilization of water-power development, for the adequate protection, mitigation, and enhancement of fish and wildlife . . . , and for other beneficial public uses," 16 U.S.C. § 803(a)(1).

On July 15, 1994, FERC . . . granted Tunbridge a 40-year license "to construct, operate, and maintain the Tunbridge Mill Project." However, . . . FERC found that conditions P, J, and L were beyond the scope of Vermont's authority under the CWA. Accordingly, FERC refused to incorporate them into the Tunbridge license. Vermont and American Rivers now seek review in this court of the Commission's determination.

Prior to Tunbridge Mill, FERC had held that it was required by § 401 to include in its licenses all conditions imposed by a state in its certifications notwithstanding the Commission's view that the conditions were beyond a state's authority under § 401.

In Tunbridge Mill, however, the Commission reversed field, finding that "to the extent that states include conditions that are unrelated to water quality, these conditions are beyond the scope of Section 401 and are thus unlawful." "We conclude that we have the authority to determine that such conditions do not become terms and conditions of the licenses we issue." *Id.* The Commission reasoned, in part: "We believe that, in light of Congress' determination that the Commission should have the paramount role in hydropower licensing process, whether certain state conditions are outside the scope of Section 401(d) is a federal question to be answered by the Commission."

The principal dispute between petitioners and the Commission in this case surrounds the relative scope of authority of the states and the Commission under the CWA and the FPA. Petitioners' contention is straightforward, resting on statutory language. In their view, the plain language of § 401(d) indicates that FERC has no authority to review and reject the substance of a state certification or the conditions contained therein and must incorporate into its licenses the conditions as they appear in state certifications. FERC disagrees, arguing that the language of § 401(d) is not as clear as petitioners would have it. Rather, FERC contends, it is bound to accede only to those conditions that are within a state's authority under § 401, that is, conditions that are reasonably related to water quality and that otherwise conform to the dictates of § 401. The Commission also argues that without the authority to reject state-imposed § 401 conditions its Congressionally mandated role under the FPA of ensuring comprehensive planning and development of hydropower would be undermined.

The Clean Water Act. Before considering the Commission's contentions regarding the CWA, we note that FERC's interpretation of § 401, or any other provision of the CWA, receives no judicial deference under the doctrine of Chevron USA, Inc. v. Natural Resources Defense Council, 467 U.S. 837 (1984), because the Commission is not Congressionally authorized to administer the CWA. *See* 33 U.S.C. § 1251(d) ("Except as otherwise expressly provided in this chapter, the Administrator of the Environmental Protection Agency . . . shall administer this chapter."); *see also* West v. Bowen, 879 F.2d 1122, 1137 (3d Cir. 1989) (holding that "no deference is owed an agency's interpretation of another agency's statute"). Thus, we review de novo the Commission's construction of the CWA.

We begin, as we must, with the statute itself. In this case, the statutory language is clear. Section 401(a), which is directed both to prospective licensees and to the federal licensing agency (in this case, the Commission), provides, in relevant part:

> Any applicant for a Federal license or permit to conduct any activity . . . which may result in any discharge into the navigable waters, shall provide the licensing or permitting agency a certification from the State in which the discharge originates or will originate. . . . No license or permit shall be granted until the certification required by this section has been obtained or has been waived. . . . No license or permit shall be granted if certification has been denied by the State. . . .

33 U.S.C. § 1341(a). More important, § 401(d), reads, in pertinent part:

> Any certification provided under this section . . . shall become a condition on any Federal license or permit subject to the provisions of this section.

33 U.S.C. § 1341(d).

This language is unequivocal, leaving little room for FERC to argue that it has authority to reject state conditions it finds to be ultra vires. Rather, in this case, to the extent that the Commission contends that Congress intended to vest it with authority to reject "unlawful" state conditions, the Commission faces a difficult task since it is generally assumed—absent a clearly expressed legislative intention to the contrary—"that Congress expresses its purposes through the ordinary meaning of the words it uses. . . ." *Escondido Mutual Water Co. v. La Jolla Band of Mission Indians*, 466 U.S. 765, 772 (1984).

The Commission argues that, notwithstanding the mandatory language of the provision, § 401(d) itself restricts the substantive authority of states to impose conditions: "Section 401 authorizes states to impose only conditions that relate to water quality." This is plainly true. Section 401(d), reasonably read in light of its purpose, restricts conditions that states can impose to those affecting water quality in one manner or another. *See P.U.D. No. 1 of Jefferson County*, 114 S. Ct. at 1909 (holding that a state's authority to impose conditions under § 401(d) "is not unbounded"). However, this is not tantamount to a delegation to FERC of the authority to decide which conditions are within the confines of § 401(d) and which are not. And this is the crux of the dispute in this case.

In *Escondido Mutual Water Co. v. La Jolla Band of Mission Indians*, 466 U.S. 765 (1984)—a case which the Commission goes to great lengths to distinguish—the Supreme Court was called upon to consider a strikingly analogous factual and legal scenario. At issue was a pre-license certification scheme within the FPA itself, permitting (in this instance) the Secretary of the Interior to impose requirements on licenses issued "within" any Native American "reservation." In particular, this certification scheme, § 4(e) of the FPA, 16 U.S.C. § 797(e), provides that licenses issued under this provision "shall be subject to and contain such conditions as the Secretary of the department under whose supervision such reservation falls shall deem necessary for the adequate protection and utilization of such reservation." 16 U.S.C. § 797(e). FERC, however, refused to accept the Secretary's conditions, and an aggrieved party sought review. In construing § 4(e), the Supreme Court focused closely on the provision's plain language, remarking that "the mandatory nature of the language chosen by Congress appears to require that the Commission include the Secretary's conditions in the license even if it disagrees with them." *Escondido*, 466 U.S. at 772. Consistent with this view, the Court gave effect to the plain language of 4(e), 16 U.S.C. § 797(e), finding no "clear expressions of legislative intent to the contrary." *Id.*

Although Escondido arose in a different context, it is instructive in this case for several reasons. In both contexts, FERC is required in clear statutory language to incorporate conditions imposed by an independent governmental agency with special expertise, in Escondido, the Department of the Interior, 16 U.S.C. § 797(e), and in this instance, the states, *see* 33 U.S.C. § 1251(b) ("It is the policy of the Congress to recognize, preserve, and protect the primary responsibilities and rights of States to prevent, reduce, and eliminate pollution. . . ."); *see also United States v. Puerto Rico*, 721 F.2d 832, 838 (1st Cir. 1983) ("states are the prime bulwark in the effort to abate water pollution"). In both cases, the Commission attempted to ignore this command and substitute its own judgment for that of the certifying agency. In both cases, the real issue in dispute is not whether there are limits on the certifying agency's authority to impose conditions on federal licenses, but "whether the Commission is empowered to decide when the . . . conditions exceed the permissible limits." *Escondido*, 466 U.S. at 777. In neither case do the underlying statutes or their schemes for administrative and judicial review suggest that Congress wanted the Commission to second-guess the imposition of conditions.

Finally, and most persuasively, in both cases the Commission argued that without the authority to review conditions imposed by the certifying agency its ability to carry out its statutory mission would be compromised. In *Escondido*, notwithstanding this contention, the Supreme Court found that absent a challenge by the applicant-licensee, the Interior Secretary's conditions must either be incorporated in full into any license that it issues or the Commission must deny the license altogether. 466 U.S. at 778 n.20. In reaching this conclusion, the Court expressly addressed difficulties inherent in such a statutory scheme, difficulties the Commission decries in this case:

> We note that in the unlikely event that none of the parties to the licensing proceeding seeks review, the conditions will go into effect notwithstanding the Commission's objection to them since the Commission is not authorized to seek review of its own decisions. The possibility that this might occur does not, however, dissuade us from interpreting the statute in accordance with its plain meaning. Congress apparently decided that if no party was interested in the differences between the Commission and the Secretary, the dispute would best be resolved in a nonjudicial forum. *Id.*

The Commission's efforts to distinguish Escondido are unavailing.

The Federal Power Act. Independent of FERC's concerns that Vermont's 401 conditions violate the terms of the CWA, the Commission contends that the 401 conditions run afoul of the FPA. The Commission primarily fears that "to accept the conditions proposed would give the state the kind of governance and enforcement authority that is critical and exclusive to the Commission's responsibility to administer a license under the Federal Power Act, a power the Courts have repeatedly concluded belongs exclusively to the Commission." In particular, FERC argues (1) that the conditions that impose deadlines on construction conflict with § 13 of the FPA, 16 U.S.C. § 806, which places construction deadlines largely within the discretion of the Commission and generally contemplates that construction will be commenced within two years of the date of the license, *see First Iowa Hydro-Elec. Coop. v. Federal Power Comm'n,* 328 U.S. 152, 168 n.13 (1946); (2) that the reopener conditions and pre-approval conditions violate § 6 of the FPA, 16 U.S.C. § 799, which provides that a license, once issued, "may be revoked only for the reasons and in the manner prescribed under the provisions of this chapter, and may be altered or surrendered only upon mutual agreement between the licensee and the Commission," as well as other provisions of the FPA, *see* 16 U.S.C. §§ 803(b), 820, 823b; and, (3) more generally, that the conditions "eviscerate[ ] the carefully balanced approach" to environmental concerns expressed in the Electric Consumers Protection Act ("ECPA"), *see, e.g.,* 16 U.S.C. §§ 797(e), 803(a), 803(j).

We have no quarrel with the Commission's assertion that the FPA represents a congressional intention to establish "a broad federal role in the development and licensing of hydroelectric power." *California v. FERC,* 495 U.S. 490, 496 (1990). Nor do we dispute that the FPA has a wide preemptive reach. *Id.* The CWA, however, has diminished this preemptive reach by expressly requiring the Commission to incorporate into its licenses state-imposed water-quality conditions. *See* 33 U.S.C. § 1341(a)(1). Although we are sympathetic to the Commission's suggestion that without the authority to reject states' conditions that are beyond the scope of § 401, the preemptive reach of the FPA may be narrowed at the will of the states, the Commission's concerns are overblown.

The Commission fails to acknowledge appropriately its ability to protect its mandate from incursion by exercising the authority to refuse to issue a hydropower license altogether if the Commission concludes that a license, as conditioned, sufficiently impairs its authority under the FPA. *See, e.g., Escondido,* 466 U.S. at 778 n.20. If the Commission is concerned that the conditions imposed by a state "intrude[ ] upon the Commission's exclusive authority under the FPA," nothing in the CWA prevents it from protecting its field of authority by simply refusing to issue the license as so conditioned.

The Commission, however, has chosen to forgo this route, arguing that refusing to issue a license is not a "practical option" in relicensing cases. *Id.* at 20 n.10. Although we understand that refusing to relicense a hydroelectric project would result in the disassembly of the project, presenting "serious practical and economic problems" and affecting all manner of local interests, *id.*, the Commission's dissatisfaction with the remedy of license denial is not reason enough to turn a blind eye to FERC's assumption of authority to review and reject a state's 401 conditions. Rather, the Commission must establish that the authority it proposes is rooted in a Congressional mandate. And this they have failed to do.

Finally, with respect to the ECPA amendments to the FPA, the Commission is mistaken. Under these provisions, the Commission must "give equal consideration to . . . the protection, mitigation of damage to, and enhancement of, fish and wildlife . . . and the preservation of other aspects of environmental quality," 16 U.S.C. § 797(e), and must impose conditions, based on recommendations of relevant federal agencies and affected states, to "protect, mitigate damages to, and enhance, fish and wildlife . . . affected by the development, operation, and management of the project . . . ," 16 U.S.C. § 803(j)(1). *See U.S. Dep't of Interior v. FERC,* 952 F.2d 538, 543 (D.C. Cir. 1992) (describing environmental aspects of the ECPA amendments). The Commission argues that absent the authority to reject state-imposed conditions beyond the scope of § 401 of the CWA, the carefully balanced approach of the ECPA amendments, in general, and § 10(j), 16 U.S.C. § 803(j), in particular, would be "eviscerated . . . through the simple expedient of [states'] labeling . . . recommendations 'conditions' to the Section 401 certification." In short, the Commission is concerned that it would be "held hostage" to every state imposed condition, compromising its role under the ECPA amendments of reconciling competing interests. *Id.* Such a result, the Commission contends, is impermissible under § 511(a) of the CWA, 33 U.S.C. § 1371(a), which provides, in part, that the Act "shall not be construed as . . . limiting the authority or functions of any officer or agency of the United States under any other law or regulation not inconsistent with this chapter. . . ."

The Commission's claim that the CWA—as we construe it—and the ECPA amendments are incompatible must be rejected. The Commission's concern that states will hold the Commission hostage through the § 401 process is misplaced because states' authority under § 401 is circumscribed in notable respects. First, applicants for state certification may challenge in courts of appropriate jurisdiction any state-imposed condition that exceeds a state's authority under § 401. In so doing, licensees will surely protect themselves against state-imposed ultra vires conditions. Second, even assuming that certification applicants will not always challenge ultra vires state conditions, the Commission may protect its mandate by refusing to issue a license which, as conditioned, conflicts with the FPA. In so doing, the Commission will not only protect its mandate but also signal to states and licensees the limits of its tolerance. Third, and most important, to the extent that the existence of states' authority to impose 401 conditions may otherwise conflict with the ECPA amendments, the ECPA is inconsistent with the terms of the CWA, thus, making inapplicable § 511(a) of the CWA. *See* 33 U.S.C. § 1371(a) (the Act "shall not be construed as . . . limiting the authority or functions of any officer or agency of the United States under any other law or regulation not inconsistent with this chapter . . .").

We have considered the Commission's remaining arguments and find them to be without merit. For the foregoing reasons, we grant the petition for review, vacate the orders of the Commission, and remand for proceedings consistent with this opinion. ■

NOTES AND COMMENTS

1. On remand, FERC issued the license subject to the state's conditions. *Tunbridge Mill Corporation*, 82 F.E.R.C. ¶ 61,265 (1998). For a discussion of the unusual power CWA § 401 affords states as against a federal agency, see Ann E. Carlson and Andrew Mayer, Reverse Preemption, 40 Ecology L.Q. 583 (2013).

2. The Supreme Court faced the question of the proper scope of CWA § 401 again in *S.D. Warren Co. v. Maine Environmental Protection Bd.*, 547 U.S. 370 (2006). In that case the project developer, Warren, contended that hydroelectric projects do not "discharge" to navigable waters, and therefore require no 401 certificate. The State of Maine had imposed a number of water quality conditions in granting the certificate to Warren. Warren argued that the definition of "discharge" as used on § 401 must be the same as that used in § 402 of the Act (which governs pollutant discharges), and the latter limits the term to activities involving the addition of pollutants to the waterway. The Court rejected Warren's arguments, noting that the same term can have different meanings in different contexts within the same statute.

3. American Indian Tribes share with the states the power to set conditions on water usage within reservations. Tribes have been active participants in the negotiations on many of the contested hydropower licensing proceedings. *See* Jane Marz et al., Tribal Jurisdiction over Reservation Water Quality and Quantity, 43 S.D. L. Rev. 315 (1998).

4. Just exactly which environmental issues fall within the state's 401 certification authority after *P.U.D. No. 1 of Jefferson County v. Washington Dep't of Ecology*? It is easy to see the connection between water quantity in the river below the dam and water quality issues. Of the litany of environmental concerns raised by hydroelectric projects, which affect water quality and which do not, in your view? Given our growing understanding of the interdependent relationships between flora and fauna within ecosystems, do you expect a growing number of issues to fall within the states' jurisdiction under section 401? *See* Michael C. Blumm & Viki A. Nadol, The Decline of the Hydropower Czar and the Rise of Agency Pluralism in Hydroelectric Licensing, 26 Colum. J. Envtl. L. 81 (2001) (arguing that FERC's dominance over the licensing process has been eroded by decisions like this one).

5. Certain small hydroelectric projects that are otherwise subject to FERC's jurisdiction are "exempt" from licensing under the FPA and FERC's

regulations. These exempt facilities are narrowly defined, and most require that the applicant already own all the property rights necessary to build and operate the project. The project owner files a notice with FERC, which then issues an exemption for the project. These projects are exempt from many of the licensing standards contained within the FPA, but the term "exemption" is a bit of a misnomer, since FERC-issued exemptions usually contain conditions that are very like those contained in hydroelectric licenses. *See* 18 C.F.R. §§ 4.31, 4.106. In 2013 Congress passed the Hydropower Regulatory Efficiency Act of 2013 (HREA), Pub. L. No. 113–23, 127 Stat. 493 (2013), which increased the size of small conduit facilities that are exempt from licensing (from 15 MW to 40 MW). (Conduit facilities are hydro stations that use existing water flows through a tunnel or other conveyance to generate power, without a dam.) HREA also amends the FPA to exclude entirely from FERC's FPA licensing jurisdiction certain qualifying very small conduit facilities (5 MW or less), substituting a less burdensome certification process for those facilities.

6.   Sometimes the operation of a hydroelectric facility affects the operations (and profitability) of other facilities upstream or downstream of the original facility. Section 10(f) of the FPA requires the Commission to order licensees who benefit from improvements to other projects (called "headwater benefits") to reimburse the owner of the project providing the benefits, and reimbursement provisions are now a standard condition of hydroelectric licenses. 16 U.S.C. § 803(f). States, however, may not require reimbursement above and beyond that authorized required under the FPA. *Albany Engineering v. Hudson River-Black River Regulating District,* 548 F.3d 1071 (D.C. Cir. 2008) (finding state law requiring additional compensation preempted by the FPA).

7.   In 2011 the Bureau of Reclamation concluded that there existed 191 federally owned sites at which hydropower development was feasible, and at least 70 at which such development would be economical. The sites represented more than 200 MW of generating potential. Bureau of Reclamation, Dep't. of the Interior, Reclamation, Managing Water in the West: Hydropower Resource Assessment at Existing Reclamation Facilities (2011).

8.   The Energy Policy Act of 2005 runs counter to the recent historical trend toward increasing leverage for environmental interests in the FERC licensing process. The Act adds procedural protections against (and increases the transaction costs associated with) decisions imposing environmental conditions in hydroelectric licenses. For example, section 231 of the Act provides project owners with a right to a trial-type hearing to challenge license conditions imposed by resource agencies under Section 4(e) of the FPA, as well as FERC-imposed license conditions requiring the construction of fish passage facilities. 16 U.S.C. § 797(e). The Act further weakens the leverage of federal resource agencies under Section 4(e) by authorizing FERC to select alternate license conditions over conditions proposed by resource agencies when it finds that such alternate conditions would provide "adequate protection" and be less costly or more efficient. It remains to be seen whether (or to what extent) Congress's attempt to increase the procedural costs associated with imposing environmental protection conditions in hydroelectric licenses will lead FERC to impose fewer, or weaker, environmental protection conditions in future licenses.

2.   RELICENSING AND THE ENVIRONMENT

Hundreds of the early project licenses for hydroelectric dams have now expired, and applications are pending before FERC to reissue many of these licenses. Indeed, most of the first generation of hydroelectric projects has already been relicensed. The courts long ago established that even if the relicensing application proposed to continue to operate the project unchanged, FERC must conduct a full, *de novo* review (including a full environmental review under NEPA). Yakima Indian Nation v. FERC, 746 F. 2d 466 (9th Cir. 1981). And as already mentioned, ECPA abolished the municipal preference at relicensing.

After the passage of ECPA in 1986, environmental interests argued that many of the hundreds of hydro projects up for relicensing in the 1990s and early 21st century ought to be decommissioned rather than relicensed, and their dams removed in order to restore historic fish runs and the dam sites to their natural condition. As described in the *Udall* decision, dams had destroyed historic fish runs on both the east and west coasts. For decades the Commission responded to this problem by requiring hydroelectric project owners to install fish passage facilities, which were insufficient to restore historic fish migration patterns. By the 1980s state environmental agencies and Indian tribes had established programs for restoring salmon migration routes by restocking salmon rivers, and had begun to bring pressure on FERC to do more to help. Environmental groups like American Rivers supported this effort by intervening in hydroelectric relicensing proceedings, urging FERC to deny relicensing applications and order the decommissioning of existing dams.

This cause received a boost from FERC in December of 1994 in the form of a policy statement declaring that FERC had the power to order complete removal of existing hydroelectric power generating dams. Project Decommissioning at Relicensing; Policy Statement, 60 Fed. Reg. 339 (1994). Only three years after its 1994 policy statement, FERC exercised this authority by ordering the removal of the Edwards Dam, a dam across the Kennebec River near Augusta, Maine. The site had been dammed since the early 1800s, and when Edwards Manufacturing filed its relicensing application in 1991, the application brought resistance from various environmental groups, sporting organizations, state and federal agencies, and other businesses. Several of the intervenors sought to have the dam removed in order to restore migration for anadromous fish. After a lengthy proceeding involving two EISs, FERC concluded "that the project's negative impact on fishery resources could not be mitigated except by removal of the dam," and ordered the dam removed at the owner's expense. Edward's Mfg. Co. & City of Augusta, Me.; Order Denying New License and Requiring Dam Removal, 81 F.E.R.C. ¶ 61,255 (1997).

While the courts were considering the appeal of FERC's Edwards Dam decision, the case was settled pursuant to a larger agreement among dam owners and resource agencies on the lower Kennebec River in Maine. The State of Maine had established spawning programs that were already making progress reintroducing anadromous species to the river, and sought a global settlement of the problem of dams and fish migration on the Kennebec. The Edwards Dam decision sparked hope among environmentalists that more dams would be removed, and historic fish runs restored. Experience since has tempered those hopes. The following decision, concerning the relicensing of a facility at the dam immediately upstream of the Edwards Dam, is fairly typical of recent relicensing cases.

Merimil Limited Partnership, Project No. 2574–032, Order Issuing New License
110 F.E.R.C. ¶ 61,240 (2005).

On April 29, 2002, Merimil Limited Partnership (Merimil) filed an application for a new license, pursuant to sections 4(e) and 15 of the Federal Power Act (FPA), 16 U.S.C. §§ 797(e) and 808, respectively, for the continued operation and maintenance of the existing 6.915-megawatt (MW) Lockwood Project No. 2574, located on the Kennebec River, a navigable waterway, in Kennebec County, Maine.

The Lockwood Project, located at river mile 63, is now the first dam on the mainstem of the Kennebec River. The Lockwood Project includes an 81.5-acre reservoir, an 875-foot-long and 17-foot-high dam with two spillway sections and a 160-foot-long forebay headworks section, a 450-foot-long forebay canal, two powerhouses, and two transmission lines. The dam and forebay headworks span the Kennebec River immediately upstream of the U.S. Route 201 bridge along a site originally known as Ticonic Falls. . . .

The Kennebec River in the vicinity of the Lockwood Project supports a varied fish population. The impoundment supports a warm water fish community, including naturally reproducing smallmouth bass. Migratory species in the impoundment include American shad, alewife, and American eel. The fish communities in the river below the project consist of both warm water and cold water species typical in the region, including smallmouth bass, largemouth bass, perch, black crappie and a variety of forage species. Anadromous species that could move up to the project tailwaters include striped bass, rainbow smelt, Atlantic sturgeon, shortnose sturgeon, Atlantic salmon, American shad, and alewife. Only American shad, alewife, and Atlantic salmon have historically migrated upstream of the project area. American eel have unobstructed access to the base of the dam. Large numbers of eels observed in the bypassed reach, in the impoundment, and at the Hydro-Kennebec Project (the next upstream dam) confirm that eels are successfully passing the Lockwood Project. Efforts are underway to restore American shad, alewife, Atlantic salmon, and American eel to the Kennebec River Basin.

In 1989, the license for the project was amended to include the terms of a January 1987 agreement (known as the Kennebec Hydro Developer Group [KHDG]) agreement . . . to facilitate the restoration of American shad, alewife, and Atlantic salmon in the Kennebec River Basin. The licensees agreed to provide funding to the state fishery agencies for interim trap and truck operations at the projects, to install and operate permanent downstream and upstream fish passage facilities according to a schedule, and to conduct studies related to the restoration efforts. Permanent upstream and downstream fish passage facilities were to be installed and operational at the Lockwood Project by May 1, 1999. This schedule was based on the assumption that fish passage would be provided at the Edwards Project by the late 1980s.

In April 1997, the licensees of the KHDG agreement projects requested the Commission to amend the licenses to delay installation of the permanent fishways at the projects (including Lockwood) until fish passage was available at the Edwards Project or the dam removed and restoration of salmon, shad, and alewives in the Kennebec River had proved successful. . . . On May 28, 1998, an offer of settlement, now known as the Lower Kennebec River Comprehensive Settlement Accord (1998 Accord), was filed by state and federal fisheries agencies, environmental groups, and the licensees of the Edwards Project and seven upstream projects. The 1998 Accord modified the KHDG agreement and included provisions for removing the Edwards dam and, upon the occurrence of certain triggering events, installing fish passage at the upstream projects, including the Lockwood Project. The Lockwood license was amended in September 1998 to incorporate the terms of the 1998 Accord. Merimil's relicense proposal includes these measures . . .

Friends of the Kennebec Salmon intervened in opposition to the relicensing of the project, contending that the goals of the fishery restoration programs in the Kennebec River Basin cannot be achieved using fish passage facilities at the Lockwood Project, and thus the license should be denied and the project removed.

On October 3, 2003, the Commission issued a draft environmental assessment (EA) that analyzed the impacts of relicensing the project under the terms of the 1998 Accord (Merimil's proposal), as proposed by Merimil with additional staff-recommended measures (staff alternative), and without interim and permanent upstream fishways (no-action alternative). . . .

Water Quality Certification

On April 25, 2002, Merimil applied to the Maine DEP for water quality certification. Merimil twice withdrew and refiled the application for certification (April 18, 2003, and April 16, 2004). Maine DEP issued water quality certification for the project on August 24, 2004. Ordering Paragraph (D) incorporates into the license the conditions of the certification, which is attached as Appendix A.

In summary, Merimil must: (1) operate in a run-of-river mode; (2) minimize impoundment level fluctuations (within six inches of full pond when all flashboards are in place and above the spillway crest when flashboard failure has occurred); (3) maintain minimum leakage flows of 30 to 50 cfs from the dam; (4) implement fish rescue measures during flashboard replacement or impoundment drawdown; (5) maintain the existing shoreline angler access site in the project's tailwater; and (6) comply with the requirements of the 1998 Accord. . . .

Threatened and Endangered Species

Section 7(a) of the Endangered Species Act of 1973 (ESA), 16 U.S.C. § 1536(a), requires federal agencies to ensure that their actions are not likely to jeopardize the continued existence of federally listed threatened and endangered species, or result in the destruction or adverse modification of designated critical habitat. . . . Federally listed species that occur in the project area are the threatened bald eagle and endangered shortnose sturgeon. In the final EA, staff found that relicensing the project would not be likely to adversely affect the bald eagle, but would be likely to adversely affect the shortnose sturgeon.

Adverse effects on the shortnose sturgeon result from handling during the rescue of shortnose sturgeon that may become entrapped in isolated pools in the bypassed reach during flashboard repair, and during sorting and returning to the river any sturgeon caught in the fish lift that is to be constructed. . . .

On October 16, 2003, Commission staff requested formal consultation with NOAA Fisheries under section 7(a)(2) of the ESA on the shortnose sturgeon. NOAA Fisheries requested additional information, which was provided in the final EA along with a recommendation that Merimil prepare a sturgeon rescue plan that defines handling protocols and notification procedures. . . . The plan defines procedures for handling and returning shortnose sturgeon to the Kennebec River below the project during operation of the fish lift and during fish rescue efforts associated with flashboard replacement.

On January 14, 2005, NOAA Fisheries filed its biological opinion on relicensing the Lockwood Project, which found that relicensing the project with staff's recommended measures would not jeopardize the continued existence of the Kennebec River population of the shortnose sturgeon.

Recommendations of Federal and State Fish and Wildlife Agencies

Pursuant to section 10(j) of the FPA, 16 U.S.C. § 803(j)(1), the Commission, when issuing a license, includes conditions based on the recommendations of federal and state fish and wildlife agencies submitted pursuant to the Fish and Wildlife Coordination Act, 16 U.S.C. § 661 *et seq.*, for the protection and enhancement of fish and wildlife and their habitat affected by the project. . . . For the Lockwood Project, Interior and the Maine SPO on behalf of Maine Department of Marine Resources, Maine Department of Inland Fisheries and Wildlife, and the Maine Atlantic Salmon Commission submitted a total of 15 recommendations (some of which are duplicative) that fall within the scope of section 10(j). The license contains conditions consistent with all of these recommendations.

Other Issues

Friends of the Kennebec Salmon argue that relicensing the project will prevent the restoration of Atlantic salmon, American shad, and alewives to the Kennebec River Basin. The group contends that fish passage inefficiencies at the Lockwood Project, and at other upstream dams, will reduce the number of fish that reach the upstream spawning habitat to the point that a self-sustaining population cannot be achieved. As a result, it argues that the application for a new license should be denied and that the project should be decommissioned and the dam removed.

As noted above, in 1987, Merimil, together with the other members of KHDG, entered into an agreement with fisheries resource agencies to facilitate the restoration of Atlantic salmon, American shad, and alewives to the lower Kennebec River Basin. KHDG provided funds to the agencies to help pay for acquiring and stocking fish to restore populations and studying restoration efforts. The KHDG licensees also agreed to construct and operate fish passage facilities according to a schedule that called for sequential construction of the facilities, beginning with the downstream projects and moving upstream. The licenses for the KHDG projects were amended to reflect the fish passage provisions of the agreement. In 1998, the agreement was modified (the 1998 Accord) to provide for the removal of the Edwards Dam and link the construction of fish passage facilities to biological triggers instead of to specific dates. The 1998 Accord continued the requirement for financial support by the licensees of the restoration activities.

Fishery restoration activities in the lower Kennebec River Basin have made significant progress. In 2003, the latest year for which data are available, over 135,000 alewives were trapped at the Ft. Halifax project. This provided enough fish for the resource agencies to meet all their stocking goals and have additional fish available for stocking outside the Kennebec River Basin. The alewife spawning run is now large enough to meet the stocking needs and support a commercial fishery; reports from 48 percent of the commercial fisherman showed a catch of over 128,000 alewives from the Sebasticook River at Ft. Halifax. Earlier estimates of the size of the alewife run were 1 to 2 million fish and biologists reported that there seemed to be more alewives in 2003 than in previous years.

The number of shad fry stocked above Lockwood increased from 1.75 million in 2002 to 2.54 million in 2003, and the interim downstream fish passage measures at Lockwood, Hydro Kennebec, and Shawmutt appear to be allowing juvenile shad and alewife to migrate downstream without significant injury or mortality. The existing license for the Lockwood Project requires Merimil to install and operate interim upstream fish passage facilities by May 1, 2006.

The Maine Atlantic Salmon Commission does not currently have an active salmon restoration program in the Kennebec River. No Atlantic salmon are stocked in the Kennebec above Lockwood and any adult salmon returning to the river are either strays from other rivers or the result of natural reproduction in the Kennebec or its tributaries below Lockwood.

We believe that the 1998 Accord has created an effective, comprehensive, and coordinated program for achieving the fishery restoration goals for the lower Kennebec River Basin. The Accord provides for continuing restoration activities and installation of fish passage facilities as required by the growth of the fish populations and their expansion into upstream habitat. Friends of the Kennebec Salmon argue that dam removal is needed to guarantee success of the restoration efforts. The evidence to date shows that the restoration plans are making significant progress. We believe it is too early in the restoration efforts to conclude that the plan will ultimately succeed or fail. Therefore we do not agree that we should abandon the plan embodied in the 1998 Accord.

Coastal Zone Consistency Certification

Under section 307(c)(3)(A) of the Coastal Zone Management Act, 16 U.S.C. § 1456(c)(3)(A), the Commission cannot issue a license for a project within or affecting a state's coastal zone unless the state CZMA agency concurs with the license applicant's certification of consistency with the state's CZMA program, or the agency's concurrence is conclusively presumed by its failure to act within 180 days of its receipt of the applicant's certification. . . .

The Commission orders:

(A) This license is issued to Merimil Limited Partnership (licensee) to operate and maintain the Lockwood Project, for a period of 31 years and 8 months, effective the first day of the month in which this order is issued. The license is subject to the terms and conditions of the Federal Power Act (FPA), which is incorporated by reference as part of this license, and subject to the regulations the Commission issues under the provisions of the FPA. . . . ■

NOTES AND COMMENTS

1. While proponents of dam removal have had little luck persuading FERC to order removal over the objections of relicensing applicants, they have had more success leveraging their opposition into dam removal agreements with project sponsors. American Rivers states that more than 100 dams have been removed in the 21st century, most through a series of voluntary agreements and commercial decisions. The FPA has always provided a mechanism for surrender of a hydroelectric license and several licenses are surrendered each year. Some are for projects that are no longer economical or technically feasible to run. Sometimes FERC will order dam removal as part of the surrender process. *See, e.g.*, FPL Energy Maine Hydro, LLC, 107 F.E.R.C. ¶ 61,120 (May 6, 2004) (order issued by FERC to further the objectives of the 1998 KHDG agreement, ordering the surrender of an existing license and a partial dam removal, with the licensee's agreement); *see also* Duke Energy Carolinas, LLC., 120 F.E.R.C. ¶ 61,054 (2007) (order accepting Duke Energy's surrender of a license on its Dillsboro Dam project pursuant to a similar agreement with stakeholders).

2. Dam removal proponents continue to focus on dams blocking other historic salmon runs like those on Columbia River basin in the Pacific Northwest. Environmental groups and others are seeking the removal of several dams on the Klamath and Snake Rivers in the Pacific Northwest. Relicensing proceedings in the northwest are even more contentious than those in the east, pitting developers, fishermen and Indian tribes, irrigation districts, farmers, environmental groups and resource agencies against one another in a Hobbesian war of all against all. *See* Holly Doremus & A. Dan Tarlock, Fish, Farms, and the Clash of Cultures in the Klamath Basin, 30 Ecology L.Q. 279 (2003) (detailing role played by ESA in fights over relicensing projects on the Klamath River); Michael C. Blumm et al., Symposium on Water Law: Saving Snake River Water and Salmon Simultaneously, 28 Envtl. L. 997 (1998). Following the Kennebec River model, a diverse set of interested parties have executed an agreement covering projects up for relicensing on the Klamath River. However, as reported in the New York Times, achieving unanimity in such a contentious atmosphere is difficult.

> Almost since the Bureau of Reclamation first began plumbing the Klamath River in 1906, creating a vast and fertile farming region out of arid southeastern Oregon and northeastern California, people have fought over what the river provides: water for farming, water to preserve one of the West Coast's largest salmon runs and a source of hydroelectric power.

> Then, suddenly, a truce was announced. In February 2010, after five years of confidential negotiation, an unlikely alliance of

American Indian tribes, environmentalists, farmers, fishermen, governors and the federal government signed the Klamath Basin Restoration Agreement.

The agreement was hailed as evidence of a new era in the West in which bitter divisions over natural resources could be bridged. Within a decade, it dictated, four dams would come down, enabling much of the river to flow freely and its once-mighty run of salmon to return. At the same time, farmers would be assured of water for their crops and affordable power. And Indian tribes would regain land lost decades ago.

Interior Secretary Ken Salazar said he had expected Congress to act that year to approve the agreement, known as the K.B.R.A., and to begin appropriating the more than $1 billion to carry out what he called "the largest river restoration project in the world."

Yet more than two years later, that has not happened, and it is unclear when, if ever, the agreement will be enacted.

William Yardley, Tea Party Blocks Pact to Restore a West Coast River, New York Times, July 18, 2012.

3.   Congress continues to debate whether to approve the Klamath River agreement. *See* S.2379—Klamath Basin Water Recovery and Economic Restoration Act of 2014. As of this writing the bill has not been reported to the floor of the Senate. For a comment on the agreement from the Tribes' point of view, see Thomas P. Schlosser, Dewatering Trust Responsibility: The New Klamath River Hydroelectric and Restoration Agreements, 1 Wash. J. Envtl. L. & Pol'y 42 (2011). For a broader review of the implications of the fight in the Pacific Northwest, see Michael C. Blumm & Andrew B. Erickson, Dam Removal in the Pacific Northwest: Lessons for the Nation, 42 Envtl. L. 1043 (2012).

4.   Is it possible for an agency to quantify and weigh the competing values of wild fish and electric power? Can environmental values be stated in dollars? Consider the following quote from the noted ecologist, Eugene P. Odum: "Money is related to energy, since it takes energy to make money. Money is a counterflow to energy in that money flows out of cities and farms to pay for the energy and materials that flow in. The trouble is that money tracks human-made goods and services but not the equally important natural goods and services. At the ecosystem level, money enters the picture only when a natural resource is converted into marketable goods and services, leaving unpriced (and therefore not appreciated) all the work of the natural system that sustains this resource." Eugene P. Odum, Ecology and Our Endangered Life Support Systems 105 (2d ed. 1993). As the quote from Odum indicates, our present systems of accounting assume that when we use a natural resource we are creating an asset, even though we are depleting the long-term supply of the resource. Many economists and accountants are debating ways in which our systems of cost accounting could be changed to take into account depletion of natural resources.

5.   The nature and extent of FERC's authority to require dam removal upon decommissioning has yet to be decided by the courts. Some dam operators have suggested that dam decommissioning may amount to a regulatory taking for which the licensees should be compensated. There is speculation as to how this exception would apply to dam decommissioning. Licensees

assert they have an interest in the hydro project lands, the physical structures, water use rights, and even the FERC license and should therefore be compensated if ordered to decommission a dam. However, it is difficult to say that there is a property interest in an expired license. A FERC license may be considered a "regulatory contract" between the licensee and the federal government. Existing FERC licenses may be regarded as property rights. But, once the license expires, the contract ends and the property right no longer exists. *See* United States v. Fuller, 409 U.S. 488 (1973) (taking of grazing land required no compensation for any value added to the lands by the permits). One court has held that the *Fuller* case is the relevant precedent if the federal government condemns a licensed hydroelectric project, so that the project is to be appraised as if its license will not be renewed. United States v. 42.13 Acres of Land, 73 F.3d 953 (1996). For a more detailed discussion of these limits, see Joseph Sax, Reserved Public Rights in Water, 36 Vt. L. Rev. 535 (2012).

6.   Hydropower project owners also do not have a property interest in the value of water power or the value of the land as a hydropower site. *See* Lewis Blue Point Oyster v. Briggs, 229 U.S. 82 (1913) (despite lessee's contrary interest, the Congress may pursuant to the Commerce Clause order dam removal without paying compensation); United States v. Chandler-Dunbar Water Power Co., 229 U.S. 53 (1913) (compensation not required for lost water use for power production when federal government condemned land in order to take navigable river flow for interstate commerce and revoked a hydropower license); *see also* United States v. Grand River Dam Auth., 363 U.S. 229 (1960) (the United States has a superior navigation easement that precludes private ownership of the water or its flow). But compensation for the condemnation of private riparian land was required in *United States v. Kelley,* 243 U.S. 316 (1917). *See* Comment, FERC's Dam Decommissioning Authority under the Federal Power Act, 74 Wash. L. Rev. 95 (1999); Katharine Costenbader, Damning Dams: Bearing the Cost of Restoring America's Rivers, 6 Geo. Mason L. Rev. 635 (1998).

7.   These contests are complicated further by the listing of several species of salmon as endangered under the ESA. Once a particular fish population has been listed as an endangered or threatened species under the ESA, the powerful sanctions of the Act begin to play a dominant role in the management of the river. Federal wildlife agencies need to sign off on federal projects or federal permits that affect the river. 16 U.S.C. § 1536. It becomes unlawful to "take" any such fish, 16 U.S.C. § 1538, including taking through habitat destruction. Palila v. Haw. Dep't of Land & Natural Res., 639 F.2d 495 (9th Cir. 1981). The management of the Columbia and Snake Rivers is now subject to very different legal rules than it was at the time the *Udall* case was decided. "The Columbia Basin is now awash with ESA listings of salmonids. No fewer than twelve Columbia Basin salmonid species are currently under ESA protection. [In 1990,] there were no salmonid listings at all. The ESA has assumed a dominant role in salmon law and policy in the basin." Michael C. Blumm & Greg D. Corbin, Salmon and the Endangered Species Act: Lessons from the Columbia Basin, 74 Wash. L. Rev. 519, 586 (1999); *see also* John M. Volkman, How Do You Learn From a River? Managing Uncertainty in Species Conservation Policy, 74 Wash. L. Rev. 719 (1999). Given the impact of dams on salmon migration routes, the National Wildlife Federation and other groups seek to use the ESA to compel removal of existing dams in the Pacific Northwest. *See* Nat'l Wildlife Fed'n v. Nat'l Marine Fisheries Serv., 422 F.3d 782 (9th Cir. 2005) (affirming federal

district court injunction holding that the National Marine Fisheries Service had violated the ESA when it issued a 2004 "biological opinion" that had formed the basis of the operating plans for the Federal Columbia River Power System.)

3.   HYDROKINETIC PROJECT DEVELOPMENT

Growing concern about climate change has provided an impetus for developing renewable energy projects, which in turn has spurred interest in hydrokinetic power projects. Hydrokinetic projects use wave energy or tidal/current energy to produce electricity. Wave energy technologies extract energy from the rise and fall of ocean waves and swells. The generator is either connected to a buoy or moored to the ocean floor, and uses the up-and-down motion of ocean swells to drive hydraulic pumps, or to move pistons that capture energy in compressed air. Tidal and current systems use underwater turbines to generate electricity. The turbines can be fixed to the floor of the ocean or river, or may be part of a water capture system that operates not unlike a pumped storage hydroelectric project. The DOE has produced a short video that explains the various hydrokinetic technologies simply and clearly, as part of its "Energy 101" series. DOE, Energy 101: Marine and Hydrokinetic Energy, http://www.youtube.com/watch?v=ir4XngHcohM & feature=youtu.be.

In *AquaEnergy Group, Ltd.,* 102 F.E.R.C. ¶ 61,242 (2002), FERC claimed jurisdiction, over the developer's objections, over the proposed Makah Bay Ocean Wave Energy Pilot Power Plant, off the coast of Washington State. AquaEnergy argued that its project was not a hydroelectric project as defined in the FPA. Section 4 of the FPA authorizes FERC to issue licenses for the purpose of constructing and operating "powerhouses, transmission lines, or other project works necessary and convenient for . . . the development, transmission, and utilization of power across, along, with, from, or in any of the streams or other bodies of water over which Congress has jurisdiction . . ."

Section 23(b) prohibits the construction or operation of any "dam, water conduit, reservoir, powerhouse, or other works incidental thereto across, along, or in any of the navigable waters of United States . . ." without a license. The Makah Bay Project, noted AquaEnergy, does not use dams or other conduits to drive water through a turbine, nor does it use a "powerhouse." FERC rejected these arguments, noting that the buoys used by the project will be attached to turbines, which will drive generators, and that these types of structures fall within the coverage of sections 4 and 23(b) of the FPA. FERC also rejected the developer's claims that the project, which was to be approximately 3 miles offshore, was not located in "navigable waters" as that term is used in the FPA. 102 F.E.R.C. ¶ 61,242 at P16–18; see Chapter 4 (discussing federal offshore jurisdiction).

After asserting jurisdiction over the Makah Bay Project, however, FERC initiated proceedings to develop a new process for licensing hydrokinetic projects that would better fit the needs of these new technologies. It concluded that the standard licensing process was inappropriate in many cases, since many proposed projects are experimental or pilot phase projects, for which some of the responsibilities within traditional licenses (e.g., 30 to 50 year terms) do not make sense. Instead, FERC proposed an "expedited pilot project licensing process," which would look not unlike the standard integrated licensing process, but with a shorter process timetable. This expedited process would be available only for hydrokinetic projects that are relatively small, environmentally noncontroversial, and that seek a shorter license term. *See* FERC, Licensing Hydrokinetic Pilot Projects, http://www.ferc.gov/industries/hydropower/gen-info/licensing/hydro kinetics/pdf/white_paper.pdf.

As of this writing, FERC has issued two 10-year licenses for pilot projects. In 2012 the agency issued a license to Verdant Power for its proposed 1,050 KW Roosevelt Island Tidal Project, located in the East River in New York City. Verdant Power LLC, 138 F.E.R.C. ¶ 62,049 (2012). Two years later, FERC issued its second 10-year license to P.U.D. No. 1 of Snohomish County, Washington for its 600 KW Admiralty Inlet Tidal Project located in Puget Sound. Notice that project capacity for both projects is expressed in kilowatts, not megawatts. P.U.D. No. 1 of Snohomish Cnty, Wash., 146 F.E.R.C. ¶ 61,197 (2014).

FERC has indicated that the ideal project for the pilot project licensing process would be (1) small, (2) short term, (3) located in environmentally non-sensitive areas based on the Commission's review of the record, (4) removable and able to be shut down on short notice, (5) removed, with the site restored, before the end of the license term (unless a new license is granted), and (6) initiated by a draft application in a form sufficient to support environmental analysis. The agency has also issued preliminary permits to hydrokinetic projects that are not yet ready for licensing. As of April 2014, seven such permits were in effect, five for tidal projects and two for wave projects.

Recognizing that offshore hydrokinetic developments, in particular, could require the approval of other agencies, (see the discussion of the coastal zone management and Outer Continental Shelf aspects of offshore oil and gas development in Chapter 4), FERC also declared its intention to issue "conditioned licenses" which will authorize hydrokinetic projects conditioned on the yet-to-be-obtained approval of other governmental agencies. The purpose of these conditioned licenses is to allow developers to secure financing and do other non-physical preliminary work for which no additional approvals are required; once all of the required additional approvals (including the 401 certification) are secured, the applicant must then secure a final approval from FERC before proceeding with the construction. In fact, FERC ultimately issued a conditioned license for the Makah Bay Project, over the objections of the Washington State Department of Ecology, which argued that case law prohibited conditioned licenses.

In 2012, FERC and the Department of Interior's Bureau of Ocean Energy Management (BOEM) issued joint guidelines for development of hydrokinetic projects on the outer continental shelf. The guidelines followed a 2009 Memorandum of Understanding (MOU) between BOEM and FERC. Both documents recognize that BOEM has jurisdiction to issue leases on the OCS for marine hydrokinetic projects, while FERC has jurisdiction to issue licenses for these same projects. *See* BOEM / FERC Guidelines on Regulation of Marine and Hydrokinetic Energy Projects on the OCS, http://www.ferc.gov/industries/hydropower/gen-info/licensing/hydrokinetics/pdf/mms080309.pdf. It remains to be seen whether this sharing of regulatory jurisdiction and dual approval process will prove unwieldy.

FERC's assertion of jurisdiction over hydrokinetic projects has not yet been reviewed by federal courts. However, because the FPA preempts state and local law, it is an important development, one with profound implications over the future regulation of hydrokinetic power. For more on hydrokinetic power and renewable generally, see Jon Wellinghoff & Dave Morenoff, Facilitating Hydrokinetic Energy Development through Regulatory Innovation, 29 Energy L.J. 397 (2008).

4. COMPETITION BETWEEN HYDROELECTRIC AND OTHER RENEWABLES

One increasingly common legal issue relating to hydroelectric power is the dispatching of hydroelectric power within a power system. As discussed in more detail in Chapter 10, grid operators are responsible for determining which electric generating plants should be "dispatched" (sent through the electric grid) to meet demand. Grid operators typically take the cheapest generation sources first, moving up the line to the next cheapest sources until all power needs are met. Other considerations also come into play, however. Some hydroelectric sources argue that they *must* produce a certain amount of power and send it through the grid at certain times of year. If the ESA or flood control measures mandate that a certain amount of water flow through the dam turbines, for example, managers of hydroelectric dams argue that their electricity production should not be curtailed. This issue has become increasingly complicated with the addition of yet another power source to the grid—intermittent wind and solar energy. In the Pacific Northwest, in particular, where both wind and hydroelectric power are abundant, battles have emerged between wind and hydroelectric providers both wanting to send power through the grid at the same time. Often, the transmission grid simply cannot support all of this electricity "traffic."

This type of battle was recently highlighted in a dispute involving wind generators and the Bonneville Power Administration (BPA), a federal entity. BPA owns and operates hydroelectric dams in the Pacific Northwest and a large network of transmission lines in this same region—including transmission lines that provide much-needed electricity to California markets. BPA had refused to allow wind generators to send electricity through its wires at certain times, citing the difficulty of maintaining a constant voltage in the transmission wires due to the intermittency of wind as well as the need to accommodate electricity from a variety of power sources, including wind, nuclear, and hydro, for example, within the wires. Wind energy companies filed a complaint with FERC, and FERC ordered BPA to revise its tariff—the set of rules that FERC requires BPA to follow. Specifically, BPA could not unduly discriminate against wind farms in the rates it charges for transmission service and the type of transmission service it provides, and it had to provide wind farms with transmission service comparable to the transmission service that BPA provides for its own hydroelectric power. Iberdrola Renewables, Inc. *et al.* v. FERC, 137 F.E.R.C. ¶ 61,185 (Dec. 7, 2011), http://www.bpa.gov/Projects/Initiatives/Oversupply/Oversupply Documents/OtherDocs/FERC-order-Dec7.pdf. Subsequent orders on rehearing confirmed this directive. The parties have since settled one portion of the case. For a summary of the settlement, see http://www.bpa. gov/news/newsroom/Pages/Energy-balancing-rate-settlement-signals-commitment-to-work-on-broader-solutions.aspx.

E. THE FUTURE OF HYDRO

Some see growth potential for hydropower in the emerging wave and tidal hydrokinetic technologies, the addition of capacity at federal dams, and in the use of pumped storage as a "clean" source of backup power for wind and solar (as is common in Europe). There is a tremendous amount of excitement about wave and tidal technologies in particular, and a great deal of experimentation is underway. We seem to be early in the learning curve, and perhaps technological great leaps forward are in our future.

Others are more skeptical. Hydrokinetic technologies are unproven, so far. Professor A. Dan Tarlock, one of the leading academic writers on hydroelectric licensing, argues that more conventional hydro development faces a number of important obstacles. Hydro is not carbon-free, in that dam reservoirs can be a source of carbon emissions. More importantly, we seem to be less willing to tolerate the other environmental costs associated with hydro development: hence the trend toward dam removals. A. Dan Tarlock, Hydro Law and the Future of Hydroelectric Generation in the United States, 65 Vand. L. Rev. 1723 (2012). Perhaps Europeans use pumped storage hydro to support wind because they have no cheaper alternatives. Use of pumped storage (or conventional reservoirs) to support wind or solar requires raising and lowering the reservoir frequently, which damages wetlands. Should we use hydro in that way when demand response or natural gas fired turbines can provide the same services?

Hydro's future is uncertain, but with more than 1,000 licensed projects (and additional exempted projects) still operating in the United States, it seems clear that hydro generation will remain a significant part of the energy mix.

CHAPTER 7

NUCLEAR ENERGY

A. Background on Nuclear Power
    1. Origins of Nuclear Power
    2. Governance: The Nuclear Agencies
    3. The Nuclear Fuel Cycle
    4. The First Generation of Nuclear Power Plants
    5. Changing Outlooks: The Industry Since 1979
B. Nuclear Safety and Risks
    1. Three Mile Island
    2. Chernobyl and Fukushima
C. Regulating Nuclear Power Plants
    1. New Reactor Licensing
        a. Early Site Permits
        b. Licensing Power Plant Designs
        c. Combined Operating License
        d. Current Issues in Reactor Licensing
    2. Incentivizing Reactor Construction
        a. The Cost of Nuclear Power
        b. EPAct 2005 Incentives
        c. Nuclear Power in Competitive Markets
    3. Decommissioning
D. Nuclear Wastes and Used Nuclear Fuel
    1. Uranium Mill Tailings
    2. Military Radioactive Waste
    3. Low-Level Radioactive Waste
    4. High-Level Radioactive Waste
        a. The Nuclear Waste Policy Act
        b. Implications of the Failure of the Yucca Mountain Project
            i.   The Blue Ribbon Commission's Report
            ii. The Nuclear Waste Fund and Breach of Contract Claims
            iii. Interim Storage Methods
            iv. The Waste Confidence Decision

Perhaps more than any other fuel source for electricity, nuclear power attracts attention for its place at the intersection of technological achievement, hope for combatting climate change, and a legacy of negative risk perception and strong opposition. As introduced in Chapter 1, nuclear power accounts for about 20% of electricity generation in the United States. Because nuclear fission is achieved by a chain reaction that is difficult to stop and start, nuclear power is particularly suited to supplying baseload generation. This feature of nuclear power promotes reliability, especially as intermittent renewable generation grows. (See Chapter 11.)

Nuclear power generation itself produces neither greenhouse gases (GHGs) nor criteria air pollutants like particulate matter, nitrogen oxides, and sulfur dioxide, making it an attractive source of baseload when compared to coal, oil, and natural gas. (*See* Chapter 5.) Indeed, the small carbon footprint of nuclear power makes it an important player in policy discussions regarding climate change mitigation. Refer back to the carbon wedge concepts in Chapter 1; recall that increasing nuclear generation is one of the wedge options. EPA's proposed Clean Power Plan, described in Chapter 5, also contemplates nuclear power as a means of reducing GHG emissions from the power sector. Even over the entire nuclear fuel cycle (which includes uranium mining and used fuel management), the carbon footprint of nuclear power is similar to that of renewables like hydropower and wind. *See, e.g.*, Dep't of Energy, Nat'l Renewable Energy Lab., Fact Sheet, Lifecycle Greenhouse Gas Emissions from Electricity Generation (2012), http://www.nrel.gov/docs/fy13osti/57187.pdf.

But the persistent challenge of nuclear power lies in the risks, both measurable and perceived, associated with radiation. These risks contribute to high construction costs for new reactors, high used-fuel and waste-management costs, and high transaction costs in the form of procedural requirements, stakeholder engagement, and political battles. Further, the nature of these risks makes the perception of nuclear power susceptible to "punctuating events," that is, events like Three Mile Island, Chernobyl, and Fukushima (see discussion below). Such punctuating events amplify already-present negative risk perceptions such that the costs of such events—whether on industry in the form of stricter measures or on society in the form of inefficient electric-fuel-supply choices—go well beyond the actual costs of the events themselves. *See* Paul Slovic, Perception of Risk, 236 Sci. 280, 283–84 (Apr. 17, 1987).

As you consider the legal and policy framework for nuclear power generation, ask yourself: How does nuclear power compare with other sources of fuel for electricity? Should it be easier, or harder, to add new nuclear generation capacity in the future? What should be done with nuclear waste? Is the existing, heavily federal, governance scheme the best way forward?

A. BACKGROUND ON NUCLEAR POWER

This chapter details the law and policy of civilian nuclear power generation; except where noted, issues specific to military uses (as well as other peaceful uses of nuclear power like nuclear medicine) are beyond the scope of this book. Nevertheless, the military roots of nuclear energy influence the legal and policy framework for nuclear power that exists today. Thus, we begin with a brief overview of that history.

1. ORIGINS OF NUCLEAR POWER

Nuclear energy in explosive form was first brought into being in the latter days of World War II, when the United States developed and used the atomic bomb against the Japanese cities of Hiroshima and Nagasaki.

In retrospect, these events made "environmental" concerns a serious domestic issue for the first time, as Judge Richard Cudahy recalls:

> In the war years, a healthy environment was one free of five hundred pound bombs and long-range artillery fire. There was a flickering of concern about radioactivity when A-bombs and H-bombs began exploding. In fact, I think in principle nuclear explosions raised the basic environmental question. Here was an awesome source of primal energy released by sophisticated human calculation, but spreading a whole battery of mysterious and severe health hazards in its wake.

Richard D. Cudahy, Coming of Age in the Environment, 30 Envtl. L. 15 (2000).

In the years immediately following the war, the United States was the only nation that had demonstrated its ability to create nuclear fission. The government hoped that it could maintain that monopoly, but it soon became apparent that the Soviet Union was also capable of producing nuclear weapons. As nuclear capabilities spread, the United States gave up hope of isolating nuclear technology and decided to encourage the spread of peaceful uses of nuclear energy. The "Atoms for Peace" program, initiated by President Eisenhower shortly after his election, was meant to deter nuclear weapons proliferation in exchange for sharing information worldwide.

2. GOVERNANCE: THE NUCLEAR AGENCIES

Responsibility for nuclear technology was originally vested in the Manhattan Engineer District of the U.S. Army Corps of Engineers. In a major victory for civilian uses, however, Congress created the Atomic Energy Commission (AEC) in 1946; this agency was the predecessor to both the Nuclear Regulatory Commission (NRC) and the Department of Energy (DOE). Consider the evolving roles of these agencies and their relationship to the development of nuclear power and policy:

> At its creation in 1946, the AEC was tasked with broad authority over the entire nuclear field; its mandate included developing nuclear energy, ensuring its safety, and developing the nation's nuclear-weapons arsenal. At the time, the AEC was the only agency with expertise in nuclear science and technology. In 1946, just after its creation, the AEC had "complete domination over atomic energy development in this country." Given the gravity of this subject matter, Congress chose a commission framework for the agency to ensure that such important powers were not concentrated in a single agency head. As a Senate report said, "The framers of the [1946 Act] deliberately established a five-man directorate, rather than a single administrator, to control our atomic enterprise for the very purpose of assuring that diverse viewpoints would be brought to bear upon issues so far reaching as those here involved." . . . Despite the civilian side of its mandate, the AEC was nevertheless largely occupied with military applications in its early years. Not until the passage of the Atomic Energy Act of 1954 did privately owned nuclear-fuel and production facilities become both possible and subject to the AEC's

regulation. . . . Indeed, a primary policy function of the AEC in the ensuing years was to encourage private industry to construct nuclear-power plants and thereby facilitate the emergence of that entire industry. But increasingly, this role seemed at odds with ensuring safety and environmental responsibility. . . . [T]he mixed mission of the AEC raised serious concerns that the agency was far too cozy with industry. Responding to concerns about this dual expert/policy function, Congress enacted the Energy Reorganization Act of 1974, which abolished the AEC and created three successor agencies. These included the NRC, tasked with licensing and regulation; the Energy Research and Development Administration (ERDA), tasked with research, development, and production; and the Federal Energy Administration, tasked with data collection and analysis. The last two were combined in 1977 to become the DOE. The legislative history of the split reveals particular attention to detail with respect to separating expertise and policy.

For example, Congress carefully delineated the NRC's licensing authority. The conference report emphasized Congress's intent that the NRC was to be responsible for licensing in an oversight role, as opposed to being responsible for developing research to support licensing in the first place: "The regulatory agency should never be placed in a position to generate, and then have to defend, basic design data of its own. The regulatory agency must insist on the submission of all of the data required to demonstrate the adequacy of the design contained in a license application or amendments thereto." . . .

A look at the functions of the ERDA reveals a contrasting broad focus on policymaking generally, as well as on the congressional desire that that administrator work directly with the president. Further, the DOE's authorizing statute reveals a purpose to develop a coordinated national energy policy and to assess energy-research priorities, among other policy-oriented goals.

Emily Hammond, Presidential Control, Expertise, and the Deference Dilemma, 61 Duke L.J. 1763, 1771–89 (2012).

As you study the laws governing nuclear power, consider whether Congress's institutional design choice—splitting AEC and ultimately forming NRC and DOE—meets the goals of separating expertise from policy. Notice too the lack of state involvement in nuclear power regulation. With its deep military roots, nuclear energy is perhaps the most federalized of all the fuels for electricity. Is that approach still justified? Finally, as the excerpted material above hints, the environmental externalities of nuclear power have attracted significant attention. But to what extent has the nuclear industry internalized those costs?

3. THE NUCLEAR FUEL CYCLE

Like oil, coal, and some gas-fired generation, nuclear power uses steam to turn turbines that generate electricity. The fuel cycle begins with uranium, which exists in nature primarily as two isotopes: U–238 and U–235. The latter is the most useful for nuclear chain reactions, but the former is far more prevalent in the environment. Thus, U–238 must be processed and then "enriched" to produce sufficient quantities of U–235 for commercial reactors. About 90% of the United States' supply of uranium comes from mines in other countries, but there are a few domestic mining facilities in America. The Office of Surface Mining, housed within the Department of the Interior, oversees conventional uranium mining in the United States. After the uranium is processed and enriched, it is converted into ceramic pellets. These pellets are loaded into fuel rods that comprise the final fuel assemblies. NRC has regulatory oversight responsibility at these latter steps.

At the heart of commercial nuclear power plants in the United States are reactor vessels, which house the fuel assemblies and in which nuclear fission takes place in a chain reaction. The chain reaction releases heat, which turns water to steam, drives a turbine, and generates electricity. In addition to being used for steam, water also helps moderate the chain reaction and cool the reactor. Cooling towers, which help condense steam back into water, are also prominent features of nuclear power plants. These plants include numerous and redundant design features meant to stop the chain reaction in emergencies, contain radiation, and protect the containment structure from being breached. The applicable standards, located in Title 10 of the Code of Federal Regulations, are constantly being updated. For example, following the September 11, 2001 terrorist attacks, NRC requires that reactors constructed after 2009 must be designed to withstand the impact of a fully loaded passenger jet without being breached.

Nuclear reactor fuel rod assemblies must be removed from reactors and replaced after about 18 months to 2 years. The assemblies are cooled initially in spent fuel pools, after which they are often moved to dry casks. These large, reinforced-concrete structures are housed either onsite at the nuclear power plant, or at dedicated temporary storage facilities across the United States. Although used nuclear fuel can be reprocessed and used again, this technology was banned in the United States beginning in the 1970s, amid concerns about nuclear weapons proliferation. The ban has been lifted, but the technology has not yet been developed in this country. The Nuclear Waste Policy Act maintains that permanent geological disposal in Yucca Mountain, Nevada, is the end point for the nuclear fuel cycle (see below). But that alternative has not come to fruition, and used nuclear fuel remains in temporary storage while policymakers assess other options. All told, over 70,000 metric tons of used fuel are in storage, and about 2,000 metric tons are added annually.

4. THE FIRST GENERATION OF NUCLEAR POWER PLANTS

In 1951, an experimental "breeder" reactor in Idaho powered four light bulbs and demonstrated to the world that nuclear power was an option for electricity generation. In 1954, the Soviet Union opened the first nuclear power plant connected to the electric grid; Britain and France quickly followed suit. As the excerpt above suggests, in the United States the federal government regulates all domestic uses of nuclear power under the Atomic Energy Act of 1954 (AEA), 42 U.S.C. §§ 2011 et seq. The AEA encouraged the private development of nuclear power, and two designs emerged as dominant in the United States: (a) boiling water reactors (BWRs), which typically heat water to a boil in a single loop to drive a steam turbine, and (b) pressurized water reactors (PWRs), which superheat water under pressure and use a heat exchanger to boil unpressurized water in a second loop, which in turn drives a steam turbine. Other designs flourished in other countries. "Heavy water reactors," which require less enrichment of uranium fuel, predominated in Canada. The former Soviet Union and Warsaw Pact nations employed the "RBMK" reactor designs, which use graphite rather than water to moderate the nuclear reaction, and which did not have a separate containment building around the reactor vessel. And while the United States did not pursue the commercial development of breeder reactors, which can produce more fissile material than they consume, some other countries (France, India, and several others) have.

Despite competition over reactor designs in the private sector, Admiral Hyman Rickover's efforts to design reactors to power the American Navy are credited with yielding the design of the first U.S. commercial nuclear power plant, which came on line in 1957 (a PWR system) in Shippingport, Pennsylvania, near Pittsburgh. Initial experience suggested that the cost of nuclear power would decline steadily with improvements in the technology. In the mid-1960s, optimistic supporters of nuclear power extrapolated that decline into the future and encouraged new construction in hopes of obtaining a cheap source of power to meet projected increased demand.

Power companies throughout the world rushed to jump on the bandwagon. From 1965 until 1975, they ordered almost 300 nuclear power plants. Companies in Japan, Sweden, Britain, France, Germany and Canada joined four big American companies in the race to build nuclear plants as fast as the orders could be filled. In the United States, nuclear power was seen as an important element in America's ability to maintain energy self-reliance. With existing and potential regional wars disrupting world trade, American industry was increasingly nervous about its growing reliance on oil that had to be imported from the Middle East. Throughout this period the United States was continuing to develop and test nuclear weapons. Moreover, other nations including the Soviet Union, China and France were actively testing such weapons.

In the United States, public reaction to nuclear power plants was initially positive, dominated by patriotic pride in American technology that submerged fears about accidental or hostile misuse of the power. As the public became aware of the long-range impact of radiation sickness on residents of Hiroshima and Nagasaki, however, the fear of nuclear power plants began to spread. NRC reacted to the growing doubts about the risks associated with nuclear power by repeatedly adding new safety requirements, which were often applied to plants already under construction. In addition, interested parties enjoyed numerous procedural protections during the licensing process. The delays accompanying NRC's substantive changes and the various procedural layers contributed to significant cost overruns, as described in more detail below.

5. CHANGING OUTLOOKS: THE INDUSTRY SINCE 1979

Two important events in 1979 dealt serious blows to the American nuclear power industry. The first was when Ayatollah Khomeni took power in Iran, leading to the "second oil shock," which reduced oil supplies and inflated the price of all energy sources, including electricity. This caused electricity users to institute conservation measures, thus reducing the demand for electricity. This in turn made some of the nuclear power plants under construction appear to be unnecessary, and a number of plants were canceled before they were completed. The second major event was the accident at Metropolitan Edison's Three Mile Island (TMI) nuclear power plant, near Harrisburg, Pennsylvania (discussed below), which brought extended media attention to the risks associated with the potential malfunction of nuclear power plants.

Other factors contributed to nuclear power's demise after 1979. The earlier rush to embrace nuclear technology produced economic factors that drove up costs. The shortage of trained labor led to enough faulty construction to scare even the most loyal advocates of nuclear power. And the dominance of a few firms limited competition and contributed to dramatic cost increases. *See* Robert J. Duffy, Nuclear Politics in America (University Press of Kansas, 1997).

The utilities were forced to raise electric rates sharply during this period, to cover both the costs of the nuclear plants and the rise in the prices of other fuels. Consumer resistance to these increases put great pressure on state utility commissions, which often forced utility shareholders—rather than ratepayers—to swallow expenditures for plants that went dramatically over budget or were never completed. The result was that many electric utilities were forced to cut dividends and face the wrath of both unhappy shareholders and unhappy customers. And their attempts to challenge state regulatory denials of rate increases under the Taking Clause of the U.S. Constitution proved largely fruitless after the Supreme Court's decision in *Duquesne Light Co. v. Barasch*, 488 U.S. 299 (1988). (As discussed in Chapter 6, that decision rejected a Takings Clause challenge to a state statute under which the costs of canceled nuclear power plants were excluded from utilities' rates, thus requiring the utlities and their shareholders to shoulder the costs of unused plants themselves without help from ratepayers.) *But see* Richard J. Pierce, Jr., The Regulatory Treatment of Mistakes in Retrospect: Canceled Plants and Excess Capacity, 132 U. Penn. L. Rev. 497, 517–21 (1984) (describing how some states permitted at least some recovery).

In a few short years, therefore, the utilities' attitude toward nuclear power went from sweet to sour. "The massive disallowances of utility investments in nuclear power plants dramatically changed utility incentives. The high perceived risk of future disallowances reversed utilities' incentives to overinvest, and made utilities extremely reluctant to build new power plants. Shareholders are not compensated for this risk through the allowed rate of return. Disallowances also place utility managers' jobs in jeopardy." Bernard S. Black & Richard J. Pierce, Jr., The Choice Between Markets and Central Planning in Regulating the U.S. Electricity Industry, 93 Colum. L. Rev. 1339 (1993).

By the end of the 1970s, over 120 new reactor orders in the United States had been cancelled. And in 1986, the Chernobyl disaster (see below) further intensified environmental opposition to nuclear power. In the next decades, only one new reactor was completed—the Tennessee Valley Authority's Watts Bar 1, which came online in 1996 but had been ordered in 1970.

Despite the sharp decline in reactor orders, since the early 1970s, nuclear power production in the United States has increased over 20% as plants have become more efficient. As of April 2014, NRC had approved 154 "uprates" in power, resulting in a cumulative increase of generating capacity equivalent to about 7 new reactors. *See* NRC, Backgrounder on Power Uprates for Nuclear Plants, http://www.nrc.gov/reading-rm/doc-collections/fact-sheets/power-uprates.html.   Further,   industry consolidations have created additional efficiencies. Average operating and maintenance costs for reactors have dropped, and increasing concerns about GHG emissions have all combined to promote the attractiveness of nuclear power. Indeed, as of 2013, 73 reactors had received 20-year license extensions from NRC, and dozens more had pending applications or announced their intentions to seek renewals. Finally, in 2012, NRC granted construction licenses for two new reactors in Georgia; as of 2014, 3 additional reactors were under construction and several other applications were pending. *See* Congressional Research Serv., Nuclear Power: Outlook for New U.S. Reactors, RL33442 (2007).

Three other factors have contributed to this resurgence in nuclear power. First, NRC streamlined its permitting process in 1989, and in 2002 DOE provided various incentives to would-be licensees, including an offer to pay up to half the licensing costs incurred by applicants. Second, as discussed below, Congress established several important initiatives in the Energy Policy Act of 2005 (EPAct 2005), including a nuclear tax production credit, regulatory risk insurance, and loan guarantees. Finally, the increasing urgency of climate change has drawn attention to nuclear power as an important non-emitting power generation option.

But countervailing considerations cannot be overlooked. First, the 2012 Fukushima Daiichi disaster in Japan (discussed below) provided a forceful reminder that risk can never be eliminated. It also prompted renewed efforts by various groups to oppose nuclear power. Second, the United States has so far been unable to implement its chosen policy option for spent nuclear fuel disposal—the Yucca Mountain Project (YMP)—which temporarily forced new reactor license applications to a halt. Finally, the nuclear industry is increasingly expressing concern about competition in restructured markets—from low-priced natural gas as well as from renewables like wind that have priority access to the grid. The Nuclear Energy Institute (NEI), an industry group, has warned that without significant market reforms, nuclear power plants will not be economically viable—and if baseload power plants are forced to shut down the reliability of the grid will be threatened. *See* NEI News Release, NEI Warns Wall Street Analysts of Flawed Electricity Markets (Feb. 13, 2014), at http://www.nei.org/News-Media/Media-Room/News-Releases/NEI-Warns-Wall-Street-Analysts-of-Flawed-Electrici.

What is the future of nuclear power?

B. NUCLEAR SAFETY AND RISKS

Of all the perceived risks of nuclear power, safety is perhaps the most salient. Humans and other animals are exposed to radioactivity in small amounts in everyday life from numerous sources, including cosmic rays, elements such as radon in the soil, consumer products, and medical procedures. But when radiation exceeds certain levels it can be very hazardous to health and even deadly. As radioactive material emits radiation it gradually loses its radioactive property. Some materials become safe within a matter of days, while other materials will remain dangerously radioactive for thousands of years. The safety of nuclear power is given high priority across the fuel cycle, and nuclear power has one of the best safety records of all the fuel sources for electricity. *See* Forbes, How Deadly is Your Kilowatt? We Rank the Killer Energy Sources (June 10, 2012), http://www.forbes.com/sites/jamesconca/2012/06/10/energys-deathprint-a-price-always-paid/. Still, three important incidents have shaped the regulatory landscape, technical specifications, management practices, and public opinion of nuclear power: Three Mile Island, Chernobyl, and Fukushima. This section provides a brief overview of those incidents.

While you read, keep in mind that in the United States, the AEA grants NRC exclusive authority to regulate the safety of nuclear facilities. Thus, as with hydroelectric licensing, federal law preempts state and local regulation of the safety of nuclear power. Although federal law governs nuclear power plant safety regulation, nuclear power plants must comply with state laws that are not safety-related. Indeed, Congress recognized that the electric industry was heavily regulated by state public utility commissions (PUCs), and intended to leave this regulatory system in place. As explored in Chapter 8, for example, a state PUC's decisions about what nuclear-related costs can be recovered from customers can have a significant impact on the viability of nuclear power in that state. But some states have sought other ways to discourage the construction of plants within their borders.

In *Pacific Gas & Elec. Co. v. Energy Resources & Development Comm'n*, 461 U.S. 190 (1983), the Supreme Court upheld a California law that conditioned nuclear plant construction on findings by the State Energy Resources Conservation and Development Commission that adequate storage facilities and means of disposal are available for nuclear waste. The court accepted California's avowed economic purpose as the rationale for enacting the statute, and held that the statute lay outside the federally occupied field of nuclear safety regulation:

> There is little doubt that a primary purpose of the Atomic Energy Act was, and continues to be, the promotion of nuclear power . . . [But] the promotion of nuclear power is not to be accomplished "at all costs." The elaborate licensing and safety provisions and the continued preservation of state regulation in traditional areas belie that. Moreover, Congress has allowed the States to determine—as a matter of economics—whether a nuclear plant vis-a-vis a fossil fuel plant should be built. The decision of California to exercise that authority does not, in itself, constitute a basis for pre-emption. Therefore, while the argument of petitioners and the United States has considerable force, the legal reality remains that Congress has left sufficient

authority in the States to allow the development of nuclear power to be slowed or even stopped for economic reasons. Given this statutory scheme, it is for Congress to rethink the division of regulatory authority in light of its possible exercise by the States to undercut a federal objective. The courts should not assume the role which our system assigns to Congress.

Id. at 221. Would a state's attempts to discourage nuclear power violate the dormant Commerce Clause? *See* Entergy Nuclear Vt. Yankee, LLC v. Shumlin, 733 F.3d 393 (2d Cir. 2013) (distinguishing *Pacific Gas* and holding Vermont statutes were preempted; dormant Commerce Clause challenge was not ripe). As you read the material that follows, note the tension between federal and state authority.

1.   THREE MILE ISLAND

In 1979, the United States experienced a nuclear power incident that continues to shape perceptions of the fuel source even today.

In re TMI Litigation

193 F.3d 613 (3d Cir. 1999).

■ MCKEE, J.: [Plaintiffs sued the owners, operators and contractors of the Three Mile Island nuclear power plant, alleging that they suffered neoplasms as a result of radiation released into the environment as a result of an accident at the plant. For background purposes, the court described the accident as follows:] What has been described as the "nation's worst nuclear accident" began at about 4:00 a.m. on Wednesday, March 28, 1979. Ironically, the "nation's worst nuclear accident" grew out of a minor malfunction, or transient that occurred in the nonnuclear part of the system. For some reason, several feedwater pumps, that normally drew heat from the pressurized water reactor's (PWR's) cooling water, shut-off automatically. The system was designed so that when the feedwater pumps tripped, the main turbine and electrical generator also tripped. Thus, by design, the turbine and generator tripped approximately one second later. Three seconds after the turbine tripped, the pressure in the reactor coolant system increased to a level that caused the power-operated relief valve (PORV) to open in order to release the pressure. When the PORV opened, the fission process in the reactor core automatically shut down. Consequently, the heat generation in the reactor core dropped to decay heat levels.

However, the PORV did not close as it should have when the system pressure was reduced to acceptable levels. Instead, it remained open for approximately 2 hours. Unfortunately, the personnel operating Unit 2 did not realize that the PORV had not closed. They believed that it had automatically closed when the system was depressurized. Because the PORV remained open, reactor coolant water flowed from the reactor coolant system into the reactor coolant drain tank, which is designed to collect reactor coolant that is released from the reactor coolant system through the PORV during power operation. The continued flow of reactor coolant water into the reactor coolant drain tank caused a safety valve to lift on the drain tank and a drain tank rupture disk to burst. This rupture disk burst allowed the reactor coolant water to be discharged directly into the reactor building, which overfilled along with its sump pumps. The reactor building sump pumps were on automatic and aligned with the auxiliary building sump tank. When the reactor building sump pumps overfilled, some coolant water was transferred to the aligned auxiliary building sump tank. For some reason, there was no rupture disk on the sump tank and reactor coolant water was discharged directly into the auxiliary building. The contaminated coolant water continued to flow from the reactor building into the auxiliary building for several days. Estimates of the amount of radioactive water discharged into the reactor and auxiliary buildings range from 700,000 gallons to 5,000,000 gallons.

Approximately 2 minutes into the accident, the emergency core cooling system ("ECCS") began pumping water into the reactor core. However, operations personnel, still believing that the PORV had closed, and therefore unaware that reactor coolant water was escaping from the reactor coolant system, turned off most of the water flowing to the core through the ECCS. They did so believing that they were preventing the reactor system from becoming filled with water—a condition they were required to prevent.

However, there was not enough coolant water being circulated through the reactor coolant system to cool the reactor core because reactor coolant water was being discharged into the reactor building. Consequently, the core reaction was producing more heat than the coolant system was removing, and the core began to heat up. The loss of reactor coolant water allowed the reactor core to become uncovered. Within three hours of the beginning of the accident, as much as two-thirds of the twelve-foot high core was uncovered. Temperatures reached as high as 3500 to 4000 degrees Fahrenheit or more in parts of the core during its maximum exposure.

About 2-1/2 hours into the accident, some of the fuel rods in the reactor cracked, releasing xenon and other fission product gases, which had accumulated in the fuel rod gap between the fuel and the cladding, into the coolant water. Over the next few hours, more fuel rods cracked, releasing radioactive iodine and cesium into the primary coolant water as well as additional noble gases.

A series of events then unfolded involving various reactions, valves and controls. The end result was that, nearly 10 hours into the accident, there was a sudden spike of pressure and temperature in the reactor building. Initially, the spike was dismissed as some type of instrument malfunction. However, operations personnel learned on March 29th that the spike was caused by the explosion of hydrogen gas in the reactor building. Fears of another hydrogen explosion developed when a hydrogen gas bubble was later found in the reactor system. Presumably, there was a concern that another hydrogen explosion would damage the reactor vessel, leading to further releases of radioactive material. However, the fears about another hydrogen explosion were later learned to be unfounded.

During the last days of March and the first week of April, operations personnel began to regain control and contain the radioactive releases caused by the accident. However, it was not until the afternoon of April 27, 1979 that stable conditions were finally established in TMI–2.

The parties generally agree that the radioactive fission products released to the environment as a result of the accident escaped from the damaged fuel and were transported in the coolant through the letdown line into the auxiliary building. Once in the auxiliary building, the radioactive fission products were released into the environment through the building's ventilation system. Because of the volatility of noble gases and radioiodines, those elements were the primary radionuclides available for release from the auxiliary building. Two krypton isotopes, 87 and 85, were not released in significant quantities because of the short half-life of 87Kr and because of the small amount of 85Kr in the reactor core. Nonetheless, despite the various filters, radioiodines were released. After the first day, the quantities of 88Kr and 135Xe were reduced by radioactive decay. All of the 133I contained in the coolant which was released to the auxiliary building eventually decayed to 133Xe and 133mXe. These radionuclides were the predominate ones released from the plant to the environment. TMI–2 also contained a treatment system, called the "liquid radwaste treatment system", which was designed to collect, process, monitor and recycle or dispose of radioactive liquid wastes prior to discharge to the environment. After the system processed the liquid radwaste, it was discharged into the Susquehanna River. However, because the primary coolant water flowed into the auxiliary building during the accident, the liquid radwaste treatment system was overwhelmed and radioactive materials were released to the Susquehanna River. The Nuclear Regulatory Commission's Special Inquiry Group concluded that the quantity of radioactive materials contained in the liquid released into the Susquehanna River was not significant. None of the plaintiffs here claim harm as a result of the releases of liquid radwaste into the river.

[In an exhaustive opinion, covering 116 pages in the Federal Reporter, the court affirmed the district court's grant of summary judgment in favor of defendants in regard to ten plaintiffs who had been selected as trial plaintiffs. It held that the district court properly excluded much of the plaintiffs' expert testimony under the standard set forth in *Daubert v. Merrell Dow Pharmaceuticals, Inc.*, 509 U.S. 579 (1993).] ■

NOTES AND COMMENTS

1. Public support for nuclear power was drastically reduced by the TMI accident. A thorough analysis of the TMI accident and its aftermath is found in J. Samuel Walker, Three Mile Island: A Nuclear Crisis in Historical Perspective (2004). See also Bonnie A. Osif et al., TMI 25 Years Later (2004). Although these and most other assessments of the impact of TMI have found no evidence of long-term health impacts, critics of nuclear power maintain that "remarkably few questions about the health effects of that near-catastrophe have been asked, let alone answered." Joseph Mangano, Three Mile Island: Health Study Meltdown, 60 Bull. Atomic Scientists 30 (2004).

2. In 1957, Congress passed the Price-Anderson Act, which caps the liability of private companies and provides federal reinsurance for the nuclear industry. The Act does not only limit liabilities arising out of any nuclear incident or precautionary evacuation, 42 U.S.C. § 2014(w); it also provides a mechanism for consolidating all claims in the nature of any "public liability action arising out of or resulting from a nuclear accident" in

a single federal court proceeding. 42 U.S.C. § 2210(n)(2). Congress extended these protections until the end of 2025 in § 602 of EPAct 2005.

3. The TMI accident focused attention on the issue of emergency evacuation of the area around a nuclear power plant in case of an accident. In 1980, Congress added new requirements for emergency evacuation plans as a condition for issuing power plant licenses. This new requirement led to a series of conflicts between utilities and nearby local governments, which hoped to prevent new plants from being constructed by refusing to participate in the evacuation planning process. The Shoreham nuclear plant on the south shore of Long Island, for example, was abandoned after completion because the local governments were unable to come up with an evacuation plan (and didn't want to). In New Hampshire, the Seabrook plant took so long to build that the company went bankrupt, although the plant is still in operation today. Neighboring states created construction delays for Seabrook by refusing to participate in evacuation planning.

Eventually, after additional legislation, NRC adopted the "realism doctrine," and concluded that the Commission could assume that each local government would really cooperate in the utility's evacuation plan if an emergency arose, even if the local government claimed that it wouldn't. NRC rules incorporating these assumptions were upheld in *Massachusetts v. United States*, 856 F.2d 378 (1st Cir. 1988). But even modernly, evacuation concerns are raised in policy debates. For example, these concerns have featured heavily in discussion regarding the proposed extension of Entergy's Indian Point nuclear power plant, located in the Hudson Valley in New York State. *See* Peter Applebome, Fukushima, Indian Point and Fantasy, N.Y. Times (Mar. 20, 2011) (arguing 50-mile evacuation radius would extend into most of New York City).

2. CHERNOBYL AND FUKUSHIMA

The accidents at the nuclear power plants in Chernobyl, Ukraine, in the former Soviet Union, and in Fukushima, Japan, have had wide-ranging impacts on nuclear power policy and regulation around the world. The following two excerpts briefly describe both accidents.

Backgrounder on Chernobyl Nuclear Power Plant Accident NRC Fact Sheet

(last updated May 2013).

Background

On April 26, 1986, a sudden surge of power during a reactor systems test destroyed Unit 4 of the nuclear power station at Chernobyl, Ukraine, in the former Soviet Union. The accident and the fire that followed released massive amounts of radioactive material into the environment.

Emergency crews responding to the accident used helicopters to pour sand and boron on the reactor debris. The sand was to stop the fire and additional releases of radioactive material; the boron was to prevent additional nuclear reactions. A few weeks after the accident, the crews completely covered the damaged unit in a temporary concrete structure, called the "sarcophagus," to limit further release of radioactive material. The Soviet government also cut down and buried about a square mile of pine forest near the plant to reduce radioactive contamination at and near the site. Chernobyl's three other reactors were subsequently restarted but all eventually shut down for good, with the last reactor closing in 1999. The Soviet nuclear power authorities presented their initial accident report to an International Atomic Energy Agency meeting in Vienna, Austria, in August 1986.

After the accident, officials closed off the area within 30 kilometers (18 miles) of the plant, except for persons with official business at the plant and those people evaluating and dealing with the consequences of the accident and operating the undamaged reactors. The Soviet (and later on, Russian) government evacuated about 115,000 people from the most heavily contaminated areas in 1986, and another 220,000 people in subsequent years.

Health Effects from the Accident

The Chernobyl accident's severe radiation effects killed 28 of the site's 600 workers in the first four months after the event. Another 106 workers received high enough doses to cause acute radiation sickness. Two workers died within hours of the reactor explosion from non-radiological causes. Another 200,000 cleanup workers in 1986 and 1987 received doses of between 1 and 100 rem (The average annual radiation dose for a U.S. citizen is about .6 rem). Chernobyl cleanup activities eventually required about 600,000 workers, although only a small fraction of these workers were exposed to elevated levels of radiation. Government agencies continue to monitor cleanup and recovery workers' health.

The Chernobyl accident contaminated wide areas of Belarus, the Russian Federation, and Ukraine inhabited by millions of residents. Agencies such as the World Health Organization have been concerned about radiation exposure to people evacuated from these areas. The majority of the five million residents living in contaminated areas, however, received very small radiation doses comparable to natural background levels (0.1 rem per year). Today the available evidence does not strongly connect the accident to radiation-induced increases of leukemia or solid cancer, other than thyroid cancer. Many children and adolescents in the area in 1986 drank milk contaminated with radioactive iodine, which delivered substantial doses to their thyroid glands. To date, about 6,000 thyroid cancer cases have been detected among these children. Ninety-nine percent of these children were successfully treated; 15 children and adolescents in the three countries died from thyroid cancer by 2005. The available evidence does not show any effect on the number of adverse pregnancy outcomes, delivery complications, stillbirths or overall health of children among the families living in the most contaminated areas.

Experts conclude some cancer deaths may eventually be attributed to Chernobyl over the lifetime of the emergency workers, evacuees and residents living in the most contaminated areas. These health effects are far lower than initial speculations of tens of thousands of radiation-related deaths.

US Reactors and NRC's Response

The NRC continues to conclude that many factors protect U.S. reactors against the combination of lapses that led to the accident at

Chernobyl. Differences in plant design, broader safe shutdown capabilities and strong structures to hold in radioactive materials all help ensure U.S. reactors can keep the public safe. When the NRC reviews new information it takes into account possible major accidents; these reviews consider whether safety requirements should be enhanced to ensure ongoing protection of the public and the environment.

The NRC's post-Chernobyl assessment emphasized the importance of several concepts, including:

- designing reactor systems properly on the drawing board and implementing them correctly during construction and maintenance;
- maintaining proper procedures and controls for normal operations and emergencies;
- having competent and motivated plant management and operating staff; and
- ensuring the availability of backup safety systems to deal with potential accidents.

The post-Chernobyl assessment also examined whether changes were needed to NRC regulations or guidance on accidents involving control of the chain reaction, accidents when the reactor is at low or zero power, operator training, and emergency planning.

The NRC's Chernobyl response included three major phases: (1) determining the facts of the accident, (2) assessing the accident's implications for regulating U.S. commercial nuclear power plants, and (3) conducting longer-term studies suggested by the assessment.

. . . The agency concluded that the lessons learned from Chernobyl fell short of requiring immediate changes in the NRC's regulations. ■

Backgrounder on NRC Response to Lessons Learned From Fukushima NRC Fact Sheet
(last updated Apr. 2014).

The Fukushima Dai-ichi Nuclear Accident

On March 11, 2011, a 9.0-magnitude earthquake struck Japan about 231 miles (372 kilometers) northeast of Tokyo off the Honshu Island coast. Eleven reactors at four sites (Fukushima Dai-ichi, Fukushima Dai-ni, Onagawa, and Tokai) along the northeast coast automatically shut down after the quake. Fukushima Dai-ichi lost all power from the electric grid, with diesel generators providing power for about 40 minutes. At that point an estimated 45-foot-high (14 meter) tsunami hit the site, damaging many of the generators. Four of six Fukushima Dai-ichi reactors lost all power from the generators. The tsunami also damaged some of the site's battery backup systems.

Units 1, 2 and 3 at Fukushima Dai-ichi were operating when the earthquake hit. Units 4, 5 and 6 were shut down for routine refueling and maintenance. One of Unit 6's diesel generators continued working, providing power to keep both Units 5 and 6 (at right in the photo) safely shut down. Steam-driven and battery-powered safety systems at Units 1, 2 and 3 worked for several hours (and more than a day in some cases). Those systems eventually failed and all three reactors overheated, melting their cores to some degree. The conditions in the reactors generated extreme pressure, causing leaks of radioactive gas as well as hydrogen. The hydrogen exploded in Units 1, 2 and 4, damaging the buildings and releasing more radioactive material from Units 1 and 2. Radioactive contamination spread over a large area of Japan, requiring the relocation of tens of thousands of people. The Japanese government has reopened a very limited area for residents to return to, but many communities remain off-limits. Japanese authorities eventually stabilized the damaged reactors with alternate water sources. Work continues to isolate the damaged reactors and radioactive contamination from the environment.

NRC's Short-Term Actions

The NRC's 24-hour Operations Center in Rockville, Md., began monitoring the situation shortly after the earthquake and tsunami occurred. The NRC's first focus was potential tsunami effects on California's nuclear power plants and other nuclear materials users on the West Coast and in Hawaii, Alaska, and U.S. Pacific Territories. By the afternoon of March 11 the agency had fully staffed the Operations Center and begun interactions with Japanese regulators. The NRC sent two experts that weekend to assist the U.S. Embassy in Tokyo. By March 14, the agency had sent additional staff to provide technical support to the U.S. Embassy and the Japanese government. The NRC maintained its presence at the U.S. Embassy through December 2011.

On March 16, the NRC, along with other U.S. government agencies, provided technical information supporting the U.S. Embassy's advisory for American citizens to avoid the area within 50 miles of Fukushima Dai-ichi. The 50-mile recommendation expired in October 2011. The NRC also ensured U.S. nuclear power plants took action to prepare for a Fukushima-like event. The NRC told its inspectors to independently assess each plant's level of preparedness. The inspections covered procedures to compensate for extensive onsite damage, loss of all alternating current power, and seismic and flooding issues, as well as procedures for dealing with a damaged reactor.

NRC's Long-Term Response

In April 2011 the Commission named a formal task force of senior NRC experts to examine information from the accident. The task force then reviewed NRC regulations to determine whether any actions were needed to ensure the safety of U.S. nuclear power plants. The task force's July 2011 report concluded U.S. reactors can continue operating safely while the NRC considers enhancements to existing safety and emergency preparedness requirements. The task force recommended a dozen broad enhancement areas for the Commission to consider. Later in 2011 the Commission approved staff proposals for prioritizing the specific actions suggested by the task force, as well as six additional topics related to the events at Fukushima.

The agency also created the Japan Lessons Learned Project Directorate, or JLD, to lead implementation of the task force recommendations. This approach lets the remainder of the agency focus on overseeing safety at operating reactors. The JLD's approximately 20 full-time employees work with experts from across the agency. The JLD is directed by a steering committee made up of NRC senior managers.

The agency issued three Orders in March 2012, requiring U.S. reactors to:

- Obtain and protect additional emergency equipment, such as pumps and generators, to support all reactors at a given site simultaneously following a natural disaster (pictured below).

- Install enhanced equipment for monitoring water levels in each plant's spent fuel pool.

- Improve/install emergency venting systems that can relieve pressure in the event of a serious accident (only for reactors with designs similar to the Fukushima plant).

The NRC strengthened the venting Order in 2013, requiring the vents to handle the pressures, temperatures and radiation levels from a damaged reactor. The revised Order also calls for plants to ensure their personnel could operate the vents under those conditions. As part of the same action, the staff is using the NRC's rulemaking process to consider filtering methods to prevent radioactive material from escaping containment in an accident. The staff is looking at new filter systems or a combination of existing systems.

The NRC has also asked all U.S. reactors to re-confirm their flooding and earthquake preparedness, as well as re-analyze their earthquake and flooding hazards. Other NRC activities include creating or revising rules related to maintaining key safety functions if a plant loses all alternating-current power, and several aspects of emergency preparedness. The NRC's website includes more information on Fukushima-related actions. ■

NOTES AND COMMENTS

1. The International Atomic Energy Agency (IAEA) maintains an International Nuclear and Radiological Event Scale (INES), which is a tool for communicating with the public, in a consistent and prompt manner, the safety significance of a nuclear event. *See* IAEA, The INES, http://www-ns. iaea.org/tech-areas/emergency/ines.asp. The classification system considers impacts in three categories: people and the environment, radiological barriers and controls, and "defence-in-depth," which refers to events that did not impact the first two categories but for which accident-prevention measures did not properly function. *Id.* The scale ranges from a low of 0 (no safety significance) to a high of 7 (major accident). TMI was rated at 5—an accident with wider consequences—because of damage to the reactor core. Chernobyl and Fukushima were both rated at 7. Despite having the same INES rating, what were the differences between Chernobyl and Fukushima?

2. In the aftermath of Chernobyl and Fukushima, many wondered whether similar accidents could happen in the United States. The Chernobyl reactor design was an RBMK-design (referring to a light, water-cooled, graphite-moderated reactor). This design, which includes flammable graphite and produces weapons-grade plutonium in addition to electricity, is far less stable than those approved for use in the United States. Further, the reactor did not have a steel-reinforced containment structure, which is a requirement in the United States. In short, the RBMK design could not be licensed in this country.

But could natural disasters cause problems even for well-designed reactors? Fukushima brought such concerns to the forefront of safety discussions in the United States. Older cases had rejected challenges to specific licensing decisions grounded in concerns about seismology. E.g., Ohio v. NRC, 814 F.2d 258 (6th Cir. 1987); Carstens v. NRC, 742 F.2d 1546 (D.C. Cir. 1984). After Fukushima, NRC convened a task force to review NRC regulations and determine whether new measures needed to be taken to ensure the safety of domestic plants. The task force concluded there was no immediate risk to U.S. power plants, but it issued a series of recommendations for NRC's consideration. *See* Recommendations for Enhancing Reactor Safety in the 21st Century: The Near-Term Task Force Review of Insights from the Fukushima Dai-ichi Accident (July 12, 2011), http://www.nrc.gov/reactors/operating/ops-experience/japan-info.html. On March 12, 2012, NRC adopted new requirements for power plant safety and requested each reactor to reevaluate the site-specific seismic and flooding hazards using present-day methods. NRC, Order Modifying Licenses with Regard to Requirements for Mitigation Strategies for Beyond-Design-Basis External Events, EA–12–049 (Mar. 12, 2012); *see also* Emily Hammond, Nuclear Power, Risk, and Retroactivity, ___ Vand. J. Transnat'l L. ___ (forthcoming 2015) (providing critical assessment of Fukushima response).

3.   The type of reactor involved in the Chernobyl accident is still in use in parts of the former Soviet Union today. *See* ASME, Chernobyl 25 Years Later, https://www.asme.org/engineering-topics/articles/nuclear/chernobyl-25-years-later. Japan, on the other hand, closed dozens of reactors following Fukushima, despite that the country had, prior to the accident, relied on nuclear power for 30% of its electricity. Brian Walsh, Japan Mulls Nuclear Revival Not Even 3 Years after Fukushima, Time (Feb. 25, 2014). Other countries, such as Germany, began to dial back their nuclear power operations and plans as well. But in 2014, the Japanese Prime Minister announced an energy plan that envisioned restarting many of the shuttered plants. Economics played a role: without nuclear, Japan increased its imports of oil and natural gas, leading to a $204 billion trade deficit. *Id.* Further, electricity costs and CO_2 emissions in Japan both increased significantly following the nuclear shutdown. *Id.* Though Germany continues to denuclearize, China, India, and smaller emerging countries like Turkey and Poland are contributing to an overall small, but increasing growth trend for nuclear power—as is the United States, discussed below. *Id.*

4.   Should the world be more cautious about nuclear power? Even if Chernobyl was primarily design-related, TMI illustrated the cost of human error while Fukushima revealed the force of natural disasters. How might such risks be mitigated?

C. REGULATING NUCLEAR POWER PLANTS

1. NEW REACTOR LICENSING

All 100 nuclear reactors in operation as of 2014 were licensed by NRC under 10 C.F.R. part 50. Under this process, an applicant obtained (1) a construction permit authorizing construction of a new nuclear power plant; and (2) a license to operate the new plant. This two-step process did not always work as envisioned. Many in the nuclear power industry criticized part 50 because issues they thought were resolved in the construction permit stage were reopened in the operating permit stage. The licensing process was inefficient, and cost overruns were frequent where finality on issues such as design, safety, and construction were not reached until the applicant had already designed and built the reactor.

Parties opposed to constructing new plants also criticized the part 50 process. They contended that the window of opportunity to raise issues either came too early during the construction permitting stage, when not much was known about the final design, or far too late when the plant was nearly ready to operate. Last-minute concerns involving adequacy of an emergency plan, safety concerns with operation, quality of construction, and many other issues put both sides at risk of either missing the ability to challenge or, conversely, the ability to resolve such issues earlier in the process.

In response to numerous urgings from industry and Congress, and with a keen awareness that change was needed if new reactors were ever to be built in the United States again, in 1989 the NRC adopted a new reactor licensing process. 10 C.F.R. part 52; *see* Nuclear Info. Res. Serv. v. NRC, 969 F.2d 1169 (D.C. Cir. 1992) (en banc) (upholding part 52).

Underlying part 52 is the simple aim of standardizing the licensing process. With few limited exceptions, issues resolved at each standardized stage cannot be revisited at any other stage in the licensing process. Importantly, part 52 sets forth the policy that safety and environmental issues are to be resolved early on in the licensing process. Meanwhile, an applicant to build a new reactor could still apply using the traditional two-step approach under part 50.

Under part 52, new reactor licensing is divided into three standardized licenses: the Early Site Permit (ESP), the Design Certification (DC), and the Combined Operating License (COL). Procedurally, part 52 defines each standardized stage, what types of legal challenges ("contentions") can be raised at each stage, and how the stages interact with each other throughout the licensing process. Courts have upheld this licensing scheme against challenges that it violates the AEA. See Nuclear Info. Resource Serv. v. NRC, 969 F.2d 1169 (D.C. Cir. 1992); Nuclear Info. Resource Serv. v. NRC, 918 F.2d 189 (D.C. Cir. 1990).

Although promulgated in 1989, it wasn't until additional regulatory and statutory incentives (see below) were put into place that part 52 was used. As of this writing, part 52 has been partially tested through a handful of completed DCs, four issued ESPs, and many COL reviews still underway. With a refined understanding of part 52, NRC promulgated comprehensive amendments to the rule in 2007. 72 Fed. Reg. 49,351 (Aug. 28, 2007). Despite these recent changes, many in the industry remain skeptical of the new licensing process. Numerous parties on both sides of the table continue to point out potential, preventable, and unjustified burdens. Thus, persistent yet divergent urging for more comprehensive reform continues to burden NRC with the impossible task of making all parties happy.

As you read about the components of part 52 below, keep in mind that NRC is tasked with promoting security, safety, and environmental protection not just under the AEA, but also under the National Environmental Policy Act of 1969 (NEPA). NRC's regulations for implementing NEPA are located at 10 C.F.R. part 51. Licensing any nuclear facility is considered a "major federal action," which triggers the need for an Environmental Impact Statement (EIS). (For a detailed discussion of NEPA, see Chapter 6.) Under both the AEA and NEPA, final agency actions are subject to judicial review. Further, these actions are reviewable under the Administrative Procedure Act (APA), which itself provides a cause of action against federal agencies for failure to comply with, among other things, various procedural and substantive requirements. Litigants often allege violations of all three statutes—the AEA, NEPA, and the APA—when they challenge NRC's actions. You will see several examples in the materials that follow.

Finally, it is helpful to note that NRC has made changes to its hearing procedures. These changes again reflect a move toward procedural efficiency by streamlining the hearing process. NRC's procedures are located in 10 C.F.R. part 2. Until 1989, reactor licensing procedures were very formal, meaning they resembled a judicial trial. However, such procedures are often criticized (not just in energy law) for being too time-consuming and inflexible. Thus, NRC amended its regulations to provide for less-formal reactor licensing procedures, and changed the available mechanisms for participation. For example, the new procedures limited opportunities for cross-examination and the variety of discovery tools. Antinuclear groups unsuccessfully challenged the rulemaking as contrary to NRC's mandate in the AEA in *Citizens Awareness Network v. NRC*, 391 F.3d 338 (1st Cir. 2004).

Procedurally, most reactor licensing matters are presided over by an official from the Atomic Safety & Licensing Board Panel (ASLBP, ASLB, or the Board), which is an independent, trial-level adjudicatory body within NRC. The Board manages the proceeding, rules on evidentiary matters and other motions, and issues a preliminary decision. Its decisions may be appealed to the full Commission. Final decisions of NRC may be appealed to the U.S. Courts of Appeal. See 10 C.F.R. part 2; NRC, The Hearing Process, http://www.nrc.gov/about-nrc/regulatory/adjudicatory/hearing-pro.html.

a.   EARLY SITE PERMITS

Under the traditional two-step approach of part 50, all new power plant applicants had to undergo a safety and environmental review by NRC staff. The Safety Analysis Report (SAR) was the applicant's primary document assessing the safety requirements needed for issuing a construction permit. The SAR evaluated all safety characteristics related to siting such as emergency planning, site geography, and site stability. Any related challenges could be raised during the construction permitting stage. But because another complete safety review was also conducted before issuing an operating license, all siting criteria related to safety could be challenged again at that stage. The multiple opportunities to challenge such issues contributed to cost overruns and delays for would-be license holders.

The ESP process is meant to resolve safety, environmental, and emergency preparedness issues related to siting before an applicant commits resources to construction. Therefore, whenever an ESP holder subsequently applies for a COL it can simply reference an already approved ESP with regard to all siting issues related to that particular site in the COL application. Except in very limited circumstances, parties contesting a COL application referencing an ESP cannot challenge any site-related characteristics. 10 C.F.R. § 52.39. It is important to note, however, that an ESP is optional: an applicant can skip the ESP process and take up siting issues in conjunction with an application for a COL.

Once an ESP is issued for a specific site, the holder of the ESP may "bank" that site for future construction of a new nuclear power plant. The ESP is valid 10 to 20 years from the date it is issued, and may be renewed for an additional 10 to 20 years. Thus, an applicant can file for an ESP long before filing for a COL. As of mid-2014, NRC had issued 4 ESPs, and was reviewing one additional application (another, submitted in 2010, was withdrawn in fall 2012). For updates, see NRC, http://www.nrc.gov/reactors/new-reactors/esp.html.

With so few ESP applications having been filed, experience is limited, but the following observations can be made about how the process has worked. First, like most nuclear reactor licensing, EPSs have been strongly opposed by citizens, public interest groups, and anti-nuclear organizations in particular. In each of the proceedings for the 4 granted ESPs, such parties intervened and raised many concerns, termed "contentions," involving technical issues, NEPA, and environmental justice.

Of the many safety-related contentions raised, the Board held very few to be admissible, either because the applicant had thoroughly addressed issues related to siting in its safety report, or because the Board found that the contention did not relate to siting. Several environmental contentions involving siting were ruled to be admissible, however. One set of issues—relating to whether NRC's analysis of alternative energy sources satisfied NEPA's requirements—made its way to the Seventh Circuit Court of Appeals.

Environmental Law & Policy Center v. NRC

470 F.3d 676 (7th Cir. 2006).

■ PFLAUM, J. . . . Federal Guidelines require any entity commencing construction of a nuclear power plant to obtain a construction permit and an operating license. Permit applicants must submit information related to the plant's design, a safety assessment of the site, and a report that assesses the environmental impact of the plant's construction and operation. After reviewing a permit application, the NRC prepares an Environmental Impact Statement ("EIS") for the construction permit. If an entity is not yet ready to construct a nuclear power plant but desires to seek early approval for a potential construction site, NRC regulations permit the person to apply for an ESP. The ESP application process resolves key site-related safety, environmental, and emergency preparedness issues before the NRC authorizes (or declines to authorize) construction on that site. If granted, the ESP allows an applicant to maintain a site for possible future construction of new nuclear power facilities for up to twenty years. Moreover, an applicant may renew the ESP for an additional twenty-year term. However, an ESP does not authorize the holder to construct a nuclear plant. NRC regulations require applicants to obtain additional permits before commencing such construction. Under 10 C.F.R. § 52.17 and § 52.18, an ESP applicant must submit a complete environmental report and the NRC must issue an EIS that addresses all issues NEPA identifies regarding the construction and operation of a nuclear power plant on the proposed site, but a project's benefits need not be discussed at the ESP stage. If the benefits are not discussed, they must be evaluated at later permit or licensing stages before construction may begin.

. . .

In this case, Exelon Generation Company ("Exelon") applied for an early site permit (ESP), seeking approval for the construction of one or two new nuclear reactors on an existing Clinton nuclear power station site. Exelon is a merchant generator, which means that it sells power on the open wholesale market. Unlike a traditional regulated utility, Exelon is not required to supply the energy needs of any particular area. In its ESP application, Exelon stated that it sought to reserve the proposed site for future large-scale, baseload nuclear energy generation; that is, the creation of new energy intended to continuously produce electricity at or near full capacity, with high availability. Exelon intended to sell any new energy it generated on the open wholesale market.

Exelon evaluated alternative sources in terms of their ability to produce a baseload power equivalent to the amount of electricity that the proposed nuclear facility would produce. In its initial report, Exelon evaluated wind power coupled with energy storage mechanisms, solar power coupled with energy storage mechanisms, fuel cells, geothermal power, hydropower, burning wood waste or other biomass, burning municipal solid water, burning energy crops, oil-fired plants, coal-fired plants, and natural gas-fired plants. The report concluded that several of the alternatives were not viable baseload energy alternatives because, for example, they involved insufficiently matured technology (fuel cells) or the state lacked sufficient available fuel supplies (geothermal power, hydropower, woodwaste, and biomass). The report stated that wind and solar power, by themselves, were not reasonable baseload alternatives because they are intermittent energy sources and therefore cannot maintain continuous full rated capacity (the sun is not always shining, and the wind is not always blowing). In addition, the report concluded that power generated from natural gas and coal had greater environmental impacts on air quality than a nuclear plant.

. . .

Exelon [also provided a revised] report evaluating facilities that combined wind or solar power with fossil fuel. Exelon's revised evaluation concluded that coal-fired facilities, gas-fired facilities, or facilities using a combination of these alternatives were not environmentally preferable to the proposed nuclear facility, because the combination would produce environmental impacts greater than or equal to a new nuclear facility.

After reviewing the submitted information, the NRC issued a draft EIS, which evaluated a wide range of reasonable alternatives to nuclear baseload energy. The draft EIS reached conclusions similar to those reached by Exelon. Specifically, the draft EIS found that individual wind and solar facilities were not sufficient on their own to generate baseload power. The draft EIS also concluded that, from an environmental standpoint, the nuclear facility would be preferable or equivalent to a combination facility using wind or solar power and fossil fuel. The draft also concluded that a new nuclear unit was preferable in terms of air resources, ecological resources, water resources, and aesthetics.

After the NRC issued the draft EIS, . . . the board granted summary disposition . . . in favor of Exelon and terminated the contested portion of the ESP proceeding. The [plaintiff] Environmental Groups then appealed the Board's decision to the NRC. The NRC affirmed the Board's ruling, and the Environmental Groups appealed.

II. Discussion

[In **Part A** of the court's opinion, it held that it had jurisdiction to consider the Environmental Group's appeal.]

B. Failure to Consider Energy Efficiency

. . .

This Court's review of agency action under NEPA is governed by the Administrative Procedure Act ("APA"). The APA instructs courts to set aside agency action only if it is "arbitrary, capricious, an abuse of discretion, or otherwise not in accordance with the law." . . . This Court cannot substitute its own judgment for that of the agency as to the environmental consequences of its actions. In fact, in applying the arbitrary and capricious standard, this Court's only role is to ensure that the agency has taken a hard look at environmental consequences.

The Environmental Groups challenge two aspects of the Board's decision to decline consideration of energy efficiency alternatives. First, they contend that the Board unnecessarily excluded reasonable alternatives like energy efficiency measures by adopting Exelon's goal of generating baseload energy. In any case, the Environmental Groups argue that the Board should have considered energy efficiency alternatives in a "need for power" analysis—an analysis that the Board refused to conduct altogether.

The Environmental Groups claim that the Board's rejection of reasonable energy efficiency alternatives is contrary to the "searching inquiry into alternatives" required by NEPA. We have held that blindly adopting the applicant's goals is "a losing proposition" because it does not allow for the full consideration of alternatives required by NEPA. NEPA requires an agency to "exercise a degree of skepticism in dealing with self-serving statements from a prime beneficiary of the project" and to look at the general goal of the project rather than only those alternatives by which a particular applicant can reach its own specific goals.

. . . The Environmental Groups argue that . . . the Board "stacked the deck" against reasonable alternatives by adopting Exelon's limited business purpose of generating baseload power. According to the Environmental Groups, this purpose favors Exelon's proposed new nuclear plant by rendering energy efficiency alternatives inconsistent with the project's goal.

. . .

The Board's decision relied on case law supporting the proposition that a reviewing agency can take an applicant's goals for a project into account. For example, in Citizens Against Burlington, Inc. v. Busey, the court noted that an agency's evaluation of reasonable alternatives is "shaped by the application at issue." 938 F.2d 190, 199 (D.C.Cir.1991). The Board also noted that where a federal agency is not the sponsor of a project, the "consideration of alternatives may accord substantial weight to the preferences of the applicant and/or sponsor in the siting and design of the project." City of Grapevine v. Dep't of Transp., 17 F.3d 1502, 1506 (D.C.Cir.1994).

We are persuaded by the Board's analysis. Because Exelon was a private company engaged in generating energy for the wholesale market, the Board's adoption of baseload energy generation as the purpose behind the ESP was not arbitrary, capricious, an abuse of discretion or otherwise not in accordance with law. See APA § 706(2)(A). The adopted purpose was broad enough to permit consideration of a host of energy generating alternatives. Moreover, it was reasonable for the Board to conclude that NEPA did not require consideration of energy efficiency alternatives when Exelon was in no position to implement such measures. The Environmental Groups further contend that the Board should have independently analyzed energy efficiency alternatives, regardless of the project's stated purpose because NEPA requires consideration of the need for power as part of any alternatives analysis. The NRC responds that the Board equated analysis of energy efficiency alternatives to a "need for power" analysis and that under NRC regulations 10 C.F.R. §§ 52.17(a)(2) and 52.18, Exelon and the NRC did not need to conduct a "need for power" analysis at the ESP stage. Instead, the Board reasoned, it could defer that analysis until a later combined licensing proceeding.

Under NRC regulations, an applicant may defer an analysis of the need for power until a combined license application, when construction will be authorized. See 10 C.F.R. § 52.21. Because an ESP does not authorize construction, the evaluations conducted at the ESP stage are intended to provide early resolution to some—but not all—of the environmental issues. 10 C.F.R. §§ 52.79(a)(1) and 52.89 (stating that "any significant environmental issue not considered" at the ESP stage must be addressed when the holder of an ESP applies to commence construction). Although the Environmental Groups contend that the NRC regulations violate NEPA, the agency regulations at issue are not inconsistent with the environmental law, because all relevant issues will eventually be considered. Courts have permitted agencies to defer certain issues in an EIS for a multistage project when detailed useful information on a given topic is not "meaningfully possible" to obtain, and the unavailable information is not essential to determination at the earlier stage. In this case, it is especially reasonable to defer the "need for power" analysis to a later stage considering that construction on the nuclear reactor could begin as late as forty years from now. The need for power could vary considerably over that time period, so any analysis at this stage is speculative at best. The NRC, in its broad discretion to implement procedural rules under the APA, see, e.g., Vermont Yankee Nuclear Power Corps. v. Natural Res. Def. Council, Inc., 435 U.S. 519, 543–44, (1978), deferred analysis that would be merely speculative at such an early stage. That decision was not arbitrary, capricious, an abuse of discretion, or otherwise not in accordance with the law. We therefore affirm the NRC's dismissal of the Environmental Groups' energy efficiency contention.

C. Summary Disposition of Contention 3.1
[Clean Energy Alternatives]

The final claim that the Environmental Groups advance is that the Board should not have granted summary disposition in favor of Exelon regarding [clean energy alternatives]. The Environmental Groups argue that the NRC should have held a full evidentiary hearing in order to conduct a rigorous exploration and objective evaluation of clean energy alternatives and should have considered the comparative costs of the nuclear plant and the clean energy alternatives. They also claim that the NRC violated NEPA by distorting the combinations of clean energy alternatives.

It is true that NEPA requires an agency to "rigorously explore and objectively evaluate all reasonable alternatives," 40 C.F.R. § 1502.14(a), and to take a "hard look" at the environmental impacts of the proposed action and its alternatives. However, "it is not our role to second-guess. We merely consider whether the [agency] followed required procedures, evaluated relevant factors and reached a reasoned decision." The Environmental Groups' claims regarding clean energy alternatives go to the substantive judgments made by the Board and the NRC—judgments this Court will defer to as long as they satisfy NEPA procedures and are not clearly wrong.

The Board's 57-page memorandum and order granting summary disposition in favor of Exelon demonstrates that the Board rigorously explored all reasonable alternatives and took a hard look at the environmental impacts of the proposed action. The Board addressed the Environmental Groups' concerns point by point, carefully considering each issue and providing reasons for each decision it made. It is unnecessary to repeat the Board's analysis here. Whether or not this court would have made the same substantive judgment is irrelevant so long as the decision is not arbitrary. It is clear that the Board satisfied NEPA's procedural requirements and rendered a decision that thoughtfully considered all reasonable alternatives. We therefore affirm the decisions of the Board and the NRC.

III. Conclusion

For the foregoing reasons, we AFFIRM the NRC and its Board on all matters. ∎

NOTES AND COMMENTS

1.   Why did Exelon's purpose, baseload generation, matter for obtaining an ESP? See 42 U.S.C. § 4332 (requiring consideration of reasonable alternatives as part of EIS). By characterizing the project purpose as baseload generation, was Exelon able to narrow the possible reasonable alternatives?

2.   As the Seventh Circuit held, the need for power is an issue that can be considered at the COL stage of the process. Were you convinced by the court's reasoning? If Exelon waits to consider the need for power until it decides to pursue a COL, has it robbed itself of the benefit of the streamlined licensing procedures?

Some commentators argue that the NRC's desire to streamline and standardize licensing proceedings is in conflict with the purpose of NEPA and the NRC. Vincent Manapat, Seeking An Informed Decision: Early Site Permits And Energy Alternatives In *Environmental Law And Policy Center v. United States Nuclear Regulatory Commission*, 19 Vill. Envtl. L.J. 335, 338 (2008). Will issues similar to those presented in the above case make ineffective the NRC's streamlined process of new reactor licensing? Did the court weaken NEPA's effectiveness by allowing the Board to interpret the new streamlined regulations in a way that narrowly construes the purpose of the EIS in a licensing proceeding? Is one of NRC's core purposes of promoting human health weakened when the reach of the EIS is contracted? How deliberate should the NRC be when deciding on such issues in light of the costs and relative burdens? These environmental concerns and others like them will continue to be at the heart of the debate over the legitimacy and legality of the new ESP process.

3.   What role did restructured wholesale markets play in this case? Given that Exelon is a merchant generator, how would you expect the need-for-power analysis to be different if Exelon were a regulated utility? Whose interests does the need-for-power analysis protect? For further discussion, see Chapter 10.

4.   One other important regulatory change with respect to ESPs is an amendment to the Limited Work Authorization (LWA) process under 10 C.F.R. § 50.10. The purpose of the LWA is to allow an applicant to commence certain defined and limited pre-construction activities before the issuance of a construction permit or a COL. The limit is based on what activities on a site could be easily negated by restoring a site to its original condition. Under the traditional two-step approach, construction permit applicants could be approved to perform limited pre-construction activities before the permit was obtained. Under the new approach, NRC expanded the LWA in two ways. First, under the amended regulation ESP holders may obtain an LWA without applying for a COL. Second, NRC expanded the definition of the word "construction" in the new LWA regulation to include a broader array of pre-construction activities.

    What is the practical effect of these changes? In August 2009, Southern Nuclear Operating Co. ("Southern Company") became the fourth applicant (Exelon Corporation's Clinton Plant, Entergy's Grand Gulf Plant and Dominion's North Anna Plant were the first three) to receive an ESP from the NRC for its Vogtle site, located in Georgia. However, Southern Company was the first applicant to receive a technology-specific ESP (that is, siting issues were considered in the context of a specified reactor design) and an ESP that included a LWA. The LWA allowed limited construction to begin on the reactors, including placing backfill and constructing retaining walls, prior to Southern Company's receipt of its COL. The Company received its COL in 2012, and expects operations to begin in 2017 and 2018.

b.   LICENSING POWER PLANT DESIGNS

    In developing the part 52 procedures, NRC recognized that design issues needed significant attention for three main reasons. First, significant advancements in reactor design technology had taken place since the construction of the reactors currently operating in the United States. Second, the older two-step approach allowed identical design issues to be questioned needlessly a second time at the operating license application stage. Finally, standardizing design criteria through a certification sought by vendors would considerably lessen the overall burden on a company constructing a new reactor that had already been designed and certified by another company.

With the DC, NRC's goal is streamlining new reactor licensing without sacrificing security and safety concerns. The DC therefore allows NRC to issue certifications for standard reactor designs. Essentially, a reactor vendor or "designer" may apply for a DC for one of its designs and, once issued, sell its "pre-approved," "off-the-shelf" standard design to a company seeking to build a new nuclear power plant. The company purchasing the rights to use the DC will need only to reference that particular DC in its COL application. This new approach to design issues places a strong emphasis on standardization because an applicant to construct and operate a new reactor holding a DC should not have any design requirements under review; all NRC and public scrutiny related to design should have taken place during DC rulemaking. The DC must contain all of the design information related to safety matters that is required in the final SAR during the operating licensing stage of the traditional two-step process. Therefore, the DC is effectively a complete reactor design except that site-related information is set to generic parameters.

The DC application process is much different than its predecessor. Whereas the two-step approach included design issues in both the construction and operating licensing processes (which were adjudications), part 52 makes the design certification a rulemaking process. This is administratively significant because NRC rulemaking follows different and more limited procedures for public involvement than NRC adjudications. Only after NRC has reviewed the entire DC application and issued a Safety Evaluation Report (SER) for the design, will it begin the rulemaking process. The SER is the NRC equivalent to the SAR; essentially, the NRC staff generates its own internal safety review as an answer and critique to the SAR. At that point, the public may request an informal hearing; however, unlike the licensing process where administrative hearings are required, during rulemaking the Commission may adapt a hearing process as it sees fit in accordance with the subject matter. Though the difference may seem subtle, public participation may be less effective in a much less structured, restricted, and relatively informal hearing proceeding. After the conclusion of the hearing process, NRC will issue a standard DC in the form of a rule that is added as an appendix to part 52 and is valid for 15 years.

NRC maintains that the DC process adequately attends to the need for public involvement, but some public interest groups question the fairness of the DC process. They claim that the relaxed hearing process leaves little room for real public participation. Opponents of the DC further contend that fragmenting reactor licensing proceedings deeply limits a party's capacity to understand the many overlapping licensing issues that would be more apparent if all aspects of licensing remained juxtaposed. *See* Neal H. Lewis, Interpreting The Oracle: Licensing Modifications, Economics, Safety, Politics, and the Future of Nuclear Power in the United States, 16 Alb. L.J. Sci. & Tech. 27, 33 (2005–2006). Some also argue that the DC process disconnects local involvement when a new reactor is being licensed in a particular location. Because design proceedings are not attached to a particular site, those who live near sites under consideration for a new reactor are unlikely to challenge a proposed DC that is not yet attached to their site, and unable to challenge design issues at a subsequent public hearing.

To date, NRC has approved 4 designs; 6 others are under review. The main purpose of the DC was to standardize and streamline new reactor design. Consequently, the pre-approved DCs enable companies seeking a DC to focus only on design issues rather than dealing with peripheral concerns partially related to design. It also allows companies seeking a COL to entirely avoid design issues or at least resolve design issues much earlier in the licensing process. But what if a reactor design needs to be changed?

Indeed, the most costly and time-consuming setback in the DC process involves significant changes to uncertified designs that are still under review, or proposed modifications of a DC referenced in a COL. Whenever a DC holder or applicant determines that a change is needed to a particular design, NRC must conduct a thorough analysis of the modification to determine whether the change must go through an extensive amendment process or can be dealt with during the COL licensing process. For example, Westinghouse's AP1000 design underwent at least sixteen revisions, the last of which the required Westinghouse to seek a DC amendment. Moreover, any COL applicant that referenced an AP1000 design must deal with the associated delays and extra costs.

This issue arose in connection with Southern Company's Vogtle site referenced above. In *Blue Ridge Environmental Defense League v. NRC*, 716 F.3d 183 (D.C. Cir. 2013), petitioners challenged both NRC's grant of a COL to Southern Company, and its approval of an amendment to the AP1000 design upon which the COL application relied. In particular, the petitioners contended that the design amendment should have triggered a supplement to the design's Environmental Assessment (EA) under NEPA. The DC process requires that an EA encompass cost-benefit analyses of design alternatives for mitigating severe accidents. *See* 10 C.F.R. § 51.30(d). However, the court rejected the petitioners' argument with little analysis, concluding that NRC had reasonably evaluated severe accidents in the original EA, and that the petitioners had failed to identify any specific shortcomings created by the design amendment. 716 F.3d at 200. Because the court also upheld NRC's issuance of the COL, it remains to be seen in what other ways amended DCs may interact with pending COL applications. For example, are there circumstances under which design issues will be reborn in the later review phases of the COL application process?

NOTE ON ADVANCED NUCLEAR POWER REACTORS

Research and development for new nuclear reactor designs are underway across the world. In the United States, DOE funds research on five such reactors: the thermal neutron, gas cooled very high temperature reactor (VHTR); the super-critical water cooled reactor (SCWR); the gas-cooled fast neutron reactor (GFR); and the sodium-cooled fast neutron reactor. In the EPAct 2005, Congress established the Next Generation Nuclear Plant (NGNP) project to develop a working prototype VHTR, which is led by the Idaho National Laboratory in cooperation with the private sector. The project has experienced funding setbacks but continues to attract interest. *See*

https://inlportal.inl.gov/portal/server.pt/community/nuclear_energy/277/
next_generation_of_reactors_home.

In addition, DOE has prioritized the commercial development of small
modular reactors (SMRs), which require lower capital investment and offer
siting flexibility for applications where large plants are not needed, such as
for isolated areas, smaller grids, or specific industrial needs. DOE's program
seeks to support certification and licensing requirements at NRC. For
information on current projects, see http://www.energy.gov/ne/nuclear-
reactor-technologies/small-modular-nuclear-reactors.

c. COMBINED OPERATING LICENSES

A COL is defined as a combination of a construction permit and
operating license. Therefore, unlike the old approach of requiring two
separate and lengthy licensing applications, part 52 applicants need
attain only a single COL before commencing plant operation.
Furthermore, if design requirements and siting criteria are resolved with
a DC and ESP respectively, COL applicants holding one or both of these
licenses can simply reference either or both in a COL application to
satisfy those requirements.

To take advantage of a DC and ESP, a COL applicant must make
various showings; among other things, the facility must meet design
interface requirements as well as fall within the parameters referenced
by the ESP. In addition, COL applicants must comply with requirements
new to the part 52 process called the Inspections, Tests, Analyses, and
Acceptance Criteria (ITAAC). This final phase of the COL application
process involves a wide range of detailed last-minute tests that must be
conducted to reassure NRC that the plant has been constructed and will
operate in conformance with COL, ESP and DC requirements. Under
part 2, fuel loading cannot commence until the Commission finds that all
ITAAC have been met. Even after NRC approves an applicant's ITAAC
requirements, the new rule requires an applicant to perform
maintenance of its ITAAC after operation has commenced through
testing, documentation, and reporting back to NRC.

NRC's rationale for adopting the ITAAC phase was twofold. First, it
asserted that it was reinforcing the Commission's main purposes by
providing reasonable assurance that all major safety, security, and
environmental requirements continued to be met right before issuance of
a COL. By doing so, NRC furthered its second goal, which was to preclude
last-minute issues from arising at any pre-fueling hearings that would
otherwise stall commencement of operation. Thus, if an applicant has
passed all ITAAC tests related to siting, no party can raise a last-minute
contention related to siting.

Once a COL is granted, the COL holder must inform NRC of its
expected fuel loading date no less than 270 days before loading. 10 C.F.R.
§ 52.103. NRC must issue a notice of intended operation within not less
than 180 days prior to the fuel loading date. *Id.* At that point, the public
has its last opportunity to raise any issues through a hearing, but may
only do so through a showing of noncompliance with ITAAC. NRC must
render decisions quickly. These requirements greatly reduce the scope of
issues that can be raised just before fuel loading. In Spring 2014, NRC
proposed procedures for conducting this final pre-fueling hearing. *See*

Proposed Procedures for Conducting Hearings on Whether Acceptance Criteria in Combined Licenses are Met, 79 Fed. Reg. 21,958 (Apr. 18, 2014). The proposal modifies the part 2 procedures to permit NRC to comply with the timing requirements and substantive obligations for pre-fueling hearings.

d.   CURRENT ISSUES IN REACTOR LICENSING

For many years, NRC did not receive a single COL application. Thus, for a long time the administrative burdens and boundaries of litigation that the new COL process might bring remained untested and unknown. Then, between 2007 and 2009, NRC received 17 applications to build a total of 24 new reactors, with more expected. (Why? See below.) So far, 4 reactors have received COLs: 2 to Southern Company for their Vogtle Units 3 and 4, and 2 to South Carolina for their Virgil C. Summer Units 2 and 3. As the names imply, all four units are located at the sites of existing nuclear facilities, and (as discussed below) benefit from state incentives. One additional reactor has been licensed under the older part 50 procedures. Although COL applications for 8 sites are listed as under review, an additional 8 sites' proceedings have been either suspended or withdrawn. For the most current update, including links to the proceedings, see http://www.nrc.gov/reactors/new-reactors/col.html.

In COL proceedings, some of the opponents' contentions parallel the types raised 30–40 years ago, but other concerns reflect current events. Following the September 11, 2001 terrorist attacks, for example, petitioners challenged NRC's decision not to consider potential commercial aircraft attacks in its DC or COL decisions in *Public Citizen v. NRC*, 573 F.3d 916 (9th Cir. 2009). The Ninth Circuit rejected the challenge, reasoning that NRC had considered the possibility of such attacks and implemented many mitigatory measures; it acted in a manner consistent with its statutory mandate and was not required to include such attacks as a factor in its final rule. As described above, however, NRC ultimately did require new reactors to take this risk into account.

A related concern involves the safety of spent fuel pools from terrorist attacks. A National Research Council study suggested that on-site water pool storage of spent fuel rods raised security concerns in some existing plants where the spent fuel rods were stored above the reactor. Nat'l Research Council, Safety and Security of Commercial Spent Nuclear Fuel Storage: Public Report (National Academies Press, 2006). In 2008, New York and two other states filed a rulemaking petition with NRC asking it to find that spent fuel at nuclear power plants creates a significant environmental impact within the meaning of NEPA. NRC denied the petition, and the states appealed:

State of New York v. NRC

589 F.3d 551 (2d Cir. 2009).

Under the National Environmental Policy Act ("NEPA"), each federal agency must prepare an Environmental Impact Statement ("EIS") before taking a major action that significantly affects the quality of the "human environment." 42 U.S.C. § 4332(2)(C). The renewal of a license for a nuclear power plant is a major action requiring an EIS under NRC regulations. *See* 10 C.F.R. § 51.20.

The EIS required for license issuance and renewal at nuclear power plants covers both generic and plant-specific environmental impacts. The NRC has decided that these two kinds of impacts are to be treated separately. Category I impacts are those that: 1) are common to all nuclear power plants; 2) can be assigned a uniform significance level of small, moderate, or large (even if the impact is not precisely the same at each plant); and 3) do not require plant-specific kinds of mitigation. Category II impacts require site-by-site evaluation. Since Category I impacts are common to each license renewal, the NRC has produced a Generic Environmental Impact Statement ("GEIS") that applies to these common issues. Massachusetts v. United States, 522 F.3d 115, 120 (1st Cir. 2008). The GEIS, combined with a site-specific EIS, constitutes the complete EIS required by NEPA for the major federal action of a plant's license renewal. *Id.* (noting also that the GEIS was codified as a final rule in Environmental Review for Renewal of Nuclear Power Plant Operating Licenses, 61 Fed. Reg. 28,467 (June 5, 1996)).

The NRC classifies on-site storage of spent fuel in pools as a Category I issue that causes a small environmental impact. Massachusetts and California contended that the information in their rulemaking petitions showed a greater risk of fire from this source than previously appreciated, and that therefore the environmental impact should no longer be discounted as small; they further contended that the risk should be evaluated plant-by-plant (rather than be considered within Category I). New York and Connecticut supported these original petitions. The NRC considered both petitions together, and concluded that its initial determination was correct. After these petitions were denied in August 2008, this petition for review followed.

The States' primary arguments on appeal are that: 1) new information submitted by Massachusetts and California in their petitions (and New York in support of those petitions) show that the risk of a spent fuel pool fire is not so remote that, when considered in light of the potentially devastating effects, on-site storage in pools has a low environmental impact; and 2) the NRC's decision to deny the rulemaking petitions was arbitrary and capricious because it relied on plant-specific mitigation and security to support a finding that spent fuel pools generically have low environmental impacts.

A.   The risks posed by keeping nuclear fuel on site in spent fuel pools—including the risk of fire—have been considered in studies prepared over the past four decades. The studies relied on by the NRC all found that the risk of a fire was low. These studies (including those conducted since September 2001) consider the risk of fire precipitated by a terrorist attack, and classify that risk as low.

The NRC had already analyzed most of the studies submitted in connection with Massachusetts and California's petitions; the petitioners simply disagree with the NRC's interpretation of those studies. Massachusetts and California did submit one study that the NRC had not previously considered; but the NRC—having examined this study in considering whether to grant the petitions—concluded that it was not as accurate as the studies on which the NRC had previously relied.

These are technical and scientific studies. "Courts should be particularly reluctant to second-guess agency choices involving scientific disputes that are in the agency's province of expertise. Deference is desirable." . . . "Particularly when we consider a purely factual question within the area of competence of an administrative agency created by Congress, and when resolution of that question depends on 'engineering and scientific' considerations, we recognize the relevant agency's technical expertise and experience, and defer to its analysis unless it is without substantial basis in fact." Fed. Power Comm'n v. Fla. Power & Light Co., 404 U.S. 453, 463 (1972). The relevant studies cited by the NRC in this case constitute a sufficient "substantial basis in fact" for its conclusion that the overall risk is low. *See id.* We therefore conclude the NRC's decision was not an abuse of its discretion.

B.   The States on appeal contend that the risk of a spent fuel pool fire must be a Category II rather than a Category I risk, because the risk is affected by mitigation that varies from plant to plant. It is true that the NRC relies in part upon mitigation at nuclear power plants—including various coolant sprays and makeup water systems in case of pool drainage—to conclude that the risk of an accidental or terrorist-caused fire in the pools is uniformly low. However, the NRC has mandated that these mitigation tactics be implemented at all nuclear power plants. The NRC decision states that the agency has "approved license amendments and issued safety evaluations to incorporate these [mitigation] strategies into the plant licensing bases of all operating nuclear power plants in the United States." The NRC also requires heightened security at all plants as part of its licensing process in the wake of the September 11, 2001 attacks. *See* 10 C.F.R. § 50.54(hh); Power Reactor Security Requirements, 74 Fed. Reg. 13,975 (Mar. 27, 2009). An agency may take into account attempts to mitigate an environmental impact when determining that an environmental impact is small enough to not require an EIS, so long as the effectiveness of the mitigation is demonstrated by substantial evidence. Nat'l Audubon Soc'y v. Hoffman, 132 F.3d 7, 17 (2d Cir. 1997). The NRC relies on numerous studies detailing the effectiveness of its required mitigation measures; these studies constitute substantial evidence.

Conclusion

We conclude that the NRC's decision denying the rulemaking petitions was reasoned; it considered the relevant studies, and it took account of the relevant factors. We therefore must conclude that the agency acted within its broad discretion. We find the States' other arguments to be without merit. The States' petition to review the NRC's denial of the rulemaking petitions is denied. ∎

NOTES AND COMMENTS

1.   What standard of review did the Second Circuit apply? Consider this statement of administrative law, which arose from the nuclear licensing context: "[A] reviewing court must remember that the Commission is making predictions, within its area of special expertise, at the frontiers of science. When examining this kind of scientific determination . . . a reviewing court must generally be at its most deferential." Balt. Gas & Elec. Co. v. Natural Res. Def. Council, Inc., 467 U.S. 87, 103 (1983). Is the expertise of an agency like NRC sufficiently greater than that of the courts that such "super

deference" is justified? Or do the high stakes involved in nuclear technology warrant increased judicial scrutiny? *See generally* Emily Hammond, Super Deference, the Science Obsession, and Judicial Review as Translation of Agency Science, 109 Mich. L. Rev. 733 (2011).

2. Another licensing consideration relates to § 103d of the AEA, which provides that no new reactor license may be issued to "an alien or any corporation or other entity . . . owned, controlled, or dominated by an alien, a foreign corporation, or a foreign government." The purpose of this provision is to ensure the security and safety of nuclear resources within the United States. Thus, in 2013 NRC upheld a Board decision that UniStar Nuclear Energy was ineligible for a new reactor license because it was wholly owned by a French company. In the Matter of Calvert Cliffs 3 Nuclear Project, LLC, No. 52–016–COL (NRC Mar. 11, 2013). Should this policy be reconsidered in light of the globalization of the U.S. economy? Or is that all the more reason to keep it in place? What approach would best attract investors?

3. Greenhouse gas issues increasingly find their way into licensing proceedings related to new energy production. To what extent should NRC evaluate the carbon footprint of new reactors? NRC has stated, "We expect the Staff to include consideration of carbon dioxide and other greenhouse gas emissions in its environmental reviews for major licensing actions under the National Environmental Policy Act. The Staff's analysis for reactor applications should encompass emissions from the uranium fuel cycle as well as from construction and operation of the facility to be licensed. The Staff should ensure that these issues are addressed consistently in agency NEPA evaluations and, as appropriate, update Staff guidance documents to address greenhouse gas emissions." In the Matter of Duke Energy Carolinas, LLC, CLI–09–21 (NRC Nov. 3, 2009). This policy in essence declares that the environmental review process at NRC with regard to carbon emissions is consistent with the current science on the issue and should be upgraded only upon a changed understanding of climate change.

4. Under the AEA, operating licenses for nuclear power plants are issued for up to 40 years. However, operators may renew their licenses for up to an additional 20 years under procedures set forth in 10 C.F.R. parts 51 & 54. The process requires evaluations of the safety of aging plant structures as well as environmental impacts pursuant to NEPA. Numerous plants have completed renewal applications; others are under consideration or have submitted letters of intent to renew. A complete list is available at http://www.nrc.gov/reactors/operating/licensing/renewal/applications.html.

5. When a reactor is licensed, it will produce nuclear waste and spent nuclear fuel, as the principal case indicates. How should the environmental ramifications of the back end of the fuel cycle be accounted for in reactor licensing proceedings? Since the early 1980s, NRC's Waste Confidence Decision has essentially provided that uncertainty about nuclear waste disposal will not be considered at individual licensing proceedings. *See* New York v. NRC, 681 F.3d 471, 474–75 (D.C. Cir. 2009) (providing history). Challenges to this approach have been largely rejected in the past, but in June 2012, the D.C. Circuit issued a major decision that resulted in NRC suspending final licensing decisions. In New York v. NRC, 681 F.3d 471 (D.C. Cir. 2012), which is excerpted below, the court held that NRC failed to meet the requirements of NEPA when, in a revision to the Waste Confidence Decision, it did not consider the environmental effects of failing to establish a nuclear waste repository. The U.S. history of nuclear waste policy is

discussed below. For now, understand that following the D.C. Circuit's decision, NRC halted its consideration of new reactor license applications until it could develop a new rule concerning the environmental impacts of spent nuclear fuel and their relationship to reactor licensing. NRC issued its final rule and supporting Generic EIS in August 2014; it also issued an Order lifting the suspension of its consideration of pending license applications. *See* In re Matter of Calvert Cliffs et al., CLI–14–08 (NRC Aug. 26, 2014) (describing history and lifting suspension).

2. INCENTIVIZING REACTOR CONSTRUCTION

a. THE COST OF NUCLEAR POWER

In many ways, nuclear power projects are no different from other large, capital-intensive construction projects. But nuclear projects also present unique issues: very high technical and legal complexity; heightened environmental considerations; special liability, insurance, and waste management requirements; costly decommissioning; and public opinion that is both mixed and strident. *See* Helen Cook, The Law of Nuclear Energy 305 (2013).

Perceptions about nuclear power relate to its financial viability as well as to its political feasibility. Plagued by the experience of cost overruns and regulatory and litigation-related delays during the construction phase in the 1980s and early 1990s, investors have been hesitant to back new nuclear construction. With little contemporary experience, construction costs are hard to predict. The failed promise of electricity "too cheap to meter" has also fed investor skepticism. An influential study by the Massachusetts Institute for Technology (MIT), for example, noted that although nuclear power plants today exceed 90% efficiency, if one takes into account the life-cycle availability of the entire nuclear fleet (including those that closed early), the number is much lower. See MIT, The Future of Nuclear Power 38 (2003); MIT, 2009 Updates to the Future of Nuclear Power, both at http://web.mit.edu/nuclearpower/. The same study's 2009 updates put the overall life cycle costs (including construction, operation and maintenance of nuclear power) at 8.4 cents/kWe-h, compared to 4.3 for coal and 4.1 for natural gas. 2009 Updates at 6–7.

In a deregulated market where utilities do not pass such costs to consumers through ratemaking, these figures are unlikely to attract investors compared with coal and natural gas. How could nuclear life-cycle costs be reduced? The MIT study suggests that the cost of capital could be reduced by shortening the construction time with fewer delays, more regulatory certainty, and less litigation. *Id.* at 7. In addition, if fossil-fueled power were to pay a carbon tax or otherwise pay for more of its GHG externalities, nuclear might also be more competitive. *Id.* at 6.

b. EPAct 2005 INCENTIVES

As described above, the part 52 licensing structure is intended to reduce regulatory uncertainty and minimize regulatory delays. But it was not until EPAct 2005 included three provisions meant to lower the cost of capital for nuclear that new COL applications began coming in.

The three key provisions were: (1) regulatory risk insurance; (2) a nuclear production tax credit; and (3) loan guarantees.

First, the regulatory risk insurance is provided for in § 638 of EPAct 2005. Entitled "Standby Support for Certain Nuclear Plant Delays," this provision is meant to alleviate concerns that the untested COL procedures would result in too many delays. The Act authorizes DOE to enter into up to six contracts with sponsors of new nuclear power plants, under which the federal government promises to pay the principal and interest on debt and extra costs incurred for purchasing replacement power due to licensing delays. Licensing delays include NRC's failure to follow its own procedures and licensing-related litigation (regardless of the ultimate prevailing party).

Under the program, DOE is to pay 100% of these costs up to a limit of $500 million per reactor for each of the first two licensed reactors, and 50% of the costs up to a limit of $250 million after a 180 day delay for the next four reactors. In other words, the first reactors that face the most uncertainty stand to obtain the largest benefit. The sponsors of these reactors must, for their part, promise to use due diligence to minimize delay. See Standby Support for Certain Nuclear Plant Delays, 71 Fed. Reg. 46,306 (Aug. 11, 2006) (DOE's final rule implementing § 638). After you read the material below on the role of nuclear waste policy on licensing, ask yourself whether the current delays would meet the criteria for standby support.

Second, EPAct 2005 provided a 1.8 cents/kWh tax credit for up to 6000 MW of new nuclear capacity for the first 8 years of operation. The Internal Revenue Service (IRS) was tasked with allocating the tax credit among reactors, in consultation with DOE. Under the IRS's resulting guidance document, reactors were required to apply for combined licenses by December 31, 2008, begin construction by January 1, 2014, and meet DOE eligibility requirements. See Internal Revenue Bulletin, No. 2006–18 (May 1, 2006). Early uncertainties included how the production tax credit would be allocated among eligible reactors (recall that numerous COL applications were filed in 2008). The IRS guidance detailed a method for such allocation, but the issue became moot a few years later. With nuclear reactors' license applications stalled pending the need for a new Waste Confidence Decision, only four reactors met the eligibility criteria. IRS's updated guidelines issued in 2013 made no changes to the criteria, so absent new guidance or changes in law, no other reactors would qualify. *See* Internal Revenue Bulletin, No. 2013–68 (Nov. 12, 2013).

Finally, § 1703 of EPAct 2005 authorized loan guarantees for "clean energy" projects, which include nuclear as well as wind, solar, hydropower, and carbon sequestration, among others. Under the program, which is administered by DOE, the federal government can guarantee up to 80% of a plant's estimated cost. In 2009, Congress authorized $18.5 billion for nuclear projects and an additional $2 million for nuclear front-end projects (such as uranium enrichment). In 2014, DOE closed on loans for the Vogtle project in Georgia ($8.33 billion), and for a uranium enrichment facility in Idaho ($2 billion). To be eligible for a loan guarantee for a nuclear power plant, applicants must have obtained a COL from NRC. Once again, however, because current applications are on hold pending a new Waste Confidence Decision, DOE has not been able to move forward with additional loan guarantees for nuclear power. *See* Gov't Accountability Ofc., Status of DOE Loan Programs, Briefing to Appropriations Committees, at 17 (Feb. 2013).

c.   NUCLEAR POWER IN COMPETITIVE MARKETS

As noted above, nuclear power is an important contributor to baseload generation. This is true for both technological reasons—the fission chain reaction is difficult to stop and start—and for economic reasons—the marginal cost of nuclear power is very low. But as mentioned above, hydraulic fracturing has opened up new natural gas reserves and led to declining natural gas prices. In restructured markets (*see* Chapter 10), nuclear industry representatives state that they are unable to bid in power at prices sufficient to support continued operation of nuclear power plants. *See* Greenwire, Nuclear giants urge market changes to thwart closures (Feb. 6, 2014). The industry is increasingly voicing concerns that existing generation cannot compete in such markets because subsidized renewables generation is disrupting the balance of supply and demand, making baseload less important and sacrificing grid reliability. *Id.* Indeed, new construction thus far is taking place only in traditionally regulated locations, which are able to offer cost recovery for construction works in progress, for example (*see* Chapter 8).

On the other hand, supporters of renewables, deregulation, distributed generation, and demand response argue that baseload is of declining importance for a grid that can increasingly fine-tune the balance of supply and demand. *See* Mark Cooper, Old Reactors v. New Renewables: The First Nuclear War of the 21st Century (June 6, 2014), renewableenergyworld.com. They further contend that nuclear energy has been artificially subsidized for decades, including EPAct 2005's incentives for new construction. *Id.*

Who is right? The ultimate outcome likely depends on a host of variables, many of which are explored throughout this book. In the meantime, one of the largest nuclear power companies, Entergy Corp., announced in 2013 that it was closing the Vermont Yankee nuclear plant; other plant closures have also been announced. *See* Elizabeth Douglass, First U.S. Nuclear Power Closures in 15 Years Signal Wider Problems for Industry, InsideClimate News (Sept. 24 2013), at insideclimatenews.org. For a full analysis of these issues, see Emily Hammond & David B. Spence, The Regulatory Contract in the Marketplace, available at http://ssrn.com/abstract=2584619 (forthcoming 2016).

3.   DECOMMISSIONING

When a nuclear power plant closes, the facility must be decommissioned. This process can be achieved in one of three ways. The first option is immediate dismantling, which requires removing or decontaminating the radioactive portions of the facility so that the property can be "released" and the NRC license terminated. The second option is called "deferred dismantling," which involves maintaining the site while the radioactivity decays, after which dismantling occurs. The third option involves entombment of all radioactive contaminants on-site until the radioactivity decays to a level that would permit restricted release of the property. No facilities to date have sought this final option. NRC regulations governing decommissioning are located in Title 10 of the C.F.R., Part 20 Subpart E. Updates on all reactor sites undergoing decommissioning can be found at www.nrc.gov/info-finder/ decommissioning/power-reactor/.

Decommissioning nuclear power sites is extremely expensive. To ensure that nuclear power plant can be properly decommissioned, plant operators must provide financial assurances to NRC. A typical way of meeting this obligation is to establish and contribute to a decommissioning trust fund. *See* 10 C.F.R. § 50.75. The following decision provides context and examples of the types of issues that can arise.

Pennington v. ZionSolutions LLC

742 F.3d 715 (7th Cir. 2014).

■ POSNER, CIRCUIT JUDGE. This is a class action suit on behalf of purported beneficiaries of a "decommissioning trust" created by Commonwealth Edison, the large electrical utility, to fund the decommissioning of its now-shuttered nuclear power plant in Zion, Illinois. Jurisdiction is based on diversity of citizenship and the applicable substantive law is Illinois's, though federal regulation of decommissioning lurks in the background. The plaintiffs and the other class members are ComEd customers. The two defendants are the current trustee (BNY Mellon) of a trust (the Zion Trust) containing the assets that were originally in the ComEd trust, and the company that is doing the decommissioning (ZionSolutions) and drawing on the assets of the Zion Trust to pay for its work.

ComEd closed the Zion plant in 1998. When a nuclear facility is closed, it must be "decommissioned," which means rendered harmless, that is, cease to be dangerously radioactive. The process of decommissioning is supervised by a federal agency, the Nuclear Regulatory Commission. There are several methods of decommissioning. The one originally chosen for the Zion plant is called SAFSTOR (short for "safe storage"). That method requires that the defunct plant be enclosed in a way that prevents radioactive leakage, and that it remain in this state for many years—usually 40 to 60. By the end of that period the natural decay of radioactive materials will have rendered the plant much less radioactive, thereby reducing the cost of dismantling the plant and eliminating any dangerous radioactive residue. Thus in SAFSTOR the dismantlement and decontamination of a nuclear power plant are deferred for decades.

But then it was decided to substitute for SAFSTOR as the method of decommissioning the Zion plant a method called DECON (short for decontamination). In DECON, as much as possible of the radioactive material is removed from the site and sent to a [disposal facility] to decay in peace, enabling the decontamination of the site to be completed much more rapidly than if SAFSTOR were used. *See* U.S. NRC, "Decommissioning Nuclear Power Plants," July 10, 2013, www.nrc.gov/ reading-rm/doc-collections/fact-sheets/decommissioning.html (visited Jan. 31, 2014); Matthew L. Wald, "After the Nuclear Plant Powers Down," New York Times, Nov. 23, 2010, p. B1.

Regulations of the Nuclear Regulatory Commission require a nuclear plant operator, at the very outset of operations, to begin accumulating money—typically by creating a decommissioning trust funded by charges to ratepayers—sufficient to finance the eventual decommissioning, which is likely to cost hundreds of millions of dollars. *See* 10 C.F.R. § 50.75; 18 C.F.R. § 35.32. But the details of the creation of the trust fund are left to the state agency that regulates the utility, in this case the Illinois Commerce Commission, which pursuant to a provision of the Illinois Public Utilities Act, authorized ComEd to create a trust (with Northern Trust Company as trustee) to be funded by some $700 million in charges levied by ComEd on its customers. The Act entitles ComEd's customers to the return of any money that has not been spent when the decommissioning is completed, because financing the decommissioning was the only purpose for which the charges deposited in the ComEd trust had been levied on the utility's customers.

In 2001, with the permission of the Illinois Commerce Commission, ComEd transferred ownership of the Zion plant, together with the trust assets, to ComEd's parent, Exelon. Neither Exelon nor its subsidiary is a public utility. Ordinarily the utility (ComEd) would have retained the plant after shutting it down, and hired a contractor to decommission the plant. But economies were anticipated from getting the utility out of the picture; transaction costs would be reduced by uniting financing and decommissioning in the same company. (See Wald, supra, for a fuller discussion.) Another step was necessary, however: Exelon transferred plant and trust assets to a company created to do the actual decommissioning—ZionSolutions. This enabled a further economy, besides uniting financing and decommissioning, inasmuch as ZionSolutions' parent, EnergySolutions, owns a nuclear waste site, which plays an essential role in the DECON decommissioning method; for it is to such a site that radioactive material removed from the shuttered plant is taken. Because neither party to the transfer of the trust assets was an Illinois public utility, the permission of the Illinois Commerce Commission to make the transfer was not required.

By the terms of the transfer, the assets originally in ComEd's trust were placed in a new trust, the Zion Trust, with BNY Mellon as trustee. The trust assets are to be used to pay ZionSolutions' decommissioning costs. The transfer agreement provides that should there be unspent money in the trust when the decommissioning is complete, that money will be returned to Exelon, which in turn will remit it to ComEd for distribution to ComEd's customers, just as if the money had been in ComEd's trust all the time. The transfer agreement also provides that if the decommissioning costs exceed the trust's remaining assets (as the Illinois commission thought likely), ZionSolutions must swallow them; it will not be permitted to seek reimbursement of any excess costs from ComEd or ComEd's customers.

The plaintiffs brought this suit against ZionSolutions and the bank in 2011, claiming that the trust funds are being misused in violation of both the Illinois Public Utilities Act and Illinois's common law of trusts. The suit seeks the appointment of a new trustee, an accounting, an injunction against improper expenditure of trust funds, an order directing that "at least some of the trust funds" be disbursed to ComEd customers at once, and other relief. The district court, without deciding whether to certify a class, dismissed the complaint for failure to state a claim.

There's been no determination that ZionSolutions or BNY Mellon has mismanaged trust assets, but suppose one or both of them have. The plaintiffs and other class members are not beneficiaries of the Zion Trust. The only beneficiary is Exelon, the source of the trust money. ComEd's customers have rights only to the money, if any, left unspent in the Zion Trust and therefore returned via Exelon to ComEd when the decommissioning of the Zion plant has been completed.

The Illinois Public Utilities Act does impose duties on trusts administered by the utility companies regulated by the Illinois Commerce Commission, but the plaintiffs are not complaining about the administration of the ComEd trust, which in any event is an empty shell. They haven't named ComEd, ComEd's trust, or Northern Trust Company as defendants. How could they? Their rights, as we said, are limited to any Zion Trust assets that remain after the decommissioning is completed.

The Illinois Commerce Commission's approval was required for the transfer of the assets from the ComEd trust to Exelon, ComEd's parent, and that approval was given after an administrative proceeding in which the plaintiffs could have objected to the transfer, but did not, though other ComEd customers did. With that approval, ComEd and its customers are out of the picture unless and until there is money left over from the decommissioning.

Still, the plaintiffs and the other class members have a residual interest in the assets now in the hands of ZionSolutions and BNY Mellon. A theft or squandering of any of those assets will reduce the probability that ComEd customers will receive any refunds when the decommissioning is complete. But there is a difference between an interest and a right. Imagine there is hanky-panky in the management of a company, resulting in a deterioration in service. A consumer who had planned to buy goods produced by the company and cannot find an adequate substitute will be harmed. Yet assuming he has no contractual rights against the company—no promise by the company to sell him goods of a specified quantity and quality at a specified price—he'll have no legal claim against the company, or whoever in the company was responsible for its deterioration. It is the same here. The plaintiffs and class members are not the beneficiaries of the Zion Trust and have no contractual relationship with it, ZionSolutions, or BNY Mellon, and therefore no basis for asserting legal claims against any of those entities.

And for good reason: had ComEd's customers a cause of action against the decommissioner of the Zion nuclear plant for mismanaging the project, no reputable firm would have agreed to undertake the project or act as trustee of the project assets without an ironclad agreement by ComEd or Exelon to indemnify the decommissioning company and the trustee for any damages and litigation expenses. ComEd has more than three and a half million customers. On the plaintiffs' legal theory any or all of them could sue ZionSolutions or BNY Mellon for breach of trust.

. . .

At the oral argument the plaintiffs' lawyer made the wild and unsubstantiated claim that the NRC cares only about safety and not at all about money (contrary to the regulations we've cited), that the cost of decommissioning Zion will be only $450 million, and that the Commission will simply ignore ZionSolutions' pocketing of $250 million ($700 million, the original trust money, minus $450 million) that of rights belong to ComEd's customers. But not only is the Nuclear Regulatory Commission the designated policeman of decommissioners; its competence to assess the management of the complex, technologically sophisticated process of nuclear decommissioning exceeds that of state or federal judges, who are generalists. Rulings on decommissioning, including rulings on the financial issues involved in decommissioning, are within the commission's primary jurisdiction.

. . .

Our plaintiffs, having sued only companies against which they have no rights, have failed to present a judicially cognizable claim. The litigation must be, not suspended, but dismissed, as the district court ruled.

Affirmed. ■

NOTES AND COMMENTS

1. How do the issues raised in ZionSolutions relate to ratemaking? (See Chapter 8.) Restructuring of electricity markets? (See Chapter 10.) What about governance choices inherent in the decommissioning requirements—should states have a greater role?

2. Decommissioning requires approval from NRC and triggers NEPA. See 10 C.F.R. § 51.95 (postconstruction environmental impact statements); Citizens Awareness Network, Inc. v. NRC, 59 F.3d 281 (1st Cir. 1995) (holding arbitrary and capricious NRC's action allowing operator to complete 90% of decommissioning prior to NEPA compliance).

3. You may be familiar with the famous administrative law decision *Vermont Yankee Nuclear Power Corp. v. Natural Resources Def. Council, Inc.*, 435 U.S. 519 (1978), which involved NEPA compliance, waste disposal and licensing issues, and the courts' ability to impose procedural requirements on administrative agencies. The Vermont Yankee power plant continued to attract attention over time, some of which is detailed in *Entergy Nuclear Vt. Yankee, LLC v. Shumlin*, 733 F.3d 393 (2d Cir. 2013), discussed above in the preemption context. There, the Second Circuit held that a Vermont statute requiring state legislative approval to operate Vermont Yankee after 2012 was preempted by the AEA. *Id.* at 422. In the meantime, NRC had extended the plant's operating license for 20 years in 2011. But as noted above, in 2013, the plant's owner announced that it would cease operations due to economic factors (including the competition of lower-cost natural gas-fueled electricity). Decommissioning is scheduled to begin in late 2014. *See* PR Newswire, Entergy to Close, Decommission Vermont Yankee, http://www. marketwatch.com/story/entergy-to-close-decommission-vermont-yankee-2013-08-27 (Aug. 27, 2013).

As of Fall 2014, NRC listed 17 power reactors undergoing decommissioning in the United States. http://www.nrc.gov/info-finder/ decommissioning/power-reactor/.

D. NUCLEAR WASTES AND USED NUCLEAR FUEL

The most troublesome issue dogging nuclear power continues to be managing nuclear fuel that has lost its usefulness but remains radioactive. This section describes the overall legal framework for managing and disposing of radioactive materials before focusing on the biggest issue for our purposes—disposal of civilian nuclear waste from reactors. In the United States, separate statutes and regulations create and govern four categories of waste: (1) uranium mill tailings; (2) military waste; (3) low-level radioactive waste (LLRW); and (4) high-level waste (HLW).

A few notes on terminology may be helpful here. With respect to HLW in particular, there is increasing recognition that if such material were reprocessed and reused, considerable efficiencies would be gained and the need for long-term disposal options would be at least mitigated. Thus, outside the legal framework, many refer to HLW as "spent nuclear fuel" or "used nuclear fuel." We use all three terms interchangeably throughout this chapter, but you will no doubt see that each term is laden with policy implications.

1. URANIUM MILL TAILINGS

When ore is processed to remove uranium, the ore that remains is referred to as uranium mill tailings. Such tailings contain low but significant levels of radioactivity. Most uranium mining in the United States has ceased production, but large amounts of mill tailings remain near the mining sites. *See* Abandoned Uranium Mines, http://www.abandonedmines.gov/wbd_um.html. The Uranium Mill Tailings Radiation Control Act of 1978, 42 U.S.C. § 2000 et seq. (UMTRCA) vests NRC with responsibility to issue permits for disposing of uranium mill tailings, while EPA has responsibility to adopt standards with which disposal facilities must comply. *See* Am. Mining Cong. v. Thomas, 772 F.2d 640 (10th Cir. 1985); *see also* Waste Action Project v. Dawn Mining Corp., 137 F.3d 1426 (9th Cir. 1998) (holding UMTRCA precludes joint jurisdiction under Clean Water Act).

2. MILITARY RADIOACTIVE WASTE

As you will recall from the first part of this chapter, nuclear energy's origin was in military applications; defense-related research and development continued even after civilian power was developed, and it is currently ongoing. Large amounts of waste are currently being stored at various defense-related sites, most of which are under the control of DOE.

The world's first operating underground repository for nuclear waste is the Waste Isolation Pilot Plant (WIPP), located in Carlsbad, New Mexico, and operated by DOE. Congress authorized the facility in 1979, and it was constructed during the 1980s. The facility is designed to store transuranic, or TRU, waste. In 1998, EPA certified WIPP for disposal of TRU wastes, and it accepted its first shipment in 1999. WIPP accepts shipments from DOE sites that arrive by truck, which are tracked by satellite and strictly regulated.

WIPP encountered significant litigation prior to its operation. *See* WIPP Chronology, http://www.wipp.energy.gov/fctshts/Chronology.pdf.

However, it enjoys widespread support from the community of Carlsbad and is frequently cited as an example of a successful geologic repository. *See* Blue Ribbon Commission, Report to the Sec'y of Energy 48 (Jan. 2012) ("unwavering local support helped to sustain the project during periods when federal and state agencies had to work through disagreements over issues such as the nature of the wastes to be disposed, the role of different entities in providing oversight, and the standards that the facility would be required to meet").

In February 2014, WIPP experienced two unrelated events that caused it to temporarily stop accepting shipments pending investigations. First, a salt-hauling truck caught on fire underground due to contact between hydraulic fluid or diesel fuel and the truck's catalytic converter. Eighty-six workers were successfully evacuated; several were treated for smoke inhalation. The fire did not result in the release of radioactive materials. DOE convened an Accident Investigation Board, which issued an independent report and made numerous recommendations to prevent future similar accidents. *See* DOE, Accident Investigation Report, Underground Salt Haul Truck Fire at the Waste Isolation Pilot Plant, Feb. 5, 2014 (Mar. 2014), http://www. wipp.energy.gov/Special/AIB% 20Report.pdf.

Then on February 14, 2014, an air monitor measured radioactivity near the underground operating location where waste was being placed. The air monitor set off an alarm that automatically caused the air circulating from the repository to the outside surface to circulate through high efficiency particulate air (HEPA) filter that removes radioactive particles. Then the next day, an above-ground air monitor detected very low levels of radioactivity. Components of the air system have since been sealed, and no further measurements of radioactivity have been observed. DOE also appointed an Accident Investigation Board for this incident, which is operating in two phases. The first phase considered the health and environmental implications of the incident, concluding that the release was well below a level of public or environmental hazard. However, the Board made numerous recommendations to prevent future occurrences. *See* DOE, Accident Investigation Report, Phase I: Radiological Release Event at the Waste Isolation Pilot Plant on Feb. 14, 2014 (Apr. 2014), http://www.wipp.energy.gov/Special/AIB_Final_WIPP_ Rad_Release_Phase1_04_22_2014.pdf.

The second phase of the investigation will involve manned entry into the repository, which has not been scheduled as of this writing. Meanwhile, aboveground work at the site continues and WIPP officials are committed to reopening the repository for shipments as soon as possible. Updates are available at http://www.wipp.energy.gov/wipp recovery/recovery.html.

3.   LOW-LEVEL RADIOACTIVE WASTE

Radioactive material is generated at all of the various stages of the nuclear fuel cycle, but much of it contains only small amounts of radioactive material. LLRW includes a wide range of material such as tools, clothing, and equipment from uranium production; lab coats, cloths, materials used in power plants where radioactive material is present; materials from hospitals used in connection with radioactive material; carcasses of animals treated with radioactive materials; and research equipment from laboratories. When these materials need to be disposed of, they become categorized as LLRW. For almost half a century, Americans have been debating what to do with this waste.

Low-level radioactive wastes are ranked in increasing order of hazard level and must be disposed of according to regulations tailored to the relevant hazard levels. *See* 10 C.F.R. § 61.55 (waste classification). The Low-Level Radioactive Waste Policy Amendments Act of 1985 provides that States are responsible for disposal of waste generated within their borders, while the Federal Government is responsible for LLRW that it generates. See 42 U.S.C. § 2021c. Under the AEA, states may assume limited regulatory authority over some nuclear materials. The Act further encouraged states to form Interstate Compacts to create regional disposal sites for LLRW. See id. § 2021d. Both individual states and state compacts had difficulty siting LLRW disposal sites due to intense local opposition. After years of unsuccessful attempts to approve a site, the State of New York challenged the Act, leading the Supreme Court ultimately to invalidate portions of the Act on 10th Amendment grounds. *New York v. United States,* 405 U.S. 144 (1992). In several of the regional compacts, once a member state was selected to host a disposal site, the state would withdraw from the compact. Despite these difficulties, there are currently four active LLRW sites, all of which are operated by states that have obtained such authority from NRC.

The four LLRW sites are located in South Carolina, Texas, Utah, and Washington. The volume and radioactivity of waste at each site varies from year to year based on the types and quantities of waste shipped. In 2011, over 1.8 million cubic feet of radioactive materials were disposed of at the South Carolina, Utah, and Washington sites. The Texas facility, which opened in 2012 and is reported separately, disposed of over 20,000 cubic feet in the third quarter of 2014.

4. HIGH-LEVEL RADIOACTIVE WASTE

HLWs are the byproducts of the reactions that occur inside nuclear reactors. The waste comes in two forms. The first is spent fuel, which has been used to operate the reactor for up to two years and is still radioactive, but not at the intensity needed to fuel the reactor. 42 U.S.C. § 10101(12). The second type of HLW is the waste material that remains after reprocessing spent fuel in defense or energy department facilities. All spent fuel from commercial power plants is thermally hot and potentially harmful, but it cannot be converted to bomb-making material without elaborate reprocessing facilities. http://www.nrc.gov/waste/high-level-waste.html.

a. THE NUCLEAR WASTE POLICY ACT

For more than three decades, commercial nuclear waste disposal has been governed by the Nuclear Waste Policy Act of 1982 (NWPA), which anticipates a deep geologic repository for permanent disposal of such waste. 42 U.S.C. §§ 10101–10270. Under the Act, DOE and NRC share responsibility: DOE must characterize the chosen site and construct and operate the facility, while NRC must issue compliance standards and the appropriate licenses to DOE. To cover the costs of this work, nuclear

power generators must make payments to a Nuclear Waste Fund. *Id.*
§ 10131(b)(4).

Despite the nuclear industry's having contributed some $30 billion to the
Nuclear Waste Fund since 1983, the United States still does not have its
geologic repository. As you read the following excerpt, consider why.
What lessons can be applied for future management of spent nuclear
fuel?

> As originally enacted in 1982, the NWPA directed the DOE
> to consider five different sites for their suitability as potential
> nuclear-waste repositories, three of which were to be forwarded
> to the president for review. The three sites suggested for the
> first repository were in Texas, Washington, and Nevada. Texas
> and Washington had far more political clout than the sparsely
> populated Nevada, however, and in 1987, Congress amended
> the NWPA to specify that Yucca Mountain would be the only
> site characterized.
>
> The DOE thereafter completed its characterization of the
> Yucca Mountain site and submitted to President George H.W.
> Bush its recommendation that the site be selected. President
> Bush notified Congress that he considered Yucca Mountain to
> be qualified for a construction-license application. Nevada filed
> a notice of disapproval, as contemplated by the statute.
> Congress responded with a joint resolution approving the site's
> development.
>
> After proceeding through various technical phases and
> surviving a battery of lawsuits, the Yucca Mountain Project
> looked poised to advance to construction licensing. The DOE had
> submitted its safety report for the NRC's review, as well as its
> construction-license application. Before the application was
> approved, however, then-Senator Obama made a campaign
> promise to Nevada, the home state of Senate Majority Leader
> Harry Reid, stating that he would shut down Yucca Mountain if
> elected. After his election, President Obama first eliminated
> funding for the project in his 2009 proposed budget. Then, in
> 2010, he directed the DOE to file a motion to withdraw the
> construction-license application, while also directing it to
> establish a Blue Ribbon Commission to evaluate the country's
> nuclear-waste policy.

Hammond, Deference Dilemma, *supra*, at 1783–84 (footnotes omitted).
The ASLB denied DOE's motion to withdraw its construction-license
application, reasoning that DOE's reasons were not grounded in the
statute:

> Did Congress, which so carefully preserved ultimate control
> over the multi-stage process that it crafted, intend—without
> ever saying so—that DOE could unilaterally withdraw the
> Application and prevent the NRC from considering it? We think
> not. When Congress selected the Yucca Mountain site over
> Nevada's objection in 2002, it reinforced the expectation in the
> 1982 Act that the project would be removed from the political
> process and that the NRC would complete an evaluation of the
> technical merits. . . .

U.S. Dep't of Energy, No. LBP–10–11, at 9 (Atomic Safety & Licensing Bd., Nuclear Regulatory Comm'n June 29, 2010). DOE appealed that decision to the full NRC, but meanwhile, various other entities (including states that were storing spent nuclear fuel and awaiting a repository) sued DOE, contending that it was violating the NWPA by abandoning the Yucca Mountain site. *See* In re Aiken County, 645 F.3d 428 (D.C. Cir. 2011). The D.C. Circuit held the claim was unripe and remanded the matter to NRC. *Id.* at 435–36.

On remand, NRC was evenly divided on whether to uphold the ASLB's denial of the DOE motion to dismiss; under NRC rules, the ASLB order therefore stood. *See* http://pbadupws.nrc.gov/docs/ML1006/ ML100621397.pdf. Nevertheless, NRC directed ASLB to suspend its consideration of the DOE application because of a predicted lack of funding. NRC was promptly sued.

In re Aiken County

725 F.3d 255 (D.C. Cir. 2013).

■ KAVANAUGH, CIRCUIT JUDGE. This case raises significant questions about the scope of the Executive's authority to disregard federal statutes. The case arises out of a longstanding dispute about nuclear waste storage at Yucca Mountain in Nevada. The underlying policy debate is not our concern. The policy is for Congress and the President to establish as they see fit in enacting statutes, and for the President and subordinate executive agencies (as well as relevant independent agencies such as the Nuclear Regulatory Commission) to implement within statutory boundaries. Our more modest task is to ensure, in justiciable cases, that agencies comply with the law as it has been set by Congress. Here, the Nuclear Regulatory Commission has continued to violate the law governing the Yucca Mountain licensing process. We therefore grant the petition for a writ of mandamus.

I

This case involves the Nuclear Waste Policy Act, which was passed by Congress and then signed by President Reagan in 1983. That law provides that the Nuclear Regulatory Commission "shall consider" the Department of Energy's license application to store nuclear waste at Yucca Mountain and "shall issue a final decision approving or disapproving" the application within three years of its submission. 42 U.S.C. § 10134(d). The statute allows the Commission to extend the deadline by an additional year if it issues a written report explaining the reason for the delay and providing the estimated time for completion. Id. § 10134(d), (e)(2).

In June 2008, the Department of Energy submitted its license application to the Nuclear Regulatory Commission. As recently as Fiscal Year 2011, Congress appropriated funds to the Commission so that the Commission could conduct the statutorily mandated licensing process. Importantly, the Commission has at least $11.1 million in appropriated funds to continue consideration of the license application.

But the statutory deadline for the Commission to complete the licensing process and approve or disapprove the Department of Energy's application has long since passed. Yet the Commission still has not issued the decision required by statute. Indeed, by its own admission, the Commission has no current intention of complying with the law. Rather, the Commission has simply shut down its review and consideration of the Department of Energy's license application.

Petitioners include the States of South Carolina and Washington, as well as entities and individuals in those States. Nuclear waste is currently stored in those States in the absence of a long-term storage site such as Yucca Mountain. Since 2010, petitioners have sought a writ of mandamus requiring the Commission to comply with the law and to resume processing the Department of Energy's pending license application for Yucca Mountain. Mandamus is an extraordinary remedy that takes account of equitable considerations. The writ may be granted "to correct transparent violations of a clear duty to act." . . .

In 2011, a prior panel of this Court indicated that, if the Commission failed to act on the Department of Energy's license application within the deadlines specified by the Nuclear Waste Policy Act, mandamus likely would be appropriate. See In re Aiken County, 645 F.3d 428, 436 (D.C. Cir. 2011). In 2012, after a new mandamus petition had been filed, this panel issued an order holding the case in abeyance and directing that the parties file status updates regarding Fiscal Year 2013 appropriations. At that time, we did not issue the writ of mandamus. Instead, in light of the Commission's strenuous claims that Congress did not want the licensing process to continue and the equitable considerations appropriately taken into account in mandamus cases, we allowed time for Congress to clarify this issue if it wished to do so. But a majority of the Court also made clear that, given the current statutory language and the funds available to the Commission, the Commission was violating federal law by declining to further process the license application. And the Court's majority further indicated that the mandamus petition eventually would have to be granted if the Commission did not act or Congress did not enact new legislation either terminating the Commission's licensing process or otherwise making clear that the Commission may not expend funds on the licensing process.

Since we issued that order more than a year ago on August 3, 2012, the Commission has not acted, and Congress has not altered the legal landscape. As things stand, therefore, the Commission is simply flouting the law. In light of the constitutional respect owed to Congress, and having fully exhausted the alternatives available to us, we now grant the petition for writ of mandamus against the Nuclear Regulatory Commission.

II

Our analysis begins with settled, bedrock principles of constitutional law. Under Article II of the Constitution and relevant Supreme Court precedents, the President must follow statutory mandates so long as there is appropriated money available and the President has no constitutional objection to the statute. So, too, the President must abide by statutory prohibitions unless the President has a constitutional objection to the prohibition. If the President has a constitutional objection to a statutory mandate or prohibition, the President may decline to follow the law unless and until a final Court order dictates otherwise. But the President may not decline to follow a statutory mandate or prohibition simply because of policy objections. Of course, if

Congress appropriates no money for a statutorily mandated program, the Executive obviously cannot move forward. But absent a lack of funds or a claim of unconstitutionality that has not been rejected by final Court order, the Executive must abide by statutory mandates and prohibitions.

Those basic constitutional principles apply to the President and subordinate executive agencies. And they apply at least as much to independent agencies such as the Nuclear Regulatory Commission. . . .

In this case, however, the Nuclear Regulatory Commission has declined to continue the statutorily mandated Yucca Mountain licensing process. Several justifications have been suggested in support of the Commission's actions in this case. None is persuasive.

First, the Commission claims that Congress has not yet appropriated the full amount of funding necessary for the Commission to complete the licensing proceeding. But Congress often appropriates money on a step-by-step basis, especially for long-term projects. Federal agencies may not ignore statutory mandates simply because Congress has not yet appropriated all of the money necessary to complete a project. For present purposes, the key point is this: The Commission is under a legal obligation to continue the licensing process, and it has at least $11.1 million in appropriated funds—a significant amount of money—to do so.

Second, and relatedly, the Commission speculates that Congress, in the future, will not appropriate the additional funds necessary for the Commission to complete the licensing process. So it would be a waste, the Commission theorizes, to continue to conduct the process now. The Commission's political prognostication may or may not ultimately prove to be correct. Regardless, an agency may not rely on political guesswork about future congressional appropriations as a basis for violating existing legal mandates. A judicial green light for such a step—allowing agencies to ignore statutory mandates and prohibitions based on agency speculation about future congressional action—would gravely upset the balance of powers between the Branches and represent a major and unwarranted expansion of the Executive's power at the expense of Congress.

Third, the Commission points to Congress's recent appropriations to the Commission and to the Department of Energy for the Yucca Mountain project. In the last three years, those appropriations have been relatively low or zero. The Commission argues that those appropriations levels demonstrate a congressional desire for the Commission to shut down the licensing process.

But Congress speaks through the laws it enacts. No law states that the Commission should decline to spend previously appropriated funds on the licensing process. No law states that the Commission should shut down the licensing process. And the fact that Congress hasn't yet made additional appropriations over the existing $11.1 million available to the Commission to continue the licensing process tells us nothing definitive about what a future Congress may do. As the Supreme Court has explained, courts generally should not infer that Congress has implicitly repealed or suspended statutory mandates based simply on the amount of money Congress has appropriated. See TVA v. Hill, 437 U.S. 153, 190, 98 S.Ct. 2279, 57 L.Ed.2d 117 (1978) (doctrine that repeals by implication are disfavored "applies with even greater force when the claimed repeal rests solely on an Appropriations Act"). . . .

In these circumstances, where previously appropriated money is available for an agency to perform a statutorily mandated activity, we see no basis for a court to excuse the agency from that statutory mandate.

Fourth, the record suggests that the Commission, as a policy matter, simply may not want to pursue Yucca Mountain as a possible site for storage of nuclear waste. But Congress sets the policy, not the Commission. And policy disagreement with Congress's decision about nuclear waste storage is not a lawful ground for the Commission to decline to continue the congressionally mandated licensing process. To reiterate, the President and federal agencies may not ignore statutory mandates or prohibitions merely because of policy disagreement with Congress.

III

We thus far have concluded that the Commission's inaction violates the Nuclear Waste Policy Act. To be sure, there are also two principles rooted in Article II of the Constitution that give the Executive authority, in certain circumstances, to decline to act in the face of a clear statute. But neither of those principles applies here. [The court explained that the President's independent authority to assess the constitutionality of a statute was not at issue. Nor could NRC rely on the Executive's Article II prosecutorial discretion.]

. . . .

IV

At the behest of the Commission, we have repeatedly gone out of our way over the last several years to defer a mandamus order against the Commission and thereby give Congress time to pass new legislation that would clarify this matter if it so wished. In our decision in August 2012, the Court's majority made clear, however, that mandamus likely would have to be granted at some point if Congress took no further action. Since then, Congress has taken no further action on this matter. At this point, the Commission is simply defying a law enacted by Congress, and the Commission is doing so without any legal basis.

We therefore have no good choice but to grant the petition for a writ of mandamus against the Commission. This case has serious implications for our constitutional structure. It is no overstatement to say that our constitutional system of separation of powers would be significantly altered if we were to allow executive and independent agencies to disregard federal law in the manner asserted in this case by the Nuclear Regulatory Commission. Our decision today rests on the constitutional authority of Congress, and the respect that the Executive and the Judiciary properly owe to Congress in the circumstances here. To be sure, if Congress determines in the wake of our decision that it will never fund the Commission's licensing process to completion, we would certainly hope that Congress would step in before the current $11.1 million is expended, so as to avoid wasting that taxpayer money. And Congress, of course, is under no obligation to appropriate additional money for the Yucca Mountain project. Moreover, our decision here does not prejudge the merits of the Commission's consideration or decision on the Department of Energy's license application, or the Commission's consideration or decision on any Department of Energy attempt to withdraw the license application. But unless and until Congress authoritatively says otherwise or there are no appropriated funds remaining, the Nuclear Regulatory Commission must promptly continue with the legally mandated licensing process. The petition for a writ of mandamus is granted.

So ordered. ∎

NOTES AND COMMENTS

1. Recall that after *Massachusetts v. EPA*, EPA evidenced reluctance to engage in greenhouse gas regulation under the CAA. (*See* Chapter 5.) Had EPA refused to act, what would have been the result?

2. On remand, NRC set forth a schedule of activities to be conducted in connection with the licensing proceeding. These activities were limited due to the lack of projected funds, and included consideration of a Safety Evaluation Report and NEPA compliance activities. NRC issued a portion of the Safety Evaluation Report on October 16, 2014; other portions are expected to be issued as they are completed. *See* NRC Press Release, NRC Staff Issues Volume 3 of Yucca Mountain Safety Evaluation Report (Oct. 16, 2014). The adjudication, however, continued to be held in abeyance. *See* In the Matter of U.S. DOE (High-Level Waste Repository), CLI 63–001, 2013 WL 7046350 (NRC Nov. 18, 2013).

3. The Yucca Mountain Project is designed to hold over 70,000 metric tons of spent nuclear fuel. However, industry data as of 2009 showed nearly 63,000 tons of spent nuclear fuel in temporary storage across the United States, with an additional 2000-to-2400 tons being added annually. Even if Yucca Mountain were to go forward, what should be done with the spent nuclear fuel in excess of the project's design capacity?

4. Over $15 billion has been spent on the Yucca Mountain Project. As of this writing, it is fenced and closed. With the funding cutbacks mentioned above, staffing for the site was eliminated, and officials were forced to shut off the lights and ventilation. Many of the scientists and engineers associated with Yucca Mountain have retired or moved to other jobs. Were the site to reopen, how could sufficient human expertise be re-mobilized?

b.   IMPLICATIONS OF THE FAILURE OF THE YUCCA MOUNTAIN PROJECT

i.   *The Blue Ribbon Commission's Report*

On January 29, 2010, DOE announced the formation of a Blue Ribbon Commission (BRC) on America's Nuclear Future. As mentioned above, the BRC was formed following the Obama Administration's decision not to proceed with Yucca Mountain. In fact, the BRC was specifically mandated *not* to consider Yucca Mountain. The BRC issued its full report in 2012, and made eight key recommendations:

     (1) A consent-based approach to siting future nuclear waste facilities.

     (2) A new organization or agency whose sole mission is to implement a waste management program.

     (3) Access to the money in the Nuclear Waste Fund.

(4) Prompt efforts to develop a geologic repository.

(5) Prompt efforts to develop a consolidated storage facility.

(6) Prompt efforts to prepare for shipping massive amounts of spent nuclear to a consolidated facility or geologic repository.

(7) Funding for nuclear technology and workforce development.

(8) Active U.S. leadership in peaceful uses of nuclear power and non-proliferation activities.

See BRC on America's Nuclear Future, Report to the Secretary of Energy (Jan. 2012), http://cybercemetery.unt.edu/archive/brc/201206 20211605/http:/brc.gov/. Which of these recommendations seems most urgent to you? If implemented, which would best alleviate the many impacts of Yucca Mountain's failure? Consider this question as you read the following materials.

ii.   The Nuclear Waste Fund and Breach of Contract Claims

As described above, the NWPA enabled DOE to enter into contracts with nuclear power plant operators under which DOE agreed to gather and dispose of spent nuclear fuel in exchange for payments into the Nuclear Waste Fund. Utilities—and their customers through rates— thus paid substantial fees to DOE for many years to cover the costs of permanent geological disposal. But with Yucca Mountain's closure, nuclear power operators were faced with unanticipated costs of on-site storage of spent nuclear fuel. In two landmark suits against DOE, the D.C. Circuit held that DOE was liable under a breach-of-contract theory for costs incurred by DOE's delayed performance. N. States Power Co. v. DOE, 128 F.3d 754 (D.C. Cir. 1997); Ind. Mich. Power Co. v. DOE, 88 F.3d 1272 (D.C. Cir. 1996); *see also* Neb. Pub. Power Dist. v. United States, 590 F.3d 1357 (Fed. Cir. 2010) (holding proper D.C. Circuit's assertion of jurisdiction).

As of a 2009 report by the Congressional Research Service, 71 breach-of-contract claims had been filed against DOE, resulting in over a billion in damages so far with estimates of potential liability exceeding $50 billion. *See* Todd Garvey, The Yucca Mountain Litigation: Breach of Contract Under the Nuclear Waste Policy Act of 1982, CRS 7–5700 (Dec. 2009). And in an unusually forceful opinion, the D.C. Circuit in 2013 ordered DOE to stop collecting fees for the Nuclear Waste Fund: "[T]he Secretary is ordered to submit to Congress a proposal to change the fee to zero until such a time as either the Secretary chooses to comply with the Act as it is currently written, or until Congress enacts an alternative waste management plan." Nat'l Ass'n of Regulatory Util. Comm'rs v. DOE, 736 F.3d 517, 521 (D.C. Cir. 2013). Currently, the Fund contains about $31 billion, interest upon which accrues at about $1.3 billion per year. For a variety of reasons, the money in the fund is difficult to access for its intended purpose, and is instead used to offset the federal budget deficit. *See* BRC, *supra*, at 72–76. Although the BRC recommended changes to the structure of the Fund, its future has not been decided as of this writing; meanwhile, the breach-of-contract litigation continues.

iii. Interim Storage Methods

Recall that spent nuclear fuel is initially stored in water pools on the site of each nuclear power plant in which the fuel was used. Water pool storage of spent nuclear fuel is needed for 3 to 10 years in order to cool the fuel and protect against releases of radiation. At some sites, water pool storage continues indefinitely; at others, dry cask storage provides an option after the fuel is sufficiently cool. Industry reported in 2009 that over 48,000 metric tons were stored in pools, while nearly 14,000 metric tons (about 22 percent) were stored in dry casks.[1]

One might ask whether private fuel storage could be a possibility. One group tried. Private Fuel Storage (PFS) was a joint venture of electric utility companies that sought permits for a facility that would accept spent fuel to be stored onsite in dry cask storage. PFS contracted with a Native American Tribe to build a facility on Tribal property in Tooele County, Utah. The County, located west of Great Salt Lake, was already home to two Air Force bombing ranges, the Dugway Proving Grounds and Chemical Demolition Center (where stocks of nerve gas are being incinerated), and the Tooele Army Depot, which is a storage site for war reserve and training ammunition.

NRC approved permits, but the State of Utah opposed the project. The State adopted legislation trying to prevent PFS from building the facility, but Tribal land is exempt from many kinds of state regulation. And in *Skull Valley Band of Goshute Indians v. Nielson*, 376 F.3d 1223 (10th Cir. 2004), the Tenth Circuit held that Utah was trying to regulate nuclear safety, which was preempted by the federal law. But Utah's congressional delegation slipped into a budget bill a clause designating a small piece of land on the access route to the site as wilderness. This designation prevented construction of a rail line to the site, and the project collapsed.

With spent nuclear fuel in storage at nuclear power plants across the country and no geologic repository in sight, NRC issued an updated Waste Confidence Decision. The new rule departed from the prior Waste Confidence Decision in that it no longer attempted to specify a date certain by which a geologic repository would be available. Waste Confidence Decision Update, 75 Fed. Reg. 81,037 (Dec. 23, 2010). Instead, NRC revised its timeframes within which spent fuel could be stored onsite from 30 years after the expiration of a facility's license to 60 years past that date. The decision excerpted below, *New York v. NRC*, 681 F.3d 471 (D.C. Cir. 2012), sets forth the D.C. Circuit's response.

iv. The Waste Confidence Decision

New York v. NRC

681 F.3d 471 (D.C. Cir. 2012).

■ SENTELLE, C.J. Four states, an Indian community, and a number of environmental groups petition this Court for review of a Nuclear

---

[1] For security reasons, the federal government does not share data on nuclear waste storage. The industry releases its own data periodically, but as of this writing has not done so since 2009.

Regulatory Commission ("NRC" or "Commission") rulemaking regarding temporary storage and permanent disposal of nuclear waste. . . .

I.   Background

This is another in the growing line of cases involving the federal government's failure to establish a permanent repository for civilian nuclear waste. *See, e.g.*, In re Aiken County, 645 F.3d 428, 430–31 (D.C.Cir.2011) (recounting prior cases). We address the Commission's recent rulemaking regarding the prospects for permanent disposal of nuclear waste and the environmental effects of temporarily storing such material on site at nuclear plants until a permanent disposal facility is available.

After four to six years of use in a reactor, nuclear fuel rods can no longer efficiently produce energy and are considered "spent nuclear fuel" ("SNF"). Fuel rods are thermally hot when removed from reactors and emit great amounts of radiation—enough to be fatal in minutes to someone in the immediate vicinity. Therefore, the rods are transferred to racks within deep, water-filled pools for cooling and to protect workers from radiation. After the fuel has cooled, it may be transferred to dry storage, which consists of large concrete and steel "casks." Most SNF, however, will remain in spent-fuel pools until a permanent disposal solution is available.

Even though it is no longer useful for nuclear power, SNF poses a dangerous, long-term health and environmental risk. It will remain dangerous "for time spans seemingly beyond human comprehension." Nuclear Energy Inst., Inc. v. Envtl. Prot. Agency, 373 F.3d 1251, 1258 (D.C. Cir. 2004) (per curiam). Determining how to dispose of the growing volume of SNF, which may reach 150,000 metric tons by the year 2050, is a serious problem. Yet despite years of "blue ribbon" commissions, congressional hearings, agency reports, and site investigations, the United States has not yet developed a permanent solution. That failure, declared the most recent "blue ribbon" panel, is the "central flaw of the U.S. nuclear waste management program to date." Experts agree that the ultimate solution will be a "geologic repository," in which SNF is stored deep within the earth, protected by a combination of natural and engineered barriers. Twenty years of work on establishing such a repository at Yucca Mountain was recently abandoned when the Department of Energy decided to withdraw its license application for the facility. At this time, there is not even a prospective site for a repository, let alone progress toward the actual construction of one.

Due to the government's failure to establish a final resting place for spent fuel, SNF is currently stored on site at nuclear plants. This type of storage, optimistically labeled "temporary storage," has been used for decades longer than originally anticipated. The delay has required plants to expand storage pools and to pack SNF more densely within them. The lack of progress on a permanent repository has caused considerable uncertainty regarding the environmental effects of temporary SNF storage and the reasonableness of continuing to license and relicense nuclear reactors.

In this case, petitioners challenge a 2010 update to the NRC's Waste Confidence Decision ("WCD"). The original WCD came as the result of a 1979 decision by this court remanding the Commission's decision to allow the expansion of spent-fuel pools at two nuclear plants. Minnesota v. NRC, 602 F.2d 412 (D.C. Cir. 1979). In *Minnesota*, we directed the Commission to consider "whether there is reasonable assurance that an off-site storage solution [for spent fuel] will be available by . . . the expiration of the plants' operating licenses, and if not, whether there is reasonable assurance that the fuel can be stored safely at the sites beyond those dates." The WCD is the Commission's determination of those risks and assurances.

The original WCD was published in 1984 and included five "Waste Confidence Findings." Briefly, those findings declared that: 1) safe disposal in a mined geologic repository is technically feasible, 2) such a repository will be available by 2007–2009, 3) waste will be managed safely until the repository is available, 4) SNF can be stored safely at nuclear plants for at least thirty years beyond the licensed life of each plant, and 5) safe, independent storage will be made available if needed. The Commission updated the WCD in 1990 to reflect new understandings about waste disposal and to predict the availability of a repository by 2025. The Commission reviewed the WCD again in 1999 without altering it.

In 2008, the Commission proposed revisions to the Waste Confidence Findings, and, after considering public comments, made revisions in 2010. Waste Confidence Decision Update, 75 Fed. Reg. 81,037 (Dec. 23, 2010). That decision, under review in this case, reaffirmed three of the Waste Confidence Findings and updated two. First, the Commission revised Finding 2, which, as of 1990, expected that a permanent geologic repository would be available in the first quarter of the twenty-first century. As amended, Finding 2 now states that a suitable repository will be available "when necessary," rather than by a date certain. *Id.* at 81,038. In reaching that conclusion, the Commission examined the political and technical obstacles to permanent storage and determined that a permanent repository will be ready by the time the safety of temporary on-site storage can no longer be assured. *Id.*

Finding 4 originally held that SNF could be safely stored at nuclear reactor sites without significant environmental effects for at least thirty years beyond each plant's licensed life, including the license-renewal period. *Id.* at 81,039. In revising that finding, the Commission examined the potential environmental effects from temporary storage, such as leakages from the spent-fuel pools and fires caused by the SNF becoming exposed to the air. Concluding that previous leaks had only a negligible near-term health effect and that recent regulatory enhancements will further reduce the risk of leaks, the Commission determined that leaks do not pose the threat of a significant environmental impact. *Id.* at 81,069–71. The Commission also found that pool fires are sufficiently unlikely as to pose no significant environmental threat. *Id.* at 81,070–71. As amended, Finding 4 now holds that SNF can be safely stored at plants for at least sixty years beyond the licensed life of a plant, instead of thirty. *Id.* at 81,074. In addition, the Commission noted in its final rule that it will be developing a plan for longer-term storage and will conduct a full assessment of the environmental impact of storage beyond the sixty-year post-license period. *Id.* at 81,040. Based on the revised WCD, the Commission released a new Temporary Storage Rule ("TSR") enacting its conclusions and updating its regulations accordingly. *See* Consideration of Environmental Impacts of Temporary Storage of Spent Fuel after Cessation of Reactor Operation, 75 Fed. Reg. 81,032 (Dec. 23, 2010); 10 C.F.R. § 51.23(a). Petitioners challenge the amended 10 C.F.R. § 51.23(a) based on both Finding 2 and Finding 4.

II. The Commission's Obligations Under NEPA

The National Environmental Policy Act of 1969 ("NEPA"), 42 U.S.C. § 4321 et seq., requires federal agencies such as the Commission to examine and report on the environmental consequences of their actions. NEPA is an "essentially procedural" statute intended to ensure "fully informed and well-considered" decisionmaking, but not necessarily the best decision. Vermont Yankee Nuclear Power Corp. v. NRDC, 435 U.S. 519, 558 (1978). Under NEPA, each federal agency must prepare an Environmental Impact Statement ("EIS") before taking a "major Federal action[ ] significantly affecting the quality of the human environment." 42 U.S.C. § 4332(2)(C). An agency can avoid preparing an EIS, however, if it conducts an Environmental Assessment ("EA") and makes a Finding of No Significant Impact ("FONSI"). . . . The issuance or reissuance of a reactor license is a major federal action affecting the quality of the human environment.

The parties here dispute whether the WCD itself constitutes a major federal action. . . . [The court held that the WCD constituted a major federal action because its generic findings have a preclusive effect in all future licensing decisions. Thus, the agency was required to follow the NEPA process.]

III. Availability of a Permanent Repository

With these NEPA obligations in mind, we turn to the Commission's conclusion that a permanent repository for SNF will be available "when necessary." In so concluding, the Commission examined the historical difficulty—now measured in decades rather than years—in establishing a permanent facility. Though a number of commenters suggested that the social and political barriers to building a geologic repository are too great to conclude that a facility could be built in any reasonable timeframe, the Commission believes that the lessons learned from the Yucca Mountain program and the Blue Ribbon Commission on America's Nuclear Future will ensure that, through "open and transparent" decisionmaking, a consensus would be reached. Further, the Commission noted that the Nuclear Waste Policy Act mandates a repository program, demonstrating the continued commitment and obligation of the federal government to pursue one. The scientific and experiential knowledge of the past decades, the Commission explained, would enable the government to create a suitable repository by the time one is needed.

A.

Petitioners argue that the Commission's conclusion regarding permanent storage violates NEPA in two ways: First, it fails to fully account for the significant societal and political barriers that may delay or prevent the opening of a repository. Second, the Commission's conclusion that a permanent repository will be available "when necessary" fails to define the term "necessary" in any meaningful way and does not address the effects of a failure to establish a repository in time. Petitioners further contest the Commission's claim that the WCD constitutes an EA for permanent disposal, let alone the EIS they contend is required here.

The Commission responds by contending that it "candidly acknowledged" the societal and political challenges, and crafted the WCD to account for those risks. Overcoming political obstacles is not the responsibility of the Commission, it contends, and the NRC's conclusion that institutional obstacles will not prevent a repository from being built is entitled to substantial deference. The Commission contends that the selection of a precise date for Finding 2 is not required by NEPA or any other laws governing the NRC, and the Commission used the "when necessary" formulation as far back as 1977.

As for examining the environmental effects of failing to establish a repository, the Commission contends that the WCD is an EA supporting the revision of 10 C.F.R. § 51.23(a). No EIS is necessary regarding permanent disposal because, the Commission argues, the WCD is not a major federal action, and conducting an EIS for this issue would be the sort of "abstract exercise" the Supreme Court declined to require in Baltimore Gas and Electric Company v. NRDC, 462 U.S. 87, 100 (1983). Further, the Commission's existing "Table S–3" already considers the environmental effects of the nuclear fuel cycle generally and found no significant impacts. Therefore, the Commission believes, no EIS is required.

B.

The Commission's "when necessary" finding is already imperiled by our conclusion that the WCD is a major federal action. We hold that the WCD must be vacated as to its revision to Finding 2 because the WCD fails to properly analyze the environmental effects of its permanent disposal conclusion.

While we share petitioners' considerable skepticism as to whether a permanent facility can be built given the societal and political barriers to selecting a site, we need not resolve whether the Commission adequately considered those barriers. Likewise, we need not decide whether, as the Commission contends, an agency's interpretation of the political landscape surrounding its field of expertise merits deference. Instead, we hold the WCD is defective on far simpler grounds: As we have determined, the WCD is a major federal action because it is used to allow the licensing of nuclear plants. Therefore, the WCD requires an EIS or, alternatively, an EA that concludes with a finding of no significant impact. The Commission did not supply a suitable FONSI here because it did not examine the environmental effects of failing to establish a repository.

Even taking the Commission's word that the WCD constitutes an EA for the permanent storage conclusion, the EA is insufficient because a finding that "reasonable assurance exists that sufficient mined geologic repository capacity will be available when necessary," does not describe a probability of failure so low as to dismiss the potential consequences of such a failure. Under NEPA, an agency must look at both the probabilities of potentially harmful events and the consequences if those events come to pass. An agency may find no significant impact if the probability is so low as to be "remote and speculative," or if the combination of probability and harm is sufficiently minimal. *See, e.g.,*

City of New York v. Dep't of Transp., 715 F.2d 732, 738 (2d Cir.1983) ("The concept of overall risk incorporates the significance of possible adverse consequences discounted by the improbability of their occurrence."). Here, a "reasonable assurance" that permanent storage will be available is a far cry from finding the likelihood of nonavailability to be "remote and speculative." The Commission failed to examine the environmental consequences of failing to establish a repository when one is needed.

The Commission argues that its "Table S–3" already accounts for the environmental effects of the nuclear fuel cycle and finds no significant impact. Not so. Table S–3, like the Commission itself, presumes the existence of a geologic repository. Therefore, it cannot explain the environmental effects of a failure to secure a permanent facility. The Commission also complains that conducting a full analysis regarding permanent storage would be an "abstract exercise." Perhaps the Commission thinks so because it perceives the required analysis to be of the effects of the permanent repository itself. But we are focused on the effects of a failure to secure permanent storage. The Commission apparently has no long-term plan other than hoping for a geologic repository. If the government continues to fail in its quest to establish one, then SNF will seemingly be stored on site at nuclear plants on a permanent basis. The Commission can and must assess the potential environmental effects of such a failure.

IV. Temporary On-Site Storage of SNF

In concluding that SNF can safely be stored in on-site storage pools for a period of sixty years after the end of a plant's life, instead of thirty, the Commission conducted what it purports to be an EA, which found that extending the time for storage would have no significant environmental impact. This analysis was conducted in generic fashion by looking to environmental risks across the board at nuclear plants, rather than by conducting a site-by-site analysis of each specific nuclear plant. Two key risks the Commission examined in its EA were the risk of environmental harm due to pool leakage and the risk of a fire resulting from the fuel rods becoming exposed to air. We conclude that the Commission's EA and resulting FONSI are not supported by substantial evidence on the record because the Commission failed to properly examine the risk of leaks in a forward-looking fashion and failed to examine the potential consequences of pool fires.

. . .

Both the Supreme Court and this court have endorsed the Commission's longstanding practice of considering environmental issues through general rulemaking in appropriate circumstances. *See, e.g.,* Baltimore Gas, 462 U.S. at 100 ("The generic method chosen by the agency is clearly an appropriate method of conducting the hard look required by NEPA."). Though *Baltimore Gas* dealt with the nuclear fuel cycle itself, which is generally focused on things that occur outside of individual plants, we see no reason that a comprehensive general analysis would be insufficient to examine on-site risks that are essentially common to all plants. This is particularly true given the Commission's use of conservative bounding assumptions and the opportunity for concerned parties to raise site-specific differences at the time of a specific site's licensing. Nonetheless, whether the analysis is generic or site-by-site, it must be thorough and comprehensive. Even though the Commission's application of its technical expertise demands the "most deferential" treatment by the courts, *Baltimore Gas*, 462 U.S. at 103, we conclude that the Commission has failed to conduct a thorough enough analysis here to merit our deference.

1.

The Commission admits in the WCD Update that there have been "several incidents of groundwater contamination originating from leaking reactor spent fuel pools and associated structures." The Commission brushes away that concern by stating that the past leaks had only a negligible near-term health impact. Even setting aside the fact that near-term health effects are not the only type of environmental impacts, the harm from past leaks—without more—tells us very little about the potential for future leaks or the harm such leaks might portend. The WCD Update seeks to extend the period of time for which pools are considered safe for storage; therefore, a proper analysis of the risks would necessarily look forward to examine the effects of the additional time in storage, as well as examining past leaks in a manner that would allow the Commission to rule out the possibility that those leaks were only harmless because of site-specific factors or even sheer luck. The WCD Update has no analysis of those possibilities other than to say that past leaks had "negligible" near-term health effects. A study of the impact of thirty additional years of SNF storage must actually concern itself with the extra years of storage.

Despite giving our "most deferential" treatment to the Commission's application of its technical and scientific expertise, we cannot reconcile a finding that past leaks have been harmless with a conclusion that future leaks at all sites will be harmless as well. The Commission's task here was to determine whether the pools could be considered safe for an additional thirty years in the future. That past leaks have not been harmful with respect to groundwater does not speak to whether and how future leaks might occur, and what the effects of those leaks might be. The Commission's analysis of leaks, therefore, was insufficient.

2.

Even though the Commission engaged in a more substantial analysis of fires than it did of leaks, that analysis is plagued by a failure to examine the consequences of pool fires in addition to the probabilities. Petitioners . . . argue that the Commission could only avoid conducting an EIS if it found the risk of fires to be "remote and speculative." The Commission argues that it did not need to examine the consequences of fires because it found the risk of fires to be very low.

We disagree with both parties. As should be clear by this point in our opinion, an agency conducting an EA generally must examine both the probability of a given harm occurring and the consequences of that harm if it does occur. Only if the harm in question is so "remote and speculative" as to reduce the effective probability of its occurrence to zero may the agency dispense with the consequences portion of the analysis. But, contra petitioners, the finding that the probability of a given harm is nonzero does not, by itself, mandate an EIS: after the agency examines the consequences of the harm in proportion to the likelihood of its occurrence, the overall expected harm could still be insignificant and thus could support a FONSI. Here, however, the Commission did not undertake to examine the consequences of pool fires at all. Depending on the weighing of the probability and the consequences, an EIS may or may not be required, and such a determination would merit considerable deference. But unless the risk is "remote and speculative," the Commission must put the weights on both sides of the scale before it can make a determination.

. . .

Overall, we cannot defer to the Commission's conclusions regarding temporary storage because the Commission did not conduct a sufficient analysis of the environmental risks. In so holding, we do not require, as petitioners would prefer, that the Commission examine each site individually. However, a generic analysis must be forward looking and have enough breadth to support the Commission's conclusions. Furthermore, as NEPA requires, the Commission must conduct a true EA regarding the extension of temporary storage. Such an analysis must, unless it finds the probability of a given risk to be effectively zero, account for the consequences of each risk. On remand, the Commission will have the opportunity to conduct exactly such an analysis.

V.   Conclusion

We recognize that the Commission is in a difficult position given the political problems concerning the storage of spent nuclear fuel. Nonetheless, the Commission's obligations under NEPA require a more thorough analysis than provided for in the WCD Update. We note that the Commission is currently conducting an EIS regarding the environmental impacts of SNF storage beyond the sixty-year post-license period at issue in this case, and some or all of the problems here may be addressed in such a rulemaking. In any event, we grant the petitions for review, vacate the WCD Update and TSR, and remand for further proceedings consistent with this opinion.

So ordered.

NOTES AND COMMENTS

1.   As noted previously, the Waste Confidence Decision formed the basis of power plant licensing since the 1970s. Generic rulemaking is a method by which many agencies—not just NRC—can resolve issues that would be recurring and redundant in licensing decisions. It played a role in several of the decisions in this Chapter. Did the D.C. Circuit hold that NRC could not proceed by generic rulemaking? What were the flaws in NRC's approach? What are its obligations on remand?

2.   The principal case speaks in terms of risk assessment; that is, risk is a function of both the likelihood of a hazard occurring and the magnitude of that hazard. What were the flaws in the agency's risk assessment approach with respect to temporary pool storage? Consider another aspect of risk theory—that of risk perception. As noted throughout this book, a variety of mechanisms contribute to perceptions of risk that over-or under-predict the measurable risk at issue. How does the principal case account for the impacts of risk perception? Does it?

3.   Following *New York v. NRC*, NRC announced its decision not to issue licenses for activities that were dependent on the Waste Confidence Decision.

The result was that most COL applications were suspended. Finally, in 2014, NRC issued a new rule with a new name: the Continued Storage of Spent Nuclear Fuel. *See* Continued Storage of Spent Nuclear Fuel, 79 Fed. Reg. 56,238 (Sept. 19, 2014). The new rule is accompanied by a new Generic Environmental Impact Statement. *See id.* It analyzes the environmental effects of spent fuel storage for three timeframes: (1) up to 60 years following the expiration of a reactor license; (2) up to 160 years following the expiration of a reactor license; and (3) indefinite storage. *Id.* at 56,245. Key assumptions include replacing storage containers every 100 years and removing all spent fuel from pools at the end of the shortest 60-year timeframe. The GEIS continues to conclude that geologic storage will continue to be feasible and will at some point be available. *Id.* at 56,251–52. The final rule is effective October 20, 2014. Do you expect a legal challenge?

4.   Review the mix of incentives for nuclear power and many hurdles it continues to face. What is your view of its continuing role in the electricity sector?

CHAPTER 8

RATE REGULATION PRINCIPLES

As discussed in Chapter 2, electric power distributors and many other energy facilities (such as gas distribution lines) have long been considered natural monopolies. Many firms providing gas and electric services to customers are regulated as public utilities and granted an exclusive monopoly franchise in exchange for controlled rates. A public utility's rates are typically set based on cost, to ensure that it does not engage in monopolistic conduct, such as overcharging customers or unfairly discriminating across customer groups.

This chapter discusses the operation and challenges created by cost-of-service rate regulation, setting the stage for discussion of the opening up of gas and electric power markets in Chapters 9 and 10, respectively. As is discussed in the following two chapters, even though many states today have "deregulated" gas and electric power, the ratemaking principles discussed in these chapters continue to apply in a majority of states—and effectively apply in even deregulated states to the distribution utility's "wires" services.

A. AN OVERVIEW OF RATES BASED ON COST-OF-SERVICE

The establishment of a monopoly franchise for any energy firm will raise the specter of monopoly pricing, at potential harm to consumers. Justice Stephen Breyer wrote an important book on the topic of economic regulation prior to his elevation to Justice of the U.S. Supreme Court. According to him:

> In a perfectly competitive market, firms expand output to the point where price equals incremental cost—the cost of producing an additional unit of their product. A monopolist, if unregulated, curtails production in order to raise prices. Higher prices mean less demand, but the monopolist willingly forgoes sales—to the extent that he can more than compensate for the lost revenue (from fewer sales) by gaining revenue through increased price on the units that are still sold.

Stephen Breyer, Regulation and Its Reform 15–16 (1982). It is well understood that, left unchecked, the monopolist who does not face a competitive market has incentives to charge a price above the competitive level, produce less output than a competitive market, and transfer wealth from consumers to itself.

Price regulation is designed to serve as a check on the monopolist. In economic terms, price regulation aims to produce the mix of price, output, and profits approximating that which a competitive market would produce. Price regulation began with the local railroad and gas boards of the late nineteenth century. Today, most state public utility commissions (PUCs) or public service commissions (PSCs), as well as the Federal Energy Regulatory Commission (FERC) (the Federal Power Commission's (FPC) successor agency), continue (to varying degrees) to regulate the prices public utilities charge their customers on the basis of the cost incurred to provide service.

Cost-of-service rate regulation is a widely accepted way of limiting the losses to society associated with a monopolist's higher price and reduced output. Much cost-of-service regulation is designed with this consumer protection goal in mind. No less important, granting a monopoly and setting rates is designed to assure that a regulated firm earns what it needs to remain in business. For example, as discussed later in this chapter, under the Takings Clause of the Fifth Amendment of the U.S. Constitution, a utility's investors are allowed to earn an adequate rate of return on their investments.

Regulators achieve these goals by attempting to set price at a level that—at least in theory—would approximate a competitive market. What works in theory, however, does not always work in practice. By definition, no comparable competitive market for a natural monopoly service exists; the very presence of such a competitive market would call into question whether such a "natural" monopoly exists in the first place. (Why? Think back to Chapter 2.) Given the lack of a competitive market against which the monopolist's prices can be compared, regulators are forced to look at the firm's costs of providing service to customers. Consequently, rates are typically set to cover reasonably incurred costs, including a fair rate of return on investment for the firm's investors.

This approach to setting rates based on cost of servive is typically based on a simple formula, representing the firm's *revenue requirements*—that is, the costs a firm needs to recover in order to stay in business into the foreseeable future. The formula includes the amount the firm needs to cover both its fixed and variable costs, plus the cost of capital, including a reasonable rate of return for its investors.

Revenue requirements (R) can be stated as the following formula:

$$R = B*r + O$$

The variables to this formula include:

R the utility's *revenue requirement*—the total amount the firm needs to recover from its customers to cover its costs.

B the utility's *rate base*, representing its capital investment in plant and other assets.

R the *rate of return* regulators allow the utility to earn on its rate base to compensate its investors.

O the utility's *operating expenses*, or expenses such as fuel and labor that vary with its level of production.

B and O are typically determined based on "test year" data—a representative, recent year that shows the utility's typical capital investment and operating expenses. Data from this year are modified to reflect any abnormal circumstances that arose during that year. The rate of return is typically established based on testimony from economists and other experts about the return on investment produced by entities similar to the corporation that operate in approximately the same geographic area as the utility.

This formula is deceptively simple. In the real world, however, the calculation of each variable involves difficult economic and policy judgments. For example, calculating R involves a range of difficult financial and policy judgments, as well as many legal issues that are discussed below.

One each variable has been calculated for the utility, a revenue requirement and rate, or price, for servive can be determined. For example, if rates are set on a per unit basis for customers, $P = R/V$ where P is the price per unit the firm is permitted to charge, R is the firm's allowed revenue requirement, and V is the number of units of volume of the product the firm expects to sell. Note that the rates that a utility may charge based on this formula do not provide a guaranteed profit for the utility and its investors. Rather, if the utility operates as expected and sells a certain quantity of electricity, charging the allowed rate, it has the opportunity to cover its expenses and provide a return for its investors.

As a much-simplified example, consider the following hypothetical set of facts: Assume that Florida Power & Light (FP&L), an electric utility that operates a monopoly franchise serving retail customers, in the state of Florida, is submitting its rates for approval by Florida regulators. FP&L incurs $10,000,000 in operating expenses, including purchasing coal or natural gas and paying its employees, and builds its power plant and transmission lines at a cost of $250,000,000 in order to provide 28,000,000 kWh of service to a single class of residential customers in a given year. Further assume that the average cost of FP&L's various sources of capital—the interest it pays on its debt and the rate of return on its equity—is 10%. FP&L's revenue requirement is $10,000,000 + ($250,000,000 x .10), or $35,000,000. The Florida PSC will set its residential rates at $35,000,000/28,000,000, or $1.25 a kWh.

NOTE ON THE ECONOMICS OF PRICE REGULATION

As discussed in Chapter 2, gas and electric utilities were long considered to be natural monopolies, in which a single seller represents the most efficient way to provide service within a designated geographical market. Public utility regulation has historically protected gas and electric utilities against competitive entrants. Absent price regulation, the protected monopolist will be able to charge more than a competitive price—though it cannot charge an infinite price for its services, since consumers will eventually find substitutes. Indeed, the rational monopolist will charge a higher price and produce a lower quantity than a firm that is subject to competition. Therefore, one key objective of public utility regulation is to force the utility's price to be closer to the competitive price.

Within most markets, including gas and electric service markets, the market demand curve is downward sloping, because consumers purchase more of a product as price decreases. As the only seller in a given market, the monopolist facing this downward-sloping demand curve can increase price without losing customers to competitors, to the extent that the revenue realized from a price increase is greater than the revenue lost from (those few) customers who exit the system in response to a price increase. In perfect competition (where there are many sellers, not a single monopolist), an individual firm does not face a downward-sloping demand source. Instead, its demand curve is flat: the firm is a price taker, meaning that is the firm raises its prices consumers can always find a competitive firm willing to sell at the lower, competitive price. Thus, even though the industry-wide demand curve is downward sloping under both monopoly and competition, under competition the firm is only presented with a flat demand curve, representing demand at a competitive price. In this way, the monopoly seller has the power to control price and quantity in competitive market in ways competitive sellers do not.

This basic phenomenon is the result of differences in the *elasticity of demand* between a competitive market and a monopolist one. In most industries, the demand curve is downward sloping, representing that consumers purchase more of a product as price decreases. While such demand curves are common in both competitive and monopolistic markets, there are differences between a competitive and monopolistic *firm*. A perfectly competitive firm does not face a downward sloping demand curve. Instead, its demand curve is flat, or *elastic*, representing that the single firm has little or no control over price, even though the industry-wide demand curve may be downward sloping; if a competitive firm increases its price above the market price, it risks losing all of its customers, as they substitute away to other firms charging lower prices.

In contrast, the monopolist firm faces a more *inelastic* demand curve (since it faces the same demand curve as the industry), allowing it the ability to increase price without losing as many customers. Elasticity of demand for a firm reflects the willingness of consumers to respond to changes in price and, when a firm faces an inelastic demand curve (as the monopolist does) the degree of market power the firm possesses over price is substantially larger than a firm facing an elastic demand curve.

As a technical illustration of this phenomenon, consider **Figure 8–1**. Assume that the monopolist seeks to maximize its profits and that it charges all consumers the same price. Because the monopolist is the only firm serving the market, the firm's demand curve is the industry demand curve; it is downward sloping, reflecting that consumers will buy more of a product if the price is lower. The monopolist, like any other firm, must choose the level of output to produce and the price to charge. Like any other firm, it will produce to the point where marginal revenues equal marginal costs. If the firm gains $1 by selling 1 more unit and its marginal costs are only $.80, the firm will expand production because marginal revenues exceed marginal costs, bringing the firm a profit.

Of course, firms in a competitive market would also produce up to the point where marginal revenue (including a rate of return, to ensure the firm can provide a return to its investors) equals marginal cost; however, a competitive firm would face a very different demand curve; again, if a market is competitive the firm's demand curve is relatively flat, or *elastic*, since the competitive firm will not be able to increase its price significantly without losing all or most of its customers to its competitors. (Unlike the firm's demand curve, in a competitive market the industry's demand curve remains downward sloping.) By contrast, the firm in a monopolistic market faces the same downward sloping demand curve as the industry in that market, reflecting its degree of market power over price. Since demand for this firm is relatively price *inelastic*, it can increase its prices through output restrictions to the point where it maximizes profits (again where marginal revenue equals marginal cost).

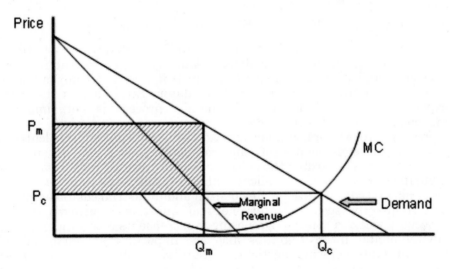

Figure 8–1

The profit-maximizing strategies of a firm in a monopolistic market will yield a different quantity of production and price than the strategy of a competitive firm. Although the monopolist will follow a basic decision-making process very similar to the competitive firm—it will produce at an output level up to the point additional revenues (including a rate of return) equal additional costs—the characteristics of monopolist markets make the outcomes of this process very different. A competitive market would produce the quantity QC and charge price PC. The monopolist will produce less and charge a higher price than a competitive market would yield. It will produce the quantity QM and charge price PM. In so doing it maximizes its profits.

There are some well-recognized economic losses produced by such monopoly pricing that may make government regulation desirable. One such loss is reduced access to products and higher prices, as is reflected in the shaded box of **Figure 8–1**. This shaded box may represent monopoly profits, or money spent by the monopolist to exclude potential rivals. Government might regulate monopoly pricing for a variety of purposes, including protection of consumers against pricing abuses, ensuring monopoly rents are spent on socially valuable items, protecting against the risks of political influence, and limiting the size of the firm and encouraging small business. For further discussion of the basics, see Richard A. Posner, Economic Analysis of Law 343–66 (Little Brown, 4th ed. 1992); Mark Seidenfeld, Microeconomic Predicates to Law and Economics 61–62 (1996); W. Kip Viscusi, John M. Vernon & Joseph E. Harrington, Jr., Economics of Regulation and Antitrust (1992). While rather technical in nature, this economic explanation of the losses associated with monopoly pricing explains a simple intuition that undergirds the principles of price regulation and the legal issues surrounding it: The monopolist will typically be inclined to price its services higher and produce less of them than a competitive market. This comes at a cost to consumers and to society.

B. COMMON LEGAL ISSUES IN COST-OF-SERVICE REGULATION

1. A HYPOTHETICAL RATEMAKING PROBLEM

While the cost-of-service formula is well accepted in the practice of ratemaking, the devil is in the details. A utility's expenses and financial decisions, and its claims about how much it needs to compensate its investors, are a starting point, but regulators rarely accept the firm's expenses at face value. The ratemaking process is not simple or inexpensive for utilities, consumers or regulators, but instead economists, regulators, and lawyers expend significant effort calculating the various components of the ratemaking formula. In making determinations regarding the calculation of the cost-of-service variables, regulators need to strike a delicate balance to address a range of societal and financial considerations. Residential and industrial customer groups will frequently seek to intervene and question a utility's rates—especially where a utility is proposing to increase its rates. Increasingly, environmental interest groups also are important stakeholders and frequently intervene and participate in utility ratemaking proceedings.

A ratemaking proceeding typically begins with a utility's proposal to increase rates, though the process can also be initiated by regulators in their role as monitors of previously-approved rates. By the time a utility makes a rate proposal to regulators, it typically has amassed a considerable amount of data to support its requested rates, and often will also have expert testimony to back up the policy judgments that lie beneath its request. A calculation of the various cost-of-service components typically is determined by an agency following an adjudicative hearing, in which the utility and intervenors submit evidence and present various arguments for consideration. These ratemaking proceedings are important because—along with proceedings related to the "need" for new generation, transmission and distribution facilities ("need" proceedings are discussed in Chapter 11)—they determine basic infrastructure decisions that will affect society, sometimes for decades into the future.

Effective energy lawyers, whether they represent utilities or other stakeholders, need to understand the basic policy, constitutional, and statutory considerations that typically arise in ratemaking proceedings. To give these issues some context, the following problem is designed to present a (somewhat simplified) example of some issues that can arise in a typical rate case. The problem is designed to survey the range of legal and policy issues that rate cases present for modern energy lawyers.

Throughout the remainder of the chapter, many questions presented following excerpted cases connect back to this problem, which is designed to survey a range of issues associated with cost of service ratemaking. Following the problem, some background cases are used to introduce important legal principles that inform debates about the value of the various calculations in utility rate cases. Later, the chapter also highlights how jurisdictional issues also play an important role in utility ratemaking.

COST-OF-SERVICE RATEMAKING PROBLEM

Edison Electric (EE), an investor-owned public utility in the State of New York, is seeking a rate increase from the New York State Public Service Commission (PSC). The rate increase is designed to address some costly new projects EE is pursuing to address the environmental impacts of its approach to generating electric power and to improve the reliability of the service it provides to its customer. EE is maintaining that these investments would result in a 20% increase in the average residential customer's annual power costs, and is seeking a rate increase.

A portion of EE's request focuses on the cost of retrofitting the power generation turbines at one of its oldest coal-fired power plants to allow the plant to convert from burning coal to natural gas as a way of generating power in the future. Assume that the capital expenditures to allow these base load plants to remain in operation and burn natural gas instead of coal total $30 million. EE's request would include these expenses in rate base. These costs would be allocated primarily to "firm" residential and commercial customers, since these customers require reliable power. Industrial ratepayers, who have interruptible tariffs (allowing the utility to turn off their power in shortage situations with some notice), will not be allocated any costs associated with these capital expenditures, since there is no obligation to provide service to them during peak periods where notice of interruption has been provided.

As EE retires its coal plant, it also needs to clean up the stored waste at the site from past power generation to comply with state hazardous waste laws. EE is requesting $10 million for these cleanup costs in its rate base, as well as an additional $1 million annually (as an operating expense) for the next 5 years for the costs of monitoring and studying the risks associated with the past storage of coal waste. EE maintains that a fuel adjustment clause (FAC) decrease due to low natural gas prices will likely offset this monitoring expense. (An FAC is a provision separate from a rate that, unlike the rate that may be charged per kWh of electricity provided, may be automatically adjusted up or down depending on the price of fuel. Under this adjustment clause, the utility is compensated for its costs (the costs of fuel) by ratepayers on a penny-for-penny basis. The rate that may be charged per kWh of electricity, on the other hand, might over- or under-compensate the utility for its costs depending on how efficiently the utility operates.)

EE has also requested to include in the rate base the cost of new software to help it analyze consumer consumption patterns, with an eye towards encouraging conservation through future reductions in demand. This new software, which will be deployed on EE's residential smart meters, is expected to cost $15 million.

In addition, EE is requesting to invest $30 million in a multi-state transmission line project that will improve the reliability of the grid throughout the Northeastern United States and allow it to use more renewable energy resources in its generation portfolio, as New York law requires. FERC has approved the cost allocation of this project in wholesale rates as part of a transmission planning process initiated by the New York Independent System Operator (a regional transmission organization (RTO), of which EE is a voluntary member). The proposed cost allocation would require the RTO's members, including EE, to pay for the new lines to purchase and sell electricity in the bulk power market. Renewable energy suppliers in the wind industry are excited about this new line, which will allow them to sell their power to a larger geographic market. EE will own the portion of these new lines in its service territory. The lines will provide some congestion relief that will benefit customers of EE by improving the reliability of EE's grid, as well as the grid of other utilities throughout the Northeast—an important goal in addressing the increased risk of hurricanes and other storm outages associated with climate change adaptation.

EE's allowable current return on rate base, representing the cost of capital, was last approved by the PSC in 2008, and is currently 10.5%. EE is requesting a 12% cost of capital. Part of the reason for the increase is the increased volatility of risk in the energy industry given federal regulation of emissions from coal plants and a more robust interstate market for electric power.

Here is a summary of how EE's overall rate increase request breaks down:

Rate base increase request:	$85 million
New cost of capital:	12 percent
Annual operating expenses:	$1 million increase
FAC adjustment:	anticipated $1 million reduction per year

The stakeholders:

New York's Consumer Advocate has intervened and opposes the increase as an unnecessary luxury and believes that rate increases are especially unnecessary in an era of historically low interest rates. They also argue that the cost of capital should be reduced to 9%, to represent lower interest rates.

The New York chapter of the Sierra Club has intervened and supports the increase, as helping to reduce New York's dependence on dirty sources of energy.

New Yorkers for Energy Efficiency (NYEE), an advocacy group promoting new technologies for energy conservation, has intervened and opposes the increase, maintaining that lower cost and more reliable options are available for New York—including purchasing natural gas power and investing in reducing the demand for electric power.

New York Industrial Power Users Group (NYIPUG) has intervened in support of the increase but argues that none of the costs should be allocated to industrial customers and should be borne entirely by residential customers.

The New York Wind Energy Association (NYWEA) has intervened and favors the increase but also argues that the portions of the increase related to the transmission line is mandated under federal law.

For purposes of the present chapter, assume that EE generates and distributes electric power as a public utility in the relevant market (i.e., that it is operating in what is often called a "regulated" market).[1] As you read the materials below and in the following sections, consider the support for each stakeholder's arguments for and against the rate increase. Do the arguments support the particular cost-of-service components EE is requesting in its rate proposal? If you worked for agency staff and were assigned the task of making a recommendation to the Commission, what would you propose?

Supporting statutes:

N.Y. Pub. Serv. L. §§ 65 and 5(2):

§ 65. Safe and adequate service; just and reasonable charges; unjust discrimination; unreasonable preference; protection of privacy.

1.   Every gas corporation, every electric corporation and every municipality shall furnish and provide such service, instrumentalities and facilities as shall be safe and adequate and in all respects just and reasonable. All charges made or demanded by any such gas corporation, electric corporation or municipality for gas, electricity or any service rendered or to be rendered, shall be just and reasonable and not more than allowed by law or by order of the commission. Every unjust or unreasonable charge made or demanded for gas, electricity or any such service, or in connection therewith, or in excess of that allowed by law or by the order of the commission is prohibited.

2.   No gas corporation, electric corporation or municipality shall directly or indirectly, by any special rate, rebate, drawback or other device or method, charge, demand, collect or receive from any person or corporation a greater or less compensation for gas or electricity or for any service rendered or to be rendered or in connection therewith, except as authorized in this chapter, than it charges, demands, collects or receives from any other person or corporation for doing a like and contemporaneous service with respect thereto under the same or substantially similar circumstances or conditions.

3.   No gas corporation, electric corporation or municipality shall make or grant any undue or unreasonable preference or advantage to any person,

---

[1]   As is discussed in Chapter 10, New York is one of many states that have "deregulated" the provision of retail electric power sales. Once you read the materials in Chapter 10, you should consider how, if at all, deregulation would change the issues in this rate case.

corporation or locality, or to any particular description of service in any respect whatsoever, or subject any particular person, corporation or locality or any particular description of service to any undue or unreasonable prejudice or disadvantage in any respect whatsoever.

. . .

5.   Nothing in this chapter shall be taken to prohibit a gas corporation or electrical corporation from establishing classifications of service based upon the quantity used, the time when used, the purpose for which used, the duration of use or upon any other reasonable consideration, and providing schedules of just and reasonable graduated rates applicable thereto. No such classification, schedule, rate or charge shall be lawful unless it shall be filed with and approved by the commission, and every such classification, rate or charge shall be subject to change, alteration and modification by the commission.

§ 5: Jurisdiction, powers and duties of public service commission.

2.   The commission shall encourage all persons and corporations subject to its jurisdiction to formulate and carry out long-range programs, individually or cooperatively, for the performance of their public service responsibilities with economy, efficiency, and care for the public safety, the preservation of environmental values and the conservation of natural resources.

2.   COST-OF-SERVICE REGULATION PRINCIPLES

a.   THE "END RESULTS" TEST

Rate base, B, and rate of return, r, are often treated as distinct issues in rate cases before regulatory commissions. Each of these elements has been the subject of an enormous amount of litigation. What legal protections constrain application of this formula for the protection of consumers? For investors and utilities? When is a regulator limited in what it can approve or fail to include in B or r?

The Supreme Court decided the following case in an era when it was beginning to recognize stronger constitutional protections of private property under the doctrine of "substantive due process." The case illustrates some of the more significant historic limitations courts have imposed on setting utility rates.

Smyth v. Ames
169 U.S. 466 (1898).

[Railroads argued that a Nebraska statute establishing maximum rates applicable to rail service within the state violated the constitutional prohibition on taking private property without just compensation. After comparing the revenues each railroad would have earned by charging the prescribed rate with each railroad's operating costs for each of several years, the Court addressed the issue of rate base.]

■ HARLAN, J.—A corporation maintaining a public highway, although it owns the property it employs for accomplishing public objects, must be held to have accepted its rights, privileges and franchises subject to the condition that the government creating it, or the government within whose limits it conducts its business, may by legislation protect the people against unreasonable charges for the services rendered by it. It cannot be assumed that any railroad corporation, accepting franchises, rights and privileges at the hands of the public, ever supposed that it acquired, or that it was intended to grant to it, the power to construct and maintain a public highway simply for its benefit, without regard to the rights of the public. But it is equally true that the corporation performing such public services and the people financially interested in its business and affairs have rights that may not be invaded by legislative enactment in disregard of the fundamental guarantees for the protection of property. The corporation may not be required to use its property for the benefit of the public without receiving just compensation for the services rendered by it. How such compensation may be ascertained, and what are the necessary elements in such an inquiry, will always be an embarrassing question. As said in the case last cited:

> Each case must depend upon its special facts; and when a court, without assuming itself to prescribe rates, is required to determine whether the rates prescribed by the legislature for a corporation controlling a public highway are, as an entirety, so unjust as to destroy the value of its property for all the purposes for which it was acquired, its duty is to take into consideration the interests both of the public and of the owner of the property, together with all other circumstances that are fairly to be considered in determining whether the legislature has, under the guise of regulating rates, exceeded its constitutional authority, and practically deprived the owner of property without due process of law. . . . The utmost that any corporation operating a public highway can rightfully demand at the hands of the legislature, when exerting its general powers, is that it receive what, under all the circumstances, is such compensation for the use of its property as will be just both to it and to the public.

We hold, however, that the basis of all calculations as to the reasonableness of rates to be charged by a corporation maintaining a highway under legislative sanction must be the fair value of the property being used by it for the convenience of the public. And in order to ascertain that value, the original cost of construction, the amount expended in permanent improvements, the amount and market value of its bonds and stock, the present as compared with the original cost of construction, the probable earning capacity of the property under particular rates prescribed by statute, and the sum required to meet operating expenses, are all matters for consideration, and are to be given such weight as may be just and right in each case. We do not say that there may not be other matters to be regarded in estimating the value of the property. What the company is entitled to ask is a fair return upon the value of that which it employs for the public convenience. On the other hand, what the public is entitled to demand is that no more be exacted from it for the use of a public highway than the services rendered by it are reasonably worth. But even upon this basis, and determining the probable effect of the act of 1893 by ascertaining what could have been its effect if it had been in operation during the three years immediately preceding its passage, we perceive no ground on the record for reversing the decree of the Circuit Court. On the contrary, we are of opinion that as to most of the companies in question there would have been, under such rates as were established by the act of 1893, an actual loss in each of the years ending June 30, 1891, 1892 and 1893; and that, in the exceptional cases above stated, when two of the companies would have earned something above operating expenses, in particular years, the receipts or gains, above operating expenses, would have been too small to affect the general conclusion that the act, if enforced, would have deprived each of the railroad companies involved in these suits of the just compensation secured to them by the Constitution. Under the evidence there is no ground for saying that the operating expenses of any of the companies were greater than necessary. ■

NOTES AND COMMENTS

1.   Does this case concern rate base or rate of return? Because *Smyth v. Ames* is generally concerned with the "fair value of the property being used," it is more concerned with a utility's assets, or rate base, than its rate of return, or the cost the utility must pay to attract investors.

2.   How helpful is the term "fair value" as a substantive legal requirement? The Court suggests that four criteria are relevant in the determination of "fair value": (1) "original cost of construction"; (2) "the amount and market values of [the utility's] bonds and stocks"; (3) "the present as compared with the original cost of construction"; and (4) "the probable earning capacity of the property under particular rates prescribed." Does this give PUCs and subsequent courts a meaningful standard to apply? Is there any difference between (2) and (4)? Are these really concerns in calculating rate base? Are reviewing courts really competent to evaluate any of these things, or are they better determined by agency experts or by a finder of fact in an adjudicative hearing?

3.   As is discussed below, later cases repudiate the "fair value" doctrine. The doctrine did, however, reign during the *Lochner* era until immediately after the New Deal. *See* Stephen A. Siegel, Understanding the *Lochner* Era: Lessons from the Controversy Over Railroad and Utility Rate Regulation, 70 Va. L. Rev. 187 (1984).

With the end of the *Lochner* era, *Smyth v. Ames* is now only history (though like *Lochner*, it is not the kind of history that can be ignored). The following cases, which are cited in virtually every appeal concerning a utility's rates, present the "end results" approach to judicial review of ratemaking, which has replaced the "fair value" doctrine.

Bluefield Water Works & Improvement Co. v. Public Service Commission

262 U.S. 679 (1923).

■ BUTLER, J.—The company contends that the rate of return is too low and confiscatory. What annual rate will constitute just compensation depends upon many circumstances and must be determined by the exercise of a fair and enlightened judgment, having regard to all relevant facts. A public utility is entitled to such rates as will permit it to earn a return on the value of the property which it employs for the convenience of the public equal to that generally being made at the same time and in the same general part of the country on investments in other business undertakings which are attended by corresponding risks and uncertainties; but it has no constitutional right to profits such as are realized or anticipated in highly profitable enterprises or speculative ventures. The return should be reasonably sufficient to assure confidence in the financial soundness of the utility and should be adequate, under efficient and economical management, to maintain and support its credit and enable it to raise the money necessary for the proper discharge of its public duties. A rate of return may be reasonable at one time and become too high or too low by changes affecting opportunities for investment, the money market and business conditions generally. ∎

Federal Power Commission v. Hope Natural Gas Co.

320 U.S. 591 (1944).

∎ DOUGLAS, J.—The primary issue in these cases concerns the validity under the Natural Gas Act of 1938 (52 Stat. 821, 15 U.S.C. 717) of a rate order issued by the Federal Power Commission reducing the rates chargeable by Hope Natural Gas Co. . . .

The Commission established an interstate rate base of $33,712,526 which, it found, represented the "actual legitimate cost" of the company's interstate property less depletion and depreciation and plus unoperated acreage, working capital and future net capital additions. The Commission, beginning with book cost, made certain adjustments not necessary to relate here and found the "actual legitimate cost" of the plant in interstate service to be $51,957,416, as of December 31, 1940. It deducted accrued depletion and depreciation, which it found to be $22,328,016 on an "economic-service-life" basis. . . .

Hope introduced evidence from which it estimated reproduction cost of the property at $97,000,000. It also presented a so-called trended "original cost" estimate which exceeded $105,000,000. The latter was designed "to indicate what the original cost of the property would have been if 1938 material and labor prices had prevailed throughout the whole period of the piecemeal construction of the company's property since 1898." 44 PUR. (N. S.), pp. 8–9. Hope estimated by the "per cent condition" method accrued depreciation at about 35% of reproduction cost new. On that basis Hope contended for a rate base of $66,000,000. The Commission refused to place any reliance on reproduction cost new, saying that it was "not predicated upon facts" and was "too conjectural and illusory to be given any weight in these proceedings." *Id.*, p. 8. It likewise refused to give any "probative value" to trended "original cost" since it was "not founded in fact" but was "basically erroneous" and produced "irrational results." . . .

The fixing of prices, like other applications of the police power, may reduce the value of the property which is being regulated. But the fact that the value is reduced does not mean that the regulation is invalid. *Block v. Hirsh*, 256 U.S. 135, 155–157; *Nebbia v. New York*, 291 U.S. 502, 523–539 and cases cited. It does, however, indicate that "fair value" is the end product of the process of rate-making not the starting point as the Circuit Court of Appeals held. The heart of the matter is that rates cannot be made to depend upon "fair value" when the value of the going enterprise depends on earnings under whatever rates may be anticipated.

We held in *Federal Power Commission v. Natural Gas Pipeline Co.*, *supra*, that the Commission was not bound to the use of any single formula or combination of formulae in determining rates. Its rate-making function, moreover, involves the making of "pragmatic adjustments." p. 586. And when the Commission's order is challenged in the courts, the question is whether that order "viewed in its entirety" meets the requirements of the Act. *Id.*, p. 586. Under the statutory standard of "just and reasonable" it is the result reached not the method employed which is controlling. *Cf. Los Angeles Gas & Electric Corp. v. Railroad Commission*, 289 U.S. 287, 304–305, 314; *West Ohio Gas Co. v. Public Utilities Commission (No. 1)*, 294 U.S. 63, 70; *West v. Chesapeake & Potomac Tel. Co.*, 295 U.S. 662, 692–693 (dissenting opinion). It is not theory but the impact of the rate order which counts. If the total effect of the rate order cannot be said to be unjust and unreasonable, judicial inquiry under the Act is at an end. The fact that the method employed to reach that result may contain infirmities is not then important. Moreover, the Commission's order does not become suspect by reason of the fact that it is challenged. It is the product of expert judgment which carries a presumption of validity. And he who would upset the rate order under the Act carries the heavy burden of making a convincing showing that it is invalid because it is unjust and unreasonable in its consequences. . . .

The rate-making process under the Act, i.e., the fixing of "just and reasonable" rates, involves a balancing of the investor and the consumer interests. Thus we stated in the *Natural Gas Pipeline Co.* case that "regulation does not insure that the business shall produce net revenues." 315 U.S. p. 590. But such considerations aside, the investor interest has a legitimate concern with the financial integrity of the company whose rates are being regulated. From the investor or company point of view it is important that there be enough revenue not only for operating expenses but also for the capital costs of the business. These include service on the debt and dividends on the stock. *Cf. Chicago & Grand Trunk Ry. Co. v. Wellman*, 143 U.S. 339, 345–346. By that standard the return to the equity owner should be commensurate with returns on investments in other enterprises having corresponding risks. That return, moreover, should be sufficient to assure confidence in the financial integrity of the enterprise, so as to maintain its credit and to attract capital. *See Missouri ex rel. Southwestern Bell Tel. Co. v. Public Service Commission*, 262 U.S. 276, 291 (Mr. Justice Brandeis concurring). The conditions under which more or less might be allowed are not important here. Nor is it important to this case to determine the various permissible ways in which any rate base on which the return is computed might be arrived at. For we are of the view that the end result in this case cannot be condemned under the Act as unjust and unreasonable from the investor or company viewpoint. . . .

As we have noted, the Commission fixed a rate of return which permits Hope to earn $2,191,314 annually. In determining that amount it stressed the importance of maintaining the financial integrity of the company. It considered the financial history of Hope and a vast array of data bearing on the natural gas industry, related businesses, and general economic conditions. . . .

In view of these various considerations we cannot say that an annual return of $2,191,314 is not "just and reasonable" within the meaning of the Act. Rates which enable the company to operate successfully, to maintain its financial integrity, to attract capital, and to compensate its investors for the risks assumed certainly cannot be condemned as invalid, even though they might produce only a meager return on the so-called "fair value" rate base. ■

NOTES AND COMMENTS

1.   *Smyth* required regulators to use "fair value" in determining rate base. Generally the choice for determining "fair value" comes down to two alternatives: original cost (or historical cost) and reproduction cost (or present cost). Early on, the Court read *Smyth* to require a regulator to consider both. In several cases decided between 1898 and 1944, the Supreme Court held rate decisions unconstitutionally confiscatory where an agency gave undue consideration to original cost and insufficient consideration to reproduction cost. *See, e.g.*, Missouri ex rel. Sw. Bell Tel. Co. v. Mo. PSC, 262 U.S. 276 (1923). Holmes and Brandeis, in a concurrence to that case, dissented from the majority's reliance on the indeterminate "fair value" standard of *Smyth*.

One significance of the 1944 *Hope* case is that a majority agreed with Holmes and Brandeis' 1923 concurrence: "If the total effect of the rate order cannot be said to be unjust and unreasonable, judicial inquiry under the Act is at an end. . . . Rates which enable the company to operate successfully . . . cannot be condemned as invalid, even though they might produce only a meager return on the so-called 'fair value' rate base." 320 U.S. at 602–05. *Hope* marks a departure from *Smyth's* "fair value" standard—a standard first enunciated during the rise of the substantive due process era of the late nineteenth and early twentieth centuries. *See* Basil L. Copeland, Jr. & Walter W. Nixon, III, Procedural Versus Substantive Economic Due Process for Public Utilities, 12 Energy L.J. 81 (1991).

2.   The modern "end results" test suggests that courts will focus more on the output, or end results, of the ratemaking process, than on monitoring the details of the calculation of inputs—as *Smyth* endorsed. Notice how the modern "end results" test is also not entirely grounded in some abstract constitutional limit on rates, but is connected to the "just and reasonable" standard that appears in a statute. Also notice that to the extent that the "end results"—not the exact calculation of B, O or r—is the test that matters for appellate review of rates, courts typically focus their review on factual determinations and procedures, and less on the actual substantive policy choices, behind utility ratemaking. Most agency determinations that involve factual determinations or policy choices are subject to high levels of deference on appeal.

3.   Still, is there any remaining role for appellate courts applying a substantive standard in the review of agency rate determinations and what is it? Other than the "end results" test, what language (if any) do these cases give to constrain agencies in setting utility rates, and who among the stakeholders in a ratemaking process does that language tend to favor?

4.   An interested party aggrieved by the procedural consideration or end result of a utility rate case may appeal. Under the FPA and NGA, FERC rate cases are appealed to the U.S. Court of Appeals for the D.C. Circuit or the circuit within which the utility or aggrieved party sits. State rate determination by a PUC or PSC are appealed to state courts and then, if an appropriate federal or constitutional issue is raised, to the U.S. Supreme Court. The Johnston Act, 28 U.S.C. § 1342, prohibits a U.S. District Court from exercising jurisdiction over a rate appeal from a state PUC where there is an adequate remedy in state court.

5.   On appeal, challenges to rate proceedings may focus not only on the substance of public utility law, under statutory and constitutional principles, but also on the procedures by which agencies make their factual, policy, and legal determinations. Rate cases often involve hearings before an adjudicative decision-making body, during which the utility and intervening parties are given an opportunity to present expert testimony in support of their positions in both oral and written form and are given an opportunity to seek discovery of and cross-exam the testimony of other parties. These adjudicative hearings can last from a period of days to months. Normally, uncontested factual findings do not require a full-fledged adjudicative hearing before an agency. However, an adjudicative hearing is typically required where an agency is making a factual determination under contest by a party or where the agency is making a new policy or legal decision. *See* Cajun Electric Power Coop. v. FERC, 28 F.3d 173 (D.C. Cir. 1994). Often, an agency will make generic policy and legal decisions through a process called notice-and-comment rulemaking—allowing adoption of generally policies (including policies about the setting of rates) without a full-fledged adjudicative hearing.

6.   Thinking back to the ratemaking hypothetical, assume that more than 20 years ago EE was required by regulators to build new plants to serve customers in the state of New York, and that state regulators approved building coal plants to serve these customers. Once the plants are built, would it be unconstitutional for regulators to refuse to allow EE to recover these costs in its rate base? What are the arguments for and against inclusion? Which arguments are better in light of the materials above and the *Charles River Bridge* case? (See Chapter 2.)

7.   If, in the hypothetical ratemaking problem, EE is allowed to include its coal plants in rate base, doesn't it also follow that it also should be constitutionally entitled to include the costs of converting these plants to natural gas in rate base? Why or why not?

b.   RATE OF RETURN AND UNCONSTITUTIONAL TAKINGS

Important language in both *Bluefield* and *Hope* recognizes that there are some substantive constitutional limits on how a regulator determines the utility's cost of capital. The setting of a rate of return (r), like most ratemaking issues, raises complex accounting, economics, and forecasting matters. It is an extremely important issue, since its calculation reflects the time value of the investors' money and a utility's capital investments are often financed over long periods of time.

At its most basic level, a rate of return represents the utility's cost of capital—i.e., the opportunity it forgoes by using its capital to provide utility services rather than engaging in some other profitable activity. Cost of capital can be broken into two main components: 1) the cost of money that is borrowed on both a long- and short-term basis, also known as "debt"; and 2) money received by the utility in exchange for its stock, or "equity."

The equity capital of a public utility is generally of two types: (1) preferred and (2) common. The former is essentially the same as long-term debt capital as regards specified and agreed rates of return or dividends and times of payment. While the consequences of nonpayment are not as onerous, dividends on or the cost of the preferred stock capital of a public utility nevertheless must be paid before any dividends may be paid on common stock.

The common equity capital of a public utility is that which incurs the highest risk. Unlike most debt capital, its ultimate recovery by those who furnished the funds is not secured by liens against the property of the utility, and, unlike both debt capital and preferred stock investors, those who hold common stock are not entitled to any agreed or assured rate of return on their investment. In short, their earnings consist of the net remaining from revenues after all other creditors of the public utility, including long-term debt and preferred stock investors, have been paid. While the return on this type of capital is actually measured by the amount of net income from gross receipts so remaining, this actual return is not necessarily synonymous with the cost of this category of capital. The cost or rate of return a public utility must pay or be able to pay in order to obtain common equity funds from the private capital markets is set for the company by the market, not by this commission or the company. It is particularly important to stress and recognize that the cost of a public utility's common equity capital is simply another cost of furnishing service, which is not generically different from any of its other costs. Those who furnish common equity capital to a utility, whether by purchasing new stock of the company or by permitting the company to retain and invest their earnings in new plant and equipment, expect and are entitled to a return or earnings for the use of their money by the utility. In an economic sense, this return represents the company's cost of the common equity capital employed, just as rent on an office building leased by the company or wages to those who work for the company constitute costs to it.

In re Pub. Serv. Co. of New Mexico, N. Mex. PUC, Case No. 1196, 8 P.U.R. 4th 113 (1975).

Equity is the more difficult capital cost for regulators to determine. Since there is rarely a fixed commitment to a stock dividend rate, the actual cost of floating a stock issue is uncertain. "Investors' decisions are largely based on a utility's expected earnings and upon their stability, as well as upon alternative uses of investment funds. Yet, since the allowable amount of earnings is the object of a rate case, a commission's decision, in turn, will affect investors' decisions." Charles F. Phillips, Jr., The Regulation of Public Utilities 394 (3d ed. 1993). Two principal methods are used to estimate the cost of equity capital: the "market-determined" standard, which focuses on investor expectations in terms of the utility's earnings, dividends and market prices; and a "comparable earnings" standard, which focuses on what capital can earn in various alternative investments with comparable risks. *Id.*

A related issue in measuring cost of capital is determining the appropriate capital structure for the utility. Since the interest rate on debt is normally lower than the cost of equity capital (why?), the overall cost of capital will be lower when the debt-equity ratio (the ratio represented by dividing a firm's total liabilities by its equity) is high. Some argue that regulators should look to the ideal rather than actual capital structure, in order to minimize the possibility that utility capitalization decisions are made based on rate regulation decisions. As the natural gas and electric utility industries have moved towards competition, as is discussed in Chapters 9 and 10, risks have increased and many utilities have been required to rely more heavily on equity to raise capital.

As the Supreme Court acknowledged in *Bluefield*, there are some substantive constitutional limits on how regulators set the cost of common equity capital for a firm:

> A public utility is entitled to such rates as will permit it to earn a return on the value of the property which it employs for the convenience of the public equal to that generally being made at the same time and in the same general part of the country on investments in other business undertakings which are attended by corresponding risks and uncertainties; but it has no constitutional right to profits such as are realized or anticipated in highly profitable enterprises or speculative ventures. The return should be reasonably sufficient to assure confidence in the financial soundness of the utility, and should be adequate under efficient and economical management, to maintain and support its credit and to enable it to raise the money necessary for the proper discharge of its public duty. A rate of return may be reasonable at one time, and become too high or too low by change affecting opportunities for investment, the money market and business conditions generally.

In *Federal Power Commission v. Hope Natural Gas Co.*, 320 U.S. 591 (1944), where the court endorsed an "end result" test, it also specified three conditions of a fair return on the invested capital of a public utility: (1) it should be sufficient to maintain the financial integrity of the utility; (2) it should be sufficient to compensate the utility's investors for the risks assumed; (3) it should be sufficient to enable the utility to attract needed new capital.

NOTES AND COMMENTS

1.   Regulated firms can use a two-step strategy to maximize their returns to shareholders. First, they attempt to obtain a rate of return, r, that exceeds the actual cost of capital. Second, they may overinvest in capital, producing a product of B and r that is greater than the actual cost of capital used. *See* Harvey Averch & Leland L. Johnson, Behavior of the Firm Under Regulatory Constraint, 52 Am. Econ. Rev. 1052 (1962).

2.   What are the capital sources available to a firm? Like any other business enterprise, an energy utility needs to attract investors. Generally a firm has two options in raising capital: debt (bond obligations) and equity (stock).

Capital structure refers to a firm's mix of debt and equity. Would an unregulated firm ever intentionally choose a suboptimal mix of capital? No. Because it competes in markets as a buyer of capital, the unregulated firm faces strong economic incentives to choose the debt-equity ratio that minimizes its risk-adjusted cost of capital. However, cost-of-service regulation, by guaranteeing a utility a minimum rate of return, reduces the strength of this incentive. How likely are regulators to determine a firm's correct capital structure—i.e., the mix of debt and equity the regulated firm would face in a competitive market?

3.   In *Permian Basin Area Rate Cases*, 390 U.S. 747 (1968), the Court reviewed FPC orders setting area-wide (regional) rates for gas producers. Writing for the majority, Justice Harlan affirmed *Hope*, stating that a court reviewing rate orders must assure itself both that "each of the order's essential elements is supported by substantial evidence" and that "the order may reasonably be expected to maintain financial integrity, attract necessary capital, and fairly compensate investors for the risks they have assumed, and yet provide appropriate protection to the relevant public interests, both existing and foreseeable." *Id.* at 792. In examining the end result of the rate order, a court cannot affirm simply because each subpart of that order, taken in isolation, was permissible; it must be the case "that they do not together produce arbitrary or unreasonable consequences." The reviewing court, according to Harlan, must determine that "the record before the Commission contained evidence sufficient to establish that these rates, as adjusted, will maintain the industry's credit and continue to attract capital." *Id.* at 812.

4.   FERC has recently clarified its approach for determining the return on equity (ROE) for electric utilities in a proceeding involving the calculation of rate of return for ISO-New England's Transmission system. For over 30 years, FERC based ROEs on the rate of return required by investors to invest in a company. Over this period, FERC relied primarily on what is known as the "discounted cash flow" model to provide an estimate of investors' required rate of return. The underlying premise of this model is that an investment in common stock is worth the present value of the infinite stream of dividends discounted at a market rate commensurate with the investment's risk. FERC's approach to using this model for electric utilities departed from an approach it took for natural gas pipelines (which used the DCF model but accounted for long-term growth projections). For electric utilities, FERC had traditionally used an approach that emphasized short-term growth projections—primarily because of a concern that long-term growth rates would overcompensate utilities and inflate their ROEs.

However, in 2014 FERC observed that given electric utility internal growth rates now more closely approximate long-term growth rates so there is no longer "a reason to use long-term growth projection for public utilities that is less than [ ] projected long-term growth. . . ." FERC's revised DCF methodology is the same used for natural gas and oil pipeline ROEs: incorporating both short-term and long-term measures of growth in dividends. FERC has applied this new methodology to the New England transmission owners' ROEs, finding that based on the record, including the unusual capital market conditions (particularly historically low interest rates), the just and reasonable base ROE for the New England transmission owners should be set halfway between the midpoint of the zone of reasonableness and the top of the zone of reasonableness. As an illustration, the New England transmission owners' base ROE assuming a long term growth rate based on GDP would be 10.57 percent, the point halfway between the 9.39 percent midpoint of the zone of reasonableness and the 11.74 percent top of that zone. *See* Martha Coakley v. Bangor Hydro-Electric Co. 147 F.E.R.C. ¶ 61,234 (2014).

5.   Consider the hypothetical ratemaking problem presented earlier in this chapter. Given uncertainties facing the energy industry and a need to invest in new infrastructure such as transmission lines, many electric utilities request rate increases based on a higher cost of capital or rate of return reflecting the higher risks utilities face in today's equity markets than in previous eras where there was less competition and need for new investments. Yet, as of early 2015, interest rates in financial markets are at historical lows (and many other utilities are facing requests for rate decreases due to overcharges from inflated rates of return). What kind of evidence would regulators consider in making a rate of return determination for EE? Who has the better of the arguments regarding rate of return in the EE rate case? Is there a way for regulators to set the rate of return to take into account uncertainty and changing market conditions?

6.   Again considering this hypothetical problem, if the New York State PSC denies EE's requested 12% rate of return and allows it only a 10.5% rate of return, and EE appeals, would this be considered confiscatory? What factors will the reviewing court consider in determining whether it is confiscatory? Suppose that the rationale for this is that 10.5% is simply the average of the 12% EE is requesting and the 9% that the Consumer Advocate believes to be appropriate?

c.   ASSESSING THE PRUDENCE OF COSTS

Beyond some of the constitutional constraints discussed above, most state agencies have a statutory responsibility to set rates for public utilities based on a "just and reasonable" standard, which typically appears in a statute. For example, the statute that applies to the New York PSC explicitly prohibits a utility subject to the agency's jurisdiction from charging rates that are not "just and reasonable." In a similar manner, Section 205 of the FPA requires FERC to determine whether rates for wholesale sales of electric energy in interstate commerce are "just and reasonable," and Section 206 empowers FERC to set aside wholesale rates that are "unjust, unreasonable, unduly discriminatory or preferential."

What interests should an agency regulator take into account in determining whether rates are just and reasonable? Certainly, as the above excerpt suggests, regulators are concerned with ensuring that the utility and its investors are provided with sufficient revenue to keep the utility operating. However, as in the case of EE, utility rate filings are often subject to challenge by a myriad of non-utility interest groups with a stake in the outcome: consumers who seek the lowest possible rates; environmental groups who may seek to increase rates to discourage wasteful consumption, or have regulators force the utility to adopt conservation-enhancing mechanisms; and public advocates, such as state attorneys general or consumer protection offices, who may advocate some version of the public interest. The preferences of these interest groups often clash.

So in refereeing this clash of preferences, what policy objectives should guide regulators in setting rates? First, as the readings have suggested, regulators should attempt to ensure that the utility meets its revenue requirement. This includes not only the payment of operating expenses, but the cost of capital as well. The cost of capital does not reflect pure profit or gain for the utility and its shareholders; instead maintenance of a minimum cost of capital to attract investment for the utility's infrastructure is in the public interest as well. As the New Mexico PUC suggests in *In re Pub. Serv. Co. of New Mexico* (above), if a utility does not receive a competitive rate of return, existing investors may find alternative investments. While consumers are justifiably concerned with paying high rates to subsidize utility profits, they certainly would not want to see their local utility struggling to stay one step away from bankruptcy.

A second policy objective of rate-setting is economic efficiency. Rates should encourage the regulated enterprise to provide service at the lowest economic cost and explore ways to further reduce costs through better management and the adoption of newer, more efficient technological processes.

A third policy objective relates to environmental concerns. Approved rates should not encourage waste or encourage uses that are threatening to the environment or the energy resource base. Approved rates should allow utilities to comply with pollution mandates imposed by other state or federal agencies, and should also encourage utilities to take initiative to minimize the environmental degradation caused by their energy activities. This is certainly related to the second objective: If all social costs (including environmental costs) are fully internalized in the rate making process, then efficient rates will reflect environmental costs as well as the financial costs necessary for a utility to continue to provide service. However, the environmental impacts of energy activities are often not fully internalized as costs for energy firms for two reasons. As a practical matter, it is difficult to quantify the actual impact of a certain energy conversion or distribution process on the environment. In addition, many environmental costs affect parties or deplete resources that are addressed outside of the jurisdiction of the regulatory body setting the utility's rates. Does this mean that economic regulators who are focusing on energy markets, such as FERC or the New York PSC, should give special weight to environmental concerns addressed by other state or federal agencies, or should economic regulators make some effort to address these environmental impacts on their own?

A final regulatory objective is social and distributional. Should some customers—say wealthy or middle-class suburban customers—pay higher rates to subsidize other customers—say low income urban customers—or to build a distribution network to serve rural customers? Should a state that has adopted a policy of encouraging manufacturing set low rates for industrial customers?

There are several classic treatises on rate regulation. *See, e.g.*, James C. Bonbright, Albert L. Danielson & David R. Kamerschien, Principles of Public Utility Rates (2d ed. 1988); Paul J. Garfield & Wallace F. Lovejoy, Public Utility Economics (1964); Phillips, Jr., *supra*. Some common issues raised in utility rate cases include the following:

The Test Year Approach. The purpose of a utility's rate application and hearing before a regulatory commission is to set utility rates for the future. A utility is seeking approval for the rate it will charge its customers for months or years to come—at least until another rate increase is approved. However, it is impossible to obtain exact financial information for a future year. For this reason, as briefly introduced above, regulators use what is known as a "test year" in setting rates. This is a hypothetical future period into which regulators attempt to forecast a utility's revenue requirements for purposes of the cost-of-service equation set forth above. Like any forecast, use of a test year depends upon certain assumptions about consumer demand, input prices, and the state of the economy in general. In actuality, some years may provide for over-recovery of costs and other years may provide for under-recovery. PUCs typically attempt to subtract unusual costs from a test year—costs that they deem to not represent a utility's annual expenses.

Policy Concerns in Determining Rate Base. Recall the two alternatives presented in *Smyth v. Ames*: reproduction cost or original (historical) cost. In *Union Electric Company v. Illinois Commerce Commission*, the Illinois Supreme Court adopted an original cost approach. Union Elec. Co. v. Ill. Com. Comm'n, 396 N.E.2d 510 (1979). The Court noted: ". . . [A] cost based rate reflects the amount of capital whereas a value rate base reflects the value of assets which the utility has devoted to serving the public." *Id.* at 516. FERC bases property valuations on original cost, as do the vast majority of state PUCs.

Does the calculation of rate base on reproduction cost give utility shareholders a windfall? Or does it encourage an efficient allocation of resources? During a period of inflation, the rates of regulated utilities may be lower than the rates of non-regulated enterprises with which they compete (which would reflect reproduction cost). This could increase the demand for the services of a regulated utility and lead to an uneconomical expansion of capacity. For discussion of the merits of reproduction cost versus original cost, see Phillips, Jr., *supra*, at 299–307.

i.   Determination of "Used and Useful" Property

Recall that *Smyth v. Ames* refers to "the fair value of the property being used" in its definition of rate base. In *Denver Union Stock Yard Co. v. United States*, 304 U.S. 470, 475 (1938), the Court held that property not used or useful in providing regulated services does not have to be included in rate base. What has come to be known as the "used and useful" doctrine prohibits the inclusion in rate base of assets used exclusively to provide unregulated goods or services, or assets that are technologically or economically obsolete. The doctrine has its origins in statutory or regulatory requirements that exist at the state or federal level. While the test seems rather simple, in application it can be difficult. How does a regulator determine whether property is used and useful and who are the relevant customers?

The clearest example of a used and useful asset is where a utility has placed the most economical plant into operation to meet a specific customer demand. It is beyond dispute that such a facility is used and useful. Beyond this, however, determining whether a cost a utility expects to incur is used and useful can be very difficulty. Regulators are typically flexible as they apply the used and useful doctrine on an ad hoc basis, and they usually are attentive to customer benefits in applying the test. But which customers are relevant and how do we assess when they benefit? Some regulators try to sort this out by focusing on what "costs" each customer class causes for the utility—a principle sometimes referred to as "the cost causer pays."

As the following two cases address, however, in addition to the issues of policy and statutory construction there can also be some constitutional limitations if a regulator refused to deem property used and useful.

Jersey Central Power & Light Co. v. FERC

810 F.2d 1168 (D.C. Cir. 1987).

[FERC allowed Jersey Central Power and Light Co. to amortize a $397 million investment in a canceled nuclear plant over a fifteen-year period. Jersey Central was not allowed, however, to include the unamortized balance in its rate base, because FERC determined the plant was not "used and useful." The effect of this treatment meant that the interest costs of the $397 million were charged to shareholders while the principal costs were charged to ratepayers over a fifteen-year period.]

■ BORK, J.—Jersey Central Power and Light Company petitions for review of Federal Energy Regulatory Commission orders modifying the electric utility's proposed rate schedules and requiring the company to file reduced rates. Jersey Central charges that it alleged facts which, if proven, show that the reduced rates are confiscatory and violate its statutory and constitutional rights as defined by the Supreme Court in *FPC v. Hope Natural Gas Co.*, 320 U.S. 591 (1944). Though it is probable that the facts alleged, if true, would establish an invasion of the company's rights, the Commission refused the company a hearing and reduced its rates summarily.

The decision of the Commission is vacated and the case remanded for a hearing at which Jersey Central may finally have its claim addressed. . . .

The teaching of [*Hope* and *Permian Basin*] is straightforward. In reviewing a rate order courts must determine whether or not the end result of that order constitutes a reasonable balancing, based on factual findings, of the investor interest in maintaining financial integrity and access to capital markets and the consumer interest in being charged non-exploitative rates. Moreover, an order cannot be justified simply by a showing that each of the choices underlying it was reasonable; those choices must still add up to a reasonable result. . . .

The allegations made by Jersey Central and the testimony it offered track the standards of *Hope* and *Permian Basin* exactly. The *Hope* Court stated that the return ought to be "sufficient to ensure confidence in the financial integrity of the enterprise, so as to maintain its credit and to attract capital," and that "it is important that there be enough revenue not only for operating expenses but also for the capital costs of the business. These include service on the debt and dividends on the stock." 320 U.S. at 603. *Permian Basin* reaffirmed that the reviewing court "must determine" whether the Commission's rate order may reasonably be expected to "maintain financial integrity" and "attract necessary capital." 390 U.S. at 792. Jersey Central alleged that it had paid no dividends on its common stock for four years and faced a further prolonged inability to pay such dividends. [It also alleged] that the company was unable to sell senior securities; that its only source of external capital was the Revolving Credit Agreement, which was subject to termination and which placed the outstanding bank loans the company was allowed to maintain below the level necessary for the upcoming year; that the need to pay interest on the company's debt and dividends on its preferred stock meant that common equity investors not only were earning a zero return, but were also forced to pay these interest costs and dividends and that "continued confiscation of earnings from the common equity holder . . . will prolong the Company's inability to restore itself to a recognized level of credit worthiness"; that its "inability to realize fully its operating and capital costs so as to provide a fair rate of return on its invested capital has pushed its financial capability to the limits"; that "adequate and prompt relief is necessary in order to maintain the past high quality of service"; and that the rate increase requested was "the minimum necessary to restore the financial integrity of the Company."

The Commission maintains that because excluding the unamortized portion of a canceled plant investment from the rate base had previously been upheld as permissible, any rate order that rests on such a decision is unimpeachable. But that would turn our focus from the end result to the methodology, and evade the question whether the component decisions together produce just and reasonable consequences. We would be back with the assertion made in *Jersey Central I* that "the end result test is to be applied . . . only to those assets which valid Commission rules permit to be included in the rate base." 730 F.2d at 823. That statement was one which neither party endorsed. It was incorrect. The fact that a particular ratemaking standard is generally permissible does not per se legitimate the end result of the rate orders it produces. . . .

In addition to prohibiting rates so low as to be confiscatory, the holding of *Hope Natural Gas* makes clear that exploitative rates are illegal as well. If the inclusion of property not currently used and useful in the rate base automatically constituted exploitation of consumers, as one of the amici maintains, then the commission would be justified in excluding such property summarily even in cases where the utility pleads acute financial distress. A regulated utility has no constitutional right to a profit, see *FPC v. Natural Gas Pipeline Co.*, 315 U.S. at 590, and a company that is unable to survive without charging exploitative rates has no entitlement to such rates. *Market Street Ry. v. Railroad Comm'n of Cal.*, 324 U.S. 548 (1945). But we have already held that including prudent investments in the rate base is not in and of itself exploitative, and no party has denied that the Forked River investment was prudent. Indeed, when the regulated company is permitted to earn a return not on the market value of the property used by the public, *see Smyth v. Ames*, but rather on the original cost of the investment, placing prudent investments in the rate base would seem a more sensible policy than a strict application of "used and useful," for under this approach it is the investment, and not the property used, which is viewed as having been taken by the public. The investor interest described in *Hope*, after all, is an interest in return on investment. *Hope*, 320 U.S. at 603.

The central point, however, is this: it is impossible for us to say at this juncture whether including the unamortized portion of Forked River in the rate base would exploit consumers in this case, or whether its exclusion, on the facts of this case, constitutes confiscation, for no findings of fact have been made concerning the consequences of the rate order. Nor, for the same reason, can we make a judgment about the higher rate of return the utility sought as an alternative to inclusion in the rate base of its unamortized investment. Jersey Central has presented allegations which, if true, suggest that the rate order almost certainly does not meet the requirements of *Hope Natural Gas*, for the company has been shut off from long-term capital, is wholly dependent for short-term capital on a revolving credit arrangement that can be canceled at any time, and has been unable to pay dividends for four years. In addition, Jersey Central points out that the rates proposed in its filing would remain lower than those of neighboring utilities, which at least suggests, though it does not demonstrate, that the proposed rates would not exploit consumers. The Commission treated those allegations as irrelevant and hence has presented us with no basis on which to affirm its rate order. The necessary findings are simply not there for us to review. When the Commission conducts the requisite balancing of consumer and investor interests, based upon factual findings, that balancing will be judicially reviewable and will be affirmed if supported by substantial evidence. That is the point at which deference to agency expertise will be appropriate and necessary. But where, as here, the Commission has reached its determination by flatly refusing to consider a factor to which it is undeniably required to give some weight, its decision cannot stand. *Citizens to Preserve Overton Park, Inc. v. Volpe*, 401 U.S. 402, 416 (1971). The case should therefore be remanded to the Commission for a hearing at which the Commission can determine whether the rate order it issued constituted a reasonable balancing of the interests the Supreme Court has designated as relevant to the setting of a just and reasonable rate.

■ STARR, J., concurring—The Commission's stated justification for summarily dismissing these allegations was the weight of its prior "used and useful" precedent. But as the court's opinion shows, that body of precedent did not constitute as iron-clad a rule as the Commission would have us believe. It is certainly not evident from those precedents that the rule could be summarily applied in the face of the financial demise of the regulated entity.

Indeed, the Commission as a matter of policy has departed over the years from the strictures of the "used and useful" rule. This is illustrated by its treatment of "construction work in progress" (CWIP), part of which, the Commission recently determined, can be included in a utility's rate base. *See Mid-Tex Electric Cooperative v. FERC*, 773 F.2d 327 (D.C. Cir. 1985). In that proceeding, the Commission recognized that its own practice admits of "widely recognized exceptions and departures" from the "used and useful" rule, "particularly when there are countervailing public interest considerations." *See* 48 Fed. Reg. 24,323, 24,335 (June 1, 1983) (CWIP final rule). In that setting, financial difficulties in the electric utility industry played a significant role in the Commission's decision to bend the rule. *See id.* at 24,332; 773 F.2d at 332–34; *see also, e.g., Tennessee Gas Pipeline Co. v. FERC*, 606 F.2d 1094, 1109–10 (D.C. Cir. 1979) (departure from "used and useful" to permit rate base treatment of natural gas prepayment is justified as means of encouraging development of additional gas reserves), *cert. denied*, 445 U.S. 920 (1980).

This policy of flexibility, it seems to me, reflects the practical reality of the electric utility industry, namely that investments in plant and equipment are enormously costly. Rigid adherence to "used and useful" doctrines would doubtless imperil the viability of some utilities; thus, while not articulating its results in *Hope* or "takings" terms, the Commission—whether as a matter of policy or perceived constitutional obligation—has in the past taken these realities into account and provided relief for utilities in various forms.

The utility business represents a compact of sorts; a monopoly on service in a particular geographical area (coupled with state-conferred rights of eminent domain or condemnation) is granted to the utility in exchange for a regime of intensive regulation, including price regulation, quite alien to the free market. *Cf. Permian Basin*, 390 U.S. at 756–57 (unlike public utilities, producers of natural gas "enjoy no franchises or guaranteed areas of service" and are "intensely competitive"). Each party to the compact gets something in the bargain. As a general rule, utility investors are provided a level of stability in earnings and value less likely to be attained in the unregulated or moderately regulated sector; in turn, ratepayers are afforded universal, non-discriminatory service and protection from monopolistic profits through political control over an economic enterprise. Whether this regime is wise or not is, needless to say, not before us.

In the setting of rate regulation, when does a taking from the investors occur? It seems to me that it occurs only when a regulated rate is confiscatory, which is a short-hand way of saying that an unreasonable balance has been struck in the regulation process so as unreasonably to favor ratepayer interests at the substantial expense of investor interests. Thus, in my view, a taking does not occur when financial resources are committed to the enterprise. That is especially so since a utility's capital investment is made not simply in satisfaction of legal obligations to provide service to the public but in anticipation of profits on the investment. The utility is not a servant to the state; it is a for-profit enterprise which incurs legal obligations in exchange for state-conferred benefits. A profit-seeking capital investment is scarcely the sort of deprivation of possession, use, enjoyment, and ownership of property which can conceptually be deemed a taking. *See generally* R. Epstein, Takings 63–92 (1985). Indeed, it would seem odd to consider as a taking government's disavowal of any interest in property which remains unregulated and which reflects a profit-seeking investment.

For me, the prudent investment rule is, taken alone, too weighted for constitutional analysis in favor of the utility. It lacks balance. But so too, the "used and useful" rule, taken alone, is skewed heavily in favor of ratepayers. It also lacks balance. In the modern setting, neither regime, mechanically applied with full rigor, will likely achieve justice among the competing interests of investor and ratepayers so as to avoid confiscation of the utility's property or a taking of the property of ratepayers through unjustifiably exorbitant rates. Each approach, however, provides important insights about the ultimate object of the regulatory process, which is to achieve a just result in rate regulation. And that is the mission commanded by the Fifth Amendment. Unlike garden-variety takings, the requirements of the Takings Clause are satisfied in the rate regulatory setting when justice is done, that is to say the striking of a reasonable balance between competing interests.

Thus it is that a taking occurs not when an investment is made (even one under legal obligation), but when the balance between investor and ratepayer interests—the very function of utility regulation—is struck unjustly. Although the agency has broad latitude in striking the balance, the Constitution nonetheless requires that the end result reflect a reasonable balancing of the interests of investors and ratepayers. As we have seen, both investors and ratepayers were the intended beneficiaries of the Forked River investment; both should presumptively have to share in the loss. Filling in the gaps, the making of the specific judgments that constitutes the difficult part of this enterprise, belongs in the first instance to the politically accountable branches, specifically to the experts in the agency, not to generalist judges.

■ MIKVA, J., with whom CHIEF JUDGE WALD, and JUDGES ROBINSON and EDWARDS join, dissenting—The real mischief of today's decision lies not in the majority's belief that the utility has raised an issue of fact necessitating a hearing, but in its determination that Jersey Central has actually made out a case of constitutional confiscation. As Justice Douglas remarked, "he who would upset the rate order under the Act carries the heavy burden of making a convincing showing that it is invalid because it is unjust and unreasonable in its consequences." *Hope*, 320 U.S. at 602. The majority believes that Jersey Central can meet this burden. We simply cannot swallow the majority's assertion that "it is probable that the facts alleged [by Jersey Central], if true, would establish an invasion of the company's rights." In our view, it is beyond cavil that Jersey Central has not presented allegations which, if true, would establish that the Commission's orders result in unjust and unreasonable rates.

Permian Basin teaches that if the Commission reasonably balances consumer and investor interests, then the resulting rate is not confiscatory. The separate opinion ably translates this into a working definition of a confiscatory rate: it exists when "an unreasonable balance has been struck in the regulation process so as unreasonably to favor ratepayer interests at the substantial expense of investor interests." The majority appears to agree with the teaching of *Permian Basin*. The lesson it gleans, however, is incongruous. According to the majority, balancing competing interests is not enough; a rate is confiscatory if it does not satisfy the "legitimate investor interest" outlined by the Court in *Hope*. This interpretation of *Hope* and *Permian Basin* is implausible.

. . . The *Hope* court did not define "unjust or unreasonable"; nor did it articulate when a rate would be confiscatory. It certainly did not hold that the end result could be condemned if the investor criteria defined in the case were not fulfilled. Indeed, it expressly noted that its holding made no suggestion that more or less might not be allowed. 320 U.S. at 603; *see Market Street*, 324 U.S. at 566.

This understanding of *Hope* is the only way to reconcile the Court's recitation of investor interests with its avowal that "regulation does not insure that the business shall produce net revenues." *See Hope*, 320 U.S. at 603 (*quoting Natural Gas Pipeline*, 315 U.S. at 590). Investor interests are only one factor in the assessment of constitutionally reasonable, therefore non-confiscatory, rates. *Permian Basin*, 390 U.S. at 769. In any instance, the rate must also "provide appropriate protection to the relevant public interests, both existing and foreseeable." *Id*. at 792. A just and reasonable rate which results from balancing these conflicting interests might not provide "enough revenue not only for operating expenses but also for the capital costs of the business . . . includ[ing] service on the debt and dividends on the stock." *See Hope*, 320 U.S. at 603.

The Court made this abundantly clear in *Market Street*. . . . Neither the regulatory process nor the fifth amendment shelter a utility from market forces. Thus, contrary to the majority's intimations, rates do not fall outside the zone of reasonableness merely because they do not enable the company to operate at a profit or do not permit investors to recover all their losses. . . .

Application of this principle is readily apparent in the Commission's current treatment of electric utility plants, investments prudent when made but sometimes frustrated in fruition. If the investment is successful, the customer benefits from controlled rates for the service provided. But the ratepayer also shares the costs if the investment fails; he must pay for the expenditure made on an unproductive facility from which he obtains no service. From the investor's viewpoint, price regulation cabins both his upside and downside risk. He cannot collect the windfall benefits if the project is a boon; he does not bear all costs if the project is a bust. Electric utility stockholders do not lose equity in the non-serviceable facility, as they might in the marketplace. They simply do not procure a return on the investment.

The majority quibbles with this risk allocation; it would prefer a world in which the investor is guaranteed a return on his investment, if prudent when made. Its resultant holding today is directly at odds with fundamental principles laid out in *Hope* and its progeny. Adherence to the majority's insistence on the inclusion of prudent investments in the rate base would virtually insulate investors in public utilities from the risks involved in free market business. This would drastically diminish protection of the public interest by thrusting the entire risk of a failed investment onto the ratepayers. . . . ■

Duquesne Light Company v. Barasch
488 U.S. 299 (1989).

■ REHNQUIST, C. J.—Pennsylvania law required that rates for electricity be fixed without consideration of a utility's expenditures for electrical generating facilities which were planned but never built, even though the expenditures were prudent and reasonable when made. The Supreme Court of Pennsylvania held that such a law did not take the utilities' property in violation of the Fifth Amendment to the United States Constitution. We agree with that conclusion, and hold that a state scheme of utility regulation does not "take" property simply because it disallows recovery of capital investments that are not "used and useful in service to the public." 66 Pa. Const. Stat. § 1315 (Supp.1988).

I

In response to predictions of increased demand for electricity, Duquesne Light Company (Duquesne) and Pennsylvania Power

Company (Penn Power) joined a venture in 1967 to build more generating capacity. The project, known as the Central Area Power Coordination Group (CAPCO), involved three other electric utilities and had as its objective the construction of seven large nuclear generating units. In 1980 the participants canceled plans for construction of four of the plants. Intervening events, including the Arab oil embargo and the accident at Three Mile Island, had radically changed the outlook both for growth in the demand for electricity and for nuclear energy as a desirable way of meeting that demand. At the time of the cancellation, Duquesne's share of the preliminary construction costs associated with the four halted plants was $34,697,389. Penn Power had invested $9,569,665.

In 1980, and again in 1981, Duquesne sought permission from the Pennsylvania Public Utility Commission (PSC) to recoup its expenditures for the unbuilt plants over a 10-year period. The Commission deferred ruling on the request until it received the report from its investigation of the CAPCO construction. That report was issued in late 1982. The report found that Duquesne and Penn Power could not be faulted for initiating the construction of more nuclear generating capacity at the time they joined the CAPCO project in 1967. The projections at that time indicated a growing demand for electricity and a cost advantage to nuclear capacity. It also found that the intervening events which ultimately confounded the predictions could not have been predicted, and that work on the four nuclear plants was stopped at the proper time. In summing up, the Administrative Law Judge found "that the CAPCO decisions in regard to the [canceled plants] at every stage to their cancellation, were reasonable and prudent." He recommended that Duquesne and Penn Power be allowed to amortize their sunk costs in the project over a 10-year period. The PSC adopted the conclusions of the report.

In 1982, Duquesne again came before the PSC to obtain a rate increase. Again, it sought to amortize its expenditures on the canceled plants over 10 years. In January 1983, the PSC issued a final order which granted Duquesne the authority to increase its revenues $105.8 million to a total yearly revenue in excess of $800 million. The rate increase included $3.5 million in revenue representing the first payment of the 10-year amortization of Duquesne's $35 million loss in the CAPCO plants.

The Pennsylvania Office of the Consumer Advocate (Consumer Advocate) moved the PSC for reconsideration in light of a state law enacted about a month before the close of the 1982 Duquesne rate proceeding. The Act amended the Pennsylvania Utility Code by limiting "the consideration of certain costs in the rate base." It provided that "the cost of construction or expansion of a facility undertaken by a public utility producing . . . electricity shall not be made a part of the rate base nor otherwise included in the rates charged by the electric utility until such time as the facility is used and useful in service to the public." On reconsideration, the PSC affirmed its original rate order. It read the new law as excluding the costs of canceled plants (obviously not used and useful) from the rate base, but not as preventing their recovery through amortization. . . . [On an appeal brought by the Consumer Advocate, the Pennsylvania Supreme Court held that the controlling language of the Act prohibited recovery of the costs in question *either* by inclusion in the rate base *or* by amortization and remanded the case to the PSC for further proceedings based on this holding. Duquesne and Penn Power appealed to the U.S. Supreme Court, claiming that this interpretation of the statute was a taking, in violation of the Fifth Amendment of the U.S. Constitution]

III

As public utilities, both Duquesne and Penn Power are under a state statutory duty to serve the public. A Pennsylvania statute provides that "[e]very public utility shall furnish and maintain adequate, efficient, safe, and reasonable service and facilities" and that "[s]uch service also shall be reasonably continuous and without unreasonable interruptions or delay." 66 Pa. Const. Stat. § 1501 (1986). Although their assets are employed in the public interest to provide consumers of the State with electric power, they are owned and operated by private investors. This partly public, partly private status of utility property creates its own set of questions under the Takings Clause of the Fifth Amendment.

The guiding principle has been that the Constitution protects utilities from being limited to a charge for their property serving the public which is so "unjust" as to be confiscatory. If the rate does not afford sufficient compensation, the State has taken the use of utility property without paying just compensation and so violated the Fifth and Fourteenth Amendments. As has been observed, however, "[h]ow such compensation may be ascertained, and what are the necessary elements in such an inquiry, will always be an embarrassing question." *Smyth v. Ames*, 169 U.S. 466, 546 (1898). *See also Permian Basin Area Rate Cases*, 390 U.S. 747, 790 (1968) ("[N]either law nor economics has yet devised generally accepted standards for the evaluation of rate-making orders").

At one time, it was thought that the Constitution required rates to be set according to the actual present value of the assets employed in the public service. This method, known as the "fair value" rule, is exemplified by the decision in *Smyth v. Ames, supra.* Under the fair value approach, a "company is entitled to ask . . . a fair return upon the value of that which it employs for the public convenience," while on the other hand, "the public is entitled to demand . . . that no more be exacted from it for the use of [utility property] than the services rendered by it are reasonably worth." 169 U.S., at 547. In theory the *Smyth v. Ames* fair value standard mimics the operation of the competitive market. To the extent utilities' investments in plants are good ones (because their benefits exceed their costs) they are rewarded with an opportunity to earn an "above-cost" return, that is, a fair return on the current "market value" of the plant. To the extent utilities' investments turn out to be bad ones (such as plants that are canceled and so never used and useful to the public), the utilities suffer because the investments have no fair value and so justify no return.

Although the fair value rule gives utilities strong incentive to manage their affairs well and to provide efficient service to the public, it suffered from practical difficulties which ultimately led to its abandonment as a constitutional requirement.[5][2] In response to these

---

[2]   Perhaps the most serious problem associated with the fair value rule was the "laborious and baffling task of finding the present value of the utility." The exchange value of a utility's assets, such as powerplants, could not be set by a market price because such assets were rarely bought and sold. Nor could the capital assets be valued by the stream of income they produced because setting that stream of income was the very object of the rate proceeding. According to

problems, Justice Brandeis had advocated an alternative approach as the constitutional minimum, what has become known as the "prudent investment" or "historical cost" rule. He accepted the *Smyth v. Ames* eminent domain analogy, but concluded that what was "taken" by public utility regulation is not specific physical assets that are to be individually valued, but the capital prudently devoted to the public utility enterprise by the utilities' owners. *Missouri ex rel. Southwestern Bell Telephone Co. v. Public Service Comm'n,* 262 U.S. 276, 291 (1923) (dissenting opinion). Under the prudent investment rule, the utility is compensated for all prudent investments at their actual cost when made (their "historical" cost), irrespective of whether individual investments are deemed necessary or beneficial in hindsight. The utilities incur fewer risks, but are limited to a standard rate of return on the actual amount of money reasonably invested.[6][3]

Forty-five years ago in the landmark case of *FPC v. Hope Natural Gas Co.,* 320 U.S. 591 (1944), this Court abandoned the rule of *Smyth v. Ames,* and held that the "fair value" rule is not the only constitutionally acceptable method of fixing utility rates. In *Hope* we ruled that historical cost was a valid basis on which to calculate utility compensation. 320 U.S., at 605 ("Rates which enable [a] company to operate successfully, to maintain its financial integrity, to attract capital, and to compensate its investors for the risk assumed certainly cannot be condemned as invalid, even though they might produce only a meager return on the so called 'fair value' rate base"). We also acknowledged in that case that all of the subsidiary aspects of valuation for ratemaking purposes could not properly be characterized as having a constitutional dimension, despite the fact that they might affect property rights to some degree. Today we reaffirm these teachings of *Hope Natural Gas:* "[I]t is not theory but the impact of the rate order which counts. If the total effect of the rate order cannot be said to be unreasonable, judicial inquiry . . . is at an end. The fact that the method employed to reach that result may contain infirmities is not then important." *Id.,* at 602. This language, of course, does not dispense with all of the constitutional difficulties when a utility raises a claim that the rate which it is permitted to charge is so low as to be confiscatory: whether a particular rate is "unjust" or "unreasonable" will depend to some extent on what is a fair rate of return given the risks under a particular rate-setting system, and on the amount of capital upon which the investors are entitled to earn that return. At the margins, these questions have constitutional overtones.

Pennsylvania determines rates under a slightly modified form of the historical cost/prudent investment system. Neither Duquesne nor Penn Power alleges that the total effect of the rate order arrived at within this system is unjust or unreasonable. In fact the overall effect is well within the bounds of *Hope,* even with total exclusion of the CAPCO costs. Duquesne was authorized to earn a 16.14% return on common equity and an 11.64% overall return on a rate base of nearly $1.8 billion. Its $35 million investment in the canceled plants comprises roughly 1.9% of its

---

Brandeis, the *Smyth v. Ames* test usually degenerated to proofs about how much it would cost to reconstruct the asset in question, a hopelessly hypothetical, complex, and inexact process.

[3] The system avoids the difficult valuation problems encountered under the *Smyth v. Ames* test because it relies on the actual historical cost of investments as the basis for setting the rate. The amount of a utility's actual outlays for assets in the public service is more easily ascertained by a ratemaking body because less judgment is required than in valuing an asset.

total base. The denial of plant amortization will reduce its annual allowance by 0.4%. Similarly, Penn Power was allowed a charge of 15.72% return on common equity and a 12.02% overall return. Its investment in the CAPCO plants comprises only 2.4% of its $401.8 million rate base. The denial of amortized recovery of its $9.6 million investment in CAPCO will reduce its annual revenue allowance by only 0.5%.

Given these numbers, it appears that the PSC would have acted within the constitutional range of reasonableness if it had allowed amortization of the CAPCO costs but set a lower rate of return on equity with the result that Duquesne and Penn Power received the same revenue they will under the instant orders on remand. The overall impact of the rate orders, then, is not constitutionally objectionable. No argument has been made that these slightly reduced rates jeopardize the financial integrity of the companies, either by leaving them insufficient operating capital or by impeding their ability to raise future capital. Nor has it been demonstrated that these rates are inadequate to compensate current equity holders for the risk associated with their investments under a modified prudent investment scheme.

Instead, appellants argue that the Constitution requires that subsidiary aspects of Pennsylvania's ratemaking methodology be examined piecemeal. One aspect which they find objectionable is the constraint Act 335 places on the PSC's decisions. They urge that such legislative direction to the PSC impermissibly interferes with the PSC's duty to balance consumer and investor interest under *Permian Basin*, 390 U.S., at 792. Appellants also note the theoretical inconsistency of Act 335, suddenly and selectively applying the used and useful requirement, normally associated with the fair value approach, in the context of Pennsylvania's system based on historical cost. Neither of the errors appellants perceive in this case is of constitutional magnitude.

It cannot seriously be contended that the Constitution prevents state legislatures from giving specific instructions to their utility commissions. We have never doubted that state legislatures are competent bodies to set utility rates. And the Pennsylvania PSC is essentially an administrative arm of the legislature. This is not to say that any system of ratemaking applied by a utilities commission, including the specific instructions it has received from its legislature, will necessarily be constitutional. But if the system fails to pass muster, it will not be because the legislature has performed part of the work.

Similarly, an otherwise reasonable rate is not subject to constitutional attack by questioning the theoretical consistency of the method that produced it. "It is not theory, but the impact of the rate order which counts." *Hope*, 320 U.S., at 602. The economic judgments required in rate proceedings are often hopelessly complex and do not admit of a single correct result. The Constitution is not designed to arbitrate these economic niceties. Errors to the detriment of one party may well be canceled out by countervailing errors or allowances in another part of the rate proceeding. The Constitution protects the utility from the net effect of the rate order on its property. Inconsistencies in one aspect of the methodology have no constitutional effect on the utility's property if they are compensated by countervailing factors in some other aspect.

Admittedly, the impact of certain rates can only be evaluated in the context of the system under which they are imposed. One of the elements always relevant to setting the rate under Hope is the return investors expect given the risk of the enterprise. *Id.*, at 603 ("[R]eturn to the equity owner should be commensurate with returns on investments in other enterprises having corresponding risks"); *Bluefield Water Works & Improvement Co. v. Public Service Comm'n of West Virginia*, 262 U.S. 679, 692–693 (1923) ("A public utility is entitled to such rates as will permit it to earn a return . . . equal to that generally being made at the same time and in the same general part of the country on investments in other business undertakings which are attended by corresponding risks and uncertainties"). The risks a utility faces are in large part defined by the rate methodology because utilities are virtually always public monopolies dealing in an essential service, and so relatively immune to the usual market risks. Consequently, a State's decision to arbitrarily switch back and forth between methodologies in a way which required investors to bear the risk of bad investments at some times while denying them the benefit of good investments at others would raise serious constitutional questions. But the instant case does not present this question. At all relevant times, Pennsylvania's rate system has been predominantly but not entirely based on historical cost and it has not been shown that the rate orders as modified by Act 335 fail to give a reasonable rate of return on equity given the risks under such a regime. We therefore hold that Act 335's limited effect on the rate order at issue does not result in a constitutionally impermissible rate. Finally we address the suggestion of the Pennsylvania Electric Association as amicus that the prudent investment rule should be adopted as the constitutional standard. We think that the adoption of any such rule would signal a retreat from 45 years of decisional law in this area which would be as unwarranted as it would be unsettling. *Hope* clearly held that "the Commission was not bound to the use of any single formula or combination of formulae in determining rates." 320 U.S., at 602. ■

NOTES AND COMMENTS

1.   How utilities "depreciate" their assets, such as power plants, can have a major impact on the structure of the energy industry. If utilities depreciate plants at 3% a year, this means that these assets are expected to remain in operation, and used and useful for ratepayers, for 30 to 40 years. As a result, the decision whether to build a plant in the first place is a very significant capital decision for the firm, current and future customers.

2.   On rehearing in *Jersey Central III*, the Commission sustained the amortization scheme after holding a hearing. *See* Jersey Cent. Power & Light, 49 F.E.R.C. ¶ 63,004 (1989).

3.   Does *Duquesne* resolve the differences between the majority and dissent in *Jersey Central III*? Would the Supreme Court have sided with the majority, the dissent, or Judge Starr's concurrence? The *Duquesne* case raises the relationship between regulatory takings and takings in the ratemaking context. Should utility regulation that is found to satisfy the *Hope* "end results" test be subjected to additional tests to determine whether or not the regulation results in "confiscation" and is a "regulatory taking"? *See* Richard Goldsmith, Utility Rates and 'Takings,' 10 Energy L.J. 241 (1989). Judge Starr, in his concurrence to *Jersey Central III*, suggests that

the *Hope* test operates independent of the takings tests that might apply in other contexts, and the dissent appears to agree.

Duquesne purports to reaffirm *Hope*, but there is considerable disagreement over whether the Court opened the door to second-guessing regulators' choices. According to some commentators, "a wolf in sheep's clothing, the *Duquesne* opinion has resurrected the language of substantive economic due process, and has the potential for undoing everything for which *Hope* stood." Basil M. Copeland, Jr. & Walter W. Nixon, III, Procedural Versus Substantive Economic Due Process for Public Utilities, 12 Energy L.J. 81, 89 (1991). Does the language of *Duquesne* support Copeland and Nixon's argument? Others disagree with this reading, maintaining that *Hope* and *Duquesne* effectively remove the judiciary from constitutional review of ratemaking. *See* Richard J. Pierce, Jr., Public Utility Regulatory Takings: Should the Judiciary Attempt to Police the Political Institutions?, 77 Geo. L.J. 2031, 2062 (1989). The approach of lower courts in adjudicating recent takings challenges in the ratemaking context seem to lend more support for Pierce's views on the issue.

4.   *Depreciation Expenses*: Even if original cost is chosen as the method for valuing rate base, there is still a significant question as to how original cost should be determined. As an accounting matter, rate base, B, does not remain constant from year-to-year; rather, a utility's investments in capital assets depreciate over their useful lives and are eventually retired, scrapped, or sold. Assets are capitalized over their useful years, not expensed in a single year. By contrast, variable expenses are expensed during the periods in which they are consumed.

For example, many modern consumers finance automobiles over a 4- or 5-year period; in doing this, the consumer spreads the cost of the automobile over its most useful years. By contrast, in buying a hamburger, the cost is incurred immediately. If the hamburger is bought on a credit card, it is charged simultaneously with consumption of the hamburger. Only an unwise or financially irresponsible consumer would pay for hamburger over a 4- or 5-year period. When assets are paid for over time, their original value needs to be adjusted to take into account what has already been paid and used. Depreciation, d, represents the cumulative amount of assets that have been retired for accounting purposes. Rate base, B, is typically adjusted by d, by subtracting d from V, the gross value of the utility's capital investment.

In *Jersey Central III*, briefly excerpted above, Jersey Central's investment of $397 million in the canceled Forked River nuclear plant was at issue. FERC allowed Jersey Central to amortize its $397 million investment over a fifteen-year period. (Amortization is the functional equivalent of depreciation; it expenses a portion of an intangible asset's value over its useful life.) It did not, however, allow Jersey Central to recover the unamortized balance in rate base, because the plant was not "used and useful." As a result, interest costs were charged to shareholders while principal costs were recovered from ratepayers, but only over the fifteen-year period. In other words, the firm lost the time value of its money by only recovering a portion of the $397 million as an operating expense. To a utility, failure to recover depreciation as part rate base can make a large difference in revenue requirements, as it may deny the utility (and its investors) the ability to earn a rate of return on the entire capital investment for a large project (such as a canceled nuclear plant).

5.   *Depreciated v. Trended Original Costs*: If depreciation is included in rate base, there are basically two approaches available to regulators in applying d to B: depreciated original cost (DOC) and trended original cost (TOC). Both measure the amount of fixed investment for the provision of utility service in actual dollars, as adjusted, not only for depreciation, but also for some complicated accounting concepts—e.g., allowance for funds used during construction and normalized taxes—which are beyond the scope of our discussion.

Under DOC, assets are depreciated on what accountants call a "straight-line" basis—i.e., rate base declines at a steady rate over the useful life of the asset as d increases at a steady rate. Under DOC a front-end asset load is created: investors in early years pay higher rates on the new assets, while investors in later years pay lower rates on the depreciated plant. (As rate base is depreciated, smaller and smaller portions of rate base are left to which to apply the cost of capital.)

With TOC, rate base is increased by an inflation factor at the same time that the facilities are depreciated over their remaining useful life of the asset. FERC has given the following example to illustrate the TOC method:

> Assume a new pipeline with an original equity investment of $1,000. Also assume that a just and reasonable overall rate of return on equity would be 16 percent and that 7 percent of that represents inflation. That leaves 9 percent as a so-called "real" rate of return. In its first year of service, the pipeline would be entitled to earn $90 (9 percent times $1,000) and $70 (7 percent times $1,000) would be capitalized into its equity rate base to be amortized over the life of the property starting with the first year, along with the depreciation on the $1,000. If that life were twenty years, in addition to the return of $90, the pipeline would be entitled to recover, in the first year, $3.50 as amortization ($70 divided by 20), $50 as depreciation ($1,000 divided by 20), its embedded debt cost, and depreciation associated with debt investment. This process would continue over the life of the property until the rate base (assuming no salvage value) hit zero. Unless changed in a rate case, the real rate, which should be relatively stable, would be 9 percent each year. The inflation rate would vary as the chosen inflation index varies.

Williams Pipe Line Co., 31 F.E.R.C. ¶ 61,377 at 61,834 (1985).

Unlike DOC, application of TOC results in a rate base that increases in the initial year of operation and then turns downward until the facilities are fully depreciated. TOC and DOC are essentially the same except for their treatment of inflation. TOC has been advanced as a mechanism that will more closely replicate competitive markets, by avoiding the front-loading problem of DOC. For criticism, see Henry E. Kilpatrick, Jr. & Dennis H. Melvin, The Trended Vs. Depreciated Original Cost Controversy: How Real Are the Real Returns?, 12 Energy L. J. 323 (1991).

6.   *Construction Work In Progress (CWIP)*: Application of the used and useful doctrine is controversial in instances where a utility has invested in plants that are never completed or when a utility builds plants beyond its needs to serve customers. Are power plants under construction "used and useful"? On one hand, the electric generating plant that is not yet producing

electricity is not "used and useful" to customers. On the other hand, the construction expense and length of time required to create the new generating facility suggests the utility should get at least some recovery for its expenses from the commission.

As Judge Starr notes in his concurrence to *Jersey Central III*, FERC has departed from the used and useful rule to allow utilities to include a portion of the costs of CWIP in rate base. Utilities in every state are allowed under state law to include at least a portion of CWIP in rate base. FERC allowed utilities to include in rate base up to 50 percent of CWIP allocable to electric power sales and 100 percent of CWIP associated with pollution control and fuel conversion facilities. Construction Work In Progress for Public Utilities; Inclusion of Costs in Rate Base, 48 Fed. Reg. 24,323 (June 1, 1983) (codified at 18 C.F.R. §§ 35.12, 35.13, 35.26), *remanded* in Mid-Tex Elec. Coop. v. FERC, 773 F.2d 327 (D.C. Cir. 1985); Mid-Tex Elec. Coop. v. FERC, 864 F.2d 156 (D.C. Cir. 1988).

In *Legislative Utility Consumers' Council v. Public Service Co.*, 402 A.2d 626 (1979), the New Hampshire Supreme Court upheld the state PSC's inclusion in rate base of construction work in progress of $111,258,428 to finance construction of the Seabrook nuclear generating plant. The Legislative Utility Consumer's Council, a legislative agency comprised of state legislators statutorily authorized to intervene in rate proceedings on behalf of consumers, contested the commission's inclusion of construction work in progress in the company's rate base as contravening the "used and useful" requirement, which was codified in New Hampshire. The court noted:

> . . . The commission should consider whether the CWIP asked to be included in the rate base represents the cost of money expended for raising capital to finance construction that is undertaken upon sound business judgment and in accordance with a definite plan to meet the needs of future utility consumers. . . .

> The factual determination that the commission had to make in its used and useful analysis was whether the company's CWIP represents an expenditure incurred in raising capital to finance a reasonable construction program that will inure to the benefit of energy consumers by assuring a future supply of electricity. . . .

> We next consider the LUCC's argument that inclusion of CWIP in the company's rate base violates the basic "just and reasonable" principle of RSA ch. 378. The thrust of the LUCC's position is that including CWIP in the rate base forces present ratepayers to pay costs that should fall on future ratepayers who will actually benefit from the plant under construction when it comes on line. The LUCC argues that the traditional [Allowance for Funds Used During Construction] AFUDC treatment of CWIP, whereby it is capitalized and collected from future ratepayers via inclusion in the rate base over the period of the useful life of the plant when it comes on line, is required by the "just and reasonable" principle. The LUCC suggests that "the inclusion of CWIP [in the current rate base] is detrimental to present consumers while providing a windfall to future consumers."

> We reject the LUCC's contention that AFUDC treatment of CWIP is mandated by law. The commission's decision to include

CWIP in the rate base instead of capitalizing it in an AFUDC account is a factual one to be made on a case-by-case basis. Incorporating the burden of proof standard of RSA 378:8, we hold that "the burden of proving the necessity" of including CWIP in the rate base instead of employing traditional AFUDC treatment is upon the public utility. In the present case, we cannot say that "a clear preponderance of the evidence before [us]," demonstrates that the commission erroneously decided that the company has met its burden. RSA 541:13.

. . . The building of a nuclear powered generating facility requires very substantial lines of bank credit for the early construction stages. Immediate financing must be available. If credit is not forthcoming, the construction program will be jeopardized. *Amyot, supra* at 281. Because it is fundamental that rate making must take into account the need for the utility to maintain the confidence of investors, *Bluefield Water Works & Improvement Co. v. Pub. Serv. Comm'n*, 262 U.S. 679, 693 (1923); *accord, Federal Power Comm'n v. Hope Natural Gas Co.*, 320 U.S. 591, 603 (1944), the commission properly exercised its regulatory function by allowing the company to prove the necessity of including its CWIP in the rate base. . . .

Ratepayers like taxpayers come and go but ratepayers like taxpayers cannot expect to be charged solely on the basis of their individual benefit. Schools and other public buildings are benefitting the taxpayers today but were fully paid for by taxpayers of yesterday. . . .

Id. at 633–48.

If CWIP is not allowed in rate base, a firm cannot earn a current rate of return on its investment. However, it is permitted to use an alternative method of recovering the cost of capital invested in CWIP during the period before the new plant is placed into service through an account referenced in the passage above, known as Allowance for Funds Used During Construction (AFUDC); the firm accumulates in AFUDC an amount each year that represents the annual cost of capital in its CWIP account. Once a plant is completed and placed in service, all costs of the plant, including the accumulated AFUDC, are transferred to the firm's rate base. This allows the firm to earn a return on its CWIP, but the receipt of that money is deferred until after the plant is in service. In the above case, the New Hampshire Supreme Court rejected this approach:

The commission also evaluated alternative ratemaking approaches to that of including CWIP in the rate base. It considered full normalization of tax benefits of accelerated depreciation and allowing a higher return on equity capital. It found that these methods were "disadvantageous and undesirable in many respects." The commission relied on witness Trawicki's testimony to reject the alternative of allowing a higher return on equity capital. Trawicki stated "that such an alternative would result in an inflated return which is unrealistic when compared to other utilities and it could have the effect of establishing an inappropriate precedent." In rejecting the option of full normalization of tax benefits from accelerated depreciation, the commission found that this method would not generate enough funds to remedy the company's revenue deficiency and also that this procedure is imprecise and not readily controllable. The commission's report elaborated on the reasoning favoring CWIP in the rate base as the most desirable ratemaking approach.

We find that setting a rate of return higher than normal [on equity capital] would impose the same burdens on customers, that is, the rates would be the same while providing none of the advantages of the CWIP method, that is, a future reduction in rates because of a smaller future rate base. In other words, if the interest on the CWIP component is paid for today, it will not be included in the rate tomorrow. If CWIP were not allowed and the needed cash revenue were generated through a rate of return, the Company would continue to accumulate AFUDC along conventional accounting principles and eventually add this total amount to the total capitalization of plant. Thus, there would be no future reduction in rates stemming from discontinuance of AFUDC. . . .

7.   Used and useful, as a criterion for including costs in rate base, serves to protect current generations from bearing the burden of paying for the capital necessary to generate energy for future generations. Does this create the right incentives for energy consumption? What are the effects of the doctrine on technological innovation? Does allowing recovery of CWIP serve any useful distributive or economic purpose?

8.   In light of these materials, think back to the hypothetical case problem presented earlier in the chapter. Is it appropriate for EE to require current residential customers to pay for the cleanup costs associated with coal plants that they are not currently using? Why or why not? May EE also require residential customers to pay for the costs of smart metering software that has not yet been installed and is thus not yet used and useful? See Chapter 13 for further consideration of this issue.

ii.   Calculation of Operating Expenses

The day-to-day operational decisions of a regulated utility, such as the number of employees to hire and benefits to offer employees, or how many trucks to send out to trim trees around transmission wires, remain largely in the hands of its management, although they are impacted by federal reliability requirements such as minimum vegetation maintenance mandates as well as state requirements. Operating and maintenance expenses are often recorded in the utility's actual books and records, so their identification and measurement does not pose the same challenge as other aspects of the ratemaking formula. FERC and state PUCs generally defer to private management regarding the utility's decisions as to what type of fuel to purchase, the need for more service workers, or a salary increase for management. Still, the ratemaking process also can allow consumer groups to challenge the fiscal prudency of utility operation expense decisions, as well as whether customers actually benefit from the costs incurred to meet operating expenses.

For most utilities, depreciation and taxes are treated as operating expenses. Although, as is noted above, depreciation is typically deducted from capital investment to determine rate base, depreciation for the relevant period is also included as an operating expense. So, although the utility's rate base may be declining with time, the utility is able to recover the value of the reduction from customers as they benefit from the use of the plant.

Although operating expenses sometimes can comprise 75% or more of a utility's revenue requirements, in practice operating expenses may be the least controversial of the costs in the ratemaking formula. Deference is the standard with respect to operating expenses, but not every expense item is rubber-stamped for rate inclusion by FERC or state PUCs. In dictum, *Smyth v. Ames* qualified its description of the operating costs, *O*, a utility must be allowed to recover: "Under the evidence there is no ground for saying that the operating expenses of any companies were greater than necessary." This has come to be known as the "prudent expenditure" and "prudent investment" doctrines. Regulators will disallow operating expenses or investments that do not meet the prudence standards. These two standards are distinct, and the "prudence" issue affects both rate base (capital expenditures) and operating expenses. A decision to build (prudent investment) is evaluated separately—under rate base—from the reasonableness of operating costs once that decision has been made (prudent expenditure). In evaluating prudence, regulators apply a general presumption of managerial competence. *See* Missouri ex rel. Sw. Bell Tel. Co. v. Pub. Serv. Comm'n, 262 U.S. 276 (1923).

While the prudent investment doctrine is primarily a rate base issue, FERC and state PUCs have disallowed many operating expenses under the prudent expenditure standard. Sometimes the basis for this is economic waste. For example, state commissions have disallowed from rate recovery portions of wages they deem to be excessive. *See, e.g.,* Sw. Bell Tel. Co. v. Ar. Pub. Serv. Comm'n, 715 S.W.2d 451 (Ark. Ct. App. 1986) (en banc); S. Cal. Edison Co. v. Pub. Util. Comm'n, 576 P.2d 945 (Cal. 1978). In addition, the costs of unnecessary charitable contributions and advertising have regularly been disallowed. *See, e.g.,* Cleveland v. PUC, 406 N.E.2d 1370 (Ohio 1980) (disallowing charitable contributions "not reasonably necessary to produce safe, reliable service to utility customers"); Cent. Me. Power Co., 26 P.U.R.4th 388 (Me. PSC 1978) (disallowing advertisements designed to influence pending rate proceedings as "political").

Should the prudence of each of a utility's charitable contributions be evaluated, or is it the overall amount of the contribution that should be subject to a reasonableness standard? In *Business & Professional People v. Illinois Commerce Comm'n*, 585 N.E.2d 1032 (Ill. 1991), the Illinois Supreme Court held that the overall amount of expenses is important to the assessment of just and reasonable rates. Commonwealth Edison argued that the Commission arbitrarily disallowed $1.269 million of charitable contributions from Edison's operating expenses. The Court reasoned:

> Edison is correct that the Act prohibits the Commission from "disallowing by rule, as an operating expense, any portion of a reasonable donation for public welfare or charitable purposes." (Ill. Rev. Stat. 1987, ch. 111 2/3, par. 9–227.) However, section 9–227 does not provide that every donation Edison makes to a qualified organization is presumed reasonable. Edison still has

the burden of showing that a donation is reasonable in amount. When this burden of proof is considered, the Act merely states that the Commission shall not disallow any portion of that amount which Edison has shown to be reasonable in amount. Contrary to Edison's position, we believe that the Commission must determine the reasonableness of the amount of contributions based on the total contributions rather than on an individualized basis. There are numerous charitable organizations worthy of Edison's support. If Edison were to make a reasonable donation to each of these organizations, the aggregate total of the donations could very easily exceed a reasonable amount.

Id. at 1066. The court refused to substitute its judgment for the Commission's on which requested charitable expenses to exclude from an overall reasonable amount.

Another prevalent operational expense is fuel costs or the costs of purchased power (i.e., wholesale power bought by a utility for resale to its customers). As is discussed above, utility rates are typically based on a "test year"—a description of costs over a period of time that are used to set rates into the future. This creates the potential for a regulatory gap between approved rates and the costs a utility actually incurs. Since it is burdensome for regulators to evaluate rates on a continuing basis, it is common to automatically make adjustments to rates for cost variations in the price and quantity of fuel or purchased power through a regulatory instrument known as a "Fuel Adjustment Clause" (FAC). A FAC is a statutory or regulatory rule that allows a utility to automatically pass through to rates increased fuel or purchased power costs, without the need for a formal rate proceeding. One of the must most significant operating expenses incurred by utilities is the cost of fuel. Volatilities in fuel prices can create a gap between the actual cost of service and approved rates based on test-year projections. For example, a four-fold increase in petroleum prices in 1973, coupled with the escalation of coal and natural gas prices, left utilities facing costs that exceeded test-year projections in approved rates. Utilities faced a revenue shortfall and many lobbied for a FAC to automatically adjust their rates to reflect these fuel costs increases. With increased variations in the price of purchased electric power supply in the wholesale power market, FACs have also become important for many utilities that do not generate their own electricity.

FACs may reduce incentives for utilities to negotiate lower fuel or purchased power costs, but consumers can also benefit from a FAC if the costs of fuel decrease between regulatory approval of rates. For a FAC to effectively close the regulatory gap created by a difference between approved rates and actual costs, however, the cost data used in FACs must be accurate. For example, the California Supreme Court has observed how using a FAC on the basis of entirely forecasts or projections about fuel costs may lead to over-collection of revenues by utilities, to the extent fuel cost estimates overstate actual costs:

Not surprisingly, at the hearings below [Southern California] Edison's witness was extremely reluctant to admit that the company in fact treated such overcollections as earnings; rather, he took refuge in the repeated assertion that the funds could not be "isolated" from Edison's overall revenues. It clearly appears from published figures, however, that Edison's overcollections pursuant to the fuel clause were not only large in the absolute sense, they amounted to a very significant proportion of the company's general revenue picture. For example, for the year 1974 Edison reported a total net income from all sources of $218.3 million; yet during the same 12-month period, according to Edison's own figures filed with the commission in compliance with the decision under review, Edison's net fuel clause overcollections were $122.5 million—in other words, they constituted more than 56 percent of the company's system-wide net income for the entire year. Moreover, that net income was itself 47.8 percent higher than in the previous year, even though sales were lower; Edison's reported earnings per share were $4.10 for 1974, as compared with $2.70 for 1973; and the company's board of directors voted to increase the common stock dividend in 1974, the first such raise in three years. (Annual Rep., p. 4.) In announcing all these benefits to the shareholders, Edison acknowledged that the fuel clause adjustments, together with a general rate increase in late 1973, "contributed substantially to higher revenues."

These continuing overcollections by Edison and other electric utility companies did not pass unnoticed. On the contrary, they triggered a sequence of public complaints, investigations, and proposals for reform or abolition of the entire fuel clause procedure. Among the most vocal critics were consumer groups (e.g., The Fuel-Adjustment Caper (Nov. 1974) 39 Consumer Rep. 836) and organs of the Congress (*see* Rep. of Subcom. on Oversight and Investigations of House Com. on Interstate and Foreign Commerce on Electric Utility Automatic Fuel Adjustment Clauses (Oct. 1975) passim).

While sharing many of the concerns voiced by critics of the clause, the commission determined that the cost adjustment concept should be preserved but the clause should be modified to eliminate the defects revealed by experience. The principal such defect, as we have seen, was the provision authorizing Edison to base its calculations on a prediction of its fossil fuel needs for the 12-month period following each application for a billing adjustment, premised on the assumption that "average" weather conditions would prevail throughout that time. The commission abandoned this procedure, and in lieu thereof adopted a clause which operates on a "recorded data" basis, i.e., on the actual fuel expenses incurred by the utility during the period preceding its application for a billing adjustment. The utility is now required to maintain a monthly "balancing account," into which it will enter the amount by which its actual energy cost for the month was greater or less than the revenue generated by the clause; and on each occasion hereafter that the clause is invoked, the billing factor will be adjusted so as to bring the balance of this account back to zero. By this device the possibility of large over- or under-collections accumulating in the future is eliminated. And because the commission expanded the clause to include all sources of purchased energy—e.g.,

nuclear and geothermal, in addition to fossil fuels—it renamed
the device the "energy cost adjustment clause."

S. Cal. Edison Co. v. Pub. Utils. Comm'n, 576 P.2d 945, 949–50 (Cal.
1978). The Court held that adjustment clause did not result in retroactive
ratemaking. *Id.*

NOTES AND COMMENTS

1.   Operating expenses from a utility's test year—the year that is supposed
to show typical costs and thus the amount of money the utility needs to
recover through rates—may also be disallowed if they are under
representative (or non-recurring). Generally non-recurring expenses, such as
repair expenses attributable to a hurricane or excess fuel costs incurred
during an excessively hot summer, will not be used as a basis for test year
recovery of expenses, but will be allowed one-time recovery as extraordinary
expenses. In addition, some operating expenses simply may not qualify for
inclusion in the rate. *See* Sandstone Resources, Inc. v. FERC, 973 F.2d 956
(D.C. Cir. 1992) (costs incurred in removing liquid brine from natural gas
held to be nonrecoverable production costs).

2.   How would you oppose or defend the inclusion of the following as
legitimate utility operating expenses? Are all of these best characterized as
operating expenses, or should some of them be included in rate base?

—   A contribution to an industry-wide Gas Research Institute. *See*
PUC of Colo. v. FERC, 660 F.2d 821 (D.C. Cir. 1981).

—   Research programs in solar energy and nuclear reactor
technology standards. *See* Caldwell v. PUC, 613 P.2d 328 (Colo.
1980).

—   A discount on electric charges for company employees. *See*
Cent. Me. Power Co. v. PUC, 405 A.2d 153 (Me. 1979).

—   A commercial scale plant demonstrating a new coal
gasification technique. See Transwestern Pipeline Co. v. FERC,
626 F.2d 1266 (5th Cir. 1980).

—   Expenses incurred when a plant under construction is
abandoned. *See* Office of Consumers' Counsel v. Pub. Util. Comm'n,
423 N.E.2d 820 (Ohio 1981).

3.   One of the most controversial expense issues regulators currently face
is the intergenerational allocation of costs in utility rates. The general
principle of cost-of-service ratemaking is that customers should pay for the
costs of the services they consume. However, as issues such as CWIP,
depreciation, and the FAC illustrate, it is much simpler to state that
principle than make it work in practice. Consumers today, through items
such as CWIP, may pay for services that benefit future generations.
Although commissions generally frown upon "retroactive ratemaking," there
is no hard and fast rule that commissions or courts use to match costs and
benefits across generations. It generally comes down to balancing the various
interests before the regulator.

In this balancing of interests, since future generations are not
represented it might be expected that often the costs associated with benefits
to today's ratepayers are passed on to future generations. Ratepayers today
are paying for services that may have unanticipated costs for future

generations. As a result, future generations may pay greater rates to benefit today's consumers.

As an example, billions of dollars are at stake in the recovery of nuclear "decommissioning" costs—the costs utilities must incur when nuclear plants producing power today are retired 10, 20, or 30 years into the future to seal off radioactive waste and return nuclear facilities to a low-risk status. Regulators failed to account for most of these costs in initially determining the prudence of nuclear construction. Because it would be unfair to impose these costs on future ratepayers, utilities have been required to seek recovery in current rates.

In other cases, current ratepayers might pay for benefits received only by future generations. When ratepayers pay for CWIP associated with nuclear plants, they are not yet receiving the power that will eventually be produced by that nuclear plant. If these ratepayers move out of the state before the nuclear plant is up and running, they will never benefit from this relatively inexpensive power.

4.   The intergenerational problem illustrates one aspect of the issue of what is known as "rate design." Even once cost or revenue requirements are determined, regulators must decide who, among the various customer classes, should pay the costs of service. Several rate design issues may arise, among them the allocation of demand and energy charges, marginal cost pricing, or seasonal or peak load pricing.

In terms of the cost-of-service rate formula, distinct costs of service can be allocated to distinct customer classes. For example, it may be more costly for a utility to build the distribution infrastructure to serve the hundreds of residential customers in a development than to serve one or two very large industrials customers, even though the two classes—residential and industrial—may consume similar total amounts of energy.

In allocating costs to classes of customers, including residential, industrial, and small business customers, regulators use two billing components: demand and energy charges. Demand charges generally refer to the portion of utility costs allocated to a customer group to meet the aggregate demand of that group. In other words, these costs represent the amount of plant and other fixed assets allocated to a customer group through a utility rate base $(B*r)$. Energy charges generally refer to the cost of providing a certain amount of kWh to a class of customers. These costs vary with the amount of power consumed (e.g., fuel) and thus represent the amount of a utility's operating expenses allocated to a class of customers (O). On a customer's bill, distinct charges for demand and energy will appear. Depending on how "firm" the customer's service is—i.e., the level of reliability the utility has guaranteed—the appropriate charges will be assessed. Because many industrial customers take service on an "interruptible" basis, their bills have small demand components relative to the portion of their bill attributed to energy charges (given the large number of units that they consume). By contrast, residential customers generally have high demand components (given that they need "firm" power) relative to the energy charges on their bills. See the discussion in Chapter 2.

5.   Many states have experimented with low-income or lifeline rates, in which some customers pay less than the cost of service to serve social welfare goals. Is there any sound economic rationale for subsidizing low-income customers? Is this an instance of market failure for which some regulatory

solution may be justified? Or is this a pure redistributive program that serves non-cost goals?

Charging and collecting rates are two different actions. Many customers who are charged rates may never pay them, and utilities are often required to undergo costly collection efforts, sometimes at a cost to all customers. One way to conceptualize low-income rates is based on cost. As Roger Colton describes:

> The National Consumer Law Center has developed the energy assurance program (EAP) to address these dual problems [charging as opposed to collecting rates]. The EAP recognizes that some households simply do not have sufficient income to pay for the basic necessities of life, including energy. There is no question but that this inability to pay is a social problem. There is no question, however, that this inability to pay also represents a business problem for utilities. For these households, regardless of the number of disconnect notices sent, regardless of the number of times service is disconnected, regardless of the type of payment plan that is offered, there will be insufficient household funds available to pay utility bills. A utility can recognize this fact and seek to collect what it can, while minimizing collection expenses, or a utility can deny this fact and devote its time, energy, and attention to what will prove to be fruitless and expensive collection attempts. . . .
>
> The EAP is not simply sound social policy. It is based on sound regulatory principles as well. A utility is required to operate with all reasonable efficiency. This is part and parcel of the obligation to provide least-cost service. Accordingly, utilities should pursue all reasonable means of minimizing the total revenue requirement, including the adoption of innovative credit and collection techniques.

Roger D. Colton, "A Cost-based Response to Low-income Energy Problems," Pub. Util. Fortnightly, Mar. 1, 1991. As Colton sees it, this type of program "is not designed to serve as a social program providing rate discounts to low-income households." Instead, it "is intended to be a collection device. It is a means of collection that will maximize the receipt of revenue from customers who cannot afford to pay their bills, while at the same time minimizing all of the expenses associated with delinquent payments." This makes some sense in a rate-regulated system: since fixed costs do not vary with the amount of service consumed, if a customer can cover at least the variable costs attributed to that customer, in the short-run other customers are not made any worse off. Colton states:

> The concept behind this statement is simple: It is better to collect 95 percent of a $70 bill than it is to collect 50 percent of a $100 bill. . . .
>
> Removing a nonpaying customer from the utility system does not necessarily result in the least-cost provision of service to all remaining ratepayers. Whenever a customer's service is disconnected, two things happen. The company does avoid the variable cost of delivering that unit of energy to the household. However, the company also foregoes the revenue that would have

been collected from the household but for the disconnection of service.

To the extent that the revenue would have exceeded the variable cost of delivering the energy (whether it be gas or electricity), other ratepayers lose a contribution toward the payment of the fixed charges of the company. In this instance, the disconnection of service leaves remaining, paying customers worse off than had the disconnection not occurred.

In general, there is an advantage to all ratepayers from keeping as many households on the system as possible. So long as households pay the variable costs of delivering the energy they consume, other ratepayers are no worse off. To the extent that households pay anything beyond the variable cost of the energy they consume, they are making a contribution toward the fixed costs of the system and all ratepayers are better off than they would have been had those households been disconnected. It is thus cost-effective for the utility, and for all remaining ratepayers, to provide payment-troubled customers with an incentive to make reduced payments (even when full payment cannot be made) by deciding not to disconnect so long as these customers continue to pay more than the variable cost of providing service. In essence, this proposal is no different than the treatment that many states accord their large natural gas and telecommunications customers who have the ability and inclination to engage in bypass. In effect, these residential customers who, because of their inability to pay their utility bill, would be disconnected from the utility system and forced to move to alternative sources of home energy, would be treated as opportunity sales by the utility.

Id. Roger Colton wrote this article in response to Howard M. Spinner's article, "Choosing an Efficient Energy Assistance Program," which appeared in the December 20, 1990 issue of the Public Utilities Fortnightly. For further development of the concept, see Roger D. Colton, The Duty of a Public Utility to Mitigate 'Damages' from Nonpayment Through the Offer of Conservation Programs, 3 B.U. Pub. Int. L.J. 239 (1993); Roger D. Colton & Mike Sheehan, A New Basis for Conservation Programs for the Poor: Expanding the Concept of Avoided Costs, 21 Clearinghouse Rev. 135 (1987).

Subsidies for low-income energy consumers have received congressional attention. The Public Utility Regulatory Policies Act (PURPA) supported low-income rate concepts. *See* 16 U.S.C. § 2624. In addition, federal agencies, such as the formerly-named Department of Housing and Urban Development (HUD), provide assistance (approximately one billion dollars annually) to the poor in meeting their energy needs through a number of federal programs. *See* Steven Ferrey, In from the Cold: Energy Efficiency and the Reform of HUD's Utility Allowance System, 32 Harv. J. on Legis. 145 (1995); Steven Ferrey, Cold Power: Energy and Public Housing, 23 Harv. J. on Legis. 33 (1986). For examples of state low-income energy assistance programs, see Ind. Housing and Commun. Dev't Auth., Energy Assist. Prog. (LIHEAP), http://www.in.gov/ihcda/2329.htm; Pa. Pub. Util. Comm'n, Energy Assist. Prog., http://www.puc.state.pa.us/consumer_info/electricity/energy_assistance_programs.aspx; Pub. Util. Comm'n of Texas, Paying Your Bill, https://www.puc.texas.gov/consumer/lowincome/Assistance.aspx.

Do the benefits of administering any low-income rate program exceed the potential costs? For example, how will a PUC distinguish between low-income and middle-income and wealthy residential customers? Can it establish an eligibility test? What is the best way to do this?

6.   Thinking back to the EE case study presented earlier in the chapter, are costs associated with software for implementing smart meters best recovered in rate base, or as operating expenses? How would the consumer advocate likely respond to EE's claims regarding the FAC offsetting the environmental monitoring expense?

Is it appropriate for EE to allocate none of the capital costs for converting its coal plants to industrial customers (who presumably would only pay for the fuel for each kWh of energy that they consume from the converted plants)? How would you anticipate that consumer advocates representing residential customers will respond to this argument?

C. ALTERNATIVES TO COST-OF-SERVICE RATE REGULATION

In recent years, many observers have expressed dissatisfaction with cost-based rate regulation. Both in this country and abroad, legislatures and regulatory agencies have been exploring completely different approaches to the subject of utility pricing.

There are several critiques to the traditional cost-based approach to rate regulation:

Rate regulation relies on case-by-case determinations that are firm specific, rather than on evaluation of industry-wide conditions. The process is information intensive and is very costly to both firms and to regulators.

There is also a likelihood of mistakes in the calculation of rates. If a regulator or a firm makes a mistake in estimating costs, this could be frozen into utility rates until the next rate determination. While the ratemaking process may be self-correcting if firms face regular rate evaluation, in many jurisdictions a decade or more will pass between rate adjustments. Regulated rates may not be sensitive to adjustments in fuel costs and other economic variables, such as interest rates or the rate of inflation.

Rate proceedings also create incentives for firms to exaggerate costs and to engage in strategic manipulation of the types of information presented to regulators. Even if manipulation of the system is not intentional, there is evidence to suggest that rate regulation has led to a higher than optimal capital to labor ratio in the industry. *See* Harvey Averch & Leland L. Johnson, Behavior of the Firm Under Regulatory Constraint, 52 Am. Econ. Rev. 1052 (1962). As a result, there may be overinvestment in certain infrastructure or technology, a cost that is borne by consumers in higher rates, by shareholders in reduced returns, or both.

Finally, to the extent that regulated rates are tied to specific capital decisions, such as a specific power plant or transmission line, rate regulation disfavors new investment and may work to thwart innovation. While this is a potential cost to rate regulation, regulated utilities also may be more likely to invest in newer, higher risk technologies to the extent that they are guaranteed cost recovery in their rates.

1. PRICE-CAP REGULATION

One of the most popular non-cost-based methods of pricing utility service is price ceilings or caps. To counteract the effects of inflation and save the regulatory costs associated with calculating revenue requirements, regulators will limit the charges utilities can pass on to certain customers. For instance, the British government adopted price ceilings when it privatized its telecommunications industry in 1984, and several federal and state regulators in the United States have experimented with price level regulation as well. In some instances, utilities may favor price caps since they give utilities the ability to make their own decisions about expenditures without regulatory oversight. If a utility can find ways to decrease its costs, it may keep some or all of the additional revenue it generates as profit. Regulators may find price caps attractive too, since they may create incentives for utilities to become productive.

Nevertheless, price level regulation has not been widespread in the United States. Regulators are unable to accurately set ceiling prices: when utilities make excess profits public pressure leads regulators to return to cost of service regulation, yet if utilities are making little or no profits they will pressure regulators to raise ceiling prices.

A price cap limits the retail or wholesale price that a supplier can charge. Many price caps are benchmarked to inflation, allowing some flexibility in their implementation. Regulators have experimented with price caps in the context of nearly every energy resource, from gasoline to natural gas and electricity. In nearly every context in the energy sector, they have failed to achieve their overall policy goal, yet they are often embraced by federal and state regulators as a way of keeping energy prices low. Consider the following critique:

Richard J. Pierce, Price Level Regulation Based on Inflation Is Not an Attractive Alternative to Profit Level Regulation
84 Nw. U. L. Rev. 665 (1990).

When the British government privatized its telecommunications industry in 1984, it was forced to confront for the first time the issue of how, if at all, to regulate that industry. It rejected traditional cost-of-service regulation in favor of a system of price level regulation. Price level regulation relies entirely on a price cap that changes automatically over time in accordance with a formula that incorporates expected future changes in costs and in productivity. The changes in regulated price are unrelated to actual changes in firm costs or profits. British Telecommunication's ceiling price at any time is determined through application of a simple formula: present price equals initial price, plus inflation, minus a three percent productivity adjustment factor (CPI–3). . . .

In their 1989 book, *Price Level Regulation for Diversified Public Utilities*, Professors Jordan Jay Hillman and Ronald Braeutigam of Northwestern University urge serious consideration of price level regulation as a substitute for profit level regulation of all natural monopolies. . . . I conclude that price level regulation based on the CPI–3 formula holds little realistic promise of yielding acceptable results.

Proponents of price level regulation refer to the British Telecom experience to demonstrate the viability of the concept. I doubt the predictive value of this experience for three reasons: (1) it is limited to a single context; (2) we have only four years of experience; and (3) it may constitute de facto profit level regulation disguised as price level regulation.

Recent experience with real price level regulation has much greater predictive power. The United States adopted price level regulation for important purposes in the Natural Gas Policy Act ("NGPA"), Crude Oil Windfall Profits Tax Act ("COWPT"), and the Public Utility Regulatory Policies Act ("PURPA"). The experience under each of those statutes is not encouraging.

In the NGPA Congress imposed price ceilings at varying levels on each of several categories of natural gas. Each price ceiling consisted of an initial price and an automatic price adjustment mechanism designed to further several goals simultaneously. The price ceiling applicable to "new natural gas' " illustrates the NGPA approach. In 1978, Congress chose an initial price ceiling slightly higher than the pre-existing price ceiling derived from profit level regulation and somewhat lower than what Congress perceived to be the price that would exist in a competitive market. Congress then selected a price adjustment mechanism based on its desire to achieve parity between the "new gas' " ceiling price and the market-clearing price of gas by 1985. To accomplish this purpose the price adjustment clause was designed to reflect simultaneously four factors: (1) expected increases in nominal costs; (2) expected increases in real costs attributable to the depleting resource effect; (3) expected productivity increases; and (4) the need to close the perceived gap between the initial ceiling price and the efficient price. Based on extensive testimony, Congress ultimately selected a price adjustment mechanism that consisted of the Gross National Product implicit price deflator minus 0.2%, plus 3.5%. The first term in the adjustment mechanism was intended to reflect changes in nominal costs, while the second term was intended to reflect the net effect of the other three factors.

Even with perfect hindsight, it is difficult to determine the relationship between the initial price level Congress chose and the "efficient price' " in 1978. It is easy, however, to assess the performance of the automatic price adjustment mechanism Congress chose. That mechanism performed miserably, largely because it was incapable of reflecting major changes in demand factors. The quantity of gas demanded at the new gas ceiling price soared in 1979 in response to changes in the closely related oil market in the wake of the Iranian Revolution. For two years, it appeared that Congress had seriously underestimated the rate of change in the "new gas' " ceiling price necessary to yield an efficient price.

That concern was replaced quickly in 1981 with the opposite concern. The world price of oil began to decline, yielding a rapid decrease in the quantity of gas demanded at the "new gas' " ceiling price. In the meantime, that ceiling price continued its inexorable climb as a function of the operation of the automatic adjustment mechanism. The costs of the factors of production later declined in response to the change in demand factors. The automatic adjustment mechanism was incapable of reflecting either the downward changes in demand or the ensuing reductions in factor costs. The ceiling price kept increasing as the efficient price decreased rapidly. Eventually, the ceiling price was more than double the efficient price.

This experiment with price level regulation in the gas industry had devastating effects on all market participants. Gas consumers were particularly hard hit, faring far worse than they would have if the government had withdrawn completely from any attempt to regulate even those components of the gas industry that possess some degree of natural monopoly power. Regulation through the use of price ceilings yielded prices higher than would have resulted from the unconstrained exercise of natural monopoly power by pipelines and distributors. Ineffective price regulation was combined with the typical anticompetitive features of economic regulation to minimize both regulatory and market constraints on prices and output. The regulated market intermediaries, pipelines and distributors, enjoyed considerable insulation from competitive pressures through the usual array of tariff provisions, regulatory barriers to entry, and regulatory barriers to exit that create barriers to entry.

This experience suggests the possibility that adoption of price level regulation in other contexts also has the potential to create allocative inefficiencies worse than those resulting from unconstrained monopoly if the typical anticompetitive features of economic regulation are retained. This raises an important issue—if we move from profit level regulation to price level regulation, do we simultaneously discard all of the constraints on competition that usually accompany regulation based on perceived natural monopoly? If we do not, the NGPA experience suggests the existence of one set of significant risks. Yet, if we abandon those aspects of economic regulation, we risk the very problems that originally caused us to impose regulatory barriers to entry, exit, and competition in natural monopoly markets.

It is tempting to dismiss the NGPA experience with price level regulation as attributable merely to a one-time error in selecting an appropriate price adjustment formula. Yet, it is not so easy to suggest ways in which Congress could have avoided its error. Congress assumed that the real costs of exploration and production attributable to the depleting resource effect would increase at a level sufficient to offset any productivity gains and to yield a net real cost increase of 3.5% per year. That assumption seemed plausible at the time. Congress can be criticized for failing to incorporate changes in demand factors in the automatic adjustment mechanism. It is difficult even today, however, to conceive of any method of accomplishing that important goal through a price adjustment mechanism designed to further the primary goal of tracking expected changes in costs.

Congress was not alone in making enormous errors in the process of implementing price level regulation under NGPA. Congress delegated authority to the Federal Energy Regulatory Commission (FERC) to identify new categories of gas produced under conditions that justified a price ceiling at or near the market price. FERC exercised this authority in 1980. It determined that gas produced from "tight sands' " merited a special price ceiling. FERC decided that the incentive price applicable to this new category should be based on FERC's approximation of the present and expected future market price of gas—the "efficient price' " in the parlance of price level regulation. It chose for this purpose an initial price level of $4.50 per million Btus, subject to an automatic price adjustment of twice the level of inflation. Ex post, it is easy to conclude that both the initial price and the automatic adjustment mechanism chosen by FERC were wrong. The ceiling price rose to $7.00, while the efficient price declined to less than $2.00. In this case it is also easy to criticize FERC's decision ex ante. Its estimates were naive even in 1980. It is much more difficult, however, to suggest a price adjustment mechanism that would have performed acceptably. Any of the mechanisms used or proposed for use in the new systems of price level regulation would have produced a ceiling price far higher than the efficient price.

The federal government tried a different version of price level regulation in COWPT. The "windfall profit' " subject to tax was based on the difference between the market price at which a barrel of oil was sold and the "adjusted base price' " applicable to that barrel. Each of three "tiers" of oil was subject to a different adjusted base price. The initial base prices selected in 1979 were $16.55, $15.20, and $12.81 per barrel. In the case of the lower two base prices, the automatic price adjustment mechanism was the level of inflation. For the higher base price category, the adjustment mechanism was inflation plus two percent, again reflecting the expected net effect of real cost increases and expected productivity increases.

The adjusted base price in this system was not intended to be the "efficient price' "; Congress relied on the market for that purpose. The adjusted base price applicable to the high base price category—$16.55 plus inflation plus two percent—was intended, however, to parallel the market price, thereby yielding a steady flow of tax revenue each year. Thus, the automatic price adjustment mechanism applicable to Tier Three Oil in COWPT was designed to perform a function analogous to the automatic price adjustment mechanism in a system of price level regulation. The government expected to raise revenues of $227.3 billion through COWPT between 1979 and 1991. Its total revenues to date are a tiny fraction of that amount. The large disparity between expected and actual tax revenues is attributable entirely to one feature of COWPT. The automatic price adjustment mechanism Congress chose as a surrogate for expected future changes in the costs of finding and producing crude oil was incapable of reflecting changes in demand factors. Demand for domestically produced crude oil plummeted, while the adjusted base price increased. Eventually, finding costs also fell significantly, but the price adjustment mechanism was incapable of reflecting that change either. The adjusted base price applicable to Tier Three Oil, which was intended always to lie below the market price, has been well above the market price since 1981.

The final recent experience with a version of price level regulation arose under PURPA. Section 210 of PURPA requires state utility commissions to compel electric utilities to purchase power from qualified cogenerators and small power producers at a price that represents each utility's "full avoided cost' " of generating electricity. Since cogeneration and small power production projects depend for their financial viability on continuity of markets at predictable prices, the statute required each state agency to reflect in long-term contracts the agency's projection of the utility's "full avoided cost' " of generation for the next several decades. The pricing provisions of the mandated contracts typically included an initial price and an automatic price adjustment mechanism based on the agency's best estimate of expected future changes in the utility's costs. In a high proportion of cases, the price adjustment mechanism chosen by the agency produced a mandatory price to the utility far above the utility's actual avoided cost. Again, the adjustment mechanism was incapable of reflecting either major changes in demand factors or the resulting major changes in firm costs.

All of these descriptions of recent disastrous experiences with inflation-based price level regulation are drawn from the energy context. Based on these experiences, I feel confident in urging complete rejection of any inflation-based form of price level regulation for potential application to electric and gas utilities. This experience also explains in part my extreme skepticism that the CPI–3 version of price level regulation represents an alternative to profit level regulation worthy of serious consideration in any context. . . .

Having acknowledged the high social costs of profit level regulation and criticized the theoretically promising alternative of CPI–3 price level regulation, I feel obligated to identify other alternatives that offer greater promise. The approach that offers the highest probability of improving allocative and productive efficiency depends critically on the present and expected future characteristics of a market that is now subject to profit level regulation. The alternatives to price level regulation that are likely to enhance social welfare in some contexts include: (1) plain vanilla deregulation; (2) deregulation of sales markets combined with mandatory equal access to significant sunk cost facilities; (3) deregulation combined with reliance on relational contracts; and (4) flexible pricing within boundaries. . . . ■

NOTES AND COMMENTS

1.   Price caps have effectively been integrated into many state retail restructuring plans, to the extent they limit the prices that can be charged for power. Many of the state retail electric plans discussed in Chapter 10 guarantee residential consumers a rate decrease or set limits on future rate increases. Do you think that price caps in this context will pose some of the problems Professor Pierce discusses? Why or why not?

2.   Jordan Jay Hillman and Ronald Braeutigam responded to Professor Pierce:

> Our position can be described more fully as follows: Given the serious deficiencies of profit level regulation and the potential efficiency benefits of price level regulation, especially in the case of diversified public utilities serving both natural monopolies and

other markets with varying price elasticities, we should continue efforts to minimize certain impediments to the success of price level regulation in the natural monopolly markets.

Pierce initially seems to agree with us about the serious deficiencies of profit level regulation and the substantial potential benefits of price level regulation. In the end, however, his views and ours on the potential comparative efficacy of the two systems diverge in two major respects: (1) we attach greater weight to the identified deficiencies of profit level regulation, and (2) we are more hopeful that credible economic standards and decisional processes important to the success of a price level regime can be established. . . .

We do not differ from Pierce in finding substantial impediments to the success of price level regulation. In the case of our shared concerns, however, we sense a greater possibility of workable solutions. Other of his concerns to us seem inapposite. In particular, we find little predictive value in the notable failures he cites in the regulation or taxation of energy commodities by rigid price formula. As Pierce notes, these prices were subject to unusual volatility. These energy commodities involve competitive markets in which the price of any single commodity is greatly affected by changes in alternative fuel prices. In the case of natural gas, the question is whether any regulation was warranted in 1978, when Congress imposed a rigid, wholly formulaic price adjustment mechanism on a commodity whose market price was driven by the price of oil. We find no analogy in this experience to the more flexible price adjustment mechanisms proposed for the retail markets of regulated public utilities with relatively stable demand. . . .

Jordan Jay Hillman & Ronald Braeutigam, The Potential Benefits and Problems of Price Level Regulation: A More Hopeful Perspective, 84 N.W. U. L. Rev. 695 (1990). But, if competition is presented as an alternative to cost-of-service regulation, do Hillman and Braeutigam's proposals still have relevance for regulators?

3.   Other non-cost methods of pricing include what is known as "incentive regulation." Regulators may achieve some of their goals by building incentives into the components of the ratemaking process without basing these entirely on cost. For example, to reward a utility encouraging conservation and efficiency, some regulators have given utilities rewards in the calculation of cost-of-capital.

2. MARKET-BASED RATES

Especially as competition has been introduced into various energy industries (discussed further in Chapter 10), FERC and many states have experimented with market-based rates. These rates are not based on cost-of-service, but are negotiated by supplier firms and purchasers. Section 205 of the Federal Power Act (FPA), 16 U.S.C. § 824d, states:

(a) Just and reasonable rates

All rates and charges made, demanded, or received by any public utility for or in connection with the transmission or sale of electric energy subject to the jurisdiction of the Commission, and all rules and regulations affecting or pertaining to such rates or charges shall be just and reasonable, and any such rate or charge that is not just and reasonable is hereby declared to be unlawful.

(b) Preference or advantage unlawful

No public utility shall, with respect to any transmission or sale subject to the jurisdiction of the Commission, (1) make or grant any undue preference or advantage to any person or subject any person to any undue prejudice or disadvantage, or (2) maintain any unreasonable difference in rates, charges, service, facilities, or in any other respect, either as between localities or as between classes of service.

Notwithstanding this language, courts have allowed FERC to set market-based rates so long as FERC engages in sufficient oversight to ensure that rates do not run afoul of Section 206 of the FPA; that is, they are not unjust, discriminatory, or otherwise preferential. *See* Lockyer v. FERC, 383 F.3d 1006 (9th Cir. 2004).

For example, electric power marketers can qualify for market-based rates for their sales in interstate power markets if they demonstrate a lack of market power in generation or transmission and file quarterly reports with FERC that disclose ownership and affiliation with other facilities. FERC's guidelines on how to receive market-based rate authority are available online at FERC, Electric Market-Based Rates: How do I get authorization?, http://www.ferc.gov/industries/electric/gen-info/mbr/authorization/app.asp.

Market power is the ability of a firm to set prices above competitive rates. FERC has reduced this process to reliance on a market screening test. In a 2007 rule FERC adopted two screens to indicate which applicants for market-based in wholesale energy sales would require more detailed scrutiny of market power.

The first screen, the pivotal-supplier screen, looks at whether a supplier is pivotal to the market. Will supplies (including imports) from other entities be sufficient to meet wholesale demand in the market? The second screen, the market-share screen, calculates an applicant's share of uncommitted generation capacity in the wholesale market. If the applicant's share exceeds 20 percent, the applicant fails the screen. As has been pointed out, the market-share screen can be a challenge for traditional vertically-integrated utilities that own and control transmission. *See* John R. Morris, FERC's Market Test: The Good, The Bad and the Ugly, Pub. Util. Fortnightly, July 2005, at 37.

Failing one or both of the screens creates a rebuttable presumption of market power. The commission then initiates a Section 206 hearing, where applicants can provide evidence that they do not possess market power. For those who cannot, they then either can accept the commission's default cost-based rates, or they can propose a mitigation plan that would address the commission's market-power concerns.

Once market-based rates are approved, FERC's monitoring of market power in wholesale energy markets occurs through the disclosure of information in quarterly reports. In addition, every three years firms qualifying for market-based rates are required to file a market analysis. If FERC finds that a firm charging market-based rates has exercised market power, FERC has the authority to require the refunding of prices charged above the competitively set prices.

In 2002, FERC recognized that the traditional rate hearing would no longer be the primary mechanism for evaluating the firms it regulates, especially in wholesale energy markets. (What about transmission? See Chapter 11.) Today, FERC's Office of Market Oversight and Investigations assesses market performance, assures conformance with Commission rules and reports its findings to the Commission and the public. The office is made up of economists, engineers, attorneys, auditors, data management specialists, financial analysts, and regulatory and energy policy analysts. The Office analyzes overall energy markets to identify and remedy energy market problems, discourage improper behavior and maintain just and reasonable rates. A more complete discussion of the challenge presented by market-based rates in wholesale interstate energy markets, including some of the federalism issues it presents, appears in Chapter 10.

D. JURISDICTIONAL ISSUES

Normally, regulators are asked to balance a variety of different interests in utility ratemaking. The evidence presented at a hearing is a complex combination of accounting and finance data. Not surprisingly, many lawyers find this intimidating and even uncomfortable territory—though familiarity with the cost-of-service formula and the common issues it presents can help. Sometimes lawyers are successful in raising statutory or constitutional objections to a rate determination, but often in ratemaking proceedings lawyers focus on the fairness of procedures and the weight and credibility of the evidence supporting a particular position behind a rate determination in a hearing context. For example, some energy lawyers have made major contributions to utility rate cases by working to support or oppose expert witnesses in the hearing process.

However (and fortunately for many of us!), utility ratemaking raises another cluster of legal issues where lawyers feel much more at home. In determining rates an agency may be asked to make decisions that overlap with another agency's programs or initiatives, with other statutes, or with judicial proceedings. To name a few of these jurisdictional issues: To what extent can regulators approving rates consider environmental concerns in determining what is "just and reasonable" and how far can they go with this? How is authority divided between the federal government and states? What is the connection between antitrust disputes, which are typically litigated in federal courts, and rate regulation? The following sections address these important questions.

1. ENVIRONMENTAL CONSIDERATIONS

Although public utility regulation arose from a different era and set of concerns than modern environmental statutes affecting electric power, environmental and economic regulation of public utilities often overlap significantly. Not only do they overlap, but different regulators may be charged with implementing environmental and economic goals. What is the effect of this overlap on regulatory objectives? On the industry? On consumers? On the environment?

In *Grand Council of the Crees (of Quebec) v. Federal Energy Regulatory Commission*, 198 F.3d 950 (D.C. Cir. 2000), a panel for the U.S. Court of Appeals for the D.C. Circuit addressed the issue under federal economic regulation. As noted above, the FPA charges FERC to set rates for electric utilities within its jurisdiction at a "just and reasonable" level. *See* 16 U.S.C. § 824d(a). Groups appealing FERC's rate decisions based their standing on allegations that the agency's decision, by impacting the uses of electricity, will "devastate the lives, environment, culture and economy of the Crees" and "will destroy fish and wildlife upon which Cree fisherman, trappers and hunters depend." 198 F.3d at 954. The D.C. Circuit, however, denied administrative standing to these groups, holding that the environmental concerns they raised are outside of the zone of interests of FERC's statutory mandate to set "just and reasonable" rates. The panel reasoned that "the fixing of 'just and reasonable' rates[ ] involves a balancing of the investor and consumer interests," but that "[b]oth interests are economic and tied directly to the transaction regulated." *Id.* at 956. The D.C. Circuit also noted that "[t]he Supreme Court has never indicated that the discretion of an agency setting 'just and reasonable' rates for sale of a simple, fungible product or service should, or even could, encompass considerations of environmental impact (except, of course, as the need to meet environmental requirements may affect the firm's costs)." *Id.* at 957. The court also gave weight to the fact that FERC had affirmatively forsworn environmental considerations in adjudicating rates.

Should the fact that other agencies have jurisdiction over environmental considerations necessarily limit FERC's authority to take environmental goals into account in making its policy decisions? Is FERC limited to considering environmental goals only where it is authorized to do so? Peter Huber argues that the multiple agencies regulating the utility industry result in "only a cycle of ecstasy and agony." According to him, "Utilities may be pleased with regulatory inertia when the issue is emissions from older, coal-fired power plants, but they are dismayed when regulatory paralysis smothers a half-built nuclear power station." Environmentalists fare no better: "Those who favor more electricity production are pleased that it is enormously difficult to shut down older power plants, regardless of how unsafe or dirty those plants may be." Huber concludes: "There is something in the system for everyone, but always something negative. Where can any of the contending parties turn for affirmative regulatory leadership?" *See* Peter Huber, Electricity and the Environment: In Search of Regulatory Authority, 100 Harv. L. Rev. 1002, 1054 (1987). Is there a better way to regulate a utility industry? Do other activities that are subject to regulation, such as immigration, food and product safety, suffer the same problem?

One side of the coin is to consider an expansion of how FERC or state regulators approach their ratemaking function. For example, it has been argued that FERC may have more expansive jurisdiction to consider the carbon costs associated with generating electricity in setting "just and reasonable" rates. In other words, "costs" used in setting cost-of-service rates could conceivably include social costs as well as costs incurred in purchasing good and services that are already reflected in market prices. Consider this argument:

> The time has come to rethink FERC's policy of excluding environmental considerations from its wide-ranging regulation of the electricity industry under sections 205 and 206 of the FPA (what we have referred to as FERC's "rate regulation" for convenience's sake). FERC's rationales for its current policy are unconvincing. Its narrow view of its authority to consider environmental consequences is arguably too restrictive. Its policy is also increasingly at odds with its own embrace and pursuit, however tacit, of environmental goals. Finally and most fundamentally, it is difficult to justify FERC's neglect of environmental considerations as good policy today. Although it may once have seemed defensible to divide energy or economic regulation (i.e., by FERC) from environmental regulation (i.e., by EPA) of the electricity industry and pit them against each other to some degree, such an approach seems deeply wrong in an era in which we increasingly view sustainability and economic growth as interrelated and inseparable, and when we face an environmental threat of unprecedented proportions in climate change. In the absence of adequate congressional action to correct this problem, FERC would do well to explore the possibility that its "just and reasonable" mandate must evolve to encompass these defining issues of our time.

Christopher J. Bateman & James T.B. Tripp, Toward Greener FERC Regulation of the Power Industry, 38 Harv. Envtl. L. Rev. 276, 333 (2014). Similar views have been advanced by others. *See* Jeremy Knee, Rational Electricity Regulation: Environmental Impacts and the "Public Interest," 113 W. Va. L. Rev. 739 (2011); Steven Weissman & Romany Webb, Addressing Climate Change Without Legislation: How the Federal Energy Regulatory Commission Can Use Its Existing Legal Authority to Reduce Greenhouse Gas Emissions and Increase Clean Energy Use (University of California-Berkeley Center for Law, Energy and the Environment Report July 2014), https://www.law.berkeley.edu/files/CLEE/FERC_Report_FINAL.pdf.

To date, FERC has not adopted such a broad "cost-internalization" approach in setting rates for electric power generation. Most states that take environmental concerns into account in setting rates do it by either passing through the rates associated with environmental compliance or through environmental adders with explicit legislative authorization. If FERC or states were to engage in carbon pricing of electricity in determining just and reasonable rates are you convinced that they would have the statutory jurisdiction to do so? The pricing of carbon costs associated with various power generation activities is of course complex, and would require FERC to make such tough policy decisions. If FERC were to consider such costs, would it limit cost impacts of carbon to the United States, or would considering global cost impacts be more appropriate? Should such cost calculations include life-cycle carbon impacts of various fuel sources, and how would costs impacts for future generations be weighed? As is discussed in Chapter 11, FERC has moved to considering broader social costs and environmental goals in transmission cost allocation, though its approach falls considerably short of considering full social costs.

Going beyond rate regulation, Professor William Boyd has recently drawn on the progressive history of the public utility to argue that state regulatory commissions could reassess the basic understanding of public utilities to move beyond protecting traditional investor owned utilities to encourage greater innovation and investments in renewable energy, and to promote planning the utility system to reduce carbon emissions. William Boyd, Public Utility and the Low-Carbon Future, 61 UCLA L. Rev. 1614 (2014). For Professor Boyd, much of the solution lies in how we approach planning and coordination in the industry, as well as ensuring that public utility encourage, rather than discourage, innovation. See also Chapter 11 for a discussion of how jurisdictional aspects of "public utility" regulation are being treated by state regulators and courts in addressing new innovations in renewable energy provision. Considering environmental costs associated with power generation is common in the utility planning process, and many states have increasingly used this process to take into account carbon costs.

Another side of the coin is to not consider expanding the determination of "cost" in ratemaking, but to better recognize how ratemaking agencies interact with environmental regulations. For example, if environmental regulators mandate pollution controls for power plants, should utility regulators be required to allow for recovery of these costs in rates? When environmental regulators are imposing new pollution controls, such as EPA's initiative to regulate the carbon emissions from existing coal plants, what is the obligation of agencies to consult with each other? See Chapter 5.

Consider the ratemaking problem presented above. Is it relevant for the PSC to take into account environmental concerns, including conservation, in assessing EE's rate request? Do environmental groups have prudential standing to participate and how, if at all, may this differ from the *Grand Council of the Crees* case? Absent a statute authorizing it to consider values such as conservation, would the agency have the authority to do this in determining "just and reasonable rates"? What are the arguments and their implications for cost-of-service utility ratemaking?

2. WHOLESALE V. RETAIL RATES

In addition to questions of federal and state environmental law and the extent to which they may be considered in ratemaking and other utility-related cases, one of the most important issues that arises in utility rate cases relates to federalism. The cases that follow illustrate some of the issues that pervade the borderline between federal and state regulation of the electric industry—a topic oft-disputed topic.

The relationship of investor-owned utilities with federal agencies, municipals and rural electrical co-ops has had its ups and downs. *FPC v. Southern California Edison*, presented below, introduces the relationship of the various segments of the industry in addressing basic jurisdictional issues related to the FPA. Southern California Edison is a major investor-owned electric utility that generates, transmits, and distributes electricity. The federal government generates power from its hydroelectric facilities, some of which is sold to Edison. The City of Colton is a small municipality-owned facility; like many municipal utilities, it distributes, but does not generate, electricity. This case involves Colton's attempt to obtain federal regulation of the price it had to pay to buy power from Edison. The case involves the interpretation of section 201 of the FPA, 16 U.S.C. § 824. Subsection (a) declares that the business of transmitting and selling electric energy for ultimate distribution to the public is affected with a public interest, and that federal regulation of matters relating to certain generation, the transmission of electric energy in interstate commerce, and the sale of such energy at wholesale in interstate commerce is necessary in the public interest. Such federal regulation, however, extends only to those matters that are not subject to regulation by the states. Subsection (b)(1) of section 201 provides that:

> The provisions of this Part shall apply to the transmission of electric energy in interstate commerce and to the sale of electric energy at wholesale in interstate commerce, but except as provided in paragraph (2) shall not apply to any other sale of electric energy or deprive a State or State commission of its lawful authority now exercised over the exportation of hydroelectric energy which is transmitted across a State line. The Commission shall have jurisdiction over all facilities for such transmission or sale of electric energy, but shall not have jurisdiction, except as specifically provided in [cited sections], over facilities used for the generation of electric energy or over facilities used in local distribution or only for the transmission of electric energy in intrastate commerce, or over facilities for the transmission of electric energy consumed wholly by the transmitter. . . .

> (d) The term "sale of electric energy at wholesale" when used in this subchapter, means a sale of electric energy to any person for resale. . . .

Federal Power Comm'n v. Southern California Edison Co.

376 U.S. 205 (1964).

■ BRENNAN, J.—Petitioner City of Colton, California (Colton), purchases its entire requirements of electric power from respondent Southern California Edison Company (Edison), a California electric utility company which operates in central and southern California and sells energy only to customers located there. Colton applies some of the power purchased to municipal uses, but resells the bulk of it to thousands of residential, commercial, and industrial customers in Colton and its environs. Respondent Public Utilities Commission of California (PUC) had for some years exercised jurisdiction over the Edison-Colton sale, but petitioner Federal Power Commission (FPC), on Colton's petition filed in 1958, asserted jurisdiction under § 201(b) of the Federal Power Act which extends federal regulatory power to the "sale of electric energy at wholesale in interstate commerce." 16 U.S.C. §§ 791a, 824–824h.

Some of the energy which Edison markets in California originates in Nevada and Arizona. Edison has a contract with the Secretary of the Interior under which, as agent for the United States, it generates energy at the Hoover power plants located in Nevada. This contract allocates to Edison 7% of the total firm generating capacity of Hoover Dam. Edison is also a party to a 1945 contract with the United States and the Metropolitan Water District of Southern California under which it is entitled to a portion of the unused firm energy allocated to the Water District from Hoover Dam. Payment for this energy is made to the United States for the credit of the Water District. Also, Hoover Dam, Davis Dam in Arizona, and Parker Dam in California are interconnected by a transmission line from which Edison has drawn energy by agreement with the Water District.

The FPC found, on the extensive record made before a Hearing Examiner, that out-of-state energy from Hoover Dam was included in the energy delivered by Edison to Colton, and ruled that the "sale to Colton is a sale of electric energy at wholesale in interstate commerce subject to Sections 201, 205 and 206 of the Federal Power Act." 26 F.P.C. 223, 231.

The Court of Appeals did not pass upon the question whether the finding that out-of-state energy reached Colton has support in the record. The court assumed that the finding had such support, but held nevertheless that § 201 (b) did not grant jurisdiction over the rates to the FPC. It ruled that the concluding words of § 201 (a)—"such Federal regulation, however, [is] to extend only to those matters which are not subject to regulation by the States"—confined FPC jurisdiction to those interstate wholesales constitutionally beyond the power of state regulation by force of the Commerce Clause, Art. I, § 8, of the Constitution. Accordingly, it held that the FPC had no jurisdiction because PUC regulation of the Edison-Colton sale was permissible under the Commerce Clause. Because of the importance of the question in the administration of the Federal Power Act we granted the separate petitions for certiorari of the FPC and Colton. 372 U.S. 958. We reverse. We hold that § 201 (b) grants the FPC jurisdiction of all sales of electric energy at wholesale in interstate commerce not expressly exempted by the Act itself, and that the FPC properly asserted jurisdiction of the Edison-Colton sale.

The view of the Court of Appeals was that the limiting language of § 201(a), read together with the jurisdictional grant in § 201(b), meant that the FPC could not assert its jurisdiction over a sale which the Commerce Clause allowed a State to regulate. Such a determination of the permissibility of state regulation would require, the Court of Appeals said, an analysis of the impact of state regulation of the sale upon the national interest in commerce. The court held that such an analysis here compelled the conclusion that the FPC lacked jurisdiction, because state regulation of the Edison-Colton sale would not prejudice the interests of any other State. This conclusion was rested upon the view that the interests of Arizona and Nevada, the only States other than California which might claim to be concerned with the Edison-Colton sale, were already given federal protection by the Secretary of the Interior's control of the initial sales of Hoover and Davis energy. Since the first sale was subject to federal regulation, and since the energy subsequently sold by Edison to Colton for resale was to be consumed wholly within California, there was said to be a "complete lack of interest on the part of any other state," and the sale was therefore held to be subject to state regulation and exempt from FPC regulation. 310 F.2d, at 789.

The Court of Appeals expressly rejected the argument that § 201(b) incorporated a congressional decision against determining the FPC's jurisdiction by such a case-by-case analysis, and in favor of employing a more mechanical test which would bring under federal regulation all sales of electric energy in interstate commerce at wholesale except those specifically exempted, and would exclude all retail sales. In reviewing the court's ruling on this question we do not write on a clean slate. In decisions over the past quarter century we have held that Congress, in enacting the Federal Power Act and the Natural Gas Act, apportioned regulatory power between state and federal governments according to a test which this Court had developed in a series of cases under the Commerce Clause. The Natural Gas Act grew out of the same judicial history as did the part of the Federal Power Act with which we are here concerned; and § 201(b) of the Power Act has its counterpart in § 1(b) of the Gas Act, 15 U.S.C. § 717(b), which became law three years later in 1938.

The test adopted by Congress was developed in a line of decisions, [the last of which] and the one which directly led to congressional intervention, was *Public Utilities Comm'n v. Attleboro Steam & Elec. Co.,* 273 U.S. 83. There the Public Utilities Commission of Rhode Island asserted jurisdiction over the rates at which a Rhode Island company sold energy generated at its Rhode Island plant to a Massachusetts company, which took delivery at the state line for resale to the City of Attleboro. The Court held that the case did not involve "a regulation of the rates charged to local consumers," and that since the sale was of concern to both Rhode Island and Massachusetts it was "national in character." Consequently, "if such regulation is required it can only be attained by the exercise of the power vested in Congress." 273 U.S., at 89–90.

Congress undertook federal regulation through the Federal Power Act in 1935 and the Natural Gas Act in 1938. The premise was that constitutional limitations upon state regulatory power made federal regulation essential if major aspects of interstate transmission and sale were not to go unregulated. *Attleboro*, with the other cases cited, figured prominently in the debates and congressional reports. In *Illinois Natural Gas Co. v. Central Illinois Public Service Co.,* 314 U.S. 498, we were first required to determine the scope of the federal power which Congress had asserted to meet the problem revealed by Attleboro and the other cases. The specific question in that case was whether a company selling interstate gas at wholesale to distributors for resale in a single State could be required by that State's regulatory commission to extend its facilities and connect them with those of a local distributor, or whether such extensions were exclusively a matter for the FPC. The Court noted that prior to the Natural Gas Act there had been another line of cases which adopted a more flexible approach to state power under the Commerce Clause; these cases had been "less concerned to find a point in time and space where the interstate commerce in gas ends and intrastate commerce begins, and [have] looked to the nature of the state regulation involved, the objective of the state, and the effect of the regulation upon the national interest in the commerce." 314 U.S., at 505. But the Court held that Congress, rather than adopting this flexible approach, which was applied by the Court of Appeals in the instant case, "undertook to regulate . . . without the necessity, where Congress has not acted, of drawing the precise line between state and federal power by the litigation of particular cases." *Id.*, at 506–507. What Congress did was to adopt the test developed in the Attleboro line which denied state power to regulate a sale "at wholesale to local distributing companies" and allowed state regulation of a sale at "local retail rates to ultimate consumers." 314 U.S., at 504.

In short, our decisions have squarely rejected the view of the Court of Appeals that the scope of FPC jurisdiction over interstate sales of gas or electricity at wholesale is to be determined by a case-by-case analysis of the impact of state regulation upon the national interest. Rather, Congress meant to draw a bright line easily ascertained, between state and federal jurisdiction, making unnecessary such case-by-case analysis. This was done in the Power Act by making FPC jurisdiction plenary and extending it to all wholesale sales in interstate commerce except those which Congress has made explicitly subject to regulation by the States. There is no such exception covering the Edison-Colton sale. . . . [The Court also rejected the argument that Congress had exempted sales of Hoover Dam Power from FPC jurisdiction.] ∎

NOTES AND COMMENTS

1.   The words "wholesale" and "retail" are important terms of art in energy law. The rule in the *Colton* case still remains in effect under the FPA. A wholesale transaction is one between two entities who are not the ultimate users of the electricity. A retail sale is a sale directly to an end user. Wholesale sales are regulated by FERC (the successor to the FPC, see Chapter 2), while retail sales are regulated by the state in which the transfer occurs. This important jurisdictional distinction is discussed throughout the book—for example, *New York v. FERC* (see Chapter 10) involves a clash between states and FERC over FERC jurisdiction to promote open access on the transmission grid, and *Electric Power Supply Association v. FERC* (see Chapter 13) involves whether FERC had jurisdiction to make a rule governing "demand response" (techniques to reduce electricity consumption during periods of high demand).

2.   The other qualifier that limits federal jurisdiction is that the sale must be in interstate commerce. What if a generator exists purely within a particular state, but it connects its power to transmission lines that cross state borders? When power is generated by a source that does not also own transmission lines, or by a source that owns transmission lines but these lines do not reach the geographic area in which customers are located, it is necessary for a utility to interconnect its lines with the source. In addition, it is common for adjacent utilities that own transmission lines to interconnect in order to coordinate power generation and distribution.

In *FPC v. Florida Power & Light Co.*, 404 U.S. 453 (1972), the Supreme Court allowed FPC to exercise jurisdiction over power sold by Florida Power & Light (FP&L), the major investor-owned utility serving South Florida. All of FP&L's generation and transmission facilities were located within the state of Florida and none of its facilities connected directly with out-of-state utilities, customers, or power sources. Nevertheless, FPC contended that FP&L-generated electrons[4] reached the interstate market in Georgia

---

[4]   The term "electrons," as commonly used in energy law, is meant to denote electricity traceable to a particular source of generation. As a matter of physics, however, electrons do not travel through wires so much as transmit electromagnetic force, or voltage.

because FP&L's transmission lines were connected with those of another Florida utility, Florida Power Corporation (Corp), which in turn connected with Georgia Power Company.

The Court addressed what would determine FPC jurisdiction over the interstate transmission of electricity:

> . . . The FPC may exercise jurisdiction only if there is substantial evidentiary support for the Commission's conclusion that FP&L power has reached Georgia via Corp or that Georgia's power has reached FP&L because of exchanges with Corp. What happens when FP&L gives power to Corp and Corp gives power to Georgia (or vice versa)? Is FP&L power commingled with Corp's own supply, and thus passed on with that supply, as the Commission contends? Or is it diverted to handle Corp's independent power needs, displacing a like amount of Corp power that is then passed on, as respondent argues? Or, as the Commission also contends, do changes in FP&L's load or generation, or that of others in the interconnected system, stimulate a reaction up and down the line by a signal or chain reaction that is, in essence electricity moving in interstate commerce?

Federal jurisdiction clearly would have been present if FP&L directly exchanged power with Georgia. Jurisdiction would also have been present, the Court held, if Corp, the intermediate utility, "could be shown to be sometimes no more than a funnel." Even though neither of these circumstances was true in this case, the Court held that FP&L's power was commingled with Corp power and exported across the Georgia line. As the Court observed, "the elusive nature of electrons renders experimental evidence that might draw the fine distinctions in this case practically unobtainable." The Court upheld FPC's assertion of jurisdiction.

3.   Utilities in the State of Texas are exempt from much federal regulation of energy sales and transmission under the FPA because they do not ship power across state lines. Many of their activities, however, are regulated by the Electric Reliability Council of Texas (ERCOT). In 1996 the Texas PUC established ERCOT as an Independent System Operator (ISO) that is separate from, and largely independent of, the utilities that own the transmission network. The reconstituted ERCOT board established policies for operating the transmission network on a nondiscriminatory basis for all power producers and users. See Chapter 10.

The following case, *FPC v. Conway Corp.*, examines the scope of federal ratemaking authority and introduces the tensions between investor-owned utilities (IOUs) and smaller municipal and co-op systems that do not generate power. Although these municipals and co-ops tend to be small in relation to the typical IOU, they have always exerted considerable influence on energy policy in Congress and the executive branch through the American Public Power Association. *See* Am. Pub. Power Ass'n, www.appanet.org.

Federal Power Comm'n v. Conway Corp.

426 U.S. 271 (1976).

■ WHITE, J.—The question in this case is this: When a power company that sells electricity at both wholesale and retail seeks to raise its wholesale rates, does the Federal Power Commission (Commission) have jurisdiction to consider the allegations of the company's wholesale customers that the proposed wholesale rates, which are within the Commission's jurisdiction, are discriminatory and noncompetitive when considered in relation to the company's retail rates, which are not within the jurisdiction of the Commission? We hold that it does.

Arkansas Power & Light Co. (Company) is a public utility engaged in the sale of electric energy at wholesale in interstate commerce under the meaning of § 201 of the Federal Power Act, 16 U.S.C. § 824. Its wholesale rates are thus within reach of the Commission's powers under § 206(a) of the Act to establish rates which are just, reasonable, and nondiscriminatory. 16 U.S.C. § 824e(a). The Company also sells at retail and seeks industrial sales in competition with some of its wholesale customers. These wholesale customers include the seven municipally owned electric systems and the two electric power cooperatives which are respondents here. Each of these respondents (Customers) operates in the State of Arkansas and each borders on or is surrounded by the territory served by the Company.

In June 1973, the Company filed with the Commission a wholesale rate increase pursuant to § 205(d). The Customers sought to intervene before the Commission, urging that the rate increase be rejected. Among other grounds, it was asserted that the Customers and the Company were in competition for industrial retail accounts and that the rate increase was "an attempt to squeeze [the Customers] or some of them out of competition and to make them more susceptible to the persistent attempts of the company to take over the public[ly] owned systems in the State." It was alleged that the proposed wholesale rates would make it "impossible for the [Customers] to sell power to an industrial load of any size at a competitive price with [the Company], since, in many cases, the revenues therefrom would not even cover the incremental power costs to [the Customers]." It was also asserted that the rate filing was "plainly discriminatory against the single class of customer which [the Company] has historically attempted to drive out of business, without justification on any ordinary cost of service basis. . . ."

The Company opposed the petition. The Commission permitted the Customers to intervene but ruled that it would "limit Customers' participation in this proceeding to matters other than the alleged anticompetitive activities" because the Customers had failed to demonstrate that the relief sought was "within this Commission's authority to direct." The Commission also denied the Customers' amended petition to intervene, again refusing to consider the tendered anticompetitive and discrimination issues. Inasmuch as the Commission's authority is limited to wholesale rates and does not reach sales at retail, the Commission's opinion was that "the relief sought by [the Customers] is beyond the authority granted to us under the Federal Power Act."

Section 201(b) of the Act, 16 U.S.C. § 824(b), confers jurisdiction on the Commission with respect to the sale of electric energy at wholesale in interstate commerce. The prohibition against discriminatory or preferential rates or services imposed by § 205(b) and the Commission's power to set just and reasonable rates under § 206(a) are accordingly limited to sales "subject to the jurisdiction of the Commission," that is, to sales of electric energy at wholesale. The Commission has no power to prescribe the rates for retail sales of power companies. Nor, accordingly, would it have power to remedy an alleged discriminatory or anticompetitive relationship between wholesale and retail rates by ordering the company to increase its retail rates.

As the Commission is at great pains to establish, this is the proper construction of the Act, the legislative history of § 205 indicating that the section was expressly limited to jurisdictional sales to foreclose the possibility that the Commission would seek to correct an alleged discriminatory relationship between wholesale and retail rates by raising or otherwise regulating the nonjurisdictional, retail price. Insofar as we are advised, no party to this case contends otherwise.

Building on this history, the Commission makes a skillful argument that it may neither consider nor remedy any alleged discrimination resting on a difference between jurisdictional and nonjurisdictional rates. But the argument, in the end, is untenable. Section 205(b) forbids the maintenance of any "unreasonable difference in rates" or service "with respect to any . . . sale subject to the jurisdiction of the Commission." A jurisdictional sale is necessarily implicated in any charge that the difference between wholesale and retail rates is unreasonable or anticompetitive. If the undue preference or discrimination is in any way traceable to the level of the jurisdictional rate, it is plain enough that the section would to that extent apply; and to that extent the Commission would have power to effect a remedy under § 206 by an appropriate order directed to the jurisdictional rate. This was the view of the Court of Appeals, and we agree with it.

The Commission appears to insist that a just and reasonable wholesale rate can never be a contributing factor to an undue discrimination: Once the jurisdictional rate is determined to be just and reasonable, inquiry into discrimination is irrelevant for § 206(a) purposes, for if the discrimination continues to exist, it is traceable wholly to the nonjurisdictional, retail rate. This argument assumes, however, that ratemaking is an exact science and that there is only one level at which a wholesale rate can be said to be just and reasonable and that any attempt to remedy a discrimination by lowering the jurisdictional rate would always result in an unjustly low rate that would fail to recover fully allocated wholesale costs. As the Court of Appeals pointed out and as this Court has held, however, there is no single cost-recovering rate, but a zone of reasonableness: "Statutory reasonableness is an abstract quality represented by an area rather than a pinpoint. It allows a substantial spread between what is unreasonable because too low and what is unreasonable because too high." *Montana-Dakota Util. Co. v. Northwestern Pub. Serv. Co.*, 341 U.S. 246, 251 (1951). The Commission itself explained the matter in *In re Otter Tail Power Co.*, 2 F.P.C. 134, 149 (1940):

> It occurs to us that one rate in its relation to another rate may be discriminatory, although each rate per se, if considered independently, might fall within the zone of reasonableness.

> There is considerable latitude within the zone of reasonableness insofar as the level of a particular rate is concerned. The relationship of rates within such a zone, however, may result in an undue advantage in favor of one rate and be discriminatory insofar as another rate is concerned. When such a situation exists, the discrimination found to exist must be removed.

The Commission thus cannot so easily satisfy its obligation to eliminate unreasonable discriminations or put aside its duty to consider whether a proposed rate will have anticompetitive effects. The exercise by the Commission of powers otherwise within its jurisdiction "clearly carries with it the responsibility to consider, in appropriate circumstances, the anticompetitive effects of regulated aspects of interstate utility operations pursuant to . . . directives contained in §§ 205, 206. . . ." *Gulf States Util. Co. v. FPC*, 411 U.S. 747, 758–759 (1973). The Commission must arrive at a rate level deemed by it to be just and reasonable, but in doing so it must consider the tendered allegations that the proposed rates are discriminatory and anticompetitive in effect.

We think the Court of Appeals was quite correct in concluding:

> When costs are fully allocated, both the retail rate and the proposed wholesale rate may fall within a zone of reasonableness, yet create a price squeeze between themselves. There would, at the very least, be latitude in the FPC to put wholesale rates in the lower range of the zone of reasonableness, without concern that overall results would be impaired, in view of the utility's own decision to depress certain retail revenues in order to curb the retail competition of its wholesale customers.

510 F. 2d, at 1274. Because the Commission had raised a jurisdictional barrier and refused to consider or hear evidence concerning the Customers' allegations, the Court of Appeals could not determine whether a wholesale rate, if set low enough partially or wholly to abolish any discriminatory effects found to exist, would fail to recover wholesale costs. The case was therefore remanded to the Commission for further proceedings.

We agree with this disposition. It does not invade a nonjurisdictional area. The remedy, if any, would operate only against the rate for jurisdictional sales. Whether that rate would be affected at all would involve, as the Court of Appeals indicated, an examination of the entire "factual context in which the proposed wholesale rate will function." *Id.*, at 52, 510 F. 2d, at 1273. These facts will naturally include those related to nonjurisdictional transactions, but consideration of such facts would appear to be an everyday affair. As the Commission concedes, in determining whether the proposed wholesale rates are just and reasonable, it would in any event be necessary to determine which of the Company's costs are allocable to its nonjurisdictional, retail sales and which to its jurisdictional, wholesale sales—this in order to insure that the wholesale rate is paying its way, but no more. . . .

Furthermore, § 206(a) provides that whenever the Commission finds that any rate, charge, or classification, demanded, observed, charged, or collected by any public utility for any transmission or sale subject to the jurisdiction of the Commission, or that any rule, regulation, practice, or contract affecting such rate, charge, or classification is unjust, unreasonable, unduly discriminatory or preferential, the Commission shall determine the just and reasonable rate, charge, classification, rule, regulation, practice, or contract to be thereafter observed and in force, and shall fix the same by order.

The rules, practices, or contracts "affecting" the jurisdictional rate are not themselves limited to the jurisdictional context. In the *Panhandle* case, supra, decided under the almost identical provision of the Natural Gas Act, 15 U.S.C. § 717d(a), the Court emphasized the same aspect of the section, and went on to hold that because it was "clear" that a gas company's "contracts covering direct industrial sales" are contracts "affecting" jurisdictional rates, [t]he Commission, while it lacks authority to fix rates for direct industrial sales, may take those rates into consideration when it fixes the rates for interstate wholesale sales which are subject to its jurisdiction. 324 U.S., at 646. ■

NOTES AND COMMENTS

1.   When one utility tries to pick off the best customers of another utility it is commonly referred to in the trade as "cherry-picking." The *Conway* case made it quite difficult for IOUs to pick off the best customers of the municipals by offering lower rates because IOUs might be forced to offer the same rates to the municipal itself.

2.   Municipal utilities sometimes get into conflicts with rural cooperatives as well as with investor-owned utilities. For example, if a city served by a municipal utility expands into an area formerly served by a rural cooperative, state statutes may authorize the municipal utility to use eminent domain power to acquire the existing facilities of the co-op that are located in the expansion area. This can give rise to difficult issues of valuation of the acquired facilities and the measurement of the damages incurred by the co-op. *See, e.g.,* City of Stilwell v. Ozarks Rural Elec. Coop. Corp., 166 F.3d 1064 (10th Cir. 1999).

3.   Does the expansion of jurisdiction to practices "affecting" FERC jurisdictional rates suggest that, in effect, there is no limiting principle on FERC's exercise of jurisdiction over rates? For example, does this authorize FERC to regulate aspects of retail energy markets? And if this is a "brightline" test, does FERC completely preempt the state's ability to regulated in areas where there is an affect on wholesale rates? This issue is addressed in chapter 9 (discussing the *Oneok* case) and continues to be litigated in electricity markets. See Chapters 10 (discussing state incentives for new generators) and 13 (discussing demand response).

3. REGULATION V. CONTRACT: THE FILED RATE DOCTRINE

Wholesale electricity rates are determined in two different ways: (1) by contracts between utilities, or between utilities and customers, such as industrial customers; or (2) by the regulatory provisions of the FPA, which now typically allow utilities to charge market rates (whatever the market will bear) for wholesale transactions. Traditionally, energy companies have relied just as heavily on long-term contracts called power purchase agreements, or PPAs, as they have on rates set following a hearing. Financial institutions often insist on such contracts as a condition for financing major capital facilities. Chapter 11 contains an example of the factors considered in writing a PPA.

The U.S. Supreme Court has held that wholesale rates arrived at by contract are presumed to reflect fair bargaining. Therefore, under the Court's so-called "*Mobile-Sierra* doctrine," FERC cannot change a rate set by contract unless it first finds that the contract rate is "unjust, unreasonable, unduly discriminatory or preferential." *See* United Gas Pipeline v. Mobile Gas Serv. Corp., 350 U.S. 332 (1956); FPC v. Sierra Pac. Power Co., 350 U.S. 348 (1956). The *Mobile-Sierra* doctrine applies to both the gas and electric sides of FERC's operations.[5]

Today, electric utilities are less likely to prefer long-term contracts than they were in earlier times. The volatility of energy prices that began in the mid-1970s meant that many electric utilities, like the natural gas utilities, found themselves stuck with long-term contracts that had been entered into under much different market conditions. The *Mobile-Sierra* doctrine made it difficult to modify or terminate these contracts. The following case addresses the application of this doctrine in the context of a contract between two electric utilities.

San Diego Electric & Gas Co. v. FERC

904 F.2d 727 (D.C. Cir. 1990).

■ WILLIAMS, J.—This dispute arises out of the lurching energy prices of the past two decades. An energy purchase contract that looked good for both parties on the date signed (November 4, 1985) soon afterwards looked dismal to the buyer. The Federal Energy Regulatory Commission declined to lower the price, but at the same time declined to relieve the seller from a delay of the effective date stemming from what may seem a technical default. We affirm the Commission against attack by both sides.

The contract obligates San Diego Gas & Electric Company to buy 100 megawatts of generating capacity and associated energy from Public Service Company of New Mexico for a 13-year period starting May 1, 1988. At the time it was entered into, the seller was awash in excess generating capacity and the state Public Service Commission had ordered the unnecessary capacity excluded from its retail rate base. Worse still, more unwanted capacity loomed from New Mexico's interest in a nuclear generating station whose three reactors would start up over the next two years. San Diego needed more capacity and wanted to diversify its mix of power sources by securing entitlements to power from coal and nuclear plants. The price offered by New Mexico was the most favorable available to San Diego and was in line with then prevailing market prices.

---

[5] Today, wholesale contracts may specify that they are subject to FERC regulation. For example, in *Union Pacific Fuels v. FERC,* 129 F.3d 157 (D.C. Cir. 1997) the court upheld FERC's power to change the rate for transportation on the Kern River gas pipeline from modified fixed/variable to straight fixed/variable in response to the industry-wide shift mandated by Order 636. The Court held that where the contract between the shippers and the pipeline contained a clause specifying that rates were subject to FERC regulation, the *Mobile-Sierra* doctrine allowed regulatory rate revisions initiated by FERC even though the contract also contained a clause by which the parties agreed not to initiate any such changes themselves. Note, however, that most wholesale rates both for gas and electricity are now market rates— whatever the market will bear—because FERC has approved the use of market rates in these transactions.

November 1985 proved, however, to be something of a crest in the wave of energy prices. Oil prices fell from nearly $30 a barrel in November 1985 to $12 in March 1986. The plunge triggered a drop in the bulk electric power market as well. As oil is used to produce electricity, a fall in its price (and that of close substitutes such as natural gas, whose price is directly affected by that of oil) drives power production costs down; variable costs fall and electricity producers are able to shift away from relatively capital-intensive nuclear and coal sources. . . . New contracts in 1988 evidently called for much lower prices—with demand charges (the charge for the purchasing utility's entitlement to take electricity) about half or one-third that specified in the contract.

Under § 205 of the Federal Power Act, 16 U.S.C. § 824d (1988), New Mexico could not collect rates under the contract until it had been accepted for filing with the Commission. When New Mexico filed, San Diego tried to persuade FERC to reject the contract as unjust and unreasonable, but the Commission refused. On the other hand, it also refused New Mexico a waiver that proved necessary if New Mexico was to be able to collect the demand charge starting on the date provided by contract, May 1, 1988. As a result of the refusal New Mexico was unable to collect the $3.3 million contract demand charge accrued from May 1 to June 13. Both parties appeal. . . .

San Diego claims that the Commission did not give enough weight to market changes between the execution of the agreement and the time for its performance. These changes were so great, it argues, as to require that the Commission set the contracts aside under its statutory obligation to ensure that interstate wholesale power rates are just and reasonable. *See* Federal Power Act § 205, 16 U.S.C. § 824d.

In fact the Commission was far from blind to the prevailing market conditions:

> Given our statutory obligation to judge the justness and reasonableness of the rate in the Agreement, we are required to explore [San Diego's arguments]. The freedom of the parties to contract in this instance must yield to the Commission's duty to ascertain the justness and reasonableness of the rates.

43 FERC at ¶ 62,153. Against this it placed great weight on the policy considerations behind contract stability:

> The certainty and stability which stems from contract performance and enforcement is essential to an orderly bulk power market. If the integrity of contracts is undermined, business would be transacted without legally enforceable assurances and we believe that the market, the industry and ultimately the consumer would suffer.

Id.

This has long been the Commission's position. . . . Indeed, the Supreme Court has insisted on great Commission deference to freely arrived at contract prices. *See United Gas Pipe Line Co. v. Mobile Gas Service Corp.*, 350 U.S. 332 (1956); *FPC v. Sierra Pacific Power Co.*, 350 U.S. 348 (1956).

As the Commission recognized, the purpose of this contract was to allocate the risk of market price changes between the parties:

The volatility of oil and gas prices, often reflecting large and dramatic swings, is old news. Indeed, this is the very reason that San Diego pursued a long-term purchase from [New Mexico] at rates reflecting [New Mexico's] nuclear and coal units.

Order, 43 FERC at 62,153.

San Diego wanted to diversify its mix of power sources, so to reduce the risk from further surges in the cost of oil and gas. J.A. 256. But each source carries its own set of risks. That is an inevitable part of energy production in a world where sources are varied and their relative prices subject to constant change. Scanning all the sources to which it had access, San Diego selected what it viewed as the optimal mix. On the other side, the contract gave New Mexico partial protection from the risk it had taken in investing heavily in precisely the sources that San Diego (in 1985) felt it needed. San Diego's current conclusion that it got the mix wrong is no reason to allow it to shift the risk (now the loss) back to New Mexico.

We note that New Mexico is no great winner either. The capital-intensive coal and nuclear plants to which it committed itself cannot generate the once-expected revenues. Nothing suggests that New Mexico is a more efficient bearer of the risks that the literal terms of the contract shifted to San Diego. Indeed, San Diego's participation in the 1985 contract as part of a systematic, deliberate program of diversifying risks would seem to mark it as an efficient risk bearer. *See* Richard A. Posner and Andrew M. Rosenfield, Impossibility and Related Doctrines in Contract Law: An Economic Analysis, 6 J. Legal Stud. 83, 91–92 (1977) (promisor's inferior ability to diversify risks may make it less efficient risk bearer and justify its discharge).

San Diego invokes our decision in *Associated Gas Distributors v. FERC,* 824 F.2d 981 (D.C. Cir. 1987), where this court required FERC to proffer adequately "reasoned decisionmaking" for its decision not to use § 5 of the Natural Gas Act, 15 U.S.C. § 717d (1988), to relieve pipelines of enormous take-or-pay liabilities under contracts that had become uneconomic. But the root of that decision was the Commission's failure to face directly the effects of its own decision, Order No. 436, restructuring the gas pipeline industry and for the first time subjecting pipelines as gas-sellers to competition from gas sold by others but transported by the pipelines themselves. . . . Our ultimate conclusion was that on remand the Commission "must more convincingly address the magnitude of the problem and the adverse consequences likely to result from the nondiscriminatory access and CD adjustment conditions [i.e., the Commission's own regulatory interventions]." *Id.* at 1044. And, although asking for more reasoned decisionmaking, we acknowledged that even in the context of risks that the Commission itself had severely exacerbated, FERC's pro-contract policy arguments were "powerful and well grounded in the statutes it is authorized to enforce." *Id.* at 1027. San Diego here offers nothing remotely comparable to the AGD petitioners' plea for regulatory relief; the Commission's reasoning amply served the case at hand.

The petitions for review are Denied. ∎

NOTES AND COMMENTS

1.   As the above case illustrates, the oil shocks of the 1970s and 1980s also had a significant impact on the electricity sector. Many utilities saw the rising fuel prices of the 1970s and early 1980s as a signal to increase their investment in nuclear power. When fuel prices fell in the mid-1980s (What else happened? See Chapter 7), that signal changed, but many utilities thought they were too far down the nuclear road to respond. Today, the expansion of domestic natural gas production from shales and tight sandstones has made utilities more confident about investing in gas plants, although they remain concerned about potential price volatility. Although gas prices will continue to fluctuate, U.S. Energy Information Administration (EIA) projections and other data suggest that there might be less gas price volatility over the next several decades.

2.   In an earlier case, *Metropolitan Edison Co. v. FERC*, 595 F.2d 851 (D.C. Cir. 1979), the court considered a contract entered into in the year 1906 by which an IOU agreed to provide electricity to the Borough of Middletown, Pennsylvania, for one cent per kilowatt-hour until such time as the Borough chose to terminate the contract. The court upheld FERC's determination that the contract was not subject to revision under the *Mobile-Sierra* doctrine despite that the price was far below current market rates. The court found that the overall impact of the contract on the utility's revenues was minimal.

3.   As *San Diego Electric & Gas Co.* indicates, the courts tended to read the NGA and the FPA *in pari materia*.

4.   The issue of contract versus regulation is perhaps most frequently litigated under what is known as the "filed rate doctrine." Under this doctrine, the filed and approved rate controls over any requested deviation, which is typically being requested from a court. The filed rate doctrine has historically worked to protect firms with a "filed rate" (approved by a federal or state agency) from contract and torts suits, such as fraud claims. It also has been applied to block federal antitrust claims where a federal agency has approved the pricing scheme that is alleged to be monopolistic. When a rate is "filed," antitrust often may not be used to challenge its validity; rather, challengers must use the processes offered by the agency that approved the price. Even market rates are considered "filed" if FERC has allowed a utility to charge market rates—meaning the utility may charge whatever the going market price is for its product. Thus, although FERC now allows most utilities to charge a market rate for the wholesale electricity that they sell to other utilities, that rate is considered "filed." When Enron and other power marketers manipulated wholesale energy prices in the early 2000s, causing them to dramatically rise, California and other states, utilities, and retail customers affected by high wholesale rates could not, for the most part, use antitrust claims but were limited to proceedings before FERC. *See* PUC District No. 1 of Snohomish v. Dynegy Power Mktg., 375 F.3d 831 (9th Cir. 2004). Just as the *Mobile-Sierra* doctrine did not allow FERC to deviate from a just and reasonable rate, the filed rate doctrine is a defense that precludes a judicial damages remedy that would, in effect, deviate from a just and reasonable rate.

This doctrine serves to protect consumers against discrimination in the setting of rates, by not allowing a firm to provide some customer discounts due to a legal judgment. In addition, the doctrine serves to advance goals such as deference to agency regulators and federalism. *See* Jim Rossi,

Lowering the Filed Tariff Shield: Judicial Enforcement for a Deregulatory Era, 56 Vand. L. Rev. 1591 (2003). The doctrine does not apply automatically, however. The filed rate doctrine serves as a valid defense only if the relevant regulator carefully evaluates and sets prices. In addition, there are recognized exceptions to the doctrine in the contexts of claims for injunctive relief and in price-squeeze antitrust cases.

Nantahala P & L v. Thornburg, 476 U.S. 953 (1976), held North Carolina regulators setting retail rates cannot "trap" FERC-approved wholesale power generation costs by refusing to include them in retail rates. The Court reasoned that North Carolina's decision to reject FERC-approved costs as imprudent is inconsistent with the filed rate doctrine: "Once FERC sets such a rate, a State may not conclude in setting retail rates that the FERC-approved wholesale rates are unreasonable. A State must rather give effect to Congress' desire to give FERC plenary authority over interstate wholesale rates, and to ensure that States do not interfere with this authority." However, what is known as the "Pike County exception" would have allowed state regulators to reject a wholesale purchase of electric power from a particular source if the state deemed it imprudent. In *Nantahala* the Court held that this did not apply to the transaction at issue because the utility did not have a choice of power supply sources that would have presented a lower-cost option.

5. Think back again to the EE case study presented earlier in this chapter. Is the New York State PSC required to approve the increase in EE's retail rates that can be attributed to the FERC-approved allocation of transmission line costs? What if the state rejects passing through the costs of transmission on the rationale that consumers in the state do not benefit? What if it rejects the costs of transmission lines on the rationale that state efficiency and conservation programs will offset any future need for new power transmission? These tensions between federal transmission policies and state rate regulation have become more prominent as FERC approves the cost allocation for multi-state transmission line projects—a topic discussed further in Chapters 11 and 12.

4. RELATIONSHIP TO ANTITRUST LAWS

Treating firms in the electricity industry as regulated public utilities was viewed as an appropriate to the extent that the industry constitutes a "natural monopoly." In fact, however, that monopoly was never complete. Since its initial development as an energy resource, competition has existed between electricity and alternative energy sources, such as oil and natural gas. For example, as the price of electricity rises, residential consumers in many areas have the option of switching from electricity to natural gas for purposes of heating and cooling. In this sense, the availability of alternative energy sources worked as a competitive check on electricity. In addition, competition among various suppliers of electricity has always existed to some degree.

The power of federal regulators to enhance competition in the electric utility industry is limited, largely because federal jurisdiction over competition policy has largely been restricted by statute to wholesale utilities and transactions. Still, as is discussed in Chapter 10, federal policy has significantly expanded the role of markets in allocating and pricing bulk power supplies in interstate commerce. Even where energy markets are not completely deregulated, the antitrust laws can play an important role in reinforcing competition norms and in promoting consumer welfare.

Antitrust statutes are designed to protect against anti-competitive and monopolistic conduct, and the overarching purpose of antitrust law is to promote competition. Most modern antitrust laws in the United States (including many state antitrust laws) derive from federal antitrust statutes passed during the late nineteenth and early twentieth centuries, such as the Sherman Antitrust Act of 1890 (the "Sherman Act"). The wording of the Sherman Act's two substantive sections— Sections 1 and 2—reflects Congress's broad public policy against anti-competitive behavior. Another statute, the Clayton Act, was adopted several years later. A variety of offenses are included under the Sherman Act and Clayton Act, including combinations in restraint of trade, price fixing, price squeeze, and other anticompetitive acts. Regulation of public utilities may implicate legal concerns under sections 1 and 2 of the Sherman Act, which address agreements in restraint of trade and illegal monopolization, respectively. For example, utility rate cases may raise concerns of about price fixing (a section 1 problem) and price squeeze (a section 2 problem). *See, e.g.*, Lawrence J. Spiwak, Is the Price Squeeze Doctrine Still Viable in Fully Regulated Energy Markets?, 14 Energy L.J. 75 (1993).

But how should these antitrust statutes, largely enforced in claims brought in federal court, co-exist with statutes such as the FPA, which authorizes FERC to police utility rates, or where state regulators have set retail rates for a utility? The following two cases illustrate the basic challenge when an antitrust claim is brought in federal court, by highlighting a) the tension between federal courts and federal agencies, and b) the tension between federal courts and state regulators.

Otter Tail Power v. United States
410 U.S. 366 (1973).

[Otter Tail Power was the major IOU in Minnesota, North Dakota, and South Dakota. Like most IOUs, it engaged in the generation, transmission, and distribution of power. It served the large majority of towns in these three states, but in a number of towns power was distributed through a municipal power company that did not generate power itself. These municipal distribution utilities could purchase power at a low rate from federal Bureau of Reclamation projects. However, the purchased power had to be transmitted ("wheeled") over the lines owned by Otter Tail. The municipals alleged that Otter Tail had sought to take over service in the municipal areas by anticompetitive means in violation of the Sherman Act. The civil antitrust suit alleged that Otter Tail had refused to sell wholesale power, had refused to wheel power, had discouraged other suppliers from dealing with the municipals, and had begun litigation to delay the establishment of municipal power systems. The District Court found in favor of the United States and the municipals.]

I.

■ DOUGLAS, J.—Otter Tail contends that by reason of the Federal Power Act it is not subject to antitrust regulation with respect to its refusal to deal. We disagree with that position.

"Repeals of the antitrust laws by implication from a regulatory statute are strongly disfavored, and have only been found in cases of plain repugnancy between the antitrust and regulatory provisions." *United States v. Philadelphia National Bank*, 374 U.S. 321, 350–351. *See also Silver v. New York Stock Exchange*, 373 U.S. 341, 357–361. Activities which come under the jurisdiction of a regulatory agency nevertheless may be subject to scrutiny under the antitrust laws.

In *California v. FPC*, 369 U.S. 482, 489, the Court held that approval of an acquisition of the assets of a natural gas company by the Federal Power Commission pursuant to § 7 of the Natural Gas Act "would be no bar to [an] antitrust suit." Under § 7, the standard for approving such acquisitions is "public convenience and necessity." Although the impact on competition is relevant to the Commission's determination, the Court noted that there was "no 'pervasive regulatory scheme' including the antitrust laws that ha[d] been entrusted to the Commission." *Id.*, at 485. Similarly, in *United States v. Radio Corp. of America*, 358 U.S. 334, the Court held that an exchange of radio stations that had been approved by the Federal Communications Commission as in the "public interest" was subject to attack in an antitrust proceeding.

The District Court determined that Otter Tail's consistent refusals to wholesale or wheel power to its municipal customers constituted illegal monopolization. Otter Tail maintains here that its refusals to deal should be immune from antitrust prosecution because the Federal Power Commission has the authority to compel involuntary interconnections of power pursuant to § 202 (b) of the Federal Power Act. The essential thrust of § 202, however, is to encourage voluntary interconnections of power. *See* S. Rep. No. 621, 74th Cong., 1st Sess., 19–20, 48–49; H. R. Rep. No. 1318, 74th Cong., 1st Sess., 8. Only if a power company refuses to interconnect voluntarily may the Federal Power Commission, subject to limitations unrelated to antitrust considerations, order the interconnection. The standard which governs its decision is whether such action is "necessary or appropriate in the public interest." Although antitrust considerations may be relevant, they are not determinative.

There is nothing in the legislative history which reveals a purpose to insulate electric power companies from the operation of the antitrust laws. To the contrary, the history of Part II of the Federal Power Act indicates an overriding policy of maintaining competition to the maximum extent possible consistent with the public interest. As originally conceived, Part II would have included a "common carrier" provision making it "the duty of every public utility to . . . transmit energy for any person upon reasonable request. . . ." In addition, it would have empowered the Federal Power Commission to order wheeling if it found such action to be "necessary or desirable in the public interest." H. R. 5423, 74th Cong., 1st Sess.; S. 1725, 74th Cong., 1st Sess. These provisions were eliminated to preserve "the voluntary action of the utilities." S. Rep. No. 621, 74th Cong., 1st Sess., 19.

It is clear, then, that Congress rejected a pervasive regulatory scheme for controlling the interstate distribution of power in favor of voluntary commercial relationships. When these relationships are governed in the first instance by business judgment and not regulatory coercion, courts must be hesitant to conclude that Congress intended to override the fundamental national policies embodied in the antitrust laws. *See United States v. Radio Corp. of America*, supra, at 351. This is particularly true in this instance because Congress, in passing the Public Utility Holding Company Act, which included Part II of the Federal Power Act, was concerned with "restraint of free and independent competition" among public utility holding companies. *See* 15 U.S.C. § 79a(b)(2).

Thus, there is no basis for concluding that the limited authority of the Federal Power Commission to order interconnections was intended to be a substitute for, or to immunize Otter Tail from, antitrust regulation for refusing to deal with municipal corporations.

II.

The decree of the District Court enjoins Otter Tail from "refusing to sell electric power at wholesale to existing or proposed municipal electric power systems in cities and towns located in [its service area]" and from refusing to wheel electric power over its transmission lines from other electric power lines to such cities and towns. But the decree goes on to provide:

The defendant shall not be compelled by the Judgment in this case to furnish wholesale electric service or wheeling service to a municipality except at rates which are compensatory and under terms and conditions which are filed with and subject to approval by the Federal Power Commission.

So far as wheeling is concerned, there is no authority granted the Commission under Part II of the Federal Power Act to order it, for the bills originally introduced contained common carrier provisions which were deleted. The Act as passed contained only the interconnection provision set forth in § 202(b). The common carrier provision in the original bill and the power to direct wheeling were left to the "voluntary coordination of electric facilities." Insofar as the District Court ordered wheeling to correct anticompetitive and monopolistic practices of Otter Tail, there is no conflict with the authority of the Federal Power Commission.

III.

The record makes abundantly clear that Otter Tail used its monopoly power in the towns in its service area to foreclose competition or gain a competitive advantage, or to destroy a competitor, all in violation of the antitrust laws. *See United States v. Griffith*, 334 U.S. 100, 107. The District Court determined that Otter Tail has "a strategic dominance in the transmission of power in most of its service area" and that it used this dominance to foreclose potential entrants into the retail area from obtaining electric power from outside sources of supply. 331 F. Supp., at 60. Use of monopoly power "to destroy threatened competition" is a violation of the "attempt to monopolize" clause of § 2 of the Sherman Act. *Lorain Journal v. United States*, 342 U.S. 143, 154; *Eastman Kodak Co. v. Southern Photo Materials Co.*, 273 U.S. 359, 375. So are agreements not to compete, with the aim of preserving or extending a monopoly. *Schine Chain Theatres v. United States*, 334 U.S. 110, 119. In *Associated Press v. United States*, 326 U.S. 1, a cooperative news association had bylaws that permitted member newspapers to bar competitors from joining the association. We held that practice violated the Sherman Act, even though the transgressor "had not yet achieved a complete monopoly." *Id.*, at 13.

When a community serviced by Otter Tail decides not to renew Otter Tail's retail franchise when it expires, it may generate, transmit, and distribute its own electric power. We recently described the difficulties and problems of those isolated electric power systems. *See Gainesville Utilities v. Florida Power Corp.*, 402 U.S. 515, 517–520. Interconnection with other utilities is frequently the only solution. *Id.*, at 519 n. 3. That is what Elbow Lake in the present case did. There were no engineering factors that prevented Otter Tail from selling power at wholesale to those towns that wanted municipal plants or wheeling the power. The District Court found—and its findings are supported—that Otter Tail's refusals to sell at wholesale or to wheel were solely to prevent municipal power systems from eroding its monopolistic position.

Otter Tail relies on its wheeling contracts with the Bureau of Reclamation and with cooperatives which it says relieve it of any duty to wheel power to municipalities served at retail by Otter Tail at the time the contracts were made. The District Court held that these restrictive provisions were "in reality, territorial allocation schemes," 331 F. Supp., at 63, and were per se violations of the Sherman Act, *citing Northern Pacific R. Co. v. United States*, 356 U.S. 1. Like covenants were there held to "deny defendant's competitors access to the fenced-off market on the same terms as the defendant." *Id.*, at 12. We recently re-emphasized the vice under the Sherman Act of territorial restrictions among potential competitors. *United States v. Topco Associates*, 405 U.S. 596, 608. The fact that some of the restrictive provisions were contained in a contract with the Bureau of Reclamation is not material to our problem for, as the Solicitor General says, "government contracting officers do not have the power to grant immunity from the Sherman Act." Such contracts stand on their own footing and are valid or not, depending on the statutory framework within which the federal agency operates. The Solicitor General tells us that these restrictive provisions operate as a "hindrance" to the Bureau and were "agreed to by the Bureau only at Otter Tail's insistence," as the District Court found. The evidence supports that finding. . . .

V.

Otter Tail argues that, without the weapons which it used, more and more municipalities will turn to public power and Otter Tail will go downhill. The argument is a familiar one. It was made in *United States v. Arnold, Schwinn & Co.*, 388 U.S. 365, a civil suit under section 1 of the Sherman Act dealing with a restrictive distribution program and practices of a bicycle manufacturer. We said: "The promotion of self-interest alone does not invoke the rule of reason to immunize otherwise illegal conduct." *Id.*, at 375.

The same may properly be said of section 2 cases under the Sherman Act. That Act assumes that an enterprise will protect itself against loss by operating with superior service, lower costs, and improved efficiency.

Otter Tail's theory collided with the Sherman Act as it sought to substitute for competition anticompetitive uses of its dominant economic power.

The fact that three municipalities which Otter Tail opposed finally got their municipal systems does not excuse Otter Tail's conduct. That fact does not condone the antitrust tactics which Otter Tail sought to impose. Moreover, the District Court repeated what we said in *FTC v. National Lead Co.*, 352 U.S. 419, 431, "those caught violating the Act must expect some fencing in." The proclivity for predatory practices has always been a consideration for the District Court in fashioning its antitrust decree. *See United States v. Crescent Amusement Co.*, 323 U.S. 173, 190.

We do not suggest, however, that the District Court, concluding that Otter Tail violated the antitrust laws, should be impervious to Otter Tail's assertion that compulsory interconnection or wheeling will erode its integrated system and threaten its capacity to serve adequately the public. As the dissent properly notes, the Commission may not order interconnection if to do so "would impair [the utility's] ability to render adequate service to its customers." 16 U.S.C. § 824a(b). The District Court in this case found that the "pessimistic view" advanced in Otter Tail's "erosion study" "is not supported by the record." Furthermore, it concluded that "it does not appear that Bureau of Reclamation power is a serious threat to the defendant nor that it will be in the foreseeable future." Since the District Court has made future connections subject to Commission approval and in any event has retained jurisdiction to enable the parties to apply for "necessary or appropriate" relief and presumably will give effect to the policies embodied in the Federal Power Act, we cannot say under these circumstances that it has abused its discretion. ■

NOTES AND COMMENTS

1.   *Otter Tail* considered the authority of FPC to order interconnection or wheeling of power. The benefits of interconnection are summarized in *Gainesville Utilities v. Florida Power Corp.*, 402 U.S. 515 (1971):

> The demand upon an electric utility for electric power fluctuates significantly from hour to hour, day to day, and season to season. For this reason, generating facilities cannot be maintained on the basis of constant demand. Rather, the utility's generating capacity must be geared to the utility's peak load of demand, and also take into account the fact that generating equipment must occasionally be out of service for overhaul, or because of breakdowns. In consequence, the utility builds certain "reserves" of generating capacity in excess of peak load requirements into its system. The practice of a utility that relies completely on its own generating resources (an "isolated" system in industry jargon) is to maintain equipment capable of producing its peak load requirements plus equipment that produces a "reserve" capacity equal to the capacity of its largest generating unit.

> The major importance of an interconnection is that it reduces the need for the "isolated" utility to build and maintain "reserve" generating capacity. An interconnection is simply a transmission

line connecting two utilities. Electric power may move freely through the line up to the line's capacity. Ordinarily, however, the energy generated by each system is sufficient to supply the requirements of the system's customers and no substantial amount of power flows through the interconnection. It is only at the times when one of the connected utilities is unable for some reason to produce sufficient power to meet its customers' needs that the deficiency may be supplied by power that automatically flows through the interconnection from the other utility. To the extent that the utility may rely upon the interconnection to supply this deficiency, the utility is freed of the necessity of constructing and maintaining its own equipment for the purpose.

Gainesville Utilities upheld an FPC order that directed interconnection between a municipal utility and a larger, adjacent investor-owned system. The Court reversed the Court of Appeals' decision, which required the municipal system to provide substantially greater compensation for the interconnection than the FPC had required.

2. In PURPA, Congress expanded FERC's authority to order interconnection, even where it was not voluntary. The Energy Policy Act of 1992 further expanded FERC's authority to mandate wholesale transmission (also known as "wheeling") to promote competition. Order 888 later required all FERC-jurisdictional transmission lines to wheel power, with very limited exceptions. See Chapter 10. If FERC has the statutory authority to do this, would the plaintiffs' claim today in *Otter Tail* fail? Or are there still aspects of transmission access and pricing that could qualify for a Sherman Act claim? For discussion, see Note, Saving *Otter Tail*, The Essential Facilities Doctrine and Electric Power Post-*Trinko*, 33 Fla. St. U. L. Rev. 231 (2005).

3. The Public Utilities Holding Company Act of 1935 (PUHCA), mentioned in *Otter Tail*, regulated the ownership structure of public utilities. During the 1920s and 1930s, public utility holding companies had gained effective control over many operating electric utility companies, primarily by controlling voting with far less than 100 percent ownership. PUHCA was aimed at breaking up the trusts that controlled U.S. gas and electric utilities. At the time PUHCA was enacted into law, financial pyramid schemes were common. These schemes allowed utilities in many different areas of the country to fall under the control of a small number of holding companies. Before PUHCA, almost half of all electricity was controlled by three huge holding companies.

Samuel Insull's investments in the industry, a target during the hearing that led to the enactment of PUHCA, are a good example:

> The Insull interests (which operated in 32 states and owned electric companies, textile mills, ice houses, a paper mill, and a hotel) controlled 69 percent of the stock of Corporation Securities and 64 percent of the stock of Insull Utility Investments. Those two companies together owned 28 percent of the voting stock of Middle West Utilities. Middle West Utilities owned eight holding companies, five investment companies, two service companies, two securities companies, and 14 operating companies. It also owned 99 percent of the voting stock of National Electric Power. National, in turn, owned one holding company, one service company, one paper

company, and two operating companies. It also owned 93 percent of the voting stock of National Public Service. National Public Service owned three building companies, three miscellaneous firms, and four operating utilities. It also owned 100 percent of the voting stock of Seaboard Public Service. Seaboard Public Service owned the voting stock of five utility operating companies and one ice company. The utilities, in turn, owned eighteen subsidiaries.

L.S. Hyman, America's Electric Utilities: Past, Present and Future 102 (5th ed. 1994).

The Securities and Exchange Commission (SEC) was charged with administering PUHCA, including regulating holding companies. PUHCA authorized SEC to break up the massive utility holding companies by requiring them to divest their holdings until each was a single consolidated system serving a defined geographic area. PUHCA also limited the businesses in which utility holding companies could engage to utility-related functions. All holding companies were required to register with SEC. Through the registration process, SEC determined whether each holding company would be regulated or exempt from the requirements of PUHCA. SEC defined a utility holding company as a company that directly or indirectly owned 10 percent or more of the outstanding securities of a single utility company. The agency took a very aggressive approach to interpreting this requirement, but there was a safety valve in PUHCA for holding companies that were entirely intrastate in character. *See* EIA, The Public Utility Holding Company Act of 1935: 1935–1992 (1993).

Congress repealed PUHCA in the Energy Policy Act of 2005. With PUHCA repeal, utilities and unregulated entities are able to buy any utility asset or utility company regardless of location. Mergers between utilities that are located far from each other are possible for the first time since PUHCA was enacted. It is also much less burdensome for multistate, for-profit transmission companies to form. The Energy Policy Act of 2005 also directed FERC to issue rules providing for expedited treatment of mergers, allowing for complete review of mergers with 360 days. For discussion of the significance of PUHCA as a barrier to mergers in the industry, see Judge Richard Cudahy, Consolidation: Key to the Future?, Pub. Util. Fortnightly, Aug. 2005, at 15.

4.   In *Otter Tail*, Otter Tail claimed that it was exempt from the Sherman Act because of what is known as the "regulated industries" exception. Where an enterprise's competitive activities are already scrutinized under a pervasive regulatory scheme, courts may look to the doctrine of primary jurisdiction, deferring to that regulatory scheme rather than applying the antitrust laws. As the Court notes, however, such deference is unlikely where a regulatory scheme is not directly concerned with the anticompetitive implications of an enterprise's activities.

———

A similar exemption applies to regulated enterprises at the state level, where retail transactions in the electricity industry have historically been regulated. The "state action" doctrine exempts from federal antitrust laws anticompetitive conduct where a state has explicitly adopted an active regulatory policy to displace competition with regulation or a monopoly franchise. Thus, state PUC price regulation of a state-franchised public utility may be exempt from antitrust challenge. However, like the regulated industries exception, the state action doctrine is not automatic. *See, e.g.,* City of Lafayette v. La. Power & Light Co., 435 U.S. 389 (1978); Cantor v. Detroit Edison Co., 428 U.S. 579 (1976). The following case illustrates this doctrine and the challenges courts increasingly are facing in deciding when to apply it to conduct that is potentially regulated at the state level:

TEC Cogeneration, Inc. v. Florida Power & Light Co.

76 F.3d 1560 (11th Cir. 1996).

■ This is an appeal from the denial of a motion for summary judgment by the district court. Two questions are presented: first, whether a public utility is immune from antitrust liability under the state-action doctrine of Parker v. Brown, 317 U.S. 341 (1943), for its allegedly anti-competitive conduct concerning a cogenerator in the areas of wheeling, rates, and interconnection; and second, whether lobbying of a county legislative body by the utility is protected from antitrust liability under the Noerr/Pennington doctrine. *Eastern R.R. Presidents Conference v. Noerr Motor Freight, Inc.*, 365 U.S. 127 (1961); *United Mine Workers of America v. Pennington*, 381 U.S. 657 (1965). The district court found that the utility was not entitled to immunity from antitrust sanctions for its actions. We disagree. The denial by the district court of the utility's motion for summary judgment is reversed.

Appellant Florida Power & Light Company ("FPL") is an investor-owned public electric utility engaged in three functions: generation, transmission, and distribution and sale of electric energy. It services southern and eastern Florida, including most of Dade [County]. FPL is regulated by the Florida Public Service Commission ("PSC"). It owns and controls ninety percent of the total electrical generating capacity in its service area and the electrical grid with which [the Miami Downtown Government] Center can interconnect. FPL has monopoly power within its service area both as to the purchase of wholesale power and the sale of retail power.

In 1981, Dade issued requests to bid on the Center cogeneration facility. Cogenerators' proposal was selected and in late 1983, Dade and the Cogenerators entered into contracts providing for the construction and operation of a twenty-seven megawatt cogeneration facility at Center and for the supply of cogeneration equipment for the project. The Cogenerators agreed to operate Center for Dade for sixteen years. The Cogenerators also contracted to supply electrical and thermal power to Dade. Dade and the Cogenerators were to share in the profits, if any, from operating the Center; the Cogenerators were to absorb the losses. The final contract allowed for excess power, if any, from Center, to be dispensed to Dade facilities outside Center, such as to the Jackson Memorial Hospital/Civic Center complex (Hospital). Practically speaking, excess power could be dispensed only one of two ways, either via a wheeling arrangement with FPL or by constructing a separate transmission line. A separate line would require the approval of the local legislative body, i.e., the Dade County Board of Commissioners (Commission). With these parameters in place, construction of the cogeneration facility commenced in mid-1984 and the facility became fully operational at the end of 1986.

To reduce their losses, the Cogenerators sought a logical use for the excess power. Under rules promulgated by the PSC, two options were immediately available: (1) the Cogenerators could either sell the surplus electricity to FPL at a rate equal to FPL's avoided cost; or (2) the Cogenerators could force FPL to transmit or wheel the excess power to another Florida utility, who in turn would purchase it at its own avoided cost rate.

At avoided cost rates, it appeared that the Cogenerators could not break even with either option. FPL alleges that the Cogenerators deliberately ignored their two legitimate options and pursued a third, allegedly illegitimate, alternative in order to obtain higher prices for their power: the Cogenerators approached FPL to wheel their surplus power to other Dade facilities outside Center, most notably, to Hospital, two miles northwest. Believing that the Cogenerators' request violated the PSC's self-service wheeling rules,[17][6] FPL declined to wheel.

Rebuffed by FPL, the Cogenerators then turned to the best efforts clause in its contract with Dade. They directed Dade, in effect, to petition the PSC for an order compelling FPL to wheel power from Center to other Dade facilities, including Hospital.

After an eleven-month administrative proceeding, the PSC denied Dade's petition. The PSC found that Dade could not comply with the PSC's self-service wheeling rules because Dade did not actually own the generating equipment that produced the power to be wheeled; did not generate the power to be wheeled; and was contractually bound to purchase the electricity from the Cogenerators. Hence, the PSC found, by definition, that Dade could not "serve oneself." Petition of Metropolitan Dade County for Expedited Consideration of Request for Provision of Self-Service Transmission, Order No. 17510, Docket No. 860786–EI, 87 FPSC 5:32, 35–37 (May 5, 1987).

After the PSC wheeling disallowance, the Cogenerators played their fourth and final card: what can't be sent indirectly, send directly. They approached Dade with a proposal to construct a separate transmission line from Center to Hospital. A separate line would reduce surplus electricity without being dependent upon wheeling by FPL at avoided cost rates. A joint submission was made by the Cogenerators and Dade to Commission for its approval. The Cogenerators lobbied Commission for approval; FPL lobbied against. The Commission voted five-to-one against the construction of the separate transmission line.

Within weeks, the Cogenerators filed this suit. . . .

FPL's motion for summary judgment relies principally on two immunity doctrines: the state action immunity doctrine and the Noerr/Pennington immunity doctrine. The district court denied summary judgment under both.

---

6   Under PSC regulations, the Cogenerators can ask FPL to wheel electricity from Center to Hospital only if they qualify under the self-service wheeling rules: (1) there must be an exact identity of ownership between the generator and the consumer of the electricity; and (2) wheeling will not increase rates to utility, i.e., FPL ratepayers. Fla. Admin. Code R. 25–17.0882. Under Florida law, a cogenerator may not sell electricity at retail. PW Ventures, 533 So.2d at 281.

We review each of these findings de novo. . . .

The Supreme Court first articulated the state-action immunity doctrine in *Parker v. Brown*, 317 U.S. 341 (1943). In Parker, the Court grappled with the applicability of the Sherman Act to a California agricultural statutory program intended to restrict competition among private producers of raisins in order to stabilize prices and prevent economic waste. Relying on principles of federalism and state sovereignty, the Court refused to find that the Sherman Act was "intended to restrain state action or official action directed by a state" and determined that "[t]here is no suggestion of a purpose to restrain state action in the Act's legislative history." *Id.* at 351. The Court held, therefore, that federal antitrust laws were not intended to reach state-regulated anticompetitive activities. *Id.* at 350–52; *City of Columbia v. Omni Outdoor Advertising, Inc.*, 499 U.S. 365, 370 (1991).

Thirty-seven years later, in *California Retail Liquor Dealers Ass'n. v. Midcal Aluminum, Inc.*, 445 U.S. 97 (1980), a unanimous Court established a two-pronged test to determine when private party anticompetitive conduct is entitled to state action immunity from antitrust liability: (1) the conduct had to be performed pursuant to a clearly articulated policy of the state to displace competition with regulation; and (2) the conduct had to be closely supervised by the state. *Id.* at 105; *see also* F.T.C. v. Ticor Title Ins. Co., 504 U.S. 621 (1992). These two prongs are addressed below. . . .

1. Clearly Articulated Policy of the State

The Court set out the first element of state action immunity in *Southern Motor Carriers Rate Conference, Inc. v. U.S.*, 471 U.S. 48 (1985). There, the Court determined that a private party acting pursuant to an anticompetitive regulatory program need not "point to a specific, detailed legislative authorization" for its challenged conduct. *Id.* at 57. As long as the State as sovereign clearly intends to displace competition in a particular field with a regulatory structure, the first prong of the Midcal test is satisfied. *Id.* at 64.

In this case, the district court found that Florida has two statutory policies regarding power generation and transmission: a policy favoring monopoly power in Florida electric utilities, and a policy of encouraging development of Florida cogeneration facilities, complemented by the implementation of PSC regulatory guidelines. Fla. Stat. § 366.051 (1991). The district court found that these statutes set out clearly articulated policies regarding utilities and cogenerators. Accordingly, the district court found that FPL had satisfied the first prong of the Midcal test, except as to its Strategic Energy Business Study or SEBS.

We agree with the district court that Florida has an obvious and clearly articulated policy to displace competition with regulation in the area of power generation and transmission and that FPL's conduct has been performed pursuant to that policy. The Florida legislature gave the PSC broad authority to regulate FPL. *See* Ch. 366, Fla. Stat. Further, the relationship between Florida utilities and cogenerators has been subject to pervasive state regulation through statute and regulatory rules. Fla. Stat. § 366.05(1), .04(1), (5), .06(1), .051 (1994); Fla. Admin. Code R. 25–17.080–.091 (1988). A myriad of agency proceedings have transpired. The field has not been left to the parties' unfettered business discretion. In addition, the Florida Supreme Court has been active in its role of judicial review. *See* C.F. Industries, Inc. v. Nichols, 536 So.2d 234 (Fla.1988) (standby rates for qualifying facilities); PW Ventures, Inc. v. Nichols, 533 So.2d 281 (Fla.1988) (third-party sales by qualifying facilities); Storey v. Mayo, 217 So.2d 304, 307 (Fla.1968), cert. denied, 395 U.S. 909 (1969) ("The powers of the Commission over . . . privately-owned utilities [are] omnipotent within the confines of the statute and the limits of organic law.").

We disagree, however, with the district court's exclusion of SEBS from its finding. It is clear that Florida intended to displace competition in the utility industry with a regulatory structure, Southern Motor Carriers, 471 U.S. at 64, and FPL's internal SEBS study has no relevance to the issue of Florida's clearly articulated policy of regulation. Contrary to the district court's ruling, we conclude that the first prong of the state action defense is satisfied here, without qualification, that is, including SEBS.

2.   Conduct Actively Supervised by the State.

This second prong of the state action defense applies when the challenged conduct is by a private party rather than a government official. Ticor, 504 U.S. at 630. Active state involvement is the second precondition for antitrust immunity; the conduct by the private party has to be closely supervised by the state. Midcal, 445 U.S. at 105–06. The active supervision requirement is designed to ensure that the state has "ultimate control" over the private party's conduct, with the power to review and disapprove, if necessary, particular anticompetitive acts that may offend state policy. *Patrick v. Burget*, 486 U.S. 94, 101 (1988).

The district court considered FPL's conduct in three areas alleged to be anticompetitive by the Cogenerators: (1) FPL's refusal to wheel; (2) its use of rates; and (3) its alleged interference with interconnection. It determined that for FPL to meet the second prong of the state action defense, Florida, through the PSC, must have "actively supervised, substantially reviewed, or independently exercised judgment and control" over FPL's "overall anti-competitive campaign."

In each of the three areas, the district court found that, while the PSC had the power to review FPL's conduct, it was not given the opportunity to exercise its power to review FPL's conduct. Therefore, the district court determined that the PSC's regulatory authority (in application or as applied) did not satisfy the second prong of the state action immunity standard.

As we conclude that the PSC did in fact exercise active supervision over FPL, we do not discuss these areas separately, as the same rationale applies to each.

3.   The Active Supervision in this Case

In 1987, the PSC denied Dade's petition to allow the Cogenerators to wheel power to Hospital because they could not satisfy the PSC self-service wheeling rules. In re: Petition of Metropolitan Date County, Order No. 17510 (1987).

The district court notes that FPL stands behind this PSC ruling as conclusive evidence of active state supervision. The district court finds this reliance misplaced. It focuses instead on the circumstances leading up to the PSC hearing: FPL's acts that have their genesis in the embryonic stages of Center when FPL participated in the early negotiations of the Cogenerator-Dade agreement. That is, under an estoppel-like analysis, the district court found that, when FPL ostensibly gave its blessing to the contract (with full knowledge that it contemplated: (1) the wheeling of excess power by FPL to other Dade locations; (2) the conveyance of power to other Dade facilities through a direct transmission line; or (3) the sale of excess power to FPL at avoided cost rates), it can't be heard to complain now. The district court's determination is based, not on whether the PSC had the power to actively supervise and review FPL's conduct, but on whether it was ever given the opportunity to exercise its power to supervise and review (and possibly disapprove), these early acts of FPL.

That is not the issue. The issue is this: Has the State of Florida, through its state regulatory agency, the PSC, actively supervised FPL in the areas of wheeling, rates and interconnection? The answer is clearly yes, as to each. The fact that FPL didn't complain about wheeling or rates or interconnection when it first reviewed the Center contract is not material as to whether or not the PSC had the power to actively supervise FPL. That power is insulated. FPL's failure to object does not take away from the PSC its opportunity to exercise the power of active supervision. Failure by the parties to commence an action or proceeding (at the time when the district court apparently thought they should have objected), does not constitute the nullification of the PSC's power to act.

The PSC exercises its powers only when called upon to do so. No call was made. For example, the decisions of this circuit govern or control a plethora of legal issues—but if a particular issue is never brought before us—it doesn't mean we don't have control. We don't have opportunity—but we still have control. We still have active supervision.

The record is clear—the doors to the PSC were open to all with standing to complain. Being met with a complaint, the PSC had the full power to actively supervise. Whether or not the State, through the PSC, exercises its control sua sponte is not material, unless, of course, there is an apparent devious design to abdicate or obstruct control, and that is not the case here. The record shows that, when the PSC was called upon, they acted. We, the judiciary, do not have to take a walk with the PSC members to see if they visit FPL's offices every morning.

In sum, Florida has clearly articulated policies regarding the relationship between FPL and the Cogenerators. In addition, the record is clear that the PSC actively supervised all aspects of FPL's alleged anti-competitive conduct. We conclude, therefore, that both prongs of the state action immunity doctrine are satisfied here and FPL's conduct is immune from antitrust liability in each of the three areas of wheeling, rates and interconnection. ∎

NOTES AND COMMENTS

1.   If an agency's approval of activity initiated by a firm is only pro forma, or if the agency failed to evaluate fully the effects of the firm's activities on competition, there still appears to be some room for antitrust enforcement. *See* Hughes Tool Co. v. Trans World Airlines, 409 U.S. 363 (1973). If the costs of pervasive agency regulation are higher than the costs of competition as

enforced through antitrust litigation, what is the most efficient regulatory scheme? Do the legal tests courts consider in deciding whether to pursue antitrust claims take into account this kind of cost comparison?

2.   The issue of state action immunity from antitrust enforcement is increasingly made relevant by state laws that were designed to promote new entrants in power generation and state law designed to deregulate retail customer rates. For discussion of this, see Chapter 10. As deregulation of energy markets becomes more prominent, and states abandon rate hearings and move towards market-based rates, should the tradition of refusing antitrust enforcement against utilities continue?

3.   Think back one more time to the EE case study presented earlier in the chapter. Suppose that EE's proposal is accepted in its entirety by the PSC, allowing EE's rate increase to go into effect. Groups representing competing power suppliers bring an antitrust claim alleging that EE violated the Sherman Act by offering the power generators it owns lower cost access to its transmission lines than it offered to competing sources of electric power that are not owned by EE. They maintain that if EE priced transmission appropriately, other generators could sell power to meet customer demand and it would not be necessary to retrofit EE's coal plants to burn natural gas, and that as a result consumers are harmed by the rate increase. Assuming these groups have standing, should a court entertain this claim under the Sherman Act? Why or why not?

CHAPTER 9

OIL AND GAS PIPELINES: OPENING MARKETS

A. SOME BASICS

Without a transport system, oil and gas markets cannot develop to deliver these fuels to customers, often located hundreds of miles from the wells. This chapter discusses the federal regulation of the transportation of oil and gas after they leave the well head. Congress regulated natural gas pipelines in 1938 quite differently from its regulation of oil pipelines in 1906. Oil pipelines were treated as common carrier, open-access pipelines from the start, whereas gas pipelines had to be restructured in the 1970s and 1980s to achieve this result and allow more competitive gas markets. Both types of pipelines are regulated by the Federal Energy Regulatory Commission (FERC), but the regulatory regimes are different. With the boom in light tight oil from shale plays, oil pipeline regulation has received new attention, quite aside from the "media hot" issue whether the Keystone XL pipeline will ever secure approval to bring Canadian oil from the oil sands into the United States. Cross-border energy issues, such as approvals for exports of crude oil, LNG, and oil and gas products are treated in Chapter 14.

The chapter will first look at natural gas pipeline regulation, and then at oil pipelines. The physical flow of oil from well head to refinery is described in Chapter 4.

1.   THE FLOW OF GAS FROM WELL HEAD TO DOWNSTREAM END USERS

Natural gas flows through a continuous chain of links as follows:

Producers. About 400,000 gas wells produce in the United States today, operated by about 7,000 producers. Ken Costello, The Natural Gas Industry at a Glance 4 (Nat'l Regulatory Research Inst. Oct. 2010). Gas comes from two types of fields: Associated gas (also called casinghead gas) is gas that is produced along with oil from oil wells, separated from the oil, and then sent into gas pipelines. Non-associated gas wells produce from gas-only fields that have no accompanying oil production. Gas is gathered in small-diameter pipelines (called gathering lines) from all the wells in a field; run through processing facilities in the field to remove water and impurities; compressed to boost its pressure so that it will flow into a large transmission pipeline; and transported to storage or marketing centers, as depicted in **Figure 9–1**:

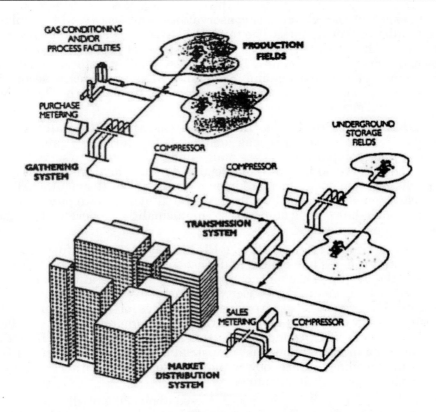

Figure 9–1
Typical Natural Gas Pipeline System
Source: 2 Energy Law and Transactions, Ch. 50, p. 50–107 (David J. Muchow &
William A. Mogel eds. 2002)

Gatherers and Gas Processing. Producers may also construct and operate the gathering lines and field processing facilities, but the increased size of this market in recent years has brought new entrants into this business. It is sometimes difficult to differentiate a gathering facility, which is largely regulated at the state level by public utility commissions, from a transmission pipeline that can fall under federal jurisdiction. *See* Kurt L. Krieger, Gathering and Transporting Marcellus and Utica Shale and the Regulation of Midstream Companies—the Case for a Uniform Federal and State Definition of Gathering in the Context of Economic and Siting Regulation, 19 Tex. Wesleyan L. Rev. 49–75 (2012).

Transmission Pipelines. These large pipelines of high-strength steel (20 inches to 42 inches in diameter) form an "interstate highway" system of over 280,000 miles for natural gas to travel. Interstate pipeline companies have, for antitrust reasons, been independent from the gas producing companies. Interstate pipelines are regulated by FERC using many of the principles of utility rate regulation discussed in Chapter 8, such as conditioning new pipeline construction on certificates of public convenience and regulating rates of service. In large producing and consuming states like Texas, many intrastate pipelines also exist. These are regulated by a state agency, often the public utility commission. State agencies, often the oil and gas conservation commissions, also regulate the smaller gathering lines. The term "midstream" is used to refer to the activities that occur between the upstream producers and the downstream end users, mainly transmission pipelines, storage facilities and sometimes gathering and processing. The midstream sector is experiencing boom-like expansion in an effort to match the flow from shale oil and gas fields.

Distributors or LDCs. In urban areas, there is usually a "gas company" that distributes gas delivered to the "city gate" by a transmission company, using gas mains under the streets to serve homes for heating and cooking and commercial and industrial businesses. These local distribution companies are known as "LDCs" or distributors. They are usually investor-owned utilities regulated by the state public utility commission, but, in some cases, municipalities operate the gas distribution business.

Industrial Users and Power Plants. Gas is used as fuel in many industrial processes like boilers and blast furnaces. During the 1990s, it became the fuel of choice for most new electricity generation plants and the fate of both gas and electricity restructuring became intertwined. Industrial users often use very large volumes of gas and are quite sensitive to its price. Unlike residential and commercial users who buy gas from the area's LDC, industrial users may take gas directly from the pipeline, in a practice known as "industrial bypass" (bypassing the LDC as an intermediary). Most power plants also take gas directly from a pipeline or a spur off the pipeline.

In 2012, the electric power sector used about 39% of all the natural gas consumed in the United States; the industrial sector used about 31%; and the residential and commercial sectors combined used about 30%.

2.   BASIC GAS PIPELINE OPERATIONS AND RATES

The market for natural gas has wide seasonal variations. In the Northern states, where gas is commonly used for space heating, residential gas usage is seven times as high in the winter as in the summer. The electricity sector's demand for gas as a generation fuel for residential electricity use is 50% higher in the summer than in the fall and spring because air conditioning has become so prevalent. Thus, different pipelines face differing seasonal demand patterns. The laws of physics limit how much gas can be pushed through a pipe, depending on the size and strength of the pipe. Compressor stations posted about every 70 miles along a transmission line keep the gas under considerable pressure, but there are limits on the extent to which it can be compressed without risking a rupture, which can be disastrous. A pipeline system must be designed to have enough capacity to meet the demands of customers on the most extreme cold-or hot-weather day, known as the "peak." On off-peak days, there will be room in the pipeline for other users.

To address this variability in demand, two different methods are often employed. First, depleted reservoirs nearer to consuming areas are converted into gas storage units by injecting gas into the reservoir during off-peak days, and drawing it out during peak days. (The ownership of stored gas was discussed in Chapter 4 in the context of the rule of capture.) As gas has become the premier fuel for power plants, gas storage facilities have greatly expanded and this alleviates, but does not eliminate, the problem of supplying peak demand.

Second, many industrial users that use very large quantities of gas year-round, such as petrochemical plants or steel mills, maintain alternative coal or fuel oil facilities to which they can switch if gas is not available or becomes relatively expensive compared to substitute fuels. These large, flexible customers are quite desirable for a pipeline company, which is always seeking to maximize the use of its facilities every day of the year. To attract such customers, pipeline companies designed "interruptible" rates which allow industrial users to buy gas at low rates on condition that they can be cut off if the pipeline space is needed, say, for residential gas heating on very cold days. An industrial user with a steady demand has a "high load factor." Load factors are the ratio of average demand to peak demand. Thus, if a firm has an average demand of 8 units and a peak demand of 10 units, the load factor is 80%. Residential space heating customers have low load factors, *i.e.*, volatile demand swings due to weather.

An interruptible customer pays a rate based primarily on the amount of gas it actually transports through the pipeline, called the "usage" or "commodity" charge. A commodity charge is defined as the charge per unit of gas (measured by volume or heat content) delivered to the buyer. This customer pays little of the fixed cost of the pipeline because the pipeline serves the user only when spare capacity exists.

The "firm" customer (like the residential consumer) pays a two-part rate. The first part is based on the actual amount of gas used, *i.e.*, the usage or commodity rate. In addition, the firm customer pays for the right to demand service even on the coldest day. This second part of the rate is called a "reservation" or "demand" charge because the pipeline reserves space to meet this customer's demand at all times. The customer pays this charge whether it uses the service or not. The charge is often based on the actual or estimated peak usage of the customer over a certain time period. (Review Chapter 8 on rate design.)

If the weather becomes so extreme that even a cutoff of the industrial customers is inadequate to free up enough gas to serve the firm customers, LDCs typically establish priority lists to allocate gas among the firm customers. Usually, the customers that will suffer the least damage from a shutdown are the first to be cut off, but any such action is an emergency situation to be avoided if at all possible.

3.   CHANGING INDUSTRY LANDSCAPES

The business relationships among the companies in Figure 9–1 were well established until the energy shocks of the 1970s forced a radical restructuring of the industry. Historically, the pipelines bought gas from producers, transported it to markets, and sold it to distributors and industrial users. Because financing to construct a pipeline was not available unless the company could show that it had an assured source of supply and demand for twenty years or so, pipeline companies entered into long-term contracts to buy gas from producers, usually at relatively fixed prices. Similarly, distributors entered into long-term agreements to buy gas from the pipelines at rates approved by the state public utility commission.

The physical flow of gas and the straightforward buy/sell arrangements in the gas chain from the "upstream" wells to the "downstream" consumer before the restructuring are depicted in **Figure 9–2**. The pipeline was both a merchant—buying gas from the producer on one end and then selling it to the LDC at the other—and the sole provider of the transportation service to move the gas. All the gas in the pipeline belonged to the pipeline company.

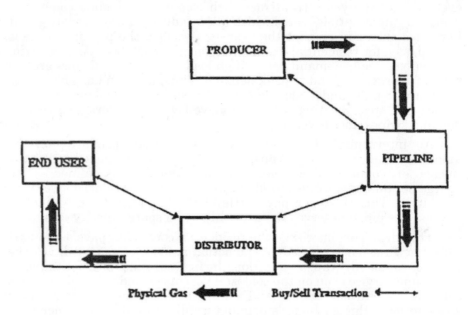

Figure 9–2
Historical Marketplace for Gas

Today, gas still flows in pipelines from the well to the users, but the buy/sell financial transactions involve new players and new risk management tools created in response to fast-moving market forces. The new landscape is depicted in **Figure 9–3 below**. The evolution from the "merchant pipeline" model in **Figure 9–2**, which used public utility regulation to control monopolistic pipelines, to the "open access," market-oriented model of **Figure 9–3** took place without a change in the Natural Gas Act of 1938, through the efforts of FERC and the District of Columbia Circuit Court of Appeals (which has exclusive jurisdiction over FERC orders) from the 1970s through 1990.

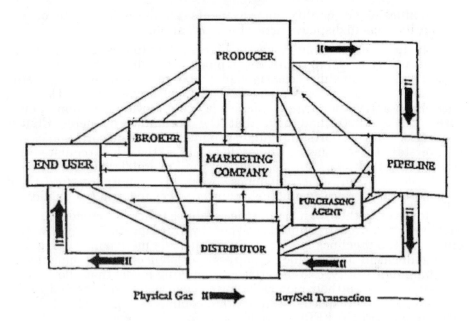

Figure 9–3
Today's Marketplace for Gas

B. FEDERAL FRAMEWORK OF NATURAL GAS REGULATION

1. THE NATURAL GAS ACT OF 1938

The Natural Gas Act of 1938 still operates today, largely unchanged, but it is now clothed in almost eight decades of case law interpretation, including the famous, or rather infamous, case of *Phillips v. Wisconsin* that has been blamed for creating the serious gas shortages of the 1960s and 1970s. A second statute, the Natural Gas Policy Act (NGPA) of 1978, was enacted to overrule the *Phillips* case and undo the gas shortages. This Act died a well-deserved death (in the opinion of most observers) when Congress passed the Wellhead Decontrol Act of 1989, decreeing the end of federal price controls on all gas as of 1993.

A cogent scholar of natural gas regulation summarizes the transition in Richard J. Pierce, Jr., The Evolution of Natural Gas Regulatory Policy, Nat. Resources & Env't 53 (Summer 1995):

> Deregulation of the market for natural gas surely ranks as one of the most significant accomplishments in natural resources law over the past decade. During the period 1985 to 1995, the Federal Energy Regulatory Commission (FERC) accomplished this massive task by, in effect, reversing through regulatory decisionmaking a pair of unfortunate public policy errors made by Congress in 1938 and by the U.S. Supreme Court in 1954. The results of FERC's carefully constructed deregulatory program are impressive. They include at least a $5 billion annual improvement in aggregate social welfare and

significant air quality improvements attributable to use of natural gas to displace dirtier fuels. *Id.* at 53.

The first mistake that Professor Pierce refers to was the adoption of a public utility model to regulate gas pipelines in the 1938 Natural Gas Act. Interstate pipelines clearly had to be regulated by the federal government because they were natural monopolies characterized by high barriers to entry and large economies of scale. Several Supreme Court cases in the 1920s had held that the dormant Commerce Clause preempted states' efforts to regulate the interstate transportation of gas or interstate sales of gas at wholesale to LDCs (that then regulated the retail market for gas). A 1935 study by the Federal Trade Commission (FTC) found that the pipelines were over-charging for their transportation services using their market power to harm the public.

However, rather than forcing the pipelines to act as common carriers that were required to ship gas owned by third parties (which would eliminate the pipelines' power to act as the sole merchant, buying and selling all gas in the pipeline), Congress was lobbied by the companies to adopt a public utility, cost-of-service ratemaking model that allowed the companies to keep their monopoly power over gas producers and LDCs for gas sold or transported in interstate commerce. The Federal Power Commission (FPC), FERC's predecessor, had been created in 1935 to license hydropower facilities and the transmission and sale of electricity in interstate commerce (see Chapter 6). Congress gave FPC similar powers to regulate natural gas pipelines and wholesale sales of gas.

Here is the jurisdictional authority of FERC under section 1(b) of the Natural Gas Act (15 U.S.C. § 717(b)):

> [T]his chapter shall apply to the transportation of natural gas in interstate commerce, to the sale in interstate commerce of natural gas for resale for ultimate public consumption for domestic, commercial, industrial, or any other use, and to natural-gas companies engaged in such transportation or sale, . . . but shall not apply to any other transportation or sale of natural gas or to the local distribution of natural gas or to the facilities used for such distribution or to the production or gathering of natural gas.

The second major mistake identified by Professor Pierce was made by the Supreme Court, not Congress. In a close decision (5–4) in *Phillips Petroleum Co. v. Wisconsin*, 347 U.S. 672 (1954), the majority held that the NGA required FPC to regulate the price of natural gas sold by independent gas producers at the well head into interstate commerce.

The *Phillips* case arose in the following setting: Phillips Petroleum was a gas producer engaged in the production, gathering, processing and sale of gas. It did not engage in the interstate transmission of gas and it was not affiliated with any interstate pipeline company. Phillips simply sold its gas to five different interstate pipeline companies that then transported and resold it to consumers and LDCs in 14 different states.

For more than two decades, many end users had been buying gas under 20-year contracts at prices fixed in the 1930s when gas supplies were in huge excess. Prices in many of these contracts were set at about one cent per thousand cubic feet (MCF). After World War II, new pipelines opened up large Eastern markets. The demand for gas increased briskly and the amount available to market slowed as producers reinjected gas back into reservoirs in order to increase oil recovery. Gas prices responded to the forces of supply and demand and started to advance. By the mid-1950s, many old gas contracts came up for renewal, and prices were jumping as much as ten-fold to about 15 cents per MCF. Lawyers in the cold state of Wisconsin argued that FPC was required to regulate the wellhead price of gas under the language of section 1(b) quoted above.

FPC issued an order denying jurisdiction over independent producers like Phillips, based on the express exemption of "production and gathering" in the statute. The FPC therefore refused to investigate the reasonableness of Phillips's gas prices. This set the stage for the Supreme Court's majority opinion interpreting section 1(b) as follows:

> In general, petitioners [Phillips, and the state of Texas] contend that Congress intended to regulate only the interstate pipeline companies since certain alleged excesses of those companies were the evil which brought about the legislation. If such were the case, we have difficulty in perceiving why the Commission's jurisdiction over the transportation *or* sale for resale in interstate commerce of natural gas is granted in the disjunctive. It would have sufficed to give the Commission jurisdiction over only those natural-gas companies that engage in "transportation" or "transportation and sale for resale" in interstate commerce, if only interstate pipeline companies were intended to be covered.

> Rather we believe that the legislative history indicates a congressional intent to give the Commission jurisdiction over the rates of all wholesales of natural gas in interstate commerce, whether by a pipeline company or not and whether occurring before, during or after transmission by an interstate pipeline company. There can be no dispute that the overriding congressional purpose was to plug the "gap" in regulation of natural-gas companies resulting from judicial decisions prohibiting on federal constitutional grounds, state regulation of many of the interstate commerce aspects of the natural-gas business.

>   * * *

> Regulation of the sales in interstate commerce for resale made by a so-called independent natural-gas producer is not essentially different from regulation of such sales when made by an affiliate of an interstate pipeline company. In both cases, the rates charged may have a direct and substantial effect on the price paid by the ultimate consumers. Protection of consumers against exploitation at the hands of natural-gas companies was the primary aim of the Natural Gas Act.

Id. at 682–83, 685. Justice Douglas dissented:

> The sale by this independent producer is a "sale in interstate commerce . . . for resale." It is also an integral part of "the production or gathering of natural gas." So we must make a choice. . . .

There are practical considerations which . . . lead me to conclude that we should not reverse the Commission in the present case. If Phillips' sales can be regulated, then the Commission can set a rate base for Phillips. A rate base for Phillips must of necessity include all of Phillips' producing and gathering properties; and supervision over its operating expenses. . . . The fastening of rate regulation on this independent producer brings "the production or gathering of natural gas" under effective federal control, in spite of the fact that Congress has made that phase exempt from regulation. The effect is certain to be profound. . . . The sales price determines his profits. And his profits and the profits of all the other gatherers, whose gas moves into the interstate pipelines, have profound effects on the rate of production, the methods of production, the old wells that are continued in production, the new ones explored, etc. Regulating the price at which the independent producer can sell his gas regulates his business in the most vital way any business can be regulated. That regulation largely nullifies the exemption granted by Congress.

Id. at 690. Justices Clark and Burton also dissented, citing additional concerns:

The states have been for over 35 years and are now enforcing regulatory laws covering production and gathering, proration of gas, ratable taking, unitization of fields, processing of casinghead gas, . . . well spacing, repressuring, abandonment of wells, . . . and other devices. There can be no doubt that federal regulation of production and gathering will collide and substantially interfere with and hinder the enforcement of these state regulatory measures. We cannot square this result with the House Report on this Act which states that the subsequently enacted bill "is so drawn as to complement and in no manner usurp State regulatory authority."

Id. at 695–96.

Thus, by the vote of one justice, producers in the United States became subject to FPC cost-of-service ratemaking for any gas they sold at the well head to an interstate pipeline. Yet producers were not natural monopolists; hundreds of producers in Texas alone competed to acquire leases and to produce and sell the oil and gas they discovered. The effect of imposing price controls on the first sale of gas into interstate commerce became readily evident over the next few years. Shortages of gas developed in the interstate market because the price was set at below-market rates that did not reflect the increased demand for gas in the post-war economy. Moreover, FPC shortly faced a backlog of 2,900 rate cases as hundreds of producers sought FPC authorization for their sales. Pierce, *supra,* at 54. By 1969, interstate pipelines were forced to decrease their deliveries to LDCs. Gas service was curtailed to thousands of manufacturing plants in the harsh winter of 1976–1977, schools were closed, and workers went unpaid because their companies closed. The natural gas shortages added to the pain consumers were feeling at the gasoline pump and in heating oil bills because of tumultuous Mideast events in the 1970s (see Chapter 4).

The *Phillips* decision foreseeably led to a dual system for selling natural gas: an intrastate and an interstate market. By 1978, producers' sales into the interstate market, with its low federally regulated prices, had dried up. Gas was available to intrastate users in the producing states, but only at a higher price. The 1976 gas delivery shortages to the East coast led to the popular Texas bumper sticker "Drive 70 and freeze a Yankee in the dark."

Congress had to act. It passed the Natural Gas Policy Act of 1978 (NGPA), instructing FERC to gradually deregulate the wellhead price of gas. Here is Professor Pierce's summary of the NGPA:

Richard J. Pierce, Jr., The Evolution of Natural Gas Regulatory Policy

Nat. Resources & Env't 53, 55, 84–85 (Summer 1995).

* * *

The NGPA regulatory regime was extraordinarily complicated: it divided gas supplies into over a score of different categories, each subject to different rules and statutory price ceilings. . . .

In one sense, NGPA was a major breakthrough. It was designed ultimately to deregulate the wellhead gas market, and it did create the conditions in which FERC ultimately was able to accomplish that task. In another sense however, NGPA was a catastrophe. Congress drafted NGPA based on the assumption that market forces are relatively weak and require many years to yield beneficial results. Congress assumed that the quantity of gas demanded and supplied would change slowly in response to changes in the price of gas. Thus, for instance, Congress scheduled deregulation to take place gradually over a period of many years, with most gas subject to constantly increasing statutory price ceilings for a decade or more. Congress expected the statutory ceiling prices to remain below the market price of gas for the entire period in which the NGPA authorized gradual replacement of ceiling prices with prices determined by market forces. Congress also expected the shortage to persist for many years. Instead, as the price of gas increased, the quantity of gas demanded fell rapidly, the quantity of gas supplied rose rapidly, and the market price of gas plummeted to well below the statutory ceiling prices.

* * *

Between 1985 and 1992, FERC took a series of regulatory actions that had the effect of reversing the many disastrous policy decisions that were made between 1938 and 1978. The details of FERC's successful strategy are too intricate to recount in this summary, but two regulatory actions formed the core of that strategy. The first took place in 1985 when FERC issued Order 436. That order used regulatory sticks and carrots to coerce interstate pipelines into agreeing to become "equal access" carriers; pipelines obligated themselves to transport gas owned by third parties on terms equivalent to the terms on which the pipelines transported their own gas. A year later, in Order 451, FERC changed the rules with respect to ceiling prices in ways that allowed producers and pipelines to adjust their prices to be compatible with the new relationship between gas supply and demand. The Order 436 equal access policy and the Order 451 flexible pricing policy went a long way toward eliminating pipelines' monopoly power in the wholesale gas market and toward forcing producers and pipelines to sell gas at market-based prices. With pipelines operating under equal access tariffs, LDCs and industrial consumers were free to buy gas directly from thousands of producers and independent marketers. That access to competing suppliers forced pipelines and producers to lower their prices significantly. Consumer prices plummeted; the quantity of gas consumed increased; and, the gas surplus began to dissipate.

* * *

By 1989, Congress was sufficiently impressed with the results of FERC's regulatory restructuring that it enacted the Natural Gas Wellhead Decontrol Act. That statute ratified FERC's de facto deregulation of the gas sales market, formally eliminated all wellhead price ceilings effective on January 1, 1993, and encouraged FERC to take such further actions as it deemed appropriate to create a fully competitive gas sales market. . . . In 1992 FERC issued Order 636. That order completed the process of deregulating the gas sales market. It required interstate pipelines to provide fully unbundled services; henceforth, pipelines were required to sell separately transportation services, storage services, and natural gas. After Order 636, LDCs and industrial consumers were free to purchase gas, storage services, and even transportation services from scores of potential suppliers.

The participants in the gas market have responded to the spur of competition by implementing numerous efficiency-enhancing commercial and technological innovations. Gas is being found, produced, stored, and transported at much lower cost than was the case a decade ago. Gas is traded constantly at dozens of market hubs at constantly changing spot prices. Hundreds of new pipeline interconnections have transformed the previously fragmented transportation system into a closely integrated network that links all North American supplies with all markets in the United States and Canada. Electronic bulletin boards allow market participants to engage in continuous trade with respect to transportation capacity so that all gas can move from supply areas to market areas over the least expensive route. Market participants have changed their methods of using storage in a variety of ways that have simultaneously reduced costs and increased service reliability. ■

The NGPA unified FERC control over all natural gas production, both intrastate and interstate, so that a national policy could be exerted over all gas sales. The Act deregulated most gas prices gradually by January 1, 1985, protecting residential and commercial consumers from huge, abrupt price shocks. At the same time, the NGPA sought to prevent producers from collecting monopoly rents or excess profits on "old" gas from already existing wells, while still encouraging producers to drill new wells to alleviate shortages by offering incentive prices on newly discovered gas, especially from high-cost areas, such as offshore. Finally, the Act sought to promote the flow of gas from the intrastate market into the interstate market where shortages were most severe.

In the long run, natural gas prices were freed from the utility-type, cost-of-service ratemaking imposed on it by the *Phillips* case. The path to this end result was rocky, however, because of the multi-billion dollar take-or-pay (TOP) problem which grew out of the private system of long-term contracts that pipeline merchants had with producers. A brief discussion of TOP contracts is worth noting because TOP provisions appear today in wind power leases and also in the long-term sales contracts used internationally. For example, utilities and end users in European nations have TOP contracts to buy gas from Russia's Gazprom for many years.

2. TAKE-OR-PAY CONTRACTS, RATE DESIGN AND MARKET FORCES UNDER THE NGPA

Most contracts between selling producers and pipeline purchasers negotiated in the 1970s were for long-term sales commitments and contained a TOP provision similar to the following:

> Seller agrees to sell and deliver to Buyer, and Buyer agrees to purchase and take, or pay for if available and not taken, Seller's pro rata part of the following quantities of gas produced from the reserves committed to this contract, to wit, a Quantity of gas equal to 85% of Seller's delivery capacity.

The TOP provision guaranteed producers a minimum cash flow in return for dedicating the producer's gas to one pipeline purchaser. Once dedicated, the gas could not be sold to others, even if the contracted purchaser did not take the gas. Producers wanted assurance against the risk that the dedicated purchaser would keep the gas in the ground, as a "bank" account of reserve gas. If the purchaser did so, the TOP clause assured the producer that it would nonetheless be paid for the gas not taken. The interstate pipelines were desperate for additional gas supplies and were sure that gas shortages would last forever. They had not been able to compete for more supplies on the basis of price because of federal price controls. Thus, they competed by giving producers other favorable contract provisions to lure them into signing up. Pipelines were happy to pay this non-price premium for gas because they expected to take all the gas that was dedicated and pay little or nothing as TOP payments. TOP percentages increased from 35% to 90% during the gas shortages of the 1970s. *See* John Lowe, Oil and Gas Law 288–90 (West 1995).

These long-term TOP contracts, coupled with FERC policies and utility rate design, prevented the pricing of natural gas in the newly deregulating markets from reflecting its true market price. FERC allowed "rolled-in" gas pricing. Under the NGPA, old gas continued to be underpriced to protect consumers. Rolled-in pricing allowed pipelines to average the price of low-cost gas with the price of new, much higher-priced gas. Thinking that shortages would last forever, the pipelines eagerly bid higher prices for new gas that was largely price-deregulated by 1979 under the NGPA's regime. Thus, the price of decontrolled "deep" gas category soared to $9.00 per MCF by 1980, while old gas vintages sold for 50 cents per MCF. The pipelines passed the higher weighted average cost of old and new gas along to the LDCs, which then passed the cost on to consumers. From 1978 to 1984, natural gas prices increased substantially.

The higher prices had two effects: On the supply side, they spurred considerable additional drilling and new production. On the demand side, end users of natural gas that could switch to a cheaper fuel source, such as coal or heavy fuel oil, did so (although gas could command a premium under newly strengthened clean air act laws because it burned more cleanly). Other end users adopted conservation practices, such as more efficient furnaces or better insulation. By 1981, high oil prices caused by the Arab oil embargo had resulted in large-scale energy conservation, and oil prices started to fall. Gas prices, however, continued to rise under the combination of the NGPA's provisions and the TOP contracts. By 1982, excess demand for gas no longer existed; twenty years of gas shortages had ended. James M. Griffin & Henry B. Steele, Energy Economics and Policy 301–303 (2d ed. 1986).

Indeed, by 1982, a gas supply surplus, called the "bubble" appeared. Yet, the TOP contracts had the perverse market effect of causing a rise in gas prices even though there was now a glut of gas. Industrial users in particular no longer demanded as much natural gas, but pipeline purchasers had committed to buy high volumes of gas from producers at high prices or pay for the gas not taken. As Griffin and Steele vividly note, the TOP contracts "became the casket in which pipelines were to be buried." *Id.* at 301. Pipeline bankruptcy loomed large.

Because pipelines had to pay for gas that they could not sell in a shrunken gas market, they strove to minimize their TOP liabilities to producers by shutting in the lowest-cost gas (and paying producers for not taking that gas) and producing the highest-cost gas. This policy maximized the pipelines' supply costs, the exact opposite of what competitive firms usually strive to do, but, it was a perfectly logical approach given the regulatory, contractual and market constraints confronting the pipelines. Griffin and Steele continue: "As the January 1, 1985 deadline for gas price deregulation approached, demand was falling, prices to consumers were rising, gas producers were suffering from a burden of shut-in production, many pipelines were grasping at the straws of legal doctrines such as force majeure to save them from ruin, and the FERC was having difficulties explaining how gas prices could have risen so rapidly under continued price regulation." *Id.* at 303.

Consider this scenario, which FERC confronted on its march to restructure natural gas markets. "Transco" pipeline, the only pipeline serving the "Harper field," signed long-term contracts during the first years under the NGPA when gas shortages still existed. Transco offered to buy gas from all the producers in the Harper gas field for $5 per MCF with a 90% TOP provision. The NGPA allowed this price, which was far above historical prices, because the cost was price-deregulated, "high cost" gas. One independent producer, "SpotCo," the owner of 5% of the reserves in the field, refused to sign a long-term contract. Instead it sold all of its gas to Transco on short-term (30-day) contracts at a spot-market price. For a while after 1979, the spot market price rose to $8 per MCF, significantly higher than the long-term contract price of $5. SpotCo was glad that it had refused Transco's offer of a long-term, fixed price contract. However, as the gas shortage became a surplus, the spot market price dropped to $2 an MCF. The LDC that bought Transco's gas lost industrial customers that switched to lower-priced fuels. Without this demand source, Transco no longer had a market to supply 90% of the deliverability of the wells in the Harper field and it had to cut back production. If Transco reduced its purchases under the long-term contracts, it would still have to pay for the $5 gas not taken because of the TOP provision. So Transco opted not to renew its short-term contract with SpotCo. In short, Transco had the incentive to buy high-cost gas under its TOP contracts, not low-cost gas at the current market price.

Truly, natural gas markets were tied into a Gordian knot of dysfunction. Two parties in particular were losers in this scenario: SpotCo, the low-priced producer whose wells were shut in because it had no pipeline access to a market; and Transco, whose TOP liability to high-priced producers was driving it into bankruptcy because it had no end users willing to pay for high-priced gas. A third group, those producers that did have TOP contracts with Transco, were also unhappy because Transco was not taking their high-priced gas, but also was not honoring its TOP obligation. Transco owed them billions of dollars.

Surely there was room to maneuver a workable solution that would move market participants away from the brink of bankruptcy caused by dysfunctional contracts and regulation.

In one of the first cases to address this Gordian knot scenario, the U.S. Supreme Court held that an order issued by the State Oil and Gas Board of Mississippi (the state's conservation commission), directing an interstate pipeline like Transco to take gas offered by an independent producer like SpotCo, impermissibly intruded on the Congressional mandate that FERC comprehensively regulate the natural gas market that it had now been charged with deregulating. Transcontinental Gas Pipe Line Corp. v. State Oil & Gas Board of Mississippi, 474 U.S. 409 (1986). The Court offered its view of what post-NGPA federal regulation was now to accomplish compared to its earlier view in *Phillips* that FERC's mandate was to keep prices to consumers low:

> The aim of federal regulation remains to assure adequate supplies of natural gas at fair prices, but the NGPA reflects a congressional belief that a new system of natural gas pricing was needed to balance supply and demand. The new federal role is to "overse[e] a national market price regulatory scheme." *See* S.Rep. No. 95–436, at 21 (NGPA implements "a new commodity value pricing approach").

> That FERC can no longer step in to regulate directly the prices at which pipelines purchase [price-deregulated] gas, however, has little to do with whether state regulations that affect a pipeline's cost and purchasing patterns impermissibly intrude upon federal concerns. Mississippi's action directly undermines Congress' determination that the supply, the demand, and the price of [NGPA-deregulated] gas be determined by market forces. . . . [Congress wanted] to leave determination of supply and first-sale [i.e., wellhead] price to the market. 474 U.S. at 421–22.

The Court further explained that Mississippi's order would disturb the "uniformity of the federal scheme" envisioned by Congress under the NGPA. Congress had enacted a "comprehensive federal regulatory scheme to give market forces a more significant role in determining the supply, the demand, and the price of natural gas." *Id*. at 422. The Mississippi order would have the effect of increasing prices to consumers by forcing Transco to take delivery of the noncontract gas offered by SpotCo. Because pipelines were already committed to take gas in excess of market demand, Transco would have to reduce its purchases of gas from its contract customers, thus increasing the pipeline's take-or-pay liabilities. Transco's customers would ultimately have to bear this cost. In short, Mississippi's order was preempted by the new federal scheme.

The task of unwinding the TOP contracts and opening up pipeline access to allow market forces to determine the price of natural gas production now fell to FERC, unimpeded by state conservation orders.

3. OPEN ACCESS FOR ALL: ORDER 636

By 1985, natural gas production had been freed of the pervasive price regulation once imposed on gas producers. Now it was time to tackle the gas transportation sector. In 1985, FERC began issuing a series of orders to transform gas pipelines into open-access common carriers, the regulatory model which Congress had failed to enact in 1938.

Today, the natural gas business would hardly be recognized by the people who knew it in the 1970s. A highly regulated, conservative industry has been transformed into a competitive business featuring entrepreneurs and marketers who would be equally at home on Wall Street. (Refer back to **Figures 9–2** and **9–3** to view the changing landscape.) However, the transformation took more than a decade and had major obstacles to overcome, especially because of the rigidity of long-term contracts entered into under the Natural Gas Act and during the early years of the NGPA.

The FERC order that crowned its efforts to transform pipelines into common carriers was Order 636. Before its issuance, FERC had cautiously opened up opportunities for producers that had TOP contracts with pipelines to deal directly with large industrial end users that wanted to buy gas at its low market price, not the high contract price in the producers' contracts with the pipeline. The "carrot" offered to the pipeline by the producer to induce it to carry third-party gas was a credit against its TOP liability to the producer for every unit of gas released from the long-term contract and then sold to the industrial end user. These voluntary "Special Marketing Programs" were a start, but much more was needed. Full-scale restructuring of the industry demanded that all pipelines become open-access pipelines, obligated to transport the gas owned by all groups of end users (not just industrials) without discrimination, on the same basic rates and terms as any gas still owned by the pipeline as a merchant. In 1992, FERC issued its famous Order 636: Full restructuring had arrived. Pipelines would become like railroads and trucks, obligated to carry goods owned by others.

Here is an overview of the key provisions of Order 636:

a. Functional unbundling. The widely used term for the separation of one line of business from another is "unbundling." The pipelines were directed to separate their gas merchant sales services from their transportation services. This required changes in the internal organization of the companies that, in the past, had primarily transported only gas they bought and sold themselves. Because the pipelines were not required to actually divest themselves of one of these two divisions, Order 636 did not require a true unbundling, although the pipelines had the option to do so. The Order only demanded that an internal "fire wall" be created within the company to prevent the exchange of information between the two divisions, except on the same terms as available to competitors. For this reason, the process became known as "functional" unbundling.

b.   Storage access. Most pipelines operate storage fields near their major markets, consisting of depleted oil or gas reservoirs into which gas can be pumped in the summer and withdrawn in the winter. Order 636 directed the pipelines to provide equal access to these storage fields to all shippers of gas and on terms comparable to the pipeline's own gas.

c.   Transportation access. Pipelines were required to file rate schedules ("tariffs") allowing all gas shippers to buy transportation services at the same rate that the pipeline charged customers who bought gas owned by the pipeline.

d.   Electronic notification. Pipelines were required to install information technology that would give their customers equal and timely access to the prices and conditions of transportation service. These are referred to as "electronic bulletin boards," or "EBBs."

e.   Capacity release. Pipelines were required to implement a "capacity release" program so that firm shippers, *i.e.,* those who have committed to pay for reserved space in the pipeline, can release unneeded space to others who can use the capacity to ship their own gas. Contracts for pipeline capacity are bought and sold on the EBBs.

f.   Common rate design. All pipelines were required to compute their rates for transportation services on the basis of the same formula, which shifted pipeline capital costs to the class of firm shippers rather than interruptible shippers. Cross-subsidizing residential customers by extracting revenues from interruptible industrial users to pay for the pipeline's fixed costs became a thing of the past.

g.   Market hubs. FERC prohibited practices that discouraged the formation of "market centers," or "hubs" where pipelines intersect, allowing customers to access many more transportation routes and choose between sellers from different natural gas production areas.

Order 636 was largely upheld on appeal in *United Distribution Companies v. FERC,* 88 F.3d 1105 (D.C. Cir. 1996). Despite its 150-page length, the court's opinion is largely congratulatory of FERC's effort to convert pipelines to common carriers and adopt more "light-handed" regulation while still meeting its mandate to protect consumers against pipelines' monopoly power. The D.C. Circuit plays an important policy-making role in administrative law, particularly in natural gas regulation where this court has often overruled FERC. FERC decisions are appealable directly to a circuit court of appeals, not to a district court. As a result of Byzantine multi-district litigation procedures, this case came to oral argument 3 1/2 years after Order 636 was issued and after most of the restructuring had already taken place.

4.   ISSUES ARISING UNDER ORDER 636 RESTRUCTURING

This section reviews some of the larger issues that FERC, and the courts reviewing its orders, confront in restructured gas markets.

The prickly issue of who would bear the burden of the staggering take-or-pay (TOP) liabilities that resulted from the restructuring has now been resolved, but the dollar sums show just how massive some of the transition costs were. Although producers and pipelines had settled many TOP claims before Order 636, after the order was issued, more customers canceled contracts to buy gas from the pipelines, forcing the pipelines to pay more TOP charges to producers. Orders 436 and 636 created massive TOP liabilities for those pipelines that converted to open access transportation service because their once-bundled customers mostly elected to convert bundled sales into a separate firm transportation contract and then make their own arrangements to buy cheaper gas from sources other than the pipeline's merchant gas. In Order 636, FERC authorized the pipelines to pass along all of these charges to customers, unlike its earlier orders which sought to force pipelines (and indirectly producers) to share some of the realignment costs. FERC's pre-Order 636 policy had permitted pipelines to surcharge their transportation customers for TOP costs only if the pipelines agreed to absorb between 25 and 50 percent of those costs.

In the end, it appears that many groups shared the TOP transition costs which totaled about $50 billion, or almost 60 percent of the 1985 value of final gas sales to end users. Interstate pipeline companies filed to recover about $10.4 billion in TOP costs, of which about $3.6 billion would be absorbed by pipeline company shareholders. The bulk of the debt was negotiated away in settlements between the pipeline companies and producers over the years. In many cases, the gas producers, or the parties who held the gas contracts as collateral, had to accept lower values for the contracts they held. Some costs were spread to the creditors of those pipelines that went bankrupt, and some costs may have been partially shifted to general taxpayers if losses were used as credits in calculating income taxes. Margaret Jess, Restructuring Energy Industries: Lessons from Natural Gas, in EIA, Natural Gas Monthly, at vii (May 1997).

These TOP costs clearly presented a "pig-in-the-python" problem for state public utility commissions. (PUCs). Suppose, for example, that a pipeline paid $500 million to producers to settle TOP lawsuits and that FERC allowed the pipeline to pass these costs along to its customers, many of whom were LDCs. LDCs then sought to recoup these costs from their end-use customers in retail rates regulated by the state PUC. The state courts were called upon to police the rate formulas that the PUCs designed to allow their LDCs to recover the costs of what Professor Pierce rightly called "two unfortunate policy mistakes" made at the federal level. *See, e.g.*, Hamm v. Pub. Serv. Comm'n of S.C., 425 S.E.2d 28 (S.C. 1992).

Lest one think that TOP contracts are now a thing of the past in the United States, some recent wind power purchase agreements with electricity providers include fixed-price, long-term TOP provisions favoring the wind generator. One commenter warns that electricity providers in competitive retail markets are setting themselves up for large losses, when cheaper wind power from newer, bigger turbines and power from low-cost shale gas render their purchase obligations uneconomic. Scott Looper, Take-or-Pay Crisis V2.0: What Wind Power Generators and Providers Failed to Learn from Gas Pipeline's 1980 Dilemma, 33 Hous. J. Int'l L. 303 (2011).

TOP contracts do not cause prolonged distress if the price that the buyer promises to pay adjusts flexibly when market conditions change.

Real hardship ensues when buyers promise to take or pay for minimum quantities of gas (or wind) at a fixed price that then becomes uncompetitive. Long-term sales-and-purchase agreements, such as those for LNG, may contain price reopener clauses that allow the parties to adjust the price if unforeseeable market conditions arise. Outside of the United States, buyers of LNG (such as a public utility in Japan or Korea) often agree to pay a gas price based linked to the prices of crude oil or competing fuels in the domestic market of the buyer. Since 2009 and the shale gas production boom in the United States, the price of domestic U.S. natural gas has become delinked from the price of oil. While U.S. buyers paid about $4 per MMBTU for gas in 2013, Asian buyers often paid $14 per MMBTU under their long-term LNG contracts. A global spot market for LNG has begun to open up that offers LNG at prices much lower than $14. Price reopener clauses in the Asian LNG contracts may be triggered by the new market conditions, arising from the U.S. shale revolution and projected exports of LNG from the United States. *See* James Baily & Rachel Lidgate, 7 J. World Energy L. & Bus. 140 (2014) (discussing the types of triggers and procedures contained in price reopener provisions of long-term gas contracts).

The following sections address some continuing issues that arise in restructured gas markets.

a. FUNCTIONAL UNBUNDLING AND AFFILIATES

To comply with Order 636's functional unbundling requirements, most pipelines set up separate marketing entities. These marketing entities were not to receive any information from their pipeline affiliate that was not also made available to competitors. Shippers filed a number of complaints with FERC alleging violations by pipelines and their marketing affiliates of the "fire wall" requirements. Most complaints were resolved through negotiations (*see, e.g.,* In re Transcontinental Gas Pipe Line Corp., 55 F.E.R.C. ¶ 61,318 (1991)), but a few resulted in the assessment of penalties against the pipelines. For example, in *Amoco Prod. Co. v. Natural Gas Pipeline Co. of Am.,* 82 F.E.R.C. ¶ 61,038 (1998), shippers alleged that the pipeline had violated Standard of Conduct G which states that "to the maximum extent practicable [a pipeline's] operating employees and the operating employees of its marketing affiliate must function independently of each other." 18 C.F.R. § 161.3(g) (1997). FERC found that the pipeline had created a System Optimization Group, composed of employees who had day-to-day duties and responsibilities for planning, directing, and carrying out gas-related operations including gas transportation, gas sales, or gas marketing activities for both the pipeline and its marketing affiliate. 82 F.E.R.C. ¶ 61,038. FERC also found that the System Optimization Group decided whether to accept transportation discounts from nonaffiliated shippers, provided its marketing affiliate with pricing inputs for its auction bids, and then evaluated the bids received. FERC assessed civil penalties of $8,840,000 against the pipeline but suspended half the penalty if the pipeline did not violate the rules again during the next two years. 83 F.E.R.C ¶ 61,197 at 3 (1998).

Implicit in the natural gas restructuring policy discussion is the premise that unbundling, or separating, services traditionally performed by the same pipeline is desirable as a matter of economic efficiency. As

FERC noted, the rationale for unbundling was to minimize distortions in the sales market caused by the market power that pipeline companies possessed in the transportation market. Yet, it is well recognized that vertical integration can be efficient. Vertical integration internalizes within the firm those transactions costs which otherwise must be incurred through contracting in the open market with third parties. In industries that demand high degrees of fixed capital, the internalization of such transactions costs by building company-owned production or distribution infrastructures is often an efficient response to market uncertainties that cannot be easily contracted away. *See* Ronald H. Coase, The Nature of the Firm, 4 Economica 386 (1937); Oliver E. Williamson, The Mechanisms of Governance (1996); Oliver E. Williamson, Transaction Cost Economics: The Governance of Contractual Relationships, 22 J. L. & Econ. 233 (1979). In addition, operating and engineering (or network) efficiencies can be gained through vertical integration. *See* Alfred E. Kahn, The Economics of Regulation: Principles and Institutions 157–58 (1988).

From the perspective of economic efficiency, then, it is not so clear that unbundling the market is more efficient than allowing vertical integration. Mandatory unbundling was FERC's response to taming the power and incentive of pipelines to favor their own gas shipments. But FERC has struggled to control the marketing affiliates of the unbundled pipelines, as discussed in the assessment of restructured gas markets in Section C, *infra* (Order 2004).

b.   RATE DESIGN: ROLLED-IN RATES FOR NEW PIPELINE CAPACITY

Another contentious issue of rate design is rolled-in versus incremental rates. When a pipeline builds a new segment of its system, should the cost of that segment be paid solely by the customers who will be served by it, or should those costs be "rolled-in" to the overall rate base and distributed among all of the pipeline's customers?

In *Midcoast Interstate Transmission, Inc. v. FERC,* 198 F.3d 960 (D.C. Cir. 2000), the court held that FERC had properly authorized rolling-in the cost of new pipeline construction into the company's system-wide rates because there would be system-wide benefits to consumers and because the impact on system-wide rates would be minimal. This case starkly illustrates how the choice between rolled-in and incremental rates can affect competing pipelines. Midcoast and Southern Colonial were both competing to bring new pipeline capacity to the same Alabama market. FERC granted Southern's application to construct a new pipeline. Midcoast appealed this FERC order as an aggrieved party. It argued that if FERC had required incremental pricing, Southern would have had to charge users of the new pipeline an incremental rate of $10.00 in addition to its system-wide rate of $8.80 per decatherm per month. Midcoast proposed to charge a total rate of only $8.60 to the users of the new pipeline. If Southern were allowed to roll in the costs of the new pipeline, rates would not rise by more than five percent because large pipeline systems like Southern's can spread the costs over its existing system-wide customers. The cost of the new facilities is subsidized by existing users, to the detriment of smaller competitors like Midcoast. *See also* Transcontinental Gas Pipeline Corp. v. FERC, 518 F.3d 916 (D.C. Cir. 2008) (absent proof of any specific, direct benefits to existing customers from additional compressors installed to serve new customers, FERC's order allocating all expansion costs, both construction costs and additional electricity costs for new compressors, to new customers was just and reasonable; strong dissent arguing that incremental pricing for the additional electricity costs of the new compressors would disrupt integrated operations and result in grossly unfair charges to the new customers).

c.   SPOT AND FUTURES MARKETS: OVER-RELIANCE ON SHORT-TERM CONTRACTS?

Today, most natural gas is purchased through contracts on the spot market. These transactions are short-term (*i.e.*, for a term of less than a year, usually 30 days) and are generally interruptible. These contracts respond to current market prices, but also expose the parties to the risks of price volatility or service interruption. In fact, price spikes have become part of the restructured gas markets.

The development of spot markets in physical sales of gas went hand-in-hand with the creation of a natural gas futures market on the New York Mercantile Exchange (NYMEX), which allows buyers and sellers of physical volumes of gas to hedge their price risks on a clearinghouse exchange, thus reducing their exposure to price volatility. NYMEX prices are quoted daily and provide price signals to all market participants. Visit www.nymex.com. Futures markets also allow speculators to invest in complex financial derivatives tied to commodity prices, such as swaps, options, caps, floors and collars. Speculators willingly take on price risk in the hope that they can "beat the market." Unlike hedgers, financial speculators have no interest in owning actual physical volumes of natural gas. Financial derivatives are not traded on NYMEX or other such regulated exchanges; they were exempted from regulation by the Commodities Futures Trading Commission (CFTC) in what was called the "Enron loophole" (which the Dodd-Frank Act later closed). Derivatives can create more efficient markets by transferring risk from hedgers to speculators, promoting information dissemination and price discovery, and creating a broader, more liquid market. For a more complete analysis of natural gas derivatives, see Mark E. Haedicke, Gas Commodity Markets, in 4 Energy Law and Transactions, Ch. 88 (David J. Muchow & William A. Mogel eds., 2014).

The array of new financial products created after restructuring can help large users of natural gas insure their operations against losses from rapid fluctuations in the price of natural gas. The value of these financial risk management tools was not tested until after 2000 because prices were quite stable in the 1990s, compared to the price shocks of the 1970s and 1980s.

When tested during the California energy crisis of 2000–2001, serious problems were discovered with the linkages between the physical sales of natural gas and these financial markets, as explained in Section C(2) *infra*.

Even before then, Professor Pierce, a strong advocate of deregulated markets, worried about over-reliance of market participants on short-term contracts both for gas purchases and for transportation service. The switch to a competitive gas market became possible because so many new pipelines had been built that most market areas had reasonably good access to more than one pipeline and because pipeline capacity had largely caught up with demand. Thus, few pipelines had monopoly positions and there was less need for major new capital facilities that could be financed only on the basis of long-term contracts. Still, Professor Pierce argued that this reliance on the spot market and interruptible transportation would not encourage adequate future investment in the gas chain from production to pipelines to power plants that used gas as a fuel. The financing of major capacity additions, especially for pipelines, would require long-term, firm contracts between the actors in this value chain. Private parties seemed overly reluctant to enter into these long-term contracts because of "bad experiences" with regulators who nullified or modified contracts or who passed regulations that had the effect of altering contracts, which many parties then refused to honor. Richard J. Pierce, Jr., Experiences with Natural Gas Regulation and Competition in the U.S. Federal System: Lessons for Europe, in Natural Gas in the Internal Market 125 (Ernst J. Mestmäcker, ed., 1993); *see also* Jeffrey Petrash, Long-Term Natural Gas Contracts: Dead, Dying, or Merely Resting?, 27 Energy L.J. 545 (2006) (arguing that regulators should assess ways to encourage longer-term contracts for both gas transportation service and supplies).

This anxiety about reliance on short-term markets spills over into the bigger issue of reliability. Will deregulated markets reliably supply both the natural gas molecules and the pipeline services that are needed to bring gas to end users when untoward events occur, such as an Arctic blast that hangs over half of the landmass of the United States for a week, or a major pipeline rupture that shuts down a transmission line for days? Section C(5) *infra* discusses the post-2000 problems that have indeed developed with the interface between gas pipelines and generating plants using natural gas during extreme weather events.

Meanwhile, the two cases that follow immediately below discuss FERC's approach to natural gas curtailments in Order 636's restructured industry.

d.   WHAT HAPPENS IN A SHORTAGE? CURTAILMENT AND THE MARKET

In its Order 636, FERC displayed a nearly unbridled faith in the power of markets to assure reliability and to protect citizens from the real harm caused by disruptions to gas service that could leave homes and hospitals without heat. The D.C. Circuit, in its review of Order 636, was not quite so sanguine about the issue. The following is an excerpt from the opinion in the case reviewing Order 636's "curtailment" policy, in which the court cautions FERC not to overly embrace markets, private contracts and self-help forms of relief in times when pipelines are constrained from carrying all of the gas demanded by its customers. The court carefully contrasts curtailments caused by a shortage of natural gas supply from curtailments caused by a shortage of pipeline capacity.

United Distribution Companies v. FERC
88 F.3d 1105 (D.C. Cir. 1996).

■ PER CURIAM. In Order No. 636, the Federal Energy Regulatory Commission (Commission or FERC) took the latest step in its decade-long restructuring of the natural gas industry, in which the Commission has gradually withdrawn from direct regulation of certain industry sectors in favor of a policy of "light-handed regulation" when market forces make that possible. . . .

II.C.   Curtailment

When supply shortages arose in the natural gas industry during the 1970s, the Commission adopted end-use curtailment plans to protect high-priority customers from an interruption of supply. *See generally Consolidated Edison Co. v. FERC*, 676 F.2d 763, 765–67 (D.C. Cir. 1982); *North Carolina v. FERC*, 584 F.2d 1003, 1006–08 (D.C. Cir. 1978). In 1973, the Commission found itself "impelled to direct curtailment on the basis of end use rather than on the basis of contract simply because contracts do not necessarily serve the public interest requirement of efficient allocation of this wasting resource." Order No. 467, 49 F.P.C. 85, 86. The Commission's end-use curtailment schemes were essentially enacted into law by title IV of the Natural Gas Policy Act of 1978 (NGPA), which establishes the following priority system:

Whenever there is an insufficient supply, under the Act first in line to receive gas are schools, small business, residences, hospitals, and all others for whom a curtailment of natural gas could endanger life, health, or the maintenance of physical property. After these "high-priority" users have been satisfied, next in line are those who will put the gas to "essential agricultural uses," followed by those who will use the gas for "essential industrial process or feedstock uses," followed by everyone else.

With the introduction of stand-alone firm-transportation service in Order No. 436, the Commission distinguished for the first time between supply curtailment and capacity curtailment. Transportation service can suffer from a capacity interruption (such as a force majeure loss of capacity due to pipeline system failure or a pipeline's overbooking of capacity), whereas sales service can suffer from a shortage in the supply of gas. The Commission's subsequent approach was to allow pipelines to adopt pro rata capacity curtailment (allocation proportional to the amount reserved, without regard to end use), *see, e.g.*, Texas Eastern Transmission Corp., 37 F.E.R.C. ¶ 61,260, at 61,692–93 (1986), *order on reh'g*, 41 F.E.R.C. ¶ 61,015 (1987), *aff'd sub nom.* Texaco, Inc. v. FERC, 886 F.2d 749 (5th Cir. 1989), unless the parties agreed to end-use capacity curtailment on a particular pipeline, *see, e.g.*, Florida Gas Transmission Co., 51 F.E.R.C. ¶ 61,309, at 62,010–11, *order on reh'g*, 53 F.E.R.C. ¶ 61,396 (1990).

[The court then explained why supply curtailments due to shortages of natural gas often affected the parties differently from capacity curtailments due to a pipeline not having enough space for all its customers. Gas shortages usually affect a broader market and are longer lasting than a pipeline capacity shortage, which is usually caused by some temporary bottleneck that appears unexpectedly in part of pipeline system. These capacity shortages often affect gas flows on only one segment of a pipeline and the customers can receive their gas by re-routing it to another pipeline or taking other self-help measures,]

[This court has] acknowledged that the NGA provided protections for capacity shortages. The court stated that "implicit in the consumer protection mandate is a duty to assure that consumers, especially high-priority consumers, have continuous access to needed supplies of natural gas." 993 F.2d at 895. This duty arises because " 'no single factor in the Commission's duty to protect the public can be more important to the public than the continuity of service provided.' " *Id.* (*quoting Sunray Mid-Continent Oil Co. v. Fed. Power Comm'n*, 239 F.2d 97, 101 (10th Cir. 1956), *rev'd on other grounds*, 353 U.S. 944 (1957)). . . .

In Order No. 636, . . . the Commission continued without change its curtailment policies [which required end-use curtailment, placing high-priority customers at the top of the list to get gas]. . . . [T]he Commission maintained that self-help measures would allow the consumer-protection mandate of the NGA to be satisfied by pro rata capacity curtailment:

> The Commission believes that with deregulated wellhead sales and a growing menu of options for unbundled pipeline service, customers should rely on prudent planning, private contracts, and the marketplace to the maximum extent practicable to secure both their capacity and supply needs. In today's environment, LDC's [sic] and end users no longer need to rely exclusively on their traditional pipeline supplier. Rather, to an ever-increasing degree they rely on private contracts with gas sellers, storage providers, and others; a more diverse portfolio of pipeline suppliers, where possible; local self-help measures (e.g., local production, peak shaving and storage); and their own gas supply planning through choosing between an increasing array of unbundled service options.

Id. at 30,590.

* * *

We review the Commission's policy on pro rata curtailment to determine whether it is "just and reasonable" under § 4 and whether it serves the "present or future public convenience and necessity" under § 7(e). The Commission decided that the consumer-protection mandate of the NGA did not require it to adopt end-use capacity curtailment across the board and promised to address the issue in each pipeline restructuring proceeding. Order No. 636–A, ¶ 30,950, at 30,591–92. Indeed, the Commission has broad latitude on whether to effectuate its policies in generic rulemakings or in individual-pipeline adjudications. The issue presented to us, then, is whether the Commission's decision that the NGA does not require end-use curtailment in all circumstances is "reasoned, principled, and based upon the record."

The Commission explained that Order No. 636 had allowed the development of market structures that would enable customers to take independent, market-based steps to avoid the need for Commission-mandated end-use curtailment. Order No. 636–A, ¶ 30,950, at 30,590. Moreover, the Commission found that since the enactment of the NGPA in 1978 "the industry has not experienced shortages beyond isolated, short-lived dislocation," *id.* at 30, 591, and "gas has always flowed according to the dictate of the market, i.e., to the heat sensitive users who need it most and who are thus willing to pay the prevailing market price for it." *Id.* at 30,592. This experience with the industry provides substantial evidence for the Commission's conclusion that end-use curtailment is not required in all circumstances.

We are unpersuaded, particularly in light of the Commission's own actions in the restructuring proceedings, that pro rata capacity curtailment would adequately protect all high-priority customers on all pipelines. The Commission's market-based alternatives for customers to avoid curtailment fall into the following categories: (1) arrangements with other pipelines; (2) arrangements with other gas sellers; (3) arrangements for gas storage; (4) arrangements with other customers (including the capacity-release mechanism); and (5) "peak shaving." First, arrangements with other pipelines are more widely available after Order No. 636, such as by using different pipelines that connect to one "market center," but a capacity constraint on a pipeline will still cut off delivery to any "captive customers," no matter how many transportation options some other customers may have. Second, arrangements with other gas sellers are by definition relevant only to supply curtailment, not to capacity curtailment. Third, arrangements for gas storage are unhelpful if the capacity interruption occurs at a point between the contract-storage area and the customer's receipt point. Fourth, obtaining gas from other customers, whether through the capacity-release mechanism or otherwise, depends upon the willingness of lower-priority customers to forgo deliveries. Fifth, practices such as "peak shaving" (letting a little gas go a longer way) can temporarily help to alleviate curtailment problems but cannot ensure continuous service if the interruption lasts too long. [Ed. note: Peak shaving adds propane-air mixtures to augment supplies of natural gas during peak demand.] None of these market-based solutions, therefore, can guarantee continuous service to all high-priority customers in cases of capacity interruptions. Many of the market-based solutions fail to acknowledge that many customers have far less control over access to pipeline capacity than they do over gas supply. In addition, some of the self-help mechanisms will be more readily available to larger pipeline customers. *City of Mesa*, 993 F.2d at 897.

[While FERC had clearly indicated that it strongly preferred pro rata curtailment to end-use curtailment in Order 636, the court noted that Order 636 did not preclude the use of curtailment plans that better protected high-priority customers. FERC had indicated that it would review each pipeline's curtailment policies on a case-by-case basis rather than in a generic rulemaking. In previous curtailment plans aimed at natural gas shortages rather than pipeline constraints, FERC had ordered pipelines to include provisions giving relief to any high priority shipper when that shipper had exercised all other self-help remedies in times of bona fide emergencies, or whenever necessary to avoid irreparable injury to life or property. FERC had even suggested that "there may be extraordinary circumstances when reasonable self-help efforts are insufficient, even for large customers," such that some emergency protections may always be required for certain force majeure capacity interruptions. *El Paso*, 69 F.E.R.C. ¶ 61,164, at 61,624; see also *United Gas Pipe Line Co.*, 65 F.E.R.C. ¶ 61,006, at 61,092, *reh'g denied sub nom. Koch Gateway Pipeline Co.*, 65 F.E.R.C. ¶ 61,338, at 62,630–31 (1993). Thus, the court concluded]:

We uphold the Commission's decision not to require end-use curtailment on a generic basis for capacity curtailment, but to proceed instead on a case-by-case basis. ∎

Two years later, in 1998, the same D.C. Circuit court confronted a case in which FERC had approved a tariff filing that included an "emergency" exception to pro rata capacity curtailment, in keeping with the admonition of the court in the *United Distributors* case that FERC had a duty to protect high-priority users. FERC included in its approval of the tariff a compensation formula that would reimburse the other users who were cut back more than their pro rata share in order to route gas to the user with the emergency. The D.C. Circuit again remanded aspects of FERC's curtailment policy for more reasoned decision making. In defense of its order, FERC raised the issue of its ability to monitor conditions in the fast-changing gas markets. This issue became a very real one from 2000 onwards when the California energy crisis revealed major problems with relying on short-term markets for gas and electricity.

Process Gas Consumers Group v. FERC

158 F.3d 591 (D.C. Cir. 1998).

■ WILLIAMS, J. In Order No. 636, FERC exercised its authority under § 5 of the Natural Gas Act, 15 U.S.C. § 717d, to require that natural gas pipeline companies unbundle their gas transportation and sales services and file tariffs in compliance with the order. The tariff filing at issue here provides that in the event of certain curtailments, customers with specified emergency conditions can secure exemption from curtailment. This of course increases the curtailment of the pipeline's other customers, which would otherwise have been pro rata. The tariff also calls for some compensation to be paid by the exempted customers to the customers who are additionally deprived. But the petitioners argue that the compensation approved by the Commission is so limited that it gives customers inadequate incentives to plan ahead to reduce the likelihood and severity of gas curtailment emergencies. . . .

Texas Eastern Transmission Corporation ("Tetco") made its compliance filing in 1992. The proposed tariff would have allowed Tetco to curtail service—even to "firm" transportation customers—in certain situations of force majeure or operational necessity. Such "capacity curtailment" was to be borne pro rata with two exceptions: first, to protect high priority end-uses, as defined by §§ 401 and 402 of the Natural Gas Policy Act, 15 U.S.C. §§ 3391–92, and second, to provide gas to customers for "emergency" situations, defined as ones where gas was necessary "to avoid irreparable injury to life or property (including environmental emergencies) or to provide for minimum plant protection." Prompted by the comments of NUI Corporation (Elizabethtown Gas Division) ("NUI/Elizabethtown"), the Commission rejected Tetco's first proposed exception to pro rata curtailment, finding that the priorities in the NGPA did not apply to capacity curtailment. *See Texas Eastern Transmission Corp.*, 62 F.E.R.C. ¶ 61,015 at 61,119 (1993). The Commission allowed the second exception, but required that Tetco's revised tariff "include compensation by the customer seeking the short term [emergency] exception to any other customer receiving more than its pro rata share of the capacity curtailment." *Id.* Tetco filed a revised tariff, including such a compensation measure, in February 1993.

The compensation provided, however, was quite limited. The tariff calls for increases in the exempted customer's bill by "the aggregate curtailment adjustment quantity requested by the Customer pursuant to [the emergency exemption] multiplied by the Reservation Charge Adjustment for the applicable rate schedule per Dth [Dekatherm] for the applicable zone"; this amount is then distributed to the customers who were curtailed more than pro rata because of the exemption. As we understand this, it means that although the advantaged customers have already paid a reservation charge for their entitlement to transportation, they pay a premium, proportional to that charge, for the transportation they enjoy above pro rata curtailment levels by virtue of their emergency condition. The proceeds go to the more deprived customers, in proportion to their deprivation.

[Petitioners NUI/ Elizabethtown, joined by large industrial users, petitioned for review of FERC's order on two grounds.] NUI/Elizabethtown argued that the compensation was inadequate, particularly for local distribution companies ("LDCs"). The increased curtailment for non-exempt customers removes these customers' regular access to part of their gas supply; this supply must be rerouted or replaced, often at a much higher cost. If no replacement can be found, the LDC customers lose the profit they would have made on the resale of the gas. NUI/Elizabethtown therefore proposed setting compensation either by these actual damage amounts (net replacement cost or lost margin) or by a "generic cost" calculated as "a stated percentage in excess of the spot gas price." The Industrial Groups raised an additional argument: that Tetco's compensation scheme gave bad incentives to its customers. Because an emergency exemption aids only customers without some backup capabilities of their own (such as "peak shaving" facilities), the low compensation rate allows these customers to free-ride on the costly contingency preparations of others. Between the grasshopper and the ant, in other words, Tetco's scheme favors the grasshopper and thus encourages his feckless ways. To correct this incentive problem, the Industrial Groups proposed compensation at "a predetermined amount that exceeds the cost of the most expensive gas sources or alternative fuels available to customers."

The Commission gave two reasons for rejecting these suggestions. First, the Commission pointed to the tariff's imbalance resolution procedures as an "adequate remedy" for the loss of gas supply. 63 F.E.R.C. ¶ 61,100 at 61,496; 64 F.E.R.C. ¶ 61,305 at 63,301. This seems to be a red herring. So far as appears, the imbalance procedures impose no cost on customers receiving emergency relief.

Second, the Commission claimed that "no party has put forth a plausible compensation scheme that could be adequately monitored by the Commission." 64 F.E.R.C. ¶ 61,305 at 63,301. But the Commission's opinions say nothing to explain how any of the petitioners' proposals is either implausible or impractical to monitor. . . . [T]he Commission itself has in related contexts embraced a compensation device tied to the spot gas price as the cash-out price used to resolve imbalances, see 62 F.E.R.C. ¶ 61,015 at 61,116–17, and, as compensation paid by those enjoying an emergency exemption from gas supply curtailment, see *Transcontinental Gas Pipe Line Corp.,* 72 F.E.R.C. ¶ 61,037 at 61,237–38 (1995). While we recognize that capacity curtailment and supply curtailment are not identical, the Commission has nowhere explained why the differences render use of a spot-price solution inappropriate here. Nor, to repeat, has it offered any explanation of the supposed deficiencies of the petitioners' other proposals.

If the Commission had grounds to reject petitioners' proposed alternatives, it has not revealed them. We accordingly remand the case for reconsideration.

So ordered. ∎

C. ASSESSMENT OF RESTRUCTURED GAS MARKETS

1. PRE-2000 ASSESSMENT

Professor Richard Pierce's assessment of gas restructuring, quoted at the start of this chapter, concluded that gas restructuring had succeeded by 1995. Restructuring had brought a $5 billion *annual* improvement in aggregate efficiency; cleaner air; commercial and technical innovations; and competitive markets that performed well in the harsh winter of 1993–1994. Another enthusiastic supporter of FERC Order 636 marveled that federal regulators—of all people!—had restructured the pipelines into competitive entities, no longer operating under "incompetent regulation and redistributionist politics." Robert J. Michaels, The New Age of Natural Gas: How the Regulators Brought Competition, Reg. 68 (Winter 1993). Their former captive customers could now customize their own deals with gas producers, using the pipeline only for delivery:

> Smaller producers and inexperienced customers have at their disposal a growing industry of gas marketers and brokers, who can familiarize them with the market and individualize their transactions. Over two-thirds of all gas sales are now effectively in "spot" markets, with terms of thirty days or less. Pipeline interconnections have grown in capacity and complexity to open up a national market. Futures contracts and options are traded on the New York Mercantile Exchange. *Id.*

Some commentators were not so happy about the changes. Joseph Fagan worried about the fate of the small consumer in the restructuring process. With industrial bypass by large, sophisticated players, the cost of gas would increase for the captive consumer who lacked the flexibility to switch suppliers. This captive core would suffer a disproportionate share of transition costs (in the form of higher prices charged by the pipelines to customers to recover the pipelines' take-or-pay settlement costs and because FERC's rate design no longer allowed cross-subsidies from industrial and other interruptible users in favor of residential consumers). In his view, parts of Order 636 undermined FERC's duty to protect the natural gas consumer. Joseph Fagan, From Regulation to Deregulation: The Diminishing Role of the Small Consumer within the Natural Gas Industry, 29 Tulsa L.J. 707, 726–27 (1994). Even Fagan agreed, however, that pain to the residential consumer notwithstanding, in the end, "a free, unregulated market for natural gas will benefit all concerned." *Id.*

NOTES AND COMMENTS

1.   What is the best measure of the success of gas restructuring? A decrease in natural gas prices? Are there non-price factors that should be rated to measure the success of gas restructuring? What are they? Reliability? Reduced pipeline explosions and accidents? Equity? In fact, big industrial users and power plants experienced much greater price reductions than retail consumers. Jess, Restructuring Energy Industries, *supra*, at xxi.

2.   One commentator warned LDCs and state utility commissioners that they would soon be forced to follow the federal path blazed at the wholesale level for gas sales and transportation in their local, retail franchise areas. Industrial customers would no longer tolerate cross-subsidies to residential consumers and industry would use the new federal open-access rules to bypass LDCs that did not adapt to more competitive markets. The LDCs should become open-access carriers themselves, allowing retail customers to choose their own gas supplier and use the local gas mains to have their gas delivered rather than be captive to the LDC's monopoly status. Michaels, *supra* at 72. Indeed, by 2010, 21 states allowed retail customers to choose their gas-commodity supplier. Ken Costello, The Natural Gas Industry at a Glance 14 (Nat'l Regulatory Research Inst., Oct. 2010). The issues that arise in retail competition are discussed in Chapter 10 in the context of the electric industry. Many of the issues discussed in this chapter on federal gas regulation have their counterpoint in electricity restructuring, such as who will bear the transition costs (called "stranded costs"), rate design, curtailment policies, and the price volatility of spot markets in electricity. In other ways, electricity restructuring has proven to be significantly different and often more difficult at the wholesale level than gas restructuring.

2.   COMMODITY MARKETS, PRICE VOLATILITY AND MANIPULATION

Two events upset the pre-2000 equanimity that restructured gas markets were working successfully. First, extraordinary price spikes in natural gas occurred in the Northeast in the cold winter of 2000–2001; and second, at the same time, California was in the throes of a full-blown energy crisis with unimaginably high electricity prices and brownouts. Legislators called on the Government Accountability Office (GAO) to do a three-part study of (1) the factors underlying the gas price spike; (2) FERC's role in ensuring that gas prices were being set in a competitive, informed marketplace; and (3) the options available to gas distributing companies (LDCs) to mitigate the effects of price spikes on residential customers. In *Natural Gas: Analysis of Changes in Market Price* (GAO–03–46, Dec. 2002), GAO concluded:

•   Price spikes occur in natural gas markets because supplies cannot adjust quickly to demand increases and demand is inelastic. In the cold winter of 2000–2001, gas supplies were constrained and demand soared in the Northeast, leading to the "perfect environment" for price spikes. There were "some indications" that prices had been manipulated in the Western United States, but investigations were not yet complete. *Id.* at 5

•   FERC did not have an adequate monitoring system in place to provide assurance that gas prices were being set competitively. FERC's oversight initiatives were "incomplete or ineffective" and "served more to help educate FERC's staff about the new markets than [t]o produce effective oversight." *Id.* at 28. FERC staff had not used data available to it to conduct an investigation into allegations of market manipulation and FERC faced "significant human capital challenges" in acquiring a qualified staff that understood the restructured markets. FERC's belated investigation into improper behavior by energy companies such as Enron was "largely reactive to complaints" rather than pro-active, and relied heavily on requests for information from the energy companies because FERC itself lacked systems to collect or monitor market information. *Id.* at 29.

- FERC's regulations governing the conduct of gas pipeline companies with affiliates were outdated. The 1988 rules did not reflect the significant changes in unbundling, capacity release, E-commerce and online trading systems, and market consolidation that had expanded the number and types of pipeline affiliates. *Id.* at 30.

As to the third requested item, the GAO report provided a guide to local gas utilities describing tools that could be used to protect the LDC and its customers against price spikes. Physical tools include: (1) gas storage; and (2) fixed-price contracts (also called forward contracts) to take physical delivery of a set quantity of gas over time at a set price. This price may, of course, be either higher or lower than spot prices at any specific time, but the fixed price provides price stability. Financial tools include: (1) futures contracts traded on NYMEX to lock in a future price for up to 72 months in the future; (2) option contracts that can be used to guarantee a future price; and (3) swaps, which are futures contracts that are usually individually negotiated and traded in the over-the-counter ("OTC") market rather than on an organized exchange like NYMEX.[46] An extended discussion of such financial tools is presented in Chapter 10. For now, consider this example of price hedging from the GAO report, *id.* at 35–37:

> Suppose, *e.g.,* in March, a utility company wants to hedge against a possible future price increase by buying a futures contract for gas to be delivered the next January at $4.60 (per million BTUs). If the actual January cash price of gas later increases to $5.15, the company can buy the gas on the spot market at $5.15 and sell its futures contract on NYMEX for $5.15. Since it bought the futures contract for only $4.60, the company gains 55 cents on the futures contract in the financial markets, and the net price of the physical gas that is delivered to the utility is $4.60 (the $5.15 spot price in the physical market minus the gain of 55 cents in the financial market). Conversely, if the January cash price for gas has dropped to $4.25, the company can buy the gas at this spot price for delivery in the physical market that month, sell the futures contract at a loss of 35 cents, and still pay a net gas cost of $4.60.

---

[46] As described in more detail in Chapter 10, OTC markets were not regulated by the CFTC at the time.

The example makes clear that hedging does not guarantee the lowest gas price in the market. Rather, hedging allows the utility to mitigate price volatility and gain certainty with respect to its future gas costs. Trying to "beat the market" by making a one-way bet on which way future gas prices will head is an entirely different strategy, one performed by speculators rather than hedgers.

In March 2003, FERC completed its fact-finding review and analysis of the California gas and electric markets. In its Final Report on Price Manipulation in Western Markets (Docket No. PA02–2–000), FERC reported its key conclusions: "[M]arkets for natural gas and electricity in California are inextricably linked, and . . . dysfunctions in each fed off one another during the crisis. Spot gas prices rose to extraordinary levels, facilitating the unprecedented price increase in the electricity market." *Id.* at ES–1. "While soaring demand for gas and flawed electric power market rules were the primary drivers of high gas prices, spot market manipulations contributed significantly." *Id.* at I–1.

How had spot gas prices, so crucial to the efficient (and fair) functioning of restructured gas and electric markets, been manipulated? The FERC report documented two ways:

First, trading in natural gas at Topock (a major delivery hub near the border where El Paso's interstate pipeline met the intrastate pipeline of Southern California Gas Company, a LDC), exhibited an anomalous pattern of "churning" between two traders—one from (the now infamously defunct) EnronOnline (EOL) and the other from Reliant Energy Services, a trading affiliate of a large Texas-based company that had restructured into a regulated utility company (called Centerpoint) and an unregulated affiliate (Reliant) that sought to provide new services to participants in new gas markets. Churning is the rapid execution of buy/sell trades between two traders in a very short period of time, designed to produce sharp upward price movements. (*E,g.,* on one day, Reliant traded gas at the rate of one transaction every 10 seconds over a 30-minute period.) These price movements were seen by all traders using the EOL electronic bulletin board, which was the dominant trading platform in the industry. These traders, not knowing that the price of gas was being churned, would start bidding up the gas price also, thinking that the price of gas they saw on EOL's screen reflected real market factors. Then, later, Reliant would profit as a net buyer of spot gas when the prices fell (which, of course, Enron knew they would). Enron traders used EOL to take large positions in the market as an active speculator. Enron had an enormous information advantage over other traders: it was both a buyer and seller on its EnronOnline trading platform. Using its information advantage from the physical gas trading market, Enron earned huge profits in the derivatives and other financial products markets, as did Reliant in its churning game. *Id.* at ES–12. The EOL/Reliant churning at Topock was large enough to affect the prices of natural gas at the Henry Hub, the largest trading hub in the U.S. *Id.* at III–36, IX–12 to IX–14.

The second method of manipulating the spot price of gas was far more widespread. Reliant and many other traders participated in false reporting of natural gas prices to the publishers of the gas price indices widely used by market participants to settle their contract obligations to buy and sell gas. Two trade publications, Platts *Gas Daily* and Platts

Inside FERC were widely used by the industry to determine what gas had actually sold for on both a daily and monthly basis. This price was assumed to reflect the "market price" or "market value" of gas that buyers would owe to sellers under the short-term contracts signed to buy and sell physical volumes of gas. To collect the data, Platts employees would call the trading desks of various energy companies that traded gas at hubs throughout the United States. The traders would then report to Platts what the weighted average daily price had been that day (weighted by the volumes sold at each price in each trade) for gas bought and sold in the physical market. As FERC staff lamentably concluded in its investigation, false reporting was "epidemic" and "price index manipulation was part of the price formation process." *Id.* at Ch. III.

The motives for reporting false information were several: to influence the published price indices to enhance the value of the trading company's financial position in the derivatives markets or its purchase obligations; to increase reported volumes to create the impression of more liquid markets, thus attracting more customers; and to influence the spot market price of electricity which was based on the price of gas used by the generators, especially if the traders also sold power in California or were affiliated with such sellers. *Id.* at ES–6 & Ch. III. The false data reporting was not limited to the Western markets. El Paso Merchant's reported price trades in the Northeast and Gulf Coast failed to match actual trades 99% of the time. Instead, El Paso reported data according to its "book bias," *i.e.*, its trading book position in the financial markets where it could earn large profits.

In sum, the gas and electricity commodity markets that were so carefully created and nurtured by FERC over years of sometimes painful transitioning to competitive markets were being manipulated by many actors, in many ways, to produce prices that were not "just and reasonable," as required under the NGA or, as discussed in Chapter 10, under the Federal Power Act. With respect to natural gas, FERC's analyses found that the price of gas would have been lower by almost $8.54 per MMBtu in December 2000 if Reliant had not churned the market. Customers of Southern California Gas Co. paid hundreds of millions of dollars in excessive gas costs which, under reasonable assumptions, inflated electric prices by some $1.6 billion in December 2000 alone. *Id.* at II–60.

In response to this 2003 FERC Staff Report, FERC created the Office of Market Oversight and Investigation (OMOI), now moved to the Office of Enforcement's Division of Energy Market Oversight or "DEMO," staffed by highly qualified professionals (including some former employees of trading companies that were dissolved by their affiliated parents in the face of class action litigation, multi-agency investigations, and plummeting stock values). The Energy Policy Act of 2005 (EPAct 2005) strengthened FERC's regulatory authority over gas and electricity price information and manipulation, as is discussed briefly in Section C(4) below and in more detail in Chapter 10.

3. AFFILIATE ABUSE AND TRANSPARENCY

As we have seen, FERC required only "functional unbundling," not the physical divestiture of pipelines, from the merchant trading arms. FERC's task was to enforce rules of nondiscrimination to prevent a pipeline company from favoring its own marketing affiliate with sweetheart deals that gave the affiliate an advantage in securing pipeline space, especially during shortages, or which gave price discounts only to its affiliate. In April 2000, a month before the California energy crisis began, the California Public Utility Commission (CPUC) complained to FERC that El Paso Pipeline and its affiliate were engaged in anticompetitive practices that violated FERC's Standards of Conduct for pipeline operations. El Paso Pipeline had put a large block of capacity up for auction. Two of its own merchant affiliates outbid other bidders and won all 1.22 billion cubic feet of capacity at rates below the level set in El Paso Pipeline's published tariff. The auction allowed El Paso Merchant to hold one-sixth of the pipeline capacity into California, allegedly allowing El Paso to exercise market power and raise the price of gas to the state.

After months of investigations and hearings, the chief FERC administrative law judge found evidence of affiliate abuse in transcripts of phone conversations between El Paso Pipeline personnel and El Paso Merchant personnel, which violated the "firewall" that FERC rules required between the two. The judge concluded that El Paso Pipeline had failed to post and schedule all the capacity that it controlled to transport gas to California, thus artificially raising the price of natural gas delivered there. The evidence also showed that El Paso officials discussed the "ability to influence the physical market to the benefit of any financial hedge/position" and ways to boost profits by "idling large blocks of transport." *See* Jacqueline L. Weaver, Can Energy Markets Be Trusted? The Effect of the Rise and Fall of Enron on Energy Markets, 4 Hous. Bus. & Tax L. J. 1, 55 (2003). Just days before FERC was to issue a final order on the case, El Paso agreed to a $1.7 billion payment to the state of California to settle the charges of withholding capacity to that state. At the same time, Williams Company agreed to pay a $20 million fine to FERC to resolve allegations that its Transco pipeline gave preferential treatment to its energy-trading affiliate. FERC had discovered that Williams' computer system allowed marketing personnel to gain access to Transco's confidential shipping information, giving it an advantage over other competitors. *Id.* at 56. The lengthy hearings in the El Paso case (culminating in 14 volumes of evidence) showed the difficulty of detecting and proving the exercise of market power and affiliate abuse. ABA Section on Env't, Energy & Resources, Electric & Natural Gas Comm., Year in Review 2001 Report, Tab A, at 6–10 (2002).

To remedy these types of problems, FERC issued Order 2004, imposing more stringent and detailed standards of conduct to govern the relationship between transmission providers of both "pipes and wires," *i.e.,* both gas and electricity shippers. The order broadened the definition of affiliate to cover a wide range of non-marketing activities performed by affiliates in areas such as gas processing, gathering, producing, and trading, even when the affiliate did not hold or control any capacity on the pipeline. However, in *National Fuel Gas Supply Corp. v. FERC*, 468 F.3d 831 (D.C. Cir. 2006), the court vacated and remanded Order 2004 because FERC had not presented any evidence of complaints or abuse between pipelines and their non-marketing affiliates. The court noted that vertical integration could be efficient and therefore "FERC cannot impede vertical integration between a pipeline and its affiliates without 'adequate justification' " (citing Tenneco Gas v. FERC, 969 F.2d 1187

(D.C. Cir. 1992)). The court allowed FERC to try to support its rule by elucidating its "best case for relying *solely* on a theoretical threat of abuse," in the absence of complaints and actual evidence of abuse, and gave some illustrative guidance to FERC, should it choose this route. *Id.* at 844.

FERC then initiated a rulemaking to amend its Standards of Conduct in Docket No. RM07–1–000, resulting in the adoption of Orders 717 (18 C.F.R. Part 358) (Oct. 16, 2008) and 717–A (18 C.F.R Part 358) (Oct. 15, 2009). The new standards create three *per se* rules, violation of which would automatically be sanctionable. The "Independent Functioning Rule" requires that pipeline employees operate independently of marketing employees and defines the two categories, with *de minimis* exceptions. The "No-Conduit Rule" expands the prohibition against disclosing pipeline information to marketing employees or using any conduit to pass restricted information. The "Transparency Rule" requires that the pipeline post any inadvertent disclosure of nonpublic information on the electronic bulletin board or its website and requires contemporaneous records of conversations between pipeline employees and marketing employees. *See* Natural Gas Reg. Comm. Report, 29 Energy L.J. 715, 719–22 (2008).

Other rules enacted in 2007–2008, such as FERC Order No. 710 requiring interstate natural gas companies to submit forms with more current market and cost information, showed FERC's much more active stance as a regulator of natural gas markets. *Id.* at 717. This stance prompted some companies to self-report violations so that penalties would be reduced. For example, BP Energy Co. conducted a self-assessment of its compliance with FERC's capacity release rules and discovered widespread violations, including "flipping" short-term releases of discounted rate capacity to affiliated replacement shippers to avoid competitive bidding requirements for longer term capacity releases. BP entered into an agreement to pay a civil penalty of $7 million and instituted better internal compliance measures. *Id.* at 728.

4.   EPACT 2005 AND BEYOND

By 2005, FERC cautiously asserted that gas markets were functioning reasonably well. Granted that natural gas prices had risen 63% in 2003 and another 7% in 2004, market forces were working: Gas producers were responding to higher prices by increasing efforts to find new supplies, investment in gas pipeline infrastructure was proceeding apace, financial gas markets had developed new risk management tools that allowed traders and companies to hedge risks more robustly, and natural gas price indices had improved, although the collection and publication of key market data (such as reports on the amount of gas in storage) still needed improvement. *Id.* at 138. FERC, Staff Report, 2004 State of the Markets Report, Natural Gas Markets 138–158 (2005). Traders were reporting gas prices to publishers under new procedures established by the trade press (with strong input from FERC) to ensure honest reporting. Still, "popular confidence" in natural gas pricing remained uncertain. *Id.* at 147. With rapid price increases in 2003–2004, pricing mechanisms remained under close scrutiny by Congress and other policymakers.

Indeed, Congress did react to the commodity trading scandals that were unearthed. The Energy Policy Act of 2005 amended the NGA in three ways that aimed at increasing public confidence in natural gas markets and trading. First, Section 315 of EPAct added Section 4A to the NGA (15 U.S.C. § 717c–1) to prohibit any entity, directly or indirectly, from using "any manipulative or deceptive device or contrivance" in the purchase or sale of natural gas or gas transportation services in violation of any rules that FERC might prescribe as necessary to protect gas ratepayers. (This language is modeled after section 10(b) of the Securities Exchange Act.) Second, Section 314 of EPAct amended Sections 21 and 22 of the NGA by greatly enhancing civil and criminal penalties for violations, including authorizing fines of up to $1 million per day (increased from $5,000) and five years of imprisonment. 15 U.S.C §§ 717t, t–1.

Third, Section 316 of EPAct 2005 directed FERC to "facilitate price transparency in markets for the sale or transportation of physical natural gas in interstate commerce" by adding Section 23 to the NGA. 15 U.S.C. § 717t–2. FERC is given the power to obtain pricing information from "participants" in the gas markets and FERC may itself establish an electronic information system if it determines that existing price publications are not adequately providing price discovery or market transparency. In other words, if the gas industry and the price index publishers do not adequately police themselves, FERC will step in.

Several years after FERC's many successful efforts to dispel its image as an incompetent regulator of gas and electricity markets, FERC's State of the Markets Report 2008 showed that problems still existed in the interrelationship between the physical commodity market and the financial trading market. One of the 2008 Report's major conclusions was that "physical fundamentals alone cannot explain natural gas prices experienced during the year." Supply and demand factors could not explain why Henry Hub prices reached $13.32/MMBtu on July 3, 2008 and then fell below $6 at year's end. FERC 2008 Report at 6–9, and 25–35. The Report concluded that an unprecedented increase in financial trading in gas markets by passive investors (i.e., institutional investors who had placed $260 billion into commodity index trading vehicles in March 2008 compared to $13 billion in 2003) coupled with "technical trading strategies" of commodity traders induced "commodity bubble-like markets." *Id.* at 26, 32–33. Further:

> Financial natural gas prices provide a basis for the formation of physical natural gas prices. Prior to growth in the use of natural gas futures, swaps and other derivatives, market participants established short-term natural gas price expectations by assessing physical supply and demand conditions. . . . The prices of [these] financial instruments are now used by physical markets to form price indexes. . . . The lack of real-time transparency can lead to misperceptions that lead to skewed price signals and prices that can over- or under-shoot underlying values based on physical fundamentals. An example of this occurred in 2008, when many market observers missed the extraordinary growth in unconventional gas production.

Id. at 32.

When the financial bubble burst in the fall of 2008, triggering a global financial recession, energy market participants were faced with much less available credit and a higher cost of borrowing from banks that were financially troubled themselves. Many oil and gas companies announced cutbacks in future capital expenditures. The domestic drilling rig count plummeted. *Id.* at 14–15. Bad market outcomes occurred, not just for the industry, but for almost all Americans when the market bubbles burst, leading to deep recession in 2009 and into 2010.

As described in more detail in Chapter 10, the massive Dodd-Frank Act of 2010 (Pub. L. 111–203) was enacted to prevent another financial meltdown in the banking sector and among Wall Street trading firms like the now-defunct Lehman Brothers. Title VII of the Act, known as the Wall Street Transparency and Accountability Act of 2010, is directed at regulating derivatives trading by requiring certain derivative trades, mainly swap trades, to be made on regulated exchanges (rather than over the counter in private negotiations) and mandating more transparent reporting and records and greater margins to reduce speculation. Dodd-Frank is aimed at regulating the financial sector, not at parties buying and selling physical volumes of oil and gas (such as producers and end users) to hedge against price volatility. *See* Matthew J. Agen, Dodd-Frank and Electric Utilities, 151 Pub. Util. Fortnightly 18 (Dec. 23, 2013). Non-financial companies, such as refiners, utilities and airlines, are now entering into privately negotiated futures contracts that are then publicly reported to clearinghouse exchanges, such as the Intercontinental Exchange (ICE) or CME Group. Matthew Leising, Energy Swaps Migrating to Futures on Dodd-Frank Rules (Jan. 25, 2013), http://www.bloomberg.com/news/print/2013–01–25/energy-swaps-migrating-to-futures-as-dodd-frank-rules-take-hold.html. This practice brings more transparency.

Physical gas trading by banks has declined since 2008 and several large financial players have exited the business in light of increased trading restrictions. *See generally* FERC 2012 State of the Markets Report 56–65 (discussing the interplay between physical and financial gas and power markets). J.P. Morgan, a large Wall Street player, announced an agreement to sell its physical commodities trading business to a Swiss trading firm in March 2014. This action followed shortly after J.P Morgan paid $410 million to settle FERC charges that it had gamed the energy markets in California and the Midwest from September 2010 to November 2012. In settling, J.P. Morgan admitted the facts described in FERC's charge, but did not admit to wrongdoing. Hannah Northey, JP Morgan to Sell Physical Commodities Arm, E&E News PM, Mar. 19, 2014.

Three federal agencies have jurisdiction over market manipulation in the physical and financial energy markets. FERC regulates physical markets in electricity and gas, CFTC regulates commodity exchanges and futures contracts, and the Federal Trade Commission (FTC) covers crude oil, gasoline and distillates markets. The 2008 Farm Bill (Pub. L. 110–234, amending 7 U.S.C. § 2(h)(7)) granted the CFTC the power to regulate derivative contracts (like Henry Hub gas swaps) that had been exempt from regulation under the "Enron loophole." The CFTC now regulates those over-the-counter (OTC) gas contracts that have a "significant price discovery function" that could affect prices on the regulated exchanges. The respective roles of the three agencies are discussed in more detail in Chapter 10.

Two cases conclude this section. The first involves FERC's efforts to increase transparency in the physical gas markets under Section 316 of EPAct 2005 discussed *supra*. The second introduces yet another group of regulators to police the manipulation of energy markets, should this group be found to have jurisdiction after FERC's (possibly pre-emptive) restructuring of gas markets.

In late 2008, FERC issued Order 720 requiring the posting of gas flow information to improve price transparency in the interstate natural gas markets. Order 720 required that postings be made by major non-interstate pipelines in states like Texas and Oklahoma, so that market participants could better understand the impact of new discoveries such as the Barnett Shale in Texas which was served by both inter-and intra-state pipelines. The Texas Pipeline Association quickly brought suit challenging FERC's jurisdiction to require postings by intrastate pipelines. The Fifth Circuit Court of Appeals made short work of FERC's assertion of a new "transparency authority" over intrastate pipelines that "participated" in interstate markets:

Texas Pipeline Association v. FERC

661 F.3d 258 (5th Cir. 2011).

■ JERRY E. SMITH, CIRCUIT JUDGE:

    * * *

The central question is whether [§ 316] of EPAct 2005 permits FERC to compel owners and operators of intrastate pipelines . . . to post flow, capacity and scheduling information on the Internet. The relevant portions of [§ 316] direct FERC to promulgate rules that facilitate transparency in the interstate market for natural gas:

    (2) . . . The rules shall provide for the dissemination, on a timely basis, of information about the availability and prices of natural gas sold at wholesale and in interstate commerce to the Commission, State commissions, buyers and sellers of wholesale natural gas, and the public.

    (3) the Commission may—(A) obtain the information described in paragraph (2) from any market participant. . . . 15 U.S.C. § 717t–2(a)(2)–(3).

In support of its position that it had the authority to promulgate the Posting Rule, FERC focuses on the language . . . that includes "any market participant" within the ambit of regulable entities. FERC argues that broad phrase is ambiguous but can reasonably be interpreted to include major intrastate pipelines because they are so integrated with the interstate market, being links between interstate pipelines and through participation in national market hubs (which service both interstate and intrastate pipelines), that interstate and intrastate markets functionally operate as one large interconnected market. Thus, FERC contends it can fulfill Congress's directive of facilitating price transparency in the interstate market only by requiring this information from major intrastate pipelines. . . . In short, FERC argues that major intrastate pipelines "participate" in the interstate market so that [§ 316] can reasonably be interpreted to apply to them—an interpretation that, urges FERC, warrants *Chevron* deference.

[The court then discussed the context of § 316: that it was codified in Chapter 15B of the Natural Gas Act, which commences with § 1(b), as quoted *supra* in the *Phillips* decision, that the chapter "shall apply to the "transportation of natural gas in interstate commerce, to the sale in interstate commerce of natural gas for resale, . . . but shall not apply to any other transportation or sale of natural gas. . . ."]

That provision unambiguously denies FERC the power to regulate entities specifically excluded from Chapter 15B, including wholly-intrastate pipelines. . . . ■

In short, FERC could not "manufacture statutory ambiguity with semantics" to enlarge its Congressional mandate. *Id.* at 264. The court vacated FERC's Order 720.

Until vacated, Order 720 made 97% of all daily natural gas production visible to the market, including gas from fast-growing shale plays. Order 720 also made daily changes in market dynamics visible, such as allowing market participants to assess quickly the extent and impact of natural gas wells freezing up in February 2011. Here is FERC's graphic depiction of the before-and-after effect of its Order 720:

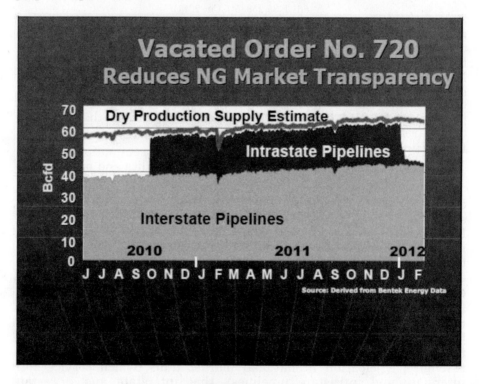

Figure 9–4
Item No. A–3 (Apr. 19, 2012), URL: http://www.ferc.gov/market-oversight/reports-analyses/st-mkt-ovr/som-rpt-2011.pdf

A second case challenging FERC's jurisdiction also arose in the aftermath of the California energy crisis. This time, the defendant companies asserted that FERC did have jurisdiction over their practices under the Natural Gas Act, and that this NGA jurisdiction thereby preempted any claims brought by the plaintiffs for state antitrust violations related to market manipulation. The U.S. Supreme Court granted the petition for certiorari in this case, after the Ninth Circuit Court of Appeals held that the NGA did not preempt the antitrust claims and allowed the case to proceed to trial. As you read *Learjet*, consider whether the holding in *Texas Pipeline Association v. FERC, supra*, helps or hurts the defendant companies.

Learjet, Inc. v. Oneok, Inc. (In re W. States Wholesale Natural Gas Antitrust Litig.)

715 F.3d 716 (9th Cir. 2012), *cert. granted,* 134 S.Ct. 2899 (July 4, 2014).

■ BEA, CIRCUIT JUDGE:

These cases arise out of the energy crisis of 2000–2002. Plaintiffs (retail buyers of natural gas) allege that Defendants (natural gas traders) manipulated the price of natural gas by reporting false information to price indices published by trade publications and engaging in wash sales. Plaintiffs brought various claims in state and federal court beginning in 2005, and all cases were eventually consolidated into the underlying multidistrict litigation proceeding. In July 2011, the district court entered summary judgment against Plaintiffs in most of the cases, finding that their state law antitrust claims were preempted by the Natural Gas Act, 15 U.S.C. § 717 et seq. ("NGA"). Plaintiffs appeal the district court's order granting summary judgment. . . .

We reverse the district court's order granting summary judgment to the Defendants.

I.   Facts and Regulatory Framework

A.   Energy Crisis of 2000–2002

A brief recitation of the background of this litigation, as well as a description of the regulatory framework governing this case, is useful to set the stage for our holding. These cases arise out of claims that the Defendants violated antitrust laws by manipulating the natural gas market and selling natural gas at artificially inflated prices, leading to the energy crisis of 2000–2002. The Federal Energy Regulatory Commission ("FERC") conducted a fact-finding investigation of the energy crisis, and concluded that "[s]pot gas prices rose to extraordinary levels, facilitating the unprecedented price increase in the electricity market." This market distortion stemmed in part from efforts of energy trading companies to manipulate price indices compiled by trade publications.

The natural gas industry relied on two trade publications, *Gas Daily* and *Inside FERC*, which published the most widely-used price indices. *Gas Daily* published a daily gas price index, while *Inside FERC* published a monthly gas price index. *Gas Daily* relied on telephone interviews with natural gas market participants (traders, end users, and producers) to collect pricing data. *Inside FERC* collected pricing data through standardized spreadsheets, which traders filled out and emailed to *Inside FERC*. Buyers and sellers relied on these indices as reference points to determine the market price for natural gas transactions. In short, the prices for actual transactions were pegged to price indices that were subject to manipulation by energy traders.

After the energy crisis of 2000–2002, a number of energy trading companies admitted that their employees provided false pricing data to *Gas Daily* and *Inside FERC*. Government investigations revealed that the companies had few, if any, internal controls in place to ensure the accuracy of the data reported to the trade publications. A 2003 FERC report described the process as follows:

> Traders from all companies describe a typical trading day as hectic, pressure packed, and frenetic. One of their many tasks was to report trading data to the Trade Press; this was viewed as bothersome but necessary. Often it was a job given to the newest employee. Many companies report passing around a form and using a spreadsheet on a shared drive. . . . There was nothing to stop a trader from changing the numbers someone else had entered. In other cases, traders took an oral "survey" to get a sense of where the market was trading. Sometimes they represented it to the Trade Press as an actual survey, but in other cases they made up trades to average out to a number that was consistent with this "survey." In addition to reporting false data to the price indices, traders also manipulated the market by engaging in "wash sales," or prearranged sales in which traders "agreed to execute a buy or a sell on an electronic trading platform . . . and then to immediately reverse or offset the first trade by bilaterally executing over the telephone an equal and opposite buy or sell."

B.   Overview of Natural Gas Regulation

Whether Plaintiffs' state law antitrust claims are cognizable depends, for one thing, on whether the field of natural gas regulation has been preempted by federal regulation. This court's preemption analysis is governed by the framework of natural gas regulation, and more importantly, the distinction between categories of sales that fall within FERC's jurisdiction ("jurisdictional sales") and the categories of sales that fall outside of FERC's jurisdiction ("non-jurisdictional sales").

. . . Put simply, the NGA applies to: (1) transportation of natural gas in interstate commerce, (2) natural gas sales in interstate commerce for resale (i.e., wholesale sales), and (3) natural gas companies engaged in such transportation or sale. The NGA does *not* apply to retail sales (i.e., direct sales for consumptive use). . . .

Since the passage of the NGA, Congress has removed other categories of sales from the scope of FERC's jurisdiction as part of a general effort to reduce federal regulation of the natural gas industry. In 1989, Congress passed the Natural Gas Wellhead Decontrol Act of 1989, Pub. L. No. 101–60, which removed "first sales" from FERC's jurisdiction, therefore completely eliminating FERC's authority to set prices at the wellhead. . . .

The final aspect of the natural gas regulatory scheme relevant to this appeal is FERC's practice of issuing "blanket marketing certificates."[6][47] Following congressional efforts to reduce federal regulation of the industry, FERC began its own deregulation process. In 1992, FERC promulgated Order 636, which "required all interstate pipelines to 'unbundle' their transportation from their own natural gas sales." FERC also issued blanket sale certificates to interstate pipelines that allowed them to offer "unbundled" natural gas at market-based rates, rather than at rates filed with FERC. *See* 57 Fed. Reg. at 13,270. FERC continued its own deregulation process by issuing blanket sales certificates for all other resales of natural gas. *See* Regulations Governing Blanket Marketer Sales Certificates, 57 Fed. Reg. 57,952; 57,957–58 (Dec. 8, 1992). These blanket certificates had the effect of allowing all natural gas companies subject to FERC's jurisdiction to charge market-based rates, as opposed to rates filed with and approved by FERC.

II. Procedural History

[The court summarized the Defendants' successful argument in the district court that the NGA preempted the state antitrust claims. The Defendants had argued that FERC had jurisdiction to regulate "any practice" affecting a rate subject to the jurisdiction of the Commission under Section 5(a) of the NGA. Section 5(a) states that whenever FERC finds that any "rate, . . . regulation, practice, or contract affecting such rate is unjust, unreasonable, unduly discriminatory, or preferential, the Commission shall determine the just and reasonable rate, . . . regulation, practice, or contract to be thereafter observed or in force." 15 U.S.C. § 717d. Because the price indices were used to set the prices of natural gas sold both within and outside of FERC's jurisdiction, any manipulation of these indices fell within FERC's exclusive jurisdiction.]

III. The Natural Gas Act and Preemption

     * * *

B. Preemption

The "touchstone in every pre-emption case" is expressed congressional intent. Wyeth v. Levine, 555 U.S. 555, 565 (2009). The Supreme Court recently emphasized that in preemption cases, courts should "start with the assumption that the historic police powers of the States were not to be superseded by the Federal Act unless that was the clear and manifest purpose of Congress." *Id.* In the present case, the presumption against preemption applies with particular force in light of Congress's deliberate efforts to preserve traditional areas of state regulation of the natural gas industry.

The question presented by this appeal is as follows: does Section 5(a) of the NGA, which provides FERC with jurisdiction over any "practice" affecting jurisdictional rates, preempt state antitrust claims arising out

---

[47] Under blanket certificates issued pursuant to Section 7(c) of the NGA, "a natural gas company may undertake a restricted array of routine activities without the need to obtain a case-specific certificate for each individual project." *See* Blanket Certificates, Federal Energy Regulatory Commission (last visited on March 25, 2013), http://www.ferc.gov/industries/gas/indus-act/blank-cert.asp. A company with a blanket certificate may "construct, modify, acquire, operate, and abandon a limited set of natural gas facilities, and offer a limited set of services, provided each activity complies with constraints on costs and environmental impacts set forth in the Commission's regulations." *Id.*

of price manipulation associated with transactions falling outside of FERC's jurisdiction? We conclude that such an expansive reading of Section 5(a) conflicts with Congress's express intent to delineate carefully the scope of federal jurisdiction through the express jurisdictional provisions of Section 1(b) of the Act. Our analysis is guided by several circuit court decisions counseling in favor of a narrow reading of Section 5(a). As a result, we hold that the NGA does not preempt the Plaintiffs' state antitrust claims, and reverse the district court's order granting summary judgment to the Defendants. When Congress enacted the NGA in 1938, it expressly limited federal jurisdiction over natural gas to "the sale in interstate commerce of natural gas for resale." 15 U.S.C. § 717(b). An early Supreme Court case interpreting the scope of the NGA described Congress's intent as follows:

> The omission of any reference to other sales, that is, to direct sales for consumptive use, in the affirmative declaration of coverage was not inadvertent. It was deliberate. For Congress made sure its intent could not be mistaken by adding the explicit prohibition that the Act "shall not apply to any other . . . sale." Panhandle Eastern Pipe Line Co. v. Pub. Serv. Comm'n of Ind., 332 U.S. 507, 516 (1947).

> * * *

Since the passage of the NGA, Congress has further demonstrated its intent to limit the scope of federal regulation by enacting statutes removing first sales from FERC's jurisdiction. *See* Natural Gas Wellhead Decontrol Act of 1989, Pub. L. No. 101–60, 103 Stat. 157.

This court's decision in *E&J Gallo Winery v. Encana Corp.*, 503 F.3d 1027 (9th Cir. 2007) provides further support for our holding that the NGA does not preempt all state antitrust claims. The claims in *Gallo* were essentially the same as the Plaintiffs' claims in the present case. E. & J. Gallo Winery alleged that EnCana Corp., a natural gas supplier, conspired to inflate the price of natural gas by manipulating the prices reported to private indices published by natural gas trade publications and the execution of wash trades. Gallo's complaint consisted of federal and state antitrust actions, as well as state-law damages claims. Encana Corp. moved for summary judgment, claiming that . . . federal preemption principles barred Gallo's state claims. *Id.* at 1032. The district court denied EnCana's summary judgment motion, and this court affirmed the district court. *Id.* at 1030.

We noted in *Gallo* that although FERC did not set the rates charged by the natural gas companies, it did engage in market oversight by granting blanket market certificates after determining that the seller lacked market power. *Id.* at 1041. As a result of FERC's market oversight, the court found "that the market-based rate for natural gas transactions *under FERC's jurisdiction* are FERC-authorized rates, and cannot be the basis of a federal antitrust or state damage action" because of the filed-rate doctrine. *Id.* at 1043 (emphasis added). [Ed. note: The court explained the filed-rate doctrine as a judicially created doctrine that when federal statutes give federal agencies exclusive jurisdiction to set rates for certain utilities, this jurisdiction bars challenges under state law and federal antitrust laws to rates set by federal agencies.]

Although this court found that the filed-rate doctrine barred claims based on FERC-authorized rates, it distinguished claims based on FERC-authorized rates from claims based on the rates reported in the price indices. *Id.* at 1045. It stated that the record reflected that "the indices potentially include transactions that are under FERC's jurisdiction as well as transactions outside FERC's jurisdiction." *Id.* There were two relevant categories of non-FERC-authorized rates included in the challenged price indices:

> First, there is evidence in the record some index pricing inputs were misreported or wholly fictitious. Misreported rates and rates reported for fictitious transactions are not FERC-approved rates, and barring claims that such fictitious transactions damaged purchasers in the natural gas market would not further the purpose of the filed rate doctrine.

> Moreover, as part of its investigation of the indices, FERC concluded that it "has jurisdiction over *most* of the transactions that form the basis for the indices." . . . This language indicates that at least some of the transactions included in the indices are not subject to FERC's jurisdiction, and thus would be subject to challenge by Gallo. *Id.* at 1045. The non-jurisdictional transactions included in the price indices included first sales at the wellhead or via imports from Canada or Mexico. *Id.*

We explained in depth why the removal of certain transactions from FERC's jurisdiction meant that claims arising out of those transactions were not preempted by the NGA. Id. at 1046. Most importantly, we assumed that Congress was aware of the existing context of state and federal antitrust law when it enacted the Wellhead Decontrol Act and other statutes limiting FERC's jurisdiction. *Id.* State and federal antitrust laws complement Congress's intent to move to a less regulated market, because such laws support fair competition. *Id.* ("By enabling private parties to combat market manipulation and other anti-competitive actions, the laws under which Gallo brought its claim support Congress's determination that the supply, the demand, and the price of high-cost, first sale gas be determined by market forces.") (internal quotations omitted). For these reasons, we concluded that "Congress did not preclude plaintiffs from basing damage claims on rates associated with first sales." *Id.* Our reasoning in *Gallo* applies with equal force to the question presented by this case: federal preemption doctrines do not preclude state law claims arising out of transactions outside of FERC's jurisdiction.

C. The NGA's Jurisdictional Limitations

The district court in the present case acknowledged this court's holding in *Gallo*, but distinguished that case on the grounds that "*Gallo* did not address whether FERC's exclusive jurisdiction over natural gas companies *and their practices which affect jurisdictional rates* preempts state jurisdiction over the same subject matter." It reasoned that Defendants' status as FERC-regulated entities, combined with FERC's authority under Section 5(a) of the NGA to regulate "any rule, regulation, practice, or contract" affecting a jurisdictional rate, conferred exclusive jurisdiction on FERC to regulate the conduct at issue in this case.

The district court read the word "practices" in Section 5(a) of the NGA to preempt impliedly the application of state laws to the same transactions (first sales and retail sales) that Congress expressly exempted from the scope of FERC's jurisdiction in Section 1(b) of the Act. However, this reading runs afoul of the canon of statutory construction that statutory provisions should not be read in isolation, and the meaning of a statutory provision must be consistent with the structure of the statute of which it is a part. . . . While the Ninth Circuit has not had the opportunity to define the scope of Section 5(a), the Supreme Court and other circuits have read Section 5(a) narrowly to define the scope of FERC's jurisdiction within the limitations imposed by Section 1(b). [The court then discussed three cases that had read Section 5(a) narrowly.]

* * *

D.   FERC's Regulatory Authority

One final issue dividing the parties in this appeal is the extent to which FERC had authority to regulate the market manipulation that gave rise to the energy crisis in 2000–2001. The Defendants point to the Code of Conduct promulgated by FERC in 2003 as evidence that FERC had regulatory authority over the anticompetitive conduct at issue, including the false price reporting and wash sales. FERC promulgated the Code of Conduct by amending the blanket market certificates governing jurisdictional sellers. *See* Amendments to Blanket Sales Certificates, 68 Fed. Reg. 66,323 (Nov. 26, 2003). The Commission stated that the need for the Code of Conduct "was informed by the types of behavior that occurred in the Western markets during 2000 and 2001." *Id.* ¶ 2. The Code prohibited *jurisdictional* sellers "from engaging in actions without a legitimate business purpose that manipulate or attempt to manipulate market conditions, including wash trades and collusion." *Id.* ¶ 4. The Code further provides that jurisdictional sellers are required to provide complete and accurate transactional information to publishers of gas price indices. *Id.* ¶ 5.

While Defendants rely on the promulgation of the Code of Conduct as evidence that FERC had jurisdiction over the market manipulation at issue, there are two significant flaws in their argument. First, two years after the promulgation of the Code, Congress enacted the Energy Policy Act of 2005 ("EPA"),[15][48] which prohibits market manipulation and authorizes FERC to promulgate rules and regulations to protect natural gas ratepayers. There is a canon of statutory interpretation that counsels against reading acts of Congress to be superfluous. This canon suggests that Congress enacted the relevant provision of the EPA *because* FERC did not already have regulatory authority over the anticompetitive conduct at issue.

The second flaw in Defendants' argument is more relevant to our jurisdictional analysis. Even if FERC did have the statutory authority to

---

[48]   The EPA provides, in relevant part:

It shall be unlawful for any entity, directly or indirectly, to use or employ, in connection with the purchase or sale of natural gas or the purchase or sale of transportation services subject to the jurisdiction of the Commission, any manipulative or deceptive device or contrivance. . . . in contravention of such rules and regulations as the Commission may prescribe as necessary in the public interest or for the protection of natural gas ratepayers. Pub. L. No. 109–58 tit. III, § 315 (codified at 15 U.S.C. § 717c–1).

promulgate the 2003 Code of Conduct and to make it applicable to "first sales" and other nonjurisdictional sales, a close reading of the Code reveals that FERC limited the application of the Code to sales within its jurisdiction. FERC acknowledged that because of acts deregulating first sales of natural gas, such sales were outside the scope of FERC's jurisdiction. Amendments to Blanket Sales Certificates, 68 Fed. Reg. 66,323 ¶ 14 (Nov. 26, 2003). FERC further noted that some commenters had raised "concerns regarding the potential adverse effect of imposing the proposed code of conduct only on the portion of the natural gas market under the Commission's jurisdiction," *id.* ¶ 16, and responded by stating, "The fact that the Commission does not regulate the entire natural gas market does not compel the Commission to refrain from exercising its authority over that portion of the gas market which is within its jurisdiction to prevent the manipulation of prices." *Id.* ¶ 21. The discussion of jurisdictional limitations within the Code of Conduct itself suggests that the Code does *not* support the Defendants' argument that FERC had jurisdiction over the anticompetitive behavior related to nonjurisdictional sales. For these reasons, the 2003 enactment of the Code of Conduct does not affect our conclusion that the NGA does not grant FERC jurisdiction over claims arising out of false price reporting and other anticompetitive behavior associated with nonjurisdictional sales.

* * *

VII. Conclusion

We REVERSE the district court's order granting summary judgment to Defendants on preemption grounds. . . . We REMAND to the district for further proceedings consistent with this opinion. ∎

NOTES AND COMMENTS

1.   If FERC does not have the authority to regulate "market participants" whose acts can affect interstate gas markets or to regulate all "practices" that affect these markets, then what agencies or other actors fill this regulatory gap?

2.   While FERC worked hard from 2001 onwards to restore confidence in gas markets, it also focused tremendous efforts on facilitating what was then considered the most promising new source of natural gas for U.S. consumers: LNG imported across the ocean from gas fields in foreign lands. EPAct 2005 had given FERC authority to permit imports and exports of natural gas and had adopted a proprietary "merchant" model rather than a public utility model of regulation for permitting LNG import terminals. Section 311 of EPAct 2005 (amending § 3 of the NGA, 15 U.S.C § 717b) specifically forbade FERC from requiring the terminal operator to offer service to any users other than itself or from regulating any rates or terms or conditions of service for using the terminals, The rush to build import terminals ended abruptly when the "shale gale" led investors in these terminals to seek permits to convert them to export terminals.

5.   GAS AND ELECTRICITY CONVERGENCE: RELIABILITY CONCERNS

Most new power generation built in the United States after 2013 will be fueled by natural gas. Between 1990 and 2012, gas-fired plants comprised 74% of all additions to new U.S. electricity generating capacity; wind power generation supplied another 14% of new capacity; and the remaining 12% of new additions was fueled by coal, nuclear, hydropower and solar. EIA, Annual Energy Outlook 2014, Market Trends: Electricity Demand (May 7, 2014), http://www.eia.gov/forecasts/aeo/MT_electric.cfm#cap_natgas. FERC has restructured wholesale electricity markets using the same model as that used for natural gas. However, gas pipelines are not controlled centrally by a large regional entity, as in electricity markets. Each pipeline controls its own operations. Some marketing affiliates of functionally unbundled pipeline companies trade both gas and power. They are traded as commodities in short-term markets that are closely linked: the marginal cost of producing electricity is often based on the marginal cost of using gas as fuel, as vividly illustrated by Enron's manipulation of the Topock hub in 2001, discussed in Section C(2) *supra*. Recall that Professor Pierce, a strong supporter of competitive gas markets, worried that the post-Order 636 world had become too reliant on short-term contracts that would not provide incentives for long-term investments in production facilities, pipelines and power plants. (Review section B(4)(c) *supra*.)

The shale revolution shows that the upstream end of the gas supply chain has not been discouraged from making massive investments in new production. However, the convergence of gas and electricity markets has raised key issues of reliability in other parts of the gas supply chain. First, many new gas-fired power plants have not contracted for firm transportation service on the pipeline system, meaning that they will be "bumped off" if there is a shortage of pipeline capacity needed to serve the firm customers (usually LDCs) that have paid for premium service, unless FERC's curtailment regulations or the pipeline's tariff structure allow these power plant customers to elbow their way back in during an emergency. (Curtailment policies were discussed in Section B(4)(d) *supra*.) Second, many new gas plants lack fuel-switching capability (although some larger units do hold fuel oil in storage). Third, regulators today must account for the addition of significant amounts of intermittent generation from wind and solar. Gas-fired plants are the only generating facility that can ramp up (do a "black start") or down quickly to accommodate the growing renewable portfolios of many states. At the same time, many coal plants are being retired. These plants used long-term supply contracts and held large onsite coal inventories to reliably supply base-load electricity. In short, the U.S. grid is shifting toward intermittent sources and to gas-fired power that is not supported with long-term contracts for gas supply or gas transportation.

The Southwest Cold Snap in early 2011 starkly exposed reliability problems in the gas/electric interface. Sub-freezing temperatures hit the Texas-New Mexico-Arizona region between February 1 and February 5, 2011. In Texas, 210 unenclosed generating units (built for extreme heat, not extreme cold) suffered an outage, failed to start, or operated only at reduced rates. More than 4.4 million electricity customers lost service. The water co-produced with gas froze inside the wells, blocking gas flow and resulting in gas curtailments; 50,000 gas customers lost service in wide areas of New Mexico. Jennifer E. Gardner, The Southwest Cold Snap: Extreme Weather at the Gas/Electric Interface, 27 Nat. Res. & Env't 8 (2012). Both FERC and NERC (the North American Electric Reliability Council) launched an extensive investigation, concluding that gas producers and generators had adequate notice of the coming Arctic blast, but poor weatherization of equipment and lack of communication in coordinating emergency protocols between generators, the electric reliability coordinator and gas pipelines greatly exacerbated the severity of the storm's impact. The event made it "alarmingly clear" that the gas and electric industries were tightly tied to each other and needed much better coordination. *Id.* at 9.

As an example: Even a brief power loss to electric-powered gas compressors, pumps, and processing plants in the field can put the equipment out of service for long periods. Gas outages then escalate the power outages by reducing fuel supplies to generators. FERC/NERC, Report on Outages and Curtailments during the Southwest Cold Weather Event of February 1–5, 2011, at 215 (Aug. 2011) (recommending that regulators consider exempting critical gas facilities from rolling blackouts).

In 2012, FERC initiated five technical conferences to solicit comments from both the gas and electricity sectors to enhance coordination between them. One obvious shortcoming in integrating the two sectors was the time difference between scheduling the next day's flows and generation. The "gas scheduling day" runs from 9:00 a.m. to 9:00 a.m. of the next day (Central Time). During this time, supplier nominations, confirmation, scheduling, and any needed line packing occur to serve the next-day's markets. The "electric scheduling day" runs from midnight to midnight in local time. Thus, a time gap of up to eight hours is built into the current scheduling patterns, hindering a coordinated response to sudden, severe weather events. The effect of the different schedules is well-described in FERC's Order Initiating Investigation into ISO and RTO Scheduling Practices, 146 F.E.R.C. ¶ 61,202 (Mar. 20, 2014). Gas-fired generators must commit to gas supplies across two gas operating days. Once committed, they must rely on intra-day nomination gas cycles to change nominations for an electric day. This mismatch means that generators are depleting their available gas supplies during the peak morning period for electricity demand. Even worse, the scheduling mismatch means the generators cannot obtain gas supply or transportation capacity during the time period when these markets are most liquid. *Id.* at 4–5, ¶¶ 7–9. FERC has issued a Notice of Proposed Rulemaking to coordinate the schedules better by changing the natural gas nomination times and providing additional intra-day gas nomination opportunities to generators. *Id.* at 6–7, ¶¶ 12–13. Clearly, FERC is concerned that gas-fired power plants, many of which have not bought firm gas transportation service, will be left "out in the cold" during the next severe winter weather event.

The gas and power industries expressed concern that FERC's Standards of Conduct governing communications between pipelines and their marketing affiliates, and between public utilities that own or operate transmission and their affiliates, hindered industry's coordinated response to emergencies. FERC reminded industry players that its Standards of Conduct authorize communication of sensitive information to address emergency conditions and then called for additional work in this area. Order Directing Further Conferences and Reports, FERC Docket No. AD12–12–000, 141 F.E.R.C. ¶ 61,125 (Nov. 15, 2012). *See also* NERC, 2013 Special Reliability Assessment: Accommodating an Increased Dependence on Natural Gas for Electric Power (May 2013). In November 2013, FERC issued Order No. 787 expressly authorizing the sharing of non-public, operational information between interstate gas pipelines and electric transmission operators to strengthen reliability. The order adopted a No-Conduit Rule to protect the confidentiality of the information so that no party can use it to obtain an undue preference for itself or its affiliates. FERC Order No. 787, Communication of Operational Information between Natural Gas Pipelines and Electric Transmission Operators, 145 F.E.R.C. ¶ 61,134 (Nov. 15, 2014). The No-Conduit Rule is discussed in C(3) *supra*.

The Polar Vortex that hit the Northeast in January 2014 did not result in the widespread natural gas and power shortages of the Southwest Cold Snap. However, a FERC report on the severe weather events of 2014 documented the "extreme stress" on the grid caused by the bitter cold: Significant generator outages did occur, often related to gas curtailments, lack of fuel oil delivery, and frozen coal. FERC Staff, Winter 2013–2014 Operations and Market Performance in RTOs and ISOs, AD14–8–000, at 8 (Apr. 1, 2014). Some users voluntarily curtailed use under demand response programs, and soon-to-retire coal plants served much of the increased demand for power while natural gas generation actually declined slightly. *Id.* at 7, 9.

FERC's orders on better scheduling and communication between gas pipeline operators and power generators do not address a key problem in the gas/electric interface. Gas-fired generators will not commit to long-term gas purchases or to purchase firm gas transportation capacity when they sell into competitive, short-term electricity markets. Echoing Professor Pierce's concern, one commentator sees trouble ahead. Judah Rose, Waiting for the Next Polar Vortex, 152 Pub. Util. Fort. 32 (June 2014). In Rose's view, FERC's market rules have not properly valued reliability. Most gas-fired power plants in deregulated markets do not have long-term firm gas supplies and they are unwilling to commit to firm service. Without such a commitment, new pipeline expansions will not be forthcoming to serve them.

The highest-ever spot price for gas in the Northeast area occurred during the Polar Vortex, while much lower and more stable prices existed in the gas-supply area of the Marcellus shale field. *Id.* at 35. Such a price difference shows that a lack of pipeline capacity constrained gas from moving northward to the areas hit hardest by the Polar Vortex. Up to one-fourth of the outages at power plants in the Northeast were due to a lack of natural gas, and gas-fired power plants were half of the total outages. *Id.* The gas-fired power plants that are replacing retired coal plants in the Northeast have not contracted for firm pipeline space and lack back-up fuel. *Id.* at 37. While all power plants with firm gas transportation service received gas during the Polar Vortex, plants with interruptible service literally can be left out in the cold. Rose describes how, in his view, FERC's policies in the electric sector are sending the market signal that reliability is not valued. *Id.* at 37. Unless generators are assured that they can recover the cost of contracting for firm pipeline capacity, even in markets without merchant power plants, reliability of the electricity grid is at risk.

Here is where the pipeline industry and the merchant power sector are on a "collision course" over the need to expand gas infrastructure. Peter Behr, Who Pays for New Pipeline Infrastructure?, EnergyWire, July 16, 2012. The gas pipeline industry requires customers to commit to long-term contracts for gas delivery before pipelines are built. It blames the power generators for not "stepping up" and contracting for reliability. The generators argue that they cannot afford to hold firm pipeline capacity if they do not get paid for doing so in the electricity markets. Eighty percent of merchant power plants' revenues comes from sales of short-term power into competitive markets where fuel costs and delivery costs determine whether the plant will be called upon to run. As the president of the Electric Power Supply Association (EPSA, the trade group for merchant power plants) has stated: "You can't force somebody to pay for something over the longer term than the product they're selling." *Id.* The head of the Interstate Natural Gas Association of America (INGAA) agrees with EPSA—and points to FERC to make it all work out.

NOTES AND COMMENTS

1.   The Polar Vortex caused spot gas prices to soar to over $120 per MMBtu at key trading points in the Mid-Atlantic and Northeast (compared to the Henry Hub, Louisiana price of $5.70 per MMBtu). FERC Staff, Winter 2013–2014 Operations, *supra* at 5. FERC's Office of Enforcement actively monitored the wholesale prices of gas and power and found no evidence of market manipulation. FERC staff reported that using data feeds from the clearinghouse exchanges and from CFTC's Large Trader Report (now shared with FERC) helped its market surveillance. *Id.* at 19–20. It does appear that FERC is a much more adept market monitor than during the California energy crisis.

Price volatility is a common feature of commodity markets. With forecasts commonly agreeing that bounteous shale gas supplies will keep U.S. gas prices low for the next 15 years at least, commenters have urged LDCs and other gas users to consider longer-term contracts for gas supplies and a greater use of financial instruments to hedge against price volatility. *See* Ken Costello, Going "Long" with Natural Gas?, 24 Electricity J. 42 (2011); Bipartisan Policy Center and Amer. Clean Skies Found., Task Force on Ensuring Stable Gas Markets (2014). The latter report lists a full page of new gas pipeline expansions underway in the Northeast, mostly to serve the Marcellus field. *Id.* at 47. The conflict between power generators and pipeline operators over funding new lines by committing to firm transportation has clearly not prevented many new projects.

2.   The Polar Vortex also led FERC, for the first time in its history, to exercise its emergency powers under the Interstate Commerce Act to direct liquid pipelines to ship propane, used for space heating in rural areas, on a priority basis to alleviate shortages in the Midwest and Northeast. FERC Staff, Winter 2013–2014 Operations, *supra* at 15 (Apr. 1, 2014). The political reaction to the propane shortage and its resulting high price was intense. Congress quickly passed the Home Heating Emergency Assistance through

Transportation Act of 2014, Pub. L. 113–90, authorizing the Secretary of Transportation to allow propane truck drivers to work longer hours when a propane shortage exists. *Query:* Does this Act trade one type of public safety for another? Trucker fatigue is a major cause of serious accidents and roads are icy in winter.

After Superstorm Sandy exposed the vulnerability of energy infrastructure along the Atlantic coast in 2012, the Department of Energy announced that it would establish two gasoline reserves, holding 500,000 barrels each, near New York harbor and in northern New England. Nick Snow, DOE to Establish Northeast Gasoline Reserve, Oil & Gas J. 31 (May 12, 2014). This is one form of adapting to severe weather events without relying on the market. Who does bear the cost of these reserves? Who will benefit from them?

If you live in an area served by merchant power plants that do not have firm gas supplies, would you consider buying a diesel generator, assuming that you have room to place it in your backyard? What are the safety and reliability records for these devices?

D. OIL PIPELINE REGULATORY FRAMEWORK

FERC regulates almost 200,000 miles of pipelines that ship liquids, such as crude oil and refined products, throughout the United States. The regulation of pipelines carrying oil and liquid petroleum products has a "complex and somewhat tortured history," as summarized by James H. McGrew in FERC: Federal Energy Regulatory Commission 227–34 (2d ed. 2009). The Hepburn Act of 1906 placed oil pipelines under the jurisdiction of the Interstate Commerce Commission (ICC), an agency created in 1887 to regulate railroads and telegraph companies. In 1977, jurisdiction over pipelines was transferred to the newly created FERC, to be regulated under the provisions of the Interstate Commerce Act (ICA). *Id.* at 227. FERC's website provides a copy of the October 1, 1977 version of the ICA's oil pipeline regulations (which no longer appear in the U.S. Code; indeed the ICC no longer exists, having been replaced in 1995 with the Surface Transportation Board). This 1977 ICA law is the foundation of the oil pipeline regulatory framework used today. *See* http://www.ferc. gov/legal/maj-ord-reg/ica.pdf.

Oil pipeline regulation shares one critical characteristic with natural gas pipeline regulation: FERC is required to assure that pipeline rates are fair and reasonable and nondiscriminatory. ICA, §§ 1(5), 2, & 3(1). Under Section 15(1) of the ICA, FERC must "determine and prescribe what will be the just and reasonable" rate for transportation services. However, in many other respects, oil pipeline regulation differs greatly from the gas side:

> The FERC has no authority over an interstate oil or liquids pipeline's decision to build a new pipeline, to expand a pipeline, or to abandon service, . . . or interconnect with another pipeline. The FERC has no jurisdiction over the decision by a pipeline to reverse the direction of its service, to discontinue offering transportation to particular commodities, or to lease all or a part of its pipeline system to another pipeline. The limited scope of FERC's regulation of oil pipelines stands in stark contrast to its pervasive role in pipeline infrastructure under the Natural Gas

Act, which even prohibits a would-be pipeline sponsor from putting a shovel in the ground until a certificate of public convenience and necessity is issued. The developer of a massive new multi-state oil pipeline could (in theory) choose not to inform the FERC of its plan to construct and operate a pipeline until it files an initial tariff thirty to sixty days prior to commencing service.

Christopher J. Barr, Unfinished Business: FERC's Evolving Standard for Capacity Rights on Oil Pipelines, 32 Energy L. J. 563, 564–65 (2011)(Barr 2011); *see also* Judith M. Matlock, Federal Oil and Gas Pipeline Regulation: An Overview, 48 Rocky Mtn. Min. L. F. J. 95, 173–74 (2011) (comparing the two frameworks and charting the different jurisdictional tests for FERC authority over interstate oil pipelines compared to gas pipelines).

Because oil pipelines are not required to have certificates of public convenience from FERC or any other federal agency, oil pipelines are not subject to federal siting authority, and thus are exempt from the need to comply with NEPA's environmental impact planning. This exemption also means that oil pipelines do not have the power of federally-granted eminent domain, as do gas pipelines. Oil pipeline siting and condemnation fall within the jurisdiction of state authorities. Section E discusses condemnation authority for oil pipelines under state law. Section F loops back to natural gas pipelines and the siting issues that arise when FERC issues certificates of public convenience for new gas facilities. Before moving to these sections, this section addresses two key features of oil pipeline regulation: the common carrier obligation and ratemaking.

Common Carrier Obligation. Under Section 1(4) of the ICA (Title 49, Ch. 1, Pt. 1, Sec. 1(4)(1977)), every common carrier must "provide and furnish transportation upon reasonable request." Thus, even if an oil pipeline is full, space must be made available to a new shipper tendering oil by cutting back the volumes shipped by existing users. This is called "prorationing" the oil pipeline's capacity. Until 1984, shippers typically nominated monthly volumes of crude to ship on a pipeline. If the nominations exceeded the pipeline's capacity, all shippers' nominations were reduced pro rata based on the percentage by which nominations exceeded pipeline space. Barr 2011, *supra* at 575. After 1984, FERC's tariff orders began to expressly include pipeline prorationing provisions based on historical volumes shipped over a certain period. Under this method, if three shippers had historically used 50%, 30% and 20% of a pipeline's capacity, and a new shipper requested service to use 10% of the pipeline's space, each historical shipper's volumes would be reduced ratably by 10%. The pipeline space would now be allocated to four shippers, with 45%, 27%, 18%, and 10% shares. *Id.* at 575. In its orders authorizing prorationing based on historical shipments on existing pipelines, FERC has consistently required that some of the pipeline's capacity (typically, at least 10%) be reserved for new shippers so that incumbents cannot monopolize the pipeline space. *Id.*

FERC's view of its duty to maintain open access on existing pipelines is also demonstrated in a 1996 decision in which FERC rejected a pipeline company's request to offer firm service to certain "contract" shippers. These contract shippers were willing to guarantee a monthly payment to the pipeline in return for the right to guaranteed throughput capacity, not subject to prorationing. FERC viewed this proposed tariff filing as a violation of the common carrier obligation that all shippers, including new entrants, have access to pipeline space, and also as a violation of Section 3(1) of the ICA that disallows any "undue or unreasonable preference" to any shipper. Matlock, *supra*, at 149–151. More recently, in 2014, FERC refused to approve a requested order granting Colonial Pipeline Company the right to create two classes of service on an existing pipeline that to date had offered the same service and rates to all shippers. Colonial proposed to create a class of committed shippers with priority access and another class of uncommitted shippers without such access. The committed shippers would gain first access to the allocation of any available excess system capacity in exchange for committing to ship a specific volume or pay a deficiency charge for not shipping that amount (a "ship or pay" contract). Colonial would also offer discounted rates to shippers making volume commitments for space on its existing line. FERC found the proposed terms of service to be unduly discriminatory. Colonial Pipeline Company, 146 F.E.R.C. ¶ 61,206 (2014). Note that Colonial was not requesting this new two-tiered tariff structure in order to finance an expansion of the pipeline's capacity, although Colonial argued that its proposed tariff would enhance its "confidence" in the soundness of a major investment in new capacity in the future by assuring throughput guarantees on its existing line.

In today's changed business environment, FERC has had to adapt its prorationing policies in two ways: First, to accommodate a virtual flood of new shippers seeking to use certain existing lines; and second, to respond to the commercial reality that contracts between shippers and pipeline owners are often necessary to fund new pipeline capacity.

The first scenario is well illustrated by a pipeline carrying Bakken crude. In *Enbridge Pipeline (North Dakota) LLC*, 140 F.E.R.C. ¶ 61,193 (2012), Enbridge sought an order revising its prorationing tariff. Between 2006 and 2012, 246 new shippers had registered to get on board Enbridge's North Dakota line. In October 2010, FERC granted an emergency two-year freeze on the ability of new shippers to become regular shippers on this pipeline, limiting new shippers to 10% of the pipeline's capacity. With the freeze about to end, Enbridge requested that FERC approve the following prorationing policy: (1) shippers with a history of shipping in nine of the most recent twelve months were "historical" shippers entitled to receive 95% of total capacity based on past use; (2) all other shippers were "new" shippers, with 5% of existing capacity reserved for them; (3) any expansion of capacity would guarantee new shippers a priority to at least 10% of total capacity; (4) affiliates of historical shippers could not become new shippers; and (5) minimum batch sizes were imposed to assure efficient operations. FERC found the proposed tariff to be just and reasonable, based on its broad support from shippers and the unique circumstances facing Enbridge. *See* Report of the Oil & Liquids Pipeline Regulation Comm., 34 Energy L.J. 1, 17–18 (2013).

In a second case with a scenario similar to Enbridge's Bakken line, the proliferation of new shippers and over-nominations on its pipeline led Seaway Pipeline to propose a creative approach to allocating 10% of capacity to new shippers: a lottery system using a software program to generate random "winners" of pipeline space. Seaway argued that the proposed system would set a fair and nondiscriminatory method of allocating minimum-batch size tenders to the many new shippers clamoring for access. Seaway also asked that the definition of affiliate be revised so that no affiliates could win space in the same lottery and that nominations be limited to no more than the total reserved space set aside for new shippers. Some new shippers protested that the tariff essentially locked them out because a new shipper would have to win the lottery for twelve successive months in order to gain the status of a regular shipper. FERC accepted the tariff as a good faith attempt to balance the interests of the bona fide, long-term shippers on the system with the interests of new shippers that were not abusing the nominations process by submitting speculative requests for service. Any lottery winner had to deliver volumes equal to the minimum tender or pay a tariff charge. Seaway Crude Pipeline Company LLC, 143 F.E.R.C. ¶ 61,036 (2013); Report of Oil Pipeline Comm., *supra*, at 16–17. Note that neither of these FERC orders authorized any type of firm service to a new class of contract shippers operating under a special rate; rather, the orders established new methods of allocating existing pipeline space among all shippers.

FERC's second accommodation to the ICA's mandated common carrier duty involves new pipelines and pipeline capacity expansions. Recall that long-term contracts between gas pipeline owners and shippers are a cornerstone of FERC regulation of the gas industry. Those shippers who buy firm (i.e., non-interruptible) service are guaranteed the pipeline capacity that they have committed to buy by paying a reservation fee in addition to the usage charge based on the volume of gas actually shipped. See Section A.2, above. Companies building new gas pipelines request certificates of public convenience and necessity from FERC only after almost all proposed new capacity is committed to contracts with firm shippers. Christopher Barr, Growing Pains: FERC's Response to Challenges to the Development of Oil Pipeline Infrastructure, 28 Energy L.J. 43, 66 (2007) (Barr 2007). This regulatory framework provides considerable certainty to investors to fund new gas pipelines. By contrast, most shippers on oil pipelines do not enter into a written contract with the pipeline; rather they nominate and tender shipments under the terms of the FERC-approved tariff. Barr 2011, *supra*, at 568.

For many decades, oil pipelines simply filed tariffs after construction. Litigation over rates or service between shippers and the pipeline owners was rare because the two parties were affiliates, doing business together as separately incorporated companies, under the common ownership of a vertically integrated major. Shippers signed "throughput and deficiency" (T&D) agreements with pipeline owners, requiring shippers to use pipeline capacity or pay a deficiency charge. However, starting in the 1980s, independent pipeline companies have entered the market because of spin-offs by integrated companies or divestments required by regulators in approving mergers, and also because of the tax-related attractiveness to large investment funds of forming master limited partnerships and other such vehicles. With the increase in unaffiliated shippers, pipeline investors sought some sort of advance approval of tariff and service terms, including terms that granted priority rights to pipeline space to those shippers who signed long-term contracts that helped to finance a new pipeline. Barr 2007, *supra*, at 52.

In response, FERC has adopted a policy that allows priority access to shippers that make long-term commitments to use a proposed new pipeline. FERC's approval of such a tariff structure is done in a declaratory order, issued in advance of constructing the pipeline, to provide some assurance to the investors in the proposed expansion that their investment (often totaling many hundreds of millions of dollars) will be financially secure. In this regard, these declaratory orders are analogous to FERC's certification procedure for new gas pipelines.

The first project to use such an order was a proposed new pipeline transporting oil from Western Canada to the Rockies and Midwest. In *Express Pipeline P'ship*, 75 F.E.R.C. ¶ 61,303 (1996), the pipeline company held an "open season," allowing any shipper to commit to long-term use of the pipeline (varying from five years to fifteen years) in return for locking in lower pipeline rates. The pipeline company asked FERC for a declaratory order pre-approving the committed shippers' rates and also approving key rate components to use in setting the cost-based rate available to the non-contract shippers who declined to commit during the open season. FERC's declaratory order approved this dual rate structure, finding that the two different rates were not discriminatory because the two types of shippers were differently situated. While this order did not involve a priority right for contract shippers that would allow them to escape prorationing if pipeline space was oversubscribed, it did establish a way to secure advance approval of pipeline rates prior to construction. It also showed that FERC now interpreted the ICA as allowing special contract rate rights for contract shippers in the context of pipeline expansions, a decided change from its 1996 stance that contract rates would violate the ICA's prohibition against undue or unreasonable preferences. Barr 2011, *supra*, at 574. FERC does require that contract shippers pay a higher premium rate, reflecting the priority service that they receive, but the premium may be quite small.

Subsequent orders have allowed priority rights to expanded pipeline space for committed shippers. For example, in 1999, FERC approved a tariff providing that 80% of the expanded capacity of Mid-America's pipeline could be allocated to contract shippers that were willing to pay a rate premium in return for not being subject to prorationing during their seven-year commitment to use the pipeline. In a 2006 order, this 80%/20% split was retained in another expansion of capacity by Mid-America, after FERC carefully noted that a majority of total capacity was still offered on a common carrier basis and that all shippers had the same opportunity to participate in the contract program. Barr 2011, *supra*, at 579.

How much capacity can a pipeline owner contract away in advance when pipelines are statutorily required to be common carriers and to prorate existing users to make room for new shippers? FERC has required that pipeline owners leave at least 10% of their expanded capacity open to new shippers so that incumbent shippers cannot squeeze out new competitors that need access to markets. Barr 2011, *supra*, at 580–583. FERC now views these long-term contracts with "anchor" shippers as essential for assuring pipeline owners that construction of a new pipeline will be a financially secure investment. As Barr notes,

"FERC's policy regarding priority rights for contract shippers has developed dramatically in recent years . . . to the rapid and seemingly routine approval of substantial priority rights for contract shippers." *Id.* at 583.

Declaratory orders are now used for many projects seeking advance approval of many actions, including rolled-in versus incremental ratemaking, surcharges to fund expansions, and even line abandonment. FERC orders have also approved "settlement offer" rates, negotiated and agreed to by pipelines and shippers, to avert future rate disputes over expansion projects. Barr 2007, *supra*, at 54–55. FERC's ratemaking principles are discussed next.

Ratemaking. When FERC inherited authority over oil pipelines in 1977, it struggled to understand the ICC's arcane, cost-based regulation of oil pipelines, which differed significantly from FERC's regulation of gas pipelines. In 1982, FERC decided to adopt a "clean slate" approach to oil pipeline ratemaking. McGrew, *supra*, at 228–29. FERC issued Opinion No. 154 in the *Williams Pipe Line Co.* case in 1982, which departed quite radically from the methodology and assumptions of the ICC. FERC based its approach on a finding that the ICA did not require traditional cost-based regulation because oil markets were competitive enough to keep rates within a reasonable zone. Therefore, FERC simply set a rate cap to prevent "egregious price exploitation." McGrew, *supra*, at 229. However, the reviewing court found that FERC's approach did not ensure that rates would be just and reasonable, as required by the ICA, because there was no nexus to cost of service and no demonstrable evidence that competitive forces would result in just and reasonable rates. Farmers Union Central Exch., Inc. v. FERC, 734 F.2d 1486 (D. C. Cir. 1984)(Farmers Union II).

On remand, FERC tried again and issued Opinion No. 154–B in the *Williams* case in 1985, adopting a "trended original cost" methodology to ratemaking that accorded with traditional ratemaking principles. Order No. 154–B is the ratemaking standard for cost-based rates today. It sets a ceiling rate that may not be surpassed, although rates may be (and often are) lower than the ceiling. However, oil pipeline regulation continued to be plagued by uncertainties and protracted litigation over rates. Congress stepped into the fray with EPAct 1992. First, Congress declared that unprotested pipeline rates in existence for at least a year at the time of passage of EPAct on October 23, 1992 were "deemed to be just and reasonable." Thus, many rates were grandfathered into the new regulatory framework.

Second, EPAct 1992 directed FERC to issue a "simplified and generally applicable ratemaking methodology" for oil pipelines that would meet the "just and reasonable" standard, using streamlined procedures to reduce delays in future proceedings. *Barr 2007, supra, at 57.* In response, FERC promulgated three orders, Orders No. 561, 571, and 572 in 1993 and 1994, to simplify ratemaking. Order No. 561 created a cost-of-service ratemaking method for new services and also set a generic indexing methodology to govern rate changes. A pipeline's base year rate is multiplied by a factor based on the Producer Price Index (PPI) for Finished Goods to establish a ceiling for just and reasonable rates. This generic index is applied to EPAct 1992's grandfathered rates as well. Thus, FERC asserted that it met the Congressional mandate to set a simple and generally applicable way of regulating oil pipeline rates. The grandfathered rates, adjusted by the index, would establish many oil pipeline rates in the future. Barr 2007, *supra*, at 58. This Order survived judicial review in *Association of Oil Pipelines v. FERC*, 281 F.3d 239 (D.C. Cir. 2002) and most pipeline rate changes have used the ceiling index.

FERC also adopted three alternatives to the generally applicable use of this indexed ratemaking:

1.   Cost-based rates, higher than the index rate, that can apply if a pipeline shows that its actual costs diverge substantially from the indexed rate. 18 C.F.R. § 342.4(a).

2.   Market-based rates (MBRs) that are permitted only after FERC has made a finding that the pipeline lacks significant market power. 18 C.F.R. § 342(b).

3.   "Settlement" rates, also called "negotiated" rates, that are based on a written agreement with shippers. 18 C.F.R. § 342.4(c). If some shippers refuse to agree to the settlement rate negotiated by other shippers, a cost-based rate will apply to the non-contract shippers. 18 C.F.R. § 342.2.

These efforts by Congress and FERC have simplified oil pipeline ratemaking. Still, some areas of significant uncertainty remain, including challenges to the use of grandfathered rates based on a substantial change in circumstances. One of the "hottest" areas of concern involves the application of market-based rates in place of cost-based rates. The following case illustrates the economic principles used by FERC to decide if market-based rates should be granted to an oil pipeline; the same principles are used for gas pipelines. As background, the FERC staff supported Mobil Pipe Line's request for market-based rates, but the Administrative Law Judge and the FERC commissioners did not agree with the staff's view. The court adopted the FERC staff's "slam dunk" view of the case, leaving the reader to wonder why the commissioners had rejected market-based rates. The notes after the case offer some additional perspective.

Mobil Pipe Line Co. v. FERC

676 F.3d 1098 (D.C. Cir. 2012).

■ KAVANAUGH, CIRCUIT JUDGE:

Congress has directed the Federal Energy Regulatory Commission to ensure that oil pipeline rates are "just and reasonable." When the market in which a pipeline operates is not competitive, the Commission caps the pipeline's rates. When the market in which a pipeline operates is competitive, however, the Commission generally allows the pipeline to charge market-based rates.

Mobil owns and operates the Pegasus crude oil pipeline, which runs from Illinois to Texas. The pipeline transports mostly Western Canadian crude oil. Out of the 2.2 million barrels of Western Canadian crude oil produced each day, Pegasus transports only about three percent—about 66,000 barrels each day.

In light of the competitiveness of the Western Canadian crude oil market and Pegasus's minor role in it, Mobil applied to FERC for permission to charge market-based rates on Pegasus. FERC's expert staff examined the market and deemed this case a "slam dunk" for allowing Mobil to charge market-based rates. But the Commission itself came out the other way and denied Mobil's application on the ground that Pegasus possessed market power.

We conclude that the Commission's decision was unreasonable. . . .

I.A.

Congress has directed FERC to ensure that oil pipelines charge "just and reasonable" rates. 49 U.S.C. app. § 1(5) (1988); *see* Frontier Pipeline Co. v. FERC, 452 F.3d 774, 776 (D.C. Cir. 2006).

To implement that command, the Commission regulates rates via an indexing system. *See* Revisions to Oil Pipeline Regulations Pursuant to the Energy Policy Act of 1992 (Order No. 561), 58 Fed. Reg. 58,753, 58,754 (Nov. 4, 1993). Under FERC's indexing system, an oil pipeline must establish an initial baseline rate with the Commission. 18 C.F.R. § 342.1(a). That rate is usually determined by a pipeline's cost of providing service, including a reasonable return on investment. 18 C.F.R. § 342.2; *see also* 58 Fed. Reg. at 58,758. After FERC accepts a pipeline's initial baseline rate, the pipeline may increase that rate up to a ceiling set by the Commission's indexing formula. 18 C.F.R. § 342.3. FERC's indexing system allows oil pipelines to adjust their rates to account for inflation, while protecting shippers from large rate increases. 58 Fed. Reg. at 58,758.

But rates set by indexing "do not function well to signal individuals how to efficiently respond to changes in market conditions." Market-Based Ratemaking for Oil Pipelines (Order No. 572), 59 Fed. Reg. 59,148, 59,150 (Nov. 16, 1994). To address that shortcoming, FERC may authorize pipelines to charge rates established by market competition instead of indexing. *See* 18 C.F.R. §§ 342.4(b), 348.1, 348.2. Market-based rates "can result in pricing that is both efficient and just and reasonable." 59 Fed. Reg. at 59,150.

A pipeline does not have a unilateral right to charge market-based rates. Rather, in order to charge market-based rates, a pipeline must obtain approval from the Commission. *See* 18 C.F.R. §§ 342.4(b), 348.1, 348.2.

FERC Order No. 572 guides the Commission's consideration of applications for market-based rate authority. 59 Fed. Reg. at 59,149. Under Order No. 572, FERC's inquiry centers on whether a pipeline possesses market power. *Id.* at 59,150. To qualify for market-based rate authority, a pipeline must demonstrate that it lacks market power in its product and geographic markets. 18 C.F.R. §§ 342.4(b), 348.1(c)(1), (2). FERC has said that market power is "the ability profitably to maintain prices above competitive levels for a significant period of time." *See* Department of Justice & Federal Trade Commission, Horizontal Merger Guidelines § 0.1 (rev. ed. 1997). . . . As that standard formulation suggests, FERC has decided to adhere to well-settled economic and competition principles in determining whether an oil pipeline possesses market power.

B

Pegasus is an 858-mile, 20-inch-diameter crude oil pipeline owned and operated by Mobil. Until April 2006, Pegasus transported about 66,000 barrels of crude oil per day from Nederland, Texas, to Patoka, Illinois. Rapid development of the Western Canadian oil sands, however, made transportation of Western Canadian crude oil to new markets an attractive proposition. To take advantage of that opportunity, in April 2006, Mobil reversed the direction of the flow of crude oil on Pegasus so that it could transport Western Canadian crude oil southward.

Pegasus now transports almost entirely Western Canadian crude oil from Illinois to Texas. The crude oil comes to the Pegasus pipeline in Illinois by pipelines from Western Canada. Importantly, Pegasus transports only about 66,000 barrels of Western Canadian crude oil each day—which is only about three percent of the 2.2 million barrels of Western Canadian crude oil produced each day.

Mobil filed an application with FERC to charge market-based rates on Pegasus. The Commission scheduled an initial hearing before an administrative law judge to determine whether Pegasus possessed market power. At the hearing, FERC's expert staff strongly supported Mobil's application for market-based rate authority, concluding that Pegasus's origin and destination markets were plainly competitive.

The contested issue here concerns Pegasus's origin market, consisting of the competitive alternatives available for producers and shippers of Western Canadian crude oil to transport and sell their crude oil. Those alternatives include local refineries in Western Canada and refineries throughout Canada and the United States that can be reached by pipelines. [Ed. note: No party contested FERC's finding that Pegasus's Gulf Coast destination market was extremely competitive.]

In arguing that Mobil should be allowed to charge market-based rates on the Pegasus pipeline, FERC's expert staff did not think this a close case. To get a flavor of the expert staff's views, we here quote some of their observations:

* * *

- "[H]ow can a small pipeline exert market power over a large origin market?" J.A. 617.
- "Pegasus clearly cannot be a monopolist for the transportation" of "Western Canadian crude . . . as the supply of such products vastly exceeds Pegasus's capacity." J.A. 825.
- "[I]t is literally impossible for a recent entrant to be a monopolist if it is entering an already established market." J.A. 640.

* * *

II

FERC denied Mobil's application for market-based rate authority on the ground that Pegasus possessed market power in its origin market. . . . We find FERC's decision unsustainable.

The Pegasus pipeline transports almost exclusively Western Canadian crude oil. The proper question, therefore, is whether producers and shippers of Western Canadian crude oil must rely so heavily on Pegasus for transportation of their crude oil that Pegasus can be said to possess market power—that is, whether Mobil could profitably raise rates on Pegasus above competitive levels for a significant period of time because of a lack of competition. . . .

Market-power analysis focuses on whether there are alternatives to a firm's services that constrain its ability to profitably charge prices above competitive levels for a significant period of time. The inquiry examines the alternatives reasonably available to consumers and the cross-elasticity of demand—that is, the extent to which consumers will respond to an increase in the price of one good by substituting or switching to another. . . .

* * *

Here, in considering the relevant market, FERC's expert staff identified many local refineries that process Western Canadian crude oil, as well as several pipelines that move Western Canadian crude oil to other refineries in Canada and the United States. As the staff noted, the critical statistic is that about 97 percent of Western Canadian crude oil gets to refineries by means other than Pegasus.

. . . Mobil rightly asks: How can Pegasus be said to possess market power over producers and shippers of Western Canadian crude oil when Pegasus transports only about three percent of Western Canadian crude oil? FERC has no good answer to that simple question. And the absence of a good answer is why FERC's expert staff concluded that this case was a "slam dunk" for market-based rates.

The hole in the Commission's analysis is highlighted by the fact that Pegasus is a new entrant into a previously competitive market. Before Pegasus started transporting Western Canadian crude oil in 2006, producers and shippers of Western Canadian crude oil had numerous competitive alternatives for transporting and selling their crude oil. When Pegasus came onto the scene, it simply provided an additional alternative for Western Canadian crude oil producers and shippers. Basic economic logic dictates that the introduction of a new alternative into a highly competitive market further increases competition; it does not suddenly render a previously competitive market uncompetitive.

Put simply, we fail to understand how the entry of Pegasus, which transports only about 66,000 barrels per day, into a previously competitive 2.2 million barrel per day market makes that market suddenly uncompetitive. As FERC's expert staff explained, "If you evaluate the market with no Pegasus, and it's clearly competitive, adding one more option can't possibly make the market less competitive." Tr. of Admin. Hrg. at 2216. The Commission's contrary conclusion is analogous to saying that a new shoe store in a city has monopoly power even though there are already numerous shoe stores in the same city. That doesn't make much sense.

The Commission may have been led astray by its assessment that Mobil, if granted market-based rate authority, could raise rates on Pegasus by 15 percent or more. But the Commission calculated that figure by using Pegasus's *regulated* rate as the baseline. As FERC's expert staff explained, the 15 percent figure demonstrates only that Pegasus's regulated rate is below the competitive rate. The regulated rate does not reflect Pegasus's full value to Western Canadian crude oil producers and shippers. Therefore, the possibility that the market rate might be higher than the regulated rate does not show that Pegasus possesses market power.

FERC also seemed concerned that producers and shippers of Western Canadian crude oil could obtain higher prices on the Gulf Coast, thereby giving Pegasus undue leverage over producers and shippers of Western Canadian crude oil who sought that particular outlet. It is true that Pegasus is the primary avenue for producers and shippers of Western Canadian crude oil to get their crude oil to *Gulf Coast* refineries. But from the perspective of producers and shippers of Western Canadian crude oil, there is nothing unique about *Gulf Coast* refineries, as distinct from other refineries available to them in Canada and the United States. . . . The overall picture here, as FERC's expert staff emphasized, is one of robust competition for Western Canadian crude oil: Producers and shippers of Western Canadian crude oil have numerous competitive alternatives to get their crude oil to refineries. If Pegasus raised its rates above competitive levels, then producers and shippers of Western Canadian crude oil would choose one of the many alternative outlets available to them. Those other outlets thereby constrain the rates that Pegasus can charge. There is thus no plausible way, as we see it and as FERC's expert staff saw it, to say that Pegasus holds a hammer over Western Canadian crude oil producers and shippers.

Moreover, contrary to FERC's suggestion, short-term price variations—which may temporarily make Gulf Coast refineries (and thus Pegasus) an attractive outlet for Western Canadian crude oil producers and shippers—are consistent with competition. . . . As FERC has previously explained, short-term price variations that result in regional price differentials do not establish market power. *See* Explorer Pipeline Co., 87 FERC at 62,394 ("Differential pricing, when constrained by effective competition, can materially improve the efficiency of transportation markets by allocating capacity to those shippers who value it the most, particularly in markets involving different degrees of geographic or seasonal variation."); Longhorn Partners Pipeline, L.P., 83 FERC at 62,380 ("[A]ny price differential between the origin and destination markets does not confer monopolistic power upon [the pipeline], but rather it promotes competition.").

In sum, when an agency is statutorily required to adhere to basic economic and competition principles—or when it has exercised its discretion and chosen basic economic and competition principles as the guide for agency decisionmaking in a particular area, as FERC did in Order No. 572—the agency must adhere to those principles when deciding individual cases. Here, the Commission jumped the rails by treating the Pegasus pipeline as the rough equivalent of a bottleneck or essential facility for transportation of Western Canadian crude oil. As we have explained, the record thoroughly undermines FERC's conclusion. The Commission's decision thus cannot stand.

. . . We grant Mobil's petition for review, vacate FERC's order, and remand for further proceedings consistent with this opinion. *So ordered.* ■

NOTE AND COMMENT

1.   All five FERC Commissioners, both Democrats and Republicans, had adopted the reasoning of the Administrative Law Judge (ALJ) that Mobil Pipeline had monopoly power and therefore should not be granted market-based rates (MBRs). *See* 133 F.E.R.C. ¶ 61,192 (Dec. 1, 2010) (affirming the ALJ's decision to deny MBRs). The ALJ had found that the origin market was confined to the Upper Midwest area and that shippers had no good competitive alternatives to sending their crude south to markets. Thus, nothing constrained Mobil's ability to charge more than a reasonable rate. All parties agreed on the definition of market power as the ability to profitably sustain "a small but significant and nontransitory increase in price," the "SSNIP" test. 133 F.E.R.C. ¶ 61,192, at ¶ 12. How could such disparate conclusions be reached?

The ALJ had determined that the benchmark, long-term competitive price for applying the SSNIP test was Pegasus's prevailing tariff rate of $1.218 per barrel because FERC had accepted this tariff as a fair and reasonable reflection of Pegasus's long-run average costs. *Id.* at ¶ 13. The ALJ, using earlier FERC precedents, found that a 15% threshold test for a price increase under the SSNIP test would properly allow Mobil to raise its rate by $0.1827 per barrel (15% of $1.218). The data showed that the price differential between crude oil stored in the Midwest and crude oil sold on the Gulf Coast was about $4.50. *Id.* at ¶¶ 34–35. Clearly, a shipper would want to get its oil to the Gulf Coast if it cost less than $4.50 to ship it there, unless some other alternative could be used that would give the shipper a higher "netback" price. The netback price is the price to the producer/shipper after paying the transportation costs to a delivery point. Mobil's position was that it owned the scarce resource that allowed the oil to flow south, and so Mobil should be able to capture the $4.50 price differential in a market-based rate. This rate would clearly be a dramatic increase over its existing tariff. The ALJ and FERC commissioners found that a market-based rate would put Pegasus shippers "at the mercy of Mobil" for a persistent period of time due to high demand for Pegasus's service. *Id.* at ¶ 51.

How did the D.C. Circuit court dismantle this reasoning?

While the Pegasus pipeline was a relatively small one, FERC faced an impending rate case in 2012 involving a pipeline flow reversal for the much larger Seaway pipeline owned by Enterprise and Enbridge ("E&E"). Large amounts of crude oil were bottled up at the Cushing hub in Oklahoma and shippers were eager to move it south to the Gulf Coast. E&E requested market-based rates for the reversed pipeline, which would flow 150,000 barrels per day at first, but increase to 375,000 bpd by 2013 because of pump additions and modifications. Twenty parties, including the Canadian Association of Petroleum Producers, Chevron and the Independent Petroleum Association of America, moved to intervene to protest the proposed MBRs. FERC Commissioners denied MBRs for the Reversed Seaway pipeline in *Enterprise Products Partners L.P. and Enbridge*, Docket No. OR12–4–000, 139 F.E.R.C. ¶ 61,099 (May 7, 2012), on the basis that E&E had failed to provide the necessary data to evaluate competitive alternatives in terms of price.

The D.C. Circuit opinion in *Mobil Pipeline* had been issued just three weeks before FERC's denial of MBRs to Seaway. In June 2012, the Commission granted an Order for Rehearing in the *Seaway* case, seeking comments from all parties about the proper interpretation of the Court of Appeals' decision in the *Mobil* case.

On February 20, 2014, the FERC Commissioners again denied MBRs to the reversed Seaway pipeline in a continuation of Docket No. OR12–4–000, 146 F.E.R.C. ¶ 61,115 (Feb. 20, 2014). FERC's order contains an extensive analysis of the impact of *Mobil* on FERC policies and procedures for market-power determinations going forward. FERC first summarized the position of the pipeline companies, represented by the Association of Oil Pipelines (AOPL), with those of many shipper groups, such as the Domestic Energy Producers Alliance (DEPA). The following material quotes directly from FERC's order by numbered paragraphs, interspersed with bracketed paraphrasing of FERC's reasoning:

Enterprise Products Partners L.P. and Enbridge, Inc.

Docket No. OR12–4–000, 146 FERC ¶ 61,115 (Feb. 20, 2014).

* * *

10. . . . AOPL states that the Commission's recent rulings appear to indicate a diminished faith in markets and an unwarranted retreat from the Commission's longstanding market-based rate policies. AOPL believes that the holding in *Mobil* is consistent with the Commission's previously articulated goals, and it urges the Commission to return to the core principles of Order No. 572 and its decisions in *Explorer* and *Longhorn*: (1) that the market-based rate analysis must be solely rooted in, and not stray from, the concept that a good alternative for the pipeline-applicant's shippers is an alternative that is reasonably available to those shippers in such market; (2) the level of the pipeline-applicant's regulated rate is irrelevant to rendering a decision on an application for market based rates; and (3) an entrant into a previously competitive market typically will make that market more competitive, rather than render a previously competitive market uncompetitive.

11. The Domestic Energy Producers Alliance (DEPA) submits that *Mobil* should have no effect on the May 7, 2012 Order [denying MBRs to Seaway], which the Commission should reaffirm on rehearing. DEPA states that the Commission correctly found that Enterprise/Enbridge's application for permission to charge market-based rates . . . must be denied "given the applicant's failure to provide detailed cost data, a fundamental element of market power analysis, which Enterprise/Enbridge acknowledges cannot be provided at this time."

* * * [The positions of other intervenors are omitted.]

32. The court in *Mobil* first identified Order No. 572 as the guide for the Commission's consideration of applications for market-based rate authority. The court then set forth the Commission's definition of market power as "the ability profitably to maintain prices above competitive levels for a significant period of time." The court stated that in adopting this definition of market power, the Commission "decided to adhere to

well-settled economic and competition principles in determining whether an oil pipeline possesses market power." Ultimately, the court held that when the Commission decided to follow basic economic and competition principles, as it has under Order No. 572, the Commission must adhere to these principles in deciding individual cases. The language concerning Order No. 572 and the Commission's approach to market power applications clearly show that the court in no way intended to overturn or fundamentally alter the Commission's long-standing procedures. . . . [T]he court instead faulted the Commission for failing to properly apply this framework to Pegasus' application.

33. . . . To ensure those policies are followed in the present and future proceedings, the Commission will reiterate the steps necessary for an oil pipeline to demonstrate a lack of market power.

[¶ 34. A pipeline requesting MBRs must show that it lacks significant market power. Under Order No. 572, it must (1) define the relevant markets; (2) identify competitive alternatives to shippers; and (3) compute the market concentration for the relevant market.]

[¶¶ 35–44. The proper geographic origin market for oil pipelines is the production field in which the pipeline is physically located, but an applicant may offer other evidence to establish the origin market for market hubs. FERC will continue to make case-by-case determinations of the relevant market. The relevant product market consists of products being shipped in the origin market that can discipline the exercise of market power, based on cross-elasticities of demand.

Competitive alternatives must be described and may include other pipelines, rail, barges, and local refiners or users.]

[¶¶ 45–46. Data is required for an alternative to be deemed "good" in terms of availability and price. The methodology for determining whether an alternative was competitive constituted the single largest point of contention in the *Mobil* proceeding. Trial Staff and the applicant found numerous alternatives; shippers and the ALJ found none that could effectively constrain rates on the Pegasus pipeline.]

[¶ 47. Competitive alternatives are determined using prices. A shipper will choose a higher-priced transportation route if the price of crude in a destination market exceeds the transportation price differential. That is, a shipper will spend $2 more to transport crude if the destination point's price for crude exceeds by $2 any other destination's price.]

[¶ 48. In *Mobil*, the Pegasus tariff rate was used as a proxy for the competitive price, but this was not an appropriate proxy under the market conditions presented in the case.]

49. The primary concern over using Pegasus' tariff rate as a proxy for the competitive price centered on the excess demand for transportation on Pegasus, and how this excess demand demonstrated that the tariff rate was below, perhaps far below, the competitive price. Absent a price restraint such as a tariff that prevents a pipeline from raising its transportation rate, a pipeline facing excess demand for access to its pipeline will increase price to a point where the demand for transportation equals the capacity, or supply, of the pipeline. As a competitive price is by definition at the point where supply and demand intersect, excess demand occurs when a price is below the competitive

level. Using a proxy that is significantly below the competitive price in a traditional netback analysis could yield improper results, for any price increase from the point of the tariff rate up to the competitive level could be mistaken for an exercise of market power where no such market power exists.

[¶¶ 50–54. As shown in *Mobil*, a pipeline's regulated rate can be far below a competitive price level. FERC's prior orders on MBRs have explicitly stated that MBRs will exceed cost-of-service rates, which only serve as a floor. Still it is necessary, as a fundamental element of market-power analysis, to find that competitive alternatives exist in terms of price. For an alternative to be a good alternative, it must be competitively priced.]

[¶ 55. In *Mobil*, Trial Staff found that all alternatives being used in the origin market were good alternatives in terms of price. A competitive price is the netback of the alternative that provides the lowest netback among all alternatives, called the "marginal netback," Shippers will seek to ship on the alternative that earns the highest netback. When that alternative is full, shippers will seek the alternative that offers the next highest netback, etc. The marginal netback is the lowest netback generated among alternatives being used by shippers. Thus, all used alternatives represent netbacks above the marginal netback and are therefore competitively priced. The fact that a shipper uses an alternative shows that this alternative is economically viable for the producer-shipper.]

[¶¶ 56–59. Usage is the necessary proxy to determine good alternatives in terms of price. Usage data will satisfy FERC's requirement that price data be provided by the applicant to demonstrate good alternatives and lack of market power.]

60. The question in market power analyses is whether an alternative can discipline an increase in price above the competitive level. As demonstrated in *Mobil*, it is not necessarily a question of whether the applicant can raise its current rates. By measuring market power by use of the marginal netback, all alternatives that could prevent an anti-competitive increase in price will be included as competitive alternatives.

[¶¶ 61–64 omitted.]

[¶¶ 65–68. Unused alternatives offer lower netbacks than the marginal netback. A detailed price analysis is necessary to overcome the implication from shipper behavior (i.e., its non-use of an available alternative) that the alternative is not price competitive.]

69. [In sum], . . . the competitive price in an origin market analysis will equal the lowest netback provided by used alternatives, also known as the marginal netback. The marginal netback is calculated by ranking the netbacks offered by used alternatives until the lowest is reached. Once the marginal netback is determined, any available [but currently unused] alternatives providing a lower netback are analyzed to determine whether a sub-marginal netback is within an acceptable range to still discipline a potential price increase by the applicant pipeline above the competitive level.

70. Th[e] list of competitive alternatives within a geographic market will thus include used alternatives, and useable alternatives that are shown to be competitive alternatives in terms of price. Usage provides

justification for determining that an alternative is a good alternative in terms of price. Comparison with the marginal netback provides justification for including unused but useable alternatives in the list of competitive alternatives. Pipelines and other participants may offer detailed price analyses to include or challenge the inclusion of any alternative on a case-by-case basis.

[¶¶ 71–76 on Market Share and Market Concentration Measures omitted.]■

FERC concluded its order by denying E&E's request for MBRs because E&E had not met its burden of proof that it did not have market power in the origin market. E&E had not presented any operational data, as required above, to allow a MBR determination. However, FERC noted that E&E could file an application for MBR authority under the policies and procedures explained by FERC above.

NOTES AND COMMENTS

1. Review the positions of AOPL and the producers in the two first paragraphs quoted above in this FERC decision about the effect of *Mobil Pipeline*. Whose position did FERC adopt?

2. The burden of proof is on the applicant to present the cost and price data under the economic principles outlined above. Test your understanding of FERC's economic principles in the following scenario. Assume a shipper-producer can sell its crude to five existing market outlets via pipeline shipments from its wells in the field to these destination markets. After transporting the oil, the producer's netback price of a barrel of crude oil sold is as follows for each of the five used alternatives. Two other currently unused alternatives are also presented in the scenario:

    1. **$59 netback for sales to Refinery A,** located near the producing field, but not able to process heavy crude without significant costs added to the refining process.

    2. **$70 netback for sales to Refinery B**, located further from the producing field, but able to process heavy crude into gasoline and sell it using pipelines that do not have excess demand.

    3. **$60 netback using Pipeline X** to Gulf Coast markets.

    4. **$62 netback using Pipeline Y** to Gulf Coast markets.

    5. **$64 netback using Pipeline Z** to Gulf Coast markets.

    6. **Pipeline Caliph headed West** to California markets is currently not being used, but if used, would result in a netback to the producers of **$55 per barrel**.

    7. **Railroad RRCo.** will be completed in six months; the netback price using RRCo. to the Gulf Coast is **$57 per barrel.**

    (a) What is the marginal netback price that will be the proxy for the competitive benchmark price in a market-based rate analysis?

    (b) If Seaway were granted MBRs and producers receive a netback price of $59.50 on Seaway, is this a just and reasonable price under FERC's methodology outlined above?

If the market-based shipping rates on Seaway are 10 times higher than a cost-based rate, are they still just and reasonable under FERC's Order No. 572 and the economic principles applicable to implementing this order?

(c) If Seaway were granted MBRs, resulting in producers receiving a netback price of $55, is this just and reasonable under FERC's policies? What test are you using?

(d) The soon-to-be Railroad results in a *higher* shipper netback. Won't this new entrant put pressure on Seaway to reduce its shipping rates to meet or beat this competition from rail? The FERC Opinion does not discuss the role of possible new entrants. One pipeline company cancelled plans to build a new line to handle Bakken crude because of tepid interest from producers. Rail is more expensive, but it offers greater route flexibility, especially to East Coast refiners. Oil from the Eagle Ford in South Texas can reach Gulf Coast refineries much more easily than Bakken crude. Bakken crude may be forced to head East or West, not South. For a dizzying account of what crude may go where and when and by what shipping mode, see Trisha Curtis *et al*, Oil & Gas J. 100 (Mar. 3, 2014).

3.   What if (desperate) producers, who would be drained under the Rule of Capture if they leave their oil in the ground, are willing to accept a netback price of $51, which gives them no profit on their production, but is still better than being drained by those with access to other outlets? Should Seaway be able to collect all that economic rent from producers? For how long? What if the MBRs are 20 times higher than the existing cost-based rates? Isn't Seaway making a "monopoly" profit by having such a strategic pipeline in the right place at the right time? What does this high profit signal to investors?

4.   FERC granted market-based rates to Pegasus. Its new tariff, effective October 1, 2012, is $5.0791 per barrel compared to its old tariff of $1.571 per barrel. Order Accepting Tariff, 140 F.E.R.C. ¶ 61,249, Docket No. IS12–553–000 (Sept. 27, 2012). Shippers protested, arguing that the new rates were outside any possible "zone of reasonableness" and that market conditions had changed in three fundamental ways since the *Mobil* case was decided: (i) Midwest markets were saturated with crude; (ii) infrastructure to markets in the West where crude could be sold at international prices was lacking; and (iii) current differentials in crude prices will be lengthy, sustained and will increase for an indefinite period of time. Also, the MBRs allowed the pipeline to receive returns on equity of 45% or more. FERC denied all shippers' requests to reopen the hearing. Order Denying Rehearing, 142 F.E.R.C. ¶ 61,175, Docket No. IS12–553–001 (Mar. 5, 2013). In essence, FERC's response to the shippers using the Pegasus pipeline was "the court made us do this" because the court had found that Pegasus lacked market power and competitive alternatives existed in the origin market in Canada.

5.   Another part of the Seaway saga involved committed shippers' rates. Committed shippers had agreed in writing to pay new rates on the reversed Seaway pipeline. Seaway requested a declaratory order from FERC that the committed shippers' tariff would be governed by the transportation agreements signed with the committed shippers during the open season. Under Order No. 561, if non-contract shippers protest these contract rates, FERC requires that the applicant submit cost-of-service data (*see* 18 C.F.R. § 342.2(a)). Seaway rued its request to FERC when an Initial Decision of an

ALJ declared that Seaway's committed shipper rates were unjust and unreasonable. The uncommitted shippers appear to have convincingly argued that the committed rates were inflated by market power and generated excessive returns to Seaway.

The FERC Commissioners reversed the Initial Decision in *Seaway Crude Pipeline Co. LLC*, 146 F.E.R.C. ¶ 61,151, Docket No. IS12–226–000 (Feb. 28, 2014) because it conflicted with established FERC policy. While asserting the authority under the ICA to review or modify committed rates, when appropriate, FERC explained:

> 29. FERC has always expressed concern that a pipeline with market power may establish an unjustly high rate through negotiation. The Commission therefore established a requirement that an alternative cost-based rate be available to any shipper unwilling or unable to pay the negotiated rate. While the Commission allows negotiated rates to exceed a pipeline's cost of service, the Commission requires that a cost-of-service alternative be available for any party unwilling to pay the negotiated rate.

In short, concerns about market power in a committed rate context are remedied by providing a cost-based alternative to uncommitted shippers. FERC contrasted this result with a pipeline's request for MBRs, which always require a finding that the pipeline lacks market power because *all* shippers would be subject to these higher MBRs. Absent a "compelling reason," FERC would not second guess the decisions made by savvy players when negotiating committed rates. Seaway's rate structure did not link committed rates in any way to uncommitted rates, so there was no burden on uncommitted shippers regardless of what the sophisticated parties agreed to. *Id.* at ¶¶ 31–33. Moreover, not a single uncommitted shipper or potential shipper had asserted that they were unfairly denied an opportunity to become a committed shipper in the open season process. *Id.* at ¶ 36. A "general distaste" over the high returns to the pipeline could not trump approval of the committed rates, absent some "clearly unreasonable" impact on others or some "important policy purpose." *Id.* at ¶ 36.

The Permian Basin in West Texas is undergoing an oil shale play expected to be larger than the Eagle Ford play. Because of a lack of infrastructure, Permian producers were selling their crude oil for $21 less than that sold at the Cushing, Oklahoma hub in late August 2014. Robert Grattan, Bottleneck Keeps Permian Oil Far Below Benchmark, Hous. Chron. Aug. 20, 2014, at B1.

To keep up with FERC developments, read the annual Reports of the Oil & Liquids Pipeline Regulation Committee of the Energy Bar Ass'n in the Energy Law Journal. *See, e.g.*, http://www.felj.org/sites/default/files/docs/elj342/5.OilLiquidsPipelineRegulation.pdf.

Oil pipeline ratemaking is hardly the staid backwater of FERC's workload today.

6. On March 29, 2013, homeowners in Mayflower, Arkansas had to evacuate their neighborhood when many thousands of barrels of heavy Canadian crude oil flowed into their yards, streets and the town's storm drains. The southward-flowing Pegasus pipeline had ruptured. Nora Caplan-Bricker, This Is What Happens When a Pipeline Bursts in Your Town, New Republic, Nov. 18, 2013, http://www.newrepublic.com/article/115624/exxon-

oil-spill-arkansas-2013-how-pipeline-burst-mayflower. The siting of oil and gas pipelines and their safety are discussed in the final three sections of this chapter.

E. SITING OIL PIPELINES: EMINENT DOMAIN AND STATE LAW

FERC lacks any statutory authority under the ICA to issue a certificate of public convenience to construct a new oil pipeline or to issue an order approving abandonment of such a pipeline. McGraw, *supra*, at 235–36. Instead, oil pipeline owners must look to each state's statutes to determine if that state offers a condemnation procedure to oil pipelines and, if so, comply with its provisions. State laws differ greatly. Some states grant condemnation power to all pipelines, some only to pipelines that are public utilities or that carry crude oil (not refined products), and some states, such as Colorado, provide no eminent domain authority at all. *See* Barr 2007, *supra*, at 50.

The following case illustrates how one state polices the regulatory bargain that gives a pipeline condemnation power if it is a common carrier pipeline. The case occurs in the context of a pipeline owner seeking to build a CO2 pipeline to transport CO2 to a depleted oil field where it will be injected to release additional oil from the reservoir rock in an Enhanced Oil Recovery (EOR) operation. However, the common carrier status of other pipelines often depends on whether they transport oil "for the public for hire."

Texas Rice Land Partners, Ltd. v. Denbury Green Pipeline—Texas, LLC

363 S.W.3d 192 (Tex. 2012).

■ JUDGE WILLET delivered the opinion of the Court.

* * *

The Texas Constitution safeguards private property by declaring that eminent domain can only be exercised for "public use." Even when the Legislature grants certain private entities "the right and power of eminent domain," the overarching constitutional rule controls: no taking of property for private use. Accordingly, the [Texas] Natural Resources Code [Sec. 111.019(B)] requires so-called "common carrier" pipeline companies to transport carbon dioxide "to or for the public for hire." In other words, a CO2 pipeline company cannot wield eminent domain to build a *private* pipeline, one "limited in [its] use to the wells, stations, plants, and refineries of the owner." A common carrier transporting gas for hire implies a customer other than the pipeline owner itself.

This property-rights dispute asks whether a landowner can challenge in court the eminent-domain power of a CO2 pipeline owner that has been granted a common-carrier permit from the Railroad Commission. The court of appeals answered no, holding that (1) a pipeline owner can conclusively acquire the right to condemn private property by checking the right boxes on a one-page form filed with the Railroad Commission, and (2) a landowner cannot challenge in court whether the proposed pipeline will in fact be public rather than private. We disagree. Unadorned assertions of public use are constitutionally insufficient. Merely registering as a common carrier does not conclusively convey the extraordinary power of eminent domain or bar landowners from contesting in court whether a planned pipeline meets statutory common-carrier requirements. Nothing in Texas law leaves landowners so vulnerable to unconstitutional private takings. We reverse the court of appeals' judgment and remand to the district court for further proceedings consistent with this opinion.

I. Background

Denbury is engaged in tertiary recovery operations that involve the injection of CO2 into existing oil wells to increase production. Denbury owns a naturally occurring CO2 reserve in Mississippi known as Jackson Dome, and desired to build a CO2 pipeline from Jackson Dome to Texas oil wells to facilitate tertiary operations on the wells. The record contains some evidence that, in the future, Denbury might purchase man-made or "anthropogenic" CO2 from third parties and transport it in the pipeline.

In March 2008, Denbury Green [a subsidiary] applied with the Railroad Commission to operate a CO2 pipeline in Texas. This pipeline would be a continuation of a pipeline originating at Jackson Dome in Mississippi and traversing Louisiana. Denbury Green's portion of the pipeline would extend from the Texas-Louisiana border to the Hastings Field in Brazoria and Galveston counties. The one-page permit application, designated a Form T–4, has two boxes for the applicant to indicate whether the pipeline will be operated as "a common carrier" or "a private line." Denbury Green placed an "x" in the common-carrier box. Separately and also relevant to common-carrier status, applicants are directed to mark one of three boxes if the pipeline will not be transporting "only the gas and/or liquids produced by pipeline owner or operator." Of the three boxes, indicating the gas will be "[p]urchased from others," "[o]wned by others, but transported for a fee," or "[b]oth purchased and transported for others," Denbury Green marked the box for "[o]wned by others, but transported for a fee." Denbury Green also submitted a letter, pursuant to Section 111.002(6) of the Natural Resources Code, stating that it "accepts the provisions of Chapter 111 of the Natural Resources Code and expressly agrees that it is a common carrier subject to duties and obligations conferred by Chapter 111."

In April 2008, eight days after Denbury Green filed its application, the Commission granted the T–4 permit. In July 2008, the Commission furnished a letter to Denbury Green [confirming its status as a common carrier pipeline].

Texas Rice Land Partners, Ltd. has an ownership interest in two tracts along the pipeline route. When Denbury Green came to survey the land in preparation for condemning a pipeline easement, Texas Rice Land Partners and a lessee, rice farmer Mike Latta (collectively Texas Rice), refused entry. Denbury Green sued Texas Rice for an injunction allowing access to the tracts. On cross-motions for summary judgment, the trial court rendered judgment in favor of Denbury Green. The trial court found that Denbury Green "is a 'common carrier' pursuant to Section 111.002(6) of the Texas Natural Resources Code" and "has the power of eminent domain/authority to condemn/right-to-take pursuant to Section 111.019 of the Texas Natural Resources Code." The court permanently enjoined Texas Rice from (1) interfering with Denbury Green's "right to enter and survey" its proposed pipeline route across Texas Rice's land, and (2) harassing Denbury Green or its agents and contractors while conducting the surveys.

[The court of appeals affirmed, concluding that Denbury Green had established its common-carrier status as a matter of law, with one justice dissenting on the basis that "[m]erely offering a transportation service for a profit does not distinguish a private use from a public use."]

A.   Common Carriers and the Power of Eminent Domain

The Natural Resources Code regulates CO_2 pipelines serving as common carriers. Three Code provisions are particularly relevant.

> Section 111.002(6) states a person is a common carrier if he: owns, operates, or manages, wholly or partially, pipelines for the transportation of carbon dioxide . . . to or for the public for hire, but only if such person files with the commission a written acceptance of the provisions of this chapter expressly agreeing that, in consideration of the rights acquired, it becomes a common carrier subject to the duties and obligations conferred or imposed by this chapter.

> Section 111.003(a) states: The provisions of this chapter do not apply to pipelines that are limited in their use to the wells, stations, plants, and refineries of the owner and that are not a part of the pipeline transportation system of a common carrier as defined in Section 111.002 of this code.

> Section 111.019 states in part: (a) Common carriers have the right and power of eminent domain.

* * *

While these provisions plainly give private pipeline companies the power of eminent domain, that authority is subject to special scrutiny by the courts. The power of eminent domain is substantial but constitutionally circumscribed. Article 1, Section 17 of the Texas Constitution provides, "No person's property shall be taken . . . for or applied to public use without adequate compensation. . . ." This provision not only requires just compensation to the property owner, but also "prohibits the taking of property for *private* use."

The legislative grant of eminent-domain power is strictly construed in two regards. First, strict compliance with all statutory requirements is required. Second, in instances of doubt as to the scope of the power, the statute granting such power is "strictly construed in favor of the landowner and against those corporations and arms of the State vested therewith" [citing Coastal States Gas Producing Co. v. Pate, 309 S.W.2d 828, 831 (Tex. 1958)].

B.   The T–4 Permit . . . Does Not Conclusively Establish Eminent-Domain Power

The parties dispute whether Denbury Green was entitled to summary judgment on the issue of whether it is a common carrier. We hold at the outset that the T–4 permit alone did not conclusively establish Denbury Green's status as a common carrier and confer the power of eminent domain.

Nothing in the statutory scheme indicates that the [Railroad] Commission's decision to grant a common-carrier permit carries conclusive effect and thus bars landowners from disputing in court a pipeline company's naked assertion of public use. As stated above, the right to condemn property is constitutionally limited and turns in part on whether the use of the property is public or private. We have long held that "the ultimate question of whether a particular use is a public use is a judicial question to be decided by the courts." We have also held in numerous contexts that the Commission does not have authority to determine property rights. We presume the Legislature is aware of relevant caselaw when it enacts statutes. Had the Legislature intended a T–4 permit to render a company's common-carrier status and eminent-domain power unchallengeable, it would have said so explicitly. "[W]hen an action is inherently judicial in nature, the courts retain jurisdiction to determine the controversy unless the legislature by valid statute has expressly granted exclusive jurisdiction to the administrative body."

Further, the record, rules, and statutes before us indicate that the Commission's process for granting a T–4 permit undertakes no effort to confirm that the applicant's pipeline will be public rather than private. . . . [T]he applicant need only place an "x" in a box indicating that the pipeline will be operated as a common carrier, and to agree under Section 111.002(6) to subject itself to "duties and obligations conferred or imposed" by Chapter 111. Under these minimal requirements, Denbury Green reported itself as a common carrier and obtained a permit a few days later. There was no investigation, and certainly no adversarial testing, of whether Denbury Green was indeed entitled to common-carrier status and the extraordinary power to condemn private property. Denbury Green concedes in its brief that the Commission "did not adjudicate anything." Private property cannot be imperiled with such nonchalance, via an irrefutable presumption created by checking a certain box on a one-page government form. Our Constitution demands far more.

The Railroad Commission's process for handling T–4 permits appears to be one of registration, not of application. The record suggests that in accepting an entity's paperwork, the Commission performs a clerical rather than an adjudicative act. . . . No notice is given to affected parties. No hearing is held, no evidence is presented, no investigation is conducted. . . . [A]s for the core constitutional concern—the pipeline's public vs. private use—the parties point to no regulation or enabling legislation directing the Commission to investigate and determine whether a pipeline will in fact serve the public. Given this scant legislative and administrative scheme, we cannot conceive that the Legislature intended the granting of a T–4 permit alone to prohibit a landowner—who was not a party to the Commission permitting process and had no notice of it—from challenging in court the eminent-domain power of a permit holder.

C.   The Test for Common-Carrier Status

Denbury Green contends that merely making the pipeline available for public use is sufficient to confer common-carrier status. We disagree. . . . Denbury Green's reading of Section 111.002(6) would confer common-carrier status and eminent-domain power even when the pipeline will never serve the public by transporting CO_2 "to or for the public for hire" under the statute—and indeed when there was never any reasonable possibility of such service—so long as the owner agrees to be subject to the Chapter 111 common-carrier regime. As we read the statute, the language that the pipeline be owned or operated "to or for the public for hire" is a separate requirement for common-carrier status, and the statute, *in addition*, requires the owner or operator to agree to subject itself to Chapter 111. Denbury Green's interpretation would read out of the statute the language that the pipeline be operated "to or for the public for hire". . . .

Second, Denbury Green's construction leads to a result that we cannot believe the Legislature intended, namely a gaming of the permitting process to allow a private carrier to wield the power of eminent domain. Suppose an oil company has a well on one property and a refinery on another. A farmer's property lies between the oil company's two properties. The oil company wishes to build a pipeline for the exclusive purpose of transporting its production from its well to its refinery. Only about 50 feet of the proposed pipeline will traverse the farmer's property. The farmer refuses to allow construction of the pipeline across his property. The oil company knows that no party other than itself will ever desire to use the pipeline. In these circumstances, the application for a common-carrier permit is essentially a ruse to obtain eminent-domain power. The oil company should not be able to seize power over the farmer's property simply by applying for a crude oil pipeline permit with the Commission, agreeing to subject itself to the jurisdiction of the Commission and all requirements of Chapter 111, and offering the use of the pipeline to non-existent takers. . . . Hence, we conclude that Denbury Green is not entitled to common-carrier status simply because it obtained a common-carrier permit, filed a tariff, and agreed to make the pipeline available to any third party wishing to transport its gas in the pipeline and willing to pay the tariff. . . .

We accordingly hold that for a person intending to build a CO2 pipeline to qualify as a common carrier under Section 111.002(6), a reasonable probability[29][49] must exist that the pipeline will at some point after construction serve the public by transporting gas for one or more customers who will either retain ownership of their gas or sell it to parties other than the carrier.

Consistent with judicial review of Commission determinations generally, a permit granting common-carrier status is prima facie valid. But once a landowner challenges that status, the burden falls upon the pipeline company to establish its common-carrier bona fides if it wishes to exercise the power of eminent domain.

D.   Denbury Green Was Not Entitled to Summary Judgment

Under our test, Denbury Green did not establish common-carrier status as a matter of law. A Denbury Green vice president attested that Denbury Green was negotiating with other parties to transport anthropogenic CO2 in the pipeline, and that the pipeline "can transport carbon dioxide tendered by Denbury entities as well as carbon dioxide tendered from other entities and facilities not owned by Denbury." . . . He did not identify any possible customers and was unaware of any other entity unaffiliated with Denbury Green that owned CO2 near the

---

[49]   In this context, a reasonable probability is one that is more likely than not.

pipeline route in Louisiana and Mississippi. This evidence does not establish a reasonable probability that such transportation would ever occur.

Further, the record includes portions of Denbury's own website that suggest the pipeline would be exclusively for private use. In describing the pipeline project, the site states:

> We like these tertiary operations because . . . to date, in our region of the United States, we have not encountered any industry competition. Generally, from the Texas Gulf Coast to Florida, there are no known significant natural sources of carbon dioxide except our own, and these large volumes of CO2 are the foundation for our entire tertiary program. . . .

> We have entered into three agreements, and are having various levels of discussions with many others, to purchase (if the plants are built) all of the CO2 production from man-made (anthropogenic) sources of CO2 from planned solid carbon gasification projects.

> [W]e believe that our potential ability to tie these sources together with pipelines will give us a significant advantage over our competitors, in our geographic area, in acquiring additional oil fields and these future potential man-made sources of CO2.

. . . Denbury Green's representations suggesting that it (1) owns most or all of the naturally occurring CO_2 in the region, (2) intends to purchase all the man-made CO_2 that might be produced under current and future agreements, (3) sees its access to CO_2 as giving it a significant advantage over its competitors, and (4) intends to fully utilize the pipeline for its own purposes, are all inconsistent with public use of the pipeline. As Denbury Green did not establish common-carrier status as a matter of law, it was not entitled to summary judgment.

III. Conclusion

Pipeline development is indisputably important given our State's fast-growing energy needs, but economic dynamism—and more fundamentally, freedom itself—also demand strong protections for individual property rights. Locke deemed the preservation of property rights "[t]he great and chief end" of government, a view this Court echoed almost 300 years later, calling it "one of the most important purposes of government."[34][50] Indeed, our Constitution and laws enshrine landownership as a keystone right, rather than one "relegated to the status of a poor relation."[35][51]

A private enterprise cannot acquire unchallengeable condemnation power under Section 111.002(6) merely by checking boxes on a one-page form and self-declaring its common-carrier status. Merely holding oneself out is insufficient under Texas law to thwart judicial review. While neighboring states impose fewer restrictions on the level of public use required for such takings [citing La. Rev. Stat. Ann. § 19:2; Miss. Code

---

[50] Eggemeyer v. Eggemeyer, 554 S.W.2d 137, 140 (Tex. 1977). Private property rights have been described as "fundamental, natural, inherent, inalienable, not derived from the legislature and as preexisting even constitutions." *Id.* They are, in short, a foundational liberty, not a contingent privilege.

[51] Dolan v. City of Tigard, 512 U.S. 374, 392 (1994); . . .

Ann. § 11–27–47], meaning companies may seize land to build pipelines for their exclusive use, the Texas Legislature enacted a regime more protective of landowners. If a landowner challenges an entity's common-carrier designation, the company must present reasonable proof of a future customer, thus demonstrating that the pipeline will indeed transport "to or for the public for hire" and is not "limited in [its] use to the wells, stations, plants, and refineries of the owner." We reverse the court of appeals' judgment, and remand this case to the district court for further proceedings consistent with this opinion. ■

NOTES AND COMMENTS

1.   As noted in *Denbury*, some states are even more relaxed about the "public use" limit on a developer's condemnation powers. For a thorough discussion, see Alexandra B. Klass, The Frontier of Eminent Domain, 79 U. Colo. L. Rev. 651 (2008)(describing many Western states' Constitutions or laws that grant mining and other resource developers the right of eminent domain for privately owned infrastructure to further economic development; and recent and proposed reforms that provide more protections to landowners and more balance between resource development with other land uses).

2.   Do you think Denbury will succeed in its quest to obtain common carrier status? What must it demonstrate to succeed? Denbury does envision a future of capturing anthropogenic CO_2. Visit its website at http://www. denbury.com/operations/operations-overview/default.aspx.   The CO_2-EOR business is set to flourish. Will Denbury's business model be even more profitable if a tax is placed on CO2 emitted into the air? *See* Vello Kuuskraa & Matt Wallace, CO_2-EOR Set for Growth as New CO2 Supplies Emerge, Oil & Gas J., May 5, 2014, at 92–104. CO_2 pipelines are essential to building large-scale carbon capture and storage (CCS) facilities to mitigate climate warming, but CO_2 pipelines do not have federal condemnation authority. *See* Robert R. Nordhaus & Emily Pitlick, Carbon Dioxide Pipeline Regulation, 30 Energy L.J. 85 (2009) (recommending that such authority be granted, preempting any state laws that may apply).

3.   Because of the different regulatory frameworks, it clearly matters whether an interstate pipeline is defined as a natural gas pipeline or an oil pipeline. This issue has become important with the rising production of "natural gas liquids" (NGLs), such as butane and ethane from shale fields (see Chapter 4). NGLs typically bring a higher price than natural gas because they are liquids, condensed from gas, and thus are more easily transported. The ICA does not define "oil." In determining whether a substance flowing through a pipeline is oil, FERC uses several tests, such as asking whether the substance competes with oil for pipeline space and/or is used as an alternative for heating oil. If so, it is more likely to be defined as oil. Michelle T. Boudreaux and Amy L. Hoff, Determining the Jurisdictional Status of NGL Pipeline Transportation Service, http://cblpipelinelaw.com/news/articles/DeterminingJurisdictionalStatusNGLPipelines_09242013.pdf.

    FERC has determined that raw NGLs are oil for the purposes of pipeline transportation, but various derivatives of NGLs have left lingering jurisdictional questions. In a 2013 case, a company that wanted to construct a pipeline to carry ethane, an NGL component, argued that the ethane was a feedstock in an industrial process and should not be considered "oil." FERC disagreed, concluding that ethane can be and sometimes is used for fuel purposes, like oil. Williams Olefins Feedstock Pipelines, L.L.C., Declaratory Order, 145 F.E.R.C. ¶ 61,303 (Dec. 31, 2013).

If a state's laws authorize eminent domain for "crude oil" or "oil," do pipelines carrying NGLs or bitumen from the Canadian oil sands fall under this authority? *See* Crosstex NGL Pipeline L.P. v. Reins Road Farms-1, Ltd. 404 S.W.3d 754 (Tex. App. 2013) (holding that "crude oil" as defined in Texas statutes does not include NGLs and so condemnation authority and common carrier status were properly denied). However, a segment of the Keystone XL pipeline was held to be a common carrier carrying crude oil under Texas law. Crawford Family Farm P'ship v. TransCanada Keystone Pipeline, L.P., 409 S.W.3d 908 (Tex. App. 2013).

The president of the Interstate Natural Gas Association of America (INGAA) reports that 95% of all right-of-way agreements with landowners are negotiated; only 5% require court proceedings. Eminent Domain an Issue as Industry Plans 450,000 miles of New Lines, Greenwire, Feb. 4, 2013.

4. ***The Keystone XL Pipeline:*** TransCanada has been trying to obtain approval since 2008 to carry Canadian oil-sands crude via its Keystone XL pipeline across the U.S. border to Cushing, Oklahoma and then south to the Gulf Coast. The pipeline would pick up Bakken crude along the way. While the Cushing-to-Gulf Coast segment has been built, the northern cross-border segment requires a "Presidential Permit," approved by the U.S. Department of State. *See* Exec. Order 13,337 (Apr. 30, 2004), building on Exec. Order 1953, which provides that "[t]he proper conduct of the foreign relations of the United States requires that executive permission be obtained for the construction and maintenance at the borders of the United States of facilities for the exportation or importation of electric energy and natural gas." A Presidential Permit triggers NEPA and the need for an environmental impact statement. The 2004 Executive Order also requires that EPA and DOE review the application and allow public comments on it.

As of February 2015, this cross-border permit had not been issued by the President. However, some of the initial delay in permitting the pipeline arose from strong opposition by Nebraskan citizens over the pipeline's proposed route above the Sand Hills Aquifer. In 2011, Nebraska modified its state laws for oil pipeline siting. First, it passed L.B. 1, the Major Oil Pipeline Siting Act, http://nebraskalegislature.gov/FloorDocs/102/PDF/Slip/LB1_S1. pdf (approved by the Governor on November 22, 2011). This Act confirmed that oil pipeline companies have eminent domain authority, but that they must first obtain state approval of a pipeline application. L.B. 1 required that the pipeline company apply to the state's Public Service Commission (PSC) and provide information on its planned route and methods to minimize or mitigate potential impacts of a major pipeline. L.B. 1 also required the PSC to hold a public hearing on the application and allowed other input from the state's Department of Environmental Quality (DEQ) and Department of Natural Resources. The PSC was required to approve the pipeline application if it was found to be in the public interest, considering environmental, economic, and social factors, as well as impacts on counties.

L.B. 1 did not apply to Keystone XL, however, because the bill stated that it did not apply to major pipeline carriers that had submitted an application for a Presidential Permit to the Department of State prior to the bill's effective date, which TransCanada had done for Keystone XL. *See* Thompson v. Heineman, 289 Neb. 798, 805 (2015) (discussing the bill).

In addition to L.B. 1, Nebraska's L.B. 4 allowed the DEQ to collaborate with federal agencies to prepare a supplemental environmental review of the pipeline under NEPA. *See* Legislative Bill 4, http://nebraskalegislature.gov/FloorDocs/102/PDF/Slip/LB4_S1.pdf (approved by the Governor on November 22, 2011). The DEQ and the federal agencies were to enter into a memorandum of understanding setting forth the responsibilities of each agency in conducting this review. After the supplemental review was prepared, it was to be submitted to the Nebraskan Governor for his approval of the routes reviewed in the document. This bill applied to Keystone XL and did not require that a pipeline carrier obtain routing approval from the PSC prior to exercising eminent domain authority. *See Thompson*, 289 Neb. at 806.

In 2012, the Nebraska Legislature approved another bill, L.B. 1161, applicable to Keystone XL. This bill amended the statute produced by L.B. 4 to allow the Nebraska DEQ to conduct its own independent environmental review of a proposed pipeline route. Under L.B. 1161, pipeline owners like TransCanada could now choose to go through the S.B. 4 route review process with the DEQ (including a process involving independent review by the DEQ), with final route approval decided by the Governor. This process would be in lieu of a siting determination by the Nebraska PSC. Alternatively, pipeline owners could choose to go through the PSC process. Legislative Bill 1161, http://nebraskalegislature.gov/FloorDocs/102/PDF/Slip/LB1161.pdf (approved by the Governor on April 17, 2012). Landowners who opposed the pipeline argued that allowing pipeline owners to bypass the PSC and receive route approval from the Governor was unconstitutional under Nebraska Constitution Article IV, § 20. This Article provides that the Nebraska Public Service Commission's "powers and duties" include "general control of common carriers." The District Court of Nebraska, Lancaster County, agreed, finding that oil pipelines are common carriers and that L.B. 1161 "unlawfully divests the PSC of control over routing decisions involving such common carriers." Thompson v. Heineman, No. CI122060, 2014 WL 631609 at *29 (D. Neb. Feb. 19, 2014). The Nebraska Supreme Court vacated the district court's judgment. In Nebraska, the vote of five judges is required to find legislation unconstitutional, and only four judges determined that the landowners had standing. *Thompson* 289 Neb. at 802. Thus, at the state level, the Keystone XL had cleared all hurdles, but the supreme court did not issue a binding ruling on the substantive issue of whether bypassing the PSC was constitutional.

Meanwhile, at the federal level, in January 2012, the Department of State had denied TransCanada's Presidential Permit application. In April 2012, TransCanada proposed alternative routes around the Sand Hills Region to Nebraska's DEQ, and in May 2012, it submitted a new application for a Presidential Permit to the Department of State, including the alternative Nebraskan routes. Later in May, the Nebraska DEQ and the Department of State entered into a memorandum of understanding to conduct a collaborative analysis of the Nebraska routes under NEPA and other applicable federal laws. In January 2013, the DEQ submitted its Final Evaluation Report on the proposed pipeline to the Governor, who approved the new route on January 22, 2013. Letter from Governor Dave Heineman to President Barack Obama and Secretary Hillary Rodham Clinton, Jan. 22,

2013, available at http://keystone-xl.com/wp-content/uploads/2012/11/Governor_Pipeline_Approval.pdf.

In 2014, the Department of State issued a Final Supplemental Environmental Impact Statement (SEIS) assessing the new Presidential Permit application. U.S. Department of State, Final Supplemental Environmental Impact Statement (SEIS), http://keystonepipeline-xl.state.gov/finalseis/index.htm. The SEIS described a variety of potentially significant adverse environmental impacts of the pipeline, including oil spills and impacts on wildlife, and noted the various mitigation measures that the company had agreed to make. The SEIS further concluded that denying the Presidential Permit would probably not reduce carbon emissions from the production and use of oil sands crude because the oil would be shipped by rail as an alternative, albeit a less safe one.

The U.S. House of Representatives has repeatedly attempted to require the President to approve the U.S.-Canada portion of Keystone XL, to no avail. A bill passed on May 22, 2013, declaring that "no Presidential permit shall be required for the pipeline." H.R. 3, Northern Route Approval Act, https://www.congress.gov/bill/113th-congress/house-bill/3. Another bill to approve the pipeline failed by one vote in the Senate in November 2014. *See* Ashley Parker and Coral Davenport, Senate Defeats Bill on Keystone XL Pipeline in Narrow Vote, N.Y. Times, Nov. 18, 2014, http://www.nytimes.com/2014/11/19/us/politics/keystone-xl-pipeline.html.

Chapter 14 on international trade law discusses whether Canada could challenge the long delay by the United States in approving the Keystone XL pipeline under the North American Free Trade Agreement (NAFTA).

Section G below continues the discussion of pipeline safety and crude-by-rail. It is worth noting that many Canadians, especially those to the West of the oil sands, including First Nations tribes, oppose pipelines across Canada that could serve as alternatives to the Keystone XL. Suffice it to say that there is a vast amount of oil sands production yearning for a pipeline to an export market. *See* Nat'l Energy Board of Canada, Canadian Pipeline Transportation Report (Apr. 10, 2014) (showing the depressed price differentials of bottled-up Canadian oil).

F. SITING GAS PIPELINES: FERC CERTIFICATES OF PUBLIC CONVENIENCE

As noted *supra*, FERC authority over interstate gas pipeline infrastructure is quite extensive, especially compared to its lack of such authority over oil pipelines. Under Section 7(c) of the NGA (15 U.S.C § 717f(c)), any new interstate pipeline facility must receive a FERC certificate of public convenience and necessity before commencing construction. This provision requires that FERC find that the applicant is "able and willing properly to do the acts and to perform the proposed service" that "is or will be required by the present or future public convenience and necessity." *Id.* at § 717f(e).

The following case traces the roles of FERC and of state and local authorities in certificating a new compressor facility to handle the booming gas production from the Marcellus. Unlike pipelines, compressors cannot be buried; they make noise, emit air pollutants, and may clash with the rural ambience of small towns. Must a FERC-certificated compressor conform to the local zoning code of a small town and to the clean air requirements of the state?

Dominion Transmission, Inc. v. Summers
723 F.3d 238 (2013).

■ GRIFFITH, CIRCUIT JUDGE:

Hoping to construct a natural gas compressor station in Myersville, Maryland, Dominion Transmission, Inc., applied for and received a certificate of public convenience and necessity from the Federal Energy Regulatory Commission. To proceed with construction, however, Dominion must also obtain an air quality permit from the Maryland Department of the Environment (the Department). After the Department twice refused to process Dominion's application for a permit, Dominion sought expedited review by this court. Because we hold that the Department's failure to act is inconsistent with federal law, we remand the case to the Department and direct it to adhere to a schedule to ensure prompt action on Dominion's application.

I. A

The Natural Gas Act (NGA), 15 U.S.C. §§ 717–717z, establishes a "comprehensive scheme of federal regulation" that vests FERC with "exclusive jurisdiction over the transportation . . . of natural gas in interstate commerce for resale." Before a company may construct a facility that transports natural gas, it must obtain from FERC "a certificate of public convenience and necessity," 15 U.S.C. § 717f(c), and comply with all other federal, state, and local regulations not preempted by the NGA.

One regulatory regime the NGA expressly does not preempt is the system of state emissions regulations established by the Clean Air Act (CAA), 42 U.S.C. §§ 7401–7671q. *See* 15 U.S.C. § 717b(d)(2). Air quality regulation under the CAA is an exercise in cooperative federalism: The Environmental Protection Agency "promulgates national ambient air quality standards ('NAAQS') for air pollutants." If states wish to have a hand in air quality regulation, they "must then adopt state implementation plans ('SIPs') providing for the implementation, maintenance, and enforcement of the NAAQS; such plans are then submitted to EPA for approval." *Id.* To win approval, a SIP must include an air quality permit program for the "construction of any stationary source within the areas covered by the plan [in order] to assure that [NAAQS] are achieved." 42 U.S.C. § 7410(a)(2)(C).

Maryland's SIP consists of a collection of regulations and requirements that are incorporated by reference into the Code of Federal Regulations. *See* 40 C.F.R. § 52.1070. The Department, headed by respondent Secretary Robert Summers, administers Maryland's air quality control program, including Maryland Code § 2–404, which governs the issuance of permits to construct emissions sources. The present controversy centers on § 2–404(b)(1), which prohibits the Department from processing an application for a permit until the applicant submits documentation:

(i) That demonstrates that the [proposed source] has been approved by the local jurisdiction for all zoning and land use requirements; or

(ii) That the source meets all applicable zoning and land use requirements. Md. Code § 2–404(b)(1).

In other words, the successful applicant must show that the project has received approval from the local authority or otherwise satisfies local law.

Because the administrative demands of these various requirements can impede "public convenience and necessity," 15 U.S.C. § 717f(e), Congress designated FERC as "the lead agency for the purposes of coordinating all applicable Federal authorizations," including air quality permits. 15 U.S.C. § 717n(b). Additionally, Congress provided for expedited judicial review of federal or state agency action or inaction that deprives a company building a FERC-certified natural gas facility of an authorization it requires to proceed with construction. 15 U.S.C. § 717r(d). We proceed under § 717r(d) in this case.

B

Dominion, which stores and transports natural gas across the Northeast and Mid-Atlantic regions, is in the process of building infrastructure and facilities in Maryland, Ohio, Pennsylvania, and West Virginia as part of a long-range plan to increase its capacity. One such facility is a compressor station that Dominion hopes to build in Myersville, Maryland. The compressor station will include equipment that emits pollutants.

On February 1, 2012, Dominion submitted an air quality permit application to the Department. A week later, the Department notified Dominion that it had failed to provide the documentation of zoning compliance required by § 2–404(b)(1). Dominion replied on March 8 with a letter explaining that the compressor station would comply with zoning and land use requirements. The next month, Dominion filed a zoning application with the Town of Myersville. Pet'r's Br. 11. A group of residents organized the Myersville Citizens for a Rural Community (MCRC), the Intervenor in this case, to oppose the application. On June 5, while the zoning application was pending, the Department returned Dominion's air quality permit application "for lack of documentation that demonstrates that the project has been approved by the local jurisdiction for all zoning and land use requirements." Sup. J.A. 101. In August, the Town of Myersville denied Dominion's zoning application on the grounds that the proposed compressor station was contrary to the local development plan, endangered public health, and posed a nuisance.

On December 20, 2012, FERC issued a certificate of public convenience and necessity for a number of Dominion facilities, including the compressor station in *Myersville. Dominion Transmission, Inc.*, 141 F.E.R.C. ¶ 61,240 (2012). FERC concluded that there was "strong evidence of market demand" for natural gas transportation capacity, demonstrating the need for the facility. *Id.* at 62,297. FERC's detailed order addressed comments critical of the proposed location but ultimately concluded that "the Myersville site is the more appropriate site for the Maryland compressor station." *Id.*

The next day, with FERC's certificate in hand, Dominion applied to the Department once again for an air quality permit. Its cover letter stated it now satisfied § 2–404(b)(1) because all local zoning and land use requirements had been preempted by FERC's certificate and were therefore not "applicable." J.A. 3–5. On January 15, 2013, the Department verbally informed Dominion that it would not be able to process the application. On January 17, responding to a protest MCRC sent to the Governor, the Department sent a letter reassuring the group that it would not proceed with the application because Dominion had failed to provide the documentation of compliance required by § 2–404(b)(1). The Department sent a copy of the letter to Dominion, as well. After receiving the letter, Dominion petitioned this court for review of the Department's reasons for refusing to process its application.

II

Turning to the merits, we must determine whether the Department's failure to act on Dominion's application for an air quality permit was "inconsistent with . . . Federal law." 15 U.S.C. § 717r(d)(3). The parties agree that, in this context, we must ask whether the Department's failure was arbitrary, capricious, an abuse of discretion, or otherwise contrary to law.

A.   Dominion argues that the Department acted contrary to law by requiring a demonstration under § 2–404(b)(1) that the proposed compressor station was in compliance with local law. The NGA preempted that state law requirement, Dominion argues, to the extent that it calls for more from a natural gas facility than does FERC. We disagree that the NGA preempted § 2–404(b)(1). It is true, as the Supreme Court observed, that Congress intended to occupy the field to the exclusion of state law by establishing through the NGA a "comprehensive scheme of federal regulation of all wholesales of natural gas in interstate commerce." *Schneidewind*, 485 U.S. at 300. But Congress expressly saved states' CAA powers from preemption. 15 U.S.C. § 717b(d)(2). In other words, laws that are part of a state's SIP are not preempted, unless the NGA says otherwise. Our inquiry therefore turns on whether § 2–404(b)(1) is part of Maryland's SIP. [The court finds that this provision was incorporated by reference into the C.F.R. and is part of the SIP.]

B.   Even so, Dominion asserts, the Department's argument cannot rely on § 2–404(b)(1) because Dominion has in fact complied with its terms. Recall that § 2–404(b)(1) requires an applicant to provide documentation that establishes that its project has been approved by local authorities or, lacking that approval, demonstrates how that project nevertheless meets "all applicable zoning and land use requirements." Unable to show local approval, Dominion attempted to show compliance with zoning and land use requirements. With its second application for an air quality permit, Dominion included FERC's certificate of public convenience and necessity and a letter arguing "that the requirements of § 2–404(b)(1) are satisfied." J.A. 5. Dominion's letter points out that § 2–404(b)(1) requires documentation of compliance with "applicable" local requirements, then argues, correctly, that local law preempted by a federal law is not "applicable" because the Supremacy Clause bars its enforcement by a state agency. FERC's certificate preempts all local requirements that regulate in the same field as the NGA—including, according to Dominion, those requirements on which the Myersville Town Council based its zoning decision. Because those local requirements are preempted by federal law, they are no longer "applicable," and Dominion reasons that it need not demonstrate compliance with them to satisfy § 2–404(b)(1).

In its January 17 letter to MCRC and in its briefs to this court, the Department relied on two reasons for rejecting Dominion's analysis. In the Department's view, a letter from a permit applicant is not the type of documentation called for by § 2–404(b)(1), and FERC's certificate did not do all that Dominion claims because it did not expressly preempt Myersville's zoning and land use requirements.

According to the Department, a statement of compliance from the local zoning authority is the only documentation that satisfies § 2–404(b)(1). The Department asserts that it "has consistently interpreted the documentation requirement in § 2–404(b) [as] requiring a letter or statement from a local zoning authority that any proposed construction project has local zoning approval or otherwise meets local zoning and land use requirements." Resp. Br. At 24. But this interpretation is inconsistent with the plain meaning of § 2–404, which expressly permits the applicant to avoid involvement by the local zoning authority altogether. Subsection (ii) states that § 2–404(b)(1) may be satisfied by documentation "that the source meets all applicable zoning and land use requirements." If subsection (ii) required a statement or letter from the local zoning authority, then it would differ in no meaningful respect from subsection (i), which permits applicants to satisfy § 2–404(b)(1) with documented approval by the local zoning authority. This is not a sensible reading of the statute, . . . The Department's purported requirement of a written statement from the local zoning authority is therefore contrary to law.

Although it is true that the FERC certificate "does not definitively state that all of Myersville's applicable zoning requirements are preempted in this particular case . . . ," J.A. 1, that does not relieve the Department of its obligation to explain why it has refused to process Dominion's application. Section 2–404(b)(1) forbids the Department from processing only those applications for projects that do not comply with "applicable" local laws, so the Department may not rely on that provision to refuse to process an application if the only local laws with which an applicant fails to demonstrate compliance are preempted. As FERC explained, "state and local regulation is preempted by the NGA to the extent they [sic] conflict with federal regulation, or would delay the construction and operation of facilities approved by" FERC. *Dominion Transmission*, 141 F.E.R.C. at 62,298. Presented with a FERC certificate that approves Dominion's compressor station, the Department must apply this standard to determine which of Myersville's zoning and land use requirements it preempts, and which remain "applicable" to Dominion's compressor station. The absence of express preemption in FERC's certificate should play no role in that analysis. FERC properly chose to let the Department—the agency charged with administering § 2–404(b)(1)—determine in the first instance which of Myersville's requirements are preempted, and which are "applicable." *Dominion Transmission*, 141 F.E.R.C. at 62,298.

Believing, like FERC, that the Department is better situated to determine whether Dominion has complied with § 2–404(b)(1), we remand. . . . On remand, the Department must either identify one or more "applicable" (that is, not preempted) zoning or land use requirements with which Dominion has not demonstrated compliance, or it must process Dominion's application for an air quality permit. An order directing the parties to propose a schedule for prompt action on remand accompanies this decision.

III

Because the Department's failure to act to grant, condition, or deny Dominion's air quality permit was inconsistent with federal law, we grant Dominion's petition and remand for further action consistent with this opinion. *So ordered.* ■

NOTES AND COMMENTS

1.   FERC's grant of a certificate to construct facilities under its jurisdiction triggers the possible applicability of NEPA and the need for an Environmental Impact Statement if the certificate is a "major federal action" affecting the environment. (See Chapter 6.) Compressors in other small towns have also faced strong citizen opposition. In *Minisink Residents for Environmental Preservation and Safety v. FERC*, 762 F.3d 97 (D.C. Cir. 2014), the court upheld a 3–2 decision by FERC Commissioners to certificate a large compressor in the town of Minisink, New York. Two Commissioners had dissented from FERC's choice of the Minisink site compared to a less populated location a few miles away where a smaller compressor would reduce air emissions and fuel costs, improve reliability and capacity constraints, and result in only short-term disruption to agricultural land. *See* Order Issuing Certificate, Millennium Pipeline Co., L.L.C., FERC Docket No. CP11–515–000 (July 17, 2012). The reviewing court refused to second-guess FERC and held that FERC had taken a hard look at both alternatives and made a tough judgment. The Millennium Docket Order provides a nice description of FERC's certification process, including the conditions attached to the certificate to mitigate impacts.

In *Delaware Riverkeeper Network v. FERC*, 753 F.3d 1304 (D.C. Cir. 2014), the court found that FERC had violated NEPA when it treated four Tennessee Gas pipeline projects as separate projects with insignificant environmental impacts, even though the evidence clearly showed that the four projects were interrelated and contemporaneous. The court held that FERC violated NEPA by failing to address the cumulative impacts of what was, in effect, a functionally integrated project. FERC argued that the four projects could be judged separately because each had its own shipper contract commitments and were financially independent of each other. On the other hand, FERC's environmental review of pipeline projects need not include the impacts of natural gas production or processing. Coalition for Responsible Growth & Res. Conservation v. FERC, 485 Fed. Appx. 472 (2d Cir. 2012). NEPA's cumulative impacts analysis is more fully discussed in Chapter 14 in the context of federal approval of coal and LNG export terminals.

2.   Project developers complain that delays in government permitting hinders, thwarts, and raises the costs of modernizing necessary infrastructure in the United States. Some very public examples of seemingly endless delays include both "green" energy projects, such as the Cape Wind project in Nantucket Sound, and fossil fuel projects, such as the Keystone XL pipeline bringing oil from Canada to U.S. markets. A summary of possible remedies for unreasonable delays and their effectiveness in approving

energy projects appears in Michael B. Gerrard, Expedited Approval of Energy Projects: Toward Assessing the Forms of Procedural Relief, 4 San Diego J. of Climate & Energy L. 105 (2012–13). In May 2014, the Obama Administration released a report describing four strategies to modernize U.S. infrastructure needs by reducing uncertainty for project applicants, cutting review times in half, and producing measurably better environmental and community outcomes. Steering Committee on Federal Infrastructure Permitting and Review Process Improvement, Implementation Plan for the Presidential Memorandum on Modernizing Infrastructure Permitting (May 2014).

Whatever permitting delays may exist, capital spending on oil and gas midstream and downstream oil and gas infrastructure has expanded by 60% in just three years (from $56 billion in 2010 to almost $90 billion in 2013). IHS Global Inc., Oil & Natural Gas Transportation & Storage Infrastructure: Status, Trends, & Economic Benefits 3 (Dec. 2013) (prepared for the American Petroleum Inst.). Further, the industry seems quite confident about future infrastructure investments, expected to average about $80 billion per year through 2020. *Id.* at 4.

This infrastructure expansion, huge as it has been since 2010, has not kept up with surging shale gas and oil production. A quick-acting competitor has filled some of the gap—the railroads. Rail transport since 1980 has been largely deregulated from federal ratemaking authority, although common carrier obligations exist. John Fritelli *et al.*, Cong. Research Service, U.S. Rail Transportation of Crude Oil: Background and Issues for Congress 6 (2014) (Report 7–5700). "Crude-by-rail" shipments in the United States have increased from 9,500 tank car loads in 2008 to 400,000 car loads in 2013, a remarkable 40-fold increase, despite the fact that moving oil by rail typically costs $5 to $10 more per barrel than the average $5 per barrel charged by pipelines. *Id.* at 6.

Moving oil by rail from North Dakota to the Gulf Coast takes about seven days versus about 40 days by pipeline. *Id.* Over two-thirds of North Dakota's oil is shipped by rail. Mike Lee, N.D. Considers Rules on Stabilizing Bakken Oil before Transportation, EnergyWire (Aug. 11, 2014). Some North Dakota crude rides by rail to Albany (the capital of New York State) and then is shipped down the scenic Hudson River to refining and market centers. Colin Sullivan, Could Albany Be the Next Crude Futures Trading Hub? EnergyWire, Apr. 10, 2014. Barge operators have seen a thirteen-fold increase in barrels of Bakken and Canadian oil-sand crudes shipped down the Mississippi every month from 2010. Tom Fowler, Oil Boom a Boon for Barge Operators, Wall St. J. Feb. 3, 2014, at B3. The safety of rail and barge shipments is of considerable concern, as are oil spills.

G. PIPELINE SAFETY; CRUDE-BY-RAIL

Pipelines are controlled by continuous, remote sensing units which monitor flows and pressures and detect releases, but only after they have occurred. Prevention is the key to pipeline safety, but the best integrity testing measures (such as the use of "smart pigs," which are instruments placed inside the pipe to detect corrosion) are difficult to use in older lines and require highly skilled engineers to interpret the data. Often, operators inspect a small sample of pipe by excavating in suspect places and examining the pipe directly. Large transmission lines for liquids or natural gas most commonly rupture because of corrosion; smaller gas distribution lines (usually near customers in urban areas) most often rupture because an outside force damages the pipe. *See* Carol M. Parker, The Pipeline Industry Meets Grief Unimaginable: Congress Reacts with the Pipeline Safety Improvement Act of 2002, 44 Natural Res. J. 243, 252–57 (2004).

In August 2000, twelve members of an extended family were camping on the banks of the Pecos River in a rural part of New Mexico when an El Paso gas pipeline ruptured 675 feet away, instantly burning six members alive and ultimately killing all of them. The gas was being transported under high pressure in a major transmission line to California, which was in the throes of an energy crisis now best known for its exposure of market manipulation by Enron and other parties involved in that state's newly opened retail electricity markets. The year before, in Bellingham, Washington, a pipeline released 250,000 gallons of gasoline which exploded and sent a fireball more than 1 1/2 miles long through the an urban area, killing three children. In 2002, Congress enacted the Pipeline Safety Improvement Act of 2002 (Pub. L. No. 107–355, 49 U.S.C. §§ 6103–6107 and 60104–60133), following years of industry inertia and agency incompetence. These disasters led to lawmaking.

In Parker, *supra*, the author documents the doleful history of pipeline safety before this 2002 legislation and then describes the reforms made by the new Act. The reforms include giving the federal Petroleum and Hazardous Materials Safety Administration (PHMSA) and the Office of Pipeline Safety (OPS), which reside inside the Department of Transportation, the authority to order immediate corrective action for potential safety conditions; increased penalties for violations; stronger training for PHMSA employees; and a requirement that industry perform Risk Analysis and Integrity Management Programs that inspect all natural gas pipelines on a scheduled basis.

The new Act required that all pipeline operators provide geospatial data to the National Pipeline Mapping System within six months of passage; however, a Community-Right-to-Know section which would alert citizens to the location of pipelines near them was omitted because of security concerns after 9–11 that such information would help terrorists. Parker also makes recommendations for improving the Act, including imposing financial responsibility on the parent corporation of often-undercapitalized pipeline subsidiaries. In 2006, Congress passed the Pipeline Inspection, Protection, Enforcement and Safety Act of 2006, (Pub. L. No. 112–90, 49 U.S.C. §§ 6103–6104, and §§ 60101–60140), which required minimum standards for Integrity Management Programs (IMPs) for distribution lines, standards for reducing risks from human factors such as fatigue, updated incident reporting mandates, and enhancing the use of the "One Call" system that prohibits digging until excavators contact the state One Call system to locate any underground pipes.

In 2011, the boom in domestic oil and gas production and the heated debate over the Keystone XL and other pipelines led to passage of another act directed at pipeline safety. The Pipeline Safety, Regulatory Certainty, and Job Creation Act (codified at 49 U.S.C. §§ 60101 *et seq.*) aimed to improve pipeline performance in light of several other very public events. In 2010, a gas pipeline exploded in San Bruno, California, creating an inferno that killed eight people, injured many more, and destroyed many homes. In July 2011, an oil pipeline rupture spilled 1,000 barrels of oil into the historic Yellowstone River. However, the 2011 Act did not include many changes proposed by the National Transportation Safety Board (NTSB), an independent federal agency charged with investigating significant accidents in all modes of transportation, including aircraft, pipelines, rail, marine and highway. The 2011 Act mainly increased PHMSA's budget by 60% and added 120 new federal inspectors. More inspections do not necessarily result in greater safety. *See* Sarah L. Stafford, Will Additional Federal Enforcement Improve the Performance of Pipelines in the U.S.?, 37 Int'l Rev. L. & Econ. 137 (2013) (finding scant empirical evidence of a correlation).

The NTSB's report on the San Bruno explosion concluded that the probable cause was the failure of Pacific Gas & Electric (PG&E), the pipeline's owner, to perform quality assurance in 1956 when the pipeline was installed with visible seam weld flaws; and PG&E's inadequate integrity management system over the years. Nat'l Trans. Bd, Pacific Gas and Electric Company Natural Gas Transmission Pipeline Rupture and Fire, San Bruno, Calif., Sept. 9, 2010 (NTSB/PAR–11/01) (2011). PG&E had not been required to install, and had not voluntarily installed as part of its safety system, automatic shutoff valves and remote control valves that could have reduced the volume of flammable gas released, even though these devices were available. *See id.* at 56–57. This NTSB report reads depressingly like the Presidential Commission's report on the Deepwater Horizon blowout and spill, discussed in Chapter 4. Safety management systems are crucial to pipeline safety, especially because the greater public is often in harm's way.

A 2013 field hearing on pipeline safety includes statements and testimony of the Chair of the NTSB, the head of PHMSA, and others on the latest efforts by federal regulators to prevent gas pipeline explosions, following the 2011 Act. Senate Comm. on Commerce, Science, and Transportation, Field Hearing, Pipeline Safety: An On-the-Ground Look at Safeguarding the Public (113th Cong. 1st Sess., Jan 28, 2013). The hearing was held near a town in Kentucky that had suffered a gas pipeline explosion in December 2012. One resident's testimony about the wall of fire outside her front window is hair-raising. *Id.* at 5–7. The statement of the president of the Pipeline Safety Trust details many remaining gaps in pipeline safety regulation, including the 2011 Act's failure to require automatic shutoff and remote control valves on existing pipelines in High Consequence Areas, as recommended by the NTSB's San Bruno report. *See* NTSB Report, *supra,* at 129. (The Department of Transportation has authority to require these valves for new pipelines. 49 U.S.C. § 60102.) The Pipeline Safety Trust is a national organization, created from settlement monies paid in the Bellingham, Washington incident. The Department of Justice, in settling that case, was shocked by both the pipeline's lax safety practices and by the lax federal supervision over it. The Trust was created as a watchdog over both industry and its regulators. Field Hearing, *supra,* at 74–81; http://www.pstrust.org.

PHMSA data show that less than 16% of all gas pipeline leaks and less than 50% of major releases are initially identified by leak detection systems. Field Hearing, *supra*, at 75. This means that someone other than the pipeline controller, perhaps a local resident or emergency response personnel, is the first to discover the pipeline failure. Time is required to then communicate the problem to the pipeline control room. Industry is testing new leak and spill detection systems, such as aerial drones. The "best available technology" for detecting gas leaks in the field has been trained dogs whose acute sense of smell lets them find pinhole size leaks in pipe buried eight feet under frozen clay. Judy Carr, Going to the Dogs, Oil & Gas J., Dec. 6, 2004, at 17.

One study shows that pipeline transportation of oil and liquids is safer than shipment by road, barge or rail. A pipeline incident must be reported to PHMSA if it involves an explosion or fire, the release of more than five gallons of petroleum or petroleum products, a fatality, serious personal injury, or property damage. Data from 2005–09 show that U.S. safety incidents per billion ton-miles of product shipped average 2.08 for rail, 0.58 for hazardous liquid pipelines and 0.89 for gas pipelines. Diana Furchtgott-Roth & Kenneth P. Green, Intermodal Safety in the Transport of Oil 11 (Table 8) (Fraser Inst. 2013). Fatalities and injury data alone follow the same pattern. *Id.* at 11–12.

A runaway train carrying 72 carloads of Bakken crude oil derailed in the center of the town of Lac-Megantic, Quebec on July 6, 2013, killing 47 people and destroying most of the town. Canada's Transportation Safety Board's subsequent investigation found 18 factors played a role in the accident, but a weak corporate safety culture, lack of a safety management system, and lax regulation all played central roles. Trans. Safety Bd. of Canada, Report R13D0054, Runaway and Main-track Derailment, Montreal, Maine & Atlantic Railway, Freight train MMA–002, Mile 0.23, Sherbrooke Subdivision, Lac-Mégantic, Quebec, available at http://www.tsb.gc.ca/eng/rapports-reports/rail. Four other trains carrying crude oil, mostly from North Dakota and Canada, have derailed and caught fire in 2013 through January 2014. The Federal Railroad Administration handles rail safety, such as grade crossings and operating practices. PHMSA issues requirements for safe transport of hazardous materials that are enforced by the Federal Railroad Authority. CRS Report, *supra*, at 12–14.

The Lac-Mégantic disaster has triggered discussion of many reforms, some of which have been enacted in Canada and are quite likely to be followed in the United States. Changes in minimum standards for railcar construction, removal from service of the model DOT–111 railcars that were found to be inadequately impact-resistant, route selection to avoid populated areas, community notification rules, limiting engine speeds, addressing fatigue management, reducing the volatility of the oil before shipping, requiring thorough audits by regulators of safety systems—all are in the process of being implemented or are under serious discussion. CRS Report, *supra*, 14–19. To those knowledgeable about the Exxon Valdez and Deepwater Horizon incidents, it is déjà vu all over again.

CHAPTER 10

ELECTRIC POWER MARKETS

A. ELECTRIC POWER COMPETITION

Over the past forty years, lifting barriers to entry in electric power supply and expanding transmission infrastructure have enabled the rise of competitive, robust electric power markets. This chapter discusses the laws and regulations that have increased competition in electric power production, allowed access to transmission facilities, and shaped interstate electric power markets. This chapter also explores approaches several states have taken in introducing retail competition in electric power supply markets and other energy services.

Historically, it was widely assumed that electric power should be provided by a price-regulated public utility. See Chapter 8 for details on the various approaches to setting rates. Since the time of Samuel Insull (whose influence on the development of electric power is discussed in Chapter 2), it was widely assumed that vertical integration of generation, transmission and distribution services was efficient, and so the public utility's franchise ought to be protected from new entrants. The absence of competition, in turn, necessitated price regulation. Even at the wholesale level, where the Federal Energy Regulatory Commission (FERC) exercised jurisdiction, these assumptions prevailed and cost-of-service principles were applied to most power supply arrangements between utilities. See Chapter 8.

This conventional approach has been challenged by firms and policymakers alike, and over the years the assumption that electric power is most efficiently provided by a price-regulated public utility has changed substantially. Much of the change was precipitated by poor investment decisions by firms under cost-of-service regulation, miscalculations and lagging reactions by regulators to changes in technologies and market conditions, volatilities in fuel prices, and opportunities for new technological innovations that could improve efficiency and benefit consumers. These changes challenged an inflexible and rigid regulatory approach, designed to promote certainty and keep the risks associated with providing reliable and cheap electric power services low. The appearance of new firms known as non-utility generators (NUGs) or independent power producers (IPPs) also challenged the traditional predominance of the investor-owned utility. Today NUGs and IPPs provide over 40% of power supply in the United States.

While debates about "deregulation" of electric power continue to occur, today these debates are not about whether some competition in the electric power industry is desirable. Almost everyone agrees that it is. Rather, these debates focus on how much regulation should occur, of what activities, and by whom. At the federal level, competition in electric power is now considered a well-established tenet of federal policy, endorsed by Congress and by presidential administrations of both political parties. But that does not mean the regulatory apparatus for federal power markets has been disassembled. As FERC states on its website:

> National policy for many years has been, and continues to be, to foster competition in wholesale power markets. In each major energy bill over the last few decades, Congress has acted to open up the wholesale electric power market by facilitating entry of new generators to compete with traditional utilities. As the third major federal law enacted in the last 30 years to embrace wholesale competition, the Energy Policy Act of 2005 strengthened the legal framework for continuing wholesale competition as federal policy for this country. The Commission has acted quickly and strongly over the years to implement this national policy. The Commission's core responsibility is to "guard the consumer from exploitation by non-competitive electric power companies." The Commission has always used the following two general approaches to meet this responsibility:
>
> **Regulation**—was the primary approach for most of the last century and remains the primary approach for wholesale transmission service.

Competition—has been the primary approach in recent years for wholesale generation service.

Advances in technology, exhaustion of economies of scale in most electric generation, and new federal and state laws have changed the Commission's views of the right mix of these two approaches. The Commission's goal has always been to find the best possible mix of regulation and competition to protect consumers from the exercise of monopoly power.

FERC, Electric Competition, http://www.ferc.gov/industries/electric/indus-act/competition.asp. As this excerpt highlights, today electric power *transmission* remains a natural monopoly and is regulated. However, electric power *generation*, also sometimes referred to as "power supply," is recognized to be competitive in nature and thus has been deregulated in many key respects. What do you believe accounts for the difference between the two?

The partial deregulation of the electric utility industry is often called "restructuring," to reflect that some aspects continue to be regulated, and some have been deregulated. The two terms are often used (wrongly) as synonymous: "While policymakers sought to 'deregulate' the industry, the laws and regulations they used were intended and designed to 'restructure,' not deregulate, electricity." Joseph P. Tomain, 2002 Energy Law Symposium: The Past and Future of Electricity Regulation, 32 Envtl. L. 435, 437–38 (2002).

Professor David Spence describes the impetus for market restructuring of electric utility industries in the United States as follows:

> The theoretical case for restructuring was and is simple, straightforward, and based on two related propositions. First, the sale of electricity is not a "natural monopoly"; rather, it can and should be an industry in which sellers compete for customers. Second, and partly therefore, markets can set electricity prices better and more efficiently than governments can. Both of these propositions represent departures not only from traditional thinking but also from the assumptions that underlay the creation of the federal and state electric utility regulatory regimes during the first half of the twentieth century.
>
> Federal public-utility statutes like the FPA and its state analogs were created amid public worry over the concentration of economic power in the utility industries. Indeed, it is no coincidence that state regulation of electric utilities arose concurrently with American antitrust law. In the late nineteenth and early twentieth centuries, public demand for electric power grew, and electric systems grew up in major metropolitan areas. Some were publicly owned, others privately owned. Some used central-station technology, delivering power over a grid; others employed smaller, geographically distributed generators. A lengthy political fight eventually yielded the system we have today, dominated by state-chartered, vertically integrated, investor-owned utilities ("IOUs") providing monopoly electric service within their designated service areas, using their own central-station technology and distribution grid.

However, the price of political victory included two important restrictions on IOUs' freedom: the obligation of universal service and limits on the sale price of electricity. Since IOUs were monopoly providers within their service areas, price regulation was necessary to prevent the deadweight losses and producer surpluses associated with monopoly pricing. Thus, by 1930, state public-utility commissions had begun to regulate the rates charged by IOUs for electric service, using various forms of "cost-plus-fair-return" approaches. The "duty to serve" restriction forced IOUs to serve not only the most attractive customers—industrial users with large stable loads and geographically clustered residential and commercial customers—but also customers for whom the provision of service was more expensive. Since the tariffs according to which IOUs provided universal service did not permit price discrimination within customer classes, this duty to serve limited IOUs' ability to control average costs. . . .

[Federal and State statutes] created a legal foundation for electricity pricing that remained fairly stable for the next five or six decades. State public service commissions regulated retail rates, and FERC regulated wholesale rates. Under this system, most twentieth-century IOUs were vertically integrated companies, generating most of their own power (and buying some power in wholesale markets), transmitting it over their own distribution system, and selling it directly to their retail customers. This remains the norm in most states today. Traditional regulation guarantees licensed monopoly electric service providers administratively established rates that allow the companies a "fair" return on their prudently made investments. In return, electric utilities agree to meet a variety of service obligations to the general public, including the obligation to serve all eligible customers and to provide a reliable source of supply.

The potential for inefficiency in this approach has long been evident. Regulators must depend upon the regulated [utilities] to divulge their cost information. Commission staff and ratepayer advocate groups intervene in rate cases and review this information with a fine-tooth comb, but they cannot hope to overcome the information asymmetries inherent in the process. The regulated, in turn, have very little incentive to minimize costs, and every incentive to maximize the size of the rate base because under traditional ratemaking a larger rate base means more revenues. Finally, the regulatory oversight process entails its own considerable transaction costs. To its critics, a system characterized by high transaction costs, information asymmetries, and perverse incentives is bound to yield unnecessarily high electric rates in both wholesale and retail markets.

If the traditional system is inefficient, can the market do better? Yes, say proponents of restructuring. Traditional regulation has been based on a false premise: that the provision of electric service is a natural monopoly. That might be true if the sale and delivery of energy were one bundled product, but they are not. Rather, we can conceive of (and price) electricity sales, on the one hand, and the delivery of electricity, on the other, as two separate products. Delivery—transmission and distribution service—is a natural monopoly because the construction of duplicate electricity-delivery systems between two points is inefficient. However, the sale of the product that is delivered over such a system—electricity—is not a natural monopoly. We can unbundle sales and distribution so that buyers in wholesale and retail markets can choose their electricity supplier. Thus, said proponents of restructuring, transmission and distribution service should remain regulated, but prices of electricity sales should be set by the market. Competition among electricity sellers will force sellers to minimize (rather than maximize) costs, thereby driving prices down. The market will eventually weed out those who cannot provide reliable service at a competitive price, and consumers— broadly defined to include all consumer classes—will benefit. In this way, competitive markets should represent a Kaldor-Hicks improvement over regulated markets.[1]

David B. Spence, The Politics of Electricity Restructuring: Theory vs. Practice, 40 Wake Forest L. Rev. 417 (2005).

What are the goals of competitive restructuring (or so-called "deregulation") of the electric power industry? A predominant populist measure of success is lower prices for consumers, but perhaps this criterion is too narrow a measure of success, as some prices may increase while other decrease. There are many other goals, among them:

—Diversification of firms in the industry.

—Increased flexibility in firm investments.

—Increased adaptability to technological change.

—Increased efficiencies.

—Diversification of risk.

—Increased accountability and decreased reliance on government.

There are also many barriers to pursuing these goals as well as costs to restructuring. Among these are the following:

—Increased price volatility for consumers.

—Potential decreases in reliability.

—Reduced incentives for new entrants and innovation as price approaches marginal cost.

—Greater risks for investors and consumers.

—Potential concerns about consumer welfare and environmental programs.

—Increased costs of regulatory oversight for market conduct as firms increasingly engage in strategic profit-maximizing behavior.

---

[1] [Editors' Note: A Kaldor-Hicks improvement makes many people better off, and although it makes some people worse off, the surplus created by the improvement could be used to compensate the losers.]

—More intractable jurisdictional problems, as federal, state and local regulators each interact with the same firms.

Throughout this chapter, think carefully: how successful have restructuring and introducing competition in electric power been in the United States? Do they gauge well against these various policy goals? How, if at all should they be changed? What in the legal and regulatory approach to electric power enables or serves as a barrier to these kinds of changes?

B. COMPETITION IN POWER SUPPLY

Although competition in electricity generation is often embraced as a way to improve economic efficiency, the net degree of efficiency improvement is a subject of considerable controversy. A 1997 report by the U.S. Energy Information Administration (EIA) concluded that if full-scale competition in electricity generation began, retail prices for electricity would be reduced as much as 6 to 13 percent within 2 years compared to prices under the current approach to regulation. Under conditions of intense competition, the same study predicted that prices could fall as much as 24 percent. The same study noted, however, that there are significant differences across regions of the U.S. *See* EIA, Electricity Prices in a Competitive Environment: Marginal Cost Pricing of Generation Services and Financial Status of Electric Utilities—A Preliminary Analysis Through 2015 (Aug. 1997).

To understand the current degree and future growth of competition in the electric power industry, it is useful to explore some of the legal and policy issues that have been addressed at the federal level since the 1970s. In evaluating these legal and policy issues it is important to recognize how the services historically provided by a single, vertically-integrated utility—generation, transmission, and distribution—are no longer regarded as possessing similar economic characteristics. Generation or power supply is seen as a structurally competitive industry, one that can accommodate multiple competing suppliers. At the very least, electric power markets require (a) removing some barriers to entry that conventional utilities imposed—barriers that limited competition in electric power supply; and (b) moving away from cost-of-service hearings as a way of determining electric power prices.

1. RELAXING BARRIERS TO ENTRY

The various factors that caused electricity prices to increase in the 1970s and 1980s—increased oil prices, environmental standards, and nuclear costs—created pressure for increasing competition in the electric industry. Higher costs (many attributed to nuclear plant investments; see Chapter 7) did not impact electric utilities uniformly, increasing the disparity of electric rates among different utilities and causing some customers to look enviously at the rates their neighbors were paying.

The Public Utilities Regulatory Policies Act (PURPA) was enacted in 1978, as a part of President Carter's national energy plan. PURPA's enactment showed that Congress was responsive to the desire of customers to explore new options. According to Richard Hirsh, "Through its mostly unintended consequences, PURPA inaugurated the process by which the traditional structure of the utility system disintegrated."

Richard F. Hirsh, Power Loss: The Origins of Deregulation and Restructuring in the American Electric Utility System 119 (1999). As discussed below, PURPA endorsed the potential for efficiency and conservation in the energy conversion process and the promotion of efficiency in pooling, interconnecting, and "wheeling" (i.e., off-system customer or supplier transmission) power. It also represented the first explicit endorsement by Congress of competition policies for the electric power industry. *See* Hon. Richard D. Cudahy, PURPA: The Intersection of Competition and Regulatory Policy, 16 Energy L.J. 419 (1995). Since 1978, Congress has amended PURPA several times, most recently in the Energy Independence and Security Act of 2007 (EISAct 2007). See Chapter 13 for further discussion of EISAct 2007 amendments to PURPA in connection with achieving greater energy efficiency.

One of PURPA's most important provisions for introducing competition (as well as promoting other goals, such as conservation) is Section 210, through which Congress intended to remove the barriers that the monopoly of the traditional, vertical-integrated utility presented to new entrants in the generation sector of the electric power industry. Congress authorized FERC to prescribe rules to encourage new entrants in the power generation sector (known as "qualifying facilities," or QFs) by requiring utilities to purchase or sell electricity from such facilities. No mandatory purchase of QF power could be at "a rate which exceeds the incremental cost to the electric utility of alternative energy," known as the "avoided cost." Avoided cost was further defined by statute as "the cost to the electric utility of the electric energy which, but for the purchase from such cogenerator or small power producer, such utility would generate or purchase from another source." That is, if a utility does not purchase power from a QF, it has to generate it itself or buy it from another producer. What would be the cost of that next MW of electricity?

As described below, the statute left that question largely to the states. First, the states would typically set avoided cost rates in regulatory proceedings. Next, individual QFs would make showings that they were entitled to contracts with utilities at avoided cost rates. Finally, utilities would then be required to interconnect with the QFs and pay them avoided cost rates for power the utilities purchases. Note that utilities were therefore required to purchase QF power even if, on a given day, the utility did not need that additional power. In such circumstances, utilities had to ramp down their own production. Though as discussed below these requirements could lead to market inefficiencies, for now it is important to understand the growth of small power production and how it was facilitated by the setting of avoided-costs.

PURPA provided that the rate at which utilities purchased power from QFs: (1) would be just and reasonable and in the public interest; and (2) shall not discriminate against cogenerators (such as gas- or biomass-fired generators that produce electricity and useful heat simultaneously, often recycling their thermal output to enhance efficiency) or small power producers (small-scale facilities based on renewable sources, such as solar, wind, geothermal, hydro, and biomass). The impact of PURPA on the development of renewable resources is discussed further in Chapter 11.

FERC promulgated rules under PURPA in 1980, encouraging the growth of QFs by requiring utilities to purchase their power at avoided costs, requiring interconnection with the electric utility's grid (recall that at the time, utilities were vertically integrated), and exempting the new facilities from certain federal and state regulations, including traditional rate regulation. According to the FERC rules, the states and federal government shared responsibility for implementing this basic mandate. FERC determined whether a facility qualified as a QF, in certification proceedings based on fairly detailed operational criteria. State PUCs then determined what constituted "avoided cost" for utilities they regulated, with state regulators having wide latitude in establishing the procedures to assign avoided costs. *See* 18 C.F.R. Pt. 292. FERC's rules were challenged but upheld by the U.S. Supreme Court. *See* Am. Paper Inst., Inc. v. Am. Electric Power Serv. Corp., 461 U.S. 402 (1983) (holding FERC's avoided cost rules not arbitrary, capricious or an abuse of discretion); *see also* FERC v. Mississippi, 456 U.S. 742 (1982) (holding Congress, in enacting PURPA, did not exceed its power under the Commerce Clause or violate states' rights under the Tenth Amendment).

How should states calculate avoided costs? Over time, they settled on a variety of approaches, including: administrative (holding administrative proceedings designed to quantify avoided costs); competitive solicitation (bidding); and combinations of the two. Avoided cost rates are typically not based on actual costs incurred in the production of electricity, and, not surprisingly, they vary greatly between states. It is readily apparent that avoided cost calculations are fraught with uncertainty. States did not have carte blanche in establishing avoided cost rates. For example, efforts to base avoided costs on a fixed price rule, such New York's effort to establish a 6-cent flat rate for avoided costs, were the subject of much legal controversy, and were eventually abandoned or rejected by courts. Consider these, among other questions the states faced:

(1) Would the electric capacity "avoided' by a purchase from a renewable power facility come from a new power plant (and if so, how much would it cost)? Or would it come through a purchase from another supplier? Or demand reduction? FERC provided that utilities could be required to pay for the "capacity value" only when new resources allowed the utilities to reduce their own capacity-related costs by deferring construction of new plants or by deferring commitments to "firm" power purchase contracts (that is, contracts in which a generator commits to provide a pre-established amount of electricity within a certain time period, and in which this service is not interruptible and cannot be "curtailed" or cut off except in extreme circumstances). But states could— and did—diverge in deciding when that would happen. (See Chapter 11.)

(2) Could the "avoided cost" be zero because the utility would have excess capacity, not be planning to construct new plants, and not need to purchase more electricity from a QF to meet anticipated demand? FERC provided that even if the purchasing utility had excess capacity, a QF would always be entitled to energy payments except during times when the utility actually would incur higher costs (i.e., negative avoided costs) as a result of purchasing from a QF because such purchases would cause the utility to operate an existing plant at a lower and less efficient level.

Despite uncertainties over the definition of avoided costs, PURPA's QF certification scheme jump-started the growth of an independent energy sector. After decades of declining electricity prices, between 1973 and 1982 electricity prices had increased by about 60 percent in real (inflation adjusted) terms. DOE, Energy Security, A Report to the President of the U.S., DOE/S–0057, at 154 (1987). This created strong economic incentives for large consumers of electricity to reduce their energy costs. These developments, combined with PURPA's incentives, meant that cogeneration (primarily gas-fired), which had supplied nearly 50 percent of power produced in the United States around the turn of the century, again became a viable economic alternative for many industrial and commercial energy users. By 1990, non-utility generation had grown to supply more than half of the marginal generation capacity added to the industry, and more than 10% of cumulative generation capacity. As introduced above, today these non-utility generators (including PURPA QFs) provide more than 40% of power generation supply in the United States. For a discussion of states' roles in implementing this aspect of PURPA, see Deirdre Callaghan & Steve Greenwald, PURPA from Coast to Coast: America's Great Electricity Experiment, Nat. Resources & Env't, Winter 1996, at 17.

2. PRICE COMPETITION

With the rise of new entrants in power supply markets, federal regulators began to consider moving away from the traditional approach of setting rates, and to allow electric power supply prices to be based on market pressures rather than cost-of-service ratemaking. See Chapter 8. Two common approaches, both still dependent on some degree of regulatory oversight by FERC, are market-based rates and incentive rates. As introduced in Chapter 8, FERC currently allows nearly all utilities that sell wholesale power (sales of power from one utility to another for eventual resale to customers) to charge market-based rates— whatever rate the market will bear. As is discussed below, a minority of states have also restructured their retail electric power industries, and allow retail electricity providers to charge their customers market-based rates. These states often implement transition periods in which there is a ceiling (and/or a floor) on the rate that utilities may charge retail customers, avoiding excessive prices for retail customers through the price ceiling and excessive undercutting of prices and market disruptions through the price floor. These states also often provide a default utility and default rate for customers who choose not to move to a competitive supplier. Some of these states have opted to phase out these temporary controls in order to allow fully competitive pricing. This section describes both market-based rates and incentive rates.

a. MARKET-BASED RATES

In the late 1980s, FERC adopted additional regulatory strategies to increase competition in the independent energy sector, jump-started by PURPA. Two significant measures adopted by FERC were: (1) the approval of market-based rates for independent power producers that lacked significant market power, effectively relieving these generators of the regulatory burden imposed by cost-of-service regulation; and (2) the exercise of "light-handed" regulation for independent power producers, which relieved these generators from other costly reporting requirements. Several states have adopted similar market-based rate and light-handed regulation mechanisms. In addition, state programs designed to encourage or require competitive bidding for approval of new generation capacity increased from only a few in 1988 to more than 30 by 1993. As discussed in Chapter 8, market-based rates remain an important tool for FERC, which engages in active monitoring of such rates for the sales of energy at wholesale in interstate commerce. FERC's *Dartmouth Power* order provides an overview of some of the concerns raised by market-based and light-handed regulation at the federal level:

Dartmouth Power Associates Limited Partnership
53 F.E.R.C. ¶ 61,117 (1990).

■ Before Commissioners: MARTIN L. ALLDAY, CHAIRMAN; CHARLES A. TRABANDT, ELIZABETH ANNE MOLER and JERRY J. LANGDON.

On March 21, 1990, as completed on October 5, 1990, Dartmouth Power Associates Limited Partnership (Dartmouth) submitted a Power Purchase Agreement (the Agreement) between Dartmouth and Commonwealth Electric Company (Commonwealth Electric), and an Amendment to the Agreement (Amendment). The rates from Dartmouth to Commonwealth Electric were negotiated between the parties and, as discussed infra, Dartmouth requests that the Commission find that its rates are just and reasonable as market-based rates. . . .

Negotiations leading up to the Agreement began in the spring of 1987. The Agreement was executed September 5, 1989, and was filed March 21, 1990. The Agreement originally provided that Dartmouth would construct, own and operate a 168.8-MW combined cycle, gas-fired unit, and would sell 50 MW of capacity and energy to Commonwealth Electric. Dartmouth states that in February 1990, it decided to reconfigure the unit to reflect a smaller, 67.6-MW combined cycle unit, and notified Commonwealth Electric of this proposed change. . . .

According to Dartmouth, the unit will be located in Commonwealth Electric's service territory and will be fully dispatchable by the New England Power Pool ("NEPOOL"). Dartmouth states that it will own only those transmission facilities used to interconnect the unit with Commonwealth Electric's system. . . .

Dartmouth is a limited partnership. Dartmouth's sole general partner, EMI Dartmouth, Inc., is a Massachusetts Corporation owned entirely by an individual, James Gordon. According to Dartmouth, Mr. Gordon "will also own at least 50% of the limited partnership interests in Dartmouth." Currently, five other individuals hold limited partnership interests in Dartmouth, and Dartmouth states that other limited partnership interests may be sold in the future. In this regard, the respective interests of Dartmouth's general and limited partners have yet to be determined.

Through Mr. Gordon, Dartmouth will be affiliated with Pawtucket Power Associates Limited Partnership (Pawtucket), an entity which will own a 62-MW cogeneration facility. Dartmouth states that Mr. Gordon owns a 100% interest in EMI Management, Inc. ("EMI"), the developer of Dartmouth and Pawtucket. According to Dartmouth, EMI has also developed a cogeneration facility which will sell electricity to Commonwealth Electric. . . .

Dartmouth states its price to Commonwealth Electric "was negotiated over an extended period of time," and that "[t]he history of the negotiations between [Commonwealth Electric] and Dartmouth and [Commonwealth Electric's] access to alternative sources of wholesale electric power demonstrate the existence of a competitive market supporting market-based rates." In this regard, in support of its request for approval of market-based rates, Dartmouth argues that the New England electricity market is characterized by an active market for new QF capacity, and that Commonwealth Electric participates in this market both through formal QF bid solicitations and through nonbid negotiations. . . .

Dartmouth argues that negotiations between Dartmouth and Commonwealth Electric took place in the context of a competitive market in which Commonwealth Electric had numerous supply alternatives. In this regard, Dartmouth notes that Commonwealth Electric has had numerous supply alternatives to choose from as evidenced by: (1) the responses to Commonwealth Electric's solicitation for QF capacity in RFP 1 (where bids totaling over 920 MW were received, constituting more than ten times the amount of capacity sought); (2) the responses eight other New England utilities received to 1987 and 1988 solicitations (where bids totaled over 11,000 MW, twelve times the capacity solicited); (3) the response Boston Edison Company (BECO) received in its fall 1989 QF solicitation (where bids totaled 2,837 MW, fourteen times the capacity solicited); and (4) the fact that, according to Dartmouth, 6,200 MW of independent power capacity is currently under construction or development in New England. . . .

Dartmouth argues that, since neither it nor its parent or affiliates own or control transmission facilities (other than those required to interconnect the facility with the purchaser's system), it cannot restrict Commonwealth Electric's access to competing suppliers. Furthermore, Dartmouth states that it does not control any other resources by which it could erect barriers against the entry of other suppliers. Dartmouth also states that it has no affiliations or business relationships which could result in self dealing.

Based on the foregoing arguments, Dartmouth concludes that it lacks market power over Commonwealth Electric, when its proposal is judged against the standards used by the Commission in approving other market-based rates.

Dartmouth requests that the Commission grant waivers of its regulations, considering the market-based nature of Dartmouth's rates. . . .

In Commonwealth Atlantic Limited Partnership (*Commonwealth Atlantic*), the Commission determined that market-based rates are acceptable if the seller can demonstrate that it lacks market power over the buyer. In addition, the Commission has carefully scrutinized transactions involving nontraditional sellers affiliated with franchised utilities, or affiliated with any other entities that own or control resources that could be used to create barriers to other suppliers who seek to enter the market. Accordingly, we have analyzed Dartmouth's proposal consistent with the analysis used in our prior cases.

In both *Enron* and *Commonwealth Atlantic*, the Commission noted that it had previously approved long-term power sales at market-based rates where the seller demonstrated that it had no market power over the buyer (or that the seller had adequately mitigated its market power) and where there was no evidence of potential affiliate abuse. *E.g., Enron*, 52 FERC at p. 61,708 & n.41 (*citing Commonwealth Atlantic*, 51 FERC P61,368 (1990)). In *Enron* and *Commonwealth Atlantic*, the Commission noted that it had previously stated that a seller has market power when it can significantly influence the price in the market by restricting supply or by denying access to alternative sellers. *E.g., id.* (*citing Commonwealth Atlantic*, 51 FERC at p. 62,244 & n.43.

Specifically, the criteria set forth in the Commission's prior decisions require that the seller provide evidence that: (1) neither the seller nor any of its affiliates is a dominant firm in the sale of generation services in the relevant market; (2) neither the seller nor any of its affiliates owns or controls transmission facilities which could be used by the buyer in reaching alternative generation suppliers, or they have adequately mitigated their ability to block the buyer in reaching such alternative suppliers; and (3) neither the seller nor any of its affiliates is able to erect or otherwise control any other barrier to entry. The Commission has also analyzed whether there is evidence of potential abuses of self dealing or reciprocal dealing. As discussed below, we find that Dartmouth's filing meets these standards, and thus we will accept Dartmouth's rates for filing. . . .

Neither Dartmouth nor its affiliates own or are affiliated with utilities that own transmission facilities in the region. Neither Dartmouth nor its QF affiliates can erect barriers preventing others from entering the relevant market; in this regard, Dartmouth has stated that it controls no major input factors (e.g., land sites, gas pipelines, or fuel supplies).

Finally, we find that there is no evidence of self dealing or reciprocal dealing abuse. Dartmouth is not affiliated with Commonwealth Electric. Although Dartmouth is affiliated with a developer which is constructing a QF which will serve Commonwealth Electric, there is no evidence that Dartmouth, because of this affiliation, was able to influence the price at which Commonwealth Electric purchased power. . . .

We find that Dartmouth's market-pricing proposal will result in rates to Commonwealth Electric that are within the legally mandated zone of reasonableness. We note that we will have the opportunity to reassess this finding if changes to the rate are proposed. The Dartmouth/Commonwealth Electric Agreement is a formula rate. While the rate charged Commonwealth Electric will vary over time, the adjustments will be pursuant to the approved formulae, which our review has shown were determined through negotiations in which Dartmouth lacked market power. The formulae cannot be changed without a further filing with the Commission. Accordingly, if Dartmouth in the future acquires market power over Commonwealth Electric and tries to exercise that power through modifications to the formula rate, it will need the Commission's approval for such changes. The Commission would review Dartmouth's proposal de novo in light of the then existing circumstances, and would not approve continuation of a market-based rate unless we were assured that Dartmouth continued to lack market power, or had adequately mitigated its market power.

■ CHARLES A. TRABANDT, COMMISSIONER, concurring:

I join in approving the market rate that Dartmouth Power Associates Limited Partnership (Dartmouth Power) proposes to charge Commonwealth Electric Company under the contract before us. I write in order briefly to explain why.

[I take] issue with the majority's approach to approving market rates for independent power producers (IPPs), generators unaffiliated with utilities. [T]he Federal Power Act and the cases contain three requirements: finding a workable competitive market; imposing a just and reasonable price ceiling; and creating a monitoring mechanism to account for changed conditions. Specifically, I disagreed with the Commonwealth holding that we need not subject rates IPPs negotiate to just and reasonable ceilings.

Here, we all agree that the Dartmouth Power contract emerged from a competitive market. As to the second criterion, in this case, the majority keeps to its rejection of a rate ceiling. I adhere to my view. Nevertheless, I agree with approving the contract before us. . . . ■

Market-based rates and FERC's role in monitoring market power are discussed in Chapter 8. Recall that FERC has a statutory obligation to ensure that rates are "just and reasonable." Are market-based rates consistent with this obligation? Two appellate courts have determined that market-based rates are consistent with FERC's mandate to ensure "just and reasonable" rates under the Federal Power Act (FPA). *See* California ex rel. Lockyer v. FERC, 383 F.3d 1006, 1013 (9th Cir. 2004); La. Energy & Power Auth. v. FERC, 141 F.3d 364, 365 (D.C. Cir. 1998). The U.S. Supreme Court has yet to speak to the issue, and has consistently ducked it, most recently in the *Morgan Stanley* case, discussed below.

b. INCENTIVE REGULATION

While FERC and many state PUCs will allow market-based rates where a firm lacks market power, most utilities with market power continue to base rates on the cost of service. However, in recent years new regulatory mechanisms designed to encourage more efficient utility rate setting have emerged. One of the most popular of these is incentive rates, which focus on setting rates to include more efficient conduct by the firm.

In a 1992 policy statement, FERC announced that it would allow electric utilities with market power to propose incentive rate systems to advance two efficiency-enhancing results: lower rates to consumers; and increased shareholder returns. Incentive Ratemaking for Interstate Natural Gas Pipelines, Oil Pipelines, and Electric Utilities, 61 FERC ¶ 61,168 (Mar. 13, 1992).

This policy statement permitted electric utilities and natural gas pipelines to propose incentive rate mechanisms as alternatives to cost-of-service ratemaking. The Commission's incentive rate policy was premised on two overriding principles. First, incentive rate mechanisms should encourage efficiency by optimizing operating efficiency, allocating services to the highest valued uses, investing new capital when economically warranted, and capturing expanding markets. Second, the initial rates under the incentive rate mechanism must conform to the Commission's just and reasonable standard.

FERC required incentive rates to adhere to five principles. They must:

    (1) be prospective;

    (2) be voluntary;

    (3) be understandable;

    (4) result in quantifiable benefits for consumers, subject to the constraint that they not exceed the rates that would apply under cost-of-service regulation; and

    (5) maintain or enhance incentives to improve the quality of service.

FERC indicated that it would rely on incentive rates on a case-by-case basis. To date, few utilities have availed themselves of the incentive rate mechanisms FERC has made available for power supply—mostly because market-based rates have come to predominate in competitive bulk power markets. However, the Energy Policy Act of 2005 (EPAct 2005) added a new section 219 to the FPA, directing FERC to develop incentive-based rate treatments for *transmission* of electric energy in interstate commerce.

Most experimentation with incentive rates has occurred at the state level. In addition to cost-of-service regulation, discussed at length in Chapter 8, state PUC rate experiments include: benchmarking—giving rewards or penalties to a utility's earning opportunity based on comparison with a pre-set standard, the value of which becomes known in the future; and price caps—setting a maximum price to be charged, which is determined by formula based on factors not within the utilities' control, such as inflation, or factors under the utilities' control, such as costs. *See* J. Robert Malko & Richard J. Williams, Traditional and New Regulatory Tools, 93, 99 in Reinventing Electric Utility Regulation (Gregory B. Enholm & J. Robert Malko, eds. 1995).

For example, Central Maine Power Co.'s incentive rates impose a price cap, utilizing current rates as a starting point. The utility is not able to recover dollar-for-dollar through its fuel adjustment clause or for purchased power, as it has in the past. The incentive rates contain a service reliability component that establishes an earnings-reduction mechanism, allowing imposition of penalties ranging from $250,000 to $3 million if net service quality or customer satisfaction declines. In addition, the utility is allowed to pass through to ratepayers a share of the savings and costs associated with the buyout of (QF) power purchase contracts. The utility has also secured a pricing flexibility component, which allows it to select from a variety of pricing options, typically between a marginal cost floor and the price cap, subject to safeguards designed to protect core customers, avoid undue discrimination, and preserve its previously-established rate design policy. Central Me. Power Co., Proposed Increase in Rates, Docket No. 92–345, Jan. 10, 1995 (Me. PUC). A similar price flexibility program without a full-fledged price cap was approved in *Re Bangor-Hydro Electric Co.*, Docket Nos. 94–125, 94–273, Feb. 14, 1995 (Me. PUC).

NOTES AND COMMENTS

1.   Might incentive rate mechanisms run afoul of the traditional "just and reasonable" cost-of-service principles? In *Stewart v. Utah Public Service Comm'n,* 885 P.2d 759 (Utah 1994), the Utah Supreme Court held that incentive rates that were designed to encourage investment in the Utah telecommunications infrastructure by providing for an adjustable rate of return and revenue sharing between shareholders and customers of U.S. West, a regulated utility, violated these principles:

> We turn now to the legality of the plan promulgated by the Commission under § 54–4–4.1(1). The Commission made no findings in support of the percentage breakdowns that determine the sharing of revenues between the utility and the ratepayers. Revenue sharing begins at a rate of return of 12.2%, the rate the Commission erroneously found to be just and reasonable based on cost-of-service standards. Under the plan, USWC [U.S. West Communications] retains 20% of all overearnings between 12.2% and 13.2%; 40% of all overearnings between 13.2% and 14.2%; and 50% of all overearnings between 14.2% and 17%. Earnings in excess of 17% were to be returned to the ratepayers. Thus, notwithstanding the 12.2% authorized rate of return fixed by the Commission, USWC has an incentive to earn up to a 17% rate of return.
>
> The Commission's order is defective for a number of reasons. First, it was entered without notice to any party or a hearing on the merits of the plan. Second, the plan essentially forsakes cost-of-service principles as required by Title 54 of the Public Utilities Code. The sharing of revenue begins at 12.2%, but all earnings over and above that percentage that USWC can retain are necessarily excessive because they are not justified by any cost-of-service principle. Nor can they be justified on the ground that they provide an "incentive" for USWC to invest in Utah. . . . In fact, the incentive to earn higher profits can be achieved as easily, or more easily, by false economics such as cutting maintenance expenses, reducing customer services, and deferring necessary investments. On that score, we emphatically note that the Commission has allowed USWC accelerated depreciation rates to induce USWC to invest in Utah and USWC has not made the investments contemplated. Unjustifiable accelerated depreciation rates translate into unjustifiable charges against ratepayers that inure to the benefit of the shareholders.
>
> Nor can the Commission's plan be justified on the ground that it enables ratepayers to share in some of USWC's excess earnings. Given the Commission's extraordinary default in the regulation of USWC's earnings over the past years, that might well seem a desirable objective, but it is hardly a rationale for institutionalizing and legalizing exorbitant rates. Even if it is possible to justify a sharing of earnings in excess of an authorized rate of return

because of a necessary and inevitable lag in rate-fixing procedures, it is certainly not justifiable for a utility to retain excess earnings in increasingly larger percentages above the authorized rate of return on equity. Finally, the Commission's plan in effect assumes that another rate-making proceeding need not take place unless and until USWC earns in excess of 17%, a prescription for regulatory neglect and exploitive rates.

For all the above reasons, the Commission's incentive plan is arbitrary, capricious, and unlawful.

2. Performance-based incentive rates focus on incentives for the utility to improve performance. Some other "incentive" rates are more concerned with local economic development than improved utility performance. These economic development incentive rates are designed to entice new and preserve existing industries and business. To the extent that these allow the pricing flexibility necessary for utilities to continue to compete in emerging power markets, such rates are not necessarily inefficient. For example, the North Carolina Utilities Commission adopted interim guidelines for such economic development incentive rates to give utilities pricing flexibility necessary for competition. Re Self-generation, Deferral Rates, Dispersed Energy Facilities and Economic Incentive Rates, Docket No. E–100, Sub. 73, Nov. 28, 1994 (N.C.U.C.).

3. EXPANSION OF FERC'S AUTHORITY OVER TRANSMISSION

With the enactment of the federal Energy Policy Act of 1992 (EPAct 1992), a statute adopted following the initial U.S. crisis with Iraq, Congress gave even more emphasis to the promotion of competition among various components of the electric power industry. Two developments were significant in promoting more widespread wholesale power supply competition. EPAct 1992 expanded FERC's historically limited authority over wholesale transmission, allowing FERC to introduce more competition-based policies within this sector. In addition, EPAct 1992 removed some of the restrictions on the growth of the independent power industry imposed by the Public Utility Holding Company Act of 1935 (PUHCA).

As the Supreme Court observed in *Otter Tail* (see Chapter 8), the FPA did not originally authorize the Commission to require one utility to transmit power generated outside of the utility's own system. In 1978, however, PURPA authorized FERC to mandate "wheeling" (that is, transmission access) for wholesale customers and suppliers, by adding §§ 211 and 212 to the FPA. These new provisions allowed FERC to mandate wholesale wheeling, but only where it would not result in a "reasonably ascertainable uncompensated economic loss," would not impose "an undue burden" or "unreasonably impair the reliability" for any affected utility, and would not impair adequate service to customers.

However, in part because of narrow agency and judicial interpretations, the version of §§ 211 and 212 enacted in 1978 was never fully used to require a utility to transmit power from an off-system source. The Second Circuit held that § 211 clearly indicated that wheeling could not be ordered solely on the basis of the public interest in enhanced competition. New York Elec. & Gas Corp. v. FERC, 638 F.2d

388, 402 (2d Cir. 1980). In addition, the Fifth Circuit rebuked an effort by FERC to foster competition through mandatory wheeling, noting that although FERC's goal was "laudable," the agency "is without authority under the FPA to compel wheeling." Fla. Power & Light Co. v. FERC, 660 F.2d 668, 677–779 (5th Cir. 1981). Following these decisions, FERC itself interpreted § 211 to "prohibit[ ] the issuance of wheeling orders that have a significant procompetitive effect." Se. Power Admin., 26 F.E.R.C. ¶ 61,127, 61,323 (1984). Although FERC had earlier noted that it may have been willing to require wholesale wheeling to address fuel shortages or to promote the coordination of electricity among utilities, Se. Power Admin., 25 F.E.R.C. ¶ 61,204, 61,539 (1983), FERC did not issue a single order requiring procompetitive wheeling.

Even though the 1978 version of §§ 211 and 212 were never directly used to enhance competition, they may have had some indirect effect on competition in the industry. First, the threat of compulsory wheeling may have nudged utilities to negotiate voluntary transmission agreements with other suppliers and wholesale customers. Second, FERC used indirect regulatory mechanisms to implement §§ 211 and 212. Under this statutory framework FERC's ability to implement open access in transmission was perceived as severely limited by § 211(c)(1) of the FPA, which barred FERC from requiring wholesale wheeling service "unless the Commission determined that such order would reasonably preserve existing competitive relationships." Despite these jurisdictional limits, FERC did issue procompetitive transmission access orders in the adjudicative context as a voluntary condition to a benefit or approval conferred under other sections of the FPA. FERC developed a general market-based pricing policy in a number of adjudicative cases, routinely requiring wholesale transmission access as a condition to its approval of market-based rates. FERC also used its merger approval authority to develop transmission policy on a case-by-case basis. *See* Jim Rossi, Redeeming Judicial Review: The Hard Look Doctrine and Federal Regulatory Efforts to Restructure the Electric Utility Industry, 1994 Wis. L. Rev. 763 (1994).

The EPAct 1992 explicitly expanded FERC's authority to mandate transmission access, thus opening up broader possibilities for open access. After passage of the EPAct 1992, dozens of requests for wholesale transmission service were filed with FERC. Despite a spirited opposition by the utility industry, FERC's treatment of these requests erased any remaining doubt that it would, in certain circumstances, use its new authority under § 211 of the FPA to push the industry towards open access and increased competition.

In a watershed decision issued in October 1993, FERC voted unanimously to require Florida Power & Light (FP & L) to provide network transmission service to members of the Florida Municipal Power Agency, thus requiring the utility to wheel other utilities' power using its transmission lines. Fla. Mun. Power Agency, 65 F.E.R.C. ¶ 61,125 (1993) (granting request for transmission service as establishing further proceedings to investigate the rates, terms, and conditions of such service). Interpreting its new authority broadly, FERC noted that § 211(c)(2) of the FPA did not bar issuance of a wheeling order due to pre-existing transmission contracts, effectively allowing existing transmission customers the opportunity to "upgrade" the service they received under existing contracts. Given the FPA's purpose of "encourag[ing] the orderly development of plentiful supplies of electricity . . . at reasonable prices," FERC found the public interest in favor of issuing a wheeling order to be compelling under the circumstances:

> As a general matter, the availability of transmission service (or increased flexibility to use transmission) will enhance competition in the market for power supplies over the long run because it will increase both the power supply options available to transmission customers (thereby benefitting their customers) and the sales options available to sellers. This should result in lower costs to consumers. In addition, if a transmission customer determines that flexible service, such as network service, will allow it to serve its customers more efficiently, we believe that the public interest will be served by requiring that service to be provided so long as the transmitting utility is fully and fairly compensated and there is no unreasonable impairment of reliability.

Id. FERC's order emphasized that the rates, terms, and conditions under which the service is offered must be nondiscriminatory and comparable to what the utility provides other customers.

This represented the first step in imposing on the industry the "comparability" standard that FERC first endorsed in the natural gas context, as is discussed in Chapter 9. [This requires a utility to offer pipeline or transmission service to other customers on terms that are "comparable" to what it offers to its own gas or power supply.] This precedent-setting decision was widely recognized by industry experts as a clear message that FERC was serious about "leveling the competitive playing field" between transmission users and transmission-owning utilities. FERC has continued to adopt competitive transmission mechanisms by requiring transmission to the distribution level and requiring the open access tariffs filed in merger proceedings to provide network service. Following the 1993 FP & L order, FERC required all providers of transmission service to open their transmission lines to generators on a first-come, first-served, nondiscriminatory basis, as discussed in the following section.

C. OPEN ACCESS TRANSMISSION

1. ORDER NO. 888

After the EPAct 1992, competitive reforms of the electric power industry have evolved significantly. FERC endorsed the idea of shifting the wholesale electric power market in the direction of competition when it adopted landmark regulations in a notice-and-comment rulemaking culminating in Order No. 888 in 1996. Order No. 888 requires all public utilities that own, control or operate facilities used for transmitting electric energy in interstate commerce to file open access non-discriminatory transmission tariffs with FERC. The basic idea behind this rule was to open up power supply markets to competition. FERC's rules were challenged and largely affirmed by the Supreme Court.

New York v. Federal Energy Regulatory Comm'n

535 U.S. 1 (2002).

■ STEVENS, J. These cases raise two important questions concerning the jurisdiction of the Federal Energy Regulatory Commission (FERC or Commission) over the transmission of electricity. First, if a public utility "unbundles"—*i.e.,* separates—the cost of transmission from the cost of electrical energy when billing its retail customers, may FERC require the utility to transmit competitors' electricity over its lines on the same terms that the utility applies to its own energy transmissions? Second, must FERC impose that requirement on utilities that continue to offer only "bundled" retail sales?

In Order No. 888, issued in 1996 with the stated purpose of "Promoting Wholesale Competition Through Open Access Non-Discriminatory Transmission Services by Public Utilities," FERC answered yes to the first question and no to the second. It based its answers on provisions of the Federal Power Act (FPA), as added by § 213, 49 Stat. 847, and as amended, 16 U.S.C. § 824 *et seq.,* enacted in 1935. Whether or not the 1935 Congress foresaw the dramatic changes in the power industry that have occurred in recent decades, we are persuaded, as was the Court of Appeals, that FERC properly construed its statutory authority.

I

In 1935, when the FPA became law, most electricity was sold by vertically integrated utilities that had constructed their own power plants, transmission lines, and local delivery systems. Although there were some interconnections among utilities, most operated as separate, local monopolies subject to state or local regulation. Their sales were "bundled," meaning that consumers paid a single charge that included both the cost of the electric energy and the cost of its delivery. Competition among utilities was not prevalent.

Prior to 1935, the States possessed broad authority to regulate public utilities, but this power was limited by our cases holding that the negative impact of the Commerce Clause prohibits state regulation that directly burdens interstate commerce. When confronted with an attempt by Rhode Island to regulate the rates charged by a Rhode Island plant selling electricity to a Massachusetts company, which resold the electricity to the city of Attleboro, Massachusetts, we invalidated the regulation because it imposed a "direct burden upon interstate commerce." Creating what has become known as the "*Attleboro* gap," we held that this interstate transaction was not subject to regulation by either Rhode Island or Massachusetts, but only "by the exercise of the power vested in Congress."

When it enacted the FPA in 1935, Congress authorized federal regulation of electricity in areas beyond the reach of state power, such as the gap identified in *Attleboro,* but it also extended federal coverage to some areas that previously had been state regulated. The FPA charged the Federal Power Commission ("FPC"), the predecessor of FERC, "to provide effective federal regulation of the expanding business of transmitting and selling electric power in interstate commerce." Specifically, in § 201(b) of the FPA, Congress recognized the FPC's jurisdiction as including "the transmission of electric energy in interstate commerce" and "the sale of electric energy at wholesale in interstate commerce." Furthermore, § 205 of the FPA prohibited, among other things, unreasonable rates and undue discrimination "with respect to any transmission or sale subject to the jurisdiction of the Commission," and § 206 gave the FPC the power to correct such unlawful practices.

[I]n 1995, FERC initiated the rulemaking proceeding that led to the adoption of the order presently under review. FERC proposed a rule that would "require that public utilities owning and/or controlling facilities used for the transmission of electric energy in interstate commerce have on file tariffs providing for nondiscriminatory open-access transmission services." The stated purpose of the proposed rule was "to encourage lower electricity rates by structuring an orderly transition to competitive bulk power markets." Rather than grounding its legal authority in Congress' more recent electricity legislation, FERC cited §§ 205–206 of the 1935 FPA—the provisions concerning FERC's power to remedy unduly discriminatory practices—as providing the authority for its rulemaking.

[FERC] found that electric utilities were discriminating in the "bulk power markets," in violation of § 205 of the FPA, by providing either inferior access to their transmission networks or no access at all to third-party wholesalers of power. Invoking its authority under § 206, it prescribed a remedy containing three parts that are presently relevant.

First, FERC ordered "functional unbundling" of wholesale generation and transmission services. FERC defined "functional unbundling" as requiring each utility to state separate rates for its wholesale generation, transmission, and ancillary services, and to take transmission of its own wholesale sales and purchases under a single general tariff applicable equally to itself and to others.

Second, FERC imposed a similar open access requirement on unbundled *retail* transmissions in interstate commerce. . . . FERC ultimately concluded that it was "irrelevant to the Commission's jurisdiction whether the customer receiving the unbundled transmission service in interstate commerce is a wholesale or retail customer." Thus, "if a public utility voluntarily offers unbundled retail access," or if a State requires unbundled retail access, "the affected retail customer *must* obtain its unbundled transmission service under a non-discriminatory transmission tariff on file with the Commission."

Third, FERC rejected a proposal that the open access requirement should apply to "the transmission component of bundled retail sales." Although FERC noted that "the unbundling of retail transmission and generation . . . would be helpful in achieving comparability," it concluded that such unbundling was not "necessary" and would raise "difficult jurisdictional issues" that could be "more appropriately considered" in other proceedings.

In its analysis of the jurisdictional issues, FERC distinguished between transmissions and sales. It explained:

> [Our statutory jurisdiction] over sales of electric energy extends only to wholesale sales. However, when a retail transaction is broken into two products that are sold separately (perhaps by two different suppliers: an electric energy supplier and a transmission supplier), we believe the jurisdictional lines

change. In this situation, the state clearly retains jurisdiction over the sale of power. However, the unbundled transmission service involves *only* the provision of 'transmission in interstate commerce' which, under the FPA, is exclusively within the jurisdiction of the Commission. Therefore, when a bundled retail sale is unbundled and becomes separate transmission and power sales transactions, the resulting transmission transaction falls within the Federal sphere of regulation.

With respect to various challenges to its jurisdiction, FERC acknowledged that it did not have the "authority to order, *sua sponte,* open-access transmission services by public utilities," but explained that § 206 of the FPA explicitly required it to remedy the undue discrimination that it had found. FERC also rejected the argument that its failure to assert jurisdiction over bundled retail transmissions was inconsistent with its assertion of jurisdiction over unbundled retail transmissions. FERC repeated its explanation that it did not believe that regulation of bundled retail transmissions (*i.e.,* the "functional unbundling" of retail transmissions) "was necessary," and again stated that such unbundling would raise serious jurisdictional questions. FERC did not, however, state that it had no power to regulate the transmission component of bundled retail sales. Rather, FERC reiterated that States have jurisdiction over the retail *sale* of power, and stated that, as a result, "[o]ur assertion of jurisdiction . . . arises only if the [unbundled] retail transmission in interstate commerce by a public utility occurs voluntarily or as a result of a state retail program.". . .

III

The first question is whether FERC exceeded its jurisdiction by including unbundled retail transmissions within the scope of its open access requirements in Order No. 888. New York argues that FERC overstepped in this regard, and that such transmissions—because they are part of retail transactions—are properly the subject of state regulation. New York insists that the jurisdictional line between the States and FERC falls between the wholesale and retail markets.

As the Court of Appeals explained, however, the landscape of the electric industry has changed since the enactment of the FPA, when the electricity universe was "neatly divided into spheres of retail versus wholesale sales." As the Court of Appeals also explained, the plain language of the FPA readily supports FERC's claim of jurisdiction. Section 201(b) of the FPA states that FERC's jurisdiction includes "the transmission of electric energy in interstate commerce" and "the sale of electric energy at wholesale in interstate commerce." The unbundled retail transmissions targeted by FERC are indeed transmissions of "electric energy in interstate commerce," because of the nature of the national grid. There is no language in the statute limiting FERC's *transmission* jurisdiction to the wholesale market, although the statute does limit FERC's *sale* jurisdiction to that at wholesale. . . .

New York is correct to point out that the legislative history is replete with statements describing Congress' intent to preserve state jurisdiction over local facilities. The sentiment expressed in those statements is incorporated in the second sentence of § 201(b) of the FPA, as codified in which provides:

The Commission shall have jurisdiction over all facilities for such transmission or sale of electric energy, but shall not have jurisdiction, except as specifically provided in this subchapter and subchapter III of this chapter, over facilities used for the generation of electric energy or over facilities used in local distribution or only for the transmission of electric energy in intrastate commerce, or over facilities for the transmission of electric energy consumed wholly by the transmitter.

Yet, Order No. 888 does not even arguably affect the States' jurisdiction over three of these subjects: generation facilities, transmissions in intrastate commerce, or transmissions consumed by the transmitter. Order No. 888 does discuss local distribution facilities, and New York argues that, as a result, FERC has improperly invaded the States' authority "over facilities used in local distribution." However, FERC has not attempted to control local distribution facilities through Order No. 888. To the contrary, FERC has made clear that it does not have jurisdiction over such facilities and has merely set forth a seven-factor test for identifying these facilities, without purporting to regulate them.

New York also correctly states that the legislative history demonstrates Congress' interest in retaining state jurisdiction over retail sales. But again, FERC has carefully avoided assuming such jurisdiction, noting repeatedly that "the FPA does not give the Commission jurisdiction over sales of electric energy at retail." Because federal authority has been asserted only over unbundled *transmissions,* New York retains jurisdiction of the ultimate sale of the *energy.* And, as discussed below, FERC did not assert jurisdiction over bundled retail transmissions, leaving New York with control over even the transmission component of bundled retail sales. . . .

IV

Objecting to FERC's order from the opposite direction, Enron argues that the FPA gives FERC the power to apply its open access remedy to *bundled* retail transmissions of electricity, and, given FERC's findings of undue discrimination, that FERC had a duty to do so. In making this argument, Enron persistently claims that FERC held that it had no jurisdiction to grant the relief that Enron seeks. That assumption is incorrect: FERC chose not to assert such jurisdiction, but it did not hold itself powerless to claim jurisdiction. Indeed, FERC explicitly reserved decision on the jurisdictional issue that Enron claims FERC decided. *See* Order No. 888, at 31,699 (explaining that Enron's position raises "numerous difficult jurisdictional issues that we believe are more appropriately considered when the Commission reviews unbundled retail transmission tariffs that may come before us in the context of a state retail wheeling program"). Absent Enron's flawed assumption, FERC's ruling is clearly acceptable.

As noted above, in both Order No. 888 and rehearing Order No. 888–A, FERC gave two reasons for refusing to extend its open access remedy to bundled retail transmissions. First, FERC explained that such relief was not "necessary." Second, FERC noted that the regulation of bundled retail transmissions "raises numerous difficult jurisdictional issues" that did not need to be resolved in the present context. Both of these reasons provide valid support for FERC's decision not to regulate bundled retail transmissions.

First, with respect to FERC's determination that it was not "necessary" to include bundled retail transmissions in its remedy, it must be kept in mind exactly what it was that FERC sought to remedy in the first place: a problem with the *wholesale* power market. FERC's findings, as Enron itself recognizes, concerned electric utilities' use of their market power to " 'deny their *wholesale* customers access to competitively priced electric generation,' " thereby " 'deny[ing] consumers the substantial benefits of lower electricity prices.' "

To remedy the wholesale discrimination it found, FERC chose to regulate all wholesale transmissions. It also regulated unbundled retail transmissions, as was within its power to do. However, merely because FERC believed that those steps were appropriate to remedy discrimination in the wholesale electricity market does not, as Enron alleges, lead to the conclusion that the regulation of *bundled* retail transmissions was "necessary" as well. Because FERC determined that the remedy it ordered constituted a sufficient response to the problems FERC had identified in the wholesale market, FERC had no § 206 obligation to regulate bundled retail transmissions or to order universal unbundling.

Of course, it may be true that FERC's findings concerning discrimination in the wholesale electricity market suggest that such discrimination exists in the retail electricity market as well, as Enron alleges. Were FERC to investigate this alleged discrimination and make findings concerning undue discrimination in the retail electricity market, § 206 of the FPA would require FERC to provide a remedy for that discrimination. And such a remedy could very well involve FERC's decision to regulate bundled retail transmissions—Enron's desired outcome. However, because the scope of the order presently under review did not concern discrimination in the retail market, Enron is wrong to argue that § 206 requires FERC to provide a full array of retail-market remedies.

Second, we can agree with FERC's conclusion that Enron's desired remedy "raises numerous difficult jurisdictional issues," without deciding whether Enron's ultimate position on those issues is correct. The issues raised by New York concerning FERC's jurisdiction over unbundled retail transmissions are themselves serious. It is obvious that a federal order claiming jurisdiction over *all* retail transmissions would have even greater implications for the States' regulation of retail sales—a state regulatory power recognized by the same statutory provision that authorizes FERC's transmission jurisdiction. But even if we assume, for present purposes, that Enron is *correct* in its claim that the FPA gives FERC the authority to regulate the transmission component of a bundled retail sale, we nevertheless conclude that the agency had discretion to decline to assert such jurisdiction in this proceeding in part because of the complicated nature of the jurisdictional issues. Like the Court of Appeals, we are satisfied that FERC's choice not to assert jurisdiction over bundled retail transmissions in a rulemaking proceeding focusing on the wholesale market "represents a statutorily permissible policy choice."

■ JUSTICE THOMAS concurred in part and dissented in part, joined by JUSTICE SCALIA and JUSTICE KENNEDY—. . . Given that it is impossible to identify which utility's lines are used for any given transmission, FERC's decision to exclude transmission because it is associated with a particular type of transaction appears to make little sense. And this decision may conflict with FERC's statutory mandate to regulate when it finds unjust, unreasonable, unduly discriminatory, or preferential treatment with respect to any transmission subject to its jurisdiction. FERC clearly recognizes the statute's mandate, stating in Order No. 888–A that "our authorities under the FPA not only permit us to adapt to changing economic realities in the electric industry, but also require us to do so, as necessary to eliminate undue discrimination and protect electricity customers." And it is certainly possible that utilities that own or control lines on the grid discriminate against entities that seek to use their transmission lines regardless of whether the utilities themselves bundle or unbundle their transactions. The fact that FERC found undue discrimination with respect to transmission used in connection with both bundled and unbundled wholesale sales and unbundled retail sales indicates that such discrimination exists regardless of whether the transmission is used in bundled or unbundled sales. Without more, FERC's conclusory statement that "unbundling of retail transmission" is not "necessary" lends little support to its decision not to regulate such transmission. And it simply cannot be the case that the nature of the commercial transaction controls the scope of FERC's jurisdiction.

To be sure, I would not prejudge whether FERC *must* require that transmission used for bundled retail sales be subject to FERC's open access tariff. At a minimum, however, FERC should have determined whether regulating transmission used in connection with bundled retail sales was in fact "necessary to eliminate undue discrimination and protect electricity customers." FERC's conclusory statement instills little confidence that it either made this determination or that it complied with the unambiguous dictates of the statute. While the Court essentially ignores the statute's mandatory prescription by approving of FERC's decision as a permissible "policy choice," the FPA simply does not give FERC discretion to base its decision not to remedy undue discrimination on a "policy choice."

. . . . By refusing to regulate the transmission associated with retail sales in States that have chosen not to unbundle retail sales, FERC has set up a system under which: (a) each State's internal policy decisions concerning whether to require unbundling controls the nature of federal jurisdiction; (b) a utility's voluntary decision to unbundle determines whether FERC has jurisdiction; and (c) utilities that are allowed to continue bundling may discriminate against other companies attempting to use their transmission lines. The statute neither draws these distinctions nor provides that the jurisdictional lines shift based on actions taken by the States, the public utilities, or FERC itself. While Congress understood that transmission is a necessary component of all energy sales, it granted FERC jurisdiction over all interstate transmission, without qualification. As such, these distinctions belie the statutory text.

As the foregoing demonstrates, I disagree with the deference the Court gives to FERC's decision not to regulate transmission connected to bundled retail sales. Because the statute unambiguously grants FERC jurisdiction over all interstate transmission and mandates that FERC remedy undue discrimination with respect to all transmission within its jurisdiction, at a minimum the statute required FERC to consider whether there was discrimination in the marketplace warranting application of either the OATT or some other remedy.

I would not, as petitioner Enron requests, compel FERC to apply the OATT to bundled retail transmissions. I would vacate the Court of Appeals' judgment and require FERC on remand to engage in reasoned decisionmaking to determine whether there is undue discrimination with respect to transmission associated with retail bundled sales, and if so, what remedy is appropriate. ∎

NOTES AND COMMENTS

1.   The three significant reforms adopted by Order No. 888 are (1) open access transmission, (2) functional unbundling, and (3) stranded cost recovery (discussed further below, in the context of state restructuring). How does FERC approach each of these specific issues? Does the Supreme Court uphold each of them and under what legal authority?

2.   Following Order No. 888, FERC issued Order No. 889, requiring transmission utility participation in its Open Access Same-Time Information System (OASIS), an electronic bulletin board system for selling and scheduling transmission service. The OASIS requirements apply to public utilities and non-public utilities that provide reciprocal open access transmission service, unless a waiver is granted. Order No. 889 requires that such utilities establish, maintain, and operate (either individually or jointly with other utilities) a real-time information network on which available transmission capacity will be posted and on which capacity reservations may be made. Information about a utility's transmission system must be made available to all transmission customers at the same times. OASIS makes that information available to all customers, ensuring that utilities do not use their ownership, operation, or control of transmission to unfairly deny access to their competitors or competitors of their affiliates. Order No. 889 also requires a public utility and non-public utility providing reciprocal service to adopt standards of conduct. These standards are designed to ensure that the utility's employees engaged in transmission system operations function act independently of the utility's employees engaged in wholesale purchases and sales of electric energy in interstate commerce.

3.   Under the FPA, FERC's authority over the electric power supply industry is limited to wholesale transactions. Later statutes, such as the EPAct 1992, continue to endorse jurisdictional limitations over FERC's authority to completely deregulate the industry—especially regarding the provision of retail services—but FERC has obviously played a major role in moving the wholesale power industry towards a competitive structure, much as it played a major role in restructuring natural gas. Even with respect to FERC's jurisdiction over the wholesale operations of the industry, however, FERC's ability to successfully implement a competitive and reliable industry may fall short absent congressional expansion of its authority. How does the U.S. Supreme Court approach these issues in its decision upholding Order No. 888?

4.   Prior to *New York v. FERC*, the Eighth Circuit held that FERC's attempt in Order No. 888 "to regulate the curtailment of electrical transmission on native/retail consumers is unlawful, as it falls outside of the FPA's specific grant of authority to FERC." N. States Power Co. v. FERC, 176 F.3d 1090 (8th Cir. 1999). Consider the following authors' assessment of the *Northern States Power* case:

> [I]f it survives, the Eighth Circuit's decision poses a serious threat of state interference with interstate transmission of electricity. The resulting balkanization of electricity markets would be a major setback both to existing electricity markets and to evolving electric power markets, ultimately undermining, not enhancing, service reliability for both wholesale and retail customers.

William H. Penniman & Paul B. Turner, A Jurisdictional Clash Over Electricity Transmission: Northern States Power v. FERC, 20 Energy L.J. 205 (1999). Does this ruling survive *New York v. FERC*?

5.   Restructuring of the European Union electric power market has embraced "open access" principles similar to those endorsed by FERC for the United States. A series of E.U. directives issued in 1996, 2003, and 2009 require open access to transmission and financial separation of generation, transmission and distribution activities. The 2009 directive calls for the establishment of an EU-wide coordinator of national regulators. *See* Directive   2009/72/EC,   http://eur-lex.europa.eu/legal-content/EN/TXT/ HTML/?uri=CELEX:32009L0072&from=EN.   Progress toward a single market in electricity has been halting, however, in part because national governments have some discretion as to how they implement directives. For example, the United Kingdom and Germany have implemented full wholesale and retail competition, while Spain has implemented wholesale but not retail competition. However, the French government is actively studying competition for its markets, in part because the European Commission has taken legal action against France for its failure to end the monopoly of Electricité de France. The E.U. experience illustrates the practical implications of the legal constraints faced by federal regulators in the United States:

> The E.C.'s French compliance action illustrates one of the [ ] most striking differences in U.S. and E.U. power markets. In Europe, the E.C. has ultimate authority over member states to compel the market opening, whereas in the United States there is no national authority nor federal law to require states to open their retail markets. That is rather ironic since a united Europe is a relatively new phenomenon by comparison to the U.S. federal structure.

Shannon Burchett, A Continent United? Some Thoughts on Prospects for a Single Energy Market in Europe, Pub. Util. Fortnightly, Jan. 15, 2000, at 32.

6.   One of Order No. 888's most significant features is that it requires each FERC jurisdictional utility to file with FERC, and for FERC to approve, an open access tariff. This tariff lays out the basic terms and conditions for access to transmission at the wholesale level. Typically, the price for such transmission is set by the utility (or as is discussed below regional managers of utility transmission) and approved by FERC.

This seems similar to the open access approach FERC endorsed for natural gas pipelines. (See Chapter 9.) Importantly, however, the transmission of electricity differs in many respects from the transportation of natural gas. Transmission lines, unlike natural gas pipelines, have no valves. Although it is possible to install technology to control the physical flow of power on transmission lines, extreme caution must be exercised to determine the optimum location of such flow control devices to avoid sacrificing reliable service. Absent some sort of flow control, electric current flows in the path of least resistance. Thus, a transmission transaction that appears to involve the flow of electricity from New York to New Jersey may use transmission lines located in other states, such as Ohio, even though these states do not lie in the direct physical path between the generator and customer. Such physical geographical diversions in electricity transmission are called "loop flows."

Under traditional cost-of-service regulation, regulators have been able to avoid most of the economic, operational, and policy problems raised by loop flows. Because most utilities were vertically integrated and did not engage in a large number of transactions with third parties, this was not a significant issue. Where utilities were exchanging power, they tended to rely on informal cooperative mechanisms, such a regional power pools, to monitor loop flow problems. The transition to competition, however, and the attendant rise in generators from numerous states accessing transmission lines, raises the specter of larger-scale loop flow problems. While FERC has been able to implement competition in natural gas markets on a model of bilateral trading, in which consumers negotiate directly with pipelines for natural gas transportation, such a simple market model is likely to be problematic where transmission capacity constraints lead to large and constantly changing congestion costs.

7.   Is the main difference between electricity transmission and natural gas pipelines technological, or are there also significant legal differences in the scope of FERC's authority? For discussion of the legal barriers to restructuring the electric power industry at the federal level, see Richard J. Pierce, Jr., Completing the Process of Restructuring of the Electricity Market, 40 Wake Forest L. Rev. 451 (2005). Writing before FERC adopted Order No. 888, Professor Pierce observed, "The FERC cannot control the path and rate of progress of the electricity transition to the extent it exercised control over the gas transition because it lacks many of the regulatory tools it applied to the gas industry." Richard J. Pierce, Jr., The State of the Transition to Competitive Markets in Natural Gas and Electricity, 15 Energy L. J. 323 (1994).

2.   THE RISE OF REGIONAL GOVERNANCE OF TRANSMISSION

Although Order No. 888 required open access based on utility-specific tariff filings, FERC has also encouraged inter-utility open access plans. In many areas of the country, regional entities called independent system operators (ISOs) and regional transmission organizations (RTOs) now operate transmission lines. FERC first encouraged the formation of regional transmission entities in Order 888 in 1996, in which FERC called these entities ISOs. It established standards for organizations wishing to be approved by FERC as ISOs. FERC further encouraged the formation of regional organizations in Order 2000 in 1999 (finalized in the year 2000 as Order 2000–A), in which FERC slightly updated the standards for regional entities to be approved and now called these regional entities "RTOs." With a few exceptions noted below, ISOs and RTOs are essentially the same—RTOs are simply those organizations approved by FERC under the year 2000 standards, as opposed to the 1999 standards.

Both ISOs and RTOs are non-profit organizations that control large portions of the transmission grid. As described below, to be certified as an RTO or ISO by FERC, these organizations must meet certain standards, showing that they in fact have regional control of a transmission grid and act independently of generators and will thus not favor certain generators over others for use of the grid.

Many RTOs and ISOs do not own the physical transmission wires, but they *operate* the wires. Utilities that own transmission lines give up control of these lines to the ISO or the RTO. The ISO or RTO then obtains a tariff from FERC that allows the ISO or RTO to operate the transmission lines. Within the tariff, the ISO or RTO, like any other transmission line owner, must ensure that the lines will be open access and will be open to generators on a first-come, first-served nondiscriminatory basis. The tariff also sets the price the ISO or RTO may charge generators for the use of transmission lines. (The ISO or RTO then sends the money it collects for the use of the transmission lines back to the utilities that own the lines.) Further, FERC requires that the RTO or ISO conduct long-term planning for needed grid expansions that will ensure grid reliability. While RTOs and ISOs do not have the power to site new transmission lines, they work with states to determine where new lines are needed and to develop plans for line expansion.

When we say here that RTOs and ISOs "operate" transmission lines, we mean the following: specifically, they determine which generators may send electricity through the wires, and when; and they run markets for electricity, accepting bids from generators who want to send electricity through the wire and bids from "load serving entities" (LSEs) who want to purchase electricity sent by generators through the wires. Generators bid in the amount of power they want to send through the grid at a particular price, and LSEs place bids for how much power they need. The ISO or RTO then accepts the generation bids up to the point at which all LSE demand will be fulfilled, taking the lowest-priced bids first and moving up.

ISOs and RTOs typically run these markets on a day-ahead, fifteen-minute, and real-time basis, taking bids ahead of time and also last minute in order to ensure that the exact amount of electricity needed by LSEs flows through the lines. Some RTOs and ISOs also operate capacity markets in which generators commit to providing electricity years in advance, thus demonstrating that there will be enough power for growing demand in the region as populations rise and electricity use expands.

The idea behind ISOs and RTOs was to further encourage competition in the electric industry by making electricity more regional—pulling in a variety of competitive generators from around a region and thus giving utilities more access to potentially inexpensive generation. As independent, third-party operators of regional, multi-utility transmission systems, ISOs and RTOs offer assurance to customers of transmission that access is truly nondiscriminatory. Despite the structure of member utilities, since ISOs and RTOs are independently operated, they have fewer incentives to favor the wholesale generation supply provided by any incumbent utility, and they can therefore support competitive generation. FERC also believed that regional rather than state-based control of the grid would better ensure transmission reliability.

As introduced above, in Order No. 888, FERC identified eleven principles of ISO governance and operation, in hopes that multiple utilities would coordinate to develop and produce filings that satisfy these principles:

Promoting Wholesale Competition Through Open Access Non-Discriminatory Transmission Services By Public Utilities; Recovery of Stranded Costs by Public Utilities and Transmitting Utilities

61 Fed. Reg. 21,540 (May 10, 1996) (codified at 18 C.F.R. Parts 35 & 385)

ISO Principles

The Commission recognizes that some utilities are exploring the concept of an Independent System Operator and that the tight power pools are considering restructuring proposals that involve an ISO. While the Commission is not requiring any utility to form an ISO at this time, we wish to encourage the formation of properly-structured ISOs. To this end, we believe it is important to give the industry some guidance on ISOs at this time. Accordingly, we here set out certain principles that will be used in assessing ISO proposals that may be submitted to the Commission in the future. These principles are applicable only to ISOs that would be control area operators, including any ISO established in the restructuring of power pools. We recognize that some utilities are exploring concepts that do not involve full operational control of the grid. Without in any way prejudging the merits of such arrangements, the following principles do not apply to independent administrators or coordinators that lack operational control. We do not have enough information at this time to offer guidance about such entities, but recognize that they could perform a useful role in a restructured industry. Because an ISO will be a public utility subject to our jurisdiction, the ISO's operating standards and procedures must be approved by the Commission. In addition, a properly constituted ISO is a means by which public utilities can comply with the Commission's non-discriminatory transmission tariff requirements. The principles for ISOs are:

1.   The ISO's governance should be structured in a fair and non-discriminatory manner. The primary purpose of an ISO is to ensure fair and non-discriminatory access to transmission services and ancillary services for all users of the system. As such, an ISO should be independent of any individual market participant or any one class of participants (e.g., transmission owners or end-users). A governance structure that includes fair representation of all types of users of the system would help ensure that the ISO formulates policies, operates the system, and resolves disputes in a fair and non-discriminatory manner. The ISO's rules of governance, however, should prevent control, and appearance of control, of decision-making by any class of participants.

2.   An ISO and its employees should have no financial interest in the economic performance of any power market participant. An ISO should adopt and enforce strict conflict of interest standards. To be truly independent, an ISO cannot be owned by any market participant. We recognize that transmission owners need to be able to hold the ISO accountable in its fiduciary role, but should not be able to dictate day-to-day operational matters. Employees of the ISO should also be financially independent of market participants. We recognize, however, that a short transition period (we believe 6 months would be adequate) will be needed for employees of a newly formed ISO to sever all ties with former transmission owners and to make appropriate arrangements for pension plans, health programs and so on. In addition, an ISO should not undertake any contractual arrangement with generation or transmission owners or transmission users that is not at arm's length. In order to ensure independence, a strict conflict of interest standard should be adopted and enforced.

3.   In the absence of an ISO or RTO, the owner of each transmission line segment would charge for the use of its line. For long distance transmissions over many line segments, this causes the stacking or "pancaking" of rates. An ISO should provide open access to the transmission system and all services under its control at non-pancaked rates pursuant to a single, unbundled, grid-wide tariff that applies to all eligible users in a non-discriminatory manner. An ISO should be responsible for ensuring that all users have non-discriminatory access to the transmission system and all services under ISO control. The portion of the transmission grid operated by a single ISO should be as large as possible, consistent with the agreement of market participants, and the ISO should schedule all transmission on the portion of the grid it controls. An ISO should have clear tariffs for services that neither favor nor disfavor any user or class of users.

4.   An ISO should have the primary responsibility in ensuring short-term reliability of grid operations. Its role in this responsibility should be well-defined and comply with applicable standards set by NERC and the regional reliability council. Reliability and security of the transmission system are critical functions for a system operator. As part of this responsibility an ISO should oversee all maintenance of the transmission facilities under its control, including any day-to-day maintenance contracted to be performed by others. An ISO may also have a role with respect to reliability planning. In any case, the ISO should be responsible for ensuring that services (for all users, including new users) can be provided reliably, and for developing and implementing policies related to curtailment to ensure the ongoing reliability and security of the system.

5.   An ISO should have control over the operation of interconnected transmission facilities within its region. An ISO is an operator of a designated set of transmission facilities.

6.   An ISO should identify constraints on the system and be able to take operational actions to relieve those constraints within the trading rules established by the governing body. These rules should promote efficient trading. A key function of an ISO will be to accommodate transactions made in a free and competitive market while remaining at arm's length from those transactions. The ISO may need to exercise some

level of operational control over generation facilities in order to regulate and balance the power system, especially when transmission constraints limit trading over interfaces in some circumstances. It is important that the ISO's operational control be exercised in accordance with the trading rules established by the governing body. The trading rules should promote efficiency in the marketplace. In addition, we would expect that an ISO would provide, or cause to be provided, the ancillary services described in this Rule.

7. The ISO should have appropriate incentives for efficient management and administration and should procure the services needed for such management and administration in an open competitive market. Management and administration of the ISO should be carried out in an efficient manner. In addition to personnel and administrative functions, an ISO could perform certain operational functions, such as: determination of appropriate system expansions, transmission maintenance, administering transmission contracts, operation of a settlements system, and operation of an energy auction. The ISO should use competitive procurement, to the extent possible, for all services provided by the ISO that are needed to operate the system. All procedures and protocols should be publicly available.

8. An ISO's transmission and ancillary services pricing policies should promote the efficient use of and investment in generation, transmission, and consumption. An ISO . . . should conduct such studies as may be necessary to identify operational problems or appropriate expansions. Appropriate price signals are essential to achieve efficient investment in generation and transmission and consumption of energy. The pricing policies pursued by the ISO should reflect a number of attributes, including affording non-discriminatory access to services, ensuring cost recovery for transmission owners and those providing ancillary services, ensuring reliability and stability of the system and providing efficient price signals of the costs of using the transmission grid. In particular, the Commission would consider transmission pricing proposals for addressing network congestion that are consistent with our Transmission Pricing Policy Statement. In addition, an ISO should conduct such studies and coordinate with market participants including RTGs, as may be necessary to identify transmission constraints on its system, loop flow impacts between its system and neighboring systems, and other factors that might affect system operation or expansion.

9. An ISO should make transmission system information publicly available on a timely basis via an electronic information network consistent with the Commission's requirements. A free flow of information between the ISO and market participants is required for an ISO to perform its functions and for market participants to efficiently participate in the market. At a minimum, information on system operation, conditions, available capacity and constraints, and all contracts or other service arrangements of the ISO should be made publicly available. This information should be made available on an OASIS operated by the ISO.

10. An ISO should develop mechanisms to coordinate with neighboring control areas. An ISO will be required to coordinate power scheduling with other entities operating transmission systems. Such coordination is necessary to ensure provision of transmission services

that cross system boundaries and to ensure reliability and stability of the systems. The mechanisms by which ISOs and other transmission operators coordinate can be left to those parties to determine.

11. An ISO should establish an ADR process to resolve disputes in the first instance. An ISO should provide for a voluntary dispute resolution process that allows parties to resolve technical, financial, and other issues without resort to filing complaints at the Commission. We would encourage the ISO to establish rules and procedures to implement alternative dispute resolution processes. ∎

Following Order No. 888, many utilities filed multi-utility transmission proposals with FERC, including groups of utilities located in California and New York. In addition, many utilities announced their intent to form for-profit single-utility or multiple utility "Transcos," combining ownership with operational control of for-profit, stand-alone transmission companies.

As briefly noted above, FERC has also encouraged geographically broader approaches to transmission management and operation. Most notably, FERC Order No. 2000 focused on the promotion of RTOs, which are voluntary (at least as far as FERC is concerned) and serve an overlapping function with ISOs in the promotion of wholesale competition. However, they differ in their degree of tightness and their geographic dispersion (RTOs are by definition multi-state). Below are excerpts from the proposed rule, which describes the necessity for FERC's rule, as well as a description of the final RTO rule adopted in Order 2000 from FERC's order on rehearing on the rule.

Regional Transmission Organizations; Notice of Proposed Rulemaking

Fed. Reg. 31,390 (June 10, 1999).

The Federal Energy Regulatory Commission (Commission) is proposing to amend its regulations under the Federal Power Act (FPA) to facilitate the formation of Regional Transmission Organizations ("RTOs"). The Commission proposes to require that each public utility that owns, operates, or controls facilities for the transmission of electric energy in interstate commerce make certain filings with respect to forming and participating in an RTO. The Commission also proposes minimum characteristics and functions that a transmission entity must satisfy in order to be considered to be an RTO.

As a result [of Order No. 888 and ensuing developments], the traditional means of grid management is showing signs of strain and may be inadequate to support the efficient and reliable operation that is needed for the continued development of competitive electricity markets. In addition, there are indications that continued discrimination in the provision of transmission services by vertically integrated utilities may also be impeding fully competitive electricity markets. These problems may be depriving the Nation of the benefits of lower prices, more reliance on market solutions, and lighter-handed regulation that competitive markets can bring.

If electricity consumers are to realize the full benefits that competition can bring to wholesale markets, the Commission must address the extent of these problems and appropriate ways of mitigating them. Competition in wholesale electricity markets is the best way to protect the public interest and ensure that electricity consumers pay the lowest price possible for reliable service. We believe that further steps may need to be taken to address grid management if we are to achieve fully competitive power markets. We further believe that regional approaches to the numerous issues affecting the industry may be the best means to eliminate remaining impediments to properly functioning competitive markets.

Our objective is for all transmission owning entities in the Nation, including non-public utility entities, to place their transmission facilities under the control of appropriate regional transmission institutions in a timely manner. We seek to accomplish our objective by encouraging voluntary participation. We are therefore proposing in this rulemaking minimum characteristics and functions for appropriate regional transmission institutions; a collaborative process by which public utilities and non-public utilities that own, operate or control interstate transmission facilities, in consultation with the state officials as appropriate, will consider and develop regional transmission institutions; a willingness to consider incentive pricing on a case-specific basis and an offer of non-monetary regulatory benefits, such as deference in dispute resolution, reduced or eliminated codes of conduct, and streamlined filing and approval procedures; and a time line for public utilities to make appropriate filings with the Commission and initiate operation of regional transmission institutions. As a result, we expect jurisdictional utilities to form Regional Transmission Organizations (RTOs).

As discussed in detail herein, regional institutions can address the operational and reliability issues now confronting the industry, and any residual discrimination in transmission services that can occur when the operation of the transmission system remains in the control of a vertically integrated utility. Appropriate regional transmission institutions could: (1) improve efficiencies in transmission grid management; (2) improve grid reliability; (3) remove the remaining opportunities for discriminatory transmission practices; (4) improve market performance; and (5) facilitate lighter handed regulation. . . .

In light of important questions regarding the complexity of grid regionalization raised by state regulators and applicants in individual cases, we are proposing a flexible approach. We are not proposing to mandate that utilities participate in a regional transmission institution by a date certain. Instead, we act now to ensure that they consider doing so in good faith. Moreover, the Commission is not proposing a "cookie cutter" organizational format for regional transmission institutions or the establishment of fixed or specific regional boundaries under section 202(a) of the FPA.

Rather, the Commission is proposing to establish fundamental characteristics and functions for appropriate regional transmission institutions. We will designate institutions that satisfy all of the minimum characteristics and functions as Regional Transmission Organizations (RTOs). Hereinafter, the term Regional Transmission Organization, or RTO, will refer to an organization that satisfies all of the minimum characteristics and functions. . . .

In light of the comments received [from state regulators and other parties in a previous proceeding], we wish to respond to several concerns that were raised.

First, we are not proposing to mandate RTOs, nor are we proposing detailed specifications on a particular organizational form for RTOs. The goal of this rulemaking is to get RTOs in place through voluntary participation. While this Commission has specific authorities and responsibilities under the FPA to protect against undue discrimination and remove impediments to wholesale competition, we believe it is preferable to meet these responsibilities in the first instance through an open and collaborative process that allows for regional flexibility and induces voluntary behavior.

Second, the development of RTOs is not intended to interfere with state prerogatives in setting retail competition policy. The Commission believes that RTOs can successfully accommodate the transmission systems of all states, whether or not a particular state has adopted retail competition. However, for those states that have chosen to adopt retail wheeling, RTOs can play a critical role in the realization of full competition at the retail level as well as at the wholesale level. In addition, the Commission believes that RTOs will not interfere with a state's prerogative to keep the benefits of low-cost power for the state's own retail consumers.

Third, we propose to allow RTOs to prevent transmission cost shifting by continuing our policy of flexibility with respect to recovery of sunk transmission costs, such as the "license plate" approach.

Fourth, the existence of RTOs has not, and will not in the future, interfere with traditional state and local regulatory responsibilities such as transmission siting, local reliability matters, and regulation of retail sales of generation and local distribution. In fact, RTOs offer the potential to assist the states in their regulation of retail markets and in resolving matters among states on a regional basis. They also provide a vehicle for amicably resolving state and Federal jurisdictional issues.

Finally, we do not propose to establish regional boundaries in this rulemaking. Our foremost concern is that a proposed RTO's regional configuration is sufficient to ensure that the required RTO characteristics and functions are satisfied. To this end, the Commission proposes guidance regarding the scope and regional configuration of RTOs. . . .

Various reasons have been advanced to explain why it is difficult to form a voluntary, multi-state ISO. These include cost shifting in transmission capital costs; disagreements about sharing of ISO transmission revenues among transmission owners; difficulties in obtaining the participation of publicly-owned transmission facilities; concerns about the loss of transmission rights and prices embedded in existing transmission agreements; the likelihood of not being able to maintain or gain a competitive advantage in power markets through the use of transmission facilities; and the preference of certain transmission owners to sell or transfer their transmission assets to a for-profit transmission company in lieu of handing over control to a non-profit ISO. . . . ■

FERC Order 2000—A Regional Transmission Organizations; Order on Rehearing

90 F.E.R.C. ¶ 61,201 (Feb. 25, 2000).

The Federal Energy Regulatory Commission (Commission) reaffirms its basic determinations in Order No. 2000 and clarifies certain terms. Order No. 2000 requires that each public utility that owns, operates, or controls facilities for the transmission of electric energy in interstate commerce make certain filings with respect to forming and participating in an Regional Transmission Organization (RTO). Order No. 2000 also codifies minimum characteristics and functions that a transmission entity must satisfy in order to be considered an RTO. The Commission's goal is to promote efficiency in wholesale electricity markets and to ensure that electricity consumers pay the lowest price possible for reliable service.

In Order No. 2000, the Commission concluded that regional institutions could address the operational and reliability issues confronting the industry, and eliminate undue discrimination in transmission services that can occur when the operation of the transmission system remains in the control of a vertically integrated utility. Furthermore, we found that appropriate regional transmission institutions could: (1) improve efficiencies in transmission grid management; (2) improve grid reliability; (3) remove remaining opportunities for discriminatory transmission practices; (4) improve market performance; and (5) facilitate lighter handed regulation. We stated our belief that appropriate RTOs can successfully address the existing impediments to efficient grid operation and competition and can consequently benefit consumers through lower electricity rates and a wider choice of services and service providers. In addition, substantial cost savings are likely to result from the formation of RTOs.

Order No. 2000 established minimum characteristics and functions that an RTO must satisfy in the following areas:

Minimum Characteristics:

1. Independence
2. Scope and Regional Configuration
3. Operational Authority
4. Short-term Reliability

Minimum Functions:

1. Tariff Administration and Design
2. Congestion Management
3. Parallel Path Flow
4. Ancillary Services
5. OASIS and Total Transmission Capability (TTC) and Available Transmission Capability (ATC)
6. Market Monitoring
7. Planning and Expansion
8. Interregional Coordination

In the Final Rule, we noted that the characteristics and functions could be satisfied by different organizational forms, such as ISOs, transcos, combinations of the two, or even new organizational forms not yet discussed in the industry or Docket No. RM99–2–001–3 proposed to the Commission. Likewise, the Commission did not propose a "cookie cutter" organizational format for regional transmission institutions or the establishment of fixed or specific regional boundaries under section 202(a) of the Federal Power Act (FPA).

We also established an "open architecture" policy regarding RTOs, whereby all RTO proposals must allow the RTO and its members the flexibility to improve their organizations in the future in terms of structure, operations, market support and geographic scope to meet market needs.

In addition, the Commission provided guidance on flexible transmission ratemaking that may be proposed by RTOs, including ratemaking treatments that address congestion pricing and performance-based regulation. The Commission stated that it would consider, on a case-by-case basis, innovative rates that may be appropriate for transmission facilities under RTO control. Furthermore, to facilitate RTO formation in all regions of the Nation, the Final Rule outlined a collaborative process to take place in the Spring of 2000. Under this process, we expect that public utilities and non-public utilities, in coordination with state officials, Commission staff, and all affected interest groups, will actively work toward the voluntary development of RTOs. Lastly, under Order No. 2000, all public utilities that own, operate or control interstate transmission facilities must file with the Commission by October 15, 2000 (or January 15, 2001) a proposal to participate in an RTO with the minimum characteristics and functions to be operational by December 15, 2001, or, alternatively, a description of efforts to participate in an RTO, any existing obstacles to RTO participation, and any plans to work toward RTO participation. That filing must explain the extent to which the transmission entity in which it proposes to participate meets the minimum characteristics and functions for an RTO, and either propose to modify the existing institution to the extent necessary to become an RTO, or explain the efforts, obstacles and plans with respect to conforming to these characteristics and functions. ■

NOTES AND QUESTIONS

1.   Many commented on FERC's proposed rule to promote RTOs. The economist Paul Joskow argued that FERC's approach risks shortchanging consumers. His position has been summarized as follows:

> "Transmission regulatory reform," says Joskow, "should not be viewed primarily as a 'carrot' . . . to entice reluctant utilities to form and participate in RTOs." . . . "Regulators," Joskow notes, "will not be doing consumers any favor at all if the small price reduction they receive in the short run as a result of cutting a couple of points off the expected rate of return . . . destroys the transmission owner's incentives to invest." But even if the FERC should offer higher rates of return, as the industry wants, Joskow still warns against putting too much faith in rate incentives as a way of enticing grid

> expansion: "Indeed, proceeding under the assumption that, at the present time, 'the market' will provide needed transmission network enhancements is the road to ruin. There is abundant evidence that market forces are drawing tens of thousands of megawatts of new generating capacity into the system [but] there is not evidence that market forces are drawing . . . entrepreneurial investments in new transmission capacity."

See Bruce W. Radford, RTOs: Road to Ruin, Pub. Util. Fortnightly, Sept. 15, 1999, at 4.

2.   Other commentators focus on the form of the transmission operator. Professor Charles Koch favors the ISO/RTO over a for-profit Transco model, because he believed that the ISO/RTO would be less inclined to act as a monopolist. He argues, however, that ISOs/RTOs need enhanced authority and carefully structured governance design. *See* Charles H. Koch, Jr., Control and Governance of Transmission Organizations in the Restructured Electricity Industry, 27 Fla. St. U. L. Rev. 569 (1999).

By contrast, Professor Robert Michaels believes that the ISO/RTO faces very similar incentives to the for-profit Transco, since in the end any ISO/RTO is also made up of for-profit utilities, which face market incentives. He believes that the focus on the form of the transmission operator has focused too much on profit versus not-for-profit. Instead, he urges attention to the nature and consequences of the governance of ISOs/RTOs and Transcos. According to Professor Michaels, "ISOs are supported by those who have been best at playing the politics of traditional regulation, and opposed by those who have generally been less successful." Professor Michaels fears that ISOs/RTOs are likely to become barriers to entry (see discussion of California's ISO in this chapter), and that they may impair innovation vis-a-vis a Transco. *See* Robert J. Michaels, The Governance of Transmission Operators, 20 Energy L.J. 233 (1999).

In the end, does FERC favor either the ISO/RTO or Transco model? One author has argued that, despite Order No. 2000's professed neutrality on the issue, FERC favors ISOs/RTOs over Transcos. *See* Jeremiah D. Lambert, Order 2000: A Subtle But Clear Preference for ISOs, Pub. Util. Fortnightly, Mar. 1, 2000, at 36. But others, including a member of FERC during Order No. 2000's adoption, argue that FERC has paved the way for Transcos. *See* Curt L. Hebert, Jr. & Joshua Z. Rokach, Order 2000: Exposing Myths on What the FERC Really Wants, Pub. Util. Fortnightly, Mar. 1, 2000, at 42.

3.   The availability of transmission access means little to generators and customers if they do not have information regarding a transmitting utility's transmission capacity and load. The EPAct 1992 also required FERC to promulgate rules on reporting transmission information. FERC's regulations require transmission-owning utilities to report hourly "system lambda" data, which is closely associated with the marginal cost of producing power and provides a good indicator of the price for competitive energy. This information, once available only to the transmission owning firm and power pool operators, undoubtedly provides vital information for both buyers and sellers of power. *See* William C. Booth & Judah L. Rose, Using Hourly System Lambda to Gauge Bulk Power Prices, Pub. Util. Fortnightly, May 1, 1995. With the integration of renewable resources into the grid, FERC has begun to require more frequent reporting of transmission capacity data.

4. The implementation of ISOs and RTOs has been one of the more controversial issues faced by FERC. Not every transmission owning utility has seen it beneficial to participate in ISOs/RTOs. States, especially in the Southern and Western United States, have been resistant to the idea of ceding any authority to regional bodies. FERC does not have authority to mandate participation in ISOs/RTOs, so it has to rely on voluntary participation by ISO/RTO members. However, there may be industry pressure to participate, and FERC also has a variety of powers that can be used to nudge utilities and states towards participation. Professor Joel Eisen describes one high-profile conflict:

Under the FPA, FERC has authority to review and approve mergers involving utilities under its jurisdiction. In 2000, FERC approved the proposed merger between AEP [American Electric Power] and Central and South West Corporation on the condition that AEP transfer operational control of its transmission facilities to a fully functioning FERC-approved RTO by December 15, 2001. AEP then made two unsuccessful attempts to join an RTO. FERC denied RTO status to the Alliance Companies, a group of companies (including AEP), and subsequently, AEP negotiated unsuccessfully to join the Midwest Independent System Operator. In April 2002, FERC ordered AEP to state which RTO it intended to join, and in response, AEP filed with FERC a document stating its intent to join PJM. Later that year, AEP filed for approval to transfer control of its transmission facilities to PJM, and FERC approved the application on April 1, 2003.

AEP serves eleven states and needed approval from the PUCs in those states before control could be transferred. Two of those states—Kentucky and Virginia—took actions to block or delay the transfer. On April 2, 2003 (one day after FERC approved AEP's application to transfer control to PJM), Virginia amended its Restructuring Act to preclude Virginia incumbent electric utilities from transferring control of their transmission facilities to RTOs until July 1, 2004 but, interestingly, to require that they do so by January 2005. Three months later, the Kentucky Public Service Commission ("KPSC") denied AEP's request to transfer control of its Kentucky transmission facilities to PJM.

At this point, the case became sui generis. AEP had been ordered to join an RTO (itself unusual) but then had been unable to do so. It now faced conflicting deadlines that could not be resolved. AEP was in a pickle, to say the least. In response, FERC initiated an inquiry designed " 'to gather sufficient information for moving forward in resolving the voluntary commitment made by several entities to increase regional coordination by joining RTOs' and to 'explore ways to resolve the interstate disputes . . . and enhance regional coordination to establish a joint and common market in the Midwest and PJM region.' " On November 25, 2003, FERC used section 205(a) of PURPA to make preliminary findings that the proposed transfer should be approved. This subsection authorizes FERC to exempt electric utilities, in whole or in part, from any provision of state law or regulation [that] prohibits "the voluntary coordination of electric utilities" if FERC determines that such voluntary coordination is "designed to obtain economic utilization of facilities and resources in any area." It contains a savings clause limiting FERC's authority to provide this exemption if the state law or regulation "is designed to protect public health, safety, or welfare, or the environment or conserve energy or is designed to mitigate the effects of emergencies resulting from fuel shortages."

Because FERC had thrown down the gauntlet to states using their power to oppose its drive toward mandatory RTO formation, the case quickly became a lightning rod for pro-deregulation and anti-deregulation states. Some, already suspicious of FERC's market initiatives, saw FERC's trumping of state law as diminishing their authority to regulate the industry and leading to a loss of cost control—historically the province of state regulators. The novel use of PURPA section 205(a) to achieve this purpose led other states to criticize FERC's reasoning. A number of Northern and Midwestern states (including Michigan, Indiana, Illinois, Pennsylvania, and New Jersey), however, supported FERC and called for regional coordination to take place without delay, which would prevent the benefits to be gained from integrating utilities into RTOs. The Texas PUC, not a player in this debate because of its unique status in the electricity regulatory environment, joined the battle anyway, arguing that RTOs "are a critical element for vibrant wholesale competition."

In March 2004, a FERC Administrative Law Judge ("ALJ") made an order rejecting the arguments of Virginia and Kentucky. The Virginia State Corporation Commission ("VSCC") had argued that PURPA was inapplicable, stating that "voluntary coordination" under PURPA meant only "the cost-based, tight power pools then known to the industry." The ALJ rejected this argument, stating that the transfer would create exactly the type of coordinated effort that Congress contemplated when it enacted PURPA a quarter-century earlier. The ALJ also rejected arguments by Virginia and Kentucky that AEP's decision to join was not voluntary because AEP had made other RTO proposals, stating it was "far more reasonable" to conclude that AEP was maneuvering to avoid "jurisdictional conflict." Virginia and Kentucky also claimed that the decision was not voluntary because AEP was forced to accept RTO membership as a merger condition. This argument, too, was rejected, with the ALJ noting that AEP was free to contest FERC's position in the courts.

Next, the ALJ turned to the central issue of whether the transfer would "obtain economic utilization of facilities and resources" in any area. This issue had generated reams of testimony from those (including the VSCC staff) who argued about the benefits of RTO membership. The ALJ disagreed with the VSCC on the proposed merger's benefits, finding that that there was "an impressive array of consistent expert testimony as to the benefits of the planned integration of AEP into PJM." Unfortunately, none of this testimony consisted of hard evidence.

Instead, the ALJ relied on estimates from witnesses for PJM and AEP who argued that the proposed integration would result in a net efficiency gain under every conceivable forecasting scenario. The VSCC staff also argued that the costs of implementing the transaction had to be considered. The ALJ agreed with the VSCC staff and concluded that "consideration of the costs . . . that will result from the planned integration is a relevant and necessary element of a determination whether the planned coordination is designed to obtain economic utilization," but declined to find that this cost outweighed the benefits to be derived from integration.

The second major issue in the case—whether the state laws, rules, or regulations of Virginia and Kentucky were preventing AEP from fulfilling its voluntary commitment to join an RTO—was also decided in FERC's favor. The ALJ noted that while PURPA did not allow FERC to mandate coordination, it did grant FERC authority to prevent states from "blocking or frustrating coordination efforts." The ALJ concluded that the Virginia state law clearly impeded AEP from joining PJM and was "precisely the kind of state action that PURPA Section 205(a) was enacted to prevent—a state law, rule, or regulation which prohibits or prevents the voluntary coordination of electric utilities for the benefit of regional and national interests." The ALJ also concluded that while Kentucky did not directly prevent the transfer of control, its statement that it would not act in contravention of a state statute requiring preference to be given to native load customers "freezes integration in its tracks."

In June 2004, FERC affirmed the ALJ's decision, and the case took on an entirely new twist. Kentucky settled out of the case. The VSCC approved the integration of AEP into PJM, as its hands were effectively tied under Virginia's restructuring statute. At that point, a casual observer would be forgiven for thinking the case had become moot. But the VSCC, understandably, remained troubled by the existence of precedent under PURPA that would support orders to other utilities to join RTOs. It offered to settle the case with FERC, if FERC would vacate the opinion affirming the ALJ's decision. The VSCC argued that, "[i]f not vacated, Opinion No. 472 would represent an unfortunate precedent that will continue to contribute to federal-state tension and mistrust that will harm ongoing collaborative efforts between this Commission[, FERC,] and state utility commissions."

The VSCC's offer received a considerable number of comments from state PUCs and utility companies, including those that had intervened in the case originally. The intervenors generally supported the VSCC, arguing for the most part that FERC had achieved what it set out to do when Virginia approved the AEP-PJM integration and that leaving the opinion on the books was not necessary. Other commenters supported Virginia's position that vacating the decision would ameliorate federalism concerns and argued that because it had not been cited in any forum, vacating the decision would create a "no harm, no foul" case.

Not surprisingly, FERC disagreed. It issued an order dismissing the rehearing requests due to mootness, rejecting the settlement offer, and refusing to vacate the opinion. It also stated that "[o]ur decision not to vacate Opinion No. 472 does not reflect a retreat from our commitment to federal-state comity on RTO or other issues," which of course is a statement the VSCC and its allies are unlikely to endorse. But if the VSCC was to proceed further at this point, it would face a serious hurdle. PURPA section 205(a) gives administrative deference to FERC, allowing the exemption from state law which prohibits voluntary coordination of electric utilities "if the Commission determines" that such coordination is designed to obtain said benefits. And, of course, that is exactly what FERC has done. For this reason, the FERC staff's findings, confirmed by the ALJ, would almost certainly be given great latitude in any federal-court proceedings. It may well take another case to decide whether the evidence about problems in load pockets and potential price spikes in wholesale markets outweigh the forecasts of pro-deregulation proponents.

This hardly means, however, that this case was unimportant. In holding that the Virginia and Kentucky laws did not fit the PURPA savings clause, the ALJ revealed that the states disagreed strongly with FERC about the costs and benefits of RTO membership and thus highlighted a central issue. The ALJ believed Virginia wanted to amend its restructuring statute "essentially to prevent the integration of AEP into PJM" and "protect the economic interests of Virginia ratepayers by shielding them from the impact of the Commission's Standard Market Design . . . [and to] maintain the preferential treatment for Virginia consumers in the operation of an interstate transmission grid by securing an opportunity to second-guess the Commission's decisions on RTOs." The ALJ also held that the record demonstrated that "the primary reason KPSC denied AEP's application to join PJM was the KPSC's belief that costs to Kentucky's ratepayers would increase." According to the ALJ, the "KPSC's denial of AEP's application to transfer functional control of transmission assets from AEP to PJM was largely based upon AEP's alleged failure to show that Kentucky ratepayers would receive any benefits from such transfer." The ALJ further concluded that "while economic regulation may be a valid exercise of traditional state utility regulatory authority, in this proceeding, such state regulatory actions cannot be allowed to fall under the savings clause because those actions would prevent the voluntary coordination that is the purpose of PURPA Section 205(a)."

Because PJM uses LMP [locational marginal pricing; see below for description] to make fundamental decisions, Virginia and Kentucky clearly viewed AEP's integration into PJM as the lamb lying down with the lion. The core of FERC's argument was the notion that RTOs yield economic benefits to consumers. But the ultimate point is not whether or not this will happen. It is that the parties are fighting at great length and over a period of years about whether RTOs will yield benefits. This fight is costly to ratepayers. The time and effort spent litigating this battle—not to mention the time and effort spent in earlier efforts to integrate AEP into an RTO—could have been spent far more productively in crafting an alternative scenario that would have been more palatable to the utility, FERC, and other stakeholders.

Looking at this outcome, Professor Pierce and others probably blame the Southern states and their allies for dilatory tactics. The proceedings in The New PJM Cos. might indeed afford some support for this view that the protracted litigation was an example of state regulators captured by parochial interest groups. On reflection, that conclusion might be worth some re-examination. The states, it would seem, are not without blame. But neither is FERC. Its estimates that RTOs will yield benefits to the industry are just that—estimates—and have been challenged strongly. In the face of hard evidence, states should be entitled to assert their statutory and regulatory mandate to ensure that their ratepayers are protected.

It is perhaps even more revealing to look at the fate of the VSCC's settlement offer. Section 205(a) of PURPA is "obscure" and had not been relied upon in any recorded case since the 1980s, when the electric utility industry was far different from that of today. In these earlier cases, it was not used for the purpose advanced by FERC in The New PJM Cos. and of course could not have been, as the development and implementation of the concept of a regional transmission entity was still many years away. Even when the case was essentially over, it was not; FERC insisted on letting its decision stand as a message to later negotiators and litigants. And the message this sends is clear. FERC has exacerbated the difficulties of moving toward the market by taking the PJM model, making it the basis for the "one-size-fits-all" market design and promoting it to the rest of the country. The VSCC (and even the FERC ALJ, for that matter, in confirming some of the states' arguments) made it clear that the severe disagreements about this issue have been brought about in part by FERC's insistence on marginal price-based models for electricity markets. But its stance in this case is a signal from FERC that it believes in the economics of SMD so strongly that it will contest them in any forum—even with ill-fitting arguments if necessary—with anyone who disagrees. That only guarantees more time and effort will be spent hashing out this issue, rather than working toward constructive solutions.

Joel B. Eisen, Regulatory Linearity, Commerce Clause Brinkmanship, and Retrenchment in Electric Utility Deregulation, 40 Wake Forest L. Rev. 545 (2005). Can a state legislature concerned with the impact of an ISO/RTO on consumers prohibit a utility from participating in such an entity, or does FERC have the authority to preempt this?

5.   While ISOs/RTOs have become the primary governance mechanism for multi-utility transmission in deregulated wholesale markets in many areas of the country, some regions of the country have consistently opposed the RTO model, instead relying on in-state ISOs or on individual utility tariffs filings with FERC to govern transmission. Below (**Figure 10-1**) is a map that

provides a snapshot of the current approach to ISOs/RTOs throughout the United States. Note that much of the Southeastern and Northwestern United States do not have RTOs. However, even outside of RTO areas multi-state transmission-owning entities such as the Tennessee Valley Authority (which operates 16,000 miles of transmission lines in seven southeastern states) or the Bonneville Power Authority (which operates more than 15,000 miles of transmission lines in eight northeastern states) can in effect serve a similar function to RTOs—even if they are not regulated in the same manner. Elsewhere in the United States, transmission is largely managed through individual utilities, although many utilities are members of power pools that provide coordination independent of an ISO/RTO.

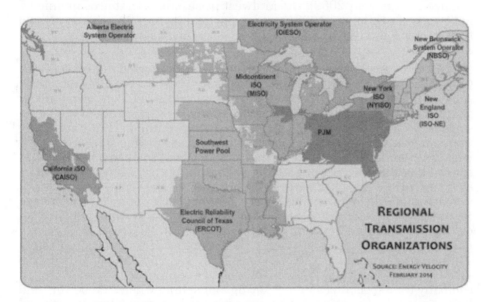

Figure 10–1
Regional Transmission Organizations
Source: http://www.ferc.gov/industries/electric/indus-act/rto.asp

6.   Do states lose some authority when their electric utilities join an RTO? In the early 2000s, two states in the eastern portion of the PJM RTO, New Jersey and Maryland, grew dissatisfied with wholesale electricity prices in eastern PJM. As noted above, PJM operates a capacity market to organize the procurement of sufficient capacity to meet future demand within the RTO. Policymakers in New Jersey and Maryland concluded that the PJM capacity market was not inducing sufficient investment in new generation facilities in eastern PJM, and undertook to subsidize construction of new generation within their state borders. Reasoning that these subsidies would distort prices in the PJM market, federal circuit courts overturned each of these two subsidy programs as preempted by the Federal Power Act, which grants the FERC exclusive authority to regulate wholesale rates. PPL EnergyPlus, LLC v. Nazarian, 753 F.3d 467 (4th Cir. 2014), petition for cert. filed, No. 14-614, No. 14-623 (Nov. 25 & 26, 2014); and PPL EnergyPlus, LLC v. Solomon, 766 F.3d 241 (3d Cir. 2014), petition for cert. filed, No. 14-634, No. 14-694 (Nov. 26, 2014 & Dec. 10, 2014).

As is discussed below, New Jersey and Maryland both have deregulated retail markets. Does this mean that states with deregulated markets lack the authority to adopt subsidies for new generation, while states with traditional rate regulation have broader leeway to adopt subsidies? What do these judicial decisions mean for state incentives to promote investments in nuclear energy (see Chapter 7) or in renewable power (see Chapter 11).

3. GRID RELIABILITY ISSUES

One of the major challenges competitive power markets face today is reliability. As is mentioned in FERC's proposed rule on RTOs (which was finalized in the year 2000), the Midwest price spikes that accompanied a heat wave in Summer 1998 posed a particular stress to the wholesale transmission system. Did emerging new markets in power supply contribute to this problem, or did they help utilities avoid disaster?

As the events of Summer 1998 were reported, operators for Commonwealth Edison Company, the utility that serves Chicago, faced some difficult choices. Although Commonwealth Edison owns many generation facilities, it still depends on bulk power purchases to serve some of its customer load. With the heat wave during Summer 1998, Commonwealth Edison was required to purchase power on a short-term basis from bulk power markets. In a single hour, Commonwealth Edison spent $4 million for power that would normally cost $200,000. At their extreme, prices surged to nearly 100 times their normal level. Utility managers faced the following choice: "either black out areas of Chicago to conserve power during a severe heat wave, just as storms had knocked out some plants and key transmission lines in the Midwest, or buy extra power at sky-high prices." *See* Agis Salpukas, Deregulation Fosters Turmoil in Power Market, N.Y. Times, July 15, 1998, at D1. During the same period, other companies made some very profitable sales. Enron, a company that specializes in marketing and selling wholesale power, sold large amounts of power to utilities at high prices, and when it reported its earnings, it had a doubling of revenue to $5.86 billion, and an 85 percent rise in income, to $241 million. As has been described, "This was all a marked contrast with the old days, when utilities sold power to one another at reasonable prices during emergencies, and it provides a vivid glimpse of the challenges facing this industry." *Id.* While some of this volatility may be due to the growth of competition, there were other events contributing to the power shortage. "A heat wave was moving across the region, causing a surge in demand for electricity. Violent storms had knocked out key transmission lines and a nuclear plant in Ohio, causing further shortages." *Id.*

Following the Midwest power shortage, FERC investigated the reliability of emerging competitive markets in wholesale power and issued a report. *See* Staff Report to the Federal Energy Regulatory Commission on the Causes of the Wholesale Electric Pricing Abnormalities in the Midwest During June 1998, http://www.ferc.gov/legal/maj-ord-reg/land-docs/mastback.pdf. FERC's report acknowledged that in competitive markets the price of wholesale power will be high in periods of peak demand, but determined that the conditions during the Summer of 1998 were "unusual." Some criticized FERC for downplaying the lesson of the Summer 1998 shortage, leading to calls for more regulation of transmission and generation reliability, as well as alternative calls for more deregulation with warnings to the public about impacts on reliability:

> If we continue to move forward half-regulated and half-unregulated (i.e., with the wholesale market deregulated and the retail market regulated), then one of two transition strategies is required. Planning reserve margins sufficient to protect endusers should be put in place and enforced with clear penalties, as in NEPOOL. In the alternative, policy makers should rely on the market alone to set reserves. If the market route is chosen, the public should be warned of the potential for rolling generation shortage-caused blackouts, especially in major urban areas, and especially during the transition.

Judah L. Rose, Missed Opportunity: What's Right and Wrong in the FERC Staff Report on the Midwest Price Spikes, Pub. Util. Fortnightly, Nov. 15, 1998, at 48. Others saw the events of Summer 1998 as the new wholesale power market working itself pure:

> Certainly it is true that bulk power markets in the Midwest are relatively underdeveloped. However, our data show that they functioned quite effectively under extreme conditions. A relatively undeveloped market adapted quickly and efficiently to events never before seen. Buyers and sellers reacted rationally to those events in the face of great uncertainty and unfamiliar limits on their abilities to transact.

Robert J. Michaels & Jerry Ellig, Price Spike Redux: A Market Emerged, Pub. Util. Fortnightly, Feb. 1, 1999, at p. 40.

Although the bulk power markets in the Midwest are no longer relatively underdeveloped, the debate over the Summer 1998 price spikes continues to have some impact on the regulatory discussion. The North American Electric Reliability Council (NERC) has implemented new procedures to relieve line overloading, known as transmission load relief (TLR) protocols. These TLR protocols would relieve the impact of parallel flows on grid systems not located directly on the contract path of the curtailed transaction (since electrons simply flow in the path of least resistance, not based on contractual obligations). FERC encouraged utilities to apply the TLR rules within the Eastern Interconnection pending a final decision, so they were in operation during the period of the Summer 1998 price spikes. The TLR procedures were a significant issue in the rulemaking that culminated in Order 2000, but FERC has consistently looked to NERC in setting protocols, rather than adopting its own independent protocols. FERC's Order 2000 also requires transmission utilities that do not use the NERC TLR protocols to post their own protocol on FERC's OASIS system, so that customers have information regarding TLR.

Does FERC's lack of power over generation load impair its ability to ensure reliable transmission markets? TLR produces a type of rationing. Is it better to let a market determine the prices of transmission service? Can this happen? How should transmission be priced? Are there any other jurisdictional weaknesses that might make FERC's job in ensuring a reliable transmission market more difficult? Issues related to RTOs and transmission planning and pricing—perhaps one of the most fundamental issues confronting the power grid today—are discussed further in Chapter 11, on renewable power.

In 2003, another substantial blackout hit the Northeastern United States. *See* Nat. Resources Canada & DOE, U.S.-Canada Power System Outage Task Force, Final Report on the Implementation of the Task Force Recommendations (2006), http://energy.gov/sites/prod/files/oeprod/ DocumentsandMedia/BlackoutFinalImplementationReport(2).pdf.   The blackout was largely attributed to a single event: A coal-fired power plant operated by FirstEnergy Corp. began to behave oddly and had to be taken off-line, or "tripped." An hour later, one of the company's major transmission lines failed. The alarm system intended to warn the utility of such problems did not operate properly, so FirstEnergy did not give regional regulators and organizations in adjacent states any warning of the mishap. Over the next 45 minutes, three more transmission lines failed. The problem cascaded and, within hours most people in Ohio, Michigan, Ontario, New York State, New Jersey, and Connecticut were without power.

Following the 2003 blackout, the EPAct 2005 made significant changes to federal jurisdiction, particularly over electric power transmission and the enforcement of reliability standards. As is discussed in Chapter 11, one of the most significant changes concerns federal jurisdiction over transmission siting in what DOE deems to be "national interest electric transmission corridors"—areas where, among other things, transmission congestion is a significant problem. The EPAct 2005 authorized FERC "backstop authority" in limited circumstances to order the acquisition and siting of rights-of-way for developing transmission in these corridors. Chapter 11 briefly describes how two Ninth Circuit cases have substantially limited this authority, rendering it nearly meaningless.

The EPAct 2005 also amended the FPA to provide expansive new mandatory and enforceable electric reliability standards for interstate wholesale markets. Since 1968 NERC and regional reliability councils called regional entities or REs—subentities of NERC—had been authorized to implement a voluntary, industry-based process to maintain reliability of the interstate transmission system. The new amendments to the FPA provide for FERC to certify an Electric Reliability Organization (ERO) with the authority to develop and enforce reliability standards, subject to FERC review. EPAct 2005 required the reliability standards to be mandatory, not voluntary, and enforcement of the standards was also to be subject to FERC review.

NERC was designated as the ERO and assumed the following responsibilities:

— An obligation to maintain independence from users, owners and operators of the bulk power system while assuring fair stakeholder representation on its board of directors.

— The right to charge and collect fees, dues and charges from endusers to pay for the ERO's administrative costs.

— A duty to promulgate reliability standards after notice and opportunity for public comments subject to FERC approval.

— The authority to impose penalties for violations of reliability standards, also subject to FERC review.

The ERO was authorized to delegate authority to develop and enforce reliability standards to a regional entity like an RTO if the regional entity met the same criteria as the ERO. (A regional entity was permitted to be governed by an independent stakeholder board or a balanced stakeholder board or both.) Existing regional reliability councils have sought and obtained delegation agreements with RTOs to serve as the reliability organizations for the RTOs.

The EPAct 2005 also bolstered FERC's enforcement jurisdiction by giving it jurisdiction over all users, owners, and operators of the "bulk power system," including traditional utilities, power marketers, independent power producers and utilities not otherwise subject to FERC jurisdiction (such as municipal systems and ERCOT utilities). The "bulk power system" was defined to include the interconnected transmission network as well as "electric energy from the generation facilities needed to maintain transmission system reliability." FERC was otherwise expressly denied jurisdiction over generation facilities. The statute did not give FERC authority over the adequacy of generation or of transmission capacity and FERC cannot require the construction or enlargement of transmission facilities.

FERC was also given explicit authority to impose penalties if FERC found that a user, owner or operator of the bulk power system had engaged in or was about to engage in any act that constituted or would constitute a violation of an ERO reliability standard. FERC was authorized to impose civil penalties of up to $1 million per day for each day of a violation of any provision of the FPA continues, and criminal penalties and jail sentences were also available. The ERO, and regional entities by delegation from the ERO, also had the authority to impose penalties subject to FERC review, but only for actual violations.

A savings clause in the EPAct 2005 protected the rights of states to take actions to ensure the reliability of electric service within a state so long as the action was not inconsistent with the reliability standards promulgated by FERC or the ERO. The state of New York was granted special status allowing it to establish its own reliability rules so long as those rules provided for greater reliability within the state and no lesser reliability outside of New York. All of these provisions remain in place today.

Despite these significant changes to federal energy statutes, however, the limited jurisdiction of federal regulators in the United States remains a central issue. For example, proposals to authorize FERC to mandate RTO participation are controversial and have failed to become law. See also Chapter 11 (discussing Order 1000 and transmission); Chapter 13 (discussing demand response).

D. OPERATION AND GOVERNANCE OF WHOLESALE ELECTRIC POWER MARKETS

Organized power markets operating within ISOs and RTOs, as well other restructured wholesale markets, have proved to be tumultuous for consumers and investors and challenging for regulators.

California deregulated its retail power market before 2000 (as is discussed below, in the survey of state retail competition plans), but much of California's power supply is purchased on the wholesale market (California imports more than one-third of the electricity it consumes.) Consequently, the success or failure of California's retail competition policies depended to a large degree on effective wholesale markets. Early problems with power markets in California were a sign that much more difficult challenges would lie ahead for interstate power markets.

Through its restructuring and deregulation efforts, California required most of its vertically integrated utilities to divest all of their generation resources. These generation resources were to be offered up in a competitive wholesale power market called a Power Exchange, or PX. The transmission service required to transport electricity from PX generators was to be run through an ISO. The California market was not simply atypical; it was atypical in ways that led directly to a severe crisis during 2000–2001. Indeed, California's wholesale power market handed market power to major wholesale sellers on a silver platter. How? First, California had inadequate supply reserve margins in 2000, irrespective of the drought in the Northwest. According to FERC, California's average electricity demand grew by 11% during the 1990s, while installed generating capacity shrunk by about 2%. This reduced California's reserve margins to very low levels, giving sellers of wholesale power the ability to charge very high prices when power demand spiked and there was inadequate reserve to meet demand. Second, California forced wholesale buyers—providers of retail services to end users—to purchase nearly all of their power on the short-term markets through the PX. They were not permitted to enter into bilateral long-term power-purchase arrangements, which maximized their exposure to price fluctuations in short-term markets; rather, all buyers and sellers received the market clearing price. This was done in part to prevent the still somewhat vertically integrated, incumbent providers like Pacific Gas and Electric (PG & E) and Southern California Edison (SCE) from self-dealing in the contest for wholesale power from major generating units. Third, the California restructuring plan (discussed below) called for a cap on the retail rates incumbent providers could charge during the first phase of restructuring, which lasted until the incumbent had recovered all of its so-called "stranded costs" through rates.

With hindsight, the errors of California's ways seem obvious. When reserve margins are low, supply is scarce. When supply is scarce, prices on the spot market will go up. Not only did this system offer large players in the spot market the opportunity to manipulate the market, but during periods of peak demand sellers of electricity from large plants could assume that their plants would be necessary to serve demand on the spot market and that their bids would be taken even if they demanded exorbitant prices (at least, by historical standards in California). Why? Price elasticity of demand for electricity is relatively low at certain points on the demand curve, because some consumers cannot effectively substitute other energy sources for electricity, at least in the short term. More importantly, retail price caps prevented end user demand (and so, wholesale buyer demand) from responding to high wholesale prices. The price caps sustained high levels of demand, and incumbent utilities like SCE and PG & E had no choice but to purchase the amount of power they needed to serve that demand, often at exhorbitant prices. All of these characteristics helped to keep open the opportunities to manipulate the market and/or exact enormous scarcity rents.

FERC's 2003 Final Report on Price Manipulations in Western Markets contains a somber analysis of the manipulative practices. Order Directing the Release of Information, Fact Finding Investigation of Potential Manipulation of Electric and Natural Gas Prices, 102 F.E.R.C. ¶ 61,311 (2003). The involvement of Enron in power supply and transmission markets in California, as well as other power marketers and sellers, created four separate problems in California, each of which has been the subject of extensive after-the-fact investigation: (1) gaming of the flawed regulatory system; (2) withholding of generating capacity; (3) affiliate abuse of pipeline capacity; and (4) manipulation of gas and power price indexes. The following excerpt describes Enron's gaming practices and their devastating impact on the California market.

Jeffrey D. Van Niel, Enron—The Primer *in* Enron: Corporate Fiascos and Their Implications
18–25 (2004).

California's market design had flaws, but the crisis was caused more precisely by a failure to understand the inherent rationale of regulation or to regulate despite those flaws. Some of Enron's schemes appear to violate ISO rules, which expressly prohibit gaming the system. The ISO tariff prohibits (1) "gaming" (defined as "taking unfair advantage of the rules and procedures") of either the PX or ISO; (2) "taking undue advantage" of congestion or other conditions that may affect the grid's reliability or render the system "vulnerable to price manipulation to the detriment of [the ISO Markets'] efficiency"; or (3) engaging in anomalous market behavior, such as "pricing and bidding patterns that are inconsistent with prevailing supply and demand conditions." Contrary to these express prohibitions, Enron and other companies created and tested techniques that did all of the above. These techniques had names like Death Star (a phantom power transfer), Fat Boy (an artificial increase in demand), Ricochet (see Ricochet Chart and description below), Load Shift (megawatt laundering—see Load Shift Chart below) and others to extract huge profits from the California market. Let's look at some of these games in a bit more detail.

Under several of the schemes, companies would intentionally over-schedule power into a transmission and power transfer interface in order to take advantage of the most obvious loophole in the system, in which the ISO would pay congestion relief charges to companies that failed to deliver power to the interface. In other words, the companies would schedule loads for delivery that they had *no intention* of providing, so that they could be paid by the ISO not to deliver that power. Enron called this particular scheme "Load Shift." . . .

Enron had another game called "Ricochet." Enron and others simply bought power from the PX, shipped it out of state to a confederate, then when prices were high enough in California, wheeled that same power back into California at prices that were sometimes 200 times higher than the price that was paid for the same power earlier that day. . . .

One of the most popular abuses employed was "wash trades," "swap trades," or "roundtrip trades." Under this mechanism, there appears [*sic*] to be two purchases and two sales between two market participants. In reality, these trades exist only on paper: no power or money ever changes hands, as the two transactions take place simultaneously and cancel each other out completely. Electricity was not the only commodity manipulated using the roundtrip trade method; roundtrip trading was also used for natural gas and broadband capacity. Dynegy, AEP, CMS, El Paso, and Williams admitted that some of their traders had engaged in roundtrip trades. ∎

The aftermath of the Enron debacle featured high-profile investigations of the company's practices, with the company's bankruptcy proceeding and corporate scandals dominating national news for a considerable period of time. Manipulation of energy markets provoked enforcement actions by the FERC, the U.S. Commodities Futures Trading Commission, and the U.S. Justice Department that have resulted in more than 3 billion dollars in refunds, hundreds of millions of dollars in civil and criminal fines, and criminal prosecution of some individuals involved in the scandal. Pub. Citizen, Largest Fines, Penalties and Refunds Ordered by Federal and State Authorities Against Corporations for Manipulation of the West Coast Energy Market and Natural Gas Price Index Manipulation, http://www.citizen.org/documents/camarketfines.pdf. We take up the broader regulatory response to the market manipulation problem below.

1.   BALANCING CONTRACT WITH THE PUBLIC INTEREST

Morgan Stanley Capital Group, Inc. v. Public Utility District No. 1 of Snohomish County
554 U.S. 527 (2008).

∎ SCALIA, J.—Under the *Mobile-Sierra* doctrine, the Federal Energy Regulatory Commission (FERC or Commission) must presume that the rate set out in a freely negotiated wholesale-energy contract meets the "just and reasonable" requirement imposed by law. The presumption may be overcome only if FERC concludes that the contract seriously harms the public interest. These cases present two questions about the scope of the *Mobile-Sierra* doctrine: First, does the presumption apply only when FERC has had an initial opportunity to review a contract rate without the presumption? Second, does the presumption impose as high a bar to challenges by purchasers of wholesale electricity as it does to challenges by sellers?

The Federal Power Act (FPA) gives the Commission the authority to regulate the sale of electricity in interstate commerce—a market historically characterized by natural monopoly and therefore subject to abuses of market power. Modeled on the Interstate Commerce Act, the FPA requires regulated utilities to file compilations of their rate schedules, or "tariffs," with the Commission, and to provide service to electricity purchasers on the terms and prices there set forth. Utilities wishing to change their tariffs must notify the Commission 60 days before the change is to go into effect. Unlike the Interstate Commerce Act, however, the FPA also permits utilities to set rates with individual electricity purchasers through bilateral contracts. As we have explained elsewhere, the FPA "departed from the scheme of purely tariff-based regulation and acknowledged that contracts between commercial buyers and sellers could be used in ratesetting." Like tariffs, contracts must be filed with the Commission before they go into effect.

The FPA requires all wholesale-electricity rates to be "just and reasonable." When a utility files a new rate with the Commission, through a change to its tariff or a new contract, the Commission may suspend the rate for up to five months while it investigates whether the rate is just and reasonable. The Commission may, however, decline to investigate and permit the rate to go into effect-which does not amount to a determination that the rate is "just and reasonable." After a rate goes into effect, whether or not the Commission deemed it just and reasonable when filed, the Commission may conclude, in response to a complaint or on its own motion, that the rate is not just and reasonable and replace it with a lawful rate. . . .

In two cases decided on the same day in 1956, we addressed the authority of the Commission to modify rates set bilaterally by contract rather than unilaterally by tariff. In *United Gas Pipe Line Co. v. Mobile Gas Service Corp.*, 350 U.S. 332 (1956), we rejected a natural-gas utility's argument that the Natural Gas Act's requirement that it file all new rates with the Commission authorized it to abrogate a lawful contract with a purchaser simply by filing a new tariff. The filing requirement, we explained, is merely a *precondition* to changing a rate, not an *authorization* to change rates in violation of a lawful contract (*i.e.*, a contract that sets a just and reasonable rate

In *FPC v. Sierra Pacific Power Co.*, 350 U.S. 348 (1956), we applied the holding of *Mobile* to the analogous provisions of the FPA, concluding that the complaining utility could not supersede a contract rate simply by filing a new tariff. In *Sierra*, however, the Commission had concluded not only (contrary to our holding) that the newly filed tariff superseded the contract, but also that the contract rate itself was not just and reasonable, "solely because it yield[ed] less than a fair return on the net invested capital" of the utility. Thus, we were confronted with the question of how the Commission may evaluate whether a contract rate is just and reasonable.

We answered that question in the following way:

> "[T]he Commission's conclusion appears on its face to be based on an erroneous standard. . . . [W]hile it may be that the Commission may not normally impose upon a public utility a rate which would produce less than a fair return, it does not follow that the public utility may not itself agree by contract to a rate affording less than a fair return or that, if it does so, it is entitled to be relieved of its improvident bargain. . . . In such circumstances the sole concern of the Commission would seem to be whether the rate is so low as to adversely affect the public interest-as where it might impair the financial ability of the public utility to continue its service, cast upon other consumers an excessive burden, or be unduly discriminatory." . . .

Over the past 50 years, decisions of this Court and the Courts of Appeals have refined the *Mobile-Sierra* presumption to allow greater freedom of contract . . . Thus, as the *Mobile-Sierra* doctrine has developed, regulated parties have retained broad authority to specify whether FERC can review a contract rate solely for whether it violates the public interest or also for whether it results in an unfair rate of return. But the *Mobile-Sierra* presumption remains the default rule. . . .

Over the years, the Commission began to refer to the two modes of review-one with the *Mobile-Sierra* presumption and the other without-as the "public interest standard" and the "just and reasonable standard." We do not take this nomenclature to stand for the obviously indefensible proposition that a standard different from the statutory just-and-reasonable standard applies to contract rates. Rather, the term "public interest standard" refers to the differing *application* of that just-and-reasonable standard to contract rates. . . .

FERC will grant approval of a market-based tariff only if a utility demonstrates that it lacks or has adequately mitigated market power, lacks the capacity to erect other barriers to entry, and has avoided giving preferences to its affiliates. In addition to the initial authorization of a market-based tariff, FERC imposes ongoing reporting requirements. A seller must file quarterly reports summarizing the contracts that it has entered into, even extremely short-term contracts. It must also demonstrate every four months that it still lacks or has adequately mitigated market power. If FERC determines from these filings that a seller has reattained market power, it may revoke the authority prospectively. And if the Commission finds that a seller has violated its Regional Transmission Organization's market rules, its tariff, or Commission orders, the Commission may take appropriate remedial action, such as ordering refunds, requiring disgorgement of profits, and imposing civil penalties.

Both the Ninth Circuit and the D.C. Circuit have generally approved FERC's scheme of market-based tariffs. *See California ex rel. Lockyer v. FERC*, 383 F.3d 1006, 1013 (9th Cir. 2004); *Louisiana Energy & Power Authority v. FERC*, 141 F.3d 364, 365 (D.C. Cir. 1998). We have not hitherto approved, and express no opinion today, on the lawfulness of the market-based-tariff system, which is not one of the issues before us. It suffices for the present cases to recognize that when a seller files a market-based tariff, purchasers no longer have the option of buying electricity at a rate set by tariff and contracts no longer need to be filed with FERC (and subjected to its investigatory power) before going into effect.

In 1996, California enacted Assembly Bill 1890 (AB 1890), which massively restructured the California electricity market. [This is discussed further in this chapter, below.] The bill transferred operational control of the transmission facilities of California's three largest investor-owned utilities to an Independent Service Operator (Cal-ISO). It also established the California Power Exchange (CalPX), a nonprofit entity that operated a short-term market-or "spot market"-for electricity. The bill required California's three largest investor-owned utilities to divest most of their electricity-generation facilities. It then required those utilities to purchase and sell the bulk of their electricity from and to the CalPX's spot market, permitting only limited leeway for them to enter into long-term contracts. . . .

That diminishment of the role of long-term contracts in the California electricity market turned out to be one of the seeds of an energy crisis. In the summer of 2000, the price of electricity in the CalPX's spot market jumped dramatically-more than fifteenfold. . . . Because California's investor-owned utilities had for the most part been forbidden to obtain their power through long-term contracts, the turmoil in the spot market hit them hard. The high prices led to rolling blackouts and saddled utilities with mounting debt.

In late 2000, the Commission took action. A central plank of its emergency effort was to eliminate the utilities' reliance on the CalPX's spot market and to shift their purchases to the forward market. To that end, FERC abolished the requirement that investor-owned utilities purchase and sell all power through the CalPX and encouraged them to enter into long-term contracts. The Commission also put price caps on wholesale electricity. By June 2001, electricity prices began to decline to normal levels.

The principal respondents in these cases are western utilities that purchased power under long-term contracts during that tumultuous period in 2000 and 2001. Although they are not located in California, the high prices in California spilled over into other Western States. Petitioners are the sellers that entered into the contracts with respondents.

The contracts between the parties included rates that were very high by historical standards. For example, respondent Snohomish signed a 9-year contract to purchase electricity from petitioner Morgan Stanley at a rate of $105/megawatt hour (MWh), whereas prices in the Pacific Northwest have historically averaged $24/MWh. The contract prices were substantially lower, however, than the prices that Snohomish would have paid in the spot market during the energy crisis, when prices peaked at $3,300/MWh.

After the crisis had passed, buyer's remorse set in and respondents asked FERC to modify the contracts. They contended that the rates in the contracts should not be presumed to be just and reasonable under *Mobile-Sierra* because, given the sellers' market-based tariffs, the contracts had never been initially approved by the Commission without the presumption. Respondents also argued that contract modification was warranted even under the *Mobile-Sierra* presumption because the contract rates were so high that they violated the public interest. . . .

[FERC affirmed the ALJ's finding that the *Mobile-Sierra* presumption should apply to the contracts]. The Commission first held that the *Mobile-Sierra* presumption did apply to the contracts at issue. Although agreeing with respondents that the presumption applies only where FERC has had an initial opportunity to review a contract rate, the Commission relied on the somewhat metaphysical ground that the grant of market-based authority to petitioners qualified as that initial opportunity. The Commission then held that respondents could not overcome the *Mobile-Sierra* presumption. It recognized that the Staff Report had "found that spot market distortions flowed through to forward power prices," but concluded that this finding, even if true, was not "determinative" because:

"a finding that the unjust and unreasonable spot market caused forward bilateral prices to be unjust and unreasonable would be relevant to contract modification only where there is a 'just and reasonable' standard of review. . . . Under the 'public interest' standard, to justify contract modification it is not enough to show that forward prices became unjust and unreasonable due to the impact of spot market dysfunctions; it must be shown that the rates, terms and conditions are contrary to the public interest."

The Commission determined that under the factors identified in *Sierra*, as well as under a totality-of-the-circumstances test, respondents had not demonstrated that the contracts threatened the public interest. On rehearing, respondents reiterated their complaints, including their charge that "their contracts were the product of market manipulation by Enron. The Commission answered that there was "no evidence to support a finding of market manipulation that specifically affected the contracts at issue."

[The Ninth Circuit] agreed with respondents that rates set by contract (whether pursuant to a market-based tariff or not) are presumptively reasonable only where FERC has had an initial opportunity to review the contracts without applying the *Mobile-Sierra* presumption. To satisfy that prerequisite under the market-based tariff regime, the court said, the Commission must promptly review the terms of contracts after their formation and must modify those that do not appear to be just and reasonable when evaluated without the *Mobile-Sierra* presumption (rather than merely revoking market-based authority prospectively but leaving pre-existing contracts intact). This initial review must include an inquiry into "the market conditions in which the contracts at issue were formed," and market "dysfunction" is a ground for finding a contract not to be just and reasonable. Second, the Ninth Circuit held that even assuming that the *Mobile-Sierra* presumption applied, the standard for overcoming that presumption is different for a *purchaser's* challenge to a contract, namely, whether the contract rate exceeds a "zone of reasonableness."

II.

A. Application of Mobile-Sierra Presumption to Contracts Concluded Under Market-Based Rate Authority

As noted earlier, the FERC order under review here agreed with the Ninth Circuit's premise that the Commission must have an initial opportunity to review a contract without the *Mobile-Sierra* presumption, but maintained that the authorization for market-based rate authority qualified as that initial review. . . .

We are in broad agreement with the Ninth Circuit on a central premise: There is only one statutory standard for assessing wholesale electricity rates, whether set by contract or tariff-the just-and-reasonable standard. The plain text of the FPA states that "[a]ll rates . . . shall be just and reasonable." But we disagree with the Ninth Circuit's interpretation of *Sierra* as requiring (contrary to the statute) that the Commission apply the standard differently, depending on *when* a contract rate is challenged. . . .

That is a misreading of *Sierra*. *Sierra* was grounded in the commonsense notion that "[i]n wholesale markets, the party charging the rate and the party charged [are] often sophisticated businesses enjoying presumptively equal bargaining power, who could be expected to negotiate a 'just and reasonable' rate as between the two of them." Therefore, only when the mutually agreed-upon contract rate seriously harms the consuming public may the Commission declare it not to be just and reasonable. *Sierra* thus provided a definition of what it means for a rate to satisfy the just-and-reasonable standard in the contract context- a definition that applies regardless of when the contract is reviewed. The Ninth Circuit, by contrast, essentially read *Sierra* "as the equivalent of an estoppel doctrine," whereby an initial Commission opportunity for review prevents the Commission from modifying the rates absent serious future harm to the public interest. But *Sierra* said nothing of the sort. And given that the Commission's passive permission for a rate to go into effect does not constitute a finding that the rate is just and reasonable, it would be odd to treat that initial "opportunity for review" as curtailing later challenges. . . .

Nor do we agree with the Ninth Circuit that FERC must inquire into whether a contract was formed in an environment of market "dysfunction" before applying the *Mobile-Sierra* presumption. Markets are not perfect, and one of the reasons that parties enter into wholesale-power contracts is precisely to hedge against the volatility that market imperfections produce. That is why one of the Commission's responses to the energy crisis was to remove regulatory barriers to long-term contracts. It would be a perverse rule that rendered contracts less likely to be enforced when there is volatility in the market. (Such a rule would come into play, after all, *only* when a contract formed in a period of "dysfunction" did *not* significantly harm the consuming public, since contracts that seriously harm the public should be set aside even under the *Mobile-Sierra* presumption.) By enabling sophisticated parties who weathered market turmoil by entering long-term contracts to renounce those contracts once the storm has passed, the Ninth Circuit's holding would reduce the incentive to conclude such contracts in the future. Such a rule has no support in our case law and plainly undermines the role of contracts in the FPA's statutory scheme.

To be sure, FERC has ample authority to set aside a contract where there is unfair dealing at the contract formation stage-for instance, if it finds traditional grounds for the abrogation of the contract such as fraud or duress. . . . But the mere fact that the market is imperfect, or even chaotic, is no reason to undermine the stabilizing force of contracts that the FPA embraced as an alternative to "purely tariff-based regulation. We may add that evaluating market "dysfunction" is a very difficult and highly speculative task-not one that the FPA would likely require the agency to engage in before holding sophisticated parties to their bargains.

We reiterate that we do not address the lawfulness of FERC's market-based-rates scheme, which assuredly has its critics. But any needed revision in that scheme is properly addressed in a challenge to the scheme itself, not through a disfigurement of the venerable *Mobile-Sierra* doctrine. We hold only that FERC may abrogate a valid contract only if it harms the public interest.

B.   Application of "Excessive Burden" Exception to High-Rate Challenges

We turn now to the Ninth Circuit's second holding: that a "zone of reasonableness" test should be used to evaluate a buyer's challenge that a rate is too high. In our view that fails to accord an adequate level of protection to contracts. The standard for a buyer's challenge must be the same, generally speaking, as the standard for a seller's challenge: The contract rate must seriously harm the public interest. That is the standard that the Commission applied in the proceedings below. . . .

Where we disagree with the Ninth Circuit is on the overarching "zone of reasonableness" standard it established for evaluating a high-rate challenge and setting aside a contract rate: whether consumers' electricity bills "are higher than they would otherwise have been had the challenged contracts called for rates within the just and reasonable range," *i.e.,* rates that equal "marginal cost." The Ninth Circuit derived this test from our statement in *Sierra* that a contract rate would have to be modified if it were so low that it imposed an "excessive burden" on other wholesale purchasers. The Ninth Circuit took "excessive burden" to mean merely the burden caused when one set of consumers is forced to pay above marginal cost to compensate for below-marginal-cost rates charged other consumers. And it proceeded to apply a similar notion of "excessive burden" to high-rate challenges (where all the burden of the above-marginal-cost contract rate falls on the purchaser's own customers, and does not affect the customers of third parties). That is a misreading of *Sierra* and our later cases. A presumption of validity that disappears when the rate is above marginal cost is no presumption of validity at all, but a reinstitution of cost-based rather than contract-based regulation. We have said that, under the *Mobile-Sierra* presumption, setting aside a contract rate requires a finding of "unequivocal public necessity," or "extraordinary circumstances." In no way can these descriptions be thought to refer to the mere exceeding of marginal cost.

The Ninth Circuit's standard would give short shrift to the important role of contracts in the FPA, as reflected in our decision in *Sierra*, and would threaten to inject more volatility into the electricity market by undermining a key source of stability. The FPA recognizes that contract stability ultimately benefits consumers, even if short-term rates for a subset of the public might be high by historical standards-which is why it permits rates to be set by contract and not just by tariff. As the Commission has recently put it, its "first and foremost duty is to protect consumers from unjust and unreasonable rates; however, . . . uncertainties regarding rate stability and contract sanctity can have a chilling effect on investments and a seller's willingness to enter into long-term contracts and this, in turn, can harm customers in the long run."

Besides being wrong in principle, in its practical effect the Ninth Circuit's rule would impose an onerous new burden on the Commission, requiring it to calculate the marginal cost of the power sold under a market-based contract. Assuming that FERC even ventured to undertake such an analysis, rather than reverting to the *ancien régime* of cost-of-service ratesetting, the regulatory costs would be enormous. We think that the FPA intended to reserve the Commission's contract-abrogation power for those extraordinary circumstances where the public will be severely harmed.

III. Defects in FERC's Analysis Supporting Remand

Despite our significant disagreement with the Ninth Circuit, we find two errors in the Commission's analysis, and we therefore affirm the judgment below on alternative grounds.

First, it appears, as the Ninth Circuit concluded, that the Commission may have looked simply to whether consumers' rates increased immediately upon the relevant contracts' going into effect, rather than determining whether the contracts imposed an excessive burden on consumers "down the line," relative to the rates they could have obtained (but for the contracts) after elimination of the dysfunctional market . . . As the Ninth Circuit put it, "[i]t is entirely possible that rates had increased so high during the energy crises because of dysfunction in the spot market that, even with the acknowledged decrease in rates, consumers still paid more under the forward contracts than they otherwise would have." If that is so, and if that increase is so great that, even taking into account the desirability of fostering market-stabilizing long-term contracts, the rates impose an excessive burden on consumers or otherwise seriously harm the public interest, the rates must be disallowed.

Second, respondents alleged before FERC that some of the petitioners in these cases had engaged in market manipulation in the spot market. . . . We are unable to determine from the Commission's orders whether it found the evidence inadequate to support the claim that respondents' alleged unlawful activities affected the contracts at issue here. . . .

We emphasize that the mere fact of a party's engaging in unlawful activity in the spot market does not deprive its forward contracts of the benefit of the *Mobile-Sierra* presumption. There is no reason why FERC should be able to abrogate a contract on these grounds without finding a causal connection between unlawful activity and the contract rate. Where, however, causality has been established, the *Mobile-Sierra* presumption should not apply.

STEVENS, J., and SOUTER, J., dissenting—The basic question presented by these complicated cases is whether "the Federal Energy Regulatory Commission (FERC or Commission) must presume that the rate set out in a freely negotiated wholesale-energy contract meets the 'just and reasonable' requirement imposed by law." . . .

The Court purports to acknowledge that "[t]here is only one statutory standard for assessing wholesale electricity rates, whether set by contract or tariff-the just-and-reasonable standard." Unlike rates set by tariff, however, the Court holds that any "freely negotiated" contract rate is presumptively just and reasonable unless it "seriously harms" the public interest. According to the Court, this presumption represents a "differing *application* of [the] just-and-reasonable standard," but not a different standard altogether. I disagree. There is no significant difference between requiring a heightened showing to overcome an otherwise conclusive presumption and imposing a heightened standard of review. I agree that applying a separate standard of review to contract rates is "obviously indefensible," but that is also true with respect to the Court's presumption.

Even if the *"Mobile-Sierra* presumption" were not tantamount to a separate standard, nothing in the statute mandates "differing *application*" of the statutory standard to rates set by contract. Section 206(a) of the FPA provides, "without qualification or exception," that FERC may replace any unjust or unreasonable contract with a lawful contract. The statute does not say anything about a mandatory presumption for contracts, much less define the burden of proof for overcoming it or delineate the circumstances for its nonapplication. Nor does the statute prohibit FERC from considering marginal cost when reviewing rates set by contract.

Neither of the eponymous cases in the *"Mobile-Sierra* presumption," nor our subsequent decisions, substantiates the Court's atextual reading of §§ 205 and 206.

As the Court acknowledges, *Mobile* itself says nothing about what standard of review applies to rates established by contract. Rather, *Mobile* merely held that utilities cannot unilaterally abrogate contracts with purchasers by filing new rate schedules with the Commission. The Court neglects to mention, however, that although *Mobile* had no occasion to comment on the standard of review, it did imply that Congress would not have permitted parties to establish rates by contract but for "the protection of the public interest being afforded by supervision of the individual contracts, which to that end must be filed with the Commission and made public."

[According to *Sierra*] When the seller has agreed to a rate that it later challenges as too low, "the sole concern of the Commission would seem to be whether the rate is so low as to adversely affect the public interest-as where it might impair the financial ability of the public utility to continue its service, cast upon other consumers an excessive burden, or be unduly discriminatory." The Court further elaborated on what it meant by the "public interest":

> "That the purpose of the power given the Commission by § 206(a) is the protection of the public interest, as distinguished from the private interests of the utilities, is evidenced by the recital in § 201 of the Act that the scheme of regulation imposed 'is necessary in the public interest.' When § 206(a) is read in the light of this purpose, it is clear that a contract may not be said to be either 'unjust' or 'unreasonable' simply because it is unprofitable to the public utility."

Sierra therefore held that, in accordance with the statement of policy in the FPA, whether a rate is "just and reasonable" is measured against the public interest, not the private interests of regulated sellers. Contrary to the opinion of the Court, *Sierra* instructs that the public interest is the touchstone for just-and-reasonable review of *all* rates, not just contract rates. *Sierra* drew a distinction between the Commission's authority to *impose* low rates on utilities and its authority to *abrogate* low rates agreed to by utilities because these actions impact the public interest differently, not because the public interest governs rates set bilaterally but not rates set unilaterally. When the Commission imposes rates that afford less than a fair return, it compromises the public's interest in attracting necessary capital. The impact is different, however, if a utility has agreed to a low rate because investors recognize that the utility, not the regulator, is responsible for the unattractive rate of return. . . .

The decision of the Court of Appeals for the Ninth Circuit deserves praise for its efforts to bring the freewheeling *Mobile-Sierra* doctrine back in line with the FPA and this Court's cases. I cannot endorse the opinion in its entirety, however, because it verges into the same sort of improper policymaking that I have criticized in the Court's opinion. Both decisions would hobble the Commission, albeit from different sides. Congress has not authorized courts to prescribe energy policy by imposing presumptions or prerequisites, or by making marginal cost the sole concern or no concern at all. I would therefore vacate and remand the cases in order to give the Commission an opportunity to evaluate the contract rates in light of a proper understanding of its discretion.

I respectfully dissent. ∎

NOTES AND COMMENTS

1.   The FPA "just and reasonable" standard is discussed further in Chapter 8. Do market-based rates violate the FPA's "just and reasonable" rate standard? Why or why not?

2.   Despite the Supreme Court's effort to articulate a presumption in favor of contract, the intersection of contract and the public interest remains a significant issue. At the same time that the *Morgan Stanley* case was before the Supreme Court, the U.S. Court of Appeals for the D.C. Circuit considered whether the *Mobile-Sierra* doctrine precludes non-contracting third parties from raising public interest challenges to a contract. In *Maine Pub. Util. Comm'n v. FERC*, 454 F.3d 278 (D.C. 2006), the D.C. Circuit concluded that the *Mobile-Sierra* doctrine could not be applied to parties who opposed a settlement, since this would violate the public interest. In 2010, the Supreme Court reversed, in *NRG Power Marketing, LLC v. Maine Pub. Util. Comm'n*, 558 U.S. 165 (2010), holding that the *Mobile-Sierra* doctrine applies even to third parties who do not participate in a settlement and that there is no public interest standard independent of the "just and reasonable" requirement.

3.   *PURPA Revisited*: Interest in competition and restructuring led in turn to calls for repeal or modification of PURPA's "avoided cost" purchase requirement. Some proponents of PURPA repeal—primarily IOUs in the Northeast and in California—argued that their state regulators' implementation of PURPA in the early 1980s had locked them into long-term contracts that might have been appropriate at the time, but forced them to pay above-market rates by the 1990s:

> By the late 1980s and early 1990s, however, oil prices had stabilized, natural gas prices had declined, and excess generating capacity in most regions of the country allowed utilities to buy capacity and energy at much lower prices than had been forecast a decade earlier. The utilities' actual avoided costs dropped lower than in the mid-1980s and were considerably lower than the levels required by the long-term contracts imposed by some State Commissions. Many utilities contend that PURPA has caused dramatic hikes in retail electric rates, and many groups along with

these utilities now believe that new regulatory action must be taken to correct past misjudgments.

EIA, The Changing Structure of the Electric Power Industry 2000: An Update, http://www.eia.doe.gov. While FERC had taken action in some cases, it had expressly refused to overturn utilities' contracts with QFs "simply because avoided-cost rates have changed and the deals have gone sour in changing electricity markets." Michael J. Zucchet, Renewable Resource Electricity in the Changing Regulatory Environment, EIA (1995).

Other proponents of PURPA repeal argued that the mandatory purchase obligation was not realistic in a competitive retail market. The local utility would no longer have the obligation to serve, as that obligation traditionally was defined, and would not have a captive customer base to which it could pass through the cost of QF purchases. Aggrieved utilities felt above-market rates being paid to QFs would put them at a competitive disadvantage compared to their new competitors, who could choose their power suppliers and the rates they paid them. In short, these above-market rates would be a type of "stranded cost." Still others felt the QF industry had matured to the point where a federal program was no longer necessary. *See* S. Cal. Edison v. San Diego Gas & Elec. Co., 70 F.E.R.C. ¶ 61,215 (1995) (William L. Massey, Commissioner, concurring) (noting that "The power supply industry has become much more competitive since the enactment of PURPA. PURPA has been a success in this respect. The QF industry has matured sufficiently that QFs can and should compete on the merits with other supply options.").

Opponents of PURPA repeal—industrial power customers, some natural gas producers, renewable energy facility owners and developers, and environmental groups—claimed that PURPA not only introduced competition in the electric generating sector but also helped promote environmental values. Repealing PURPA would allow utilities to purchase from any source, and perhaps impede the development of the renewable energy industry and hamper the achievement of the objectives Congress sought to promote. As one observer noted,

> A good bit of the commentary on PURPA, including arguments made in its defense, seems to assume that in a perfectly competitive world, PURPA, as a regulatory intervention, would no longer be "necessary." It is not clear whether this means that PURPA's goals would be advanced by unconstrained market competition or that the market will simply sort out modes of generation according to its own values. If these values corresponded with those of PURPA, so much the better. If they did not, too bad for PURPA—PURPA would then be the first lamb slaughtered on the altar of competition. This sort of analysis more clearly reflects the frailties of thinking about competition than it does the frailties of PURPA.

Cudahy, *supra*.

4.   *PURPA Repealed?:* In the 1990s and early 2000s, a wide variety of bills were introduced in Congress to restructure the electric utility industry. Most included some provision for modification or repeal of PURPA section 210's avoided cost mandate. Some repeal proponents linked their proposals or support for them to only those regions where there were sufficiently competitive markets for QFs to sell their power. For example, Elizabeth

Moler, a Vice President for utility Exelon Corp. and former FERC Commissioner, testified on behalf of the Electric Power Supply Association (the national trade association representing competitive power suppliers) in 2003 that "EPSA supports prospective PURPA repeal in regions where competitive wholesale markets exist." Statement of Elizabeth A. Moler on Behalf of EPSA Before the Senate Energy & Natural Resources Committee, Mar. 27, 2003.

Congress took this position in section 1252 of EPAct 2005, which added new PURPA Section 210(m). That section mandated elimination of the purchase obligation where QFs have "nondiscriminatory access" to "wholesale markets for long-term sales of capacity and electric energy." In 2006, the FERC promulgated new regulations under PURPA to implement Section 210(m). *See* 18 C.F.R. § 292.303. The FERC found that the markets operated by the Midwest Independent Transmission System Operator, PJM Interconnection, ISO-New England and the New York Independent System Operator met the statutory criteria set forth by EPAct 2005 for member utilities to apply for relief from PURPA's mandatory purchase obligations. FERC also found that ERCOT's markets in Texas were sufficiently comparable to allow for applications for relief from the mandatory purchase obligation.

The rule creates a rebuttable presumption that for QFs larger than 20 MWs, unimpeded, nondiscriminatory access to markets and transmission exists in these markets and as a result, utilities in these markets may apply to FERC for an order relieving them from the obligation to purchase QF power. However, QFs may seek to rebut the presumption of access to markets based on operational characteristics or transmission constraints. In 2008, the FERC regulations survived a legal challenge in *American Forest & Paper Ass'n v. FERC*, 550 F.3d 1179 (D.C. Cir. 2008). The court upheld FERC's interpretation of the term "markets" under a *Chevron* analysis.

In areas without regional wholesale markets, the mandatory purchase provisions of Section 210 of PURPA continue as before.

2. THE RELATIONSHIP BETWEEN ENERGY MARKETS AND FINANCIAL MARKETS

FERC has recently taken several large enforcement actions against banks and other entities alleged to have manipulated electricity commodities markets and futures markets. *See* Gretchen Morgensen, Off Limits, But Blessed by the Fed, N.Y. Times, Dec. 21, 2013. These actions have highlighted the interconnections between electricity markets (and as discussed in Chapter 9, natural gas markets and markets for other energy commodities), on the one hand, and financial markets— particularly the market for energy derivatives—on the other.

a. ENERGY TRADING AND HEDGING PRICE RISK

It should be evident that restructured (price competitive) electricity markets expose market participants to more price risk than traditionally regulated markets.[2] Each organized wholesale market manages trading in electricity—so-called "physical" or "spot" markets. Since electricity cannot be stored, and it takes time to bring new supply into the system, the forces of supply and demand can, on occasion, cause sharp, abrupt changes in the spot price, as the 2000–01 California wholesale market demonstrated. One way to avoid (or to hedge against) the price risk associated with spot markets is to enter into bilateral, long-term power purchase contracts. However, even where market participants use long-term bilateral contracts, spot markets are necessary to balance markets in real time—that is, to organize sales necessary to supplement sales covered by long-term contracts. By discouraging the use of long-term contracts in the California wholesale market in 2000–01, California removed an important tool wholesale buyers could have used to protect themselves against price risk.

To see why this is, assume retail provider XYZ Electric buys 75% of its power—750 MWh per day—under a long-term contract establishing a fixed price of $40 per MWh. Assume further that XYZ Electric relies on the daily spot market to secure the remainder of its daily power needs (250 MWh per day), and that the spot market price fluctuates. Over a ten-day period, XYZ Electric's total power purchase costs are $470,000 (the sum of the last row of Figure 10–2). The average spot market price over that period is greater than the fixed price under XYZ's long-term power purchase contract. If XYZ had been forced to rely exclusively on the spot market for all its power needs, then its costs would have been $680,000 (the sum of the products of the daily market prices multiplied by XYZ's 1000 MWh needs). On the other hand, when the spot market price is lower than the long-term contract price, XYZ's power purchase costs are more than if it had relied exclusively on short-term markets. Thus, while long-term bilateral contracts are not always cheaper than exclusive reliance on spot markets, their use provides more price certainty. Since most retail providers in restructured states enter into contracts with their customers to provide power at a specified rate, or according to a specified rate schedule, they welcome this additional price certainty on the wholesale market.

---

[2]   Indeed, this issue is also important in the natural gas context, as was discussed in Chapter 9.

DAY	1	2	3	4	5	6	7	8	9	10
Spot Market Price ($/MWh)	30	30	40	40	60	100	180	110	50	40
Spot Market Purchase Costs ($) (250MWh/day x Spot Market Price)	7500	7500	10,000	10,000	15,000	25,000	45,000	27,500	12,500	10,000
Long-Term Power Purchase Costs ($) (750MWh/day @ $40/MWh)	30,000	30,000	30,000	30,000	30,000	30,000	30,000	30,000	30,000	30,000
Total Costs ($)	37,500	37,500	40,000	40,000	45,000	55,000	75,000	57,500	42,500	40,000

Figure 10–2[3]

Modern energy market participants use energy derivatives contracts, like futures or options, to hedge price risk. An energy futures contract is a contract in which one party agrees to provide the other party with energy on a future date at a specified price; an option contract is a contract in which one party purchases the right to make a future purchase or sale at an agreed-upon price. Traders in other commodities markets have used derivatives to hedge price risk for centuries, and the Commodities Exchange Act (CEA), 7 U.S.C. § 1 *et seq.*, has regulated commodities futures since the time of the New Deal. Energy derivatives markets are relatively recent vintage, and emerged as a response to increased price risk—in oil and gas markets in the late 20th century, and in electricity markets early in the 21st century.

Traders in energy derivatives markets may be energy companies interested in the physical delivery of energy (oil, gas or electricity), or they may be banks and other financial speculators interested purely in the possibility of making money by speculating in the market. In essence, derivatives are bets based on projections of the future price of the commodity: typically, at settlement, the party who bet wrong pays the party who bet right. Some derivatives (including futures or options contracts) are standardized contracts traded on exchanges like the New York Mercantile Exchange (NYMEX); these have traditionally been regulated by the CFTC. Other so-called "over-the-counter" (OTC) energy derivatives, like forward contracts or swaps, were not traditionally traded on exchanges, and have been less closely regulated. Forward contracts are like futures contracts except that they are not traded on commodities exchanges; swaps represent a bet on future market prices whereby the contracting parties agree to exchange their interest-payment obligations.

Exchange trading of commodities entails relatively little risk of counterparty default, since exchange members must meet specified capital requirements and exchange-traded derivatives (including energy futures) are settled daily: that is, as the market price of the commodity

---

[3] This figure and the accompanying discussion have been adapted from David B. Spence, The Politics of Electricity Restructuring: Theory vs. Practice, 40 Wake Forest L. Rev. 411 (2005).

moves relative to the futures contract price, the parties' accounts are debited or credited to account for the difference. The exchanges may also impose "position limits" which restrict the amount any single trader can participate in a product market (e.g., to prevent manipulation, or reduce system risk). Nowadays, most futures contracts do not contemplate delivery of the commodity at expiration; instead, the parties settle only their financial differences. If one party was hedging and needs to buy or sell the underlying physical commodity, it does so in the spot or "cash" markets. For a good explanation of exchange trading of energy derivatives, see Alexia Brunet and Meredith Schafe, Beyond Enron: Regulation in Energy Derivatives Trading, 27 Nw. J. Int'l L. & Bus. 665, 670–1 (2007). Forwards and swaps need not be standardized products, and because they were not traditionally traded on exchanges, they exposed the parties to the contract to more credit or default risk

Regulation of OTC derivatives has changed over the years. The CEA prohibits both manipulation and "cornering" of commodities markets, 7 U.S.C. § 13(a)(2). However, in 2000 Congress passed the Commodities Futures Modernization Act, exempting from most CFTC regulation OTC trading of energy derivatives by sophisticated or institutional parties. See 7 U.S.C.§ 2(h)(1). This provision became known as "the Enron loophole," and passage of the CFMA sparked a rapid expansion in OTC trading, including trading of both the standardized and non-standardized derivatives on electronic exchanges, particularly London's Intercontinental Exchange (ICE). For example, the U.S. Government Accountability Office (GAO) reported a more than fourfold increase in trading of energy derivatives on the ICE between the years 2003 and 2006. See GAO, Commodity Futures Trading Commission: Trends in Energy Derivatives Markets Raise Questions about CFTC's Oversight, Oct. 2007, http://www.gao.gov/new.items/d0825.pdf.

However, the run up in energy prices from 2003–07 and subsequent crash sparked concern about the operation of derivatives markets, and fears that speculators had driven up prices in physical energy markets. In 2010 Congress passed the Dodd-Frank Wall Street Reform and Consumer Protection Act (Dodd-Frank), Pub. L. No. 111–203 (2010), Title VII of which closed what had become known as the "swaps loophole." Prior to the legislation, swaps dealers had been selling investors (such as hedge funds) swaps contracts the returns of which were tied to (energy) commodity price indices, exposing the dealers to significant price risk. To hedge that risk, swaps dealers purchased exchange-traded futures contracts in the corresponding commodities. Reasoning that in this instance swaps dealers were acting as hedgers—that is, that they needed to hedge commodity price risk (just as commercial traders do)—the CFTC and NYMEX had extended to swaps dealers the same exemptions (from position limits and other requirements) that they extended to commercial traders. This enabled non-commercial traders to speculate on energy prices in much larger volumes than they would have been able to but for the exemptions. Dodd-Frank required standardized swaps to be traded on regulated exchanges, and directed the CFTC to set position limits and margin requirements for swaps transactions.

Dodd-Frank subjects swap dealers and major swap participants to registration requirements, margin requirements, and reporting, recordkeeping, and business conduct rules requirements established under § 4 of the CEA. Registration of Swap Dealers and Major Swap Participants, 77 Fed. Reg. 2613 (Nov. 23, 2010) (codified at 17 C.F.R. Parts 3, 23, 100 & 170). Under Dodd-Frank, all swaps accepted for clearing by derivatives clearing organizations (DCOs) are subject to mandatory clearing, and the CFTC has established rules governing what a DCO must do to register and maintain status as a DCO. Derivatives Clearing Organizations and International Standards, 78 Fed. Reg. 72476 (2013). Dodd-Frank also creates an end-user exception for certain swaps that are "used to hedge or mitigate commercial risk."

b. REGULATING MANIPULATION IN ENERGY AND DERIVATIVES MARKETS

The California crisis highlighted some of the ways in which traders can trade strategically in both physical markets for energy and energy derivatives markets. Traders' ability to exploit positions in one market to their benefit in another market has sometimes tested FERC's ability to ensure smoothly functioning markets.

After the California crisis, FERC's initial reaction to the problem of market power in dysfunctional markets was to try to tighten the conditions under which it granted the authority to charge market-based rates, and to improve its ability to monitor and detect the acquisition of market power by sellers. In 2003 it adopted new conditions—called "market behavior rules"—applicable to any wholesale seller of electricity authorized to charge market-based rates. FERC, Order Amending Market-Based Rate Tariffs and Authorizations, Investigation of Terms and Conditions of Public Utility Market-Based Rate Authorizations, 105 F.E.R.C. ¶ 61,218 (2003). Rule 2, in particular, prohibited "[a]ctions or transactions that are without a legitimate business purpose . . . [which] . . . foreseeably could manipulate market prices." *Id.* at 9, 35. The FERC also sought to strengthen the checks it used to determine whether a seller has market power before any grant of authority to charge market-based rates, by adopting "market power screens" to assess generators' or sellers' market power. The new screens examined not only a sellers' market share, but also the question of whether it is a "pivotal supplier" within its geographic markets during times of peak demand. *See* FERC, News Release: Commission Revises Interim Generation Market Power Screen and Mitigation Policy; Seeks Public Input on Future Market Power Rulemaking 1–2 (2004), http://www.ferc.gov/media/news-releases/2004/2004-2/04-14-04-market.pdf.

Congress intervened on the question of how to police competition in energy markets in the EPAct 2005, § 315, which directed the FERC to adopt an approach to regulating electricity markets that focuses on fraud, and prohibits the use of "any manipulative or deceptive device or contrivance" by market participants. *See* 15 U.S.C. § 717c–1. (Congress enacted simultaneous, identical changes in the Natural Gas Act as well.) This fraud/manipulation language was explicitly borrowed from § 10(b) of the Securities and Exchange Act of 1934, and incorporated into the FPA (and NGA) the same scienter requirements found in the securities laws, criminalizing "willful and knowing" violations. FERC subsequently implemented these requirements through Order 670, making it illegal to "use or employ any device, scheme, or artifice to defraud" and to engage in "any act, practice, or course of business that operates or would operate as a fraud or deceit upon any entity" in connection with the purchase or sale of energy subject to FERC jurisdiction. *See* 18 C.F.R. § 1c.2. FERC indicated that it would incorporate case law interpreting § 10(b) and Rule 10b–5 into its understanding of this new rule, where appropriate and relevant. Prohibition of Energy Market Manipulation, Order No. 670, 71 Fed. Reg. 4244 (Jan. 26, 2006).

This fraud/deceit language seems to exclude from its coverage the mere use of innocently acquired market power (in dysfunctional markets like California's 2000–01 markets) to capture scarcity rents (no matter how dysfunctional the market), and raised the question of whether physical withholding or economic withholding would be covered by the rule. FERC answered some of these questions shortly after issuing Order 670 when it rescinded Rule 2 of its market behavior rules. FERC specifically rejected the notion that Rule 2 had been aimed at curbing market power or at anticompetitive conduct not involving deception and fraud:

> [M]arket power is a structural issue to be remedied, not by behavioral prohibitions, but by processes to identify and, where necessary, mitigate market power that a tariff applicant may possess or acquire. This occurs in the screening process before the Commission grants an application for market-based rate authority, on consideration of changes in the seller's status or operations, and in the triennial review of market-based rate authorization . . .

17 C.F.R. § 240.10b–5. On the other hand, the Order 670 fraud and deceit language does cover many of the other forms of anticompetitive conduct witnessed in the California markets, including the use of so-called "wash trades," the artificial creation and relief of transmission congestion, various forms of collusion, and the submission of false information.

Since the implementation of this new approach borrowed from securities regulation, FERC has continued to scrutinize market conditions in electric and gas markets. *See* Order 697, Market-Based Rates for Wholesale Sales of Electric Energy, Capacity and Ancillary Services by Electric Utilities, 119 F.E.R.C. ¶ 61,295 (June 21, 2007). In organized electricity markets FERC has enlisted the ISOs and RTOs to monitor markets and detect the existence of market power in individual firms, with FERC oversight. Wholesale Competition in Regions with Organized Electric Markets, Order 719, 73 Fed. Reg. 64,100 (Oct. 28, 2008) (codified at 18 C.F.R. pt. 35). Each ISO/RTO employs a market monitor that focuses on the operation of the relevant markets overseen by the ISO/RTO—electricity spot markets, transmission capacity, and markets for new electric generating capacity—to ensure that prices reflect a well-functioning competitive market, and to detect manipulation. Each year FERC publishes an assessment of each ISO/RTO market, including an assessment of its competitiveness.

Detecting and punishing manipulation remains a challenge, one that is sometimes complicated by jurisdictional complexities and the interrelationship of physical and derivatives markets. Of course, the value of an energy derivative contract is, by definition, a function of the price of the underlying physical energy commodity, which in turn is determined by operation of the physical market. CFTC regulates energy derivatives markets, and FERC regulates physical energy markets. After the passage of the EPAct 2005, CFTC and FERC signed a memorandum of understanding aimed at coordinating their regulation of energy markets. FERC, News Release: FERC Chairman Kelliher and CFTC Chairman Jeffery sign MOU on information sharing, confidentiality (2005), http://www.ferc.gov/media/news-releases/2005/2005–4/10–12–05.pdf. The agencies subsequently brought a coordinated enforcement action against Amaranth, a hedge fund charged with manipulating the price of NYMEX natural gas futures in order to influence the settlement prices on other contracts it held. That case was settled in 2009 for $7.5 million. However, the principal individual defendant charged by FERC, Brian Hunter, fought the charges against him. The following opinion addresses the jurisdictional boundary between FERC and CFTC.

Brian Hunter v. FERC

711 F.3d 155 (D.C. Cir. 2013).

■ TATEL, CIRCUIT JUDGE:

Pursuant to the Energy Policy Act of 2005, the Federal Energy Regulatory Commission fined petitioner $30 million for manipulating natural gas futures contracts. According to petitioner, FERC lacks authority to fine him because the Commodity Futures Trading Commission has exclusive jurisdiction over all transactions involving commodity futures contracts. Because manipulation of natural gas futures contracts falls within the CFTC's exclusive jurisdiction and because nothing in the Energy Policy Act clearly and manifestly repeals the CFTC's exclusive jurisdiction, we grant the petition for review.

I.

Petitioner Brian Hunter, an employee of the hedge fund Amaranth, traded natural gas futures contracts on the New York Mercantile Exchange (NYMEX), a CFTC-regulated exchange. For those unfamiliar with the complexities of commodity futures trading, the Second Circuit offers a crisp explanation:

> A commodities futures contract is an executory contract for the sale of a commodity executed at a specific point in time with delivery of the commodity postponed to a future date. Every commodities futures contract has a seller and a buyer. The seller, called a "short," agrees for a price, fixed at the time of contract, to deliver a specified quantity and grade of an identified commodity at a date in the future. The buyer, or "long," agrees to accept delivery at that future date at the price fixed in the contract. It is the rare case when buyers and sellers settle their obligations under futures contracts by actually delivering the commodity. Rather, they routinely take a short or long position in order to speculate on the future price of the commodity.

Strobl v. New York Mercantile Exchange, 768 F.2d 22, 24 (2d Cir. 1985).

This case arises from Hunter's alleged manipulation of the "settlement price" for natural gas futures contracts, which is determined by the volume-weighted average price of trades during the "settlement period" for natural gas futures. The settlement price may affect the price of natural gas for the following month.

According to FERC, Hunter sold a significant number of natural gas futures contracts during the February, March, and April 2006 settlement periods. During these settlement periods, Hunter's sales ranged from 14.4% to 19.4% of market volume. Given their volume and timing, Hunter's sales reduced the settlement price for natural gas. Hunter's portfolio benefited from these sales because he had positioned his assets in the natural gas market to capitalize on a price decrease—that is, he shorted the price for natural gas.

Hunter's trades caught the attention of federal regulators. On July 25, 2007, the CFTC filed a civil enforcement action against Hunter, alleging that he violated section 13(a)(2) of the Commodity Exchange Act by manipulating the price of natural gas futures contracts. 7 U.S.C. § 13(a)(2). The next day, FERC filed an administrative enforcement action against Hunter, alleging that he violated section 4A of the Natural Gas Act, which prohibits manipulation. 15 U.S.C. § 717c–1. FERC claimed that Hunter's manipulation of the settlement price affected the price of natural gas in FERC-regulated markets. Following a lengthy administrative process, FERC ruled against Hunter and imposed a $30 million fine.

II.

. . . Most significantly for this case, CEA section 2(a)(1)(A) provided, at the time of Hunter's trades, that:

> The Commission shall have exclusive jurisdiction . . . with respect to accounts, agreements(including any transaction which is of the character of, or is commonly known to the trade as, an "option", "privilege", "indemnity", "bid", "offer", "put", "call", "advance guaranty", or "decline guaranty"), and transactions involving contracts of sale of a commodity for future delivery, traded or executed on a contract market designated or derivatives transaction execution facility registered pursuant to section 7 or 7a of this title or any other board of trade, exchange, or market, and transactions subject to regulation by the Commission. . . . Except as hereinabove provided, nothing contained in this section shall (I) supersede or limit the jurisdiction at any time conferred on the Securities and Exchange Commission or other regulatory authorities under the laws of the United States or of any State, or (II) restrict the Securities and Exchange Commission and such other authorities from carrying out their duties and responsibilities in accordance with such laws.

7 U.S.C.§ 2(a)(1)(A) (emphases added).

Stated simply, Congress crafted CEA section 2(a)(1)(A) to give the CFTC exclusive jurisdiction over transactions conducted on futures markets like the NYMEX. In response to the California energy crisis, Congress enacted the Energy Policy Act of 2005, which [expanded FERC's authority to regulate manipulation in energy markets and directed FERC and CFTC to enter into a memorandum of understanding about information sharing]. . . .

As we see it, this case reduces to two questions. First, does CEA section 2(a)(1)(A) encompass manipulation of natural gas futures contracts? If yes, then we need to answer the second question: did

Congress clearly and manifestly intend to impliedly repeal CEA section 2(a)(1)(A) when it enacted the Energy Policy Act of 2005? A quick glance at the statute's text answers the first question. CEA section 2(a)(1)(A) vests the CFTC with "exclusive jurisdiction . . . with respect to accounts, agreements[,] . . . and transactions involving contracts of sale of a commodity for future delivery, traded or executed" on a CFTC-regulated exchange. 7 U.S.C. § 2(a)(1)(A). Here, FERC fined Hunter for trading natural gas futures contracts with the intent to manipulate the price of natural gas in another market. Hunter's scheme, therefore, involved transactions of a commodity futures contract. By CEA section 2(a)(1)(A)'s plain terms, the CFTC has exclusive jurisdiction over the manipulation of natural gas futures contracts.

. . . According to FERC, although it and the CFTC "each have exclusive jurisdiction over the day-to-day regulation of their respective physical energy and financial markets, where, as here, there is manipulation in one market that directly or indirectly affects the other market, both agencies have an enforcement role." But FERC's contention that the CFTC may exclusively regulate only day-to-day trading activities—not an overarching scheme like manipulation—finds no support in CEA section 2(a)(1)(A)'s text. Moreover, as the CFTC points out, "[a]cceptance of FERC's jurisdictional test would allow any agency having authority to prosecute manipulation of the spot price of a commodity to lawfully exercise jurisdiction with respect to the trading of futures contracts in that commodity." Such an interpretation would eviscerate the CFTC's exclusive jurisdiction over commodity futures contracts and defeat Congress's very clear goal of centralizing oversight of futures contracts. . . .

FERC argues that the Energy Policy Act of 2005 contemplates complementary jurisdiction between it and the CFTC. FERC contends that it is empowered to prohibit manipulation not only in FERC-regulated markets but also when the manipulation "coincides with—i.e., is 'in connection with,' 'directly or indirectly'—FERC-jurisdictional gas transactions." (quoting 15 U.S.C. § 717c–1). But [that section's] text fails to answer the question whether FERC may intrude upon the CFTC's exclusive jurisdiction. More importantly, because FERC is free to prohibit manipulative trading in markets outside the CFTC's exclusive jurisdiction, there is no "irreconcilable conflict" between the two statutes and therefore no repeal by implication. *Posadas v. National City Bank*, 296 U.S. 497, 503 (1936).

FERC next relies on [the 2005 Energy Policy Act] section 23's savings clause, which states that "[n]othing in this section may be construed to limit or affect the exclusive jurisdiction of the [CFTC] under the Commodity Exchange Act." 15 U.S.C. § 717t–2(c)(2). FERC interprets this clause as applying only to section 23's requirement that it and the CFTC enter into a memorandum of understanding. In addition to section 23's text, FERC points to legislative history indicating that Congress rejected a universal savings clause that would have applied to the Energy Policy Act as a whole. But section 23 is far more ambiguous than FERC admits. By requiring the two agencies to enter into a memorandum of understanding to "ensur[e] that information requests to markets within the respective jurisdiction of each agency are properly coordinated," § 717t–2(c)(1) (emphasis added), section 23 indicates that the CFTC and

FERC regulate separate markets. Given this ambiguity, a universal savings clause may have been unnecessary, especially given the strong presumption against implied repeals. . . .

For the foregoing reasons, we grant the petition for review. ■

NOTES AND COMMENTS

1.   The type of manipulation in which Brian Hunter was engaged was typical of the cases that arose out of the California energy crisis: that is, an attempt to manipulate one market in order to benefit a position in another market. But many of those cases involved attempts to manipulate the physical spot price in order to achieve better daily settlement terms for exchange-traded futures or options contracts. Consider another recent FERC enforcement action. On July 16, 2013, FERC issued an order finding Barclays Bank PLC and several of its traders in violation of FERC's anti-manipulation regulations in connection with electricity trading. The Order charges the defendants with:

> manipulating the energy markets in and around California through the use of a coordinated, fraudulent scheme. Respondents intentionally engaged in an unlawful scheme to manipulate prices on 655 product days over 35 product months in the period between November 2006 to December 2008 in the Commission-regulated physical markets at the four most liquid trading points in the western United States. Respondents conducted the manipulation by building substantial monthly physical index positions in the opposite direction of the financial swap positions they assembled at the same points and then trading a next-day fixed price, or "cash," product at those points to "flatten" their physical index obligations in a manner intentionally designed to increase or lower the daily index (Index) (representing a daily volume-weighted average of prices paid for the fixed-price trades conducted each day) at that point. By intentionally increasing or decreasing the Index, Respondents benefited Barclays' financial swap positions whose value was ultimately determined by the same Index. Put simply, Respondents traded fixed price products not in an attempt to profit from the relationship between the market fundamentals of supply and demand, but instead for the fraudulent purpose of moving the Index price at a particular point so that Barclays' financial swap positions at that same trading point would benefit.

Barclays Bank, Order Assessing Civil Penalties, 144 F.E.R.C. ¶ 61,041 (July 16, 2013). What does the holding in *Hunter* say about agency jurisdiction in this case? The defendants sought a trial in federal district court, and the judge has stayed the effective date of the $453 million in fines and penalties FERC assessed against the defendants.

2.   If the government must prove "fraud" and "deceit" in bringing enforcement actions against market manipulators, does a trader who openly tries to corner a market violate the FPA's anti-manipulation provisions? Does it matter if the attempted corner is on the physical market or the derivatives market? For a discussion of this issue, see David B. Spence & Robert Prentice, *The Transformation of American Energy Markets and the Problem of Market Power*, 53 B.C. L. Rev. 131 (2012). Economist Craig

Pirrong contends that when it comes to manipulation of derivatives markets, the CEA is ill-suited to deal with market power manipulations that exploit scarcity conditions created in part by the trader's own positions, or to invite courts to look for the presence of deception or fraud in such cases (just as courts have done in securities cases). *See* Craig Pirrong, Energy Market Manipulation: Definition, Diagnosis, and Deterrence, 31 Energy L.J. 1 (2010).

3. If the government must prove "fraud" and "deceit" in bringing enforcement actions against market manipulators, is a trader who exercises market power as a pivotal supplier violating the FPA's anti-manipulation provisions? A mere two weeks after the Barclays complaint, FERC and J.P. Morgan agreed to settle a case in which FERC charged Morgan subsidiaries with manipulating the MISO and California ISO wholesale electricity markets by engaging in bidding practices (in connection with generating plants they owned) that did not reflect the plants' true costs and were designed to influence the market-clearing price. *See* J.P. Morgan, Order Approving Stipulation and Consent Agreement, 144 F.E.R.C. ¶ 61,068 (July 30, 2013). Is it "fraud" or "deceit," for example, to withhold generation from the market in order to create shortages that will increase the market clearing price? If not, is it a violation of some other legal requirement?

4. While FERC is considered the more aggressive enforcer, CFTC has initiated some high-profile enforcement actions outside the electricity context, including actions against ConAgra Trade Group for false reporting of trades on the NYMEX crude oil exchange, a case that was settled for $12 million (ConAgra Trade Group, Inc. C.F.T.C. Docket No. 10–14 (2010)), and Cantor Fitzgerald for fraudulent wash sales in gasoline markets, which was settled with the payment of a $100,000 fine. Cantor Fitzgerald & Co., C.F.T.C. Docket No. 11–08 (2011). Since passage of the Dodd-Frank Act, CFTC promulgated additional rules on market manipulation, which subject end-users to disclosure requirements. It has also clarified that "reckless behavior could constitute manipulation," and has prohibited "attempted manipulation." Prohibition on the Employment, or Attempted Employment, of Manipulative and Deceptive Devices and Prohibition on Price Manipulation, 76 Fed. Reg. 41,398 (July 14, 2011). More recently, FERC and CFTC have focused on coordinating information sharing related to enforcement and harmonizing market-manipulation regulation, but there is still a potential for conflicts between them.

3. LEAST-COST DISPATCH

To develop a full appreciation of the risks associated with selling power in competitive wholesale electricity markets, it is useful to understand how the grid operator (say, an RTO or ISO) makes decisions to dispatch power from individual electric generating facilities to the grid. One of the longstanding, bedrock principles of grid management is that power plants should be dispatched on a least-cost basis. That is, as the next increment of power is needed to satisfy additional demand, the grid operator should dispatch power from the available generating facility that can provide the needed power at the lowest marginal cost. This principle holds for the first megawatt of capacity brought online during periods of low demand to the last megawatt of capacity brought online during periods of peak demand. Generally, grid operators deviate from this priority rule only to ensure the security of the power system—

that is, to avoid severe congestion or other operational problems associated with dispatching the least-cost unit. Thus, we say that the grid operates on a "security-constrained, least-cost dispatch" or "security constrained economic dispatch" (SCED) rule.

This rule applies both in traditionally regulated systems controlled by a single vertically integrated IOU, and in competitive, organized wholesale markets characterized by arms-length sales between generators/wholesalers and retailers. The rule is consistent with the FPA mandate that wholesale rates be "just and reasonable," and protects ratepayers from having to pay more than is necessary for power. In most competitive spot markets (which tend to be those managed by an RTO or ISO), sellers submit day-ahead bids indicating the price at which they will be willing to sell power into the system at various time increments the following day. Buyers do the same, submitting bids representing the amount they are willing to pay for power during those same time increments. For each time increment, the ISO or RTO matches buyers' and sellers' bids and determines the market clearing price, which all sellers will receive for power dispatched to the system.

Theoretically, in a pure competitive market, sellers should bid into the market at a price that reflects their marginal cost of supplying power. In practice, a large number of factors can influence the marginal cost of dispatching a particular plant at a particular time. A thermal plant operating at less than full capacity will have a lower marginal cost of providing the next unit of power than it would if it had to provide the additional power from a cold start, for example. Furthermore, congestion conditions on the grid can affect the "security" part of the equation. Sometimes, the plant with the lowest marginal cost is located in the wrong place, such that dispatching power from that plant will cause congestion that threatens security of the system. Taking these and other factors into consideration, the ISO/RTO may perform this market clearing function for multiple locations (nodes) within the system, and may adjust prices to reflect congestion. This is "locational marginal pricing": marginal cost pricing that takes into account the added costs of congestion at various nodes (locations) on a regional grid at a given moment.

Putting these complexities aside for the moment, consider the following stylized, hypothetical electric system. **Figure 10–3** lists all of the power plants available on our hypothetical grid. The information in the table includes each plant's technology (coal, combined cycle natural gas, run-of-river hydro, wind or solar), its generating capacity (in megawatts), and its marginal cost of dispatch.[4] Assume for simplicity that each plant's marginal cost is constant across its full range of operation, from the first megawatt hour it produces to the last (operating at full capacity). The table also indicates other potential sources of revenue for the plant in the form of government subsidies (such as a production tax credit) or a power purchase agreement (PPA). PPAs are discussed further in Chapters 11 and 12.

---

[4] In reality, plants guard their cost information jealously; but it is generally true that marginal cost is correlated with fuel costs. Hence the zero marginal cost for wind and solar in our hypothetical.

Plant Type	Capacity	Marginal cost of dispatch ($/kwh)	Per kwh subsidy	PPA price ($/kwh)
Coal-fired Plant 1	700 MW	0.03		0.06
Coal-fired Plant 2	700 MW	0.04		0.06
CCNG Plant 1	300 MW	0.04		0.06
CCNG Plant 2	300 MW	0.04		0.06
CCNG Plant 3	300 MW	0.05		0.08
CCNG Plant 4	300 MW	0.05		0.08
CCNG Plant 5	300 MW	0.08		0.10
CCNG Plant 6	300 MW	0.08		0.10
RoR Hydro Plant 1	80 MW	0.02		0.04
RoR Hydro Plant 2	80 MW	0.02		0.04
RoR Hydro Plant 3	80 MW	0.02		0.04
Wind Farm 1	200 MW	0	0.02	0.08
Wind Farm2	200 MW	0	0.02	0.08
Wind Farm 3	200 MW	0	0.02	0.08
Solar Farm 1	200 MW	0	0.02	0.08
Solar Farm 2	200 MW	0	0.02	0.08
Solar Farm 3	200 MW	0	0.02	0.08

Figure 10–3

Assume that all plants are available to provide power (if needed) at full capacity, and the owners of the generation facilities all bid into the market at their marginal cost. Consider, then, the following questions:

QUESTION 1: What is the "merit order" of dispatch using the SCED rule? That is, in what order will these plants be dispatched as demand grows from 0 to 4500 MW on this system?

QUESTION 2: What will the market clearing price be if system demand is 3000 MW?

QUESTION 3: If demand falls to 1000 MW, what will the market clearing price be then?

On many systems, wind and solar facilities are recent additions to the system. How would your answers to Questions 2 and 3 have been different prior to these renewables coming online on our hypothetical system?[5]

---

[5] Of course, in reality, wind and solar generation is intermittent. These plants are available to be dispatched only when the wind blows and the sun shines, respectively. When they become available, however, they will displace sources already providing power to the grid: those sources will be ramped down to make room for cheaper, zero-marginal cost renewable power. This is efficient for ratepayers, but can be inefficient in other ways, depending on the type of generating facility being ramped down. Many older fossil fueled-plants, particularly coal-fired plants, were designed to run at full capacity, not to be ramped up and down. The ramping process exerts wear and tear on the facility, reducing its useful life and causing it to emit more pollutants per unit of energy dispatched (in part because the facility has now become partly a reserve unit). *See, e.g.,* Bentek Energy, How Less Became More: Wind, Power and Unintended Consequences in the Colorado Energy Market (Apr. 2010), http://docs.wind-watch.org/BENTEK-How-Less-Became-More.pdf. The National Renewable Energy Laboratory (NREL) has since provided a more nuanced analysis of wear and tear on plants due to ramping and on the emissions impacts of ramping, noting on page 13 of the following report that some studies have disagreed with Bentek's conclusions. D. Lew et al., NREL, The Western Wind and Solar Integration Study Part 2 (2013), http://www.nrel.gov/docs/fy13osti/55588.pdf.

It should be evident that the introduction of more renewables on to the system reduces the market clearing price, all else equal. When renewables are available and demand is low, prices may even be negative, as they sometimes are in places like west Texas, where the wind blows at night, during periods of very low demand. Even when renewables are not determining the market clearing price directly, they do so indirectly. By moving to the top of the merit order, they displace facilities lower in the merit order that would have been necessary to serve load, but are no longer. Thus, on our hypothetical system, with all facilities available to operate at full capacity, and demand at 3000 MW, and putting aside subsidies and contracts, the marginal plant is either Coal-fired Plant 2 or CCNG Plants 1 or 2 (all of whose marginal costs are 4 cents/kwh). The marginal plant determines the market clearing price, which will be 4 cents/kwh under our assumptions, and all sellers whose plants are dispatched will earn that price for sales of power during that time period. Had there been no wind or solar on the system, the marginal plant at 3000 MW of demand would have been CCNG Plant 5 or 6, and the market clearing price 8 cents/kwh.

In this way, the presence of any new, cheaper source of power (in this case, renewables) benefits buyers in the wholesale markets, and so benefits their retail customers. At the same time, these cheaper sources make it more difficult for the remaining plant owners to recover their costs. Remember, in order to profit from electric generation, owners must recover not simply their marginal costs, but their *average costs* over the long run, including the cost of servicing debt. All generators, renewables included, have long-run average costs greater than zero. If the market clearing price is consistently less than a plant's average cost, or if the plant is so far down in merit order that it is rarely dispatched, it will not make money. Generators in competitive markets depend upon market-clearing prices being high enough over the long run to allow them to recover their costs and earn a competitive return. Renewables and cheaper natural gas tend to depress the market clearing price in the long run. For current and prospective generators of power, this is the harsh reality of modern competitive markets. Under traditional regulation this was not a problem, since plant owners (IOUs) were guaranteed a fair return on their prudently made investments. Indeed, fears that competitive markets do not provide a sufficient incentive to invest in generating capacity have given rise to the capacity markets (in which owners of capacity are paid merely to make the capacity available to the system, regardless of whether it ever provides that power) described earlier in this chapter.

Finally, in a system governed by security-constrained least-cost dispatch, long-term PPAs do not determine which plants actually supply power to the grid. Rather, the agreements become nothing more than hedging devices, equivalent to derivative contracts. If a wholesale buyer has agreed to pay 10 cents/kwh for the output of CCNG Plant 6 in Figure 10–3 above, and that plant is not dispatched, the buyer must secure (and pay for) its power needs from a different plant. Thus, PPAs act as forward contracts and/or contracts for differences: the contract establishes a price against which the spot price is compared, with the seller or buyer paying the difference to the other party. Nevertheless, if the plant owner can secure a long-term PPA in advance of construction, that guaranteed stream of revenue can help attract the capital necessary to build a plant in the first place.

E. RETAIL COMPETITION IN ELECTRIC POWER

1. HISTORY AND RATIONALE OF RETAIL RESTRUCTURING

While FERC has extensive jurisdiction over interstate and wholesale sales of electricity, state PUCs (and legislatures) took on the task of designing and implementing retail competition. States have authority over retail rates, local distribution of electricity, and construction and siting of power plants and transmission lines within their boundaries. By the turn of the 21st century, nearly one-half of all states had introduced retail competition, although several have since abandoned their restructuring programs, partially in response to the Enron crisis and California's restructuring problems.

For a number of years, states had considered plans to implement retail wheeling, or direct access to electricity supply markets, mostly for large retail customers such as industrial plants. By the mid-1990s, however, state retail wheeling plans were being displaced by much more comprehensive efforts to implement "retail competition." Unlike retail wheeling, which focuses solely on the issue of retail transmission access, retail competition plans address a range of additional issues, including consumer protection, stranded cost recovery, and green pricing. The basic approach has been to encourage competitive markets to evolve through the "unbundling" of generation, transmission and distribution: splitting the incumbent utility company into its component parts either functionally or legally.

Some aspects of this decentralized industry remain fully regulated by the states, and others are governed by new, market-oriented regimes. Thus, states' laws and regulations have not achieved complete deregulation; instead, they have pursued restructuring of their electricity markets. In a competitive retail market, the incumbent distribution utility continues to provide service to retail customers and remains a regulated natural monopoly. On the other hand, retail customers are afforded the opportunity to choose the company from which they buy electricity—customers choose generators, in other words. In some states, like Texas, a retail electric provider (REP) connects customers to a variety of generation options, so customers in choosing a REP also choose a particular bundle of generation options. The REP also provides metering and billing service but uses the incumbent, regulated utility's distribution lines. This opens the incumbent utility's distribution network to access by its competitors, and introduces several levels of complexity in setting up restructuring plans. Think of the many questions involved in defining the relationship between the incumbent utility and the new entrants in the generation and transmission business. Under what terms and conditions would the incumbent utility provide open access? Could the incumbent utility keep some customers and jettison others? Regulators needed to carefully address these and many other issues.

Each restructuring state has taken its own approach to the question of retail restructuring, and there are even regional differences.

Generally, retail restructuring was more likely to happen where retail prices were high, due to smaller, balkanized utility systems, greater state-imposed obligations to buy power from renewable sources, and the cost burden of imprudent investments (e.g., in costly nuclear plants). Thus, electricity prices were higher in California, the Northeast, and the upper Midwest than in the Northwest, lower Midwest, and Southeast. That, in turn, created a political environment more conducive (politically and economically) to restructuring in California, the Northeast, and the upper Midwest, than in the southeast, lower Midwest, and Northwest. *See* Richard J. Pierce, Jr., Completing the Process of Restructuring the Electricity Market, 40 Wake Forest L. Rev. 101, 108–09 (2005). Some states, including several in the Southeast, however, continue to refer to themselves as "low cost power" states in which retail electric prices are fully regulated and capped, suggesting that retail competition is far off on the regulatory horizon. Low cost power states see no need to restructure, as they do not believe that consumers will be better off with retail competition. Will these states be able to continue to avoid implementing retail access markets, or will the failure to do so impair the development of wholesale competition?

States pursuing restructuring face a bewildering array of complex policy questions. One primary set of issues involves consumer protection. Despite promises of lower prices, with the rise of retail competition many consumer protections taken for granted under the traditional approach to state utility regulation would be at risk. Under the traditional approach, as discussed in Chapter 8, regulation of utilities by state PUCs struck a balance between private gain and the public interest. The prospect of retail competition creates a tension between these two interests, requiring regulators to reassess their role and transform their regulatory structures.

This in turn creates major uncertainties. How would market mechanisms control supply and demand for electricity? Would retail rates decrease or would consumers be vulnerable to price spikes in a restructured market? How would markets be structured so that participants would not take advantage of consumers? Would price signals from the market be sufficiently clear to encourage the appropriate level of investment in generation and transmission? Or would it be more likely that "the current group [of generators] is seeing strong incentives to limit capacity additions, and maximize profits"? Alan H. Richardson, Can A Free Market Work For Electricity?, Pub. Power, Nov.–Dec. 2000, at 6.

Another set of concerns came from utilities most directly affected by a transition from a regulated monopoly environment to a competitive marketplace. They contended they would not be able to recover investments they had made under the assumption that state regulation of their activities would continue. These so-called "stranded costs," they argued, needed to be accounted for in the restructuring process. If the states were to accept this argument and compensate utilities in whole or part for their stranded costs, who would bear the responsibility for paying them and by what mechanism would the stranded costs be recovered? Would the recovery of stranded costs be limited to the period of transition to competition or would it last longer?

There were (and continue to be) issues related to the general division of power between the federal government and the states regarding competition policy. Would states modify or even scrap their traditional regulatory authority over utilities based in their states? In this transitional environment, what would be the limits of state ability to implement retail competition? What would be the relationship between FERC's initiatives to restructure the wholesale power market and state retail competition policies? There were other federalism issues to consider: Would federal antitrust laws continue to protect consumers in light of state restructuring, or would states need to develop their own active consumer protection programs to replace the traditional protections that accompanied price regulation?

In the quarter-century since the enactment of PURPA, a number of innovative programs had been developed to interject environmental concerns into the utility industry, thus raising more questions for state restructuring and the federal-state relationship. These programs, such as "demand side management" (DSM) and "integrated resource planning" (IRP) (see Chapter 13), had just begun to be adopted on a widespread basis in the industry. Would restructuring and the advent of competition slow the adoption of these programs or stall it altogether? There were other environmental concerns, such as impacts on enforcement of the federal Clean Air Act (CAA) to reduce pollution from the utility industry. With the industry fragmenting and introducing a whole new set of competitors, how would better air quality be ensured? EPA's proposed Clean Power Plan to reduce carbon emissions from power plants (Carbon Pollution Emission Guidelines for Existing Stationary Sources: Electric Utility Generating Units, 79 Fed. Reg. 34,829 (June 18, 2014)) further complicates this issue, raising questions as to whether certain plants will simply no longer be feasible because they will be unable to meet the carbon standard, or whether "dirty" plants can offset their carbon emissions with clean, renewable plants elsewhere in the state. What if state regulations associated with power plant and transmission line siting posed a tension with federal or state competition policy? Would they yield or retain primacy?

2. COMMON FEATURES OF STATE RESTRUCTURING PLANS

State restructuring laws are complex and are usually the result of lengthy discussions, negotiations, task force reports, and inevitable political compromises, given the billions of dollars at stake. As a result, the features of restructuring programs differ widely from state to state. On the whole, however, each state typically addresses the following common issues:

(1) *Choice of alternate provider*: Retail electricity customers in most states have their choice of electricity generators but no choice of distribution utility. As mentioned above, for example, in Texas customers choose a REP that in turn selects the generators and sells electricity to retail consumers.

(2) *"Standard offer" or "default" service and protections for customers not selecting alternate providers*: The "duty to serve" has evolved in the competitive environment (see discussion below), and states use different ways of protecting customers who choose to stay with their incumbent electricity providers:

Four models, with variations, illustrate the major approaches used thus far: (a) the incumbent utility continues to provide service [to non-switchers] under a rate that essentially passes through the utility's wholesale cost of power; (b) the utility remains a service provider to some customers but not to others; (c) the utility continues to provide service but does so under a rate structure designed to gradually wean customers away from utility service and towards market-based prices; and (d) the privilege of serving non-choosing customers is bid out, while the utility's role is to deliver power.

Nat'l Coun. on Elec. Pol'y, A Comprehensive View of U.S. Electric Restructuring with Policy Options for the Future 33 (2003).

(3) *Stranded costs*: Most states established some sort of "competitive transition charge" (CTC) that customers pay to incumbent utilities to cover stranded costs. The restructuring laws set up transition periods during which utilities are able to assess these charges; the charges end after the end of these periods. The CTC may apply to all consumers, or, in states such as Virginia (under its now-repealed restructuring law), only to those consumers who switch to another supplier of power.

(4) *Consumer rate protections*: Many state restructuring plans promised consumers rate reductions or attempted to hold residential consumers harmless, recognizing from the outset that retail power markets would not begin full operation immediately or for a period of years. Illinois and California, for example, promised customers rate reductions with the adoption of retail competition. Many, such as Maryland, established rate caps designed to last for the period of years during which the state was undergoing a transition to full competition. Rate caps have been criticized for dampening the competitive market: if consumers have the protection of guaranteed low rates, what incentive is there to switch electricity providers? As customers leaving their current utility would give up the rate caps' protection, it is not surprising that this has been a factor in keeping switching rates low. Yet if a state did not protect its consumers, it would be gambling that a new and untested retail market would keep rates low over time. States were not willing to take this risk, as shown by subsequent events. Many of these retail rate caps have since expired, though wholesale rate caps (imposed by RTOs and ISOs) remain in place in most organized wholesale markets.

(5) *Other consumer protections*: Most restructuring states set up systems designed to protect consumers in their states from abusive behavior by marketers of electricity. As retail markets emerged, state regulators needed to actively police against abuses such as "slamming" and "cramming," deceptive practices designed to induce customers to switch providers used early in the transition to competitive telecommunications markets. Practices like these have taken place in some states but are not common in the electric utility industry; nevertheless, states felt the need to put specific protections into place.

The Maine Public Utilities Commission's (MPUC's) scheme is typical. Electricity marketers are required to secure a license from the state. To obtain the license, they must show evidence of financial capability, demonstrate that they could enter into binding interconnection agreements with utilities that would transmit and distribute their power, disclose all pending legal actions or consumer complaints from the previous year, and disclose names of affiliates. Providers furnishing power to retail customers cannot terminate service without at least 30 days' notice, and cannot make telemarketing calls to those customers who have made written "do not call" requests. The MPUC may revoke a license of a marketer that violates its terms, and can impose penalties of as much as $5,000 per day for each violation. *See* Me. Rev. Stat. Ann. tit. 35–A, § 3203.

With the adoption of comprehensive retail competition plans, state regulators have also embarked on massive consumer education programs.

(6) *System benefits charges*: Either in the restructuring law itself or in a separate law, a number of states have established system benefits charges designed to ensure that the environmental programs underway in the electric utility industry would be continued in a restructuring environment. These charges are discussed more fully in Chapter 13. Other environmental laws such as air pollution regulation impacted the utility industry as it restructured. See Chapter 5.

(7) *Exit fees and switching penalties*: If too many customers "switch"—leave the incumbent utility to purchase in a competitive market—or switch power supply providers due to short term changes in price, this could cause serious problems with the reliability of distribution. What constraints, if any, are there on the customer's ability to leave or return to the original incumbent utility? One way some states are addressing this issue is to assess exit fees (also used to compensate for stranded costs), or penalties for customers who switch power suppliers too often and thus impose costs on other customers of the power distribution system. What impact will these fees have on "distributed generation"? See Chapter 11.

Other states require a minimum period in power purchase options offered by the utility or others. In Illinois, where power purchase options offered by utilities were required by law to run for at least twelve months, competitive markets were slow to develop because the prices for such contracts (determined by an independent consulting firm) were set at what many consider artificially low levels, deterring many customers from leaving the incumbent utilities and encouraging some customers that once used other retail suppliers to return to the utility. *See* Steve Daniels, A Jolt to Electricity Deregulation: Pricing Glitch is Restoring ComEd's Market Power, Crain's Chicago Bus., Mar. 13, 2000.

(8) *Functional separation (unbundling)*: States typically require that utilities separate the generation function of their businesses from the transmission and distribution functions, with detailed rules about conduct to prohibit inappropriate self-dealing. This is an attempt to control the potential exercise by utilities of their market power. For further discussion of this issue, see the analysis of the "state action doctrine," below.

a.   THE TREATMENT OF "STRANDED COSTS"

"Stranded costs" refer to the transition costs of implementing competition in a previously regulated industry. Regulation protected the utility's capital investments, by allowing for rate base recovery in rates, but a firm may risk losing guaranteed recovery of its capital investments if they are no longer competitive when valued in the market. It is often claimed that competitive electricity markets will lead toward increased efficiencies and (perhaps) lower electricity prices overall, but the move towards competitive markets is not what economists would call a "Pareto" superior move: Competition does not always not make everyone better off and at least some persons or groups will be harmed in the transition. Stranded costs are not specific to energy, and have plagued regulatory transitions in the arisen in the telecommunications, railroad and airline industries too. Regulators face important distributional questions in addressing stranded costs.

To understand stranded costs, consider a utility's decision to build a build a new power under rate regulation. The utility may have significant costs under rate regulation by investing in a power plant, expecting that these costs would be recovered through regulated rates over a long period of time, typically 20 to 50 years. The basic ratemaking principle that consumers who benefit from a plant pay for it requires long depreciation schedules. Yet a lot can happen in a time period that spans half a human life. The "stranded cost" problem arises as regulators announce new policies (such as restructuring plans) that do not guarantee rate base or other rate recovery of the costs of utilities' assets. "Stranded" is an apt metaphor for this phenomenon: These assets or costs are effectively "shipwrecked," isolated from the traditional revenue streams used to pay for them. While this problem can exist in any industry (think about how the calculator displaced the slide rule), utility regulation may exacerbate the problem by setting rate recovery expectations over 20 to 50 years (allowing new entrants to undercut incumbents with new technology) and burdening incumbents with obligations, such as the duty to serve, not faced by new entrants.

Gregory Sidak and Daniel Spurber, who advocate for full stranded cost recovery for utilities, define stranded costs as, "the inability of utility shareholders to secure the return of, and a competitive rate of return on, their investment." J. Gregory Sidak & Daniel F. Spulber, Deregulatory Takings and the Regulatory Contract 27 (1997). This definition would include both utilities' operating expenses and capital outlays. Timothy Brennan and James Boyd identify four basic types of stranded costs for electric utilities: "(1) Undepreciated investments in power plants that are more expensive than generators today. (2) Long-term contracts—most if not all mandated by [PURPA]. (3) Generators built but not used, primarily nuclear. (4) Expenses related to [DSM] and other conservation programs that, as substitutes for new plant construction, were charged to the generation side of the business." Timothy J. Brennan & James Boyd, Stranded Costs, Takings, and the Law and Economics of Implicit Contracts, 11 J. Reg. Econ. 41 (1997). Other commentators focused on the actual capital outlays made by utilities. Herbert Hovenkamp defines stranded costs as "investments in specialized, durable assets that may seem necessary, or at least justifiable, when constructed and placed into service under a regime of price and entry controls but that have become underutilized or useless under deregulation." Herbert Hovenkamp, The Takings Clause and Improvident Regulatory Bargains, 108 Yale L.J. 801 (1999).

At the beginning of the transition to competition in electric power, EIA estimated that stranded costs could lead to an increase in bankruptcies in the industry if regulators did not find a way to address them. EIA, Electricity Prices in a Competitive Environment: Marginal Cost Pricing of Generation Services and Financial Status of Electric Utilities—A Preliminary Analysis Through 2015 ix (1997). Not surprisingly, then, utilities have made vigorous arguments in favor of full or near-full recovery of stranded costs. Utilities and many commentators have argued that compensation for these costs is efficient because it sends investors a signal that governmental commitments are credible and will be honored. Sidak & Spulber, *supra*. Some advocates believe that disallowing stranded costs recovery would put incumbent utilities at a competitive disadvantage with new entrants, working essentially as a "negative barrier to entry." *See* William B. Tye & Frank C. Graves, The Economics of Negative Barriers to Entry: How to Recover Stranded Costs and Achieve Competition on Equal Terms in the Electric Utility Industry, 37 Nat. Resources J. 175 (1997).

Sidak and Spulber compiled their arguments for stranded cost recovery in a book titled Deregulatory Takings and the Regulatory Contract: The Competitive Transformation of Network Industries in the United States (1997). Their book, more than 500 pages of legal and regulatory analysis, has been invoked in regulatory proceedings and judicial cases across the country. It was compared in its importance to Robert Bork's The Antitrust Paradox (1978) as proposing a comprehensive reorientation of legal principles (in this case, those governing regulated industries). For reviews of the arguments made in the book, see Jim Rossi, The Irony of Deregulatory Takings, 77 Tex. L. Rev. 297, 311–13 (1998); Hovenkamp, *supra*.

Consider Sidak and Spulber's use of the term "regulatory contract" in the title of their book. Part of this traditional "bargain" between utilities, customers, and regulators was that utilities are allowed to recover prudently incurred costs through their rates. Utilities that own generation assets insist on stranded cost recovery in part because they expected the regulatory contract to continue. But is it fair to provide stranded cost recovery no matter what the efficiency consequences? Sidak and Spulber's opponents, such as Oliver Williamson, argued that stranded cost compensation ignored "strategic opportunism" by utilities. Williamson stated that he was not necessarily convinced that investments by utilities were "prudently incurred" or that "regulated firms are operated in least-cost ways (*i.e.*, with an absence of slack)," and called Sidak and Spulber "unduly sanguine." Oliver Williamson, Response: Deregulatory Takings and the Breach of the Regulatory Contract: Some Precautions, 71 N.Y.U. L. Rev. 1007 (1996). As one prevailing view suggests, utilities (with the acquiescence of regulators) may have overinvested in capital. If they were overcompensated, opponents of stranded cost recovery argued, they would be sent a signal that they could overinvest in the future. *See* Elizabeth Nowicki, Denial of Regulatory Assistance in Stranded Cost Recovery in a Deregulated Electricity Industry, 32 Loy. L.A. L. Rev. 431 (1999) (arguing that monopolists should not be rewarded for their inefficient investments). Opponents also felt that stranded cost recovery would recreate many of the same problems with ratemaking that led some to view restructuring and competition as potentially more efficient. As occurred with cost-of-service regulation, utilities might seek inclusion of many items in stranded cost recovery that consumer advocates and others might find questionable. *See* Robert J. Michaels, Stranded Investment Surcharges: Inequitable and Inefficient, Pub. Util. Fortnightly, May 15, 1999, at 21.

Putting all these arguments together, the case against stranded cost recovery was perhaps expressed best by Peter Bradford, a former state PSC chair in Maine and New York:

> I want particularly to dispel the claim that some societal "compact" compels the [regulator] to assure the recovery of every dollar not found to have been spent imprudently. My conclusion is based on several propositions:
>
> 1) There never was a regulatory compact.
>
> 2) Investors have long been aware that serious losses, even bankruptcy, were possible in the electric utility industry and that no compact protected them from technological or regulatory change.
>
> 3) Electric utility investors have for many years been compensated at levels sufficient to cover the risk of some loss of their strandable investment.
>
> 4) Not all strandable commitments were prudently incurred.

Peter Bradford, Testimony Before the Vermont PSB, Investigation into the Restructuring of the Electric Utility Industry in Vermont, Docket No. 5854 (1996).

Sidak and Spulber's reference to "deregulatory takings" suggests a possible constitutional problem with denying a utility stranded cost recovery. In recent years the term "regulatory takings" has come in vogue in such Supreme Court cases as *Lucas v. South Carolina Coastal Council*, 505 U.S. 1003 (1992). It refers to governmental regulation that goes so far as to deprive the regulated party of the economic value of its property interest as to be the equivalent of the government physically taking property for public use without just compensation (prohibited by the Takings Clause of the Fifth Amendment as applied by the Fourteenth Amendment to the states). Sidak and Spulber argued that deregulating the industry would operate as a "taking" if stranded costs were not completely recovered by utilities. Sidak and Spulber, Deregulatory Takings, *supra*, at 857–58.

However, the "regulatory takings" theory turned out to be overstated; in subsequent cases (*see* In the Matter of Energy Ass'n of N.Y. State v. Public Serv. Comm'n, 653 N.Y.S.2d 502 (Sup. Ct., Albany Cty. 1996)) and commentary it was criticized as giving short shrift to the history of utility regulation. As one commentator put it, "the 'end results' test announced in *Hope* can be seen as a decision to allocate to the political institutions of government near total power to protect the constitutional values underlying the takings clause in the ratemaking context." Richard J. Pierce, Jr., Public Utility Regulatory Takings: Should the Judiciary Attempt to Police the Political Institutions?, 77 Geo. L.J. 2031 (1989); *see also* Jim Chen, The Second Coming of *Smyth v. Ames*, 77 Tex. L. Rev. 1535 (1999) (arguing that "Judicial endorsement of Deregulatory Takings would reinvigorate . . . the confiscatory ratemaking doctrine [of *Smyth v. Ames*"]); Hovenkamp, *supra*.

In Order No. 888, FERC allowed utilities to recover a large portion of their stranded costs. FERC's decision to allow stranded cost recovery for electric utilities appears to conflict with its policies in the natural gas market, where Order No. 500 articulated a principle for resolving how the costs of uneconomic "take or pay" contracts would be shared. In Order No. 500, FERC opted for cost sharing of the stranded costs in the natural gas pipeline industry pursuant to an equitable formula. FERC made pipelines (and their shareholders) absorb between twenty-five and fifty percent of high-priced natural gas costs and allowed them to pass on an equal amount to their customers through a fixed charge. Any residual costs (for instance, fifty percent if a pipeline chose to absorb just twenty-five percent and pass through twenty-five percent) could be added to the ordinary rate and recouped to the extent that customers would buy the pipeline's expensive gas. Regulation of Natural Gas Pipelines After Partial Wellhead Decontrol, Order No. 500, 52 Fed. Reg. 30,334, 30,337 (Aug. 14, 1987). The difference between the two Orders led to criticism of FERC's allowance of stranded costs recovery in the electric utility industry. *See* John Burritt McArthur, The Irreconcilable Differences Between FERC's Natural Gas and Electricity Stranded Cost Treatments, 46 Buff. L. Rev. 71 (1998) (noting that "such a marked difference in approach, with outcomes so contradictory, justifies at least the presumption that something is wrong with Order No. 888.").

Is stranded cost recovery fair because of our societal obligations to utilities, or is it unfair because it rewards them for their past business mistakes? In the states, this question was addressed in highly charged, politicized proceedings. Most states chose to allow utilities to recover all or most of their stranded costs. The most common mechanism used, as noted above, was a nonbypassable charge imposed on all utility customers (typically known as a CTC or "wires charge") for a transitional period of time. Pennsylvania imposed a CTC on "every customer accessing the transmission or distribution network," but in no event to last beyond 2005. 66 Pa. C.S. § 2808(a)–(b); *compare* Va. Code § 56–583 (imposing a "wires charge"). Regulators and legislatures have also considered "exit fees" for customers leaving incumbent utilities and often combined stranded cost recovery with rate freezes or reductions for consumers; in Pennsylvania's case the rate cap lasted for nine years.

Differences among states primarily related to the process of calculating stranded costs and their amount. To some extent, states' restructuring laws listed specific categories of costs to be treated as stranded costs. Pennsylvania's law includes "regulatory assets and other deferred charges" and "the unfounded portion of projected nuclear decommissioning costs," among others, as allowable stranded costs. Other states (such as Virginia) left this decision to the PUC. States typically disallowed costs that were not prudent investments when made, and imposed a duty on utilities to mitigate their costs by reducing them as much as possible before claiming them (renegotiating above-market power supply contracts, for example).

Beyond this, there were differences in how stranded costs were to be calculated, which was not surprising given the massive uncertainty in forecasting them. Estimating a utility's cost profile in the competitive environment was difficult. What would a utility's assets be worth in the future? Didn't that depend on knowing how competition would turn out (and in turn on knowing who would be the utility's competitors and what their costs would be)? Forecasting could be done *ex ante*—before the start of competition—or *ex post*, after competition began. *See* EIA, The Changing Structure of the Electric Power Industry: An Update, Methodologies for Estimating Stranded Costs, Appendix E (1997) (Modified 1999), http://www.eia.doe.gov. Using the *ex ante* approach could lead to windfall gains or losses if calculations were incorrect; using the *ex post* approach might be more accurate but leave the uncertainty to be worked out down the line. Calculations could be done "bottom-up" (computing the value of each investment that would be stranded) or "top-down" (calculating the difference in revenue likely to occur with competition).

Some states, like California, used an administrative determination of stranded costs. Massachusetts established an administratively determined stranded cost number, but then adjusted it downwards once utilities sold their power plants for much more than had originally been anticipated. Consequently, many states adopted formulae that allowed them to adjust the stranded cost recovery periodically. Some states permitted stranded cost recovery to be "securitized," an approach whereby all or a portion of the utility's right to receive future competition transition charges could be converted into a current, fully vested property right that could be pledged or sold as security for the issuance of transition bonds. *See e.g.*, 66 Pa. C.S. § 2812 (securitization provision). Securitization of stranded costs enabled a utility to receive cash "today, as opposed to a revenue stream generated . . . over time." Calvin R. Wong, Emerging and Nonstandard Products: A Rating Agency's Perspective, 759 PLI/Comm 347, 371 (1999). Some utilities found this attractive. It also had some benefits from a cost mitigation perspective: proceeds from the sale of "rate reduction bonds" (bonds issued to finance the stranded costs) could reduce the utility's interest expenses. Because the legislature and the PUC guaranteed the CTC (and therefore the underlying revenue stream used to retire the bonds), the capital markets could provide certainty and lower interest rates. *See* J. Gregory Sidak & Daniel F. Spulber, Givings, Takings, and the Fallacy of Forward-Looking Costs, 72 N.Y.U. L. Rev. 1068, 1154–55 (1997).

Securitization is controversial for a number of reasons. It is different from conventional asset securitization in that traditional securitized assets are "already an enforceable contract right at the time of their securitization and require only collection by the servicing organization." Walter R. Hall, Securitization and Stranded Cost Recovery, 18 Energy L.J. 363, 385 (1997). Fixing the level of stranded costs up front, as would be necessary for securitization, has all the potential drawbacks of the *ex ante* estimation approach: if stranded costs turn out to be more or less than the fixed amount, there might be a windfall or loss to the utility. *See* Kenneth Rose, Securitization of Uneconomic Costs: Whom Does It Secure?, Pub. Util. Fortnightly, June 1, 1997, at 32. Consumer advocates and others have objected to securitization because it gives utilities an immediate payment up front, removing any future risk. Another objection to securitization is that it would put incumbent utilities in a stronger competitive position than new entrants. Rose, *supra*, at 32.

b.   SURVEY OF STATE COMPETITION PLANS

As of 2014, 13 states and the District of Columbia have fully restructured their retail electricity markets—that is, they have implemented retail competition across all customer segments (industrial, commercial and residential). Another 6 states have implemented partial restructuring: they offer competition across some but not all market segments, or have otherwise limited competition to a specified portion of the market. Finally, 5 more states have suspended or repealed their restructuring laws in the wake of the California electricity crisis of 2000–01. The momentum behind retail restructuring was dissipated by the California electricity crisis; however, in the last few years, Ohio, Michigan and a few other states have begun to explore the expansion of retail competition within their borders. And California has reinstated competition for some customer classes, though not residential customers.

In its 2014 assessment of retail competition in U.S. states and Canadian provinces, the Compete Coalition (which advocates retail competition) concluded that competition is maturing in competitive jurisdictions, as evidenced by diversification of product offerings (mostly contracts and contract features) to customers by retailers, and the creation of more market niches. Compete also produced the following table, which offers one measure of the robustness of competition across jurisdictions:

Residential Customers Taking Competitive Electric Service

Jurisdiction	Customers
Texas	5,854,000
Illinois	3,077,000
Ohio	2,106,000
Pennsylvania	1,877,000
New York	1,389,000
Connecticut	605,000
Alberta	542,000
New Jersey	536,000
Maryland	524,000
Massachusetts	399,000
Maine	214,000

Figure 10–4

Compete Coalition, Annual Baseline Assessment of Choice in Canada and the United States (2014), http://www.competecoalition.com/files/ABACCUS-2014-vf.pdf. Customer switching is a key indicator of the vitality of a retail market. While one or two states saw significant rates of customer switching early in the restructuring process, others (including some near the top of this list) did not, and had to work hard to develop their markets. Competition has indeed matured in some states, but the specter of California's spectacular failure still hangs over retail competition. (Notice California's absence from the Compete Coalition list.)

To get a flavor for the variety of approaches states have taken to restructure their retail electricity markets, consider the restructuring experience in four states: we will revisit California, and take a brief look at restructuring in New York, Pennsylvania, and Texas.

i.   California

In the 1990s, Californians paid more for electricity than their neighbors in Oregon and Washington. As in other states, the pressure to reduce electric rates in California came in the first instance from major industrial users that believed competition would lower their electric rates. California's efforts to adopt retail competition began in 1994, when the California Public Utilities Commission (CPUC) adopted a rule designed to allow all customers in the state a choice of their electricity supplier by the year 2002. In May 1995, after analysis of the changing electricity industry and many hearings around the state to get input from industry experts, utilities, consumer organizations, and the public, the CPUC proposed a policy for introducing competition in California's electric industry. Later that year, after additional public comment, the CPUC adopted a final policy and began to plan the transition to the new market.

In 1996, California Governor Pete Wilson signed AB 1890, a bill designed to facilitate the transition to retail competition in the state. The California act spelled out in detail provisions designed to address (1) stranded cost recovery, (2) organization of the new industry structure, (3) protection of system reliability, (4) funding of public purpose and environmental programs, and (5) consumer protection. To facilitate the transition to retail competition, the California act envisioned that state-chartered, non-profit institutions would play an integral role in the new industry structure. An ISO would "ensure efficient use and reliable operation of the transmission grid." A power exchange (CalPX), open to all buyers and sellers on a nondiscriminatory basis, would operate an "efficient, competitive auction" for the buying and selling of power. There would also be an Oversight Board for the ISO and the CalPX. The Act required both investor-owned and publicly-owned utilities to commit control of their transmission facilities to the ISO and jointly file transmission rates with FERC. After prolonged negotiations, the three major utilities and some larger electricity users agreed on a proposal for an ISO and submitted it to FERC for approval in April of 1996. The California legislature effectively endorsed that proposal by passing AB 1890.

The three primary companies that distribute electricity in California were Pacific Gas and Electric Co. (PG & E), which covers northern California, Southern California Edison (SCE) and San Diego Gas & Electric (SDG & E), which serve the southern parts of the state. In addition, there are some substantial municipal systems, including the City of Los Angeles. By law, PG & E, SCE, and SDG & E were required to reduce residential and small commercial electric rates by 10 percent on January 1, 1998. This seemed to provide protection to retail customers in California, and indeed was promoted that way. In addition, PG & E, Edison and SDG & E would now have to purchase electricity from the CalPX at market prices that fluctuated by the day, hour, and even by ten-minute segments, depending on demand and supply conditions.

The CPUC reviewed and approved incumbent utilities' stranded costs as reasonable, and authorized utilities to recover them through a competitive transition charge between 1998 and 2001. The CalPX began trading on April 1, 1998. Under its rules, distribution utilities that also own generation were required to sell their generated electricity to the power exchange and repurchase it at the spot market price prior to selling it to their incumbent customers. This paper transaction was meant to effectively unbundle generation and distribution. *See* Peter Fox-Penner, Electric Utility Restructuring: A Guide to the Competitive Era 211–13 (1997).

As has been noted above, the years 2000 and 2001 were disastrous for California's electricity market. During the early summer of 2000, electricity prices began a rapid increase. The high prices and system emergencies threatened by the fall and winter of 2001 to send the state's electricity system into total failure. The crisis sent two of the state's largest companies to the edge of bankruptcy and derailed the state's retail competition plan. On September 20, 2001, the CPUC suspended retail competition in the state. CPUC, Interim Opinion Suspending Direct Access, D. 01–09–060 (Sept. 20, 2001).

Much has been written about the failure of retail competition in California, and the causes of the crisis are both well-known and multiple. So many events came together to bring the state into crisis that commentators have referred to them as the "perfect storm," after the then-popular movie of the same name. California relied on electricity imported from other states for up to 25 percent of its generation needs. However, the surrounding states (which exported power to California) were growing rapidly themselves, and needed more power. Second, the Pacific Northwest, from which California bought power, experienced a drought that adversely affected generation of hydroelectric power (prevalent in the region) at just the time that California needed it most. Much of California's in-state electricity generation depends on natural gas, which skyrocketed in price during 2000–2001. California's gas prices rose to three and four times the national average, contributing to higher electricity prices. Restrictions on long-term contracts meant that the CalPX was a spot market, and the utilities could only buy power one day ahead, which exposed them even more to the fluctuations in electricity prices. California's largest utilities, encouraged by regulations to do so, had sold off their generation assets (although they were not required to do so), and that left them even more exposed to the spot market. The rate freeze protected customers from rising rates but put utilities in a terrible bind. When wholesale prices skyrocketed, the utilities were purchasing power at high wholesale rates, but selling it at low frozen retail rates. And we have already discussed another problem with the California market in 2000–01: namely, the manipulation of the California market by Enron and other power traders and sellers.

California served as a cautionary tale for other states (and nations) considering the move to retail competition. Several states abandoned restructuring after the crisis, and a few even returned to traditional regulation from retail competition. However, in the ensuing years we have settled into a kind of equilibrium in which a large number of states remain comfortable with traditional retail regulation, another sizeable group have grown comfortable with markets and competition, and a few seem inclined to explore expanding competition within their borders.

ii.   New York and Pennsylvania

The road to the upper reaches of the Compete Coalition's list of efficient retail electricity markets was much less exciting for the states of New York and Pennsylvania. Both states now boast competitive retail markets in which retail customers can choose their power supplier at a power shopping web site: the http://www.newyorkpowertochoose.com/ site in New York, and the www.papowerswitch.com website in Pennsylvania.

New York has the distinction of being the only state whose PUC effected the transition to competitive retail markets without the necessity of state legislation. The state's retail prices in the 1990s were above the national average, like much of the rest of the northeast. As part of a process it initiated in 1996, the PUC approved individual utility transition plans proposed by incumbent IOUs, and put in place procedures that gave electric customers access to competitive retailers, known in New York as energy service companies or "ESCOs." New York assigned to the incumbent distribution company the obligation to provide default service to customers who did not switch suppliers. By 2002 the competition plans had been implemented in each of the incumbent IOUs' service territories. The transition to competition in New York has generated relatively little controversy, and customer switching has happened gradually. According to the Independent Power Producers of New York, a trade group, competition has spurred investment of nearly $6 billion in New York power plants since 1999, and an additional 2,000 megawatts of generation is currently under construction.

Like New York, Pennsylvania moved forward with retail competition in the late 1990s. The state's retail electricity rates in the 1990s were 15% over the national average, the eleventh highest average electricity price of the 50 states. The Pennsylvania PUC believed that moving toward a competitive market might result in savings of as much as 25% for consumers in the state. As noted above in the description of the Pennsylvania plan, the state proposed to allow consumers to choose an electricity generation supplier. A local distribution company would continue to provide transmission and distribution, and would continue to be regulated.

Hearing on Status of Electric Restructuring in Pennsylvania and H.B. 1841 Pennsylvania House Consumer Affairs Committee (Mar. 4, 2004), Testimony of Sonny Popowsky, Consumer Advocate

Several weeks ago I had the opportunity to speak at a conference . . . that was entitled: Pennsylvania's *Electric Restructuring at its Midpoint: Is it on the Right Track?* As the statutory representative of

Pennsylvania's electricity consumers, my answer to that question was: *Yes.* Now, if the question had been phrased differently, that is: *Is Pennsylvania Electric Restructuring on the Track That You Expected?*, my answer would have been: *No.*

So, how was it possible for me to conclude that we are going in the right direction, even though it is not the direction that I anticipated? I think . . . the framework that we developed has continued to work even as the retail market that we anticipated has not developed in the manner that many of us expected. I would contrast the Pennsylvania experience with the contemporaneous experience in California. . . . In Pennsylvania, we established a framework that may have lacked the ideological purity of the spot market design of California, but had a sufficient level of protection for consumers and flexibility for utilities that, even as unexpected setbacks occurred, the restructuring program as a whole has continued to advance. Also, it is important to note that we had the good fortune in Pennsylvania of building our restructured retail electric model on the foundation of what was at the time, and remains today, the most sophisticated and reliable wholesale electricity structure in the Nation— the PJM Interconnection.

So what did I expect would happen after 1996, and why do I think we are still on the right track even though it is not the track I expected us to be on? Basically, by 2004, I had expected that the majority of Pennsylvania consumers, including residential consumers, would be receiving their generation service from someone other than their local electric distribution company. In the electric pilot program in 1996, more than a million Pennsylvania consumers volunteered for the 230,000 slots in that program. There was a tremendous amount of excitement about electric choice, generated in part by a humorous and informative public education campaign. Our utilities even insisted on a "phase-in" provision in the restructuring act so that no more than a third of Pennsylvania consumers would be able to switch suppliers on the first day the market opened. Indeed, some of those early expectations were not that far off. By April 2000, just 15 months after the market opened throughout Pennsylvania, more than 500,000 Pennsylvania consumers were being served by alternative providers, including more than 25% of the residential customers of Duquesne Light Company and 15% of the residential customers of PECO Energy. In the PECO service territory alone, there were 17 active electric generation suppliers offering 23 different products to residential customers. As to industrial customers, by April 2000, more than 60% of the industrial load for PECO, PPL and GPU was being served by alternative suppliers.

By the beginning of 2004, however, most of the competitive suppliers who had been serving residential customers in Pennsylvania had either gone bankrupt or had simply abandoned the market. Except for PECO and Duquesne, the combined market share of all the competitive suppliers in the residential market of all the other electric utilities was less than 0.5%. The industrial market share for competitive suppliers in the PECO service territory dropped from 63% to less than 5%.

While I expect that shopping for industrial customers will rebound in the future, I now believe that the vast majority of residential customers in Pennsylvania will continue to receive generation service through their electric distribution company indefinitely.

Is that such a terrible thing? Not in my opinion. As I mentioned earlier, the Pennsylvania restructuring plan was flexible enough to protect consumers even if things didn't work out the way we may have hoped or expected. The most obvious protection was our long-term rate caps. . . . With rate caps in place, customers have not suffered as a result of the lack of robust retail competition. Rates paid by nearly all Pennsylvania electric consumers are no higher than the rates paid by those customers in 1996. In the case of Duquesne Light Company, where stranded cost recovery and the initial rate caps expired in 2002, rates were actually reduced at that time to a level that was more than 20% lower than they were prior to restructuring. In other words, just because the original rate caps expired, that didn't mean that Duquesne ratepayers lost their regulatory protections. On the contrary, Duquesne filed a new rate plan to serve those customers who did not shop in the competitive market and the overall prices under that plan were 20% less than they had been prior to the passage of our restructuring law in 1996.

Some people have argued that our rate caps themselves prevent robust competition and that we should let our utilities raise their prices as high as the market will bear, and then competitors will appear. The problem with that argument, I believe, is that it confuses ends with means. The goal of restructuring was not to force consumers to pay ever higher rates to their utilities until they were forced into the market. In my view, to the extent that competitive suppliers offer benefits to consumers, either in the form of lower prices or value-added services, such as "green" or renewable power, then that is a benefit we should seek to obtain. But the "default" service that customers have a right to continue to receive from their utility under Pennsylvania law should be at least as good as the service they were receiving prior to restructuring. Our goal in 1996 was to make consumers better off, not worse off. And I think consumers are better off. As I said, customers across Pennsylvania today are paying no more than, and, in the case of Duquesne, substantially less than, they were paying under our prior form of regulation. In real, inflation-adjusted terms, of course, virtually all Pennsylvania consumers are paying lower rates today than they were in 1996.

While shopping has dropped substantially, nearly all Pennsylvania consumers continue to be able to choose a "green" alternative, and I believe more than 100,000 Pennsylvania consumers have taken advantage of that choice even though they recognize that the green supplier is typically more expensive than the standard utility service. I also do not think it is a coincidence that as generation choice became available to retail consumers in Pennsylvania, the choices made by generation builders in Pennsylvania changed as well. So today, when you drive along the Pennsylvania Turnpike, you can not only see smokestacks and cooling towers in the distance, but you can also see powerful windmills serving a still small but increasing portion of our electric needs. I would also add that a less-noticed provision of both our electric and natural gas restructuring laws in Pennsylvania was the addition of the concept of "universal service" to our energy vocabulary and a requirement that all of our utilities either maintain or expand vital programs needed to keep low-income and payment troubled customers connected to these vital life-giving services.

Finally, as I noted earlier, the Pennsylvania restructuring program has meshed well with the wholesale market that has thrived in the PJM Interconnection. I have long believed that the greatest benefits of generation competition would be reflected in the wholesale market. Those wholesale market benefits flow through directly to those retail customers who choose alternate suppliers. But even for customers who stay with their electric distribution company, a robust wholesale market will be essential when generation rate caps expire and the default service that is provided by our electric distribution companies will almost certainly be based in large part on wholesale market prices.

I am not testifying that everything has worked perfectly in Pennsylvania's electric restructuring. Far from it. I am particularly concerned that, despite the explicit requirement in our 1996 legislation that service reliability must be maintained at least at the levels that were present prior to restructuring, we have seen a deterioration in service quality statistics for some of our major utilities. The PUC has recently opened a formal investigation into that issue for three of our companies. I am also concerned about the impact on certain of our utilities resulting from unregulated investments around the Nation and around the world that have led to real damage to those companies' financial standing even as they have continued, to their credit, to meet their obligations to their Pennsylvania ratepayers. In the wholesale market, I am concerned with the continuing lack of a robust reliability and market structure in the Midwest region, which I believe contributed to the inexcusable Northeast Blackout of August 14, 2003. Finally, I am concerned that our increasing reliance on natural gas as the fuel of choice for nearly all new generating plants could leave electric consumers exposed to higher and increasingly volatile wholesale energy prices in the future and at the same time result in higher prices for natural gas customers who use natural gas for home heating and other industrial processes. Overall, however, I remain optimistic that we will continue on a track that will serve the long-term interests of Pennsylvania consumers and that the benefits of restructuring to consumers will continue to exceed the costs . . . ∎

Since that testimony by the Pennsylvania Consumer Advocate, customer switching and choice has grown in Pennsylvania. The state now has about 50 competitive retail suppliers, whose sales represent about 60 percent of the electricity sold at retail in the state. The Retail Energy Supply Association, a trade group, agrees with Compete Coalition's characterization of the Pennsylvania market as a successful one. Pennsylvania's retail rate caps expired in 2011.

As part of the process of transitioning to retail competition, Pennsylvania required that utilities bid out the privilege of serving non-switching consumers. The "Competitive Default Service" program required 20% of a utility's residential customers—determined by random selection, including low-income and inability-to-pay customers—to be assigned to a default supplier other than the utility. A lack of interest in competitive bidding for these customers prompted PECO Energy to develop a program (with PUC approval) under which non-shoppers were assigned to a new supplier for service. In 2003, customers were randomly assigned to the winning bidders and received a 1.25 percent discount from PECO's generation and transmission rates for at least one year. Those who wished to decline the switch could do so with no penalty.

iii. Texas

Texas took yet a different route to retail competition, one that spurred the creation of a robust, competitive market much more quickly than other states. The following excerpt describes the unique features of the Texas market.

Lynne Kiesling, Retail Restructuring and Market Design in Texas Electricity Restructuring: The Texas Story
154–73 (2009).

Retail competition became law in Texas on June 18, 1999, when Governor George W. Bush signed Senate Bill 7. SB7 provided for a phased-in transition to full retail choice in the Electric Reliability Council of Texas (ERCOT) region by January 1, 2002, with a transition period, including pilot programs, commencing in 2001, and the institution of a retail price transition mechanism for residential and small commercial customers called the "price to beat" (PTB). Although the implementation of SB 7 has faced challenges, most notably the political difficulty of designing and implementing retail restructuring and competition during a period of rising fuel input costs, it has successfully expanded choice for Texas consumers of all sizes, increased cost savings and production efficiency in the industry, and delivered improvements in environmental quality in Texas. . . .

SB 7's Retail Market Design

The retail market design in Texas focused on several dimensions of making the transition from a vertically integrated, regulated utility to an unbundled industry with competitive generation and retail, using regulated transmission and distribution wire services. The market design focused both on structural rules leading to changes in the firms themselves and behavioral rules that shaped the incentives facing incumbents and new entrants.

Unbundling and Participation. SB 7 lead to the foundation for opening the Texas markets to rival retail electricity providers (REPs). REPs are parties that purchase power from generators and provide customer service to the final customer. SB 7 required incumbent utilities to unbundle the four components of the traditional vertically integrated supply chain: generation, transmission, distribution, and retail marketing. . . . The form of unbundling was largely functional, not structural; incumbents could retain ownership of unregulated retail affiliates and of generation capacity, but had to create separate functional units for power generation, power delivery (the transmission and distribution utility, or TDU), and retail sales. They were also required to divest their generation assets in excess of 20 percent of their native service territory load. Municipal utilities and cooperatives were not required to participate, but they could choose to do so.

The Price-to-Beat Transition Mechanism. The "price to beat" mechanism included in SB 7 provided some retail rate stability by ensuring that a fixed, regulated rate would be available for small customers during the transition. Under it, an affiliated retail electric provider (AREP) could not charge its native residential and small commercial customers a rate lower than its PTB rate. This price floor remained in effect until January 1, 2005, or until the AREP lost 40% of its residential and small commercial load, at which point the AREP could lower its prices. Between January 1, 2002, and December 31, 2006, the PTB would also act as a price ceiling, providing a default service contract for small customers in the AREP's native service territory. As the end of the transition period approached, the PUCT [Public Utility Commission of Texas] could evaluate whether a retail market was sufficiently competitive to allow the PTB to expire on January 1, 2007, as planned. . . .

Provider of Last Resort. SB 7 also required the PUCT to designate provider of last resort (POLR) REPs for each area to serve residential customers who did not actively choose a REP, or whose REP had left the market. Each POLR would offer a standard retail service package at a fixed rate and serve the customers of REPs that exited the market or otherwise failed to serve them. . . .

Renewable Energy. The issues of renewable energy and the environmental impact of increasing electricity demand also drew the attention of legislators and regulators. SB 7 contained a renewable portfolio standard (RPS), which was designed and implemented in late 1999. The legislation required the construction of 400 MW of renewable energy resources by 2003 and 850 MW by January 2005, scaling up to installation of 2000 MW in total by 2009. . . .

Consumer Education, Protection, and the System Benefit Fund. Retail restructuring had the potential to create unanticipated and hitherto unknown outcomes for consumers, particularly for residential consumers who had not previously had opportunities for retail choice. . . . These concerns led to provisions in SB 7 for consumer education and protection, with the objective of ensuring that consumers, including low income and non-English-speaking consumers, were sufficiently knowledgeable about retail competition and choice to make informed decisions. . . . The provisions in SB 7 for creating and funding a system benefit fund (SBF) were intended to assist low income consumers with budget difficulties. Although each utility established its own assistance plan for low income customers under regulation, such a plan was not likely to be feasible under retail competition. The SBF included in the wires charge a mandatory customer charge per kilowatt hour to fund [consumer education and low income benefit programs] . . .

Transition Period, 2002–6. The transition period began on January 1, 2002. Large commercial and industrial customers (with peak demand greater than 1 MW) were already prepared for their rapid transition, as they had neither a PTB price transition mechanism nor designated POLRs with which to contend. All residential and small commercial and industrial customers who had not chosen a REP were transferred from the utility to the AREP on January 1, 2002, at the PTB rate.

Although the PTB rate represented a 6 percent discount on the regulated rate, new REPs were entering the market in all regions and could compete against the AREP's PTB. The fact that REPs were entering the market and providing competitive residential services suggests that they anticipated being able to compete against the discounted PTB rate, which was consistent with the objectives of the PTB and the inclusion of headroom in it.

Current Snapshot: Outcomes and Consequences of Retail Competition

The PTB mechanism expired on January 1, 2007, opening the full Texas market to retail competition. How are consumers and producers faring now, compared to the regulated environment in 1999? Is there evidence that total surplus has increased? . . .

Although the high natural gas prices and hurricanes in 2005 induced increases in both the PTB and the prices offered by REPs, the Texas retail market design adapted to those strains, and today it shows demonstrable evidence of success. Many competitors have entered and offered a variety of products, customer switching has been active, AREPs have changed their product offerings to retain customers, and new investment has occurred, with more planned. . . .

Texas customers can choose from a wide range of retailers and products, amounting to over 95 products from more than 25 providers in each region, and enough switching has occurred that REPs now provide the majority of energy sold (across all consumer classes) in the ERCOT region. In comparison both to the performance of a regulated market and that of retail restructuring in other states, the extent and variety of choice in Texas are impressive. Judging by entry, rivalry, and product differentiation, this institutional change has been successful. When performance is measured by number of customers instead of by energy consumption, 40 percent of residential customers have chosen a REP, which also indicates the success of retail competition in Texas under difficult circumstances.

The most striking differences between current market conditions and regulated conditions are evident in both retail and wholesale prices. Recall that the last regulated rate in 2001 included a 6 percent discount on previous rates, and that since 2001 natural gas prices had tripled. Six years later, three of the five regions with retail competition had competitive offers available in the market that were lower than the last regulated rate—a reflection of the competitive pressure exerted by retail competition on wholesale markets as well. ■

NOTES AND COMMENTS

1.   Wholesale and retail electricity prices did increase, as Kiesling notes, until around 2010, after which prices fell somewhat. Texas was one of the few low-cost states to move to retail competition, and the movement of rates may be attributable in large part to variation in the market price of natural gas, because the majority of generation in ERCOT is fueled by natural gas. From the 2002 opening of the retail market to competition through 2008, natural gas prices increased approximately 150% and wholesale electricity prices more than doubled. Since then, the drop in gas prices has been accompanied by a less steep drop in electricity prices.

2.   The "price to beat" was a form of government intervention in the market, one designed to promote competition among and with the incumbent utilities. The Texas market has eschewed (so far) another form of intervention common to other organized markets: namely, capacity payments. Generators of power must recover their costs on the competitive wholesale market, and cannot earn capacity payments, as generators can in places (NE RTO, NY ISO, PJM) with capacity markets that reward

generators for their commitments to provide electricity in the future. Because retail customers typically sign contracts of no more than 1 year with their retailers, generators typically cannot secure long term PPAs with retailers. All of which creates a natural experiment. Will wholesale prices offer sufficient incentive for prospective investors to invest in Texas markets, or will reserve margins dwindle below target levels? Will regulators and politicians allow the experiment to continue, or will they intervene to provide an additional incentive to build or provide reserve capacity? A 2012 report by the economic consultants Brattle Group projected that reserves would fall below target levels by 2015. *See* Samuel Newell, et al., ERCOT Investment Incentives and Resource Adequacy, June 1, 2012, http://www.ercot.com/content/news/presentations/2013/Brattle%20ERCOT%20Resource%20Adequacy%20Review%20-%202012-06-01.pdf. As of this writing, in lieu of a capacity market the PUC of Texas is exploring intervening in the market in a different way: it is considering changing the way ancillary services are priced in the ERCOT market, and imposing an administratively-determined price for operating reserves. Ancillary services are last-minute services, such as rerouting power through different lines or sending additional power through the grid from a peaker plant, which are provided to ensure that supply is balanced with demand, and a constant voltage in the grid maintained.

3. THE FUTURE OF STATE RESTRUCTURING

There is no consensus answer to the question whether restructuring will be beneficial in the long run. In the nearly two decades of restructuring, scholars and interest groups have maintained a continual and unresolved debate over the question of whether restructuring is working as intended. The American Public Power Association (APPA), an association of municipal utilities, published an analysis showing that between 1997 and 2011, increases in retail electric prices were significantly greater in states with deregulated electric markets than in regulated states. APPA, Retail Electric Rates in Regulated and Deregulated States: 2011 Update (2012). Using the same EIA data, the Electric Power Suppliers Association claims that "organized wholesale markets have seen dramatic price declines as a result of competitive forces," and have provided a variety of other benefits to consumers. John E. Shelk & Glen Thomas, How Consumers are Benefiting, and Will Continue to Benefit, From Competitive Electricity Markets, Electricity Pol'y J. 1 (Mar. 2013). The Compete Coalition has also published analyses supporting the idea that competitive markets bring lower prices and more consumer choice.

The crux of the disagreement seems to be over what to do about the aspects of electricity markets that promote price volatility—the inability to store the product in commercial quantities, the relative inelasticity of demand, barriers to (rapid) entry, etc. While the California market was uniquely susceptible to the acquisition and abuse of market power, these characteristics mean that some version of the California problem can arise in any market where there are sufficiently few sellers and/or sufficiently small supply margins. Indeed, regulators, RTOs/ISOs and market monitors remain focused on these issues. There is a high degree of agreement that the road to the marketplace will be bumpy, but disagreement over whether electricity markets can be structured to realize the promise of competition. The following two excerpts address these questions.

Jacqueline Lang Weaver, Can Energy Markets Be Trusted? The Effect of the Rise and Fall of Enron on Energy Markets

Houston Bus. & Tax L. J. 1, 131–140 (2004).

After California, retail electricity deregulation is a much harder political sell. But even before that state's chaos made headlines for so many months, thoughtful commentators had questioned whether the small consumer would benefit from deregulated energy markets in contrast to large industrial and commercial users. It is very difficult to allow incumbent utilities to recover their stranded costs and also prevent prices to the consumer from rising, while simultaneously providing enough profit margin for new competitors to enter the markets and erode the monopoly power of the local incumbent. Even for larger users, price volatility is a serious business risk for companies that no longer rely completely on long-term contracts for their energy supplies. Risk management tools may not be adequate to hedge against risk that extends beyond a few years.

Small wonder, then, that in electricity—with its peculiar needs for spare capacity and real-time balancing of the grid minute by minute—the transition to competitive markets will be much more difficult than in other industries. The federal/state jurisdictional issues, stranded costs, inelastic demand for electricity, and the ineffectiveness of antitrust laws and other regulatory reviews to assess and curb monopoly power add enormously to the complexity of the sheer physics of electricity markets. In a widely publicized report, Consumers Union looked at the effects of deregulation in the airlines, trucking, cable TV, banking, telephone, and electricity markets, and scored deregulation in terms of price savings, consumer rights, safety, consumer choice, and innovation. All industries present a mixed picture, ranging from the woeful $160 billion government bailout of 1,600 bank failures in the savings-and-loan crisis of the early 1990s, to the success of Southwest Airlines as an efficient, low-cost carrier. Yes—prices have dropped in most of the deregulated industries, but prices were falling before deregulation, often at a faster rate, a fact seldom recognized by proponents of deregulation.

In longer reports, this consumer organization looked more closely at electricity deregulation. Electricity deregulation in many states, not just California, had been too often accompanied by abuse of market power, excessive scarcity overcharges, inefficient transactions costs of coordinating the complex system, and a sharp increase in the cost of capital, all of which may have swamped any conceivable efficiency gains. Lower electricity prices to date are often due to mandated regulatory price decreases, not to deregulation. In major respects, the Consumer Federation is right: deregulation has produced decidedly mixed results. The question is: Do we move forward in electricity markets, learning from past mistakes, or do we go back to a less complex system that, whatever its inefficiencies, never produced the chaos that now enshrouds the entire industry? The public utility model, for all its faults, generally delivered reliable power and reserve margins at reasonable prices. How can competition and deregulation provide this essential reliability without a high degree of coordination, interrelatedness, and centralized planning? Even the top utility regulator in Texas sounded like a central planner the minute that power companies in the state started shutting down plants in the midst of a surplus of generating capacity, saying, "We can't take for granted these blessed reserves," so new rules would be needed to protect against future power shortages. In essence, have markets met their match in electricity?

. . . So, should we plunge forward, as Alfred Kahn suggests, or engage in dialogue first about the morality and rationality of markets? . . . The ultimate test of electricity markets will be how industry participants, regulators, and consumers react to shortages that may arise after 2005. It is relatively easy to regulate when excess capacity exists—and quite difficult when it disappears, as California discovered. It is still not clear whether FERC's proposed Standard Market Design or Wholesale Market Platform has provided adequate market incentives and regulatory mandates to assure investment in transmission assets and reserve generating capacity.

. . . The new paradigm views the goals of regulation as the promotion of competition and consumer choice. Once in place, competition and choice will police the markets without much need for a regulatory bureaucracy. "Light-handed" regulation will suffice. The reasons for this paradigm shift have been found to be twofold: first, key interest groups, notably large business interests, discovered that deregulation was to their advantage; and second, economists and other policy elites reached an ideological consensus that the risks of regulatory failure under the original paradigm exceeded the risk of market failure under the new paradigm.

As noted earlier, large industrial and commercial users are the chief recipients of benefits from competition in electricity and natural gas (although these lower prices should ultimately "trickle through" to lower-priced manufactured products for consumers). Furthermore, there is so much money being spent on political lobbying by every major group within the electricity industry that cynics say Congress has little incentive to resolve energy issues quickly. As to the ideological consensus, strongly fostered by economists, that markets are superior to regulation, there is little doubt that that this has been a major factor in electricity restructuring. This ideology explains FERC's long reluctance to intervene in the chaos of California and California's own embrace of a Power Exchange as the ultimate market of all power markets. The California crisis precipitated an extraordinary round of competing "manifestos" by prominent economists. The true believers urged officials to resist any form of price cap, while those who recognized the reality of dysfunctional markets, including Alfred Kahn, urged regulatory intervention. Another manifesto was issued in early 2003, urging California to create commodity market institutions, to implement real-time pricing, and to "rely on markets whenever possible."

But when are markets "possible"? . . . The primary lesson of California is that . . . light-handed regulation combined with the entrepreneurial, profit-maximizing behavior of private participants in electricity markets does not serve the public well. So, can electricity markets be trusted? Here again is Fukuyama's definition of trust as "the expectation that arises within a community of regular, honest, and cooperative behavior." I think the easy answer is: no. They cannot be trusted to work without a high degree of government intervention that true believers will continue to find "offensive" and continue to criticize as retarding the "dazzling benefits" that markets can provide. In this conclusion, I have the company of others:

[T]he process of deregulation is more corruptible than the process of regulation. . . . [I]t is absolutely clear that if we are to pursue "deregulation," then we must be willing to regulate deregulation.

Alan Richardson, American Public Power Association President, June 2002.

The curious paradox of a market-based regulatory reform [in electricity] is that we may end up with more rather than less regulation.

Joseph P. Tomain, Dean and Professor of Law, 2002

And will the government intervention be well-designed even when it incorporates lessons learned from experience? FERC has learned this lesson from its study of market problems in California and the Northeast:

Small details of market design can turn out to have major effects on market performance.

FERC's proposal for Standard Market Design, July 2002.

If the "devil is in the details," but the details are so difficult to get right because electricity has such unique attributes, then it is time to say that markets have met their match in this arena. In even simpler markets, such as one-time auctions for the telecommunications spectrum, "disastrous" results have occurred because "superficially trivial" distinctions between policy proposals were actually quite important and because the economic consultants' market design, while sound in theory, could not translate into good policymaking, given real-world political pressures, including lobbying from the regulated industry.

Certainly, electricity markets can and will be designed to avoid the more obvious flaws in California's noble, but failed, experiment. But, the real question is whether deregulated energy markets will produce a better grade than the C+ that [FERC Chairman] Pat Wood gave to traditional utility regulation. The FERC Chairman is hoping for a grade of B for restructured markets. In my mind, the mid-term grade to date for deregulation is a U for "unsatisfactory." Residential consumers have for too long been wooed with hyperbolic promises of great benefits from electricity deregulation—lower rates, more reliability, and greater choice. There is little evidence that restructured markets will reduce electricity rates in any meaningful amount for the residential consumer.

The poor performance of retail competition hinders the development of wholesale markets by undermining investment incentives for distribution companies and other retail providers to enter into long-term contracts with new investors for generation and transmission service. Without new entrants, incumbents are left with market power that regulators will intervene to suppress when prices rise as supply margins narrow. Reliability becomes more precarious as the industry "de-integrates" into competitive rather than coordinated units. In addition, no one in these new markets—except traders, sometimes—appears to like the volatility that has accompanied deregulation. The dreadful

"Averch-Johnson inefficiency" of regulated utilities does not seem to have been so large that deregulation will capture significant gains that regulators were not already capturing through incentive-based performance standards, mandatory competitive bidding by utilities for new generation supplies, and other mechanisms that were lowering electricity rates before restructuring began. ∎

David B. Spence, Can Law Manage Competitive Energy Markets?
93 Cornell L. Rev. 765, 809–17 (2008).

While there is some disagreement about the particular effects of restructuring on prices, restructuring has not brought the kind of general decline in energy prices across customer classes that many expected. . . . Whether or not prices are lower than they would have been but for restructuring, they certainly are not lower than they were before restructuring. It is clear that prices remain high in many places and large price disparities persist across regions. In the fourth quarter of 2006, residential retail customers in New England paid . . . about twice as much for electricity as their counterparts in the central part of the country. More importantly, those consumers facing the highest prices reside in the very states that pursued electricity restructuring, while their counterparts living in regions where retail restructuring was not the norm continue to pay less. . . .

To what factors can we attribute the persistence of high prices and regional rate disparities? Some analysts ascribe the bulk of the problem to increases in the cost of inputs. . . . Others ascribe high prices to [the] general problem of too few sellers chasing too many customers, a problem that offers the few sellers in the market the opportunity to exert market power over prices. This "too few sellers" problem, in turn, may result from regulators' inability to prevent incumbents sellers from imposing entry barriers on prospective competitors. If this analysis is correct, there is a broken market equilibrium in energy, one in which incumbents' market power is self-sustaining; in other words, incumbents' market power may be both cause and consequence of barriers to entry in energy markets. Regulators and policymakers are devoting a great deal of effort to understanding this dynamic and to replacing the current broken market equilibrium with a functioning competitive market equilibrium. . . .

If markets are to achieve efficiency benefits, they will do so through price signals spurred by market forces. That does not mean prices will simply decline monotonically; to the contrary, they will move in both directions, reflecting the forces of supply and demand. When prices are low, demand will rise and supply will fall; when prices are high, demand will fall and new sellers will enter the market, increasing supply. Economic theory tells us that in this way, the up and down movement of prices yields an efficient result over the long run, yet it remains unclear whether we are actually realizing any of the efficiency in energy markets. Restructuring is apparently nearing a crossroads where market skeptics and markets proponents will have to confront one another more openly.

Market skeptics look at the current state of energy markets and wonder why this experiment in restructuring has gone as far as it has. They compare current energy prices to prices before restructuring and conclude that market efficiency is a chimera, at least in energy markets. They doubt that energy markets *can* work efficiently. Perhaps, they say, vertical integration is the more efficient approach in energy markets: in a market where good network management requires flexibility and speed, perhaps unbundling and arms length transactions create *in*efficiency rather than efficiency. These market skeptics see regulators attempts to fine tune markets as a poor substitute for regulation. All this fine tuning, they say, seeks to do what price regulation or state ownership used to do: namely to guarantee prospective investors in new capacity a sufficient return on investment to assure adequate capacity reserves over the long run. Furthermore, while fine tuning markets may be able to induce investors to invest in new capacity, it does not necessarily protect consumers from all short-term price fluctuations. . . .

Proponents of markets, on the other hand, many argue that it takes time for markets to mature. To compare current prices to pre-restructuring prices is to compare apples to oranges, they say. Rather, we should compare current prices under restructuring to what current prices would have been under regulated markets. The jury is still out on that question, but in any case, energy markets are young, and regulators deserve time to set the conditions that will allow those markets to realize the promise of lower prices for average consumers. We may find that some vertical integration is efficient and that markets can accommodate that efficiency. For example, it may be efficient to permit sellers of energy to own some sources of supply (such as production facilities). On the other hand, integrating transmission and production is probably not efficient, and well-designed, independently managed transmission service operators can probably provide network management services more efficiently than a vertically integrated firm can. If politicians can resist the temptation to distort price signals, markets can work, say their proponents. The proponents' view, however, offers no comfort to politicians concerned about protecting consumers from high prices.

There is no reasonable way to proceed until regulators and politicians acknowledge both the economic and political imperatives of restructuring: (i) that market efficiency cannot be realized if politicians intervene to protect consumers from price increases caused by energy scarcity (or if there is a significant risk that politicians will do so); and (ii) that vulnerable customers cannot be subjected to unaffordable energy costs. Thus, politicians must find alternative ways to protect vulnerable consumers from price volatility—ways that do not distort price signals. If politicians (responding to voter preferences) cannot or will not find those alternatives, then markets will continue to struggle with shortages, seller market power, and price volatility. Such a case may indicate that voters prefer the certainty of (potentially higher) regulated prices to the risks (and potential benefits) that market prices bring. ∎

NOTES AND COMMENTS

1. Interest groups as widely divergent in their perspective on governmental regulation as the libertarian think tank Cato Institute and the consumer group National Association of State PIRGs have criticized retail competition in electricity. The Cato report from 2004, "Rethinking Electricity Restructuring," prefers full deregulation of the industry but, noting it would be politically difficult, calls for the electric power industry to embrace an

updated version of its former regulated, vertically integrated structure because restructuring has led to spectacular failures in the states. Cato Inst., Rethinking Electricity Restructuring, http://www.cato.org/pubs/pas/pa530. pdf. Others strongly disagree. Laura Murrell and Ken Malloy, Ctr. for the Advancement of Energy Markets, Throwing the Baby out with the Bathwater: A Rebuttal to Cato's Report 'Rethinking Electricity Restructuring' (2004), http://www.caem.org, offer this criticism:

> "Adam Smith must be rolling over in his grave. . . . Rather than constructively engaging on making the open access model work—a model of competition that is both politically feasible and has delivered significant benefits to in telecom and natural gas—CATO takes the bizarre position that the U.S. return to the monopoly model," said Malloy.

> The open access model in electricity has unquestionably suffered setbacks in the last several years. "This is no time to cut and run. It is a time for the supporters of competitive electric markets to regroup and develop an action plan that learns from the past setbacks. The Cato report is a wake-up call that we have a lot of work to do," said Malloy.

2.   Should electricity retailers be able to avail themselves of traditional antitrust immunity enjoyed by public utilities under traditional regulation? Recall from Chapter 8 that the actions of private companies may be exempt from antitrust liability if they fall under the so-called "state action" exemption. *Cal. Retail Liquor Dealers Ass'n. v. Midcal Aluminum, Inc.*, 445 U.S. 97 (1980) established a two-pronged test to determine when private party anticompetitive conduct is entitled to state action immunity from antitrust liability: (1) the conduct had to be performed pursuant to a clearly articulated policy of the state to displace competition with regulation; and (2) the conduct had to be closely supervised by the state. Recall the discussion of the applicability of the filed rate doctrine to market-based rates above. Should the state action exemption apply to market-based retail rates? An official with the U.S. Department of Justice antitrust division has stated:

> If a state opens its retail market to competition, then the state action doctrine would not apply to conduct that relates directly to retail competition," says the attorney, Milton A. Marquis. "So I think it's becoming less relevant in electricity, certainly with respect to wholesale [power], which is not a state matter anyway, but with respect to retail competition in those states that have decided to open their retail markets to competition. Because you can't have both. You can't have the state action doctrine and retail competition.

Joseph F. Schuler, State Action Doctrine Losing Relevance, Department of Justice Attorney Says, Pub. Util. Fortnightly, May 15, 1999, at 70. For further discussion of application of the state action doctrine to a deregulated electric power industry, see Jeffery D. Schwartz, The Use of the Antitrust State Action Doctrine in the Deregulated Electric Utility Industry, 48 Am. U. L. Rev. 1449 (1999).

3.   In thinking about the future of electric power markets, consider the new technologies presented by renewable energy, energy storage or demand response (discussed in Chapters 11–13). Some argue that these technologies are likely to create a disruption of the traditional electric utility industry.

Does traditional utility regulation encourage or discourage renewable and clean energy projects? Or do states with traditional regulated utilities have some tools to pursue renewable energy that may not be available in reregulated states? Can issues of retail competition be separated from issues related to innovation in renewable and clean energy? Do the approaches states are taking to encourage renewable energy technologies facilitate greater competition, or do they risk recreating their own "stranded cost" problems? For example, if enough customers who can afford it opt to use distributed generation such as rooftop solar panels to generate electricity, might that leave the remaining customers, including some of the lowest income customers, bearing the stranded costs of operating the distribution grid?

CHAPTER 11

RENEWABLE POWER

A. RENEWABLE SOURCES: AN INTRODUCTION

As you have learned in earlier chapters, one of the greatest challenges in energy policy is the need to provide a reliable, continuous supply of energy while limiting externalities, such as security concerns and environmental harms. Renewable energy resources—those that are not depleted when used, or replenish very quickly—are often touted as the answer to this challenge. Renewable energy can be used to produce electric power or for transportation. This chapter addresses renewable power production, the next chapter presents two case studies related to renewable power projects, and Chapter 15 addresses renewable energy issues in the transportation sector.

Renewable resources that can generate large quantities of electricity from centralized plants include the following:

- Solar photovoltaic (PV) technology, which uses solar panels to transform sunlight into electricity;
- solar thermal, which heats water to generate steam and turn a turbine;
- solar dish, which uses heat to expand air in an engine chamber and move a piston;
- wind energy, in which wind directly turns a turbine;
- hydroelectric power, in which water directly turns a turbine;
- wave power, in which waves turn a turbine;
- tidal power, in which tidal ebb and flow turns a turbine;
- methane (natural gas) from manure digesters and landfills used for heat or the heating of water to turn a turbine;
- waste to energy—heat or electricity generated from burning waste;
- biomass—trees and other material burned to generate steam to turn a turbine; and
- geothermal energy, which uses heat from beneath the earth to generate steam for use in heating, or steam to turn a turbine.

Most of these technologies can be deployed on a "utility" scale, meaning that they produce large amounts of electricity that is sold at wholesale or retail to many customers. Hydroelectric power and forms of hydrokinetic power from waves or tides are discussed in Chapter 6, although some of these may confront some of the same issues as other renewable power projects discussed in this chapter.

Some renewable resources—especially solar and wind—also can be deployed at the smaller "distributed" scale. "Distributed generation" or DG involves smaller-scale technologies that produce less electricity than utility-scale plants and often serve just one or several buildings, or a single customer. "Community-scale" renewables exist between the levels of utility scale and distributed renewables. These medium-sized installations serve a neighborhood, rather than one home or a larger customer base. The most common forms of distributed and community-scale renewable power include the following:

- solar PV panels on rooftops or parking garages;
- passive solar—in which rather than generating electricity using solar panels, buildings are constructed and positioned on lots to reduce energy demand (through natural shading on hot days, for example);
- small wind turbines;
- small hydroelectric dams; and

- geothermal heating and cooling systems, which use tubes buried beneath buildings to heat or cool a refrigerant, which then travels through the buildings.

In addition to being categorized by the resource that produces electricity and by their size, renewable energy technologies are also often described as "hot" or "cool," meaning that they generate electricity by combusting a fuel like biomass and are "hot," or they generate electricity from sunlight, wind, water, or another resource without having to burn anything and are thus "cool." Not all of these resources are in wide use—wave and tidal power, for example, are largely in the developmental phase in the United States, and solar dish technologies are not common here. Some governments and scholars also do not include all of the above resources in the renewable energy category. All share a common theme, in that they use fuel that replenishes quickly after use, but some are considered more environmentally destructive than others.

When considered on a life-cycle basis, which assesses the impacts of manufacturing, transporting, and operating renewable energy equipment, many renewable resources have far fewer environmental impacts than fossil fuel resources have. As compared to fossil fuels, many produce substantially less air and water pollution. Wind energy and dish and photovoltaic solar also use negligible amounts of water (primarily only for rinsing dust off equipment) as compared to fossil fuel-fired plants—an increasingly important consideration in areas experiencing drought and water shortages. *See* U.S. Dept. of Energy (DOE), Energy Demands on Water Resources (2006), http://www.sandia.gov/energy-water/docs/121-RptToCongress-EWwEIAcomments-FINAL.pdf.

Renewable resources are also key to addressing the increasingly clear, and problematic, impacts of climate change, including more severe storms, rising seas, deaths from heat waves and diseases that spread in heat, the expanded range of pests like pine beetles that destroy forests, and a faster rate of species extinction. The International Energy Agency (IEA) indicates that "low-carbon energy resources" and "much improved energy efficiency" will be necessary if we are to meet certain climate targets, such as limiting global temperature rise to 2 degrees Celsius. IEA, Are We Entering a Golden Age of Gas? 43 (2012), http://www.world energyoutlook.org/media/weowebsite/2011/WEO2011_GoldenAgeofGas Report.pdf.

The appeal of renewable energy resources extends beyond combating climate change. Environmental and security concerns have led to widespread interest in small-scale generation facilities that might diversify the types of fuel used to generate electricity and reduce reliance on large, centralized power plants. Renewable energy advocates envision solar panels on every roof, wind turbines on top of commercial buildings and at windy locations on land and at sea, and other innovative ways to generate electricity. Proponents of a "green economy" argue further that investing in renewable energy technology and expanding green energy production has the potential for a "watt-com" boom that would create jobs and stimulate the U. S. economy.

Renewable power also has drawbacks, and no renewable resource can produce power without also producing its own set of externalities. At the utility scale, technologies like large wind and solar farms, which are often considered the most "green" of the renewable resources, require large swaths of land—in some cases, even more land than is occupied by fossil fuel plants and associated mineral extraction. *See* Sara C. Bronin, Curbing Energy Sprawl with Microgrids, 43 Conn. L. Rev. 547, 553–557 (2010). Residents near wind farms complain of "shadow flicker"—the strobe-like shadow effect caused by turning blades—which they argue causes headaches and other health problems. And in cold climates, wind turbines can throw icicles for miles. Some people also view wind farms as ugly, and the blinking lights on wind turbines, which are required for aviation safety, can be an annoyance. Wind farms also kill birds, although not nearly as many as are killed by house cats or cars each year. Bat deaths are also a problem, which may be caused by "barotrauma"— a pressure change that occurs as bats fly close to wind turbines. Utility-scale solar farms, in turn, are likely to impact endangered species like the desert tortoise.

Beyond the impacts of generation, utility-scale renewable technologies also often require the construction of new transmission lines, as some of the most abundant wind and sunlight in the United States is located far from population centers. *See* Alexandra B. Klass & Elizabeth J. Wilson, Interstate Transmission Challenges for Renewable Energy: A Federalism Mismatch, 65 Vand. L. Rev. 1801 (2012). Transmission lines fragment wildlife habitat, are unsightly, and, like other energy equipment, kill some wildlife. Some landowners who live near proposed or existing transmission lines also worry that electric and magnetic field radiation from transmission lines causes health problems, although there is no scientific consensus supporting this view.

From an efficiency perspective, substantial amounts of electricity also are lost when electricity travels long distances over transmission lines: the U.S. Energy Information Administration (EIA) estimates a 7% average annual loss of electricity from transmission and distribution of electricity in the United States. EIA, How Much Electricity is Lost in Transmission and Distribution in the United States?, http://www.eia.gov/tools/faqs/how-much-electricity-lost-transmission-and-distribution-united-states. Further, transmission lines are costly, and they may be increasingly so as a result of weather patterns driven by climate change: many utilities are proposing expensive "storm hardening" programs to reduce the likelihood of damage to lines by severe storms, and some are even considering the more expensive option of burying lines.

Distributed and community-scale generation such as geothermal, solar, and wind avoids many of these negative impacts. It does not typically require the construction of new transmission lines, and it often does not take up valuable green space. Smaller-scale renewable generation has additional benefits. By producing electricity for a building rather than drawing electricity from the grid during certain times of the day, it can reduce the need for utility-scale "peaker" plants that come online when electricity demand is high. It also can enhance energy security. After Hurricane Sandy in 2013, campuses like New York University (NYU) continued to have electricity while much of the rest of New York remained in the dark, in part because NYU relied on its own, smaller (albeit not renewable) electricity system. This is not always the case—distributed generation, like the larger transmission grid, can also go down after large storms, but if carefully installed, it can provide an important back-up resource when the larger grid fails due to a cybersecurity attack, bad weather, or other grid interruption. Large utilities tend to oppose the expansion of distributed generation, however, because it often requires grid upgrades. Solar panels and other distributed generation must be equipped with a proper inverter, for example, to control the flow of excess electricity back into the grid, and distribution wires often must be upgraded to accommodate this flow. Utilities also view distributed generation as unwanted competition. *See* Joel B. Eisen, Residential Renewable Energy: By Whom?, 31 Utah Envtl. L. Rev. 339 (2011).

The greatest challenge associated with all renewable technologies— both large and small scale—is affordability. In part because we do not currently price all of the externalities of fossil fuels (such as their contribution to climate change), and in part because some renewable technologies are still developing, they are often still more expensive than their less green counterparts. Federal, state, and local governments, as well as regional collectives of governmental actors, have engaged in various programs to support, encourage, or subsidize renewable technologies; once deployed on a large scale, they are more likely to become cost-competitive. In Texas and parts of the Midwest, wind energy on good days is equal in price to or cheaper than natural gas-fired generation, even ignoring the various unaccounted-for externalities of natural gas generation. And the price of solar photovoltaic (PV) panels has recently plummeted, in part due to rapidly expanding Chinese production of panels. But because many renewable energy sources are more expensive than fossil fuel-fired electricity on a "sticker price" basis at utility-scale, there is ongoing debate about the desirable level of government support. Project proponents often complain that government incentives and subsidies are insufficient, especially given long-standing subsidies for fossil fuels. Others question whether any government incentives or subsidies to favor renewable resources or select new technologies are desirable.

Even where government support is available, developers of renewable energy projects must use creative financing mechanisms. Some financing schemes allow companies to engage in tax equity financing, in which a lender provides money to a renewable project and takes at least some short-term ownership interest in it and acquires the project's tax benefits in return. Yet financing must look beyond the tax benefits. A company with low amounts of capital or relatively low tax bills might not be able to benefit much from tax savings. Even companies with higher tax liability will eventually run out of ways to use tax benefits. So other financing models have become increasingly popular. On the distributed energy level, more companies are using a third-party ownership model, in which a company contracts with a homeowner or business to install the company's solar panels on a roof. The company sells electricity to the homeowner or business over the long term and sells excess electricity back to the grid. The homeowner, in turn, benefits from a long-term, stable electricity price, and from avoiding the cost of installing the generation him or herself.

The debate surrounding the cost of renewables, and the need to provide subsidies and creative financing mechanisms for renewables, has been heightened by recent declines in the price of natural gas. As gas prices have plummeted and become less volatile as a result of the shale gas boom, many utilities are switching to gas. This appears to be displacing not only coal, but also, potentially, investment in renewables. Natural gas alone, however, will not allow us to reach basic climate goals, thus leading some groups to argue that gas should be a "bridge fuel" that will lead us to renewables. There is also concern that the focus on gas will lead to stalled innovation in other areas, possibly including renewables. On the other hand, many point to the lower air and water emissions of natural gas-fired generation—as compared to coal—as a major environmental improvement in energy. The affordability challenge in renewable energy as compared to other energy sources, and associated government support and creative financing schemes, are a focus of this chapter.

A second area of focus in this chapter is a major challenge in renewable energy: zoning and land use issues, and other regulatory requirements. Although all forms of electricity generation face various permitting and land use requirements, renewables are in some ways unique, as described in more detail below. Utility-scale solar and wind farms require large amounts of land and therefore require complex land assembly schemes. These facilities cross town boundaries and even tribal-state boundaries, thus triggering so many different regulations that an "anticommons" can emerge. In this situation, so many entities have competing rights to a resource that underdevelopment of the resource occurs. An example might be several localities' rights to prohibit certain necessary development stages of a wind farm through permit denials, combined with state and federal agencies' abilities to deny several environmental permits. *See* Hannah Wiseman, Expanding Regional Renewable Governance, 35 Harv. Envtl. L. Rev. 477 (2011). The siting of small-scale renewables can be similarly difficult. Some neighborhoods and private communities ban rooftop solar panels because they are considered unsightly, although some states prohibit these bans. In other cases, zoning codes do not include any mention of distributed generation such as solar panels or small wind turbines, thus creating uncertainty and requiring case-by-case approval, or full code revisions, for projects to move forward.

This chapter addresses these core financial and land use challenges associated with renewable energy. It begins by describing renewable technologies in more detail, and then explores the government programs and private financing efforts that have made renewables possible. Next, the chapter describes the land use approvals and permitting required for renewable energy.

B. UNDERSTANDING RENEWABLE TECHNOLOGIES

1. COOL RENEWABLES

The extent to which any energy resource is "renewable" depends on the time scale you use. The sun itself will presumably fade gradually over millions of years. Uranium and related minerals usable as fuel for nuclear power might be exhausted in a few millennia. Coal resources will apparently last for a century or more, as will oil and gas—due in large part to recent improvements in production techniques for shales.

In today's terminology, renewable energy resources have come to be defined as those that can be utilized without any discernable reduction in their future availability. A common technical definition is whether a resource can be restored within a generation of its use in converting energy, which is why most fossil fuels are not considered renewable resources (even though biomass, which sometimes involves harvesting large amounts of vegetation and burning it to create energy, is considered renewable). Does this definition make sense? Are there some technologies that we have not mentioned so far in this chapter that you might consider to be renewable resources? Or some resources we have mentioned that are not renewable? Why or why not?

As explained in the introduction, renewable energy resources are often classified into two basic categories: (a) cool resources, which can produce energy without being burned; and (2) hot resources, which require combustion.

a.   SOLAR ENERGY

Solar energy is the prototype of a cool renewable energy resource. This may seem odd given the heat of the sun's rays, but that heat means that solar energy does not have to be burned and is thus classified as a cool resource.

Energy from the sun is virtually unlimited. By some estimates, there is enough sunshine falling on the Earth to meet the world's entire energy needs many times over, but the critical challenges have been to harness that energy in useful, cost-effective ways. There are several ways to produce energy from the sun. At the utility-scale level, solar thermal plants collect heat from the sun and use the heat to boil water and produce steam, which turns a turbine.

There are three types of solar thermal plants: parabolic troughs, concentrated solar power (CSP) or "power towers," and solar dish/engine. Parabolic trough systems involve long, trough-like structures that run parallel to each other and are close to the ground. Oil-filled tubes run down the middle of the troughs, where the sunlight is focused (at the center of the parabola). The heat collected within the tubes is used to heat water at a centralized facility to produce steam and turn a turbine. CSP uses an array of mirrors to concentrate sunlight on one receiver—a tall, central tower, which collects heat that then boils water. Solar dish technology concentrates heat within the center of large structures that look like satellite dishes. Some solar dish systems collect the heat and send it to a central facility to heat water to produce steam and turn a turbine, while others have an engine in the middle of each dish. Within this "stirling engine," heat in an engine chamber causes air to expand within the chamber and move a piston, which spins a turbine and produces electricity. EIA, Renewable Solar, http://www.eia.gov/kids/energy.cfm?page=solar_home-basics-k.cfm.

Unlike solar thermal technologies, which concentrate heat to generate steam (or, in the case of stirling engines, use heat to move a piston), solar PV technology generates electricity directly from sunlight using semiconductors such as silicon. PV is more flexible than solar thermal technologies, as it can be deployed at the utility, community, or distributed scale. One large PV plant in Arcadia, Florida—the DeSoto Next Generation Solar Energy Center—can generate 25 MW of electricity, which powers approximately 3,000 homes annually. Fla. Power & Light, Solar Energy Centers, https://www.fpl.com/clean-energy/solar/energy-centers.html.

Finally, at the smallest scale, there are solar heating and cooling systems for homes, and solar lighting. Solar heating and cooling of homes can be active or passive. Active systems use solar collectors—structures of glass and metal—to trap heat and send it through the home using fans and other devices. Another active system—solar hot water heaters—uses the sun's energy to heat hot water, which is stored in an insulated tank to be kept warm until it is used. Passive systems use the components of the building, such as walls and windows, to trap or release heat. Passive solar buildings are also sometimes situated on lots for maximum shade or sunlight exposure (depending on the climate). DOE, Passive Solar Home Design (2013), http://energy.gov/energysaver/articles/passive-solar-home-design.

Passive solar technology is finding increasing use in residential and commercial buildings. In regions a long way from the equator, reliance on solar energy as a sole source for heating a home would be impractical, but builders are discovering that passive solar heating can dramatically reduce heating costs. Active solar technology's current promise is also great in a wide variety of applications. The fastest growth in residential solar is in "grid connected" PV systems in residential or commercial applications where buildings have solar panels in place but remain connected to the electric grid.

Producing electricity with solar energy has considerable environmental benefits: it is pollution-free (except in the device manufacturing and transport process) and relies on an inexhaustible resource. In 2013, total installed solar capacity in the U.S. was about 9,370 megawatts (MW). Solar Energy Indus. Ass'n (SEIA), http://www.seia.org/research-resources/solar-industry-data. States with the most installed solar capacity (commercial, residential, and utility combined) included California, Arizona, New Jersey, and Nevada. The SEIA predicted that solar installations in the United States would increase by 30% between 2012 and 2013. *Id.* Solar energy is still a drop in the bucket compared to other energy resources, though, representing only 0.11% of total 2012 U.S. electricity generation. EIA, What is U.S. Electricity Generation by Energy Source?. http://www.eia.gov/tools/faqs/what-us-electricity-generation-energy-source.

This may change in the near future, as solar in the U.S. is moving rapidly toward "grid parity"—generating electricity at a price that competes with the price of electricity generated from traditional fossil fuel sources. Technology costs are dropping quickly. The SEIA reported in 2013 that "[t]he average price of a solar panel has declined by 60 percent since the beginning of 2011." SEIA, Solar Industry Data, http://www.seia.org/research-resources/solar-industry-data. In part due to this drop in equipment price, the "installed price" of all PV systems—residential, commercial, and utility-scale—has also declined in recent years. Between 2011 and 2012, the installed price, which is the "up-front price paid by the PV system owner, prior to receipt of incentives," dropped by 14 percent for PV systems less than or equal to 10 kilowatts (kW), 13% for 10–100 kW systems, and 6% for systems larger than 100kW. Galen

Barbose et al., Lawrence Berkeley Natl. Lab., Tracking the Sun VI (2013), http://emp.lbl.gov/sites/all/files/lbnl-6350e.pdf.

Utility-scale solar is still expensive compared to other types of plants, despite declining costs. A convenient way to compare the costs of energy sources, including solar, is the levelized cost—the "per-kilowatthour cost (in real dollars) of building and operating a generating plant over an assumed financial life and duty cycle." EIA, Levelized Cost and Levelized Avoided Cost of New Generation Resources in the Annual Energy Outlook 2014, http://www.eia.gov/forecasts/aeo/pdf/electricity_generation.pdf. The following table compares the total system levelized cost of power plants coming online in 2019. The total system levelized cost includes fixed and variable operations and maintenance, capital costs, and transmission investment, of various types of power plants in the United States in 2012 dollars per megawatt hour.

Plant type	Total system levelized cost in 2012$/megawatt hour
Conventional coal	95.6
Conventional combined-cycle natural gas	66.3
Advanced nuclear	96.1
Geothermal	47.9
Biomass	102.6
Wind-onshore	80.3
Solar PV	130.0
Solar Thermal	243.1
Hydro	84.5

Figure 11–1
U.S. Average Levelized Costs (2012$/megawatthour)
For plants entering service in 2019
Source: EIA, Levelized Cost and Levelized Avoided Cost of New Generation
Resources in the Annual Energy Outlook 2014, http://www.eia.gov/forecasts/aeo/pdf/
electricity_generation.pdf

Although the relative costs of large-scale solar remain high, declining solar panel prices have greatly benefited small-scale PV systems on homes and businesses, as evidenced by the 14% decline in installed costs for smaller systems between 2011 and 2012. The following excerpt discusses the promise for active, small-scale solar PV in places such as parking lots, as well as the potential for larger-scale solar projects to expand.

Arjun Makhijani, Carbon-Free and Nuclear-Free: A Roadmap for U.S. Energy Policy 37–45

Inst. For Energy and Env't Research (2007, 2010 printing).

The average solar energy incident on the continental United States is far greater than the wind energy potential. At about 5 kilowatt hours per square meter per day (annual average, 24 hours-per-day basis), the total is four thousand times the annual electricity generation in 2005. Of course, only a small part of the area can be used, and less than half of the incident energy is converted into usable electricity even under the best circumstances in a laboratory. But even at 20 percent efficiency and with one percent of the land area, the total potential for solar electricity generated by photovoltaic cells (solar PV) is about eight times the total U.S. electricity generation, and about three times greater than the wind energy potential. . . .

It turns out that a considerable part of the potential for solar electricity generation can be achieved on an intermediate-scale at the point of use—on rooftops, over parking lots, and if thin films get thin enough and cheap enough, simply by covering south-facing walls of buildings with photocells. . . .

. . . . Parking lot solar PV makes a great deal of sense for several reasons. Among them:

1.   It does not require roof penetrations, reducing maintenance and the risk of leaks.

2.   It does not require any new dedicated land.

3.   It can be implemented on a scale that provides significant economies in installation costs.

4.   It provides shade to parked vehicles, increasing comfort and reducing the need for air-conditioning at full blast when vehicles are started after being parked on bright summer days.

5.   It increases the value of the parking lot.

6.   Not least, grid connections in large parking lots (and rooftops) can be made compatible with vehicle-to-grid storage systems. In these systems, parked electric vehicles or plug-in hybrids can supply power to the grid during peak daytime hours (for instance, on hot summer days), having been charged during off-peak hours at night. They could also be charged in the workplace during off-peak hours (for instance during night shifts or the early morning hours), with the same result. This also increases the value of the vehicles parked in the lot.

The land area devoted to parking spaces in the United States is very large. It has been estimated by the Earth Policy Institute at about 1.9 million hectares, or 19 billion square meters. Most of these are not multi-story parking lots, but rather vast expanses of asphalt at shopping centers, offices, high schools, universities, airports, strip malls, supermarkets and other large stores, and the like, as well as private parking spaces. At 15 percent conversion efficiency, available today, parking lot PV installations could supply much of the electricity generated in the United States. . . .

Solar electric systems can also be used in more centralized installations. At 15 percent efficiency, a 1,000 MW plant in the Southwest (that is, in a favorable area for solar) would occupy about 20 square kilometers for a flat plate, non-tracking system. . . . The semi-arid and desert areas in the Southwest and West not only have the greatest incident energy, but also the greatest number of cloudless days. Those regions are therefore excellent candidates for central station solar PV, especially since this technology, unlike fossil fuel and nuclear plants, does not require cooling water. At 15 percent efficiency, the area requirements in the Southwest for generating one-fourth of the 2007 U.S. electricity output would be on the order of 3,000 to 4,000 square miles, for non-tracking systems. The area for tracking systems would be considerably larger.

Solar energy, of course, has in some measure a problem of intermittency, but in arid and semi-arid climates, this is not a significant issue, especially if solar PV is integrated with other energy sources. Solar insolation is much more predictable than wind on an hour-ahead, day-ahead, and seasonal basis. Moreover, it does not have the same kinds of micro-fluctuations that can create regulation problems on a time scale of seconds or minutes that wind energy does. Finally, being available in the daytime, it covers many of the peak hours, notably in the summer.

However, there are also certain periods of no sunshine when solar PV output is zero. Hence the problem of storage occurs on a diurnal time scale. . . . A part of the problem of diurnal and seasonal variation in solar energy can be dealt with by combining solar thermal power plants with heat storage as well as supplemental fuel use with solar thermal generation. Central station solar thermal plants use concentrators to focus heat on long pipes (parabolic troughs) or on a small area ("power towers"). . . . A variety of heat storage devices ranging from concrete and bricks to molten salt are being investigated, but none have been demonstrated in conjunction with a commercial solar thermal power plant. . . .

Every energy source has its environmental costs, but when all is said and done, those associated with solar energy, even at a very large-scale of deployment, would be small. At present, the main environmental problems associated with solar energy arise from the emissions from fossil fuel plants that provide the energy to make the photovoltaic cells. Since crystalline silicon cells are the most energy intensive, the largest emissions, whether of heavy metals or CO_2, are associated with them. ∎

NOTES AND COMMENTS

1.   As shown in **Figure 11–1**, the price per megawatt-hour of electricity generated from the sun is currently above that of electricity generated from fossil fuels (natural gas and coal) or from nuclear power plants, though the gap is closing rapidly. Then why should the government offer any incentives at all to solar power producers? After all, opponents of what they call unwarranted "subsidies" claim we don't support higher-priced grocers or plastics manufacturers; if they cannot produce their wares more cheaply than their competitors, they run the risk of failing. Why should solar power producers be treated differently?

One frequent answer is that traditional rate regulation of electricity generation from fossil fuels and transmission does not reflect the full social costs of power production and delivery. These activities create externalities in two distinct ways: (1) they may impose costs on adjacent or nearby users by emitting pollutants, influencing property prices or creating risks; and (2) they may fail to fully reflect the actual costs of the fuel inputs utilized for production, leading to overuse and potential depletion of these inputs. In addition, it is frequently observed that many fossil fuels have received significant government support in the past, and continue to receive government subsidies and support today. Maura Allaire and Stephen Brown, Eliminating Subsidies for Fossil Fuel Production: Implications for U.S. Oil and Natural Gas Markets (Resources For the Future, 2009), http://rff.org/

RFF/Documents/RFF-IB-09-10.pdf; and Cong. Budget Ofc., Federal Financial Support for the Development and Production of Fuels and Energy Policies 3 (2012), http://www.cbo.gov/sites/default/files/cbofiles/attachments/03-06-FuelsandEnergy_Brief.pdf discuss the tax preferences and other subsidies for fossil fuel industries. For explanations and criticisms of oil and gas subsidies, see Calvin H. Johnson, Accurate and Honest Tax Accounting for Oil and Gas, 125 Tax Notes 573 (2009).

2.   As early (comparatively speaking) in solar's development as 1999, a study found that a PV system can recoup its original cost in as little as one to four years. Nat'l Renewable Energy Lab. (NREL), Energy Payback: Clean Energy From PV, http://www.nrel.gov/docs/fy99osti/24619.pdf. That payback period can be shorter if state net metering laws, which allow generators of power using renewable resources to sell their excess power back to the utility, are taken into account. See Chapter 12 for further discussion of net metering.

3.   The California Solar Initiative (CSI), which gives cash incentives for solar installed on "roof or ground space that gets unobstructed sunlight from 11 a.m. to sunset year round" has driven rapid growth of residential PV in the state. The California Solar Initiative—CSI, http://www.gosolarcalifornia.ca.gov/csi/index.php. As of March 2015, 245,838 solar projects representing 2,353 megawatts of electricity have been installed in the state, and the cost per watt has steadily declined from 2007 to the present, with an average cost of $5.56 per watt for projects less than 10kW. Go Solar California, http://www.californiasolarstatistics.ca.gov/.

4.   Green power can mean green jobs and investments. Although numbers provided by proponents of industry tend to err on the high side, The Solar Foundation estimated that in 2012 the U.S. solar industry employed "119,016 workers in the United States including an addition of 13,872 new solar workers in 2012—a 13.2 percent increase from 2011." The most worker additions were in the area of solar installation. The Solar Found., Nat'l Solar Jobs Census 2012, http://thesolarfoundation.org/sites/thesolarfoundation.org/files/TSF%20Solar%20Jobs%20Census%202012%20Final.pdf.

However, creating new jobs is possible only if the United States provides adequate government support for renewables industries, says noted New York Times columnist Thomas L. Friedman. On a visit to Applied Materials, a Texas-based company that builds solar panel factories, Friedman bemoaned the fact that all 14 factories that Applied Materials built in a two-year period were outside of the United States. He added:

> The reason that all these other countries are building solar-panel industries today is because most of their governments have put in place the three prerequisites for growing a renewable energy industry: 1) any business or homeowner can generate solar energy; 2) if they decide to do so, the power utility has to connect them to the grid; and 3) the utility has to buy the power for a predictable period at a price that is a no-brainer good deal for the family or business putting the solar panels on their rooftop.

Thomas L. Friedman, Have a Nice Day, N.Y. Times, Sept. 15, 2009.

The SEIA similarly worries about the oversupply of solar panels from countries like China, which has caused solar panel prices to plummet but has also, it believes, "put a serious strain on solar manufacturers worldwide."

SEIA, Solar Industry Data, http://www.seia.org/research-resources/solar-industry-data. Trade wars have erupted in this area, with the U.S. imposing 31.4% tariffs on PV cells from China in 2012 and China announcing a 6.5% tariff on U.S. solar materials in 2013. U.S. Dept. of Commerce, Intl. Trade Comm'n., Fact Sheet, Commerce Preliminarily Finds Dumping of Crystalline Silicon Photovoltaic Cells, Whether or Not Assembled into Modules from the People's Republic of China, http://ia.ita.doc.gov/download/factsheets/fact sheet-prc-solar-cells-ad-prelim-20120517.pdf; Wayne Ma, China Levies 6.5% Tariff on U.S. Solar-Panel Materials, Wall St. J., Sept. 18, 2013, http://online.wsj.com/article/SB10001424127887323527004579079070572200630.html. We discuss one World Trade Organization dispute related to certain solar technologies in Chapter 14.

Section C of this chapter evaluates the variety of state and federal government programs designed to encourage the solar industry and other renewables industries. For now, ask why these three goals might or might not be the most important goals of government renewables programs, and what government programs you would like to see to achieve them. Goals such as jobs and economic development are not unique to renewable energy resources, of course. Are there reasons we should favor these kinds of jobs over jobs produced by coal or other fossil fuel production?

5.   With respect to one possible government program that could spur more rapid deployment of renewables, Arjun Makhijani notes,

> [T]ime-of-use pricing [in which electricity prices rise and fall in real time depending on the quantity of electricity demanded and the types of resources available to meet that demand at a given time] is an important policy tool for a transition to a renewable electricity system. It also best reflects market considerations in terms of cost of supply. A lack of time-of-use pricing is a reflection of improper market signals and the cause of significant market failures in the electricity sector.

Arjun Makhijani, Carbon-Free and Nuclear-Free: A Roadmap for U.S. Energy Policy 40, Inst. For Energy and Env't Research (2007). See Chapter 13 for a discussion of time-of-use (or "real-time") pricing of electricity, as one of the technologies and policies necessary for a "Smart Grid."

b.   Wind Power

Wind power has become one of the most attractive sources of renewable energy in certain parts of the world, including in the United States. Huge farms of windmills with blades exceeding 100 feet in length are used to generate electricity. The use of wind power for electricity generation has been growing at a rapid rate in the past decade, albeit from a low baseline.

About 2% of the solar energy that reaches the earth is ultimately converted to the kinetic energy of wind. Joseph M. Moran et al., Meteorology: The Atmosphere and the Science of Weather 204 (5th ed., Prentice Hall 1997). Wind blows when there is uneven air pressure, which is caused by variations in the temperature in the Earth's atmosphere. See George Bomar, Texas Weather 176–198 (1995).

Wind power has its greatest potential where average wind speeds are relatively strong and consistent in direction. In the United States, such "regions include the western High Plains, the Pacific Northwest coast, portions of coastal California, the eastern Great Lakes, the south coast of Texas, and exposed summits and passes in the Rockies and Appalachians." Moran et al., *supra,* at 205. The use of wind power for the generation of electricity in these resource-rich regions has become a big business. Giant "wind farms" that contain dozens of linked windmills have been erected in many locations. In Europe between 2000 and 2012, 51.2% of all new generation installations have been renewable installations, with wind making up 27.7% of new installations. The European Union had 106 gigawatts (GW) of installed wind capacity in 2012, covering "7% of the EU's electricity consumption." European Wind Energy Ass'n, Wind in Power: 2012 European Statistics, Feb. 2013, http://www.ewea.org/fileadmin/files/library/publications/statistics/ Wind_in_power_annual_statistics_2012.pdf.

In comparison, the United States had 60,007 MW of installed wind energy capacity by 2012, a dramatic increase from 2,539 MW in 2000. Windpoweringamerica.gov, Installed Wind Capacity by State, www.wind poweringamerica.gov/docs/installed_wind_capacity_by_state.xls. Texas led the states with 12,212 MW, followed by California (5,549 MW), Iowa (5,137 MW), Illinois (3,568 MW), and Oregon (3,153 MW). This installed capacity comprised 3.46% of total U.S. electricity generation. EIA, What is U.S. Electricity Generation by Energy Source?. http://www.eia.gov/ tools/faqs/what-us-electricity-generation-energy-source. The EIA reports that "[i]n 2012, wind energy became the number one source of new U.S. electricity generation capacity for the first time—representing 43 percent of all new electric additions and accounting for $25 billion in U.S. investment." EIA, Energy Dep't Reports: U.S. Wind Energy Production and Manufacturing Reaches Record Highs, Aug. 6, 2013, http://energy. gov/articles/energy-dept-reports-us-wind-energy-production-and- manufacturing-reaches-record-highs.

The following excerpt discusses the opportunities and challenges of using wind power to replace fossil fuels in electricity generation.

Arjun Makhijani, Carbon-Free and Nuclear-Free: A Roadmap for U.S. Energy Policy 30–36

Inst. For Energy and Env't Research (2007, 2010 printing).

Wind-generated electricity has been growing very rapidly. . . .

It is clear that overall potential is vast—over two-and-a-half times total U.S. electricity generation in the United States in 2005. . . . The wind energy resource is quite sufficient to supply the entire electricity requirement of the country for some time to come under any scenario, if total potential were the only consideration.

Of course, it is not. Intermittency is a critical issue. Secondly, the geographic location of the wind resource is another potential constraint. It is concentrated in the Midwest and the Rocky Mountain states while the population of the United States is concentrated along the coasts. . . .

Tapping into a large amount of the high-density landbased wind resource will require transmission infrastructure to take the electricity to transmission system hubs from where it would be taken to population centers. Transmission corridors exist going eastwards and westwards from the center of the country. But the wind resource is dispersed and it must be delivered to the hubs. Second, the capacity of some of the lines to carry the electricity would have to be expanded. . . .

One advantage of the geographic concentration of wind resources in the continental United States is that much of it is located in the Midwestern Farm Belt. Since crops can be planted and cattle can graze right up to the wind turbine towers, wind farms are quite compatible with growing crops and ranching. They can provide a reliable and steady source of income to farmers and ranchers, insulating them, to some extent, from the vagaries of commodity markets. The largest single problem with wind energy is intermittency. This intermittency affects the system at many levels: short-term wind fluctuations, hourly or daily variations, and week-to-week and seasonal variations. . . . The variability of wind energy necessitates the addition of reserve capacity other than wind that can be tapped when the wind falls below the forecasted level over a period of hours or days. . . .

Besides the need for extra reserves, there are other costs of wind integration with electricity grids. Winds fluctuate over very short periods of time (seconds to minutes) creating disturbances in the system that could affect the stability of the frequency of the electricity supply. A constant frequency (in the United States, 60 cycles per second, called 60 hertz) is essential for much consuming equipment, such as clocks and computers and automated controls in industry dependent on electronic timing systems. The frequency of the electricity supply is therefore maintained within narrow limits at all times. The added cost of maintaining constant frequency as the proportion of wind energy in the system increases is called the regulation cost.

In between these two times scales (seconds to about a day) is the issue of load following. As we turn lights on and off and industries are brought on line or taken off, as millions of televisions are turned on in the evening when people return home from work, the electricity system must be able to follow the load and increase or decrease the output according to the demand. This is more complex if there is no actual control of the fuel supply that can change the output, which is the case with wind energy. It is analogous to a third party controlling the accelerator of a car.

These issues are managed by having some form of added reserve capacity and the reserves have to increase as the proportion of wind-supplied electricity increases. This is obviously an added cost that must be attributed to wind energy. It is the grid equivalent of having a battery storage for solar or wind energy in off-grid systems. Since loads can fluctuate rapidly over periods of minutes, every electricity system must have spinning reserve capacity—that is capacity that is available whenever the demand goes up—somewhat like electricity "on tap."

The additions to reserve capacity needed for maintaining the reliability of supply are a critical aspect of wind energy integration into electrical grids and represent part of the costs of this energy source. These costs are low when the proportion of wind-generated electricity is small, and tend to rise as that proportion increases.

* * *

A great deal of effort, study, and practical experience has gone into addressing problems such as wind integration to rather high levels of generation—up to about 20 percent—mainly in Europe (Denmark, Germany, Spain) and Texas. Though the penetration of wind in the U.S. electricity market is still very low (about 0.7 percent of electricity generation) (*Eds. Note*: the percentage in 2014 is 3.5%), there have been many rigorous studies of wind integration costs. Overall, these have been assessed to be modest—in the range of 0.25 to 0.5 cents per kilowatt hour ($2.50 to $5 per megawatt-hour (MWh)). . . .

A complementary approach, and one that would greatly increase geographic diversity, would be to develop offshore wind resources. This has been a topic of some controversy in the United States in a period when several European countries have developed significant offshore capacity and expertise. . . . Higher penetration of wind energy can and should be optimized with other renewable energy sources to take advantage of the diversity of supply and the greater ability of combinations of sources to more closely match demand. . . .

. . . The main constraints lie in a lack of transmission infrastructure and an overall policy to reduce CO_2 emissions that would give rise to more rapid investments in this area. ∎

NOTES AND COMMENTS

1.   53% of the U.S. population lives near the coast—and thus closer to the strongest wind energy potential in the United States (offshore wind). The U.S. government study of offshore wind potential within 50 nautical miles of shore (excluding Alaska and Florida), and excluding shipping lanes, marine sanctuaries, or other areas where development would not be permitted, shows promising results. Anthony Lopez et al., NREL, U.S. Renewable Energy Technical Potentials: A GIS-Based Analysis (July 2012), http://www. nrel.gov/docs/fy12osti/51946.pdf. By one U.S. government estimate, offshore wind capacity could be 4,223 GW, enough to power at least 950 million homes (1 GW supplies 225,000–300,000 homes annually). (Putting this in context, the United States had approximately 115 million occupied homes in 2011.) U.S. Dept. of Interior (DOI), Bureau of Ocean Energy Mgmt., Offshore Wave Energy,   http://www.boem.gov/Renewable-Energy-Program/Renewable-Energy-Guide/Offshore-Wind-Energy.aspx; American Housing Survey FAQ, http://www.census.gov/housing/ahs/about/faq.html#Q5.

2.   The issues raised in this excerpt regarding further wind power development are addressed elsewhere in this chapter. Section C.4 analyzes siting of wind power projects and briefly addresses offshore wind permitting. Transmission siting issues are also covered in Section C.4.

3.   In addition to the objections to wind mentioned in the introduction to this chapter, wind power projects may also be challenged for their claimed adverse impacts on existing land uses. Jennifer Schwab, Renewable Energy—Not in My Backyard!, Huffington Post, Sept. 11, 2009, http://www. huffingtonpost.com/. The high-profile Highlands wind power project in southwest Virginia, a planned 19-turbine wind farm, ran into a host of objections. One unusual one, lodged by another Virginia state agency against the State Corporation Commission (the state's PSC), was that the project would have an adverse impact on a Civil War battlefield across the border in

West Virginia. Battlefield complicates Va. wind dispute, Charleston Daily Mail, Sept. 21, 2009.

4. The federal Endangered Species Act, 16 U.S.C. §§ 1531–1544, is a potentially powerful obstacle to construction of a wind power facility. When a species (or a subspecies or population of a species) is listed under the Act, all federal agencies must consult with the U.S. Fish and Wildlife Service (FWS) before taking any action that might jeopardize the continued existence of the species. Moreover, any person that harms a listed species may be guilty of "taking" the species, which carries criminal penalties under the act. Destruction of the habitat of a listed species can also constitute a taking. For a thorough analysis of the Endangered Species Act, see John Copeland Nagle, J.B. Ruhl, and Kalyani Robbins, The Law of Biodiversity and Ecosystem Management (Foundation Press 3rd ed. 2012).

The discovery of an endangered species near a proposed wind power facility can have a dramatic impact. In 1999, a planned wind farm in California was relocated after the National Audubon Society objected that the turbines might pose a threat to the endangered California Condor. Andrew Broman, Environmentalists Pressure Houston-Based Firm to Drop Plans for Wind Farm, Houston Chronicle, Nov. 4, 1999. In 2012 FWS issued Land-Based Wind Energy Guidelines, which specify the procedures that wind developers should follow to identify, prevent, mitigate, and monitor potential species impacts. FWS, Land-Based Wind Energy Guidelines, http://www.fws.gov/windenergy/docs/weg_final.pdf.

c. SUBTERRANEAN ENERGY

Geothermal energy is another cool renewable resource. In those limited locations in which underground steam produces hot springs or geysers, this steam can be used for electric generation. Geothermal heat originates from the earth's core, where temperatures reach over 9,000 degrees F. Magma that remains beneath the earth's crust heats rock and water. The hot water sometimes travels to the earth's surface as hot springs and geysers, although most stays underground in cracks and porous rocks. Such a formation is known as a geothermal reservoir, and such reservoirs, where available, provide a source of geothermal energy. Generating electricity from geothermal sources requires heat, water, and permeability (ability of water to travel underground). Reservoirs meeting all three of the requirements are "hydrothermal" or conventional reservoirs. DOE estimates that "if 1% of the thermal energy contained within the Earth's uppermost crust (10 kilometers or less) were tapped for use, that output would be equivalent to 500 times the energy contained in all the oil and gas resources known in the world." DOE, Office of Energy Effc'y and Renewable Energy, Nat'l Geothermal Action Plan (2009).

Geothermal power plant developers drill wells into geothermal reservoirs and use steam, heat or hot water from geothermal reservoirs to spin turbine generators that produce electricity. The water is then returned through an injection well to be reheated and sustain the reservoir. There are three kinds of geothermal power plants. A "dry" steam reservoir produces steam, but very little water. The steam is piped into a "dry" steam power plant that provides the force to spin the turbine generator. A "flash" power plant uses water ranging from 300–700 degrees F. The water is brought to the surface through a production well where some of the water "flashes" into steam, which powers a turbine. A binary power plant uses water that is not hot enough to flash into steam. The water is passed through a heat exchanger, where the heat is transferred to a second liquid that has a lower boiling point than water. The binary liquid flashes to vapor when heated and is used to spin the turbine. The vapor is then condensed and used again.

Geothermal power is a very clean source of energy. The land required for utility-scale geothermal power plants is generally smaller per megawatt than most any other type of power plant. There is also much less physical damage to the environment. Rivers do not need to be dammed or forests cut down. Geothermal power is reliable: the plants are located on top of the power source. This eliminates the uncertainties associated with weather and natural disasters, and possible political conflicts that often affect the importation of fossil fuels.

However, not many places in the world happen to be situated in locations where hydrothermal reservoirs are sufficiently close to the surface of the earth that they can be utilized efficiently with current technology. In 2012, the United States had a total installed capacity of 3,386 MW of geothermal electricity production, most of which was in California and Nevada. Geothermal Energy Ass'n, 2013 Annual US Geothermal Power Production and Development Report 4 (2013), http://geo-energy.org/pdf/reports/2013AnnualUSGeothermalPowerProduction andDevelopmentReport_Final.pdf. Where it is available, the rights to access this energy have sometimes created disputes not unlike those involving the right to sunlight. *See* Parks v. Watson, 716 F.2d 646 (9th Cir. 1983). Some geothermal reservoirs are located on federal lands, and DOI's Bureau of Land Management is the lead federal agency for geothermal leasing on federal lands, sometimes working with the United States Forest Service. The Energy Policy Act of 2005 (EPAct 2005) required these federal agencies to draft a Programmatic Environmental Impact Statement (PEIS) to expedite leasing activities on federal lands. In part due to the limited locations available for geothermal energy, this has often meant monopolization of the resource by a single supplier, as it is most efficiently developed by large facilities that provide economies of scale. This reduces competition and the economies that competition typically creates.

Even though geothermal production today is restricted to hydrothermal reservoirs, often located in remote areas, it could one day be far more widespread. In recent years, research into a new generation of geothermal technology, known as Enhanced Geothermal Systems (EGS), has shown promise for extending geothermal's reach to more unconventional resources. EGS involves the "development of a geothermal system where the natural flow capacity of the system is not sufficient to support adequate power production but where hydraulic fracturing of the system can allow production at a commercial level." Geothermal Energy Ass'n, *supra*, at 5. While EGS is still a young technology, if the challenges can be addressed successfully, the potential is enormous. DOE estimates that "[o]f the roughly 556,890 MWe of estimated recoverable resources, 93% is expected to be achieved through EGS technology." Nat'l Geothermal Action Plan, *supra* at 9. As of 2012, three EGS projects have begun in Alaska, Arizona, and Nevada. Geothermal Energy Ass'n, *supra* at 19–20, 26. Some believe, however, that EGS technology creates increased risks of inducing earthquakes. Domenico Giardini, Geothermal quake risks must be faced, 462 Nature 848, Dec. 17, 2009.

On a smaller scale, geothermal technology is used as a form of localized energy storage for household heating and/or cooling through a "geothermal heat pump" (GHP). A GHP takes advantage of the fact that the temperature of the ground or ground water a few feet below the earth's surface remains relatively constant throughout the year. The GHP uses a refrigerant fluid contained in a field of loop pipes buried beneath the surface to draw heat from the relatively warm ground when the air temperature is much colder, and in summer transfer waste heat to the relatively cool ground. Depending on the temperature of the ground and the ground area available, this can be more efficient than conventional heat pumps or air conditioners that use the outdoor air. Because they require burying of pipes, GHPs are generally more expensive to install than outside air heat pumps. However, they can reduce energy consumption by more than 20 percent compared to even high-efficiency outside air heat pumps. As a bonus, they also use the waste heat from air-conditioning to provide free hot water heating in the summer.

d. OTHER RESOURCES

Hydropower is by far the largest source of cool renewable energy currently being used. Water stored behind dams is released to turn turbines that generate electricity. Because of the extensive environmental impacts of these facilities, however, they are often controversial. Hydropower is discussed in Chapter 6.

Unlike long-established hydropower, deepwater energy is an experimental form of renewable energy. Three forms have been the subject of various test projects: (a) tidal power plants, if located in areas where there is a big range in the tides, could be built to operate on the energy generated by the tidal movement; (b) generation of electricity from ocean wave energy (through floating buoys and other technologies); and (c) convection plants, which would build up a circulation of cold deep water that could be used to cool buildings. Compared with other forms of renewable energy, such as solar and wind, these forms of marine energy are continuous but highly variable, although wave levels at specific locations can be predicted well in advance. In recent years, various wave energy system designs have been developed and tested, and several are now moving forward. In 2004, the British government announced a project to harness tidal power. The prototype Pelamis "wave energy converter," deployed off the coast of Scotland, had generated 160 megawatt-hours of electricity as of October 2013 at one offshore site. Erica Rex, Clean, green, and unobtrusive, wave and tidal products appeal to Scots, ClimateWire, Oct. 1, 2013, http://www.eenews.net/climatewire/stories/1059988095.

At present, wave energy systems are at an early stage of development in the United States. Over the past decade, the federal government has become involved in evaluating these projects and entering into agreements with states to smooth the permitting and siting process. The EPAct 2005 gave the Department of Interior jurisdiction over evaluating renewables projects (including wave energy projects) that make use of federal waters. In 2009, the agency then called MMS released proposed rules for all forms of renewable energy development on the Outer Continental Shelf (OCS), and in 2012, DOE announced $16 million in funding for seventeen projects to "capture energy from waves, tides, and currents." DOE, Energy Department Invests $16 Million to Harness Wave and Tidal Energy, Aug. 29, 2013, http://energy.gov/ articles/energy-department-invests-16-million-harness-wave-and-tidal-energy.

Oregon has included ocean energy in its Territorial Sea Plan, which includes policies for offshore siting and development. Oregon Territorial Sea Plan Part 5, http://www.oregon.gov/LCD/OCMP/docs/ocean/otsp_5. pdf. The Oregon Territorial Sea Plan Advisory Committee is working to identify "areas for responsible wave energy," and a company called Ocean Power Technologies and its affiliate is deploying a wave energy system 2.5 miles off the coast of Reedsport, Oregon. This facility will be "North America's first commercial wave power station." Ocean Power Technologies, Reedsport Wave Energy Project, July 2012, http://www. oceanpowertechnologies.com/PDF/Reedsport_Newsletter_July_2012_ Vol2.pdf. The Federal Energy Regulatory Commission (FERC) has also entered into various memoranda of understanding with states to coordinate the review of ocean energy projects. FERC, Hydrokinetic Projects, http://www.ferc.gov/industries/hydropower/gen-info/licensing/ hydrokinetics.asp.

Hydrogen-powered fuel cells are currently the form of cool renewable technology that is attracting some of the most attention:

> Fuel cells use an electrochemical process that combines hydrogen and oxygen, producing water and electricity. Avoiding the inherent inefficiency of combustion, today's top fuel cells are roughly twice as efficient as conventional engines, have no moving parts, require little maintenance, are silent, and emit only water vapor. Unlike today's power plants, they are nearly as economical on a small scale as on a large one. Indeed, they could turn the very notion of a power plant into something more closely resembling a home appliance.

Brown et al., *supra,* at 28–29. Whether this assessment is overly optimistic remains to be seen. Fuel cell technology for transportation is discussed in more detail in Chapter 15.

2.   HOT RENEWABLES

Among the so-called "hot" renewable resources, the term biomass includes a wide variety of renewable plant materials that can be converted to provide various sources of energy. The state of Oregon describes biomass and its potential this way:

> Biomass is the organic matter in trees, agricultural crops and other living plant material. It is made up of carbohydrates— organic compounds that are formed in growing plant life . . . Biomass is solar energy stored in organic matter. As trees and plants grow, the process of photosynthesis uses energy from the sun to convert carbon dioxide into carbohydrates (sugars, starches and cellulose). Carbohydrates are the organic compounds that make up biomass. When plants die, the process

of decay releases the energy stored in carbohydrates and discharges carbon dioxide back into the atmosphere. Biomass is a renewable energy source because the growth of new plants and trees replenishes the supply.

Oregon Biomass Energy Home Page, http://www.oregon.gov/ ENERGY. Biomass can be used to fuel transportation (through liquid fuels like ethanol), or it can be burned to produce electricity. Relying on biomass-based energy is controversial, due to a debate about whether certain materials should be considered food or fuel. However, there are many kinds of biomass and not all are foodstuffs. Biomass feedstocks include a variety of food products (primarily starches from corn kernels, sugars from sugar cane or sugar beets, and vegetable oils such as palm, sunflower, canola and soy oils). The fibrous, woody, and generally inedible portions of plants are called "cellulosic" or "lignocellulosic" biomass because they contain cellulose, hemicellulose, and lignin—key structural components of plant cell walls. Cellulosic biomass is the most plentiful biological material on earth, and includes plants like jatropha, rapeseed, duckweed and jojoba, refuse plant matter such as remnant lumber byproducts, and post-harvest plant stover. Other materials considered biomass include botanical microorganisms (such as algae and cyanobacteria), and animal waste products (such as livestock manure). Stanford's Global Climate and Energy Project homepage features information about the technical aspects of many forms of agricultural biomass. Stanford Global Climate and Energy Project, http://gcep. stanford.edu/.

In undeveloped regions, wood and animal manure are often still primary sources of energy. Is wood a renewable resource? Are livestock chips? They are if used in moderation and accompanied by effective replanting or ecological recuperation by leaving land fallow. In many undeveloped regions, however, these fuel resources are being depleted faster than they are being replaced.

Biomass consumption statistics show that the United States biomass sector has grown substantially since 2003, with electricity generation from wood, wood-derived fuels, and other biomass like solid waste increasing by 7.9% between 2003 and 2012. EIA, Electric Power Monthly with Data for July 2013, Sept. 2013, http://www.eia.gov/ electricity/monthly/pdf/epm.pdf. Production of U.S. fuel ethanol, in turn, rose from 1.62 billion gallons in 2000 to 13.30 billion gallons in 2012. EIA, U.S. Ethanol Production, Imports, and Consumption, http://www.eia.gov/ tools/faqs/how-much-ethanol-produced-imported-and-consumed-us. These gains have come from aggressive government R&D and regulatory support. In the United States, the Biomass Research and Development Initiative (BRDI) is a multi-agency effort established in 2000 to coordinate bioenergy research and development funding from targeted legislation, government agencies, and public grants. Biomass Research and Dev't, http://www.biomassboard.gov/. This program provides financial assistance to institutions of higher education, national laboratories, federal research agencies, state research agencies, private sector entities, and nonprofit organizations.

The 2008 Food, Conservation and Energy Act (Pub. L. No. 110–246 (2008), known as the "farm bill") extended funding for the BRDI and amended the program to ensure a cooperative effort between the

Departments of Energy and Agriculture in deploying adequate financial resources to conduct biomass research. Biomass R&D projects are ongoing at universities throughout the nation. At a state level, Iowa's Energy Center's Biomass Energy Conversion Facility (BECON) has become an innovator. BECON, http://www.energy.iastate.edu/. Private sector investments have also targeted the various technologies that convert fuel resources into energy.

The most common form of biomass conversion to energy in developing regions is through direct combustion. Burning of waste vegetation from agricultural crops is a potential energy source that is beginning to find commercial uses. In tropical climates, for example, after sugar is exacted from sugar cane for use in foods or to be converted to biofuel, the remainder of the plant has traditionally been burned into biochar. If burned to generate electricity, it remains renewable so long as the soil maintains viable nutrient levels to continue producing crops. Converting biomass to energy can happen in three major ways besides burning: biochemical (via microorganism digestion and fermentation), thermochemical (commonly by either gasification or pyrolysis), and chemical (via refineries). The end products have many potential uses and can be adapted to many end users' needs, from biomethane gas to heat homes to bioethanol for cars and solid algae cake used to replace coal in power plants.

The most controversial means of transforming biomass into energy is through fermentation of feedstocks into bioalcohols (such as biobutanol, bioethanol and biomethanol), mainly because it requires the input of large amounts of water and energy. However, this process can produce energy-positive outputs (where less energy is put into the system to create the total energy output potential in the alcohol-derived fuel). A hot renewable resource created through fermentation that is attracting increased attention in its own right is "biodiesel," which is diesel fuel derived from fermenting waste vegetable oils or animal fats for use in vehicles. Biodiesel itself contains no petroleum products, but can be used alone or in combination with other fuels to power vehicles, in many cases without any modifications to the vehicles. Unless used in its "neat" form (B100, or pure biodiesel), biodiesel is not strictly speaking a purely renewable resource because vehicles running on it also burn a petroleum product. However, there are environmental benefits associated with the use of the B20 blend (fuel that is 20% biodiesel and 80% regular diesel fuel), particularly in reducing air emissions associated with diesel engines. The latest available figures show that 991 million gallons of biodiesel was produced in the United States in 2012. EIA, Monthly Biodiesel Production Report, Sept. 2013, http://www.eia.gov/biofuels/bio diesel/production/biodiesel.pdf.

A wide variety of federal programs, including various tax credits, promote biodiesel. *See* http://www.afdc.energy.gov. The EPAct 2005 and the Energy Independence and Security Act of 2007 (EISAct 2007) established and increased a Renewable Fuels Standard that requires all transportation fuels to contain a minimum amount of renewable fuel. The EISAct 2007 requires the overall volume of renewable fuels that must be blended into transportation fuels each year to increase to 36 billion gallons per year by 2022. In addition, beginning in 2013, a certain percentage of the renewable fuels must be advanced and/or cellulosic-based biofuels and biomass-based diesel. For more on biodiesel, see Chapter 15.

C. SUPPORTING AND FINANCING RENEWABLES

As introduced at the beginning of this chapter, renewable power projects can be difficult to fund and finance. Although most renewable fuels are free, the equipment required to capture these fuels is expensive. Large capital expenditures and lengthy permitting processes are of course required for any large energy project, renewable or not: electricity generation and fuel extraction is a very capital- and regulation-intensive endeavor, as perhaps best demonstrated by nuclear energy projects, which have multi-billion dollar price tags. But as compared to fossil fuel plants, renewable energy projects can be more expensive than their fossil fuel counterparts, in that at either the small or large scale they sometimes require larger up-front investments and have longer payback periods.

The federal government has long had a role in encouraging renewable energy development. More recently, regional, state, and local governments have led a sustained push toward renewable energy. This governmental support comes in five primary forms:

(a) creating renewable markets by requiring utilities to interconnect with renewable generators and purchase power from them at developers' requests, or requiring them to build renewable plants themselves;

(b) providing financial support to renewable energy developers in the form of grants, loans, or tax relief;

(c) conducting or funding research and development;

(d) encouraging or requiring transmission lines that either directly or indirectly support renewable energy projects; and

(e) streamlining or lessening the burdens of certain land use and permitting rules.

Private financing mechanisms augment certain of these government programs by making it easier for renewable developers to take advantage of government grants and tax benefits, as discussed in this part.

1. CREATING RENEWABLE ENERGY MARKETS

One of the most direct support mechanisms for renewable energy is the creation of a market in renewables. Some argue that governments need to spur renewable markets due to diseconomies of scale: when an industry is not sufficiently large, it lacks widespread manufacturing support, lower supply costs, employee expertise and training, and "network effects" that tend to accompany larger industries. A large industry like coal-fired generation has a battalion of trained plant operators and construction companies to choose from, and abundant supply chains for needed parts, but newer industries lack this type of support.

Nascent generating industries also face high coordination problems: they need shared transmission lines to transport wind or solar energy from a particular region to a customer base, for example. Yet companies are hesitant to build transmission lines until they know that generators will use the lines, and generators are hesitant to build before they know that transmission lines will be available. Furthermore, newer markets cannot benefit from knowledge generated by earlier failed and successful markets—someone must take the leap first. All of these serve as impediments to the growth of a new energy market in renewables, and governments can directly encourage the creation of renewable markets in two ways. First, they can require utilities to purchase renewable energy if it is offered to them, and at a certain price—thus providing guaranteed buyers if renewable energy developers happen to construct projects. More directly, governments can require that utilities build or purchase a certain amount of renewable energy, thus essentially mandating that renewable projects move forward.

a.   REQUIRING INTERCONNECTION AND PURCHASE AT A SET PRICE: THE PUBLIC UTILITY REGULATORY POLICIES ACT AND FEED-IN TARIFFS

One historical obstacle to renewable energy projects was the lack of access to vertically integrated utilities—those that generated, transported, and distributed electricity themselves and had little incentive to purchase electricity from new renewable producers. In the 1970s, the idea of wind farms and solar power arrays hooked into the electric power grid and supplying customers was the stuff of fantasy. There was virtually no such thing as a non-utility generator in the United States, as traditional electric utilities generated electricity from their resources and refused to purchase from outsiders. There were many reasons for this. As monopolies, electric utilities were the only potential buyers for power generated by renewable energy facilities, and were in no hurry to deal with potential competitors. It was rare for utilities to agree to purchase power from outsiders. When they did, they offered unattractive prices and unfavorable terms on important issues, notably on interconnecting to the electric power grid and ensuring that facilities would have standby and backup power when the sun did not shine or the wind did not blow. A renewable energy producer that provided electricity to a utility's grid also ran the risk of being considered a public utility and thus being subjected to extensive state and federal regulation.

i.   *Public Utility Regulatory Policies Act*

As described in more detail in Chapter 10, Congress addressed the monopoly power of incumbent utilities and barriers to new entrants in power supply with the Public Utility Regulatory Policies Act of 1978 (PURPA). Section 210 of PURPA aimed to remove the obstacles that qualifying renewable energy project developers encountered when attempting to sell their power to utilities and connect to the grid. Full grid access for independent generators, including renewable power plants, did not emerge until the issuance of FERC Order 888 in 1996, which required that generators have open access to utilities' transmission lines. See Chapter 10 for a fuller discussion of the open access orders. As also discussed in more detail in Chapter 10, Section 1252 of the EPAct 2005 added new PURPA Section 210(m), which mandated elimination of the purchase obligation in circumstances where

QFs have "nondiscriminatory access" to "wholesale markets for long-term sales of capacity and electric energy."

ii. Feed-In Tariffs

While PURPA required utilities to interconnect with and purchase electricity from small utility projects at avoided cost, a more recent mechanism, the feed-in tariff, has arguably created even greater incentives for renewable energy development. The term "feed-in tariff" refers to incentives modeled after those adopted (most notably) by Germany to promote renewable energy resources. Under the typical FIT structure, renewable energy projects are guaranteed interconnection with the electricity grid, and project owners are paid an above-market rate locked in for a specific term of years (in Germany, 20 years). The rate can take one of several forms, such as a fixed amount defined in advance, or a premium over the wholesale price of electricity. Some American proponents refer to FITs as renewable energy payments.

The FIT is different from previous approaches in the United States for promoting renewables because it is a fixed amount paid to the electricity generator, determined up front on the basis of the generator's cost and profit expectations. Conceptually, this stands in contrast to the avoided cost approach of PURPA, which fixes payments based on the utility's costs. The security of a direct payment to project owners is meant to generate a reasonable profit for project investors and make it easier to secure project financing. Also, a recipient of a FIT payment can be anyone with a renewable energy system, not just a PURPA QF. This prompts many to support the FIT idea for its potential to spur a boom in local and community-based small-scale solar and wind projects. Of course, what some see as a boon, others view less favorably. Paying above-market rates to help overcome the cost disadvantages of renewable energy can be viewed as "anti-competitive." Zac Anderson, As Florida shifts to solar, a fight looms, HeraldTribune.com, Mar. 22. 2009 (citing comments opposing a FIT proposal in Florida by utility Florida Power & Light Company).

There is an obvious overlap between a FIT and net metering. The two are different but related. Net metering rewards a business or homeowner for installing a renewable energy system that sometimes provides more than enough electricity to meet the customer's needs (in which case the meter "spins backwards" and the customer sells power to the grid) and sometimes does not. FITs, by comparison, pay anyone for electricity generated from renewables, whether or not it is sent back to the grid.

The German FIT is designed to encourage the deployment of onshore and offshore wind, biomass, hydropower, geothermal and solar PV. Germany had a national renewable energy target of 12.5% of gross electricity consumption in 2010 and has a 20% for 2020, and the FIT supports achieving these targets. The rates paid are differentiated by resource type (e.g. solar, wind, biomass, etc.) and by project size, with rates decreasing each year by 1% to 6.5%. The German FIT has caused explosive growth in renewable energy generation during the past decade. Germany more than doubled its national supply of electricity produced from renewables between 2000 and 2007, and met its 2010 target three years ahead of schedule. See Envtl. and Energy Study Inst., Issue Brief,

Feed-in Tariffs, Mar. 2010, http://www.eesi.org/files/feedintariff_
033110.pdf. The costs of the FIT program have been controversial,
however. Other European Union countries have also adopted FITs, and
in 2006, Ontario became the first government in North America to
establish one, in its Standard Offer Contract. International trade-based
legal challenges to FITs in Canada are discussed in Chapter 14.

In the United States, a federal FIT was proposed in 2008 but not
enacted. A number of states have considered FITs, but by 2013, only
five—Washington, Vermont, Oregon, Rhode Island, and Hawaii—had
adopted them in some fashion, and California had a similar law with
different characteristics. Of the states with European-like FITs,
Vermont's law is the most like the German model, with different rates
paid for different technologies and project sizes, and set at the cost of
generation plus profit at a "reasonable rate of return" for long contract
terms. Paul Gipe, Vermont FITs Become Law: The Mouse That Roared,
RenewableEnergyWorld.com, June 1, 2009.

Several cities also have feed-in tariffs. For example, Gainesville,
Florida, has perhaps the most aggressive European-style FIT in the
nation, with its regional utility paying as much as $0.21 per kWh in 2013
for solar PV. Gainesville adopted a solar FIT in 2009 for its regional
utility (a "municipal" utility, meaning that it is a utility owned by the
city, not private sector investors). The FIT applies to all connections in
the muni's service territory with qualified solar PV resources, although
the program's capacity is capped, and applicants for non-residential feed-
in projects exceeded program capacity. For those applicants accepted,
residential and commercial entities install their own solar systems, sell
the electricity directly to the Gainesville municipal utility, and receive a
fixed-price payment for the electricity under a 20-year contract. For a
description of other municipal FITs, see Felix Mormann, Enhancing the
Investor Appeal of Renewable Energy, 42 ENVTL. L. 681, 694 n.85 (2012).

California's FIT, unlike those elsewhere, originally guaranteed
generators a price "based on the value of electrical generation provided,"
and "not intended to embed a subsidy or rebate in the price offering." Cal.
Pub. Util. Comm'n (CPUC), Summary of Feed-In Tariffs, http://www.
cpuc.ca.gov/PUC/energy/Renewables/feedintariffssum.htm. The most
recent guaranteed price structure for renewable generators under the
tariff—the "renewable market adjusting tariff," or "ReMat"—went into
effect on November 1, 2013. CPUC, Renewable Feed-in Tariff (FIT)
Program, http://www.cpuc.ca.gov/PUC/energy/Renewables/hot/feedin
tariffs.htm. This tariff embodies the same principles as other FITs—
capturing the value of renewable generation provided to a utility—but
also contains a cap on price adjustments to avoid "unreasonable price
increases." CPUC, Decision Adopting Joint Standard Contract for
Section 399.20 Feed-In Tariff Program and Granting, in Part, Petitions
for Modification of Decision 12–05–035, May 23, 2013, http://docs.cpuc.
ca.gov/PublishedDocs/Published/G000/M066/K060/66060837.PDF.

California's utilities must take electricity offered by projects up to 3
MW involving renewable energy resources under California's RPS
program—those that contribute to California's requirement that 33% of
electricity come from renewable resources by 2020. These resources also
must be "strategically located" in terms of providing baseload or peak

generation. Utilities need not take *all* of this offered generation, however; they may limit the total MW accepted based on their percentage share of retail electricity sales, and requested contracts to sell generation under the tariff are accepted on a first-come, first-served basis. Decision Adopting Joint Standard Contract, *supra*.

The FIT approach seems to provide a stronger incentive for renewable energy investment than PURPA's avoided cost requirement, as the FIT is typically designed to cover the renewable investor's capital costs and to sometimes guarantee profits. By contrast, avoided cost simply pays the renewable generator what the purchasing utility would have otherwise paid someone else. There may be a conflict between the federal avoided cost requirement and the state and local FIT approach, however, because FERC—although not required to do so by case law—has interpreted the avoided cost requirement as both a floor and a ceiling. FERC views avoided costs as both the minimum and maximum rate utilities can be required to pay renewable developers, despite the fact that PURPA is optional: generators might choose to use PURPA to require utilities to purchase their electricity, but they are free to pursue other avenues instead. FERC still allows states some discretion in crafting their FIT, however, as shown by the following order.

California Public Utilities Comm'n et al. Order Granting Clarification and Dismissing Rehearing (Oct. 21, 2010)
133 F.E.R.C. ¶ 61,059.

On July 15, 2010, the Commission issued an order addressing the California Public Utilities Commission's (CPUC) petition for declaratory order and the separate petition for declaratory order filed by Pacific Gas and Electric Company (PG & E), Southern California Edison Company (SCE), and San Diego Gas & Electric Company (SDG & E) (collectively, Joint Utilities). On August 16, 2010, the CPUC filed a request for clarification, or, in the alternative, a request for rehearing of the July 15 Order.

In this order, the Commission grants the CPUC's request for clarification, and dismisses rehearing of the July 15 Order, as discussed below.

Background

On May 4, 2010, in Docket No. EL10–64–000, the CPUC submitted a petition for declaratory order requesting that the Commission find that sections 205 and 206 of the Federal Power Act (FPA), and section 210 of the Public Utility Regulatory Policies Act of 1978 (PURPA) and Commission regulations do not preempt the CPUC's decision to require California utilities to offer a certain price to combined heat and power (CHP) generating facilities of 20 MW or less that meet energy efficiency and environmental compliance requirements. On May 11, 2010, in Docket No. EL10–66–000, the Joint Utilities filed a separate petition for declaratory order arguing that the CPUC's decision is preempted by the FPA insofar as it sets rates for electric energy that is sold at wholesale.

The California "Waste Heat and Carbon Emissions Reduction Act," Assembly Bill (AB) 1613, amended the California Public Utilities Code to require "electrical corporations" in California (i.e., investor-owned utilities (IOU) regulated by the CPUC) to offer to purchase, at a price to be set by the CPUC, electricity that is generated by certain CHP generators and delivered to the grid. CHP generators eligible for the price set by the CPUC must have a generating capacity of not more than 20 MW and must meet certain efficiency and emissions standards. The legislation requires CPUC-jurisdictional utilities to file standard ten-year purchase contracts (AB 1613 feed-in tariffs) with the CPUC that require them to offer to purchase at the CPUC-set price electricity generated by eligible CHP generators. As amended, the California Public Utilities Code states that this tariff shall "provide for payment for every kilowatt hour delivered to the electrical grid by the combined heat and power system at a price determined by the commission." In addition, AB 1613 requires that the CPUC set the rates at which the utilities must offer to purchase from CHP generators at a level that "ensure[s] that ratepayers not using [CHP] systems are held indifferent to the existence of [the AB 1613 feed-in] tariff."

The July 15 Order found that the CPUC's decision to require California utilities to offer a certain price to CHP generating facilities of 20 MW or less that meet energy efficiency and environmental compliance requirements would not be preempted by the FPA, PURPA, or Commission regulations, as long as the program meets certain requirements. The Commission explained that a state commission may, pursuant to PURPA, determine avoided cost rates for qualifying facilities (QF). The Commission found that although the CPUC did not argue that its AB 1613 program is an implementation of PURPA, to the extent the CHP generators that can take part in the AB 1613 program obtain QF status pursuant to the Commission's regulations, the CPUC's AB 1613 feed-in tariff would *not* be preempted by the FPA, PURPA, or Commission's regulations as long as: (1) the CHP generators from which the CPUC is requiring the Joint Utilities to purchase energy and capacity are QFs pursuant to PURPA; and (2) the rate established by the CPUC does not exceed the avoided cost of the purchasing utility. In addition, the July 15 Order explained that there is no record in these proceedings upon which the Commission may determine whether the CPUC's offer price is consistent with the avoided cost rate requirements of section 210 of PURPA.

Request for Clarification or Rehearing

In its request for clarification, or, in the alternative, rehearing, the CPUC states that, based upon the findings of the Commission in the July 15 Order, the CPUC intends to reexamine the basis of its implementation of AB 1613 by implementing it under section 210 of PURPA. The CPUC therefore requests clarification that the State of California enjoys sufficient flexibility with regard to calculating avoided cost rates so that it can achieve the goals of AB 1613 to promote the development of efficient CHP generation. The CPUC contends that the basic purpose of AB 1613, "to encourage cogeneration by requiring utilities to sign contracts with CHP QFs of 20 MW or less" would be undermined if the Joint Utilities could continue to litigate or attempt to prevent California from implementing AB 1613.

The CPUC requests clarification that: (1) the CPUC can require retail utilities to consider different factors in the avoided cost calculation in order to promote development of more efficient CHP facilities; and (2) "full avoided cost" need not be the lowest possible avoided cost and can properly take into account real limitations on "alternate" sources of energy imposed by state law. The CPUC argues that the answers to these questions are necessary to determine "whether it would violate PURPA if the CPUC were to require a flexible pricing mechanism in contract offers from California retail utilities to potential AB 1613 CHP-QF systems that would entitle the CHP–QF systems to charge full avoided cost rates when the CHP-QF facility is operating at the significantly high *state* efficiency standards under AB 1613, but to also entitle the QFs to charge the established short-run avoided cost rate to the extent they were no longer operating at these high state efficiency standards.". . . .

With respect to the CPUC's request for clarification, as discussed below, we find that the concept of a multi-tiered avoided cost rate structure is consistent with the avoided cost requirements set forth in section 210 of PURPA and in the Commission's regulations.

* * *

The CPUC asks whether it may implement a two-tiered rate structure, where AB 1613-compliant QFs receive rates based on higher, long-run avoided cost rates reflecting more stringent efficiency standards, and non-AB 1613 compliant QFs continue to receive rates based on lower short-run avoided costs.

Pursuant to section 210(a) of PURPA, the Commission prescribed rules imposing on electric utilities the obligation to offer to purchase electric energy from QFs. Section 210(b) of PURPA provides that such purchases must be at rates that are: (1) just and reasonable to electric consumers and in the public interest; (2) not discriminatory against QFs; and (3) not in excess of "the incremental cost to the electric utility of alternative electric energy." Section 210(d) of PURPA, in turn, defines "incremental cost of alternative electric energy" as "the cost to the electric utility of the electric energy which, but for the purchase from [the QF], such utility would generate or purchase from another source."

The Commission implemented this so-called mandatory purchase obligation set forth in PURPA in section 292.303 of its regulations, which provides that "[e]ach electric utility shall purchase, in accordance with § 292.304, . . . any energy and capacity which is made available from a qualifying facility. . . ." The regulation further provides that nothing in the regulation requires any electric utility to pay more than the "avoided costs for purchases." "Avoided costs" is defined as "the incremental costs to an electric utility of electric energy or capacity or both which, but for the purchase from the qualifying facility. . . , such utility would generate itself or purchase from another utility's system cost data; (2) the terms of any contract including the duration of the obligation; (3) the availability of capacity or energy from a QF during the system daily and seasonal peak periods; (4) the relationship of the availability of energy or capacity from the QF to the ability of the electric utility to avoid costs; and (5) the costs or savings resulting from variations in [transmission] line losses from those that would have existed in the absence of purchases from the QF. Avoided cost rates may also "differentiate among qualifying facilities using various technologies on the basis of the supply characteristics of the different technologies."

As the Commission has previously explained, "states are allowed a wide degree of latitude in establishing an implementation plan for section 210 of PURPA, as long as such plans are consistent with our regulations. Similarly, with regard to review and enforcement of avoided cost determinations under such implementation plans, we have said that our role is generally limited to ensuring that the plans are consistent with section 210 of PURPA. . . ." In this regard, the determinations that a state commission makes to implement the rate provisions of section 210 of PURPA are by their nature fact-specific and include consideration of many factors, and we are reluctant to second guess the state commission's determinations; our regulations thus provide state commissions with guidelines on factors to be taken into account, "to the extent practicable," in determining a utility's avoided cost of acquiring the next unit of generation. . . .

The CPUC, in its request for clarification, seeks guidance on a proposal to explicitly implement AB 1613 pursuant to the provisions of PURPA, and, in particular, a proposal to explicitly set new avoided cost rates using a multi-tiered avoided cost rate structure. We find that the concept of a multi-tiered avoided cost rate structure can be consistent with the avoided cost rate requirements set forth in PURPA and our regulations. Both section 210 of PURPA and our regulations define avoided costs in terms of costs that the electric utility avoids by virtue of purchasing from the QF. The question, then, is what costs the electric utility is avoiding. Under the Commission's regulations, a state may determine that capacity is being avoided, and so may rely on the cost of such avoided capacity to determine the avoided cost rate. Further, in determining the avoided cost rate, just as a state may take into account the cost of the next marginal unit of generation, so as well the state may take into account obligations imposed by the state that, for example, utilities purchase energy from particular sources of energy or for a long duration. Therefore, the CPUC may take into account actual procurement requirements, and resulting costs, imposed on utilities in California. ■

* * *

As Professor Jim Rossi and Thomas Hutton have observed, it is odd to treat PURPA and avoided costs as a mandatory price ceiling when renewable developers can avoid PURPA altogether if they wish. States can partly avoid this conflict, though, by implementing the avoided cost requirement in a flexible manner. If avoided costs are sufficiently high and vary based on state requirements for electricity purchases, requirements for the payment of a feed-in tariff can fit within avoided costs.

Jim Rossi & Thomas Hutton, Federal Preemption and Clean Energy Floors
91 N.C. L. Rev. 1283, 1310–1312 (2013).

[FERC's unitary approach of] treating PURPA's avoided costs as a ceiling on state-mandated incentive rates in order to advance consumer protection purposes has not clearly been required by judicial decisions. Courts considering the preemptive effect of the avoided cost standard have not ruled on whether states can require a utility to pay favored generation sources more than the utility's avoided costs. In *Independent Energy Producers, Inc. v. California Public Utilities Commission*, the Ninth Circuit reviewed California rules implementing PURPA, which allowed utilities to dock their payments to QFs by twenty percent if the QF did not comply with certain operating and efficiency standards to advance clean energy goals. The court rejected this procedure, concluding that "the [California] program is preempted by PURPA insofar as it authorizes the Utilities to determine that a QF is not in compliance with . . . operating and efficiency standards and to impose a reduced avoided cost rate on that QF." This Ninth Circuit decision resulted in rejection of a state effort to allow utilities to pay less than avoided cost. However, the court left open the question whether utilities can be compelled by a state to pay more than their avoided cost. Still, to the extent that the Ninth Circuit treated PURPA's avoided cost language as requiring the setting of rates by both federal and state regulators on the very same terms, it may be interpreted as endorsing the idea of a preemption ceiling in the determination of avoided costs.

FERC itself seems to have adopted this unitary standard approach in avoided cost determinations, and a recent FERC ruling arising from a California clean energy policy illustrates its significance for state clean energy policies generally. California had enacted feed-in tariff legislation, A.B. 1613, which directed the California Public Utility Commission ("CPUC") to promulgate the details of a state-administered feed-in tariff for combined heat and power ("CHP") and renewable facilities. However, affected utilities complained that California had exceeded its authority by requiring them to pay for power from these facilities at a rate that was more than their avoided costs. The CPUC applied to FERC for a declaratory order to the effect that the California feed-in tariff was not preempted by PURPA or the Federal Power Act. FERC sided with the complaining utilities rather than the state of California. As to PURPA, FERC construed the statute to preempt any state feed-in tariffs mandating that utilities pay prices that exceed the avoided cost under PURPA, consistent with its position in Connecticut Light & Power Co. The FERC viewed itself as confined to this result, because if the feed-in tariff beneficiaries were to operate outside of PURPA, they would then be selling energy for resale, and this would bring them within another statute FERC is charged to implement, the FPA. . . . In all, FERC's approach treated PURPA avoided costs as a statutory ceiling on California feed-in-tariffs.

Although FERC's decision on California's feed-in tariff was largely mitigated by an order on motions for clarification as described below, the ruling effectively caps state and local feed-in tariffs at PURPA's avoided costs and brings compliance with that cap within FERC's regulatory purview. It reflects an approach to preemption that is more in line with ceiling preemption and a unitary federal standard for utility rates under PURPA than a floor preemption approach.

3.   Reclaiming PURPA's Clean Energy Floor

FERC's decision on California's feed-in tariff and its prior decisions in the same vein risk extending PURPA's preemptive reach to a length that is not required or even envisioned by the statute. Initially, PURPA does not even direct that any state-administered feed-in tariff needs to operate under the auspices of the federal statute. The rationale is that such a state policy could operate entirely independently of PURPA, as FERC appreciated shortly after the statute was enacted. Indeed, California's feed-in tariff program did not limit its beneficiaries to facilities eligible for QF status under PURPA. ∎

* * *

b.   MANDATING RENEWABLE GENERATION: RENEWABLE PORTFOLIO STANDARDS

Rather than requiring utilities to pay avoided cost or the fixed rate under a set tariff if a renewable energy developer offers electricity for sale, governments can also mandate renewable energy purchases or generation through a renewable portfolio standard (RPS), clean energy standard (CES), or renewable electricity standard (RES) (the terms are largely interchangeable). A RPS typically requires a specified percentage of power sold by electricity retailers operating in a state to be derived from renewable power sources. Many RPS plans are accompanied by markets in tradable renewable credits, allowing suppliers with excess credits to sell them to those who need them. The RPS typically has twin sets of goals: to reap the energy, environmental, and economic benefits of renewable energy and stimulate market and technology development; and to help make electricity generated from renewables.

At the beginning of 2015, 29 states had RPS mandates and an additional nine had voluntary goals or other RPS-like programs for renewable energy deployment. A number of municipalities have also adopted RPS programs. For example, Austin, Texas requires that 35% of electricity needs be met by renewable sources by 2020, using 200 MW of solar. City of Austin Climate Protection Resolution No. 20070215–0232 (2012 Update), http://www.austintexas.gov/sites/default/files/files/Sustainability/2012%20Resolution%20Matrix.pdf.

State RPSs will be increasingly important under greenhouse gas regulations promulgated by the U.S. Environmental Protection Agency (EPA) under Section 111 of the federal Clean Air Act (CAA). As discussed further in Chapter 5, EPA released proposed carbon regulations for existing power plants under section 111(d) on June 2, 2014. These regulations, called the Clean Power Plan, apply to power plants in operation or having commenced construction as of January 8, 2014. The regulations set goals for reducing GHG emissions from these plants and direct the states to implement plans that achieve these goals. Specifically, states must implement plans under which existing power plants achieve the "best system of emission reduction . . . adequately demonstrated" to reduce carbon emissions. EPA indicates that four different strategies will form the foundation of this technological standard:

1.   Reducing the carbon intensity of generation at individual affected EGUs through heat rate improvements. "Heat rate" is defined as "the amount of energy used by an electrical generator or power plant to generate one kilowatthour (kWh) of electricity." EIA, Frequently Asked Questions, http://www.eia.gov/tools/faqs/faq.cfm?id=107&t=3.

2.   Reducing emissions from the most carbon-intensive affected EGUs in the amount that results from substituting generation at those EGUs with generation from less carbon-intensive affected EGUs (including NGCC [natural gas combined cycle] units under construction).

3.   Reducing emissions from affected EGUs in the amount that results from substituting generation at those EGUs with expanded low- or zero-carbon generation.

4.   Reducing emissions from affected EGUs in the amount that results from the use of demand-side energy efficiency that reduces the amount of generation required.

Carbon Pollution Emission Guidelines for Existing Stationary Sources: Electric Utility Generating Units, 79 Fed. Reg. 34,829 (June 18, 2014). See Chapter 5 for more on the Clean Power Plan.

Item 3 above, in particular, shows that state RPSs will be a core building block in assuring that existing power plants achieve the best system of emissions reduction adequately demonstrated. With the exception of nuclear power, renewable technologies are the only sources of zero-carbon generation, a type of generation that EPA defines as a core building block of its CAA carbon regulations. EPA notes in its proposed rule that RPSs "reduce utilization of fossil fuel-fired EGUs and, thereby, lead to reductions in GHG emissions by meeting a portion of the demand for electricity through renewable or other energy sources," highlighting Minnesota's and Oregon's RPSs as examples of successful programs.

State RPSs vary substantially, however, and it is not yet clear which will meet EPA's requirements for carbon emission reductions from existing sources. As highlighted in the excerpts below, state plans vary with respect to the targets they set, the types of sources that count as renewable, and methods for obtaining compliance, among other differences. In states with competition in retail electricity markets, utilities typically meet the RPS requirements on their own. In other states, PUCs oversee utility procurement and contracting under the RPS, and two states, New York and Illinois, have specific state agencies with direct responsibility for RPS procurement.

U.S. Environmental Protection Agency
Renewable Portfolio Standards Fact Sheet (2009).

How Does a Renewable Portfolio Standard Encourage Clean Energy?

An RPS creates market demand for renewable and clean energy supplies. Currently, states with RPS requirements mandate that between 4 and 30 percent of electricity be generated from renewable sources by a specified date. While RPS requirements differ across states, there are generally three ways that electricity suppliers can comply with the RPS:

- Owning a renewable energy facility and its output generation.
- Purchasing Renewable Energy Certificates (RECs).
- Purchasing electricity from a renewable facility inclusive of all renewable attributes (sometimes called "bundled renewable electricity").

What Are the Benefits of a Renewable Portfolio Standard?

The policy benefits of an RPS are the same as those from renewable energy:

• Environmental improvement (e.g., avoided air pollution, global climate change mitigation, waste reduction, habitat preservation, conservation of valuable natural resources).

• Increased diversity and security of energy supply.

• Lower natural gas prices due to displacement of some gas-fired generation, or a more efficient use of natural gas due to significantly increased fuel conversion efficiencies.

• Reduced volatility of power prices, given stable or non-existent fuel costs for renewables.

• Local economic development resulting from new jobs, taxes, and revenue associated with new renewable capacity.

• Because it is a market-based program, an RPS also has several operational benefits:

• Achieves policy objectives efficiently and at a relatively modest cost (ratepayer impacts range from less than 1 percent increases to 0.5 percent savings).

• Spreads compliance costs among all customers.

• Minimizes the need for ongoing government intervention.

• Functions in both regulated and unregulated state electricity markets.

• Provides a clear and long-term target for renewable energy generation that can increase investors' and developers' confidence in the prospects for renewable energy. ∎

* * *

i.   State RPS Experience

Requirements of state RPS programs differ widely. States have grappled with these difficult questions in designing their RPS plans:

(1) *What is the appropriate percentage target*? As the EPA notes, target percentages vary from as low as 4% to as high as 30%. Too low a target, and no new generation is stimulated. Too high, and utilities might find it impossible to meet the standard.

(2) *Which renewable resources count toward the RPS percentage requirement*? Solar, wind, geothermal, and some biomass typically count. What about burning wood from old-growth forests, which might have negative environmental impacts? Should that count? On the other end of the spectrum, should projects perceived to have extra environmental benefits, such as parking lot solar PV, count even more? (Sometimes they do.) Some RPSs do not count existing hydropower and municipal solid waste projects, finding them to be not as green as other renewables. Sometimes, though, both are subtracted from the generation total to which the RPS target is applied. If existing sources are counted, the RPS may be easier to meet (for example, Maine's 30% RPS requirement includes existing hydropower projects) and can therefore be less

ambitious than it appears on the surface. Do you agree with this approach?

Should other clean energy approaches count, even if they are not renewables and would do nothing to stimulate the market for renewable power projects? If so, what would count? How about improvements in energy efficiency, which decrease the need for electricity generation and have many of the same environmental benefits? If mitigating global warming impacts is important, what about nuclear energy or carbon capture and storage (CCS)?

(3) *Should the state allow electricity generated from out-of-state renewable resources to count toward a state RPS?* Might it even be *required* to do so? (See the discussion of the Dormant Commerce Clause, below.) If a utility operates in the territory of an RTO, would it be appropriate for the state to count resources from generators in that territory, but not those from other regions?

(4) *How should market mechanisms be incorporated?* RPS policies can incorporate market-based mechanisms that enable utilities to buy or sell tradable renewable energy certificates or credits ("RECs") to demonstrate compliance. Many economists contend that the flexibility of market-based trading systems lowers the overall cost in meeting environmental goals.

As you read through this analysis of design issues associated with state RPS, consider how different states have addressed these questions, and whether a federal standard might be better than having multiple state standards (and, if so, why).

K.S. Cory and B.G. Swezey, Renewable Portfolio Standards in the States: Balancing Goals and Implementation Strategies

Nat'l Renewable Energy Lab. (2007)
http://www.nrel.gov/docs/fy08osti/41409.pdf.

There are significant differences in state RPS design—such as technology and geographic eligibility, methods that can be used to achieve compliance, and implementation specifics—that make it difficult to generalize about RPS policies nationally.

The RPS implementation issues covered here can be divided into the following categories: resource availability, resource-specific provisions, political and regulatory consistency, and ability to finance new renewable projects.

Resource Availability

To successfully implement an RPS policy, sufficient renewable energy resources must be available. However, renewable resource availability varies widely across the regional climates and geographies of the United States, and the lowest-cost resources may not be accessible within any particular RPS state. Using renewable energy certificates or credits is one mechanism for tapping into the best resources. At the same time, officials must have confidence in both the quality and the legitimacy of RECs.

Renewable Energy Certificates

RECs are a relatively new market instrument created by separating the "attributes" of renewable electricity generation from the physical electricity produced, thus making RECs a tradable commodity separate from the actual electrons. One REC typically represents the attributes of 1 megawatt-hour (MWh) of renewable electricity generation.

RECs have many advantages. The use of RECs frees renewable energy sellers from the need to deliver the renewable electricity in real time to the ultimate users. Rather, the electricity, devoid of any attributes, is injected into the grid while the RECs are retained for other uses. The RECs provide an accurate, durable record of what was produced and a fungible commodity that can be traded among suppliers.

The use of RECs can reduce the cost of RPS compliance by lowering transmission and distribution costs, while also providing access to a larger quantity of resource options. Finally, RECs provide compliance flexibility by facilitating market trading and increasing market liquidity. As a result, RECs have become the dominant mechanism of RPS compliance. However, the manner in which RECs are defined and treated in RPS policies varies by state and region.

REC Definitions

State-specific definitions of renewable energy or RECs eligibility tend to segment renewable energy markets across the United States, which results in markets that are smaller and less liquid than they would be if common eligibility definitions were used. This can increase the cost of RPS compliance by limiting the types and sources of renewable energy that can be used for compliance. State-specific definitions also work against the development of a larger spot market for renewable energy attributes. The result is that today, with few exceptions, the majority of REC sales are bilateral (i.e., conducted between one buyer and one seller in a private transaction in which pricing information remains confidential). And differences in REC shelf lives between markets can create an additional challenge.

REC Shelf Life

The shelf life of a REC (i.e., the length of time during which a REC can be used for compliance) can be as short as three months (in New England) to as long as four years (in Nevada and Wisconsin). Because renewable energy generation can vary on both a seasonal and an annual basis due to changing weather patterns, longer REC lives increase the ability of the market to smooth out these variations. In addition, the ability to "bank" RECs helps address supply and demand imbalances that result from project construction intervals as well as the "lumpiness" of new supply additions. Whether states adopt longer REC lives or banking, it is important to place some finite limit on REC life; otherwise an oversupply of vintage RECs could reduce demand for new production.

Double Counting

Double counting occurs when more than one entity claims ownership of a REC or of the REC and its associated power. This can be a serious issue in RPS implementation and for renewable energy markets in general. Policy makers may be tempted to count any and all renewable energy generated in a state toward RPS compliance. This is a particularly serious issue where markets exist for voluntary renewable energy (or "green power") purchases. Counting voluntary market sales toward RPS compliance undermines one of the fundamental tenets of these markets—that an individual consumers' voluntary purchase supports renewable energy development over and above the development that occurs otherwise. An RPS is designed to "prime the pump" and enable a wider market for renewable power; it is not designed to limit total demand.

Most states with an RPS policy have determined that voluntary green power purchases should not be counted toward RPS compliance.

REC Tracking Systems

REC tracking systems provide a mechanism for regulators to easily verify and trace REC ownership. REC tracking systems are now operating in Texas/ERCOT, New Jersey (solar-only), New England, the Pennsylvania-New Jersey-Maryland (PJM) interconnect, the Midwest, and Western grid regions. These REC tracking platforms have been designed for the specific state or regional circumstances. As more states employ REC tracking systems to monitor RPS compliance, the trading of RECs between systems with divergent definitions and tracking structures will have to be addressed. Key challenges relate to whether and how to allow for interregional trading, and how to protect against double counting between states and regions. . . .

Limiting Out-of-State Generator Eligibility

Geographic eligibility rules differ widely among states. Some RPS policies require that certain renewable facilities be built within the state or require a facility to be directly interconnected to the state grid. Other states are less restrictive, requiring only that the energy be delivered to the state. Still others allow energy and REC delivery to a regional control area or regional transmission organization (RTO). Finally, a small number of states allow the use of RECs without electricity delivery if certain conditions are met. Some states and regions are limiting out-of-state renewable energy delivery, not through RPS policies but through the design of their REC tracking systems. For example, the New England Power Pool's Generation Information System (NEPOOL-GIS) restricts the participation of out-of-region projects by requiring that firm transmission into the region be purchased to match a renewable facility's generation on an hourly basis. . . . Some states have designed their RPS policy specifically to favor in-state facilities, such as providing extra compliance credit to in-state facilities or by creating set-asides for customer-owned systems. And some states employ complementary policies that encourage in-state renewable generation; these include rebates, state tax incentives, public benefit funding, and net metering. [See discussion of potential dormant commerce clause problems in Note 1.]

Solar-Specific Provisions

Some states have established RPS carve-outs or set-asides for particular renewable energy technologies to support promising technologies with valuable characteristics that might otherwise be shut out of the market because of their higher costs. Solar energy has been the primary recipient of most RPS set-aside rules.

For example, states can specify a certain quantity or percentage of the RPS that must be met with solar resources so that solar does not have to compete with other renewables. Another tactic used in RPS programs is to have set-asides for customer-sited or distributed systems, which tend to favor solar. Many RPS policies offer extra credit to either solar or distributed generation (DG); for example, DG and/or solar RECs are assigned greater weight toward compliance than other RECs. Washington, Nevada, Utah (RPS goal), Texas, Michigan, Delaware, and West Virginia (RPS goal) offer double credit or multipliers for "non-wind," solar or DG. *See* Database of State Incentives For Renewables & Efficiency, www.dsireusa.org/documents/summarymaps/Solar_DG_RPS_map.ppt.

Because solar energy remains relatively expensive when compared with other renewable energy technologies, states with solar set-asides may also offer financial incentives to assist with solar compliance.

Most solar systems are customer-owned and sited, which presents certain challenges for verifying system output. [*Note from authors*: In states like California, the majority of distributed solar systems are now owned by companies, not homeowners. These companies own solar panels, and they enter into numerous individual contracts with homeowners in which the companies promise to install, operate, and maintain the panels and the homeowners promise to purchase electricity from the panels under a long-term contract. The installer/operator also sells excess electricity back to the grid. Verification can still be difficult within this "third-party" system, however.]

Political and Regulatory Consistency

The success of any RPS policy depends not only on implementation specifics but also on the strength and consistency of the policy over time. The strongest RPS policies incorporate noncompliance penalties, either in the form of fines or an alternative compliance payment (ACP). An ACP requires suppliers to pay a predetermined amount (per kilowatt-hour) if they fall short in meeting the RPS. The ACP funds collected are normally used to support new renewable energy development. Penalties and ACP systems become even stronger motivators if load-serving entities are prohibited from recovering these costs from ratepayers or customers.

On the other end of the spectrum are states that enact ambiguous RPS regulations or definitions, allow frequent or major rule changes, or have weak enforcement mechanisms. Also, compliance waivers are available in many states. These provisions tend to be vague as to when and how a waiver is to be granted. For example, the Arizona statute allows a utility to request a waiver from any provision, "for good cause." Some waivers are based on, "economic and competitive pressure" (Minnesota), or whether renewable resources are, "reasonably available" (Pennsylvania).

RPS Cost Caps

Many states concerned about the potential rate impacts of an RPS have instituted cost caps which limit the exposure of ratepayers to higher costs associated with RPS implementation. In general, if a cost cap is reached, suppliers are exempted from further compliance requirements.

Changing Eligibility Rules

RPS policies that are subject to frequent changes introduce uncertainty into the market. In particular, some states have modified their renewable resource and technology eligibility definitions, or the manner in which renewable energy production, and thus compliance, is measured. This has resulted in large REC market price swings. For example, resource eligibility changes in Connecticut allowed a number of preexisting biomass plants to sell into the compliance market, causing REC market prices to fall sharply in 2005. Such uncertainty is a disincentive to investment in new renewable energy projects.

Summary and Conclusions

In the end, a successful RPS policy is one that meets a particular state's policy goals. States may enact an RPS with any number of policy goals in mind, such as fuel diversity, economic development, electricity price stability, environmental benefits, and others. However, policy makers should keep in mind that the pursuit of some goals, such as maximizing in-state development, could come at the expense of the achievement of other goals, such as minimizing the cost impacts of an RPS. ∎

NOTES AND COMMENTS

1. Professor Kirsten Engel notes that "a state acts unconstitutionally if it creates a marketable permit or obligation scheme and employs facial discrimination to retain the environmental public goods for its own residents," and states therefore may not prohibit the "use of out-of-state renewable energy credits" to meet an RPS. States also may not implement statutes or regulations that are "facially neutral and yet place[ ] an excessive burden on interstate trade." A state is likely to be permitted, however, to "restrict the legal value of a tradable environmental permit according to the location of the ultimate use of the permit (for example, limiting renewable energy credits that satisfy a renewable portfolio standard to credits that are sold to in-state consumers)." This type of policy would not prohibit the use of out-of-state credits, but it would require these credits to be "spent" in-state for in-state RPS credit. Kirsten H. Engel, The Dormant Commerce Clause Threat to Market-Based Environmental Regulation: The Case of Electricity Deregulation, 26 Ecology L.Q. 243 (1999). For a detailed exploration of how states should be able to enact RPSs while avoiding dormant Commerce Clause problems, see Daniel K. Lee & Timothy P. Duane, Putting the Dormant Commerce Clause Back to Sleep: Adapting the Doctrine to Support State Renewable Portfolio Standards, 43 Envtl. L. 295 (2013). Dormant Commerce Clause issues are addressed in more depth in Section b.ii., *infra*.

2. State RPS policies appear to have stimulated the development of new renewable energy facilities. In 2012, the U.S. Partnership for Renewable Energy Finance estimated that "RPS mandates have driven creation of one-third of current U.S. non-hydro renewable electricity." U.S. Partnership for Renewable Energy Finance, Ramping up Renewables: Leveraging State RPS Programs amid Uncertain Federal Support (2012), http://www.uspref.org/wp-content/uploads/2012/06/Ramping-up-Renewables-Leveraging-State-RPS-Programs-Summary.pdf. In addition, most states met their initial RPS targets rather quickly after they were established. *Id.*

It is debatable how much of that growth can be attributed to the RPS. Indeed, there is substantial evidence that a state RPS by itself is ineffective in promoting renewable power projects without other programs (such as rebates and financial incentives) in place. (Section 4, below, discusses these incentive programs.) Moreover, as state targets increase over time, they may be more difficult to meet in the long run.

3.   Any state with a RPS typically has renewable energy facilities that are QFs under PURPA and entered into long-term energy purchase contracts with utilities well before the RPS was first established. FERC emphasized in its final PURPA Section 210(m) rule (see Section C.1 above) that its rule preserved existing contracts and did not terminate any utility's mandatory purchase obligation under those contracts.

This creates an interesting issue in some cases: who owns the REC? In newer contracts the parties tend to be aware of RECs and contract for their transfer. However, in some older contracts the concept of a REC did not exist when the contracts were signed, so it is not obvious whether selling the energy to the utilities conveyed the "attributes" that make up a REC. *See, e.g.*, Wheelabrator Lisbon v. Dep't of Pub. Util. Control, 531 F.3d 183 (2d Cir. 2008). In American Ref-Fuel Company, 105 FERC ¶ 61,004 (2003), FERC declared that state law governs this issue, noting that "contracts for the sale of . . . energy entered into pursuant to PURPA do not convey RECs to the purchasing utility . . . absent [an] express provision in [the relevant] contract" or a rule of state law to the contrary. FERC also observed that "RECs are created by the States. They exist outside the confines of PURPA. PURPA thus does not address the ownership of [the credits]." *Id.* at ¶ 61,007.

Most courts ruling on this issue (including the *Wheelabrator* court and the New Jersey Superior Court (In re Ownership of Renewable Energy Certificates, 913 A.2d 825 (N.J. Super. Ct. App. Div. 2007)) have held that renewable QF project attributes are conveyed to power purchasers, allowing them to count the generation toward RPS compliance. On the other hand, states ruling on net metered projects have decided that the RECs belong to customer-generators.

4.   State RPSs operate at the state level, but utilities are increasingly purchasing power in regional marketplaces. As the excerpt notes, tracking RECs is increasingly done on ISO/RTOs' generation tracking systems. *See* Joel B. Eisen, The Environmental Responsibility of the Regionalizing Electric Utility Industry, 15 Duke Envtl. L. & Pol'y F. 295 (2005).

5.   As this excerpt notes, "green pricing" programs for residential, commercial, and industrial consumers have emerged to promote environmentally safer ways of generating electricity. These programs allow customers to choose to purchase electricity based on its green attributes (particularly its fuel source and emissions profile) and enable consumers to pay premiums for electricity generated from renewable sources.

DOE, Ofc. of Energy Effc'y and Renewable Energy, Guide to Purchasing Green Power 15 (2004), http://emp.lbl.gov/sites/all/files/purchasing_guide_for_web.pdf.

An important element of any "green pricing" program is information. Consumers need to know that they are getting "green power" and that those marketing "green" power are not deceiving consumers. However, the nature of electricity and the grid makes it impossible to prove that actual electrons flowing to a consumer came from "green" sources. Some states have disclosure rules designed to address this issue through labeling about power's green attributes. States' disclosure rules work with certification programs such as the Green-e stamp, which are independent assessments of "green" power products that ensure that the power provided is in fact "green." *See* Green-e, http://www.green-e.org. The Database of State Incentives for Renewables and Efficiency (DSIRE) and DOE's Office of Energy Efficiency and Renewable Energy's "Green Power Network" maintain comprehensive lists of states' disclosure provisions. DSIRE, http://www.dsireusa.org/; DOE, Office of Energy Efficiency and Renewable Energy, http://www.eere.energy.gov.

In general, the voluntary nature of "green pricing"—states may require utilities to offer green pricing but do not compel consumers to choose it—limits its effectiveness and suggests why most states do not include power chosen through "green pricing" in the RPS percentage.

6.   States differ in how they implement cost caps for RPS plans. The most common is a reasonable cost threshold beyond which utilities are no longer required to acquire renewable supply. Some states, such as Colorado and New Mexico, limit costs to a total percentage of an electric customer's bill, regardless of whether that makes it possible to meet the RPS. Cory and Swezey, *supra*.

7.   There has been extensive discussion about whether FITs are superior to RPSs for promoting renewables. Most observers conclude that they are. For example, when Florida was considering adopting a RPS, the environmental group Environmental Defense Fund wrote to the state's PSC that it objected to the RPS design and in any event the state should consider a FIT instead because "[e]vidence is mounting that a REP policy far outweighs other procurement models for the large-scale adoption of renewable energy technologies." Letter from Kellyn Eberhardt, Envtl. Defense Fund, to Fla. Pub. Svc. Comm'n, Aug. 26, 2008, *available at* http://www.wind-works.org/. Federal researchers note that "RPS mandates prescribe *how much customer demand* must be met with renewables, while properly structured FIT policies attempt to support *new supply development* by providing investor certainty." Karlynn Cory et al., NREL, Feed-in Tariff Policy: Design, Implementation, and RPS Policy Interactions 8–9 (2009). They add that "[e]xperience in Europe is beginning to demonstrate that due to the stable investment environment created under well-designed FIT policies, renewable energy development and financing can happen more quickly and often more cost-effectively than under competitive solicitations" that utilities use for RPS mandates. The long-term contracts associated with FITs, in which a utility agrees to buy renewable energy at a fixed rate for a certain period of years, also provide investor certainty, and countries with FITs have cheaper electricity generated from renewables than those with RPS plans. *Id.* Researcher Toby Couture, one of the NREL report co-authors, observed in a 2009 interview, "We deal with data and the evidence is very clear. Feed-in tariffs have consistently proven to be cheaper for consumers. That's the bottom line." *Id.*

ii.   *Barriers to State Goals: Dormant Commerce Clause and Preemption Concerns*

While states' RPS and other programs to promote renewables are increasingly popular, do they violate the dormant Commerce Clause, which protects commerce from protectionist regulation by states?

California's Low Carbon Fuel Standard was challenged on this basis, as shown in the following case.

Rocky Mountain Farmers Union v. Corey

730 F.3d 1070 (9th Cir. 2013).

■ GOULD, CIRCUIT JUDGE: Whether global warming is caused by carbon emissions from our industrialized societies is a question for scientists to ponder. Whether, if such a causal relationship exists, the world can fight or retard global warming by implementing taxes or regulations that deter carbon emissions is a question for economists and politicians to decide. Whether one such regulatory scheme, implemented by the State of California, is constitutional under the United States Constitution's Commerce Clause is the question that we consider in this opinion.

Plaintiffs-Appellees Rocky Mountain Farmers' Union et al. ("Rocky Mountain") . . . sued Defendant-Appellant California Air Resources Board ("CARB"), contending that the Low Carbon Fuel Standard ("Fuel Standard"), Cal.Code Regs. tit. 17, §§ 95480–90 (2011), violated the dormant Commerce Clause and was preempted by Section 211(*o*) of the Clean Air Act, 42 U.S.C. § 7545(*o*), known as the federal Renewable Fuel Standard ("RFS"). In three rulings issued in December 2011, the district court held that the Fuel Standard (1) facially discriminated against out-of-state ethanol; (2) impermissibly engaged in the extraterritorial regulation of ethanol production; (3) discriminated against out-of-state crude oil in purpose and effect [note from authors: this issue is omitted in the case excerpts below]; and (4) was not saved by California's preemption waiver in the Clean Air Act. The district court applied strict scrutiny, and although it reasoned that the Fuel Standard served a legitimate state purpose, it concluded that CARB had not shown that its purpose could not be achieved in a nondiscriminatory way.

We hold that the Fuel Standard's regulation of ethanol does not facially discriminate against out-of-state commerce. . . . We vacate the preliminary injunction and remand to the district court to consider whether the Fuel Standard's ethanol provisions discriminate in purpose or in practical effect. If so, then the district court should apply strict scrutiny to those provisions. If not, then the district court should apply the balancing test established in *Pike v. Bruce Church, Inc.,* to the Fuel Standard's ethanol provisions. . . . To prevail under that test, Plaintiffs-Appellees must show that the Fuel Standard imposes a burden on interstate commerce that is "clearly excessive" in relation to its local benefits.

I

A

. . . . When instituting uniform federal regulations for air pollution in the Clean Air Act, "Congress consciously chose to permit California to blaze its own trail with a minimum of federal oversight." Section 209(a) of the Clean Air Act expressly prohibited state regulation of emissions from motor vehicles. 42 U.S.C. § 7543(a). But the same section allowed California to adopt its own standards if it "determine[d] that the State standards will be, in the aggregate, at least as protective of public health and welfare as applicable Federal standards." *Id.* § 7543(b). Other states could choose to follow either the federal or the California standards, but they could not adopt standards of their own. *Id.* § 7507. . . .

Continuing its tradition of leadership, the California legislature enacted Assembly Bill 32, the Global Warming Solutions Act of 2006. The legislature found that "[g]lobal warming poses a serious threat to the economic well-being, public health, natural resources, and the environment of California." Cal. Health & Safety Code § 38501(a). . . .

Faced with these threats, California resolved to reduce its greenhouse gas ("GHG") emissions to their 1990 level by the year 2020, and it empowered CARB to design emissions-reduction measures to meet this goal. . . . CARB adopted a three-part approach designed to lower GHG emissions from the transportation sector: (1) reducing emissions at the tailpipe by establishing progressively stricter emissions limits for new vehicles ("Tailpipe Standards"); (2) integrating regional land use, housing, and transportation planning to reduce the number of "vehicle miles traveled" each year; and (3) lowering the embedded GHGs in transportation fuel by adopting the Fuel Standard to reduce the quantity of GHGs emitted in the production of transportation fuel. . . . The Fuel Standard, . . . is directed at the supply side, creating an alternate path to emissions reduction by reducing the carbon intensity of transportation fuels that are burned in California. [The case explains in a footnote that "[a] fuel's carbon intensity is the amount of lifecycle greenhouse gas emissions caused by production and transportation of the fuel, per unit of energy of fuel delivered, expressed in grams of carbon dioxide equivalent per megajoule (gCO_2e/MJ)."]

B

On January 18, 2007, the California governor issued Executive Order S–01–07, which directed CARB to adopt regulations that would reduce the average GHG emissions attributable to California's fuel market by ten percent by 2020. The Fuel Standard, developed in response, applies to nearly all transportation fuels currently consumed in California and any fuels developed in the future. In 2010, regulated parties [distibutors and blenders of fuels] were required to meet the Fuel Standard's reporting requirements but were not bound by a carbon intensity cap. Beginning in 2011, the Fuel Standard established a declining annual cap on the average carbon intensity of California's transportation-fuel market. By setting a predictable path for emissions reduction, the Fuel Standard is intended to spur the development and production of low-carbon fuels, reducing overall emissions from transportation.

To comply with the Fuel Standard, a fuel blender must keep the average carbon intensity of its total volume of fuel below the Fuel Standard's annual limit. Fuels generate credits or deficits, depending on whether their carbon intensity is higher or lower than the annual cap. Credits may be used to offset deficits, may be sold to other blenders, or may be carried forward to comply with the carbon intensity cap in later years. With these offsets, a blender selling high carbon intensity fuels can comply with the Fuel Standard by purchasing credits from other regulated parties; no regulated party is required to sell any particular fuel or blend of fuels with a certain carbon intensity or origin. . . .

i

The Fuel Standard uses a "lifecycle analysis" to determine the total carbon intensity of a given transportation fuel. Because GHGs mix in the atmosphere, all emissions related to transportation fuels used in California pose the same local risk to California citizens. One ton of carbon dioxide emitted when fuel is produced in Iowa or Brazil harms Californians as much as one emitted when fuel is consumed in Sacramento. The Tailpipe Standards control only emissions within California. Without lifecycle analysis, all GHGs emitted before the fuel enters a vehicle's gas tank would be excluded from California's regulation. Similarly, the climate-change benefits of biofuels such as ethanol, which mostly come before combustion, would be ignored if CARB's regulatory focus were limited to emissions produced when fuels are consumed in California.

With a one-sided focus on consumption, even strong tailpipe-emissions standards would let GHG emissions rise during fuel production. Tailpipe standards could sharply reduce emissions from each individual vehicle without reducing net GHG emissions. In the extreme, rising emissions from production could raise total GHG emissions, completely subverting tailpipe-emissions limits. . . . To avoid these perverse shifts, CARB designed the Fuel Standard to account for emissions associated with all aspects of the production, refining, and transportation of a fuel, with the aim of reducing total, well-to-wheel GHG emissions. When these emissions are measured, CARB assigns a cumulative carbon intensity value to an individual fuel lifecycle, which is called a "pathway."

The importance of lifecycle analysis is shown clearly by the diversity of the California fuel market, which includes fuels made with many different source materials, called "feedstocks," and production processes. As of June 2011, CARB has performed lifecycle analyses of fuels made from petroleum, natural gas, hydrogen, electricity, corn, sugarcane, used cooking oil, and tallow. Fuels made from these feedstocks generate or avoid emissions at different stages of their production, transportation, and use, depending on when the conversion to fuel requires or displaces energy.

* * *

ii

Ethanol is an alcohol produced through fermentation and distillation of a variety of organic feedstocks. Most domestic ethanol comes from corn. Brazilian sugarcane dominates the import market. Ethanol production is a resource-intensive process, requiring electricity and steam. Steam is usually produced on site with coal or natural gas in dedicated boilers. The choices of type of feedstock, source of electricity, and source of thermal energy affect the carbon intensity of the fuel pathway. To illustrate, ethanol made with sugarcane, hydroelectricity, and natural gas would produce lower emissions than ethanol made from corn and coal. To determine the total carbon intensity values for each ethanol pathway, the [California] model considers the carbon intensity of factors including: (1) growth and transportation of the feedstock, with a credit for the GHGs absorbed during photosynthesis; (2) efficiency of production; (3) type of electricity used to power the plant; (4) fuel used for thermal energy; (5) milling process used; (6) offsetting value of an animal-feed co-product called distillers' grains, that displaces demand for feed that would generate its own emissions in production; (7) transportation of the fuel to the blender in California; and (8) conversion of land to agricultural use.

[In one table] CARB separates these factors into those that are correlated with location and those that are not, using a regional identifier as a shorthand for the factors correlated with location. The milling process, co-product, and source of thermal energy are not correlated with region, so they are labeled individually. Factors related to transportation, efficiency, and electricity are correlated with a plant's location in the Midwest, Brazil, or California. For example, California ethanol plants are newer and more efficient on average than those in the Midwest, using less thermal energy and electricity in the production process. Also, the electricity available on the grid in the Midwest produces more emissions in generation than electricity in California or Brazil because much of the electricity in the Midwest is generated by coal-fired power plants. By contrast, California receives most of its power from renewable sources and natural gas, and Brazil relies almost entirely on hydroelectricity.

Emissions from transporting the feedstock and the refined fuel are related to location, but they are not directly proportionate to distance traveled. Transportation emissions reflect a combination of: (1) distance traveled, including distance traveled inside California to the fuel blender; (2) total mass and volume transported; and (3) efficiency of the method of transport. California ethanol produces the most transportation emissions because California grows no corn for ethanol, so its producers import raw corn, which is bulkier and heavier than the refined ethanol shipped by producers in Brazil and the Midwest. Brazilian ethanol produces fewer emissions than the 7,500 miles it travels would suggest because ocean tankers are very efficient. Midwest ethanol, going one third of that distance, produces the least.

* * *

III

Plaintiffs contend that the Fuel Standard's ethanol . . . provisions discriminate against out-of-state commerce and regulate extraterritorial activity. CARB disagrees and, in the alternative, contends that Section 211(c)(4)(B) of the Clean Air Act authorizes the Fuel Standard under the Commerce Clause. We address each claim in turn.

The Commerce Clause provides that "Congress shall have Power . . . [t]o regulate Commerce . . . among the several States." U.S. Const., art. I, § 8, cl. 3. This affirmative grant of power does not explicitly control the several states, but it "has long been understood to have a 'negative' aspect that denies the States the power unjustifiably to discriminate against or burden the interstate flow of articles of commerce." Known as the "negative" or "dormant" Commerce Clause, this aspect is not a perfect negative, as "the Framers' distrust of economic Balkanization was limited by their federalism favoring a degree of local autonomy.". . . .

"The modern law of what has come to be called the dormant Commerce Clause is driven by concern about 'economic protectionism— that is, regulatory measures designed to benefit in-state economic interests by burdening out-of-state competitors.' " For dormant Commerce Clause purposes, economic protectionism, or discrimination, "simply means differential treatment of in-state and out-of-state economic interests that benefits the former and burdens the latter." "[O]f course, any notion of discrimination assumes a comparison of substantially similar entities." If a statute discriminates against out-of-state entities on its face, in its purpose, or in its practical effect, it is unconstitutional unless it "serves a legitimate local purpose, and this purpose could not be served as well by available nondiscriminatory means." Absent discrimination, we will uphold the law "unless the burden imposed on [interstate] commerce is clearly excessive in relation to the putative local benefits." *Pike,* 397 U.S. at 142.

A

The district court concluded that the Fuel Standard facially discriminated against out-of-state corn ethanol by (1) differentiating between ethanol pathways based on origin and (2) discriminating against out-of-state ethanol based on factors within the CA–GREET formula that were "inextricably intertwined with origin."

i

Before we consider whether the Fuel Standard discriminates against out-of-state ethanol, we must determine which ethanol pathways are suitable for comparison. Entities are similarly situated for constitutional purposes if their products compete against each other in a single market. If they do, it is irrelevant whether they are made from different materials or if one poses a substantial competitive threat to another.

The district court concluded that all Brazilian ethanol pathways and all [of California's model's] factors correlated with origin were outside the bounds of comparison. The . . . district court defined "production processes" as only those factors not correlated with origin in the default pathways. After excluding sugar cane ethanol and all GHG emissions related to transportation, electricity, and plant efficiency from comparison, the district court concluded that "the [Fuel Standard] discriminates on the basis of origin." But this selective comparison, which excludes relevant fuel pathways and important contributors to GHG emissions, cannot support the district court's finding of discrimination.

As Plaintiffs strenuously maintain and all parties agree, ethanol from every source has "identical physical and chemical properties." Indeed, the market relies on this undifferentiated structure because ethanol from different regions made with different feedstocks is regularly mixed together in the fuel supply. Ethanol from Brazil, the Midwest, and California may end up blended in the same gallon of fuel. Because of this close competition, all sources of ethanol in the California market should be compared, and the district court erred in excluding Brazilian ethanol from its analysis.

The district court also erred by ignoring GHG emissions related to: (1) the electricity used to power the conversion process, (2) the efficiency of the ethanol plant, and (3) the transportation of the feedstock, ethanol, and co-products. Those factors contribute to the actual GHG emissions from every ethanol pathway, even if the size of their contribution is correlated with their location. Instead of considering all sources of GHG emissions, the district court concluded that different pathways were equivalent if they used the same feedstock and what the court called the "production process"—the type of milling process, treatment of the co-product, and source of thermal energy—regardless of their carbon intensity values for the remaining factors.

But these pathways are not equivalent. As the district court concluded, their carbon intensities are "different according to lifecycle analysis." Each factor in the default pathways is an average based on scientific data, not an ungrounded presumption that unfairly prejudices out-of-state ethanol, whether it is an average value for the use of coal in a boiler or for the shipment of raw corn from the Midwest to California. To the atmosphere, emissions related to an ethanol plant's source of electrical energy are no less important than those caused by a plant's source of thermal energy. If we ignore these real differences between ethanol pathways, we cannot understand whether the challenged regulation responds to genuine threats of harm or to the mere out-of-state status of an ethanol pathway. . . .

ii

Under the dormant Commerce Clause, distinctions that benefit in-state producers cannot be based on state boundaries alone. But a regulation is not facially discriminatory simply because it affects in-state and out-of-state interests unequally. If California is to assign different carbon intensities to ethanol from different regions, there must be "some reason, apart from their origin, to treat them differently."

Following this logic, the Supreme Court has consistently recognized facial discrimination where a statute or regulation distinguished between in-state and out-of-state products and no nondiscriminatory reason for the distinction was shown. For example, in *Oregon Waste,* the Supreme Court considered an Oregon statute that imposed a $2.25 per ton surcharge on out-of-state waste but charged in-state waste only 85 cents. 511 U.S. at 96, 114 S.Ct. 1345. This fee differential was discriminatory because out-of-state waste was no more harmful or costly than waste generated within the state, leaving no basis for differential treatment other than the state of origin. The Court explained, however, that "if out-of-state waste did impose higher costs on Oregon than instate waste, Oregon could recover the increased cost through a differential charge on out-of-state waste." In a similar case, the Court struck down as discriminatory an Alabama law that imposed a fee on imports of hazardous waste from out of state when there was no association between place of origin and risk to Alabama. *Chem. Waste v. Hunt,* 504 U.S. 334 (1992). Rather, Alabama admitted that "[t]he risk created by hazardous waste and other similarly dangerous waste materials [was] proportional to the *volume* of such waste." As it did in *Oregon Waste,* the Court explained that a disposal fee calibrated to the actual risk imposed by hazardous waste, whether imported or domestic, would have been appropriate.

Unlike these discriminatory statutes, the Fuel Standard does not base its treatment on a fuel's origin but on its carbon intensity. The Fuel Standard performs lifecycle analysis to measure the carbon intensity of all fuel pathways. When it is relevant to that measurement, the Fuel

Standard considers location, but only to the extent that location affects the actual GHG emissions attributable to a default pathway. Under dormant Commerce Clause precedent, if an out-of-state ethanol pathway does impose higher costs on California by virtue of its greater GHG emissions, there is a nondiscriminatory reason for its higher carbon intensity value. . . .

iii

The district court held that two of the CA–GREET factors, transportation and electricity source, were "inextricably intertwined with origin" and that CARB's use of those factors was impermissible under the dormant Commerce Clause. To reach this conclusion, the district court reasoned first that any factor correlated with origin is "inextricably intertwined with geography" and second that any otherwise neutral factor becomes discriminatory if it is intertwined with geography, even if that factor measures real variations in emissions from different methods and locations of ethanol production. This reasoning is incorrect.

As explained above, these factors bear on the reality of GHG emissions, with resulting consequences for California. . . .

Plaintiffs contend that any consideration of emissions from the transportation of feedstocks and fuels is forbidden. They cite *Fort Gratiot Sanitary Landfill, Inc. v. Michigan Department of Natural Resources,* 504 U.S. 353 (1992), and *Dean Milk Co. v. City of Madison,* 340 U.S. 349 (1951), but neither case stands for that proposition. In *Fort Gratiot,* a Michigan law allowed each county to refuse solid waste from another county, state, or country. The Court held that the statute discriminated against interstate commerce by authorizing each county to isolate itself from the national economy, "afford[ing] local waste producers complete protection from out-of-state waste." Michigan argued that the law did not discriminate because the county was also authorized to isolate itself from the rest of the state, but the Court explained that a state "may not avoid the strictures of the Commerce Clause by curtailing the movement of articles of commerce through subdivisions of the State, rather than through the State itself." In *Dean Milk,* the Court struck down a Madison, Wisconsin, ordinance that prohibited the sale of milk unless the milk was bottled within five miles of the town central square. The Court held that the regulation had the practical effect of "exclud[ing] from distribution in Madison wholesome milk produced and pasteurized in Illinois." That Madison also excluded milk from Milwaukee was irrelevant. In both of these cases, the Supreme Court found discrimination based on the communities' decision to isolate themselves and direct business to local processors, not based on the use of distance for sound reasons correlating with the purposes of the regulation.

CARB's attention to emissions from transportation has no such isolating effect. We "view[ ] with particular suspicion state statutes requiring business operations to be performed in the home State that could more efficiently be performed elsewhere." *Pike,* 397 U.S. at 145. But transporting raw corn produces more emissions than importing refined ethanol, driving up a fuel pathway's carbon intensity and making local processing less attractive. This is not a form of discrimination against out-of-state producers. Even if California were to someday produce significant amounts of corn for ethanol, the [California model's] transportation factor would remain non-discriminatory to the extent it applies evenly to all pathways and measures real differences in the harmful effects of ethanol production.

Plaintiffs also contend that the carbon intensity of electricity is "inextricably intertwined with geography." California's mix of electricity generation is weighted toward lower-carbon sources such as natural gas, nuclear, and hydroelectric, and California ethanol producers pay more for electricity with fewer emissions than the national average. By contrast, Midwest producers have largely located their plants near cheap and carbon-intensive sources of coal-fired electricity generation. The default pathways reflect the resulting difference in the average carbon intensity of electricity available in the region where producers are located.

But ethanol producers in the Midwest are not hostage to these regional electricity-generating portfolios. Many ethanol plants in the Midwest generate some or all of their own electricity and use the waste heat as a source of thermal energy, reducing emissions. . . .

We conclude . . . that the CA–GREET lifecycle analysis used by CARB, including the specific factors to which Plaintiffs object, does not discriminate against out-of-state commerce. . . .

V

CARB contends that Section 211(c)(4)(b) of the Clean Air Act authorized the Fuel Standard under the Commerce Clause. Although we reverse the district court's conclusions on the dormant Commerce Clause, this claim is not moot because the district court will consider further dormant Commerce Clause issues on remand. Rejecting CARB's contention, the district court concluded that CARB "failed to establish that the savings clause [ ] demonstrate [s] express exemption from Commerce Clause scrutiny." We agree.

Section 211(c)(4)(a) of the Clean Air Act preempts state laws prescribing, "for purposes of motor vehicle emission control, any control or prohibition respecting any characteristic or component of a fuel or fuel additive." 42 U.S.C. § 7545(c)(4)(A). The next subsection of the Act exempts California from that explicit preemption. *Id.* § 7545(c)(4)(B) (Section 211(c)(4)(b)). The Fuel Standard falls within this exemption because it is "a control respecting a fuel or fuel additive and was enacted for the purpose of emissions control." But we have previously held that "the sole purpose of [Section 211(c)(4)(B)] is to waive for California the express preemption provision found in § 7545(c)(4)(A)." On this point, our precedent forecloses CARB's argument. . . .

The Fuel Standard's ethanol provisions are not facially discriminatory, so we reverse that portion of the district court's decision and remand for entry of partial summary judgment in favor of CARB. We also reverse the district court's decision that the Fuel Standard is an impermissible extraterritorial regulation and we direct that an order of partial summary judgment be entered in favor of CARB on those grounds. We remand the case for the district court to determine whether the ethanol provisions discriminate in purpose or effect and, if not, to apply the *Pike* balancing test. ∎

On June 30, 2014, the U.S. Supreme Court denied the Rocky Mountain Farmers Union's petition for certiorari, which, *inter alia*, asserted that the Ninth Circuit erred in finding that California's LCFS did not facially discriminate against interstate commerce. This win for California might give other states hope for their renewables standards, but the area remains unsettled.

The dormant commerce clause also arose in the following challenge to Minnesota's RPS—a challenge likely to be increasingly common in light of other states' similar standards. This case assessed whether states are permitted to require both in-state and imported electricity to be generated from sources that do not contribute to the state's carbon dioxide emissions in the power sector.

North Dakota v. Heydinger

15 F. Supp. 3d 891 (D. Minn. 2014).

This matter is before the Court on Defendants' Motion for Summary Judgment and Plaintiffs' Motion for Summary Judgment. . . . For the reasons set forth below, Defendants' Motion for Summary Judgment is denied in part and denied as moot in part, [and] Plaintiffs' Motion for Summary Judgment is granted in part and denied as moot in part.

This lawsuit arose from Minnesota's enactment of a statute regulating certain aspects of the use and generation of electric energy, and thus affecting the United States electric utility sector.

* * *

At one point in time, "most electricity was sold by vertically-integrated utilities that had constructed their own power plants, transmission lines, and local delivery systems." In 1935, however, under the Federal Power Act ("FPA"), Congress granted to the Federal Energy Regulatory Commission ("FERC") the "exclusive authority to regulate the transmission and sale at wholesale of electric energy in interstate commerce." And, FERC issued an order in 1999 encouraging the creation of regional transmission organizations ("RTOs"). . . . (hereinafter "FERC Order 2000"). RTOs coordinate and monitor the minute-to-minute transmission of energy on the grid in a region or large state. They also ensure open access to the grid and coordinate transmission planning, as well as oversee the safety and reliability of the regional electric system.

The Midcontinent Independent System Operator (formerly, the Midwest Independent System Operator) ("MISO") was approved as an RTO in 2001. MISO is an independent, non-profit organization whose members include transmission owners, investor-owned utilities, public power utilities, independent power producers, and cooperatives. It operates and controls transmission facilities in the Midwest (including in Minnesota, North Dakota, Wisconsin, and Iowa). . . .

The statute at issue in this lawsuit is Minnesota's Next Generation Energy Act ("NGEA"). The Minnesota legislature passed the NGEA in 2007, establishing energy and environmental standards related to carbon dioxide emissions. Minn.Stat. § 216H.03, subd. 3, seeks to limit increases in "statewide power sector carbon dioxide emissions." That provision states:

Unless preempted by federal law, until a comprehensive and enforceable state law or rule pertaining to greenhouse gases that directly limits and substantially reduces, over time, statewide power sector carbon dioxide emissions is enacted and in effect, . . . *no person shall:*

(1) construct within the state a new large energy facility that would contribute to statewide power sector carbon dioxide emissions;

(2) import or commit to import from outside the state power from a new large energy facility that would contribute to statewide power sector carbon dioxide emissions; or

(3) enter into a new long-term power purchase agreement that would increase statewide power sector carbon dioxide emissions. For purposes of this section, a long-term power purchase agreement means an agreement to purchase 50 megawatts of capacity or more for a term exceeding five years.

Minn.Stat. § 216H.03, subd. 3 (emphasis added). "Statewide power sector carbon dioxide emissions" are defined in the statute as "the total annual emissions of carbon dioxide from the generation of electricity within the state and all emissions of carbon dioxide from the generation of electricity imported from outside the state and consumed in Minnesota."

Certain persons are exempt from the prohibitions contained in Minn.Stat. § 216H.03, subd. 3. For example, "[t]he prohibitions in subdivision 3 do not apply if the project proponent demonstrates to the [Minnesota] Public Utilities Commission's satisfaction that it will offset the new contribution to statewide power sector carbon dioxide emissions with a carbon dioxide reduction project." The carbon dioxide reduction project must: offset in an amount equal to or greater than the proposed new contribution to statewide power sector carbon dioxide emissions in either, or a combination of both, of the following ways:

(1) by reducing an existing facility's contribution to statewide power sector carbon dioxide emissions; or

(2) by purchasing carbon dioxide allowances from a state or group of states that has a carbon dioxide cap and trade system in place that produces verifiable emissions reductions.

The MPUC must ensure that proposed carbon dioxide emissions offsets are "permanent, quantifiable, verifiable, enforceable, and would not have otherwise occurred."

* * *

Plaintiffs are the State of North Dakota, the Industrial Commission of North Dakota, the Lignite Energy Council, Basin Electric Power Cooperative, the North American Coal Corporation, Great Northern Properties Limited Partnership, Missouri Basin Municipal Power Agency d/b/a Missouri River Energy Services, and Minnkota Power Cooperative, Inc. Defendants are the Commissioners of the Minnesota Public Utilities Commission and the Commissioner of the Minnesota Department of Commerce, each in their official capacities.

* * *

Neither the parties, nor this Court, dispute that carbon dioxide emissions are a problem that this country needs to address. The question here is not the environmental issue. The question is whether the Minnesota Legislature has the power, under the U.S. Constitution, to address that issue through the means articulated in Minn.Stat. § 216H.03. Because the Court finds that Minn.Stat. § 216H.03, subd. 3(2)–(3), violates the dormant Commerce Clause, the answer to that question is "no."

* * *

"The Commerce Clause . . . grants Congress the authority to regulate interstate commerce." "The dormant Commerce Clause is the negative implication of the Commerce Clause: states may not enact laws that discriminate against or unduly burden interstate commerce." There are three levels of analysis under the dormant Commerce Clause. First, a state statute that has "an 'extraterritorial reach,' that is, . . . the statute has the practical effect of controlling conduct beyond the boundaries of the state," is per se invalid. Second, a state statute that is discriminatory on its face, in practical effect, or in purpose is subject to strict scrutiny. Third, a state statute that is not discriminatory, but indirectly burdens interstate commerce, is evaluated under the balancing test set forth in *Pike v. Bruce Church* (1970).

* * *

The Court finds that [the Minnesota statute] violates the extraterritoriality doctrine and is per se invalid and, therefore, the Court need not address whether the statute is discriminatory or fails a *Pike* analysis. Under the extraterritoriality doctrine, "[t]he Commerce Clause precludes application of a state statute to commerce that takes place wholly outside of the state's borders." In other words, a state statute is invalid "when the statute requires people or businesses to conduct their out-of-state commerce in a certain way." This is true regardless of whether the commerce has effects within the state, and regardless of whether the legislature intended for the statute to have an extraterritorial effect. "The critical inquiry is whether the *practical effect* of the regulation is to control conduct beyond the boundaries of the State."

The practical effect of a statute is evaluated by looking not only at "the consequences of the statute itself," but also at "how the challenged statute may interact with the legitimate regulatory regimes of other States and what effect would arise if not one, but many or every, State adopted similar legislation." As noted by the U.S. Supreme Court, "[g]enerally speaking, the Commerce Clause protects against inconsistent legislation arising from the projection of one state regulatory regime into the jurisdiction of another State." Thus, for example, "no State may force an out-of-state merchant to seek regulatory approval in one State before undertaking a transaction in another." The rationale is that "any attempt directly to assert extraterritorial jurisdiction over persons or property would offend sister States and exceed the inherent limits of the State's power."

* * *

In *Edgar v. MITE Corp.,* the Court considered a Commerce Clause challenge to the Illinois Business Take-Over Act, which required that any takeover offer for the shares of an Illinois company with its executive offices in Illinois be registered with the Illinois Secretary of State. The

Court found that the statute could prevent an out-of-state offeror from engaging in interstate transactions not only with Illinois residents, but also with non-Illinois residents, and that the statute could be applied in situations in which no Illinois residents were involved. Thus, the Court invalidated the statute, finding that it "purport[ed] to regulate directly and to interdict interstate commerce, including commerce wholly outside the State" and that it had a "sweeping extraterritorial effect." The Court later described its opinion in *Edgar* as an "extraterritorial decision" that "significantly illuminates the contours of the constitutional prohibition on extraterritorial legislation."

Likewise, the Eighth Circuit has applied the extraterritoriality doctrine to statutes other than price control laws. For example, in *Cotto Waxo Co.*, the court considered the extraterritorial effect of a Minnesota statute prohibiting the sale of petroleum-based sweeping compounds. Although the Eighth Circuit did not ultimately invalidate the statute on extraterritoriality grounds, it did not limit application of that doctrine to price control statutes.

Other Circuits have similarly applied the extraterritoriality doctrine to non-price control statutes. In *National Solid Wastes Management Ass'n v. Meyer,* the Seventh Circuit analyzed a Wisconsin statute stating that "no person may" dispose of certain materials in Wisconsin's landfills unless the waste was generated in a region that had an "effective recycling program" as detailed under the statute. Relying on the extraterritoriality principles set forth in *Healy* and *Edgar,* the Seventh Circuit found that the statute was unconstitutional:

> Wisconsin's solid waste legislation conditions the use of Wisconsin landfills by non-Wisconsin waste generators on their home communities' adoption and enforcement of Wisconsin recycling standards; all persons in that non-Wisconsin community must adhere to the Wisconsin standards whether or not they dump their waste in Wisconsin. If the out-of-state community does not conform to the Wisconsin way of doing things, no waste generator in that community may utilize a Wisconsin disposal site. The practical impact of the Wisconsin statute on economic activity completely outside the State reveals its basic infirmity: It essentially controls the conduct of those engaged in commerce occurring wholly outside the State of Wisconsin and therefore directly regulates interstate commerce.

Id. at 658.

* * *

In *American Booksellers Foundation v. Dean,* the Second Circuit [similarly] analyzed a Vermont statute stating that "[n]o person may, . . . with actual knowledge that the recipient is a minor," disseminate through the internet material that is harmful to minors. 342 F.3d at 100. After determining that the statute could be read to apply to material posted on a website or shared in an email or discussion group, the court evaluated the statute's extraterritorial effects and found that it violated the dormant Commerce Clause. The court explained its reasoning as follows:

Because the internet does not recognize geographic boundaries, it is difficult, if not impossible, for a state to regulate internet activities without "project[ing] its legislation into other States."

A person outside Vermont who posts information on a website or on an electronic discussion group cannot prevent people in Vermont from accessing the material. If someone in Connecticut posts material for the intended benefit of other people in Connecticut, that person must assume that someone from Vermont may also view the material. This means that those outside Vermont must comply with [the statute] or risk prosecution by Vermont. Vermont has "project[ed]" [the statute] onto the rest of the nation.

* * *

As a final example of an extraterritoriality analysis of a non-price control statute, the Ninth Circuit recently considered California's Low Carbon Fuel Standard ("Fuel Standard") statute in *Rocky Mountain Farmers Union v. Corey,* 730 F.3d 1070 (9th Cir.2013), *reh'g denied.* The Fuel Standard applies to transportation fuels consumed in California and requires a fuel blender to keep the average carbon intensity of its fuel below a specified annual limit. . . .

At issue in *Rocky Mountain* was the Fuel Standard's regulation of the production and sale of ethanol, a fuel that is shipped to California on ocean tankers, trains, and trucks, or passed through pipelines. After summarizing the Supreme Court's extraterritoriality precedent, . . . the Ninth Circuit found that "[t]he Fuel Standard impose[d] no analogous conditions on the importation of ethanol" warranting its invalidation under the extraterritoriality doctrine. Among other things, the court noted that the Fuel Standard imposed no penalties on non-compliant, wholly out-of-state transactions. Rather, the statute applied only to fuel blenders in California and the producers who contracted with them. The court noted that, "[w]hen presented with similar rules in the past, [it has] distinguished statutes 'that regulate out-of-state parties directly' from those *that regulate[ ] contractual relationships in which at least one party is located in [the regulating state]."*

* * *

. . . . [B]ased on the U.S. Supreme Court and Circuit Court precedent discussed above, the Court finds that [the Minnesota statute] is a classic example of extraterritorial regulation because of the manner in which the electricity industry operates. . . . [T]he statute . . . requires out-of-state entities to seek regulatory approval in Minnesota before undertaking transactions in other states. This statute overreaches and, if other states adopt similar legislation, it could lead to balkanization.

[The statute] violates the extraterritoriality doctrine because its plain language applies to power and capacity transactions occurring wholly outside of Minnesota's borders. While the statute draws strong parallels to those at issue in all of the cases discussed above in which the courts found a violation of the extraterritoriality doctrine, it is most directly analogous to the internet use regulation found to violate the dormant Commerce Clause in *American Booksellers*. Like the Vermont statute at issue in that case, which—by its plain language—regulated non-Vermont residents' internet use outside of Vermont's borders, the practical effect of [the Minnesota statute] is to control non-Minnesota entities' conduct occurring wholly outside of Minnesota.

As discussed above, MISO is the RTO responsible for operating and controlling the transmission of electricity in and among several states, including Minnesota. Like the transmission of information over the internet, the transmission of electricity over the MISO grid does not recognize state boundaries. Therefore, when a non-Minnesota entity injects electricity into the grid to satisfy its obligations to a non-Minnesota member, it cannot ensure that the electricity will not travel to and be removed in—in other words, be imported to and contribute to statewide power sector carbon dioxide emissions in—Minnesota. . . . Likewise, non-Minnesota entities that enter into long-term power purchase agreements for capacity to satisfy their non-Minnesota load cannot ensure that the electricity, when bid into the MISO market and dispatched, will not travel to and be removed in—in other words, increase statewide power sector carbon dioxide emissions in—Minnesota. The MDOC has already verified as much in the Dairyland proceedings: "all of a utility's resources are matched to all of a utility's load, regardless of state boundaries." And, this means that those entities, although located outside of Minnesota and attempting to engage in commerce with other non-Minnesota entities, must comply with [the Minnesota statute], or risk legal action.

Because of the boundary-less nature of the electricity grid, the effect of [the Minnesota statute's regulatory scheme on interstate commerce is much different than that of the statutes at issue in *Cotto Waxo Co., National Electrical Manufacturers Ass'n,* and *Rocky Mountain,* where the Circuit Courts declined to invalidate the regulations on extraterritoriality grounds. Those cases dealt with the regulation of tangible products (sweeping compounds, light bulbs, and ethanol, respectively) that could be shipped directly from point A to point B. Therefore, in each of those cases, the courts found that the statute at issue did not require out-of-state parties to transact out-of-state business according to the regulating state's terms because the manufacturers could simply avoid engaging in the prohibited conduct when transacting out-of-state business.

* * *

In addition to regulating wholly out-of-state transactions, which is itself a violation of the extraterritoriality doctrine, [the Minnesota statute] also improperly requires non-Minnesota merchants to seek regulatory approval before undertaking transactions with other non-Minnesota entities. [The statute] provides an exemption from the prohibitions in [the statute] if an entity can demonstrate to the MPUC's satisfaction that it will offset the prohibited carbon dioxide emissions. Thus, only by undertaking a "carbon dioxide reduction project" approved by a Minnesota agency can, for example, a North Dakota generation-and-transmission cooperative inject coal-generated electricity into the MISO grid to serve its North Dakota members.

If any or every state were to adopt similar legislation (e.g., prohibiting the use of electricity generated by different fuels or requiring compliance with unique, statutorily-mandated exemption programs subject to state approval), the current marketplace for electricity would come to a grinding halt. In an interconnected system like MISO, entities involved at each step of the process—generation, transmission, and distribution of electricity—would potentially be subject to multiple state laws regardless of whether they were transacting commerce outside of their home state. Such a scenario is "just the kind of competing and interlocking local economic regulation that the Commerce Clause was meant to preclude."

For these reasons, the Court finds that, while the State of Minnesota's goals in enacting [the statute] may have been admirable, Minnesota has projected its legislation into other states and directly regulated commerce therein. Accordingly [the statute] constitutes impermissible extraterritorial legislation and is a per se violation of the dormant Commerce Clause. ∎

NOTES AND COMMENTS

1.   The *Heydinger* case might call a number of state RPSs into questions, thus suggesting that new state approaches to encouraging renewables may be needed—or perhaps solutions at other levels of government. If you were a state legislator in one of the states that currently does not have an RPS, how might you propose to design one to avoid the problem discussed in *Heydinger*?

2.   Did the court in *Heydinger* accurately characterize electricity markets? Within a regional grid like the grid operated by MISO, utilities frequently contract with each other to sell and purchase wholesale electricity under long-term power purchase agreements. The transmission operator—MISO—schedules the flow of electricity through the grid based on these long-term contracts as well as last-minute sales needed to fulfill electricity demands. Say a coal-fired utility in North Dakota has a power purchase agreement under which it sells 2 megawatts of electricity daily to Utility A in South Dakota. Similarly, a wind farm in Minnesota has a power purchase agreement under which it sells 1 megawatt of electricity daily to Utility B in Minnesota. As long as the coal-fired utility in North Dakota sends 2 megawatts of electricity through the grid and the wind farm in Minnesota sends 1 megawatt of electricity through the grid, each utility has fulfilled its contractual obligations. If it happens that some of the 2 megawatts of electricity from the coal-fired plant in North Dakota flows to Utility B in Minnesota, Utility B will not pay that coal-fired power plant. Similarly, if it happens that some of the electricity from the Minnesota wind farm flows to Utility A in South Dakota, Utility A will not pay the wind farm. Rather, each utility receiving electricity will pay the utility with which it contracted to buy electricity. Utility B in Minnesota did not, it seems, "import" electricity from the coal-fired power plant in North Dakota simply because some electricity from the plant happened to flow through the grid into Minnesota. Electricity within the grid flows to the point of least resistance. Picture a hose with many connections. If you send water through the hose, the water will flow into the connected hoses that have the most space. Does the term "import" include an element of intent?

iii.   Federal RPS Proposals

Should the current patchwork of state RPSs be replaced with a single federal RPS? On the international level, a number of countries, especially in Europe, have already had considerable success setting national targets for renewables. Germany's Renewable Energy Sources Act of 2000 set a goal of doubling the country's share of electricity derived from renewable sources by 2010, and China's Renewable Energy Law sets national targets.

Why a national standard for the United States instead of a state one? For one, some argue that state policies alone simply have not prompted the development of enough renewable energy projects. With the total share of the nation's non-hydro electricity coming from renewables still less than 4%, "States alone cannot adequately address the need for increased renewable energy." Robin J. Lunt, Recharging U.S. Energy Policy: Advocating for a National Renewable Portfolio Standard, 25 UCLA J. Envtl. L. & Pol'y 371, 402–03 (2006/2007). In this view, the availability of a national marketplace (presumably, with RECs tradable nationwide) would support renewable energy facilities in a way that individual states cannot. *Id.* One proponent of a federal RPS cites the numerous studies on the issue and notes that "federal intervention can help create a more just, diverse, and predictable national market for renewable resources without significantly increasing aggregate electricity prices." Christopher Cooper, A National Renewable Portfolio Standard: Politically Correct or Just Plain Correct?, 21 The Electricity J. 9 (2008).

Others disagree, believing that a streamlined national market would not promote renewable energy deployment more than state RPSs. Economist Robert Michaels, for example, sees no evidence that small renewable energy facilities of the sort currently existing today need a national market to prosper. Robert J. Michaels, National Renewable Portfolio Standard: Smart Policy or Misguided Gesture?, 29 Energy L.J. 79 (2008). Still others note that if renewable energy facilities would be selling into a national market, transmission capacity is a big concern, with some noting that a federal RPS would require massive upgrades. One observer notes: "We have national transmission corridors that have been identified, but I think you have to take that to a whole new level in order to implement something like RPS. Any kind of federal RPS is going to need more state-to-state transmission." Jeff Postelwait, A U.S. Federal Renewable Portfolio Standard: Potentials and Pitfalls, RenewableEnergyWorld.com, Mar. 27, 2009.

Proponents of a federal RPS also make a "race to the bottom" argument like those often used to justify uniform federal environmental standards. In the absence of a federal standard, some states would set low targets to avoid punishing their industries. States most likely to do this would be those without a wealth of renewable resources or those that are located upwind from air pollution sources. Benjamin K. Sovacool and Christopher Cooper, The Hidden Costs of State Renewable Portfolio Standards (RPS), 15 Buff. Envt'l. L.J. 1, 9–10 (2007–2008). This problem is exacerbated in states where utilities participate in wholesale markets for electricity. With some states having RPS and some not, operators of plants fired by fossil fuels could continue to sell to the regional grid and their power would flow to those states without mandates. (This, it appears, was a problem that Minnesota attempted to address through the legislation discussed in the *Heydinger* case, in which the state prohibited both in-state and out-of-state generation that contributed to the state's carbon emissions.)

Professor Lincoln Davies explores the benefits and challenges of a federal RPS in detail in Power Forward: The Argument for a National RPS, 42 Conn. L. Rev. 1337 (2010).

2. PROVIDING GRANTS, LOANS, AND BENEFITS

In addition to mandating or encouraging the construction of renewable generation through guaranteed rates, direct requirements for renewables (RPS, for example) and plans that encourage renewables, governments sometimes directly fund renewables by providing construction grants and loans, tax benefits, rebates, and other financial rewards. Law and accounting firms, in turn—with the help of federal and state statutes—also develop financing mechanisms that allow renewable developers to benefit as much as possible from these financial carrots.

a. TAX INCENTIVES FOR PROJECT OWNERS

Federal policies promoting renewables through the tax code with tax credits and accelerated depreciation rates are deemed critical to the industries' success. Perhaps the most important financial incentive is the production tax credit (PTC) for power produced from renewables, which allows renewable energy facility owners to take a credit per kWh of power produced. The Renewable Energy Production Incentive (REPI) is the counterpart to the PTC for entities such as state and local governments that do not pay corporate income taxes, offering a payment instead of a tax credit. The PTC has garnered criticism from some who see it as a pure subsidy to the industry, but without it renewables producers claim they would not succeed.

The PTC's record is a sad story of "Same Time, Next Year." Over the years, it has been renewed for short periods (often as little as one year), requiring its backers to come back to Congress anew to push for its extension. The PTC was up for renewal three times in the seven years through 2007; as an example, it was extended for only one year as part of an omnibus tax bill in 2004. See Working Families Tax Relief Act of 2004, Pub. L. No. 108–311, 118 Stat. 1166 (2004) (restoring PTC retroactively to January 1, 2004); American Jobs Creation Act of 2004, Pub. L. No. 108–357, 118 Stat. 1418 (2004) (expanding resources eligible for PTC). When the PTC's future is uncertain or in doubt, projects stall. In 2004, before that year's tax bill's enactment, wind power projects slated to add 2,000 MW of new domestic capacity at a cost of $2 billion were postponed, according to an industry spokeswoman. Industry growth slowed by cost hurdles, Greenwire, June 14, 2004; Jeff Nesmith, Some see a way to produce new energy at competitive rates, but investors are few because a tax credit has expired, Atl. J.–Const., Sept. 13, 2004 (discussing a project in Oklahoma put on hold).

The American Recovery and Reinvestment Act of 2009 (ARRA, popularly known as the "stimulus law") put a four-year end to the tenuous situation caused in the renewables industry by uncertainty about the PTC. The ARRA extended the PTC to facilities placed in service on or before December 31, 2013 at an inflation-adjusted rate starting at 2.1¢ per kWh for 2009. In the 2013 fiscal cliff deal, Congress renewed the

PTC again, but for only one year. Diane Cardwell, Renewed Tax Credit Buoys Wind-Power Projects, N.Y. Times, Mar. 21. 2013. Congress extended the credit for an additional year (2013–2014), but the credit had expired at the time of textbook publication. American Wind Energy Ass'n, Congress extends policy critical to the success of wind energy; industry continues to seek long-term stability to scale up, Dec. 17, 2014, http://www.awea.org/MediaCenter/pressrelease.aspx?ItemNumber= 7057.

The ARRA also created a number of other financial incentives for developers of renewable energy facilities. If it was more advantageous, project developers could choose to receive a 30% investment tax credit (ITC) in place of the PTC. The ITC has become a popular tax benefit for developers of renewable power projects. It amounts to 30 percent of the cost of the "energy property" that is "placed in service" during the taxable year. To be "placed in service," the property must be ready for use. This typically requires that all tests have been completed, all licenses and permits have been obtained, and the project is synchronized with the transmission system and is operational. The ITC is therefore unlike the PTC, which is based on the amount of electricity produced and sold.

Under federal tax law, a developer may elect to claim either the ITC or the PTC for facilities qualifying for the PTC. That is, to be eligible for the ITC, the developer may not claim the PTC for electricity generated by the project. See 26 U.S.C. § 48(a)(3). The choice between the two tax credits can be an important one in deciding whether a project is financially viable. It is also complex. To decide whether to take the ITC, the developer needs to know the project's estimated cost. To decide whether to take the PTC, the developer needs to know how much power the project is expected to generate. It also needs some certainty about the price that it will receive for the power over and above the PTC, including prices under any power purchase agreement (PPA). A PPA, as discussed further in Chapter 12, fixes the price that the host of a renewable power project pays the firm that installs and maintains that system. The PPA typically requires the host to pay a set price for a term of years, often 10– 15 or more.

Another consideration for a developer choosing between the two tax credits is that the ITC vests 20 percent per year over five years. If the property is disposed of or otherwise becomes ineligible for the ITC prior to the expiration of this five-year period, the unvested portion is recaptured. (Q: How might this affect an investor's perspective on how long the term should be set for a PPA?)

The ARRA also created a renewable energy grant program in the U.S. Department of the Treasury. This cash grant could be taken in lieu of the ITC. In July 2009, the Department of the Treasury issued guidelines for the grants, terms and conditions and a sample application. U.S. Dep't of the Treasury, 1603 Program: Payments for Specified Energy Property in Lieu of Tax Credits, http://www.treasury.gov/initiatives/ recovery/Pages/1603.aspx.

The ARRA created a new 30% tax credit for a business investing in a "qualified advanced energy manufacturing project." It increased the amount of funds available for issuing new clean renewable energy bonds to finance public sector renewable energy projects (a program first established in the EPAct 2005), and added $6 billion into an existing DOE

Loan Guarantee Program, also first established in the EPAct 2005. In July 2014, the DOE added $2.5 billion to the Loan Guarantee Program. DOE, Loan Guarantee Solicitation for Applications for Renewable Energy Projects and Efficient Energy Projects, July 3, 2014, http://energy.gov/lpo/services/solicitations/renewable-energy-efficient-energy-projects-solicitation.

b.   TAX AND FINANCING INCENTIVES FOR CONSUMERS

Providing a tax break to homeowners purchasing renewable energy systems was a cornerstone of the initial push to promote renewables in the late 1970s and early 1980s. The Energy Tax Act of 1978 created tax credits for residential solar and wind installations, but the credits expired at the end of 1985. This lapse in federal tax breaks for homeowners is widely believed to have contributed significantly to the decline of renewables industries in the mid-to late-1980s.

The EPAct 2005 reinstated a federal tax credit for residential renewable energy systems, which is currently set to expire in 2016. A taxpayer may claim a credit of 30% of qualified expenditures for a residential renewable energy system. The credit was initially applied to only solar electric systems, solar water heating systems and fuel cells, but the Energy Improvement and Extension Act of 2008 extended it to small wind energy systems and geothermal heat pumps. The ARRA expanded the availability of the credit by removing the maximum credit amount for all eligible technologies except fuel cells placed in service after 2008. This is significant because the credit had been capped at $2,000, and many systems cost far more than the credit amount. For the increasing number of American taxpayers subject to the alternative minimum tax (AMT), the ARRA also provided that the renewable energy tax credit could be used to offset tax liability under the AMT.

c.   STATE AND MUNICIPAL FINANCIAL INCENTIVES

States, like the federal government, offer a range of direct financial incentives to renewable energy developers and consumers, including rebates or tax credits for the cost of installing residential renewable energy equipment, for example.

i.   *Public Benefit Funds / Systems Benefits Charges*

One common method for states to pay for renewable energy projects is the public benefit fund (also known as a system benefit charge fund), discussed further in Chapter 13 in connection with its use in funding energy efficiency programs.

Public benefit funds are often used to help develop new renewable energy systems, increase consumer demand, and support in-state renewable energy industry development. They are funded through a small charge, established in fifteen states and the District of Columbia, through a fee imposed on all electricity customers' bills, regardless of the entity selling power to those customers. DSIRE maintains a state-by-state map with current information about state programs. Database of State Incentives For Renewables & Efficiency, http://programs.dsireusa.org/system/program/maps. The provision establishing the system benefits charge was often included in a state electricity restructuring law. While the fee imposed is typically small, the funds raised can amount to millions of dollars.

States use these funds for rebates on renewable energy systems, funding for research and development of renewable energy, and development of renewable energy education programs. The design of the program (particularly the size of the fees imposed and the purposes for which the funds are used) varies considerably from state to state:

> The form of administration of renewable trust funds varies. Many states administer them through a state agency, while others use a quasi-public business development organization. Some funds are managed by independent third-party organizations, some by existing utilities, while two states allow large customers to self-direct the funds. For distribution, some states utilize an investment model, making loans and equity investments. Other states provide financial incentives for production or grants to stimulate supply-side development. Some other states use research and development grants, technical assistance, education, and demonstration projects.

Steven Ferrey, Sustainable Energy, Environmental Policy, and States' Rights: Discerning the Energy Future Through the Eye of the Dormant Commerce Clause, 12 N.Y.U. Envtl. L.J. 507, 523–25 (2004). Two typical funds are the Connecticut Clean Energy Fund (CCEF) and the Massachusetts Renewable Energy Trust (RET). The CCEF has operated since 2000, with funding expected to total $444 million by 2017. It has invested in biomass gasification projects, fuel cell companies, and ocean wave technologies. One creative use of the CCEF is a solar lease program, which provides assistance in financing of solar systems to homeowners making less than 200% of the annual median income in their areas. Connecticut Announces Solar Lease Program, RenewableEnergyWorld.com, Aug. 18, 2008. The RET was created in 1993 as part of Massachusetts' restructuring law, and is funded with approximately $25 million annually. It has invested in solar PV manufacturers and fuel cell companies, and it provided $54 million for a waste-to-energy program affecting 138 communities.

ii. Municipal Funding

At the municipal level, property tax financing or property assessed clean energy (PACE), which is also referred to as municipal financing, allows local governments to provide property owners the option of installing renewable energy projects and paying for them over a period of years by adding specified amounts to their property tax bills. In states that allow property tax financing, municipalities use funds from special tax bonds to install renewable projects on individuals' homes. The individuals then pay the city for the cost of installation over time through taxes collected on the property tax bill.

While this approach is not yet widespread, it could catch on quickly as it has several key advantages. First, the homeowner pays nothing up front, as the city or county offers 100 percent financing. Second, because the debt is repaid through the property tax, if the homeowner moves before the payoff period of the system, the debt simply continues to be repaid by the next owner. This can go a long way toward convincing homeowners who think they will move before the renewable energy system is paid off. California's Clean Energy Municipal Financing Law pioneered this approach, and as of 2009, ten states had amended their laws to allow their counties and cities to establish special assessment districts for energy financing. *See, e.g.,* Va. Code § 15.2–958.3. These laws typically permit cities and counties to create energy financing districts, define types of projects eligible for financing, and give authority to the cities and counties to issue the bonds for financing.

In 2008, Berkeley, California became the first city in the nation to establish an energy financing program using local public funds. One year later, the Berkeley FIRST program had funded 38 solar projects. City of Berkeley, Office of Energy and Sustainable Development, http://www.ci. berkeley.ca.us. By mid-2009, five other cities and counties nationwide had established similar programs. Vice President Joseph Biden announced a "Recovery Through Retrofit" initiative to create a national program based on the Berkeley model. Carolyn Jones, Biden to model solar finance plan on Berkeley's, SFGate.com (Oct. 20, 2009).

In 2009, the ARRA removed one potential disincentive to municipal financing. Previously, the federal tax code prohibited individuals or businesses receiving "subsidized energy financing" from receiving federal incentives for renewable energy projects, such as the tax credits above. The ARRA contains a provision that ends this prohibition for home and business owners who finance their projects with taxable municipal bonds. Congress is considering legislation that would extend this provision to tax exempt municipal bonds.

Despite the benefits of property tax financing and the removal of some obstacles to it, the Federal Housing Finance Authority (FHFA) has discouraged this funding mechanism in the residential context. FHFA, which is the conservator of Fannie Mae and Freddie Mac (government-sponsored entities that purchase mortgages from private lenders and that suffered large financial losses in the Great Recession that put them into conservatorship), initially stated that Fannie Mae and Freddie Mac would not purchase any mortgage that is subject to a PACE obligation. Later, it issued a proposed rule to clarify its directive and to "offer alternatives that might permit some alteration of those Agency actions." However, in subsequent litigation, several federal courts held that the directive was a proper exercise of FHFA's powers as a conservator, and FHFA withdrew the proposed rule. Fed. Housing Fin. Agc'y, Enterprise Underwriting Standards, 78 Fed. Reg. 46,295 (July 31, 2013) (explaining the rule's withdrawal and citing case decisions). The FHFA's concerns about PACE have not stopped PACE financing efforts. PACE bonds worth more than $104 million were recently issued to investors. Adam Tempkin, First energy-efficiency bonds sold to investors, Reuters, Mar. 7, 2014, http://www.reuters.com/article/2014/03/07/pace-bond-abs-idUSL1N0M41J920140307.

3. CONDUCTING OR FUNDING RESEARCH AND DEVELOPMENT

Not all renewable energy technologies are alike. Some are mature, but further research and development is needed to improve their cost and performance and to effectively use them for electricity generation, transportation, or residential or commercial use. Others (such as enhanced geothermal systems) are at an early stage and require further work to overcome current technical limitations. Still others are considered promising, but fundamental breakthroughs must take place before they can be considered commercially viable.

The federal government has funded this work since the 1970s. Federal subsidies for renewable energy R&D were included in the EPAct 2005, EPAct 1992, Renewable Energy and Energy Efficiency Technology Competitiveness Act of 1989, Solar Energy and Energy Conservation Act of 1980, Solar Photovoltaic Energy Research, Development, and Demonstration Act of 1978, and Solar Energy Research Development and Demonstration Act of 1974. The federal renewables R&D program atrophied in the 1990s and 2000s, and amounts devoted to it were so small that in the 2000s they lagged even behind the R&D levels of the late 1970s. The DOE wind R&D program, for example, was funded at about $50 million in fiscal year 2008, below its high of $63 million in 1980.

The ARRA contained a number of provisions designed to reverse this trend. It allocated a total of $16.8 billion for renewable energy and energy efficiency programs over ten years, with $2.5 billion going to support DOE's research, development and deployment activities. The ARRA also provided funds for the Advanced Research Projects Agency-Energy (ARPA-E) within DOE, first established in 2007. The ARPA-E, like the highly successful cutting-edge military research agency DARPA, is meant to invest in "high risk, high payoff concepts—technologies promising true energy transformations." ARPA-E, http://arpa-e.energy. gov/.

4. POTENTIAL TRANSMISSION BARRIERS: SITING AND COST ALLOCATION

One of the largest hurdles to utility-scale renewable development is the need for transmission to link new generation to electricity consumers. Transmission lines often serve multiple generators—thus posing coordination problems for the construction of new lines—and introduce a chicken and egg problem: a transmission line company will not build the line until it is assured that generators will use it and pay it, and generators won't build facilities until they know that a line is available. This problem can be overcome in at least two ways. Governments can require large utilities, including transmission-only utilities, to build lines, guaranteeing the builders a return on their investment. This requires governments to first identify where clustered renewable energy generation is likely to be built. Governments can alternatively simply identify the most productive areas for renewable energy and hope that utilities will build transmission lines to them.

Efforts at enhancing federal authority over the siting of transmission lines have been largely squelched by the courts. In the EPAct 2005, Congress directed DOE to identify National Interest Electric Transmission Corridors (NIETCs) where transmission was congested. FERC would then have "backstop" siting authority in these NIETCs, which would allow FERC to grant construction certificates for transmission lines within an NIETC if a state had "withheld" approval for the line for more than one year. In *California Wilderness Coalition v.*

DOE, 631 F.3d 1072 (9th Cir. 2011), the Ninth Circuit held that the DOE had not adequately consulted with states in designating NIETCs, and had erred in failing to conduct adequate environmental review under the National Environmental Policy Act. Further, in *Piedmont Envtl. Council v. FERC*, 558 F.3d 304 (4th Cir. 2009), the Fourth Circuit held that a state's *denial* of a construction certificate for a transmission line does not amount to "withholding" of approval. Rather, FERC may only grant construction certificates where a state has *failed to act* within a year of receiving a request to build transmission. These decisions have rendered the EPAct 2005 federal siting provisions ineffective.

Some states have stepped up to fill the transmission line siting vacuum that exists at the federal level. Texas engaged in this process through its Competitive Renewable Energy Zone (CREZ) project. Through CREZ, the Texas Legislature required the state's PUC to identify the zones where large numbers of wind farms could be built. Decision-making criteria included the finances of various renewable energy developers and their likely commitment to building, and the areas with the largest amount of wind energy potential. The legislature then required the PUC to select utilities to build priority transmission lines to these zones. The PUC has selected the location of many of the line routes, and the lines are currently being built. The utilities building the lines negotiated with landowners for easements and used eminent domain where necessary.

California is engaging in a similar effort through its Renewable Energy Transmission Initiative (RETI). The Western Governors' Association (WGA)—a regional group—has also identified the best areas for renewable energy development through its Western Renewable Energy Zone process. The WGA identified the most likely areas based on an assessment of wind, solar, and other resources; the location of conflicting land uses or designations, such as protected wildlife habitat; and other likely impediments to development. It then selected those zones in which development should be prioritized in an effort to encourage transmission utilities to build to those zones. Because the Association lacks eminent domain authority, however, or the authority to require construction of the lines, it cannot guarantee construction, unlike the CREZ and RETI projects. For discussions of the difficulties of relying on states to approve the siting of transmission lines, see Alexandra B. Klass & Elizabeth Wilson, Interstate Transmission Challenges for Renewable Energy: A Federalism Mismatch, 65 Vand. L. Rev. 1801 (2012).

An additional impediment to the construction of transmission lines for renewable energy is the issue of cost allocation. Because transmission lines for renewables are often regional—crossing local and state lines— and do not benefit everyone equally, there are extensive battles over which ratepayers should have to pay to finance the new lines, and how much they should have to pay. In Texas's ERCOT region, which is beyond FERC's Federal Power Act jurisdiction over transmission rates, the transmission utilities' costs will be shared by all ERCOT ratepayers, regardless of whether they benefit directly from the new lines or not. However, in the rest of the lower 48 states, the Federal Power Act requires that cost allocation be just, reasonable and nondiscriminatory.

Is Texas's method of spreading the costs of CREZ lines among all ERCOT ratepayers just, reasonable and nondiscriminatory?

In 2011, FERC issued Order 1000, which attempted to solve many of these cost allocation issues. The Order directs utilities to participate in regional transmission planning processes and consider regional transmission needs, and it includes six cost allocation principles for regional transmission projects.

Another aspect of Order 1000, which we do not include in the case excerpt below, attempted to encourage more competition in the construction of new transmission lines. Certain federally- and state-granted rights of first refusal previously allowed transmission line providers already operating in a territory to have the first opportunity to build new transmission lines in an area. Order 1000 endeavored to largely remove these rights, and the court found this to be acceptable.

Several parties challenged FERC Order 1000 and related Orders. The D.C. Circuit issued the following decision:

South Carolina Public Service Auth. v. FERC

762 F.3d 41 (D.C. Cir. 2014).

■ Before: ROGERS, GRIFFITH and PILLARD, CIRCUIT JUDGES.

■ PER CURIAM: This case involves challenges to the most recent reforms of electric transmission planning and cost allocation adopted by the Federal Energy Regulatory Commission pursuant to the Federal Power Act. In Order No. 1000, as reaffirmed and clarified in Order Nos. 1000–A and 1000–B (together, "the Final Rule"), the Commission required each transmission owning and operating public utility to participate in regional transmission planning that satisfies specific planning principles designed to prevent undue discrimination and preference in transmission service, and that produces a regional transmission plan. The local and regional transmission planning processes must consider transmission needs that are driven by public policy requirements. Transmission providers in neighboring planning regions must collectively determine if there are more efficient or cost-effective solutions to their mutual transmission needs.

The Final Rule also requires each planning process to have a method for allocating ex ante among beneficiaries the costs of new transmission facilities in the regional transmission plan, and the method must satisfy six regional cost allocation principles. Neighboring transmission planning regions also must have a common interregional cost allocation method for new interregional transmission facilities that satisfies six similar allocation principles. Additionally transmission providers are required to remove from their jurisdictional tariffs and agreements any provisions that establish a federal right of first refusal to develop transmission facilities in a regional transmission plan, subject to individualized compliance review.

[Petitioners] include state regulatory agencies, electric transmission providers, regional transmission organizations, and electric industry trade associations. They challenge the Commission's authority to adopt these reforms, and they contend that the Final Rule is arbitrary and capricious and unsupported by substantial evidence. For the following reasons, we conclude their contentions are unpersuasive.

We hold in Part II, that the Commission had authority under Section 206 of the Federal Power Act to require transmission providers to participate in a regional planning process. In Part III, we conclude that there was substantial evidence of a theoretical threat to support adoption of the reforms in the Final Rule. In Part IV, we hold that the Commission had authority under Section 206 to require removal of federal rights of first refusal provisions upon determining they were unjust and unreasonable practices affecting rates, and that determination was supported by substantial evidence and was not arbitrary or capricious. . . . In Part V, we hold that the Commission had authority under Section 206 to require the ex ante allocation of the costs of new transmission facilities among beneficiaries, and that its decision regarding scope was not arbitrary or capricious. In Part VI, we hold that the Commission reasonably determined that regional planning must include consideration of transmission needs driven by public policy requirements. . . .

Accordingly, we deny the petitions for review of the Final Rule.

* * * I.

Upon enacting the FPA, Congress determined that federal regulation of interstate electric energy transmission and its sale at wholesale is "necessary in the public interest," FPA § 201(a), 16 U.S.C. § 824(a), and vested the Commission with "jurisdiction over all facilities for such transmission or sale," id. § 201(b)(1), 16 U.S.C. § 824(b)(1). The States would retain authority over "any other sale of electric energy" and facilities used for "generation of electric energy," "local distribution," or "transmission of electric energy in intrastate commerce." Id.

Congress directed that "[a]ll rates and charges made, demanded, or received by any public utility for or in connection with the [jurisdictional] transmission or sale of electric energy . . . shall be just and reasonable," and that "[n]o public utility shall, with respect to any [jurisdictional] transmission or sale . . . subject any person to any undue prejudice or disadvantage" or "maintain any unreasonable difference in rates, charges, service, facilities, or in any other respect, either as between localities or as between classes of service." FPA § 205(a)–(b), 16 U.S.C. § 824d(a)–(b).

Additionally, Congress empowered the Commission to take action on its own motion in order to ensure that such rates, charges, and classifications, as well as "any rule, regulation, practice, or contract affecting such rate, charge, or classification," are not "unjust, unreasonable, unduly discriminatory or preferential." FPA § 206(a), 16 U.S.C. § 824e(a).

In Order No. 888, the Commission required each jurisdictional electric public transmission provider to "functional[ly] unbundl[e]" its wholesale generation and transmission services and file an open-access transmission tariff ("OATT") containing minimum terms of non-discriminatory transmission service. Through these structural changes, the Commission sought to open the electric grid to all sources of electric power and thereby "ensure that customers have the benefits of competitively priced generation." To promote development of competitive markets, the Commission encouraged the formation of regional transmission organizations ("RTOs") and independent system operators ("ISOs") to coordinate transmission planning, operation, and use on a regional and interregional basis.

In 2007, the Commission issued Order No. 890, Preventing Undue Discrimination and Preference in Transmission Service, F.E.R.C. Stats. & Regs. ¶ 31,241, 72 Fed. Reg. 12,266 (2007). Noting that the United States had "witnessed a decline in transmission investment relative to load growth," the Commission found that the resulting grid congestion "can have significant cost impacts on consumers."

Concluding that transmission providers lacked incentives to plan and develop new transmission facilities in a manner consistent with the public interest, the Commission found that the "lack of coordination, openness, and transparency" in transmission planning had "result[ed] in opportunities for undue discrimination" because "participants ha[d] no means to determine whether the plan developed by the transmission provider in isolation is unduly discriminatory." To "remedy these transmission planning deficiencies" and "prevent undue discrimination in the rates, terms and conditions of public utility transmission service," Order No. 890 required each transmission provider to establish an open, transparent, and coordinated transmission planning process that complied with nine planning principles. Transmission providers were also required "to open their transmission planning process to customers, coordinate with customers regarding future system plans, and share necessary planning information with customers."

By late 2008, the electric industry was reporting that an estimated $298 billion of investment in new electric transmission facilities would be needed between 2010 and 2030 to maintain current levels of reliable electric service across the United States. NERC, the electric industry's self-regulator, projected that in the next decade a 9.5% to 15% increase in circuit miles of transmission would be needed to maintain reliability and to "unlock" and integrate renewable resources like wind generation that are likely to be remote from demand centers. The Energy Department had similarly determined that "under any future electric industry scenario," a "[s]ignificant expansion of the transmission grid will be required" to "increase reliability, reduce costly congestion and line losses, and supply access to low-cost remote resources, including renewables."

In June 2010, the Commission published a Notice of Proposed Rulemaking. The Commission explained that although substantial improvements in the transmission planning process had occurred as a result of compliance with Order No. 890, "significant changes in the nation's electric power industry" since then required consideration of additional reforms. Among other things, the Commission identified "a trend of increased investment in the country's transmission infrastructure" due principally to investment in transmission of renewable energy sources. Although governmental reforms and market forces had resulted in expansion of the transmission grid, the Commission concluded that this positive trend highlighted deficiencies in existing transmission planning and cost allocation processes that would inhibit the construction of new transmission facilities and adversely affect rates if left unremedied.

The Commission identified five general deficiencies in Order No. 890, and proposed additional reforms "to correct [those] deficiencies . . . so that the transmission grid can better support wholesale power markets and thereby ensure that Commission-jurisdictional services are provided at rates, terms and conditions that are just and reasonable and not unduly discriminatory or preferential," In August 2011, the Commission issued Order No. 1000, which adopted the proposed reforms. Transmission Planning and Cost Allocation by Transmission Owning and Operating Public Utilities, F.E.R.C. Stats. & Regs. ¶ 31,323, 76 Fed. Reg. 49,842 (2011).

Under Order No. 1000: (1) Each transmission provider must participate in a regional transmission planning process that complies with the planning principles in Order No. 890, produces a regional transmission plan for development of new regional transmission facilities, and includes procedures to identify transmission needs driven by public policy requirements established by federal, state, or local laws or regulations and evaluate potential 14 solutions to those needs. (2) Neighboring transmission planning regions must establish interregional coordination procedures that provide for sharing information and planning data as well as the identification and joint evaluation of interregional transmission facilities that could address transmission needs more efficiently or cost-effectively than separate regional transmission facilities. (3) Transmission providers must remove from jurisdictional tariffs and agreements any provisions that establish a federal right of first refusal for an incumbent transmission developer to construct new regional transmission facilities included in a regional transmission plan. An "incumbent" transmission provider refers to a public utility transmission provider that develops a transmission project within its own retail distribution service territory, while a "non-incumbent" transmission provider refers to either a transmission developer without a retail distribution service territory or a public utility transmission provider that proposes a transmission project outside its existing retail distribution service territory. (4) Each transmission provider must demonstrate that the regional planning process in which it participates has established appropriate qualification criteria for transmission developers, identified the information that a transmission developer must submit in proposing a regional transmission project, and has a selection process for transmission projects that is transparent and not unduly discriminatory.

The cost-allocation reforms in Order No. 1000 require each transmission provider to include in its OATT a method (or set of methods) for allocating ex ante the costs of new regional transmission facilities that complies with six regional cost allocation principles. Those principles include cost causation, under which "[t]he cost of transmission facilities must be allocated to those within the transmission planning region that benefit from those facilities in a manner that is at least roughly commensurate with estimated benefits." Transmission providers in neighboring transmission planning regions are similarly required to establish a common method (or set of methods) for allocating ex ante the costs of a new transmission facility to be located in both planning regions that complies with interregional cost allocation principles closely tracking the regional cost allocation principles. Participant funding of new transmission facilities (i.e., allocating the costs of a transmission facility only to entities that volunteer to bear those costs) is not permitted as a regional or interregional cost allocation method.

Upon rehearing, the Commission clarified and reaffirmed the reforms in Order No. 1000. In Order No. 1000–B, the Commission provided clarifications and restated that the obligation to remove federal rights of first refusal would arise only after an individualized determination.

Petitioners challenge the Final Rule on the grounds that the Commission lacked statutory authority, made factual findings that were unsupported by substantial evidence, and acted in a manner that was arbitrary or capricious or contrary to law. In addressing these contentions, the court is bound to apply the following standards of review. The court reviews challenges to the Commission's interpretation of the FPA under the familiar two-step framework of [*Chevron*] . . . "No matter how it is framed, the question a court faces when confronted with an agency's interpretation of a statute it administers is always, simply, whether the agency has stayed within the bounds of its statutory authority," City of Arlington v. FCC, 133 S. Ct. 1863, 1868 (2013) (emphasis omitted), and the court will defer to the Commission's reasonable interpretation of statutory ambiguities concerning both the scope of its statutory authority and the application of that authority, see id. The court must uphold the Final Rule unless it is arbitrary, capricious, an abuse of discretion, or otherwise not in accordance with law.

Furthermore, in rate-related matters, the court's review of the Commission's determinations is particularly deferential because such matters are either fairly technical or "involve policy judgments that lie at the core of the regulatory mission." The court owes the Commission "great deference" in this realm because "[t]he statutory requirement that rates be 'just and reasonable' is obviously incapable of precise judicial definition," and "the Commission must have considerable latitude in developing a methodology responsive to its regulatory challenge."

II.   Mandatory Regional Planning: Statutory Authority.

In adopting the transmission planning reforms in the Final Rule, the Commission relied on FPA Section 206. Petitioners contend that the Commission lacks authority "to mandate transmission planning in the first instance" because the FPA "only allows [the Commission] to regulate existing voluntary commercial relationships."

A.

Section 206(a) provides, in relevant part: Whenever the Commission, after a hearing held upon its own motion or upon complaint, shall find that any rate, charge, or classification, demanded, observed, charged, or collected by any public utility for any transmission or sale subject to the jurisdiction of the Commission, or that any rule, regulation, practice, or contract affecting such rate, charge, or classification is unjust, unreasonable, unduly discriminatory or preferential, the Commission shall determine the just and reasonable rate, charge, classification, rule, regulation, practice, or contract to be thereafter observed and in force, and shall fix the same by order.

By its plain terms, Section 206 instructs the Commission to remedy "any . . . practice" that "affect[s]" a rate for interstate electricity transmission services "demanded" or "charged" by "any public utility" if such practice "is unjust, unreasonable, unduly discriminatory or preferential." Id. The text does not define "practice," although use of the word "any" amplifies the breadth of the delegation to the Commission. See United States v. Gonzales, 520 U.S. 1, 5 (1997).

Petitioners challenge neither the Commission's conclusion that the current transmission planning processes are "practices" under Section 206, nor its conclusion that such transmission planning practices directly affect rates. Neither can they dispute that the Commission is obligated by the plain text of Section 206 to ensure that such practices are just and reasonable and not unduly discriminatory or preferential. Instead petitioners maintain essentially that a lack of regional transmission planning was not an existing practice subject to the Commission's authority under Section 206, and that "the decision whether to coordinate planning is left, in the first instance, to utilities." Petitioners rely on Atlantic City Electric Co. v. FERC, 295 F.3d 1, 10 (D.C. Cir. 2002), for the proposition that the Commission is "limited under section 206 to investigat[ing] the reasonableness of the terms of existing utility-customer relationships."

Petitioners' reliance on Atlantic City is misplaced because it begs the question of what "practice" means. The authority and obligation that Congress vested in the Commission to remedy certain practices is broadly stated and the only question is what limits are fairly implied. On the one hand, Section 206 cannot be fairly viewed as the type of "subtle device" at issue in MCI Telecommunications Corp. v. AT & T Co., 512 U.S. 218, 224, 231 (1994), on which petitioners rely. There, the Supreme Court rejected the agency's attempt to interpret its statutory authority to "modify any requirement" to extend to a fundamental change to a tariff-filing requirement of "enormous importance to the statutory scheme." Id.

On the other hand, in California Independent System Operator Corp. v. FERC, 372 F.3d 395, 398 (D.C. Cir. 2004) ("CAISO"), this court held that the Commission had exceeded its authority under Section 206 by calling for the replacement of a public utility's board of directors. The court explained that "[t]he word 'practices' is a word of sufficiently diverse definitions that the only realistic approach to determining Congress's 'plain meaning,' if any, is to regard the word in its context." Understood in the context of Section 206's transactional terms, the court observed, "[i]t is quite a leap" to move from the authority to regulate rates, charges, classifications and closely related matters to "an implication that by the word 'practice,' Congress empowered the Commission . . . to reform completely the governing structure of [an ISO]." Id.

Reforming the practices of failing to engage in regional planning and ex ante cost allocation for development of new regional transmission facilities is not the kind of interpretive "leap" that concerned the court in CAISO but rather involves a core reason underlying Congress' instruction in Section 206.

For the reasons discussed, we conclude, consistent with the deferential standard in step two of the Chevron analysis, 467 U.S. at 843, that the Commission reasonably interpreted Section 206 to authorize the Final Rule's planning mandate.

B.

[The court rejects the petitioners' argument that FPA Section 202(a), dealing with voluntary interconnection, "bars the Commission from mandating transmission planning," holding that "coordination" refers to the coordinated operation of existing transmission facilities, not to the planning of future facilities.]

C.

Petitioners contend that even if Section 206 does not bar the Commission from mandating regional transmission planning, FPA Section 201(a) does. Section 201(a) authorizes the Commission to regulate "transmission of electric energy in interstate commerce" but also provides that this authority "extend[s] only to those matters which are not subject to regulation by the States." Petitioners assert that the mandate infringes on the States' traditional regulation of transmission planning, siting, and construction, violating the federalism principle recognized in Section 201(a).

We disagree. Petitioners' contention that the challenged orders intrude on the States' traditional role in regulating siting and construction requires little discussion. Even assuming arguendo that siting and construction are matters "subject to regulation by the States" within the meaning of Section 201(a), petitioners' contention simply cannot be squared with the language of the orders, which expressly and repeatedly disclaim authority over those matters. The orders neither require facility construction nor allow a party to build without securing necessary state approvals.

Petitioners' argument that the orders interfere with state regulation of planning, however, poses a closer question. Petitioners correctly contend that the Commission used the challenged orders to further regulate the transmission planning process. And, petitioners maintain, because state regulators were already substantially involved in regulating that process, the orders encroach on their authority in violation of Section 201(a)'s statement that the Commission's authority "extend[s] only to those matters which are not subject to regulation by the States." 16 U.S.C. § 824(a). But while petitioners' argument is not without force, relevant precedent suggests that Section 201(a) does not stand in the way of the orders' planning mandate. In New York v. FERC, 535 U.S. 1, the Court rejected a state's argument that Section 201(a) barred the Commission from ordering certain utilities to "transmit competitors' electricity over [their] lines on the same terms that the utilit[ies] applie[d] to [their] own energy transmissions."

Even though Section 201(b) does "limit FERC's sale jurisdiction to that at wholesale," there is no textual warrant for the suggestion that the Commission lacks jurisdiction over retail transmission. That is, the FPA preserves for the States relatively more sales authority than transmission authority. Second, Section 201(a)'s reference to a sphere of state authority is "a mere policy declaration" that should not be read in derogation of other specific provisions granting the Commission authority, including Section 201(b)'s grant of authority over "transmission of electric energy in interstate commerce."

As long as the Commission's activity falls within one of these specific jurisdictional grants, the "prefatory language of section 201(a)" does "not undermine FERC's jurisdiction." And the authority that Section 201(b) affords to the Commission has expanded over time because transmissions on the interconnected grids that have now developed "constitute transmissions in interstate commerce." Taken together, these points support the Commission's assertion of authority over transmission planning matters in the challenged orders, notwithstanding petitioners' contention that the orders intrude on the States' authority. First, because the planning mandate relates wholly to electricity transmission, as opposed to electricity sales, it involves a subject matter over which the Commission has relatively broader authority.[4][1]

Second, because the orders' planning mandate is directed at ensuring the proper functioning of the interconnected grid spanning state lines, the mandate fits comfortably within Section 201(b)'s grant of jurisdiction over "the transmission of electric energy in interstate commerce."

Accordingly, we reject petitioners' challenge because Section 201 does not preclude the Commission's regulation of transmission planning in the Final Rule. . . .

V. Cost Allocation.

As a key element of the regional planning process, the Final Rule requires transmission providers to devise methods for allocating the costs of certain new transmission facilities to those entities that benefit from them. In keeping with the overall approach of the transmission planning reforms, the Final Rule uses a light touch: it does not dictate how costs are to be allocated. Rather, the Rule provides for general cost allocation principles and leaves the details to transmission providers to determine in the planning processes.

Two groups of petitioners challenge the cost allocation provisions on nearly opposite grounds. One, the Joint Petitioners, contends that the Commission lacks sufficient statutory authority to adopt the cost allocation requirements. The other, the International Transmission Company Petitioners ("ITC Petitioners"), asserts that the Commission acted arbitrarily and capriciously in adopting them, essentially because the agency did not go far enough. We disagree on both counts.

A.

Before the current reforms, the Commission did not mandate that the costs of new transmission facilities be allocated ex ante to those who would benefit from those facilities. The Commission has since concluded that the lack of any method or process to ensure that new facilities were paid for by those that benefitted from them created perverse incentives—indeed, a sort of tragedy of the transmission commons. As the Commission explained, the challenges associated with allocating the cost of new or improved transmission facilities have become more pressing as the need for such infrastructure has grown. That is because "constructing new transmission facilities requires a significant amount of capital and, therefore, a threshold consideration for any company considering

---

[1]   This fact distinguishes this case from Electric Power Supply Ass'n v. FERC, 753 F.3d 216 (D.C. Cir. 2014), a case cited by petitioners where this court struck down a Commission attempt to regulate an aspect of retail electricity sales.

investing in transmission is whether it will have a reasonable opportunity to recover its costs."

In the Commission's view, the lack of methods that ascertain the beneficiaries of new and improved transmission facilities and allocate costs to entities that benefit "creates significant risk for transmission developers that they will have no identified group of customers from which to recover the cost of their investment." Id. In addition, the Commission noted that the "increasing adoption of state resource policies, such as renewable portfolio standards, has contributed to the rapid growth of renewable energy resources that are frequently remote from load centers." Id. In short, the Commission recognized that, unless costs were allocated to those who benefit, needed expansion and improvement of the power grid would not likely occur. The Commission accordingly concluded that "existing cost allocation methods may not appropriately account for benefits associated with new transmission facilities and, thus, may result in rates that are not just and reasonable or are unduly discriminatory or preferential."

For these reasons, in the Final Rule, the Commission required each public utility transmission provider to participate in a regional transmission planning process that includes, with regard to cost allocation, both: (1) "[a] regional cost allocation method for the cost of new transmission facilities selected in a regional transmission plan for purposes of cost allocation"; and (2) "an interregional cost allocation method for the cost of certain new transmission facilities that are located in two or more neighboring transmission planning regions and are jointly evaluated by the regions in the interregional transmission coordination procedures required by this Final Rule."

The reforms do not require any particular provider to pay for new facilities or dictate precisely how costs must be allocated. Instead, the Commission requires public utilities to have in place a method or methods for allocating the costs of new transmission facilities "in a manner that is at least roughly commensurate with the benefits received by those who will pay those costs," and for ensuring that costs are not "involuntarily allocated to entities that do not receive benefits." To implement these reforms, the Commission requires each public utility transmission provider to include in its OATT both "a method, or set of methods, for allocating the costs of new transmission facilities selected in the regional transmission plan" and "a method or set of methods for allocating the costs of new interregional transmission facilities." Each utility in a region "must include the same cost allocation method or methods adopted by the region." The Commission also required both regional and interregional cost allocation method(s) to adhere to six specified principles, including, for example, that costs must be allocated roughly commensurately with benefits, that those entities that receive no benefit must not be involuntarily allocated costs, and that the allocation method(s) for the costs of a regional facility must assign costs within the transmission planning region unless entities outside the region voluntarily assume them.

Thus, although the Final Rule requires each public utility in a region to include the same cost allocation method(s) in its OATT, it does not dictate either how the costs should be allocated in any more detail than those general principles, nor does the Rule specify how costs should be recovered (i.e., how the new facilities should be paid for). The Commission, moreover, requires cost allocation only for new transmission facilities that are chosen for cost allocation during the regional planning process—meaning that cost allocation will be triggered only in cases in which the transmission providers in a region, in consultation with stakeholders, evaluate a given facility and determine that its benefits merit cost allocation under the regional cost allocation method(s).

B.

Petitioners dispute the Commission's authority to adopt the cost allocation reforms under Section 206 of the FPA. The key inquiry here, as in Parts II.A and IV.B supra is whether cost allocation constitutes a "practice" "affecting . . . rate[s]" under Section 206 of the FPA such that the Commission may fix it by order. 16 U.S.C. § 824e(a). Petitioners do not dispute that the allocation of costs of new transmission facilities is a "practice" that at least in principle can "affect" a "rate." This court has previously held that the Commission has "clear" authority to reallocate capacity and production costs. Indeed, quite recently we noted that "in principle, a 'beneficiary pays' approach is a just and reasonable basis for allocating the costs of regional transmission projects, even if it leads to reallocating sunk costs." FirstEnergy Serv. Co. v. FERC, ___ F.3d ___, No. 12–1461, 2014 WL 3538062, at *7 (D.C. Cir. July 18, 2014). The central thrust of Joint Petitioners' statutory argument is that Section 206 does not authorize the Commission to require utilities to pay for the costs of transmission facilities developed by entities with whom they have no prior contractual or customer relationship and from whom they do not take transmission service. Joint Br. of Pet'rs/Intervenors Concerning Cost Allocation 2 ("Joint Pet'rs' Br.").

In the Joint Petitioners' view, Section 206 unambiguously forecloses the Commission from mandating the allocation of costs beyond pre-existing commercial relationships, and the cost allocation reforms thus fail at Chevron step one. No such limitation exists in the statutory text. Section 206 empowers the Commission to fix any "practice" affecting rates, and the Commission reasonably understood beneficiary-based cost allocation—or its absence—to be a practice affecting rates. Section 206 nowhere limits cost allocation to entities with preexisting commercial relationships. To the contrary, it empowers the Commission to fix "any rate" "demanded, observed, charged, or collected by any public utility for any transmission . . . subject to the jurisdiction of the Commission," and "any . . . practice" "affecting such rate." 16 U.S.C. § 824e(a) (emphasis added). The use of "any" to describe "rate," "public utility," and "transmission" bestows authority on the Commission that is not cabined to pre-existing commercial relationships of any given utility. See Gonzales, 520 U.S. at 5. The beneficiary-based cost allocation reforms are not clearly a "remote thing[ ] beyond the rate structure," as was the personnel and structure of the corporate board in CAISO, 372 F.3d at 403. Instead, "the statute is silent or ambiguous with respect to the specific issue." We therefore defer, at Chevron step two, to the Commission's interpretation of the Act if it is permissible.

We believe that it is. First, as noted above, nothing in the statutory language or context limits the Commission's authority to fixing only practices affecting pre-existing commercial relationships. Second, the

Commission's adoption of a beneficiary-based cost allocation method is a logical extension of the cost causation principle. Under that basic tenet, which we have repeatedly embraced, "costs are to be allocated to those who cause the costs to be incurred and reap the resulting benefits." And we have "endorsed the approach of 'assign[ing] the costs of system-wide benefits to all customers on an integrated transmission grid.' " The physics of electrical transmission supports the Commission's conclusion that even transmission providers distant from new transmission facilities—including those that do not have pre-existing commercial relationships with a transmission developer—may benefit from those new facilities. Because "there is no way to determine what path electricity actually takes between two points [on a power grid] or indeed whether the electricity at the point of delivery was ever at the point of origin," "all of the individual facilities used to transmit electricity are treated as if they were part of a single machine."

And because "a transmission system performs as a whole[,] the availability of multiple paths for electricity to flow from one point to another contributes to the reliability of the system as a whole." Id. The Commission accordingly determined that "in an interconnected electric transmission system, the enlargement of one path between two points can provide greater system stability, lower line losses, reduce reactive power needs, and improve the throughput capacity on other facilities." There is a strong scientific basis for the Commission's conclusion that "[e]ntities that contract for service on the transmission grid cannot 'choose' to affect only the transmission facilities for which they have entered into a contract" and "cannot claim that they are not using or benefiting from such transmission facilities simply because they did not enter a contract to use them." As the Commission recognized, the free rider problem it identified stems from the fact that an entity that uses part of the transmission grid may obtain benefits from improvements to and expansion of transmission facilities on another part of that grid, regardless of whether that entity has a contract for service on the improved part of the grid. The Commission therefore reasonably identified the lack of beneficiary-based cost allocation as a practice likely to result in rates that are not just and reasonable or are unduly discriminatory or preferential. And, as explained in Part II.A supra, whether a threat of unjust or unreasonable rates derives from a practice or the absence thereof, Section 206 empowers the Commission to address it.

The plain text of the statute and the Commission's reasoning show the Commission's construction to be wholly reasonable.

VI. Public Policy Requirement.

Petitioners raise three challenges to the orders' requirement that regions establish procedures that account for the impact federal, state, and local laws and regulations (i.e., public policy requirements) will have on transmission systems. None is persuasive. According to the Commission, this mandate responds to a recent proliferation of laws and regulations affecting the power grid. For example, the Commission expects that many States will require construction of new transmission infrastructure to integrate sources of renewable energy, such as wind farms, into the grid and that new federal environmental regulations will shape utilities' decisions about when to retire old coal-based generators.

Plans that fail to account for such laws and regulations, the Commission reasoned, would not adequately reflect future needs. Plans are not required to take every need into account; instead, regions must only create procedures to "identify, out of the larger set of potential transmission needs driven by public policy requirements that may be proposed, those transmission needs for which transmission solutions will be evaluated in the . . . regional transmission planning process."

A.

Petitioners assert that the Commission lacks statutory authority to promote the public welfare. The mandate simply recognizes that state and federal policies might affect the transmission market and directs transmission providers to consider that impact in their planning decisions. In this regard, the requirement is no different from other facets of the planning process. Petitioners' argument that the orders seek to unlawfully promote the general welfare is misplaced. . . .

Accordingly, we deny the petitions for review. ∎

NOTES AND COMMENTS

1.   As Professors Alexandra Klass and Elizabeth Wilson have noted, Order 1000 explicitly focuses on the environmental benefits of adding clean energy sources to the nation's electric grid. They observe that the "public policy benefits" requirement favors "transmission lines that make it easier to achieve the goals of a public policy—say, a state renewable energy standard" because they "have a clear public benefit that should be considered in planning and cost-allocation processes." Klass and Wilson, *supra*, at 1824.

Yet this aspect of Order 1000 was extremely controversial, as critics charged that FERC had dramatically overstepped its statutory mandate by promoting clean energy. *See, e.g.*, Bruce Edelston, FERC Under Fire, The Hill, June 26, 2014, http://thehill.com/blogs/congress-blog/energy-environment/210584-ferc-under-fire. FERC, of course, is not primarily tasked with protecting the environment. As Professor Todd Aagaard has noted, "The Federal Power Act gives FERC little if any authority to regulate energy transactions . . . for the direct purpose of accomplishing environmental objectives." Todd S. Aagaard, Using Non-Environmental Law To Achieve Environmental Objectives, 30 J. Land Use & Envtl. L. (forthcoming 2015).

How did the court in this case address the concern that FERC had exceeded its mandate by requiring RTOs to consider environmental benefits of new transmission projects?

2.   Chapter 13 sets forth the *Electric Power Supply Association v. FERC* decision on FERC's Order 745. That decision, involving compensation in the wholesale markets for "demand response," was issued shortly before this case. In *Electric Power Supply Association* (decided by a three-judge panel split 2–1, with a vigorous dissent by Judge Harry Edwards), the majority also analyzed the extent of FERC's authority under FPA § 206 to regulate "practices" that are "affecting" the wholesale markets. It rejected FERC's authority over demand response compensation, holding in part that "FERC can regulate practices affecting the wholesale market under §§ 205 and 206, provided the Commission is not directly regulating a matter subject to state

control, such as the retail market." Elec. Power Supply Ass'n v. FERC, 753 F.3d 216, 222 (D.C. Cir. 2014).

How does this decision distinguish that one? In particular, this decision reaches a different conclusion than *Electric Power Supply Association* on matters traditionally reserved to the states, such as states' involvement in transmission planning, rejecting challenges to Order 1000 on the basis that these aspects of the Order intrude on states' authority. Can the two decisions be reconciled, and if so, how?

The Midcontinent Independent System Operator (MISO) followed Order 1000 in planning expanded transmission lines to connect to numerous wind energy facilities throughout the Midwest. It termed these lines "multi-value projects" and allocated their costs based on the amount of electricity used in each region. The Seventh Circuit affirmed this approach in the following case.

Illinois Commerce Comm'n v. FERC
721 F.3d 764 (7th Cir. 2013).

Control of more than half the nation's electrical grid is divided among seven Regional Transmission Organizations. These are voluntary associations of utilities that own electrical transmission lines interconnected to form a regional grid and that agree to delegate operational control of the grid to the association. Power plants that do not own any part of the grid but generate electricity transmitted by it are also members of these associations, as are other electrical companies involved in one way or another with the regional grid.

The RTOs play a key role in the effort by the Federal Energy Regulatory Commission "to promote competition in those areas of the industry amenable to competition, such as the segment that generates electric power, while ensuring that the segment of the industry characterized by natural monopoly—namely, the transmission grid that conveys the generated electricity—cannot exert monopolistic influence over other areas. . . . To further pry open the wholesale-electricity market and to reduce technical inefficiencies caused when different utilities operate different portions of the grid independently, the Commission has encouraged transmission providers to establish 'Regional Transmission Organizations'—entities to which transmission providers would transfer operational control of their facilities for the purpose of efficient coordination . . . [and] has encouraged the management of those entities by 'Independent System Operators,' not-for-profit entities that operate transmission facilities in a nondiscriminatory manner."

Two Regional Transmission Organizations are involved in this case—Midwest Independent Transmission System Operator, Inc. (MISO) and PJM Interconnection, LLC (PJM). As shown in Figure 1, MISO operates in the midwest and in the Great Plains states while PJM operates in the mid-Atlantic region but has midwestern enclaves in and surrounding Chicago and in southwestern Michigan.

Each RTO is responsible for planning and directing expansions and upgrades of its grid. It finances these activities by adding a fee to the price of wholesale electricity transmitted on the grid. 18 C.F.R. § 35.34(k)(1), (7). The Federal Power Act requires that the fee be "just and reasonable," 16 U.S.C. § 824d(a), and therefore at least roughly proportionate to the anticipated benefits to a utility of being able to use the grid. *Illinois Commerce Commission v. FERC,* 576 F.3d 470 (7th Cir.2009). Thus "all approved rates [must] reflect to some degree the costs actually caused by the customer who must pay them." Courts "evaluate compliance [with this principle, which is called 'cost causation'] by comparing the costs assessed against a party to the burdens imposed or benefits drawn by that party."

MISO began operating in 2002 and soon grew to have 130 members. In 2010 it sought FERC's approval to impose a tariff on its members to fund the construction of new high-voltage power lines that it calls "multi-value projects" (MVPs), beginning with 16 pilot projects. The tariff is mainly intended to finance the construction of transmission lines for electricity generated by remote wind farms. Every state in MISO's region except Kentucky (which is barely in the region, see Figure 1) encourages or even requires utilities to obtain a specified percentage of their electricity supply from renewable sources, mainly wind farms. Indiana, North Dakota, and South Dakota have aspirational goals; the rest have mandates. The details vary but most of the states expect or require utilities to obtain between 10 and 25 percent of their electricity needs from renewable sources by 2025—and by then there may be federal renewable energy requirements as well.

"The dirty secret of clean energy is that while generating it is getting easier, moving it to market is not. . . . Achieving [a 20% renewable energy quota] would require moving large amounts of power over long distances, from the windy, lightly populated plains in the middle of the country to the coasts where many people live . . . The grid's limitations are putting a damper on such projects already."

To begin with, it has identified what it believes to be the best sites in its region for wind farms that will meet the region's demand for wind power. Most are in the Great Plains, because electricity produced by wind farms there is cheaper despite the longer transmission distance; the wind flow is stronger and steadier and land is cheaper because population density is low (wind farms require significant amounts of land).

MISO has estimated that the cost of the transmission lines necessary both to bring electricity to its urban centers from the Great Plains and to integrate the existing wind farms elsewhere in its region with transmission lines from the Great Plains—transmission lines that the multi-value projects will create—will be more than offset by the lower cost of electricity produced by western wind farms. The new transmission lines will also increase the reliability of the electricity supply in the MISO region and thus reduce brownouts and outages, and also increase the efficiency with which electricity is distributed throughout the region.

The cost of the multi-value projects is to be allocated among utilities drawing power from MISO's grid in proportion to each utility's share of the region's total wholesale consumption of electricity. Before 2010, MISO allocated the cost of expanding or upgrading the transmission grid to the utilities nearest a proposed transmission line, on the theory that they would benefit the most from the new line. But wind farms in the Great Plains can generate far more power than that sparsely populated region needs. So MISO decided to allocate MVP costs among all utilities drawing power from the grid according to the amount of electrical energy used, thus placing most of those costs on urban centers, where demand for energy is greatest.

FERC approved (with a few exceptions, one discussed later in this opinion) MISO's rate design and pilot projects in two orders (for simplicity we'll pretend they're just one), precipitating the petitions for review that we have consolidated.

* * *

MISO used to allocate the cost of an upgrade to its grid to the local area ("pricing zone") in which the upgrade was located. (There are 24 pricing zones in MISO.) But those were upgrades to low-voltage lines, which transmit power short distances and thus benefit only the local area served by the lines. MISO contends (and FERC agrees) that the multi-value projects, which involve high-voltage lines that transmit electricity over long distances, will benefit all members of MISO and so the projects' costs should be shared among all members.

* * *

Illinois . . . complains that MISO has failed to show that the multi-value projects as a whole will confer benefits greater than their costs, and it complains too about FERC's failure to determine the costs and benefits of the projects subregion by subregion and utility by utility. But Illinois's briefs offer no estimates of costs and benefits either, whether for the MISO region as a whole or for particular subregions or particular utilities. And in complaining that MISO and the Commission failed to calculate the full financial incidence of the MVP tariff, Illinois ignores the limitations on calculability that the uncertainty of the future imposes. MISO did estimate that there would be cost savings of some $297 million to $423 million annually because western wind power is cheaper than power from existing sources, and that these savings would be "spread almost evenly across all Midwest ISO Planning Regions." It also estimated that the projected high-voltage lines would reduce losses of electricity in transmission by $68 to $104 million, and save another $217 to $271 million by reducing "reserve margin losses." That term refers to electricity generated in excess of demand and therefore (because it can't be stored) wasted. Fewer plants will have to be kept running in reserve to meet unexpected spikes in demand if by virtue of longer transmission lines electricity can be sent from elsewhere to meet those unexpected spikes. It's impossible to allocate these cost savings with any precision across MISO members.

The promotion of wind power by the MVP program deserves emphasis. Already wind power accounts for 3.5 percent of the nation's electricity, and it is expected to continue growing despite the downsides of wind power that we summarized in *Muscarello v. Winnebago County Board,* 702 F.3d 909, 910–11 (7th Cir. 2012). The use of wind power in lieu of power generated by burning fossil fuels reduces both the nation's dependence on foreign oil and emissions of carbon dioxide. And its cost is falling as technology improves. No one can know how fast wind power will grow. But the best guess is that it will grow fast and confer substantial benefits on the region served by MISO by replacing more expensive local wind power, and power plants that burn oil or coal, with western wind power. There is no reason to think these benefits will be denied to particular subregions of MISO. Other benefits of MVPs, such as increasing the reliability of the grid, also can't be calculated in advance, especially on a subregional basis, yet are real and will benefit utilities and consumers in all of MISO's subregions.

It's not enough for Illinois to point out that MISO's and FERC's attempt to match the costs and the benefits of the MVP program is crude; if crude is all that is possible, it will have to suffice. As we explained in *Illinois Commerce Commission v. FERC, supra,* if FERC "cannot quantify the benefits [to particular utilities or a particular utility] . . . but it has an articulable and plausible reason to believe that the benefits are at least roughly commensurate with those utilities' share of total electricity sales in [the] region, then fine; the Commission can approve [the pricing scheme proposed by the Regional Transmission Organization for that region] . . . on that basis. For that matter it can presume [as it did in this case] that new transmission lines benefit the entire network by reducing the likelihood or severity of outages."

Illinois can't counter FERC without presenting evidence of imbalance of costs and benefits, which it hasn't done. When we pointed this out at oral argument, Illinois's lawyer responded that he could not obtain the necessary evidence without pretrial discovery and that FERC had refused to grant his request for an evidentiary hearing even though the Commission's rules make the grant of such a hearing a precondition to discovery. FERC refused because it already had voluminous evidentiary materials, including MISO's elaborate quantifications of costs and benefits—and these were materials to which the petitioners had access as well; they are, after all, members of MISO. The only information MISO held back was the production costs of particular power plants, which it deemed trade secrets and anyway are only tenuously related to the issue of proportionality. The need for discovery has not been shown; and for us to order it without a compelling reason two and a half years after the Commission rendered its exhaustive decision (almost 400 pages long) would create unconscionable regulatory delay. ∎

* * *

While MISO's cost allocation approach found favor in the Seventh Circuit, the approach of another RTO, the PJM Interconnection, originally did not. In 2009, the court rejected PJM's cost allocation approach. Illinois Commerce Commission v. FERC, 576 F.3d 470 (7th Cir. 2009). In June 2014, the Seventh Circuit issued another opinion, again authored by Judge Posner, which reviewed a new cost allocation scheme for the PJM RTO, instituted in response to the 2009 decision.

Illinois Commerce Comm'n v. FERC
576 F.3d 470 (7th Cir. 2014).

The petitioners are primarily the midwestern members of a Regional Transmission Organization (plus the Illinois Commerce Commission, which essentially is appearing on behalf of Commonwealth Edison, the largest electrical utility in Illinois) called PJM Interconnection. . . . [PJM] operates the grid on behalf of the members. . . . Its region stretches east and south from the Chicago area (northeastern Illinois) to western Michigan, eastern Indiana, Ohio, Kentucky, Tennessee, West Virginia, Pennsylvania, New Jersey, Delaware, Maryland, the District of Columbia, North Carolina, and Virginia.

* * *

What we'll refer to as the western region of PJM consists of the parts of Michigan, Illinois, and Indiana shown on the map as being in PJM's domain, along with all of Ohio. Electrical generating plants in the western region usually are close to the customers—Chicago, for example, a major electricity market, is ringed by power plants—and so in that region relatively low voltage transmission lines (typically 345 kilovolts) are adequate for serving most customers, although the region also has a number of high voltage—765 kV—lines for transmitting electricity with greater efficiency, mainly from Indiana to customers in Chicago. The cities in the eastern region use even lower voltage (230 kV lines) than the cities in the western region, but most of the power plants are farther away from the customers than in PJM's western region and therefore 500 kV lines are preferred even though more expensive; the reason is that higher voltage reduces the amount of electricity that is lost as a function of the distance over which it is transmitted.

The question presented by the petition for review is the extent to which the members of PJM in its western region (we'll call these the "western utilities") can be required to contribute to the costs of newly built or to be built 500 kV lines (we'll call these the "new transmission lines") even though the lines are primarily in the eastern part of PJM. Originally at issue were 18 such lines and related projects, expected to cost $6.6 billion in toto. The number of new lines has dwindled to 12 (11 already built, the other under construction; but 3 more are under study). The current estimate of the total cost of the projects that have been or will be completed is $2.7 billion.

PJM's western utilities are unlikely to obtain a significant additional supply of electricity from the new transmission lines. The capacity of the western utilities to generate electricity is already ample—so ample that they transmit a great deal of their electricity to the eastern members of PJM to help them meet the heavy eastern demand for electricity. Because the demand for electricity is so much greater in PJM's eastern subregion, it's unlikely that much electricity will be transmitted from the eastern to the western utilities via the new transmission lines.

Still, the western utilities may benefit from the new high-voltage transmission lines in PJM's eastern region, and to the extent they do they can be required to contribute to the cost of building the new lines. The Commission's order that we set aside five years ago made no effort to quantify those benefits, however; instead it allocated the costs of the new transmission lines among all the members of PJM in proportion to each utility's electricity sales, a pricing method analogous to a uniform sales tax. The Commission acknowledged that this was a crude method of cost allocation—which is to put it mildly, because without quantifying the benefits of the eastern projects to the western utilities it is impossible to determine what those utilities should be charged: charging costs greater than the benefits would overcharge the utilities, and charging costs less than the benefits would undercharge them. The Commission defended its approach by appealing to the difficulty of measuring the benefits that the western utilities would derive from the new lines. . . . We acknowledged that "if [the Commission] cannot quantify the benefits to the Midwestern utilities from new 500 kV lines in the East, . . . but it has an articulable and plausible reason to believe that the benefits are at least roughly commensurate with those utilities' share of total electricity sales in PJM's region, then fine; the Commission can approve PJM's proposed pricing scheme on that basis.". . . . But the Commission hadn't met that standard either. So we remanded.

Almost three years elapsed before the Commission issued its order on remand. A year later the Commission supplemented the order on rehearing, . . . and now, a year farther on, the western utilities are back before us, challenging the order on remand—which like the order we set aside prescribes "a region wide postage stamp allocation of the costs of new transmission facilities that operate at and above 500 kV." This is FERC speak for allocating the costs of the high-voltage lines across all the PJM utilities, east or west, in proportion to each utility's respective sales. Just as the price of sending a letter anywhere within the United States is the same, so the cost that an electrical utility must contribute to a 500 kV transmission line will, if FERC has its way, be independent of the utility's location relative to the location of the transmission line.

The postal analogy is forced. Distance doesn't figure in the price of a letter, because most of the costs of postal service are incurred in the postal facilities in which mail is sorted and in local pick up and delivery service, rather than in the transportation of the letter between distant locations. Here we're talking about the allocation of the huge costs of building high voltage transmission lines that do not provide uniform benefits to all the utilities in the region in which the lines are built.

Much of the Commission's order on remand is devoted to hand wringing over how difficult it is to estimate the benefits to PJM's western utilities of the new 500 kV lines in the east (thus reprising its original order). Yet at the same time the opinion contains detailed dollar estimates of many of the benefits—but without explaining the basis of the estimates. Studies are cited from time to time, but the evidence and analysis on which they're based are not described. Eventually the Commission threw up its hands and said in its order on rehearing that "500 kV and above transmission facilities provide a broad range of benefits, including reduced congestion, reduced outages, reduced operating reserve requirements, and reduced losses. These benefits radiate from the upgraded facility, and thus are spread throughout the PJM region." But how far they "radiate," and how equally, and with what loss of effect as the distance grows are critical questions not answered in the Commission's order. The benefits may "spread throughout" the entire domain of PJM without spreading equally, or even approximately equally, among the utilities that comprise PJM.

Of the four types of benefit listed by the Commission in the passage we just quoted, at least two—reduced electrical outages and reduced electricity losses—will definitely not be equally distributed between the utilities in the eastern region and the utilities in the western region. Outages in the eastern region will be reduced because the high voltage transmission facilities will enable electricity to be transmitted with greater reliability within the region. But outages in the western region will be reduced only trivially. The flow of electricity in PJM's domain is west to east except there is some flow the other way from eastern Indiana to the Chicago area. And the typical blackout or brownout occurs because of an outage in an individual transmission line or transformers, often because of an overload or weather damage, and the outages will persist until those lines can be repaired, rather than being offset by a new supply of electricity, whether from west or east.

As for reducing losses of electricity attributable to the distance over which it is transmitted, the new high voltage transmission lines will do that in the eastern region because high voltage is more efficient than low for transmitting electricity over long distances. The western utilities will benefit too, because they won't have to generate as much electricity to satisfy the eastern demand. And because PJM requires the western utilities to maintain reserve capacity (just as hospitals are required to install generators to provide a back up supply of electricity should there be an outage) to make up for interruptions in the supply of electricity to the eastern utilities, a reduction in those interruptions as a result of the new high voltage transmission facilities will enable the western utilities to reduce their reserve capacity.

Another benefit to the western utilities will be a reduction in congestion in their transmission lines if interruptions in transmission to the eastern utilities are reduced because transmission lines in the east will be transmitting electricity at a higher voltage. Transmission congestion occurs when customers' demand for electricity exceeds transmission capacity, resulting in what is called "curtailment": the grid operator does not allow additional supply to enter the grid because it would overload the lines. Curtailment is costly to the utilities because it means they're producing electricity that cannot be sold to their customers because it cannot be transmitted to them.

So some of the benefits of the new high voltage transmission facilities will indeed "radiate" to the western utilities, as the Commission said, but "some" is not a number and does not enable even a ballpark estimate of the benefits of the new transmission lines to the western utilities. Consider two utilities, one in northern Illinois and one in southern New Jersey, whose peak load capacity is the same. How likely is it that they benefit even roughly equally from a new 500 kV transmission facility in New Jersey? The New Jersey utility would obtain or deliver electricity using that facility; the Illinois utility could reduce its reserve capacity slightly because it would be less likely to have to help the New Jersey utility overcome an outage, as an outage would be less likely.

Those are not equivalent benefits, though treated by the Commission as equivalent. The only explanation for why it did that is that having failed to conduct a cost benefit analysis, it had no basis for treating the benefits as other than equivalent.

* * *

We conclude, with regret given the age of this case, that the Commission failed to comply with our order remanding the case to it. It must try again. If it continues to argue that a cost benefit analysis of the new transmission facilities is infeasible, it must explain why that is so and what the alternatives are. It has presented no evidence that postage stamp pricing is an acceptable, or the only possible, alternative.

We acknowledge that the benefits of the new facilities to the western utilities may prove unquantifiable because they depend on the likelihood and magnitude of outages and other contingencies, and that likelihood and that magnitude may for all we know baffle the best analysts. If the Commission after careful consideration concludes that the benefits can't be quantified even roughly, it can do something like use the western utilities' estimate of the benefits as a starting point, adjust the estimate to account for the uncertainty in benefit allocation, and pronounce the resulting estimate of benefits adequate for regulatory purposes. If best is unattainable second best will have to do, lest this case drag on forever.

To summarize, the lines at issue in this case are part of a regional grid that includes the western utilities. But the lines at issue are all located in PJM's eastern region, primarily benefit that region, and should not be allowed to shift a grossly disproportionate share of their costs to western utilities on which the eastern projects will confer only future, speculative, and limited benefits. The petitions for review are granted and the matter once again remanded to the Commission for new proceedings. ■

■ CUDAHY, CIRCUIT JUDGE, dissenting.

The issues presented here are practically identical with those that we dealt with in Illinois Commerce Comm'n v. FERC, 576 F.3d 470 (7th Cir. 2009) ("Illinois Commission I"). I filed a dissent in that case and I emphatically reiterate its contents here. The majority has expressed a need for more precise numbers about benefits, burdens and a variety of other aspects. Now it has enhanced that need by suggesting the use of cost-benefit analysis (a method, some think, of dressing up dubious numbers to reach more impressive solutions). I will say preliminarily that I think the majority is under the impression that somehow there is a mathematical solution to this problem, and I think that this is a complete illusion. Despite the frequency with which cost-benefit analysis is used, it does not resolve the difficulty of accurately or meaningfully measuring the costs and benefits involved with these grid strengthening projects. Cost allocation, particularly at these extraordinarily high voltages, is far from a precise science, and there are no mathematical solutions to determining benefits region by region or subregion by subregion. See PJM Interconnection, L.L.C., 142 FERC ¶ 61,216 (2013) ("Remand Rehearing Order") (noting the difficulty of precisely quantifying future benefits); see also Illinois Commerce Comm'n v. FERC, 721 F.3d 764, 774 (7th Cir. 2013) ("Illinois Commission II") (same). Both parties acknowledged this much at argument. Cost allocation is a judgmental matter and should be treated as such. . . . Cost allocation produces approximate results and requires selection of the most appropriate methodology among many, none of which are necessarily "right." This is one reason courts should generally be deferential to FERC's technical analysis; and, I think somewhat heretically, because the majority's notions of cost-causation and related technical concepts were not developed in a context of extra-high voltage projects forming a backbone framework, judicial precedents involving radically distinguishable arrangements, especially those involving lower voltages, are dubious guides to developing an appropriate methodology here.

In addition, the majority indulges in descriptions of many elements of the PJM grid and their functions without reference to any engineering evidence in support. For example, the majority claims that "the cities in the eastern region (of PJM) use even lower voltage (230 kv lines) than the cities in the western region, but most of the power plants are farther away from the customers than in PJM's western region and therefore 500 kv lines are preferred even though more expensive; the reason is that higher voltage reduces [line loss]." Such a statement is at best a vast oversimplification, and the comment that "it's unlikely that much electricity will be transmitted from the eastern to the western utilities via the new transmission lines" is based on ignoring the potential for future developments of generation and transmission. In fact, the entire thrust of the majority is toward precise cost causation, even in the present case, where that is indeterminate or at least obscure. The effect of the majority opinion is to emphasize functional relationships of the fragments of PJM rather than its value as a unique whole. I do not agree with the majority (or the Commission) that postage stamp cost distribution is "crude." The reason ascribed by the majority for this deficiency assumes that some other methodology, . . . can trace the benefits of additions with precision—an ability convincingly rejected by the Commission. In fact, the postage stamp methodology is the only one that can be mathematically verified. Thus, if one knows the total cost of the improvements and the total amount of the electrical output, one divided by the other provides an unarguable dividend representing the uniform burden of the various segments. Other methodologies provide approximations, but no more. The majority cites Illinois Commerce Comm'n v FERC, 721 F.3d 764,774 (7th Cir. 2013), the "wind power decision," as evidence of tolerance for postage stamp allocation but fails to indicate why that decision is not more broadly precedential for this one. In an elaborate effort to distinguish the very similar wind power decision, the majority underestimates the role of an ultra high-voltage backbone in equalizing benefits for all grid members. Why should not uniformity of benefit as provided by the postage stamp approach be the starting point in both cases?

* * *

For these reasons I respectfully dissent. ∎

NOTES AND COMMENTS

1.   The two *Illinois Commerce Commission* decisions demonstrate that even though Order 1000's principles of cost allocation have been upheld (in *South Carolina Public Service Authority*, discussed above), there is still much work to be done to decide on the precise cost allocation methods for transmission projects in individual RTOs. A fractured approach to transmission allocation is emerging in the federal courts—an approach that continues to demonstrate strong disagreement between Judges Cudahy and Posner on the Seventh Circuit.

What aspects of the different RTOs designs for cost allocation led the Seventh Circuit to uphold MISO's approach, but reject PJM's?

2.   Under the majority's decision in this case, how could PJM meet its burden to uphold its "postage stamp" cost allocation scheme against the concern articulated about its costs to western utilities? Would it have to provide a full cost-benefit analysis? What if it did, and that analysis continued to show that on balance the western utilities benefited less than it cost them?

———————

Even when transmission lines are available due to RTO planning or state CREZ-type requirements, renewable energy facilities often face challenges connecting to transmission lines. Because they are intermittent, these facilities can cause problems for transmission line operators. Renewable energy facilities wishing to connect to lines must submit interconnection requests to line operators—either an RTO or ISO or the owner of a transmission line—after which the renewable energy facility owner and line operator conduct detailed studies to ensure that the line can accommodate the electricity and to identify any upgrades that will be needed as a result of the interconnection. In an attempt to make interconnection requirements predictable for large wind farms— some of the most intermittent facilities—FERC issued Order No. 661 in 2005, which creates standard interconnection agreements for large wind energy facilities. Under this order, wind generators must show, *inter alia*, that they have certain remote capabilities to respond to grid problems, that they have the ability to "transmit data and receive instructions from the Transmission Provider," and that they can "remain on line during voltage disturbances."

5. STREAMLINING AND MODIFYING LAND USE RULES AND PERMITTING

Land use rules and various statutes and regulations present a final hurdle—or enabling factor—in the construction of both large and small renewable energy projects. Zoning codes often do not include language that acknowledges the existence small, mid-size, or large renewable projects, thus creating uncertainty for developers and often requiring case-by-case review. Other codes and ordinances have banned or placed moratoria on renewable projects.

Some state and local governments, in contrast, have updated statutes and ordinances to support development. Some states have centralized the siting and permitting process for mid-sized and large renewable installations, while others have left approval at the local level. Where municipalities retain control over most aspects of renewable project permitting and approval, some have created zones in which renewable energy installations of a certain size are a permitted use (one that is automatically allowed, once building permits or other needed permits are approved) or a conditional use (one that is likely to be allowed somewhere within a zone but requires individual approval to ensure that it will not conflict with other uses). And due to the lack of a common law right to free flowing air and sunlight over property, some states and municipalities have allowed for the creation of easements to light and air or other mechanisms to prevent shading or "wake effects"—the reduction of wind flow. State and local impediments to renewables, as well as efforts to remove these impediments, are discussed in the following excerpts.

Hannah J. Wiseman & Sara C. Bronin, Community-Scale Renewable Energy
14 San Diego J. of Climate & Energy L. 165 (2012–2013).

In existing neighborhoods, the most important change needed to accommodate and encourage community-scale renewables will be the revision of zoning codes to allow for the siting of community-scale energy infrastructure. These changes should include both provisions for rooftop solar and wind and for slightly larger equipment in common areas, such as an array of photovoltaic panels or a small wind turbine in a park. Many zoning codes have not yet recognized this type of mid-size equipment, but several initial efforts provide useful models. Howard County, Nebraska, for example, defines a small wind energy system as one "consisting of a wind turbine, a tower, and associated control or conversion electronics, which has a rated capacity of not more that [sic] 100 kW" and includes height limits, setbacks, and maximum decibel levels, among other requirements, for these systems. Howard County, Nebraska Planning and Zoning Regulation, Wind Generator Facilities Regulation, § 3 (2009), *available at* http://www.howardcounty.ne.gov/pdfs/planning_zoning/zoning_regulations.pdf. This specificity in the zoning code could both directly enable community-scale energy and ensure that it will be installed and operated safety. The county's code defines a small wind system as one that "is intended to primarily reduce on-site consumption of utility power," however, which may constrain the ability of a neighborhood to install the system in a common area and use it to both offset consumption throughout the neighborhood and to sell energy back to a utility when generation exceeds consumption.

The County of San Diego recently implemented broader zoning regulations for unincorporated areas, which support—even if inadvertently—community-scale renewables. Whereas the County previously required all off-site renewable projects to receive a Major Use Permit, it now allows offsite solar photovoltaic systems with project areas of less than ten acres to be reviewed through an administrative permitting process. County of San Diego, Planning & Development Services, Amendment to the Zoning Ordinance Related to Solar Energy Systems-Customer FAQs, http://www.sdcounty.ca.gov/pds/zoning/form fields/PDS-315.pdf (indicating approval on Sept. 15, 2010); County of San Diego Zoning Ordinance § 6952 b. (current through Nov. 2012), http://www.sdcounty.ca.gov/pds/zoning/z6000.pdf (codifying the change). The granting of an administrative permit requires the a finding by the county that the system will be "compatible with adjacent uses" and the County's General Plan, compliance with the state's California Environmental Quality Act (CEQA), and a consent letter from the property owner making clear that the operator of the solar energy system is allowed to use the property. These requirements may be needlessly stringent, however, with respect to community-scale projects that are not onsite yet are not as large as projects that the County anticipates on parcels ten acres and smaller: community-scale projects likely should be exempt from CEQA review requirements, for example, and this again highlights the need for codes to recognize the mid-level category of community-scale renewables.

San Diego County's code is more convenient for community-scale renewables that generate electricity from multiple rooftops, as "[o]nsite solar energy systems are allowed as-of-right as accessory uses to all "Agricultural, Civic, Commercial, Industrial, and Residential use types" and must meet relevant setbacks and height limits of other structures within the zone in which they are located; solar panels may, however, extend five feet "above the highest point of the roof." County of San Diego Zoning Ordinance § 6952 a. Los Angeles also recently revised its code to allow solar structures in all zones to "exceed the roof surface by 3 feet" even if the roof already is at the maximum height for the zone. Los Angeles Municipal Code amendments § 5.3.c (codified at Section 12.21.1), http://clkrep.lacity.org/onlinedocs/2011/11-1786_ord_182110.pdf. For existing buildings with required off-site parking space, the code also allows reduction of the required space in order to "accommodate a structure solely supporting a solar energy system." Los Angeles Municipal Code amendments § 2 (codified at Section 12.21), http://clkrep.lacity.org/onlinedocs/2011/11-1786_ord_182110.pdf.

In addition to ensuring that community-scale renewables can be placed on rooftops or in common areas within a community, states or municipalities must provide clearer standards for connecting these technologies to the grid. In the context of combined heat and power—another form of energy that has promise at the community-scale level—researchers at Columbia University note that interconnection can be time-consuming and costly: the utility's distribution lines may not be able to accommodate the additional electricity generated, and the utility or developer may need to install expensive technological changes to avoid system faults as additional quantities of electricity flow backward. Alexis Saba et al., The Opportunities for and Hurdles to the Development of Combined Heat and Power in New York City 4. In New York, customers can petition the public service commission for a "declaratory ruling . . . regarding the timely updating of substation circuit breakers and network protectors," but this ruling takes times. . . . As Professor Patricia Salkin has noted, however, New York has standardized the interconnection process for small-scale renewables, describing how individuals should apply for interconnection, specifying "technical interconnection standards," and requiring utilities to indicate interconnection status on the web. Patricia Salkin, The Key to Unlocking the Power of Small Scale Renewable Energy: Local Land Use *Regulation*, 27 J. Land Use & Envtl. L. 339, 354–362 (2012) at 345–46 (citing N.Y. State Pub. Serv. Comm'n, New York State Standardized Interconnection Requirements and Application Process for New Distributed Generators 2 MW or Less Connected in Parallel with Utility Distribution Systems (2010), *available at* http://www.dps.ny.gov/Modified_SIR-Dec_2011-Final.pdf. This solves some, but not all, of the interconnection challenges likely to arise for community-scale projects.

Once a zoning code enables community-scale renewables, a variety of zoning mechanisms can prevent neighboring uses from blocking light and air that must flow to installed solar and wind infrastructure. Zoning overlays, for example, which municipalities can apply to distinct neighborhoods as an addition to base zoning codes, can limit the height of new buildings and tree plantings in order to prevent shading of renewable technology. Easements, as described in the following section, are also a common and successful means of ensuring access of installed technology to light and air.

2. Easements

An effective and increasingly popular mechanism for ensuring adequate light and air for solar and wind development is an instrument that gives a property owner the right to an open "block" or "window" of air on neighboring property. Although these mechanisms are often described generally as solar or wind easements, they come in a variety of forms. Some are servitudes, which are positively or negatively worded— preventing the neighboring property owner from building to a certain height or requiring the property owner to maintain certain dimensions of open air. Others are more traditional easements, which give the dominant owner the right to use of the servient owner's airspace and can also come in positive or negative form. Some are purely private, in that legislation allows property owners to include restrictions or conditions in their deed, whereas others can be imposed on neighbors through landowner petitions. *See, e.g.*, IOWA CODE § 564A.3–A.4 (Westlaw 2012) (allowing a "city council or the county board of supervisors" to "designate a solar access regulatory board to receive and act on applications for a solar access easement" and allowing property owners to apply to the border for "an order granting a solar access easement"). Regardless of their form, easements allow communities to build renewable infrastructure even in areas with existing buildings.

As shown by the excerpt above and Congress's unsuccessful attempts to grant FERC authority over the siting of transmission lines in certain congested areas, both centralized and distributed renewables face land use challenges. Large renewable power plants located in rural areas often need tens or hundreds of miles of new transmission lines to transport their product to customers, whereas distributed renewable installations require relatively unimpeded access to light or air. Land use laws and policies will likely remain one of the primary challenges for renewable energy development moving forward, although some laws are changing to enable more of this development. ∎

CHAPTER 12

RENEWABLE POWER CASE STUDIES

The previous chapter introduced you to the types of renewable energy that are established or emerging in the United States and abroad and explored the laws that affect the emergence of these renewable resources. Renewable energy resources will likely continue to grow at a relatively rapid pace within the United States—the U.S. Energy Information Administration (EIA) reports that "[i]n 2012, wind energy became the number one source of new U.S. electricity generation capacity for the first time—representing 43 percent of all new electric additions and accounting for $25 billion in U.S. investment." EIA, Energy Dept. Reports: U.S. Wind Energy Production and Manufacturing Reaches Record Highs, Aug. 6, 2013, http://energy.gov/articles/energy-dept-reports-us-wind-energy-production-and-manufacturing-reaches-record-highs.

Although the continued availability of the production tax credit for wind is unpredictable, EIA projects that by 2040, renewable power will more than double from its current contribution to the electric power portfolio (from 8 to 16%), in large part due to the rapidly declining cost of solar energy technologies; this will depend in part, however, on natural gas prices and U.S. greenhouse gas (GHG) regulation. EIA, Annual

Energy Outlook 2013 at 5, http://www.eia.gov/forecasts/aeo/pdf/0383%2
82013%29.pdf.

Regardless of the exact rate of growth that ensues, renewables will be an increasingly important part of our electricity generation mix, and this will create complex work for attorneys. Financing, siting, permitting, and obtaining permission to interconnect renewable energy resources with the grid requires creativity, broad yet detailed knowledge of a range of legal areas, and flexibility on the part of project developers and attorneys. This chapter explores renewable energy law "on the ground," walking you through the types of issues that you might encounter working as an attorney on a renewable project—or for an organization involved in reviewing and approving, supporting, or opposing a project. It begins by exploring the legal nuances of large, utility-scale projects and continues with a case study involving permitting, interconnecting, and financing smaller distributed generation projects.

A. A UTILITY-SCALE CASE STUDY: WIND-EASE'S OKLAHOMA WIND FARM

1. INTRODUCTION

A developer contemplating a renewable energy project is focused, first and foremost, on whether the project will be economically feasible. This centrally depends on up-front capital costs and fixed and ongoing operations and maintenance costs, the cost of interconnecting with or building new transmission lines, the availability of financing, and viable options for sales of electricity. The sales can occur through a long-term power purchase agreement (PPA), in which a generator commits to sell a certain amount of electricity to a utility for a fixed period, such as twenty years. Alternatively or additionally, a company can sell its electricity generated from a renewable plant on a day-ahead or spot wholesale electricity market where these markets are available—typically in areas where there are regional transmission organizations or independent system operators operating wholesale markets for electricity. The generator can also sometimes sell generation on longer-term capacity markets that ensure—years in advance—that there will be adequate generation capacity to cover demand. The scope and amount of tax benefits, grants, and loans are also factors that are crucial to project feasibility.

Renewable generators often prefer long-term contracts for the sale of their electricity because these contracts provide a guaranteed cash flow over a period of twenty or so years. But purchasing utilities are often hesitant to agree to these contracts if they think that cheaper resources will be available in the near future. Utilities will therefore demand a commitment from the renewable generator that a certain quantity of electricity will be delivered reliably throughout the contract period and a guarantee from the developer that delivery of electricity will begin on a certain date, among other assurances. These developer-purchaser incentives create challenges in project decision-making: developers will be hesitant to embark upon a renewable energy project without a guaranteed purchaser, but the purchaser is hesitant to commit until it is clear that a certain quantity of electricity will in fact be available from the project. Potential lenders, too, will want solid data suggesting that the project is likely to be successful.

Because potential purchasers want information showing that a project will in fact produce electricity, developers that plan to sell electricity through long-term contracts negotiate PPAs while they are completing their financial analyses. Some lenders will require a PPA prior to approving loans for renewable power projects, and many investors also will require a PPA because this reduces the risks associated with a renewable power project. At the same time, the developers are hiring firms to conduct environmental reviews and transmission interconnection studies, which cost millions of dollars. The developers are also simultaneously attempting to obtain leases from multiple landowners, and to obtain zoning and building permits—often from several different municipalities (if the state does not offer a centralized permitting process), agreements from the U.S. Fish and Wildlife Service (FWS) regarding species impacts, Federal Aviation Administration (FAA) approvals, and agreements with other potential users of the surface, such as oil and gas companies and ranchers. In some cases, developers might spend several million dollars on initial studies and permitting for a project, only to discover that all utilities in the area have rejected their proposed PPAs.

The policy environment is important to the execution of PPAs for renewable power projects. Certainty in policies provides predictability to developers as they attempt to simultaneously locate purchasers, demonstrate the financial and interconnection-based feasibility of a project, and obtain the necessary approvals for the project. "Avoided cost" rates (for projects that are PURPA QFs) or feed-in-tariffs can also provide a guaranteed revenue stream for projects. Further, state renewable portfolio standards make it more likely that some form of purchase commitment will be available to generators, as utilities are required to generate or purchase a certain percentage of their electricity from renewable resources. The federal production tax credit for wind projects also provides a guaranteed amount of money per kilowatt-hour of wind energy produced if plants are operational by a certain deadline, although there is always a threat that Congress will not renew the tax credit. (As mentioned in Chapter 11, the tax credit expired at the end of 2013.)

This section discusses the many aspects of utility-scale renewable energy development and the laws and policies that affect the financing, siting, interconnection, and construction and operation of utility-scale plants. It does so using a hypothetical project in which a hypothetical wind energy company, WindEase LLC, proposes to build a large wind farm in a rural part of Oklahoma and to sell the electricity under PPAs negotiated with several large utilities in neighboring states. This section also explores how various aspects of the wind project would be different if the project were located in other states.

2. PROJECT FINANCE: DETERMINING ECONOMIC FEASIBILITY, LOCATING LENDERS AND PURCHASERS

The hypothetical wind energy company WindEase, LLC ("WindEase"), a closely held company, is headquartered in Texas and is contemplating building a large wind farm in Oklahoma. The first concern of the company is whether it will have enough money to construct and later operate the wind farm, and whether the farm will ultimately make money. Several factors are central to this analysis. First, with respect to whether the company will have the funds necessary to carry the project forward, the company may need a source of external financing, often from investors or lenders. The following reading discusses various options for renewable energy financing that WindEase might consider—including the option of finding an investor to become a partner in the project and to benefit from the tax incentives that WindEase will receive.

Paul Scharfenberger Developers and Investors Doing "Flips" for Government Tax Incentives: A Discussion of Partnership Flips (Nov. 1, 2010)

Renewable Energy Project Finance Blog, Nat'l Renewable Energy Lab., https:// financere.nrel.gov/finance/content/developers-and-investors-doing- %E2%80%9Cflips%E2%80%9D-government-tax-incentives-discussion-partnership-flip.

A "partnership flip" may sound like a Cirque du Soleil act (it isn't, I checked), but, in actuality, it is a financing arrangement between a renewable energy developer and investor. Don't be fooled by the seemingly less entertaining subject matter, though; the partnership flip is a creative and popular finance mechanism for wind (and rumored for solar) that requires careful coordination and planning. While the mechanics of the arrangement are complex, the objective is rather straightforward; to maximize the value of government tax-based incentives in order to improve the economics of renewable energy projects.

Renewable energy projects are eligible for accelerated depreciation deductions and federal tax credits. However, one must have sufficient taxable income to fully maximize the federal incentives. Why? Well, without getting too far into the weeds, accelerated depreciation deductions decrease a company's taxable income, thereby reducing its tax liability (i.e. what it owes the IRS). And, naturally, tax credits result in an even further reduction of a company's tax liability. Thus, if a company isn't producing a large enough taxable income, then it will not be in a position to make full use of the incentives (both the deductions and the credits)—for some renewable projects, this can amount to large dollar amounts. A company's ability to digest these incentives is sometimes referred to as "tax appetite."

This leads us to the various financing options available to developers. First, a developer can choose to go-it-alone by financing and building a renewable energy project and utilizing the federal incentives itself. However, such a strategy may be economically inefficient for a developer without tax appetite. Instead, it may be wiser for the developer to enter into a mutually beneficial finance arrangement with a tax investor capable of maximizing the federal incentives (think: Wall St. bank). One such arrangement is known as a partnership flip.

The title partnership flip actually describes the structure of the arrangement quite well. Essentially, a developer and a tax investor form a partnership or a Limited Liability Company (LLC) and become partners in the ownership of a project. Typically, the tax investor makes a disproportionately larger investment in the project initially, in exchange for a larger portion of the income that is generated from the project via power sales and the aforementioned federal incentives. Once an agreed upon rate of return for the tax investor is reached (after the tax credits and deductions are fully taken), the allocation of the project's income stream "flips," and the developer then earns the majority of the proceeds from the project. However, it's important to note that partnership flip structures vary significantly, especially in terms of the pre- and post-flip allocation that is negotiated at the outset of the arrangement. . . .

Simple enough, right? The arrangement makes perfect sense: the project's developer receives much needed equity financing; the investor maximizes the federal incentives (improving project economics), and receives a return on its investment (if everything goes as planned).

However, the mechanics of a partnership flip are far from simple. The developer and investor must determine an investment/return allocation strategy that not only "optimizes the after-tax economics" of the project . . . , but also adheres to IRS guidelines. Further, "partnership flip structures raise a number of tax issues that investors and developers must understand and negotiate at the outset of a business relationship. For example, allocations of depreciation deductions take on an added significance and complexity where the developer contributes appreciated equipment" (see Brown Rudnick). Ultimately, a significant amount of analysis and coordination is required in order to ensure that the arrangement achieves its economic objectives. Having said that, a partnership flip has been a very effective financing arrangement when conceived of and executed thoughtfully.

The partnership flip is just one of many mechanisms for financing renewable energy projects. Each mechanism has its unique advantages and disadvantages that should be weighed and compared before making a financing decision. ∎

Another potential means of financing renewable projects like WindEase is the use of the renewable energy credit or certificate (REC). The renewable energy developer could contract with an investor to transfer ownership of all credits formed by the generation of renewable power to the investor, allowing the investor to sell these RECs. RECs can be a valuable asset in states that, under their RPS, require utilities to: 1) generate a certain percentage of renewable power themselves, 2) show that they have purchased that percentage of renewable power, or 3) purchase and then retire RECs, which demonstrate that the required percentage of renewable power has been generated and used elsewhere and not double counted (e.g., not used by two different utilities to satisfy their renewable energy requirements).

Chapter 11 discussed the cases that make ownership of RECs a matter of state law. The inquiry does not end there. State laws vary on who may own RECs, and where there is no state law, an important question remains: if a renewable energy developer is a QF selling to a utility under PURPA, does the QF (the renewable developer) get to keep the RECs and thus transfer them to an investor, or does the utility purchasing power from the QF also get the RECs associated with that power? This issue has arisen in Idaho, where Grand View PV Solar Two (Grand View), LLC, a QF, wanted to sell electricity to Idaho Power Company (IPC), a utility. Grand View filed a complaint with the Idaho PUC arguing that it was entitled, on summary judgment, to enter into a "20 year, long-term, fixed-rate" PURPA PPA with IPC, and that within this PPA "Idaho Power would explicitly disclaim any ownership of the environmental attributes, or renewable energy certificates ('RECs'), associated with the purchase of that energy." Idaho Power responded that neither PURPA nor Idaho state law "requires it to disclaim any possible legal claim that it may have to the environmental attributes associated with the" power purchase. Grand View Solar Two, LLC v. Idaho Pwr. Co., Case No. IPC–E–11–15, Idaho Power Co.'s Answer to Mot. for Summ. J. (Dec. 13, 2011), http://www.puc.idaho.gov/fileroom/ cases/elec/IPC/IPCE1115/company/20111214ANSWER%20TO%20 MOTION%20FOR%20SUMMARY%20JUDGMENT.PDF   (showing arguments of both parties).

The Idaho PUC denied Grand View's motion for summary judgment. It cited the 2003 FERC order discussed in Chapter 11 in the *American Ref-Fuel Company* case, which stated that RECs " 'exist outside of the confines of PURPA. PURPA thus does not address the ownership of RECs. . . . States, in creating RECs, have the power to determine who owns the RECs in the initial instance, and how they may be sold or traded; it is not an issue controlled by PURPA.' " Grand View PV Solar Two, LLC v. Idaho Pwr. Co., Order No. 32,580, at 5 (2012) (*citing* American Ref-Fuel Co., 105 F.E.R.C. ¶ 61,004 (Oct. 1, 2003). The PUC also noted that both parties in the case agreed that PURPA does not govern RECs, that avoided cost rates under PURPA do not include payment for RECs, and that there is no Idaho law governing RECs. With these points of agreement in mind, the PUC went on to consider Grand View's argument that other state decisions sometimes confer ownership of RECs on QFs. The PUC noted that several other states had found, to the contrary, that "RECs belonged to the purchaser of the energy," and that the conflicting laws in other states should not control in Idaho.

Even if renewable energy developers are able to maintain ownership of the RECs and promise the RECs to investors within a financing agreement, there remains the question of whether RECs can be collateralized for purposes of financing—are they "security interests" under the Uniform Commercial Code, for example? Some attorneys have suggested that RECs are, as "collateral" under UCC § 9–102 is "the property subject to a security interest," and a "general intangible" is a type of collateral. The UCC excludes from the category of "general intangible "accounts, chattel paper, commercial tort claims, deposit accounts, documents, goods, instruments, investment property, letter-of-credit rights, letters of credit, money, and oil, gas, or minerals," but RECs do not appear to fall within any of these excluded categories. *See* Joanne Vos, Financing Solar Renewable Energy Projects, N.J. Builders' Ass'n, http:// www.njba.org/pages/?09-Financing-Solar-Renewable-Energy-Projects.

As part of the process of obtaining financing—and to ensure that its project will be a sound venture for the company itself—WindEase must also determine whether the project will make money. This requires complicated calculations, but for the purposes of this example, the basic questions are the following: how much electricity will the wind farm produce (based on complex wind forecasting conducted by the operator); how much electricity can WindEase sell from the project and at what price; what tax credits and other governmental support will produce additional income (or reduce expenses) for the project; what is the expected life of the project; what state requirements might make RECs generated from the project valuable, and to what other states could the RECs be sold; and what are the project costs, including capital, operations and maintenance, and eventual decommissioning? As the National Renewable Energy Laboratory (NREL) notes, many of the project costs are predictable, but some vary:

> The lifetime cost of wind energy is comprised of a number of components including the investment cost, operation and maintenance costs, financing costs, and annual energy production. Accurate representation of these cost streams is critical in estimating a wind plant's cost of energy. Some of these cost streams will vary over the life of a given project. From the outset of project development, investors in wind energy have relatively certain knowledge of the plant's lifetime cost of wind energy. This is because a wind energy project's installed costs and mean wind speed are known early on, and wind generation generally has low variable operation and maintenance costs, zero fuel cost, and no carbon emissions cost.

The following explanation and chart from NREL describes some of the costs typical of a wind energy project, which reflects the best available information on the cost of wind energy in 2010, along with a summary of historical trends and future projections:

> One way to express the cost of wind energy is to calculate the levelized cost of energy (LCOE). The LCOE is a metric that has been used by the U.S. Department of Energy (DOE) for many years to evaluate the life-cycle costs of generation for energy projects and the total system impact of technology design changes. In simple terms, LCOE is defined as the ratio:

$$\text{LCOE} \quad = \quad \frac{\text{present value of total costs (\$)}}{\substack{\text{present value of all} \\ \text{energy produced} \\ \text{over project lifetime} \\ \text{(megawatt-hours)}}}$$

> The LCOE equation used by NREL for this report is a standard method used to compare energy technologies. . . . There are four basic inputs to any LCOE equation: installed capital cost, annual operating expenses, annual energy production, and fixed charge rate (an annualized presentation of the cost of financing a wind project)

> . . . . Annual operating expenses include land-lease costs (LLC), O & M wages and materials, and levelized replacement costs (LRC). Operation and maintenance costs are generally expressed in two categories: 1) *Fixed* O & M which includes known operations costs (e.g., insurance) and typically does not change depending on how much electricity is generated, and 2) *Variable* O & M, which includes planned and unplanned maintenance and other costs that may vary throughout the project. Variable O & M costs can vary depending how much

electricity is generated by the project. Property taxes or payments in lieu of taxes may be included in O & M.

. . . . Annual Energy Production (AEP) for this analysis was computed by the NREL Wind Turbine Design Cost and Scaling Model's AEP spreadsheet. The AEP spreadsheet is designed to compute annual energy capture and other related factors such as capacity factor for a wind turbine specified by certain generic input parameters. . . . The input parameters for calculating AEP can be grouped into three general categories: turbine parameters, wind resource characteristics, and losses.

S. Tegan et al., 2010 Cost of Wind Energy Review iv–v, NREL (2012), http://www.nrel.gov/docs/fy12osti/52920.pdf.

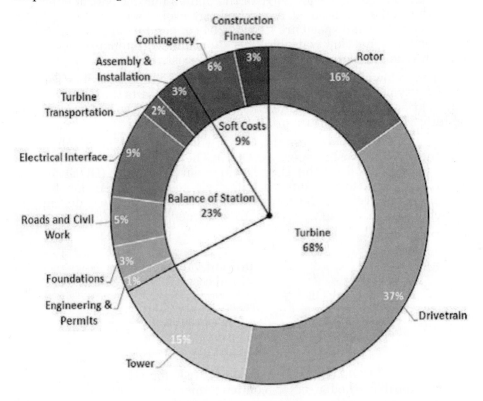

Figure 12–1
Installed capital costs for the land-based wind reference turbine
Source: S. Tegan et al., 2010 Cost of Wind Energy Review
NREL (2012), http://www.nrel.gov/docs/fy12osti/52920.pdf.

Once it has identified the likely cost of the project over its lifetime, WindEase must also understand how much money the project will generate to know whether the project will be profitable. As introduced above, this depends on tax incentives as well as how much wind energy will be produced and sold at a particular price. The amount of wind energy that will be produced over time is somewhat predictable based on wind forecasting and knowledge of the turbine. The price at which electricity will be sold is very predictable if WindEase can find a willing buyer. Early in the project, WindEase likely will approach a number of large utilities and attempt to negotiate a PPA with them. As introduced above, the PPA would include a commitment by WindEase to sell a certain quantity of electricity to the utility over a long period of time, such as twenty years, at specified times. This commitment to sell power would be either "firm," in which case the generator would commit to providing a set quantity of electricity, or interruptible, in which case WindEase could avoid supplying electricity when it was unavailable. A contract for firm power would require the WindEase to show that it had back-up contracts to purchase additional power (typically from a natural gas generator) when there was inadequate wind to provide the power demanded by the buyer.

The PPA would also guarantee that deliveries of electricity would begin on a certain date, and the PPA would contain a set price for the electricity—perhaps providing for slight price increases annually. WindEase likely would approach utilities not only in Oklahoma but also utilities in neighboring states, provided that it has access to an interstate transmission line. Because Oklahoma is within the territory of the Southwest Power Pool (SPP)—a regional transmission organization— and because SPP has planned for certain regional transmission lines and states have approved the lines, selling to an out-of-state utility likely will not be particularly difficult. WindEase also could choose to forego a PPA and sell electricity in the auctions offered by the SPP, in which generators may place bids for providing generation a day or even minutes before it is provided.

The ability of WindEase to negotiate a PPA, and the price ultimately set within the PPA, will depend on a variety of factors. First, if WindEase is a PURPA QF in an area where a utility has market power, it can force the utility to execute a contract at avoided cost—which in many states is competitive for wind. Where the PURPA purchase obligation applies, the utility is obligated to purchase the power if needed at avoided cost; this serves as a floor in that the utility cannot offer anything less than this or impose additional obligations on the seller. But it also serves as a ceiling for any PPA executed pursuant to PURPA. In areas of the country with RTOs, however, waivers from this purchase obligation are available under PURPA 210(m).

If WindEase operates in an area where SPP has a waiver under PURPA 210(m), it may not be able to force the hand of the purchasing utility, and whether a contract is executed will depend more on state policies. Because Oklahoma lacks a mandatory RPS, state policies do not provide much incentive for utilities to purchase wind power. Assuming the project is not a PURPA QF or is not subject to a PURPA purchase obligation, the ability of WindEase to negotiate a PPA will depend on what kind of energy it is offering to sell and on what terms and conditions. A wind project developer can command a premium rate from a buyer if it offers "firm" power, but, as introduced above, it would have to purchase power from alternative sources in order to provide this firm commitment.

Also note that if WindEase wanted to sell wind power in non-restructured states, it might run into difficulties—even if it was only selling at wholesale. Many of these states require all generators of electricity to obtain a certificate of public convenience and necessity from the state PUC, and sometimes these states limit certificates to utilities that provide in-state power. For example, in Florida in the late 1990s, the Public Service Commission attempted to approve several independent power producers' proposed plants (natural gas-fired plants—not renewable plants), finding that they were "needed," but the Florida Supreme Court overturned the approvals. The Supreme Court found that the PSC could only grant need determinations to generator applicants that would commit all of their electrical power to a utility that served retail customers within Florida. Tampa Electric Co. v. Garcia, 767 So. 2d 428 (Fla. 2000).

3. INTERCONNECTION WITH TRANSMISSION LINES

As WindEase is working toward obtaining financing for its Wind Energy project and locating purchases, it must also determine the exact location of its wind farm. Three primary factors influence location choice: the strength of the wind at particular locations, the availability of open land surface beneath a relatively strong wind resource, and the availability of transmission lines. Wind developers prefer to build as close to existing transmission lines as possible because building long transmission lines is an expensive and time-consuming process; in some states, independent developers like our hypothetical company WindEase do not have eminent domain authority to site transmission lines, which makes building a line nearly impossible if landowners will not negotiate for easements. (In some states, only "public utilities" have eminent domain powers, and in some cases independent generators do not count as public utilities.) For a thorough discussion of the eminent domain challenges for independent renewable energy developers, as well as for companies attempting to build interstate transmission lines and use state eminent domain authority, see Alexandra Klass, Takings and Transmission, 91 N.C. L. Rev. 1079 (2013).

Most renewable energy developers have to build at least a short line in order to interconnect with a nearby transmission line, even if they locate close to an existing line. The greatest challenge, however, is the interconnection approval process. Any generator proposing to connect to a transmission line must request interconnection approval from the entity that operates the line. As part of this interconnection process, the applicant and the entity that operates the line determine the network upgrades that will be necessary for the transmission grid if the generator interconnects, and the generator must pay for these often expensive upgrades. In places like Oklahoma, which are within an RTO area, the RTO operates the lines and approves or rejects interconnection requests. In Texas, the Electric Reliability Council of Texas receives the request, and in areas without RTOs, the transmission line owner and operator receives the request. Most transmission line operators receive interconnection requests from multiple generators in a given year, so a company like WindEase ends up in what is called an "interconnection queue." Generators in the queue are put in line based on the time at which they made the request (earlier requesters are closer to the head of the line), and the queue can often delay development for years at a time. FERC has tried to reform interconnection procedures and has allowed some RTOs to use creative mechanisms for allowing generators who are very committed to their projects to jump ahead in the line. For example, some RTOs have used "open seasons" in which during a certain period in the year, generators who want to interconnect as soon as possible can indicate their commitment by paying up front for an interconnection study and proving that it will connect to the line if approved.

Interconnection studies are the key prerequisites for connecting WindEase's proposed farm to SPP's transmission lines. These studies involve complex and expensive technical investigations and sets of tests that show that if the generation is added to the transmission line, there will be enough "room" for the electricity and it will not interfere with line operations. There are at least two types of interconnection studies required: one showing that the generation will not negatively affect the transmission system and its reliability, and another identifying the interconnection facilities that must be built and network upgrades required to ensure that the generator will be properly interconnected and will not interfere with the transmission system.

If WindEase manages to finally get to the head of the queue and to successfully complete the (very expensive) interconnection studies, the transmission line operator (in this case SPP—the RTO) then determines whether to grant the interconnection request through an "interconnection agreement." For large wind generators like Wind Ease, transmission line operators like SPP must follow FERC-specific standards in deciding whether or not to grant the request. FERC Orders 661 and 661A (order on rehearing) set out these standards, which were intended to make approvals or rejections of wind interconnection more uniform, and to ensure that wind resources, which are intermittent (the wind does not blow constantly or at the same speed), do not overly interfere with the grid. These standard interconnection procedures for large wind farms require, among other things, that WindEase can show that it has supervisory control and data acquisition (SCADA) capabilities, meaning that WindEase has technologies at its wind farm that allow it to "transmit data and receive instructions from the Transmission Provider" (SPP). Interconnection For Wind Energy, Order on Reh'g and Clarification, 113 F.E.R.C. ¶ 61,254 (2005). This is important in the event that certain turbine output needs to be temporarily reduced in order to maintain steady voltages in the line, for example. See Chapter 13 for further discussion of SCADA and its role in the Smart Grid.

Within the interconnection agreement between WindEase and SPP, the specific SCADA required would depend on "what SCADA information is essential for the proposed wind plant, taking into account the size of the plant and its characteristics, location, and importance in maintaining generation resource adequacy and transmission system reliability in its area." FERC Large Generator Interconnection Agreement (LGIA), Appendix G, https://www.ferc.gov/industries/electric/indus-act/gi/wind. asp. Within this agreement, WindEase is referred to as the interconnection customer, and SPP is referred to as the transmission provider. The transmission provider operates under a "tariff" approved by FERC. This tariff sets out all of the rules that the transmission provider must follow in operating the transmission lines, the rate that it may charge for use of the lines, and the procedures that it must follow for reviewing interconnection requests. Excerpts of the type of interconnection agreement that WindEase and SPP would enter into are included below.

Southwest Power Pool, Inc., Open Access Transmission Tariff Sixth Revised Volume No. 1 Attachment V Generator Interconnection Procedures-Attachment V Appendix 6 Generator Interconnection

http://sppoasis.spp.org/documents/swpp/transmission/studies/
GIA_Attachment_V_Appendix% 206_2_15_2013.pdf.

GENERATOR INTERCONNECTION AGREEMENT
THIS GENERATOR INTERCONNECTION AGREEMENT

("Agreement") is made and entered into this ____ day of _____ 20___, by and among _____, a _____ organized and existing under the laws of the State/Commonwealth of _____ ("Interconnection Customer" with a Generating Facility), Southwest Power Pool, Inc., a corporation organized and existing under the laws of the State of Arkansas ("Transmission Provider") and _____, a _____ organized and existing under the laws of the State/Commonwealth of _____ ("Transmission Owner"). Interconnection Customer, Transmission Provider and Transmission Owner each may be referred to as a "Party" or collectively as the "Parties."

Recitals

WHEREAS, Transmission Provider functionally controls the operation of the Transmission System; and,

WHEREAS, Interconnection Customer intends to own, lease and/or control and operate the Generating Facility identified as a Generating Facility in Appendix C to this Agreement; and,

WHEREAS, Transmission Owner owns facilities to which the Generating Facility is to be interconnected and may be constructing facilities to allow the interconnection; and,

WHEREAS, Interconnection Customer, Transmission Provider and Transmission Owner have agreed to enter into this Agreement for the purpose of interconnecting the Generating Facility with the Transmission System;

NOW, THEREFORE, in consideration of and subject to the mutual covenants contained herein, it is agreed:

When used in this Generator Interconnection Agreement, terms with initial capitalization that are not defined in Article 1 shall have the meanings specified in the Article in which they are used or the Open Access Transmission Tariff (Tariff).

* * *

Definitive Interconnection System Impact Study shall mean an engineering study that evaluates the impact of the proposed interconnection on the safety and reliability of Transmission System and, if applicable, an Affected System. The study shall identify and detail the system impacts that would result if the Generating Facility were interconnected without project modifications or system modifications, focusing on the Adverse System Impacts identified in a Preliminary Interconnection System Impact Study or that may be caused by the withdrawal or addition of an Interconnection Request, or to study potential impacts, including but not limited to those identified in the Scoping Meeting as described in the Generator Interconnection Procedures.

Definitive Interconnection System Impact Study Agreement shall mean the form of agreement contained in Appendix 3A of the Generator Interconnection Procedures for conducting the Definitive Interconnection System Impact Study.

Definitive Interconnection System Impact Study Queue shall mean a Transmission Provider separately maintained queue for valid Interconnection Requests for a Definitive Interconnection System Impact Study.

* * *

Generator Interconnection Agreement (GIA) shall mean the form of interconnection agreement applicable to an Interconnection Request pertaining to a Generating Facility that is included in the Transmission Provider's Tariff.

Generator Interconnection Procedures (GIP) shall mean the interconnection procedures applicable to an Interconnection Request pertaining to a Generating Facility that are included in the Transmission Provider's Tariff.

* * *

Interconnection Facilities Study shall mean a study conducted by the Transmission Provider or a third party consultant for the Interconnection Customer to determine a list of facilities (including Transmission Owner's Interconnection Facilities and Network Upgrades as identified in the Definitive Interconnection System Impact Study), the cost of those facilities, and the time required to interconnect the Generating Facility with the Transmission System. The scope of the study is defined in Section 8 of the Generator Interconnection Procedures.

Interconnection Facilities Study Agreement shall mean the form of agreement contained in Appendix 4 of the Generator Interconnection Procedures for conducting the Interconnection Facilities Study.

Interconnection Feasibility Study shall mean a preliminary evaluation of the system impact and cost of interconnecting the Generating Facility to the Transmission System, the scope of which is described in Section 6 of the Generator Interconnection Procedures.

Interconnection Feasibility Study Agreement shall mean the form of agreement contained in Appendix 2 of the Generator Interconnection Procedures for conducting the Interconnection Feasibility Study. ■

* * *

Interconnection agreements for wind farms have led to growing disputes before FERC. In a case involving several wind energy developers and MISO, MISO (the transmission service provider) and the owner of the transmission line entered into generator interconnection agreements (GIAs) with wind developers that needed to use the transmission lines. After entering into these GIAs, MISO informed the wind energy operators of a modeling error in the system impact study (SIS), which predicts how the connection of the wind farms to the transmission line will impact the entire transmission system and what network upgrades will be necessary to address these impacts. In the SIS, the generating capacity of two generators ahead of the wind developers in the interconnection queue had been mistakenly understated. These generators that were ahead of the wind developers would place more stress on the transmission system, and when the wind developers later connected to the same lines, more upgrades might be required to avoid impacts that could cause grid reliability problems. After having entered into the GIAs with the wind developers, MISO, on the basis of this new information about a previous omission in the SIS model, determined that the wind developers would have to pay an additional $10.26 million in network upgrades, and an additional $1.485 million would be required to pay for a "Common Use Upgrade." MISO tendered "Amended and Restated Generator Interconnection Agreements" to the wind developers—agreements that included these additional costs.

The wind developers objected to the additional costs and the delay in interconnection caused by the amended GIAs. They argued that the customers using the transmission line owner's lines should bear the costs of the network upgrades—in other words, that everyone using the transmission lines should pay for the cost of network upgrades through the "base rates" charged for transmission service. They also argued that they should not be responsible for network upgrade costs not included in the original SIS. Further, the wind developers argued that they needed to be able to connect to the lines more quickly and avoid an additional 2 or 2.5-year interconnection delay. FERC conditionally found that the wind developers could be required to pay for the additional network upgrade costs, although it determined that certain upgrade costs should not have been included in the GIAs. It also found that connecting the wind developers at the earlier time that they requested interconnection and allowing the wind developers to send the quantity of power through the lines that they requested would violate North American Electric Reliability Corporation (NERC) reliability standards. Further, the *pro forma* GIA that MISO uses anticipates that certain construction delays might be necessary in the event of reliability concerns. The wind energy developers and American Wind Energy Association filed requests for rehearing, which FERC denied in April 2013. Midwest Independent Transmission System Operator, Inc., Order on Rehearing and Compliance Finding, 143 F.E.R.C. ¶ 61,050 (Apr. 18, 2013).

The wind developers filed an appeal in June 2013, and the case is currently in abeyance. As more intermittent sources like WindEase request grid interconnections, disputes like this will likely continue.

4. OBTAINING PROPERTY RIGHTS AND LAND USE/OPERATING APPROVALS

As WindEase is working on financing its project and completing interconnection studies, it is also busy compiling the necessary property rights for its wind farms. These issues are no less important than executing a PPA and interconnection agreement, as without the ability to use land the project may never produce a single electron of power. These challenges were highlighted by the Cape Wind offshore project, in which Cape Wind required approvals from and/or consultations with the Department of the Interior (DOI), Advisory Council on Historic Preservation, Army Corps of Engineers (Corps), National Marine Fisheries Service, and state highway departments, environmental agencies, and fish and wildlife services, among other approvals. Onshore projects sometimes require just as many consultations and permits, however, as described in this section. They also pose more difficult property issues than do offshore projects: although it is not a simple process to obtain a lease from the Bureau of Ocean Energy Management—the DOI department that approves the use of the ocean floor beyond 3 nautical miles from the coast (or farther out in Texas and the Florida Gulf)—it might be easier than obtaining property rights from numerous onshore landowners. See Section 6 below for more discussion of offshore wind energy projects.

Wind farms are large—often several hundreds to thousands of acres—and therefore typically cross private property lines and city, county, and even state lines. For example, NextEra Energy Resources' Stateline Wind Energy Center straddles the Oregon-Washington border. NextEra Energy Res., Stateline Wind Energy Ctr., http://www.nextera energyresources.com/content/where/portfolio/pdf/stateline.pdf. The difficulty of compiling property rights will in part depend on whether eminent domain is available. As mentioned above in the context of interconnection, many states do not define independent generators like WindEase as public utilities, and in some states, only public utilities may use eminent domain authority within the energy sector. Regardless of whether a company like WindEase has eminent domain authority, it must negotiate with landowners regarding the leasing or sale of property rights, as eminent domain is a last-resort strategy.

To negotiate property rights, WindEase, after locating the site with the best wind resources, available land, and nearby transmission lines, will have to knock on landowners' doors, and on the doors of city, tribal or even federal government officials, to persuade them to convey an easement to their land for the wind farm and enter into various agreements regarding surface use. (Wind farms are sometimes built on a patchwork of private and public lands.) If part of the farm falls on Bureau of Land Management (BLM) lands, WindEase will have to go through a competitive BLM auction for a "right of way" (ROW), which is a lease to use federal lands, and will also have to submit a development plan.

In states like Texas, some wind companies have attempted to purchase or lease only the air rights above property, just as oil and gas developers lease mineral rights. These wind companies then sign a memorandum with the surface owner indicating that use of the surface for the wind towers and turbines to capture the flowing air is acceptable.

These might be risky instruments, as the memoranda might not be binding on future surface owners, and surface owners might object to the wind company's use of the surface. Professor Ernest Smith and co-author Becky Diffen believe, however, that just as Texas courts recognize the right of mineral lessees to use the surface as is reasonably necessary to capture minerals, the courts will likely at least recognize the validity of a severed air right. Ernest E. Smith & Becky H. Diffen, Winds of Change: The Creation of Wind Law, 5 Tex. J. Oil, Gas, and Energy L. 165 (2009-2010). It is not clear, though, just how much implied right to use of the surface would accompany a severed air right. In Oklahoma and several other states, WindEase would be limited in the extent to which it could rely on severed air rights. 60 Okla. Stat. § 820.1 provides: "No interest in any resource located on a tract of land and solely associated with the production or potential production of wind or solar-generated energy on the tract of land may be severed from the surface estate except that such rights may be leased for a definite term pursuant to the provisions of this act." Under the Act, WindEase could enter into an agreement with each landowner, which would have to comply with the following requirements in the statute:

> A wind or solar energy agreement shall run with the land benefitted and burdened and shall terminate upon the conditions stated in the wind or solar agreement.

> E.   An instrument entered into subsequent to July 1, 2010, that creates a land right or an option to secure a land right in real property or the vertical space above real property for a solar energy system, for a wind or solar energy conversion system, or for wind measurement equipment, shall be created in writing, and the instrument, or related memorandum of easement, or an abstract, shall be filed, duly recorded, and indexed in the office of the county clerk in the county in which the real property subject to the instrument is located. The instrument, but not the related memorandum of easement or abstract, shall include but not be limited to:

> 1.   The names of the parties;

> 2.   A legal description of the real property involved;

> 3.   The nature of the interest created;

> 4.   The consideration paid for the transfer;

> 5.   A description of the improvements the developer intends to make on the real property, including, but not limited to, roads, transmission lines, substations, wind turbines and meteorological towers;

> 6.   A description of any decommissioning security as defined in subsection B of this section, or other requirements related to decommissioning; and

> 7.   The terms or conditions, if any, under which the interest may be revised or terminated.

Id. For discussion of other states that limit or prohibit severance of air rights, see Troy A. Rule, Wind Rights Under Property Law: Answers Still Blowing in the Wind, 26 Prob. & Prop. 56, 59 (Nov./Dec. 2012). In all states, it is advisable for companies like WindEase to acquire easements to the surface, as this will provide the clearest surface use. The drafting, conveyancing, and recording requirements for easements that you learned about in your Property Law class, apply here—WindEase must ensure that it properly records the deed. WindEase also must work with title insurers to obtain title insurance, which sometimes requires creativity. Some title insurers are rewriting policies to address the patchwork of properties associated with wind farms.

In addition to acquiring property rights, WindEase would have to consider potential competing uses of the surface. Oil and gas operators might have leased mineral rights beneath the property that they are currently developing or plan to develop, for example. Construction and operation of the roads, towers, and underground electricity collection wires for the wind farm could interfere with oil and gas development, just as oil and gas rigs, truck traffic, and surface waste pits could interfere with the wind farm. WindEase would need to contact these oil and gas operators and attempt to enter surface use agreements with them, in which the parties agreed to who would use the land for what purpose, and when.

If the parties could not agree—with WindEase and the oil and gas operators each claiming a right to the surface—it is not always clear who would win. In Oklahoma, Osage Nation sued a wind developer alleging that proposed wind development would interfere with oil drilling. Osage Nation v. Wind Capital Grp., No. 11–CV–643–GKF–PJC, 2011 WL 6371384 (N.D. Okla. Dec. 20, 2011), *appeal dismissed*, No. 12–5007 (10th Cir. Feb. 23, 2012). The federal district court dismissed the case and found that it did not appear that the wind farm would "unreasonably interfere with plaintiff's right to make reasonable use of the surface estate." *Id*. at 6. The Oklahoma Legislature has partially clarified renewable-oil and gas disputes, requiring renewable developers to provide at least 30 days' written notice to an oil and gas operator and oil and gas lessees before beginning construction. 52 Okla. Stat. § 803. It also requires that "[n]otwithstanding any provision in a wind or solar energy agreement. . . . the lessee of a wind or solar energy agreement or the wind energy developer shall not unreasonably interfere with the mineral owner's right to make reasonable use of the surface estate, including the right of ingress and egress therefor, for the purpose of exploring, severing, capturing and producing the minerals." *Id*.

In addition to obtaining property rights and resolving conflicts with other surface users, WindEase must get a variety of land use and safety-related approvals before constructing its wind farm. There are three primary governance models for utility-scale siting approvals:

1) States fully or partially preempt local siting authority for certain types of renewable energy projects above a minimum size (defined by megawatts of capacity or the value of the project), although they often allow municipalities to adopt additional standards for renewable energy facilities that are not more stringent than the state standards, and they allow municipalities to participate in the state proceedings. Examples include Florida, Minnesota, Oregon, Wisconsin, and Wyoming. *See* Fla. Stat. Ann. § 403.511; Minn. Stat. Ann. § 216F.07; Or. Dep't of Energy, Guidelines for Applicants for Energy Facility

Site Certificates 1 (July 2008), http://www.oregon.gov/
ENERGY/SITING/docs/2008Guidelines.pdf?ga=t;   W.S.A.
§ 66.041; W.S.1977 § 35–12–106.

2) Other states allow two options: the renewable energy developer
may pursue local siting approval or seek a state-issued permit,
and local preemption if necessary. Washington is one such
state. Energy Facility Site Evaluation Council, Siting/Review
Process, Access Washington, http://www.efsec.wa.gov/cert.
shtml#Certification).

3) Still other states leave most siting approval to the local
government. These states include, among others, Kansas,
Oklahoma, and Texas.

In states where siting approvals are left to the local government,
some municipalities have been proactive about designating the types of
zones in which utility-scale wind development is a permitted use (a use
that is automatically allowed within the zone, provided proper building
permits and other needed permissions are obtained) or a conditional or
special use (a use that is allowed on a case-by-case basis after showing
that the use will be compatible with other uses in the zone). Others have
banned certain renewable energy development. In Kansas, the Supreme
Court allowed a town to ban wind development on aesthetic and other
grounds. Zimmerman v. Bd. of Cnty. Comm'rs, 218 P.3d 400 (Kan. 2009).
And in Oklahoma, WindEase might also encounter some hurdles. The
City of Piedmont, for example, banned all large wind energy systems in
December 2012. City of Piedmont, Oklahoma, Ordinance No. 581, http://
www.piedmont-ok.gov/ordinances/581.pdf.

Under all three of the above models, regardless of the siting approval
required (state, local, or a combination of both), some states—typically
those that have not restructured their retail electric industries or have
only partially restructured—require a generator to obtain a certificate of
need indicating that the infrastructure is "needed" in terms of meeting
electricity demand and is a relatively efficient way of meeting that
demand. Some states also require the wind developer to post a
decommissioning bond with the state in the event that the developer
abandons the renewable facility without properly removing equipment
and making the site safe; this might be required prior to project
construction, or after the plant has operated for some time. In Oklahoma,
after operating its plant for 15 years, WindEase would have to "file with
the Corporation Commission evidence of financial security to cover the
anticipated costs of decommissioning the wind energy facility. . . .
Evidence of financial security may be in the form of a surety bond,
collateral bond, parent guaranty, or letter of credit." 17 Okl. Stat. Ann.
§ 160.15. Some municipalities also require decommissioning bonds, as
shown by Md. Local Govt. Code § 13–706 for Garrett County:

Before an occupancy permit is issued for an industrial wind
energy conversion system in Garrett County, the Garrett
County Department of Planning and Land Development shall:

(i) at the applicant's expense, retain an independent and
certified professional engineer to prepare a net cost estimate for
decommissioning and restoration of the pad site . . . ; and

(ii) require the applicant to post a bond equal to 100% of the [decommissioning] cost estimate . . . and adjusted . . . to ensure that cost increases during the following 5-year interval will not decrease the value of the bond.

In addition to zoning approvals, siting permits, certificates of need, and/or decommissioning bonds, renewable energy developers often must work with state and local governments to comply with various safety and health related standards. State or local codes often set maximum allowed decibel levels at a certain distance from the site and require renewable energy developers to comply with various building codes—sometimes requiring an engineer's certificate showing that the facility is soundly built.

5.   OBTAINING ENVIRONMENTAL AND OTHER PERMITS

Environmental laws add more work to the many hours of labor and millions of dollars WindEase already has invested in interconnection studies, obtaining property rights, and applying for land use and siting approvals. If any of the property on which WindEase proposes to build is federal land, WindEase will likely have to provide an environmental report to the BLM, with which the BLM will prepare an environmental impact statement under the National Environmental Policy Act (NEPA). Although Oklahoma will not require a similar environmental review, some states like California do, thus requiring the developer to conduct expensive environmental studies for both the state and federal government. (California has entered into a memorandum of understanding with the BLM to try to avoid requiring duplicative efforts by the developer.)

Regardless of where WindEase locates its farm, a number of other federal laws apply. For wind towers and turbines 200 feet and higher, it must get permission from FAA before building the towers, and FAA will require the developer to use certain lights to alert air traffic to the location of the top of each tower. If any wetlands will be impacted, a dredge and fill permit from the Corps will be required under Section 404 of the Clean Water Act, and if WindEase will have to construct any transmission or distribution lines or towers in a stream or other surface water, a Section 10 Rivers and Harbors Act permit also will be required from the Corps. WindEase will have to consult with FWS about impacts on endangered bats and birds, for which it could be liable under the Endangered Species Act and, for birds, the Migratory Bird Treaty Act or the Bald and Golden Eagle Protection Act. Developers like WindEase sometimes conduct wildlife surveys long before deciding on a particular site, and if they know that an area has a large number of bat caves or is directly within a bird migration path, they tend to avoid it.

To the extent that developers cannot avoid certain wildlife impacts, they typically enter into agreements with FWS to stop certain turbines from spinning on certain days or during times of the day when birds are known to be in the area. FWS's Land-Based Wind Energy Guidelines provide extensive directives to developers for avoiding illegal "takes" of endangered and threatened species and for monitoring impacts, including, among many other steps, conducting extensive pre-and post-construction surveys and counting wildlife carcasses near turbines. Although car accidents and household cats kill far more birds each year than wind turbines do, *see* U.S. v. Brigham Oil and Gas, L.P., 840 F. Supp. 2d 1202 (D.N.D. 2012), wildlife impacts are one of the most important considerations for wind energy developers.

A final permit that WindEase will have to obtain before constructing its wind farm is a stormwater permit under the Clean Water Act, which requires the developer to implement certain practices to reduce erosion during site construction.

6. RENEWABLE ENERGY DEVELOPMENT ON PUBLIC LANDS: ONSHORE AND OFFSHORE

Depending on the location of the best wind resources and proximity to transmission lines, WindEase might consider developing a wind farm solely on federal lands. This would allow WindEase to avoid the need to consolidate property rights from multiple owners and to skirt certain state requirements. It might also expedite the permitting process. Under the Obama Administration, DOI has encouraged the development of renewable energy on federal lands, providing for streamlined approval and better coordination with FERC and other agencies. DOI Order No. 3285A1, issued in 2010 formed the Task Force on Energy and Climate to better coordinate all of the agencies involved in environmental review of renewable projects on public lands (onshore and offshore), to prioritize certain review and permitting, and to locate the best areas for renewable energy development. DOI, Renewable Energy Development by the Department of the Interior, Feb. 22, 2010, http://elips.doi.gov/ELIPS/0/ doc/151/Page1.aspx. On November 27, 2012, DOI issued a final rule intended to simplify the Bureau of Indian Affairs approval process for renewable projects on tribal lands and to more quickly review proposed projects. Offshore, in 2010 DOI implemented a "Smart from the Start" program for the Atlantic. This program was designed to identify offshore areas that were best for wind development and pinpoint potential environmental issues in advance, before projects moved forward. It was also intended to expedite the leasing and permitting process. Further, BLM has completed several Programmatic Environmental Impact Statements for wind and solar, which identify potential development areas and environmental impacts, thus making environmental review under NEPA potentially faster when projects are proposed.

Although the movement at the federal level has been toward streamlined permitting, leasing, and review processes, substantial obstacles remain to renewable energy projects on federal lands. Onshore, developers still must obtain approvals in the form of a ROW from a federal agency to install testing equipment like meteorological towers and to construct renewable projects. And NEPA requires numerous, costly studies on the part of renewable energy developers because when a developer proposes a project on federal lands, the approval of the lease and other permits by BLM or other federal agencies is a federal action that potentially has significant environmental impacts. This triggers the NEPA review process, in which agencies must consider impacts and alternatives to the project that might mitigate impacts. Multiple agencies are typically involved in the review process for renewable power projects on federal lands: the Fish and Wildlife Service and/or National Marine Fisheries Service (depending on whether the project is on or offshore) must consider the wildlife and habitat impacts; the Environmental

Protection Agency must review potential water quality issues, if any; the Army Corps of Engineers must consider the impacts of water crossings, and so on. More agencies are likely to be drawn into the NEPA review process for the transmission lines that must be built to carry renewable electricity from federal lands to population centers, and transmission lines will typically trigger a cumulative effects analysis under NEPA. Cumulative effects analyses are often conducted when several, similar projects are proposed and are connected, or when one project will lead to another (the construction of the transmission line might have to be considered in the approval of a wind farm, for example, or vice versa, as the construction of the wind farm will necessarily require the construction of lines to transport the electricity).

One potential benefit to renewable energy developers facing a cumulative effects analysis under NEPA is that renewable energy projects have beneficial cumulative effects by reducing carbon emissions—a factor that could help to offset the negative land use impacts. But the extent to which these should factor into a NEPA analysis is not fully clear. So far, federal agencies have been hesitant to include the *negative* impacts of carbon emissions in NEPA analyses, particularly where they lack jurisdiction over certain aspects of a project that will result in carbon emissions. The Army Corps of Engineers, for example, refused to consider the carbon emissions in Asia that will result from coal exported from several proposed terminals on the West Coast, as the agency lacks jurisdiction over Asian country's use of the coal. On the other hand, the State Department expressly considered the carbon impacts of approving the Keystone XL Pipeline, which would carry carbon-intensive oil sands oil from Canada, in its Environmental Impact Statement. And the construction of renewable energy projects often directly results in carbon emissions reductions—there is a more direct connection between federal approval of the project and reduced carbon emissions than there is in the coal export case, for example.

The permitting and development process is very different for an offshore energy developer than it would be for WindEase. Within three nautical miles of the coastline (or farther out in certain portions of Texas and Florida) state jurisdiction applies. But for development beyond three nautical miles on the outer continental shelf, the developer must obtain a lease from the Bureau of Ocean Energy Management, and the agency prior to issuing the lease must prepare an environmental impact statement under NEPA, which must cover meterological testing equipment, the offshore towers and turbines, and the transmission cable that will run along the ocean floor. The developer also must obtain a Section 10 Rivers and Harbors Act permit from the Army Corps of Engineers and a Clean Water Act dredge and fill permit, as well as National Marine Fisheries Service and FWS approvals with respect to species impacts. Further, the developer must conduct archaeological surveys and, if the wind farm might affect a historic or cultural area, approvals from the National Park Service, which administers the National Historic Preservation Act.

Even for projects in federal waters, at the state level the developer will have to get approvals for using state highways to carry heavy equipment to the coast, approvals under State Coastal Management Plans prepared pursuant to the Coastal Zone Management Act, state certifications under Section 401 of the Clean Water Act showing that federal approvals of the project will not negatively impact state water resources, and state permits for the transmission line that will run within three nautical miles of the coastline to shore. For an extensive survey of the lengthy list of environmental and other permitting requirements for offshore projects, see Jeffrey Thaler, Fiddling as the World Floods and Burns: How Climate Change Urgently Requires a Paradigm Shift in the Permitting of Renewable Energy Projects, 42 Envtl. L.J. 1101 (2012).

B. A DISTRIBUTED GENERATION CASE STUDY: FIRST PRESBYTERIAN CHURCH'S PROPOSED SOLAR PV SYSTEM

1. INTRODUCTION

This Case Study introduces you to key concepts and substantive topics (including important drafting issues) involved in the development and financing of a typical distributed generation project, in this case, a Power Purchase Agreement (PPA) proposed for the (hypothetical) First Presbyterian Church (FPC) in the (again, hypothetical) town of Calvertville, Maryland, a suburb of Baltimore. FPC intends to contract with a solar services firm, the (hypothetical) corporation Sun Systems Power (SSP), to obtain a solar PV system for its roof. SSP's website claims that SSP "manages everything you need to power your business with solar energy from custom design to project funding, installation and ongoing maintenance."

FPC has decided it is interested in meeting some of its electricity needs from renewable sources located at the church. SSP proposes to design, install, operate, and maintain a system with solar panel arrays on the church roof to produce 9 kilowatts (kW) of electricity (roughly the size of a large house's solar installation). Using data for Maryland, students at a local university estimated that under prevailing weather conditions, the SSP system would supply approximately 30 percent of the 40,000 kWh of electricity that the church uses each year. The remaining 70% would continue to be supplied by FPC's electric utility, Baltimore Gas and Electric (BGE).

We begin with readings on several key concepts:

1) What is a PPA for small-scale projects, and what type of solar services firms offer them?
2) What financial incentives are available (including "net metering" and Solar Renewable Energy Credits—SRECs—available under Maryland's RPS)?

We then present the remaining case study facts, followed by five selected provisions of a PPA for you to redraft, using this document for assistance.

Please note carefully: You are acting as counsel for SSP. While the contract should be written on SSP's behalf, it should not be one-sided. This is a simulation of a real-world exercise. In the normal course of affairs, there would have been a series of negotiations between FPC and SSP culminating in an agreement that you would memorialize in this

PPA. However, you may assume these negotiations have already taken place, and what's left for you is to draft the relevant provisions of the PPA. This means, among other considerations, that your agreement should be a balanced contract that you believe would satisfy both parties. Your goal is to craft an optimal PPA that embodies a desirable outcome for both sides without being overly favorable to SSP. It should be fair to both sides, and not an agreement that FPC would simply reject. Make whatever assumptions you feel are necessary.

When you redraft the substantive sections of the PPA, you also need to pay attention to principles of good contract drafting. With clarity in drafting, you maximize the likelihood that the PPA will be followed, or, in the worst-case scenario, that a court will interpret it as you intended. Think it all through—there is no "mere boilerplate." One goal to keep in mind is that a person of reasonable intelligence who knows nothing about the transaction should be able to understand the deal after one reading of the PPA.

You should consider the following factors, among others:

1) Did you use plain English and a simple style? (avoid needless words and lawyer-ese, and sloppy drafting fixes and tricks such as "Notwithstanding anything to the contrary in this agreement, . . .")

2) Did you use the active (not passive) voice?

3) Did you use "shall" (obligation) and "may" (right/privilege) clauses appropriately and consistently?

4) Have you created provisions that establish an appropriate framework for performance and enforcement by the parties?

5) Did you use practical, precise language? Have you chosen the right words, for the right resulting interpretations? You need to precisely define terms, or gamble later that a court would apply meaning to vague and ambiguous terms.

2. SOLAR PPAS AND SOLAR SERVICES FIRMS

A Solar PPA is a financial arrangement in which a third-party developer owns, operates, and maintains a photovoltaic solar (PV) system, and a host customer agrees to site the system on its property (typically on its roof).

U.S. Environmental Protection Agency Solar
Power Purchase Agreements

http://www.epa.gov/greenpower/buygp/solarpower.htm.

A Solar Power Purchase Agreement (SPPA) is a financial arrangement in which a third-party developer owns, operates, and maintains the photovoltaic (PV) system, and a host customer agrees to site the system on its roof or elsewhere on its property and purchases the system's electric output from the solar services provider for a predetermined period. This financial arrangement allows the host customer to receive stable, and sometimes lower cost electricity, while the solar services provider or another party acquires valuable financial benefits such as tax credits and income generated from the sale of electricity to the host customer.

With this business model, the host customer buys the services produced by the PV system rather than the PV system itself. This framework is referred to as the "solar services" model, and the developers who offer SPPAs are known as solar services providers. SPPA arrangements enable the host customer to avoid many of the traditional barriers to adoption for organizations looking to install solar systems: high up-front capital costs; system performance risk; and complex design and permitting processes. In addition, SPPA arrangements can be cash flow positive for the host customer from the day the system is commissioned.

How do SPPAs Work?

[The figure] below illustrates the roles of all participants in an SPPA.

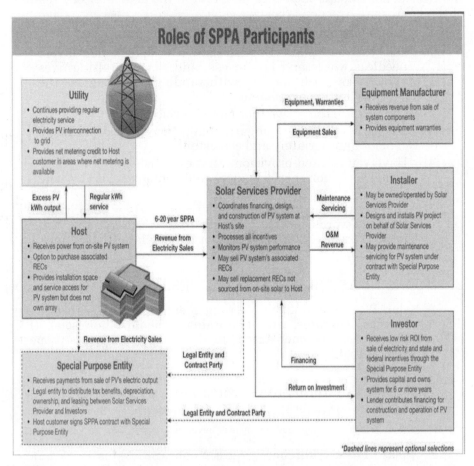

A host customer agrees to have solar panels installed on its property, typically its roof, and signs a long-term contract with the solar services provider to purchase the generated power. The host property can be either owned or leased (note that for leased properties, solar financing works best for customers that have a long-term lease). The purchase price of the generated electricity is typically at or slightly below the retail electric rate the host customer would pay its utility service provider. SPPA rates can be fixed, but they often contain an annual price escalator in the range of one to five percent to account for system efficiency decreases as the system ages and inflation-related costs increase for system operation, monitoring, maintenance, and anticipated increases in the price of grid-delivered electricity. An SPPA is a performance-based arrangement in which the host customer pays only for what the system produces. The term length of most SPPAs can range from six years (i.e., the time by which available tax benefits are fully realized) to as long as 25 years.

The solar services provider functions as the project coordinator, arranging the financing, design, permitting, and construction of the system. The solar services provider purchases the solar panels for the project from a PV manufacturer, who provides warranties for system equipment.

The installer will design the system, specify the appropriate system components, and may perform the follow-up maintenance over the life of the PV system. To install the system, the solar services provider might use an in-house team of installers or have a contractual relationship with an independent installer. Once the SPPA contract is signed, a typical installation can usually be completed in three to six months.

An investor provides equity financing and receives the federal and state tax benefits for which the system is eligible. Under certain circumstances, the investor and the solar services provider may together form a special purpose entity for the project to function as the legal entity that receives and distributes to the investor payments from the sale of the systems kWh output and tax benefits.

The utility serving the host customer provides an interconnection from the PV system to the grid, and continues its electric service with the host customer to cover the periods during which the system is producing less than the site's electric demand. Certain states have net metering requirements in place that provide a method of crediting customers who produce electricity on-site for generation in excess of their own electricity consumption. In most states, the utility will credit excess electricity produced from the PV system, although the compensation varies significantly depending on state policies. ∎

NOTES AND COMMENTS

1. The two most important terms of any PPA are the length (term) of the agreement (in years) and the price the host pays to the system owner (in cents per kWh). To the customer, these terms effectively determine whether installing a solar system will pay for itself in the long run. To the system owner, the steady, guaranteed revenue stream from a PPA customer is the foundation of its profitability. The PPA obligates the host to receive electricity at a stable and fixed cost (possibly, as the reading notes, with an escalation clause) for the PPA's entire term in return for the solar services firm's expertise. A developer typically will *not* enter into an agreement that does not obligate the host to buy the electricity and services for the full term.

2.   In states or other jurisdictions with feed-in-tariffs, the feed-in-tariff may in effect dictate the terms of a PPA, or utilities may offer a standard agreement, known as a standard offer.

Maryland Public Service Comm'n & Maryland Energy Admin. A Guidebook on Net Metering in Maryland (2013)

http://www.universityparksolar.com/Meter/MD%20NM%20Guide%20DRAFT%206-7-2013.pdf.

Net metering is a billing mechanism that credits a customer-generator for the electricity exported onto the electricity grid. When a customer generates more electricity than he or she needs, the customer receives net metering bill credits. When the customer needs more electricity than they generate, the customer can use those credits to lower his or her electricity bills. This simple billing arrangement can make a significant impact on the economic viability of a renewable energy system.

Net metering became an option for customers who also wanted to generate onsite electricity with the passage of the Federal Energy Policy Act of 2005 by mandating that "[e]ach electric utility shall make available upon request net metering service to any electric consumer that the electric utility serves," as well as install a bi-directional flow of electricity to measure net energy. Today, net metering policies have been widely adopted, and net metering is currently supporting customer-sited generation of renewable energy in 43 states, the District of Columbia, and 4 U.S. territories.

For electric customers that have installed onsite energy generation technologies, net metering allows the customer's electric meter to "spin backwards" ensuring that they receive credit for any electricity that they put back on the electricity grid rather than using themselves. Older analog meters could literally be seen spinning backwards when onsite energy was making more electricity than was needed at the house or business. The meter would spin forward as it measured the kilowatt-hours (kWh) a customer consumed; then spin backward when a solar customer generated more electricity than the customer was currently consuming, and the excess electricity is diverted back onto the grid. Modern digital meters accurately record electricity flow in both directions. Even more modern "smart meters" employ advanced metering infrastructure (AMI) architecture, enabling two-way communications back to the utility company, as well as variable tariffs, outage monitoring, prepayment and remote disconnect.

Why is Net Metering Important to Renewable Energy Systems?

Consumers with net-metered generation systems benefit financially by being able to offset conventional electricity with clean, onsite energy at full retail electric rates. This seemingly simple benefit is often cited as one of the key financial underpinnings of successful distributed, renewable energy generation systems. In some months, a customer's renewable energy system may produce more electricity over the course of the billing period than the customer uses onsite. This is typically called "net excess generation" (NEG), which is carried over as a kWh credit at the customer's full retail rate for 12 months.

What are the Specifics of Net Metering in Maryland?

Eligibility

Specific attributes related to eligibility and other parameters of net metering in Maryland are detailed below:

Eligible Customers

Commercial, Industrial, Residential, Nonprofit, Schools, Local Government, State Government, Federal Government, Agricultural, Institutional.

Eligible Generation Technologies

Photovoltaics (PV), Wind, Biomass, Fuel Cells, CHP/Cogeneration, Anaerobic Digestion, Small Hydroelectric, Fuel Cells using Renewable Fuels.

System Capacity Limit

2 MW for all technologies except 30 kW for micro-CHP, and limited to that needed to meet 200% of baseline customer electricity usage. And, the eligible customer-generator's proposed electric generating system may not exceed 200 percent of the eligible customer-generator's baseline annual usage.

System Ownership

The law permits outright ownership by the customer-generators as well as third-party ownership structures (e.g., leases and power purchase agreements (PPAs), which are discussed later in this Guide.

Electric Utility Role

Net metering rules apply to all electric utilities—investor-owned utilities (IOUs), electric cooperatives and municipal utilities. Electric utilities must make net metering available to eligible customers until the aggregate capacity of all net-metered systems statewide reaches 1,500 megawatts MW.

Tariff Oversight

State lawmakers and utility regulators generally set the rules for which types of renewable energy systems get net metering credit and how they are credited through tariffs. In Maryland, the Public Service Commission (PSC) oversees electric utilities and is responsible for administering the net metering program.

What Other Policies are related to Renewable Energy?

For each MWh of solar energy generated, a Solar Renewable Energy Credit (SREC) is also generated. In Maryland, net metering customers own and have title to all SRECs associated with electricity generation by their net-metered systems. SRECs have a useful life of three years, e.g. the year of generation and the following two years, during which the solar generator can sell the SREC to qualified electricity suppliers. SRECs provide a valuable income stream to owners of solar energy facilities, small and large, and can contribute to off-setting investment costs. Electricity suppliers must purchase and retire SRECs in order to meet their compliance obligations under the law, or pay a Solar Alternative Compliance Payment (SACP) for any shortfalls in SREC purchases. An

SREC could be defined as a tradable attribute associated with one MW of electricity generation that can be sold; in early 2013, each SREC had a value ranging from $120–135/SREC, which translates, roughly, to 12–13.5¢/kWh.

Home and business owners can sell SRECs into other states that allow PV systems to be cross-certified between states. For most Maryland generators, Pennsylvania is a viable market in mid-2013. However, home and business owners cannot sell SRECs from an out-of-state system into Maryland. Maryland recently changed the RPS to close the state off to out-of-state generators.

Renewable Energy Incentive Programs

There are a variety of Federal, State, Local, and Utility renewable energy incentives available, including the 30% Investment Tax Credit for home and business owners.

Third-Party Ownership

Maryland law permits outright ownership by the customer-generators as well as third-party ownership structures, including leases and power purchase agreements (PPAs). Third-party ownership is a financing arrangement that allows a net-metering customer to host a renewable system that is owned by a separate investor which can take advantage of tax credits which non-tax-paying entities—such as governments, schools and nonprofits—cannot. They can also be attractive to entities that either lack initial investment capital to purchase a renewable system, or the desire to own and maintain a system. Under a third-party financing arrangement, an investor monetizes available incentives, such as tax credits, rebates and depreciation deductions. The investor then sells electricity produced by a system to the host customer at lower rates than the host customer may otherwise receive. When the third-party ownership arrangement involves a PPA, the host customer agrees to purchase all the energy produced onsite. ∎

NOTES AND COMMENTS

1.   Net metering may include a sale from the customer to the incumbent utility, but net metering is not limited to sales. In some states, net metering may constitute a "credit" on a customer's bill, with no formal sale of power; in such an arrangement the electric power produced by a solar panel owned by the customer is owned by the incumbent utility once the solar panel is interconnected to the distribution grid. If there is no sale, there may be no need for a PPA; the transaction is simply a type of billing arrangement between the customer and the utility, although often this will be an arrangement that lasts for several years to provide some certainty to customers and to encourage them to invest in some renewable technologies.

2.   Unlike Maryland, some states do not allow third-party ownership of solar panels unless the owner is regulated as a public utility. In these states, most residential and smaller-scale customers need to rely entirely on customer financing of solar panels. Which approach is preferable and why?

3.   Note that there are two distinct revenue streams available in addition to tax benefits and payment for electricity generated by the project: net metering credits and revenue from the sale of SRECs. As with large-scale

projects, a good PPA in the DG context will allocate these between the host and developer, as noted below.

4.   Especially in states with traditional cost-of-service regulation, DG poses a potential threat to the very business model that many utilities operate under. There has been much discussion of a utility "death spiral," in which incumbent utilities would lose so much business to DG and other forms of competition that they would eventually become unprofitable. *See* Edison Elec. Inst., Disruptive Challenges: Financial Implications and Strategic Responses to a Changing Retail Electric Business (2013), http://www.eei.org/ourissues/finance/documents/disruptivechallenges.pdf. Why would a utility want to enter into a PPA to purchase any DG from customers? What legal and other bargaining strategies do customers have to force the hand of an incumbent utility and to require the utility to enter into negotiations regarding PPAs?

3.   BARRIERS TO THIRD-PARTY PPAS

Although many states allow net metering from distributed energy resources, states that have not restructured their retail electricity markets face a dilemma. Traditionally regulated states treat public utilities as natural monopolies that serve as the sole electricity providers within a given territory. State regulators view competition within this territory as creating wasteful, overlapping, unneeded infrastructure— the large utility that benefits from economies of scale is the most efficient electricity provider. Allowing competition will not only be wasteful, in the view of regulators, but will also take needed revenues away from the centralized utility, forcing it to spread costs among a smaller number of customers. In some of these traditionally regulated states, legislators and regulators view third-party providers of distributed electricity as competitors that will create inefficient overlap and unhealthy competition, and these states therefore treat third-party providers as "public utilities" that must obtain a certificate of need from the state and an approved rate before they may operate (if they may operate at all). This essentially blocks any efforts to build small-scale third-party generation. The following case shows how a traditionally regulated state—in this case, Florida—defines third-party providers as public utilities.

PW Ventures v. Nichols

533 So. 2d 281 (Fla. 1988).

PW Ventures, Inc. (PW Ventures) appeals from an adverse ruling of the Florida Public Service Commission (PSC). We have jurisdiction. Art. V, § 3(b)(2), Fla. Const.

PW Ventures[1][1] signed a letter of intent with Pratt and Whitney (Pratt) to provide electric and thermal power at Pratt's industrial complex in Palm Beach County. PW Ventures proposes to construct, own, and operate a cogeneration project on land leased from Pratt and to sell

---

[1]   PW Ventures is a Florida corporation, which was originally owned by FPL Energy Services, Inc. (a wholly owned subsidiary of FPL Group, Inc.) and Impell Corporation (a wholly owned subsidiary of Combustion Engineering, Inc.). After the entry of the PSC order, FPL Energy Services, Inc. transferred its 50% interest to Combustion Engineering, Inc.

its output to Pratt under a long-term take or pay contract.[3][2] Before proceeding with construction of the facility that would provide the power, PW Ventures sought a declaratory statement from the PSC that it would not be a public utility subject to PSC regulation. After a hearing, the PSC ruled that PW Ventures proposed transaction with Pratt fell within its regulatory jurisdiction.

At issue here is whether the sale of electricity to a single customer makes the provider a public utility. The decision hinges on the phrase "to the public," as it is used in section 366.02(1), Florida Statutes (1985). In pertinent part that subsection provides:

> "Public utility" means every person, corporation, partnership, association, or other legal entity and their lessees, trustees, or receivers supplying electricity or gas (natural, manufactured, or similar gaseous substance) to or for the public within this state. . . .

Distilled to their essence, the parties' views are as follows: PW Ventures says the phrase "to the public" means to the general public and was not meant to apply to a bargained-for transaction between two businesses. The PSC says the phrase means "to any member of the public." While the issue is not without doubt, we are inclined to the position of the PSC.

At the outset, we note the well established principle that the contemporaneous construction of a statute by the agency charged with its enforcement and interpretation is entitled to great weight. The courts will not depart from such a construction unless it is clearly unauthorized or erroneous.

Also, it is significant that the statute itself would permit the type of transaction proposed by PW Ventures and Pratt to be unregulated if it were for natural gas services. Section 366.02(1) provides the following exemption: "[T]he term 'public utility' as used herein does not include . . . any natural gas pipeline transmission company making only sales of natural gas at wholesale and to direct industrial consumers. . . ." The legislature did not provide a similar exemption for electricity. The express mention of one thing implies the exclusion of another.

This rationale is further illustrated in the statutory regulation of water and sewer utilities. As explained in the PSC order:

> In parallel with Section 366.02(1), Section 367.021, Florida Statutes (1985), defines a water or sewer utility as every person "providing, or who proposes to provide, water or sewer service to the public for compensation." Section 367.022(6), Florida Statutes, expressly exempts from this definition "systems with the capacity or proposed capacity to serve 100 or fewer persons". There is not a parallel numerical exemption to the statutory definition of a public utility supplying electricity. Yet the statutory interpretation advocated by PW Ventures would require a line to be drawn somewhere between sales to some members of the public, as a presumably nonjurisdictional

---

[2]   The power would be used by Pratt and several affiliated corporate entities and by the Federal Aircraft Credit Union, which is also located on the property.

activity, and sales to the public generally and indiscriminately, an admittedly jurisdictional activity.

Moreover, the PSC's interpretation is consistent with the legislative scheme of chapter 366. The regulation of the production and sale of electricity necessarily contemplates the granting of monopolies in the public interest. Section 366.04(3), Florida Statutes (1985), directs the PSC to exercise its powers to avoid "uneconomic duplication of generation, transmission, and distribution facilities." If the proposed sale of electricity by PW Ventures is outside of PSC jurisdiction, the duplication of facilities could occur. What PW Ventures proposes is to go into an area served by a utility and take one of its major customers. Under PW Ventures' interpretation, other ventures could enter into similar contracts with other high use industrial complexes on a one-to-one basis and drastically change the regulatory scheme in this state. The effect of this practice would be that revenue that otherwise would have gone to the regulated utilities which serve the affected areas would be diverted to unregulated producers. This revenue would have to be made up by the remaining customers of the regulated utilities since the fixed costs of the regulated systems would not have been reduced.

The fact that the PSC would have no jurisdiction over the proposed generating facility if Pratt exercised its option under the letter of intent to buy the facility and elected to furnish its own power is irrelevant. The expertise and investment needed to build a power plant, coupled with economies of scale, would deter many individuals from producing power for themselves rather than simply purchasing it. The legislature determined that the protection of the public interest required only limiting competition in the sale of electric service, not a prohibition against self-generation.

We approve the decision of the Public Service Commission. ∎

NOTES AND COMMENTS

1.   Do you agree with the Florida Supreme Court that the fact that the Florida Legislature exempted small utilities from the definition of "public utility" in the natural gas and water and sewer contexts but not in the electricity context indicates an intent to *not* exempt small utilities from the definition of "public utility" in the electricity context?

2.   How would a business in Florida find a third-party provider without requiring the provider to go through a full ratemaking case just to construct a small generating unit? If the business entered into a partnership with the third-party provider might this be a closer case?

3.   The Iowa Supreme Court considered *PW Ventures* and similar cases in a recent decision and reached the opposite result of *PW Ventures*, as shown in the following case.

SZ Enterprises, LLC v. Iowa Utilities Bd.

850 N.W.2d 441 (Iowa 2014).

In this case, we consider whether SZ Enterprises, LLC, d/b/a Eagle Point Solar (Eagle Point) may enter into a long term financing agreement related to the construction of a solar energy system on the property of the city of Dubuque under which the city would purchase from Eagle Point, on a per kilowatt hour (kWh) basis, all of the electricity generated by the system. Prior to proceeding with the project, Eagle Point sought a declaratory ruling from the Iowa Utilities Board (the IUB) that under the proposed agreement (1) Eagle Point would not be a "public utility" under Iowa Code section 476.1 (2011), and (2) Eagle Point would not be an "electric utility" under Iowa Code section 476.22. If Eagle Point were a public utility or an electric utility under these Code provisions, it would be prohibited from serving customers, such as the city, who were located within the exclusive service territory of another electric utility, Interstate Power and Light Company (Interstate Power). *See* Iowa Code § 476.25(3).

The IUB concluded that under the proposed business arrangement, Eagle Point would be a public utility and thus was prohibited from selling the electricity to the city under the proposed arrangement. Because of its ruling on the public utilities question, the IUB found it unnecessary to address the question of whether a party who was not a public utility could nevertheless be an electric utility under the statute.

The district court reversed. For the reasons expressed below, we affirm the decision of the district court.

I.   Factual Background and Proceedings.

A.   Introduction.

Eagle Point is in the business of providing design, installation, maintenance, monitoring, operational, and financing assistance services in connection with photovoltaic solar electric (PV) generation systems. The city of Dubuque desires to develop renewable energy for the use of the city.

Eagle Point proposed to enter into a business relationship known as a third-party power purchase agreement (PPA) with the city that would provide the city with renewable energy. Under the PPA, Eagle Point would own, install, operate, and maintain an on-site PV generation system at a city-owned building to supply a portion of the building's electric needs. The city would purchase the full electric output of Eagle Point's solar power generation facility on a per kWh basis, which escalated at a rate of three percent annually. The payments by the city would not only provide consideration for the electricity provided by the project, but would also finance the cost of acquiring the generation system, monetize offsetting renewable energy incentives related to the system, and cover Eagle Point's costs of operating and maintaining the system. Eagle Point would also own any renewable energy credits associated with the generation system but would credit to the city one third of any revenues received from the sale of those credits. At the conclusion of the agreement, Eagle Point would transfer all ownership rights of the PV generation system to the city.

The PV generation system constructed by Eagle Point would be on the customer side of the electric meter provided by the city's electric utility, Interstate Power. This means that electricity generated by the system would not pass through Interstate Power's electric meter. Due to size limitations, Eagle Point's PV generation system would not be able to generate enough electricity to power the entire building. The city would remain connected to the electric grid and continue to purchase electric power from Interstate Power to meet its remaining needs at the premises.

B.   Proceedings Before the IUB.

The IUB held that under the proposed arrangement, Eagle Point would be acting as a public utility under Iowa Code section 476.1. The IUB recognized that in Iowa State Commerce Commission v. Northern Natural Gas Co. [Northern Natural Gas I], this court held that in order to be a public utility under Iowa Code section 476. 1, the record must show "sales to sufficient of the public to clothe the operation with a public interest and not willingness to sell to each and every one of the public without discrimination." The IUB also noted that in Northern Natural Gas I the court referred to an eight-factor test in Natural Gas Service Co. v. Serv-Yu Cooperative, Inc., 219 P.2d 324, 325–26 (Ariz. 1950), to help determine whether the business was "clothed with a public interest." Northern Natural Gas I, 161 N.W.2d at 114–16.

The IUB, however, distinguished Northern Natural Gas I by noting that the exclusive service territorial statutes applicable to electric utilities do not apply to gas utilities. The IUB noted that one of the purposes of exclusive territorial arrangements was to ensure that utilities do not duplicate each other's facilities or make existing facilities unnecessary. The IUB also observed that the exception to regulation for self-generation in Iowa Code section 476.1 applies to certain electric utilities but not to gas utilities. Because Eagle Point in the proposed PPA would be selling electricity to the city, the IUB concluded that the requirement of self-generation was not present. Further, the IUB believed the limited language excluding certain self-generation units from the definition of public utility implies that other arrangements that do not fall within the scope of the exception are necessarily included in the term public utility.

C.   Proceedings Before the District Court.

On the merits, the district court concluded that Eagle Point would not be operating either as a public utility or as an electric utility. In reaching its conclusion, the district court found that the IUB's analysis of the exception contained in Iowa Code section 476.1 was flawed. According to the district court, the exception did not simply relate to the definition of public utility but provided that all provisions of "this chapter" shall not apply to qualifying self-generation. Thus, the exception was not targeted to the definition of public utility but instead to all aspects of Iowa Code chapter 476. Further, the district court found that the exception at least suggests some willingness on the part of the legislature to allow exceptions for smaller providers.

The district court next considered whether the fact that electric utilities were subject to exclusive territorial provisions provided a basis for distinguishing the Northern Natural Gas I case. The district court concluded that there was no basis for this distinction and held that the exclusive territory provisions applied only with respect to electric utilities. The district court reasoned that before the question of whether Eagle Point was an electric utility could be considered, a threshold determination needed to be made on the question of whether Eagle Point was a public utility. . . .

III.   Background of Third-Party PPAs and Public Utility Regulation.

     A.   Introduction to the Third-Party PPA.

     A fundamental legal question . . . is whether PPAs may coexist with traditional public utilities within the existing state regulatory environment. A threshold question is often whether the developer-owner in a third-party PPA is a public utility or electric supplier subject to state regulation. This definitional question often turns on whether the developer-owner in a third-party PPA is regarded as furnishing or supplying electricity "to the public."

     The consequences of this threshold determination are critical to the viability of third-party PPAs. In states where public utilities have exclusive service areas, a finding that a PPA is a public utility generally means that a PPA violates the exclusive territory provisions of state law and is thus unlawful. In states where public utilities do not have exclusive service areas, the consequence is that PPAs may be subject to substantial regulation as a public utility, including requirements to submit tariffs and to provide service to all who desire it.

     B.   State Caselaw on What Constitutes a "Public Utility" Providing Services "to the Public."

     The notion that private entities may be so affected by the public interests that public duties arise from their activities has ancient common law origins. . . . The common law tradition has influenced some state courts when construing statutes defining public utilities or service to the public. One line of authority relies on the notion that in order to be a public utility serving the public generally, the entity must directly or indirectly hold itself out as providing service to all comers. Under this theory, a business that provides sporadic services of a commodity that might ordinarily be associated with a public utility might not be drawn within the ambit of regulation.

     On the other hand, a different line of authority has developed a more flexible notion of what amounts to a public utility. These cases use a functional approach and concentrate on the nature of the underlying service and whether there is a sufficient public need for regulation.

     D.   State Precedents on Whether Third-Party PPAs Are Subject to Regulation as "Public Utilities."

[The Court noted *PW Ventures* and then addressed conflicting cases.]

2.   Decisions holding PPAs are not public utilities subject to state regulation.

     Aside from PW Ventures, the parties have not cited, and we have not found, appellate caselaw on the question of whether the developer-owner under a PPA is a public utility within the scope of regulatory statutes. There are, however, a number of regulatory decisions that address the issue. Several of them—Arizona, Nevada, New Mexico, and Oregon— have come to the conclusion that the developer-owners of PPAs are not public utilities under applicable statutes or constitutional provisions.

     We begin with a review of the decision of the Arizona Corporation Commission in SolarCity. In SolarCity, a developer sought a declaratory ruling that its method of providing solar facilities to the Scottsdale United School District did not amount to a "public service corporation" under article 15, section 2 of the Arizona Constitution. Under the stated facts, SolarCity proposed to enter into what it called a solar services agreement (SSA) whereby it would pay the upfront expenses associated with construction of the solar facility. *Id.* at 5–6. The customer would pay SolarCity "for the design, installation, and maintenance of the system based on the amount of electricity produced." *Id.* at 6. Unlike ordinary PPAs, the SSA explicitly provided that the customer was the "owner" of all electricity produced by the system. *Id.* SolarCity structured the agreement in order to comply with federal tax law and allow SolarCity to take advantage of available tax benefits. Id. The question posed was whether under the proposed transaction SolarCity would come within the scope of article 15, section 2 of the Arizona Constitution, which provides that a "corporation[ ] engaged in furnishing electricity shall be deemed [a] public service corporation[ ]."

The Arizona Corporation Commission determined that SolarCity was "furnishing electricity" to its customer. It noted that the purpose of the relationship was to sell or provide electricity. The commission found that at first, "the SSA transaction may appear to meet the textual definition of a public service corporation under the Constitution." "However, SolarCity is not in the business of selling electricity, but rather, is in the business of designing, financing, installing, and monitoring solar systems for residential and commercial customers" and therefore "[f]urther consideration must be given to the public interest and the entity's primary business purpose, activities and methods of operation."

The commission next turned to considering the second question in its analysis, namely, whether the entity's business and activities were sufficiently "clothed with the public interest" to trigger regulation. Here, the commission applied . . . eight factors. . . . [from *Natural Gas Service Co.*, 219 P.2d at 325–26]:

(1) What the corporation actually does.

(2) A dedication to public use.

(3) Articles of incorporation, authorization, and purposes.

(4) Dealing with the service of a commodity in which the public has been generally held to have an interest.

(5) Monopolizing or intending to monopolize the territory with a public service commodity.

(6) Acceptance of substantially all requests for service.

(7) Service under contracts and reserving the right to discriminate is not always controlling.

(8) Actual or potential competition with other corporations whose business is clothed with the public interest.

Applying the Serv-Yu factors, the Arizona Corporation Commission concluded that SolarCity was not "clothed with a public interest" sufficient to draw it within the scope of regulation. In reaching this conclusion, the Commission noted that (1) SolarCity did not "affect so considerable a fraction of the public," did not seek to "stand in the place of the underlying utility," and did not provide continued service to the customer (Serv-Yu factor 1); (2) the activity of SolarCity was "not integral to the public at large" (Serv-Yu factor 2); (3) SolarCity's articles of incorporation did "not reflect an intent to act as a public service corporation" (Serv-Yu factor 3); (4) SSAs never generated more than fifty percent of the power of the host and the ramifications of a shutdown were far less than that of a regulated utility (Serv-Yu factor 4); (5) SolarCity did not hold itself out to all customers and was not capable of providing comprehensive service that could expand into a monopoly (Serv-Yu factor 5); (6) SolarCity must compete with other suppliers and thus did not accept most, if not all requests for service (Serv-Yu factor 6); (7) SolarCity used individualized contracts counterbalanced by broad business solicitation (Serv-Yu factor 7); and (8) although SolarCity providers displaced power sales by incumbent utilities, they did not replace existing utilities and assist them to reach distributed generation goals (Serv-Yu factor 8).

The question of whether a PPA involving solar energy was subject to regulation as a "public utility" was also confronted by the New Mexico Public Regulation Commission. Relying on a case of the Supreme Court of New Mexico (which itself relied heavily on Northern Natural Gas I), the commission held that a "third party developer who owns renewable generation equipment, which is installed on a utility customer's premises, and uses this equipment to serve multiple customers for a portion of each customer's electricity use and, payments for which are based on a kilowatt-hour charge, is not a public utility subject to regulation by the Commission."

3.   A number of states have resolved the status of third-party PPAs by enacting legislation explicitly addressing the issue. For example, in California, Public Utilities Code section 218 specifically exempts from regulation a corporation or person employing cogeneration technology or producing power from other than a conventional power source for the generation of electricity solely for [t]he use of or sale to not more than two other corporations or persons solely for use on the real property on which the electricity is generated. New Jersey has also legislated in this area [as has] Colorado . . .

E.   Overview of Legal Issues in This Case.

The first legal issue is whether Eagle Point should be considered a public utility under Iowa Code section 476.1. This Code section provides:

> As used in this chapter, "public utility" shall include any person, partnership, business association, or corporation, domestic or foreign, owning or operating any facilities for:

IV. Is Eagle Point a Public Utility Under Iowa Code Section 476.1? . . .

B.   Failure to Apply Northern Natural Gas and Serv-Yu Factors.

A review of the IUB decision in this case reveals that the IUB did not undertake the analysis required by Northern Natural Gas I and the Serv-Yu factors, but instead sought to apply a different bright-line test, namely, a test that whenever an entity sold electricity on a per kWh basis, it would be, as a matter of law, a public utility.

We decline to introduce such an innovation into our established law. The very purpose of Northern Natural Gas I [which Iowa has followed in the past] was to escape a rigid test that required a finding that an entity was involved in providing a commodity in a fashion that gave rise to a duty to serve all members of the public.

C. Proper Application of Northern Natural Gas and Serv-Yu Factors.

We now move to consideration of the Serv-Yu factors. The first factor requires a pragmatic assessment of what is actually happening in the transaction. See Northern Natural Gas I, 161 N.W.2d at 115. The transaction may be characterized as a sale of electricity or a method of financing a solar rooftop operation. Neither characterization is inaccurate. But most importantly, we have little doubt that the transaction is an arms-length transaction between a willing buyer and a willing seller. There is no reason to suspect any unusual potential for abuse. From a consumer protection standpoint, there is no reason to impose regulation on this type of individualized and negotiated transaction.

We also note that the IUB would not seek to regulate behind-the-meter solar installations that are owned by the host or which operate pursuant to a standard lease. If this is true, the actual issue here is not the supplying of electricity through behind-the-meter solar facilities, but the method of financing. Yet, financing of renewable energy methods is not something that public utilities are required to do. As pointed out by the Consumer Advocate in this case, if providing financing for renewable energy is not required of public utilities, the converse should also be true, namely, that providing financing for solar activities should not draw an entity into the fly trap of public regulation.

With respect to the second Serv-Yu factor, we agree with the district court that it cannot be said that the solar panels on the city's rooftop are dedicated to public use. See Northern Natural Gas I, 161 P.2d at 115. The installation is no more dedicated to public use than the thermal windows or extra layers of insulation in the building itself. The behind-the-meter solar generating facility represents a private transaction between Eagle Point and the city.

On the fourth Serv-Yu factor, it seems clear that the provisions of on-site solar energy are not an indispensable service that ordinarily cries out for public regulation. See id. All of Eagle Point's customers remain connected to the public grid, so if for some reason the solar system fails, no one goes without electric service. Although some may wish it so, behind-the-meter solar equipment is not an essential commodity required by all members of the public. It is, instead, an option for those who seek to lessen their utility bills or who desire to promote "green" energy. You can take it or leave it, and, so far, it seems, many leave it.

The fifth Serv-Yu factor relating to monopoly clearly cuts against a finding that Eagle Point is a public utility. See id. There is simply nothing in the record to suggest that Eagle Point is a six hundred pound economic gorilla that has cornered defenseless city leaders in Dubuque. Indeed, the nature of the third-party PPA suggests the opposite, as the city has entered into what amounts to be a low risk transaction—it owes nothing unless the contraption on its rooftop actually produces valuable electricity.

The sixth and seventh Serv-Yu factors relate to the ability to accept all requests for service and, conversely, the ability to discriminate among members of the public. See id. These twin factors cut in favor of finding that Eagle Point is not a public utility. Eagle Point is not producing a fungible commodity that everyone needs. It is not producing a substance like water that everyone old or young will drink, or natural gas necessary to run the farms throughout the county. More specifically, Eagle Point is not providing electricity to a grid that all may plug into to power their devices and associated "aps," or, more prosaically, their ovens, refrigerators, and lights.

Instead, Eagle Point is providing a customized service to individual customers. Whether Eagle Point can even provide the service will depend on a number of factors, including the size and structure of the rooftop, the presence of shade or obstructions, and the electrical use profile of the potential customer. Further, if Eagle Point decides not to engage in a transaction with a customer, the customer is not left high and dry, but may seek another vendor while continuing to be served by a regulated electric utility. These are not characteristics ordinarily associated with activity "clothed with a public interest."

The eighth Serv-Yu factor is perhaps the most interesting. Under the eighth factor, the actual or potential competition with other corporations whose business is clothed with the public interest is considered. See id. Here, the IUB strenuously argues that allowing third-party PPAs will have decidedly negative impacts on regulated electric utilities charged with providing reliable electricity at a fair price to the public. In support of its view, the IUB cites PW Ventures. The fighting issue in this case is whether factor eight in the Serv-Yu litany trumps the preceding factors and requires that Eagle Point be treated as a public utility providing services to the public.

* * *

In the end, whether an activity is sufficient to draw an entity within the scope of utilities regulation is a matter of assessing the strength of the Serv-Yu factors on a case-by-case basis. The weighing of Serv-Yu factors is not a mathematical exercise but instead poses a question of practical judgment. In our view, in this case, the balance of factors point away from a finding that the third-party PPA for a behind-the-meter solar generation facility is sufficiently "clothed with the public interest" to trigger regulation. . . . ■

NOTES AND COMMENTS

1.   As the court in *SZ Enterprises* notes, *PW Ventures* appears to have been the only state case that had directly addressed on appeal whether a third-party electricity provider was a "public utility" in a traditionally regulated state. *SZ Enterprises* is the second case, and it reaches the opposite result of *PW Ventures*. What are the benefits of a bright-line rule, such as the one followed in *PW Ventures*, versus a case-by-case analysis followed in *SZ Enterprises*?

2.   As the court in *SZ Enterprises* notes, defining third-party electricity providers as public utilities can make or break the third-party business model. Some states, like California, have addressed potential concerns by excluding third-party providers from the definition of "public utility" by statute. Why might some regulated states alternatively want to include third-party providers within the definition of "public utility"? Might they worry that third-party providers would take advantage of customers and

charge them too high of a price? What if the providers placed a lien on property in the event that the customer failed to pay for the electricity? Would this be legal? And could the third-party provider immediately cut off electricity sales to the customer in the event of a failure to pay?

3.   In some states where third-party electricity generation is permitted, this model of electricity provision has flourished. The following case study delves into the legal details of this model.

C. CASE STUDY FACTS

First Presbyterian Church-Building and Location

FPC moved to its current location, a three-story brick building, in 1924. At the time, the area surrounding the church was mostly rural, but since then, Baltimore grew, reaching and then passing FPC, which now sits in older, inner suburbs. Over 40 years of expansion and construction has seen the addition of the present sanctuary, chapel, meeting hall, and office wing, but there is little room to expand the building's current footprint beyond the 1.5 acres it currently occupies. The worship spaces (sanctuary and chapel) were renovated in 2010.

A feasibility study has concluded that the primary roof space that could be used for the solar panel array is a mostly flat area about 55 feet wide and 80 feet long. The area has an open southern exposure that makes it ideal for solar power collection. The flat part of the roof attracts sun with few shadows throughout the day, and anything mounted to the roof would not affect the aesthetics of the building from most angles, particularly the street in front of the building.

FPC's Interest in a PPA

There are two principal reasons for FPC's interest in a solar system PPA. The first is financial. Like many churches and other nonprofit organizations, FPC's annual budget is tight. Given the recession and corresponding lower levels of weekly contributions from its members, FPC is aggressively looking for ways to cut its costs.

FPC does not have the financial resources to purchase or lease a solar system, so it has turned to SSP for assistance. FPC would not be responsible for coordinating the installation project. SSP would undertake the financing, design, permitting, and construction of the system for FPC. This is attractive to FPC, which has no members with expertise in solar system design and installation.

The second principal reason for FPC's interest in a solar system is the long-term commitment to environmental stewardship of the Presbyterian Church, U.S.A. (PCUSA), of which FPC is a member. The PCUSA is the largest Presbyterian denomination in the United States, with over 2 million members and 11,000 active congregations, and has been active in issues of environmental protection and justice since the late 1960s. In 2008, the PCUSA General Assembly adopted a statement called "The Power to Change: U.S. Energy Policy and Global Warming," with many policy recommendations. For example, the PCUSA "supports comprehensive, mandatory, and aggressive emission reductions that aim to limit the increase in Earth's temperature to 2 degrees Celsius or less from pre-industrial levels." Specific recommendations include a commitment to "[r]emoving market barriers for producers of renewable energy and encouraging decentralized and distributed power generation."

FPC's Finances

FPC's approved budget is $250,000, slightly above the median budget for all PCUSA congregations, reflecting FPC's location near a large city and corresponding expenses above the national average. The lion's share ($205,000) of the FPC budget goes to operating expenses, which is an average percentage for all congregations. Like most PCUSA churches, FPC is heavily dependent on congregant donations, receiving 80% of its income in that fashion. And, like many churches, it has seen a drop in its income, as congregants have felt squeezed during the Great Recession.

FPC's projected electric bill of almost $5,000 is 2% of the church's entire operating budget, and one of the largest individual non-personnel expenditures. In addition, Maryland is a relatively high cost state for electricity, with FPC's current electric rate of roughly $0.12 per kilowatthour (kWh) expected to increase in the near term. The process by which BGE sets FPC's price for electricity is described in more detail in "Electricity Service and Current Rates/Usage," below.

Under a PPA with SSP, FPC would not own the PV system, so it would not incur any upfront costs of purchasing or leasing a system. As this description of FPC's financial situation shows, that aspect of the PPA is extremely attractive to FPC's members and leadership. With turnkey solar systems costing well over $20,000, even with prevailing incentives, FPC cannot afford to fund the installation of a system.

SSP's Interest in the PPA

The solar systems services and installation business is relatively new. In this fast-changing industry, SSP is vulnerable to new entrants at a later date unless it has a portfolio of deals and revenue streams that insulate it from competitors. The revenue stream from PPA customers is also essential to SSP's ability to attract capital and expand its operations. However, SSP would be adversely affected if it is locked into below-market deals that would leave its profits trailing those of the competition.

Electricity Service and Current Rates/Usage

In Maryland, local electric distribution utilities provide electricity to customers. FPC's distribution utility is Baltimore Gas and Electric (BGE). BGE provides both electric and gas service in the central Maryland area, including Baltimore City, Baltimore County, and the surrounding counties.

Maryland is one of the states that have "restructured" their electricity supply markets (see Chapter 10). This means that Maryland utilities have separated their service into two parts: regulated distribution of power, which is still provided by the utility, and supply of electricity, which is open to competition. Customers can choose to receive their electric supply from their utility, or an alternate electric provider. Whether a customer chooses to have its utility or another company as its supplier, the utility company still delivers the electricity and provides all of the normal customer services.

In short, BGE customers can therefore choose whether to purchase their electricity from BGE or an alternative supplier. Customers who do not shop for supply from an alternate electric provider in Maryland receive Standard Offer Service from BGE. "Standard offer" (also known as "provider of last resort") service is the electric supply service available to non-switching customers in restructured states. See Chapter 10 for a discussion of this concept. In Maryland, state law requires utilities to use competitive bidding to buy electricity for customers who do not choose a competing electricity supplier. Customers are charged for this Standard Offer Service (SOS) under rates approved by the Maryland Public Service Commission to permit recovery of the utility's cost of purchasing power at competitive wholesale market prices. How SOS is priced depends on a customer's class and size. BGE has a variety of different SOS electric supply rates, depending on the customer size and type. BGE Elec. Rates Info., http://www.bge.com/myaccount/billsrates/ratestariffs/electric service/Pages/Electric-Rates-Information.aspx.

The total electric bill for a customer in Maryland consists of two parts:

1) Electric supply: the cost for the generation and transmission of electricity; and

2) Distribution service charges (including the cost of service and special surcharges approved by the Maryland Public Service Commission, such as allowable charges for utility energy efficiency programs).

Supply Rate (BGE Type I SOS Service)

In the most recent year, FPC used 40,000 kWh of electricity. FPC has not changed its supplier, so BGE continues to supply its electricity. FPC's size puts it in the category of a "small commercial" customer under BGE's SOS rates. The church therefore pays for supply according to "Schedule GS—Type I SOS." This is the category of "General Small Service—Electric," available to "Type I" customers like the church that consume 2,000 kWh or more in any month, but, being under 25 kW in size, are not large enough to be considered "medium-sized" commercial customers.

SOS supply rates vary by time of year, being highest in the summer months. For example, the weighted average supply price through September 2013 for Schedule GS-Type I SOS was **8.84 ¢/kWh**. Note that this was *only* the supply rate under BGE's current standard offer. SOS rates are subject to periodic adjustments, and rates for "Type I" customers change every six months. Supply for this class is "laddered" to shield customers from being directly exposed to higher wholesale market prices prevailing at any one time. The supply needs for Type I customers are split into quarters, and 25% of supply is procured every six months for a period of two years—meaning the SOS price is a revolving mix of old and current supply contracts. While intended to shield small customers from price volatility, this "laddering" can also raise prices because the SOS price does not fall as quickly when the wholesale market price falls.

Distribution Charges (BGE Schedule GS)

BGE's current electric tariff (list and full description of retail rates and terms of service) lists the charges that apply for distribution of electricity to customers governed by Schedule GS.

Schedule GS monthly rates consist of:

—a Delivery Service Customer Charge;

—Supply Charges (under the BGE SOS Schedule, as above); and

—a Delivery Service Charge in $/kWh.

This information is set forth at BGE Elec. Rates Info., http://www.bge.com/myaccount/billsrates/ratestariffs/electricservice/Pages/Electric-Rates-Information.aspx.

Total Expected Electric Bill

The following table shows FPC's total electric bill using figures from 2012–2013 from Schedule GS, factored into the annual budget (rounded up to the $5,000 figure).

First Presbyterian Church, Calvertville, MD

Estimated Annual Electricity Charges for June 2012 to June 2013

Usage (kWh)	Supply	Distribution	Total
40000	$3,536.00	$1,139.60	$4,675.60

Supply: Type I SOS @ 8.84 c/kWh

Distribution: $17.50/month plus $0.02324/kWh

D. PPA DRAFTING ISSUES

The following Articles are five selected provisions of a sample PPA, which you should redraft, using the guidelines below and materials above for assistance. There are also many sample PPAs available online. Like anything else on the Internet, they are only somewhat reliable, and you should not rely heavily upon them, but instead should engage in original drafting that conforms to the facts of this case. In some cases, you have been provided sample language for specific subsections, as a further means of assistance.

The five provisions are:

Article 1 (Term)

Article 2 (Purchase and Sale of Solar Services)

Article 3 (Access and Space Provisions)

Article 4 (Environmental Credits and System Ownership)

Article 17 (Options to Purchase)

1. CONTRACT TERM AND PRICE (PPA § 1 AND § 2)

You should propose a combination of contract term and price that would satisfy both parties.

Starting with the price, SSP proposes that FPC pay one single price for electricity and SSP's installation and maintenance services (bundled together into a purchase and sale of "Solar Services") that would be fixed for the term of the PPA. FPC will want assurance that the price is not excessive. It will not want to pay more than it does for electricity now, as its budget is tight. More importantly, it would like to ensure that it saves money in the long run. This requires some estimating, as savings depend on trends in the price of electricity over the course of the agreement, which can be difficult if not impossible to predict. (*How will you estimate the future cost of SOS service?? What factors/information would you consider?*)

SSP would like its price to be as high as possible. It has several reasons for this. Obviously, it intends to be profitable. It takes on numerous risks (including, among others, the risk of higher than expected installation and materials costs, delays in construction due to difficulties in securing the necessary permits, and others) and expects to be compensated for them. Finally, it doesn't want to be locked in for a number of years to a rate that may turn out to be a below-market price in the future.

The length (term) of the PPA is also important. A term that is too short would expose FPC to potential future increases in the price of electricity too soon, but a term that is too long might require FPC to bank on SSP continuing in business longer than it has already been in existence. For SSP's part, a term too short means possible loss of ITC benefits and a truncated revenue stream and less profitability, but a term too long increases the risk of below-market rates in the out years.

Methodology and Resources For Calculating the Solar Services Price

As noted above, FPC will pay one single Solar Services Price (Price) for electricity and SSP's installation and maintenance services in cents per kilowatt-hour (kWh), bundled together and fixed for the term of the PPA. The price per kWh is one of the most important terms of any PPA, together with the length (term) of the agreement (in years). To the customer, these terms effectively determine whether installing a solar system will pay for itself in the long run. To the system owner, the steady, guaranteed revenue stream from a PPA customer is the foundation of its profitability. This is the core of the PPA: in return for SSP's services, FPC pays for the electricity generated by SSP's solar panels for the PPA's entire term.

Please note carefully: some terms that go into calculating the Price depend on your choice of term for the PPA. Think carefully about that choice before proceeding with the rest of the calculations.

SSP has represented that the Price will compare favorably to the rates BGE currently charges FPC for conventional, utility-generated electricity. FPC will want assurance that the Price is not excessive. It will not want to pay much more—if at all—than it does for electricity now, as its budget is tight. More importantly, it would like to ensure that it saves money in the long run.

SSP would like the Price to be as high as possible. It has several reasons for this. Obviously, it intends to be profitable. It takes on numerous risks (including, among others, the risk of higher than expected installation and materials costs, delays in construction due to difficulties in securing the necessary permits, and others) and expects to be compensated for them. Finally, it doesn't want to be locked in for a number of years to a rate that may turn out to be a below-market price in the future.

Therefore, it is up to you to decide what Price, taking into account the various uncertainties associated with its calculation, would be satisfactory to both parties. This will require a bit of estimating. For example, FPC's savings depend on trends in BGE's price for electricity over the course of the PPA, which can be difficult to predict. To get a sense of whether the final Price that you have calculated is favorable to FPC, you should compare it not only against current SOS rates, but also against SOS rates you think will be in place in the future. While obviously you cannot know exactly what future rates for electricity will be, you can estimate based on historical trends. You will find the Maryland Office of People's Counsel site (http://www.opc.state.md.us/Home/Publications.aspx) to be a helpful resource for price trend information, as it lists electricity supplier prices for the last five years. Make sure to use figures for BGE, not any competitive supplier. EIA also is an excellent resource for predicting rates of growth of electricity prices over the coming years. *See* EIA, Annual Energy Outlook 2014, Table A8. Electricity supply, disposition, prices, and emissions, http://www.eia.gov/forecasts/aeo/pdf/tbla8.pdf.

Individual Terms

Figure 12–2 provides a line-by-line summary of other factors that go into calculating the Price, with links to specific resources that you may find useful.

Calculation of Solar System Price

Variable

1. TOTAL SYSTEM COST (NET OF TAX CREDITS)

Solar System Capacity (9100 Watts)

Solar System Cost per Watt

Total Cost before tax credits

Federal Tax Credits

State Tax Credits

Net System Cost

2. FINANCING

Total System Cost

Interest Rate

Number of Periods (= PPA Term in years)

Total Interest

Financing Fees (use 0.05% of Total System Cost)

Total Financing Costs

3. OTHER COSTS

Total Pre-Installed Cost of Solar System

Permitting Costs

Operating Costs

Total Installed Cost of Solar System

SSP Profit Adder @ 10%

Total Retail Cost of Solar System

4. DEDUCTIONS FROM COST

Projected Depreciated Value of System

Accelerated Depreciation Deductions

Projected Value of SRECs

Net Cost of Solar System

5. LIFETIME KWH OUTPUT

SOLAR SYSTEM PRICE (per kWh)

Figure 12–2
Calculating the Price Per kWh For the FPC Solar System

1.   System Size and Production of Electricity (lifetime kWh)

The amount of electricity a solar system will produce depends on its size, the amount of sunlight falling on the system over time (irradiation), and design criteria such as the orientation of the panels and efficiency of individual panels.

The following methods are two ways to calculate annual generation:

(1) NREL's "PV Watts Calculator" (*see* http://pvwatts.nrel.gov/) simplifies the process for you by estimating the electricity production of grid-connected PV systems at specified locations. In the "Get Started" field, type "Baltimore, MD," and then proceed to the "System Info" screen. There, use "9" for the DC system size in kW, "Premium" for the module type, and "Fixed (roof mount)" for the array type. Then, calculate the Results (annual generation in kWh).

(2) To compare and validate the PV Watts figure, calculate it based on the solar irradiation and composition of the FPC system.

NREL has published detailed maps of the amount of the solar resource available on average each day. *See* NREL, Solar Maps, http://www.nrel.gov/gis/solar.html. These maps give figures in kWh/square meter/day. Assume that this amount is available to FPC, but to account for shading or other factors that might reduce the amount of sun falling on the system, *use a figure that is 20% below the low end of the NREL range.*

SSP has specified a system consisting of 28 Kyocera solar panels, with each panel rated at a maximum of 325 watts in power (totaling 9.1 kW in capacity). The panels have an efficiency rating of 16%, meaning that they convert 16% of available sunlight into electricity, which makes them among the best-performing panels available in 2014. *See* Kyocera 325W Polycrystalline Solar Panel KD325GX-LPB, http://www.pvpower.com/kyocera-325w-polycrystalline-solar-panel-KD325GX-LPB.aspx.

The Kyocera panels measure 65" x 52" each. Total panel area is therefore 61 square meters, using proper conversion factors. Note that it is prudent to add extra area to the total area of the panels for assembly and wiring functions, but even with that extra amount, the system will be accommodated easily on FPC's roof. *See* Cal. Energy Comm'n, A Guide To Photovoltaic (PV) System Design And Installation (2001) for system design considerations.

For simplicity's sake, then calculate the total power per year (in kWh/year) as follows:

(NREL solar resource per day x 61 x efficiency factor x 365)

Compare this figure to the PV Watts figure (it should be reasonably close). Then, assuming you are satisfied that the two figures match closely enough, calculate the lifetime total system production (kWh per year x your choice of total PPA term x 0.9).

A note about that "0.9": While developers typically warrant the solar systems for the full PPA term, they also note that equipment inevitably begins to degrade over a period of years. For that reason, you should include a 10% reduction in the estimated total lifetime production to account for decreased production in later years as the system starts to age.

2.   Total System Cost (*as installed*)

You should calculate the total estimated cost for FPC's 9 kW solar system, before the application of federal and state tax credits. An excellent resource for calculating the installed cost is: Galen Barbose, Naïm Darghouth, et al., NREL, Tracking the Sun VI: An Historical Summary of the Installed Price of Photovoltaics in the United States from 1998 to 2012 (2013), http://emp.lbl.gov/sites/all/files/lbnl-6350e.pdf.

You may (and should) take into account price changes since this document was published, as the price of systems continues to drop.

3.   Federal Investment Tax Credit

The federal Investment Tax Credit would reduce the effective cost of the system. Find a resource that sets forth the amount of the credit as a percentage of the total system cost, then multiply that percentage by the total system cost (see #2). Then, deduct the credit amount from the cost before credits.

4.   State Tax Credit

The Maryland Clean Energy Production Tax Credit would also reduce the effective cost of the system. You should find a resource that sets forth the amount of the credit as an amount per kWh of generation, then establish whether the FPC system will qualify for the credit. If it does, then multiply that amount by the estimated lifetime system generation in kWh (see above). Then, deduct the credit amount from the cost before credits.

5.   System Financing (for SSP)

Assume that SSP does not pay for its systems in cash, but finances them. This cost must be added to the system cost, just as interest you might pay on an automobile increases the cost of the car. A plausible working assumption is that SSP finances half of the cost of each system at the prime interest rate for the duration of the project.

6.   Other System Costs (for SSP) ("Soft Costs")

There are resources available on the Internet to find figures for the so-called "soft costs" of solar PV, such as permitting and operating and maintenance costs. *See, e.g.,* DOE, Benchmarking Non-Hardware Balance of System (Soft) Costs for U.S. Photovoltaic Systems Using a Data-Driven Analysis from PV Installer Survey Results (2012), http://www.nrel.gov/docs/fy13osti/56806.pdf; SunRun, The Impact of Local Permitting on the Cost of Solar Power, http://www.sunrun.com/solar-lease/cost-of-solar/local-permitting/.

You should add 10% profit for SSP. The profit "adder" for SSP is important to its long-term investing strategy. Given the cost of capital to finance the initial purchase of the system, and risks that the church may not make all the payments over the PPA term, it would make sense to discount future cash flows (that is, payments by FPC to SSP for electricity). It is assumed that the 10% profit figure will take care of this. That is, you should assume that if the Price is favorable to FPC, it will (with the application of this 10% profit) also be acceptable to SSP.

7.   Deductions From System Cost (depreciation, revenue from SREC sales)

SSP can expect to use two different strategies to reduce its net cost. The first is to take depreciation deductions. Depreciation is an income tax deduction that allows SSP to recover the cost of the system over time. It is an annual allowance for the wear and tear, deterioration, or obsolescence of the system. IRS Publication 946, http://www.irs.gov/publications/p946/ch04.html, gives formulas for determining the amount of depreciation.

The second strategy is to sell the solar renewable energy credits (solar RECs, or SRECs) provided by the system. You should calculate the total value of the SRECs over the PPA term. Start by calculating the number of SREC's per year (one for each 1,000 kWh of solar electricity generated; see below).

As this chart (http://www.srectrade.com/srec_markets/maryland) shows, Maryland SREC prices at auction have been relatively constant for the past several years. There is little certainty about how the REC value might fluctuate in the future. Therefore, assume that the current SREC market price remains constant for the PPA term. The current price of Maryland SRECs, which can be found at this site: Flett Exchange, Maryland SRECs, http://markets.flettexchange.com/maryland-srec/.

Using simple calculations, the potential revenue from the SRECs over the term of the PPA to SSP would be:

(Price per SREC x number of SRECs per year x length of PPA in years)

However, given that the SREC revenue stream is **not** guaranteed, discounting these cash flows using a 5% discount rate is appropriate. You will find a calculator for this function (called "Present Value of Ordinary Annuity") at this site: Calculator Soup, Present Value of an Annuity Calculator, http://www.calculatorsoup.com/calculators/financial/present-value-annuity-calculator.php.

Use the following amounts for the variables in the calculator:

Number of Periods (t): use the length of the PPA term, in years

Rate per Period (R): use 5%

Compounding per Period (m): use 1

Payment Amount (PMT): use 1 year total SREC revenue (price per REC x 12)

Growth per Payment (G): use 0

Payments per Period (q): use 1

Payment at Period (T): leave the button as "end(ordinary)"

The result ("Present Value (PV) of the Ordinary Annuity") from the calculator should be included as a cost figure (without the dollar sign).

8.   Final Calculation of a Solar System Price

Finally, calculate the final Price. This is the Price you should compare to BGE SOS rates to determine whether it is favorable to FPC.

You may also want to contemplate whether SSP should have contractual protection in the event of rising electricity rates. Consider, for example, whether the PPA might include an escalator clause, under which rates may increase from the base PPA rate, but by no more than a specified amount (and to no more than an amount that is less than SOS rates).

* * *

Here are the Articles for redrafting.

ARTICLE 1
TERM

Section 1.1   Term.

Section 1.2   Construction Period.

ARTICLE 2
PURCHASE AND SALE OF SOLAR SERVICES

Section 2.1   Service Commencement Date.

Section 2.2   Purchase, Sale and Delivery of Electricity and Solar Services.

Section 2.3   Change in Applicable Law.

Section 2.4   Use of System to Reduce Other Electric Purchases.

Section 2.5   Sale Only to Host Customer; Net Metering.

Section 2.6   Early Termination Due To Sale of the Premises.

2.   ACCESS PROVISIONS (PPA § 3)

One important issue that a PPA normally covers is access by the developer and its designees (such as contractors) to the site, at reasonable times and upon reasonable notice, for the purposes of designing, installing, inspecting, operating, maintaining, and repairing the system. SSP will expect that in addition to providing the broadest possible access for any and all persons that will need it, FPC will grant it an easement to access the property, and record the easement so that its rights will be guaranteed in the future.

Here is the Article for redrafting.

ARTICLE 3
ACCESS AND SPACE PROVISIONS

Section 3.1   Adequate Space for Construction.

Section 3.2   Access to Premises and Related Rights.

Section 3.2.1 Access to Site.

Section 3.2.2 Lease. (**Note: simply reference the existence of a lease; do not attempt to draft one.**)

Section 3.2.3 Use of Rights.

Section 3.2.4 Rent.

Section 3.2.5 Quiet Enjoyment.

Section 3.2.6 No Interference With Insolation.

Section 3.2.7 Site Conditions and Utilities.

Section 3.2.7.1

Section 3.2.7.2 Host Customer shall provide System Owner with Station Power during the Term of this Agreement. For purposes of this Agreement, "Station Power" shall mean electric energy consumed in the start-up and operation of the System, which is distinct from the alternating current output of the System.

Section 3.3   Non-Interference By Other Customer Activities.

Section 3.4   Third Party Consents / Recording.

Section 3.4.1 In furtherance of the foregoing, Host Customer covenants that it will, upon System Owner request, obtain a subordination, non-disturbance and attornment agreement ("SNDA") from any third party who now has or may in the future obtain an interest in the Premises or the Site, including, without limitation, any lenders to Host Customer or holders of any liens or encumbrances on the Premises. Such SNDA shall (a) acknowledge and consent to System Owner's rights in connection with the Lease and this Agreement, (b) acknowledge that the third party has no interest in the System and shall not gain any interest in the System by virtue of the Parties' performance or breach of the Lease or this Agreement or the exercise of any rights by a third party, (c) subordinate any lien the third party may have in and to the System and other property that is or may from time to time hereafter be located at the Premises or Site, and (d) attorn and not disturb System Owner's rights under the Lease and this Agreement in the event that the third party forecloses on the Premises and System Owner is not in default under the Lease or this Agreement.

Section 3.4.2 Either Party may record a Memorandum of Lease, substantially in the form attached hereto as Exhibit D, in the registry or title records of the county or counties where the Premises is located or other applicable government office providing record notice of System Owner's rights under the Lease. The other Party will join in the execution of such memorandum if requested.

Section 3.5   Data Acquisition System.

Host Customer shall make available to System Owner during the Construction Period (as necessary) and the Service Term internet access at the Premises necessary for System Owner's equipment to continuously monitor the System performance, including a data acquisition system to monitor and meter System performance.

3. TAX CREDITS AND ENVIRONMENTAL BENEFITS (SRECs/MARYLAND NET METERING LAW) (PPA § 4)

It is up to you to decide, under relevant and applicable state and federal laws, how the FPC system will qualify for the maximum amount of state and federal incentives, and to craft language that ensures that SSP receives the benefits of those incentives.

As the owner of the solar system installed at FPC, SSP will receive the tax benefits (such as the federal Investment Tax Credit) that go to a system owner. As for the SRECs, the parties could decide that FPC would retain the RECs and be able to sell them. That would have an impact on the Solar Services Price: SSP would demand a higher price if FPC kept the RECs and the revenue associated with their sale. Typically, the parties to a transaction of this sort would therefore not choose this option.

Maryland's net metering law would also affect the project. At certain times of the year, notably summer months with high amounts of sunshine per day, the system might generate more electricity than FPC needs. SSP's solar systems are electrically connected to the utility grid, so it is up to you to decide how the PPA should address it to make sure that FPC can take advantage of net metering, but continues to be obligated to purchase electricity and services from SSP, even if at times FPC does not need them.

Here is the Article for redrafting.

ARTICLE 4
ENVIRONMENTAL CREDITS AND SYSTEM ATTRIBUTES

Section 4.1   Ownership of System.

Section 4.2   Ownership of Environmental Credits.

Section 4.3   Environmental Documentation.

4.   OPTION TO PURCHASE (PPA § 5)

Some PPAs permit customers to purchase solar systems and end the obligations to purchase electricity and services. Usually, the option first arises at some point after the end of the ITC recapture period (five years), at a price typically no less than fair market value. This can be a useful means of addressing some of the uncertainty associated with entering into a deal expected to last for years into the future. You should assume the parties have agreed to a purchase option, and draft accordingly. In addition, you must address the rights and responsibilities of the parties if FPC does not purchase the system under its option.

ARTICLE 5
OPTIONS UPON EXPIRATION

Section 5.1   Purchase Option.

Section 5.2   Effect of System Transfer to Host Customer.

Section 5.3   Non-Election; Removal.

CHAPTER 13

CONSERVATION, EFFICIENCY, AND THE "SMART GRID"

A. INTRODUCTION TO CONSERVATION AND EFFICIENCY

Since the 1970s, there have been numerous federal and state programs and initiatives in place to reduce energy consumption and improve energy efficiency. A wide array of techniques exists to address sectors of the economy that include household appliances, industrial equipment, and buildings. This chapter focuses on these energy efficiency and conservation programs and incentives that aim to reduce electricity demand (thereby also attempting to reduce greenhouse gas (GHG) emissions and mitigating the adverse impacts of climate change).

Often, conservation and efficiency are discussed in the context of specific energy resources. Throughout this book we have seen technology-specific applications of both concepts to electricity generation as well as transportation. However, the concepts of conservation and efficiency are significant enough that some general conceptual and policy issues merit exploration. This chapter introduces the significance and nature of conservation and efficiency, and explores legal and policy issues that arise in connection with efficiency and conservation initiatives, such as demand-reduction and load shifting, and the Smart Grid.

Policymakers may seek conservation for a variety of reasons, including the desire to conserve resources for the future, minimize environmental impacts, or save money. Efficiency is one means to that end. As a preliminary matter, we can distinguish between economic efficiency, energy efficiency, and cost efficiency. *Economic* efficiency implies a decision, or an allocation of resources, that maximizes social welfare. That is, if we could measure the costs and benefits of alternative energy policy decisions, the most economically efficient alternative would be the one that maximizes social net benefits: the difference between total benefits (including environmental benefits) and total costs. Energy production may shift some costs to society in the form of pollution and other negative externalities. Welfare economists would say that this is a form of economic inefficiency, and that those social costs ought to be internalized by the producer and reflected in the price consumers pay for energy. Environmental laws of the kind discussed in previous chapters of this book represent attempts to internalize some of these costs.

Energy companies have an ever-present financial incentive to seek greater *energy* efficiency in production and distribution. The second law of thermodynamics tells us that the process of transforming energy into more usable forms entails energy losses. To the extent that we can minimize those losses and deliver more usable energy to consumers with fewer raw material inputs, we can use less energy to produce the same benefits, thereby emitting fewer pollutants and spending less money. We sometimes seek these same benefits another way, by focusing on the energy efficiency of consumption. Consumers may be able do more with a given unit of delivered energy, by driving a more fuel-efficient car or weatherizing their houses, for example. When producers of goods and services use energy more efficiently, or when companies provide energy to those producers more efficiently, it reduces the energy intensity of the economy.

It is easy to see how the pursuit of energy efficiency may also produce greater *cost* efficiencies, but these two concepts do not always go together. Cost efficiency refers to the cost per unit of energy produced or delivered. Energy producers and distributors may find that improving the energy efficiency of their processes is costly, and will only make the necessary investment if it makes economic sense to do so. Daily and seasonal variation in energy demand can lead to cost inefficiencies in energy consumption and production. It may cost more to provide consumers with X kilowatt-hours of electricity, for example, during periods of peak usage than during off-peak periods. If consumers would just as soon consume some of those kilowatt-hours during off-peak periods, their consumption pattern is cost inefficient. (It is not necessarily energy efficient if the customer consumes just as much energy.) This kind of cost inefficiency leads to production inefficiency as well, because electric service providers must maintain generating units whose sole purpose is to serve peaks in demand. If demand could be shifted to off-peak periods, those plants would not need to be built.

1.   THE SIGNIFICANCE OF CONSERVATION AND EFFICIENCY

Robert Socolow and Stephen Pacala's "carbon triangle" model (discussed in Chapter 1) sees conservation and efficiency as a likely component of any successful effort to levelize greenhouse gas emissions. For example, their first four "wedge" solutions include:

1.   Double fuel efficiency of 2 billion cars from 30 to 60 miles per gallon (mpg).
2.   Decrease the number of car miles traveled by half.
3.   Use best efficiency practices in all residential and commercial buildings.
4.   Produce current coal-based electricity with twice today's efficiency.

Robert Socolow and Stephen Pacala, Stabilization Wedges: Solving the Climate Problem for the Next 50 Years With Current Technologies, Science, Aug. 13, 2004, at 968. Conservation and efficiency can reduce more GHG emissions than doubling reliance on nuclear (to which Socolow and Pacala attribute one wedge) or increasing reliance on wind by a factor of 50 and reliance on solar by a factor of 200 (to which they attribute three wedges).

In addition to benefits in curbing greenhouse gas emissions, the economic benefits of conservation and efficiency are very real. The U.S. Energy Information Administration (EIA) tracks a wide variety of energy consumption measures over time. The energy intensity of the U.S. economy—energy consumption per dollar of gross domestic product (GDP)—declined from $17.35 per dollar of GDP in 1949 to $7.31 per dollar of GDP in 2011 (measured in 2005 dollars). EIA, Energy Consumption, Expenditures, and Emissions Indicators Estimates, 1949–2011, http://www.eia.gov/totalenergy/data/annual/showtext.cfm?t=ptb 0105. A variety of factors contributed to this decline, including technological improvements for industrial and commercial users, more efficient residential appliances and lighting, and improvements in technology associated with electric power generation.

EIA predicts that residential energy use will continue to rise, with commercial demand leveling off and transportation use slowing. In its best-case scenario—where "consumers will install only the most efficient products available, regardless of cost, at normal replacement intervals, and . . . new buildings will meet the most energy-efficient specifications available"—EIA predicts that residential energy intensity will improve 37% through 2040. EIA, Annual Energy Outlook, 2014—Energy Demand, www.eia.gov/forecasts/aeo/pdf/0383 (2014). Improvements for energy may not approach "Moore's law" (named for Intel co-founder Gordon E. Moore) in the semiconductor industry (i.e., a doubling in the processing capacity of technology every two years). However, given the pervasiveness of energy in the economy, the impact of improvements in energy intensity is very significant. One report estimates the savings to consumers and businesses from energy intensity improvements from 1973 to 2000—when energy intensity declined at a rate of 2% per year— were more than $430 billion. Am. Council for an Energy-Efficiency

Economy, Energy Efficiency Progress and Potential-Fact Sheet, http://www.aceee.org/energy/effact.htm.

It should not be surprising that conservation and efficiency can yield significant cost savings and GHG emissions reductions. According to Professor John Dernbach:

> Individual behaviors contribute significantly to U.S. GHG emissions. Activities that are under the "direct, substantial control of the individual and that are not undertaken in the scope of the individual's employment" are responsible for about one-third of U.S. GHG emissions and eight percent of global GHG emissions. By another estimate, about one-third of the energy consumed in the United States "is directly controlled by households." About eighty percent of all U.S. carbon dioxide emissions result from the burning of fossil fuels for energy. Individuals use energy every day in a variety of ways that indirectly and less substantially affect energy use, but whose influence is nonetheless real.

> Another reason to engage individuals is the high level of per capita energy consumption in the United States, both in absolute terms and relative that of other countries. Per capita energy consumption is approximately 340 million BTUs per year in the United States. With only five percent of the world's population, the United States is responsible for about twenty-five percent of the world's annual energy consumption. Americans use twice as much energy as their European counterparts, almost seven times as much as the Chinese, and more than twenty-one times that of Africans. No one seriously argues that the rest of the world can safely consume energy at the same per capita level currently consumed by Americans.

> In the context of individual responses to climate change, two types of behaviors are especially relevant. The first is efficiency—the substitution of a more energy-efficient appliance, motor vehicle, or other device for a less energy-efficient one. Efficiency tends to require a financial investment, not an alteration, in daily behavior. The second is curtailment of energy use—for example, taking the bus to work rather than driving. Curtailment tends to require changes in daily behavior without a financial investment. Because the overall contribution of individual Americans to GHG emissions is so significant, however, almost any reduction from either approach would be of value.

John C. Dernbach, Harnessing Individual Behavior to Address Climate Change: Options for Congress, 26 Va. Envtl. L.J. 107 (2008). As Professor Dernbach emphasizes, for purposes of policy discussion it is important to distinguish between improvements in efficiency—increasing energy output for the same unit of production—and conservation—changing behavior to reduce usage of energy.

2. A SYSTEMS APPROACH TO PRODUCTION AND DELIVERY EFFICIENCY

Many of the largest energy efficiency losses are in the production and delivery of energy. Therefore, increasing the efficiency of production in the energy sector may provide one of the more significant opportunities for reducing GHG emissions. The technical conversion losses associated with generating and delivering electric power, for example, are quite substantial—exceeding 50% when the entire energy system is viewed as a whole (see **Figure 13–1**). Every energy source has a technical conversion loss; that is, at least some energy will be lost in the process of conversion. This acts as a physical limit on the ability to achieve 100% efficiency in energy conversion and delivery. However, often there is a gap between the actual conversion loss and what is technically possible, creating an opportunity for technological innovations to improve energy efficiency.

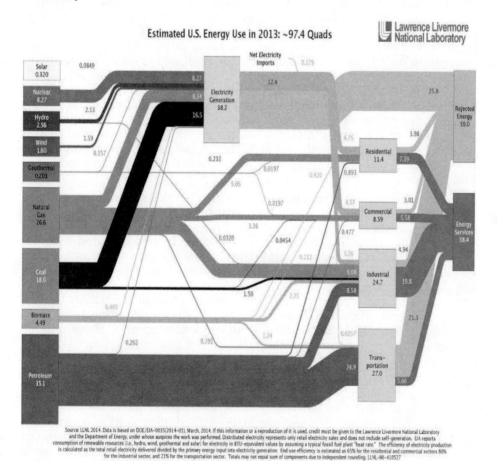

Figure 13–1
Estimated U.S. Energy Use in 2013
Source: Lawrence Livermore Nat'l Lab., https://flowcharts.llnl.gov/content/energy/
energy_archive/energy_flow_2013/2013USEnergy.png

From the perspective of conversion losses, some approaches to transferring energy are far more technologically efficient than others. A number of technological improvements in energy conversion have been discussed in individual chapters, including improvements for coal, nuclear and renewables. However, another way to pursue improvements in production efficiency focuses on understanding energy from a "systems approach," in which many interrelated components or approaches can work together to create efficiencies that may not be available in isolation.

One such example is cogeneration (discussed in Chapters 10 and 11), the process by which the burning of a fuel (typically natural gas) is combined with other uses of the thermal byproduct of power generation. Since cogeneration plants operate at 50 to 70 percent higher efficiency rates than other generation facilities, such technologies offer substantial efficiency improvements.

In addition, many inefficiencies in power generation and delivery can be reduced substantially if technologies are combined. "Hybrid" plants—generation facilities that rely on two of more primary fuel sources—are increasingly popular in the context of renewable power sources. For example, Florida Power & Light built a concentrated solar generation facility adjacent to one of its largest gas-fired power plants in Indiantown, Florida. Projects like this, or wind farms combined with natural gas, can reduce problems with intermittency and achieve greater efficiency. Likewise, renewables combined with biomass may allow more efficient operation of both technologies. All of these hybrid approaches focus on using the strength of one fuel to compensate for the weaknesses of others, especially with regards to issues such as storage and intermittency that might help to improve overall efficiency in production and delivery.

Increasingly a systems approach is also being used in assessing the interrelationship between power generation and transmission and how efficiency improvements in transmission may complement improvements in generation. The term "Smart Grid" has come to be associated with the deployment of new technologies that allow for more effective grid management at both the transmission and distribution levels. As we will see later in this chapter, it also encompasses new applications for consumers on the "smarter" grid, but a major focus of the Smart Grid is enhancing grid efficiency. This is of critical importance because as new, smaller scale projects are added to the transmission grid, there may be impacts on intermittency and the efficiency of grid management. At the extreme, this not only affects efficiency but also may pose challenges to system reliability.

For example, in New York grid managers are using flywheels to help store large amounts of electricity on a short-term basis to avoid grid surges. Other technologies include large-scale deployment of lithium ion batteries, which can provide short-term storage and grid management solutions for utilities and transmission line operators. While such technologies have yet to be deployed on a large scale, they seem to offer many efficiency improvements to high-voltage transmission and may allow better integration of power supply and transmission on a systems basis.

Perhaps the most aggressive push for grid-level storage has been made by the State of California. California statute AB 2514 mandated that the state's three largest utilities—San Diego Electric & Gas, Pacific Gas & Electric, and Southern California Edison—provide 1,325 MW of storage for the California grid by the year 2024. *See* 2010 Cal. Stat. ch. 469. The statute further directed the California Public Utility Commission (CPUC) to establish "viable and cost-effective" individual interim targets for the three utilities. In December 2013, the CPUC did so, putting the lion's share of the responsibility on the two larger utilities, Pacific Gas & Electric and Southern California Edison.

The 2013 CPUC decision further broke down the utilities' individual storage targets by storage types: transmission level bulk storage, distribution level storage, and "behind the customer meter" storage. CPUC established a timetable for achieving these interim goals, one that called for the storage procurement process to begin in mid-2014, and this process is already underway. The CPUC will provide that more than half of each utility's storage obligation must be met through bulk storage, which could include technologies such as batteries, flywheels, compressed air, small pumped storage hydro, and others. To qualify toward these targets, new storage capacity must support one or more of three goals: (1) grid optimization (increasing reliability, peak load reduction, etc.); (2) integration of renewables to the grid; and/or (3) reduction of GHG emissions. CPUC, Decision Adopting Energy Storage Procurement Framework and Design Program, D. 13–10–040 (Oct. 17, 2013).

Finally, as noted in the Smart Grid part of this chapter, rapid growth in distributed generation has sparked discussion of a "utility death spiral" in which more and more load relies less on the interstate grid altogether, relying instead on on-site generation of its own or microgrids. Therefore, the systems approach to envisioning the grid of the future will have to take these decentralizing forces into account.

3. THE CONSUMPTION SIDE

In addition to production and delivery, many efficiency improvements are available through changes to consumption levels and behaviors. Attention to consumption holds promise to improve efficiency and to change household behavior, reducing or changing overall demand for energy.

a. IMPROVING EFFICIENCY AT THE USER LEVEL

Efficiency improvements at the consumer level have the potential to substantially reduce the use of energy. A 2009 study by the McKinsey & Co. consulting firm concluded that by 2020, the United States could consume 23 percent less energy per year with aggressive investments in energy efficiency techniques. Hannah Choi Granade et al., McKinsey & Co., Unlocking Energy Efficiency in the U.S. Economy (2009). For example, improvements in motor vehicle fuel standards will reduce dependence on fossil fuels.

Often, however, improvements in technical efficiency at the consumption level are not mandated by law but depend on individual choices. For heavy industrial or commercial users of electric power, investments in efficiency in plant and facility can substantially reduce energy costs and save millions in annual energy costs. In this context, the incentives may be very salient. For individual residential customers the incentives and savings may be less salient and more remote, so additional regulatory incentives may be important. New appliances tend to use less energy than older models. Investments in insulation or air conditioning improvements can reduce energy usage, but many households may find the cost excessive and the payback period for such investments too lengthy. Often, utilities or regulators provide incentives for investment in such energy-efficient home improvements and also utilize programs such as demand-side management, discussed below.

b.   CONSERVATION

While energy efficiency represents improvements in energy output per unit of energy consumed, conservation represents a reduction in the amount of energy output consumed at the end-user stage. One might question whether individual behaviors make much of a difference, given the small impact each energy use or household may have. However, collectively individual behaviors within the United States have as significant an impact on energy use and climate change as does the industrial sector of the United States and many large countries and regions of the world. Consider the following results of a study of the impact of individual behaviors:

> [B]y merely including the behaviors over which individuals have direct, substantial control, the total emissions for the average American in 2000 equaled over 14,000 pounds (seven tons) of carbon dioxide. The total emissions for all 281 million Americans in 2000 were 4.1 trillion pounds. . . .

> Although the 4.1 trillion pound total is a tremendous amount, its importance is even more apparent in context. The 4.1 trillion pounds emitted by individuals comprise 32% of the roughly 12.7 trillion pounds emitted annually in the United States. By comparison, the entire industrial sector released 3.9 trillion pounds in 2000. The individual behavior figures also dwarf the subsectors that comprise the industrial sector. For example, the chemical-manufacturing and petroleum-refining industries, the top emitters among the manufacturing industries, emitted 686 billion pounds and 672 billion pounds of carbon, respectively, in 2002. Other industrial sectors had even lower totals, including iron and steel production (143.9 billion pounds), cement manufacture (90.8 billion), and aluminum production (13.7 billion).

> Even more striking is the comparison of emissions from individual behavior in the United States with other sources worldwide . . . The 4.1 trillion pounds attributable to U.S. individual behavior is larger than the total for sub-Saharan Africa (1.1 trillion pounds), South America (1.6 trillion), and Central America (1.0 trillion, including the Caribbean) combined, and it is roughly a third of all carbon dioxide emissions in Asia (15.6 trillion) and Europe (12.1 trillion).

Michael P. Vandenbergh & Anne C. Steinemann, The Carbon Neutral Individual, 82 N.Y.U. L. Rev. 1673, 1693–95 (2007).

Richard Thaler, a leading behavioral economist, and Cass Sunstein, the former Director of the Office of Information and Regulatory Affairs (and a former law professor), have celebrated how a novel technology called the "Ambient Orb" may help make consumers aware of their behavior and reduce energy consumption. On their view, regulators can "nudge" people to conserve simply by giving them vivid information about their current energy uses. For example, Southern California Edison encouraged consumers to conserve energy by giving them an Ambient Orb—a little ball that glows red when they are using lots of energy but green when their use is modest. Consumers using the orb reduced their energy consumption during peak periods by 40 percent. Richard J. Thaler & Cass R. Sunstein, Nudge: Improving Decisions About Health, Wealth & Happiness 194 (2008).

Implicit in the notion that regulators may be able to nudge consumers through incentives is some understanding that markets fail to do this on their own. The kinds of market failures regulators need to be prepared to respond to in addressing individual behavior include collective action problems, in which costs are focused on individuals with benefits spread among a larger group. In addition, it is well recognized that consumers lack basic information about the costs and impacts of various behaviors. Further, there are many psychological barriers to consumers making rational choices, including hyperbolic discounting of future values (in short, the human tendency to prefer smaller payoffs now over larger payoffs later), salience effects, bounded rationality, and over-optimism about the future. Consider this summary:

> [T]he rational actor theorists who study law and social norms focus on the payoffs of behavior change to the individual. These theorists typically suggest that optimal regulatory policies change the individual's opportunity set through taxes, subsidies, efficiency standards for consumer products, and other traditional measures. They reason that many behavior changes have a positive payoff for the individual, and that a rational actor—in theory—should change behavior in response to information about its payoff. Even these nominally positive-payoff behaviors, however, often face important barriers. Information may not be available or may not be noticed or understood by the individual. The individual may have adequate information but may act habitually without engaging cognitive processes. The individual may have adequate information, but her cognitive processes may suffer from bounded rationality. Even if monetary benefits will exceed costs, the effort necessary to change the behavior may outweigh such benefits. Social costs may tip a seemingly positive-payoff behavior into negative territory. Some behavior changes may be impossible for the individual because the necessary infrastructure or financial resources are not available. Other behaviors are possible but require sacrifice by the individual.

Vandenbergh & Steinmann, *supra,* at 1697. Social psychologists, such as Paul Stern and his colleagues, have put forth a Values-Beliefs-Norms theory, suggesting that information can activate norms and induce behavior change if it creates a new belief that a value is threatened and that the individual has the opportunity to reduce the threat. Paul C.

Stern et al., A Value-Belief-Norm Theory of Support for Social Movements: The Case of Environmentalism, 6 Human Ecology Rev. 81 (1999). Vandenbergh and Steinmann highlight that regulators have an opportunity to make a modest investment in "norm activation"—internalizing social norms to conform to expected social sanctions or rewards—to motivate changes in consumer behavior to address climate change problems:

> Numerous empirical studies demonstrate that norm activation could have a substantial effect on low-hanging-fruit behaviors. Many of the studies on norms and carbon-relevant behaviors involve household energy use. These studies examine the relationship between abstract norms favoring environmental protection, beliefs about energy use, and behaviors related to energy conservation. One study concluded that a belief that energy conservation has beneficial environmental effects activated a concrete norm in favor of conservation. Another study concluded that awareness of the social and environmental consequences of energy conservation decreased energy use through curtailed activities. Similarly, a third study concluded that a pro-environmental norm accounted for 11% of the variation in energy conservation activities, while the price of energy only accounted for 2% of the variation.

> Studies suggest that individuals respond to information not just about the harms arising from their specific activities but also about the harms arising from the aggregate activities of all individuals. For example, a study of utility customers demonstrated that those who felt that reduced demand would be good for people in general and believed that "households as a group could make a big difference in peak demand" reported that they felt a moral obligation to lower electricity use during periods of peak demand. The study concluded that the sense of moral obligation was more influential than price, and that, "In fact, this effect was greater than that of price even when the price differentials between peak and off-peak hours ranged as high as 8 to 1." Other studies have concluded that personal norms are reliable predictors of temperature setbacks (lower thermostat settings in winter). Studies in Europe have reached similar conclusions.

> Moreover, an extensive body of research suggests that norm activation affects recycling behavior, which can reduce individual carbon emissions by saving energy. For example, personal and social norm effects may explain why recycling programs involving block captains have more success than programs that do not, increasing recycling by 28%. The block leaders may remind individuals of their personal norms regarding recycling and may call attention to a social norm regarding recycling. A survey of participants showed that perceptions of personal and social norms favoring recycling increased in groups with block leaders but not in the others. Another study found that personal norms explained 35% of the variance in recycling behavior.

More recently, studies have examined the effects of environmental norms on transportation behaviors. A study by Annika Nordlund and Jörgen Garvill, for example, concluded that activation of abstract environmental norms through increased awareness of consequences had a positive effect on willingness to reduce personal car use. Other studies have identified more muted environmental norm effects regarding transportation. A recent analysis by Joni Hersch and W. Kip Viscusi of a survey of more than 15,000 Europeans demonstrates that individuals who believe that global warming requires immediate attention are more likely to reduce their car fuel usage, increase their public transportation usage, insulate their homes, and reduce their lighting and appliance use. Similarly, individuals who believe that fossil fuels contribute to global warming are more likely to take the first three steps, as are those who believe that transport contributes to global warming.

Vandenbergh & Steinmann, *supra,* at 1709–11.

If these studies are accurate, what regulatory approaches would be most successful in changing consumer behaviors? Is providing information to consumers sufficient to activate conservation norms, or do regulators need to adopt traditional regulatory tools such as taxes, subsidies, and changes in energy prices, to prompt changes in behavior? Is wasteful energy use always a market failure or at some level is it simply a disagreement between consumers with different individual preferences? Is there any limit on how far governmental agencies should go in taking such approaches?

Consider the following perspective:

[I]t is important to conceptualize energy as an input into the production of desired energy services (e.g., heating, lighting, motion), rather than as an end in itself. In this framework, energy efficiency is typically defined as the energy services provided per unit of energy input. For example, the energy efficiency of an air conditioner is the amount of heat removed from air per kilowatt-hour of electricity input. At the individual product level, energy efficiency can be thought of as one of a bundle of product characteristics, alongside product cost and other attributes. At a more aggregate level, the energy efficiency of a sector or of the economy as a whole can be measured as the level of Gross Domestic Product per unit of energy consumed in its production.

In contrast, energy conservation is typically defined as a reduction in the total amount of energy consumed. Thus, energy conservation may or may not be associated with an increase in energy efficiency, depending on how energy services change. That is, energy consumption may be reduced with or without an increase in energy efficiency, and energy consumption may increase alongside an increase in energy efficiency. These distinctions are important when considering issues such as the "rebound effect," whereby the demand for energy services may increase in response to energy efficiency-induced declines in the marginal cost of energy services. The distinction is also important in understanding the short-versus long-run price elasticity of energy demand, whereby short-run changes may depend principally on changes in consumption of energy services, while longer-run changes include greater changes in the energy efficiency of the equipment stock.

One must also distinguish between energy efficiency and economic efficiency. Maximizing economic efficiency—typically operationalized as maximizing net benefits to society—is generally not going to imply maximizing energy efficiency, which is a physical concept and comes at a cost. An important issue arises, however, regarding whether private economic decisions about the level of energy efficiency chosen for products are economically efficient. This will depend on both the economic efficiency of the market conditions the consumer faces (e.g., energy prices, information availability) as well as the economic behavior of the individual decisionmaker (e.g., cost-minimization).

Kenneth Gillingham, Richard G. Newell & Karen Palmer, Energy Efficiency Economics and Policy, Resources for the Future (Apr. 2009), http://www.rff.org/News/Features/Pages/WhatWeKnowAbouttheRolefor EnergyEfficiencyPolicy.aspx.

From a policy perspective, manufacturers and energy firms themselves may support efficiency efforts designed to increase use of energy, and these could crowd out any benefits associated with conservation. For example, a more efficient handheld computing device may be used for a wider range of functions, which might require more frequent recharging and could actually increase energy usage.

B. REGULATORY RESPONSES

Regulation of specific sectors of the economy (utilities, manufacturers, and buildings) is one way that efficiency and conservation improvements may be encouraged. Since the energy crises of the 1970s, the federal government and state PUCs have experimented with a variety of policy mechanisms intended to promote conservation and efficiency. These include federal fuel-efficiency standards for vehicles, product efficiency standards, utility programs to reduce demand for electricity (such as utility financed "weatherization" programs for buildings), utility tariff structures promoting reduced consumption in commercial and residential customers, state and local building codes, and many more.

Beginning with the Energy Policy and Conservation Act of 1975 (EPCA), Congress has tinkered periodically with legislation designed to encourage users of electricity to use it more efficiently. The EPCA introduced federal energy efficiency standards for appliances, which have been updated numerous times since then.

The Public Utility Regulatory Policies Act of 1978 (PURPA) was a cornerstone of the federal energy law response to the energy crises of the 1970s. PURPA aimed to promote energy independence by encouraging energy conservation and energy efficiency. Other chapters discuss this wide-ranging statute. See Chapter 11 for a discussion of PURPA's impact on generation of electricity from renewable energy sources, and Chapter

10 for a discussion of PURPA and open access to electricity markets. The section below on demand-side management looks at PURPA's policies that encouraged states to adopt different ways of setting electricity rates, and the impact on encouraging utility investments in programs designed to reduce consumption.

The federal policy on conservation and efficiency has been expanded and amended by the omnibus federal energy policy laws enacted since then, including the Energy Policy Act of 1992 (EPAct 1992), Energy Policy Act of 2005 (EPAct 2005) and Energy Independence and Security Act of 2007 (EISA 2007). States have adopted numerous laws and policies designed to promote conservation and efficiency. The American Council for an Energy-Efficient Economy (ACEEE) maintains state-specific lists of initiatives. ACEEE, http://aceee.org/sector/state-policy.

Some popular federal and state conservation and efficiency program types are described below.

1. APPLIANCE AND BUILDING ENERGY STANDARDS

Congress, the U.S. Department of Energy (DOE) and the states have recognized since the 1970s that standards requiring improved energy efficiency can reduce energy consumption of products, manufacturing processes and buildings. These account for more than half of American electricity consumption, so improving their energy efficiency can make an enormous difference. Chapter 15 discusses the federal rules that have increased vehicle fuel economy standards.

"Green" standards for products and buildings can also mitigate the adverse impacts of climate change. Professor Noah Sachs claims there is "enormous potential" for efficiency standards "as a core climate change strategy." Noah M. Sachs, Can We Regulate Our Way to Energy Efficiency? Product Standards as Climate Policy, 65 Vand. L. Rev. 1631 (2012). Others agree. By one recent estimate, federal energy efficiency standards alone could lead to reductions in GHG emissions by 2035 that would equal the annual emissions of 49 coal-fired power plants. Ctr. for Climate and Energy Solutions, Federal Action on Climate Change and Clean Energy (2013), http://www.c2es.org/publications/federal-action-climate-change-clean-energy. President Obama's 2013 Climate Action Plan set a goal of reducing GHG emissions by 3 billion metric tons cumulatively by 2030 through the use and expansion of appliance standards and energy efficiency standards for federal buildings, or "nearly one-half of the carbon pollution from the entire U.S. energy sector for one year." The White House, The President's Climate Action Plan (2013), http://www.whitehouse.gov/sites/default/files/image/president27s climateactionplan.pdf.

Federal minimum energy performance standards for major appliances and other energy consuming products made their first appearance in the EPCA. In general, DOE must set appliance efficiency standards at levels that achieve the maximum improvement in energy efficiency that is technologically feasible and economically justified. The EPAct 2005 and EISA 2007 expanded and amended the standards for numerous specific product categories. DOE's Office of Energy Efficiency and Renewable Energy (EERE) maintains the current list of covered products and standards. EERE, Covered Product Categories, http://

energy.gov/eere/femp/covered-product-categories. One standard familiar to any shopper at a home improvement store is the energy efficiency standard for light bulbs set forth in the EISA 2007. By 2020, all light bulbs must consume 60% less energy than today's bulbs.

Improving energy efficiency in non-federal buildings through new construction and retrofits is largely states' responsibility. Leading states have retooled their building codes considerably since the 1970s to set requirements for improved efficiency. California's "CALGreen" code took effect in 2011, and was the nation's first statewide mandatory green building code. Some state and local "green" building codes require LEED (Leadership in Energy and Environmental Design, a certification program developed by the U.S. Green Building Council) certification for public buildings, or tie the availability of tax credits to LEED certification for new buildings. A useful map of where each state stands on this issue is at Kriston Capps, One Nation Under LEED, Architect, May 29, 2013, http://www.architectmagazine.com/legislation/leed-and-building-rating-policies-states-map.aspx.

While states and localities have taken the lead, federal initiatives also focus on building energy efficiency. These include the U.S. Environmental Protection Agency's (EPA) Energy Star program, which allows for benchmarking that compares the energy performance of various buildings, and DOE's Better Buildings Challenge, which provides technical assistance and a forum for matching companies, municipalities, and other participants to collaborate on improving building energy efficiency.

Congress has given attention to energy efficiency in buildings as well. The Energy Savings and Industrial Competitiveness Act of 2013 was a bipartisan bill designed to promote energy savings in residential and commercial buildings and industry. It aimed to promote state compliance with model green building codes and provided funding for this purpose. It failed in the Senate in 2014, but a broad bipartisan group of Senators remained committed to energy efficiency legislation. Katie Valentine, Bipartisan Bill That Would Have Strengthened U.S. Energy Efficiency Dies In Senate, ClimateProgress, May 13, 2014. The American Climate and Energy Security Act (ACESA), the omnibus climate bill that failed to become law in 2010, went even further. ACESA Title III provided for DOE to establish national building code energy efficiency targets that states and local governments would have to adopt.

This provision raised the possibility that state and local building efficiency standards could be preempted by federal legislation. Professor Alexandra B. Klass addressed the issue of federal preemption of state and local green building codes as an issue of significant concern in implementing new regulatory standards for building efficiency. Alexandra B. Klass, State Standards for Nationwide Products Revisited: Federalism, Green Building Codes, and Appliance Efficiency Standards, 34 Harv. Envtl. L. Rev. 335 (2010) (warning against a single national uniform standard for building codes and appliances). For discussion of how federal preemption plays a parallel role in fuel efficiency standards, see Chapter 15.

One court has invalidated a local green building ordinance on the basis that it conflicts with federal law. The City of Albuquerque adopted an Energy Conservation Code, which sought to increase energy efficiency requirements for multi-family and commercial buildings by thirty percent by adopting regulations stricter than federal requirements. A U.S. District Court invalidated the Albuquerque ordinance on the grounds that the Energy Policy and Conservation Act of 1975 establishes nationwide standards for the performance of HVAC equipment and contains a preemption provision that "prohibits state regulation 'concerning' the energy efficiency, energy use or water use of any covered product with limited exceptions." The Air Conditioning, Heating & Refrigeration Inst. v. City of Albuquerque, No. 08–633, 2008 WL 5586316 (D.N.M. Oct. 3, 2008).

2. STATE ENERGY EFFICIENCY RESOURCE STANDARDS (EERS)

Chapter 11 discussed "renewable portfolio standards" (RPS) that require electric utilities to supply specified percentages of their electricity sales from wind, solar, or other qualifying renewable energy sources. Nearly three-fourths of the States and the District of Columbia have some form of RPS. Many are "clean energy standards" that allow credit for increased use of energy efficiency and conservation. For example, Nevada allows energy efficiency to meet up to one-fourth of the state's portfolio standard through 2025. Nev. Rev. Stat. § 704.7821. The ACESA would have adopted a similar approach on a national basis.

Twenty-five states have a comparable requirement applying directly to efficiency and conservation measures: an "Energy Efficiency Resource Standard" (EERS). As the ACEEE points out, these standards can have a significant impact. Achieving targets for 2020 would reduce 6.3% of 2011 national electricity consumption. ACEEE, State Energy Efficiency Resources Standards (EERS), http://aceee.org/files/pdf/policy-brief/eers-07-2013.pdf. An EERS requires that utilities achieve a specified percentage reduction in energy sales from energy efficiency and conservation measures. Like the RPS, an EERS sets specific percentages for energy savings that utilities must meet through customer energy efficiency programs. An EERS can apply to either electricity or natural gas utilities, or both, depending on the state, and can be adopted through legislation or regulation. In Massachusetts, for example, the annual savings targets of over 2.5% apply to three-year plans for energy efficiency submitted by individual utilities under the state's Green Communities Act. See Mass. Dept. of Pub. Util., Order Approving Revised Energy Efficiency Guidelines, Jan. 31, 2013, http://www.mass.gov/eea/docs/dpu/electric/dpu-11-120-a-phase-ii.pdf.

3. INTEGRATED RESOURCE PLANNING (IRP)

The EPAct 1992 amended PURPA to require state PUCs to consider requiring that all electric utilities adopt least-cost or integrated resource plans (IRP). IRP programs bridge the gap between supply and demand by requiring companies to consider demand reduction, third-party generation, and cleaner sources along with traditional supply-side alternatives to serving load.

After the EPAct 1992 encouraged IRP, a number of state PUCs adopted it and modified the process of regulating the supply of electricity provided by electric utilities. Twenty-seven states now have some form of

IRP. Synapse Energy Economics, A Brief Survey of State Integrated Resource Planning Rules and Requirements (2011), http://www.cleanskies.org/wp-content/uploads/2011/05/ACSF_IRP-Survey_Final_2011-04-28.pdf. IRP has two components: an assessment of future electric needs; and a plan to meet the projected future needs. It is "integrated" because it evaluates both traditional supply-side resources (building new power plants and transmission lines) and demand-side resources (energy efficiency and conservation) in making decisions about how best to meet projected future electric energy needs. By explicitly adding consideration of demand-side resources to utility planning, IRP aims to change the traditional pattern of building more supply to meet projected demand. This in turn can lead to conservation by utilities over the long term, and GHG emissions reductions, if more efficiency and conservation programs and incentives are included in the resulting plans.

As described by one of the leading advocates of IRP, a utility's planning program should operate as follows:

> The utility system must, in effect, take inventory of its residences, appliances, heating systems, commercial floor-space, and industrial processes, securing estimates of both absolute numbers and average efficiencies. Many utilities have made substantial progress along these lines already, although additional surveys may be needed.

> The next step is to develop low and high case projections of additions to these inventories over the forecast period. The range should bound the universe of plausible growth rates for the major end use categories. . . . Electricity needs for the high and low scenarios should then be calculated by summing existing and new uses, less anticipated retirements, over the forecast period.

> This calculation will yield a diverging "jaws" forecast comparable to that produced by the econometric methods reviewed earlier, with one crucial difference: the new forecast is rooted firmly in the instrumentalities of demand, allowing planners to track the effects of investments and policies designed to upgrade efficiencies of some or all of those instrumentalities. In parallel with this forecast, planners should develop a comprehensive assessment of opportunities for improving end use efficiencies. What is the "state of the art" existing and anticipated for delivering the services performed by the system's end uses at the lowest possible electricity consumption?

> The question then shifts to how much of this unexploited conservation resource is worth attempting to secure. The answer requires a rigorous methodology for comparing the life-cycle costs of incremental amounts of conservation for each end use with the costs of the most expensive displaceable generating unit in the utility's acquisition plans. In performing that assessment, planners should explicitly credit conservation for its advantages on indices of scale, lead-time, and uncertainty-reduction; the cost column for both the conservation options and the generation alternative should also include quantifiable

environmental costs associated with each. The calculation should take specific account of the avoidance of line losses, additional transmission construction, and additional reserve capacity that conservation makes possible when it displaces or defers a new power plant.

From this process will emerge a decision on which efficiency improvements are worth pursuing; it remains, however, to determine how much of the cost-effective conservation resource the system can count on securing. That inquiry focuses on mechanisms for getting the conservation installed; here planners can draw on numerous precedents. Options include state-imposed efficiency standards for some end uses, supplemented by direct utility investment through incentive programs. Planners must anticipate the success of such programs in convincing endusers to take advantage of efficiency opportunities. Again, substantial empirical data are already available.

Using those predictions, planners can narrow the "jaws" of the forecast by inserting assumptions about increases in the efficiency of the end use inventories for the "high" and "low" forecasts. Both forecasts will drop, but the high forecast will drop by more because there are more end uses to upgrade. The high forecast then represents the maximum plausible "post-conservation" system needs: the low forecast represents the minimum requirements that will have to be met.

The gap between the two forecasts which conservation has narrowed but not eliminated represents a range of outcomes with which the utility must be prepared to deal. The enterprise is analogous to purchasing an insurance policy; the goal is to minimize the cost of coping with contingencies of varying probability. New generating units may be one element of the response, but other options will bear close scrutiny. Load management programs that shift consumption away from peak periods, without necessarily affecting total consumption, are an obvious example. Also worth investigating is the willingness of large industrial and commercial customers to sell interruption rights to the utility system, which would provide additional reserves in the event of unexpected shortfalls.

In addition, some options, clearly inferior on cost grounds to baseload generators if markets were assured, may look more attractive as a hedge against possible but unlikely growth in demand. Combustion turbines come readily to mind as a generating alternative with relatively high fuel costs, but shorter lead-times and lower capital costs than baseload plants. Obviously, the more certain the system is that it will need significant "post-conservation" additions of energy supply, the better the high-capital-cost, low-operating-cost baseload systems will look. But the converse is also true and most existing forecasts do not permit an informed evaluation of utilities' investment alternatives.

Ralph C. Cavanagh, Least Cost Planning Imperatives for Electric Utilities and Their Regulators, 10 Harv. Envtl. L. Rev. 299–324 (1986).

As this excerpt suggests, IRP is intended to affect the process by which state PUCs regulate the supply of electricity provided by electric utilities. Traditionally, this was done through rate regulation doctrines, such as the "used and useful" principle, discussed in Chapter 8. However, supply regulation has also historically been achieved through condemnation,[1] siting, and permitting proceedings.

Many states require electric utilities to obtain a certificate-of-need (CON) (sometimes called a CPCN—"a certificate of public convenience and necessity") before building a power plant, transmission line, or pipeline. The CON is usually only issued following a siting proceeding— a hearing before the state PUC during which a utility makes its proposal and consumer and environmental groups may be allowed to participate as intervenors. The subject matter of power plant and transmission line siting proceedings was usually a specific utility-sponsored proposed project, as in the following case.

Bangor Hydro-Electric Co. v. Public Utilities Comm.

589 A.2d 38 (Me. 1991).

■ WATHEN, J.—Bangor Hydro-Electric Company ("Bangor Hydro") appeals a final order of the Maine Public Utilities Commission ("PUC") denying without prejudice Bangor Hydro's petition for certificates of public convenience and necessity for two independent hydroelectric generating projects. Bangor Hydro contends that the PUC arbitrarily ignored its own rules and precedents, made findings of fact that were not supported by the evidence, and erred in denying the certificates due to uncertainties created by their premature filing. Finding no error, we affirm the order of the PUC.

On November 22, 1989, Bangor Hydro filed petitions for certificates of public convenience and necessity requesting the PUC to approve three hydroelectric projects along the Penobscot River. The Basin Mills project, which was expected to provide 32 MW of additional capacity by 1999, involved the construction of a new dam and power facility. Construction on the project was not to begin until 1996. The Veazie project, which was expected to add 6 MW of capacity by 1996, and the Milford project, which was expected to add 2 MW of capacity by 1993, were to provide for an increase in the generating capability of currently existing hydroelectric facilities.

On August 17, 1990, the PUC denied without prejudice the Basin Mills and Veazie petitions [and approved only the Milford project]. Re Bangor Hydro-Elec. Co., Nos. 89–193 & 89–195 (Me. P.U.C. Aug. 17, 1990). While the PUC found that this decision was warranted solely on grounds of the petitions' prematurity, it also cited Bangor Hydro's failure to pursue least-cost options and demand-side resource planning as an alternative to the projects. In its order, the PUC described the standard

---

[1]   Ownership of land is often necessary for development of a power project by an electric utility. As is discussed in Chapter 2, in most states electric utilities have the power of eminent domain, which is frequently used to build transmission lines for purposes of reaching consumers.

used in evaluating petitions for certificates of public convenience and necessity:

> [T]he utility must demonstrate that the power from the new source is needed and that the resource being considered is the most economical or at least it is a part of an overall least cost plan. In addition, the utility must demonstrate that the timing is reasonable. This . . . standard . . . is consistent with the PUC's longstanding policy of encouraging the development of qualifying facilities ("QFs")[2][2] while requiring utilities to pursue a least-cost plan as required by the Maine Energy Policy Act of 1988, 35–A M.R.S.A. § 3191 (Supp.1990) ("MEPA").[3][3]

Bangor Hydro argues that the PUC erred in finding that the company did not allow independent power producers to bid against the Basin Mills and Veazie projects and it did not use the bidding process to minimize costs. . . . The PUC found that, although Bangor Hydro had issued a request for proposals, the bidding and negotiation process was far from complete, and the company had no intention of completing the process until the PUC proceeding was over. The PUC could reasonably have based these findings on the evidence presented, including the testimony of Jeffrey A. Jones, Bangor Hydro's Manager of Power Supply, who stated that, although a bidding process had begun, it would probably not be completed before this case was concluded. He further admitted that the company had not given bidders an opportunity to bid against these particular hydro projects because these projects were already priced below the avoided costs. Thus, the PUC's findings of fact were basically supported by the totality of the evidence of record and not clearly erroneous. . . .

The "All Ratepayers Test" is an analysis of the overall economic efficiency of the use of ratepayer resources to produce end uses,[4][4] to determine whether the same end uses can be provided more efficiently with a demand side energy management program than without it, considering the costs and benefits of the program to the utility and to the ratepayers, taken together. A program satisfies this test if the present

---

[2] QFs are non-utility entities of cogeneration and small power production facilities which, as unregulated electric generation sources, market their power to electric utilities. In 1978, Congress enacted the Public Utilities Regulatory Policies Act, section 210 of which was designed to encourage the development of QFs. Pursuant to section 210, the Federal Energy Regulatory Commission promulgated regulations which, among other things, required electric utilities to purchase electricity from QFS at prices not to exceed their avoided costs and required state regulatory agencies to administer the rules. "Avoided costs" are the incremental costs to an electric utility of electric energy, capacity, load management, and/or conservation measures which, but for the purchase from the QF or QFs, such utility would obtain from another source. Public Utilities Commission Rules and Regulations Chapter 36 § 1(A)(3).

[3] The MEPA states:

> The Legislature finds that it is in the best interests of the State to ensure that Maine and its electric utilities pursue a least-cost energy plan. The Legislature further finds that a least-cost energy plan takes into account many factors including cost, risk, diversity of supply and all available alternatives, including purchases of power from Canadian sources. When the available alternatives are otherwise equivalent, the commission shall give preference first to conservation and demand management and then to power purchased from qualifying facilities. 35–A M.R.S.A. § 3191.

[4] "An 'end use' is the light, heat, motor drive, industrial process, or other useful work resulting from electricity supplied by an electric utility or from a non-electric source provided through a demand side energy management program." Chapter 380 § 2(L).

value of program benefits exceeds the present value of program costs, at the time of analysis.

Chapter 380 § 2(A). Under the MEPA, a DSM program satisfying the All Ratepayers Test should be implemented in preference to additional supply-side projects, including even QFS. Applying these standards, the PUC found that Bangor Hydro had not pursued its required least-cost plan in the area of conservation and demand-side management. Bangor Hydro argues on appeal that the PUC ignored its own rules and the evidence before it in making this finding. . . .

The PUC based its finding primarily on the testimony of Steve Linnell and Carroll Lee who presented Bangor Hydro's criteria for determining the cost effectiveness of DSM programs. Bangor Hydro had the burden of persuading the PUC that its proposed projects were superior to conservation or demand-side measures. The PUC's finding may not be overturned unless Bangor Hydro can demonstrate that the finding was unreasonable, unjust, or unlawful. Examining the totality of the evidence of record, we find no error.

Bangor Hydro fails to show that the PUC ignored the evidence regarding the manner in which the company screens DSM programs. Taken in its entirety, Lee's testimony supports the conclusion that Bangor Hydro conducts its DSM planning according to its own cost-effectiveness criteria, not in compliance with Chapter 380 or the MEPA. When asked whether Bangor Hydro viewed as its responsibility the obligation to implement all cost-effective programs that it could under the All Ratepayers Test, Lee responded, "No, I don't think that is correct." He also indicated that, "as a general rule, as long as long-run marginal rates exceed a utility's long-run marginal costs, it is not appropriate to pay customers to conserve." Because, as Lee testified, Bangor Hydro's long-run marginal rates currently exceed its long-run marginal costs and are likely to continue to do so, the company would not purchase conservation even if the direct costs of conservation were less than the company's avoided cost. Linnell testified concerning the criteria Bangor Hydro uses in selecting programs for inclusion in the company's DSM plan. These criteria are clearly more stringent than the All Ratepayers Test. Bangor Hydro has failed to prove that the PUC erred in finding that its DSM resource planning was inadequate. ■

NOTES AND COMMENTS

1.   Some IRP statutes require PUCs to evaluate direct economic costs of potential new power sources and the indirect costs of the environmental damage the sources would create. One way to make utilities internalize these environmental costs is to add environmental cost values to each potential new source. Such values are sometimes referred to as "environmental adders." Two methods may be used to calculate the value of environmental externalities. One way is to calculate the environmental damage of a pollutant by examining the real world costs of future climate change, illness, and crop damage. This method is called "damage-cost estimate." Kenneth Rose et al., Nat'l Regulatory Research Inst., Public Utility Commission Treatment of Environmental Externalities 2 (1994).

PUCs often use another method in which the externality values are based on the costs to the power plants of installing air emissions control technologies. This is called the "control cost method." *Id.* Proponents of these types of regulation argue that they will show that renewable power is really cheaper than fossil fuel when all costs are taken into account. The utility companies should want to choose the resource mix that will achieve the lowest cost, and therefore will be more attracted to renewable energy sources to meet future energy needs. Clinton A. Vince et al., Integrated Resource Planning: The Case for Exporting Comprehensive Energy Planning to the Developing World, 25 Case W. Res. J. Int'l L. 371, 373 (1993).

Minnesota, which has an aggressive renewable portfolio standard (see Chapter 11), enacted renewable energy siting legislation in 1991. The law prohibited new nonrenewable energy plants unless an applicant could demonstrate renewable energy alternatives were researched and the proposed plant was "less expensive (including environmental costs) than power generated by a renewable energy source." Minn. Stat. § 216B.243(3)(a) (1994). The environmental externalities law requires the Minnesota PUC to "quantify and establish a range of environmental costs associated with each method of electricity generation." Minn. Stat. § 216B.2422(3)(a). Monetary values were set based on the values adopted by other jurisdictions and on a 1990 study of externalities. Re Quantification of Envtl. Costs, 150 Pub. Util. Rep. 4th (PUR), at 137. The Minnesota courts upheld the values on appeal. In the Matter of Quantification of Environmental Costs, 578 N.W.2d 794 (Minn. App. 1998).

2.   In the 1990s, the movement toward restructuring electric utilities to promote more competition had an adverse impact on IRP. States that partially deregulated (restructured), such as Maryland, empowered consumers to choose from among different generation options. Some of these states discontinued the use of IRPs to define how distribution utilities would meet projected demand. In some restructured states such as Connecticut, however, IRP continues in the form of procurement plans for new resources. Most states that continue with IRP have mandates for utilities to consider and incorporate energy efficiency and conservation options.

4.   DEMAND SIDE MANAGEMENT (DSM)

Dating back to the days of Thomas Edison and Samuel Insull, electric utility companies have traditionally promoted the use of electricity. As described in Chapter 8, traditional ratemaking methodologies created an incentive for companies to sell more electricity because increasing sales led to more profits. Customers also demanded more and more reliable electricity: during the 1960s, the electric utilities were criticized for failing to provide adequate, reliable service. They responded by building many more power plants.

In the 1970s it came as a shock to the industry when organized groups of ratepayers, such as major industrial users, began to complain that the utilities' emphasis on growth was driving up rates unnecessarily. If the utilities taught their customers to use electricity more efficiently, the ratepayers argued, it would not be necessary to add so many expensive new power plants. The ratepayers were supported in this argument by environmental groups that saw new nuclear power plants as too dangerous and new coal-fired plants as too dirty.

As a result, in the 1970s and 1980s electric utilities began to invest in programs aimed at reducing electricity demand. A wide array of techniques has arisen to encourage efficiency and conservation by utilities. "Demand-side management" (DSM) is the umbrella term for programs and initiatives aimed at reducing energy consumption and/or moving it from peak to off-peak periods. Curtailing usage at specific times in response to financial or other incentives, known as "demand response," can also reduce demand. Due to its distinct nature, demand response is addressed below in the Smart Grid section of this chapter.

One type of DSM focuses on energy efficiency—accomplishing the same tasks (heating a home, running an appliance, etc.) using less energy. Specific DSM techniques include encouraging consumers to use energy-saving appliances and high-efficiency heating and air conditioning systems, usually through financial incentives. Consumer characteristics such as knowledge, awareness, and motivation often influence the success of a program. External influences, such as energy prices and the market availability of relevant technologies, also affect a DSM program's success.

An example of a utility DSM program is the following:

Kauai Electric's (KE's) Commercial Retrofit (CR) Program is designed to promote energy efficiency improvements in existing commercial buildings. It targets all existing nonresidential customers. It offers energy audits (analysis), customer education, cash incentives, and low cost financing for energy efficiency measures. The primary program measures are high efficiency air conditioning systems and equipment, high efficiency lighting measures, solar water heaters and heat pumps, and energy management systems.

Commercial customers are grouped into small, medium, and large customers. Those in the small customer category are users of less than 30 kilowatts (kW); those in the medium customer category are users of 30 to 100 kW; and those in the large customer grouping are users of over 100 kW. For small and medium-sized customers, KE will conduct on-site analyses of energy usage, identify energy efficient retrofit opportunities, and assist in implementing appropriate measures through qualified installation subcontractors. KE will buy-down the installed measure cost in an amount equivalent to a two-year customer payback and provide three-year financing of customer contribution at an 8.0 per cent annual rate, with no down payment or prepayment penalty. In the event that a measure does not qualify for an incentive because the payback is two years or less, KE will, nonetheless, provide financing.

For large commercial customers, KE will conduct engineering studies to identify opportunities for increased energy efficiency and develop a phased energy improvement plan. It will negotiate the measures to be installed and the incentives with each large customer. To avoid oversubscription to the program, KE intends to (1) set the initial incentives at a relatively low level and gradually increase them over time, (2) apportion the CR program budget over the three market segments, and (3) establish a cap on the amount of incentives that any one customer can receive in a year (without KE's review).

The CR program is KE's largest DSM program and is expected to account for over one-third of its total DSM savings. KE anticipates that this program will produce energy savings of 33,064,857 kilowatt-hours (kWh) per year and demand savings of 5,583 kW. KE estimates a net resource benefit of $11,460,000 and a benefit-cost ratio of 2.42. The budget for the first year of full scale operation of the CR program is $403,723.

Re Kauai Electric Division of Citizens Utilities Co., Hawaii Pub. Util. Comm'n., No. 94–0337 (Aug. 5, 1997).

* * *

Since the 1970s, federal laws and policies have encouraged utilities' DSM programs. PURPA set forth an initial set of requirements, and the EPAct 1992, EPAct 2005, and EISA 2007 contained new requirements and amendments to PURPA. PURPA's demand-side provisions aimed to encourage conservation of energy supplied by electric utilities, optimal efficiency of electric utility facilities and resources, and equitable rates for electric consumers. PURPA did not mandate that utilities undertake specific actions, but instead encouraged the states to adopt regulatory policies. 16 U.S.C. § 2621 (2012).

PURPA originally set forth six specific federal standards for utilities' services and rates: (i) rates should reflect the actual cost of electric power generation and distribution; (ii) rates should not decline with increases in electric power use unless the cost of providing the power decreases as consumption increases; (iii) rates should reflect the daily variations in the actual cost of electric power generation; (iv) rates should reflect the seasonal variations in the actual cost of electric power generation; (v) rates should offer a special "interruptible" electric power service rate for commercial and industrial customers; and (vi) each electric utility must offer load management techniques to their electric consumers that will be practicable, cost effective and reliable, as determined by the state public utility commission. State PUCs were required to consider whether adopting these standards would further PURPA's objectives.

The EPAct 1992 added three new electric rate policies designed to encourage DSM investments. First, that "[t]he rates allowed to be charged . . . shall be such that the utility's investment in and expenditures for . . . demand[-side] management measures are at least as profitable, giving appropriate consideration to income lost from reduced sales . . . as its investments in and expenditures for the construction of new generation, transmission, and distribution equipment." Second, that "[t]he rates charged . . . shall be such that the utility is encouraged to make investments in, and expenditures for, all cost-effective improvements in the energy efficiency of power generation, transmission and distribution."

In keeping with federal encouragement of DSM investments, state PUCs had to decide whether electric utilities could recover costs associated with DSM programs using the traditional principles that apply in rate-making proceedings. See Chapter 8 for a discussion of those principles.

In the following case, a Georgia court applied ratemaking principles to decide whether a public utility could recover amounts it spent on DSM programs.

Georgia Power Company v. Georgia Industrial Group

447 S.E.2d 118 (Ga. App. 1994).

■ POPE, C.J.—Georgia Power appeals the superior court's order reversing three orders of the Georgia Public Service Commission (Commission) authorizing Georgia Power to recover through riders or surcharges the costs of certain energy conservation programs and "interruptible service credits" paid to customers to reduce their supply of electricity during peak periods.

The issue in this case is whether such costs may be recovered through riders or whether they must be recovered through base rates utilizing the accounting procedure specified in OCGA § 46–2–26.1 for determining the rates to be charged. This case arose out of the legislature's passage in 1991 of the Integrated Resource Planning Act (IRP), OCGA § 46–3A–1 et seq. The IRP requires utilities to file long-range energy plans for review and approval by the Commission. OCGA § 46–3A–2. It also requires certification by the Commission before a utility can construct or sell an electric plant, enter into a long-term power purchase, or spend money on "demand-side capacity options" (programs that reduce the demand for electricity). OCGA §§ 46–3A–1(4); 46–3A–3(a). The IRP allows a utility to recover, inter alia, its costs for any certified demand-side capacity option and an additional sum as determined by the Commission to encourage the development of such demand-side programs. OCGA § 46–3A–9.

. . . In September 1992, Georgia Power filed revised demand-side programs for its residential customers and sought a proposed residential demand-side cost recovery rider to recover the costs of such programs. The rider proposed to pass through to residential customers (except low income customers) the expected program costs through 1993, subject to a true-up against actual program costs in a future proceeding at the end of 1993. Any over or under collection would be used, together with projected costs for 1994, to set the rider for 1994. . . . On January 4, 1993, the Commission . . . held that Georgia Power should be allowed to recover the costs of its "interruptible service credits" through a rate rider since the credits were relatively new and there would be a time period necessary to determine participation levels and customer responses.

Appellee Georgia Industrial Group appealed to the Superior Court of Fulton County [from the ruling that allowed] Georgia Power to recover the costs of its demand-side programs and its "interruptible service credits" through a rider mechanism. The superior court reversed the Commission's orders, finding that such expenses are recoverable only through the test year rate case procedure prescribed by OCGA §§ 46–2–25 and 46–2–26.1, which was not followed in this case. Georgia Power brought this appeal from the superior court's order, and we reverse.

Georgia Power argues . . . that the superior court's ruling is erroneous because the future test year accounting method set forth in

OCGA § 46–2–26.1 only applies to general rate cases, which these proceedings do not involve, and because [the IRP] requires use of an accounting method different from the test year statute since the test year statute bases rates on estimated costs and the new statute requires recovery of actual costs.

OCGA § 46–2–26.1 ("Accounting methods to be used by electric utilities in ratemaking proceedings") provides in pertinent part:

"(b) In any proceeding to determine the rates to be charged by an electric utility, the electric utility shall file jurisdictionally allocated cost of service data on the basis of a test period, and the commission shall utilize a test period, consisting of actual data for the most recent 12 month period for which data are available, fully adjusted separately to reflect estimated operations during the 12 months following the utility's proposed effective date of the rates . . ."

Thus, pursuant to this future test year method, utility rates are established after an analysis of combined revenue, expenses and investment forecasted for a future 12-month period. We agree with Georgia Power that § 46–2–26.1 sets forth the accounting method to be used in determining the general rates to be charged customers rather than issue-specific rates or riders to be charged a particular group of customers. In support of this conclusion, we note that Georgia Power has cited in the record to a number of occasions in which the Commission has approved rate riders without utilizing the test year method. For the reasons discussed below, we further hold that § 46–3A–9 of the IRP gives the Commission the authority to approve recovery of demand-side costs outside of a general rate case and the test year statute.

Traditionally, electric utilities have been concerned with selling electricity and building new power plants to meet increased demands for electricity. Thus, under traditional ratemaking principles (the test year method), a utility's revenues are tied directly to how much electricity it sells. With the advent of integrated resource planning, however, the focus has been on ensuring the efficient use of electricity and the resources used to produce it. As noted earlier, demand-side programs are those that encourage customers to reduce their demand for electricity; often they involve incentives paid to customers to buy more energy efficient equipment for their homes and businesses. However, because demand-side investments result in less electricity being sold, they necessarily reduce the utility's revenues and earnings. For this reason, the legislature enacted OCGA § 46–3A–9, which allows utilities to recover the cost of demand-side programs plus an additional amount as an incentive to develop such programs:

"The approved or actual cost, whichever is less, of any certificated demand-side capacity option shall be recovered by the utility in rates, along with an additional sum as determined by the commission to encourage the development of such resources. The commission shall consider lost revenues, if any, changed risks, and an equitable sharing of benefits between the utility and its retail customers."

We read this provision to say that a utility may recover the actual or approved costs of its demand-side programs by passing along such costs directly to its ratepayers along with an additional sum or incentive (as determined by the Commission) to encourage it to develop such programs. It seems clear to us that the legislature intended to treat demand-side costs outside of general ratemaking procedures by virtue of the fact that it provided for the utility to recover through rates not only its costs of such programs but an additional financial incentive to develop such programs over and above its overall rate of return. We further note that in providing for utilities to recover the cost of constructing new power plants, the legislature specified in OCGA § 46–3A–7(a) that a utility should be permitted to include in its "rate base" the full amount of approved construction costs absent a showing of "fraud, concealment, failure to disclose a material fact, imprudence, or criminal misconduct." By contrast, § 46–3A–9 simply says that the utility shall recover its demand-side costs "in rates." Had the legislature intended for recovery of demand-side costs to be accomplished through traditional ratemaking principles, it would have specified that such costs could be put in the rate base as it did with power plant construction costs.

Finally, utilization of the test year method for calculating recovery of demand-side costs is unnecessary and would likely preclude the legislative mandate that utilities be allowed to recover their actual costs of such programs. OCGA § 46–3A–9. First, the purpose of the test year method is to analyze a utility's revenues, expenses and investment forecasted for an entire year and determine whether it is earning an appropriate return. *See* OCGA § 46–2–26.1. Since § 46–3A–9 authorizes a utility to recover the exact costs of its demand-side programs plus an incentive, there is no need to utilize the test year analysis to look at its overall earnings.

Second, use of the test year method will not allow a utility to recover its exact costs of such programs plus an additional amount as an incentive because the test year method is not tied to recovery of specific costs but to an overall rate of return. However, under the rider mechanism approved by the Commission, which contains a true-up provision for factoring in any over or under collection of program costs in setting the rider for the next year, the stated purpose of recovering the actual or approved costs of such programs will be met. *See* OCGA § 46–3A–9.

Because use of the test year statute for calculating recovery of demand-side costs would frustrate the legislature's stated intent in encouraging utilities to develop such programs, we conclude the superior court erred in holding recovery of such costs must be accomplished pursuant to OCGA § 46–2–26.1 and that the Commission could not effectuate recovery of such costs through the use of a rider mechanism.

Judgment reversed. ■

NOTES AND COMMENTS

1.   An Illinois court construed state statutes to reach the opposite result in A. Finkl & Sons Co. v. Illinois Commerce Commission, 620 N.E.2d 1141 (Ill. App.1993) ("The rule against single-issue ratemaking recognizes that the revenue formula is designed to determine the revenue requirement based on the aggregate costs and demand of the utility. Therefore, it would be

improper to consider changes to components of the revenue requirement in isolation.").

* * *

One of PURPA's six rate policies was that "rates should not decline with increases in electric power use unless the cost of providing the power decreases as consumption increases." However, by the mid-1980s, excess supply led many utilities to offer low rates (including "declining block" rates in which rates decreased with increased use) to maintain industrial customers.

In *Re Central Maine Power Company,* 150 P.U.R.4th 229 (Maine PUC 1994), the Maine Public Utility Commission declined to approve declining block rates sought by a public utility partly because it would discourage conservation:

> Should public policy allow or encourage CMP to promote load growth through a broad adoption of a rate structure known as "declining block" rates? In electric utility parlance, a rate structure in which the average price paid per kilowatt-hour remains the same at different levels of monthly usage is known as a "flat rate." If the average price per kilowatt-hour changes with usage, the rate is either "declining" or "inclining," according to whether it falls or rises with usage; because declining rates were once very common, an inclining rate has at times been known as an "inverted" rate. When the rate is flat within broad ranges or "blocks" of usage, but changes between blocks, it is either an "inclining block" or "declining block" rate. Since 1986, CMP's rate for most of its residential customers, known as Rate A, has had an "inclining block" structure, in which the price per kWh for the first 400 kWh per month is 20 percent lower than the price for usage above 400 kWh per month. Other customers, including high-use residential customers who are on time-of-use rates, and commercial and industrial customers, have a more complicated bill that includes a fixed monthly customer charge. For the higher-use rate classes, the bill includes a demand charge as well. Both of these can cause the overall average rate per kilowatt-hour paid to vary considerably with usage. However, the energy charge component of these rates is currently a flat rate per kWh used.
>
> In this case, CMP has asked us to approve the concept of replacing the inclining block structure of residential Rate A, and the flat rate energy charge of other residential and many commercial customers, with a declining block rate, so that the "tail block" monthly consumption above certain thresholds would be priced at a much lower rate. . . . In reviewing the evidence and argument developed in this case over the past year, we find that CMP has not made a convincing case for such a substantial revision to our long-standing rate design policies. . . .
>
> [A] major rate design change such as a broad move to declining block rates would be likely to cause large increases in the bills paid by many customers, in order to offset the large decreases to high-use customers; simply changing the current inclining block

structure of Rate A to a flat rate would cause the bills of the many customers using less than 400 kWh per month to go up by 12 percent, on average. (In January of 1992, the number of these customers was nearly 150,000; in August, more than 200,000.) Thus, the uncertain benefits of increased economic efficiency from the imposition of declining block rates would be bought at the certain expense of large rate changes for many customers. We find CMP's proposal especially unwise at this time of unusually high customer sensitivity to further changes in electric rates and low public confidence in the utility's ability to control its costs and charge reasonable rates.

We find that rates should continue to reflect the long-run marginal costs of service and the differences in costs between seasons and among times of day. As a general matter, making cost-based rate elements (such as variation with time of use) optional is likely to create adverse selection problems for other ratepayers, and thus would be inequitable, as customers with higher-cost usage patterns select the more beneficial rate and ultimately cause class rates to rise. In designing rates, the customer charge, if any, should reflect marginal customer costs; the demand charge, if any, should reflect the marginal capacity costs of generation, transmission, and distribution. For rate classes without a demand charge, we have seen no evidence that demand costs are disproportionately driven by usage in the lower usage blocks. If, for any rate class without a separately stated demand charge, a utility wishes to structure rates in blocks according to total energy used, then the rates for each block should reflect the total long-term cost of capacity associated with that usage.

* * *

Utility spending on DSM peaked in the early 1990s. With restructuring and the move to competitive markets in some states in the 1990s, the question arose whether investment in DSM could continue without the guaranteed returns provided by traditional ratemaking. Many utilities decreased their efforts or discontinued their programs altogether, as utilities tended to view expenditures on DSM programs as unnecessary extra costs that new competitors did not incur. Toshi H. Arimura et al., Cost-Effectiveness of Electricity Energy Efficiency, 33 Energy J. 63 (2012).

During this time period, almost every state that moved to market-based rates provided funding for the DSM programs that utilities were reducing or discontinuing. The principal mechanism for this was a "system benefits charge" (or "public benefits fund"), also discussed in Chapter 11. Fifteen states and the District of Columbia impose a small fee on all electric customers' bills. These small charges yield considerable sums for programs that can reduce consumption and achieve GHG emissions reductions, as public benefit funds were expected to hold $7.7 billion by 2017. California is responsible for nearly 2/3 of the total, but other states have multi-million-dollar funds. In most states, these funds can be used for energy efficiency, conservation, and renewable energy purposes, although program design and administration vary widely among the states. Database of State Incentives for Renewables & Efficiency, Public Benefits Funds for Renewables, http://dsireusa.org/documents/summarymaps/PBF_Map.pdf.

In recent years, declining electric generation reserve margins, growing concern over climate change, and the increasing costs associated with construction of new generation have produced a groundswell of new support for DSM investment. Spending on DSM programs, funded in part by systems benefit charges, has rebounded. In 2010, electric utilities spent $4.2 billion on DSM programs and reduced 33 GW of peak load electricity demand through the use of DSM programs. EIA, Annual Energy Review (2012), http://www.eia.gov/totalenergy/data/annual/showtext.cfm?t=ptb0813.

5. DECOUPLING

As discussed above, a well-known drawback of the traditional ratemaking process is that it discourages utilities' investments in energy efficiency and conservation. As *Georgia Power Company* indicates, under the cost of service formula for rates, utilities recover their fixed and variable costs based on the amount of electricity they project to sell. The retail electric rate is fixed between rate cases, so if the amount of electricity sold later decreases due to efficiency and conservation measures, the utility recovers less revenue unless it can lower expenses.

The concept of "decoupling," adopted by many states for electric or gas utilities or both, attempts to change this disincentive for efficiency programs. There are several formulas for implementing decoupling, but all allow for price adjustments between rate cases to tie revenue to actual expenses and break (decouple) the link between sales and revenue. California has used a form of decoupling in its rates since the mid-1980s. As of 2009, 17 states had implemented decoupling mechanisms, including 28 natural gas distribution utilities and 12 electric utilities. Nat'l Renewable Energy Lab., Decoupling Policies: Options to Encourage Energy Efficiency Policies For Utilities (2009) contains a map of states with decoupling policies, and a description of different forms of decoupling.

Here is an explanation of the different types of decoupling:

Decoupling is a slight but meaningful variation on traditional regulation, designed to ensure that utilities recover allowed amounts of revenue independent of their sales volumes. The general goal is to remove a disincentive for utilities to embrace energy efficiency or other measures that reduce consumer usage levels. Decoupling begins with a general rate case, in which a revenue requirement is determined and rates are established in the traditional way. Thereafter, rates are adjusted periodically to ensure that the utility is actually collecting the allowed amount of revenue, even if sales have varied from the assumptions used when the previous general rate case was decided. If sales decline below the level assumed, rates increase slightly, and vice-versa.

Decoupling mechanisms are divided into three categories:

- Full Decoupling: All variations in sales volumes are included in the calculation of the decoupling adjustment.

- Limited Decoupling: Only specific causes of changes in sales volume are included. For example, changes in sales due to weather may be excluded, with sales volumes recalculated based on the normal weather conditions used in the rate case.

- Partial Decoupling: Only a portion of the revenue lost or gained due to sales volume variations is included in the calculation of the decoupling adjustment.

Decoupling is relatively simple to administer. Each billing cycle, month, or year, the amount of revenue allowed in the rate case is compared to the amount actually recovered. A surcharge or credit is imposed to make up the difference.

Reg. Assist. Proj., Revenue Regulation and Decoupling: A Guide to Theory and Application 10–12 (2011).

Decoupling is controversial in part because its opponents believe it gives utilities the functional equivalent of increased rates without a rate case. Critics argue that it merely removes the risks of decreased revenues due to conservation, and represents a transfer from customers to utilities. Ken Costello, Natural Gas Revenue Decoupling: Good for the Utility or the Consumers?, Pub. Utilities Fortnightly, Apr. 2007, at 46–48. However, proponents believe it successfully removes the utilities' incentive to increase customer demand and provide an incentive for utilities to adopt efficiency and conservation programs, even if they still may not do so. Reg. Assist. Proj., *supra*, at 13.

C. THE SMART GRID

The term "Smart Grid," like "Internet," represents a wide range of infrastructure and applications on a modern network, in this case the electric grid. When President Obama introduced the stimulus package in January 2009, he called upon the nation to "update the way we get our electricity by starting to build a new Smart Grid that will save us money, protect our power sources from blackout or attack, and deliver clean, alternative forms of energy to every corner of our nation." Grant Gross, Obama includes broadband, smart grid in stimulus package, ITWorld, Jan. 8, 2009, http://www.itworld.com/.

But what is a "Smart Grid," and what technologies and changes to existing laws (or new laws) would be necessary to overhaul the existing grid to make it "Smart"? What is the relationship between Smart Grid technologies, on the one hand, and energy efficiency, generation technologies, and conservation, on the other? In the materials that follow, consider the challenges of moving from the existing grid to a Smart Grid, and what entities (federal government? state and local governments? private sector groups?) might or should have regulatory authority to oversee the transformation.

Section 1301 of the EISA 2007 (codified at 42 U.S.C. § 17381) established a national policy for grid modernization and listed a wide variety of goals and technology objectives of a Smart Grid:

1. increased use of digital information and controls technology to improve reliability, security, and efficiency of the electric grid;

2. dynamic optimization of grid operations and resources, with full cyber-security;

3. deployment and integration of distributed resources and generation, including renewable resources;

4. development and incorporation of demand response, demand-side resources, and energy efficiency resources;

5. deployment of "smart" technologies (real-time, automated, interactive technologies that optimize the physical operation of appliances and consumer devices) for metering, communications concerning grid operations and status, and distribution automation;

6. integration of "smart" appliances and consumer devices;

7. deployment and integration of advanced electricity storage and peak-shaving technologies, including plug-in electric and hybrid electric vehicles, and thermal storage air conditioning;

8. provision to consumers of timely information and control options;

9. development of standards for communication and interoperability of appliances and equipment connected to the electric grid, including the infrastructure serving the grid; and

10. identification and lowering of unreasonable or unnecessary barriers to adoption of smart grid technologies, practices, and services.

Joel B. Eisen, Smart Regulation and Federalism for the Smart Grid

37 Harv. Envtl. L. Rev. 1, 6–7, 10–12 (2013).

In 2009, the Department of Energy ("DOE") reported in its first biennial report to Congress that the Smart Grid may transform America as much as the Internet has done, redefining every aspect of electricity generation, distribution, and use.

The EISA describes the Smart Grid as a system capable of accomplishing over ten diverse objectives. Comprehensive policy frameworks from the federal government and state utility regulators, Smart Grid alliances, individual utilities and trade associations, and others contain proposals for specific actions and resource decisions. These visions are so different that they cannot be summarized or reconciled easily. Compare the electric grid to a reliable 10-year-old automobile that runs capably and enables its owner to commute each day. Improving electric utility infrastructure is like upgrading the car's systems, or replacing the car. The paradigm shift from centralized, one-directional power flow from generation resources through the transmission-distribution system, into two-way dynamic flows, is like selling the reliable car and switching to more complex but more efficient public transit.

Consider the implications of this breathtaking statement: "Just as the Internet connected commerce, banking, entertainment, digital media, voicemail systems, and all the other systems that generate or consume information, tomorrow's energy system should connect—or integrate—all of the systems and community assets that will consume or generate electricity." Advanced information and communication systems for this are largely absent. The electric grid "has a tradition of using many proprietary customized systems, and there has never been a need for information systems on the utility side of the meter to interact with systems and devices on the customer side of the meter."

Yet a Smart Grid means more than "computerizing" the grid. The upheaval we foresee must take place using the spirit of innovation that dominates our time. The "Smart" in "Smart Grid" should reflect the concept of dynamic innovation that has evolved over the past several decades. Innovation in networks takes place today on open platforms that draw on new energy, ideas, and distributed and meritocratic business practices. Disruptive technologies can produce rapid organizational changes, shifting power within an industry or displacing entire industries almost overnight. This phenomenon is ubiquitous today, and we must therefore avoid constraining the grid's Steve Jobs, who would see potential where no one has seen it before. One can imagine a Smart Grid decades from now that is entirely different from anything contemplated today. The term "Internet" (or "Internetting," as it was first called) was coined as the first network technologies were developed, but later evolved into a much different usage and understanding.

A Smart Grid is therefore different from today's grid in two fundamental ways. The first requires adding hardware and software to make the grid more intelligent, in both the utility and consumer domains. The second requires recognition of the spirit of innovation and potential for dynamic competition and new uses.

B. Disruptive Consumer Applications

The Smart Grid's potential for consumers is enormous. At present, a typical customer's interaction with a utility is limited to a wire into the house, a monthly bill, and maintenance trucks that roll in during storms. Like the dashboard of an early 20th-century automobile, a typical utility meter today has rudimentary instrumentation and only measures electricity usage. Customers receive monthly bills, often still on paper. Utility websites may not allow customers to see their usage data. Data presented are typically monthly usage totals, with little to no information on how much electricity individual appliances consume, or how consumers might alter their behavior to save energy and money.

The Smart Grid promises to dramatically change the relationship between utilities and their customers, starting with advanced communication systems. "Advanced metering infrastructure," better known as "smart meter" technology, is the Smart Grid component most visible to consumers. By 2015, 65 million American homes and businesses may have smart meters that enable two-way communication between utilities and customers. Smart meters allow customers to view their real-time electricity use. This has potential benefits for utilities, which, for example, can manage outages more efficiently, and connect new customers to the grid without sending trucks to their locations. Having near real-time information about energy usage can show consumers how to reduce consumption.

A smart meter could also show the real-time price of electricity, and help consumers save money. Demand for electricity peaks at various times during the typical day. Using a smart meter, a consumer could time shift and lower her electricity usage when demand and prices are high. As space age as it sounds, a properly-equipped washing machine could be programmed to run at lower-cost times, or the consumer could even allow the utility to control it, in return for financial incentives. Little of this is in place today, but manufacturers are scrambling to deliver advanced products to market. A smart meter can also make lower-cost charging of plug-in electric vehicles ("PEV") possible by charging cars during off-peak periods. Together with a management system, a smart meter can also link with battery technology (including the batteries in PEVs and hybrid-electric vehicles) to store electricity generated when it is inexpensive to produce. Storage is a potential game changer for the Smart Grid, if it allows consumers to buy electricity at inexpensive times and use it later.

Advanced communications systems can also expand consumers' "demand response" ("DR") opportunities. Demand response includes consumers' voluntary reductions in demand through programs that reward lower electricity use, and load control, by allowing a utility or authorized third party to control devices directly (for example, by shutting or cycling off a device such as an air conditioning unit in response to high demand on the system). Direct load control is increasingly becoming a valuable commodity of its own in wholesale electricity markets. Consumers could capture that value when a smart meter measures the reduction in demand, which today's load control equipment typically cannot do. DR can be important to a utility as part of its overall strategy to meet future anticipated demand and avoid unnecessary expenses of building new generation, transmission, and distribution infrastructure.

Yet while utilities have offered DR programs for decades, they have underinvested in them. The utility is in effect "anti-selling" its product, and state regulation traditionally rewards utilities for increased sales. State PUCs are only recently embracing "decoupling" incentives that reward utilities for promoting DR. The challenge of promoting DR will look like an opportunity to many firms. Third parties could compete with utilities by providing energy information and management services to consumers. Over time, firms that analyze customer data (data analytics firms, for example) may become adept at parsing through the massive data smart meters generate. Some are already hard at work trying to turn data into customer empowerment. Eventually, these firms might even purchase power at wholesale and supply their customers, as some firms are already doing with commercial buildings. Another possibility is that entire buildings or "micro-grids" might go off the electric grid altogether, using intelligent technologies to create local networks for distribution of electricity generated locally. ■

As this discussion suggests, a Smart Grid would have many different objectives and require many different technologies. Consider this schematic from DOE's 2009 Smart Grid report that shows the many areas of the electric grid that would be affected:

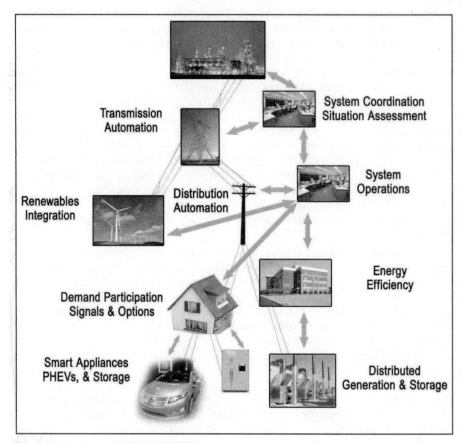

Figure 1.1. Scope of Smart-Grid Concerns

Figure 13–2
Smart Grid Impacts on the Electric Grid
Source: DOE, Smart Grid System Report 2 (2009)
http://energy.gov/oe/downloads/2009-smart-grid-system-report-july-2009

The Smart Grid could be a "nervous system" integrating all forms of generation, including distributed generation and demand reduction with traditional generation, transmission, and distribution systems in a more responsive, more environmentally friendly, less costly way. As one report puts it, the "ideal national clean-energy smart grid would use long-distance, extra-high-voltage transmission lines to move remote clean-energy resources to power load centers and connect to a distribution system that delivers energy and detailed, real-time information about the use of such energy to consumers." Bracken Hendricks, Ctr. for Am. Progress, Wired for Progress: Building a National Clean-Energy Smart Grid 12 (2009), http://cdn.americanprogress.org/wp-content/uploads/issues/2009/02/pdf/electricity_grid.pdf.

Specifically, the Smart Grid would

1)   provide expanded "Demand Participation Signals and Options" (demand response or "DR," discussed in the article above and more fully below); and

2) enable a wider and deeper deployment of distributed generation (see the icons in Figure 12.2 for "Renewables Integration," "Distributed Generation and Storage," and "Smart Appliances, PHEVs and Storage").

In addition, a Smart Grid would alleviate congestion that has become endemic, and by one estimate, currently costs consumers in the eastern United States $16.5 billion per year in the form of higher electricity prices alone. Ctr. for American Prog., *supra*, at 5. Congested transmission lines not only raise generation costs (by limiting the dispatch of low-cost resources), but also reduce grid operators' flexibility to deploy DG.

1. SMART METERS AND "DYNAMIC PRICING"

In the digital age, the existing electric grid is not as outmoded as a centralized telephone switchboard with operators pulling wires to connect calls. But it is hardly "smart." Could millions of small solar and wind generators connect to the grid and reduce the need for central power stations? Could millions of plug-in hybrid vehicles (see Chapter 15) connect to the grid, operate as sources of generation and storage and "burn" electricity rather than gasoline? All of this is possible, but requires advances in technology and new legal structures.

a. "SMART METERS"

The standard electric meter gives no information to consumers about the price of the product they are consuming. The "smart meter" and related technologies promise to change that dramatically.

U.S. Department of Energy Smart Grid
Status Report (2009)

http://energy.gov/oe/downloads/2009-smart-grid-system-report-july-2009.

3.1 Enables Informed Participation by Customers

A part of the vision of a smart grid is its ability to enable informed participation by customers, making them an integral part of the electric power system. With bi-directional flows of energy and coordination through communication mechanisms, a smart grid should help balance supply and demand and enhance reliability by modifying the manner in which customers use and purchase electricity. These modifications can be the result of consumer choices that motivate shifting patterns of behavior and consumption. These choices involve new technologies, new information regarding electricity use, and new pricing and incentive programs.

A smart grid adds consumer demand as another manageable resource, joining power generation, grid capacity, and energy storage. From the standpoint of the consumer, energy management in a smart-grid environment involves making economic choices based on the variable cost of electricity, the ability to shift load, and the ability to store or sell energy. Consumers who are presented with a variety of options when it comes to energy purchases and consumption are enabled to:

- respond to price signals and other economic incentives to make better-informed decisions regarding when to purchase electricity, when to generate energy using distributed generation, and whether to store and re-use it later with distributed storage.

- make informed investment decisions regarding more efficient and smarter appliances, equipment, and control systems.

3.1.1   Grid-Enabled Bi-Directional Communication and Energy Flows

A smart grid system relies on the accurate, up to date, and predictable delivery of data between the customer and utility company. Advanced metering infrastructure (AMI), unlike conventional metering systems, can incorporate bi-directional communication, including transmitting realtime price and consumption data between the household and utility, and coordinating with a Home Area Network. Currently, AMI composes about 4.7%, or 6.7 million, of total U.S. electric meters. The number of installed meters has been projected to grow by another 52 million by 2012. When customers are motivated by economic incentives through dynamic pricing structures or other programs, their investments in "smart" devices could facilitate reductions or shifts in energy consumption. "Smart" devices (e.g., communicating thermostats, clothes washers and dryers, microwaves, hot water heaters, refrigerators) use signaling software or firmware to communicate with the grid. For example, a "smart" water heater could be equipped with a device that coordinates with a facility's energy-management system to adjust temperature controls, within specified limits, based on energy prices.

Smart grid related technology, such as advanced meters, has enabled dynamic pricing programs implemented across the U.S. Generally, these tariffs take the following forms:

- Time of use (TOU). Under TOU, prices are differentiated based solely on a peak versus off-peak period designation, with prices set higher during peak periods. TOU pricing is not dynamic because it does not vary based on real-time conditions. It is included here though because it is viewed as an intermediate step towards a more dynamic real-time pricing (RTP) tariff.

- Critical peak pricing (CPP). Under a CPP tariff, the higher critical peak price is restricted to a small number of hours (e.g., 100 of 8,760) each year, with the peak price being set at a much higher level relative to normal conditions.

- Real-time pricing (RTP). Under RTP, hourly prices vary based on the day-of (real time) or day-ahead cost of power to the utility.

Smart grid also facilitates the bi-directional flow of energy, enabling customers to generate or store energy and sell it back to the grid during peak periods when prices are highest to the utility. In the future, as electric vehicles (EVs) and plug-in hybrid electric vehicles (PHEVs) penetrate the U.S. light-duty vehicle market, these alternative-fuel vehicles could also advance load shifting through their energy storage capabilities. The more than 12 million backup generators operated in the

U.S., representing 200 GW of generating capacity, could also be used to help alleviate peak load, provide needed system support during emergencies, and lower the cost of power provided by the utility. Most projections show increasing deployment of these resources, especially in the commercial sector where power quality and reliability are a serious consideration. Smart grid technologies may be required, along with DG-friendly regulatory structures, in order to integrate DG technologies.

3.1.2   Managing Supply and Demand

Measures, such as turning off or adjusting water heaters, dishwashers, and heating and cooling systems, result in load shifting and reduced costs through the smoothing of peak power consumption throughout the day. With appropriate metering capability in place, dynamic pricing signals received by customers can encourage greater demand response.

3.2 Accommodates All Generation and Storage Options

The ability to accommodate a diverse range of generation types, including centralized and distributed generation as well as diverse storage options, is central to the concept of a smart grid. Distributed resources can be used to help alleviate peak load, provide needed system support during emergencies, and lower the cost of power provided by the utility. Accommodating a large number of disparate generation and storage resources requires anticipation of intermittency, unavailability, while balancing costs, reliability, and environmental emissions. Accommodating the diverse nature of these options requires an interconnection process similar to the computer industry's "plug-and-play" environment.

Distributed generation and interconnection standards to accommodate generation capacity appear to be moving in positive directions. Another measure that impacts this category is dynamic pricing. Real-time tariffs would seem to drive the most efficient use of DG, bringing it on-line when prices are high and using more cost-effective central capacity when loads are more manageable. The use of smart meters, a driving force behind being able to evaluate grid load and support pricing conditions, has been increasing significantly, almost tripling between 2006 and 2008 to 19 million meters, although the increase from 2007 to 2008 was slower. Grid responsive load is just beginning to develop with 10% of utilities indicating limited entry into this field, with 45% saying it is in development and 45% having no plans. Both grid responsive load and microgrids can play a larger role once dynamic pricing and interconnection standards are universally available.

3.3.1   Enabling New Products and Services

A smart grid that incorporates real-time pricing structures and bi-directional information flow through metering and information networks is expected to support the introduction of numerous technologies into the system. Enabling AMI technology itself represents a major driver in smart-grid investment, as evidenced by several large-scale deployment programs:

- The three largest utilities in California are installing millions of smart meters at homes and businesses and charging customers $4.6 billion for the enhanced service.

- Duke Energy is installing 800,000 smart meters.
- Texas utility Oncor is installing smart meters at a cost of $690 million.
- Pacific Gas and Electric is retrofitting 9 million meters with communications electronics to enable TOU pricing.
- The Los Angeles Department of Water and Power has purchased 9,000 smart meters to enable transmission of real-time data through public wireless networks.

3.4.2   Smart-Grid Solutions to Power Quality Issues

Smart-grid-enabled distributed controls and diagnostic tools within the transmission and distribution system help dynamically balance electricity supply and demand, thereby helping the system to respond to imbalances and limiting their propagation when they occur. This reduces the occurrence of outages and power disturbances attributed to grid overload.

There are a number of technologies that serve to automate the transmission and distribution system and are enabled by a smart grid, including: Supervisory Control and Data Acquisition (SCADA) technologies, remote sensors and monitors, switches and controllers with embedded intelligence, and digital relays. Nationwide data has shown that transmission automation has penetrated the market, while distribution automation is primarily led by substation automation, with feeder automation still lagging.

The ability to track where power is going, what is being done with it, and when it is being used is paramount to addressing PQ issues. Further, the tracking of load served by service type, such as firm service or interruptible service, and their corresponding tariffs (fixed or marginal-cost based) will enable utility and government agencies to discriminate between consumer types, enable demand-curve estimation, and identify energy-consumption schedules.

3.5.2   Delivery Infrastructure

T&D automation devices communicate real-time information about the grid and their own operation and then make decisions to bring energy consumption and/or performance in line with their operator's preferences. These smart devices, which exchange information with other substation devices or area control centers, can increase asset utilization and smart-grid reliability as well as reduce operating expenses by increasing device and system responsiveness to grid events. T&D automation devices can aid in reducing the differential between average load and peak load.

Recent research found that about 60% of the control centers in North America have linkages with other utilities. Data from utilities across the nation show a clear trend of increasing T&D automation and increasing investment in these systems. Key drivers for the increase in investment include operational efficiency and reliability improvements to drive cost down and overall reliability up. With higher levels of automation in all aspects of the T&D operation, operational changes can be introduced to operate the system closer to capacity and stability constraints. ∎

b.   Dynamic Pricing

In regions with competitive wholesale markets for generation, real-time electricity prices change frequently. So with the right smart meter technologies and pricing programs in place, consumers *could* pay for electricity much as they do for airline tickets, hotel rooms, and sporting events and concerts, with prices based on the marginal cost of providing electricity under changing supply and demand conditions. If consumers had price signals in "real time"—as they do for other products like hamburgers or handkerchiefs—they could adjust their behavior accordingly. If prices were high, they could cut their demand for electricity, saving money on electric bills. As the DOE report notes above, there are several different types of "dynamic pricing," or pricing programs in which electric rates change over time, rather than being fixed.

Here is an explanation of the various types:

The most common form of time-varying prices is "time-of-use tariffs." Time-of-use rates set a time profile of prices far in advance, usually held constant over a season. For example, summer time-of-use rates might set a low off-peak rate that applies to weekday nights, early mornings, and weekend hours, and a higher peak rate for use during weekday afternoons and early evenings.

However, time-of-use prices are not truly dynamic. They do not, for example, distinguish normal July weekday afternoon conditions from those on an unusually hot day with a spike in air conditioning loads or an unexpected outage at a large generating unit. Dynamic prices can respond to those conditions, but dynamic pricing plans vary widely in the frequency of price changes.

At one end of the spectrum is "real-time pricing," in which retail prices change hourly (or more often) to reflect actual variations in the system's marginal energy cost. At the other end of the spectrum are plans that layer time-of-use tariffs with an infrequently invoked price change for so-called critical peak periods. "Critical peak pricing" programs enable utilities to designate, a day ahead, a small number of days on which demand is expected to be exceptionally high relative to available supply. On those days, they charge a price for electricity consumed during peak hours that is several times higher than the usual time-of-use peak rate. "Peak-time rebates" operate similarly to critical peak pricing programs, except that customers are given a credit for reducing consumption below their administratively determined baseline during designated critical peak hours.

Mass. Inst. of Tech., The Future of the Electric Grid 154–155 (2011), http://mitei.mit.edu/publications/reports-studies/future-electric-grid.

By some estimates, dynamic pricing could yield billions of dollars in savings for individual consumers. A survey of 24 utility pilot programs conducted in North America, Europe, and Australia between 1997 and 2011 found that programs yielded both cost savings and demand reductions, with CPP programs yielding the greatest reductions. Ahmad

Faruqui, Ryan Hledik, and Jennifer Palmer, Regulatory Assistance Project & The Brattle Grp., Time-Varying and Dynamic Rate Design (2012), http://www.hks.harvard.edu/hepg/Papers/2012/RAP_Faruqui HledikPalmer_TimeVaryingDynamicRateDesign_2012_JUL_23.pdf.

Two former PUC chairmen have stated flatly, "Smart meters don't offer value to consumers unless coupled with dynamic pricing." Phil Carson, Dynamic pricing alert! Best practices courtesy of two PUC chairmen, Intelligent Utility, Mar. 17, 2011. However, as recently as 2010, few utilities offered dynamic pricing, and only about 1% of residential consumers had time-of-use rates. FERC, 2010 Assessment of Demand Response and Advanced Metering, Staff Report 26–28 (2011), http://www.ferc.gov/legal/staff-reports/2010-dr-report.pdf.   Dynamic pricing of electricity faces continued opposition from those voicing fears that it would lead to higher electric bills for certain groups, notably senior citizens who cannot time-shift their consumption; the AARP has been a high-profile opponent of dynamic pricing. Paul L. Joskow & Catherine D. Wolfram, Dynamic Pricing of Electricity, 102 Am. Econ. Rev. 381 (2012). Press articles about dynamic pricing feed this perception, focusing on those customers who have complained that their rates are higher. Kate Galbraith, A Rough Rollout for Smart Meters in Texas, N.Y. Times, Mar. 9, 2010, http://greeninc.blogs.nytimes.com/2010/03/09/a-rough-roll-out-for-smart-meters-in-texas/; Smart Meters Raise Ire of Some PG&E Customers, KTVU.com, Nov. 18, 2009, http://www.ktvu.com/news/21660013/detail.html.

Before dynamic pricing programs are in place, consumers tend to associate them with high prices and price volatility. However, consumers who have lived with dynamic pricing, either in full-scale programs or in pilot projects, report high satisfaction. Consumer education and careful program design are critical. According to one observer, "to avoid the consumer backlash that has made headlines for two years, utilities must proactively educate their customer base on how dynamic pricing can be managed to control energy bills, provide tools such as web portals with customer energy use feedback and maintain trust and transparency as core values." Carson, *supra*.

Smart meter deployments are essential to the more widespread success of dynamic pricing programs. The federal government has provided significant incentives for the installation of smart meters and utility experimentation with dynamic pricing. The American Reinvestment and Recovery Act of 2009 (ARRA, known as the "stimulus law") appropriated about $5.0 billion to DOE for smart grid demonstration and technology deployment projects. About 130 projects were funded under the ARRA, with about $5.0 billion of matching funds from utilities and their customers. Much of the funding went to smart meters, IT and billing software, communications improvements, and other distribution network enhancements to take advantage of smart meter capabilities.

To many utilities, stimulus matching funds were critical to making the business case for AMI and dynamic pricing. Projects that appeared uneconomic looked more promising when the federal government was putting up half the money. This prompted some utilities to move quickly to establish Smart Grid programs, and Maryland-based Baltimore Gas and Electric Company (BG&E) was among the first movers. DOE

awarded BG&E $200 million under the ARRA for its Smart Grid
Initiative that included a dynamic pricing program.

Yet when BG&E sought approval of its program, the Maryland
Public Service Commission initially rejected it, sending a note of caution
to the rest of the industry.

In the Matter of the Application of Baltimore Gas and Electric Company for Authorization to Deploy a Smart Grid Initiative and to Establish a Surcharge for the Recovery of Cost Maryland Public Service Comm'n, Case No. 9208

Order No. 83410 (2010).

In this Order, we deny Baltimore Gas and Electric Company's
("BGE" or the "Company") Application for Authorization to Deploy a
Smart Grid Initiative and to Establish a Surcharge Mechanism for the
Recovery of Costs (the "Proposal"). Although we share BGE's (and
others') hopes, and even enthusiasm, for the long-run potential and
importance of the infrastructure upgrades known colloquially as the
"smart grid," we find the business case for this Proposal untenable. The
Proposal asks BGE's ratepayers to take significant financial and
technological risks and adapt to categorical changes in rate design, all in
exchange for savings that are largely indirect, highly contingent and a
long way off. We are not persuaded that this bargain is cost-effective or
serves the public interest, at least not in its current form. But we invite
BGE to revisit its Proposal in light of this Order and to submit an
alternative that addresses the issues we discuss below.

On July 13, 2009, BGE filed the Proposal with the Public Service
Commission of Maryland ("Commission"). The "Smart Grid Initiative"
aspect of the Proposal consists of three primary components: (1) universal
deployment of so-called "smart" meters and modules throughout BGE's
service territory over a three-to-five-year period, thereby replacing or
upgrading all existing electric and gas meters; (2) installation of a related
utility-to-meter-to-premise two-way communication network; and (3)
implementation of a mandatory Smart Energy Pricing rate schedule for
all residential electric customers ("RSEP") that would, among other
things, vary electricity rates during the months of June through
September based on the time of day and day of the week during which
the electricity is used (mandatory "time of use" or "TOU").

The Company estimates that the Proposal will cost $835 million–
$482 million during the initial deployment period and an additional $353
million over the expected life of the program. To be clear,
notwithstanding its name and the size of its anticipated price tag, the
Proposal would not, in and of itself, enhance the electricity transmission
grid or the Company's distribution "backbone." Rather, in order to realize
the reliability and efficiency benefits of a "smart" and "self-healing"
distribution system, the Company presumably would need to incur
significant additional expense in order to deploy an advanced automated
distribution control system that utilizes embedded sensors, intelligent
electric devices, automated substations, "smart" transformers, analytical

computer modeling tools, high-speed integrated communications, and reconfigured distribution circuits.

Nor would the Proposal result—at least not without further, substantial expenditures—in communication between the new, "smart" meters and appliances or other consumer products in BGE customers' homes to help them manage their energy use. Rather, the Company's advanced metering infrastructure ("AMI") Proposal encompasses "three foundational elements" of a broader "Smart Grid Initiative" that BGE envisions implementing at some future date.

BGE's Proposal is not solely a request for approval of the deployment of AMI. It also is a request to establish a customer surcharge for advance recovery of the costs of the Proposal, thereby shifting all financial risk to BGE customers. The Company seeks approval to recover those costs through a "tracker" surcharge that would begin appearing on BGE bills for both gas and electric customers almost immediately upon the Commission's approval of the Proposal, but before any of the infrastructure is installed or any benefits are realized. In addition to recovering the Proposal's capital and operating costs through the tracker mechanism, the Company proposes that the surcharge be used, among other things, to collect a return on the Company's net investment under the Proposal, as well as to collect Company "incentives" tied to anticipated wholesale capacity revenue, wholesale energy revenue, and wholesale capacity price mitigation resulting from anticipated changes in its customers' energy use.

The tracker virtually guarantees that the Company will recover from its ratepayers the prudently incurred costs associated with the Proposal, a profit for its investors, and a portion of certain projected benefits, if they are realized. In other words, with the proposed tracker in place, the Proposal is a "no-lose proposition" for the Company and its investors. In its filings with this Commission, BGE repeatedly has stated that cost recovery via a tracker mechanism is an "essential" element of the Proposal, and that it will withdraw the Proposal if the tracker is not approved.

It is clear that the timing of BGE's Proposal was motivated in no small measure by "[t]he availability of funding for smart grid investments from the American Recovery and Reinvestment Act ("ARRA"). We are mindful that during the pendency of its Proposal, BGE has received approval from the U.S. Department of Energy ("DOE") for $136 million in federal taxpayer funds that would partially offset the cost of the Proposal to BGE ratepayers. We are equally mindful, however, that a $136 million "discount" on an $835 million ratepayer investment cannot dictate the outcome here. Rather, in order to approve the Proposal, we must determine that it is a cost-effective means of reducing consumption and peak demand of electricity by BGE customers.

After careful consideration of the entire record in this case, we conclude that we cannot approve the Proposal in its current form. As an initial matter, we disagree with BGE that surcharge recovery is appropriate here. The proposed project is, in our view, classic utility infrastructure investment that should be recovered through distribution rates, not in a supplemental surcharge that begins long before customers could realize any benefits from the project. Just as we have declined other companies' efforts to move a broader range of expenses out of rate base and rate cases, we decline here to depart from the core principle that utilities recover the cost of infrastructure investments through distribution rates. If we were to approve a revised AMI proposal in the future, it would be appropriate to consider at that time whether to allow BGE to recognize a regulatory asset for the costs of the program.

At this time, we also will not approve a Proposal that imposes mandatory TOU rates on all BGE residential electric customers. A primary purpose of the Company's proposed TOU rates is to encourage customers to shift electricity use to less expensive, non-peak hours during the summer months. We agree with Maryland Energy Administration ("MEA") witness Fred Jennings that before transitioning to TOU rates: [I]t is critical that customers: 1) Are provided sufficient education so as to understand the new tariff and how their behavior and decisions will affect their energy bill, and 2) Are provided the equipment and technology, such as in-home displays, orbs, electronic messaging, etc. to receive the requisite information that triggers behavior changes.

Yet the Proposal contains no concrete, detailed customer education plan, includes no orbs or other in-home displays, and provides for grossly inadequate messaging, in our view, to trigger the behavior changes contemplated under the Proposal. Moreover, we are persuaded that some of the Company's most vulnerable residential customers, such as low-income households, elderly customers, customers with medical needs for electricity that cannot be shifted to off-peak hours, or other customers who are "stay at home" are less likely to realize the potential benefits of TOU pricing than would the "average" residential customer. Any future BGE AMI proposal should be supported by alternative business cases reflecting both opt-out and opt-in TOU scenarios, and should address, in detail, whether and to what extent those scenarios would affect the Company's business case.

On the benefits side of the equation, nearly 80% of the anticipated benefits of this Proposal arise not from operational savings, such as those expected to be realized from remote meter-reading capabilities, but from supply-side benefits, such as energy and capacity price mitigation, and monetizing in the PJM markets the value of projected energy and capacity reductions. Those supply-side benefits, in turn, depend upon fundamental changes in residential customers' energy use and the way most residential customers think about energy pricing, upon the operations of relatively new and difficult to predict energy and capacity markets, and upon the results of small-scale pilot programs that differed in important respects from the Proposal before us. In summary, and as discussed more fully below, the nature and magnitude of the uncertainties underlying the Company's business case raise serious doubts regarding whether the Proposal is, in fact, a cost-effective means of reducing consumption and peak demand of electricity in Maryland.

Although BGE claims that the assumptions underlying its business case are sound, the Company would have its customers bear all of the risk in the event those assumptions prove incorrect. We strongly support the overall goals of BGE's Proposal, which are consistent with many of the energy efficiency, conservation, and demand response initiatives that we have approved previously, but we conclude that BGE ratepayers should not exclusively shoulder the burden in the event that costs associated with the Proposal are greater than expected, or that anticipated benefits do not materialize. We therefore invite BGE to submit an alternative proposal that: (1) foregoes any expectation of recovery by way of a tracker surcharge mechanism; (2) provides a detailed business case that addresses the costs and benefits of proceeding without mandatory TOU pricing; (3) includes a concrete and detailed plan for how BGE intends to educate its customers regarding its new proposed rate structure; and (4) provides a workable methodology by which BGE will mitigate and more fairly allocate between the Company and its customers the risk that the proposal will not provide the benefits underlying BGE's business case, or that it will cost significantly more than BGE currently projects. ■

NOTES AND COMMENTS

1.   If dynamic pricing is so important to the success of a Smart Grid program, why did the Maryland PSC reject BG&E's proposal for it?

2.   The Maryland PSC appeared to be troubled by an asymmetry in the timing of projected costs and benefits of BG&E's Smart Grid Initiative. Operational benefits to the utility (cost savings from better capabilities to see where outages are taking place and responding to them, for example) accrue relatively quickly after smart meter installation. However, consumer savings could lag behind, especially if it takes time to design appropriate dynamic pricing and conservation programs.

How should a PSC evaluate a utility's Smart Grid proposal, if it believes the future benefits to consumers are too speculative to measure in the near term?

3.   Following this Order, BG&E amended its proposal, dropping the "tracker" and the requirement that all customers move into a time-of-use rate structure. In response, the Maryland PSC approved the proposal. Md. Pub. Svc. Comm'n, Order No. 83531, Aug. 13, 2010.

2.   PRIVACY, CYBERSECURITY, AND INTEROPERABILITY STANDARDS

The National Institute of Standards and Technology (NIST) has taken the lead in addressing a number of issues relating to Smart Grid technology. Its Conceptual Model provides a starting point for examining a wide variety of interactions among actors on the Smart Grid. Here is part of the model, showing a view of the many possible points of information flow:

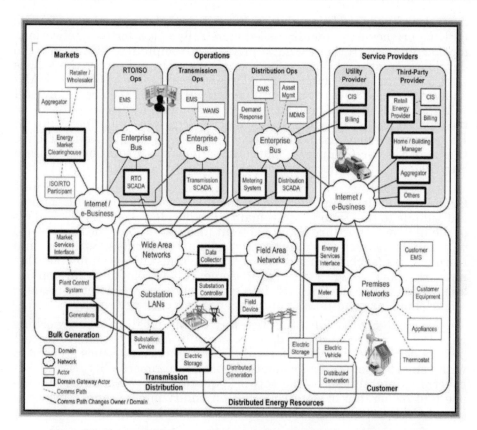

Figure 3-2. Conceptual Reference Diagram for Smart Grid Information Networks

Figure 13–3
NIST Conceptual Reference Diagram For Smart Grid Information Networks
Source: NIST Framework and Roadmap for Smart Grid Interoperability Standards, Release 2.0 (2012), http://www.nist.gov/smartgrid/upload/NIST_Framework_Release_2-0_corr.pdf

In **Figure 13–3**, note the "Energy Services Interface" at the Customer level—a gateway (separate and apart from the meter, but perhaps physically located with it) to interactions with service providers. The model anticipates that a home area network (HAN) gateway of some sort will eventually enable much more robust communications between devices inside the home and service providers outside it, and perhaps even remote control of HAN devices by a service provider.

NIST's model is for analytical purposes only. It does not mandate a particular form of the Smart Grid or prescribe the specific type of interaction. So the gateway could take a number of different forms. It could be a programmable thermostat with robust computer intelligence, an iPad, or even a cable box (as major cable companies are eyeing the energy management business). For example, the CPUC approved utilities' requests to include HAN gateways in its smart meter deployments, noting that it offers "[t]he most cost effective way . . . over the long term" of realizing the benefits of "enabling price signals, load control and near real time data for residential electric customers." The CPUC's privacy decision (discussed more fully below for its implications for keeping smart meter data private) attempted to kick-start the development of applications for the gateways by requiring the state's major utilities to file plans designed to enable a minimum of 5,000 HAN-enabled devices "to be directly connected with smart meters . . . even if full functionality and rollout to all customers awaits resolution of technology and standard issues." CPUC, Decision Adopting Rules to Protect the Privacy and Security of the Electricity Usage Data of Pacific Gas and Electric Company, Southern California Edison Company, and San Diego Gas and Electric Company, D. 11–07–056 (Jul. 29, 2011).

As California's action suggests, at this early stage of the Smart Grid's evolution, many details of the technologies that will connect individuals to the Smart Grid remain to be decided. As in the early days of the Internet, there are many different ideas about how the Smart Grid will enable two-way communication among customers, utilities, and third parties (such as energy services companies). For example, on this network, how could a utility or some other company develop an application to use fine-grained data coming off a smart meter to manage a household air-conditioning unit or charge an electric vehicle?

No matter what form this two-way communication takes, working with the new stream of big data expected to come from smart meters presents challenges never before addressed. Important issues associated with smart meter deployment involve interoperability standards governing interactions on the network, questions of privacy surrounding use and ownership of data collected on smart meters, and security of Smart Grid systems from electronic cyber-intruders.

a.   PRIVACY OF SMART METER DATA

Starting with privacy, the risks are readily apparent. The fine-grained usage data from smart meters is essential to a whole host of new uses, such as enhanced energy efficiency programs. Yet unlike the electric meters of the past, smart meters offer a direct view into household activities by providing more specific usage information and profiles about specific devices than ever before. Some worry that the information could be used to intrude on privacy, or even to regulate individual behavior. Katrina Fischer Kuh, Personal Environmental Information: The Promise and Perils of the Emerging Capacity to Identify Individual Environmental Harms, 65 Vand. L. Rev. 1565 (2012).

Consider this description of potential uses of smart meter data:

The privacy risks arising from smart meter and HAN device data are legion. Utilities may seek to monetize the information they collect from smart meters. Likewise, third parties may use this data to market products and services. In the wrong hands, this data about electricity usage may indicate when a home is occupied, exposing people and property to potential harm. Finally, legal privacy protections for utility records were developed around relatively unrevealing data—monthly aggregate consumption. Going forward, utility records will contain vastly more detailed data generated by interactions with the Smart Grid. The detailed data will make utility records a more attractive investigative tool, thus encouraging access requests by law enforcement agents and litigants in civil lawsuits, such as divorce proceedings. An analogy may be found in the use of cell phone calling records to obtain location information about criminal suspects: the steady increase in the use of cell phones has been accompanied by increasingly dense communications infrastructure that provides increasingly accurate information about a phone's location.

Deirdre K. Mulligan et al., Cal. Inst. for Energy and Env't,. Privacy in the Smart Grid: An Information Flow Analysis 6–7 (2011), http://www. law.berkeley.edu/11196.htm.

NIST had the following to say about these issues:

The constant collection and use of smart meter data has also raised potential surveillance possibilities posing physical, financial, and reputational risks that must be addressed. Many more types of data are being collected, generated and aggregated within the Smart Grid than when the only data collected was through monthly meter readings by the homeowner or utility employee. Numerous additional entities outside of the energy industry may also be collecting, accessing, and using the data, such as entities that are creating applications and services specifically for smart appliances, smart meters and other yet-to-be-identified purposes. Additionally, privacy issues arise from the question of the legal ownership of the data being collected. With ownership comes both control and rights with regard to usage. If the consumer is not considered the owner of the data obtained from metering and home automation systems, the consumer may not receive the privacy protections provided to data owners under existing laws.

NIST Framework, *supra*, at 119.

Here are two specific potential scenarios (among others) in which Smart Grid uses might pose privacy concerns:

Access by non-utility third parties to smart meters. Allowing third parties to obtain near-real-time electricity usage data could allow energy management services to compete along dimensions of price, quality, and privacy without requiring customers to purchase their own measurement devices. Establishing such third-party access will require balancing security requirements (such as the need to authenticate a party who wishes to access a meter) with a process that sets clear, non-discriminatory conditions for third-party access. It also requires privacy rules that flow with consumers' Smart Grid data.

Visibility into home area networks. Device registration or other aspects of communicating with devices on home area networks will likely expose device-specific data streams to utilities or third parties. These data streams will make it relatively simple for utilities or third parties to develop detailed customer profiles, including what kinds of devices a customer uses and when. With less precision, utilities and third parties may also be able to infer where a customer was active in the home by

> analyzing device-specific data streams or combining fine-grained energy usage information with auxiliary information about a home, such as its floor plan and the appliances inside.

Mulligan et al., *supra*, at 9.

States have taken the lead in addressing privacy concerns. The 2011 CPUC decision adopted the nation's first rules to protect Smart Grid privacy and security. CPUC, D. 11–07–056, *supra*. The decision created a consumer right of access and control, data minimization obligations, use and disclosure limitations, and data quality and integrity requirements. The new rules applied to utilities and their contractors, and provided that certain usage data used for "primary purposes" (such as use by a "third party acting under contract with the Commission to provide energy efficiency or energy efficiency evaluation services authorized pursuant to an order or resolution of the Commission") may be disclosed without a customer's consent. The "Green Button Initiative," discussed below in connection with interoperability standards, allows customers to have web-based access, including download capabilities, to their own data in a standardized format. This makes it easier for consumers—instead of utilities—to give third parties access to their information. However, the CPUC decision did not address the privacy and security of data in this situation, when consumers disclose usage data directly to third parties.

Other states have wrangled with data access and privacy issues, coming to different conclusions. For example, consider these contrasting approaches to allowing a utility to share usage data with third parties such as energy management companies. Pennsylvania provides that a utility "may not release private customer information to a third party unless the customer has been notified of the intent and has been given a convenient method of notifying the entity of the customer's desire to restrict the release of the private information." 52 Pa. Code § 54.8. On the other hand, Oklahoma allows disclosure of this information without customer consent if the third party certifies in writing that it will maintain the confidentiality of the data. 17 Okla. Stat. § 710.3.

Here is a typology of the states' different approaches to various issues relating to usage data and privacy. Which seems to be the best approach to balancing privacy concerns with the interest in making data available for productive uses? Why?

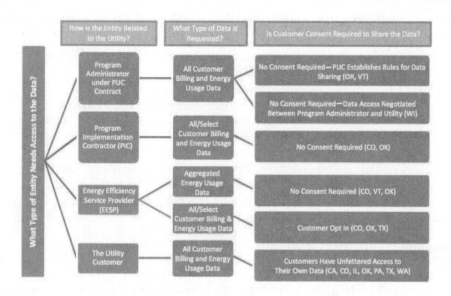

Figure 13–4
State Approaches To Privacy Of Smart Meter Data
Source: SEE Action (State and Local Energy Efficiency Action Network), A
Regulator's Privacy Guide to Third-Party Data Access for Energy Efficiency vii
(2012), https://www4.eere.energy.gov/seeaction/

b. CYBERSECURITY: KEEPING ELECTRICITY USAGE DATA SAFE

A subject related to privacy involves cybersecurity—protecting the electric grid against intrusion and data theft. Since the September 11, 2001 attacks on the United States, various studies have identified the electric grid as vulnerable to terrorist attack and called for cybersecurity improvements to protect it. Industry groups, regulators, and others have issued reports on this issue. A recent example is the comprehensive report by the National Academy of Sciences on vulnerabilities of the electric grid, including physical and cybersecurity risks. Nat'l Acad. of Sci., Terrorism and the Electric Power Delivery System (2012), http://www.nap.edu/catalog.php?record_id=12050.

The U.S. General Accountability Office (GAO) has described potential vulnerabilities on the Smart Grid that include:

- an increased number of entry points and paths that can be exploited by potential adversaries and other unauthorized users. Cybersecurity experts have demonstrated that certain smart meters can be successfully attacked, possibly resulting in disruption to the electricity grid.

- the introduction of new, unknown vulnerabilities due to an increased use of new system and network technologies. Supervisory control and data acquisition (SCADA) systems, if compromised, could allow hackers to disrupt operations and disable protective equipment. In July 2010, a sophisticated computer attack known as Stuxnet was discovered. It targeted control systems used to operate industrial processes in the energy, nuclear, and other critical sectors.

- wider access to systems and networks due to increased connectivity; and

- an increased amount of customer information being collected and transmitted, providing incentives for adversaries to attack these systems and potentially putting private information at risk of unauthorized disclosure and use.

GAO, Critical Infrastructure Protection: Cybersecurity Guidance Is Available, but More Can Be Done to Promote Its Use (2011).

If these threats sound worrisome, the lack of a coordinated response may seem even more troubling. According to former Federal Energy Regulatory Commission (FERC) Chairman Jon Wellinghoff, "Nobody has adequate authority with respect to both the electric and the gas infrastructure in this country regarding known vulnerabilities." Zack Colman, Official: Congress must establish electric grid cybersecurity authority, The Hill, Sept. 5, 2012. No single federal agency is in control of protecting the electric grid. Instead, guarding against cyber attacks is done by a patchwork of mandatory and voluntary cybersecurity standards and guidance by the North American Electric Reliability Corporation (NERC, the "electric reliability organization" (see Chapter 10) responsible for proposing reliability standards for the bulk power system for FERC's review and approval), NIST, FERC, DOE and the Department of Homeland Security.

In 2006, FERC approved NERC's Critical Infrastructure Protection (CIP) standards, making them mandatory and enforceable for all users, owners and operators of the wholesale power system. The most current version of the CIP standards is Version 5, proposed to FERC on January 31, 2013. The CIP standards consist of standards and requirements covering the security of electronic perimeters and the protection of critical cyber assets as well as personnel and training, security management, and disaster recovery planning.

NIST has identified cybersecurity standards as part of its Smart Grid interoperability standards effort (see below). In January 2011, NIST issued a first set of cybersecurity guidelines. NIST, Guidelines For Smart Grid Cyber Security: Vol. 1, Smart Grid Cyber Security Strategy, Architecture, and High-Level Requirements (2010). These guidelines addressed key cybersecurity risks and identified security requirements, but are not mandatory for utilities to follow.

Surveying the situation as a whole, GAO has criticized the "lack of a coordinated approach to monitor whether industry follows voluntary standards." GAO, supra, at 14. Recognizing the gaps in cybersecurity protection, federal agencies and President Obama have acted. In September 2012, FERC created an "Office of Energy Infrastructure Security" to coordinate its cybersecurity efforts. Ofc. of Energy Infrastructure Security, http://www.ferc.gov/about/offices/oeis.asp. A February 2013 Executive Order on cybersecurity (among other things) directed NIST to establish a Cybersecurity Framework which would identify "cross-sector security standards and guidelines applicable to critical infrastructure," and "areas for improvement that should be addressed through future collaboration with particular sectors and standards-developing organizations." Exec. Order No. 13,636, 78 Fed. Reg. 11,739 (Feb. 12, 2013).

c.   INTEROPERABILITY STANDARDS: EMPOWERING DEVICES TO COMMUNICATE

NIST's cybersecurity guideline was one product of its effort to develop "interoperability standards" governing interaction among devices and systems on the Smart Grid and allowing devices to communicate seamlessly with one another. Anyone who has visited a local coffeehouse and connected to the Internet via WiFi is familiar with interoperability standards, and their ease of use. The task of making it simple for actors on the Smart Grid to interact is a formidable one, as we don't even know yet what the Smart Grid is, let alone how to make sure of seamless interactions:

> To achieve interoperability in the Smart Grid, we are starting virtually from scratch, with hundreds of standards needed, and no common understanding of foundational matters such as what types of data are gathered or how they are exchanged. Talking about these matters is meaningless without grounding them in a broader context. It is impossible to talk about data without knowing what we are trying to accomplish with that data. Decisions about interoperability, then, are related to fundamental regulatory decisions.

> The technical challenges are daunting. Even a common vocabulary is hard to come by, as different technical disciplines use terms such as "reliability" in different ways. There is a spectrum of potential interaction among devices and systems. For example, two devices could be only physically connected, or have the ability to exchange data, or coordinate operations based on complex communication protocols and applications. The approach will be different at various locations on the Smart Grid. At some points, the quality of interaction might be loosely defined, but at others it might be tightly governed. The technology to accomplish interactions (as in the case of DG) is often not fully mature. Integrating legacy utility infrastructure, which generally lacks standardization, complicates matters further.

Eisen, *supra*, at 26–27.

The method chosen to develop interoperability standards was an unusual one, involving two different federal agencies and the private sector in a public-private partnership. Historically, private sector "standards development organizations" (SDOs) were responsible for developing technical standards. The Smart Grid standards effort would necessarily be different, as numerous factors (including the complexity of the effort, the short timeframe, and the requirement for different industries and their standards groups to work together) militated in favor of a federal solution. *Id.* at 40.

EISA 2007 did not displace SDOs, but instead tasked the federal agencies to work with them:

EISA Section 1305 gave NIST "primary responsibility to coordinate the development of a framework that includes protocols and model standards for information management to achieve interoperability of smart grid devices and systems." This section directed NIST to seek input and collaborate with FERC, the new Smart Grid entities, SDOs (including IEEE and the National Electrical Manufacturers Association), NERC, and the GridWise Architecture Council. NIST was directed to create flexible, uniform, and technology neutral standards and enable traditional resources, distributed resources, renewables, storage, efficiency, and demand response to contribute to an efficient, reliable grid.

Congress intended that FERC take an active review role, given its expertise and statutory mandates to regulate the grid. Once FERC finds that NIST has developed a "sufficient consensus" on standards, it must institute a rulemaking proceeding to "adopt" standards it deems necessary "to insure smart-grid functionality and interoperability in the interstate transmission of electric power, and regional and wholesale electricity markets." "Sufficient consensus" is therefore a threshold determination. Critically, the EISA did not give FERC any new powers to enforce any standards it might adopt, beyond its existing FPA authorities to regulate interstate transmission of electricity. Its role is limited to ensuring the standards' functionality. Congress created this two-step process because both agencies have expertise, but neither could handle the task alone. NIST has no regulatory role, and as the grid's regulator, FERC would benefit from NIST's technical expertise.

Id. at 28.

To handle the standards development effort, NIST created the "Smart Grid Interoperability Panel" (SGIP). The SGIP has thousands of members, including utilities, SDOs, companies involved in developing Smart Grid technologies, state PUCs, and others. Its various working groups do not directly develop or write standards, but instead work with SDOs that take the lead to create individual standards. In 2013, it became a private sector organization, with continued advice provided by NIST. *See* Smart Grid Interoperability Panel, www.sgip.org/.

In 2011, NIST transmitted the first five standards developed in the SGIP effort to FERC, which declined to adopt them in rulemaking, finding a lack of "sufficient consensus" in their development. Some observers felt this was a setback for the SGIP effort. Chris King, FERC says "consensus" lacking for smart grid standards: What consensus?, Smart Grid Watch, Jul. 27, 2011 (stating that "we are still at the starting line on determining the role of FERC in specifying how standards should be used, referenced, adopted or mandated in rulemaking"). Professor Eisen disagrees, noting that FERC endorsed the SGIP process. This side-stepped the problem of mandating standards. Because state PUCs have primary responsibility for deciding what standards utilities use in their projects, there would have been the potential for a jurisdictional dispute if FERC had required the states to use federally mandated standards. Eisen, *supra*, at 48. NIST has subsequently published standards in a "Catalog of Standards" that is available for state PUCs' use.

A prominent example of a new standard's use in the Smart Grid is the "Green Button Initiative," which aims to give consumers "standard, routine, easy-to-understand access to their own energy usage data." *See* Green Button, http://www.greenbuttondata.org/. A wide variety of utilities (representing nearly ¼ of all electricity consumers as of 2013) and other firms have adopted this standard, which is based on a data exchange standard developed in the SGIP process. A follow-on technology, Green Button Connect, allows households to automatically integrate their data with apps that help them analyze it, and may lead to more widespread use of the data. *See* Green Button Connect, http://www.greenbuttonconnect.com/. The Green Button websites allow consumers to download their energy usage information in a straightforward, standardized format, and share it (if they so choose and if state law authorizes it) with third parties. As Professor Eisen notes, "[t]his is as revolutionary in its significance as the Internet's first uses, for it hints at the potential for much more robust uses of the data." Eisen, *supra*, at 43.

3. SMART GRID "APP" CASE STUDY: DEMAND RESPONSE

Former FERC Chairman Jon Wellinghoff has called demand response (DR) the Smart Grid's "killer app." DR programs focus on reducing consumption at specific times when demand for electricity and its marginal cost of electricity are high. DR aims to achieve substantial benefits by reducing electricity demand at system-wide peaks.

In some DR programs, system operators, utilities, or even third parties (known as "curtailment service providers" or "aggregators") control consumption reductions. An example is "direct load control," in which customers receive some form of payment to allow a utility to reduce consumption. For example, a consumer might receive $50 per season to allow a utility to turn off an air-conditioning unit for brief periods of time at peak demand hours. In other DR programs, consumers control the reductions, reacting voluntarily to changing prices or other signals. In a "price-mediated demand response" program, the incentives established in dynamic pricing structures (discussed above) prompt customers to reduce or shift their consumption when the price is high.

The results from more widespread deployment of DR can be considerable. A 2009 FERC report estimated potential reductions in peak demand ranging from 4 percent to 20 percent, depending upon how aggressively policymakers and utilities pursue DR programs. FERC, Nat'l Assessment of Demand Response Potential, *supra*. In addition, the battles over regulatory authority over DR and the proper level of incentives for it have become an early test of how commercial development of the Smart Grid industry may evolve, testing fundamental principles along the way.

a. DR TYPES AND POTENTIAL BENEFITS

As FERC defines it, DR consists of: "Changes in electric use by demand-side resources from their normal consumption patterns in response to changes in the price of electricity, or to incentive payments designed to induce lower electricity use at times of high wholesale market prices or when system reliability is jeopardized." 18 C.F.R. § 35.28(b)(4).

Modern DR programs generally fall into three broad categories:

Historically, the most common form has been "load management or control" programs, which offer customers reduced rates or incentive payments if they agree to reduce their "interruptible" load under certain conditions. A variation of this approach allows the load-serving entity to directly control customer equipment or appliances.

A second category of demand response consists of programs administered by organized wholesale markets. ISOs and RTOs have developed a number of ways to incorporate demand response into wholesale markets as a dispatchable resource. These include allowing demand response to compete with conventional power plants as a capacity resource in forward capacity markets, offering demand buyback programs that allow customers to provide demand reductions at a specific price point, and allowing load to provide ancillary services such as spinning or regulation reserves. While such programs are generally most economic for large industrial and commercial customers, demand response aggregators have increased the participation of smaller customers, including residential customers.

The third category of demand response programs is price-mediated demand response. In these programs, customers face retail electricity rates that vary depending on the cost of electricity production at a given point in time, allowing them to reduce consumption when rates are high, or shift consumption to a time when rates are lower. The most common form of price-mediated demand response is time-of-use pricing.

While load management programs have historically accounted for the majority of demand response, the increasing penetration of technologies such as smart meters means that demand response opportunities, particularly in the residential sector, are growing substantially.

Bipartisan Pol'y Ctr., Policies for a Modern and Reliable U.S. Electric Grid 51 (2013), http://bipartisanpolicy.org/sites/default/files/Energy_Grid_Report%5B1%5D.pdf.

These programs may lead to increased conservation if usage at peak periods is eliminated rather than shifted: consider the effect of turning up an air conditioner thermostat or turning off lights during a summer weekday afternoon. The detailed, fine-grained data from smart meters may give consumers more opportunities to reduce consumption. However, whether DR will actually reduce overall electricity consumption is an open question. Some critics argue that DR will only result in time shifting of peak use, as consumers may react to high midday prices by simply shifting their clothes drying or dishwashing to other times.

Others point to a troubling aspect of DR for industrial and commercial customers: they can take less electricity from the grid, and back it up with diesel-fueled or other polluting generators. Some claim that the interplay between EPA and FERC rules may exacerbate this trend. In 2013, the EPA issued a final rule setting emissions standards under the Clean Air Act for stationary reciprocating internal combustion engines (RICE). National Emission Standards for Hazardous Air Pollutants for Reciprocating Internal Combustion Engines, Final Rule, 78 Fed. Reg. 9403 (Jan. 30, 2013). RICE includes some electrical generation facilities located on a company's premises "behind the meter" (not connected to the electric grid), like diesel engines typically used for backup, emergency, or supplemental power. The EPA's rule exempts one hundred hours of RICE operation in emergency DR programs. This, critics say, gives added incentive to large industrial and commercial customers to get paid in DR programs and satisfy their electricity generating requirements with polluting engines located behind the meter.

b.   DR IN WHOLESALE ELECTRICITY MARKETS (FERC ORDER 745)

The entities that run regional electricity markets—Independent System Operators (ISOs) and Regional Transmission Organizations (RTOs)—are increasingly incorporating DR into their systems as a dispatchable resource (one that can be called on to meet customers' demand). See Chapter 10 for a further discussion of wholesale electricity markets. Using DR as a resource in wholesale electricity markets can achieve a wide variety of financial and operational benefits. Traditionally, grid operators met increased demand on the system (peak demand on summer afternoons, say) by calling on available generation capacity—having a peaking plant run, for example. Yet under certain conditions, reducing overall system demand by 500 MW through DR could alleviate stress on the regional grid just as much as firing up a 500 MW power plant. ISOs and RTOs have realized this by allowing DR providers to bid—that is, to make specified quantities of demand reductions available at specific times—into their markets.

To understand how this works, remember that an ISO/RTO may administer multiple different types of markets, with opportunities for DR to participate in each:

(1) Capacity: In these markets, participants commit to serve future demand with (as yet unbuilt) new generating capacity. A bidder of a specific quantity of DR offers load reductions as a substitute for building the next power plants that would be built in the region.

(2) Energy: In energy markets, ISOs and RTOs offer programs that allow customers to provide DR as the equivalent of electricity sold in real time at the spot market price.

(3) Ancillary Services (such as frequency regulation): ISOs and RTOs also allow DR providers to bid DR to provide ancillary services such as regulation reserves. "Regulation" is a term of art in the electric industry that means keeping the frequency in balance on the grid. Some believe that DR can play an important role in this type of market, particularly to help in balancing out the intermittency of renewable resources added to the grid. Joel B. Eisen, Who Regulates the Smart Grid?: FERC's Authority Over Demand Response Compensation in Wholesale Electricity Markets., 4 San Diego J. of Climate and Energy L. 69, 80 (2012–2013). DR providers may also take advantage of FERC's Order 755, which changed the policies for pricing of frequency regulation service. Frequency Regulation Compensation in the Organized Wholesale Power Markets, 76 Fed. Reg. 67,260 (Oct. 20, 2011).

Professor Joel Eisen explains the mechanics of including DR as a resource in wholesale markets:

By pulling together demand reductions from a number of retail customers, an aggregator enables individual customers to take part in the market when they otherwise could not do so. Most residential customers cannot interact directly with the wholesale markets, as market rules in RTOs and ISOs require small-scale customers to do so through licensed intermediaries. The fundamental idea of curtailing an amount of demand larger than that of a typical household is not new. A traditional use of emergency DR going back several decades involves contracts between large industrial or commercial customers—such as major manufacturing facilities—and their utilities directly to allow the utilities to curtail their electricity use when necessary to balance the grid.

A wholly new business sector has arisen in the electricity market in recent years, in which firms such as EnerNOC, Comverge, and Viridity serve as intermediaries to the wholesale markets. They work with commercial customers to manage their electricity usage and handle the mechanics of bidding DR into the wholesale markets. Their portfolios to date typically consist of DR under contract with business and commercial customers. As noted above, these customers have a tradition of working with utilities to curtail electricity use on demand, so they are typically more familiar with DR and comfortable with it than residential customers. In the past few years, these companies have begun to market to the retail electricity sector, offering products and services tailored to households. The larger players in this sector are gradually becoming familiar to more customers although their reach in the residential sector is still relatively small.

Eisen, Who Regulates the Smart Grid?, *supra*, at 81–82.

DR can have numerous system-wide benefits. At present, demand on the grid peaks noticeably at a small number of hours each year. This "peakedness" can make the marginal cost of generating electricity highly variable, with the cost spiking at peak hours. Unanticipated outages or unusually high demand—think, again, of the higher use of air conditioners on a hot summer afternoon—may spike the marginal cost still further, as much as fivefold or tenfold or more. Reducing peak demand could cut these marginal costs substantially. Also, because system operators must have power plants on hand to meet peak demand, demand "peakedness" leads to oversupply of generating capacity. Many peaking plants operate for fewer than 100 hours per year, so DR could reduce peak demand and eliminate the need to build them. ISOs and RTOs increasingly rely on regional planning processes such as the PJM RTO's "Reliability Pricing Model" to decide whether new power plants are needed. PJM, Reliability Pricing Model, http://www.pjm.com/markets-and-operations/rpm.aspx. If DR were factored into these models, we could see less construction of generating capacity (and GHG emissions reductions).

However, DR faces technical and legal challenges, as it is not the same as building and running a power plant to generate electricity.

Someone must ensure that the precise quantity of demand reductions needed can be obtained at the right time from multiple consumers and controlled for as long as necessary. That can be difficult. In 2011, for example, EnerNOC petitioned the Maryland PSC to amend its contracts and reduce the amount of DR it contracted to provide, having found that it fell short of its promised amount. EnerNOC Seeks Changes to Maryland Gap RFP Contracts Due to Shortage in Meeting Obligations, Energy Choice Matters, Jun. 29, 2011.

Yet, recognizing the potential benefits, FERC has issued two rules designed to encourage more DR participation in regional wholesale markets. FERC believes that without its encouragement, there will continue to be limited participation by demand-side resources in the wholesale markets. To former FERC Chairman Jon Wellinghoff, the markets pursue a "strictly supply-side management strategy" and largely ignore the "second half" of the resources they could have available to meet demand. Jon Wellinghoff & David L. Morenoff, Recognizing the Importance of Demand Response: The Second Half of the Wholesale Market Equation, 28 Energy L.J. 389 (2007).

FERC's first rule, Order 719, required RTOs and ISOs to permit aggregators to bid DR on behalf of their retail customers directly into the wholesale energy markets, unless a state law prevented it. Wholesale Competition in Regions with Organized Electric Markets, 73 Fed. Reg. 64,100 (Oct. 28, 2008). Its second rule, Order 745, went further, requiring that DR be paid the market price:

> Order 745 governs DR bid in quantities of megawatt-hours (MWh) by intermediaries into day-ahead or real-time wholesale energy markets. These firms are known as "aggregators," "curtailment service providers," or, in Order 745's terms, "demand response resources." Under Order 745, aggregators that bundle demand reductions of individual residential and commercial customers and bid them into wholesale markets must be paid the same market price as generators, the locational marginal price (LMP).

Demand Response Compensation in Organized Wholesale Energy Markets, 76 Fed. Reg. 16,658 (Mar. 24, 2011). Complying with Order 745, grid operators have moved to implement "net benefits tests" that operate as a safety valve of sorts, precluding compensation below specific levels.

By ordering that DR resources must be paid the same as generation resources—the "locational marginal price" (discussed in Chapter 10), FERC views DR and generation as comparable because of the benefits that DR offers to wholesale energy markets. In Order 745's words, "an increment of generation is comparable to a decrement of load for purposes of balancing supply and demand in the day-ahead and real-time energy markets." Order 745, *supra*, at 16,662.

This view is highly controversial, and led to a high-profile challenge to Order 745 by a wide array of different groups, including the Electric Power Supply Association, the Edison Electric Institute, the American Public Power Association, the National Rural Electric Cooperative Association, and others. In May 2014, a split panel of the D.C. Circuit agreed with Order 745's challengers, vacating the rule over a strong dissent.

Electric Power Supply Ass'n v. FERC

753 F.3d 216 (D.C. Cir. 2014).

■ BROWN, CIRCUIT JUDGE:

Electric Power Supply Association and four other energy industry associations ("Petitioners") petition this court for review of a final rule by the Federal Energy Regulatory Commission ("FERC" or "the Commission") governing what FERC calls "demand response resources in the wholesale energy market." The rule seeks to incentivize retail customers to reduce electricity consumption when economically efficient. Petitioners complain FERC's new rule goes too far, encroaching on the states' exclusive jurisdiction to regulate the retail market. We agree and vacate the rule in its entirety.

I

Under the Federal Power Act ("FPA" or "the Act") the Commission is generally charged with regulating the transmission and sale of electric power in interstate commerce. The FPA "split[s] [jurisdiction over the sale and delivery of electricity] between the federal government and the states on the basis of the type of service being provided and the nature of the energy sale." Niagara Mohawk Power Corp. v. FERC, 452 F.3d 822, 824 (D.C. Cir. 2006). Section 201 of the Act empowers FERC to regulate "the sale of electric energy at wholesale in interstate commerce." 16 U.S.C. § 824(b)(1) (emphasis added). Thus, "FERC's jurisdiction over the sale of electricity has been specifically confined to the wholesale market." New York v. FERC, 535 U.S. 1, 19 (2002).

The Commission concedes that "demand response is a complex matter that lies at the confluence of state and federal jurisdiction." For more than a decade, FERC has permitted demand-side resources to participate in organized wholesale markets, allowing Independent System Operators (ISOs) and Regional Transmission Organizations (RTOs) to use demand-side resources to meet their systems' needs for wholesale energy, capacity, and ancillary services.

Order 745 establishes uniform compensation levels for suppliers of demand response resources who participate in the "day-ahead and real-time energy markets." The order directs ISOs and RTOs to pay those suppliers, including aggregators of retail customers, the full locational marginal price (LMP), or the marginal value of resources in each market typically used to compensate generators. The Commission conditioned the payment of full LMP on the ability of a demand response resource to replace a generation resource and required demand response to be cost effective. Cost effectiveness would be determined by a newly devised "net benefits test," which FERC directed ISOs and RTOs to implement.

Commissioner Moeller dissented, arguing the Commission's retail customer compensation scheme conflicted both with FERC's efforts to promote competitive markets and with its statutory mandate to ensure supplies of electric energy at just, reasonable, and not unduly preferential or discriminatory rates.

II

If FERC lacks authority under the Federal Power Act to promulgate a rule, its action is "plainly contrary to law and cannot stand." We address FERC's assertion of its statutory authority under the familiar Chevron doctrine. The question is "whether the statutory text forecloses the agency's assertion of authority." If, however, the statute is silent or ambiguous on the specific issue, we must defer to the agency's reasonable construction of the statute.

FERC claims when retail consumers voluntarily participate in the wholesale market, they fall within the Commission's exclusive jurisdiction to make rules for that market. Petitioners protest that retail sales of electricity are within the traditional and "exclusive jurisdiction of the States" and regulating consumption by retail electricity customers is a regulation of retail, not wholesale, activity. The problem, Petitioners say, is the Commission has no authority to draw retail customers into the wholesale markets by paying them not to make retail purchases.

FERC acknowledges "wholesale demand response" is a fiction of its own construction. Demand response resources do not actually sell into the market. Demand response does not involve a sale, and the resources "participate" only by declining to act.

As noted, and as the Commission concedes, demand response is not a wholesale sale of electricity; in fact, it is not a sale at all. Thus, FERC astutely does not rely exclusively on its wholesale jurisdiction under § 201(b)(1) for authority.

Instead, FERC argues §§ 205 and 206 grant the agency authority over demand response resources in the wholesale market. These provisions task FERC with ensuring "all rules and regulations affecting . . . rates" in connection with the wholesale sale of electric energy are "just and reasonable." 16 U.S.C. § 824d(a) (emphasis added); see also id. § 824e(a). Thus, the Commission argues it has jurisdiction over demand response because it "directly affects wholesale rates."

We agree with the Commission that demand response compensation affects the wholesale market. Reducing retail consumption—through demand response payments—will lower the wholesale price. Demand response will also increase system reliability. Because incentive-driven demand response affects the wholesale market in these ways, the Commission argues §§ 205 and 206 are clear grants of agency power to promulgate Order 745. The Commission's rationale, however, has no limiting principle. Without boundaries, §§ 205 and 206 could ostensibly authorize FERC to regulate any number of areas, including the steel, fuel, and labor markets.

States retain exclusive authority to regulate the retail market. Absent a "clear and specific grant of jurisdiction" elsewhere, see New York, 535 U.S. at 22, the agency cannot regulate areas left to the states. The broad "affecting" language of §§ 205 and 206 does not erase the specific limits of § 201. FERC can regulate practices affecting the wholesale market under §§ 205 and 206, provided the Commission is not directly regulating a matter subject to state control, such as the retail market. *Cf. Conn. Dep't of Pub. Util. Control v. FERC*, 569 F.3d 477, 479 (D.C. Cir. 2009) (finding FERC could regulate the installed capacity market under its affecting jurisdiction because FERC did not engage in direct regulation of an area subject to exclusive state control).

Demand response—simply put—is part of the retail market. It involves retail customers, their decision whether to purchase at retail, and the levels of retail electricity consumption. A buyer is a buyer, but a reduction in consumption cannot be a "wholesale sale." FERC's metaphysical distinction between price-responsive demand and incentive-based demand cannot solve its jurisdictional quandary.

Because the Federal Power Act unambiguously restricts FERC from regulating the retail market, we need not reach Chevron step two. But even if we assumed the statute was ambiguous—as Judge Edwards argues, we would find FERC's construction of it to be unreasonable for the same reasons we find the statute unambiguous. Because FERC's rule entails direct regulation of the retail market—a matter exclusively within state control—it exceeds the Commission's authority.

IV

Alternatively, even if we assume FERC had statutory authority to execute the Rule in the first place, Order 745 would still fail because it was arbitrary and capricious. A review of the record reveals FERC failed to properly consider—and engage—Commissioner Moeller's reasonable (and persuasive) arguments, reiterating the concerns of Petitioners and other parties, that Order 745 will result in unjust and discriminatory rates.

V

Ultimately, given Order 745's direct regulation of the retail market, we vacate the rule in its entirety as ultra vires agency action.

■ EDWARDS, SENIOR CIRCUIT JUDGE, dissenting:

Under the Federal Power Act, regulatory authority over the nation's electricity markets is bifurcated between the States and the federal government. In simplified terms, the Federal Energy Regulatory Commission has authority over wholesale electricity sales but not retail electricity sales, with the latter solely subject to State regulation. See 16 U.S.C. § 824(a), (b)(1). The consolidated petitions before the court call on us to parse this jurisdictional line between FERC's wholesale jurisdiction and the States' retail jurisdiction—a line which this court and the Supreme Court have recognized is neither neat nor tidy. See New York v. FERC, 535 U.S. 1, 16 (2002).

It is easy to see why FERC stated in its rulemaking that "jurisdiction over demand response is a complex matter that lies at the confluence of state and federal jurisdiction." On one view, the demand response resources subject to the rule directly affect the wholesale price of electricity. That is, the final rule's conditions operate to ensure that every negawatt of forgone consumption receiving compensation reduces both the quantity of electricity produced and its wholesale price. Focusing on this direct effect—direct, it bears repeating, because under the rule's conditions all demand response resources receiving compensation reduce the market-clearing price—it is easy to conceive of Order 745 as permissibly falling on the wholesale side of the wholesale-retail jurisdictional line. On another view, however, the electricity not consumed thanks to the rule's compensation payments would have been consumed first in a retail market. Focusing on the market in which the consumption would have occurred in the first instance, one can conceive of Order 745 as impermissibly falling on the retail side of the jurisdictional line.

The task for this court, of course, is not to divine from first principles whether a demand response resource subject to Order 745 is best considered a matter of wholesale or retail electricity regulation. Rather, our task is one of statutory interpretation within the familiar Chevron framework. The Commission has interpreted the Federal Power Act to permit it to issue Order 745. And it falls to this court to determine whether the Act unambiguously "sp[eaks] to the precise question," 467 U.S. at 842 (Chevron step one), and, if not, whether the Commission's interpretation is a permissible construction of the statute, id. at 843 (Chevron step two).

Because the Act is ambiguous regarding FERC's authority to require ISOs and RTOs to pay demand response resources, we are obliged to defer under Chevron to the Commission's permissible construction of "a statutory ambiguity that concerns the scope of the agency's statutory authority (that is, its jurisdiction)." City of Arlington v. FCC, 133 S. Ct. 1863, 1868, 1874–75 (2013). Absent an affirmative limitation under section 201, there is no doubt that demand response participation in wholesale markets and the ISOs' and RTOs' market rules concerning such participation constitute "practice[s] . . . affecting" wholesale rates under section 206 of the Act. 16 U.S.C. § 824e(a); see also id. § 824d(a) (providing that "all rules and regulations affecting or pertaining to [wholesale] rates or charges shall be just and reasonable"). Petitioners' arguments to the contrary ignore the direct effect that the ISOs' and RTOs' market rules have on wholesale electricity rates squarely within FERC's jurisdiction. The Commission has authority to "determine the just and reasonable . . . practice" by setting a level of compensation for demand response resources that, in its expert judgment, will ensure that the rates charged in wholesale electricity markets are "just and reasonable." Id. § 824e(a). It was therefore reasonable for the Commission to conclude that it could issue Order 745 under the Act's "affecting" jurisdiction. See id. §§ 824e(a), 824d(a).

In addition to challenging FERC's jurisdiction, Petitioners argue that its decision to mandate compensation equal to the LMP was arbitrary and capricious. Petitioners believe that the LMP overcompensates demand response resources since they also realize savings from not having to purchase retail electricity. The Commission, Petitioners insist, should have set the compensation level at the LMP minus the retail cost of the forgone electricity. But the Commission's decision in this regard was reasonable and adequately explained.

Having identified a problem in the wholesale electricity market, the Commission has a statutory obligation to do what it can to fix it. That is because FERC is charged under the Federal Power Act with ensuring that wholesale electricity rates are "just and reasonable." 16 U.S.C. §§ 824d(a), 824e(a). It must ensure that all "rates and charges made, demanded, or received by any public utility for *or in connection with* the . . . sale of electric energy subject to the jurisdiction of the Commission" are "just and reasonable." Id. § 824d(a) (emphasis added); see also id. § 824(a). And when FERC determines that a "practice . . . affecting" such a rate is unjust or unreasonable, it must itself determine and fix "the just and reasonable . . . practice . . . to be thereafter observed." Id. § 824e(a).

Consistent with its statutory duty and in view of the market distortions caused by inelastic wholesale demand, the Commission has initiated a series of reforms to open wholesale markets to "demand response resources."

For some years now, FERC has recognized that the direct participation of demand response resources in wholesale markets improves the functioning of these markets in several respects. First, it lowers wholesale prices because "lower demand means a lower wholesale price." Second, it mitigates the market power of suppliers of electricity because they have to compete with demand response resources and adjust their bidding strategy accordingly. See id. ("[T]he more demand response is able to reduce peak prices, the more downward pressure it places on generator bidding strategies by increasing the risk to a supplier that it will not be dispatched if it bids a price that is too high."). Third, demand response "enhances system reliability," for example, by "reducing electricity demand at critical times (e.g., when a generator or a transmission line unexpectedly fails)." Id. at **12 & n.76; see also Order 745–A, 2011 WL 6523756, at *6 ("[D]emand response generally can be dispatched by the [ISO or RTO] with a minimal notice period, helping to balance the electric system in the event that an unexpected contingency occurs.").

Petitioners argue that Order 745 is "in excess" of FERC's "statutory jurisdiction." We evaluate this contention under Chevron and defer to FERC's permissible construction of its authorizing statute, regardless of "whether the interpretive question presented is 'jurisdictional.' " City of Arlington, 133 S. Ct. at 1874–75; see also Connecticut, 569 F.3d at 481. The proper question is thus whether the Act unambiguously forecloses FERC from issuing Order 745 under its "affecting" jurisdiction. See 16 U.S.C. § 824e; Chevron, 467 U.S. at 842.

FERC's explanation of its jurisdiction under the Federal Power Act is straightforward and sensible. FERC has the authority and responsibility to correct any "practice . . . affecting" wholesale electricity rates that the Commission determines to be "unjust" or "unreasonable." 16 U.S.C. § 824e(a); see also id. § 824d(a). In its view, the ISOs' and RTOs' rules governing the participation of demand response resources in the nation's wholesale electricity markets are "practices affecting [wholesale electricity] rates." That is, an ISO's or RTO's market rules governing how a demand response resource may compete in its wholesale market, including the terms by which a demand response resource is to be compensated in the market, are "practices affecting" that wholesale market's rates for electricity. And FERC has determined that an ISO's or RTO's "practice" is unjust and unreasonable to the degree that it inadequately compensates demand response resources capable of supplanting more expensive generation resources.

FERC's explanation is consistent with our case law. In *Connecticut*, we considered whether FERC has jurisdiction to review an ISO's capacity charges. Capacity is not electricity but the ability to produce it when needed, and in *Connecticut* the ISO had established a market where capacity providers—generators, prospective generators, and demand response resources—competitively bid to meet the ISO's capacity needs three years in the future. Generation, like retail sales, is expressly the domain of State regulation under section 201, 16 U.S.C. § 824(b)(1), and the petitioners argued that by increasing the overall capacity requirement the ISO was improperly requiring the installation of new generation resources. We disagreed and held that FERC had "affecting" jurisdiction under section 206 because "capacity decisions . . . affect FERC-jurisdictional transmission rates for that system without directly implicating generation facilities." That the capacity requirement helped to "find the right price" was enough of an effect to satisfy section 206.

Order 745 does not require anything of retail electricity consumers and leaves it to the States to decide whether to permit demand response. All Order 745 says is that *if* a State's laws permit demand response to be bid into electricity markets, and *if* a demand response resource affirmatively decides to participate in an ISO's or RTO's wholesale electricity market, and *if* that demand response resource would in a particular circumstance allow the ISO or RTO to balance wholesale supply and demand, and *if* paying that demand resource would be a net benefit to the system, *then* the ISO or RTO must pay that resource the LMP. That is it. This requirement will no doubt affect how much electricity is consumed by a small subset of retail consumers who elect to participate as demand response resources *in wholesale markets*. But that fact does not render Order 745 "direct regulation" of the retail market. Authority over retail rates and over whether to permit demand response remains vested solely in the States.

To bolster their case, Petitioners invoke the specter of limitless federal authority if FERC is permitted to exercise "affecting" jurisdiction to issue Order 745. They caution that "the Commission's expansive interpretation of its 'affecting' jurisdiction would allow it to regulate any number of activities—such as the purchase or sale of steel, fuel, labor, and other inputs influencing the cost to generate or transmit electricity—merely by redefining the activities as 'practices' that affect wholesale rates."

This argument ignores the limitations we announced in CAISO, 372 F.3d 395. There, we held that FERC exceeded its jurisdiction when it replaced the board members of an ISO on the theory that the composition of the ISO's board was a "practice . . . affecting [a] rate" under section 206(a). We held that "section 206's empowering of the Commission to assess the justness and reasonableness of practices affecting rates of electric utilities is limited to those methods or ways of doing things on the part of the utility that directly affect the rate or are closely related to the rate, not all those remote things beyond the rate structure that might in some sense indirectly or ultimately do so."

These limits foreclose the parade of horribles marshaled by Petitioners. Like replacing the ISO's board of directors in CAISO, FERC could not, consistent with Circuit precedent, regulate markets in steel, fuel, labor, and other inputs for generating electricity, which constitute "remote things beyond the rate structure that might in some sense indirectly or ultimately" affect the wholesale rate of electricity. Order 745 passes the *CAISO* test quite comfortably because the demand response resources subject to the rule have a quintessentially "direct" effect on wholesale rates. There can be little doubt that FERC has the authority to review the justness and reasonableness of rates that are so closely connected with the healthy functioning of its jurisdictional markets; this, as we said in *Connecticut*, is the "heartland of the Commission's section 206 jurisdiction."

This court has no business second-guessing the Commission's judgment on the level of compensation. See La. Pub. Serv. Comm'n v. FERC, 551

F.3d 1042, 1045 (D.C. Cir. 2008) (noting that "[w]here the subject of our review is . . . a predictive judgment by FERC about the effects of a proposed remedy . . . , our deference is at its zenith"); Pub. Serv. Comm'n of Ky. v. FERC, 397 F.3d 1004, 1009 (D.C. Cir. 2005) (holding that "more than second-guessing close judgment calls is required to show that a rate order is arbitrary and capricious" (citation omitted)); Envtl. Action, Inc. v. FERC, 939 F.2d 1057, 1064 (D.C. Cir. 1991) ("[I]t is within the scope of the agency's expertise to make . . . a prediction about the market it regulates, and a reasonable prediction deserves our deference notwithstanding that there might also be another reasonable view.").

Whatever policy disagreements one might have with Order 745's decision to compensate demand response resources at the LMP (and there are legitimate disagreements to be had), the rule does not fail for want of reasoned decisionmaking. FERC's judgment is owed deference because it has put forth a reasonable multi-step explanation of its decision to mandate LMP compensation. First, responsive demand is a necessary component of a well-functioning wholesale market, and FERC understood that its obligation to ensure just and reasonable rates required it to facilitate an adequate level of demand response participation in its jurisdictional markets. Second, FERC concluded that market barriers were inhibiting an adequate level of demand response participation. *See id.* Third, FERC concluded that mandating LMP would provide the proper incentives for demand response resources to overcome these barriers to participation in the wholesale market.

FERC had jurisdiction to issue Order 745 because demand response is not unambiguously a matter of retail regulation under the Federal Power Act, and because the demand response resources subject to the rule directly affect wholesale electricity prices. And the Commission's decision to require compensation equal to the LMP, rather than LMP—G, was not arbitrary or capricious. The majority disagrees on both points. The unfortunate consequence is that a promising rule of national significance—promulgated by the agency that has been authorized by Congress to address the matters in issue—is laid aside on grounds that I think are inconsistent with the statute, at odds with applicable precedent, and impossible to square with our limited scope of review. I therefore respectfully dissent. ■

NOTES AND COMMENTS

1.   As the dissent notes, the Supreme Court has frequently rejected a bright line test for determining whether activity on the electric grid is "wholesale" or "retail," most recent observing in *New York v. FERC* (see Chapter 10) that the jurisdictional line is murky. That decision empowered FERC to regulate transmission even if it had retail level impacts. In the *Arkansas Electric Cooperative* case, also discussed in Chapter 10, the Court upheld FERC's ability to regulate wholesale rates that had impacts on retail markets. There, the Court stated, "it is difficult to square the mechanical line drawn in Attleboro and its predecessor cases, and based on a supposedly precise division between 'direct' and 'indirect' effects on interstate commerce, with the general trend in our modern Commerce Clause jurisprudence to look in every case to 'the nature of the state regulation involved, the objective of the state, and the effect of the regulation upon the national interest in the commerce.' "

Has the majority opinion followed these principles?

2.   The majority and dissent both mention *Connecticut Department of Public Utility Control v. FERC,* in which the D.C. Circuit empowered FERC to regulate capacity markets even if that impacted determinations of the need for new power plants, which is normally a state function. The majority distinguished that case on the basis that "FERC did not engage in direct regulation of an area subject to exclusive state control"; the dissent noted that DR regulation is like regulating capacity because it affects both wholesale and retail markets. Which opinion has the better of this argument?

Two circuit court decisions issued after *Electric Power Supply Association* reaffirm the principle that FERC has plenary jurisdiction over capacity markets, rejecting state laws affecting these markets. PPL EnergyPlus, LLC v. Nazarian, 753 F.3d 467 (4th Cir. 2014), petition for cert. filed, No. 14-614, No. 14-623 (Nov. 25 & 26, 2014); and PPL EnergyPlus, LLC v. Solomon, 766 F.3d 241 (3d Cir. 2014), petition for cert. filed, No. 14-634, No. 14-694 (Nov. 26, 2014 & Dec. 10, 2014). See Chapter 10 for further discussion.

3.   The majority and dissent both cite *Chevron*'s two-step analysis. How do their approaches differ, and which conclusion is more proper? Why? What is the relevance of the Supreme Court's holding in *City of Arlington* that *Chevron* deference extends to an agency's interpretation of its own jurisdiction under its statutory mandates?

4.   The D.C. Circuit's rejection of FERC's attempt to reshape the wholesale markets may be as significant as *New York v. FERC*, as it may put other FERC efforts to use the wholesale markets to advance energy and environment goals in immediate jeopardy if they are not directly related to energy sales. One is FERC Order 755 on pricing grid frequency regulation service, discussed above. FERC's emerging policies on energy storage in Orders 755 and 784 may also come under fire. *See* Third-Party Provision of Ancillary Services; Accounting and Financial Reporting for New Electric Storage Technologies, 78 Fed. Reg. 46,178 (July 30, 2013).

5.   After FERC's first DR rule, Order 719, several states regulated aggregators' business practices. A report found that this state regulation created "significant institutional and regulatory barriers" to DR aggregators' participation in wholesale markets. Peter Cappers et al., Demand Response in U.S. Electricity Markets: Empirical Evidence 26 (2009). An example is discussed in the D.C. Circuit's decision in *Indiana Utility Regulatory Commission v. FERC*, cited briefly in the *Electric Power Supply Association* majority opinion. There, side-stepping the jurisdictional issues raised in *Electric Power Supply Association*, the D.C. Circuit overturned an Indiana state law precluding customers from enrolling with aggregators without the state PUC's prior approval.

Presumably, if the panel decision in *Electric Power Supply Association* stands, some states may find it prudent to implement DR programs, but others may put up roadblocks (as Indiana did). Can the two D.C. Circuit decisions be reconciled?

6.   The future of wholesale market DR participation is cloudy. Under the panel decision in *Electric Power Supply Association*, FERC cannot require DR bids into the wholesale markets, or prices at LMP. How might it still be able to encourage DR indirectly? If a state established a DR program, what

could FERC do to encourage companies to offer DR resources into wholesale markets?

* * *

Electric Power Supply Association raises fundamental questions about the Smart Grid. Order 745 intends to put upstart DR aggregators and entrenched incumbent utilities on a level playing field. DR can be the Smart Grid's "killer app" if aggregators, spurred on by Order 745's financial incentives, kick-start the development of an industry of energy services providers, finding new and innovative ways to take advantage of smart meter data and compete with traditional utilities. But will competition come? We cannot be sure. The firms jumping headlong into DR are not household names—yet—and may suffer a setback if the *Electric Power Supply Association* panel decision stands.

The litigation over Order 745 therefore foreshadows debates yet to come about commercial use of the Smart Grid. What level of government regulates the Smart Grid's development? Should federal and state governments allow or even encourage competition to develop Smart Grid technologies—even if it threatens to disrupt the business models of incumbent utilities? These and many other questions may be unanswered for years to come.

CHAPTER 14

INTERNATIONAL ENERGY MARKETS

Energy lawyers today cannot escape the reality that energy production and delivery have global implications, and that energy markets are international in scope. This reality raises many issues regarding the scope and reach of domestic laws, the effect of international trade laws, and the impact of international environmental law treaties. It also implicates U.S. companies in the sphere of human rights violations that may take place abroad in non-democratic states and states plagued by civil war, lawlessness and extreme poverty.

This chapter begins with a discussion of the legal and policy issues that surround expansion of fossil fuel exports from the United States—a trend that is leading to increasing integration of U.S. and international energy markets. The chapter then discusses how international trade laws, such as the General Agreement on Tariffs and Trade (GATT), can affect a nation's domestic policies that subsidize or otherwise favor domestic resources. This section highlights recent disputes at the World Trade Organization (WTO) involving solar-panel dumping by China and Ontario's use of feed-in tariffs to promote renewables in a manner that favored domestic content in the provision of renewable generation. It also discusses the regional trade agreement closest to home: the North American Free Trade Agreement (NAFTA) among the United States, Mexico, and Canada and how it may apply to cross-border infrastructure projects. The third section of the chapter addresses the extraterritorial scope of U.S. laws: What U.S. laws apply to a company's operations that take place in a foreign country? The chapter concludes by examining the role of international law in governing extractive operations abroad in the areas of human rights and the environment. Both the "hard law" of treaties and the "soft law" of industry-created codes of conduct and United Nations general principles are discussed.

A. U.S. ENERGY EXPORTS: DOMESTIC LEGAL AND POLICY ISSUES

Coal, oil, and natural gas are commodities that are bought and sold on global markets. The United States both imports and exports these products, depending largely on how competitive U.S. suppliers are in pricing these commodities in global markets, but also on the policy framework. International markets, especially for oil, are often highly volatile, as prices fluctuate with geopolitical events. In 2014, despite great instability in Iraq and Libya (in addition to Western sanctions imposed on Iranian oil exports), the price of crude oil fell dramatically because Saudi Arabia refused to cut back its production and U.S. shale oil production continued to surge. *See* Ben Hubbard and Clifford Krauss, As Oil Prices Plummet, Saudi Arabia Faces a Test of Strategy, N.Y. Times, Oct. 10, 2014.

U.S. law has long imposed restrictions on the export of oil and natural gas, but not coal. Despite this policy difference, oil and coal are much more "global" commodities than natural gas. The price to American consumers of these two products is determined by international market forces of supply and demand, whereas the price of natural gas, to date, has been largely determined by regional markets because of transport constraints. Long-distance gas pipelines are very expensive to build and cannot cross the large bodies of water that often separate gas-producing countries from gas-consuming countries. However, with advances in LNG (liquefied natural gas) technology in the past 25 years, gas can now be converted to liquid by cooling it to a very low temperature. As a liquid, it can be shipped in large LNG tankers that can cross oceans and serve distant markets on other continents. Natural gas is now becoming a more global commodity, and the United States is poised to become a net LNG exporter as American shale gas producers seek international buyers for their surging production. U.S. shale oil producers also seek export markets for their crude oil supply surplus. Chapter 4 describes the boom in U.S. shale oil and gas production caused by the new technologies of horizontal drilling and hydraulic fracturing. U.S. coal producers are similarly seeking more access to international markets, particularly in Asia.

This section explores the domestic policies that control oil, natural gas, and coal exports, including the legal requirement that oil and gas exports must be found to be in the "public interest"; what environmental externalities must be considered in authorizing exports; and whether fossil fuel supplies should stay within U.S. borders for reasons of price and national security. As producers have pushed to export their burgeoning supplies of crude oil and gas, some politicians and energy users have argued that we should limit fuel exports to maintain a cheap and reliable supply of domestic energy. Some environmental groups also oppose exports because these exports will encourage the production of even more fossil fuels within the United States. *See* Russell Gold & Keith Johnson, Odd Alliance Says No to Gas Exports, Wall St. J., Mar. 9, 2012 (describing Sierra Club opposition to natural gas exports and the American Chemistry Council's concerns about "undermining the availability of domestic natural gas"). With greater access to international markets, U.S. fossil fuel producers can be expected to extract more, thereby generating more environmental externalities within the United States and more greenhouse gas emissions globally. Indeed, some commentators note that as we reduce the use of certain fossil fuels (notably coal) to improve U.S. air quality and reduce carbon emissions at home, little net environmental benefit may accrue globally if we simply export these fuels. *See* James E. Parker Flynn, A Race to the Middle in Energy Policy, 15 Sustainable Dev. L. & Pol'y 4 (2015).

U.S. producers of fossil fuels, on the other hand, point to the fact that natural gas in 2014 sells in some international markets for as much as four times its domestic price in the United States. Producers in other countries have freer access to the high-priced gas markets in Asia and Europe and these competitors may foreclose U.S. producers from access to valuable long-term contracts. *See* Christina Buurma, Asian Tigers Stalk U.S. Gas as Louisiana Shale Profits Taper, Bloomberg, Feb. 20, 2014, http://www.bloomberg.com/news/articles/2014-02-20/asian-tigers-stalk-u-s-gas-as-louisiana-shale-profits-taper. As exports of natural gas to Asia and Europe increase from a growing number of gas-producing countries (including Australia and African nations), the regional price differentials that currently exist in the global natural gas market will decline. Whether relatively high-cost shale gas producers in the United States can still compete against producers in other countries for LNG markets when prices in Europe and Asia have converged to lower levels remains to be seen.

The United States remains an energy importer despite recent attention to exports. The following text interweaves some discussion of imports with the issues arising about coal, oil and gas exports.

1. COAL

The United States has abundant coal reserves, and although U.S. coal production declined from 2011 to 2012, largely due to low natural gas prices, the Energy Information Administration (EIA) projects that U.S. coal production will gradually increase through 2030 and then stabilize. EIA, Coal Production Growth Limited by Competitive Fuel Prices and Little New Coal-Fired Capacity, Annual Energy Outlook 2014, http://www.eia.gov/forecasts/aeo/MT_coal.cfm?src=Coal-b1.   Even   if domestic use of coal declines because of the Environmental Protection Agency's (EPA) greenhouse gas (GHG) regulations and other air quality and energy-related regulations such as renewable portfolio standards discussed in Chapters 5 and 11, coal production for export is likely to continue. EIA projects that U.S. coal exports will remain stable through 2020 and then increase. *Id*.

Coal companies in the Western states view exports of coal as essential to their future due to declining U.S. demand for coal. Beth Ward, Proposed Coal Export Terminals Offer US Producers Options, Platts, Oct. 5, 2012, http://www.platts.com/news-feature/2012/coal/coal exports/index. To date, these companies have exported a limited amount of U.S. coal through three export terminals on Canada's West Coast. *Id*. But these terminals do not have enough capacity for additional U.S. coal exports. The coal export terminals already operating in the United States are primarily in the East and Southeast, with the exception of the Los Angeles/Long Beach Coal export terminal. Oxbow, Long Beach, Overview,   http://www.oxbow.com/Services_Terminals_Long_Beach. html. Due to the limited availability of Western coal export infrastructure, developers had proposed five coal export terminals in the Pacific Northwest as of 2012. Ward, *supra*. Environmental and other groups have forcefully opposed these terminals.

The proposed Gateway Pacific Terminal (GPT), to be located at Cherry Point in Whatcom County, Washington, illustrates the regulatory process that coal export developers are undergoing. The GPT includes two main developers—Pacific International Terminals (PIT) and BNSF Railway. The latter "has proposed adding rail facilities adjacent to the terminal site and installing a second track" near an existing rail spur. State of Washington Dep't of Ecology, Gateway Pacific Terminal at Cherry Point Proposal, http://www.ecy.wa.gov/geographic/gateway pacific/. The U.S. Army Corps of Engineers (Corps) describes the proposed project as follows:

> Pacific International Terminals (PIT) proposes to construct and operate the Gateway Pacific Terminal (GPT), a multimodal marine terminal for export of multiple dry-build commodities including a deep-draft wharf with access trestle and other associated upland facilities. The PIT project would be developed on approximately 350 acres of a 1,500-acre site and would include a three-berth, deep-water wharf. The new wharf would be 2,980 feet long and 105 feet wide with access provided by an approximately 1,100-foot-long and 50-foot-wide trestle built on approximately 730 steel piles, each 48 inches in diameter. Upland facilities would include two commodity storage areas, each serviced by a rail loop. Each area would contain support facilities, such as roads, maintenance buildings, and stormwater treatment systems. . . . Commodities would be delivered to the PIT project site by rail via the existing BNSF Railway (BNSF) Custer Spur line off the Bellingham subdivision main line. The initial targeted commodity is coal from Powder River Basin sources for export to Asian markets. . . .

> Interrelated to the PIT project, the existing 6.2-mile-long Custer Spur extending from the BNSF mainline down into the Cherry Point Industrial Urban Growth Area would be upgraded to support increased traffic. The upgrades to the existing rail spur are proposed to service multiple industrial users in the Cherry Point area, but the Corps considers BNSF's proposed project "connected" to the PIT's proposed project because the PIT project cannot proceed without the BNSF project. . . .

> * * *

> The wharf and trestle portion of the project site would occupy approximately 30 acres of intertidal and subtidal waters of the Strait of Georgia. . . . The overall [BNSF spur rail] corridor is approximately 6.50 miles long (approximately 200 acres) and is comprised of an existing dual rail line, switchyards, road crossings, and adjacent pastures, forests, and scrub/shrub areas. . . . The Project corridor contains approximately 9 stream crossings and 35 acres of wetlands.

U.S. Army Corps of Engineers, Mem. for R., NWS–2008–260, Pacific International Terminals, Inc.; NWS–2011–325, BNSF Railways at 1–3,

July 3, 2013, http://www.nws.usace.army.mil/Portals/27/docs/regulatory/ News/SCOPEMFRGATEWAYBNSF.pdf.

The Corps must approve this and other export terminals under Section 10 of the Rivers and Harbors Appropriation Act of 1899, 33 U.S.C. § 403, which states: "[I]t shall not be lawful to build or commence the building of any wharf, pier, dolphin, boom, weir, breakwater, bulkhead, jetty, or other structures in any port, roadstead, haven, harbor, canal, navigable river, or other water of the United States, outside established harbor lines, or where no harbor lines have been established, except on plans recommended by the Chief of Engineers and authorized by the Secretary of War." If some of the terminal infrastructure will be placed in wetlands or other waters inland, the Corps also must approve this infrastructure under Section 404 of the Clean Water Act (see Chapter 3), which prohibits the discharge of dredge or fill materials into U.S. waters without a permit from the Corps that determines where the material may be discharged. Placing posts in streams for railroad crossings requires digging up the substrate of the stream and placing that substrate somewhere and is thus "dredge and fill" activity requiring a Section 404 permit. 33 U.S.C. § 1344. Further, the GPT must receive certification from the State of Washington under Section 401 of the Clean Water Act (33 U.S.C. § 1341) that the federally-permitted project will not violate state water quality standards (see Chapter 6). *See* Letter from Mark Knudsen, Pacific International Terminals, to Michelle Walker, U.S. Army Corps of Engineers & Loree' L. Randall, State of Washington, Dep't of Ecology, June 27, 2012, http://www.ecy.wa.gov/geographic/gateway pacific/20120627_jarpaletter.pdf (describing the status of the 401 certification process).

A number of other entities are also involved in the regulatory process for approving coal export terminals. The U.S. Fish and Wildlife Service and National Marine Fisheries Services have jurisdiction over impacts on threatened and endangered species. If these species will be "taken" (harmed) by the terminal, including harm to habitat, the developer must obtain an incidental take permit from one of these agencies and implement a plan for limiting harm to the species. 16 U.S.C. § 1538. The National Marine Fisheries Service also must address impacts of the project on fish populations in the area under the Magnuson-Stevens Fishery Conservation and Management Act, and on marine mammals like seals, sea lions, whales, and dolphins under the Marine Mammal Protection Act. 16 U.S.C. § 1855; *id.* § 1372. Further, EPA regulates emissions of air and water pollutants (other than dredge and fill) from the terminals under the Clean Air and Clean Water Acts. Other federal agencies that cooperate in the approval of coal export terminals include the U.S. Coast Guard and the U.S. Department of Transportation/Federal Railroad Administration. *See, e.g.*, Corps, Mem. for Record, *supra*. As the Corps explains, "[c]ommercial vessels calling at the Gateway Pacific Terminal will be required to operate within the U.S. Coast Guard's designated vessel traffic lanes until they reach" the terminal. *Id.*

State agencies also play a role in terminal approval. Under the federal Coastal Zone Management Act (discussed in Chapter 4), states have the option to implement zoning-type laws that restrict the use of their shore lines. Washington and Oregon have done this in their state

Coastal Zone Management Program Documents, and their coastal plans have received federal approval. Federal projects that impact the state's planned use of the coastal zone and its resources (as described in these Program Documents) must be consistent with the state's coastal zone plan. This "consistency review," asking whether the project meets the state's requirements for protecting land and water resources in the coastal area, is a key component of approving coal export terminals. Other state and local requirements include shoreline development permits. In Washington state, for example, Pacific International Terminals submitted applications for a "shoreline substantial development permit and a major development permit for construction and operation of the terminal" to Whatcom County. State of Washington, Dep't of Ecology, Gateway Pacific Terminal at Cherry Point Proposal, http://www.ecy.wa.gov/geographic/gatewaypacific/. Further, Washington has a State Environmental Policy Act (SEPA), similar to the federal National Environmental Policy Act (NEPA), which requires projects that have substantial impacts to undergo environmental review prior to commencing. For the proposed Gateway Pacific Terminal, Whatcom County and the Washington Department of Ecology are working as co-leads in preparing the state environmental impact statement (EIS) for the terminal, as described in the following excerpt:

> February 2012—Determine if there will be impacts: As co-leads in the state environmental review process, Ecology and Whatcom County confirmed this and prepared to issue a determination of significance.

> March 2012—Have an informational meeting: The co-lead agencies conducted a meeting Tuesday, March 20, 2012, in Bellingham to explain the environmental review process, the agencies' roles and responsibilities, the public's opportunities to engage in the process, and to answer questions. . . .

> May 2012—Hire a contractor: The co-lead agencies selected a contractor to help prepare an [EIS]. . . .

> Sept. 24, 2012 to Jan. 21, 2013—Scoping—deciding what factors to analyze and what geographic area to consider: The co-lead agencies ask other agencies, tribes and the public to comment on what the environmental impact statement should analyze. Examples of possible factors to consider include stormwater, wetlands, air emissions, noise, and traffic. After considering comments, the lead agencies will decide what should be included in the environmental impact statement.

> March 29, 2013—Scoping Summary Report: The co-lead agencies issued a summary of the comments received during the scoping public comment period that took place Sept. 24, 2012 to January 22, 2013, as well as a description of the public meetings and the various ways that comments were received. . . .

> July 31, 2013—EIS scope announcement: Ecology, Whatcom County and the U.S. Army Corps of Engineers announced the preliminary scope—or extent of evaluation—for the EIS. . . .

> August 30, 2013—Proposal to receive separate NEPA and SEPA EISs: The U.S. Army Corps of Engineers informed Ecology and Whatcom County that it would prepare a separate NEPA EIS,

but wanted to continue to coordinate EIS development among the co-lead agencies. The Corps will prepare a NEPA EIS and Ecology and Whatcom County will prepare a SEPA EIS, each EIS with its own scope. The co-leads will revise their Memorandum Of Understanding (MOU) to incorporate the plan for parallel development of the two EISs.

September 23, 2013—Co-lead coordination agreement amended: The co-leads announced a revised MOU [memorandum of understanding] under which Ecology and Whatcom County will produce a draft SEPA EIS and the Corp will produce a draft NEPA EIS. The contractor hired in 2012 to assist the co-leads with EIS preparation will continue to do so.

Spring 2014—Begin preparing draft environmental impact statements (EISs): The contractor, under the direction of the co-lead agencies, has begun to prepare the draft NEPA and SEPA EISs according to the results of the scoping process. The purpose of an EIS is to provide the public and agency decision makers with information on likely adverse effects of a proposed project, as well as reasonable alternatives and measures to reduce those effects.

2015 or later—Issue draft EISs, open public comment period, have public hearings: The draft EISs will be circulated so that the public and other agencies are given an opportunity to comment on their accuracy and content before they are finalized. This process will include public hearings. The co-lead agencies will consider and respond to public comments in the final EISs.

2016 or later—Issue final environmental impact statements: The final EISs will include responses to the comments made on the draft EISs.

State of Washington Dep't of Ecology, Gateway Pacific Terminal at Cherry Point Proposal, *supra*. As shown above, the federal government will prepare one EIS for the terminal, and Whatcom County and the State of Washington will prepare a separate EIS under SEPA, although one contractor will draft both reports. The NEPA analysis prepared by the Corps and other agencies will address many impacts, including, among others, potential impacts on aesthetics (including the view from the shore); tribal treaty rights (particularly fishing rights); noise; "cultural, historical, archaeological, and tribal resources"; air quality; geology; biological resources, including "fish and aquatic habitat"; "wildlife and wildlife habitat"; "terrestrial vegetation communities (forests); and "federal threatened or endangered species." Corps, Mem. for R., *supra*, at 9–13.

One important issue in the EIS for the GPT was whether to consider the impacts of the railway that would carry coal to the export terminal along with the impacts of the terminal itself. Combining these two projects might make the impacts look larger and suggest that more mitigation measures were required. Determining whether projects are "connected," and which "cumulative" (combined) impacts of projects must be considered, is a contentious legal issue that environmental groups have used in many battles against developers. The Corps decided that although the BNSF railroad upgrade would benefit many activities other than the coal export terminal, it is "connected" to the GPT because the upgrade of the railroad is necessary for the GPT to operate. The coal must have a means of being transported to the terminal for export. The Corps' analysis of whether the two projects were connected is described in more detail in the following excerpt:

In determining the scope of analysis for the EIS, the Corps must identify the Corps' action under consideration and must decide for the purposes of NEPA, whether the agency has "control and responsibility" for activities outside of waters of the U.S. such that issuance of a permit would amount to approval of those activities. In this case, the proposed action to be taken by the Corps is the decision to issue, issue with conditions, or to deny a permit for various activities within the Corps' jurisdiction for the PIT and BNSF proposed projects.

The specific activity [that requires a] Corps permit may, at times, be merely one component of a larger project. As a general rule, the Corps extends its scope of analysis beyond waters of the U.S. where the environmental consequences of upland elements of the project may be considered products of either the Corps permit action or the permit action in conjunction with other Federal involvement. [This standard for analysis comes from 33 CFR Part 325 Appendix B Para 7(b)(2)).] When determining the extent to which the Corps is considered to have control and responsibility for portions of the project outside waters of the U.S., there are four typical factors set forth by regulation to consider. . . .

These four factors as considered for the combined PIT Gateway Pacific Terminal and the BNSFT Custer Spur Projects are:

a.   *Whether or not the regulated activity comprises "merely a link" in a corridor-type project*: There are no other proposed actions by either applicant outside of the combined project areas. The combined Gateway Pacific Terminal and Custer Spur Project is a "stand alone" project and is not a link or component of any linear or corridor project.

b.   *Whether there are aspects of the upland facility in the immediate vicinity of the regulated activity which affect the location and configuration of the regulated activity*: For the combined PIT/BNSF project, aspects of the proposed upland facilities would affect the location and configuration of the regulated activities. For the Gateway Pacific Terminal, the rail and commodity handling and storage facilities (plus attendant features) would need to be constructed in reasonable proximity to the proposed wharf to facilitate the transfer of commodities onto oceangoing vessels. However, while there appears to be a strong relationship between the locations of the wharf and commodity handling facilities based primarily on cost and logistics, the extent of that relationship has not been fully determined at this time. Wetlands and uplands on the Gateway Pacific Terminal project site are distributed in a mosaic pattern. Given the minimum area the applicant states it needs, constructing a functional commodity receiving, handling, and storage facility on upland portions of the project site could probably not be accomplished without impacting neighboring waters of the U.S., including wetlands. Expansion of the Custer Spur would occur within the existing BNSF right-of-way, which contains a mixture of uplands, stream crossings, and wetlands. Given the narrow, linear nature of the BNSF project area and the need to construct a continuous track the length of this corridor, there is a strong relationship among the locations of the proposed work in uplands and associated work in streams and wetlands.

c.   *The extent to which the entire project will be within the Corps' jurisdiction*: The proposed Gateway Pacific Terminal project would include installing structures in the Strait of Georgia, a navigable water of the U.S. Both projects involved the discharge of fill material into waters of the U.S. (wetlands and tributaries) requiring a [Department of the Army] DA permit. Approximately 50% of the Gateway Pacific Terminal onshore facilities would occur in waters of the U.S. (wetland fill). The other onshore portions of the project are dependent on the portions occurring in the Corps' jurisdiction. Approximately 12% of the Custer Spur project would occur in waters of the U.S.

d.   *The extent of cumulative Federal control and responsibility*: For the proposed construction of the Gateway Pacific Terminals, the Corps has authority under Clean Water Act Section 404 and Rivers and Harbors Act Section 10. For the proposed construction of the Custer Spur rail facilities, the Corps has authority under Clean Water Act Section 404. There are no other Federal agencies with control or responsibility over any aspect of the proposed shipping terminal and/or rail improvement project. The purpose of the Gateway Pacific Terminal is to export dry bulk-goods commodities which would be delivered to the site via BNSF rail lines. When considered in accordance with applicable laws and regulations, many of the activities of concern to the public, such as rail traffic, coal mining, shipping coal outside of U.S. waters and burning of coal overseas, are outside the Corps' control and responsibility. These activities are too attenuated and distant from the proposed activities being evaluated by the Corps to be considered effects of the Corps' permit actions. While other Federal agencies may have some regulatory oversight over certain aspects of a commodity's extraction of production, these activities are already occurring and will continue to be independent of the proposed projects under review by the Corps. There is limited Federal oversight of existing rail lines and traffic and no pending Federal approval or funding anticipated relating to the proposed project. Federal oversight of existing rail lines is limited to FRA authority over rail safety. There is, thus, not sufficient Federal control and responsibility over either existing main

> rail lines or use of the Custer Spur to substantiate the inclusion of these non-jurisdictional areas; therefore, portions of the Custer Spur and other rail systems (Bellingham Subdivision, etc.) outside the identified project corridor of the work requiring a DA permit are not included in the Corps' scope of analysis. There is limited federal oversight for marine vessel traffic associated with the Gateway Pacific Terminal project. Federal oversight is limited to U.S. Coast Guard authority over vessel traffic and safety in territorial waters of the U.S. Vessel traffic is already occurring in U.S. waters along routes potentially used by vessels related to the Gateway Pacific Terminal, and use of these waters will continue independent of the proposed projects under review by the Corps. There is, thus, not sufficient Federal control and responsibility over vessel traffic to substantiate the inclusion of vessel routes out to the extent of territorial boundaries (12 miles); therefore, non-project portions of marine waters are not included in the Corps' scope of analysis.

Corps, Mem. for R., *supra*, at 4–6.

Under NEPA, determining which portions of energy projects are connected and therefore should be considered cumulatively in terms of impacts analysis is important. "Cumulative" actions under Council on Environmental Quality (CEQ) regulations are actions "which when viewed with other proposed actions have cumulatively significant impacts." 40 C.F.R. § 1508.25(a)(2). (The executive-branch CEQ "oversees Federal agency implementation of the environmental impact assessment process and acts as a referee when agencies disagree over the adequacy of such assessments." Council on Environmental Quality, About CEQ, https://www.whitehouse.gov/administration/eop/ceq/about.) This definition gives little guidance on how to determine which proposed actions to consider, and thus whether these actions together have significant effects.

As shown above, the Corps applies four main factors to determine whether different components of a project should be considered cumulatively. For the GPT project, the Corps explained why it would not consider the impacts of the entire rail line used to ship coal to the export terminal, the marine vessel traffic from the terminal to overseas markets, and the burning of the coal overseas in its review of the terminal facility itself. These factors are also used to consider whether multiple, similar projects pending before the Corps, such as the other applications to construct coal export terminals in the Pacific Northwest, should be considered together under NEPA review. For the Corps, these factors include whether the regulated activity is "merely a link" in the project or is an integral part of the project; whether portions of the project are in a similar geographic area and will affect the location of the activity in question; whether the components of the project are within the jurisdiction of the agency approving the project and conducting environmental review; and "the extent of cumulative federal control and responsibility." 33 C.F.R. pt. 25 App. B.

The analysis that the agency performs under NEPA is aided by guidance from CEQ that describes when agency actions are "related" and thus must be considered together and also by the holdings of a number of cases, including *Kleppe v. Sierra Club*, 427 U.S. 390 (1976).

In *Kleppe*, the Department of the Interior (DOI) sought to approve a number of leases for coal mining on federal lands in the "Northern Great Plains region." *Kleppe*, 427 U.S. at 395. The Sierra Club argued that DOI should conduct a "comprehensive environmental impact statement" for the leases throughout the region, considering the impact of these leases cumulatively. *Id.* The Supreme Court disagreed. It recognized that "certain situations where several proposed actions are pending at the same time" might require a comprehensive impact statement and gave the following example: "[W]hen several proposals for coal-related actions that will have cumulative or synergistic environmental impact upon a region are pending concurrently before an agency, their environmental consequences must be considered together." *Id.* at 408. But the Court determined that all of these proposals had to be *related*, and that "[r]espondents can prevail only if there has been a report or recommendation on a proposal for major federal action with respect to the Northern Great Plains region," which there had not been. *Id.* at 399. Instead, there had been local DOI proposals to approve leases, as well as a national Programmatic Environmental Impact Statement for the national coal leasing program. *Id.* at 399–400. No EIS considering the regional impacts of coal leasing in the Northern Great Plains was therefore required.

Kleppe shows the importance of considering the scope of the action being approved by the agency and the scope of the impacts when determining whether a cumulative impacts analysis is required. The Court emphasized that the agency approving the action has discretion to determine the "extent and effect" of impacts, and "particularly identification of the geographic area within which they occur." *Id.* at 414. The Court also noted the importance of timing in determining whether different projects should be considered together, noting that actions "pending concurrently" would have to be considered together, but again, only if these actions were *related*. *Id.* at 410. In *Kleppe*, although many coal leases had been proposed at the same time, there was no evidence that these leases were part of a regional agency project or were sufficiently "related" to each other to require a cumulative effects analysis. *Id.* at 410. *Kleppe* did not fully clarify what it meant for projects pending before an agency to be "related," instead deferring to agencies' discretion to identify the "extent and effect" of impacts. Following *Kleppe*, the CEQ issued regulations to guide agencies in determining when agency actions were "intimately related." Actions are "intimately related" or "connected" when they:

(i)   Automatically trigger other actions which may require EISs,

(ii) Cannot or will not proceed unless other actions are taken previously or simultaneously, and

(iii) Are interdependent parts of a larger action and depend on a larger action for justification.

40 C.F.R. § 1508.25(a)(1).

NOTES AND COMMENTS

1.   In *Thomas v. Peterson*, 753 F.2d 754 (9th Cir. 1985), the court applied these CEQ factors and found that when the Forest Service planned construction of a gravel road to service a timber harvesting area, the road and timber harvesting had to be considered together. Both the road and the timber harvesting were under Forest Service jurisdiction. The court found that the Forest Service had to consider the combined impacts of the road and timber harvesting because, applying the CEQ factors for "related" projects, the road would not be built but for the timber sales, timber sales could not proceed without the road, and, considering the timber harvesting on the whole, the road and harvesting were "interdependent parts of a larger action." The road was described by the Forest Service in its environmental review as a "logging road" that formed part of a larger twenty-year timber harvesting project. With these principles in mind, do you think that the Corps was correct in deciding that vessel and rail traffic beyond the areas surrounding the GPT coal terminal, and the burning of coal overseas, were too "attenuated" to be considered in the Corps' EIS?

2.   Requiring cumulative impacts analysis in the EIS for a proposed energy project can be a make-or-break decision for the project. Extended delay caused by environmental review can cause the project to miss important contract deadlines and to lose investors. The more cumulative impacts there are, the more environmental review is likely to be required. Environmental and other groups have increasingly argued that more components of projects should be considered in agency approvals. For example, in *Delaware Riverkeeper v. FERC*, 753 F.3d 1304 (D.C. Cir. 2014), FERC issued a certificate of public convenience and necessity to Tennessee Gas Pipeline Company for the construction of an upgraded segment of a 30-inch diameter pipeline called the Northeast Project. Delaware Riverkeeper and other environmental groups argued that FERC erred under NEPA by "(1) segmenting its environmental review of the Northeast Project—*i.e.,* failing to consider the Northeast Project in conjunction with three other connected, contemporaneous, closely related, and interdependent Tennessee Gas pipeline projects—and (2) failing to provide a meaningful analysis of the cumulative impacts of these projects to show that the impacts would be insignificant." *Id.* at 1307. The Northeast Project upgrade was part of a much larger natural gas pipeline, the "300 line," and Tennessee Gas was also upgrading other portions of the 300 Line. It sought FERC approval of four separate proposals for upgrades to the 300 Line. The four projects were on the "Eastern Leg" of the pipeline. FERC completed an Environmental Analysis (EA) under NEPA for one of the four projects and recommended that the project proceed because it found no significant impacts. *Id.* at 1308. In its review, FERC did not consider the impacts of the other upgrade projects, even though one of them "was under construction during FERC's review," and FERC had already received applications for the two other projects. *Id.* The court held:

> Under applicable NEPA regulations, FERC is required to include "connected actions," "cumulative actions," and "similar actions" in a project EA and that "'[c]onnected actions' include actions that are 'interdependent parts of a larger action and depend on the larger action for their justification.'" The four pipeline improvement projects are certainly "connected actions." There is a clear physical, functional, and temporal nexus between the projects. There are no

offshoots to the Eastern Leg. The new pipeline is linear and physically interdependent; gas enters the system at one end, and passes through each of the new pipe sections and improved compressor stations on its way to extraction points beyond the Eastern Leg.

Id. at 1308–09.

Will the *Delaware Riverkeeper* decision require transmission line owners and operators that, under FERC Order 1000 must plan for regional transmission lines (including lines to support state renewable energy policies), to conduct a cumulative impacts analysis under NEPA? For discussion of Order 1000, see Chapter 11. Cumulative impacts issues also arise in the natural gas export context, as discussed in the next section.

2. NATURAL GAS

In the 1990s and through much of the early 2000s, the United States was quite concerned about declining domestic production of natural gas and the need to boost imports. The Department of Energy (DOE) and FERC—the two agencies tasked with approving gas imports and the terminals required for these imports—were thus busily approving LNG import terminals. With the rise of shale gas production, however, that situation rapidly changed. These two agencies are now busily approving LNG export terminals. As of June 11, 2014, DOE had received approximately 42 applications to export domestically-produced natural gas from the United States. DOE, Long Term Applications Received by DOE/FE to Export Domestically Produced LNG From the Lower-48 State (as of June 11, 2014), http://energy.gov/sites/prod/files/2014/06/f16/Summary%20of%20LNG%20Export%20Applications.pdf.

Both FERC and DOE are involved in approving LNG imports and exports due to complicated congressional directives. The Natural Gas Act and DOE Organization Act give DOE authority over natural gas imports and exports, while the Natural Gas Act gives FERC authority over the approval of the physical LNG import and export terminals.

Specifically, for DOE's authority, 15 U.S.C § 717b, Section 3 of the Natural Gas Act provides:

After six months from June 21, 1938, no person shall export any natural gas from the United States to a foreign country or import any natural gas from a foreign country without first having secured an order of the [Federal Power] Commission authorizing it to do so. The Commission shall issue such order upon application, unless, after opportunity for hearing, it finds that the proposed exportation or importation will not be consistent with the public interest.

Although the power to approve imports and exports was originally given to the Federal Power Commission, FERC's predecessor, the DOE Organization Act of 1977 transferred this power to the DOE, where it was further delegated to the Assistant Secretary of Fossil Energy in April 2011. *See* 42 U.S.C. § 7151 (DOE Organization Act) and Order No. 00–002.04E, Apr. 29, 2011 (for further changes involving the Atomic Energy Commission and DOE, see Chapter 7).

Under the NGA, DOE must approve the application for export license unless doing so "will not be consistent with the public interest." 15 U.S.C. § 717b(a). However, section 3(c) of the NGA makes export approval automatic for export to countries with which the United States has a free trade agreement ("FTA countries").[64] Specifically, that section states that:

> the exportation of natural gas to a nation with which there is in effect a free trade agreement . . . shall be deemed to be consistent with the public interest, and applications for such importation or exportation shall be granted without modification or delay.

15 U.S.C. § 717b(c). There is no corresponding automatic statutory approval for export to non-FTA countries. Rather, the DOE has discretion to approve or deny exports to non-FTA countries, based upon its determination whether such exports are in the public interest. As DOE explains: "Factors for consideration include economic, energy security, and environmental impacts." LNG Export Study, http://energy.gov/fe/services/natural-gas-regulation/lng-export-study.

After receiving a number of applications for LNG exports to non-FTA countries, DOE commissioned a consultant to research how exports would affect the public interest and announced that following the completion of this study, it would "begin to act on the . . . applications on a case-by-case basis." *Id.* On December 3, 2012, the consultant submitted its report to DOE. NERA Economic Consulting, Macroeconomic Impacts of LNG Exports from the United States (2012), http://energy.gov/sites/prod/files/2013/04/f0/nera_lng_report.pdf. Some key findings are excerpted below:

> This report contains an analysis of the impact of exports of LNG on the U.S. economy under a wide range of different assumptions about levels of exports, global market conditions, and the cost of producing natural gas in the U.S. These assumptions were combined first into a set of scenarios that explored the range of fundamental factors driving natural gas supply and demand. These market scenarios ranged from relatively normal conditions to stress cases with high costs of producing natural gas in the U.S. and exceptionally large demand for U.S. LNG exports in world markets. The economic impacts of different limits on LNG exports were examined under each of the market scenarios. Export limits were set at levels that ranged from zero to unlimited in each of the scenarios.

> Across all these scenarios, the U.S. was projected to gain net economic benefits from allowing LNG exports. Moreover, for every one of the market scenarios examined, net economic benefits increased as the level of LNG exports increased. In particular, scenarios with unlimited exports always had higher net economic benefits than corresponding cases with limited exports. In all of these cases, benefits that come from export expansion more than outweigh the losses from reduced capital and wage income to U.S. consumers, and hence LNG exports

---

[64] The FTA countries are Australia, Bahrain, Canada, Chile, Colombia, Dominican Republic, El Salvador, Guatemala, Honduras, Jordan, Mexico, Morocco, Nicaragua, Oman, Panama, Peru, South Korea, and Singapore.

have net economic benefits in spite of higher domestic natural gas prices. This is exactly the outcome that economic theory describes when barriers to trade are removed.

Net benefits to the U.S. would be highest if the U.S. becomes able to produce large quantities of gas from shale at low cost, if world demand for natural gas increases rapidly, and if LNG supplies from other regions are limited. If the promise of shale gas is not fulfilled and costs of producing gas in the U.S. rise substantially, or if there are ample supplies of LNG from other regions to satisfy world demand, the U.S. would not export LNG. Under these conditions, allowing exports of LNG would cause no change in natural gas prices and do no harm to the overall economy.

U.S. natural gas prices increase when the U.S. exports LNG. But the global market limits how high U.S. natural gas prices can rise under pressure of LNG exports because importers will not purchase U.S. exports if [the] U.S. wellhead price rises above the cost of competing supplies. In particular, the U.S. natural gas price does not become linked to oil prices in any of the cases examined.

Natural gas price changes attributable to LNG exports remain in a relatively narrow range across the entire range of scenarios. Natural gas price increases at the time LNG exports could begin range from zero to $0.33 (2010$/Mcf). The largest price increases that would be observed after 5 more years of potentially growing exports could range from $0.22 to $1.11 (2010$/Mcf). The higher end of the range is reached only under conditions of ample U.S. supplies and low domestic natural gas prices, with smaller price increases when U.S. supplies are more costly and domestic prices higher.

How increased LNG exports will affect different socioeconomic groups will depend on their income sources. Like other trade measures, LNG exports will cause shifts in industrial output and employment and in sources of income. Overall, both total labor compensation and income from investment are projected to decline, and income to owners of natural gas resources will increase. Different socioeconomic groups depend on different sources of income, though through retirement savings an increasingly large number of workers share in the benefits of higher income to natural resource companies whose shares they own. Nevertheless, impacts will not be positive for all groups in the economy. Households with income solely from wages or government transfers, in particular, might not participate in these benefits.

Serious competitive impacts are likely to be confined to narrow segments of industry. About 10% of U.S. manufacturing, measured by value of shipments, has both energy expenditures greater than 5% of the value of its output and serious exposure to foreign competition. Employment in industries with these characteristics is about one-half of one percent of total U.S. employment.

LNG exports are not likely to affect the overall level of employment in the U.S. There will be some shifts in the number of workers across industries, with those industries associated with natural gas production and exports attracting workers away from other industries. In no scenario is the shift in employment out of any industry projected to be larger than normal rates of turnover of employees in those industries.

Id. at 1–2 (2012).

After conducting its own analysis of the NERA report, DOE began to approve individual export terminals. Recent approvals include Dominion Cove Point, LNG in Maryland and Sabine Pass Liquefaction LLC in Louisiana, among others. *See* DOE, Long Term Applications Received by DOE/FE to Export Domestically Produced LNG From the Lower-48 States. A number of groups have criticized LNG export terminals for their environmental impacts, and some domestic industrial groups oppose exports because they worry that they will cause rising natural gas prices. *See, e.g.*, Jim Snyder, Dow Chemical Fights Ally Exxon's Natural Gas Export Push, Bloomberg, Jan. 24, 2013.

In May 2014, DOE announced that it would change its process for approving LNG export terminals. Up to that time, DOE had conditionally approved individual terminal applications, contingent upon successful completion of the EIS process under NEPA. In the future, DOE will decide whether the export of gas from a particular terminal is in the public interest only after a terminal applicant has completed full NEPA review. DOE LNG Exports Announcements, May 29, 2014, http://www. energy.gov/fe/doe-lng-exports-announcements-may-29-2014.   Further, DOE conducted a cumulative, "lifecycle" greenhouse gas analysis that investigated how gas exports might affect greenhouse gas emissions and other environmental impacts, including the displacement of coal used as a fuel abroad and the increase in the number of natural gas wells drilled and operated in the United States. The DOE analysis concluded that GHG emissions will not increase. *See* Life Cycle Greenhouse Gas Perspective on Exporting Liquefied Natural Gas from the United States, May   29,   2014,   http://www.energy.gov/fe/downloads/life-cycle-greenhouse-gas-perspective-exporting-liquefied-natural-gas-united-states.

FERC's authority over the construction and siting of LNG import and export terminals is found in the NGA, at 15 U.S.C § 717b, which provides: "The [Federal Power] Commission shall have the exclusive authority to approve or deny an application for the siting, construction, expansion, or operation of an LNG terminal."

The FERC process for approving LNG export terminals (and import terminals) is similar to the process for approving coal export terminals described above. Multiple federal agency approvals under the Endangered Species Act, Clean Water Act, Clean Air Act, and National Historic Preservation Act, among many others, are typically required. Because the terminals are along coasts and often in wet areas, the Corps usually must approve a dredge and fill permit under section 404 of the Clean Water Act, and states must approve consistency of the terminal with their Coastal Zone Management programs. As with coal terminals, FERC must conduct a detailed EIS under NEPA before approving LNG terminals, as illustrated in the following FERC order.

Cameron LNG, LLC, Order Granting Authorization Under Section 3 of the Natural Gas Act and Issuing Certificates

147 F.E.R.C. ¶ 61,230 (June 19, 2014).

On December 7, 2012, in Docket No. CP13–25–000, Cameron LNG, LLC (Cameron LNG) filed an application for authorization under section 3 of the Natural Gas Act (NGA) and Part 153 of the Commission's regulations to site, construct, and operate facilities for the liquefaction and export of domestically-produced natural gas (Liquefaction Project) at its existing liquefied natural gas (LNG) import terminal in Cameron, Louisiana. . . .

Cameron LNG seeks authorization to add natural gas processing and liquefaction capability to its existing LNG terminal in order to liquefy and export up to approximately 14.95 million metric tons per annum (MTPA), with a maximum operating capacity equivalent to pipeline receipts of up to 2.33 Bcf/d [billion cubic feet per day]. Upon placing the proposed facilities into service, the terminal will have the capacity to (i) liquefy domestically-produced natural gas for export, (ii) import LNG and regasify it for delivery to domestic markets, and (iii) import foreign-sourced LNG for subsequent export.

Discussion

. . . In support of its claim that the Liquefaction Project is inconsistent with the public interest, Sierra Club asserts that, contrary to Cameron LNG's economic arguments in support of its proposal, LNG export will have adverse and wide-ranging effects on the domestic economy, harming domestic consumers, and will not result in jobs creation. Sierra Club states that the Commission should consider how Cameron LNG's proposal, in addition to all other LNG export proposals, will affect the price of natural gas for domestic customers, as well as how these price increases will harm U.S. workers and the economy.

With respect to environmental harm, Sierra Club asserts that the project will "induce additional natural gas production in the United States, primarily hydraulic fracturing (fracking) of such production, thus causing the many environmental harms associated with such production."

We decline to address Sierra Club's economic claims, as they concern impacts associated with the exportation of the commodity natural gas, rather than the proposals before the Commission, that is, the impacts associated with Cameron LNG's export facilities used to facilitate the exports.

Section 3 of the NGA provides, in part, that "no person shall export any natural gas from the United States to a foreign country or import any natural gas from a foreign country without first having secured an order of the Commission authorizing it to do so." As noted above, in 1977, the Department of Energy Organization Act transferred the regulatory functions of section 3 of the NGA to the Secretary of Energy. Subsequently, the Secretary delegated to the Commission authority to "[a]pprove or disapprove the construction and operation of particular facilities, the site at which such facilities shall be located, and with respect to natural gas that involves the construction of new domestic facilities, the place of entry for imports or exit for exports . . ."

However, the Secretary has not delegated to the Commission any authority to approve or disapprove the import or export of the commodity itself. Nor is there any indication that the Secretary's delegation authorized the Commission to consider the types of issues raised by Sierra Club as part of the Commission's public interest determination, thus duplicating and possibly contradicting the Secretary's own decisions. Department of Energy/Office of Fossil Energy (DOE/FE), pursuant to its authority under NGA section 3, issued Cameron LNG authorization to export up to 12 MTPA, or 1.7 Bcf/d, of domestically-produced natural gas by vessel to all FTA and non-FTA nations, finding the potential export of such volumes to be not inconsistent with the public interest.

In conditionally granting Cameron LNG long-term authorization to export LNG, DOE found that there was substantial evidence of economic and other public benefits such that the authorization was not inconsistent with the public interest. We recognize DOE's public interest findings in issuing our order. Among other things, DOE found that exports from Cameron LNG's facility would result in increased production that could be used for domestic requirements if market conditions warrant such use, which would tend to enhance U.S. domestic energy security. DOE also found several other tangible economic and public benefits that are likely to follow from the requested authorization, including increased economic activity and job creation, support for continued natural gas exploration, and increased tax revenues.

Moreover, Sierra Club's claims with respect to purported adverse impacts of induced natural gas production have no bearing in this proceeding. The Commission's review is limited to the economic and environmental impacts of the proposal before us. As explained in more detail below, Sierra Club has not identified any induced production specifically connected to the Cameron LNG proposal.

The proposed Liquefaction Project is located on and adjacent to the footprint of the previously-approved and currently-operating Cameron LNG's terminal site. Much of the land in the area was previously disturbed during construction of the terminal and, as a result, we concur with the findings set forth in the EIS that the proposed project's environmental impacts are expected to be relatively small in number and well-defined.

We conclude in this order that, with the conditions we require, the Liquefaction Project results in only minimal environmental impacts and can be constructed and operated safely. Accordingly, we find that, subject to the conditions imposed in this order, Cameron LNG's proposals are not inconsistent with the public interest. . . .

The Commission orders:

. . . Cameron LNG is authorized under section 3 of the NGA to site, construct, and operate the proposed Liquefaction Project located in Cameron Parish, Louisiana, as described and conditioned herein . . . ■

Notes and Comments

1.   At least one regional EPA office has criticized FERC for limiting its review to the direct impacts of terminal construction, suggesting that FERC should follow the path of DOE and investigate cumulative impacts. Keith Goldberg, FERC Should Mull LNG Project's Enviro Effects: EPA, Law 360, Aug. 5, 2014, http://www.law360.com/articles/564205/ferc-should-mull-texas-lng-project-s-enviro-effects-epa.

2.   Protestors have also opposed FERC permits for LNG export terminals by arguing that exports will cause economic harm by increasing domestic natural gas prices. As with the environmental issues associated with increased production, FERC has responded to protestors' arguments about prices by deferring to DOE's determination that exports are in the public interest. *See, e.g.*, Dominion Cove Point LNG, 148 F.E.R.C. ¶ 61,244, at 13 (Sept. 21, 2014) (stating that "DOE found that exporting natural gas will lead to net benefits to the U.S. economy and can counteract concentration within global LNG markets, thereby diversifying international supply options and improving energy security for U.S. allies and trading partners").

3.   Environmental groups have also argued that DOE, in approving LNG exports, should consider how exporting will "induce" more domestic natural gas drilling. In April 2013, the Sierra Club and other groups petitioned DOE for updated rules, expressing concerns that the DOE's existing guidelines for approving LNG imports and exports were outdated. Sierra Club et al., Petition for Rulemaking Regarding Natural Gas Export Policy at 3–4, Apr. 8, 2013, http://vault.sierraclub.org/pressroom/downloads/2013-03-LNG-rule making-petition.pdf. Specifically, they argued: "Because roughly two-thirds . . . of gas for export would come from new unconventional gas production, export is . . . linked to intensifying environmental and public health impacts from the domestic gas boom." *Id.* at 5. DOE addressed some (but not all) of these induced effects of expanded domestic natural gas production in studies of the environmental impacts of LNG exports. These studies were not specific to each individual LNG export approval, but rather addressed the broader enterprise of LNG export from the United States. DOE emphasized that it was not required under NEPA to address the upstream (pre-pipeline) effects and that it would not, for each LNG export approval, explore the amount of natural gas production that particular export would induce. DOE cited to its approval of the Sabine Pass Liquefaction LNG export project:

> As the DOE explained in . . . [the Sabine Pass docket], lacking an understanding of where and when additional gas production will arise, the environmental impacts resulting from production activity induced by LNG exports to non-FTA countries are not "reasonably foreseeable" within the meaning of the Council on Environmental Quality's CEQ NEPA regulations.

DOE Draft Addendum to Environmental Review Documents Concerning Exports of Natural Gas from the United States at 2 (May 29, 2014), http://energy.gov/sites/prod/files/2014/05/f16/FR%20Notice%20of%20Adden dum%20%28Upstream%20Review%29.pdf. DOE further emphasized in its study of how LNG exports might induce domestic unconventional well development that "[f]undamental uncertainties constrain the ability to predict what, if any, domestic natural gas production would be induced by granting any specific authorization or authorizations to export LNG," but it assumed "for the purpose" of its broad review that "LNG export proposals would result in additional export volumes" and that these export volumes would be partially "offset" by "increasing domestic production of natural gas (principally from unconventional sources)." *Id.* at 1. DOE proceeded to address a variety of environmental impacts from domestic natural gas production, ranging from water and land use impacts to air pollutant emissions, greenhouse gas emissions from drilling and fracturing, and induced seismicity (earthquakes) from wastewater wells. *Id.* at 10–68. Again, however, DOE has not conducted individual analyses of the environmental impacts caused by enhanced unconventional gas production for its approvals of specific LNG export proposals.

4.   In another nod to growing requests of environmental groups that cumulative impacts of energy actions be considered, the Department of State considered the climate impacts of the Keystone XL pipeline, which would enable the transport of oil from the oil sands in Canada to the U.S. Gulf Coast for use domestically and for export. The Department of State asked, in its Final EIS, whether the production of this carbon-intensive oil would decline if the XL pipeline option were not available, thus lowering carbon emissions. U.S. Department of State, Keystone XL Pipeline Project, Final Environmental Impact Statement, http://keystonepipeline-xl.state.gov/documents/organization/182069.pdf. The Department concluded that the oil sands producers were already using alternative modes of transport, often rail, to move their oil, and thus that avoiding construction of the pipeline would likely not reduce carbon emissions. But the Department also noted that when the oil price drops below a certain level, transport by rail is not economic for oil-sands oil, and producers would then cut back production. *Id.* at 3.14–9, 35. The State Department also conducted a cumulative impacts analysis of existing and planned oil pipelines in the vicinity of the proposed Keystone XL pipeline, including the impacts of oil storage, natural gas and carbon dioxide pipelines, and electrical power and distribution lines near the proposed pipeline, among other analyses. *Id.* at 3.14–1 through 3.14.–14.

5.   Note the contrast between the refusal of the Corps to assess the climate impacts of burning coal exported overseas and the decisions of both the Department of State and DOE to complete relatively broad, cumulative impact analyses for the Keystone XL pipeline and LNG exports. Under *Kleppe* and other cases discussed above, is there a justification for this difference? Does DOE have more authority over exported gas than the Corps has over exported coal? Are LNG exports somehow more "connected" to the burning of natural gas globally than coal exports are connected to the burning of coal in Asia?

3. OIL

U.S. energy policy, until recently, has focused on ensuring a steady supply of oil imports to keep the U.S. economy humming. During the oil embargo of the 1970s, the Organization of the Petroleum Exporting Countries (OPEC) temporarily stopped sending oil to the United States due to U.S. support of Israel in the Arab-Israeli war, creating oil shortages and long lines at gasoline stations. Since that time, economists, scholars, and policy makers have tended to view the United States primarily as an oil importer, with foreign policy often focused on securing reliable supplies of oil abroad.

The recent surge in domestic oil production from shales and tight sandstones has started to change this picture. The United States is projected to be the world's leading producer of oil within the near future. This is not to say that the United States has an endless supply of domestic oil. Indeed, the surge in domestic production and exports might be relatively short. A 2014 International Energy Agency report projects that U.S oil production will decline again in the 2020s, and that the United States and the world will continue to rely largely on Middle Eastern markets for oil, particularly after the 2020s. International Energy Agency, Special Report: World Energy Investment Outlook, http://www.iea.org/publications/freepublications/publication/weio2014. pdf. But the United States, at least for now, has much more oil and gas than even the rosiest economic and geologic forecasts made before 2008 had ever predicted—and thus proposals for export are growing.

The surge in domestic oil production, in particular, has led to several infrastructure challenges. The United States allows exports of products refined from crude oil, such as gasoline, jet fuel, and the like. But many U.S. refineries were built for heavy (high-density) oil, and much of the oil being produced from shales and tight sandstones is in the form of very light, low-density condensate and similar light varieties. This imbalance can be resolved by constructing new   refineries (or making major modifications to existing ones) in the United States. Alternatively, the light oil could be exported to European refineries that are equipped to receive and treat light oil and that have asked the United States to send oil their way. *See* Steven Mufson, Did the Obama Administration Just Lift the Ban on U.S. Crude Oil Exports?, Wall St. J., June 25, 2014 http:// www.washingtonpost.com/blogs/wonkblog/wp/2014/06/25/did-the-oba ma-administration-just-lift-the-ban-on-u-s-crude-oil-exports/.   Indeed, analysts at Resources for the Future have concluded that this mismatch between American shale oil and American refineries causes higher gasoline prices than would be the case if the export ban were lifted. Stephen P.A. Brown et al., Crude Behavior: How Lifting the Export Ban Reduces Gasoline Prices in the United States, Resources for the Future (Feb. 2014), http://www.rff.org/RFF/Documents/RFF-IB-14-03-REV.pdf.

But exporting crude oil is no easy task due to laws enacted in the wake of the OPEC oil embargo. The Energy Policy and Conservation Act of 1975   (EPCA) prohibits the export of most crude oil, with small exceptions. This law interacts with executive branch authority over national security, as described by the Congressional Research Service:

> EPCA directs the President to "promulgate a rule prohibiting the export of crude oil and natural gas produced in the United States, except that the President may . . . exempt from such prohibition such crude oil or natural gas exports which he determines to be consistent with the national interest and the purposes of this chapter." The act further provides that the exemptions to the prohibition should be "based on the purpose for export, class of seller or purchaser, country of destination, or any other reasonable classification or basis as the President determines to be appropriate and consistent with the national interest and the purposes of this chapter. . . .
>
> Although EPCA directs the President to promulgate regulations that restrict crude oil exports, it does not provide the regulatory framework for enforcement of that restriction and the issuance

of licenses for eligible exports. . . . [T]he BIS [Bureau of Industry and Security within the Department of Commerce] is tasked with that duty, which is handled under its "short supply control" regulations. The source of this authority is somewhat complicated. The Export Administration Act of 1979 (EAA) [PL 96–72] confers upon the President the power to control exports for national security, foreign policy, or short-supply purposes, authorizes the President to establish export licensing mechanisms for certain items, and provides guidance and places certain limits on that authority. These restrictions are enforced by BIS. Crude oil restrictions and licensing are found in the BIS short supply controls authorized by the EAA. However, the EAA expired in August of 2001. The provisions of the act, and the regulations issued pursuant to it, remain in effect via yearly executive orders issued by the President under authority granted to him by the International Emergency Economic Powers Act.

That act authorizes the President to "deal with any unusual and extraordinary threat, which has its source in whole or substantial part outside the United States, to the national security, foreign policy, or economy of the United States, if the President declares a national emergency with respect to such threat." [50 U.S.C. § 1701(a).]

When the EAA first expired in 2001, the President cited this emergency authority in the issuance of Executive Order 13222, which provided for the continued execution of the EAA and the regulations issued pursuant to it. This exercise of emergency authority has been repeated annually by the President since that time, most recently in August 2013.

Phillip Brown et al., Congressional Research Service, U.S. Crude Oil Export Policy: Background and Considerations at 6–7 (2014), http://www.energy.senate.gov/public/index.cfm/files/serve?File_id=dfe108c9-cef6-43d0-9f01-dc16e6ded6b4.

As indicated in the excerpt above, the restriction on oil export specifically states that crude oil and natural gas may not be exported except for exports that the President "determines to be consistent with the national interest." While DOE makes the determination regarding whether natural gas exports are in the national interest as discussed above, the Bureau of Industry and Security (BIS) within the U.S. Department of Commerce makes the national interest determination for crude oil.

There are several steps to identifying how difficult it will be to export oil under existing statutes and Department of Commerce guidelines. First, one must identify the location from which the oil is produced, and, in very limited circumstances, its density. The Department of Commerce allows limited quantities of California heavy crude oil that has an API[65] gravity of 20 degrees or less to be exported (if a license is approved by the

---

[65] The American Petroleum Institute has developed a scale to measure the density of petroleum liquids. Oil with the highest API gravity has the lowest specific gravity. The heaviest oil, such as that in oil sand deposits, has an API gravity of 10 to 12 degrees. Most crude oil is lighter and ranges from 27 to 35 degrees on the API scale.

BIS). Beyond this California exception, however, the density of oil for export is irrelevant. Second, as shown by the California exception, the location of oil production also sometimes matters, as heavy crude oil from California is more easily exported. Under the Trans-Alaska Pipeline Authorization Act, 43 U.S.C. § 1652, oil from Alaska exported through the Trans-Alaska Pipeline may be exported without a license from the BIS, and oil produced from the Cook Inlet in Alaska may be exported if a BIS license is obtained. Any oil produced in states other than Alaska and California does not receive special exceptions from the export ban unless it is destined for certain countries and receives a license from the BIS, as described in the following regulatory text. So-called "Short Supply Controls," which are regulations of the BIS, offer special treatment to certain crude oil from California and Alaska as well as oil from all states that is sent to a limited set of countries. 15 C.F.R. § 754.2(b).

Alternatively, an exporter can avoid the ban and also avoid getting a license by taking advantage of certain enumerated exceptions to the license requirement. These exceptions include foreign-origin crude oil stored in the Strategic Petroleum Reserves, small oil samples exported for analytic and testing purposes, and exports of oil transported by pipeline over rights-of-way granted pursuant to Section 203 of the Trans-Alaska Pipeline Authorization Act.

Finally, companies that hope to export oil may request case-by-case review from the BIS to determine whether exports are in the national interest, as follows:

> The regulations [15 C.F.R. 754.2(b)(2)] also direct BIS to review applications to export crude oil that do not fall under one of these exemptions on a "case by case basis" and to approve such applications on a finding that the proposed export is "consistent with the national interest and the purposes of the Energy Policy and Conservation Act." 15 C.F.R. 754.2(b)(2). However, the regulations suggest that only certain specific exports will be authorized pursuant to this case-by-case review. The regulations provide that while BIS "will consider all applications for approval," generally BIS will only approve those applications that are either for temporary exports (e.g., a pipeline that crosses an international border before returning to the U.S.), or are for transactions (1) that result directly in importation of an equal or greater quantity and quality of crude oil; (2) that take place under contracts that can be terminated if petroleum supplies of the U.S. are threatened; and (3) for which the applicant can demonstrate that for compelling economic or technological reasons, the crude oil cannot reasonably be marketed in the U.S. 15 C.F.R. 754.2(b)(2).

Brown et al., *supra*, at 5–6.

Other than falling within the limited export-licensing exceptions, or going through case-by-case, "national interest" review, the only remaining way around the export ban is to show that the exported substance is not crude oil, but is oil that has been refined or processed into a different product. The Department of Commerce defines crude oil as follows:

> [A] mixture of hydrocarbons that existed in liquid phase in underground reservoirs and remains liquid at atmospheric pressure after passing through surface separating facilities and which has not been processed through a crude oil distillation tower [typically found in an oil refinery]. Included are reconstituted crude petroleum, and lease condensate and liquid hydrocarbons produced from tar sands, gilsonite, and oil shale. Drip gases are also included, but topped crude oil, residual oil, and other finished and unfinished oils are excluded.

15 C.F.R. § 754.2(a).

When oil flows from a well, it typically goes through initial processing at the well site (using a simple on-site unit called a "separator" or "heater treater" to separate oil from water, gas and condensate). As the Department of Commerce indicates, this initial treatment does not convert the oil from "crude" to "refined," and the oil is still classified as crude. On the other hand, oil that has been sent through a crude oil distillation tower is no longer crude. Refineries contain and operate large distillation towers to break crude oil into different products. In the distillation process, crude oil is heated and turns to gas within a distillation column (the tower). The gas is cooler near the top of the column and hotter near the bottom. Gases with various boiling points along the column become distilled back into oil product liquids when they drop below their boiling points. The different products are separated and drained off through pipes at various points along the column.

"Topped crude," which the Department of Commerce does not include in the crude oil definition, is the oil remaining after some light oils have been removed in the distillation process. "Residual oil" is also not considered to be "crude oil," and consists of the heavier products at the bottom of the distillation tower. *See* American Fuel and Petrochemical Manufacturers, http://www.afpm.org/The-Refinery-Process/#process. Importantly, the Department of Commerce defines condensate, the light oil often produced from shales and tight sandstones and typically treated to some degree near the well site, as crude oil. Condensates are thus included within the oil export ban.

In short, for oil not to be "crude" under the Department of Commerce's definition, and thus to avoid the export ban, it typically must be sent through a distillation process and thus go to a refinery. Recent Department of Commerce decisions, however, suggest that it might define other forms of light processing as converting crude oil to a refined oil product. In June 2014, the Department of Commerce issued private letter rulings to two Texas oil companies that produce condensate, also called "light oil," from shales. Christen Berthelson & Lynn Cook, U.S. Ruling Loosens Four-Decade Ban on Oil Exports, June 24, 2014, Wall St. J., http://online.wsj.com/articles/u-s-ruling-would-allow-first-shipments-of-unrefined-oil-overseas-1403644494. The letters allow these companies to export the condensate because it has been treated near the field by "stabilization units." Stabilization units remove some of the most volatile components of condensates, "making the liquids safe[r] for storage and transport and reducing atmospheric emissions of volatile hydrocarbons." Valerus, Crude Oil & Condensate Treating & Stabilization, http://www.valerus.com/products-services/production-equipment/crude-oil-condensate-treating-stabilization/.

Some analysts believe that this ruling indicates a broader intent of the Department of Commerce under the Obama Administration to allow more types of oil that have not been fully refined to avoid the crude oil export ban. *See, e.g.,* Timothy Gardner & Kristen Hays, Exclusive: Loophole for Condensate Exports May Apply to Other U.S. Crudes, Reuters, June 27, 2014, http://www.reuters.com/article/2014/06/27/us-usa-crude-exports-exclusive-idUSKBN0F226D20140627 ("The U.S. decision allowing minimally processed super-light oil known as condensate to be freely exported may open the door to doing the same with other types of crude too, according to industry and government sources who have reviewed the ruling."). But Department of Commerce spokesman Jim Hock stated that "[t]here has been no change in policy on crude oil exports," suggesting that other types of processed oil will not immediately be redefined as "non-crude." Coral Davenport, Narrow Shift by Washington on Oil Exports, N.Y. Times, June 24, 2014, http://www.nytimes.com/2014/06/25/business/energy-environment/narrow-shift-by-washington-on-oil-exports.html.

More clarity about what is "crude oil" will help investors today make better economic decisions. Rather than invest in expensive refineries and distillation towers, producers and processors could build simpler stabilization units that convert crude oil into a product that avoids the export ban. Companies today are investing in relatively costly plants called "splitters" that are small refineries that can convert condensates and light oil into naphthas and distillates that can be exported. Gardner & Hays, *supra.*

For oil that is crude and falls under the export ban, anyone wanting to export it must show that the export is consistent with the national interest to obtain a license from the Department of Commerce's BIS, as explained below:

> 15 C.F.R. § 754.2: BIS will review . . . applications to export crude oil on a case-by-case basis and . . . generally will approve such applications if BIS determines that the proposed export is consistent with the national interest and the purposes of the Energy Policy and Conservation Act (EPCA). Although BIS will consider all applications for approval, generally, the following kinds of transactions will be among those that BIS will determine to be in the national interest and consistent with the purposes of EPCA.

> (i)   The export is part of an overall transaction:

> (A) That will result directly in the importation into the United States of an equal or greater quantity and an equal or better quality of crude oil or of a quantity and quality of petroleum products listed in Supplement No. 1 to this part that is not less than the quantity and quality of commodities that would be derived from the refining of the crude oil for which an export license is sought;

> (B) That will take place only under contracts that may be terminated if the petroleum supplies of the United States are interrupted or seriously threatened; and

> (C) In which the applicant can demonstrate that, for compelling economic or technological reasons that are beyond the control of

the applicant, the crude oil cannot reasonably be marketed in the United States.

The definition of crude oil as well as BIS's criteria for which exports are in the "national interest" will likely be continuing topics of dispute in 2015 as a shale oil glut in the United States has filled up most available crude oil storage capacity. But as the International Energy Agency warns, after 2020, the United States might once again be required to import increasing supplies of crude oil from countries in the Middle East. As the U.S. shale oil and gas booms surprised many energy experts, it is difficult to predict any of these trends with a strong degree of certainty.

B. INTERNATIONAL TRADE LAW AND ENERGY MARKETS

Because modern energy markets are global in scope, international trade law also plays an important role in limiting a nation's regulatory approaches that seek to favor domestic production and domestic energy sectors. This issue has become an important topic for emerging renewable and clean energy technologies, but it also has an effect on domestic policies regarding fossil fuels.

Increasingly, the United States has become a major player in renewable energy markets, particularly with respect to the manufacturing of renewable energy equipment. The United States often faces strong competition in these global markets. For example, as China expanded its production of solar panels, prices for these panels dropped precipitously. U.S. buyers have been happy to purchase lower-priced Chinese-made panels, to the chagrin of domestic manufacturers.

Trade disputes involving international fossil fuels and renewable energy (in addition to other products) tend to arise in two forms, both of which allege that countries are unfairly favoring their own energy resources over others. First, representatives from one nation sometimes argue that other nations are unlawfully subsidizing their own energy resources through favorable tax policies, grants, and other mechanisms. Second, a nation might allege that another country is unfairly implementing "dual" or "two-tier" pricing, through which a government "keep[s] domestic prices lower (or export prices higher) than if they had been determined by market forces." United Nations Conference on Trade and Development, Trade Agreements, Petroleum and Energy Policies, Exec. Summ. at 2 (2000).

Many trade disputes involving energy are brought before the World Trade Organization (WTO). The WTO is an international organization that enforces international trade disputes under: (1) the General Agreement on Tariffs and Trade (GATT) which serves as "the WTO's 'umbrella' treaty for trade in goods," and which was formed in 1947 and reformed in GATT 1994 through the Uruguay Round negotiations; (2) the General Agreement on Trade in Services (GATS); (3) additional agreements that involve "special requirements of specific sectors or issues"; and (4) "schedules (or lists) of commitments made by individual countries allowing specific foreign products or service-providers access to their markets." Additionally, the WTO encompasses an international intellectual property agreement. WTO, Understanding the WTO: The Basics, http://www.wto.org/english/thewto_e/whatis_e/tif_e/fact5_e.htm.

Additional international and regional treaties, such as the Energy Charter Treaty and the North American Free Trade Agreement (NAFTA), and other international entities, such as the Organization of Petroleum Exporting Countries (OPEC), may also affect energy trade flows between countries. However, this section will focus on an overview of WTO law and its impact on international energy policy, as presented in the following excerpt explaining the major provisions of GATT.

Adam Vann et al., Cong. Research Serv., Federal Permitting and Oversight of Export of Fossil Fuels (2013)

http://fas.org/sgp/crs/misc/R43231.pdf.

The Marrakesh Agreement Establishing the World Trade Organization (WTO) contains the agreements relating to international trade that are binding for all WTO Members. Although there is no specific agreement relating to trade in energy products, such as liquefied natural gas, coal, or oil, the trade in these products is regulated under the General Agreement on Tariffs and Trade (GATT). Several of these sections could potentially impact a nation's ability to limit or restrict fossil fuels.

Article I—Most Favored Nation Treatment

Article I of the GATT 1994 requires that "any advantage, favour, privilege or immunity granted by any [WTO Member] to any product originating in or destined for any other country shall be accorded immediately and unconditionally to the like product originating in or destined for the territories of all other [WTO Members]." Article I applies to all rules and formalities in connection with importation and exportation. This broad category of rules and formalities appears likely to include prerequisites for exportation such as licensing requirements or other preliminary measures. More favorable treatment given to *imports* from particular countries in the context of *import* licensing requirements has been held to confer an advantage within the meaning of Article I. Generally, this means that as soon as the United States provides for certain treatment of fossil fuel exports to one country, the United States has to treat exports to all other WTO Members in the same fashion. A licensing regime that provided for more favorable treatment for exports of fossil fuels to some countries, but subjected other WTO countries to a slower process could potentially be inconsistent with Article I of the GATT.

However, there are exceptions to the Most Favored Nation Treatment requirements for Free Trade Agreements (FTA). Article XXIV of GATT 1994 allows countries to provide more favorable treatment to countries with which they have established an FTA. In order to qualify for the Article XXIV exception, the FTA must meet certain requirements outlined in the Article. Most notably, the free trade agreement must eliminate duties—such as tariffs—and restrictions on commerce between the parties to the agreement for "substantially all the trade in products originating in those territories." Therefore, in order for an agreement to qualify, it is likely that the FTA would have to cover more than just energy products flowing between the two territories. However, if the countries have a qualifying FTA, more favorable treatment towards energy products between those countries could be included in that FTA without violating the GATT.

Article XI—Export Restrictions

Article XI of the GATT covers import and export restrictions. Article XI:1 of the GATT bars the institution or maintenance of quantitative restrictions on exports to any WTO Member's territory. Quantitative restrictions limit the amount of a product that may be exported—common examples are embargoes, quotas, minimum export prices, and certain export licensing requirements. Under Article XI, duties, taxes, and other charges are the only GATT-consistent methods of restricting exports. Any government action that expressly precludes the exportation of certain goods is inconsistent with the GATT.

Although there are few WTO panel decisions on export bans, panels have consistently found that *import* bans implemented through licensing systems violate Article XI. This jurisprudence can be expected to inform any WTO panel decision on the GATT-consistency of export bans and licensing. WTO Panel decisions have also held that "discretionary" or "non-automatic" licensing requirements are prohibited under Article XI—therefore, a licensing program that gives discretion to an agency to deny an export license to potential exporters on the basis of vague or unspecified criteria would violate Article XI. Moreover, a GATT panel held that export licensing practices that cause delays in issuing licenses may be a restraint of exports that is inconsistent with Article XI.

Articles VI, XVI, and the Agreement on Subsidies and Countervailing Measures—Export Restraints as Actionable Subsidies

A fossil fuel export licensing regime that restricts exports could have the effect of keeping domestic prices of fossil fuels lower than they otherwise would be. This raises the question of whether such a licensing program could be considered an actionable subsidy to downstream users of the fossil fuels such as members of the petrochemical industry. Under the GATT 1994 and the Agreement on Subsidies and Countervailing Measures (SCM Agreement), an actionable subsidy may be the subject of countervailing measures or challenge before a panel by a WTO Member when the subsidy adversely affects the interests of that member. Adverse effects might result if export restraints on fossil fuels lead to lower input costs for downstream manufacturers that use the fuels, giving the manufacturers' products a competitive edge over the products of the other members' manufacturers in domestic or foreign markets.

The SCM Agreement defines a "subsidy" as "a financial contribution by a government or any public body within the territory of a Member" that confers a benefit. Under the agreement, one way that a "financial contribution" may occur is when a government directs a private body to sell goods to a domestic purchaser. In *U.S.—Measures Treating Export Restraints as Subsidies*, the United States Trade Representative (USTR) argued before a WTO panel that a government's restriction on exports could be considered "functionally equivalent" to that government directing private parties to sell a good to domestic purchasers. The USTR argued that this resulted in a subsidy to downstream producers that used the good as an input in their production processes. The panel rejected this argument, stating that although a restriction on exports of a good may result in lower prices for domestic users of that good, the restriction was not an explicit command or direction by the government to private parties to sell the good within the meaning of the SCM Agreement. This ruling suggests that future panels may be reluctant to find that a restriction on exports or a similar government intervention in a market is a "financial contribution" by a government. Thus, it seems unlikely that licensing procedures could constitute a subsidy under WTO rules, even if they lead to restrictions on exports.

Articles XX and XIII—General Exceptions

Article XX of the GATT provides for certain exceptions that a member country may invoke if it is found to be in violation of any GATT obligations. In order for the defense to be successful, the member country must show that its action fits under one of these general exceptions and that it satisfies Article XX's opening clauses, known as the "chapeau." When dealing with trade in energy products, a country will most likely use the exceptions under Article XX(b) or XX(g). A country may justify a GATT inconsistent practice under Article XX(b) if the practice in question is "necessary to protect human, animal, or plant life or health." Article XX(g) may permit otherwise GATT inconsistent measures that "relat[e] to the conservation of exhaustible natural resources if such measures are made effective in conjunction with restrictions on domestic production or consumption." If a WTO Member invokes an Article XX exception to the application of any quantitative export restrictions, Article XIII requires that those export restrictions must be administered in a non-discriminatory manner—that is the restrictions must comport with the most-favored nation treatment discussed above.

Article XXI—Security Exceptions

Restrictions on fossil fuels for reasons of international or domestic security that would otherwise violate the GATT 1994 may potentially be justified under the broadly worded exception for essential security interests contained in Article XXI. One paragraph of this article allows a member to take "any action which it considers necessary for the protection of its essential security interests . . . taken in time of war or other emergency in international relations."

Because there is a lack of WTO case law on Article XXI, it is necessary to consult the history of the exception's use under the General Agreement on Tariffs and Trade 1947 (GATT 1947). The GATT 1947 has been incorporated into the GATT 1994. Under the GATT 1947, the contracting parties broadly interpreted the concept of an "emergency." Thus, each party was basically the judge of what constituted an emergency in international relations. Measures that parties have sought to justify under Article XXI have included trade embargoes, import quotas, and suspensions of tariff concessions. Parties have pointed to both potential and actual dangers as "emergencies" supposedly justifying these typically GATT inconsistent measures.

With respect to who determines whether a WTO Member's use of the exception is valid, the United States has previously taken the position that Article XXI is "self-judging."79 That is, each member invoking Article XXI is the judge of whether its use of the exception is valid. As a result, there is currently no WTO case law on the use of Article XXI.

However, some scholars have speculated that, in the future, a WTO panel or the Appellate Body may decline to defer to a WTO Member's judgment about when its use of Article XXI is appropriate. One of these international quasi-judicial bodies may instead decide to more carefully scrutinize a member's use of the exception. For example, a panel may consider whether there is an emergency in international relations justifying national security screening for exports of fossil fuels to certain countries but not others. ∎

How do you think that U.S. export limits on oil and natural gas discussed in the previous section comport with these WTO requirements? It appears that current U.S. fossil fuel export policy could be challenged under some of the WTO Articles. For example, by favoring natural gas exports to countries with which we have a free trade agreement, might the United States be violating the most favored nations requirement, or will this policy fall within the free trade agreement exception to this requirement? Might our restrictions on oil and natural gas export violate the prohibition on export bans? Or might they fall under the "protection of . . . essential security interests . . . taken in time of war or other emergency in international relations" in light of our current Middle East policy, or "relate to the conservation of exhaustible natural resources"? Most of these questions have not yet been formally raised through WTO disputes, but they seem ripe for debate. The following excerpt, based on congressional testimony from a former U.S. Trade Representative, discusses how U.S. natural gas export policy might be in jeopardy under WTO rules.

Testimony of James Bacchus to the Subcommittee on Energy and Power of the Energy and Commerce Committee of the United States House of Representatives

Mar. 25, 2014.

WTO rules apply to trade in natural gas and other energy products in the same way they apply to other traded products. Some have suggested that energy products are somehow separate and apart from other traded products in how WTO rules apply to them. There is no legal basis for this view. The United States has taken no reservations from our obligations under WTO rules for exports of natural gas or other energy products.

WTO rules prohibit bans, quotas, and other forms of quantitative restrictions on exports unless those restrictions take the form of export taxes. Taxes on exports are prohibited by our Constitution, so energy export taxes are not an option for the United States. WTO rules also permit temporary restrictions on exports to prevent or relieve critical shortages of essential products, but that can hardly be said to apply to our current situation with supplies of natural gas.

A number of legal concerns occur when considering the consistency of the current US process for licensing exports of natural gas with WTO rules. First of all, the current US process gives special treatment in licensing exports of natural gas to countries with which we have a free trade agreement. Natural gas exports to these countries are deemed to be in the "public interest" and permitted without delay. In contrast, the Department of Energy has elected to subject licensing requests for LNG exports to non-FTA countries to a thorough and lengthy assessment intended to determine whether exports of natural gas to those countries serve our "public interest." In this way, applicants that will ship LNG to FTA countries are, preferentially, given expedited review in the licensing process as compared to those applicants that will ship LNG to non-FTA countries.

When seen through the prism of WTO law, these are measures affecting trade that result in discrimination between like traded products. The legal question under WTO law is whether this discrimination can be excused by an exception in WTO law that allows trade discrimination as part of a "free trade agreement." But it is not at all clear that all of the FTA's of the United States fit within the definition in the WTO treaty of a "free trade agreement. . . ."

One remaining legal concern is the question of the lengthy delays in granting export licenses. Under WTO rules, a license can clearly be a restriction on exports, and case law has defined the notion of a "restriction" broadly to include licensing procedures that pose limitations on actions or have a limiting effect, such as by creating uncertainties or by affecting investment plans. In one case, delays of up to three months in issuing export licenses were found to be inconsistent with the rules.

To be sure, liquefied natural gas is, practically speaking, not just another widget. Before it can be shipped by sea, natural gas must be transformed in a careful way that requires special facilities. Some period of deliberation in siting and evaluating LNG facilities seems reasonable. But what would WTO judges be likely to say about delays in issuing export licenses that last for several years?

A second remaining legal concern is the lack of clarity in how the Department of Energy defines the "public interest." Conceivably, even lengthy delays in the licensing process could be excused under WTO rules of it could be proven by the United States that such delays are necessary to protect life or health, or are related to the conservation of exhaustible natural resources, so long as the process is not applied in a way that results in arbitrary or unjustifiable discrimination or a disguised restriction on international trade. If, however, in determining the "public interest," the DOE considers as a factor the effect the proposed exports will have on domestic producers that use natural gas when producing their products in their competition with like foreign products, then these exceptions to WTO rules will not be available, and will not excuse a WTO violation caused by lengthy licensing delays.

A third legal [sic] remaining legal concern may arise under the WTO rules on governmental subsidies. Under WTO rules, subsidies are illegal if they are specific to certain industries and cause adverse effects in the marketplace. The questions in a WTO case would be: by restricting exports so as to reduce the domestic price of natural gas, is the United States granting a subsidy to the manufacturing firms that are the downstream users of natural gas, and, if so, does that subsidy have illegal trade effects? Here, the general exception for measures protecting life, health, and exhaustible natural resources may very well not be available to excuse such a violation of the WTO subsidy rules, even if a determination of the "public interest" excludes competitive trade concerns. ■

The testimony of James Bacchus raises the issue of whether export restrictions on fossil fuels are impermissible subsidies, but the subsidy issue also covers a much broader range of energy policies that extends beyond these export restrictions. The definition of "Subsidy" from Article 1 of the Subsidies and Countervailing Measures Agreement (a "WTO-plus" agreement that is an optional additional agreement that applies beyond GATT) is as follows:

1.1   For the purpose of this Agreement, a subsidy shall be deemed to exist if:

(a)(1) there is a financial contribution by a government or any public body within the territory of a Member (referred to in this Agreement as "government"), i.e. where:

(i)   a government practice involves a direct transfer of funds (e.g. grants, loans, equity infusion), potential direct transfers of funds or liabilities (e.g. loan guarantees);

(ii)   government revenue that is otherwise due is foregone or not collected (e.g. fiscal incentives such as tax credits);

(iii)   a government provides goods or services other than general infrastructure, or purchases goods;

(iv)   a government makes payments to a funding mechanism, or entrusts or directs a private body to carry out one or more of the type of functions illustrated in (i) to (iii) above which would normally be vested in the government and the practice, in no real sense, differs from practices normally followed by governments;

or

(a)(2) there is any form of income or price support in the sense of Article XVI of GATT 1994 [which "operates directly or indirectly to increase exports of any product from, or to reduce imports of any product into, [a contracting party's territory"]

and

(b)   a benefit is thereby conferred.

Part II of the Subsidies and Countervailing Measures Agreement defines those subsidies that are "prohibited" as including "subsidies contingent, in law or in fact, whether solely or as one of several other conditions, upon export performance" and "subsidies contingent, whether solely or as one of several other conditions, upon the use of domestic over imported goods." Further, Part III defines "Actionable Subsidies," providing:

No Member should cause, through the use of any subsidy referred to in paragraphs 1 and 2 of Article 1, adverse effects to the interests of other Members, i.e.:

(a) injury to the domestic industry of another Member;

(b) nullification or impairment of benefits accruing directly or indirectly to other Members under GATT 1994. . . .

(c) serious prejudice to the interests of another Member.

Serious prejudice occurs when a country provides (i) "subsidies to cover operating losses sustained by an industry"; (ii) "subsidies to cover operating losses sustained by an enterprise, other than one-time measures which are non-recurrent and cannot be repeated for that enterprise and which are given merely to provide time for the development of long-term solutions and to avoid acute social problems"; and (iii) "direct forgiveness of debt, i.e. forgiveness of government-held debt, and grants to cover debt repayment." SCM Article 6.1. Serious prejudice also may occur when, for example, "the effect of the subsidy is to displace or impede the imports of a like product of another Member into the market of the subsidizing Member" or other market displacement.

Energy industries have always enjoyed considerable subsidies in the United States and elsewhere throughout the world. In recent years, energy subsidies have been prominent in their support for the adoption of renewable energy. Some examples of such subsidies are discussed in Chapter 11, such as feed-in-tariffs and other direct governmental subsidies to support the production and adoption of clean energy technologies. Subsidies are not limited to renewable energy. Fossil fuels have received substantial support over the years as well, at levels that dwarf governmental support for renewable and clean energy initiatives. *See* Envtl. L. Inst., Energy Subsidies Black, Not Green, http://www.eli.org/sites/default/files/docs/Energy_Subsidies_Black_Not_Green.pdf.

Subsidies for domestically produced energy resources can give rise to trade disputes. Challenges to feed-in-tariff programs and subsidies for industries such as PV solar panel production and auto industry battery technology have already been launched. The following text discusses two trade law disputes in the renewable energy sector and then introduces a third example of a still-brewing dispute under NAFTA involving the Keystone XL pipeline. These examples highlight the types of disputes that can arise in a number of energy sectors.

International Trade Law and Solar Panel Dumping: Chinese solar panel manufacturers in recent years have greatly expanded production, leading to the export of more panels and lower prices to buyers. U.S. solar panel manufacturers, hurt by this competition, believed that Chinese manufacturers were receiving benefits from their government that gave them an unfair trade advantage. When a nation unfairly subsidizes a product, another nation may implement countervailing duties on that product. The United States imposed such duties on Chinese solar panels and wind towers, as well as on a number of other products ranging from "lawn groomers" to "kitchen shelving." *See* WTO, United States-Countervailing Duty Measures on Certain Products from China, Request for Consultations by China at 5–8, May 30, 2012 (listing the products for which the United States imposed countervailing duty measures).

Recall from the excerpt above by Adam Vann et al., that under WTO rules countries may not subsidize products by providing cheap inputs to manufacturers that produce goods for exports. As a United Nations report explains:

The provision by governments of products or services for use in the production of exported goods, on terms or conditions more favourable than for goods for domestic consumption, is considered to constitute an export subsidy if such terms or conditions are more favourable than those commercially available on world markets to their exporters. This could imply that schemes to provide petrochemical exporters with energy inputs at prices lower than world prices could be claimed to constitute a prohibited export subsidy if the same advantages were not also available as inputs into the production of goods for domestic consumption.

United Nations Conference on Trade and Development, Trade Agreements, Petroleum and Energy Policies, Exec. Summ. at 3 (2000), http://unctad.org/en/docs/poitcdtsbd9_exsum.en.pdf.

The U.S. International Trade Administration, which promotes U.S. trade and enforces trade laws and agreements, further explains:

Foreign governments subsidize industries when they provide financial assistance to benefit the production, manufacture, or exportation of goods. Subsidies can take many forms, such as direct cash payments, credits against taxes, and loans at terms that do not reflect market conditions. The statute and regulations establish standards for determining when an unfair subsidy has been conferred. The amount of subsidies the foreign producer receives from the government is the basis for the subsidy rate by which the subsidy is offset, or "countervailed," through higher import duties.

International Trade Admin., Frequently Asked Questions, http://trade.gov/faq.asp.

Under this principle, a country cannot provide a solar manufacturer that exports panels with cheaper energy and materials for production than it provides to solar manufacturers that produce domestic goods. The U.S. Department of Commerce, in imposing countervailing duty measures on Chinese solar panels and wind towers, argued that "state-owned enterprises ('SOEs') confer countervailable subsidies through their sales of inputs to downstream producers." WTO, United States-Countervailing Duty Measures on Certain Products from China, Request for Consultations by China, at 2 (summary of U.S. argument provided by China). The WTO rules that prohibit these types of subsidies define subsidies as "a financial contribution by a government or any *public body* within the territory of a Member." Agreement on Subsidies and Countervailing Measures (SCM Agreement), Article 1. China argued before the WTO that the United States "incorrectly determined, or did not have a sufficient basis to determine, that certain SOEs are 'public bodies' within the meaning" of this Article, among other arguments. WTO, United States-Countervailing Duty Measures, *supra*, at 2.

After requesting consultations on the countervailing measures imposed by the United States, China asked the WTO's Dispute Settlement Body (DSB) to establish a panel on the matter, a request that the DSB granted in September 2012. On July 14, 2014, the panel issued a report that favored China on one aspect of the solar panel issue, finding that the "United States acted inconsistently with Article 1.1(a)(1) of the SCM Agreement when the USDOC found that SOEs were public bodies." WTO, United States—Countervailing Duty Measures on Certain Products from China, Report of the Panel at 105, July 14, 2014. In response, the U.S. Trade Representative stated that "the Administration is carefully evaluating its options, and will take all appropriate steps to ensure that U.S. remedies against unfair subsidies remain strong and effective." Robert Evans, WTO Faults U.S. Over Duties on Chinese, Indian Steel Goods, Reuters, July 14, 2014, http://www.reuters.com/article/2014/07/14/us-trade-wto-usa-china-idUSKBN0FJ1S620140714.

Europe has taken a different approach to addressing Chinese solar panel exports. The European Commission entered into an agreement with China in 2013, under which Chinese manufacturers agreed not to sell panels below a minimum price and Europe agreed not to impose tariffs. But European manufacturers allege that some Chinese companies have violated the agreement and are selling below the minimum price. Matthew Dalton, EU Solar Firms Accuse Chinese Rivals of Violating Agreement, Wall St. J., June 4, 2014, http://online.wsj.com/articles/china-breaking-agreement-on-solar-panels-eu-makers-say-1401896061.

As energy becomes increasingly international and firms export and import both energy-related equipment and fuels, these types of disputes are likely to continue. And there is reason to worry that certain U.S. policies restricting exports or burdening imports could be successfully challenged as violating the WTO rules.

Renewable Feed-in-Tariffs and the WTO: Another subsidy for renewable energy policy that has been challenged through WTO processes is the feed-in-tariff (FIT). A FIT provides renewable energies with a guaranteed rate that they will receive for selling generated electricity—a rate designed to cover the costs of constructing the generation facility and guaranteeing some profit for the developer. A recent FIT debate involving Canada highlights the difficulty that FITs and other green-energy subsidies can face under international trade law.

Ontario implemented a broad FIT, covering wind, solar, bio-fuels, and other resources, which guaranteed a long-term, "above-market" price for the energy sold from renewable generators to the Ontario Power Authority. A key facet of the program, however, made it particularly suspect under international law. Ontario required that renewable generators receiving the FIT ensure that a specified percentage of their resources and labor came from Ontario, thus creating more local jobs in exchange for the higher electricity rates that the FIT program would bring. *See* Note, The World Trade Organization: A Barrier to Green Energy, 22 Transnat'l L. & Contemp. Probs. 205 (2013). As the World Trade Organization describes Ontario's FIT:

> The FIT Programme is a scheme implemented by the Government of the Province of Ontario and its agencies in 2009, through which generators of electricity produced from certain forms of renewable energy are paid a guaranteed price per kilowatt hours (kWh) of electricity delivered into the Ontario electricity system under 20-year or 40-year contracts. Participation in the FIT Programme is open to facilities located in Ontario that generate electricity exclusively from . . . wind, solar PV, renewable biomass, biogas, landfill gas, and waterpower. . . . The FIT Programme is divided into two streams: (i) The FIT stream—for projects with a capacity to produce electricity that exceeds 10 kilowatts (kW), but is no

more than 10 megawatts (MW) for solar PV projects or 50 MW in the case of waterpower projects; and (ii) the microFIT stream—for projects having a capacity to produce up to 10 kW of electricity.

WTO, Canada—Certain Measures Affecting the Renewable Energy Generation Sector at 17, May 6, 2013.

In addition to supporting renewables through guaranteed long-term contracts, Ontario's policy required wind and solar PV technologies benefiting from the FIT to follow "Minimum Required Domestic Content Levels," as summarized by the WTO:

> The "Domestic Content Level" of a facility participating in either stream of the FIT Programme is calculated pursuant to a methodology that identifies a range of different "Designated Activities" and an associated "Qualifying Percentage." For each Designated Activity that is performed in relation to a facility, an associated Qualifying Percentage will be achieved. A project's Domestic Content Level "will be determined by adding up the Qualifying Percentages associated with all of the Designated Activities performed in relation to that particular project.

WTO, Canada *supra,* at 18.

For wind, the Minimum Required Domestic Content Level was 25% from 2009–2011, rising to 50% in 2012 and thereafter. For solar PV (both FIT, and microFIT), the minimum level was 50% for 2009–2010, rising to 60% in 2011 and thereafter. *Id.*

Japan and the European Union requested that the WTO's Dispute Settlement Body establish panels to address Ontario's domestic content requirements in the FIT program. *Id.* at 15. Japan and the European Union argued that Ontario's FIT Program violated the following WTO provisions:

> 1) Articles 3.1(b) and 3.2 of the SCM agreement on subsidies, by granting subsidies "contingent upon the use of domestic over imported goods";
>
> 2) Article III:4 of the GATT 1994 on most favourable nation status through its domestic content requirements, which gave less favorable treatment to European and Japanese renewable generation equipment by favoring internal (Ontario-based) sales of the equipment (Article III:4 provides: "The products of the territory of any Member imported into the territory of any other Member shall be accorded treatment no less favourable than that accorded to like products of national origin in respect of laws, regulations and requirements affecting their internal sale, offering for sale, purchase, transportation, distribution or use."); and
>
> 3) Article III of the GATT 1994 and Article 2.1 of the trade-related investment measures (TRIMS) Agreement by implementing impermissible TRIMS "that require the purchase or use by enterprises of equipment and components for renewable energy generation facilities of Ontario origin and source."

Id. at 18–19.

The Panel found that Japan and the European Union (EU) "had failed to establish that the FIT Programme, and the individual solar PV and windpower FIT and microFIT contracts executed since the FIT Programme's inception, constituted subsidies, or envisaged the granting of subsidies" under SCM. WTO, Canada, *supra*, at 22–23. However, the Panel found that both Japan and the EU had successfully shown that Ontario violated the TRIMS Agreement [TRIMs are Trade-Related Investment Measures, now regulated by the WTO as part of GATT] and Article III:4 of the GATT 1994 by establishing "Minimum Required Domestic Content Levels" under the FIT Programme. *Id.* at 22–23. Ontario's FIT violated these provisions because Ontario made compliance with domestic content requirements "necessary" for renewable energy generators and thus allowed domestic technology producers to "obtain an advantage"—an example of an impermissible TRIMs. *Id.* at 20.

The North American Free Trade Agreement and Cross-Border Energy Infrastructure: Within North America, NAFTA serves as another important instrument that could impact certain U.S. energy subsidies and trade restrictions. Consider, for example, U.S. delays or refusals to approve siting of pipeline or transmission line infrastructure that would enable imports of oil, gas or electric power from Canada or Mexico. Part Two, Chapter Six of NAFTA addresses energy trade flows among these three countries that are Parties to NAFTA as follows:

Article 601: Principles

1. The Parties confirm their full respect for their Constitutions.

2. The Parties recognize that it is desirable to strengthen the important role that trade in energy and basic petrochemical goods plays in the free trade area and to enhance this role through sustained and gradual liberalization.

3. The Parties recognize the importance of having viable and internationally competitive energy and petrochemical sectors to further their individual national interests.

Article 603: Import and Export Restrictions

1. Subject to the further rights and obligations of this Agreement, the Parties incorporate the provisions of the *General Agreement on Tariffs and Trade* (GATT), with respect to prohibitions or restrictions on trade in energy and basic petrochemical goods.

2. The Parties understand that the provisions of the GATT incorporated in paragraph 1 prohibit, in any circumstances in which any other form of quantitative restriction is prohibited, minimum or maximum export-price requirements and, except as permitted in enforcement of countervailing and antidumping orders and undertakings, minimum or maximum import-price requirements.

3. In circumstances where a Party adopts or maintains a restriction on importation from or exportation to a non-Party of an energy or basic petrochemical good, nothing in this Agreement shall be construed to prevent the Party from:

a) limiting or prohibiting the importation from the territory of any Party of such energy or basic petrochemical good of the non-Party; or

b) requiring as a condition of export of such energy or basic petrochemical good of the Party to the territory of any other Party that the good be consumed within the territory of the other Party.

4.   In the event that a Party adopts or maintains a restriction on imports of an energy or basic petrochemical good from non-Party countries, the Parties, on request of any Party, shall consult with a view to avoiding undue interference with or distortion of pricing, marketing and distribution arrangements in another Party.

5.   Each Party may administer a system of import and export licensing for energy or basic petrochemical goods provided that such system is operated in a manner consistent with the provisions of this Agreement, including paragraph 1 and Article 1502 (Monopolies and State Enterprises).

Article 604: Export Taxes

No Party may adopt or maintain any duty, tax or other charge on the export of any energy or basic petrochemical good to the territory of another Party, unless such duty, tax or charge is adopted or maintained on:

a) exports of any such good to the territory of all other Parties; and

b) any such good when destined for domestic consumption.

Article 605: Other Export Measures

Subject to Annex 605, a Party may adopt or maintain a restriction otherwise justified under Articles XI:2(a) or XX(g), (i) or (j) of the GATT with respect to the export of an energy or basic petrochemical good to the territory of another Party, only if:

a) the restriction does not reduce the proportion of the total export shipments of the specific energy or basic petrochemical good made available to that other Party relative to the total supply of that good of the Party maintaining the restriction as compared to the proportion prevailing in the most recent 36-month period for which data are available prior to the imposition of the measure, or in such other representative period on which the Parties may agree;

b) the Party does not impose a higher price for exports of an energy or basic petrochemical good to that other Party than the price charged for such good when consumed domestically, by means of any measure such as licenses, fees, taxation and minimum price requirements. The foregoing provision does not apply to a higher price that may result from a measure taken pursuant to subparagraph (a) that only restricts the volume of exports; and

c) the restriction does not require the disruption of normal channels of supply to that other Party or normal proportions among specific energy or basic petrochemical goods supplied to that other Party, such as, for example, between crude oil and refined products and among different categories of crude oil and of refined products.

Article 606: Energy Regulatory Measures

1.   The Parties recognize that energy regulatory measures are subject to the disciplines of:

a) national treatment, as provided in Article 301;

b) import and export restrictions, as provided in Article 603; and

c) export taxes, as provided in Article 604.

2.   Each Party shall seek to ensure that in the application of any energy regulatory measure, energy regulatory bodies within its territory avoid disruption of contractual relationships to the maximum extent practicable, and provide for orderly and equitable implementation appropriate to such measures.

Article 607: National Security Measures

Subject to Annex 607, no Party may adopt or maintain a measure restricting imports of an energy or basic petrochemical good from, or exports of an energy or basic petrochemical good to, another Party under Article XXI of the GATT or under Article 2102 (National Security), except to the extent necessary to:

a) supply a military establishment of a Party or enable fulfillment of a critical defense contract of a Party;

b) respond to a situation of armed conflict involving the Party taking the measure;

c) implement national policies or international agreements relating to the non-proliferation of nuclear weapons or other nuclear explosive devices; or

d) respond to direct threats of disruption in the supply of nuclear materials for defense purposes.

Annex 602.3 of NAFTA reserves for the Mexican State unilateral allowances for investment in "exploration and production of crude oil and natural gas; refining or processing of crude oil and natural gas" and "foreign trade; transportation, storage and distribution . . . of . . . crude oil, natural and artificial gas," goods obtained from processing crude oil and natural gas, and "exploration, exploitation, and processing of radioactive minerals." Further, the Annex provides:

Where end-users or suppliers of natural gas or basic petrochemical goods consider that cross-border trade in such goods may be in their interests, each Party shall permit such end-users and suppliers, and any state enterprise of that Party as may be required under its domestic law, to negotiate supply contracts.

NAFTA also contains a general provision, Article 1105(1), which requires that NAFTA parties "accord to investments and investors of another Party treatment in accordance with international law, including fair and equitable treatment and full protection and security."

In 2014, Canada contemplated using NAFTA to challenge the U.S. delay in approving the proposed Keystone XL pipeline, which as discussed in Chapter 9 would carry crude oil from the oil sands of the Western Canadian Sedimentary basin to refineries along the U.S. Gulf Coast. Several existing pipelines already cross the U.S.-Canada border, and Canada could argue that the United States was treating Keystone XL differently. The United States, in turn, could respond that its analysis of the pipeline was not yet complete. Due to the multi-year length of the delay in approval, however (caused in part by the Department of State's issuance of several supplemental environmental impact statements and its denial of the first proposed permit), the United States might have difficulty proving that it was providing "fair and equitable treatment" to the Keystone XL project. Claudia Cattano, Ottawa mulls Keystone XL challenge under NAFTA after U.S. dodges decision again, Financial Post, Apr. 30, 2014, http://business.financialpost.com/2014/04/30/keystone-xl-nafta-challenge/?___lsa=8efb-e456.

Following a threatened challenge, Canada's Natural Resources Minister in 2014 indicated that the country would pursue alternative means to encourage approval of Keystone XL. Andrew Mayeda, Canada Won't Mount NAFTA Keystone Challenge: Rickford, Bloomberg News, May 2, 2014, http://www.bloomberg.com/news/2014-05-02/canada-won-t-mount-nafta-keystone-challenge-rickford.html.

C. SUBSTANTIVE EXTRATERRITORIAL EFFECTS OF U.S. LAW

Increasingly, U.S. companies are engaged in commercial activities involving energy resource development outside of the United States. The foreign operations of these companies may be subject to domestic laws that have extraterritorial effect. An extraterritorial law is any law of one nation (Nation X) that applies to activities outside its borders in another nation (Nation Y). To what extent can a nation be the policeman or moral guardian to the world and impose its domestic laws on other nations by regulating conduct that takes place abroad?

As discussed above in the approval procedures for energy export projects, federal agency consideration of "cumulative impacts" may include discussion of environmental effects outside U.S. borders. Litigation arises in NEPA cases over the scope of cumulative impacts required to be discussed in the EIS, a procedural issue that may delay approval of a federal permit if the EIS is found to inadequately address such impacts. NEPA does not prevent the agency from ultimately proceeding to approve a project, however.. In contrast, many federal statutes directly regulate activities outside of the United States or regulate the extra-jurisdictional impacts of U.S. activities. It is important for energy lawyers to recognize how U.S. laws involving commercial conduct can have impacts on activities that take place outside of U.S. borders.

1. PRINCIPLES OF EXTRATERRITORIALITY AND ILLUSTRATIONS

The general principles of extraterritoriality are summarized in the Restatement (Third) of the Foreign Relations Law of the United States, §§ 402–404 (Rest. 3d For. Rel.). A nation has jurisdiction to prescribe laws related to the conduct of its nationals outside its territory and to regulate conduct that occurs outside its territory that has a substantial effect within its territory, as long as the exercise of this jurisdiction is not unreasonable. A state also has jurisdiction over certain offenses recognized by the community of nations as of universal concern, such as piracy, slave trading, hijacking aircraft, genocide, and perhaps acts of terrorism.

Governments may resent one nation's policing their relationships with other countries and may enact conflicting counter-regulations designed to have the opposite extraterritorial effect. For example, the U.S. Helms-Burton Act, 22 U.S.C. §§ 6021–6091, generally bars companies doing business in the United States from trading with Cuba. In response, some countries, such as Canada, enacted laws that prohibit companies from complying with Helms-Burton, thus creating a legal dilemma for companies doing business in both the United States and in Cuba. *See* Ernest E. Smith *et al*, International Petroleum Transactions 229 (2009).

Sanctions and boycotts are a regular part of U.S. foreign policy. Sanctions, imposed by either the Executive branch or by Congress, can have serious impacts on U.S. companies. For example, Conoco was awarded a contract worth $1 billion by the National Iranian Oil Company to develop a large offshore field in 1996. After the contract was signed, President Clinton issued an executive order imposing trade sanctions on Iran, and Conoco was forced to withdraw from the project, which later was awarded to Total, the French oil company. Daily Report for Executives, Sept. 29, 1999, at A–46. More recently, Iranian oil production has fallen substantially from 2011 through 2014 because of sanctions imposed by the United States and the European Union in an effort to prevent Iran from enriching nuclear fuel. The sanctions may have assisted in moving Iran, in late 2013, to sign a Joint Plan of Action with the five permanent members of the U.N. Security Council plus Germany to scale back or freeze some of its nuclear activities while negotiating a permanent plan that allows the peaceful use of nuclear energy in Iran. *See* EIA, Iran Country Brief, July 22, 2014, http://www.eia.gov/countries/analysisbriefs/Iran/iran.pdf.

After Russia's seizure of Crimea from Ukraine, the United States imposed increasingly stringent sanctions on key Russian individuals, businesses and banks. ExxonMobil was forced to wind down its newly started drilling project in the Russian Arctic because its operations there would violate the U.S. sanctions. Sanctions have stopped almost all Western financing to Russia, causing a credit squeeze for Russian businesses and a sharp drop in the ruble price. In response to the sanctions, Russia quickly pivoted east and signed a thirty-year contract to sell gas to China. Some countries in Europe are highly dependent on Russian gas shipped by pipelines through Ukraine. Russian gas had supplied all the gas demand of Lithuania, Latvia and Estonia. These three countries arranged for a floating LNG terminal, owned by a Norwegian company, to dock in a Lithuanian port where it will be able to serve 90% of their gas demand with non-Russian imports. "Floating terminal arrives off Lithuania to aid nations dependent on Russia," EnergyWire, Oct. 29, 2014, http://www.eenews.net/energywire/2014/10/29/stories/1060008023.

Congress has enacted a number of U.S. laws that clearly are intended to have extraterritorial effect in their mandates. First, our income tax laws are borderless. Income earned anywhere in the world by a U.S. taxpayer is subject to U.S. income tax law. The foreign country where a U.S. party operates probably also imposes an income tax. Careful tax planning allows U.S. companies to avoid double taxation of the same income, either by triggering the foreign income tax credit in the U.S. tax code or by using tax treaties entered into between countries to avoid double taxation.

All companies, whether domestic or foreign, that list shares on American stock exchanges must comply with the U.S. securities laws designed to protect investors, including the Sarbanes-Oxley (SOX) Act of 2002, 15 U.S.C. § 7262 *et seq.*, which was passed after investors lost billions of dollars in corporate scandals involving Enron, WorldCom and others. The financial disclosure and compliance requirements of this act may be much more stringent than the financial accounting standards of other countries' regulators.

One particular statute, the Foreign Corrupt Practices Act of 1977 (FPCA), 15 U.S.C. §§ 78dd–1 *et seq.* has been applicable to the extraterritorial acts of all companies listed on U.S. stock exchanges for over 35 years now. Much of the world's remaining oil and gas reserves underlie countries that rank quite poorly on Transparency International (TI)'s Corruption Perceptions Index, a ranking of countries based on how pervasively corruption is embedded in business dealings in that country. TI also publishes a Bribe Payers Index ranking industrialized countries in terms of their paying bribes. *See* http://www.transparency.org. Corruption is now recognized as a serious barrier to investment, economic growth and poverty reduction. It is also a serious impediment to democratic institutions. *See generally* George Moody-Stuart, Grand Corruption: How Business Bribes Damage Developing Countries (1997); Susan Rose-Ackerman, Corruption and Government: Causes, Consequences and Reform (1999); Michael L. Ross, The Oil Curse (2012).

The FCPA was passed in the aftermath of a Securities and Exchange Commission (SEC) investigation showing that more than 400 U.S. companies, including many oil companies, had made "questionable payments" of more than $300 million abroad. The FCPA has broad extraterritorial reach. It prohibits payments, made on behalf of a company listed on an American stock exchange, to foreign officials for purposes of:

> influencing any act or decision of such foreign official in his official capacity, (ii) inducing such foreign official to do or omit to do any act in violation of the lawful duty of such official, or (iii) securing any improper advantage . . . in order to assist [the company making the payment] in obtaining or retaining business for or with, or directing business to, any person.

15 U.S.C. § 78dd–1(a)(1).

The corrupt act of bribing may have been done on foreign soil between parties, none of whom are U.S. citizens. The FCPA will nonetheless apply, subjecting individual officers, directors and employees of the listed company to fines and imprisonment for violating the act. The act also requires that corporations keep accounting records of bribes paid. A good example of the extraterritorial effect of the FCPA is found in an SEC order directed at a Norwegian oil company's payment of an unreported bribe (disguised as a "consulting contract" of $15.2 million) to an Iranian advisor to Iran's Oil Ministry to secure a contract to develop fields in Iran, *See* SEC, In the Matter of Statoil, ASA, Respondent, Administrative Proceeding File 3–12453, Release No. 54599, Oct. 13, 2006 (imposing a fine of $10,500,000 and a compliance monitor on Statoil, Norway's national oil company that is listed on the N.Y. Stock Exchange). Many other countries have now enacted similar anti-corruption statutes, such that a company operating abroad may be subject to multiple prosecutions in several jurisdictions for the same act of bribery. *See* Frank C. Razzano & Travis P. Nelson, The Expanding Criminalization of Transnational Bribery: Global Prosecution Necessitates Global Compliance, 42 Int'l Lawyer 1259 (ABA Sec. of Int'l Law 2008).

2. THE PRESUMPTION AGAINST EXTRATERRITORIALITY

It is a "longstanding principle of American law" that "legislation of Congress, unless a contrary intent appears, is meant to apply only within the territorial jurisdiction of the United States." Foley Bros. v. Filardo, 336 U.S. 281, 285 (1949). This presumption against extraterritoriality applies when Congressional intent is not clear as to the jurisdictional effect of a law. The extraterritoriality of U.S. securities laws has been litigated in a number of cases over the years, led by the Second Circuit Court of Appeals because of its location in New York City, the center of the U.S. financial markets. Over the years, this court had developed and applied two tests to determine whether the U.S. securities laws applied in a factual setting that involved predominantly foreign transactions: (1) the "effects" test, asking whether the wrongful conduct had a substantial effect inside the United States or on U.S. citizens; and (2) the "conduct" test, asking whether the wrongful conduct occurred in the United States. Other circuits generally followed this approach.

As an example, in *Consolidated Gold Fields PLC v. Minorco, S.A.*, 871 F.2d 252 (2d Cir. 1989), the court found that the anti-fraud provisions of the U.S. securities laws reached to enjoin a tender offer made outside the United States, involving two foreign companies (one South African and one British), even though American residents held only 2.5% of the outstanding shares of the company targeted for acquisition and the offering documents did not use any means or instrumentality of interstate or foreign commerce or any U.S. security exchanges. The court found that Congress intended to apply the anti-fraud provisions of the Securities Exchange Act to transactions involving even a small number of American residents. The court also found that the plaintiff-corporations successfully showed a likelihood of success on their claim that the proposed acquisition (of Gold Fields) would substantially lessen competition in violation of section 7 of the Clayton Act (15 U.S.C. §§ 18,

26 (1982)). *See also* Schoenbaum v. Firstbrook, 405 F.2d 200 (2d Cir.), *reh'g on other grounds*, 405 F.2d 215 (en banc).

However, in 2010, the U.S. Supreme Court, in *Morrison v. National Australian Bank Ltd.*, 561 U.S. 247 (2010), held that the Second Circuit's interpretation of when U.S. securities laws applied to largely foreign transactions had "excised the presumption against extraterritoriality" from its proper jurisprudential role. *Id.* at 257. Justice Scalia, writing for the majority, characterized the forty years of Second Circuit jurisprudence as "judicial-speculation-made-law," with judges "divining" what Congress intended if it had thought of the situation before the court. *Id.* at 261. Instead of applying the tests used by the Second Circuit, the majority adopted a "transactional test," asking whether the purchase or sale of securities was made in the United States or involved a security listed on a domestic exchange. *Id.* at 556. If not, the U.S. securities laws did not apply.

The *Morrison* case was brought by Australian citizens (the petitioners) who had purchased shares of an Australian bank on the Australian stock exchange. The bank's common stock was not traded on an American exchange. The petitioners alleged that the bank's officers had acquired a mortgage-servicing business in Florida and had manipulated financial models to make this acquisition appear valuable, when, in fact, its value had to be written off within three years. They sought to litigate the anti-fraud provisions of the securities law in the Southern District of New York, arguing that sufficient fraudulent conduct occurred in Florida to allow the case to proceed in New York. The district court dismissed the case and the Second Circuit affirmed this dismissal, both finding that the heart of the fraud occurred outside the United States with no evidence of injury to American investors or markets. Despite the dismissals, the Supreme Court took the case, and used it as a vehicle for strengthening the presumption against extraterritoriality.

The majority rebutted all the arguments presented over the years and in the case at hand by the petitioners for finding that the U.S. securities laws could sometimes reach conduct involving largely foreign transactions. The majority painted a broadbrush rule: "When a statute gives no clear indication of an extraterritorial application, it has none." *Id.* at 255. Two concurring justices would have kept the nuanced and flexible approach set by the Second Circuit, which allowed the presumption of extraterritoriality to be overcome when Congress had not spoken clearly on the issue. *Id.* at 559–56. How "clear" a Congressional directive must be in order to extend the extraterritorial reach of a U.S. statute, short of an express statement to that effect, awaits future litigation. It is resoundingly clear that the current Supreme Court will strongly presume no extraterritorial effect.

One oft-cited reason for judicial caution in extending U.S. laws beyond U.S. borders is the conflict that may arise with other countries' laws, triggering diplomatic tensions in the delicate area of foreign policy. In *Morrison*, the Commonwealth of Australia, the United Kingdom, and France had filed *amicus curiae* briefs, complaining of the interference with their own securities regulations from application of U.S. securities laws, especially when no clear test existed to determine extraterritoriality. U.S. courts have created doctrines, such as the Act of

State and Political Question doctrines and the doctrine of sovereign immunity, that allow judges to refuse jurisdiction over cases that implicate serious foreign policy issues and relationships with other nations. Thus, in *International Assoc. of Machinists & Aerospace Workers (IAM) v. OPEC*, 649 F.2d 1354 (9th Cir. 1981), the court dismissed a lawsuit brought by a U.S. labor union (IAM) alleging that the Organization of Petroleum Exporting Countries (OPEC) engaged in price-fixing in violation of the U.S. antitrust acts. The court first addressed the doctrine of sovereign immunity:

> In the international sphere, each state is viewed as an independent sovereign, equal in sovereignty to all other states. It is said that an equal holds no power of sovereignty over an equal. Thus the doctrine of sovereign immunity: the courts of one state generally have no jurisdiction to entertain suits against another state.

Id. at 1357.

Because some acts of states are commercial in nature, especially when conducted through National Oil Companies (NOCs) operating with private oil companies in joint ventures to develop petroleum reserves, Congress enacted the Foreign Sovereign Immunities Act, authorizing the federal courts to determine when the commercial acts of foreign states were not immune from suit in a U.S. court. The court in *IAM v. OPEC* recognized the implications of suing OPEC as it sought to maximize the value of its oil reserves: "The importance of the alleged price-fixing activity to the OPEC nations cannot be ignored. Oil revenues represent their only significant source of income. Consideration of their sovereignty cannot be separated from their near total dependence upon oil." *Id.* at 1358.

Ultimately, in *IAM v. OPEC*, the Ninth Circuit Court of Appeals dismissed the suit against OPEC, based on the Act of State doctrine:

> The act of state doctrine declares that a United States court will not adjudicate a politically sensitive dispute which would require the court to judge the legality of the sovereign act of a foreign state.

> The doctrine recognizes the institutional limitations of the courts and the peculiar requirements of successful foreign relations. To participate adeptly in the global community, the United States must speak with one voice and pursue a careful and deliberate foreign policy. The political branches of our government are able to consider the competing economic and political considerations and respond to the public will in order to carry on foreign relations in accordance with the best interests of the country as a whole. The courts, in contrast, focus on single disputes and make decisions on the basis of legal principles. The timing of our decisions is largely a result of our caseload and of the random tactical considerations which motivate parties to bring lawsuits and to seek delay or expedition. When the courts engage in piecemeal adjudication of the legality of the sovereign acts of states, they risk disruption of our country's international diplomacy. The executive may utilize protocol, economic sanction, compromise, delay, and

> persuasion to achieve international objectives. Ill-timed judicial decisions challenging the acts of foreign states could nullify these tools and embarrass the United States in the eyes of the world.

Id. at 1358.

The Political Question doctrine, based on the separation of powers in the U.S. Constitution, is an even greater hurdle to jurisdiction over certain foreign entities, as explained in *Occidental of Umm Al Qaywayn, Inc. v. A Certain Cargo of Petroleum*, 577 F.2d 1196, 1201–1203 (5th Cir. 1978):

> Throughout the history of the federal judiciary, political questions have been held to be nonjusticiable and therefore not a "case or controversy" as defined by Article III. . . . In *Marbury v. Madison*, 1 Cranch 137, 164–66, 2 L.Ed. 60 (1803), Chief Justice Marshall acknowledged the existence of a class of cases which involve a "mere political act of the executive" and which were placed by the Constitution in the hands of the executive. The Supreme Court therefore appreciated that the genesis of the political question is the constitutional separation and disbursement of powers among the branches of government.

In this case, Occidental sought to bring an action for conversion of crude oil stored in tankers that rival oil companies had shipped to the United States under the claim that they now owned the contract to develop the oil from a small Mideast island. Iran had invaded and seized the island as its own, ousting the ruler from whom Occidental had secured a concession. The rival oil companies obtained a new concession from the new rulers. The court refused to resolve the ownership of the oil because it would have required resolving a territorial dispute between foreign sovereigns.

D. INTERNATIONAL ENVIRONMENTAL AND HUMAN RIGHTS LAW

International law can also have significant implications for the activities of energy firms. This section of the chapter can provide only an introduction to international law principles, but the examples that follow provide ample evidence of the role of international law in oil and gas development activities. International law includes both "hard" (or binding) commitments imposed on nations and their citizens, as well as "soft" (nonbinding) sources of legal obligations. The sources of these legal obligations arise out of treaties, customary international law international tribunal decisions, and other transnational sources of law.

1. TREATY OBLIGATIONS

Treaties have the force of federal law. Upon ratification, a country is typically obligated to pass implementing domestic legislation. The earliest international treaties governed maritime pollution and use of the high seas, but a number of conventions now govern areas such as: (1) the conservation of various types of resources: fisheries, specific animal species (polar bears, tuna and whales), endangered flora and fauna, and World Cultural Heritage sites; (2) the transboundary movement of hazardous wastes; (3) atmospheric pollution, and nuclear testing and materials; (4) global climate change; and (5) the international use of outer space and the Antarctic.

A recent international treaty, the Minamata Convention, opened for signature in October 2013, after four years of U.N. negotiations among 140 nations. This treaty will enter into force after 50 nations sign it. It imposes binding obligations on each signatory nation to implement domestic measures to inventory and control mercury air emissions from coal-fired power plants and other large sources; to phase out certain mercury-containing products and manufacturing processes; to phase out existing mercury mining within 15 years; and to reduce, where feasible, the use and release of mercury from small-scale, artisanal gold mining. *See* Joanne Rotondi & Kim Smaczniak, The Minamata Convention on Mercury: What It Does and Does Not Mean for the United States, 29 Nat. Res. & Env't 1 (Summer 2014).

Many environmental treaties among nations are regional in nature, controlling environmental impacts only in defined geographic areas of the world. In some instances, the United States has refused to act multinationally. Recall that the United States has its own Oil Pollution Act, discussed in Chapter 4, having refused to join the International Convention on Civil Liability for Oil Pollution Damages and its supplemental International Fund for Compensation for Oil Pollution Damages, both of which entered into force in the 1970s among many other nations.

Liability under a treaty can clearly surprise some U.S. energy developers. For example, the Migratory Bird Treaty Act (MBTA), 16 U.S.C. §§ 703–12, implements a federal treaty signed by Mexico, the United States, and Canada (among others), which imposes strict liability for killing certain species of birds that migrate thousands of miles in annual winter-spring flights. Open pits containing oily water or other oilfield wastes often attract migrating birds. The birds die when they land and make contact with the polluted water. The federal Fish and Wildlife Service prosecuted 47 Texas operators because dead birds were found in their open pits. In response, the Texas oil and gas regulatory commission enacted a statewide rule requiring that operators cover their pits and certain open-top tanks with screens or nets to render them harmless to birds. *See* Ernest E. Smith & Jacqueline L. Weaver, 3 Texas Law of Oil & Gas § 14.3(B)(2) (2014). Utilities owning transmission wires that electrocute birds and wind and solar power developers can also find their facilities subject to the MBTA. However, some federal courts have refused to impose strict liability under the MBTA on operators whose pits caused bird deaths unintentionally or incidentally to their operations. *See* Shippen Howe, The Intersection of the Migratory Bird Treaty Act and Energy Companies, 41 Trends 1 (Amer. Bar Ass'n, Section of Env't, Energy & Nat. Res. Newsletter, May/June 2010).

2.   EXTRATERRITORIALITY AND THE "LAW OF NATIONS"

Oil and gas are often found in countries ruled by oppressive autocrats or by weak and unstable governments, or in countries suffering from years of civil war following post-colonial independence. Their populations are among the poorest on earth. Western oil companies go where the oil and gas are and seek contracts to develop the host government's reserves in far-flung corners of the world, from Siberia to the Sudan, Ecuador to Equatorial Guinea, Uzbekistan to Uganda (unless sanctions put these reserves off-limits to them). Many host governments do not have the capital, expertise, technology or management skills to develop their own reserves. Often, a Western oil company forms some kind of joint venture with the host government or its national oil company to develop the reserves in the area awarded under a host government contract (HGC). An oil company may find itself working with government entities that have little regard for democratic values, civil rights, or poverty reduction. Far from fuelling economic growth, oil and gas extraction has been linked to a "petro curse" of stagnation, inflation, pollution, debt, corruption, income inequality, and dictatorship. *See, e.g.*, Terry Lynn Karl, The Paradox of Plenty: Oil Booms and Petro States (1997); Michael Ross, The Oil Curse (2012).

Starting in 1980, the Alien Tort Statute (ATS) of 1789, 28 U.S.C. § 1350, emerged from 200 years of obscurity, when citizens of foreign countries successfully used the act to gain access to U.S. federal district courts as a forum to sue Western oil companies for committing human rights abuses abroad. Here is the ATS in full:

> The district courts shall have original jurisdiction of any civil action by an alien for a tort only, committed in violation of the law of nations or a treaty of the United States.

Plaintiffs seemingly needed to prove only three things to trigger the jurisdiction of the federal district courts in the United States:

1.   the plaintiff is an alien;

2.   a tort has allegedly been committed against him or her;

3.   the tort violates "the law of nations" or a treaty ratified by the U.S.

For more than thirty years, oil companies fought to dismiss such cases through procedural mechanisms, particularly by seeking summary judgments from the district court judges. Some defendants entered into settlement agreements with plaintiffs rather than proceeding to litigate further, especially when the evidence presented at the summary judgment stage showed that the companies knew that human rights abuses were occurring at the hands of government security forces or the military of the host country. Some cases were based on the companies' acceptance of apartheid policies in South Africa; others alleged acts of slave labor, torture, forcible movement of villagers from their homes to make way for pipelines or mines (without compensation), and other heinous acts. The facts coming to light during discovery in these cases presented a distressing picture of Western oil companies operating in countries with brutal regimes or corrupt leaders that were using oil monies to fund conflicts or grandiose personal projects rather than education, health and infrastructure.

In the *Unocal* case, a three-judge panel of Ninth Circuit judges had reversed the district court's grant of summary judgment to Unocal, thus allowing trial on the merits to proceed. Two of the three justices pronounced the standard of liability that would be used at trial to determine if conduct by Unocal could be found to violate the ATS. The standard declared that a company could be held liable under the ATS for "aiding and abetting" a government in committing acts that violated the law of nations. Aiding and abetting was defined as rendering "practical assistance or encouragement that has a substantial effect on the perpetration" of the acts that violate international law. DOE I v. Unocal Corp., 395 F.3d 932 (9th Cir. 2002), *reh'g granted,* 395 F.3d 978 (9th Cir. 2003), *appeal dismissed by agreement,* 403 F.3d 708 (9th Cir. 2005). The Ninth Circuit found sufficient evidence that Unocal may have aided and abetted the Myanmar military in violating international law, as shown by the following documents introduced in the summary judgment phase of the trial:

> A January 1996 meeting document lists "daily security coordination with the army" as a "working procedure." Similarly, the briefing book that Total [the French company that operated the joint project with Unocal] prepared for Unocal President Imle and Unocal CEO Beach on the occasion of their April 1996 visit to the Project mentions that "daily meeting[s]" were "held with the tactical commander" of the army. Moreover, on or about August 29, 1996, Unocal (Singapore) Director of Information Carol Scott discussed with Unocal Media Contact and Spokesperson David Garcia via e-mail how Unocal should publicly address the issue of the alleged movement of villages by the Myanmar Military in connection with the pipeline. Scott cautioned Garcia that "[b]y saying we influenced the army not to move a village, you introduce the concept that they would do such a thing; whereas, by saying that no villages have been moved, you skirt the issue of whether it could happen or not." This e-mail is some evidence that Unocal could influence the army not to commit human rights violations, that the army might otherwise commit such violations, and that Unocal knew this.

Rather than risk a trial, Unocal settled with the plaintiffs who were Myanmar villagers alleging acts of forced labor, expropriation of their property, torture and rape under the ATS. In 2004, after the *Unocal* case had settled, the U.S. Supreme Court, for the first time, interpreted the jurisdictional scope of the ATS. In *Sosa v. Alvarez-Machain,* 542 U.S. 692 (2004), the precise issue raised was whether the ATS allowed U.S. courts to assert jurisdiction over torts that violate the "law of nations," even if Congress had not passed legislation defining what specific acts constitute such violations. A majority of six justices (Justice Souter writing) interpreted the statute to allow such jurisdiction, but only for a very limited set of actions that were like those recognized as violating the law of nations in 1789. In 1789, when ATS was enacted, three specific offenses appeared to violate the law of nations: piracy, the violation of safe conduct, and infringement of the rights of ambassadors (which could affront the sovereignty of a foreign nation and give rise to serious consequences in foreign affairs, such as war). Any new claim recognized today must "rest on a norm of international character accepted by the civilized world and defined with a specificity comparable to the features of the[se] 18th-century paradigms." *Id.* at 725.

The majority opinion then urged great judicial caution when expanding claims recognizable under ATS because U.S. Constitutional jurisprudence (notably *Erie R. Co. v. Tompkins,* 304 U.S. 64 (1938)) severely limits the role of courts in making law. Laws are generally to be made by elected representatives, not by a court's "discretionary judgment" of what international custom considers a norm. Accepting new private causes of action that violate international law could have serious implications for U.S. foreign relations and impinge on the roles of the legislative and executive branches in managing foreign affairs. Thus, while the door to the courts "is still ajar," it is subject to "vigilant doorkeeping" that would often keep federal judges from recognizing new international norms under ATS as part of U.S. domestic law. *Id.* at 729. Any new claims must have the "specificity and acceptance" that the law of nations accorded to piracy. The court then noted:

> This limit upon judicial recognition is generally consistent with the reasoning of many of the courts and judges who faced the issue before it reached this Court. See *Filartiga,* 630 F.2d at 881, at 890 ("[F]or purposes of civil liability, the torturer has become—like the pirate and slave trader before him—*hostis humani generis,* an enemy of all mankind"); . . . see also *In re Estate of Marcos Human Rights Litigation,* 25 F.3d 1467, 1475 (9th Cir. 1994) ("Actionable violations of international law must be of a norm that is specific, universal, and obligatory"). [W]here there is no treaty, and no controlling executive or legislative act or judicial decision, resort must be had to the customs and usages of civilized nations. . . .

Id. at 732, 734. The majority dismissed the case at hand because the alleged violation of international law did not meet the narrow standards required to violate the law of nations under the ATS.

Justice Scalia, joined by Chief Justice Roberts and Justice Thomas, concurred in the judgment and in part of the opinion, but strongly disagreed that the door to the federal courts should be open to any new causes of action. In their view, only the elected representatives to Congress, with approval of the President, could make new federal laws. Unelected federal judges were "usurping this lawmaking power by converting what they regard as norms of international law into American law." *Id.* at 750.

In 2013, the Supreme Court took up another ATS case, brought by Nigerian nationals (now residing in the United States) who alleged that certain Dutch, British and Nigerian corporations had aided and abetted the Nigerian government in committing violations of the law of nations in their operations in Nigeria. The Court's opinion addressed the extraterritoriality of the ATS.

Kiobel v. Royal Dutch Petroleum Co.

133 S.Ct. 1659 (2013).

■ JUDGES: ROBERTS, C. J., delivered the opinion of the Court, in which SCALIA, KENNEDY, THOMAS, and ALITO, JJ., joined.

I.

Petitioners were residents of Ogoniland, an area of 250 square miles located in the Niger delta area of Nigeria and populated by roughly half a million people. When the complaint was filed, respondents Royal Dutch Petroleum Company and Shell Transport and Trading Company, p.l.c., were holding companies incorporated in the Netherlands and England, respectively. Their joint subsidiary, respondent Shell Petroleum Development Company of Nigeria, Ltd. (SPDC), was incorporated in Nigeria, and engaged in oil exploration and production in Ogoniland. According to the complaint, after concerned residents of Ogoniland began protesting the environmental effects of SPDC's practices, respondents enlisted the Nigerian Government to violently suppress the burgeoning demonstrations. Throughout the early 1990's, the complaint alleges, Nigerian military and police forces attacked Ogoni villages, beating, raping, killing, and arresting residents and destroying or looting property. Petitioners further allege that respondents aided and abetted these atrocities by, among other things, providing the Nigerian forces with food, transportation, and compensation, as well as by allowing the Nigerian military to use respondents' property as a staging ground for attacks.

Following the alleged atrocities, petitioners moved to the United States where they have been granted political asylum and now reside as legal residents. . . . They filed suit in the United States District Court for the Southern District of New York, alleging jurisdiction under the Alien Tort Statute and requesting relief under customary international law. . . . According to petitioners, respondents violated the law of nations by aiding and abetting the Nigerian Government in committing (1) extrajudicial killings; (2) crimes against humanity; (3) torture and cruel treatment; (4) arbitrary arrest and detention; (5) violations of the rights to life, liberty, security, and association; (6) forced exile; and (7) property destruction. The District Court dismissed the first, fifth, sixth, and seventh claims, reasoning that the facts alleged to support those claims did not give rise to a violation of the law of nations. The court denied respondents' motion to dismiss with respect to the remaining claims, but certified its order for interlocutory appeal. . . .

The Second Circuit dismissed the entire complaint, reasoning that the law of nations does not recognize corporate liability. We granted certiorari to consider that question. After oral argument, we directed the parties to file supplemental briefs addressing an additional question: "Whether and under what circumstances the [ATS] allows courts to recognize a cause of action for violations of the law of nations occurring within the territory of a sovereign other than the United States." . . .

II

Passed as part of the Judiciary Act of 1789, the ATS was invoked twice in the late 18th century, but then only once more over the next 167 years. . . . The statute provides district courts with jurisdiction to hear certain claims, but does not expressly provide any causes of action. We held in *Sosa* v. *Alvarez-Machain*, 542 U.S. 692 (2004), however, that the First Congress did not intend the provision to be "stillborn." The grant of jurisdiction is instead "best read as having been enacted on the understanding that the common law would provide a cause of action for [a] modest number of international law violations." *Id.*, at 724. We thus held that federal courts may "recognize private claims [for such violations] under federal common law." *Id.,* at 732. The Court in *Sosa* rejected the plaintiff's claim in that case for "arbitrary arrest and detention," on the ground that it failed to state a violation of the law of nations with the requisite "definite content and acceptance among civilized nations." *Id.,* at 699. The question here is not whether petitioners have stated a proper claim under the ATS, but whether a claim may reach conduct occurring in the territory of a foreign sovereign. Respondents contend that claims under the ATS do not, relying primarily on a canon of statutory interpretation known as the presumption against extraterritorial application. That canon provides that "[w]hen a statute gives no clear indication of an extraterritorial application, it has none," *Morrison* v. *National Australia Bank Ltd.*, 561 U.S. ___, (2010), and reflects the "presumption that United States law governs domestically but does not rule the world," *Microsoft Corp.* v. *AT&T Corp.*, 550 U.S. 437, 454 (2007).

This presumption "serves to protect against unintended clashes between our laws and those of other nations which could result in international discord." *EEOC* v. *Arabian American Oil Co.*, 499 U.S. 244 (1991) (*Aramco*). . . .

We typically apply the presumption to discern whether an Act of Congress regulating conduct applies abroad. *See, e.g., Aramco, supra,* at 246. . . . The ATS, on the other hand, is "strictly jurisdictional." *Sosa*, 542 U.S., at 713. It does not directly regulate conduct or afford relief. It instead allows federal courts to recognize certain causes of action based on sufficiently definite norms of international law. But we think the principles underlying the canon of interpretation similarly constrain courts considering causes of action that may be brought under the ATS.

* * *

. . . These concerns [of clashes with foreign policy], which are implicated in any case arising under the ATS, are all the more pressing when the question is whether a cause of action under the ATS reaches conduct within the territory of another sovereign.

* * *

III

Petitioners contend that even if the presumption applies, the text, history, and purposes of the ATS rebut it for causes of action brought under that statute. It is true that Congress, even in a jurisdictional provision, can indicate that it intends federal law to apply to conduct occurring abroad. *See, e.g.,* 18 U.S.C. § 1091(e) (2006 ed., Supp. V) (providing jurisdiction over the offense of genocide "regardless of where the offense is committed" if the alleged offender is, among other things, "present in the United States"). But to rebut the presumption, the ATS would need to evince a "clear indication of extraterritoriality." *Morrison*, 561 U.S., at ___. It does not.

To begin, nothing in the text of the statute suggests that Congress intended causes of action recognized under it to have extraterritorial reach. The ATS covers actions by aliens for violations of the law of nations, but that does not imply extraterritorial reach—such violations affecting aliens can occur either within or outside the United States. . . .

Petitioners make much of the fact that the ATS provides jurisdiction over civil actions for "torts" in violation of the law of nations. They claim that in using that word, the First Congress "necessarily meant to provide for jurisdiction over extraterritorial transitory torts that could arise on foreign soil." Supp. Brief for Petitioners 18. For support, they cite the common-law doctrine that allowed courts to assume jurisdiction over such "transitory torts," including actions for personal injury, arising abroad. *See Mostyn* v. *Fabrigas*, 1 Cowp. 161, 177, 98 Eng. Rep. 1021, 1030 (1774) (Mansfield, L.) ("[A]ll actions of a transitory nature that arise abroad may be laid as happening in an English county"). . . .

Under the transitory torts doctrine, however, "the only justification for allowing a party to recover when the cause of action arose in another civilized jurisdiction is a well founded belief that it was a cause of action in that place." *Cuba R. Co.* v. *Crosby*, 222 U.S. 473, 479 (majority opinion of Holmes, J.). . . . The reference to "tort" does not demonstrate that the First Congress "necessarily meant" for those causes of action to reach conduct in the territory of a foreign sovereign. In the end, nothing in the text of the ATS evinces the requisite clear indication of extraterritoriality.

Nor does the historical background against which the ATS was enacted overcome the presumption against application to conduct in the territory of another sovereign. . . .

[The Court then described two episodes involving violations of the law of nations that had occurred before passage of the ATS. Each involved affronts to French diplomats while on U.S. soil at a time when no U.S. law recognized the privileges of ambassadors. Shortly after the ATS was enacted, two cases invoking it concerned conduct inside U.S. territory.]

These prominent contemporary examples—immediately before and after passage of the ATS—provide no support for the proposition that Congress expected causes of action to be brought under the statute for violations of the law of nations occurring abroad.

The third example of a violation of the law of nations familiar to the Congress that enacted the ATS was piracy. Piracy typically occurs on the high seas, beyond the territorial jurisdiction of the United States or any other country. . . . Petitioners contend that because Congress surely intended the ATS to provide jurisdiction for actions against pirates, it necessarily anticipated the statute would apply to conduct occurring abroad.

Applying U.S. law to pirates, however, does not typically impose the sovereign will of the United States onto conduct occurring within the territorial jurisdiction of another sovereign, and therefore carries less direct foreign policy consequences. Pirates were fair game wherever found, by any nation, because they generally did not operate within any jurisdiction. *See* 4 Blackstone, *supra,* at 71. We do not think that the existence of a cause of action against them is a sufficient basis for concluding that other causes of action under the ATS reach conduct that does occur within the territory of another sovereign; pirates may well be a category unto themselves. *See Morrison*, 561 U.S., at ___, ("[W]hen a statute provides for some extraterritorial application, the presumption against extraterritoriality operates to limit that provision to its terms"). . . .

* * *

Finally, there is no indication that the ATS was passed to make the United States a uniquely hospitable forum for the enforcement of international norms. As Justice Story put it, "No nation has ever yet pretended to be the *custos morum* of the whole world. . . ." *United States*

v. *The La Jeune Eugenie*, 26 F. Cas. 832, 847 (No. 15,551) (CC. Mass. 1822). It is implausible to suppose that the First Congress wanted their fledgling Republic—struggling to receive international recognition—to be the first. Indeed, the parties offer no evidence that any nation, meek or mighty, presumed to do such a thing.

The United States was, however, embarrassed by its potential inability to provide judicial relief to foreign officials injured in the United States. Bradley, 42 Va. J. Int'l L., at 641. Such offenses against ambassadors violated the law of nations, "and if not adequately redressed could rise to an issue of war." *Sosa*, 542 U.S., at 715; cf. The Federalist No. 80, p. 536 (J. Cooke ed. 1961) (A. Hamilton). . . . The ATS ensured that the United States could provide a forum for adjudicating such incidents. . . . Nothing about this historical context suggests that Congress also intended federal common law under the ATS to provide a cause of action for conduct occurring in the territory of another sovereign.

Indeed, far from avoiding diplomatic strife, providing such a cause of action could have generated it. Recent experience bears this out. *See* Doe v. Exxon Mobil Corp., 654 F.3d 11, 77–78 (D.C. Cir. 2011) (Kavanaugh, J., dissenting in part) (listing recent objections to extraterritorial applications of the ATS by Canada, Germany, Indonesia, Papua New Guinea, South Africa, Switzerland, and the United Kingdom). Moreover, accepting petitioners' view would imply that other nations, also applying the law of nations, could hale our citizens into their courts for alleged violations of the law of nations occurring in the United States, or anywhere else in the world. The presumption against extraterritoriality guards against our courts triggering such serious foreign policy consequences, and instead defers such decisions, quite appropriately, to the political branches.

We therefore conclude that the presumption against extraterritoriality applies to claims under the ATS, and that nothing in the statute rebuts that presumption. [P]etitioners' case seeking relief for violations of the law of nations occurring outside the United States is barred.

IV

On these facts, all the relevant conduct took place outside the United States. And even where the claims touch and concern the territory of the United States, they must do so with sufficient force to displace the presumption against extraterritorial application. *See Morrison*, 561 U.S. ___, Corporations are often present in many countries, and it would reach too far to say that mere corporate presence suffices. If Congress were to determine otherwise, a statute more specific than the ATS would be required.

[Concurring opinions of Justices Kennedy and Alito omitted]

JUSTICE BREYER, with whom JUSTICE GINSBURG, JUSTICE SOTOMAYOR and JUSTICE KAGAN join, concurring in the judgment.

I agree with the Court's conclusion but not with its reasoning. . . .

* * *

In my view the majority's effort to answer the question by referring to the "presumption against extraterritoriality" does not work well. That presumption "rests on the perception that Congress ordinarily legislates with respect to domestic, not foreign matters." *Morrison* v. *National Australia Bank Ltd.*, 561 U.S. ___). . . . The ATS, however, was enacted with "foreign matters" in mind. The statute's text refers explicitly to "alien[s]," "treat[ies]," and "the law of nations." 28 U.S.C. § 1350. The statute's purpose was to address "violations of the law of nations, admitting of a judicial remedy and at the same time threatening serious consequences in international affairs." *Sosa*, 542 U.S., at 715. And at least one of the three kinds of activities that we found to fall within the statute's scope, namely piracy, normally takes place abroad. . . .

The majority cannot wish this piracy example away by emphasizing that piracy takes place on the high seas. . . . That is because the robbery and murder that make up piracy do not normally take place in the water; they take place on a ship. And a ship is like land, in that it falls within the jurisdiction of the nation whose flag it flies. . . .

* * *

I very much agree that pirates were fair game "wherever found." Indeed, that is the point. That is why we asked, in *Sosa*, who are today's pirates? Certainly today's pirates include torturers and perpetrators of genocide. And today, like the pirates of old, they are "fair game" where they are found. Like those pirates, they are "common enemies of all mankind and all nations have an equal interest in their apprehension and punishment." 1 Restatement § 404 Reporters' Note 1, p. 256. . . . And just as a nation that harbored pirates provoked the concern of other nations in past centuries, . . . so harboring "common enemies of all mankind" provokes similar concerns today.

Thus the Court's reasoning, as applied to the narrow class of cases that *Sosa* described, fails to provide significant support for the use of any presumption against extraterritoriality; rather, it suggests the contrary.

In any event, as the Court uses its "presumption against extraterritorial application," it offers only limited help in deciding the question presented, namely "'under what circumstances the Alien Tort Statute . . . allows courts to recognize a cause of action for violations of the law of nations occurring within the territory of a sovereign other than the United States.'" 542 U.S. ___, (2012). The majority echoes in this jurisdictional context *Sosa*'s warning to use "caution" in shaping federal common-law causes of action. But it also makes clear that a statutory claim might sometimes "touch and concern the territory of the United States . . . with sufficient force to displace the presumption." It leaves for another day the determination of just when the presumption against extraterritoriality might be "overcome."

II

In applying the ATS to acts "occurring within the territory of a[nother] sovereign," I would assume that Congress intended the statute's jurisdictional reach to match the statute's underlying substantive grasp. That grasp, defined by the statute's purposes set forth in *Sosa*, includes compensation for those injured by piracy and its modern-day equivalents, at least where allowing such compensation avoids "serious" negative international "consequences" for the United States. 542 U.S., at 715. And just as we have looked to established international substantive norms to help determine the statute's substantive reach, so we should look to international jurisdictional norms to help determine the statute's jurisdictional scope.

The Restatement (Third) of Foreign Relations Law is helpful. Section 402 recognizes that, subject to § 403's "reasonableness" requirement, a nation may apply its law (for example, federal common law, . . . not only (1) to "conduct" that "takes place [or to persons or things] within its territory" but also (2) to the "activities, interests, status, or relations of its nationals outside as well as within its territory," (3) to "conduct outside its territory that has or is intended to have substantial effect within its territory," and (4) to certain foreign "conduct outside its territory . . . that is directed against the security of the state or against a limited class of other state interests." In addition, § 404 of the Restatement explains that a "state has jurisdiction to define and prescribe punishment for certain offenses recognized by the community of nations as of universal concern, such as piracy, slave trade," and analogous behavior.

Considering these jurisdictional norms in light of both the ATS's basic purpose (to provide compensation for those injured by today's pirates) and *Sosa*'s basic caution (to avoid international friction), I believe that the statute provides jurisdiction where (1) the alleged tort occurs on American soil, (2) the defendant is an American national, or (3) the defendant's conduct substantially and adversely affects an important American national interest, and that includes a distinct interest in preventing the United States from becoming a safe harbor (free of civil as well as criminal liability) for a torturer or other common enemy of mankind.

I would interpret the statute as providing jurisdiction only where distinct American interests are at issue. . . . That restriction also should help to minimize international friction. Further limiting principles such as exhaustion, *forum non conveniens*, and comity would do the same. So would a practice of courts giving weight to the views of the Executive Branch.

    * * *

More recently two lower American courts have, in effect, rested jurisdiction primarily upon that kind of concern. In *Filartiga*, 630 F. 2d 876, an alien plaintiff brought a lawsuit against an alien defendant for damages suffered through acts of torture that the defendant allegedly inflicted in a foreign nation, Paraguay. Neither plaintiff nor defendant was an American national and the actions underlying the lawsuit took place abroad. The defendant, however, "had . . . resided in the United States for more than ninth months" before being sued, having overstayed his visitor's visa. *Id.,* at 878–879. Jurisdiction was deemed proper because the defendant's alleged conduct violated a well-established international law norm, and the suit vindicated our Nation's interest in not providing a safe harbor, free of damages claims, for those defendants who commit such conduct.

In *Marcos*, the plaintiffs were nationals of the Philippines, the defendant was a Philippine national, and the alleged wrongful act, death by torture, took place abroad. *In re Estate of Marcos, Human Rights Litigation,* 25 F.3d 1467, 1469, 1475 (CA9 1994); *In re Estate of Marcos Human Rights Litigation,* 978 F. 2d 493, 495–496, 500 (CA9 1992). A month before being sued, the defendant, "his family, . . . and others loyal to [him] fled to Hawaii," where the ATS case was heard. *Marcos*, 25 F.3d, at 1469. As in *Filartiga*, the court found ATS jurisdiction.

And in *Sosa* we referred to both cases with approval, suggesting that the ATS allowed a claim for relief in such circumstances. 542 U.S., at 732. . . . Not surprisingly, both before and after *Sosa*, courts have consistently rejected the notion that the ATS is categorically barred from extraterritorial application. *See, e.g.,* 643 F.3d, at 1025 ("[N]o court to our knowledge has ever held that it doesn't apply extraterritorially"); *Sarei* v. *Rio Tinto, PLC*, 671 F.3d 736, 747 (CA9 2011) (en banc) ("We therefore conclude that the ATS is not limited to conduct occurring within the United States"); *Doe* v. *Exxon Mobil Corp.*, 654 F.3d 11, 20, 397 U.S. App. D.C. 371 (CADC 2011) ("[W]e hold that there is no extraterritoriality bar").

Application of the statute in the way I have suggested is consistent with international law and foreign practice. Nations have long been obliged not to provide safe harbors for their own nationals who commit such serious crimes abroad. Many countries permit foreign plaintiffs to bring suits against their own nationals based on unlawful conduct that took place abroad. . . .

* * *

Thus, the jurisdictional approach that I would use is analogous to, and consistent with, the approaches of a number of other nations. It is consistent with the approaches set forth in the Restatement. Its insistence upon the presence of some distinct American interest, its reliance upon courts also invoking other related doctrines such as comity, exhaustion, and *forum non conveniens*, along with its dependence (for its workability) upon courts obtaining, and paying particular attention to, the views of the Executive Branch, all should obviate the majority's concern that our jurisdictional example would lead "other nations, also applying the law of nations," to "hale our citizens into their courts for alleged violations of the law of nations occurring in the United States, or anywhere else in the world."

Most importantly, this jurisdictional view is consistent with the substantive view of the statute that we took in *Sosa*. This approach would avoid placing the statute's jurisdictional scope at odds with its substantive objectives, holding out "the word of promise" of compensation for victims of the torturer, while "break[ing] it to the hope."

[Justice Breyer then applied these principles to the case at hand and found no jurisdiction over the two foreign corporations, whose shares were traded on the New York Stock Exchange, but whose minimal presence consisted of an office in New York City that explained their business to potential investors. The plaintiffs were nationals of other nations and the conduct occurred abroad. The allegations were not that the defendants directly engaged in acts of torture or genocide, but that they helped others (who were not American nationals) to do so. Asserting jurisdiction would not help to vindicate a distinct American interest, such as not providing a safe harbor for an "enemy of all mankind."]

I consequently join the Court's judgment but not its opinion. ■

NOTES AND COMMENTS

1.   The *Kiobel* case has been the subject of much commentary, some arguing that the majority has misread history and legislative intent and international law; others largely agreeing with the result; and others elucidating the course of future ATS litigation after *Kiobel*. Do you think that all ATS litigation in U.S. federal courts involving acts by corporations done in foreign countries has now been ended? Or, only if the acts abroad were committed by foreign corporate defendants? Or, only if the defendant, whether foreign or U.S., was accused of "aiding and abetting" a violation of international law rather than directly engaging in heinous acts?

2.   One expert commentator states that after *Kiobel*, "the old paradigm of using the Alien Tort Statute to redress human rights violations is dead." Roger P. Alford, The Future of Human Rights Litigation after *Kiobel*, 89 Notre Dame L. Rev. 749 (2014). Professor Alford then discusses the possible reach and constraints of other federal statutes (such as the Torture Victims Protection Act and RICO); state-level unfair business practices acts; state (rather than federal) tort law; and foreign tort law, including foreign law that may have international law incorporated into it. The constraints often seem broader than the reach, but he does find some avenues for human rights litigation by aliens in U.S. courts.

3.   Is it a violation of international norms to pollute the environment, leaving dangerous and toxic by-products of oil and gas drilling and production in the rainforests used by indigenous tribes for subsistence living and cultural identity? Does this amount to a form of genocide? In *Beanal v. Freeport-McMoran, Inc.*, 197 F.3d 161 (5th Cir. 1999), the court held that an Indonesian citizen failed to state claims under the ATS for international human rights violations and genocide because treaties and agreements did not contain articulable environmental standards as a basis for an international claim. For example, the Rio Declaration on Environment and Development "merely refer[s] to a general sense of environmental responsibility and state[s] abstract rights." *Id.* at 167. Although the United States has articulated standards in statutory law that apply to discharges of mine tailings and to endangered species, the federal courts should not override the environmental policies of other governments on their own lands with U.S. standards. The plaintiff alleged that Freeport's mining had destroyed his tribe's habitat, but the court held that cultural genocide was not recognized as a violation of international law. *See also* Flores v. S. Peru Copper Corp., 343 F.3d 140 (2d Cir. 2003) (personal injury and death claims brought under ATS against mining company for severe lung disease dismissed because rights to health and life were not sufficiently definite to be a binding rule of customary international law nor did such customary law prohibit pollution that stayed inside national borders). For a discussion of the ATS and climate change litigation, see Emily Hammond & David L. Markell, Private Remedies, in Global Climate Change and U.S. Law, at 256–58 (2d ed. 2014) (concluding such claims are unlikely to succeed).

4.   Can the Congressional intent behind the ATS be read as reflecting a concern to provide a remedy to aliens, especially ambassadors, who can show that violations of the law of nations were committed against them? And to provide the remedy of compensation for those aliens injured by piracy? ATS litigation may well be nearly dead, but civilized nations still have a great interest in preventing violations of international law and finding appropriate

remedies for those injured by the perpetrators of these violations, as discussed next.

3. CODES OF CONDUCT AND THE ROLE OF PRIVATE GOVERNANCE

This section examines the ways that extractive industry members, often working with entities such as non-governmental organizations (NGOs), the United Nations, and their home governments, have sought to minimize human rights abuses and, of course, to control the business risk of shareholder boycotts, violence that shuts down their foreign operations, and intensely negative media coverage. Both companies and governments have the right to protect a project's assets and to keep their workers safe from hostile acts. Many ATS cases involved the acts of public security forces that had little regard for human rights. The Unocal president, in one phase of the ATS litigation described above, is purported to have remarked: "What I'm saying is that if you threaten the pipeline, there's gonna be more military. If forced labor goes hand in glove with the military, yes there will be more forced labor. For every threat to the pipeline, there will be a reaction." Nat'l Coalition Gov't of Burma v. Unocal, 176 F.R.D 329 (C.D. Calif. 1997).

The U.S. and British governments urged their major oil companies to work with NGOs and other experts to develop a code of conduct that would discourage security forces from abusing people who live near oil projects. The resulting Voluntary Principles on Security and Human Rights have now been accepted for implementation by 26 companies, many of them in the oil or mining sector, with nine governments and eleven NGOs participating in the effort to promote respect for human rights. *See* http://www.voluntaryprinciples.org. Here are some of the key provisions, paraphrased unless otherwise indicated.

Voluntary Principles on Security and Human Rights

(first released Dec. 20, 2000 by the U.S. Department of State).

I.   RISK ASSESSMENT

The ability to assess risks is critical to the security of Company personnel, local communities and assets; to the success of the Company's short and long-term operations; and to the promotion and protection of human rights. The quality of risk assessments depends on assembling regularly updated, credible information from a broad range of local and national governments, security firms, other companies, home governments, multilateral institutions, and civil society knowledgeable about local conditions. This information may be most effective when shared to the fullest extent possible between Companies, civil society, and governments. Effective risk assessments should consider the following factors: Identification of security risks and the potential for violence; human rights records; understanding the root causes of local conflicts; assessing whether local prosecutors and judges can hold human rights violators accountable; and monitoring project equipment, both lethal and non-lethal, to prevent its diversion to those who may use it to commit human rights abuses.

II. INTERACTIONS BETWEEN COMPANIES AND PUBLIC SECURITY

Although governments have the primary role of maintaining law and order, security and respect for human rights, Companies have an interest in ensuring that actions taken by governments, particularly the actions of public security providers, are consistent with the protection and promotion of human rights. In some cases, Companies may be required or expected to contribute to, or otherwise reimburse, the costs of protecting Company facilities and personnel borne by public security. While public security is expected to act in a manner consistent with local and national laws as well as with human rights standards and international humanitarian law, abuses may nevertheless occur.

The following voluntary principles should guide relationships between Companies and public security regarding security provided to Companies:

Security Arrangements: Companies should consult regularly with host governments and local communities about the impact of their security arrangements on those communities; communicate their human rights policies to the public security providers and "express their desire that security be provided in a manner consistent with those policies by personnel with adequate and effective training."

Deployment and Conduct: Companies should "use their influence to promote the following principles:" (a) individuals credibly implicated in human rights abuses should not provide public security services for Companies; (b) force should be used only when strictly necessary; and (c) the rights of individuals should not be violated while exercising the right of peaceful assembly, collective bargaining, or other related rights of Company employees as recognized by the Universal Declaration of Human Rights and the ILO Declaration on Fundamental Principles and Rights at Work. If force is used, incidents should be reported to the appropriate authorities and to the Company, and medical aid should be provided to injured persons, including to offenders.

Companies should hold structured meetings with public security on a regular basis to discuss security, human rights concerns and should also consult regularly with other Companies, host and home governments, and civil society. In consultations with host governments, Companies should take all appropriate measures to promote observance of applicable international law enforcement principles, particularly those reflected in the UN Code of Conduct for Law Enforcement Officials and the UN Basic Principles on the Use of Force and Firearms. Companies should support efforts by governments, civil society and multilateral institutions to provide human rights training and education for public security as well as their efforts to strengthen state institutions to ensure accountability and respect for human rights.

Responses to Human Rights Abuses (quoted in full):

- Companies should record and report any credible allegations of human rights abuses by public security in their areas of operation to appropriate host government authorities. Where appropriate, Companies should urge investigation and that action be taken to prevent any recurrence.

- Companies should actively monitor the status of investigations and press for their proper resolution.
- Companies should, to the extent reasonable, monitor the use of equipment provided by the Company and to investigate properly situations in which such equipment is used in an inappropriate manner.
- Every effort should be made to ensure that information used as the basis for allegations of human rights abuses is credible and based on reliable evidence. The security and safety of sources should be protected. Additional or more accurate information that may alter previous allegations should be made available as appropriate to concerned parties.

III. INTERACTIONS BETWEEN COMPANIES AND PRIVATE SECURITY

Private security should observe the policies of the contracting Company regarding ethical conduct and human rights; the law and professional standards of the country in which they operate; emerging best practices developed by industry, civil society, and governments; and international humanitarian law. Private security should have policies regarding appropriate conduct and the local use of force. Practices of security personnel should be capable of being monitored by Companies or, where appropriate, by independent third parties. Such monitoring includes detailed investigations into allegations of abusive or unlawful acts; the availability of disciplinary measures sufficient to prevent and deter; and procedures for reporting allegations to relevant local law enforcement authorities when appropriate.

All allegations of human rights abuses by private security should be recorded. Credible allegations should be properly investigated. In those cases where allegations against private security providers are forwarded to the relevant law enforcement authorities, Companies should actively monitor the status of investigations and press for their proper resolution. In cases where physical force is used, private security should investigate and report the incident to the Company. Private security should refer the matter to local authorities and/or take disciplinary action where appropriate.

Where appropriate, Companies should include the principles outlined above as contractual provisions in agreements with private security providers and ensure that private security personnel are adequately trained to respect the rights of employees and the local community. Companies should consult and monitor private security providers to ensure they provide security in a manner consistent with these principles. Where appropriate, Companies should seek to employ private security providers that are representative of the local population. ∎

NOTE AND COMMENT

1. After a company reports credible allegations of human rights violations to the host government, has it now fully complied with the Code? If this is the extent of its obligations, isn't the Code a toothless paper tiger in the fight

to protect vulnerable people against an authoritarian and cruel host government?

The U.N. Commission on Human Rights had worked unsuccessfully for years to secure agreement among diverse stakeholder groups on a framework of norms that would guide the conduct of transnational corporations with respect to protecting human rights. The result was a set of draft norms that imposed on corporations all of the duties of States—a result lauded by NGOs, but anathema to business. The U.N. appointed John Ruggie as its Special Representative for Business and Human Rights to break the impasse and develop a workable framework that would be broadly acceptable to all groups, all of whom agreed that such a framework was urgently needed. *See* John Ruggie, Business and Human Rights: A Political Scientist's Guide to Survival in A Domain Where Lawyers and Activists Reign (2008), http://business-humanrights. org/en/pdf-business-and-human-rights-a-political-scientists-guide-to-survival-in-a-domain-where-lawyers-and-activists-reign.

After three years of multi-stakeholder meetings and studies, Dr. Ruggie presented his report to the U.N. Human Rights Council titled "Protect, Respect and Remedy: A Framework for Business and Human Rights," 8th Sess., U.N. Doc. A/HRC/8/5 (2008) available at http://www. reports-and-materials.org/sites/default/files/reports-and-materials/ Ruggie-report-7-Apr-2008.pdf (hereinafter referred to as the Final Report). The Final Report declares, as its first principle, that the "human rights regime rests upon the bedrock role of States." *Id.* at para 50. States have a duty to protect their citizens.

However, businesses must be direct and active players, independent of the State's duty and of the State's enforcement of its own duty. The second principle is the obligation of corporations to "respect human rights," summarized in three simple words: "Do No Harm." *Id.* at para. 24. This basic expectation gives business its social license to operate. The principle already appeared in many voluntary initiatives by business, in claims made by companies that they respected human rights, and in several soft law international instruments. For example, the many hundreds of companies that had joined the U.N.'s Global Compact have acknowledged a commitment to respect human rights. *Id.* at para. 22. Yet few companies had systems in place enabling them to support the claim that they do protect human rights.

The Final Report explained what corporations must do to "respect human rights." They must avoid "complicity" in the abuses that may be committed by others. *Id.* at paras 73–81. The Report acknowledged that it was not possible to specify definitive tests for complicity. But, companies could avoid complicity by employing due diligence processes to be aware of, prevent and address adverse human rights impacts. What constitutes due diligence in the Final Report?

1.   A corporate human rights policy using standards from the International Bill of Human Rights and core conventions, such as the International Labor Organization (ILO) Declaration on Fundamental Principles and Rights at Work, that are most often used to judge company conduct.

2.   Doing a human rights impact assessment, similar to environmental and social impact assessment.

3.   Integrating human rights policy throughout the company, rather than keeping it in its own institutionalized box, separate from commercial decisions.

4.   Tracking performance by monitoring and auditing.

5.   Creating an effective grievance mechanism for those who claim violations.

Id. at paras. 56–64, 93–95.

In his report, Dr. Ruggie cogently noted: "Currently, the primary means through which grievances against companies play out are litigation and public campaigns. For a company to take a bet on winning lawsuits or successfully countering hostile campaigns is at best optimistic risk management." *Id.* at para. 93.

The Final Report did not advocate or propose an overarching business and human rights treaty that many NGOs had sought as a means of imposing binding international standards on corporations. Dr. Ruggie explained why not in remarks made to the International Law Association in May 2008. In his view, international treaties suffer the same reliance on voluntary actions as do codes of conduct. A state cannot be forced to ratify a treaty, and treaty enforcement is highly problematic, often lacking any formal enforcement mechanism. *See* John Ruggie, Business and Human Rights: A Political Scientist's Guide to Survival in a Domain Where Lawyers and Activists Reign, Ann. Conf. Int'l Law Ass'n, May 17, 2008 (London). In contrast, some voluntary initiatives impose obligations on those who have joined the initiative (citing the Voluntary Principles on Security and Human Rights as an example). When coupled with third-party auditing of compliance and NGO "watch dog" reports that monitor compliance, voluntary codes can have more effective policing mechanisms than treaties. Dr. Ruggie cited as examples the Kimberley Process (aimed at deterring the sale of diamonds from conflict zones) and the Fair Labor Association's mandatory supply chain monitoring system and training of factory managers to respect workers' rights. Moreover, corporations are responsive to consumer and investor preferences and to regulatory and market forces that can bring about speedier "rights-compliant" cultures than the treaty process. In contrast, sovereigns have no legal superiors.

Dr. Ruggie was retained by the U.N. for three additional years to "operationalize" the framework summarized above. The result of that effort is the "Guiding Principles on Business and Human Rights: Implementing the United Nations 'Protect, Respect and Remedy' Framework," unanimously endorsed by the U.N. Human Rights Council in 2011, after 30 years of failed efforts. The document consists of 31 principles, with short, explanatory commentary on each. *See* http://www. ohchr.org/documents/publications/GuidingprinciplesBusinesshr_en.pdf.

The Guiding Principles (GPs) have gained considerable traction in the business sector and in law firms that advise oil companies on due diligence procedures in this and other contexts. An excellent article written by lawyers at a large London law firm and researchers from the British Institute of International and Comparative Law, asserts that these GPs are now an international standard. The article then explores the impacts of these standards on oil and gas companies. *See* Rae Lindsay et al., Human Rights Responsibilities in the Oil and Gas Sector: Applying the UN Guiding Principles, 6 J. World Energy L. & Bus. 2 (2013). The authors focus on the practices that companies should use to perform due diligence with respect to human rights. The researchers also conducted a survey of the published reports of many private oil companies, National Oil Companies (NOCs) and large service providers in the oil sector to ascertain whether they had human rights policies in place and whether they reported on human rights issues in accordance with the Global Reporting Initiative's (GRI) guidelines. (The GRI is an international non-profit organization composed of a network of professionals and organizations from many sectors and regions that has created a standard Sustainability Reporting Framework for businesses to use in reporting to stakeholders. Visit https://www.globalreporting.org/Pages/default. aspx.) While a majority of publicly listed companies had adopted human rights policies, few of the largest state-owned companies had. Lindsay et al., *supra*, at 32–34. A significant number of the publicly traded companies were using the GRI guidelines.

General Principles (GPs) 11 through 24 cover the corporate responsibility to respect human rights. GP 11 requires that businesses "seek to prevent or mitigate adverse human rights impacts that are directly linked to their operations, products or services by their business relationships, even if they have not contributed to these impacts." Private oil companies are linked by contract to a wide range of entities, including joint venture partners that are often national oil companies or host government entities, local businesses that service their operations, and a host of other suppliers in a long global supply chain. GP 19 explains that companies should use their "leverage" (defined as the ability to effect change in wrongful practices) over those entities with which they have a business relationship to prevent or mitigate adverse human rights impacts. Leverage may be increased by offering "capacity building or other incentives" to that entity, or collaborating with other actors and by seeking independent advice from expert groups.

If a company lacks any leverage over a contracting party, and cannot build any, then it should consider ending the relationship. If a relationship is deemed "crucial" to the company's business and serious human rights abuses continue to occur, the company that remains in the business relationship must show "ongoing efforts to mitigate the impact and be prepared the accept any consequences—reputational, financial or legal." *Id.* at 22. Under GP 22, companies should provide remedies for abuses that they have contributed to. GPs 25 to 31 provide considerable guidance on the types and character of grievance mechanism that companies should use to remediate human rights abuses. Lindsay et al.'s survey of oil companies in late 2011 found that few corporate human rights reports or policies included information on specific practices used as grievances mechanisms. Here is an example from ExxonMobil's 2010 Corporate Citizenship Report, as reported in the survey. *Id.* at 40, n. 92:

> We . . . recognize the need for local populations to be able to voice and resolve concerns related to a project without fear of retribution. Our Upstream Socioeconomic Management Standard includes provisions for establishing a grievance mechanism, where appropriate . . . [that can provide] a

systematic and transparent process for local people to raise concerns, which can be addressed by the company within an appropriate timeframe.

Notes and Comments

1.   Does the "leverage-based" responsibility of a business to prevent or mitigate harm caused by other entities create an active duty to protect human rights that reaches beyond the passive "do no harm" obligation? Should an international oil company include in its contracts with counter-parties, an obligation that the latter are required to adopt the company's human rights policies? The Lindsay et al. article suggests the types of covenants and assurances that oil companies might include in contracts with third parties. *Id.* at 44.

What if an oil company has reason to believe that the other party has neither the capacity nor the willingness to meet these contract terms? Are these assurances and covenants then just "empty words" that shift the burden of mitigating adverse impacts to others, absolving the company from its obligation under the GPs? Or must companies engage in capacity building that educates and trains their local contractors and other contractual partners? An Interpretative Guide to the GPs and other reports to help companies set up a human rights policy are available at http://www.ohchr.org/EN/Issues/Business/Pages/Tools.aspxAn.

The Lindsay et al. article describes the "prudent" practice of requiring that key third-party employees receive training and provide periodic certifications that they are following the codes of conduct of the company with respect to the FCPA, the ATS, and other laws and industry standards. Non-compliance by third parties breaches the contract and can result in contract termination. *Id.* at 44 & n. 206. The Human Rights Policy of one U.S.-based company, Occidental, states that contracts related to foreign activities "*shall* include provisions with respect to the observance of Human Rights, . . . and provide appropriate and practical monitoring mechanisms." *Id.* at 38.

2.   The extractive industry is itself on the "receiving end" of leverage exerted by the International Finance Corporation (IFC) and other large lending institutions that have now incorporated the GPs into their standards on environmental and social impact assessment. *Id.* at 46. Other pressure points arise from laws like California's Transparency in Supply Chains Act, which requires that certain companies report the measures used to prevent slavery and human trafficking in their supply chains. *Id.*

3.   Companies often gain access to develop oil and gas in foreign lands by entering into contracts with host governments that award them acreage. An Addendum to the General Principles, titled the "Principles for Responsible Contracts," offers guidance to negotiating and signing contracts with state-owned entities, often the state's national oil company. *See* http://www.ohchr.org/EN/Issues/TransnationalCorporations/Pages/Reports.aspx. Professor Ruggie's Final Report noted that one company included the Voluntary Principles on Security and Human Rights text into its host government contract and in another project attached the text to the project contract with its state-owned partners. In his view, this was an "important precedent" because these voluntary measures may now be legally   enforceable,   creating   a   promising   "hybrid   practice"   of

voluntary/enforceable practice. *See* Final Report, *supra,* at para 50. Why would an oil company do this?

4.   Do legal risks increase for reporting companies that now disclose more information about their due diligence in human rights protection? After *Kiobel*, the threat of ATS litigation in the United States has been greatly reduced. The Lindsay et al. authors caution that companies that knowingly provide support to perpetrators of gross abuses of human rights may still risk prosecution under international criminal law. Lindsay et al., *supra*, at 53–54. As to civil liability, while few domestic courts are open to private causes of action for breaches of international human rights laws or customary international law, domestic tort law (e.g., assault, battery, false imprisonment) may still provide a possible path to liability in some countries. *Id*. If a company implements the practices recommended in the GPs to protect and respect human rights, has it met its duty of care under traditional tort law?

Consider the answer to this last question in light of the following excerpt from the court's opinion in *Doe I v. Unocal Corp.*, 395 F.3d 932, 940–42 (9th Cir. 2002):

> Before Unocal acquired an interest in the Project, it hired a consulting company, Control Risk Group, to assess the risks involved in the investment. In May 1992, Control Risk Group informed Unocal that "[t]hroughout Burma the government habitually makes use of forced labour to construct roads." Control Risk Group concluded that "[i]n such circumstances UNOCAL and its partners will have little freedom of manoeuvre." Unocal's awareness of the risk at that time is also reflected in the deposition testimony of Unocal Vice President of International Affairs Stephen ("Unocal Vice President Lipman"):
>
> > In our discussions between Unocal and Total [preceding Unocal's acquisition of an interest in the Project], we said that the option of having the [Myanmar] [M]ilitary provide protection for the pipeline construction and operation of it would be that they might proceed in the manner that would be out of our control and not be in a manner that we would like to see them proceed, I mean, going to excess.
>
> Two months later, on March 16, 1995, Unocal Representative Robinson confirmed to Unocal President Imle that the Myanmar Military might be committing human rights violations in connection with the Project. Thus, Robinson wrote to Imle that he had received publications from human rights organizations "which depicted in more detail than I have seen before the increased encroachment of [the Myanmar Military's] activities into the villages of the pipeline area." Robinson concluded on the basis of these publications that "[o]ur assertion that [the Myanmar Military] has not expanded and amplified its usual methods around the pipeline on our behalf may not withstand much scrutiny."
>
> Later that year, on December 11, 1995, Unocal Consultant John Haseman, a former military attache at the U.S. Embassy in Rangoon, reported to Unocal that the Myanmar Military was, in fact, using forced labor and committing other human rights

violations in connection with the Project. Haseman told Unocal that "Unocal was particularly discredited when a corporate spokesman was quoted as saying that Unocal was satisfied with . . . assurances [by the Myanmar Military] that no human rights abuses were occurring in the area of pipeline construction." Haseman went on to say . . . that Unocal, "by seeming to have accepted [the Myanmar Military]'s version of events, appears at best naive and at worst a willing partner in the situation."

If Unocal (which merged with Chevron in 2005) had a human rights policy in place that accorded with the GPs, should it have acquired an interest in this Project? Having bought in, what should Unocal now do?

In September 1996, Total reported to Unocal that it had admitted to a European official investigating the use of forced labor in Myanmar that forced labor did indeed occur in connection with the pipeline. Total noted that when they knew of such occurrences, they compensated the workers. *Id.* at 942. Despite knowledge that forced labor was being used, Unocal submitted a statement to the City Counsel of New York, in response to a proposed New York City select purchasing law (imposed on firms doing business in Myanmar) that "no [human rights] violations have taken place" in the vicinity of the pipeline route. *Id.*

Why were the employees of these companies acting in these ways? What would you have done?

5.   In Chapter 4 we saw how the Recommended Practices of the American Petroleum Institute (API) were quickly incorporated into new regulations adopted by the U.S. government to improve safety and environmental management in offshore development. The "soft law" of industry-created practices became "hard law." The UN Guiding Principles on Business and Human Rights are still "soft law."

What are the weaknesses of relying on voluntary codes? Are they the best that can be done politically—but still not very good? How are the signers of these codes forced to comply? How are they monitored? Should third-party verifiers audit the company's processes, as now required by offshore regulations in the United States? Should the results be reported to the public? Do the UN Guiding Principles compromise too much in the quest for a consensus norm to guide the actions of Western multinationals abroad in the area of human rights?

The UN Global Compact (a set of ten principles, one page long, available at: http://www.unglobalcompact.org) has been signed by over 3,000 companies, committing the companies to make efforts to improve the standard of living of citizens residing in very poor countries. In 2008, to preserve the "integrity" of the Compact, the U.N. delisted 630 companies from the Compact for failing to submit progress reports. Is this "naming and shaming" an effective policing mechanism or a "costless exit"?

CHAPTER 15

TRANSPORTATION

A. A CHANGING TRANSPORTATION ECONOMY

Transportation—the use of cars, trucks, planes, trains, boats, barges, off-road vehicles, and an array of other moving devices—is often considered a separate category from energy. Indeed, as shown in Chapter 1, the majority of fuels (primary energy) that we use in the United States are used to fuel power plants to generate electricity. Yet transportation devices are also very important users of energy: we use fuels like gasoline and diesel (forms of refined oil) and natural gas to power our cars, trucks, buses, and other equipment. Increasingly, we also use electricity to power transportation: plug-in vehicles have reached consumer markets and are becoming more common, particularly in states like California with stringent limitations on air pollutant emissions from cars.

Transportation fits within our energy economy in important ways, and its role is quickly changing. First, transportation competes with power plants and other sectors for the use of fuel. As the United States produces more natural gas using horizontal drilling and hydraulic fracturing, the federal government and states have encouraged the conversion of vehicles from gasoline or diesel to natural gas. This conversion will reduce emissions from vehicles and improve air quality. If widespread vehicle conversion were to occur, however, the transportation sector might compete with the power plant sector for cheap, domestic natural gas. While supplies are abundant, there might not be much complaint, but particularly during times of peak electricity demand, the competition for natural gas between industrial users, natural gas-fired power plants, and vehicles that burn on natural gas could become more important.

Second, transportation will increasingly use energy in the form of electricity rather than fuel. Like any other "appliance," factory, or house, vehicles can now be connected to the electric grid to charge a battery that runs the vehicle. This creates important opportunities for the electric sector. As described in previous chapters, power plants face the challenge of providing the exact amount of electricity demanded by users instantaneously and maintaining a relatively constant flow of electricity in power lines. This is an expensive proposition, and the provision of electricity would be much easier, and likely substantially cheaper, if utilities could more easily store electricity and draw from storage rather than having to generate electricity whenever demand rose. Plug-in vehicles with increasingly sophisticated batteries make this storage a more realistic possibility. If thousands of car owners plugged in fully charged electric vehicles, utilities could draw from these car batteries during times of peak electric demand. Furthermore, electric vehicle owners could reduce their impact on the electric grid and avoid creating peak demand by charging their cars at night, when demand tends to be low. Indeed, electric cars, which owners can plug in at night, might constitute an important use of wind energy, which is in some areas most abundant at night yet cannot be easily stored for daytime use.

A third aspect of transportation that increasingly ties this sector with other portions of the energy sector is the movement of oil using non-pipeline infrastructure. As discussed in Chapter 4 (oil and gas) and Chapter 14 (international energy), there has been a resurgence of oil production in the United States and Canada due to the development of the oil sands in Canada and shale oil in the United States. Unlike natural gas, which generally requires pipelines for economic transport, oil can be transported via barge, train, pipeline, or truck. Indeed, as Alexandra Klass and Danielle Meinhardt note in their thorough examination of oil pipelines, oil was previously transported by teams of horses; these horse drivers formed the original "Teamsters" union. Alexandra B. Klass & Danielle Meinhardt, Transporting Oil and Gas: U.S. Infrastructure Challenges, ___ Iowa L. Rev. ___ (forthcoming 2015). As North American oil production has grown it has exceeded certain pipeline capacity, and more and more oil is transported by rail. This can displace other rail users and also raises safety concerns, as demonstrated by a recent, tragic accident in Quebec in which a rail car carrying oil turned over and exploded, resulting in numerous casualties. *See* Allan Woods et al., Lac Megantic: Death toll rises in Quebec train derailment explosion, Toronto Star, July 7, 2014.

This chapter discusses the history of transportation and its role in the energy sector, explores how that role is changing through electric vehicle use and other transitions, and describes the law that applies to the transportation sector.

B. HOW AMERICAN TRANSPORTATION EVOLVED

To understand the legal structure governing transportation in the United States it is necessary to examine how the various modes of transportation evolved and how the law changed in response.

1. TRANSPORTATION AS THE FOUNDERS KNEW IT

In the early days of the republic, animal power and wind power were the predominant sources of energy for transportation. In urban areas, horses were everywhere. Even well into the 19th century, horse-drawn vehicles were one of the main forms of urban transportation, and the livery stable, with its noise and odors, became a common target of nuisance litigation. Today, we still use "horsepower" as a measure of the ability of an engine to perform work.

The early years of the 19th century were marked by debates over the proper role of the federal government in stimulating—and financing—the improvements in transportation that the public wanted. In 1808, President Jefferson's treasury secretary, Albert Gallatin, proposed an extensive plan for the construction of turnpikes and canals, including a "national turnpike" from Maine to Georgia. The Gallatin plan was soon forgotten in the turmoil leading to the war in 1812, but because it was both a comprehensive inventory and a thoughtful assessment of geographic possibilities it set the basic framework for discussion after 1815, and continued to be debated in virtually every session of Congress for a generation. D.W. Meinig, Continental America (1993).

As the nation grew, the need for better transportation became even more obvious. From the early days of European colonization of North America, concern about linkage among the widespread sections of the country had been a matter of national debate. Could the interests of the separate states be unified without an efficient transportation network? Could we realize our "manifest destiny" of controlling the western part of the continent without effective ways to move people and goods there? How much energy should we expend in integrating the different parts of the country?

In 1816, Congressman John Calhoun introduced a bill to set up a fund to support a unified national system of roads and canals, and warned that if "we permit a low, sordid, selfish, and sectional spirit to take possession of this House . . . we will divide, and in its consequences will follow misery and despotism." Paul Chen, The Constitutional Politics of Roads and Canals: Inter-Branch Dialogue over Internal Improvements, 1800–1828, 28 Whittier L. Rev. 625, 640–41 (2006). We'll never know whether Calhoun's bill would have been the straw that kept the camel's back from breaking because regional squabbles repeatedly resulted in the defeat of national transportation legislation.

2. RAILROADS: THE MOBILE INDUSTRIAL REVOLUTION

Meanwhile, it was the private sector that took the lead in developing the new technologies that led to the construction of the transportation system that dominated the nation for almost a century—the railroad network. Steam engines fueled by coal were developed late in the 18th century, but it was not until the first half of the nineteenth century that they were installed on wheeled vehicles that came to be known as railroad trains.

The railroad engine's power proved to be the key factor in establishing the railroads' dominance in the period after the Civil War. The railroads revolutionized transportation by making it possible to carry heavy loads over long distances much faster and cheaper than older forms of transportation. Passenger travel on long distance railroads also became common. The trains provided increased comfort and convenience in comparison to the stagecoaches they replaced. The new railroads increased the volume of passengers and speed of travel while substantially reducing the cost of transportation. In 1882, just three years after the intercontinental railroad was completed, a million passengers rode between Omaha and San Francisco. Russell Bourne, Americans on the Move 97 (1995).

The steam engine also had a significant impact on water travel. Robert Fulton first attracted wide attention to the possibility of steamboats when he made his well-publicized journey up the Hudson River from New York to Albany in 1807. Within a few decades the paddlewheel steamboats became a familiar sight on rivers such as the Ohio and Mississippi, carrying passengers and towing barges. Towards the end of the century, steamships became the dominant force in international travel as well.

In the cities, electricity became the driving force in rail transportation as the old horse-drawn streetcars were replaced by electrified trolleys. Between 1890 and 1920, the use of electric streetcars rose from 2 billion to 15.5 billion trips annually. Mark S. Foster, From Streetcar to Superhighway 14 (1981).

3. THE INTERNAL COMBUSTION ENGINE

The end of the nineteenth century saw the debut of the internal combustion engine using gasoline as a fuel. Internal combustion ushered in the third phase of American transportation. Duryea Brothers opened the first American automobile manufacturing plant in 1895, followed quickly by a number of others, and by 1905 the most popular song in the country had everyone singing "Come away with me Lucille . . . in my merry Oldsmobile." Three years later, Henry Ford started producing the Model T, and the auto industry never looked back. Clay McShane, The Automobile 19–39 (1997).

It didn't take long to begin putting the internal combustion engine in trucks as well as cars, and the newly formed trucking industry quickly began to compete with railroads and barge lines for the transport of goods. In the 1950s, the efficiency of trucking was further enhanced by the widespread use of diesel engines and diesel fuel, a more economical method of transporting heavy cargoes. Between 1965 and 1980, the number of tractor-trailers in the national fleet nearly doubled, and their total miles traveled per year grew at a rate nearly double that of passenger car travel, which was itself growing significantly. Nat'l Res. Council, Transp. Res. Bd., Toward a Sustainable Future 41 (1997). By 2012, medium and heavy trucks consumed 22% of U.S. transportation energy. Stacy C. Davis et al., Oak Ridge Nat'l Lab. & Roltek, Inc.,

Transportation Energy Data Book Ed. 33 at 2-1 (2014), http://cta.ornl.gov/data/tedb33/Edition33_Full_Doc.pdf.

Automobiles brought a new mobility, unhindered by the need for extensive track systems. As the road network grew, buses replaced streetcar lines as the most common form of mass transportation. As more people acquired their own automobiles, the pattern of urban development began to change. The convenience of driving individually-owned vehicles began to dominate personal transportation decisions.

4. HOW HIGHWAY INFRASTRUCTURE GREW

With the country's attention and capital focused on railroads, roadbuilding languished in the nineteenth century. As the twentieth century began, however, pressure for better roads began to appear from a new source—bicyclists. The introduction of pneumatic tires for bicycles created heavy demand, and by 1896 a million bicycles were being sold every year. The League of American Wheelmen was formed to lobby for better roads. Bourne, *supra,* at 110–11. As quickly as 1910, however, it was apparent that the automobile would be the vehicle that most needed roadways. Today, both automobiles and bicycles compete for roads, with a growing contingent of bicyclists demanding bike lanes and other access, and with many cities working to improve access to encourage this access. Many cities welcome bicycle use as a means of reducing congestion and air pollution and improving public health.

5. THE FEDERAL ROLE IN HIGHWAY TRANSPORTATION

The U.S. Department of Agriculture (USDA) had created an Office of Road Inquiry in 1893 in response to the interests of bicyclists, and it had engaged in promotional activities to encourage local governments to build better roads. But at the outset of World War I, automobile production in America was running at about 200,000 per year, and these drivers were growing tired of being stuck in the mud. Automotive transportation began to promise the public a greater degree of flexibility than was available by rail.

In response, a stronger federal highway agency was created to tie together the road networks being developed by the various states. After the end of World War I, President Wilson implemented the act that created the Federal Bureau of Public Roads as successor to the Office of Road Inquiry. Many promoters of road construction saw themselves as providing a healthier alternative to the "teeming cities," which they saw as increasingly overcrowded. Henry Wallace, later to be USDA Secretary in President Roosevelt's cabinet, said that "decentralization properly worked out in connection with concrete roads and electricity will have a lot to do with providing a more satisfactory life for the next generation." Tom Lewis, Divided Highways 52 (1997).

The need for better roads was made apparent by the heavy influx of military-related truck traffic that had occurred during the war. The success of trucking for military goods inspired the birth of the interstate trucking industry, which joined in the demand for more and better highways. Lewis, *supra,* at 10–11. The Lincoln Highway, linking New York and San Francisco, was followed by other named routes motivated by tourism promotion.

The 1920s saw the creation of the framework of federal-state agency cooperation that continues to characterize the road-building program. By this time, each state had created a road-building agency to oversee construction of all major roads in the state.

By the end of the decade, agreement had been reached on the places where each state's roads would link up with those of their neighbors. Common systems of signage and numbering were established. As public fascination with the automobile grew, the federal money for highway construction increased each year. The chief of the Bureau of Public Roads proclaimed the goal to "be able to drive out of any county seat in the United States at thirty-five miles an hour and drive into any other county seat-and never crack a spring." Lewis, *supra,* at 19. By 1930, American auto production had reached five million vehicles per year.

The depression that began in 1929 only increased the demand for road construction as a method of providing jobs for the unemployed. Presidents Hoover and then Roosevelt continually increased the flow of federal money into highway construction during the 1930s. Congress ensured that the federal money was spread throughout every congressional district, creating a network that emphasized extensiveness rather than capacity. Federal taxes on gasoline supplemented similar state taxes to help finance the program.

The rush to spend money overrode the engineer's desire to plan a cohesive system. Traffic engineers no longer sought to create the most efficient transportation network. Their job was to identify drivers' demands and supply what they needed. Peter D. Norton, Fighting Traffic 243 (2008).

During World War II, it became apparent that American highways were quite primitive in comparison with those of Europe. After the war ended, a broad coalition of trucking companies, auto manufacturers and oil companies lobbied for better roads. President Eisenhower persuaded Congress that an extensive upgrade of the highway system was essential to national defense. Kenneth T. Jackson, Crabgrass Frontier: The Suburbanization of the United States 248–51 (1985). Extensive debate was needed, however, before a way to pay for the program was settled.

Toll roads were begun in a number of states during the postwar period. Despite opposition from the federal highway staff, Pennsylvania took the right-of-way of a defunct railroad line and used it as the basic route for the toll-financed Pennsylvania Turnpike, which proved to be surprisingly well accepted and financially sound. Mitchell E. Dakelman & Neal A. Schorr, The Pennsylvania Turnpike (2004). A few other states followed, but a boom in toll road building soon became overshadowed by President Eisenhower's strong belief in a free national highway system.

The modern federal highway program came into existence through a compromise that created a Highway Trust Fund. Dunn, *supra,* at 34–35. Congress increased taxes on gasoline, tires and other automotive supplies, but enacted legislation to sequester the tax receipts in a special fund to be used only for highway construction. Another key element of the compromise was that the new interstate system would be designed for trucks as well as automobiles. The trucking industry would be paying a significant share of the taxes going into the trust fund, so they argued that the system should be designed to meet their needs, including adequate vertical clearance and interchanges designed to enable a semi to barrel through without slowing down—a standard that greatly increased the total amount of land needed for interchanges.

Once this compromise was settled, the Interstate Highway program was shepherded through Congress in 1956 with little dissent. Lewis, *supra,* at 115–17. President Eisenhower appointed a personal friend, General Lucius Clay, to head a committee to plan the system, and that committee's report proposed that the highways extend into and through the heart of American cities as well as through rural areas. Norton, *supra,* at 253. The beginning of construction of the Interstate system in the late 1950s was a time of considerable satisfaction. There were various disputes over the location of the routes and the bypassing of small towns, but in most rural areas the recognition of the value of greater accessibility outweighed the complaints.

Controversy erupted, however, when construction began on interstate highways through urban areas. The wide highways and extensive interchanges required destruction of large amounts of housing and public facilities and the relocation of a great many unhappy people. In addition, the highways themselves were designed to move vehicles quickly, creating high noise volumes for neighboring properties. The urban interstates also cut off access to neighborhoods and destroyed the charm of many urban landscapes. The federal government transportation agencies (now consolidated in the Department of Transportation (DOT)) enlisted the help of design professionals, and some of their proposals for enhancements such as sound barriers and visual amenities gradually worked their way into the engineers' bag of tools. *See* Urban Advisors to the Fed. Highway Adm'r, The Freeway in the City: Principles of Planning and Design (1968).

In the 1960s, when it became apparent that the construction of the urban segments of the interstate highway system was going to be controversial, the federal government adopted a policy of shifting funds into the quick completion of the less controversial rural segments of the system. *See* Lewis, *supra,* at 162–63. The result was that the long stretches of rural interstate highways were largely completed by the 1970s while a few of the most difficult urban segments were never resolved, leaving some urban areas with poorly designed networks that soon became congested. Texas Transp. Inst., 2012 Urban Mobility Report, http://d2dtl5nnlpfr0r.cloudfront.net/tti.tamu.edu/documents/mobility-report-2012.pdf.

To reduce the cost of land acquisition and relocation, early highway builders often tried to map the route through low-income neighborhoods where property values and political influence were low. Coming at a time of intense concern about civil rights issues, this practice was widely condemned as racially discriminatory, and allegations of differential impact of highways on racial groups continue to pose contentious issues of environmental justice. *See, e.g.,* The Jersey Heights Neighborhood Ass'n v. Glendening, 174 F.3d 180 (4th Cir. 1999).

Even more attractive to highway builders was parkland. If the road could be built through a park no one would have to be relocated. However, this raised the ire of the advocates of urban recreation, who persuaded Congress to try to limit the use of parks for highways, as highlighted by the famous *Citizens to Preserve Overton Park v. Volpe* decision, 401 U.S.

402 (1971), which you might have read in Administrative Law or Environmental Law.

6. URBAN LAND USE FOLLOWS THE HIGHWAYS

The development of the interstate highway system greatly influenced patterns of land development. The greater mobility that people obtain from modern transportation technology led to a dramatic change in the American landscape. Americans increasingly lived in thinly scattered and decentralized locations. Roads were widened into highways and connected by interchanges that greatly increased the speed of travel, but only for a while. Retailers began to move out of downtown areas into new shopping centers scattered throughout the urban areas. Jackson, *supra,* at 257–61.

Meanwhile, the federal government stimulated new housing developments in outlying areas through federally guaranteed home loans. Federal tax law, which permitted homeowners to take a tax deduction for home mortgage interest, stimulated families and individuals to invest in a home. And if they sold the home, they were required to invest the proceeds in another equally expensive home or pay capital gains tax, thus providing further stimulation to the housing market. Christine A. Klein, A Requiem for the Rollover Rule: Capital Gains, Farmland Loss, and the Law of Unintended Consequences, 55 Wash. & Lee L. Rev. 403 (1998).

High inflation between 1970 and 1985 further stimulated homeownership as the values of homes went up dramatically. Americans came to believe that the best way to keep up with inflation was to buy a home because home prices always went up at a rate exceeding the inflation rate. Most of the new homebuilding was in outlying areas rather than in the cities. Older housing in the cities had suffered from neglected maintenance during the depression and the war, and urban renewal programs were seen as ways to clear out the slums so that people could move to a better life in new housing. Robert Moses, the master builder of transportation facilities, saw the building of highways as a means toward "slum clearance," a controversial program to move poor people into high-rise public housing, and open up access to the suburbs for the middle classes. *See* Robert A. Caro, The Power Broker: Robert Moses and the Fall of New York (1974).

Office buildings also started appearing in locations on the fringes of urban areas where land was less expensive. As traffic generators scattered throughout metropolitan areas, the radial network of rail and road routes typical of early 20th century cities became unsuited to the new non-radial travel patterns. Frequently a "beltway" circling the metropolitan area became one of the most heavily traveled routes. Highways that were built to bring workers downtown ended up carrying their heaviest traffic in the opposite direction as city workers commuted to suburban jobs. Dunphy, *supra,* at 33–35.

Such patterns of land development emphasized single-family homes at relatively low densities in subdivisions that were designed on the assumption that virtually all residents would travel by private automobile. The great amount of space needed to accommodate this pattern meant that the mileage traveled per household increased rapidly.

And with trucks replacing railways as the primary means of goods transport, the road network absorbed a growing share of American energy consumption.

7. THE RETURN OF TOLL ROADS

It did not take very long before the compromise that created the highway trust fund was no longer capable of financing the planned highway network. In California, gas tax revenues failed to meet the needs for building freeways as early as the 1970s. William Fulton, The Reluctant Metropolis 135 (1997). By the 1980s, the breakdown of the highway trust fund system was apparent. The public was resistant to gasoline tax increases while fuel prices were rising from the oil shocks. Evan N. Turgeon, Triple-Dividends: Toward Pigovian Gasoline Taxation, 30 J. Land Resources & Envtl. L. 145 (2010). At the same time, the government's encouragement of ethanol in fuel, with its dilution of gasoline and its partial exemption from the gasoline tax, was estimated by the General Accounting Office (now Government Accountability Office (GAO)) to have cost the highway trust fund $7.1 billion from 1979 to 1995. GAO, Effects of the Alcohol Fuels Tax Incentives 7 (1997). During the Reagan administration, a policy decision was made to use virtually all federal highway funds for repairs rather than new roads, with the result being that between 1981 and 1989 total highway mileage increased only 0.6% while total vehicle miles driven went up over 33%. Anthony Downs, Stuck in Traffic: Coping with Peak-Hour Traffic Congestion 11 (1992).

In addition, the public began to express increased resistance to the building of new highways. Many people perceived that more roads just led to more traffic. Tom Vanderbilt, Traffic 150–157 (2008). The result was decision-making gridlock that reduced safety, wasted time and fuel, and increased costs. The American Society of Civil Engineers estimates that in 2010 surface transportation infrastructure deficiencies generated "97 billion in vehicle operating costs, $32 billion in travel time delays, $1.2 billion in safety costs and $590 million in environmental costs." Am. Soc'y of Civil Eng'rs, Failure to Act: The Economic Impact of Current Investment Trends in Surface Transportation Infrastructure at 3 (2011), http://www.asce.org/uploadedFiles/Issues_and_Advocacy/Our_Initiatives/Infrastructure/Content_Pieces/failure-to-act-transportation-report.pdf.

The inadequacy of highway infrastructure investments is exacerbated by the way that the gas tax operates. Gasoline buyers pay a fixed number of cents per gallon; neither the cost of gasoline per gallon nor the fuel efficiency of the vehicle directly affects the amount of gas taxes paid. The National Surface Transportation Policy and Revenue Study Commission's 2008 report "Paying Our Way" concluded that the system of gasoline taxation needed to be replaced by what they called a "vehicle-mile-traveled fee system." Nat'l Surface Transp. Policy and Review Study Comm'n, Paying Our Way: A New Framework for Transportation Finance 7 (2008). But coming at the onset of a serious recession, the recommendation was slow to make headway in a Congress loath to be seen as advocating new taxes,[1] so in the interim, the

---

[1] The Commission concluded that a fee based on vehicle-miles travelled would be the preferred long-term alternative to the current fuel tax, but recognized that there was no

Commission recommended that state and local governments be given the flexibility both to charge tolls and to implement congestion pricing. *Id.* at 44.

The use of tolls as a fundraising mechanism harks back to the turnpikes of the colonial period. The Northeast and North Central states have increasingly emphasized toll roads for long-distance travel, as have a few metropolitan areas such as Chicago and Boston. Governor Rick Perry of Texas made the construction of new toll roads a major objective for his administration. Thomas L. Karnes, Asphalt and Politics 107–113 (2009). But when states rely on tolls to finance travel they seem inevitably tempted to try to place as much of the burden as possible on residents of other states, raising issues about the nation's commitment to interstate commerce.

A classic example is the Indiana Toll Road. The road runs east and west just below the northern boundary of the state, providing the fastest way for any cross-country car or truck to pass through Indiana. But an Indiana resident south of Elkhart or Gary would seem to be an unlikely candidate to use the road frequently, so the major share of the cost of the road is borne by non-residents. Is this discriminatory? Or is the fact that most of the traffic is benefiting these non-residents a reasonable justification? A state that explicitly offers lower tolls to in-state residents clearly violates the Constitution (*see, e.g.*, Selevan v. New York Thruway Authority, 584 F.3d 82 (2d Cir. 2009)), but a state that simply takes advantage of its boundary lines does not.

Of course one can't separate the policy issues relating to highway transportation from those relating to motor vehicle technology, fuel technology, and other forms of transportation, which will be discussed later in this chapter. But people who predict that the highway will someday be obsolete have a tough sell to make.

C. FUELING TRANSPORTATION

Petroleum was not the first choice of the original designers of motor vehicles for roadways. In the late 19th century, oil was scarce—the big Texas fields had not yet been discovered. Consequently, the first generation of automobiles was largely powered by electric motors. Iain Carson & Vijay V. Vaitheeswaram, Zoom: The Global Race to Fuel the Car of the Future 24 (2007). But as oil became cheaper the first generation of electric cars faded away.

There are a great many engineering differences among today's automobile, truck and airplane engines, but they have one important thing in common. Nearly all of them run on fuel derived from oil. Today diesel engines have also replaced steam engines on railroad trains and many ships, reducing the coal-fueled steam engine to the status of a nostalgic toy for rail buffs. This means that as the 21st Century began, virtually all of the mechanized transportation in the world was dependent on oil. As oil prices have risen, and domestic production has declined, interest in finding different ways of fueling transportation has grown.

---

consensus on the specific technologies that should be used, and that potential tax evasion and privacy concerns would need to be solved. *Id.* at 52.

1.   A SECOND GENERATION OF ELECTRIC CARS

In 1990, a second generation of the electric cars was born—though briefly. At that year's Los Angeles auto show General Motors introduced a concept car called the Impact. Roger Smith, the company's chairman, pledged to evaluate the car for mass production, thereby creating a groundswell of interest. The interest was especially strong in California where the California Air Resources Board (CARB) was trying to develop standards for motor vehicles with reduced tailpipe emissions.

CARB responded eagerly to the prospect of a completely electric automobile by adopting a standard for zero emission vehicles (ZEVs), and requiring automakers to produce 2% of their vehicles as ZEVs by the 1998 model year and 10% as ZEVs by 2003. General Motors (GM) proceeded to invest over $1 billion to bring the EV1 to production by 1996. Mahendra Ramsinghani, Revenge of the Electric Car, Tech. Rev., Jan. 5, 2012, http://www.technologyreview.com/news/426543/revenge-of-the-electric-car/. The car was designed from the wheels up to be an electric car; no substantial parts from other GM cars were used in its design. It featured lightweight materials, aerodynamic design, braking recharge, and sophisticated computer-controlled propulsion. The EV1 initially had a lead acid battery that provided a driving range of just over 60 miles. *Id.* GM later added a nickel metal hydride battery that increased the driving range to slightly over 100 miles. Matthew Peak, Improper Incentives: Modifying the California Zero Emission Vehicle Mandate with Regards to Regulatory, Technological, and Market Forces: 1990—2001, 7 Geo. Pub. Pol'y Rev. 137, 143 (2002).

The EV1 was not sold to customers but was leased for three years at $400–600 per month. *Id.* at 143. GM eventually built over 1100 EV1s and leased about 950 of them to drivers in Southern California. *Id.* GM never disclosed the cost of production, but it lost money on each EV1; industry experts suggested that the battery itself probably cost $35,000. GM's Junk Heap, CNNMoney, June 2, 2009, http://money.cnn.com/galleries/2009/autos/0905/gallery.gm_problem_cars/4.html.

By 2003, CARB concluded that more progress could be attained by encouraging hybrids and fuel cell vehicles instead of insisting on electric vehicles. It changed the rules so that a variety of such alternatives were available to automakers. GM quickly abandoned the production of the electric car as did the other automakers that had been beginning to promote electric vehicles. After the EV1's leases expired GM took back all of the cars and crushed them. Nat'l Museum of Am. History, America on the Move: EV1 Electric Automobile, http://amhistory.si.edu/onthemove/collection/object_1303.html. Some customers tried hard to retain their car and refused to believe the company's explanations for why it was taking the cars back. A 2008 documentary film, "Who Killed the Electric Car?," examined the claims of some customers that General Motors was bowing to the wishes of the oil industry, which had lobbied fiercely against California's ZEV program. Benjamin K. Sovacool & Richard F. Hirsh, Beyond Batteries, 37 Energy Pol'y 1095, 1101 (2009). See section F.2, *infra*, for a discussion of the current generation of electric cars. California now combines its regulation of air pollution and greenhouse gas emissions from automobiles, and its zero-emission vehicle support, within a "single coordinated package of standards."   Cal. Air Res. Bd., Zero Emission

Vehicle (ZEV) Program, http://www.arb.ca.gov/msprog/zevprog/zevprog.htm.

We are now entering what could be called the third era of electric vehicles—one that appears more promising from the perspective of creating a reliable and more widely adopted electric vehicle. The U.S. Department of Energy (DOE) explains that "[a] number of light-, medium-, and heavy-duty hybrid electric vehicles (HEVs), plug-in hybrid electric vehicles (PHEVs), and all-electric vehicles (EVs) are available from a variety of automakers or are in development." DOE, Alternative Fuels Data Ctr., Availability of Hybrid and Plug-In Electric Vehicles, http://www.afdc.energy.gov/vehicles/electric_availability.html. DOE lists ten plug-in hybrid electric vehicles (light duty) as being available for 2015 and thirteen "pure" electric vehicles for this same year. DOE, Alternative Fuels Data Ctr., Light-Duty Vehicle Search (2014). In 2011, DOE estimated that the total U.S. supply of electric vehicles between 2011 and 2015 would total 1,222,200. DOE, One Million Electric Vehicles by 2015, February 2011 Status Report at 4, http://www1.eere.energy.gov/vehicles andfuels/pdfs/1_million_electric_vehicles_rpt.pdf. While this is a drop in the bucket compared to the 15–16 million vehicles sold annually in the United States between 2005 and 2008, it represents an important change.

The extent to which electric vehicle use will increase and will offer the potential benefits described in Part A of this chapter—including benefits of electricity storage and off-peak charging—depends on many factors. All-electric vehicles require charging stations, or, even better, stations at which drivers switch out drained batteries for fully charged ones, and this requires a massive investment in new infrastructure. Should the government invest in this infrastructure, or should electric vehicle companies and consumers pay for it? If we rely on private investments, how can we avoid collective action and free riding problems that inevitably accompany investment in shared infrastructure? In some cases, private entities are investing in charging stations despite free riding, sometimes to attract a certain "brand" of customer. The Whole Foods Market grocery store chain, for example, provides free electric vehicle charging stations in its parking lots, as does the Tesla electric car company at certain rest stops along the highway. Some states are taking the need for shared charging infrastructure into their own hands, as shown by the following memorandum of understanding signed by eight U.S. states.

State Zero-Emission Vehicle Programs Memorandum of Understanding Oct. 24, 2013

http://www.nescaum.org/documents/zev-mou-8-governors-signed-20131024.pdf.

WHEREAS, the Signatory States have adopted regulations requiring increasing sales of zero-emission vehicles (ZEVs), or are considering doing so; and

WHEREAS, accelerating the ZEV market is a critical strategy for achieving our goals to reduce transportation-related air pollution, including criteria air pollutants, mobile source air toxics and greenhouse gas emissions (GHGs), enhance energy diversity, save consumers money, and promote economic growth; . . .

WHEREAS, motor vehicles are among the largest sources of GHGs and criteria air pollutants that adversely affect the health and well-being of our citizens in all of our states; and

WHEREAS, providing transportation alternatives such as ZEVs will help improve air quality, reduce the use of petroleum-based fuels in the transportation sector, protect consumers against volatile energy prices, and support the growth of jobs, businesses and services in a clean energy economy; and

WHEREAS, an increasing variety of vehicles that operate on hydrogen and low-cost electricity are commercially available and have the potential to significantly reduce emissions of criteria pollutants and GHGs, enhance consumer choice, and allow for home fueling; and

WHEREAS, states with ZEV programs collectively constitute 27 percent of the U.S. automobile market and together can help create consumer demand that will further lower ZEV costs through economies of scale and expand the range of product lines available to consumers throughout the U.S. . . . .

NOW THEREFORE, as Governors of the Signatory States we express our mutual understanding and cooperative relationship as follows:

1.   OVERALL COMMITMENT

The Signatory States agree to coordinate actions to support and ensure the successful implementation of our Zero-Emission Vehicle programs. The Signatory States agree to create and participate in a multi-state ZEV Program Implementation Task Force to serve as a forum for coordination and collaboration on the full range of program support and implementation issues to promote effective and efficient implementation of ZEV regulations. The Task Force will prepare, within six months of the date of this agreement, a plan of action to accomplish the goals identified in this MOU.

2.   MEASURABLE GOALS

Consistent with program requirements, the initial Signatory States agree to a collective target of having at least 3.3 million zero emission vehicles on the road in our states by 2025 and to work together to establish a fueling infrastructure that will adequately support this number of vehicles. On an annual basis, each Signatory State will report, within available capabilities, on the number of ZEVs registered in its jurisdiction, the number of electric/hydrogen fueling stations open to the public and available information regarding workplace fueling for ZEVs.

3.   INTER-AGENCY COORDINATION WITHIN STATES

As appropriate in each State, the Signatory States will seek to support and facilitate the successful commercialization of ZEVs and efforts to maximize the electric miles driven by these vehicles through actions such as promoting electric vehicle readiness through consistent statewide building codes and standards for installing charging infrastructure, developing streamlined metering options for homes equipped with electric vehicle chargers, evaluating opportunities to reduce vehicle operating costs and increasing electric system efficiency through time-of-use electricity rates and net metering for electric vehicles, and strengthening the connection between ZEVs and renewable energy.

4. PUBLIC FLEET PURCHASES AND FUELING STATIONS

To lead by example, each Signatory State will seek to establish ZEV purchase targets for government and quasi-governmental agency fleets and report annually on ZEV acquisitions. We will explore opportunities for coordinated vehicle and fueling station equipment procurement within and across our states. We will endeavor to provide public access to government fleet fueling stations. State contracts with auto dealers and car rental companies will, to the extent possible, include commitments to the use of ZEVs where appropriate.

5. INCENTIVES FOR ZEVS

The Signatory States agree to evaluate the need for, and effectiveness of, monetary incentives to reduce the upfront purchase price of ZEVs and non-monetary incentives, such as HOV lane access, reduced tolls and preferential parking, and to pursue such incentives as appropriate.

6. SHARED STANDARDS

The Signatory States agree, subject to their respective legislative requirements, to work to develop uniform standards to promote ZEV consumer acceptance and awareness, industry compliance, and economies of scale. Such standards may include, but are not limited to, adopting universal signage, common methods of payment and interoperability of electric vehicle charging networks, and reciprocity among states for ZEV incentives, such as preferential parking and HOV lane access.

7. PUBLIC-PRIVATE PARTNERSHIPS

The Signatory States will cooperate with automobile manufacturers, electricity and hydrogen providers, the fueling infrastructure component industry, corporate fleet owners, financial institutions and others to encourage ZEV market growth.

8. RESEARCH, EDUCATION AND OUTREACH

The Signatory States agree to share research and a coordinated education and outreach campaign to highlight the benefits of ZEVs and advance their utilization. We will collaborate with initiatives, including Clean Cities programs, the Northeast/Mid-Atlantic States Transportation Climate Initiative and the West Coast Electric Highway that are already working to raise consumer awareness and demonstrate the viability and benefits of ZEVs.

9. HYDROGEN-POWERED VEHICLES AND INFRASTRUCTURE STUDY

The Signatory States agree to pursue the assessment and development of potential deployment strategies and infrastructure requirements for the commercialization of hydrogen fuel cell vehicles.

[Signatures of the governors of California, Connecticut, Maryland, Massachusetts, New York, Oregon, Rhode Island, and Vermont followed the original text.] ■

NOTES AND COMMENTS

1. The need for the construction of shared infrastructure like electric vehicle charging stations is a familiar concept. Oil and gas producers rely on

shared pipelines; electric generators rely on shared transmission lines; and drivers of cars, trucks, bicycles, and other modes of transportation use shared highways. Do you think that just as the federal government provides ratemaking structures for natural gas pipelines and electric transmission lines, we need a federal mechanism for funding electric vehicle charging stations? Or should we leave most infrastructural investment decisions to private entities and local governments and states, as occurs for oil pipelines? How are EV charging stations similar to or different from these other types of shared infrastructure?

2.   The federal government offers a tax credit for plug-in electric vehicles and light trucks under Section 30D of the Internal Revenue Code, which phases out after "at least 200,000 qualifying vehicles have been sold for use in the United States" for a given manufacturer. *See* 26 U.S.C. § 30D. DOE also supports the construction of electric vehicle charging stations through, among other initiatives, its "Clean Cities" program. This program brings together a range of private and government experts to help provide advice and guidance regarding technical and regulatory requirements for charging stations. DOE, Plug-In Electric Vehicle Handbook for Public Charging Station Hosts (2012), http://www.afdc.energy.gov/pdfs/51227.pdf.

2.   COMPRESSED NATURAL GAS VEHICLES

Another alternative to vehicles fueled by gasoline or diesel fuel is a vehicle fueled by compressed natural gas (CNG). In the United States, there has been limited use of CNG as a fuel for vehicles, but in many countries fleet vehicles are powered by CNG more often than by gasoline. Buses also often use CNG in these countries. But those vehicles that are required to search for fueling stations are likely to use natural gas only if there is an extensive network of such fueling stations. From the most recent survey on the subject conducted in 2012, countries that have more than 1 million natural gas vehicles include Iran, Pakistan, Argentina, Brazil, China, and India. Current Natural Gas Vehicle Standards, NGV Global: Natural Gas Vehicle Knowledge Base (July 2014), http://www.iangv.org/current-ngv-stats/.

New Delhi began an aggressive natural gas vehicle program ten years ago, beginning with the conversion of approximately 60,000 auto rickshaws to CNG for fuel. Green Car Cong., Delhi Transport Orders 3,125 Natural Gas Buses with Cummins Westport B Gas Plus Engines, Oct. 16, 2008, http://www.greencarcongress.com/2008/10/delhi-transport.html. In 2002, the Indian Supreme Court ordered the city's entire bus fleet to convert to cleaner-burning CNG. A government report showed that while the number of vehicles on the road has doubled, the pollution rate has halved. Outside of New Delhi, ten other major Indian cities also have aggressive natural gas vehicle conversion programs. *Id.*

Advocates of CNG as a fuel for vehicles argue that it is the safest of all potential fuels. Natural gas has a limited range of flammability, and it is lighter than air. If a leak were to develop, the gas would rise and disperse through the atmosphere giving little chance for ignition. There have been some safety incidents associated with CNG vehicles, however. For example, in Mississippi in 2014, a CNG-fueled truck was carrying a forklift that was improperly secured to the truck. When the truck turned a corner, the forklift shifted, pierced the truck's fuel tank, and caused an explosion, killing one individual and injuring another. Nathan Phelps, 1

Dead After Natural Gas Truck Explodes in Howard, Greenbay Press Gazette, Apr. 4, 2014, http://www.greenbaypressgazette.com/article/ 20140403/GPG0101/304030314/1-dead-after-natural-gas-truck-explodes -Howard-Industrial-Park.

Raw natural gas is odorless, so a distinctive odorant that smells very much like strong sulfur is added prior to distribution. This strong odor makes the presence of a leak very easy to detect. The on-board tanks are made of steel up to one half-inch thick and often wrapped in protective reinforced fiberglass sheathing or are constructed of polymers and composites that are stronger than steel. Newer CNG systems have automatic release valves that will open and release the gas to the atmosphere if heat or pressure builds up. In the event of a fire, fuel should be safely evacuated from the car before it ever has a chance to catch fire. CNG Safety: Safety Guidelines—CNG Vehicle, Central U.P. Gas Limited, http://www.cugl.co.in/t-cngsafety.aspx.

In the United States, CNG vehicles have been introduced in a variety of commercial applications, such as taxi cabs, postal vehicles, and transit buses, and its use in these fleets and individual cars is fast growing due to the new-found abundance of unconventional gas in the United States and recent initiatives to spur vehicle conversions to CNG. DOE estimates that "[n]atural gas powers about 112,000 vehicles in the United States." DOE, Alternative Fuels Data Ctr., Natural Gas Vehicles, http://www. afdc.energy.gov/vehicles/natural_gas.html. In 2014, approximately 15 "bi-fuel" light-duty vehicles were available that could run on natural gas or gasoline. DOE, Alternative Fuels Data Ctr., Light-Duty Vehicle Search, http://www.afdc.energy.gov.

Many local governments have switched over their fleets to run on natural gas. In 2011, the Los Angeles County Metropolitan Transit Authority retired its last diesel bus, with all of its 221 buses running on CNG. L.A. Cty. Metro. Transp. Auth., Metro Retires Last Diesel Bus, Becomes World's First Major Transit Agency to Operate Only Clean Fuel Buses, Jan. 12, 2011, http://www.metro.net/news/simple_pr/metro- retires-last-diesel-bus/. An industry association, America's Natural Gas Alliance (ANGA), also refers to "[s]chool buses in Ardmore, Pennsylvania, trash trucks in Cleveland, Ohio, taxis in San Francisco, California, and airport shuttles in Phoenix, Arizona" and a number of other municipal fleets that run on natural gas. ANGA, Natural Gas Vehicles Driving Change, http://pnv-angaweb-qa.scalestaging.com/media/content/F7D144 1A-09A5-D06A-9EC93BBE46772E12/files/transportation%20brochure. pdf. Natural gas vehicles face similar infrastructural challenges to electric vehicles because there are not currently many fueling stations in place, although some states are beginning to support fueling "corridors" and other initiatives to increase the availability of fueling points. *Id.* States are also subsidizing the conversion of vehicles to natural gas and the construction of fueling stations, as shown by the following excerpt.

Texas S.B. No. 385 (2011)

AN ACT relating to the creation of programs to support the use of alternative fuels, including an alternative fuel program to be funded by the Texas emissions reduction plan fund and a grant program for certain natural gas vehicles.

BE IT ENACTED BY THE LEGISLATURE OF THE STATE OF TEXAS:

SECTION 1. Subsection (a), Section 386.252, Health and Safety Code . . . is reenacted and amended to read as follows:

(a) Money in the fund may be used only to implement and administer programs established under the plan and shall be allocated as follows:

(1) for the diesel emissions reduction incentive program, 87.5 percent of the money in the fund, of which:

(A) not more than four percent may be used for the clean school bus program;

(B) not more than 10 percent may be used for on-road diesel purchase or lease incentives;

(C) a specified amount may be used for the new technology implementation grant program, from which a defined amount may be set aside for electricity storage projects related to renewable energy;

(D) five percent shall be used for the clean fleet program;

(E) two percent may be used for the Texas alternative fueling facilities program;

(F) not less than 16 percent shall be used for the natural gas vehicle grant program; and

(G) not more than four percent may be used to provide grants for natural gas fueling stations under Section 394.010;

(2) for the new technology research and development program, nine percent of the money in the fund. . . .

* * *

SECTION 3. Subtitle C, Title 5, Health and Safety Code, is amended by adding Chapters 393 and 394 to read as follows:

CHAPTER 393. ALTERNATIVE FUELING FACILITIES PROGRAM

Sec. 393.001. DEFINITIONS. In this chapter:

(1) "Alternative fuel" means a fuel other than gasoline or diesel fuel, other than biodiesel fuel, including electricity, compressed natural gas, liquified natural gas, hydrogen, propane, or a mixture of fuels containing at least 85 percent methanol by volume.

(2) "Commission" means the Texas Commission on Environmental Quality.

(3) "Program" means the Texas alternative fueling facilities program established under this chapter.

Sec. 393.002. PROGRAM. (a) The commission shall establish and administer the Texas alternative fueling facilities program to provide fueling facilities for alternative fuel in nonattainment areas. Under the program, the commission shall provide a grant for each eligible facility to offset the cost of those facilities.

An entity that constructs, reconstructs, or acquires an alternative fueling facility is eligible to participate in the program.

Sec. 393.003. APPLICATION FOR GRANT. (a) An entity operating in this state that constructs, reconstructs, or acquires a facility to store, compress, or dispense alternative fuels may apply for and receive a grant under the program. . . .

Sec. 393.004. ELIGIBILITY OF FACILITIES FOR GRANTS. (a) The commission by rule shall establish criteria for prioritizing facilities eligible to receive grants under this chapter. The commission shall review and revise the criteria as appropriate.

(b) To be eligible for a grant under the program, the entity receiving the grant must agree to make the alternative fueling facility available to persons not associated with the entity at times designated by the grant agreement.

* * *

Sec. 393.006. AMOUNT OF GRANT. For each eligible facility for which a recipient is awarded a grant under the program, the commission shall award the grant in an amount equal to the lesser of:

(1) 50 percent of the sum of the actual eligible costs incurred by the grant recipient within deadlines established by the commission to construct, reconstruct, or acquire the facility; or

(2) $500,000.

Sec. 393.007. EXPIRATION. This chapter expires August 31, 2018.

CHAPTER 394. TEXAS NATURAL GAS VEHICLE GRANT PROGRAM

Sec. 394.001. DEFINITIONS. In this chapter:

* * *

(4) "Heavy-duty motor vehicle" means a motor vehicle with:

(A) a gross vehicle weight rating of more than 8,500 pounds; and

(B) an engine certified to the United States Environmental Protection Agency's standards for heavy-duty engines.

* * *

(6) "Medium-duty motor vehicle" means a motor vehicle with a gross vehicle weight rating of more than 8,500 pounds that:

(A) is certified to the United States Environmental Protection Agency's light-duty emissions standard; or

(B) has an engine certified to the United States Environmental Protection Agency's light-duty emissions standard.

* * *

(8) "Natural gas vehicle" means a motor vehicle that receives not less than 75 percent of its power from compressed or liquefied natural gas.

* * *

Sec. 394.002. PROGRAM. The commission shall establish and administer the Texas natural gas vehicle grant program to encourage an entity that has a heavy-duty or medium-duty motor vehicle to repower the vehicle with a natural gas engine or replace the vehicle with a natural gas vehicle. Under the program, the commission shall provide grants for eligible heavy-duty motor vehicles and medium-duty motor vehicles to offset the incremental cost for the entity of repowering or replacing the heavy-duty or medium-duty motor vehicle.

Sec. 394.003. QUALIFYING VEHICLES. (a) A vehicle is a qualifying vehicle that may be considered for a grant under the program if during the calendar year the entity:

(1) purchased, leased, or otherwise commercially financed the vehicle as a new on-road heavy-duty or medium-duty motor vehicle that:

(A) is a natural gas vehicle;

(B) is certified to current federal emissions standards;

(C) replaces an on-road heavy-duty or medium-duty motor vehicle of the same weight classification and use; and

(D) is powered by an engine certified to:

(i) emit not more than 0.2 grams of nitrogen oxides per brake horsepower hour; or

(ii) meet or exceed the United States Environmental Protection Agency's Bin 5 standard for light-duty engines when powering the vehicle; or

(2) repowered the on-road motor vehicle to a natural gas vehicle powered by a natural gas engine that:

(A) is certified to current federal emissions standards; and

(B) is:

(i) a heavy-duty engine that is certified to emit not more than 0.2 grams of nitrogen oxides per brake horsepower hour; or

(ii) certified to meet or exceed the United States Environmental Protection Agency's Bin 5 standard for light-duty engines when powering the vehicle. . . .

Sec. 394.005. ELIGIBILITY FOR GRANTS. (a) The commission by rule shall establish criteria for prioritizing qualifying vehicles eligible to receive grants under this chapter. The commission shall review and revise the criteria as appropriate after consultation with the advisory board.

(b) To be eligible for a grant under the program:

(1) the use of the qualifying vehicle must be projected to result in a reduction in emissions of nitrogen oxides of at least 25 percent as compared to the motor vehicle or engine being replaced. . . .

* * *

Sec. 394.006. RESTRICTION ON USE OF GRANT. A recipient of a grant under this chapter shall use the grant to pay the incremental costs of the replacement for which the grant is made, which may include the initial cost of the natural gas vehicle or natural gas engine and the reasonable and necessary expenses incurred for the labor needed to install emissions-reducing equipment. The recipient may not use the grant to pay the recipient's administrative expenses.

Sec. 394.007. AMOUNT OF GRANT. (a) The commission shall develop a grant schedule that:

(1) assigns a standardized grant in an amount between 60 and 90 percent of the incremental cost of a natural gas vehicle purchase, lease, other commercial finance, or repowering;

(2) is based on:

(A) the certified emission level of nitrogen oxides, or other pollutants as determined by the commission, of the engine powering the natural gas vehicle; and

(B) the usage of the natural gas vehicle; and

(3) may take into account the overall emissions reduction achieved by the natural gas vehicle. ∎

The U.S. Environmental Protection Agency (EPA) gives compressed natural gas vehicles high marks for the reduction of pollutant emissions. In comparison to gasoline or diesel fueled vehicles, NGVs dramatically reduce carbon monoxide emissions and substantially reduce emissions of nitrogen oxides, hydrocarbons, and carbon dioxide. In addition, vehicles that burn compressed natural gas emit virtually no particulate matter. A National Research Council committee found that CNG vehicles had fewer air quality impacts than other options because the technology's operations and fuel produce very few emissions. Nat'l Res. Council, Hidden Costs of Energy 10 (2009).

Why, until recently, has there been so little supply and demand for private vehicles running on natural gas? First, the compressed natural gas takes up a great deal of space in the vehicle, making it difficult to provide trunk space or room for a large number of passengers. Second, as introduced above, there are a limited number of fueling stations for natural gas vehicles (732 in the United States according to the DOE as of 2014). DOE, Natural Gas Fueling Station Locations, http://www.afdc. energy.gov/fuels/natural_gas_locations.html. Consumers are concerned about their ability to drive the cars long distances and find a location to refuel. The number of natural gas fueling stations is exceedingly small as compared to gasoline stations, for which there is "one station for every 23 miles of public roadway." Josie Garthwaite, For Natural Gas-Fueled Cars, Long Road Looms Ahead, Nat'l. Geo., Sept. 4, 2013. Natural gas vehicle owners can, however, plan trips using online tools that indicate station locations. DOE, Natural Gas Fueling Station Locations, *supra*. Third, many consumers are nervous about the safety of compressed natural gas even though the record of CNG vehicles is safer than conventional vehicles. *See* Tom Fowler, America, Start Your Natural-Gas Engines, Wall St. J., June 18, 2012, http://online.wsj.com/news/articles/ SB10001424052702304192704577406431047638416 (noting that "there's the question of consumer psychology: How do you convince drivers that it's wise or even safe to put natural gas in their cars?").

3. HYDROGEN FUEL CELL VEHICLES

Attempts to design automobile engines based on hydrogen fuel cell technology were widely assumed to be far from any current relevance until 1999, when these assumptions began to change. Daimler-Chrysler demonstrated a model of a fuel cell car that was much farther along than others in the industry had expected. The reaction in the industry was immediate: The Wall Street Journal observed that "not long ago, the fuel cell was dismissed as an environmentalist's pipe dream [but now] it is the subject of a heavily-financed research-and-development race among some of the world's biggest auto makers." Jeffrey Ball, Auto Makers Race to Sell Cars Powered by Fuel Cells, Wall St. J., Mar. 15, 1999, at 1.

Ten years later, one commentator (among others) argued that the "idea of a hydrogen-based transportation system amounts to one of the bigger hoodwinks perpetrated on Americans since smoking's health claims in the 1950s." Christopher Steiner, $20 Per Gallon: How the Rising Cost of Gasoline Will Radically Change Our Lives 95–96 (2009). Who will be proved right?

Fuel cells have been in widespread use for specialized applications ever since they began to be used in the space program. A fuel cell is a device that generates electricity from chemical reactions other than combustion. A wide variety of fuel cell technologies exist, but the technology generally used in automotive applications is the proton exchange membrane (PEM) fuel cell. PEM fuel cells use a polymer electrolyte consisting of a thin, permeable sheet that works at low temperatures. The electrolyte of the PEM must allow hydrogen protons to pass through but not electrons and heavier gases. To speed the reaction a platinum catalyst is used on both sides of the membrane. Hydrogen atoms are stripped of their electrons at the anode, and the positively charged protons pass by diffusion through one side of the porous membrane and migrate toward the cathode. The electrons pass around the electrolyte from the anode to the cathode through an exterior circuit and provide electric power along the way. At the cathode, the electrons, hydrogen protons and oxygen from the air combine to form water.

PEM fuel cells require highly purified hydrogen as a fuel. Thus, to create a PEM fuel cell vehicle, pure hydrogen must be available onboard the vehicle. If it is used to power a fuel cell, its only byproduct is pure water. A fuel cell is far more efficient than either internal combustion or steam engines, as the latter involve an intermediate mechanical step and high heat loss.

Initial development of fuel cell vehicles in the United States focused on buses. Georgetown University built and operated a fuel cell bus pursuant to a Federal Transit Administration demonstration grant, and, through the year 2000, the Chicago Transit Authority operated three hydrogen-powered fuel cell buses that stored compressed hydrogen in roof-mounted tanks that were centrally refueled by liquid hydrogen. See Jon Hilkevitch, Cta Hydrogen Bus Test Reaches End of the Line, Chicago Tribune, Mar. 23, 2000, http://articles.chicagotribune.com/2000-03-23/news/0003230378_1_cta-fuel-cells-new-natural-gas-buses. DOE can enter into grants or cooperative agreements with units of local government to promote the use of fuel cell transit buses and school buses. See 42 U.S.C. §§ 16091, 16093. In addition, Congress authorized DOT to undertake a fuel cell bus technology development program in the 2005 transportation law, the Safe, Accountable, Flexible, Efficient Transportation Equity Act (SAFETEA-LU). See 49 U.S.C. § 5308. The Federal Transit Administration provided approximately $90 million under the program, supporting both development and demonstration of fuel cell buses and supporting continued "operation of existing fuel cell buses" in places like Birmingham, Alabama and Oakland, California. Fed. Transit Admin., National Fuel Cell Bus Program Projects, http:// www.fta.dot.gov/14617_15670.html. A limited number of cars also operate on fuel cells. In 2011 and 2012, fewer than 500 fuel cell cars sold each year. Navigant Research, Fuel Cell Vehicles, http://www.navigant research.com/research/fuel-cell-vehicles. Honda has sold a very limited number of its FXC Clarity fuel cell cars since 2008—purchases are limited in part due to the lack of hydrogen fueling stations. James R. Healey, Test Drive: Honda FCX Clarity is Fuel-Cell Fab, USA Today, July 27, 2013, http://www.usatoday.com/story/money/columnist/healey/ 2013/07/27/honda-fcx-clarity-fuel-cell/2587581/; Don't Be Too Quick to Buy Into the Hydrogen Myth, Autoweek, Apr. 30, 2009, http://autoweek. com/article/car-reviews/honda-fcx-clarity-dont-be-too-quick-buy-hydrogen-myth. Several automakers are also introducing new fuel cell models in 2015. *See, e.g.*, Hyundai, Tucson Fuel Cell, https://www. hyundaiusa.com/tucsonfuelcell/; Toyota, Introducing Toyota's Fuel Cell Technology, http://www.toyota.com/fuelcell/.

California has played a leading role in promoting fuel cell vehicles. The governor of California issued an Executive Order committing the state to "achieving a clean energy and transportation future based on the rapid commercialization of hydrogen and fuel cell technologies." Cal. Executive Order S–7–04 (2004). The order designated twenty-one California highways as the "California Hydrogen Highway Network," and committed the state to take various actions to ensure a "rapid transition to a hydrogen economy." The California Fuel Cell Partnership, "a collaboration of organizations, including auto manufacturers, energy providers, government agencies and fuel cell technology companies," is working to further promote vehicles and provides a map of fueling stations. Cal. Fuel Cell P'ship, http://cafcp.org/aboutus; http://cafcp.org/ stationmap. The state now has approximately ten hydrogen fueling stations, with more than two dozen additional stations planned to go online in fall 2014 or in 2015 as a result of $46.6 million in funding from the California Energy Commission. Cal. Energy Comm'n, CEC Announces Funding for 28 Hydrogen Stations, http://cafcp.org/ getinvolved/stayconnected/blog/cec_announces_funding_28_hydrogen_ stations.

There are a number of important issues that must be resolved successfully for hydrogen-fueled vehicles to find widespread acceptance, including, among others, cost and safety. Some of the concerns about the safety of hydrogen are overstated: hydrogen is non-toxic and much lighter than air, so it will dissipate rapidly when it is released. It is also not any more flammable than gasoline or similar fuels, and the risk of fire can be managed. William Vincent, Hydrogen and Tort Law, 25 Energy L.J. 385 (2004).

D. BIOFUELS

The oil shocks of the 1970s provided an impetus to search for home-grown replacements for some of America's oil imports. As discussed in Chapter 10, biofuels—fuels derived from plant matter, such as ethanol or waste cooking oil—are one alternative to traditional fossil fuels. Congress instituted a tax benefit for the use of ethanol as an additive to gasoline. In that same period, EPA was phasing out lead in gasoline. Refiners in the United States began to mix methyl tertiary butyl ether (MTBE), an additive made from natural gas, with gasoline to comply with new EPA regulations that encouraged refiners to "oxygenate" gasoline to allow fuel to burn more completely and reduce emissions of carbon monoxide (CO) and other gases. But foul-smelling MTBE began showing up in groundwater, and soon was banned by many states. These states required refiners to add ethanol to increase oxygen. The oxygenation requirement was eliminated in 2005 after attainment of CO standards became almost universal. Bruce A. McCarl & Fred O. Boadu, Bioenergy and U.S. Renewable Fuels Standards: Law, Economic Policy/Climate Change and Implementation Concerns, 14 Drake J. Agric. L. 43, 44–48 (2009).

By the time of the elimination of the oxygenation phase-out. concerns about energy security made the idea of biofuels attractive in the United States and in many other countries. Richard Doornbosch & Ronald Steenblik, Biofuels: Is the Cure Worse than the Disease?, OECD Round Table on Sustainable Dev. 37 (2007). In 2004 Congress enacted blenders' tax credits to reduce the final cost of ethanol by $0.51 per gallon, biodiesel made from virgin oil by $1.00 per gallon, and biodiesel made from waste grease by $0.50 per gallon, and many states enacted additional state tax credits for ethanol. In 2005, and again in 2007, Congress passed legislation mandating dramatic increases in the production of biofuels, requiring that refiners produce specific amounts of specified types of biofuels by designated future years. But by then the enthusiasm for biofuels was being matched by opponents who worried about their long-term impacts. Arnold W. Reitze, Jr., Biofuels: Snake Oil for the Twenty-First Century, 87 Or. L. Rev. 1183, 1195–98 (2008).

Supporters and critics of biofuels have been engaging in a wide-ranging debate about the long-range impacts of a major switch to biofuel use. Scientists and economists have produced a wide range of projections about effects on air and water, climate, food supply, etc. In reviewing these arguments one should keep in mind that there are many potential types of biofuel and that they can be grown and processed in many different landscapes from a variety of feedstocks using constantly evolving processing methods. Broad generalizations about the impact of biofuels should be avoided

1. MANDATING BIOFUEL PRODUCTION

Section 1501 of the Energy Policy Act of 2005 required EPA to establish a Renewable Fuel Standard (RFS) to increase the volume of renewable fuel that can be blended with gasoline. The Energy Independence and Security Act (EISA) of 2007 (Pub. L. No. 110–140, 121 Stat. 1492) required EPA to revise its regulations governing the use of fuels or fuel additives "to ensure that transportation fuel sold or introduced into commerce in the United States . . . , on an annual basis, contains at least the applicable volume of renewable fuel, advanced biofuel, cellulosic biofuel, and biomass-based diesel." 42 U.S.C. § 7545(o)(2)(A)(i). EISA raised the renewable fuel standard to 9.0 billion gallons in 2008 and 36 billion gallons by 2022.

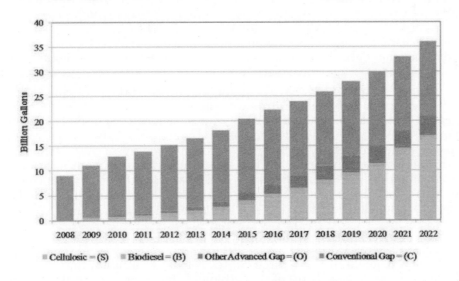

Figure 1: Biofuel Use Mandates Established by the Energy Independence and Security (EISA) Act of 2007

Figure 15–1
EISA Biofuel Use Mandates
Source: http://farmdocdaily.illinois.edu/2011/09/epa-mandate-waivers-create-new-1.
html

EISA responded to concerns about the impacts of corn-based ethanol by requiring the production of corn-based ethanol to reach a peak in 2015 and continue to match that output in future years. Growth in ethanol production after 2015 is to come from other advanced biofuels, with explicit carve-outs for cellulosic biofuels and biomass-based diesel. The EPA Administrator is given authority to temporarily waive part of the biofuels mandate, if it is determined that a significant renewable feedstock disruption or other market circumstance might occur. Renewable fuels produced from new biorefineries are required to reduce by at least 20% the life cycle greenhouse gas (GHG) emissions relative to life cycle emissions from gasoline and diesel. 42 U.S.C. § 7545(o)(7)(E)(ii). Fuels produced from biorefineries that displace more than 80% of the fossil-derived processing fuels used to operate a biofuel production facility will qualify for cash awards.[2]

---

[2]   EPA's regulations must achieve at least a 20% reduction in "lifecycle greenhouse gas emissions compared to baseline greenhouse gas emissions." 42 U.S.C. § 7545(o)(2)(A)(i). Lifecycle GHG emissions are the aggregate quantity of GHG emissions related to the full fuel cycle, including all stages of fuel and feedstock production and distribution, where the mass values for all GHGs are adjusted to account for their relative global warming potential. *Id.* § 7545(o)(1)(H). Baseline lifecycle GHG emissions are the average lifecycle GHG emissions for gasoline or diesel being replaced by the renewable fuel that was sold or distributed as transportation fuel in 2005. *Id.* § 7545(o)(4). EPA may waive the reduction requirements in response to state petitions alleging severe harm to the economy or environment. *Id.* § 7545(o)(7). The statute authorizes the trading of credits for additional renewable fuels. *Id.* § 7545(o)(5)(E). The 2007 Act provides that nothing in the statute or in regulations issued under it "shall affect or be construed to affect the regulatory status of carbon dioxide or any other greenhouse gas, or to expand or limit regulatory authority for purposes of the CAA." *Id.* § 7545(o)(12).

EISA creates its own defined terms: Transportation Fuel (i.e. motor vehicle fuel); Renewable Fuel (i.e. fuel from biomass); Advanced Biofuel (i.e. fuel from biomass other than corn starch); Conventional Biofuel (i.e. ethanol from corn starch); Additional Renewable Fuel (renewable jet or heating fuel). 42 U.S.C. § 7545(o)(1)(A),(B),(D),(F) (J), (L). The statute also specifically includes the following fuels within the category of advanced biofuel: (1) Biomass-based diesel; (2) Cellulosic biofuel; (3) Biogas[3]; and (4) Sugar-based ethanol.

Some commentators have been highly critical of the political process by which these biofuel standards were adopted. Professor Arnold Reitze argues that "the renewable fuels program is designed to put money in the pockets of corn farmers and corn-based ethanol producers at a high cost to consumers." Reitze, *supra,* at 1203. He observes that "ethanol's proponents have numerous arguments to justify government subsidies, and when they are discredited they find new arguments to convince the public there are valid reasons to support these multibillion-dollar corporate subsidies." *Id.*

2. CONVENTIONAL ETHANOL

Most biofuels in the United States consist of ethanol that is made from cornstarch. Nearly all of this ethanol is blended into gasoline at up to 15 percent by volume to produce a fuel called E15. Cars and light trucks built for the U.S. market since the late 1970s could run on a blend of 10% ethanol, and it has now been established that model year 2001 and later vehicles can run on E15 without causing exceedances of air pollution standards. Automakers also produce a limited number of Flexible Fuel Vehicles that can run on any blend of gasoline and ethanol up to 85 percent ethanol by volume (E85), but E85 is hard to find because it requires a separate supply stream to bring in the ethanol and mix it with the gasoline onsite. John Randolph, Energy for Sustainability 505 (2008).

Cornstarch-based ethanol is defined by the EISA as "conventional biofuel." The EISA sought to level off production of this ethanol and increase the production of "advanced biofuel." It also cut the tax credit for corn ethanol from $0.51 to $0.45. The 2008 farm bill authorized USDA loan guarantees for advanced biorefinery development projects and provided another $1.01 tax credit for production of cellulosic ethanol, and it renewed sugar subsidies that allow both sugar cane and sugar beets to compete as producers of "advanced biofuel." Farm Bill §§ 9003, 9005, 15321 (2008) (7 U.S.C. §§ 8103, 8105; 26 U.S.C. § 40). The 2014 Farm Bill (the Agricultural Act of 2014) provides new funding for most of the 2008 biofuel projects, thus continuing support for these projects, although it reduces mandatory funding for renewable energy projects from $1 billion over five years to $694 million for 2014–2018. Cong. Research Serv., Energy Provisions in the 2014 Farm Bill (P.L. 113–79) (2014), http://nationalaglawcenter.org/wp-content/uploads/assets/crs/R43416.pdf.

---

[3]   Although relatively ignored in the United States, biogas research in Europe is producing interesting results. Royal Society, *supra,* at 25–28.

a. ENERGY SECURITY

Will biofuels like conventional ethanol ever make a big dent in our consumption of crude oil for transportation? EIA projects that total U.S. biofuels consumption will rise from 14 billion gallons in 2012 to 16 billion gallons in 2022 (falling short of the RFS goal of 36 billion gallons), whereas diesel fuel consumption alone in 2022 will be more than 180 gallons daily (which would amount to 65.9 billion gallons in total in 2022). EIA, Annual Energy Outlook 2014, Market Trends: Liquid fuels, http://www.eia.gov/forecasts/aeo/MT_liquidfuels.cfm. And unless we find ways to reduce our use of transportation fuel, our fuel consumption will rise as our population grows. Much of the analysis and public debate about ethanol has focused on whether the manufacturing of ethanol uses more energy (much of which is imported) than the energy provided by the ethanol produced.

To make ethanol and biodiesel we burn substantial quantities of petroleum products. Farm machinery runs on gasoline or diesel fuel, biofuel refineries typically burn natural gas, and delivery of the finished biofuel is done by trucks or trains burning diesel fuel. How much energy does the manufacture of biofuels use? Will that energy need to come from imported fuels? Studies vary widely. Calculations of net energy are highly sensitive to assumptions about system boundaries, parameter values, and differences between different types of fossil energy. Alexander E. Farrell, Ethanol Can Contribute to Environmental and Energy Goals, 311 Science 56 (2006).

Cornell ecologist David Pimentel is among those who conclude that production of ethanol uses more energy than it creates. He observes: "Energy outputs from ethanol produced using corn, switchgrass, and wood biomass were each less than the respective fossil energy inputs. Ethanol production using corn grain required 29% more fossil energy than the ethanol fuel produced." David Pimentel & Tad W. Patzek, Ethanol Production Using Corn, Switchgrass, and Wood, 14 Nat. Res. Research, Mar. 2005, at 65. On the other hand, USDA relies on a study by Hosein Shapouri and Andrew McAloon that finds that corn ethanol has a favorable net energy balance, even before subtracting the energy allocated to byproducts. The net energy balance of corn ethanol adjusted for byproduct credits is 27,729 and 33,196 Btu per gallon for wet- and dry-milling, respectively, and 30,528 Btu per gallon for the industry. The study results suggest that corn ethanol is energy efficient, as indicated by an energy output/input ratio of somewhere "between 1.9 and 2.3." USDA, 2008 Energy Balance for the Corn-Ethanol Industry, http://www.usda.gov/oce/reports/energy/2008Ethanol_June_final.pdf.

Scientific analysis should also take into account the energy costs of extracting, refining and transporting gasoline. One researcher who has taken this into account has calculated an energy return on investment for gasoline of 0.76 where 1.0 is the theoretical point where no energy is expended in upstream costs, and all the energy in the gasoline is available. Using Pimentel's numbers yields an energy return on investment of 0.84, which means that ethanol is still a superior energy source compared to gasoline. *See* Roel Hammerschlag, Ethanol's Energy Return on Investment: A Survey of the Literature 1990—Present, Envtl. Sci. Tech., Feb. 2006, at 1744, http://pubs.acs.org/doi/full/10.1021/es052024h.

b.   GREENHOUSE GASES

Does ethanol production have a beneficial or harmful impact on climate change? Plants capture carbon from the atmosphere through the process of photosynthesis. Burning biomass returns this recently captured carbon to the atmosphere, a cycle that—unlike the combustion of fossil fuels—produces no net increase in atmospheric carbon. Biofuel production is typically powered by fossil fuels, so the global warming pollution from that process must be added to the equation. In addition, heat-trapping emissions generated by biomass production practices not related to combustion must be taken into account. This includes significant amounts of CO_2 and methane (CH_4) from petroleum recovery and natural gas processing, and nitrous oxide (N_2O) from fertilizers added to the soil. Nat'l Research Council, Committee on Economic and Environmental Impacts of Increasing Biofuels Production, Renewable Fuel Standard: Potential Economic and Environmental Effects of U.S. Biofuel Policy, 185–188, 195–196 (2011).

The net impact of bioenergy on global warming depends on the type of biomass being used; how the feedstock is grown; the fuel production, refining, and delivery methods; the energy resource being displaced; and how the land would have been used if it had not been converted for bioenergy use. Union of Concerned Scientists, Biofuels: An Important Part of a Low-Carbon Diet (2007), http://www.ucsusa.org/assets/documents/ clean_vehicles/ucs-biofuels-report.pdf. A 2009 report by the U.N. Environment Programme (UNEP) observes that among the four main feedstocks for production of ethanol, corn is the only one that may cause 5% more GHG emissions than fossil fuels, but may also bring benefits of about 60% GHG emissions saved—depending on the technology used, the process energy mix, and the use of co-generation products, but excluding the effects of land use change. UNEP, Toward Sustainable Production and Use of Resources: Assessing Biofuels 53 (2009), http://www.unep.org/pdf/ biofuels/Assessing_Biofuels_Full_Report.pdf. A DOE study, on the other hand, concludes that on a lifecycle basis (from the cultivation of the plant used to produce the fuel through its production and transport), corn-based ethanol emits fewer GHG emissions than do fossil fuels, and non-corn-based products perform even better. DOE, Ethanol—The Complete Lifecycle Picture (2007), https://www1.eere.energy.gov/vehiclesandfuels/ pdfs/program/ethanol_brochure_color.pdf. Despite the differences in biofuels' GHG emissions as a result of land use change, cultivation practices, and other factors, the rules under the Kyoto Protocol ignore these variations and treat all bioenergy as carbon neutral regardless of emissions created by changes in land use when biomass for energy is harvested or grown. Timothy D. Searchinger et al., Fixing a Critical Climate Accounting Error, Science, Oct. 23, 2009, at 527.

Many governments are responding to certain studies that suggest that the total emissions and environmental damage from producing "clean" biofuels might outweigh their lower emissions as compared to fossil fuels. In 2009, the European Commission (EC) enacted a Renewable Energy Directive, building from previous EC mandates to set targets for 10% of energy in the transportation sector to come from renewables by 2020 (among other targets), and a Fuel Quality Directive, which amended an earlier mandate and required a 6% reduction in GHG emissions from transportation fuels from 2010 levels by 2020. European

Parliament and Council Directive 2009/28/EC on the Promotion of the Use of Energy from Renewable Sources and Amending and Subsequently Repealing Directives 2001/77/EC and 2003/30/EC, 2009 O.J. L. 140/16, art. 3 ("Renewable Energy Directive"); European Parliament and Council Directive 2009/30/EC Amending Directive 98/70/EC As Regards the Specification of Petrol, Diesel and Gas-Oil and Introducing a Mechanism to Monitor and Reduce Greenhouse Gas Emissions and Amending Council Directive 1999/32/EC As Regards the Specification of Fuel Used by Inland Waterway Vessels and Repealing Directive 93/12/EEC 2009 O.J. L. 140/88 ("Fuel Quality Directive"). The Renewable Energy Directive required biofuels used to meet these targets to comply with certain "sustainability criteria" relating to "land with high biodiversity value" and "high carbon stock," for example. *Id.*, art. 17. *See also* Communication from the Commission on the Practical Implementation of the EU Biofuels and Bioliquids Sustainability Scheme and on Counting Rules for Biofuels, June 19, 2010, http://eurlex.europa.eu/LexUriServ/LexUriServ.do?uri=OJ:C:2010:160:0008:0016:EN:PDF. A more recent Commission proposal would "limit the contribution that conventional biofuels make . . . towards attainment of the targets in the Renewable Energy Directive" due to the indirect land use-change emissions caused by these fuels. European Commission, Proposal for a Directive of the European Parliament and of Council, amending Directive 98/70/EC relating to the quality of petrol and diesel fuels and amending Directive 2009/28/EC on the promotion of the use of energy from renewable sources, Oct. 17, 2012, http://ec.europa.eu/energy/renewables/biofuels/doc/biofuels/com_2012_0595_en.pdf.

c.   RELATIONSHIP TO FOOD PRICES

In addition to concerns about the environmental impacts of biofuels, there has been worldwide criticism of the effect of increased ethanol production on food prices. Because the cost of feedstock dominates the production cost of biofuels, all crops compete for the same inputs: land, fertilizer and irrigation water. Doornbosch & Steenblik, *supra*, at 33. EISA's promotion of advanced biofuels over corn-based ethanol reflects that criticism. Diversion of corn to ethanol in 2008 meant significantly higher prices for livestock feed, which translated to higher meat prices. Corn syrup prices rose too, which affected a wide range of processed foods that use corn syrup as a basic sweetener. For example, Texas asked EPA to waive 50% of the RFS requirement for 2008–09 because of the adverse impact of high corn prices on the livestock industry, but EPA denied that the harm was caused solely by the RFS program. McCarl & Boadu, *supra*, at 65–69.

In 2008, the head of the International Monetary Fund (IMF) argued that biofuels "posed a real moral problem" and called for a moratorium on using food crops to power cars, trucks and buses. The vital problem of global warming "has to be balanced with the fact that there are people who are going to starve to death," said Dominique Strauss-Kahn. "Producing biofuels is a crime against humanity," UN's special rapporteur for the right to food, Jean Ziegler of Switzerland, said earlier. "This is highly exaggerated," Sergio Serra, Brazil's ambassador for climate change, told AFP. "There is no real relation of cause and effect between the expansion of the production of biofuels and the raising of food prices. At least it is not happening in Brazil." Biofuels under attack as world food prices soar, Agence France Presse, Apr. 21, 2008, http://www.climateark.org/shared/reader/welcome.aspx?linkid=97392.

Crop price declines in 2009 moderated the criticism to some degree. Many farmers reduced corn acreage and increased soybean acreage. GAO, Potential Effects and Challenges of Required Increases in Production and Use 36–37 (2009), http://www.gao.gov/assets/160/157718.pdf. But as of 2014, the USDA's Economic Research Service still observes that "ethanol has a large impact on the corn market (33 percent of use)," noting that "[m]arket impacts of higher biofuel production include higher commodity prices . . . and higher retail food prices." USDA, Econ. Research Serv., Bioenergy, http://www.ers.usda.gov/topics/farm-economy/bioenergy/findings.aspx#energy.

d.   RURAL DEVELOPMENT

Farmers in the Midwest have been the most vocal supporters of biofuel development. In recent years, selling corn to ethanol plants was so profitable that many farmers switched from growing soybeans to growing corn. Farmers encouraged the construction of ethanol plants in rural communities to reduce the cost of transporting corn to the processor. The growth in ethanol production generally has provided a boost to rural economies in the corn belt states. The main benefits have come from increased crop prices and from the construction and operation of biofuel plants.

Expert views on the magnitude of these benefits to rural communities and their permanence vary. Growth in ethanol production has generated "higher farm income for most crop producers," USDA, *supra,* but it has generally hurt livestock producers, primarily by driving up feed costs. GAO, Potential Effects and Challenges of Required Increases in Production and Use, *supra*, at 47–49.

Production of corn-based ethanol in the United States may indirectly promote rural agricultural economies in developing countries. Governments in many larger developed countries, including the United States, subsidize production of many basic food crops. Agriculture in many developing countries has been severely damaged by the costs of storing surpluses, the "dumping" of those surpluses on world markets, and the economic distortions caused by the market protectionism that this demands. Royal Society, Sustainable Biofuels: Prospects and Challenges, Jan. 8, 2008, https://royalsociety.org/~/media/Royal_Society_Content/policy/publications/2008/7980.pdf, at 6–7.

e.   DELIVERY INFRASTRUCTURE

Nearly all U.S. biofuel production facilities are located close to corn and soybean acreage in the Midwest, far from coastal markets, and the current distribution system for ethanol has been dependent on rail cars and barges that deliver ethanol to fuel terminals where it is blended with gasoline before shipment via tanker truck to gasoline retailers. These transport modes lead to higher prices than pipeline transport, and the supply of current shipping options (especially rail cars) is limited.

Oil companies have always had strong objections to regulations requiring the use of ethanol. They have long averred that ethanol could not be distributed by pipeline because of its chemical composition, thus requiring that it be transported by truck or railroad tank car at considerable expense. Since most U.S. ethanol is made from corn, this imposes additional economic burdens on those regions far removed from corn-growing areas. But starting in 2008, pipeline companies successfully modified some existing pipelines to carry ethanol, and other companies are evaluating the building of new ethanol pipelines.

As non-corn biofuels play a larger role, as required by EISA, some of the supply infrastructure concerns may be alleviated. Cellulosic biofuels potentially can be produced from a variety of feedstocks, and may not be as dependent on a single crop from one region of the country. Cong. Research Serv., Selected Issues Related to an Expansion of Renewable Fuel Standard (RFS) 19 (2009), http://www.au.af.mil/au/awc/awcgate/crs/r40155.pdf. In EISA § 248, Congress authorized a study of infrastructure problems, including: (1) corrosion of pipes and storage tanks; (2) dissolving of storage tank sediments; (3) clogging of filters; (4) contamination from water or other adulterants; (5) poor flow properties in low temperatures; (6) oxidative and thermal instability in long-term storage; (7) microbial contamination; and (8) problems associated with electrical conductivity. 42 U.S.C. § 17054(b).

3. ETHANOL FROM SUGAR CANE

Ethanol made from sugar cane, which, like corn, is an alcohol-based ethanol, is the cheapest source of ethanol on the world market. Brazil, the largest producer of sugar-based ethanol, was projected to have 26.6 billion liters in total ethanol production in 2014. USDA Foreign Agric. Serv., Brazil Biofuels Annual, Annual Report 2013, http://gain.fas.usda.gov/Recent%20GAIN%20Publications/Biofuels%20Annual_Sao%20Paulo%20ATO_Brazil_9-12-2013.pdf. Brazil has also historically exported large amounts of sugar-based ethanol to the United States, and corn growers persuaded Congress to levy a tariff on imported ethanol of 54 cents per gallon. Consumer interest groups in the United States advocated repeal of the tariff so that even more sugar-based ethanol from tropical regions could be imported, and in 2012 Congress did not extend the tariff, thus ending it. *See* PR Newswire, Congressional Recess Means the End of Three Decades of US Tariffs for Imported Ethanol, Dec. 23, 2011, http://www.prnewswire.com/news-releases/congressional-recess-means-the-end-of-three-decades-of-us-tariffs-on-imported-ethanol-136143713.html.

Very few parts of the United States are suitable for growing sugar cane, which thrives in hot weather. If the embargo on trade with Cuba were to be lifted, that country might become a significant exporter of sugar-based ethanol. President Obama in 2014 began expanding U.S. relations with Cuba, and the Treasury Department was reported to be drafting regulations to "ease agricultural exports." Julie Hirschfeld Davis & Michael R. Gordon, Obama Intends to Lift Several Restrictions Against Cuba on His Own, N.Y. Times, Dec. 18, 2014, http://www.nytimes.com/2014/12/19/us/politics/obama-intends-to-lift-several-restrictions-against-cuba-on-his-own.html?_r=0. Currently, free trade agreements with other Caribbean nations allow importation of ethanol without paying the tariff. Kaylan Little, Driving the Market: The Effects on the United States Ethanol Industry if the Foreign Ethanol Tariff is Lifted, 28 Energy L.J. 693 (2007).

4. BIODIESEL

Agricultural interests have been promoting the idea of "biodiesel," a form of diesel fuel made of agricultural material. The idea of using vegetable oil for fuel has been around as long as the diesel engine. Rudolph Diesel, the inventor of the engine that bears his name, experimented with fuels ranging from powdered coal to peanut oil. In the early 20th century, diesel engines were adapted to burn petroleum distillate, which was cheap and plentiful and became known as diesel fuel. Gradually, however, the cost of diesel fuel rose, and by the end of the 1970s there was renewed interest in diesel made from many different kinds of vegetable oils by adding alcohol and a catalyst, such as sodium hydroxide to initiate a process known as transesterification in which the triglycerides in the vegetable oil are converted into alkyl esters that can be used to fuel diesel engines. Greg Pahl, Biodiesel: Growing a New Energy Economy 42–45 (2005).

Among the fuels classified as "advanced biofuels" in the EISA, biodiesel is the most commonly produced. It can be blended with petroleum diesel and used in diesel engines if the engine is compatible with the particular blend. Common blends use 2 percent, 5 percent, and 20 percent of biodiesel (B2, B5, and B20). Individual engine manufacturers' warranties generally accept B5, and some support B20. The most common feedstocks for biodiesel production are soybean oil in the United States, rapeseed and sunflower oil in Europe, and palm oil in Malaysia and Indonesia, where large tracts of tropical forest are being cleared in order to plant oil palms, the fruit of which can be refined to produce biodiesel. In Europe, biodiesel has now become quite popular and widely used. Diesel automobiles are outselling gasoline models throughout Europe. Biodiesel also can be produced from other feedstocks, including vegetable oils, tallow and animal fats, restaurant waste and trap grease. One study found that high quality biodiesel could be produced from leftover coffee grounds, and estimated that the world's total coffee consumption could theoretically produce 340 million gallons of biodiesel. Am. Chem. Soc'y, Waste Coffee Grounds Offer New Source of Biodiesel Fuel, Dec. 10, 2008, http://www.acs.org/content/acs/en/pressroom/newsreleases/2008/december/waste-coffee-grounds-offer-new-source-of-biodiesel-fuel.html. A UK company called Bio-bean is now producing this fuel and hopes to sell it to the City of London to fuel the City's biofuel buses, as well as to coffee companies and other stores for their fleets. Tim Smedley, Waste Coffee Grounds Set to Fuel London with Biodiesel and Biomass Pellets, The Guardian, Feb. 13, 2014, http://www.theguardian.com/sustainable-business/waste-coffee-grounds-fuel-london.

School bus fleets in farming communities are a key market for biodiesel. Not only are local farmers provided with a market, but the consumption of carbon-intensive vegetation does not add to the total amount of carbon dioxide that would otherwise be created. As a locally derived fuel, biodiesel avoids adding to reliance on petroleum imports, and there are indications that it can have aggregate air quality benefits. Efforts are underway to broaden the market for biodiesel.

EIA's comparison of petroleum diesel fuel and biodiesel show that biodiesel has both pluses and minuses. An important characteristic of diesel fuel is its ability to ignite on its own, as it must in a diesel engine.

This ability is quantified by the fuel's cetane number, where a higher cetane number means that the fuel ignites more quickly. The cetane number for biodiesel ranges from about 46 to 57. In comparison, the cetane index for petroleum diesel ranges from 40 to 52. Thus biodiesel tends to ignite more easily. Another important characteristic is lubricity. Fuel injectors and some types of fuel pumps rely on fuel for lubrication. Biodiesel has better lubricity than low-sulfur petroleum diesel. However, the performance of biodiesel in cold conditions is markedly worse than petroleum diesel. Finally, the energy content per gallon of biodiesel is approximately 11 percent lower than petroleum diesel, and vehicles running on a biodiesel blend will achieve fewer miles per gallon of fuel. The presence of oxygen in biodiesel improves combustion and reduces hydrocarbon, carbon monoxide, and particulate emissions, but it also increases nitrogen oxide emissions. Anthony Radich, EIA, Biodiesel: Performance, Cost and Uses (2004), http://www.eia.gov/oiaf/analysis paper/biodiesel/.

Although doubts have been expressed about the performance of biodiesel in cold weather, the industry trade association, the National Biodiesel Board, says that "biodiesel blends of 20 percent and below will work in any diesel engine without the need for modifications. These blends will operate in diesel engines just like petroleum diesel. If the blend has been properly treated by the petroleum company, it will work year round, even in cold climates. B20 also provides similar horsepower, torque, and mileage as diesel." Nat'l Biodiesel Bd., America's Advanced Biofuel, Guide to Buying Biodiesel, http://www.biodiesel.org/using-biodiesel/guide-to-buying-biodiesel.

Research is under way to find methods of producing biofuel from algae on a large scale. Dale Gardner, Nat'l Renewable Energy Lab., Looking Ahead—Biofuels, H2, & Vehicles, Oct. 28, 2008, http://www.nrel.gov/technologytransfer/pdfs/igf21_gardner.pdf. Some pilot projects start algae in enclosed photobioreactors, but photobioreactors cost about ten times as much as open ponds, so many projects grow the algae in the reactor and then inoculate open ponds with the desired species. When the pond eventually becomes contaminated with competing species the pond is drained and sterilized before being reinoculated. Scientists are still searching thousands of algae species for one that will continually dominate an open pond and have desirable biofuel properties, and biotechnologists are working to improve the productivity of microalgae in order to meet the demands of what they hope will be a rapidly growing market. Fred Bosselman, Swamp Swaps: The Second Nature of Wetlands, 39 Envtl. L. 577, 607–608 (2009).

One well-financed American venture, Sapphire Energy, hopes to make millions of barrels a day from tens of thousands of acres devoted to algae farms in states along the Gulf Coast and in the Pacific Southwest. Nevertheless, there are formidable challenges involved in the basic research on the 40,000-plus species of algae already identified, and complications in genetically engineering new varieties. Also, anyone pursuing permits for any sizable facility would need to deal with a host of government agencies. *Id.* at 608. Despite these obstacles, in 2012 Sapphire completed construction of Phase I of the "Green Crude Farm," the world's first commercial demonstration algae-to-energy facility in Columbus, New Mexico. Sapphire Energy, The Sapphire Energy Story, http://www.sapphireenergy.com/

sapphire-renewable-energy. Other companies have also made progress. In 2014, the algae-to-fuel company Algenol, which already has an Integrated Biorefinery producing "8,000 total gallons of liquid fuel per acre per year," indicated that it will announce its "first commercial scale project." Algenol Biofuels, http://www.algenol.com.

5. CELLULOSIC ETHANOL

Cellulosic ethanol is widely viewed as the successor to today's corn-based ethanol. The Clean Air Act (CAA), as amended by EISA, defines "cellulosic biofuel" as "renewable fuel derived from any cellulose, hemicellulose, or lignin that is derived from renewable biomass and that has lifecycle GHG emissions, as determined by the [EPA] Administrator, that are at least 60 percent less than the baseline lifecycle greenhouse gas emissions." 42 U.S.C. § 7545(o)(1)(E). Section 1501 of the EPAct 2005 included special incentives for the development of cellulosic ethanol as part of its general requirements that refiners increase their use of ethanol, and EISA expanded the mandate for cellulosic ethanol further. By 2022, 21 billion gallons of cellulosic ethanol will be needed to meet EISA requirements. *See* 42 U.S.C. § 7545(o)(2)(B)(i)(iii).

Much work remains to achieve the full promise of cellulosic ethanol. In particular, the true potential for cellulosic fuel is unknown because a new generation of biofuels will require scientific breakthroughs to optimize the processes for breaking down cellulosic material. Nat'l Acad. of Sci. et al., Liquid Transportation Fuels from Coal and Biomass: Technological Status, Costs, and Environmental Impacts 117–223 (2009).

As described further below, cost is also a problem. One study concluded that the cost was around $111 million for a conventional grain ethanol plant and as much as $854 million for an advanced biorefinery. Nat'l Governors Ass'n, Greener Fuels, Greener Vehicles: A State Resource Guide (2008), http://www.nga.org/files/live/sites/NGA/files/pdf/0802GREENERFUELS.PDF. Among the many possible sources for cellulose ethanol are rice straw, wheat straw, forest thinnings and switchgrass, all of which involve significant transport costs. *See* Paul A. Willems, The Biofuels Landscape through the Lens of Industrial Chemistry, 325 Science 707 (2009).

Some producers are planning larger factories now that they are more confident their technology is viable. One company, "POET," plans to open a commercial-scale cellulosic ethanol plant in Iowa—a plant that will use crop residue to make ethanol. POET, http://poet.com/cellulosic. Not all efforts are successful. For example, a demonstration-scale cellulosic ethanol facility that made ethanol from waste wood materials near Upton, Wyoming, filed for chapter 11 bankruptcy in 2012. *See* In re Western Biomass Energy, LLC, Case No. 12-21085, Chapter 11, Opinion on Trustee's Motion to Enforce the Settlement Agreement, U.S. Bankruptcy Court for the District of Wyoming, http://www.wyb.uscourts.gov/opinions-search/opinions/12-21085-400.pdf.

In part perhaps due to congressional recognition that biofuels might not be available in the volumes that Congress hopes they will be—and thus targets for the biofuel volumes to be mixed with fuel each year might not be reached—the CAA leaves EPA with a great deal of discretion to amend the targets. Specifically, the CAA, as amended by EISA, directs EPA, for each calendar year including 2005 through 2021, to estimate the "volumes of transportation fuel, biomass-based diesel, and cellulosic biofuel projected to be sold or introduced into commerce in the United States." 42 U.S.C. § 7 545(o)(3)(A).

Based on this estimate of available biofuels, by November 30 preceding the year in which compliance targets must be met, the CAA directs EPA to establish the "renewable fuel obligation" that ensures that Congress's targets for volumes of biofuels will be met. Refiners, blenders, and importers of fuel must then meet this renewable fuel obligation, which is expressed in terms of a volume percentage: "a volume percentage of transportation fuel sold or introduced into commerce in the United States." *Id.* § 7545 (o)(3)(b). If the EPA Administrator determines in his or her evaluation of the volumes of biofuel to be sold that "the projected volume of cellulosic biofuel production is less than the minimum applicable volume" established by the annual congressional target, "the Administrator shall reduce the applicable volume of cellulosic biofuel required." *Id.* § 7545 (o)(7)(D).

The EPA has repeatedly used this provision to reduce volume percentages required for cellulosic ethanol. For 2011, in 42 U.S.C. § 7545 (o)(2)(B) Congress set a target of 250 million gallons of cellulosic ethanol to be blended with fuels, whereas the EPA in its December 9, 2010 final rule required only 6 million gallons of cellulosic ethanol (as measured in ethanol-equivalent gallons, since cellulosic ethanol has a higher energy content than conventional ethanol) to be blended into the fuel supply. For 2012, EPA required only 10.45 million gallons of cellulosic ethanol to be blended as compared to 0.5 billion gallons required by Congress, and for 2013 EPA required 810,185 gallons (after industry requested a revision of the initial 6 million EPA requirement) as compared to a Congressionally-required 1 billion gallons of cellulosic ethanol. Regulation of Fuels and Fuel Additives: 2013 Cellulosic Biofuel Standard, 79 Fed. Reg. 25,025, 25,026 (May 2, 2014) (to be codified at 40 C.F.R. Part 80); Regulation of Fuels and Fuel Additives: 2012 Renewable Fuel. Standards, 77 Fed. Reg. 1320, 1321 (Jan. 9, 2012) (codified at 40 C.F.R. Part 80).

a. CAN THE 2022 CELLULOSIC ETHANOL TARGET BE REACHED?

As shown by EPA's repeated allowances for requiring less cellulosic ethanol to be blended with fuels than Congress intended, the outlook for reaching Congress's ultimate target of having 16 billion gallons of cellulosic ethanol in fuels by 2022 seems increasingly unrealistic. EIA estimates that the cellulosic ethanol industry will be unable to meet the targets set in the early years by EISA: "Although cellulosic biofuels volumes are expected to grow significantly relative to current levels, they will likely remain well below the targets envisioned in the Energy Independence and Security Act of 2007." EIA also notes: "A number of biofuels projects, including one from BP Biofuels in Highlands County, Florida, have been canceled before starting major construction." EIA, Today in Energy, Cellulosic Biofuels Begin to Flow but in Lower Volumes than Foreseen by Statutory Targets, Feb. 26, 2013, http://www.eia.gov/todayinenergy/detail.cfm?id=10131.

The Congressional Research Service has noted problems with the large-scale production of cellulosic crops. There are substantial uncertainties regarding both the costs of production for cellulosic feedstock as well as the costs of producing biofuel from them. Perennial crops are often slow to establish and can take several years before a marketable crop is produced. Crops heavy in cellulose tend to be bulky and represent significant problems in terms of harvesting, transporting, and storing. Seasonality issues involving the operation of a biofuel plant year-round based on a four- or five-month harvest period of biomass suggest that bulkiness is likely to matter a great deal. In addition, most marginal lands (i.e., the low-cost biomass production zones) are located far from major urban markets, bringing the ethanol transportation issue into play. Cong. Research Serv., Selected Issues Related to an Expansion of the Renewable Fuel Standard 8 (2009), http://www.au.af.mil/au/awc/awcgate/crs/r40155.pdf.

b.   LAND USE REQUIREMENTS

Environmental groups worry about the impact of a variety of biofuels. For sugar cane, in particular, these groups are concerned about the effect of increasing Brazilian production. The rain forest does not provide soils conducive to sugar cane, but if sugar cane plantations continue to take over grazing land, the cattle grazers may push farther into the forest, with adverse impacts on biodiversity and climate change. Frequently, the sharp leaves from the sugar cane are burned before harvesting the canes, contributing to smog problems. Habitat loss is also expected to be a major byproduct of cropland, with its accompanying decrease in biological diversity. U.N. Env't Programme, Towards Sustainable Production and Use of Resources: Assessing Biofuels at 19, http://www.unep.org/pdf/biofuels/Assessing_Biofuels_Full_Report.pdf.

The problem of analyzing GHG impact also becomes significantly more complex if the changes in land use brought about by shifting to biofuel crops are taken into account. Studies published in *Science* in early 2008 suggest that the conversion of land to crops used for biofuels can greatly increase GHG emissions:

Although biofuels have the potential to reduce CO_2 emissions, secondary effects of biofuel production must also be considered, such as how much CO_2 is released by the conversion of land to the production of biofuel stock. Fargione et al. (p. 1235) analyzed the carbon balance of the conversion of a variety of carbon-rich land types to food-based biofuel croplands and find that the carbon debt incurred by the conversion process can be as much as 420 times that of the annual greenhouse gas emission reductions that result from the displacement of fossil fuels from the energy generation process.

Biofuels made from waste biomass, or grown on abandoned agricultural lands, can avoid most, or even all, of that carbon debt, however. Searchinger et al. (p. 1238) have modeled greenhouse gas emissions in the production of corn-based ethanol. Instead of generating a roughly 20% reduction in greenhouse gases, as typically is claimed, emissions would approximately double during the first 30 years of implementation and create an emission increase that would take more than 160 years to recoup.

Timothy Searchinger et al., Use of U.S. Croplands for Biofuels Increases Greenhouse Gases Through Emissions from Land-Use Change, 319 Science 1238 (2008). Searchinger and his coauthors calculated that an ethanol increase of 56 billion liters, diverting corn from 12.8 million hectares of U.S. cropland, would in turn bring 10.8 million hectares of additional land into cultivation. Locations would include 2.8 million hectares in Brazil, 2.3 million hectares in China and India, and 2.2 million hectares in the United States. *Id.* at 1239.

6. ENVIRONMENTAL AND SOCIAL IMPACT OF BIOFUELS

In discussing the environmental impact of biofuels, one must remember that gasoline comes with its own legacy of environmental problems. Nevertheless, biofuels are not without impacts on the environment, both direct and indirect.

a. DIRECT AIR AND WATER IMPACTS

Ethanol refineries emit many of the same pollutants as other industrial facilities, such as nitrogen oxides, carbon monoxide, and VOCs, but many of them are below the thresholds at which the regulations would require intensive air pollutant emissions analysis, and are located in rural areas where air quality standards have been attained. Some factories that convert corn into ethanol have been accused of releasing carbon monoxide, methanol, and some carcinogens at dangerous levels. Some EPA officials have expressed concern that ambient levels of some hazardous air pollutants may result from increased ethanol production, especially in areas with high concentrations of ethanol refineries. Acetaldehyde, a hazardous air pollutant, forms during the ethanol conversion process and is also emitted when ethanol is used as fuel. A 2008 study by the Nebraska Department of Environmental Quality showed that some ethanol refineries may have difficulties meeting national emission standards for some hazardous air pollutants, including acetaldehyde. GAO, Potential Effects and Challenges of Required Increases in Production and Use, *supra*, at 71–72. After reviewing numerous reports, Arnold Reitze concludes that it will take more study before valid conclusions may be drawn concerning the effect (good or bad) of ethanol on toxic air emissions. Reitze, *supra*, at 1205, 1217.

Ethanol refineries also emit particulate matter, and concern about fine particulates has been increasing. A 2009 study concluded that cellulosic ethanol can offer health benefits from reduction of these particulates. Jason Hill et al., Climate Change and Health Costs of Air Emissions from Biofuels and Gasoline, 106 PNAS 2077 (2009). This suggests that a shift from gasoline or conventional ethanol to cellulosic ethanol may have greater advantages than previously recognized.

In Brazil, which manufactures large quantities of ethanol from sugar cane, the workers who cut the sugar cane are often subjected to harsh conditions. In 2007, one Brazilian mill was raided by the government's anti-slavery task force. BBC News, "Slave" Labourers Freed in Brazil, July, 3, 2007, http://news.bbc.co.uk/2/hi/americas/6266712.stm. Young sugar cane workers have a very high rate of serious chronic kidney disease, which is often fatal. Global Health Action, Climate Change, Direct Heat Exposure, Health and Well-Being in Low and Middle-Income Countries 2, http://www.globalhealthaction.net/index.php/gha/article/viewFile/1958/2182. Burning tropical forests in Asia to plant oil palms for biodiesel has produced severe air pollution affecting a wide region. A report by UNEP points to the wide-ranging impact of the Asian "brown cloud." UNEP, Wide Spread and Complex Climate Changes Outlined in New UNEP Project Atmospheric Brown Cloud Report (2008), http://www.unep.org/Documents.Multilingual/Default.asp?DocumentID=550&ArticleID=5978&l=en.

Corn, a common ingredient in U.S. ethanol, is usually heavily fertilized with nitrogen and phosphorus that run off into local waterways and cause eutrophication, which is the overenrichment and excessive growth of algae in surface waters. In some lakes, this has resulted in potentially harmful algal blooms, decreased water clarity, and hypoxia, a condition of reduced oxygen, which impairs aquatic life. Similarly, in marine waters, excessive algae growth can create a hypoxic or dead zone, a region that cannot support fish and other organisms, which require oxygen for survival. A 2007 USGS model estimated that 52 percent of the nitrogen and 25 percent of the phosphorus entering the Gulf system is from corn and soybean cultivation in the Mississippi River basin. GAO Biofuels, *supra* at 56. If cellulosic ethanol is produced from native plants that require no irrigation, the impact on water quality might be more limited, but still would not meet EPA targets for relief of hypoxia in the Gulf of Mexico. Christine Costello, Impact of Biofuel Crop Production on the Formation of Hypoxia in the Gulf of Mexico, 43 Envtl. Sci. Tech. 7985 (2009).

Some biodiesel producers have been accused of dumping glycerin contaminated with methanol into local waters, with adverse effects on wildlife. Glycerin, an alcohol that is normally nontoxic, is produced in large quantities as a byproduct of biodiesel. It can be sold for secondary uses, but it must be cleaned first, a process that is expensive and complicated. Expanded production of biodiesel has flooded the market with excess glycerin, making it less cost-effective to clean and sell.

Water quantity is also an issue in some areas where water is scarce. Studies by Argonne National Laboratory found widely varying water demands for ethanol production, but in most cases substantially in excess of the water demand for gasoline production. Argonne Nat'l Lab., Consumptive Water Use in the Production of Ethanol and Petroleum Gasoline 6, http://www.circleofblue.org/waternews/wp-content/uploads/2010/09/Water-Consumption-in-Ehtanol-and-Petroleum-Production.pdf. Another 2008 study concluded that the energy derived from biomass requires about 70 to 400 times more water than that derived from other energy carriers such as fossil fuels, wind, and solar. P.W. Gerbens-Leenes et al., Water Footprint of Bio-Energy and Other Primary Energy Carriers, UNESCO-IHE Research Report Series #29, Mar. 2008. More than 90% of the water required for biofuels is used in the production of the feedstock, UNEP, *supra,* at 56, but local biofuel production may differ widely in the amount of water consumption. Royal Society, *supra*, at 43–46. If expanded acreage is devoted to corn or soybean production requiring irrigation, it could substantially impact areas where irrigation water is scarce, such as India and China. Robert F. Service, Another Biofuels Drawback: The Demand for Irrigation, 326 Science 516 (2009).

b.   LIFE CYCLE ANALYSIS

One of the most widely debated indirect impacts of biofuels involves the extent to which increased use of biofuel crops will cause other land to be converted to uses which will have harmful effects. For example, to what extent will land be taken out of conservation reserve and planted to crops? Or will wetlands be converted to biofuel crops that will increase downstream pollution?

Models vary, with some predicting enormous shifts of land into biofuel crops. *See, e.g.,* Marshall Wise et al., Implications of Limiting CO_2 Concentrations for Land Use and Energy, 324 Science 1183 (2009). This has led some observers to call for an international certification system that would restrict biofuel trade to certified countries and allow accredited agencies to monitor the impact of biofuel production systems. Leon Marshall, The Biofuel Gamble, 62 African Wildlife 18, 21 (2008).

EISA's test of "lifecycle greenhouse gas emissions" requires that the emissions are to be measured under rules to be drafted by the EPA. The test is to measure direct and indirect emissions; significant emissions from land use changes; feedstock and fuel production; transportation of materials; and delivery to the consumer. Biofuels will be required to show that they can reduce GHG emissions in comparison to diesel and gasoline by specific percentages. Searchinger et al., *supra.*

EISA's test is designed to test lifecycle emissions of greenhouse gases, but what about impacts on workers' health, biodiversity, indigenous peoples and lots of other issues? And how do biofuels' impacts compare to the impacts of gasoline and diesel fuel? EPA's proposed RFS–2 rule triggered a debate over how to consider the effect of indirect land use changes when evaluating GHG reductions from biofuels. The primary controversy was about the impact that EPA's proposal would have on the production of grain-based ethanol. The proposed RFS–2 rule said that because of international indirect land use changes, corn and other grain ethanol will produce weak GHG emission reductions, particularly when compared with second-generation biofuels.

EPA made significant changes in the lifecycle analyses in the final rule, easing the effects on existing ethanol plants. Regulation of Fuels and Fuel Additives: Changes to Renewable Fuel Program, 75 Fed. Reg. 14,670 (Mar. 26, 2010) (codified at 40 C.F.R. Part 80). EISA specified that the lifecycle analysis of GHG emissions of each category of renewable fuel must be less than the lifecycle GHG emissions of the 2005 baseline average gasoline or diesel fuel that it replaces. The statute sets four different levels of required reductions for the four different renewable fuel categories. (1) Renewable fuel, 20%; (2) Advanced biofuel, 50%; (3) Biomass-based diesel, 50%; and (4) Cellulosic biofuel, 60%. After analyzing the existing "fuel pathways," EPA decided that the following biofuel processes met the requirements:

- Ethanol produced from corn starch at a new (or expanded capacity from an existing) natural gas-fired facility using advanced efficient technologies that we expect will be most typical of new production facilities complies with the 20% GHG emission reduction threshold;

- Biobutanol from corn starch complies with the 20% GHG threshold;

- Ethanol produced from sugarcane complies with the applicable 50% GHG reduction threshold for the advanced fuel category;

- Biodiesel from soy oil and renewable diesel from waste oils, fats, and greases complies with the 50% GHG threshold for the biomass-based diesel category;

- Diesel produced from algal oils complies with the 50% GHG threshold for the biomass-based diesel category; and

- Cellulosic ethanol and cellulosic diesel (based on currently modeled pathways) comply with the 60% GHG reduction threshold applicable to cellulosic biofuels.

Id.

As noted above, a model run by Argonne National Laboratory shows that cornstarch ethanol clearly outpaces petroleum-based fuels in terms of energy required to produce and transport the fuel and associated GHG emissions. DOE, Ethanol: The Complete Energy Lifecycle Picture, https://www1.eere.energy.gov/vehiclesandfuels/pdfs/program/ethanol_brochure_color.pdf.

Controversy remains over whether and how to analyze potential change in land use patterns, especially at the international level. Does the conversion of Brazilian soybean land to sugar cane push farmers deeper into the rain forest? Soybean production occupies more than 6 million hectares in the plateau regions of Central Brazil, primarily produced for food and feed; genetically-modified varieties are widely grown. Today, soybean oil is increasingly used for biodiesel production. The expansion of soy production into the Amazon has raised severe environmental concerns. McCarl & Boadu, *supra*, at 64–65.

EPA is not the only governmental entity to rely on life-cycle analysis, including indirect land use analysis that makes assumptions about valuable carbon-sequestering land like forestland displaced to grow corn, to regulate GHG emissions. California has taken the lead in implementing a new low carbon fuel standard (LCFS), based on the same kind of indirect land-use analysis, which the ethanol industry says already makes it difficult to sell grain-based ethanol in the state. Cal. Energy Comm'n, Low Carbon Fuel Standard, http://www.energy.ca.gov/low_carbon_fuel_standard/. See Chapter 11 for a discussion of the LCFS and the litigation involving a challenge to the LCFS under the dormant Commerce Clause of the U.S. Constitution. An industry study challenges the results of indirect life-cycle analyses, suggesting indirect effects are not as significant as EPA and California believe. A study by AIR, Inc. concludes that the indirect land-use effects of corn-based ethanol are negligible. The Renewable Fuels Association estimates that without using the "unproven assumptions" of international land use changes, corn ethanol provides a 61% reduction of GHG emissions compared to petroleum fuels. Gas2, Reprieve for Ethanol? EPA Extends Comment Period on Biofuels, July 2014, http://gas2.org/2009/07/05/reprieve-for-ethanol-epa-extends-comment-period-on-biofuels. The ability to calculate future indirect land use changes resulting from production of biofuels is limited by the lack of proven and accepted land use models and sufficient information about input data.[4] For example, future land use policies may well be major factors in determining future land use changes, and yet adequate information and approaches for calculating the effects of such as-yet-unknown policies aren't available.

E. Promoting Efficient Motor Vehicles

Beyond biofuels, for which the environmental benefits remain somewhat controversial, another means of reducing GHG emissions and limiting other environmental effects of transportation is to make vehicles more efficient: reducing the amount of fuel that vehicles consume to do the same amount of work. The primary federal regulatory mechanism for achieving this is mandatory fuel economy standards, which require auto manufacturers to increase the miles per gallon (mpg) of vehicles they sell. The National Highway Traffic Safety Administration (NHTSA), part of DOT, is the federal agency with the authority to administer the program, which is known as the Corporate Average Fuel Economy (CAFE) standards.

Attempts to require automakers to make more fuel-efficient vehicles have gone through two phases. From 1975 to 2008, the CAFE standards were politically controversial, producing expensive litigation, bitter fights in Congress, and many disputes among the states. The major automakers and the auto workers' unions bitterly opposed fuel efficiency mandates, and after 1985 successfully resisted efforts to tighten the restrictions. As a result, the CAFE standards did not increase substantially in this 30-year period. But in 2008 fuel price increases and a bad recession weakened the auto industry. Both GM and Chrysler received billions of federal dollars to enable them stay in business, making the federal government a major stakeholder in both companies. Platt's Inside Energy, Cantwell Touts 32-Page Climate Bill as 'Clean' Alternative to House Measure, Sept. 21, 2009, http://www.cantwell.senate.gov/issues/Inside%20Energy%20on%20 CLEAR%20Act%209%2021%2009.pdf. In the wake of these events, an agreement was reached that increased the CAFE standards. It appeared, at least initially, to have the support of all major interests, and might moot many of the legal battles of the past.

1. Efficient Use of Petroleum-Based Fuel

The CAFE standards are the result of a long progression of efforts aimed at improving the efficiency of vehicles, as discussed in this section.

---

[4] In its report "Assessing Biofuels," UNEP suggests that solar panels could create the same energy as biofuels with much less impact on land use. "Biomass and photovoltaic technology both make use of the solar radiation reaching the surface of the earth. However, biomass in the open field can generally store only about 1 to 6% of the solar radiation input, which still requires transformation into useful energy. Whereas technologies such as photovoltaics (PV) and solar thermal power do far better; already, they can make use of 9 to 24% of the radiation input, with recent averages of about 15%. Further, solar systems can be installed on roofs and facades, which requires no additional land. In contrast, biomass has the lowest power density of all renewable energies, and therefore requires the largest amount of land." U.N. Env't Programme, *supra*, at 84 (citations omitted).

a.   RESPONSE TO THE 1970'S OIL SHOCKS

Fuel efficiency received little attention in the 1950s and 1960s. From the 1950s to 1972 the price of gasoline gradually declined from about $1.50 to about $1.20 per gallon, the equivalent to around 35 cents in 2010 dollars. EIA, Annual Energy Review (2010), http://www.eia.doe.gov/emeu/aer/txt/ptb0524.html. The "first oil shock" awoke Americans to the global nature of the oil market. Caused by the 1973 Arab embargo, the shock sharply increased gasoline prices and caused gasoline shortages. One response, the Energy Policy and Conservation Act of 1975 (EPCA), called for a doubling in new car fuel economy in ten years. It established a fuel economy standard of 18 mpg in model year 1978, rising to 27.5 by 1985, with hopes for an even sharper improvement by 1988. EPCA also established fuel economy standards for light duty trucks, beginning at 17.2 mpg in 1979, and then to 20.7 mpg.

EPCA created much of the complexity that makes the CAFE standards difficult to understand. Congress wanted to give automakers flexibility to manufacture a wide range of types of vehicle, so EPCA established a corporate average to be met by each manufacturer. This benchmark required each company's total output of cars to average out to the minimum mpg standards, but left companies the discretion to create whatever mix of vehicles they chose as long as the average complied with the standard. NHTSA was required to set the first standards for vehicles designated as "1978 model year." (In the auto business, the 1978 model year refers to new models that came out in fall 1977.) The program set minimum mpg requirements differently for cars and "light trucks," based on total vehicle sales. That difference led to a major loophole in the standards, involving the treatment of sport utility vehicles (SUVs).

EPCA set the average fuel economy for passenger automobiles for the 1985 model year at 27.5 mpg. 49 U.S.C. § 32902. The statute enumerated exceptions for emergency vehicles, dedicated alcohol or natural gas vehicles and manufacturers of less than 10,000 autos per year. More importantly, it provided mechanisms to modify the average mpg across the board or to provide exemptions from the national standard for individual manufacturers to reflect the maximum feasible average for that model year. However, the Secretary of Transportation could only lower the average down to 26.0 mpg or increase it to 27.5 mpg. The Secretary temporarily lowered the average down to 26.0 in 1986, but the average remained at 27.5 from 1990 until the passage of EISA in 2007.

If a manufacturer is unable to meet the national standard it must either pay a $5 fine for each 0.1 mpg that the manufacturer's fleet is below the standard, multiplied by the number of cars in the fleet or it can elect to submit an alternative plan providing for future efficiency credits exceeding the national standard that may be used to remedy past standard violations. EPCA preempted state fuel economy laws unless the state adopted standards identical to the federal standard. 49 U.S.C. § 32919.

Because EPCA was enacted during the period of high gasoline prices that followed the 1973 Arab oil embargo, buyers had a good reason to be interested in fuel efficiency. That interest was heightened when the fall of the Shah of Iran in 1979 created the "second oil shock" and gasoline prices again rose dramatically. Japanese automakers were best prepared to respond to these developments because high fuel prices were a long-term fact of life in that oil-deprived country. Their cars contributed to a 40% improvement in fuel efficiency between 1978 and 1987. Carson & Vaitheeswaram, *supra,* at 175.

b. RESPONSE TO THE THIRD OIL SHOCK: THE SPORT UTILITY VEHICLE

Oil prices remained high in the early 1980s; smaller cars were selling well, and it was expected that manufacturers would have no difficulty complying with the CAFE standards. However, the "third oil shock" arrived in the mid-80s. This time the shock was a sharp fall in oil prices. Fewer people bought small cars; sport utility vehicles (SUVs) became popular; pickup truck sales boomed. The automakers saw these more expensive vehicles as a much more profitable product than small cars. They convinced the government to classify all SUVs as light trucks even if they were built on an automobile chassis. This allowed them to build more powerful SUVs that complied with the more lenient fuel efficiency standards for light trucks. A widespread marketing campaign drove up SUV and truck sales dramatically.

The special treatment of SUVs was achieved by the legerdemain of including them within the definition of "non-passenger automobile." NHTSA regulations implementing EPCA describe four categories of non-passenger automobiles: (1) automobiles designed primarily to transport more than 10 persons (large passenger vans); (2) automobiles designed primarily for purposes of transportation of property (e.g. pickup trucks); (3) automobiles derived from automobiles designed primarily for the transportation of property (e.g. truck-body camper), and (4) automobiles which are capable of off-highway operation (having high ground clearance and either having 4-wheel drive or being rated at more than 6,000 pounds gross vehicle weight (GVWR), or both). Even though most SUVs function primarily as passenger vehicles, NHTSA called them non-passenger automobiles (that is, light trucks), and regulated their mpg as such. This created a considerable incentive for manufacturers to build SUVs, as the light truck fuel economy standards were lower. *See* Ctr. for Biological Diversity v. Nat'l Highway Traffic Safety Admin., 508 F.3d 508 (9th Cir. 2007) (discussing this issue).

Light truck fuel economy requirements were first established for MY 1979 (17.2 mpg for 2-wheel drive models; 15.8 mpg for 4-wheel drive). Standards for MY 1979 light trucks were established for vehicles with a GVWR of 6,000 pounds or less. Standards for MY 1980 and beyond are for light trucks with a GVWR of 8,500 pounds or less. The light truck standard progressively increased from MY 1979 to 20.7 mpg and 19.1 mpg, respectively, by MY 1991. From MY 1982 through 1991, manufacturers were allowed to comply by either combining 2-and 4-wheel drive fleets or calculating their fuel economy separately. In MY 1992, the 2-and 4-wheel drive fleet distinction was eliminated, and fleets were required to meet a standard of 20.2 mpg. The standard progressively increased until 1996, when Congress froze the requirement at 20.7 mpg. The result was predictable: "Seduced by the short-term profits that SUVs offered during the boom years of the 1990s, GM and its

American rivals neglected to invest in more fuel efficient, environmentally friendly technologies." Carson & Vaitheeswaram, *supra*, at 287.

As the 1980s wound down, the economy improved and the boom years began. Each year, Congress told the agency that it could not tighten CAFE standards for either cars or light trucks. A small increase in light truck standards was authorized for model years after 2004, but the automakers strongly resisted even that change. So after 1985, nationwide fuel economy had remained essentially the same for twenty years.

One of the automakers' most effective arguments was the issue of safety. SUVs and light trucks were perceived by the public as providing improved safety for their occupants over other vehicles. The safety issue was discussed by Judge (later Justice) Ginsburg in the following case.

Competitive Enterprise Institute v. NHTSA

45 F.3d 481 (D.C. Cir. 1995).

GINSBURG, J.: The Competitive Enterprise Institute and Consumer Alert (hereinafter referred to jointly as the CEI) petition for review of the National Highway Traffic Safety Administration rulemaking setting the corporate average fuel economy (CAFE) standard for 1990 passenger cars. The petitioners claim that the agency arbitrarily and capriciously failed to acknowledge significant adverse safety effects of setting the standard at 27.5 rather than 26.5 miles per gallon or somewhere in between. Finding that the agency adequately rooted its decision in the record of the rulemaking, we deny the petition for review.

The CEI contends that the NHTSA failed to give adequate consideration to the petitioners' contention that [the 27.5] CAFE standard for MY 1990 would have significant adverse safety effects. Specifically, the CEI claims that the agency failed to consider that (1) the CAFE standard causes automobile manufacturers to downsize passenger cars, resulting in significantly more traffic fatalities because larger, heavier cars are safer than smaller, lighter cars; and (2) the CAFE standard constrains automobile manufacturers from upsizing cars, thereby pricing consumers out of the market for larger, heavier, and (presumably) safer cars. The substance of the CEI's position is intuitively appealing. We must deal here, however, not with our intuition and not with the petitioners' position in the abstract, but with the concrete record before us and with the conclusions that the agency drew from it. That record adequately supports the NHTSA's conclusion that maintaining the 27.5 mpg CAFE standard for MY 1990 would not significantly affect the safety of the motoring public.

First, the NHTSA reasonably concluded from the evidence before it that the MY 1990 CAFE standard did not cause automobile manufacturers either to downsize or to refrain from upsizing their cars. In its notice reopening the rulemaking proceeding, the agency asked commenters to address:

> What specific actions [manufacturers would] actually take, if any, depending upon whether the MY 1990 CAFE standard remained at 27.5 mpg or were reduced to some level between

26.5 mpg and 27.5 mpg? If the standard remained at 27.5 mpg, would manufacturers downsize vehicles, refrain from upsizing vehicles[,] or change the mix or pricing policies of the vehicles they offer for sale?

Further, recognizing that a regulatory change made in 1992 would not affect the production of vehicles in MYs 1990–92, the NHTSA asked the automobile manufacturers to state what specific actions they would take with respect to any model year (presumably by carrying credits backward or forward) were the agency to lower the 1990 standard.

No manufacturer identified any change that it would make in the size or weight of its vehicles, in its product mix, or in its pricing strategy—for any model year—if the NHTSA were to lower the MY 1990 CAFE standard. In fact, the Ford Motor Company asserted that it "did not reduce its average car size over what would have been offered absent such 1990 standard." The General Motors Corporation stated that "relaxing the standard could in some cases generate credits giving manufacturers more flexibility to offer larger, safer cars in later model years," but did not go so far as to suggest that it would be one of the beneficiaries. Accordingly, the NHTSA reasonably decided that maintaining the MY 1990 CAFE standard would have no appreciable effect upon the size or weight of automobiles offered for sale in any model year.

Second, the factual record simply does not support the CEI's contention that consumers are priced out of the market for larger, heavier cars by reason of the 27.5 mpg standard. As part of the rulemaking for the MY 1986 CAFE standard, the NHTSA analyzed the cost-effectiveness of various technological changes that manufacturers have used to meet fuel economy standards. That analysis showed that most of the technological changes paid for themselves with fuel savings over the first four years of ownership and that all but one were cost-effective over the life of the vehicle. Moreover, the NHTSA noted that the technological changes—including improved aerodynamics, substitution of lighter materials, fuel injection, electronic engine control, wide ratio gearing, reduced lubricant viscosity, and reduced rolling resistance—are widely available on large and small cars alike. Therefore, any increase in the purchase price of cars owing to those features would not impose a relative penalty upon the purchase of a large car. Finally, while the NHTSA recognized that a manufacturer could attempt to induce a shift in its product mix either by reducing the price of its small cars or by increasing the price of its large cars (or both), the agency noted that no manufacturer commented in the rulemaking on remand that it had taken either step in order to meet the MY 1990 CAFE standard of 27.5 mpg.

Finally, the NHTSA considered the study upon which the CEI rested its contention that the MY 1990 CAFE standard had a significant effect on safety. *See* Robert W. Crandall & John D. Graham, The Effect of Fuel Economy Standards on Automobile Safety, 32 J. of L. & Econ. 97, 109–10 (1989). That study suggests that in the 1980s manufacturers significantly reduced the average weight of their cars due to the CAFE standards. Using a model describing the relationship of automobile weight to safety, and explaining weight as a function solely of CAFE regulation and of the expected prices of gasoline and steel (as forecast four years in advance), Crandall and Graham estimated that the CAFE program caused a "500-pound or 14 percent reduction in the average weight of 1989 cars," which was "associated with a 14–27 percent increase in occupant fatality risk." *Id.* at 111.

The NHTSA did not directly dispute the general finding of the Crandall and Graham study, i.e., that there is a relationship between safety and the size or weight of automobiles. *See* 58 Fed. Reg. at 6946 ("The agency . . . fully agrees . . . that all other things being equal, a large car is safer than a small car"). Instead the agency faulted Crandall and Graham for failing to take account of factors in addition to gasoline and steel prices—namely, "technological advances," "increased competition," and "changes in consumer preferences"—that in the agency's view would explain almost all of the average car's weight loss that the authors instead attributed to the CAFE standard. (Indeed the agency even suggested that "any CAFE standard effect [on weight] is negligible." Id.)

Although phrased in a variety of ways, the NHTSA's response to Crandall and Graham comes down to suggesting that a change in consumers' preferences, rather than any constraining effect of the CAFE standards, accounts for vehicle downsizing over the period that they studied. (After all, "increased competition" only facilitates the satisfaction of consumers' preferences; nor, if manufacturers were not constrained by the CAFE standards to adopt them, are "technological advances" relevant unless consumers demanded them). While the agency speculated that consumers might have preferred "downsized vehicles [because they] offered better handling, easier parking, and potential cost savings associated with reduced materials usage," it offered no reason whatsoever to think that consumer preferences actually did change at all during the relevant time, much less that they changed in the direction of preferring smaller and apparently more dangerous cars. Merely to assert the existence of another possible explanation, which is all that the NHTSA has done, does nothing to undermine the significance of the findings carefully documented by Crandall and Graham. It is like asserting that regulation of the airlines had no effect because it occurred at a time when all consumers preferred amenities such as gourmet meals rather than cheaper fares; that is, of course, possible, but the only evidence is to the contrary.

The NHTSA's failure adequately to respond to the Crandall and Graham study is troubling, but it is not a basis, upon this record, for overturning the agency's decision to adhere to the 27.5 mpg CAFE standard for MY 1990. The overwhelming fact is that no automobile manufacturer is on record stating that it would have added weight to its automobiles (or taken any other action) in any model year had the NHTSA relaxed the 1990 CAFE standard. Therefore, record evidence documenting a correlation between the safety and the size or weight of a vehicle, and the contribution of the CAFE standard to determining size or weight, while potentially relevant to any future decision to retain or amend the CAFE standard, simply does not require the NHTSA to amend the MY 1990 CAFE standard. The petition for review is therefore Denied. ∎

NOTES AND COMMENTS

1.   If you were the attorney for an automobile manufacturer, and your client had received an inquiry from a federal agency asking, in effect,

whether your client could build cars that are safer than they are now building them, how would you have advised your client to answer? Was the court being fair in basing its decision on the automobile manufacturers' responses to such a loaded question?

2.   The safety argument the CEI advanced in this case continues to be a focus of public debate over CAFE standards. Nicholas Brozovic & Amy Whitenour Ando, Defensive Purchasing, the Safety (Dis)advantage of Light Trucks, and Motor-Vehicle Policy Effectiveness, 43 Transp. Res. Part B 477 (2009).

c.   "ADDICTION TO OIL"

Al Qaeda's attack on America on September 11, 2001, triggered an increasing concern about America's reliance on imported oil. The administration of George W. Bush began to push for gradual increases in fuel economy, despite strong resistance by automakers. In 2003, NHTSA issued new light truck standards, setting a standard of 21.0 mpg for MY 2005, 21.6 mpg for MY 2006, and 22.2 mpg for MY 2007. *See* 49 C.F.R. Part 553. In 2006, NHTSA adopted "reformed" CAFE standards requiring higher fuel economy performance in MY 2008 through 2011 for light duty trucks, including pickups, vans, truck-based station wagons, and SUVs. *See* 49 C.F.R. §§ 523, 533, 537.

The standards specified a continuous mathematical function that determines minimum fuel economy requirements by vehicle footprint, defined as the wheelbase (the distance from the front axle to the center of the rear axle) times the average track width (the distance between the center lines of the tires) of the vehicle in square feet. Light truck fuel economy standards vary by model year and by vehicle footprint. The rationale behind using a continuous mathematical function is that the function removes the opportunity for manufacturers to reduce fuel economy requirements by altering vehicle sizes just enough to reach lower target levels. Instead, under a continuous function approach, each footprint value has an assigned fuel economy target, and small changes in vehicle footprint are not rewarded with large decreases in target values. EIA, Fuel Economy Standards for New Light Trucks, 2007, http://www.eia.doe.gov/oiaf/aeo/otheranalysis/fuel.html#12.

In addition to revising the structure of the light truck CAFE program, NHTSA also increased the maximum GVWR of light trucks from 8,500 to 10,000 pounds. Starting in 2011, light truck CAFE standards were also applied to medium-duty passenger vehicles (MDPVs), which are defined as heavy-duty vehicles less than 10,000 pounds designed primarily for transportation of passengers. This definition includes SUVs, short-bed pickup trucks, and passenger vans that are within the specified weight and weight-rated ranges.

The 2006 CAFE standards imposed a unique fuel economy standard on each manufacturer, based on the product mix sold in a given model year. For model years 2008–2010, manufacturers had the option of complying with either the new reformed CAFE standard (the continuous mathematical function) or an unreformed CAFE standard. The unreformed CAFE standard required manufacturers to meet an average light truck fleet standard of 22.5 mpg in model year 2008, 23.1 mpg in model year 2009, and 23.5 mpg in model year 2010. All light truck manufacturers were required to adhere to the new reformed standards for model 2011 and subsequent years. EIA, Fuel Efficiency Analysis for New Light Trucks, AEO2007. On November 15, 2007, however, the Ninth Circuit ruled that the adoption of the 2006 CAFE rules violated the National Environmental Policy Act. Ctr. for Biological Diversity v. Nat'l Highway Traffic Safety Admin., 508 F.3d 508 (9th Cir. 2007). The CAFE standards program was set back just as Congress was debating its future.

d. THE SHOCK OF 2007

The autumn of 2007 marked the beginning of a severe recession. The economy tanked, and the automobile industry was one of the most severely impacted sectors of the economy; sales of vehicles dropped precipitously. Automakers reacted by closing facilities and terminating relationships with dealers. Layoffs of auto workers took place throughout the country, but particularly in the hard hit region centering on Detroit. Thomas H. Klier, From Tail Fins to Hybrids: How Detroit Lost Its Dominance of the U.S. Auto Market, Fed. Reserve Bank of Chicago, Econ. Perspectives, Vol. 33 No. 2 (May 18, 2009). Coincidentally, fears about climate change increased sharply with the release of the Intergovernmental Panel on Climate Change report in 2007. Concern over the prospect of developing a new climate treaty drew attention to the lack of progress in the United States toward reducing GHG emissions.

Another influential factor was the beginning of a rapid rise in prices of commodities, including oil, gasoline and metals, which affected both the manufacture and use of automobiles and light trucks. As the stock market declined throughout 2007, investors switched to commodity speculation that helped drive up prices. The rapid growth of China's economy, together with the economies of India, Brazil and other rapidly developing nations, also created an increased demand for oil that further exaggerated the trend toward rising prices.

Meanwhile, in the elections of November 2006 Democrats gained control of both houses of Congress, thus making it necessary to obtain bipartisan compromise to pass legislation of any type. As always, energy legislation also required compromise between a wide variety of interest groups and regional coalitions. Despite the difficulty of reaching such compromises, however, Congress succeeded in passing a revision of the CAFE standards in the EISA.

e. EISA 2007 CAFE STANDARDS

EISA imposed a wide variety of new standards relating to many kinds of energy, including the biofuels standards discussed above. Perhaps the most dramatic compromise was the resolution of long-running disputes among automakers, clean air advocates, and the state of California about vehicle fuel economy and the regulation of greenhouse gases.

Under EISA, the combined fuel economy of passenger vehicles and light trucks between model years 2011 and 2020 must grow to an average at least 35 mpg. This would increase the current fuel economy standards (which, recall, had not been successfully increased since 1975) by approximately 40 percent.

EISA amended, but did not replace EPCA, so the procedures and definitions from the earlier law were mostly unchanged, and the program continued to be administered by NHTSA. The agency was required to adopt regulations setting the standards to cover the first five years (model years 2011–15). Regulations for 2016–20 were to be published later (and have now been published).

Because EPA needed to set auto efficiency standards to respond to the Supreme Court's decision that GHGs from mobile sources were pollutants under the Clean Air Act (see Chapter 5), NHTSA and EPA jointly issued proposed rules for the 2011–15 model years for light-duty vehicles in September, 2009 and final rules in April 2010. Light-Duty Vehicle Greenhouse Gas Emission Standards and Corporate Average Fuel Economy Standards; Final Rule, 75 Fed. Reg. 25,324 (May 7, 2010) (to be codified at 40 C.F.R. Parts 85, 86, and 600; 49 CFR Parts 531, 533, and 536). They set further rules for "2017 and later model years" in 2012, covering model years 2017 through 2022. 2017 and Later Model Year Light-Duty Vehicle Greenhouse Gas Emissions and Corporate Average Fuel Economy Standards; Final Rule, 77 Fed. Reg. 62,624 (Oct. 15, 2012) (to be codified at 49 C.F.R. Parts 523, 531, 533, et al. and 600.) These agencies then issued Greenhouse Gas Emissions Standards and Fuel Efficiency Standards for Medium and Heavy-Duty Engines and Vehicles (Phase 1) in 2011 for model years 2014–2018, with EPA's GHG emission limits going into effect as of 2014 and NHTSA's fuel consumption standards becoming mandatory starting with model years 2016. Greenhouse Gas Emissions Standards and Fuel Efficiency Standards for Medium- and Heavy-Duty Engines and Vehicles; Final Rule, 76 Fed. Reg. 57,106 (Sept. 15, 2011) (to be codified at 49 C.F.R. Parts 523, 534, and 535). On February 18, 2014, President Obama directed EPA and NHTSA to "develop and issue the next phase of medium- and heavy-duty vehicle fuel efficiency and greenhouse gas standards by March 2016." The White House, Office of the Press Sec'y, Fact Sheet: Opportunity for All: Improving the Fuel Efficiency of American Trucks—Bolstering Energy Security, Cutting Carbon Pollution, Saving Money and Supporting Manufacturing Innovation, http://www.whitehouse.gov/the-press-office/2014/02/18/fact-sheet-opportunity-all-improving-fuel-efficiency-americ an-trucks-bol.

With respect to standards for light-duty vehicles, EISA required passenger car standards to be reformed by basing them on "one or more vehicle attributes related to fuel economy." 2017 and Later Model Year Light-Duty Vehicle Greenhouse Gas Emissions and Corporate Average Fuel Economy Standards, *supra*, at 62,686. This intended to "reform" the standards by establishing different standards for different sizes of vehicles, along the lines of the light truck rules adopted in 2006 but held invalid. *Id*. The 2010 and 2012 regulations varied the standard by the size of the vehicle and by the distribution of that manufacturer's vehicles among those sizes. Size was to be determined by a vehicle's "footprint": the product of the width between the tires and the length between the axles. Each company could decide for itself what mix of vehicles to build as long as the average of the aggregate of both cars and light trucks meets 92% of the standard for the year, so the actual miles per gallon requirement depends on these and a number of other variables. The rules used a continuous mathematical function that provides a separate fuel economy target for each footprint. Individual manufacturers were required to comply with a single fuel economy level that was based on the distribution of its production among the footprints of its vehicles. Light-Duty Vehicle Greenhouse Gas Emission Standards and Corporate Average Fuel Economy Standards, *supra*; 2017 and Later Model Year Light-Duty Vehicle Greenhouse Gas Emissions and Corporate Average Fuel Economy Standards, *supra*, at 62686.

Although the weight of a vehicle bears a much greater relationship to fuel efficiency than the footprint of the vehicle, weight-based standards eliminate the incentive to reduce weight by imposing a tighter standard on lighter vehicles. Automakers would be unlikely to reduce a vehicle's footprint without reducing its weight because such a reduction would reduce safety. The objective of attribute standards is to avoid the possibility that "manufacturers of small vehicles may be able to comply with the current standards without any action to improve efficiency design and technology, while manufacturers of larger vehicles, or a mix of vehicles, may have to take strong measures for compliance." Stephen E. Plotkin, Examining Fuel Economy and Carbon Standards for Light Vehicles 19–20 (2007), http://www.internationaltransportforum.org/jtrc/discussionpapers/DiscussionPaper1.pdf.

In addition to federal changes in fuel standards that limit GHG emissions from vehicles, California has been very active in pushing forward its own mobile source GHG limits. An amendment to the Clean Air Act passed in 1990 gave California the right to set its own standards for car emissions and allowed other states either to follow suit or stick to limits set by the EPA. 42 U.S.C. § 7543(b). California's attempts to make cars less polluting had been bitterly resisted by both carmakers and President Bush, but in 2009, the EPA allowed California to implement its own GHG emission limits for passenger cars, small trucks, and SUVs. California agreed to allow automobiles sold in California to follow federal greenhouse gas emissions standards for model years 2012–2016 but to implement other programs to encourage cars that released even fewer greenhouse gas emissions. "In January 2012, the [California] Air Resources Board approved a new emissions-control program for model years 2015 through 2025. The program combines the control of smog, soot and global warming gases and requirements for greater numbers of zero-emission vehicles into a single package of standards called Advanced Clean Cars." Cal. Air Res. Bd., California's Advanced Clean Car Programs, http://www.arb.ca.gov/msprog/consumer_info/advanced_clean_cars/consumer_acc.htm. Most recently, California proposed to also follow federal GHG mobile source emission limits for model years 2017–2025. *Id.* Although California has proposed to follow national standards for limits on GHG emissions from cars, under the Advanced Clean Cars program it will continue its zero emissions vehicle (ZEV) policy to encourage the sale of "battery electric vehicles, hydrogen fuel cell vehicles, and plug-in hybrid electric vehicles." Cal. Envtl. Prot. Agency, Advanced Clean Car Subsidies 3 http://www.arb.ca.gov/msprog/clean_cars/acc% 20summary-final.pdf.

California has updated its GHG emissions standards for motor vehicles to track the federal standards in part because of recent changes to the federal standards made by the EPA and NHTSA, with more aggressive limits for fuel economy and GHG emissions limits. As discussed above, in 2012, NHTSA and EPA finalized rules for light-duty vehicles for model years 2017–2025. The agencies continued to use a 2008 baseline year as well as the "footprint" method to determine vehicle size. Under the rules, by 2025 average required fleet-wide fuel economy would be 55.3 to 56.2 mpg for passenger cars, 39.3 to 40.3 mpg for light trucks, and 48.7 to 49.7 mpg combined. The 2011 rules for medium- and heavy-duty vehicles do not require mpg targets. Instead, NHTSA limits fuel consumption in terms of the amount of fuel consumed per mile or ton-mile, and the EPA limits the quantity of GHG emissions that may be produced by medium- and heavy-duty vehicles in terms of the quantity of CO_2 emitted per mile or ton-mile. CO_2 emissions measurements per ton-mile indicate "the mass of emissions from carrying a ton of cargo over a distance of one mile," and fuel consumption measurements measure the quantity of fuel consumed as a result of carrying a ton of cargo for one mile. 49 C.F.R. §§ 523, 534–35.

Will vehicles achieve the ambitious targets set forth in EPA and NHTSA standards? An MIT report suggests that this is unlikely. Depending on the model scenarios used, which make different assumptions as to whether technology improvements will be used to continue to increase fuel efficiency versus making vehicles larger or otherwise better, the likelihood of passenger cars exceeding 54.5 mpg is very low. Under EPA's and DOT's more optimistic scenario, "[t]he likelihood of meeting or exceeding the nominal CAFE" target of 54.5 mpg in 2012 is "less than 1% for passenger cars." Parisa Bastani et al., MIT Energy Init., Potential for Meeting Light-Duty Vehicle Fuel Economy Targets, 2016–2025, at 28 (2012), http://web.mit.edu/sloan-auto-lab/research/beforeh2/files/CAFE_2012.pdf.

f.   WHAT ABOUT OLDER VEHICLES?

CAFE standards apply to new vehicles sold in the United States. But there are almost 500 million motor vehicles registered in the United States. Are there ways of increasing the fuel efficiency of the existing motor vehicle fleet?

Regardless of how strict the fuel-efficiency standards for new vehicles may be, most motor vehicles have long lives. To what extent can the existing vehicles be made more fuel-efficient? A committee of the National Research Council found in 2006 that the replacement of tires could make substantial improvements in vehicle fuel efficiency. When motorists replace their tires, if they chose tires with less rolling resistance, they could gain a 1 to 2% increase in the fuel economy of their vehicles. The committee concluded that "although traction may be affected by modifying a tire's tread to reduce rolling resistance, the safety consequences are probably undetectable." Nat'l Research Coun., Tires and Passenger Vehicle Fuel Economy: Informing Consumers, Improving Performance—Special Report 286 (2006), http://www.nap.edu/openbook.php?record_id=11620&page=R3.

Congress made a short-term effort in 2009 to discourage the continued use of old cars with poor fuel efficiency. The Consumer Assistance to Recycle and Save (CARS) Act created a Car Allowance Rebate System that awarded buyers of new cars either a $3500 or $4500 voucher towards the purchase of a new, more fuel efficient car or truck from a participating dealer when the car owner traded in a less fuel efficient car or truck. 49 U.S.C. § 32901 (2009). The program was designed to boost car sales while getting gas guzzlers off the road. DOT was appropriated $1 billion for the program, which was subsequently increased to $3 billion because of high demand. When the funds were exhausted within a few months, Congress did not appropriate further funds.

2.   REGULATION OF AUTOMOTIVE AIR POLLUTION

A complete understanding of the history of automotive air pollution requires a comprehensive study of the CAA, widely regarded as one of the most complex environmental law statutes and usually a central element in courses on environmental law. Chapter 5 explores the Act's regulation of stationary sources of air pollution, and regulation of GHG emissions more generally. This section will only summarize a few of the issues relating to air pollution regulations that have particular relevance to mobile sources, and the developments relating to the energy usage of various types of transportation.

a.   REGULATION OF MOTOR VEHICLES

Driving a car is the most air polluting act an average citizen commits. Automobiles are a source of two kinds of precursors of ground level ozone: nitrogen oxides and volatile organic chemicals. More American communities are out of attainment with national standards for ozone than for any other conventional pollutant.

Since 1970, Title II of the CAA has authorized EPA to regulate emissions of harmful pollutants from mobile sources (motor vehicles) by promulgating "standards applicable to the emission of any air pollutant from any class or classes of new motor vehicles or motor vehicle engines, which in the [EPA] Administrator's judgment cause, or contribute to, air pollution which may reasonably be anticipated to endanger public health or welfare." 42 U.S.C. § 7521(a)(1). These standards apply for the useful life of the car. Currently that life is ten years or 100,000 miles (a definition that applied beginning in 1990), but vehicles are not tested after 7 years or 75,000 miles.

EPA originally was slow to establish sulfur and particulate emissions standards as required by the 1977 amendments to the CAA. EPA failed to set such standards for over six years for autos, and for even longer periods for heavier vehicles, necessitating litigation by environmental organizations that forced EPA to meet court-imposed timetables. *See, e.g.,* Natural Res. Def. Council v. Thomas, 805 F.2d 411 (D.C. Cir. 1984). EPA has since enacted a range of emissions limits on vehicles, however. In 2000, it began to address emissions from tailpipes and the content of fuels as an integrated problem, recognizing that vehicle emissions reduction systems could be impacted by the type and quality of fuels vehicles burned. Thus, beginning with its "Tier 2" rules in 2000, EPA set emissions tailpipe limits and fuel content requirements within one rule. Its latest set of mobile source rules, finalized in late April 2014, are called the "Tier 3 Motor Vehicle Emission and Fuel Standards." As described by EPA:

> The Tier 3 program is part of a comprehensive approach to reducing the impacts of motor vehicles on air quality and public health. The program considers the vehicle and its fuel as an

integrated system, setting new vehicle emissions standards and lowering the sulfur content of gasoline beginning in 2017. The vehicle standards will reduce both tailpipe and evaporative emissions from passenger cars, light-duty trucks, medium-duty passenger vehicles, and some heavy-duty vehicles. The gasoline sulfur standard will enable more stringent vehicle emissions standards and will make emissions control systems more effective."

EPA, Tier 3 Vehicle Emission and Fuel and Standards Program, http://www.epa.gov/otaq/tier3.htm.

Standards beyond those that require a reduction in the emissions from vehicles' tailpipes also apply. Under Title I of the CAA, communities that persistently violate ozone ambient air quality standards can become subject to penalties, including the withholding of federal highway funds. As a result, in places where ground level ozone levels are a problem, states and local communities undertake measures to reduce driving (e.g., toll roads, high-occupancy vehicle lanes) or promote mass transit (e.g., subsidies).

EPA's rules for ground-level ozone (smog) pollution have undergone a number of changes that have faced considerable opposition, even within the Executive Branch. In 2008 EPA adopted regulations tightening the pollution standard for ozone, expressed as the permitted ambient amount of ozone in the air measured over various periods of time. EPA lowered the ozone standard from 80 parts per billion (ppb) to 75 ppb. Compliance was based on data collected over a three-year period. States were required to submit plans for each area not in compliance, outlining how ozone pollution would be reduced. National Ambient Air Quality Standards for Ozone, 73 Fed. Reg. 16,436 (Mar. 27, 2008). Industry criticized this change as unnecessary and costly, and health and environmental groups argued that it did not go far enough.

In 2010, EPA reconsidered its 2008 ozone standard and proposed to set the ozone standard even lower, at a range of 60–70 ppb "to provide increased protection for children and other 'at risk' populations" against "adverse health effects that range from decreased lung function and increased respiratory symptoms to serious indicators of respiratory morbidity including emergency department visits and hospital admissions for respiratory causes, and possibly cardiovascular-related morbidity as well as total non-accidental and cardiopulmonary mortality." Nat'l Ambient Air Quality Standards for Ozone, 75 Fed. Reg. 11 (Jan. 19, 2010). Later in 2011, EPA issued a draft final rule incorporating this standard. Cass Sunstein, who was then the Administrator of the Office of Information and Regulatory Affairs, which reviews proposed regulations, advised EPA to "reconsider" its rule, finding that the new standard was "not mandatory and could produce needless uncertainty" and was not based on the most current science, among other concerns. Executive Office of the President, Office of Mgmt. and Budget, Letter from Cass R. Sunstein to EPA Administrator Lisa P. Jackson (Sept. 2, 2011), http://www.whitehouse.gov/sites/default/files/ozone_national_ambient_air_quality_standards_letter.pdf.   In September 2011, President Obama requested that "Administrator Jackson withdraw the draft Ozone National Ambient Air Quality

Standards at this time." *Id*. EPA then announced that it would follow the ozone standards set by the previous administration.[5]

Over time, automakers have "made impressive progress in reducing vehicle emissions as a result of innovative technology." Randolph, *supra,* at 517. Manufacturers responded to tighter emission standards by improving engine and vehicle technology, including: (1) designing highly efficient combustion systems to minimize exhaust pollution; (2) installing vapor recovery systems to capture gasoline vapors; (3) using computer technologies to regulate engine performance, and (4) adding catalytic converters and particulate filters that remove pollutants from the exhaust. EPA studies show that recently-built cars emit 75 to 90 percent less pollution per mile than 1970 cars. EPA, Milestones in Mobile Source Air Pollution Control and Regulations, http://epa.gov/otaq/consumer/milestones.htm.

For a fuller analysis of EPA's regulation of traditional pollutants emitted by motor vehicles, see Richard L. Revesz, Environmental Law and Policy (2d ed. 2012). For an analysis of EPA's regulation of GHG pollutants, see Chapter 5.

b.   REGULATION OF GASOLINE

Section 211 of the CAA (42 U.S.C. § 7545) gives EPA authority over the composition of fuels. EPA has used this authority (1) to ban certain additives, such as lead, (2) to require certain additives, such as oxygenators, (3) to set limits on impurities in gasoline, such as sulfur, (4) to regulate the volatility of gasoline, and (5) to control the emission of Mobile Source Air Toxics (MSATs).

Section 211 was first used to ban the sale of leaded gasoline. Ethyl Corp. v. EPA, 541 F.2d 1 (D.C. Cir. 1976). Leaded gasoline was phased out over many years, and now has disappeared in the United States except for certain niche uses. Today, every fuel manufacturer must register all fuels and additives that it wishes to sell. The manufacturer must provide the EPA with the name of each additive contained in the fuel, the concentration of that additive, and purpose for which the additive was added. Where the EPA finds that a fuel or additive may detrimentally affect the public health or the emission control system of any vehicle, it may control or prohibit its manufacture or sale. The 1977 amendments to the CAA explicitly authorized the EPA to regulate fuels or fuel additives "which may reasonably be anticipated to endanger the public health or welfare." Current EPA regulations adopted pursuant to § 211(f)(1)(B) of the CAA, added in 1990, impose numerous restrictions on fuel additives for the purpose of protecting emission control devices.

EPA's most controversial rule had required that gasoline used in specified high-pollution areas must contain at least 2.0% oxygen by weight. Oxygenates are added to motor vehicle fuels to make them burn more cleanly, thereby reducing toxic tailpipe pollution, particularly carbon monoxide. Oxygenates are favored not only for their vehicle emission benefits but also their blending properties in motor gasoline (e.g., octane). Ethanol was used as an oxygenate is some states, but MTBE (methyl tertiary butyl ether) was the additive favored by the oil

---

[5]   EPA proposed new ozone standards on November 25, 2014. For updates, see http://www.epa.gov/ttn/naaqs/standards/ozone/s_o3_index.html.

industry for meeting EPA's oxygen requirements. It was produced in very large quantities (more than 200,000 barrels per day in the United States in 1999) during its use as a fuel additive. However, in response to a University of California study concluding that adding MTBE to gasoline produced significant health risks while only minimally reducing emissions, California banned the use of MTBE from gasoline sold in the state beginning in 2002, and the ban was upheld in *Oxygenated Fuels Association Inc. v. Davis*, 331 F.3d 665 (9th Cir. 2003). By late 2006, most American gasoline retailers had ceased using MTBE as an oxygenate, and accordingly, production in the United States has declined sharply.

Meanwhile, carbon monoxide pollution had been steadily declining. EPAct 2005 removed the oxygenate mandate and replaced it with a renewable fuels mandate, discussed in Section D, *supra*. EISA gave EPA more time to test proposed additives. Previously, under CAA § 211(f), no new fuels or fuel additives could be introduced into commerce unless granted a waiver by EPA. If EPA did not act within 180 days of receiving a waiver request, the waiver was treated as granted. EISA section 251 tightened the waiver provision by amending the CAA to prohibit the introduction of new fuels or fuel additives unless EPA explicitly grants a waiver within 270 days of the request.

The sulfur content of motor fuel has been another contentious issue. In 2006, federal specifications for gasoline content changed from the previous 500 parts per million (ppm) to a required 30 ppm annual average and a per-gallon cap of 80 ppm for most gasoline (with some delays for gasoline produced in the Rocky Mountain area or produced by small refiners). In apparent contradiction to their early stance of opposition to emission reductions, the automakers supported EPA's plan to require oil refineries to retool to produce lower sulfur gasoline because it enables manufacturers of light trucks to lower emissions without applying new technologies. Sulfur has been shown to inhibit the performance of catalytic converters. Auto manufacturers have developed advanced emission-control technologies that can only achieve lower emissions with even lower sulfur gasoline, and they asked EPA to further reduce allowable sulfur levels. As indicated in the brief description of EPA's Tier 3 Motor Vehicle Emission and Fuel Standards finalized in 2014, the EPA has further reduced the allowed sulfur content of fuels.

Additional gasoline regulations limit volatility and content of toxic substances. *See* Revesz, *supra*.

c. REGULATION OF DIESEL FUEL

Diesel exhaust contains many fine particles that become airborne, and medical science has increasingly pinpointed ultrafine particles (less than one micrometer in diameter) as one of the most serious airborne pollutants. Jocelyn Kaiser, *Mounting Evidence Indicts Fine-Particle Pollution*, 307 Science 1858 (Mar. 25, 2005). Carbon particles appear to be the most unhealthy. Diesel exhaust exacerbates asthma attacks, heart attacks, and respiratory problems. More severely, particle pollution lessens the lifespan of individuals with lung cancer and increases the risk of getting lung cancer. Diesel particles also can contribute to premature deaths, chronic bronchitis, can restrict physical activity, increase the incidence of stroke, and cause respiratory damage. Other systems, such as immune, endocrine, reproductive, developmental, and nervous systems, are also negatively affected. *See* Clean Air Task Force, Diesel and Health in America: The Lingering Threat (2005), http://www.catf.us/resources/publications/view/83.

EPA's Highway Diesel Rule, finalized in 2001 and still effective today, required emissions controls for heavy-duty trucks and buses that burn diesel and also required reduced sulfur content in diesel fuel, with the fuel standards taking effect in 2006 and emissions controls taking effect in 2007. *See* 40 C.F.R. §§ 69, 80, 86. This rule reduced PM and NO_x emissions by 90 percent for heavy-duty trucks and by 95 percent for buses. Under the fuel portion of the rule, refiners had to meet a 15 ppm sulfur limit for at least 80% of their highway diesel fuel production, with a 500 ppm (low sulfur diesel or LSD) cap on the remaining 20%. EPA regulations reducing sulfur in diesel fuel were upheld in *Nat'l Petrochemical & Refiners Association v. EPA*, 287 F.3d 1130 (D.C. Cir. 2002). The EPA has since finalized diesel rules for nonroad vehicles and ocean-going vessels.

F. TOWARD A THIRD GENERATION OF ELECTRIC CARS?

Automakers have tried twice to sell electric cars. As the hopes for clean renewable electricity from domestic sources have grown, a new enthusiasm for the electric car has appeared. Some think that the third time is a charm, but there are still plenty of doubters.

1. HYBRID VEHICLES

Reducing a vehicle's gasoline consumption per mile should reduce fuel expenses, reduce emissions of pollutants including greenhouse gases, and decrease reliance on imported oil. The first motor vehicles that became widely used models of low gasoline consumption were the hybrids. As the term is commonly used, a hybrid vehicle is one that is powered from both a gasoline or diesel engine and an electric motor. The two sources of propulsion can work together or separately in various combinations.

a. THE PRIUS AND ITS IMITATORS

The 1976 Electric and Hybrid Vehicle Act authorized DOE to set up a demonstration project to study these vehicles and their use in federal fleets. 15 U.S.C. § 2510 (1976). When gasoline prices dropped in the 1980s interest in alternative fuels evaporated. The primary source of support for alternate-fueled vehicles then passed to the CARB, which, as introduced above, began to require that a certain percentage of cars to be sold in future years be ZEVs.

During the 1990s, CARB's emphasis was on cars exclusively powered by electric motors, which would be recharged by plugging the vehicle into the electric network. But public support for electric cars was low, and over time, CARB's interest in hybrid vehicles grew as Japanese auto manufacturers began introducing hybrid models in Japan. CARB gave manufacturers a choice of two options for meeting their low-emission vehicle requirements: (1) meeting part of their ZEV obligations by making AT–PZEVs (vehicles earning advanced technology partial ZEV credits), i.e. advanced hybrids; or (2) meeting part of their ZEV requirement by producing a sales-weighted market share of 250 fuel cell vehicles by 2008 (increasing to 2,500 from 2009–11, 25,000 from 2012–14 and 50,000 from 2015 through 2017). Currently, California has a more complex ZEV policy consisting of regulatory action by CARB and an executive order. CARB's Advanced Clean Cars program requires that by 2025, ZEVs and plug-in hybrid cars make up approximately 15.4% of new vehicle sales in California by 2025. Further, Governor Jerry Brown's Executive Order 3–23–2012 directs California's energy agency and CARB to establish benchmarks providing that by 2025, "over 1.5 million zero-emission vehicles will be on California roads and their market share will be expanding." Cal. Executive Order B–16–2012, http://www.gov.ca.gov/news.php?id=17472.

Hybrid cars on the market in the United States fall into two categories, the mild hybrid and the full hybrid. A mild hybrid uses a powerful electric starter motor to begin operation of the internal combustion or diesel engine prior to fuel injection. The internal combustion engine is shut down whenever the car is coasting, braking, or stopped, but the accessories can continue to run on electrical power. Honda uses this technology in its Insight and Civic Hybrid models, as do other manufacturers of hybrid trucks and SUVs. *See* Union of Concerned Sci., How Hybrid Cars Work, http://www.ucsusa.org/clean_vehicles/smart-transportation-solutions/advanced-vehicle-technologies/hybrid-cars/how-hybrids-work.html. A full hybrid begins to propel the vehicle using the electric motor, and the gasoline engine kicks in when more power is needed. The Toyota Prius and the Ford Escape hybrid SUV are examples of this type of hybrid vehicle. *Id.* Full hybrids achieve better gas mileage than mild hybrids for vehicles of the same weight category.

Various states have created incentives for their residents to purchase hybrid vehicles. David Diamond, The Impact of Government Incentives for Hybrid-Electric Vehicles, 37 Energy Pol'y 972 (2009). To encourage the purchase of hybrids some states have authorized owners of hybrid cars to use high occupancy vehicle lanes even if only one person is in the car. This policy has been popular with the owners of hybrids, but not always appreciated by the owners of other cars. Hybrid sales have recently increased rapidly: in 2005, an estimated 205,828 hybrids sold in the United States. These numbers remained relatively stable annually through 2011, with slightly higher sales (more than 300,000) in 2007 and 2008. In 2012, 431,798 hybrids sold in the United States. DOT, Table 1–19, Sales of Hybrid Vehicles in the United States http://www.rita.dot.gov/bts/sites/rita.dot.gov.bts/files/publications/national_transportation_statistics/html/table_01_19.html.

b.   PLUG-IN HYBRIDS

The National Commission on Energy Policy suggested more than a decade ago that renewed attention should be paid to a type of vehicle that the automakers had been avoiding, the "plug-in hybrid." Most hybrids currently on the market recharge the battery internally, and neither need to be, nor can be, plugged in to the electric grid. Given the public's historic distaste for electric cars, automakers found it important to distinguish the new hybrids from the unpopular plug-ins. Carson & Vaitheeswaram, *supra*, at 269. But the Commission pointed out that adding plug-in capability to a modern hybrid increases its energy efficiency: "These vehicles would carry more robust battery packs and be capable of being charged using the electricity grid. Since most trips are relatively short, these vehicles could operate using grid-provided electricity much of the time, while retaining the flexibility consumers desire for being able to travel longer distances without the need to recharge. To the extent they would operate more often than conventional hybrids in a pure-electric mode, plug-in hybrids could provide additional oil security and fuel diversity benefits." Nat'l Comm'n on Energy Policy, Ending the Energy Stalemate 91 (2004).

Electric utilities have also been strong supporters of plug-in vehicles. They perceive them as demanding electricity from the grid at night when generating facilities would otherwise be idle. Looking further into the future, they foresee plug-ins as potential sources of electricity: "With their large, deep-discharge batteries, PHEVs may eventually serve as distributed energy storage units that could support not only the home but the electricity grid as well. The smart infrastructure for such vehicle-to-grid setups would require advanced metering and two-way energy and information exchange, similar to that currently used in home photovoltaic electricity sales to utilities." Plug-In Hybrids, Elec. Power Research Inst. J., Spring 2008 at 15, http://mydocs.epri.com/docs/CorporateDocuments/EPRI_Journal/2008-Spring/1016422.pdf.

The nationwide electric grid is only 1% petroleum-fueled, whereas transportation is almost completely powered by oil—much of which still comes from foreign sources despite rising domestic production. Adoption of plug-in hybrids will transfer the overwhelming majority of our miles driven to nearly oil-free electricity. But a National Research Council committee suggests that as long as nearly half of U.S. electricity is generated from coal, the air pollution created indirectly by plug-ins creates more harm than that produced from gasoline burned in the vehicle. Nat'l Research Council, Hidden Costs of Energy: Unpriced Consequences of Energy Production and Use 10 (2009), http://www.nap.edu/openbook.php?record_id=12794. Supporters are beginning to see more realistic opportunities in plug-in hybrids, as the manufacturing and purchase of these vehicles in the United States has recently grown. Section 706 of the Energy Policy Act of 2005 set up a small grant program to improve technologies for plug-in hybrid or combination hybrid/flexible fuel vehicles that would achieve not less than 250 miles per gallon of petroleum fuel consumption. Under Section 721, grants were available to state and local governments for the purchase of hybrid and advanced diesel vehicles meeting certain requirements. Federal tax credits have also been available for advanced hybrids. The American Recovery and Reinvestment Act of 2009 (ARRA) provided grants for manufacturing of both traditional hybrids and plug-ins. Section 30(d) of the Internal Revenue Code, first created by the Energy Improvement and Extension Act of 2008 and amended by ARRA and the American Taxpayer Relief Act of 2013, provides a $7,500 credit for plug-in electric drive motor vehicles, including plug-in hybrids. 26 U.S.C. § 30(d).

Plug-ins currently cost more than gasoline-only vehicles mainly because batteries are expensive. But battery technology is improving steadily—especially lithium-ion batteries—and studies from the Electric Power Research Institute and the National Resources Defense Council have found that unlike gasoline cars, plug-ins will get cleaner as they get older because our power grid is getting cleaner. The EPRI study shows that under all nine scenarios for both rates of market penetration of plug-ins and the evolving power grid's characteristics (capacity/carbon intensity), plug-ins will vastly reduce greenhouse gases for the next 40 years. The NRDC study found that, for the next 20 years, even if we still use a large amount of coal, nationwide air quality for other emissions will also improve.

The F3DM was the first mass-produced plug-in hybrid. It was launched domestically by BYD Motors in China in December of 2008. It can go about 62 miles on its electric engine and has a small gasoline engine as back up. It takes nine hours to charge the battery from a regular electric outlet. Business Week, Dec. 15, 2008. Toyota sells a Prius Plug-In in Japan and plans to sell one in the U.S. in the 2010 model year. Plug-in America, Toyota Plug-in Prius, http://www.pluginamerica.org/vehicles/toyota-prius-phev.

The Chevrolet Volt first appeared in showrooms in 2011 and has since become a popular plug-in hybrid vehicle. The 2014 Volt carries drivers approximately 38 miles on battery power alone, and allows a total of 380 miles of driving "on a full charge and a full tank of gas." Chevrolet, The 2015 Volt: Electricity Travels, http://www.chevrolet.com/volt-electric-car.html. It retails for approximately $35,000. Other plug-in hybrids include the plug-in versions of the Toyota Prius and Honda Accord as well as the Ford C-MAX Energi, Ford Fusion Energi, Cadillac ELR, Porsche 918 Spyder, and the Porsche Panamera S–E.

2. ELECTRIC CARS

The growing publicity about plug-in hybrids created new interest in a third generation of electric cars. A vehicle that is fueled solely by electricity is highly dependent on a network of charging stations that is sufficiently complete to give the car owner confidence that a charging station would be available within the car's normal driving range. Substantial conversion to electric vehicles will also depend on the government's conviction that electricity is the motor fuel the best serves the national interest and on the customer's conviction that an electric vehicle will meet her needs at a reasonable cost. Electric vehicles are growing, however, like plug-in hybrids, particularly with increasing attention paid to Tesla Motors' vehicles and with growing availability of charging stations—some provided by Tesla to promote electric vehicle use. Tesla, 100 Supercharger Stations, Apr. 24, 2014, http://www.tesla motors.com/blog/100-supercharger-stations.

a. IS ELECTRICITY REALLY A SUPERIOR MOTOR FUEL?

Much of the recent surge of interest in electric cars and plug-in hybrids, which replace some gasoline use with electricity use, derives from the belief that a combination of factors makes electricity a better fuel than petroleum products:

> (1) Fewer emissions: CARB studies show that battery electric vehicles emit at least 67% lower greenhouse gases than gasoline cars—even more assuming renewables generate some of the electricity used to power them;

(2) Better acceleration: Automotive engineers believe that one of the big selling points for electric cars will be their acceleration. The low-end torque provided by electric motors means that the cars will attain high speed quickly, smoothly and quietly.

(3) Less noise: When cars run on electric power they run more quietly.[6]

(4) Time-of-use rates: Electricity rates that vary by the hour are becoming more common and will encourage charging at off-peak hours (*Authors' note*: see Chapter 11 for a discussion of this trend.)

Plug-In Hybrids, *supra*, at 11.

But even the most enthusiastic supporters of electric cars recognize that there are still significant roadblocks before the cars can become mass-market mainstays, including the following:

(1) Upfront costs: The Nissan LEAF, a popular all-electric vehicle, costs about $21,480 after tax benefits. *See* Nissan, Nissan Leaf, http://www.nissanusa.com/electric-cars/leaf/.

(2) Loss of interior space. Can batteries and electric motors be designed to occupy no more space within the vehicle than is found in current vehicles?

(3) Will the air pollution impacts of power plants improve significantly? A 2009 study by the National Research Council views the air pollution implications of electric vehicles more pessimistically than earlier studies. Nat'l Research Coun., Hidden Costs of Energy 10 (2009). The rapid replacement of coal-fired generation with natural gas-fired plants, however, might improve these numbers.

(4) Will automotive dependency on the electric grid increase the damage that could result from cyberattacks on the grid?

Richard A. Clarke and Robert K. Knake, Cyber War 98 (2010).

Nevertheless, the dramatic reductions of GHG emissions targeted in California would appear to make future use of electric cars essential. The CARB staff has concluded that to meet the state's 2050 standard, all cars sold after 2040 will need to be electric. Cal. EPA, Staff Report: Initial Statement of Reasons Advanced Clean Cars, 2012 Proposed Amendments to the California Zero Emission Vehicle Program Regulations at ES–1 (2011), http://www.arb.ca.gov/regact/2012/zev2012/zevisor.pdf.

b.   RECHARGING PLUG-IN AND ELECTRIC CARS

At what stage will the mass consumer be sufficiently confident of finding recharging opportunities that she will be willing to invest in the new technology? Will buyers be willing to assume that their lifestyle will remain so routine that they will not need a vehicle during the hour and

---

[6]   Ordinarily, people might welcome quieter cars on the roads. However, as the use of hybrid and electric vehicles grows, pedestrians and cyclists find it hard to hear them coming, especially when the cars are moving slowly. The solution, many now believe, is to fit electric and hybrid cars with external sound systems. The Sound of Silence, The Economist, May 9, 2009.

twelve minutes an advanced (Tesla) car requires to recharge at an enhanced 240 or 240-volt station? And how will people who live in apartments recharge their cars if charging stations near apartment complexes are not available? These are just a few of the issues that face developers of charging systems and networks.

A wide range of practical questions need to be answered before a charging network can become widespread. Peter Kelly Detwiler, Building Out the Electric Vehicle Charging Infrastructure: Greenlots Advocates for Open Standards, Forbes, Mar. 13, 2014, http://www.forbes.com/sites/ peterdetwiler/2014/03/13/building-out-the-electric-vehicle-charging-infrastructure-greenlots-advocates-for-open-standards/. For example, although businesses like Whole Foods Market have installed charging stations for customers in their parking lots, relatively few private businesses are likely to decide to give away electricity for free. This means that a billing system will be needed that will meter the amount of electricity consumed and ensure that the customer will pay for it. The network should also provide information that will enable a vehicle to locate charging stations that are unoccupied at a given time. Further, security systems should be provided to insure the driver against charging failures due to interruptions in the current or malicious disruption of the equipment.

A number of cities have begun to install public charging stations, with 23 installed in Minneapolis as of 2014 and 15–20 stations in Boulder, for example. Even America's oil capital, Houston, has hundreds of charging stations, although many of them are privately-operated. Green Houston Texas, List of Charging Stations, http://www.green houstontx.gov/ev/chargingstationaddresses.pdf.

c.   ADVANCES IN BATTERY TECHNOLOGY

The traditional automotive lead-acid batteries cannot store as much energy for a given weight or volume as newer technologies, but they can be extremely cost-effective. Small lead-acid battery packs provide short bursts of power to starter motors in virtually all existing cars; they are also used in large back-up power systems, and still make up about half of the worldwide rechargeable-battery market.

Toyota picked nickel-metal-hydride (NiMH) batteries for the first Prius in 1997. NiMH batteries are generally expensive and bulky, since they require high-pressure hydrogen-storage tanks, but they offer high energy-density and last a long time. Adapting the NiMH battery to motor vehicles was not easy because the work that batteries have to perform in hybrid cars is very different from the way they work in portable devices. Batteries in laptops and mobile phones are engineered to be discharged over the course of several hours or days, and they only need to last a couple of years. Hybrid-car batteries, on the other hand, are expected to work for eight to ten years and must endure hundreds of thousands of partial charge and discharge cycles as they absorb energy from regenerative braking or supply short bursts of power to aid in acceleration.

For many uses, lithium-ion batteries are replacing both lead-acid and NiMH batteries. Lithium is particularly suitable for batteries because it is the lightest metal, which means that a lithium battery of a given weight can store more energy than one based on a metal such as lead or nickel. In Search of the Perfect Battery, The Economist, Mar. 6, 2008, economist.com/PrinterFriendly.cfm?story_id=10789409. But lithium-ion batteries need to prove that they meet standards for safety, manufacturing reliability and life, and that their cost is reasonably competitive. Green Car Cong., Near-Term Prospects for Automotive Li-ion Batteries: 21% of Hybrid and EV Market by 2011, June 16, 2009.

Some companies have taken innovative approaches to battery improvement, as shown by Better Place, a firm headed by Shai Agassi that did not make cars. Instead, Agassi looked at electric transport as a system in which cars, batteries, recharging points, electrical utilities and billing systems must all work together. That is, he viewed the transportation issue as a systems-integration problem. The vision was described as follows:

> Better Place's business model involves selling electric cars provided by its partner, Renault-Nissan, using a scheme borrowed from the mobile-telecoms industry—charging not by the minute, but by the kilometer. Customers will be able to pay as they go or sign up for a contract that includes a certain number of kilometers. . . . Better Place will build networks of recharging points, plus battery-swapping stations along motorways that will, in effect, enable customers to recharge their cars in minutes in order to travel further than the 100-mile range of their cars' battery packs. Electric Evangelist, The Economist, Apr. 30, 2009, http://www.economist.com/node/13570470.

The Better Place automated battery switch, when it was briefly available, replaced a depleted electric vehicle battery with a fully charged one in just a few minutes, allowing consumers to drive long distance trips without actually recharging en route. The technology, which included the mechanisms for the switch and the control system, was part of an overall solution for electric vehicles that would provide an open network of charge spots deployed widely where cars park. The switch was controlled by three computers: one onboard the vehicle, one in the station, and one in the battery pack. The switching process occurred while the driver remained in the vehicle, used a number of integrated safety systems, and took less than 80 seconds once the car was in position. Green Car Cong., Better Place Demonstrates Battery Switch Technology, May 13, 2009, http://www.greencarcongress.com/2009/05/better-place-demo-20090513.html. Better Place filed for bankruptcy in 2013.

G. TOWARD SELF-DRIVEN AUTOMOBILES?

Electric and hybrid vehicles are not the only technologies making large inroads into the traditional vehicle market and creating new legal and policy challenges, such as the need to develop incentives for the installation of charging stations and means of charging consumers for the use of charging stations. Google's work on a self-driven or "autonomous" vehicle, in which a computer—not a human—drives the car, has brought a number of issues to the forefront. If self-driven cars become commercially available, how will traffic safety laws change? Could governments (or a computer system) avoid much of the traffic congestion currently on roads by having commuters schedule trips in advance, and how might emissions of air pollution be reduced by avoiding the idling of millions of cars? Could commuters pay extra to schedule guaranteed space on a road in advance? How would commuters' privacy be protected if the location of their vehicle was easily trackable through the car's continuous use of GPS? If a consumer converted a traditional vehicle to an autonomous vehicle and a safety issue arose, could the consumer sue the manufacturer of the traditional vehicle using a products liability claim? For updates on changes in international, federal, and state law proposed or implemented in response to the potential rise of autonomous vehicles, see Gabriel Weiner and Bryant Walker Smith, Automated Driving: Legislative and Regulatory Action, June 19, 2014, http://cyberlaw.stanford.edu/wiki/index.php/Automated_Driving:_ Legislative_and_Regulatory_Action.

Among recent changes, NHTSA in 2013 released a Preliminary Statement of Policy Concerning Automated Vehicles,[7] and California, Washington, D.C., Florida, Michigan, and Nevada have enacted statutes relating to autonomous vehicles. These statutes provide, *inter alia*, that testing of autonomous vehicles is allowed; that a human must be in an autonomous vehicle that is on a roadway, and the human must be prepared to take control if needed; that drivers of autonomous vehicles may text while driving; and that original manufacturers or cars that are converted to autonomous vehicles shall not be liable for certain damages. *See, e.g.*, Fla. Rev. Stats. §§ 316.003, 316.85, 319.145; Nev. Rev. Stats. §§ 482A.010–200; Nev. Rev. Stats. §§ 484B.165; *see also* Weiner & Smith, *supra* (providing descriptions of the legislation).

H. TRANSPORTATION IN A DECENTRALIZED SOCIETY

A final, core area of transportation policy is the land use and infrastructure planning system that drives daily transportation decisions—decisions with substantial social and environmental impacts. "Manifest Destiny" was a term used in the 1840s to justify the United States' westward expansion into such areas as Texas, Oregon, and California. The expansion fostered by the completion of the transcontinental railroads in the 1870s left no doubt that new settlements would be separated by enormous spaces. And despite the development of numerous metropolitan regions, today the nation as a whole remains highly decentralized.

1. DECENTRALIZATION'S ENERGY COST

In the twentieth century, Americans' energy choices have affected every area of production and consumption, but it is in transportation where these choices have most dramatically increased our energy consumption. As David Nye puts it, "Most farmers abandoned horses and oxen for tractors, [and] motorists preferred large cars with poor fuel economy; [while the federal government] spent billions of dollars on interstate highways instead of on mass transit. . . . As the result of all these decisions, made by the people or their institutions, the United

---

[7] The policy statement is available at http://www.nhtsa.gov/About+NHTSA/Press+ Releases/U.S.+Department+of+Transportation+Releases+Policy+on+Automated+Vehicle+ Development.

States became the largest consumer of energy in the world's history." David Nye, Consuming Power 255–56 (1998).

The reasons those living in the United States have chosen to expend such a large share of their budgets for transportation are many and complex. Is our lifestyle simply a matter of what the economists would call a "taste" for private transportation? Or are there factors about American society that make our development pattern more efficient than its critics recognize?

Much new development takes place at the edge of metropolitan areas in "a peripheral zone, perhaps as large as a county, that has emerged as a viable socioeconomic unit. . . . Its residents look to their immediate surroundings rather than to the city for their jobs and other needs, and its industries find not only the employees they need but also the specialized services." Robert Fishman, Bourgeois Utopias: The Rise and Fall of Suburbia 184 (1987).

Traditionally, Americans have sought a higher degree of personal space and privacy than people in other cultures, and the private automobile satisfies this desire. Charles L. Wright, Fast Wheels, Slow Traffic 115–18 (1992). Psychologists have observed, for example, that a group of Americans who converse with each other will stand farther apart than similar groups from most other cultures. This demand for more private space is rewarded on American roadways where the vast majority of cars carry a single occupant. The pervasiveness of air conditioning in homes and businesses has also increased the demand for the kind of air conditioned door-to-door travel that the automobile can provide.

Although over 30,000 people each year are killed in auto accidents in the United States, people tend to downplay the danger. NHTSA Data Confirms Traffic Fatalities Increased in 2012, NHTSA, Nov. 14, 2013, http://www.nhtsa.gov/About+NHTSA/Press+Releases/NHTSA+Data+Confirms+Traffic+Fatalities+Increased+In+2012; Howard Margolis, Dealing With Risk: Why the Public and the Experts Disagree on Environmental Issues 38 (1996). Despite the high risk of automobile accidents, many Americans say that they actually feel safer in their car than in public transportation. Accidents involving public transportation tend to receive more media coverage than the routine fatalities in auto accidents. And the fear of contact with criminal behavior on public transportation is a risk that ranks higher in public perception than statistics would support.

The rapid growth of advanced information technology in the 1990s has also contributed to decentralized transportation and development patterns. The need for centralized locations for "office work" has begun to diminish, and increasing numbers of people work at home for part of the week. Dunphy, *supra*, at 36–37. A growing number of individuals who work in e-commerce out of their homes have wide-ranging choices of where to live. Some Western states that once relied on resource extraction as their economic base are coming to realize that it is "resource attraction" that is bringing in new entrepreneurs who can work from any place that a satellite can see. Thomas Michael Power, Lost Landscapes and Failed Economies 41–43 (1996).

2. ALTERNATIVES TO DECENTRALIZATION

All of these factors have stimulated increasing movement into formerly rural areas, thereby stretching out the time of travel if not its frequency. If we are going to reduce our consumption of energy for transportation, we must either begin to reverse these development patterns, or find new technological ways of traveling within the current pattern without using so much energy, or both. But are current trends inevitable? Dissatisfaction with existing modes of transportation and development patterns is increasing for a variety of reasons. It has developed on two fronts: (a) attempts to accommodate the current development pattern but expend less energy, and (b) attempts to promote a more concentrated development pattern that would facilitate more use of mass transit.

a. INTERMODAL TRANSPORTATION

The historic compromise that produced the Interstate Highway Act of 1956 was interpreted by the "road lobby" as a guarantee that all of the taxes on gasoline and related equipment were to be sequestered in the Highway Trust Fund and used only for road construction. Advocates of other modes of transportation soon began to cast a covetous eye on this fund, arguing that if the fund were used to finance subways, for example, the result would be to reduce the need for highway construction by taking people off the roads.

Auto manufacturers, trucking companies and oil companies adamantly resisted these attempts. There continues to be a strenuous debate between those who think that the existing system contains built-in subsidies for automobiles (*see, e.g.,* World Resources Institute, The Going Rate: What it Really Costs to Drive (1992)) and those who believe that publicly owned transit systems are an inefficient waste of public funds *See, e.g.,* Clifford Winston & Chad Shirley, Alternate Route: Toward Efficient Urban Transportation (1998).

This debate has also been regularly heard in the halls of Congress. Since 1962, federal law has required the states to engage in a highway planning process for "urbanized areas" of more than 50,000 people. In response to the desire of local governments to play a greater role in the planning of highways, highway trust funds were given to the states to finance the creation of Metropolitan Planning Organizations, which included representatives of local governments as well as state agencies. These MPOs were staffed with engineers and planners who worked closely with state and federal highway officials in approving the layout of the highway system.

During the 1990s, Congress began to increase the funding for alternative modes of transportation. Responding to the argument that the construction of new highways just seemed to create more traffic and more traffic jams, Congress enacted the Intermodal Surface Transportation Efficiency Act of 1991 (ISTEA, or "Ice Tea"). The act adopted the policy that transportation planning should consider not only roads but also travel by train, bus, bicycle and on foot. It substantially increased the funds available for non-highway modes of transportation. It also required the states to make many detailed changes in the planning process. Each MPO had discretion in deciding how to carry out these planning processes. Some MPOs saw the need for change as a high priority, while others tried to change as little as possible. On balance, ISTEA produced a number of significant plans that brought attention to a greater variety of modes of transportation. *See* Daniel Carlson et al., At Road's End: Transportation and Land Use Choices for Communities (1995). In general, ISTEA represented a move away from the complete dominance of the highway in transportation planning. The new buzzword became "intermodalism," meaning that planners should consider all different modes of transportation and how they interrelate. Terminals at which people could interchange among transit, highway, bicycle and pedestrian facilities were encouraged. But although ISTEA was "a significant symbolic achievement for the anti highway forces," it did not cause dramatic shifts of money from highways to transit. Dunn, *supra,* at 43.

In 1998, Congress was presented with a potential surplus in the federal budget for the first time in many years. It responded by passing legislation appropriating significantly increased funds for highways and other transportation projects and making further changes in the transportation planning process. The 1998 Transportation Equity Act for the 21st Century (TEA–21) supported initiatives directed to the full range of transportation alternatives, including highways, mass transit, and bicycle paths. 23 U.S.C. § 133. TEA–21 established new programs for the design and demonstration of advanced technologies, such as fixed guideway vehicles, fuel-cell powered transit vehicles, and magnetic levitation technologies for urban public transportation.

The next major transportation bill—2005's SAFETEA–LU, discussed above—returned to traditional highway priorities. SAFETEA–LU's major thrust was the authorization of transportation projects valued in the billions of dollars—primarily highways but including other surface transportation as well. It was by far the most expensive transportation law ever enacted, and included money for many projects earmarked for the home districts of particular members of Congress. The statute made it easy for states to build roads and hard for them to build transit projects. While funds for new roads were simply distributed to states based on a formula, new transit lines had to compete with other projects from all over the country before getting a share of federal dollars. In January 2010, the Obama administration promised to speed up awards of funds for transit construction. Melanie Trottman and Josh Mitchell, New Transit—Funding Rules Make Streetcars More Desirable, Wall St. J. (Jan. 15, 2010). And in 2012, President Obama signed the Moving Ahead for Progress in the 21st Century Act (MAP–21), which, among other provisions, created the Transportation Alternatives Program (TAP). 23 U.S.C. § 213. TAP centralizes certain funding that was previously provided under separate programs and includes limited funding for alternative transportation, including construction and planning of bicycle trails.

b.   RETHINKING PUBLIC TRANSPORT

In the early part of the 20th century one of the predominant modes of travel in urban areas was the streetcar, also known as the trolley. Trolleys ran on fixed rails and shared the streets with horses, pedestrians and eventually motor vehicles. Development of streetcar networks fostered the first phase of suburbanization in many metropolitan areas. At its peak, the trolley system in the Los Angeles area ran on 1100 miles of track. Fulton, *supra*, at 129.

Today, public transit is much more widely used in Europe and Asia than in the United States. Rapidly growing countries like China and India have put significant emphasis on extending public transit lines. In Beijing, the advent of the 2008 Olympics created the incentive for the Chinese government to begin a dramatic enhancement of the subway network to help relieve the traffic congestion on the roadways. Phillip A. Hummel, Next Stop—A Cleaner and Healthier Environment: Global Strategies to Promote Public Transit, 35 Transp. L. J. 263, 269–276 (2008). American business leaders are increasingly becoming concerned about the cost of congestion in metropolitan areas. A 2008 study by the Metropolitan Planning Council of Chicago concluded that congestion in the Chicago region was costing the community $7.3 billion per year and depriving the region of 87,000 new jobs. Metro. Planning Coun., Moving at the Speed of Congestion: The True Costs of Traffic in the Chicago Metropolitan Area (Aug. 2008), http://www.metroplanning.org/multimedia/publication/272.

Subways in the United States tend to be found only in the larger metropolitan areas. During the first quarter of 2014, passengers took approximately 923 million subway trips on an average weekday, but more than 648 million of those trips were on New York subways. Am. Pub. Transp. Ass'n, Heavy Rail Public Transportation Ridership Report (2014), http://www.apta.com/resources/statistics/Documents/Ridership/2014-q1-ridership-APTA.pdf. The use of light rail rather than heavier subway construction has made transit cost-effective in many smaller communities.

An even newer mode of transit beginning to be used in the United States is what is known as bus rapid transit (BRT). The provision of dedicated lanes for buses has been a main feature of transit systems in places like Curitiba, Bogota and Mexico City. Zoom, *supra,* at 210. BRT vehicles (*e.g.*, buses, specialized BRT vehicles) can travel anywhere there is pavement, and are relatively small compared to train-based rapid transit modes. A given BRT corridor application might encompass route segments where vehicles operate both in mixed traffic and on a dedicated, fully grade-separated transitway with major stations. Nat'l BRT Inst., Characteristics of Bus Rapid Transit for Decision-Making (2009), http://www.nbrti.org/cbrt.html. Examples of BRT lines can be found along Boston's waterfront, on the orange line in Los Angeles, and on Honolulu's county express. These facilities all have special trafficways and stations for BRT buses, but they also include areas in which these buses run on the streets. Other cities such as Miami, Orlando and Pittsburgh have systems in which buses run entirely off the street right-of-way. The relatively low cost and high flexibility of the BRT systems is making them increasingly popular with local government officials.

Another very energy-efficient mode of transportation is the bicycle. Americans who had earlier been surprised to see the volume of bicycle traffic in European cities are now finding increasing bicycle traffic in many American cities as well. In his book, Pedaling Revolution, Jeff Mapes describes a new urban bike culture "that appeals to that lone rebel, an iconic part of our American DNA." Jeff Mapes, Pedaling

Revolution 143 (2009). Census Bureau statistics show that "[t]he number of U.S. workers who traveled to work by bicycle increased from about 488,000 in 2000 to about 786,000 in 2008–2012, a larger percentage increase than that of any other commuting mode." Brian McKenzie, Modes Less Traveled: Bicycling and Walking to Work in the United States: 2008–2012 (2014), http://www.census.gov/prod/2014pubs/acs-25.pdf. Increased bicycling on roadways has led to growing conflicts between motor vehicles and bicycle traffic. Injuries to bicycle riders are uncommon, but often severe. Transportation engineers debate the merits of bike lanes, separate bike paths, and free bicycle use of the roadways, without agreeing about the safest way to encourage bicycling without unduly disrupting motor vehicle traffic. Christie Aschwanden, Bikes and Cars: Can We Share the Road?, L.A. Times, Nov. 2, 2009, http://articles.latimes.com/2009/nov/02/health/he-biking2.

c.   A FUTURE FOR HIGH-SPEED RAIL?

Japan was a pioneer in the development of high-speed rail networks. Japanese bullet trains, which run on their own reserved tracks, began operation in 1964. France introduced high-speed train technology in 1981, and many European and Asian countries followed over the next two decades. Newer technologies such as Maglev trains and Talgo trains have been introduced in Europe and Japan. In general, high-speed trains achieve speeds of between 200 and 300 kilometers per hour (roughly 120–200 miles per hour). GAO, High Speed Passenger Rail, GAO–09–317 at 12–17 (2009), http://www.gao.gov/new.items/d09317.pdf[8] Recent federal U.S. funding for high-speed rail supports trains that run at "125–250+" miles per hour. U.S. Dept. of Transportation, Fed. Rail Admin., High Speed Intercity Passenger Rail (HSIPR) Program, http://www.fra.dot.gov/Page/P0134.

In the 21st century, North America has grown beyond a country of cities and suburbs to what urban studies expert Richard Florida calls "mega-regions." Central Florida's I–4 Corridor, between Orlando and Tampa, is a prime example. Mega-regions "are natural economic agglomerations whose market potential can be harnessed if they're linked up by high-speed rail," says Florida, director of the Martin Prosperity Institute at the University of Toronto. "If there's any place in the world right now where this makes sense, it's the United States. Cars and jets won't do it; high-speed rail will." Tim Padgett, U.S. Stimulus Puts Bullet Trains on the Fast Track, Time, June 22, 2009, http://content.time.com/time/nation/article/0,8599,1906025,00.html. Despite some support for high-speed rail in Florida, the governor rejected federal funds for such a project, but a private company is now developing a "fast" rather than high-speed rail project there. Alfonso Chardy, Work begins—finally—on Miami to Orlando fast train, Miami Herald, Aug. 25, 2014, http://www.miamiherald.com/2014/08/25/4308932/work-begins-finally-on-miami-to.html.

---

[8]   For further analysis, see Joshua D. Prok, High Speed Rail: Planning and Financing the Next Fifty Years of American Mobility, 36 Transp. L. J. 47 (2009); Kamaal R. Zaidi, High-Speed Rail Transit: Developing The Case For Alternative Transportation Schemes In The Context Of Innovative And Sustainable Global Transportation Law And Policy, 26 Temple J. Sci.,Tech. & Envtl. L. 301 (2007).

The Passenger Rail Investment and Improvement Act of 2008 and the ARRA offered support for the development of high-speed rail projects. The stimulus money was intended to finance "high speed rail corridors" capable of supporting trains traveling at speeds as great as 110 mph, creating the first-ever regional network of cities connected by fast rail for the first time. Jan Dennis, Gas prices, climate change revive interest in fast rail, USA Today, Sept. 8, 2007, http://usatoday30.usatoday.com/travel/2007-09-08-rail_n.htm. The Obama Administration urged states and local communities to put together plans for a network of 100 mile to 600 mile corridors, which would compete for the federal dollars.

In total, "[f]ifty-two construction projects amounting to $2.7 billion in funding are underway or complete in 21 states and the District of Columbia" as of 2014, with many of these projects funded by ARRA. Dept. of Transp., High Speed Intercity Passenger Rail Funding by Region, https://www.fra.dot.gov/Page/P0554. But many analyses of transportation's future believe the high cost of instituting high-speed rail puts it out of reach for now, and that "it will take gas prices of the most compelling magnitude to make widespread American high-speed rail a reality: $18 per gallon." Steiner, *supra,* at 202.

d. DO CITIES HAVE NEW APPEAL?

Land developers have long expressed a growing interest in promoting more dense urban development. Downs, *supra,* at 265–71. Today they are increasingly joined by advocates of sustainable living.

Some architects and planners propose a "new urbanism" in development design. The concept of new urbanism, sometimes referred to as "neotraditional" development, is based on a desire to reduce the need for automobile travel and to create communities with more social interaction. Neighborhoods are dotted with businesses accessible by foot; networks of bike paths encourage people to leave their cars at home. *See* Peter Katz, The New Urbanism (1994). For information promoting the use of community designs that minimize automotive travel, see J.H. Crawford, Carfree Design Manual (2009).

Meanwhile, a significant number of older cities are experiencing extensive revitalization as developers convert older buildings to modern housing and build new condominiums. This has attracted both young people who are bored with the suburban lifestyle and older people seeking to have more convenient access to urban amenities. Many neighborhoods in communities such as Brooklyn, Chicago, and Washington have been dramatically transformed by this "gentrification," though not without criticism from some of the poorer tenants displaced by the process. Richard Florida has attracted attention to his theory that the United States has a new class structure consisting of a creative class, a working class, and a service class, which has led many cities to try to provide the amenities that attract creative people. Richard Florida, The Rise of the Creative Class 240–48 (2002). Energy efficiency is also one of the objectives of government programs for the promotion of "infill" development on "brownfields" sites—sites that have been abandoned by earlier industries. Joel B. Eisen, Finality In Brownfields Remediation and Reuse, 41 Sw. L.J. 773, 784–786 (2013).

3. IMPROVING THE MOTOR VEHICLE NETWORK

Despite the potential for more transit and increased population in urban areas, most people believe that the congested motor vehicle network will still need to be improved to handle more road traffic in metropolitan areas. Traffic engineers have added turn lanes, restricted highway lanes to high-occupancy vehicles, and used traffic-calming strategies to divert vehicles to arterial roads. But a new generation of high-tech transportation engineers believes that the motor vehicles of the future will need a more advanced form of guidance.

a. CONGESTION ZONES AND PEAK-HOUR PRICING

"When people are forced, by means of how much it will cost them, to think about when, where, and how they are going places, interesting things begin to happen." Vanderbilt, *supra,* at 165–166. Economists have long advocated the establishment of higher prices for traveling at peak times as a way of reducing traffic congestion and improving the overall efficiency of the transportation system. Economists began to argue that "congestion pricing"—laws that would encourage people to drive during less crowded periods—would be more efficient than highway construction. Jonathan Remy Nash, Economic Efficiency Versus Public Choice: The Case of Property Rights in Road Traffic Management, 49 B.C. L. Rev. 673 (2008).

Some transit systems do provide discounts for off-peak travel, as do some toll roads and bridges, but the technical problems of implementing such a system on a large scale for automobile travel have been daunting. Tirza S. Wahrman, Breaking the Logjam, 8 Duke Env. L. & Pol'y F. 181 (1998). FHWA has encouraged states to experiment with a variety of approaches to congestion pricing. Karnes, *supra,* at 154–162.

In 2003, at the urging of Mayor Ken Livingstone, London implemented a congestion-charge program for the city center as one of the strategies designed to address the problems of traffic congestion and emissions. *See* David M. Levinson and Kevin J. Krizek, Planning for Place and Plexus, Ch. 13 (2008). The program, which levied a flat-rate, all-day area charge of £8/day for drivers entering the zone between 7:00AM–6:00PM, Monday–Friday, has proven effective. Fleet vehicles pay £7/day. Buses, taxis, motorbikes, mopeds and bicycles, emergency service vehicles and vehicles used by the disabled are exempt from the charge. Transport for London, Discount & Exemptions, http://www.tfl. gov.uk/roadusers/congestioncharging/6713.aspx. In 2007, the congestion charge zone was widened to include the West End. European motoring associations have objected strongly to congestion pricing, arguing that "placing restrictions on mobility of the individual or increasing its cost will not improve the quality of life nor enhance economic development." James Kanter, Motorist group slams "congestion pricing," N.Y. Times, Oct. 2, 2009, http://green.blogs.nytimes.com/tag/congestion-pricing/. The congestion charge remains in place, however, and is "£11.50 daily charge for driving a vehicle within the charging zone between 07:00 and 18:00, Monday to Friday" as of 2014. Certain discounts and exemptions apply. Transport for London, Congestion Charge, https://www.tfl.gov.uk/modes/driving/congestion-charge.

In 2007, New York City Mayor Michael R. Bloomberg proposed a plan to reduce traffic by charging people who drive into the busiest parts of Manhattan. The plan received significant support from the Bush administration, which noted that New York stood to gain hundreds of millions of dollars if the plan were enacted. New York would have become the first city in the United States to impose a broad system of congestion pricing. Danny Hakim and Ray Rivera, City traffic pricing wins U.S. and Spitzer's favor, N.Y. Times, June 8, 2007, http://www.nytimes.com/2007/06/08/nyregion/08congestion.html. The mayor's plan would have charged $8 for cars and $21 for commercial trucks that enter Manhattan below 86th Street between 6 a.m. and 6 p.m. on weekdays, or $4 for drivers within the congestion zone, with several exceptions. Mayor Bloomberg proposed to create a new public authority to take in the new revenue, estimated at $380 million a year, which would give the mayor more say over transportation spending.

Governor Spitzer wanted to see the money ease a looming deficit at the Metropolitan Transportation Authority. Legislators were concerned about any ripple effects the program would have on traffic in neighborhoods outside Manhattan. "One of the major problems is that districts like mine and others become possibly parking lots," said Assemblyman Joseph R. Lentol, a Democrat who represents the Brooklyn neighborhoods around the Williamsburg Bridge. The plan's backers, including civic, labor and environmental organizations, viewed the proposal as a bold step to help manage the city's growth. But the mayor's plan was strongly opposed by a broad array of politicians from Queens, Brooklyn and New York's suburbs, who viewed the proposed congestion fee as a regressive measure that overwhelmingly benefited affluent Manhattanites, and it died in the legislature. Nicholas Confessore, $8 traffic fee for Manhattan gets nowhere, N.Y. Times, Apr. 8, 2008, http://www.nytimes.com/2008/04/08/nyregion/08congest.html?pagewanted=all.

The Editors of the Economist offered some advice from London:

First, there needs to be a definite and coherent plan. Resistance to national road-pricing is as passionate as it is partly because the details are unknown. Which department will run it? What will they do with the money? When Mayor Livingstone came to the public with his plans, all this had been settled. As described below, this was the obstacle that NYC could not overcome. What to do with the money is an especially thorny issue. Mr. Livingstone's scheme was tolerated partly because he promised to spend the revenues on better public transport. London's charge brings in around £120 million/year, not enough to pay for better bus services. Most of London's public-transport improvements were financed by £1 billion of Treasury cash. The chances that the Treasury will do something similar for every city in the country are remote at best. Another option is to reduce other taxes on motoring, such as the gasoline tax, by the amount that road pricing raises. Such revenue neutrality would placate the motoring lobby, as well as make it cheaper to drive on quiet rural roads. But some models suggest that, while urban roads would improve, rural ones would clog up, producing more congestion overall.

Road pricing: a capital idea, The Economist, Feb. 22, 2007, www.economist.com/node/8746347.

Other commentators point out that congestion charges suffer from the public's tendency toward loss aversion—a reluctance to risk losing a present benefit, such as free travel, for a vaguely defined hope for a future benefit such as lower congestion. And the small group of motorists who would regularly benefit from a congestion charge are likely to be outweighed by a much larger group that would find the charge just an annoyance. King, *supra,* at 362–63.

b.   CONNECTED VEHICLES

"Connected Vehicles" is a term used to describe vehicle wireless connectivity throughout the automotive community. GM vice president Larry Burns has called for the creation of a new public/private partnership to rapidly commercialize connected vehicle technologies such as sensors, actuators, wireless communications and GPS systems, which would be integrated with future electric cars. Burns observes that electrically driven and connected vehicles offer compelling sustainability benefits: "Occupant protection is one of the key drivers of vehicle mass [the need for vehicles built with relatively dense, strong materials]. If cars don't crash, vehicle mass can be safely reduced. Lower mass, in turn, enhances the viability of electrically driven vehicles by reducing battery, hydrogen storage, and electric motor costs. Moreover, the packaging freedom associated with both electric drive (no engine compartment) and crash prevention (no front-end crash structure) can allow vehicles to be lighter and also significantly shorter, which is particularly useful where parking space is limited." Green Car Cong., GM's Burns Calls for New US Public/Private Partnership for Rapid Commercialization of Electrically Driven and Connected Vehicle Technologies; the New Automotive DNA, Jan. 14, 2009, http://www.greencarcongress.com/2009/01/gms-burns-calls.html.

In Europe, privacy advocates expressed concern about preliminary research on a Cooperative Vehicle-Infrastructure Systems (CVIS) project backed by automakers and telecoms throughout the continent. Vehicles would be equipped with devices that would emit a constant "heartbeat" revealing their location, speed and direction of travel. Objectors argue that such a system of almost total road surveillance could be tied in with mobile phone data to create a draconian personal tracking system. Paul Lewis, Big brother is watching: surveillance box to track drivers is backed, The Guardian, Mar. 31, 2009, http://www.theguardian.com/uk/2009/mar/31/surveillance-transport-communication-box. But advocates of connected vehicles say they enable predictable routing, network-wide traffic management, real-time congestion pricing, and pre-payment for parking spaces, thus making travel times shorter and more predictable and driving more convenient. Vehicle telemetry: calling all cars, The Economist, Nov. 19, 2009, http://www.economist.com/node/14902759. Connectivity allows greater knowledge of what's ahead, which can help improve fuel economy for conventional vehicles. Once cars can reliably sense hazards, they will react far faster than people. Communication between cars would allow traffic speeds to be optimized, and avoid the wasteful overtaking and slowing down that cause traffic jams. Planes, trains, and automobiles, The Economist, June 19, 2009, http://www.economist.com/node/13853060.

These types of concerns have come to the forefront with the rise of companies like Uber, a computer service that connects riders with drivers and is now one of the highest-valued products in world. It is active in more than 70 cities, but increasingly, taxi drivers and other car service employees have called for regulation of this service, arguing that it offers no needed protections for riders or training for drivers. *See, e.g.*, Martine Powers, Taxi drivers say Uber threatens their livelihoods, Boston Globe, May 22, 2014, http://www.bostonglobe.com/metro/2014/05/22/taxi-drivers-protest-uber-boston-offices/0YlRN0hHAHVhcxFIQ2X5aI/story.html. Taxi drivers and car service providers, of course, also have an anti-competitive interest in limiting the use of Uber and similar services like Lyft. Cities and some states have banned operators from using Uber and have issued cease and desist orders and fines when operators fail to comply. *See, e.g.*, David Maly, App lets riders forgo cabs and ignites debate on Dallas' code, N.T. Times/Tex. Tribune, Oct. 31, 2013, http://www.nytimes.com/2013/11/01/us/app-lets-riders-forgo-cabs-and-ignites-debate-on-dallas-code.html?_r=0.

INDEX

References are to Pages